Fighters over the Fleet

Fighters over the Fleet

Naval Air Defence from Biplanes to the Cold War

NORMAN FRIEDMAN

Seaforth

PUBLISHING

This edition first published in Great Britain in 2016 by
Seaforth Publishing,
An imprint of Pen & Sword Books Ltd,
47 Church Street,
Barnsley
South Yorkshire S70 2AS

www.seaforthpublishing.com
Email: info@seaforthpublishing.com

British Library Cataloguing in Publication Data
A catalogue record for this book is available from the British Library

ISBN 978 1 84832 404 6

Typeset and designed by Ian Hughes, Mousemat Design Limited
Printed and bound in China by 1010 Printing International Ltd

CONTENTS

ABBREVIATIONS

ACDS = Advanced Combat Data System
ACNS = Assistant Chief of the Naval Staff
ACO = Air Control Officer
ADA = Action Data Automation
ADAWS = ADA (*qv*) Weapons System
ADO = Air Defence Officer
ADNAD = Assistant Director Naval Air Department (Admiralty)
ADR = Aircraft Design Research (office in BuAer, USN)/Aircraft Direction Room (RN)
AESA = active electronically-scanned array
AEW = airborne early warning
AI = Air Intercept (radar); British designation for air-to-air radar
AIO = Action Information Organisation
AMCS = Airborne Missile Control System
APL = Applied Physics Laboratory
APO = Air Plot Officer
ARCI = Acoustic Rapid COTS (qv) Insertion
ARL = Admiralty Research Laboratory
AS = air-surface (radar)
ASE = Admiralty Signal Establishment
ASMS = Advanced Surface Missile System
ASV = Air to Surface Vessel (radar); British designation for sea-search radar
ASW = anti-submarine warfare
ASWE = Admiralty Surface Weapons Establishment
ATDS = Air Tactical Data System
BuAer = Bureau of Aeronautics (USN)
BuOrd = Bureau of Ordnance (USN)
BVP = Beacon Video Processor
CAL = Cornell Aeronautical Laboratory
CAM = Catapult Armed Merchant (ship)
CAP = combat air patrol
CCA = Carrier Controlled Approach
CDS = Comprehensive Display System/Combat Data System
CEP = Circular Error Probable
CIC = Combat Information Center
CICO = CIC (*qv*) Officer
CNA = Center for Naval Analyses
CNO = Chief of Naval Operations
CNR = Chief of Naval Requirements
CO = commanding officer
COC = Combat Operations Center
COD = Carrier-On-Board Delivery (aircraft)
COTS = commercial off-the-shelf (technology)
CW = Continuous Wave (as opposed to pulsed) radar, used mainly for missile homing (it is also used to measure the speeds of incoming aircraft for landing control)
DACR = Director Aircraft Carrier Requirements (Admiralty)
DADCAP = Dawn and Dusk Combat Air Patrol
DAE = Director of Air Equipment

DAM = Director of Air Material
DARPA = Department of Defense Advanced Research Projects agency
DAW = Director of Air Warfare (Admiralty)
DAWT = Director, Air Warfare and Training
DBR = dive bomber reconnaissance (aircraft)
DCAS = Deputy Chief of Air Staff
DCNO = Deputy Chief of Naval Operations
DDNAD = Deputy Director Naval Air Department (Admiralty)
DDR&E = Directorate for Defense Research and Engineering
D/F = (radio) direction-finding
DLCO = Deck Landing Control Officer (RN equivalent of LSO [*qv*])
DLI = deck-launched interception/interceptor
DME = Distance Measuring Equipment
DNAD = Director of Naval Air Division
DNC = Department/Director of Naval Construction
DNO = Director of Naval Ordnance (Admiralty)
D of TD = Director of Tactical Division (Admiralty)
DPT = Digital Plot Transmission
DRT = Dead-Reckoning Tracer
DTD = Director of Technical Development
DTSD = Director, Training and Staff Duties Division
ECM = electronic countermeasures
EDS = Electronic Display System
FAA = Fleet Air Arm
FBC = Future Building Committee
FDB = fighter dive bomber (aircraft)
FFAR = folding-fin aerial rockets
FLIR = forward-looking infra-red
F/R = fighter/reconnaissance (aircraft)
FY = financial year
GAO = Government Accounting Office
GDR = Gun Direction Room
GP = general purpose (aircraft)
GPS = Global Positioning System
HACS = High Angle Control System
HEAF = High Energy Aircraft Fuel
HEF = High Energy Fuel
HF = High Frequency
HPI = Height Position Indicator (radar display)
HVAR = high-velocity aircraft rocket
IACS = Interceptor Armament and Control System
IFF = Identify Friend or Foe
JATO = jet-assisted take-off
LABS = Low-Altitude Bombing System
LAP = Low Altitude Performance
LOCAP = Low Altitude Combat Air Patrol
LPD = labelled plot displays
LRC = Long Range CAP (*qv*)
LROG = Long Range Objectives Group (USN)

LSO = Landing Signals Officer
MADGE = Microwave Aircraft Digital Guidance Equipment
MADP = Main Air Display Plot
MAP = Ministry of Aircraft Production
MDAP = Mutual Defense Assistance Program
MDWP = Mutual Weapons Development Program
MEW = Microwave Early Warning (radar)
MMr = multi-mission radar
MNBO = Mobile Naval Base Organisation
MRC = Mid-Range CAP (*qv*)
MTDS = Marine Tactical Data System
MTI = moving target indication
NACA = National Advisory Committee on Aeronautics (US: prede-
    cessor of current NASA)
NAD = Naval Air Department (Admiralty)
NAF = Naval Aircraft Factory (USN)
NAMU = Naval Air Modification Unit
NASARR = North American Search and Range Radar
NAVAIR = Naval Air Systems Command (USN)
NDRC = National Defense Research Council
NEL = Naval Electronic Laboratory
NMBR = NATO Military Basic Requirement
NORAD = North American Air Defense
NOTS = Naval Ordnance Test Station
NRL = Naval Research Lab (USN)
NTDS = Naval Tactical Data System
OEG = Operational Evaluation Group
OFR = other fighter requirement
ONR = Office of Naval Research
OpDevFor = Operational Development Force
OpNav = Operations, Navy, i.e. the Office of the CNO (*qv*).
OpTevFor = Operational Test and Evaluation Force
OSD = Office of the Secretary of Defense
OSIS = Ocean Surveillance Information System
OSRD = Office of Scientific Research and Development
OTC = Officer in Tactical Command
OTH = over the horizon
P/A = pilotless aircraft
PCB = Plenum Chamber Burning (engine)
PIRAZ = Positive Identification Radar Advisory Zone
PMDS = projected map display system
PPBS = Planning, Programming, Budgeting System (US)
PPI = plan-position indicator
PSAC = President's Science Advisory Committee
RAE = Royal Aircraft Establishment

RAF = Royal Air Force
RAFAD = Research Analysis of Fleet Air Defense
RAPCAP = Radar Picket Combat Air Patrol
RDF = radio direction-finding (i.e. radar)
RDR = Radar Display Room
RIO = radar intercept officer
RNAS = Royal Naval Air Service
ROTHER = Relocatable OTH (*qv*) Radar
R/T = radio telephone, i.e. voice radio
RVP = Radar Video Processor
SA = ship-to-air (radar)
SAAICS = Semi-Automatic Air Intercept Control System
SAC = Strategic Air Command
SADZAC = Semi-Automatic Digital Analyzer and Computer
SAGE = Semi-Automatic Ground Environment (System)
SAP = semi-armour-piercing (bomb)
SBR = Space Based Radar
SCS = Sea Control Ship
SEAM = Sidewinder Expanded Acquisition Mode
SINS = Ships Inertial Navigation System
SOR = Specific Operational Requirement
S/R = spotter/reconnaissance (aircraft)
SSPK = single-shot kill probability
SSS = Strike Support Ship
SWIP = Super Weight Improvement Programme
TAC = Tactical Air Command (USAF)
TACAN = Tactical Air Navigation
TBR = torpedo/bomber/reconnaissance (aircraft)
TBS = Talk Between Ships (radio)
TCS = television camera sight
TDP = Technical Development Plan
TSR = torpedo/spotter/reconnaissance (aircraft)
TWS = Track While Scan (radar)
VCNO = Vice Chief of the Naval Staff
VDP = Visual Direction Position
VSTOL = vertical/short take-off and landing
VTO = vertical take-off
VTOL = vertical take-off and landing
WA = Warning Air (radar set)
WDS = Weapon Direction System
WIP = Weight Improvement Programme
WSEG = Weapons System Evaluation Group
W/T = wireless telegraphy, i.e. Morse-code radio
ZELMAL = Zero-Length Launch Mattress Landing

A NOTE ON SOURCES

As in other books in this series, I have depended overwhelmingly on official US and British sources for policy, tactics and the logic of aircraft and weapon choice and development. I have had to rely heavily on secondary sources for the Imperial Japanese Navy, but the bulk of this book concerns the US Navy and the Royal Navy. I have only touched on other carrier-operating navies, on the theory that they had only a limited impact on the development of naval fighters and their operation. The French Navy certainly developed and operated its own fighters, particularly before the Second World War, but only in very small numbers, because at the time it had only the single small slow carrier *Béarn*. What it would have done had it completed the two ships under construction in 1940 is thus a matter of speculation.

In the US case, research is somewhat hindered in that, because its manpower is limited, the National Archives has been unable to complete review of the Confidential Bureau of Aeronautics correspondence (which covers the period up through 1959). Correspondence through 1952 had been completely declassified and that for some later years (and some topics) has also been declassified, due largely to Freedom of Information requests, but correspondence for a few years has not been released. I am confident that what has been released, supplemented by other released material, suffices to tell nearly the whole US Navy fighter story. The only gaps of which I am aware are an account of the cancellation of the Grumman F10F Jaguar and details of revision to the F3H programme in 1954 (but in the latter case what happened is fairly obvious). I should add that what has been released includes extensive files of proposals offered to the US Navy (and, in many cases, their evaluation) and also a massive file on the parallel development of the Phantom and its rival, the Super Crusader (F8U-3).

Readers may notice some divergence between my account of fighter development and that provided by Tony Buttler in his Secret Projects series. For US subjects, Mr Buttler relied heavily on the archives of the various aircraft companies, a resource now largely shut to researchers. I have relied more on the surviving released US Navy archives, which tell a somewhat different story. The US archives include three large collections of aircraft company proposals. They are not quite complete (they omit the unsolicited proposals which became the A-4, A-5 and F-4), but they seem far more complete than any other source. The parallel correspondence series explains many of the decisions made by the US Navy's Bureau of Aeronautics and its successors. However, because of limited personnel in the National Archives, the availability of this file for 1953–9 is currently spotty. Much of the historical record is in the files of the Naval History and Heritage Command's Ships' Histories section (which merged with the former Aviation History section).

These data are supplemented by a semi-official source, the oral history/memoir produced by George A Spangenberg, a long-time aeronautical engineer at BuAer and its successor agencies, who was inducted into the Naval Aviation Museum's Hall of Fame in 1989. His comments are particularly valuable because he became the senior naval air civilian engineer at about the time of the F-111B fiasco and was heavily involved in decisions at that time (he retired in 1973, but retained his connection with naval aviation). This oral history was formerly available online from the Naval History and Heritage Command, but it is no longer available. Unfortunately the extensive attachments Mr Spangenberg cites in the oral history are not in the version I have.

For British aircraft Mr Buttler was able to combine company archives with some research in The National Archive (TNA, which I persist in calling by its old name, the Public Record Office [PRO]). I believe I have used somewhat different sources in some cases.

For characterisations of the performance of Second World War and later aircraft from a pilot's point of view, which are generally in the photo captions, I have relied heavily on the accounts given by Captain E M 'Winkle' Brown RN. His unparalleled variety of aircraft experience made it possible for him to compare different aircraft in a way no one else could. Brown's naval flying experience extended from the beginning of the Second World War through the 1970s.

ACKNOWLEDGEMENTS

This book combines three themes I have been researching and writing about for many years. One is the way in which fleets have directed fighter air defence, a theme in which I first became interested while working for the US Navy in the 1970s. I am particularly grateful to Dr John Lehman for the opportunity to serve in the Office of Program Analysis in his navy secretariat while the Maritime Strategy and the associated Outer Air Battle concept were being elaborated. My account of the Outer Air Battle reflects that experience. A second theme is the evolution of carriers and their aircraft (as they affected or were affected by, the carriers); I have written histories of both British and US carrier development. The US history came first, and I am indebted to the late Reuven Leopold, at the time the senior civilian in the then US Navy Ship Engineering Center, for early assistance. I am also indebted to the civilian engineers of the then Preliminary Design section of the Naval Sea Systems Command, particularly Herb Meier and the late Phil Sims, who provided considerable insight into US Navy thinking. The late D K Brown helped me with British carrier design, and he also made evident the considerable divide between British and American carrier operating practices, as reflected in aircraft capacity. Explaining why British carriers accommodated so many fewer aircraft than their US counterparts has proven very fruitful for me. I also benefitted (and have continued to benefit) from the assistance of the Brass Foundry outstation of the National Maritime Museum, the repository of the Ships' Covers, and in recent years particularly from the efforts of Andrew Choong and Jeremy Michell, the latest in a long line of extremely helpful curators there. In addition to the US National Archives and of the US Navy Operational Archives, I have gained considerably from access to the archive at the US Naval War College; I would particularly like to thank its long-time (now retired) archivist Dr Evelyn Cherpak. I am grateful to the personnel of the Operational Archives (of NHHC) for assistance with other US Navy files, particularly those of the Operational Evaluation Group. Other material came from the files of the immediate office of the CNO ('double-zero' files) in the Operational Archives and from the files of the General Board (now in the National Archives). For access I am grateful to the directors of that office, particularly Curtis Utz (previously chief of the aviation history branch) and Dr Dean Allard. I enjoyed many discussions with the late J D Brown, at that time head of the Royal Navy Historical Branch, but previously a naval airman and a participant in the success of the CDS/Sea Vixen combination in mock combat against the US Navy. I am also, as always, grateful to Jenny Wraight, the very knowledgeable and resourceful librarian of the Admiralty Library. I also appreciate help provided by David Hobbs, who was formerly head of the Fleet Air Arm Museum at Yeovilton.

The third strand is the aircraft themselves. While considerable historical information about the development of British naval aircraft is available in the Public Record Office/The National Archive (to whose staff I am grateful), the US situation is considerably more complicated. Many years ago the US Naval Air Systems Command maintained a historical office, headed by Dr William Armstrong, who was very helpful. Most of the files held by that office later passed into the possession of the US Naval Historical Center (now the headquarters office of the Naval History and Heritage Command [NHHC]), and I am grateful for the assistance rendered by its personnel. The situation as to aircraft information has been transformed in the last few years as files have been opened at the National Archives center at College Park, Maryland (NARA II). For access to these files, I am grateful to the naval specialists at College Park, particularly Nate Patch, and also to the declassifiers there (including Kenneth A Johnson, now retired) and to Stephanie Coon, the head of the Indexing Project (consolidating files already reviewed). I am also very grateful to Dr Thomas C Hone, particularly (but not only) for insights into choices the US Navy made in its development of carrier operations, both before and after the Second World War. He and I were involved in a study of a key question, reflected in the current book: how and why a US Navy which had little interest in technology developed elsewhere was glad to adopt three radical British innovations – the angled deck, the steam catapult, and the mirror landing sight – in short order. I am fortunate to have been allowed access to (and warmly welcomed at) the Grumman archive at Bethpage, New York; I understand it has since been closed and its contents moved to Northrop Grumman premises elsewhere.

I have benefitted from the comments and advice of many friends, particularly A D Baker III, Dana Bell, Chris Carlson, Dr Raymond Cheung, Dr Thomas C Hone, David C Isby, Mattis Ooms (for the Dutch-Indonesian crisis of 1962), Alexandre Sheldon-Dupleix (for French naval aviation), Dr Josef Straczek, and Chris Wright (editor of *Warship International*). They helped me avoid errors, but I would emphasise that I am responsible for any that remain.

For photographs I would like to thank Janis Jorgensen of the Naval Institute Photo Collection, A D Baker III (as always much more than an illustrator), Doug Siegfried of *The Hook*, the State Library of Victoria (Australia), David Hobbs, John Gourley, Dr Thomas C Hone, Richard Gimblett of the Royal Canadian Navy, and Steve Zaloga.

Because of its complexity, this book has been a more intense and difficult project than many others I have written. I could not have written completed it without the patient loving support of my wife Rhea over many years. She was also extremely helpful in developing the historical background section at the beginning of this book.

INTRODUCTION

A FEW YEARS AGO I published a history of the gunnery side of naval air defence. This is the other side of that story, fleet air defence by fighters flying from aircraft carriers. Because much the same ideas (and often much the same technology) were used before, during and after the Second World War the story extends from the beginnings of carrier aviation through the Cold War. I have concentrated on the three major carrier navies: the US Navy, the Royal Navy and the pre-1941 and Second World War Imperial Japanese Navy. Other navies, particularly the French, have certainly operated carriers and have developed their own naval fighters, but they have not developed their own doctrines and tactics to anything like the same extent. Although the detailed account ends with the end of the Cold War, fleet air defence is very much a live current issue. For the US Navy, for example, the evolving Chinese navy and its air arm present threats reminiscent of those mounted by the Soviets during the Cold War.

Naval fighters are part of a larger system which includes shipboard and airborne radar and also means of fighter direction, both shipboard and, in current incarnations, airborne. The system has to detect incoming attackers and provide fighter controllers with a tactical picture enabling them to allocate scarce fighter resources to incoming attackers. Without a sense of the whole tactical situation, the fighters can easily be concentrated against a few attackers, leaving the field free to others. Given the tactical picture, fighters have to be coached into positions from which their pilots can see and engage (not the same thing) the incoming attackers. The individual fighter pilot just cannot see enough of what is happening and he is only one of a mass of pilots who have to distribute their efforts properly. Much depends on how quickly fighters can destroy or drive off individual enemy aircraft. There was, for example, a vast difference between a relatively flimsy Second World War Japanese torpedo bomber and a heavy Cold War Soviet missile bomber. Particularly after 1945, there was also a premium on destroying enemy attackers far enough from the fleet that they could not launch their stand-off weapons effectively.

Fighter direction is a kind of fire control. In anti-aircraft fire control, a shell or missile has to be brought close enough to destroy its target. In fighter control, 'close enough' is substantially further from the incoming target aircraft, but there is still a definite limit on how far off the fighter can be. In fighter control there are, however, additional factors. If the defending fighters form a combat air patrol (CAP), the controller has to take account of how much fuel they have and also of their weapon status. As in gun fire control, a key issue is saturation: how many separate targets can the fighter-control system handle at about the same time? What determines saturation and can the operators detect that they are approaching it?

Without the whole system in place, defence fails catastrophically, as it did for the Japanese carrier striking force at Midway. Conversely, the system as a whole can achieve both fleet defence and a larger degree of air superiority. Late in the Cold War the US Navy saw its fighter defence not so much as a means of enabling its carriers to survive and to carry out their missions, but rather as a means of destroying the Soviet naval

air arm, the most potent threat to NATO shipping in the North Atlantic. In the Falklands, the Royal Navy learned that effective fleet air defence had to include fighters as well as shipboard missiles. This lesson remains valid. Conversely, carrier tactics, particularly before 1945, were heavily influenced by expectations of how well fighter defence would function.

All of this applies to land air defence just as much as to naval, but naval warfare is very different because, unlike cities ashore, ships move over a vast and trackless sea. Tracklessness and navigation no longer loom large in an era of widespread Global Positioning System (GPS) use, but well into the Second World War there were no seaborne electronic aids to navigation other than the homing beacons aboard US and British carriers. The situation ashore was only slightly better, with fixed beacons and radio beams for aircraft guidance on a limited point-to-point basis. A variety of electronic aids to navigation, such as Loran and Gee, were developed and deployed in wartime, but they seem to have had very little impact on the naval air war.

To attack a moving target at sea requires not merely detecting it once, but also tracking it so that attackers can find it when they arrive. Even if the first aircraft can determine the course and speed of the targets, there is no guarantee that they will continue on that path. That is why the *Prince of Wales* battlegroup maintained radio silence even after a Japanese scout plane detected it; Royal Navy experience in the Mediterranean had shown that nothing short of continuous tracking could enable a later air strike to find moving ships, particularly fast ones. A sharp course change after the first aircraft left would spoil its report. Subsequent radio silence in turn precluded any attempt to co-ordinate with fighters based at Singapore.[1]

Simply finding and tracking seaborne targets was and remains a major effort. Given navigational errors, a reconnaissance report might be grossly misleading.[2] Conversely, naval aircraft must find their own positions and manage to return home to their moving carriers. Before and during the Second World War, for example, US Navy pilots' briefings included the location of 'point option', where their carrier expected to be when they returned. A carrier forced to steam at slower or higher than expected speed would not be in place and pilots needed fuel reserves to search for their ships. Although both the Royal Navy and the US Navy developed homing beacons for carriers, it appears that at least in the US case pilots often failed to use them as intended. That was one reason for the substantial loss of aircraft and aircrew on the evening of the Battle of the Philippine Sea, when the aircraft returned after dusk (carrier commander Rear Admiral Marc Mitscher was very fondly remembered by many pilots for turning deck lights on, to help them land, despite the risks that entailed).

Disrupting an enemy's scouting effort could preclude an air attack altogether, as the Royal Navy found in the Mediterranean. After the Second World War, much effort was devoted to dealing with snoopers which had to find and shadow a targeted fleet as a prerequisite for an air or submarine attack. Moreover, scouting and attack had to deal with serious navigational problems. The situation for surface ships was bad enough; traditional methods using star and sun 'fixes' usually gave a ship's position to no better than 5 miles. That was good enough to make landfall and also to make a rendezvous at sea, but it was not nearly good enough for scouts working well beyond the horizon. For aircraft the situation was far worse, as they generally had to rely on dead reckoning. A pilot could estimate his air speed, but his aircraft was much affected by winds en route, which could not be measured when he took off. Considerable effort went into measuring winds at altitude, for example using balloons, but that was near a carrier, not over the long distance to a target. The navigational problem helps explain why the nominal range of carrier aircraft had so little relation to effective range. For example, aircraft returning to a carrier needed a considerable fuel reserve to allow them to search for the ship. In the early 1930s a senior US carrier officer remarked that aircraft sent more than 25 miles from a ship were often lost. The situation in 1941 was better, but it was still difficult.

The greater the distance, the more difficult it was to mount attacks on carriers. Even if scouts did find a target fleet, if their navigation was poor enough that might not matter. In the Mediterranean, the Royal Navy faced a Royal Italian Air Force which had concentrated on land operations. Its scouts might report back before they could be shot down, but often the reported positions were so wildly in error (due to inexperience navigating over the sea) that there was no point in shooting them down.

At the least, the presence of a scout was warning that an attack was brewing, hence that fighter defence had to be assembled. Conversely, a fleet operating near enemy bases presented the enemy with no great navigational problem. That is one reason it was possible for raw Kamikaze pilots off Okinawa to find and attack the US fleet there (they were convoyed to the vicinity of the fleet by experienced pilots who knew how to navigate). The Japanese also tried to follow returning strikes back to the carriers, both to evade defending fighters and simply to find their targets. Special sections of fighters, called Tomcats, had to be assigned to 'de-louse' returning strikes.

The reality of search and shadowing as prerequisites for air attack continued after the war. Much attention was paid to ways of attacking and destroying snoopers, which would generally be radar-equipped. For the US Navy of the mid-1960s, one of the great unpleasant surprises was that Soviet aircraft began to head straight for carriers instead of searching for them. It turned out that the Soviets had learned to use high-precision shore-based High Frequency Direction Finders (mainly a system called Krug) to locate carriers *without* using snoopers.

The complexity of simply finding moving targets well out to sea did not figure in most pre-war discussions of the vulnerability (or otherwise) of fleets to air attack. Advocates of air power generally concentrated on what they could achieve after the fleet was located. Analysts of fleet air defence generally began with the appearance of enemy aircraft over the fleet. The pre-war Royal Navy seems to have been unique in taking counter-scouting into account and then only when it faced a particularly difficult air attack situation in the Mediterranean.

As with any other kind of naval technology, the way in which each navy addressed fighter defence was deeply influenced by the way in which it was organised, in particular in the way in which it dealt with naval aviation. A vital factor for all three major carrier navies during the run-up to the Second World War was the view, widespread among aviators, that air operations could and would be decisive in any future war. The difference between the three navies was that in the Imperial Japanese Navy and the US Navy many of the air enthusiasts were inside the navy and saw air operations as way of enhancing sea power. In Britain the creation of a separate Royal Air Force, which took over all military air operations, placed nearly all the air enthusiasts outside the navy and indeed left many of them with the view that their arm could and should replace the conventional army and navy. Although the Royal Navy paid for the specialist naval aviators, they had no career path which would have led to their rise to senior positions (some observers were regular naval officers, however). That left the navy without the sort of air/sea knowledge which proved so useful to the US and Imperial Japanese Navies.

If anything, the course of the Second World War and its culmination in the nuclear attacks on Japan created more air enthusiasts who saw their arm as the solution to the murderously expensive problems of more conventional warfare. Although the new US Air Force did not (as it wanted to) take over all US military aviation (it did take over army support aviation), it came to share much the view that the interwar RAF had developed, that strategic air warfare could and should dominate all other efforts. The US Navy saw acquisition of a nuclear strike role as key to its survival. This view much affected the role (and the character) of carriers and of fleet air defence.

CHAPTER 1
THE CARRIER NAVIES

THE ROYAL NAVY AND CARRIERS

During most of the period covered by this book, the Royal Navy was administered by a five-man Board of Admiralty headed by the First Sea Lord. After 1917 he was both operational commander of the Royal Navy and Chief of the Naval Staff. The latter had been reorganised in 1917 specifically to emphasise the need to translate naval experience into specific Staff Requirements for, among other things, types of aircraft and air weapons. In theory, the materiel departments of the navy, the Department of Naval Construction (DNC), the Department of Naval Ordnance (DNO) and Engineer-in-Chief (propulsion) met the Staff Requirements and supervised the acquisition of ships and weapons. DNC (the same letters are used for the Director of Naval Construction) was, for example, responsible for aircraft carrier design, which in turn set the limits within which British naval aircraft were built. DNC and DNO were served by a number of laboratories, including the Admiralty Research Laboratory (ARL) and the Admiralty Signal Establishment (ASE). Initially ASE was responsible for British naval radios (a role taken away from *Vernon*, the mine/electrical school and lab, in 1917), but later

it developed radar. Other naval schools developed tactics. For this book the most important pre-war and wartime school was probably *Dryad*, which was responsible for navigation and therefore for plotting. Plotting developed into fighter direction, *Dryad* becoming the school of navigation and direction.

Before the First World War, a new Department of Naval Aircraft was created, headed by the Director of Naval Air Division (DNAD); it might be considered analogous to the DNO. A new Fifth Sea Lord was responsible for the Royal Naval Air Service (RNAS). During the war the RNAS was responsible not only for shipboard and associated land-based naval aviation, but also for some shore-based operations which might be considered only loosely naval. For example, because the Royal Navy was responsible for the defence of the British coast (beyond fixed army defences), the RNAS was largely responsible for defence against German air raids (the navy also deployed ships specifically to fire at Zeppelins approaching the British coast). The RNAS also bought the first British long-range bombers, because the navy was the closest thing the British had to a means of strategic attack.

The Royal Navy invented the carrier in several guises: strike (torpedo attack), reconnaissance and fleet air defence (initially, to drive off German snoopers). Flycatcher fighters of 401 Flight are shown over *Furious* in the 1920s. Her large main flight deck was intended for her torpedo bombers, which needed a long take-off run. The short lower flight deck, which *Furious* shared with her near-sisters *Courageous* and *Glorious*, was intended for the Flycatchers, which had a shorter take-off run. (David Hobbs)

Glorious is shown newly-completed in 1930. The windbreak on her bow protects the doors to the lower hangar housing fighters. She, her sister *Courageous* and her near-sister *Furious* operated together as the Mediterranean Fleet carrier force during the 1930s, the source of British carrier tactics. *Glorious* was sunk by the German battlecruisers *Scharnhorst* and *Gneisenau* in the North Sea in May 1940, in effect proving that carriers were both extremely powerful and extremely vulnerable. No other carriers in the Second World War were threatened by capital-ship gunfire until the battle off Samar in October 1944.

The Royal Navy employed naval aviation far more extensively than any other First World War navy. Among other things, it invented the aircraft carrier and built or converted many ships to serve aircraft. Its great aerial failure, which was inevitable, was its inability to prevent German air raids against London. To a considerable extent the 1917–18 reorganisation of British military aviation, which consolidated all air services into the Royal Air Force (RAF), was a political attempt to demonstrate the will to overcome this failure, even though there was no reason to imagine that any improved defence was possible.

On 1 April 1918 all British naval and army flying activities were merged into the Royal Air Force. In theory the new organisation would simplify aircraft production and procurement. Separate elements would support the army and the navy. In practice, after about 1920 the new air force sought an independent role based on strategic bombing. The Royal Navy continued to frame staff requirements for its aircraft and it continued to pay for them. The Admiralty also paid the pilots, but attempts to convince naval officers to become pilots foundered because such officers had few career prospects open to them. A major point of contention during the interwar period was that the new RAF was centred on pilots, whereas the Royal Navy maintained that often the executive role in an aircraft should fall on the observer or other senior officer present in a multi-seat aircraft. Naval officers were recruited into the navy's Observer Branch. An extension of this idea, particularly antithetical to the RAF, was that naval ratings were perfectly acceptable pilots (as the Admiralty proposed in 1935 as a way of solving its pilot shortage). At the time the RAF rejected the idea of non-officer pilots on what amounted to class grounds – ironically, shortly before it began recruiting non-commissioned pilots of its own in order to meet essential expansion requirements.

Without air expertise integrated into the Royal Navy, it was difficult for the Admiralty to be sure of formulating naval air policy. Staff Requirements for new aircraft, which might or might not be realistic, were submitted to the single Air Ministry, which carried out its own feasibility studies (examples of its conclusions survive). Unfortunately there was no one with naval experience to suggest that changes in the Staff Requirements, however feasible, could offer greater capability.[1] The most important consequence of this gap was probably naval acceptance, during the interwar period, of the idea that carrier fighters were inevitably inferior to land-based aircraft. That justified naval acceptance

Hermes was the first purpose-built carrier in the world, designed in 1916–17. Note her single-purpose 5.5in guns in shields, indicative of the threat presented to such a ship by enemy cruisers. There was no separate fighter hangar, because the ship was conceived entirely as a strike carrier. *Hermes* spent most of her career in the British China Fleet, the only non-Japanese carrier in the Far East. Note her T-shaped lift, which other interwar British carriers shared. It was designed to handle aircraft without folding wings. Later carriers, designed after naval aircraft had folding wings, had much narrower lifts. When the Royal Navy adopted non-folding high performance fighters in 1940–1 (Wildcats, Sea Hurricanes and early Seafires), only the earliest carriers could strike them below.

of relatively low-performance aircraft when the main objective of war plans was the Japanese fleet, whose own aircraft would also be carrier-borne. It caused serious problems when the Royal Navy had to face land-based attackers in European waters.

The Admiralty was well aware of its need for an air component. Its struggle to regain control of the Fleet Air Arm (FAA) has been well-publicised. It regained control of shipboard aviation, but not of land-based naval co-operation units (including flying boats), in April 1939. Separate air force control is often blamed for inadequacies of British naval air power after war broke out in 1939. It seems arguable that the lack of naval air experience in senior ranks associated with air force control was more significant. Pre-war Royal Navy expectations of the nature of war at sea, which are addressed in Chapter 3, may have been nearly as important. After the First World War the British Army also

argued strenuously against the loss of its aircraft, but it seems not to have been in any position to maintain an equivalent of the interwar FAA. It seems arguable that the army suffered far worse than the Royal Navy from inadequate air support when the crisis came in 1940.

From an organisational point of view, the Admiralty saw the fleet's aircraft as a single entity, spread among multiple ships. They were commanded initially by a Senior Officer (Aircraft) and then, from 1931 by a Rear Admiral (Aircraft) and then by a Vice Admiral (Aircraft).[2] The sense that aircraft were integral with the surface fleet seems to have led the British not to adopt the dispersed-carrier tactics used by the US and Imperial Japanese Navies. Also, the British seem to have been more acutely aware of navigational issues than were their foreign counter-parts, having experienced their consequences during the First World War. To the extent that they saw carrier aircraft as crucial fleet scouts, it was essential that the scouts' reports be keyed to the position of the surface fleet. That meant keeping carriers within visual signal range of the fleet flagship, which was part of a concentrated battle fleet. This thinking was probably also affected by the fact that the alternative fleet scouts, flying boats, were under RAF rather than naval control. Although it was assumed that they would co-operate with the fleet, the Royal Navy never developed the sort of mobile seaplane tender organ-isation that the US Navy and, to a slightly lesser extent, the Imperial Japanese Navy created. It did not help that flying boats (and shore-based naval co-operation in general) had a low priority in the interwar RAF. Unlike fleet aircraft, they were not funded by the Admiralty and therefore were very much subject to RAF policy. The US and Japanese situations were radically different, all naval-related aircraft, including flying boats and (in the Japanese case) land-based reconnaissance bombers coming under naval control.

The new Air Ministry created in 1918 was the RAF's equivalent to the Admiralty. It bought all RAF aircraft, including naval ones. The Admiralty continued to frame requirements on the basis of DNAD advice (i.e. staff requirements) and they were submitted to the Air Ministry for action. The Air Ministry included the centralised aircraft research establishment at Farnborough (the Royal Aircraft Establish-ment, RAE), which had a naval section. The naval section was respon-sible for, among other things, catapults and arresting gear. In 1945 its chief proposed the flexible landing deck which, although not adopted, led to the vital concept of the angled deck.

When the Royal Navy regained control of its shipboard aircraft in April 1939, it continued to rely on Farnborough and other establish-ments. The Air Ministry continued to buy aircraft for the navy. A new Ministry of Supply was created in July 1939 to centralise weapons pro-curement, but the Air Ministry retained control of aircraft design and construction, just as the Admiralty retained authority over warship design and production. The aircraft function was transferred to a new Ministry of Aircraft Production created in 1940 to emphasise the desperate need for production. In August 1945 the new Labour Govern-ment placed a single minister in charge of both the Ministry of Supply and the Ministry of Aircraft Production and they were formally merged the following year. Thus the Ministry of Supply oversaw both aircraft procurement and research post-war. That placed many key decisions, such as that to continue or abandon supersonic flight research, outside service hands. The Ministry of Supply aircraft function was moved to a new Ministry of Aviation in 1959; in 1967 it gave way to a Ministry of Technology. Anyone researching naval aircraft design will sense its range of responsibility in the 'AVIA' (Ministry of Aviation) designation of aircraft design files. Perhaps the most important point was that the

Eagle was laid down as the Chilean battleship *Almirante Cochrane* but completed as a carrier. That the Royal Navy was willing to sacrifice a battleship for this role suggests how important fleet aviation was to the wartime Grand Fleet. This photograph shows the pronounced round-down at the ship's stern, a typical feature of British carriers intended to improve airflow for landing aircraft. *Eagle*'s design was tested in a wind tunnel while she was being built. After the First World War the Admiralty hoped to build entirely new carriers and there was some discussion of completing *Eagle* as a battleship and returning her to Chile. The cost of such reconstruction (and the realisation that there would not be money for a new carrier) helped kill the project. Although she was a large ship, *Eagle* had a very limited aircraft capacity because her hangar was quite small. About 1931 the Royal Navy became aware that the US Navy kept as many as two-thirds of its aircraft continuously on deck, using a barrier and arresting gear to allow aircraft to land despite the aircraft parked forward. An attempt to increase the rated aircraft complements of carriers such as *Eagle* was resisted by the RAF in an arms-control context. The League of Nations was considering a plan to limit total numbers of military aircraft and the RAF did not want to sacrifice bombers for naval aircraft. The attempt to increase numbers had been forgotten by the time the League of Nations project collapsed. Note that at this time the ship had no arresting gear whatever.

Ministry of Supply (and its successor Ministry of Aviation) considered itself responsible not only to the service consumers of the aircraft but also to the larger central government, which might have other interests. For example, they were much concerned with the health of the British aircraft industry, which led to encouragement of joint RAF/Royal Navy tactical aircraft projects.

Perhaps most importantly, revived naval control of naval aviation created naval officer fliers with a clear career path, meaning with the potential to become senior officers with air experience and insight. The absence of such officers during the Second World War is evident in some unfortunate mis-steps, such as the exposure of *Glorious* to loss by surface fire during the Norwegian campaign in 1940. However, despite serious attempts to create air-mindedness and a very aggressive carrier-building programme, the Royal Navy did not adopt the sort of view of naval aviation typical of the US Navy or indeed of the pre-1945 Imperial Japanese Navy. At the time of crisis in 1965–6 it was unable to articulate an effective case for carrier aviation.

* * *

After the First World War the Royal Navy came to see Japan as the most likely future enemy. Admiral Jellicoe, who made an Empire cruise in 1919–20 to advise the Dominions as to future naval policy, pointed out that during the war the Japanese had sheltered anti-British subversives and had promoted their long-term policy of 'Asia for the Asians' (under Japanese tutelage). By 1924 British naval building programmes were predicated on the needs of a Far Eastern War.

At the time the major factor in overall British defence policy was the urgent need to recover from the deep wounds, particularly the financial wounds, inflicted by the war. One solution, instituted by Winston Churchill when he was at the Treasury, was the 'Ten Year Rule', the doctrine that defence budgets could be written on the assumption that there would be no war for ten years. On that basis spending on expendables such as ammunition and even quartz transducers for sonars (Asdics) could be eliminated (major capital items such as ships could still be bought). Personnel could also be cut. To some extent the Ten

Year Rule was a horizon for modernisation to reflect the technological leaps – such as air warfare and tank warfare – represented by the First World War. During the 1920s the Ten Year Rule became self-perpetuating, so the horizon for modernisation receded into the indefinite future.

The extreme financial stress inflicted by the war encouraged the British Government to seek economies through arms control. Although it was the US Government which convened the Washington Naval Conference in 1921, the British were already vitally interested in some measure of naval arms control, to the point that four new battlecruisers were approved that year with the essential justification that they were to be bargaining chips in any negotiation. At Washington, the British accepted parity with the US Navy, something which would have been inconceivable before the war. They and the Americans gained a statutory edge over the Imperial Japanese Navy, the 5:5:3 tonnage ratio.

The Royal Navy certainly wanted carriers, even though they were very much in their infancy. Its estimates showed a need for a large number of carrier aircraft. It also accepted that no carrier could accommodate many aircraft, so the need for aircraft translated into a need for substantial carrier tonnage. It was the Admiralty delegation to the Washington Conference which ensured that there would be a large tonnage allowance for what was, after all, an experimental type of warship. The Admiralty delegation also ensured that existing British carriers were classed as experimental, hence immediately replaceable.[3] All other treaty-limited warships could not be replaced until their assigned lifetimes had expired.

The effect of the Washington Treaty on naval aviation was paradoxical. In 1921 it was universally accepted that battleships and battlecruisers were the currency of seapower, so the treaty demanded large-scale scrapping and cancellation of such ships under construction. A battleship-building 'holiday' lasting until 1931 (extended by the next

Ark Royal was the first of the Second World War generation of British carriers. She had a double hangar to accommodate a large air group; British practice was to house all aircraft in the hangar. The double hangar accounts for her considerable freeboard. The pot-shaped object atop her single mast is the lantern of her Type 72 aircraft-homing beacon. The Royal Navy was very conscious of the danger of intercepted radio communication, particularly at the frequencies generally used for long-range communication. The higher frequency used by Type 72 was a lesser, but still real, concern. The tracks and end pulleys of two catapults (accelerators) are visible at her bow. The Royal Navy wanted them mainly to launch floatplanes; a carrier in the fleet would service and fuel the floatplanes launched by battleships and cruisers, so that they would not have to stop to retrieve them. The accelerator used a cumbersome four-point trolley which made for very slow launching. During the war, the Royal Navy adopted the much simpler US catapult arrangement, which did not allow for the floatplane role. *Ark Royal* was sunk by a U-boat torpedo on 14 November 1941 (she took a day to founder). The Royal Navy emphasised the submarine threat to carriers far more than did the US Navy, because it was much more significant in European waters. Two other fleet carriers were sunk by torpedoes: *Courageous* on 17 September 1939 and *Eagle* on 11 August 1942. The US Navy lost only one, *Wasp*, on 15 September 1942 (*Hornet* was finished off by submarine torpedoes but had been immobilised by air attack). The British attributed the loss of *Wasp* to what amounted to contempt for the submarine threat; she and other ships had remained in one area far too long and were proceeding at far too low a speed (the battleship *North Carolina* was torpedoed at about the same time). In addition to fleet carriers, the Royal Navy lost escort carriers to U-boat torpedoes: *Audacity* (21 December 1941), *Avenger* (15 November 1942) and *Thane* (15 January 1945, a constructive total loss). Comparable US escort carrier losses were *Block Island* (29 May 1944) and *Liscombe Bay* (24 November 1943).

treaty to 1936) was imposed.[4] However, the treaty allowed each power to convert two existing (or building) capital ships to carriers. This choice probably reflected US interest in converting two of the six large battlecruisers the US Navy was then building, *Lexington* and *Saratoga*. Japan chose the incomplete battlecruisers *Kaga* and *Amagi*, but had to substitute the battleship *Akagi* for *Amagi* after the latter was badly damaged in the massive 1923 Tokyo earthquake. The Royal Navy had no capital ships under construction. It chose the 'large light cruisers' *Courageous* and *Glorious*, which had no obvious role in the post-war battle fleet (their near-sister *Furious* had already been converted in wartime and was extensively rebuilt after the war). The treaty allowed converted ships to displace up to 33,000 tons (new carriers were limited to 27,500 tons).[5]

The existence of these huge carriers, whose size and capacity could not have been justified by wartime experience, was extremely important to interwar naval air development in all three carrier navies. US carrier operating practices provided the two ex-battlecruisers with far larger air complements than any of the other ships; it happened that the two British ships accommodated only slightly over half as many aircraft. In retrospect it was unfortunate that the Royal Navy had cancelled the three projected sister-ships to *Hood*, which would have been comparable to the two US ships. Had two of them been converted to carriers, the Royal Navy would have found itself with far larger numbers of shipboard aircraft and it might have gained a far better understanding of what large numbers of aircraft could do at sea. It is, however, only fair to say that well before the two big carriers had entered service the US Navy was experimenting with massive numbers of sea-based aircraft on the game floor at the Naval War College, to an extent that the Royal Navy's equivalent school seems not to have explored.

The provision for quick replacement of the experimental First World War ships (*Argus*, *Eagle* and *Hermes*) did the Royal Navy no good, because money was too tight. That proved unfortunate. The naval staff was painfully aware that the capacity of British carriers was insufficient, but it does not seem to have realised that the problem was a grossly inefficient way of operating, in which carrier capacity was equated to hangar capacity. The three First World War survivors had particularly small hangars for their size. With total carrier tonnage limited by treaty until 1936, the staff solution was to place aircraft on board capital ships and cruisers – not the scouts and spotters of other navies, but torpedo bombers and even, it was thought, fighters. There was considerable interest in whether carriers might be employed to rearm and refuel such aircraft after they had been launched by the surface warships. Ultimately the argument against relying on catapult aircraft was that they would

By 1936 the Royal Navy had to contemplate war in European waters, against land-based enemy air forces which could not be neutralised by a few dive bombers. With fighter defence difficult at best, the Royal Navy developed armoured-hangar carriers like *Formidable*, shown in 1943. They would stow their aircraft in the hangar to ride out an enemy air attack, relying on the massed anti-aircraft firepower of the fleet. It happened that at about the time the armoured hangar carriers were being conceived, the advent of radar made fighter defence far more practicable. Also, enemies developed dive bombers, such as the Stuka, which could deliver bombs the armoured deck over the hangar could not withstand (*Illustrious* was put out of action by such bombing in January 1941).

For most of the interwar period, the Royal Navy expected to fight the Imperial Japanese Navy in any future war. It hoped to gain air supremacy by neutralising Japanese aircraft carriers. The Blackburn Skua was intended primarily as a dive bomber, with secondary fighter capability. It was the first British naval monoplane. These Skuas of 806 NAS are shown above RNAS Eastleigh in 1940. Captain E M 'Winkle' Brown, who also flew the Dauntless and the Stuka, rated it as an excellent dive bomber, although it tended to overpower in a dive. However, it had bad deck-landing characteristics. The prototypes had Mercury engines, but because all Mercury production was then earmarked for Blenheim light bombers, production Skuas had the less satisfactory Perseus. (David Hobbs)

probably be limited to one flight, hence would be ineffective. Before that happened, aircraft requirements came to incorporate limits based partly on the limited end-speeds and weight capacities of shipboard catapults. The Royal Navy was told (and came to accept) that shipboard aircraft could not rival those based ashore.

No treaty limited the use of seaplanes or seaplane tenders. Both the United States and Japan exploited this possibility; for a time the US Navy hoped that seaplane performance would be good enough that a seaplane striking force could be created. At the very least, seaplanes based at atolls in the Pacific might be the only way to locate and track an enemy fleet. The Royal Navy had no such option, because even after April 1939 seaplanes were the province of the Royal Air Force. In theory, the British Empire offered so many potential seaplane operating areas that tenders were not essential (the Japanese viewed the Mandated Islands in much this way). However, RAF neglect of large flying boats limited the extent to which Royal Navy tacticians felt they could rely on seaplane reconnaissance. The Royal Navy never invested in seaplane tenders which would have converted atolls into temporary bases, as the Americans and the Japanese did.

The British view, then, was that carriers could and should be concentrated with the battle fleet, for which they could provide essential reconnaissance, spotting and air superiority services. The main British carrier force consisted of the three rebuilt 'large cruisers' *Courageous*, *Glorious* and *Furious*, all of which were assigned together to the Mediterranean Fleet. Not only was the Mediterranean Fleet the main organisation for tactical development, it was the core of the War Fleet which would be sent East in the event of war with Japan. One justification for concentrating the carriers in the Mediterranean was that for tactical development it was necessary that each side in a game have at least one carrier.

The British carrier concentration in the Mediterranean seems to have been the first attempt to integrate the aircraft of multiple carriers; it certainly predated Japanese attempts to do so in the form of the six-carrier First Air Fleet formed in 1941. It was roughly contemporary with the Japanese formation of two-carrier divisions which operated as a single unit. Both practices contrast with US practice, which was often to keep carriers dispersed so that a successful attack would neutralise only one of them. British pre-war practice has been forgotten because, once war broke out in 1939, the Royal Navy was compelled to disperse its limited carrier force among different operational formations.

The British Government pursued arms control in the expectation that the Ten Year Rule was valid. The 1920s were indeed an era of relatively good feeling. When money became tight, the navy's assumption that it was building a force to deal with a possible Japanese war was not difficult to attack. About 1929, when he was Chancellor of the Exchequer, Winston Churchill formally asked the Foreign Office whether there was any chance of war with Japan in the future. It said no. For the next three years the Admiralty had to find alternative justifications for the navy's existence.[6] Then Japan began to move, initially into Manchuria in 1931. The British were concerned to defend not so much the formal empire in the East as the informal or commercial empire in China and Thailand. In theory it did not much matter who controlled these countries as long as British commercial interests were undisturbed. In 1932 the Japanese briefly occupied Shanghai. Their rough handling of Britons and their property demonstrated that the era of good feelings was over. The Ten Year Rule was abandoned, not because of growing turmoil in Europe (which was recognised as a possible precursor of war), but initially because the interwar fear of Japan seemed more and more realistic. As a symbol of the change, the committee formed to develop proposals for the coming League of Nations Disarmament Conference was transformed into the Defence Requirements Committee, which was assigned to counteract the ill effects of the Ten Year Rule.

The prospect of war with Japan shaped the interwar Royal Navy and, by extension, interwar British carrier design and practice. Ultimately the naval weapon against Japan was blockade. To make that possible, the main Japanese fleet had to be destroyed, as otherwise it could sweep away any blockading craft – a submarine blockade was not envisaged. The Naval Staff looked back to the successful blockade of Germany during the First World War. That operation had been covered by a Grand Fleet based far enough from Germany that its base could not easily be attacked. Singapore was seen as a Far Eastern equivalent to Scapa Flow, far enough from Japan to be inherently secure against a naval attack or invasion. A British force at Singapore would be well placed to block Japanese imports from Europe, but not from the United States or from East Asia (Korea, already a Japanese colony, and China). Blockade had to be exercised closer to Japan.

At least in theory, in order to deal with the threat of a British fleet in the Far East, the Japanese would have to steam far to the south to confront it. Any battle would be fleet-to-fleet, without intervention by high-performance shore-based aircraft. The rub was that the British fleet could not be based at Singapore in peacetime. The place lacked infrastructure and it was hardly suited to the crews' families. British interwar policy was to base most of the War Fleet in the Mediterranean, from where it would steam East in an emergency. The British Eastern War Memorandum was concerned largely with the logistics of this lengthy movement. Another question was how to keep the Japanese from seizing Singapore before the fleet could arrive. By the 1930s that seems to have depended on a combination of a powerful submarine force in the South China Sea and coast defences at Singapore, including land-based RAF torpedo bombers. This was a feasible proposition until events in Europe placed French Indo-China (modern Vietnam, Laos and Cambodia) in Japanese hands and thus gave them airfields within range of Singapore. This proximity, incidentally, is why the Japanese movement into French Indo-China triggered the US-British-Dutch oil embargo against Japan in 1941.

The Eastern War Plan had profound implications for naval aircraft. The fleet would not be under any air threat during its lengthy deployment East. It might well encounter long-range submarines and mines they might lay. The air threat could thus be limited to the battle against the concentrated Japanese fleet, including its carriers. British carrier aircraft might well be able to neutralise the Japanese carriers, if they could strike before the Japanese found them (other navies had much the same idea of future carrier vs carrier warfare). The British even had reason to be optimistic in what they saw as superior scouting performance by their aircraft. That was not a matter of better range, but rather of better navigation over the sea, as demonstrated in exercises.

The naval situation changed dramatically from about 1934 on. That year the British formally recognised the rearming Germans as a likely future enemy; to some extent the Ten Year Rule was replaced by a new five-year rule which set 1939 as the year of maximum danger. To some extent the Royal Navy argued that Germany was only a potential enemy whereas Japan was daily attacking vital British resources in the Far East.

This new kind of problem soon became more urgent. The League of Nations, on which the British Government depended to prevent any new World War, condemned the 1935 Italian invasion of Ethiopia. For a time it seemed that Britain would have to fight Italy in the Mediterranean. Suddenly the problem of naval warfare in the face of a large land-based air force was quite real. This crisis was evident even in late 1934, before the invasion proper. The British realised that their fleet in the central or eastern Mediterranean might find itself under continuous air threat. The main fleet base at Malta suddenly seemed untenable and the fleet withdrew to Alexandria in Egypt, to an extemporised base. Although the British dominated Egypt at the time, they had never built up a permanent naval base there. Fortunately for them, since the First World War the Royal Navy had worked on what it called the Mobile Naval Base Organisation (MNBO).

British naval aircraft might well be able to neutralise the Italian fleet, but no one believed that they could permanently neutralise airfields. This change seems to have been the basis of the dramatic shift in British carrier design, from the two-hangar *Ark Royal* (which had a capacity similar to that of the largest US carriers) to the armoured-hangar carriers (*Illustrious* class), with half the capacity but with some ability to preserve an air striking force in the face of air attack.

Even after the immediate prospect of a Mediterranean war receded, growing German power and hostility raised the likelihood of a wider European war within a few years – again, against a power with a large land-based air arm. The Royal Navy began to see aircraft as a powerful anti-shipping threat. It rolled out a large programme of anti-aircraft ships specifically to defend merchant shipping.

Ironically, through at least the end of 1937 DNAD continued to concentrate on the naval air requirements of a Far Eastern war, to the extent of rejecting a question by CinC Home Fleet about provisions for naval aviation in a European war. It seems to have taken the Admiralty Board to reverse naval air policy (in favour of a heavy fighter complement for carriers) in 1938, probably because the advent of radar (then called RDF) had changed the situation dramatically.

In contemplating war against Japan and then against Germany and Italy, British naval strategists thought of battleships as the ultimate arbiters of sea power, the theory being that only a battleship could sink another battleship at sea. Particularly in the 1930s, airpower enthusiasts often challenged this view, but the Admiralty offered considerable evidence that modern battleships were survivable. Moreover, it could point to strong agreement on the part of foreign navies.[7] The available air-delivered anti-battleship weapons were torpedoes and bombs. Since the First World War considerable effort had gone into solving the problem of underwater protection. Experiments against radio-controlled target ships showed that it was unlikely that level bombers could hit ships from sufficient altitude to penetrate their armoured decks and do fatal damage. This view was also held by all other navies.

For the Royal Navy, the view that battleships would continue to be decisive shaped evaluation of naval aircraft. If the only way to contest control of the sea was to fight a surface gun battle, then aircraft were most important as scouts (to bring the battle about), as a means of maintaining a commander's situational awareness (which the Royal Navy called Action Observation) and as spotters, to maintain gunnery effectiveness in an area which, as at Jutland, might be obscured by mist and powder smoke. The most valuable offensive air role would be to slow an escaping enemy fleet by hitting some of its ships with torpedoes. Given the weight limits imposed by aircraft, it was most unlikely that airborne torpedoes could sink modern capital ships. In retrospect, particularly after the sinking of *Prince of Wales* by Japanese naval torpedo bombers (albeit land-based ones) off Malaya in 1941, this may seem very short-sighted. That the sinking of this battleship was more fluke than routine outcome suggests that the interwar Admiralty was less myopic than has been thought.[8]

The British were painfully aware that their enemies often sought to escape their battle line, so they saw the FAA as a means of finding and slowing down an enemy fleet – its motto was 'find, fix and strike'. The only realistic means of slowing an enemy battle line was aerial torpedoes, so through the interwar period the Royal Navy emphasised this weapon, although it did embrace dive bombing. Although it seemed unlikely that hits from aerial torpedoes, with their relatively small warheads, would sink enemy capital ships, it was accepted that they would slow them down. That is exactly what British torpedo bombers contributed to the destruction of the German battleship *Bismarck*: they inflicted critical damage which slowed the ship enough that British battleships could catch up and sink her. Because *Bismarck* had a torpedo protection system comparable to those of new British battleships, there was no prospect that the Swordfish could sink her, outside the possibility of a very lucky hit.

The British made a subtler error. Given the limited number of strike aircraft they could deploy, they planned to concentrate them against the most important targets, the enemy capital ships – against which they were likely to be least effective. Pre-war air weapons were much more likely to destroy the cruisers and destroyers supporting the enemy's battle line or, for that matter, to neutralise carriers by destroying their flight decks. The contemporary US Navy understood as much. The distinction was significant because during the Second World War it turned out that British cruisers and destroyers often operated by themselves. As such they were often subject to devastating enemy air attack. Too, enemy navies often did not expose their capital ships to air attack at sea.

The British mirror-imaged. Just as they planned to concentrate their effort against the enemy's battleships, they assumed that the British battleships would be the principal targets of any enemy air attacks. Thus they apparently showed little or no interest in dispersing carriers to make them difficult for enemy air patrols to detect. Enemy surface forces would thus be the main threat to British carriers (submarines were not seen as a significant problem, given the carriers' speed).[9] British pre-war tacticians wanted to keep the carriers near the British battle line as protection against enemy surface attack. They saw the fleet's concentrated anti-aircraft fire as the main defence against enemy air attack.

Attaching the carriers directly to the battle line had important implications. A carrier had to steam into the wind both to launch and to recover her aircraft. That could become a problem if the wind was blowing the wrong way or if it was so weak that the carrier had to steam at maximum speed to generate sufficient wind over the deck. That was true of all navies, but for the Royal Navy the question was how far the carrier would become separated from the cover of the rest of the fleet while launching and recovering her aircraft. As in other navies at this time, British carrier aircraft made rolling take-offs, the launching intervals being fractions of a minute. A carrier could launch her whole air group in considerably less than an hour. Landing-on was a different matter, however. Typical intervals might be more than two minutes. It might take two hours to recover a carrier's full air group and in that time the carrier might steam far from the main fleet. She would require her own escorts for protection, weakening the fleet itself. The time and separation penalty associated with aircraft recovery helped confirm the Royal Navy in its belief that carrier air groups were inherently limited.

The Royal Navy adopted arresting gear in the early 1930s. Unlike the US Navy, it saw the device as a means of simplifying carrier tactics by making it possible for a carrier to tolerate much lighter wind while recovering aircraft, hence reducing the time and separation penalty associated with a large air group. This view of arresting gear helps explain why the Royal Navy did not see much point in the sort of precision landing the US Navy adopted, with its specialist landing signal officers (LSOs). It also explains the very different landing technique used by the Royal Navy before the Second World War. British naval pilots were taught to land under power, much as they would on airfields ashore.[10] US pilots were taught to stall out over the flight deck, because that made for much quicker landings. Their LSOs ordered them to cut their engines before they reached the deck, which is why naval aircraft landings were often described as controlled crashes.

Another consequence of concentration on the fleet battle was the way in which the Royal Navy distributed functions among its limited number of carrier aircraft. The basic functions were reconnaissance (I), spotting/action observation (S), torpedo attack (T) and fighter (F). Initially limited engine power made it impossible for a torpedo bomber to carry a second crewman, so the reconnaissance role was filled by spotter-reconnaissance aircraft (S/R). There must have been some question as to whether slow long-endurance S/Rs could press home reconnaissance in the face of enemy fighters. In the early 1930s the FAA had two-seat fighters (Ospreys) described as F/Rs (the fleet also had single-seat fighters). As engine performance improved, it became possible to use torpedo bombers for reconnaissance and ultimately to build a single aircraft which could be used for either reconnaissance, spotting or torpedo attack – the Swordfish (TSR) – whose performance was certainly inferior to that of the Osprey. Soon after it was ordered the Royal Navy began work on a fighter dive bomber (FDB, the Skua) intended specifically to gain air superiority by destroying enemy carrier flight decks. It is not clear from surviving British tactical publications to what extent (if any) the Skua was also seen as a way of peeling supporting ships (destroyers and cruisers) away from an enemy battle line, as was the case with dive bombers in the US Navy.

Extensive tactical experiments convinced the Royal Navy that the best way to use torpedo bombers was in combination with other forms of air attack. Ideally all the attackers should arrive together. That was not a problem for torpedo and level bombers, since the same aircraft performed both functions (as in the US and Japanese navies). However, the dive bomber developed in the 1930s was much faster than the Swordfish and could not fly alongside it. This tactical idea may explain why the Royal Navy chose to incorporate dive-bombing capability in its next torpedo bomber, the Albacore (and, for that matter, in the much higher-performance Barracuda). Before the advent of the Barracuda, it

By 1942 the Royal Navy was painfully aware that it badly needed carriers, but the British ship-building industry could not construct armoured fleet carriers quickly enough. The solution was the unarmoured light fleet carrier, powered by cruiser engines. *Theseus* is shown in 1946, painted in peacetime light grey. The fighters on deck are Fireflies, with what seems to be a Tiger Moth biplane trainer aft. These ships were adequate for early post-war piston-engined aircraft, but could not handle jets unless they were rebuilt with angled decks and steam catapults. The greatest impact of the light fleet programme may have been created by ships transferred to friendly navies, often providing their first carrier experience. Ships of this type served, generally in modified form, in the Argentine, Australian, Brazilian, Canadian, French, Indian and Netherlands fleets.

The light carrier *Glory* in Australian waters at the end of the war, as a unit of the British Pacific Fleet. The aircraft visible on deck aft are Fireflies, showing Pacific insignia: a blue circle without the usual British red centre (to avoid being mistaken for Japanese aircraft) and US-style cross-bars. The aircraft forward are Corsairs. *Glory* shows the antennas of two different air-search radars, Type 279B on her foremast and Type 281B on her mainmast. They operated at different frequencies and as a consequence an aircraft approaching at any particular altitude would fade from the screen at different ranges. The difference could be used to estimate target height. Atop the bridge is a Type 277 antenna, which could be tipped back as a heightfinder. The short dipoles atop the air-search radars are IFF interrogators. The 'cheese' antenna about half way up the tripod foremast is a Type 293 short-range air-search set used for target indication. Unlike fleet carriers, *Glory* and her sisters were armed entirely with short-range anti-aircraft guns, in this case quadruple 2pdr pom-poms supplemented by power-driven single 40mm 'Boffin' mountings built in Australia. (Alan C Green via State Library of Victoria)

was an open question how or whether fighters could support an attack on an enemy fleet, since they had much higher performance than the Swordfish. Other navies came to similar conclusions about what amounted to combined-arms attacks. At least the US Navy of the late pre-war period and early war period found co-ordination difficult or impossible, even though its bombers had much higher performance than those of the Royal Navy.

Another important factor in interwar British thinking was its wartime experience of successful interception and exploitation of German radio signals. This success had been publicised after the war, to the extent that some interwar British officers doubted that radio would ever be used extensively at sea in a future war.[11] Again and again in the interwar *Progress in Tactics* series are to be found comments on the implications of radio silence for fleet operations. The object was always to avoid giving away the position of the fleet, assuming that the enemy could D/F (direction-find) radio up through the high frequency range. For example, for much of the interwar period carriers helped aircraft return home by D/F'ing their radio transmissions and then radioing the appropriate course.[12] Every time such an instance was described, it was followed by the comment that no such procedure would be acceptable in war, because it would result in the discovery and loss of the carrier. The homing beacon eventually adopted (Type 72) was acceptable both because it operated at a frequency so high that D/F might be difficult and because its beam rotated, denying an enemy the time to make an effective D/F 'cut'.[13] Virtually all intership signalling should, it was thought, be visual, although ship-to-air radio was certainly installed. Once war broke out, the first radar fighter controller, working on board

the radar-less *Ark Royal*, was informed by visual signals of radar detections by an accompanying cruiser.

The interwar Royal Navy considered itself sufficient for a one-ocean war, against either Japan or the European Axis powers, but hardly against both. The First Sea Lord called a two-ocean war his worst nightmare. He could imagine only one solution: to fight Japan first, then turn the surviving fleet against the European enemies, who had weaker fleets. That became impossible when war broke out in Europe but not in the Far East. Before war could break out in the Far East, the fleet had been sufficiently worn down in Europe that it was only barely superior to the Imperial Japanese Navy, even on paper. Moreover, war had broken out well before the rearmament programme of the 1930s, which included a powerful new carrier force, had gone very far towards completion. That tipped the balance even more heavily against the Royal Navy. From a naval fighter perspective, the only equaliser the Royal Navy had was a combination of radar and fighter direction, which offered a British fleet *including a carrier* a significant ability to deal with air attack. Without any carrier in company, the two capital ships sent East in hopes of deterring Japan, *Prince of Wales* and *Repulse*, had no real hope of beating off the heavy air attack ranged against them. As it happened, by the time they were sunk the Admiralty had already decided that in future capital ships should operate with carrier fighters in company. However, the necessary ships had not yet been laid down.

There is no question but that the Admiralty valued its air arm. Not only did it fight for control of its aircraft, but it maintained a large, expensive carrier force through the interwar period. It was sufficiently aware of the importance of carriers that during the interwar period it maintained one as part of the China Fleet, a costly way of supporting the prestige of Britain in the Far East. When war with Italy loomed in the mid-1930s (over the Italian invasion of Ethiopia), the Mediterranean Fleet war plans included an early carrier air strike against the Italian fleet in harbour – the plan later carried out against Taranto in November 1940.

The Royal Navy seems to have been considerably more aware of crucial navigational issues than its contemporaries. Aircraft could certainly find an enemy fleet, but for that to be useful they had to know where they were when they did so. In the Second World War, air scouting was often useless because of navigational errors. In the previous conflict the Royal Navy had learned to its cost that reports by fleet units were often wasted because of navigational errors. The solution adopted at the end of the war was for units to keep track of the position of the flagship and to report in terms of their relative positions. That was clearly far more difficult for an aircraft flying many miles beyond the flagship's horizon. It was much easier if the aircraft reported its position in terms of its position relative to the carrier and if the carrier could stay close enough to the flagship to know its own position relative to that ship. The navigational problem led the Admiralty to prefer two-seat to single-seat aircraft, the back seat being occupied by a navigator/radioman, who in some aircraft might also function as observer or bombardier (in strike aircraft there might be a third seat for a gunner).

In the 1930s Britain had a large, vigorous aircraft industry, but naval aircraft development was much affected by the limited number of aircraft the Royal Navy maintained. Most British naval aircraft had to be specially developed, so they could not benefit fully from design work on shore-based types. Moreover, in many cases naval aircraft builders

were specialists with limited capacity for expansion (the expansion schemes of the 1930s were focused on more urgent requirements: strategic bombers and home air-defence fighters). Limitations forced the Royal Navy into choices it might not have wanted to make.

Once the FAA was restored to Admiralty control in April 1939, the Royal Navy had to build up its own staff to frame requirements and its own training establishments. The lack of experienced pilots in senior staff positions must have been painful and there is some evidence that officers without air experience often did not appreciate what pilots could and could not do.[14] The necessary staff billets were created, but inevitably there were no senior officer aviators for many years. Even so, in 1939 the Royal Navy was building more fleet carriers than any other navy.

When war broke out the Royal Navy found that it did not have

When the Second World War ended, the Royal Navy had a large programme of new carriers on order. Two fleet carriers (*Ark Royal* class) and four large light fleet carriers (the *Hermes* class) survived cancellation, because all of them were already under construction. Work slowed at the end of the war, because the greatest priority was to rebuild the shattered British economy. Also, by 1947–8 the British government was convinced that it should not fear a major war until 1957, which was designated the 'year of maximum danger'. It was therefore acceptable that the new carriers, which were needed to operate even first-generation jet fighters, would not be ready for some time (construction was accelerated as the Cold War deepened and war broke out in Korea). Two of the new carriers, *Eagle* (a fleet carrier, in the foreground) and *Bulwark* (a large light carrier, in the background), are shown in Malta. The aircraft on deck are the standard Royal Navy first-generation jet fighters, Hawker Sea Hawks. This photograph was taken not long before the 1956 Suez operation, when the British and French sought unsuccessfully to reverse Egyptian President Nasser's seizure of the Suez Canal.

enough carriers or aircraft on board them to gain air superiority more than very temporarily in places like the Eastern Mediterranean. There was a growing sense that the navy had never been air-minded enough. After German bombers badly damaged the fleet trying to evacuate the army from Crete in mid-1941, Churchill asked whether German dive bombers had been able to run his navy out of the Mediterranean. Fighters seemed to be the answer. There were proposals for flight decks on battleships and cruisers. Instead of such hybrids, the Royal Navy began building fighter carriers – which became the light fleet carriers – on an emergency basis. Within the navy there was clearly a feeling of insufficient air-mindedness. As an antidote, a Future Building Committee (FBC) was created to develop an air-oriented building programme. Its ideas are apparent in ships ordered from 1942 onwards and it also developed an aircraft development programme. By 1942, however, British shipbuilding capacity was fully committed and many of the larger ships envisaged at the time were never laid down, let alone completed.

The effect of limited wartime building capacity was to focus the building programme not on the largest carriers but on light fleet carriers. Larger carriers were ordered, but their construction was delayed. As a consequence, most of them were cancelled at the end of the war. Only two of the wartime heavy carriers survived, to be completed in the early 1950s: *Ark Royal* and *Eagle*. There were also four enlarged light carriers: *Albion*, *Bulwark*, *Centaur* and *Hermes*. Again, construction was deferred for some years after 1945.

During the Second World War the Royal Navy converted a few merchant ships into escort carriers, some of them intended specifically to provide fighter protection to convoys. Many more were provided by the United States under Lend-Lease. Some of them were designated as assault carriers, specifically to provide fighter protection for landings. They were particularly important in the Mediterranean. The converted ships disappeared after the war, either because they reverted to merchant use or because they were returned to the United States, although the Royal Navy continued to contemplate the emergency use of escort carriers in a major war, but only for anti-submarine aircraft, as they could not possibly operate jet fighters. The wartime experience of fending off air attacks on shipping did lead to intense post-war interest in carrier fighters as a trade protection weapon.[15]

The war-built light carriers (and the larger escort carriers) could operate the full range of wartime naval aircraft, but their limitations became obvious as jets and even heavy propeller aircraft came into service after the war. Plans to modernise the six existing fleet carriers had to be scaled back to a single ship (*Victorious*) and by the late 1950s only she and the six ships suspended at the end of the war (and completed to modernised designs post-war) could operate modern aircraft. The balance between light fleet carriers and heavy fleet carriers made it inevitable that the British carrier force would shrink drastically after the war. That was aside from the dramatic fall in personnel numbers due to limited funding.

The wartime Royal Navy found an alternative source of aircraft supply in the United States, whose naval aircraft offered higher performance because they had not been as severely limited as their British equivalents. The wartime Lend-Lease programme provided the bulk of wartime British naval fighters, while British designers finally developed high-performance types of their own. At the end of the war, the Royal Navy was offered the aircraft, but it would have had to pay for necessary spare parts. That was difficult, because in 1945 Britain had few dollars with which to do so. Lend-Lease aircraft were destroyed (usually dumped at sea) and replaced, if at all, with British-built equivalents. There is, however, evidence that wartime planners intended to destroy Lend-Lease aircraft at the end of the war to ensure that the British aircraft industry would be supported by fresh orders.

The Royal Navy thus ended the Second World War with an awareness of what it needed but with only limited possibilities for future carriers at just the time that aircraft were changing radically. The British reaction to the new aircraft within existing limitations was a burst of remarkable creativity. Where before 1939 DNC could justly say that the FAA was little but a source of continuing apprehension, in the immediate post-war period it developed the three keys to operating jets from carriers: the steam catapult, the angled deck and the mirror landing sight (it also developed the flexdeck, which did not prove successful). At that time, moreover, Britain led the world in turbojet development. Somewhat later the Royal Navy adopted the world's first automated combat direction system, CDS. Unfortunately the war had been economically exhausting. The innovations proved most fruitful for the US Navy – which would otherwise have been unable to operate high-performance jets beyond the early 1950s. Continuing severe British economic problems led the United States rather than the United Kingdom to exploit other major British air innovations, particularly variable geometry (the 'swing wing'). The British did adopt the vertical take-off fighter, however, which saved British naval aviation after the cancellation of the next-generation carrier (CVA-01) in 1966. Perhaps it would be fair to say that in the two decades after the war there was in effect a trade of British technical innovation going to the United States and US managerial innovation, such as new ways of managing defence projects and pressure for multi-service aircraft, going to the United Kingdom.

Both in Britain and in the United States, after the Second World War the navy had to reinvent itself because the strategic situation had changed dramatically. Before the war, each navy envisaged a campaign against an enemy fleet or fleets to seize and maintain command of crucial seas. Strike aircraft were intended primarily to attack ships, with (if at all) a secondary land-attack role. After it, the most likely future enemy was a land power, the Soviet Union, which would probably seek to deny the West free use of the sea with submarines and land-based aircraft. The new atomic bomb seemed to offer a relatively inexpensive way to deter or destroy Soviet power and wartime strategic bombing campaigns suggested that the obvious way to deliver it was by land-based heavy bombers. Moreover, it seemed that only a large bomber could carry the sort of bombs which had been dropped on Japan. In Britain the RAF declared that it would deliver any atomic bomb Britain developed. Inter-service agreement already seems to have provided the RAF with authority over attacks against strategic targets. That accorded with the logic of a global British Empire which offered air bases around the periphery of the Soviet Union.

In this context, the Royal Navy could initially point to the likelihood that any war would be protracted, at the least because the Western powers had only limited numbers of nuclear weapons until well into the 1950s. An initial Soviet nuclear attack might well be devastating, but it probably would not be decisive. During the immediate post-war period British strategists envisaged a phase of 'broken-backed war' culminating in a build-up in the United Kingdom for a sort of D-Day after which the invading Soviet army would be pushed out of Western Europe. The Royal Navy would help ensure free use of the sea and access to crucial resources in the Middle East. The Soviets had had a large submarine fleet even in 1939 and by 1945 they had captured new German U-boat technology which, it seemed, might have overwhelmed existing Allied forces. The Soviets also had a substantial land-based naval air arm capable of attacking convoys at sea (as the Germans had done effectively, particularly off Norway) and also of large-scale minelaying (again, using technology they had captured from the Germans). These threats could certainly justify a substantial carrier fighter force, but its cost had to be balanced against the cost of anti-submarine modernisation and also of mine countermeasures. To the extent that surface warfare remained important, it was seen as a way of dealing with possible Soviet surface raiders comparable to the German capital ships which had bedevilled the northern convoys of the Second World War. The Royal Navy had had no experience comparable to the successful US air attacks on the two Japanese superbattleships *Yamato* and *Musashi* in 1944–5; it had never concentrated such numbers of attack aircraft.

All major defence programmes are inevitably shaped by available finances. For Britain, the war carried devastating costs. Lend-Lease had saved Britain from bankruptcy in 1941, but in effect it postponed economic disaster to the end of the war. In 1945, when Lend-Lease ended, the single most important British requirement was to revive overseas trade so as to save the economy. Virtually all naval construction was suspended. The ships which survived, to be completed later on, were those in an advanced state of construction. Entirely new carriers, which meant the huge *Malta* class ordered in wartime, were cancelled outright. For aircraft, the important projects were airliners with export prospects, work on which had begun during the war. A strong effort was made to preserve the air industrial base, which meant financing advanced prototypes, though not their production. An important factor in post-war British economics was the need to conserve dollars. Exports within the sterling area were not nearly so valuable as those outside. For example, a post-war Brazilian attempt to buy a large fleet using sterling accumulated in wartime had to be rejected.

The post-war Labour Government came into office determined to rebuild the country, at a cost which was affordable partly because it seemed that victory in the Second World War would begin an era of relative peace and thus reduced military expenses. Reconstruction, including the creation of the Welfare State, was probably considerably more expensive than expected. It did not help that many of Britain's pre-war trading partners on the Continent had been at least as badly damaged by the war and that their own economies did not begin to recover. In 1946 Britain was technically bankrupt and it needed a large loan from the United States in order to survive. Much of later British defence policy can be explained in terms of a badly overloaded economy.

Matters were further complicated by huge continuing British military commitments. They included garrisoning Germany and part of Austria, engagement in the Greek Civil War, replacing surrendered Japanese authority in much of the Far East and also policing unstable Commonwealth areas such as Palestine. In 1948 the British began more than a decade of counter-insurgency against Communists in Malaya. The British found themselves forced to maintain conscription (National Service) after the war, partly because the Indian Army, which had provided vast manpower, became unavailable once India gained independence in 1947. Overall, through most of the first post-war decade, the British spent a much larger than average share of their national product on defence.

By about 1947 it was clear that hopes that the Soviet Union would share Western commitment to a peaceful post-war world were unrealistic. The British Joint Intelligence Committee thought that the Soviet Union had been so badly damaged by the war that whatever aggressive designs Stalin might have, he would not be in a position to fight for about a decade. It also seemed that Stalin would not fight until he had sufficient nuclear weapons to counter the existing US monopoly. It was estimated that the Soviets could not have an atomic bomb before 1952 and that it would take them five years to build the necessary stockpile. Until then it seemed reasonable to assume that Stalin would limit himself to non-military forms of aggression, such as massive subversion in Western Europe. On that basis the Joint Intelligence Committee and later the British Government, designated 1957 as the 'year of maximum danger'. The idea of a critical year had been adopted pre-war; in 1934, the year 1939 was so designated. The US Government adopted this British reasoning.

Given the rush of new technology, obviously forces such as the Royal Navy had to be modernised, but that could be deferred to mature by the target year of 1957. Existing but obsolescent weapons could be retained in service while the '1957' ships and aircraft and weapons were developed. Meanwhile the British economy could recover to the point where production of the new weapons was affordable. The one R&D project which could not be deferred was also the most expensive: the creation of a nuclear bomb and a strategic bomber force to deliver it. To the British Government of the day, the bomb and associated systems were essential if Britain was to retain its place as a great power. Contemporary lists of British military requirements always began with sufficient power to retain the country's position 'in the councils of nations'. After 1945 sheer economic power (or, for that matter, manpower) no longer seemed to matter nearly as much as whether a country had nuclear weapons.

When the Soviets exploded their first atomic bomb in August 1949, confidence in the date assigned the 'year of maximum danger' was badly shaken. However, it could still be imagined that Stalin had to rebuild; to the British 1957 still seemed to be the key year. However, the US government advanced the 'year of maximum danger', which was sometimes called the target year, to 1954. Much depended on whether it was true, as sometimes reported, that the Soviets had never completely demobilised after the war (Soviet security made it difficult to say). The Soviets were certainly feverishly developing all the technology they had seized from the Germans in 1945 (as well as what they had received or stolen from the West during the war), but the question was whether they were deploying it in quantity.

The British (and US) estimate of the Soviet situation explains why the outbreak of war in Korea was so drastic a shock. Suddenly it seemed that the calculus of deterrence had been completely erroneous; the bomb was not deterring Stalin at all. Many in the West saw Korea not as a localised outbreak but as the beginning of something much larger. If Stalin felt safe launching the puppet North Koreans on an adventure in Asia, he might follow up with an attack in Germany, perhaps using puppet East Germans. Western mobilisation after Korea was directed not so much to develop forces to win that limited war, but rather to develop the forces needed to fight (or at least to deter) a much larger war. It is difficult to say whether Stalin actually had wider plans.[16] For the West, NATO (formed in 1949) was transformed from a political into a military alliance designed to resist a possible Soviet attack on Western Europe.[17]

For the British, the significance of the larger perceived threat was the sheer size of the rearmament programme ordered in August 1950: £4700 million, at that time an enormous sum. Interim aircraft, such as the Hawker Hunter, had to be put into production. Much of the enlarged naval programme was devoted to anti-submarine and mine countermeasures ships which were clearly irrelevant to the Korean War but extremely relevant to a possible new world war. Over the next few years it became painfully clear that the programme could not be executed as planned. Whether or not modernisation could have been achieved in 1957, August 1950 was far too close to the economic devastation of the Second World War. Naval modernisation projects such as carrier reconstruction and the construction of an entirely new fleet carrier (part of the mobilisation plan) could not be executed as planned.

The British Government found that it could not afford sufficient modern forces to fight a global war. Through the 1950s it asked whether such large forces were really needed. Its calculations were much affected by the need to maintain its place within NATO and, in a wider sense, to maintain its prestige. Throughout the Cold War, NATO was largely a deterrent, which meant that its more active members (such as the United Kingdom) felt compelled to maintain visible modern forces in Germany. As army technology developed, even small ground forces became increasingly expensive, their costs crowding out other investment. The NATO investment included a substantial air component based in Germany. Whether or not this component was particularly survivable in the face of air or missile attack, its existence was extremely important for NATO cohesion. So was its obvious connection to the British ground force in Germany.

At a conference in Lisbon in 1952, the new NATO staff created a list of target forces intended to face down the massive Soviet threat to Western Europe. Each NATO government was encouraged to pledge particular units to the force. These pledges in turn could be used internally by various services to justify continued investment. Although the NATO targets were never met or even approached, the existence of the pledges was an important factor for each government. NATO strategy included the use of a carrier strike force (Strike Force Atlantic) operating in the Norwegian Sea. It provided most of the air power in that region

and it was regularly demonstrated in annual exercises called Strikeback. The British commitment to NATO helped justify maintaining at least two large carriers through the early 1960s.

NATO strategy, however, was not necessarily the way the British Chiefs of Staff and their Government saw the world. In 1952, as the Korean War rearmament programme faltered, the Chiefs of Staff produced a Global Strategy paper which suggested that no protracted war was likely. Nuclear weapons would deter the sort of aggression which might trigger such a war. Through a series of defence reviews, the British came to distinguish three kinds of war. Hot War was World War III, increasingly seen as a nuclear holocaust. Cold War was the political struggle the Soviets were waging, in which reassurance to Western Europeans (through visible ground and associated air forces) was extremely important. In between was Warm War, proxy warfare in the Third World, much of it still a British responsibility. The disaster of Korean War rearmament showed that it would be difficult to fight even a large Warm War.

The culminating defence review, identified with Minister of Defence Duncan Sandys, was conducted in 1956–7. It was completed just after the Anglo-French-Israeli attack on Suez, which had been aborted under US and, to some extent, Soviet pressure. US pressure was effective largely because the British economy was still weak enough to be vulnerable to a threatened US-sponsored run on the pound. Like Korea, Suez could be seen as a demonstration of the limits of British military power (and its outcome could be seen as a demonstration of the limits of British economic power). Sandys saw nuclear deterrence as the main way to deal with the threat of Hot War. Given the potential of ballistic missiles, he doubted that manned bombers had much of a future, which in turn suggested that the big RAF investment in the fighter defence of the United Kingdom would soon be pointless. This was not a bad guess: the Soviets were already pursuing large ballistic missiles as preferable alternatives to bombers, although they maintained a large medium bomber force for use within Europe. Sandys could not eliminate the expensive ground and tactical air presence in Germany, but he ended National Service and therefore the expensive mass British forces. That in turn soon made it impossible for the British to fight manpower-intensive colonial wars like the Mau-Mau uprising in Kenya.

Another largely unmentioned force was also at work. Through the 1950s a variety of new technologies progressed from prototypes and laboratory work towards production. Forward planning, for example for the introduction of air-to-air missiles and sophisticated airborne radars, involved estimates of both schedules and costs. Since the new weapons and systems were radical extrapolations of past equipment, neither schedule nor cost could really be estimated. The late 1950s were full of unpleasant surprises. Also, the new electronics turned out to be far less reliable than anyone had imagined. Both in Britain and in the United States, defence programmes had to be cut drastically in the late 1950s

After Korea the British Chiefs of Staff came to view Warm War in the Third World as the most likely kind of future conflict. In 1964–5 the British and Australians fought exactly such a war against Indonesia, the 'Confrontation'. Powerful carrier forces were an important part of the British counter to Indonesian air power. Here British and Australian ships exercise in the Malacca Strait in 1965 to demonstrate resolve. From front to back the carriers are *Victorious*, HMAS *Melbourne*, *Bulwark* and *Eagle*. The cost of such power projection was high and the British Government decided that it could not afford to maintain forces 'East of Suez'. At about the same time Britain was paying for the expensive Polaris strategic submarine programme. Without the justification that mobile naval airpower was needed to fight far from European waters, two successive British governments decided to discard the British carrier strike force.

and early 1960s to deal with dramatic cost escalation and schedule stretch-out. Many first-generation systems, such as Sea Slug and the US '3-T' missile systems, offered impressive performance, but they functioned only occasionally. In the case of surface-to-air missiles, the US Navy paid for an expensive 'get-well' programme. The British tried to avoid this kind of effort by shifting investment to an entirely new Sea Dart missile. It turned out to have its own problems. It took a long time for the problems of such systems to become evident, so while they were under development and even for a time after they had entered service, thinking about new projects – such as fighters to operate alongside the missiles – was based on potential, rather than actual, surface missile performance.

During the 1956–7 Review First Sea Admiral Lord Louis Mountbatten argued successfully that the main problem of the future was Warm War and that the most economical way to deal with it was mobile carrier power. The mobile force had to be capable of dealing with modern Soviet weapons: in the run-up to Suez the Soviets had provided the Egyptians with current aircraft. Ballistic missiles might wipe out fixed RAF bases in the United Kingdom, but carriers had to deal with attacking aircraft seeking them out. Thus Sandys' decision to end RAF fighter development did not mean the same for the Royal Navy.

The effect of the Sandys review was a dramatic cut in the ability of the British aircraft industry to develop and build fighters and similar aircraft. Because the cost of a new aircraft is set both by the cost of de-

velopment and the cost of actually building a production aircraft, unit cost – affordability – depends very much on the length of production runs. In the 1920s, development was inexpensive, so there was not very much difference between the unit cost of an aircraft produced in lots of a hundred and one produced by the thousand. As the development share increased, that changed. Through the late 1950s and the 1960s, one great question was how to increase production runs so as to limit the cost of each combat aircraft. That applied to both the United States and the United Kingdom, but the British felt it more acutely because their

The large fleet carrier *Ark Royal* was refitted but not replaced. She is shown near the end of her life, in June 1976. As refitted she had the CDS (analogue) combat direction system and capacity for a small number of nuclear weapons (WE 177s, described in the ship's plans as '1000lb Target Markers Mk N.1'). The aircraft in the foreground forward are standard US Navy bombers cross-decked on the British ship: two A-7 Corsairs and an A-6 Intruder. Behind them are Buccaneer bombers. Aft is a Sea King helicopter. *Ark Royal* was never fitted with the big Type 984 three-dimensional radar of her sister-ship, *Victorious* and *Hermes*. Atop her island are two Type 965 'double bedstead' long range air-search radars and the combination of a shorter-range two-dimensional set (Type 982, the 'hayrake') and a heightfinder (Type 983, atop the bridge just abaft the forward 'bedstead'). The forward lattice mast carries a TACAN antenna at its head (the tall cylinder) and a Type 992 target indication radar (a short-range air-search set). Further aft on the island are radars used for carrier-controlled approach. The squat cylinder is a Type 963, the latticed radome abaft it housing a US SPN-35. The dish atop the bridge is for the Type 903 fire-control radar for Sea Cat anti-aircraft missiles.

The advent of the Sea Harrier made it possible to revive Royal Navy fixed-wing aviation, because this aircraft did not need a large carrier to support it. *Hermes* is shown on 2 September 1983. By this time she had been completed as a sophisticated fleet carrier equipped with a Type 984 radar and a computer combat system, then modified as a commando (helicopter assault) carrier, then equipped with Sea Harriers to fight in the Falklands. She shows the massive 'ski-jump' forward, which greatly increased the Sea Harriers' effective payload, by starting the aircraft already pointing up. The same device has been applied to conventional aircraft by the Chinese, Indians and Russians. A Sea Harrier is shown on the ski-jump, with other Sea Harriers and helicopters parked on deck.

air arms were so much smaller. Various alternatives were tried. One was enforced commonality, as in the P.1154 VSTOL which the Ministry of Aviation offered both the RAF and the Royal Navy in the mid-1960s (ultimately neither bought it). This particular project may have been inspired by the US decision, at the time not yet demonstrably disastrous, to force the navy and the air force to buy a common tactical aircraft in the form of the TFX/F-111. Another was an appeal to the export market (the Harrier). This alternative had the advantage of

promoting and preserving the British aerospace industry. Yet another option was to share production and cost with a partner, as in the Jaguar programme of the 1960s. Mixed with the need to cut unit prices was the continued need to limit payment outside the Sterling bloc (later, outside the European Union).[18] That is probably why the British version of the US Phantom had considerable (expensive) British content.

Events through the mid-1960s seemed to bear out Mountbatten's argument. British carrier forces found themselves embroiled in a variety of places, culminating in the Confrontation with Indonesia in 1963–6. The argument that the fleet would have to face advanced Soviet weapons was also borne out: the Soviets provided the Indonesians with the sort of missile-carrying bombers with which they threatened NATO in the Atlantic, albeit with first-generation stand-off missiles.

As might have been expected, the global Warm War capability was not inexpensive. The Confrontation coincided roughly with the need to decide on a new generation of carriers. At about the same time the bill for deterring Hot War came due in the form of construction of Polaris strategic submarines. The British Government of the day had expected to continue to rely on the existing force of medium strategic bombers, rearmed with air-launched Skybolt ballistic missiles. The crisis came about when the US government cancelled Skybolt (1962) and then felt compelled to offer the British Polaris instead. It was not as though Polaris submarines replaced a projected new (expensive) force of RAF bombers; they were an entirely new expense.

Although there was considerable discussion of the tactical virtues (or otherwise) of new carriers, it seems in retrospect that the overwhelming consideration was that some huge cut was needed to pay for Polaris. By this time the British carrier force had been identified as part of the Warm War East of Suez commitment. With the Confrontation over, the obvious cut was to Warm War; the British could afford the deterrent (including the army and tactical air arm in Germany), but little more. The Royal Navy argued that new carriers would be effective in army support, but they did not offer the alliance cohesion value which land-based tactical aircraft in Germany did. The NATO sea strike mission was not enough to keep them alive, either. In 1966 the decision was made not to build new carriers but to allow the existing force to run down, presumably as a sop to the United States and to NATO.

The Royal Navy now justified itself mainly by its contribution to NATO, particularly to resupply across the Atlantic and the North Sea. It saw the main threats to NATO shipping as submarines and missile-armed surface ships. The Royal Navy now specialised in ASW and, to some extent, in mine warfare. It justified its new 'through-deck cruisers' mainly for their contributions to Strike Fleet submarine defence. Their Harrier attack jets were justified largely by their ability to strike at Soviet surface ships and, later, by their ability to destroy long-range Soviet aircraft (snoopers) finding and tracking convoys so that submarines could attack them. The naval part of the NATO commitment included support in North Norway against a possible Soviet invasion. That justified continuing the Royal Navy amphibious fleet. In this context the Harriers would be strike bombers, armed with nuclear weapons (which made up for their very small numbers). This role did not justify any carrier fighter contribution to the defence of Norway, however.

None of this eliminated the fleet air defence problem, since if the British contribution to the Strike Fleet was effective, the Soviets would surely try to destroy the ships. They would use their most effective anti-ship weapons, including air-launched cruise missiles. To the extent that this point was raised, the answer seems to have been a combination of the ships' own anti-aircraft missiles and dedicated RAF fighters based in Scotland, directed by land-based airborne early warning aircraft. The Royal Navy argued that these aircraft could not possibly be scrambled to deal with sudden attacks hundreds of miles offshore. Given limited finances, no such argument was accepted by the Ministry of Defence. It is not clear how hard the argument was pressed.

As finances tightened, the naval roles were increasingly questioned. In 1982, on the eve of the Falklands War, Defence Minister John Nott argued that in a major war – the only situation he thought Britain could afford to handle – NATO would have no time at all to benefit from Atlantic shipping. Everything would depend on forces already in place, which meant that any available money should go into army and tactical air modernisation. He saw no value in the British surface or carrier fleet. The one completed 'through deck cruiser' was very nearly sold to Australia.

Argentina then invaded the Falklands, one of the last British dependencies and hence a British national responsibility. Prime Minister Margaret Thatcher refused to accept the loss of the islands and ordered

the Royal Navy to dispatch a task force to retake them. Whatever the virtues of land-based fighters in the North Atlantic, the Falklands were so far from other British land bases that inevitably carrier-based aircraft – Sea Harriers – were the only available fighter defence. Pre-war estimates that ship-based missiles would provide sufficient defence proved erroneous. It often took fighters to destroy attacking aircraft. The Argentines demonstrated the impotence of shipboard British missile defence by using the Exocet stand-off missile.

The Falklands War saved the British carrier force, not least by demonstrating that Britain still had real overseas commitments. The Harriers were forced into an unexpected but successful fighter role. Post-war they were modified for far greater effectiveness. Their life and death after the Cold War are outside the scope of this book.

THE US NAVY AND CARRIERS

US experience contrasts with that of the British. In April 1917 the United States entered the First World War. Although President Woodrow Wilson made much of the 'associated' rather than fully 'allied' character of the US contribution, US naval forces in Europe were often tightly integrated with the Royal Navy, offering US officers remarkable access to what was then the world's most advanced fleet. US naval officers were very impressed by British First World War naval aviation. British naval constructor Stanley Goodall (later DNC) was attached to the US Navy's Bureau of Construction & Repair during the war. He brought with him details of plans to convert a liner into the first full aircraft carrier (*Argus*) and the US Navy asked for his advice on its first carrier design (it was not built). The British hoped that the United States would be a semi-ally after the war and to this end it continued to supply details of carrier design. That is why US files contain British drawings of *Hermes* and also why the British supplied the US Navy with details of arresting gear in 1922 (with an admonition not to let any other navy know that they had been provided). This degree of co-operation ended by 1924, as the US Navy did not receive any information about the conversion of *Furious* into a large fleet carrier.

The US Navy of the interwar period and beyond was organised very differently from the Royal Navy. Operational control was vested in the Office of the Chief of Naval Operations (originally the Office of Operations, hence the abbreviation OpNav for Operations, Navy). However, materiel and personnel matters were handled by independent Bureaus responsible not to the Chief of Naval Operations but instead to the civilian Secretary of the Navy, broadly equivalent to a British First Lord of the Admiralty. The Secretary of the Navy was advised by a General Board, which framed what the British would call Staff Requirements.[19]

The General Board had been created well before OpNav, both for war planning and to co-ordinate the efforts of the Bureaus; from 1908 it was responsible for Characteristics, broadly equivalent to British Staff Requirements. From 1919 on there was tension between OpNav and the General Board (ultimately OpNav won).

Initially aircraft construction, like shipbuilding, was the responsibility of the Bureau of Construction & Repair. In 1921, however, a separate Bureau of Aeronautics (BuAer) was created. BuAer had a wider ambit than technical bureaus like Construction & Repair (for ship design and construction) and Ordnance: it was also responsible for aviation personnel and for air policy. BuAer developed aircraft and engines but not air ordnance, which was the responsibility of the Bureau of Ordnance (BuOrd). Although the General Board offered advice on aero-

By allowing the US Navy to convert two massive battlecruisers into aircraft carriers, the Washington Naval Treaty of 1922 led the US Navy to think in terms of large numbers of aircraft. The US Navy learned to operate its carriers with large numbers of aircraft permanently on deck, greatly increasing their capacity. In the 1930s, this practice, which required arresting gear and barriers, was unique among the world's navies. *Saratoga* is shown landing T4M torpedo bombers while others are parked at her bow. Once all the aircraft have been recovered, they will be moved back aft in readiness for another mass take-off. This type of operation demanded very precise timing, so that a large number of aircraft could be recovered in minimum time. That led the US Navy to emphasise tightly-controlled landings using LSOs.

nautical matters, in practice pre-war aircraft requirements were largely set by BuAer. However, drones and wartime armed drones were counted as pilotless aircraft, hence BuAer responsibility. Guided missiles created problems, because it was not clear whether they were the responsibility of BuOrd or BuAer. In 1966 the independent Bureaus were reorganised as systems commands under OpNav control; the BuAer successor was the Naval Air Systems Command (NAVAIR).

The creation of the Royal Air Force inspired some US army air officers, notably Colonel William 'Billy' Mitchell, to try to merge US naval aviation into a new unified air service. Without the political

pressure to deal with any perceived wartime failure, the navy was able to resist. Congress not only kept US naval aviation independent, but it passed a law which limited command of aviation units, including carriers, to trained aviators.[20] Senior officers were thus encouraged to take flight training so that they could enjoy the new opportunities. Examples included future Admirals King (the wartime Chief of Naval Operations) and Halsey (a future fleet commander). However, it also seems that the extensive war gaming (see below) which so many officers experienced at the Naval War College was also influential. It featured large air forces on both sides and it inculcated the most important features of air operations and large-scale tactics. Gaming probably explains why non-aviator admirals like Fletcher and Spruance proved effective in carrier operations.

To some extent giving BuAer both technical and operational responsibility was an admission that aircraft were too specialised to be part of the mainstream navy. By the middle of the Second World War, naval aviation was so dominant a part of the navy that in 1943 the operational and personnel roles of BuAer were removed to a new office of the Deputy Chief of Naval Operations (DCNO (Air) or Op-05). An Assistant Secretary of the Navy for Air was appointed. This was the one

The huge hangars of the two *Lexington*s provided enough space for future aircraft. These Boeing F3B-1s of VB-2B are shown on board *Saratoga* in 1929.

case in which direct OpNav control was exerted from the outset. DCNO (Air) was the first DCNO to be established (others, including Undersea Warfare, came later).

BuAer managed a substantial research organisation spread around the United States. That included the Naval Aircraft Factory (NAF) at the Philadelphia Navy Yard, to work alongside (and in competition with) civilian aircraft companies. The NAF aircraft design section survived as the Bureau's Aircraft Design Research (ADR) office. Like the Preliminary Design section of the Bureau of Construction & Repair (later BuShips) it developed sketch designs. In the case of ships, typical practice was to offer bidders the choice between building to the sketch design and developing an equivalent design of their own. In the case of aircraft, at least until 1930, the offer was the same, which is why in some important cases different manufacturers built different versions of the same BuAer designs. By that time, however, manufacturers were offering their own designs, sometimes as alternatives to BuAer's and sometimes as private ventures (presumably inspired by what BuAer was offering).

By the early 1930s the BuAer in-house sketch designs, at least for high-performance aircraft, were feasibility studies which indicated whether outline specifications could be met. The in-house designs were also used for guidance as to whether, for example, BuAer should abandon biplanes for monoplanes. The sketch designs also provided guidance as to whether designs offered by various manufacturers were acceptable. For example, in 1944 ADR sketched a jet fighter for which BuAer announced a design competition. Grumman's entry was rejected specifically because it did not meet that standard. Somewhat later, ADR sketched long-range carrier-based strategic bombers, which were wanted for the new carrier which became the abortive *United States* (CVA 58). Although the aircraft which won the design contest had nothing in common with the ADR sketch, the sketch did make it possible to lay out the flight deck of the new ship. ADR seems to have died with

BuAer in 1959. NAF itself gradually came to specialise in developing catapults. Its failure to develop a viable jet catapult had profound effects on the US Navy and on its relationship with British carrier technology.

Until 1934 the US Naval War College was part of OpNav rather than of the larger naval school system. For much of this period it acted much more as a seminar for senior officers – in 1941 all but one flag officer had been to the college – than as a normal school.[21] Before 1930 the War College had almost no permanent staff, its teachers being chosen from among the graduates of the previous class. War gaming seems to have been the core of the War College programme and the war games were used to help test concepts in war plans. The advantage of gaming was that the navy could grasp the possibilities and needs of its air component even before it had gained much experience of air operations. Moreover, the capabilities of the aircraft used in games could be biased towards future improvements. Games generally showed that carriers had both great offensive potential and great defensive weakness. The weakness taught the US Navy that they had to be dispersed, so that an enemy finding and neutralising one carrier would not find the others. That meant accepting some reduction in carrier firepower, since strikes from multiple dispersed carriers could not be co-ordinated.

The US Navy certainly agreed with the Royal Navy that battleships were the most effective way to sink other battleships, although both navies also took account of the possibility of loss to destroyers, submarines and even cruisers firing heavy torpedoes. The crucial difference between the US and British views was in the sort of war they contemplated, in both cases against Japan. US strategists expected war to begin with a Japanese attack on the Philippines, at that time a US possession. As with the Royal Navy, the decisive stage would be a fleet engagement. Victory would make it possible to blockade Japan. Again, as with

Like the Royal Navy, the interwar US Navy focused on a possible war with Japan. US planners envisaged a westward movement during which the fleet would have to beat off successive air, submarine and destroyer attacks, including attacks by land-based aircraft. That required high-performance carrier fighters and also the ability to repair carriers quickly after their flight decks had been bombed. The solution was a light flight deck (wood over thin metal) over an open hangar. Another part of the solution was a fixed catapult firing athwart the hangar deck, so that the ship could still launch aircraft even if her flight deck was destroyed. The sponson on hangar-deck level forward was part of this installation; the hangar deck itself is closed off by roller blinds. *Enterprise* is shown on 12 April 1939 with the usual mass of aircraft parked on her flight deck. In this photo the monoplanes are her torpedo and dive bombers; at this time her fighters were still biplanes.

the Royal Navy, much of the war plan addressed the problem of moving the fleet to the Far East.

The envisaged US fleet movement was very different from that of the British. Unlike the British War Fleet steaming east from the Mediterranean, the US fleet steaming west would pass through the Mandated Islands Japan had gained at the end of the First World War. Although the Mandate agreements banned fortification of the islands, it seemed likely that at the least the Japanese would use them to base seaplanes, light surface ships and submarines. Given excellent Japanese security, moreover, it was impossible to say whether they had been more heavily fortified. It was accepted that the Japanese strategy would be to wear down the advancing US fleet using light forces – aircraft as well as destroyers and submarines. They would withhold their own battle fleet, inferior due to the Washington Treaty, until after they had inflicted sufficient damage on the US battle fleet. This turned out to be a reasonable forecast of Japanese strategy.

Thus US war planners envisaged pitched air-sea battles to be fought before the US fleet ever reached the Far East. The US battle line would be more a target than a source of power and much of the threat would be mounted by Japanese aircraft. Although it was often said that naval

aircraft were present mainly to support the battle line (as in the Royal Navy), much attention went into the tactics to be used during the protracted pre-battle fleet phase of the war. Moreover, by the mid-1930s it seemed unlikely that the US fleet could steam unimpeded to the desired decisive battle in the Far East. A crucial 1933 war game showed that although the US battle line could probably preserve its numerical superiority, many of the ships would likely suffer underwater damage before they reached the Philippines. In this game, the fleet made for a Philippine anchorage not yet seized by the advancing Japanese.[22] Once there the fleet would lack any means of repairing the substantial damage inflicted en route. Ships would sink to the bottom if they stopped their pumps, as they would eventually have to. At that point US battle line superiority might well disappear.

Emphasis on the battles to be fought before any battle-line engagement was possible led the US Naval War College to develop circular cruising formations designed to deal with threats from any direction. The fleet adopted them. From a carrier perspective, the cruising formation generally *was* the battle formation (for battleships it was not, since they would fight as a battle line). The circular formations were well adapted to the anti-aircraft and anti-submarine defence of the carriers and they could adapt to the carriers' need to turn into the wind to launch and recover their aircraft.

After the crucial war game, US naval war plans changed. Instead of a thrust by the fleet directly to the Philippines they came to envisage a step-by-step advance through the Mandates. From 1935 on, for example, war games included a separate section on the attack (and defence) of an atoll in the Pacific. Full-scale landing exercises were conducted and specialised landing craft developed. The more gradual advance would gain air control by seizing islands and creating air bases for fleet support. Planners also envisaged the creation of intermediate bases for the fleet with sufficient repair facilities to solve the problem of battle damage without requiring ships to return to Pearl Harbor.

Pre-war US Navy thinking about war in the Pacific was dominated by the effects of the naval arms limitation treaties. The first major fleet expansion (under the Vinson-Trammell Act of 1934) approved only construction of tonnage to maintain a 'modern treaty navy' even after the quantitative limits embodied in the treaties had lapsed and Congress authorised only a single carrier, *Hornet*, before war broke out in 1939. US naval aviation was able to expand rapidly in 1942–3 because US mobilisation, ordered in 1940 after the fall of France, included a large carrier force. The *Essex* class fleet carriers, in effect much-enlarged outgrowths of the *Enterprise*, were the core of the fast carrier task force which won the carrier air war in the Western Pacific. This is the name ship of the class, on 20 May 1945 off Okinawa with Corsair (and a few Hellcat) fighters on deck. The greatest innovation in this class was the deck-edge lift amidships which replaced the midships centreline lift of the earlier designs. It was particularly useful because it did not interfere with the parking areas at bow and stern. Initially the *Essex* class was conceived as an *Enterprise* sufficiently enlarged to provide an extra fighter squadron, for a total of thirty-six such aircraft. As a result of a review of Pacific Fleet aircraft distribution, Admiral Nimitz proposed (and on 31 July 1944 Admiral King approved) an increase to fifty-four fighters. In November the air group was again revised, to seventy-three fighters. To provide enough fighters, Marine Corsairs were assigned temporarily to fast carriers, but later that year plans were made to transfer their Corsairs to the navy.

When war actually came, the base plans were transformed into plans for mobile bases, including towable floating dry docks and specialised repair ships.

In 1931 the US Navy planned to build two more carriers, which became *Yorktown* and *Enterprise*. It already had two huge general-purpose carriers in commission, with a smaller one (*Ranger*) building. The consensus at the top of the navy seems to have been that one more general-purpose carrier should be built, the second a smaller ship adapted specifically to battle-line functions. As in the Royal Navy, she would have provided the battle line with spotters and observation aircraft. Without such a carrier, these aircraft would have been floatplanes catapult-launched by battleships. They could not have been recovered in combat, because no battleship could afford to stop to do so. This was not a trivial point. The US Navy emphasised the longest possible gunnery ranges, which could not be attained without air spotting. Its war game rules showed that long range could be decisive, because there were range bands at which long-range fire could penetrate enemy deck armour.

President of the Naval War College Rear Admiral Harris Laning reversed this view based on war game experience. Although existing naval aircraft were limited, the war game rules were written to allow for maximum performance, particularly range performance and the weapons wielded by existing aircraft were already about as powerful (at least on paper) as those available when war broke out. The War College was able to try out the impact of large numbers of aircraft and carriers which could not possibly have been bought in peacetime. The Royal Navy and the Imperial Japanese Navy also used war gaming, but, it appears, not on nearly the same scale. Also, the War College could assume better aircraft performance, including much better navigation, than was being achieved in reality.

In games, carriers were both powerful and vulnerable, as one or two hits could put a flight deck out of action for the duration of any battle. The games also showed that carriers benefitted very little from the massed anti-aircraft fire of nearby battleships. What mattered was whether enemy aircraft found them. A fleet was far more visible than a carrier and a few escorts. Moreover, a fleet with multiple carriers could disperse them so that it was most unlikely that all the carriers would be caught together.

Harris won the day. The US Navy abandoned the battle-line carrier idea, although the weak *Ranger* was often cast in something like that role. Both of the new carriers were built to the same general-purpose design and US tacticians envisaged dispersed carrier operations. In such operations, the British concept that the carrier should not steam too far from the main fleet while recovering her aircraft was meaningless – and in any case US carriers recovered their more numerous aircraft much more quickly.

War games certainly brought out the vulnerability of carriers to air attack. However, in a 1925 war game, the commander of Blue aircraft managed, perhaps for the only time in interwar gaming, to beat off air attacks on his carrier. He did so largely because he had an enormous number of fighters, including many on board tankers his fleet was convoying (the idea of placing aircraft on tankers was being promoted by the Bureau of Aeronautics). He found that even with large numbers, he had to keep refuelling them to keep them in the air as needed. The Blue air leader was probably Captain Joseph M Reeves, Jr; his efforts were particularly praised in the account of the game and he became Chairman of the War College Tactics Department the following year. Reeves then went to Pensacola for flight training and was appointed Commander of Battle Force Aircraft. That meant the aircraft on board the experimental carrier *Langley*.

Langley had a small hangar, sufficient for perhaps twelve aircraft and a slow improvised lift. Reeves asked his pilots what they could do to operate much more efficiently. They and he came up with a radically new way of operating. Aircraft would land into arresting gear. Once stopped, they would be pushed to the bow rather than struck below. Aircraft in the park at the bow would be protected by a crash barrier. It was essential to slash the landing interval, which helped determine how many aircraft the carrier could operate, to a few seconds. To do that, landing had to be rigidly controlled by an LSO, which the Royal Navy later called a 'batsman'. Reeves' innovation worked, but it made carrier operation a dangerous business. Anyone who has watched movies of US carrier operations up to and through the Second World War will be aware of numerous clips of accidents, many of them fatal. It seems likely that the accident rate was acceptable in part because the pilots were part of the navy, rather than another service.

Reeves' innovation greatly increased the capacity of each US carrier and thus the production runs of naval aircraft. The sheer size of US naval

The *Essexes* were designed with the hangar-deck catapult introduced in the pre-war *Yorktowns*. The *Essex* class carrier *Yorktown* prepares to catapult a Hellcat, 20 February 1944. The catapults were eliminated so that additional quadruple Bofors guns could be mounted on a new hangar-deck sponson.

aviation guaranteed that its needs would be taken seriously by manufacturers. As an indication of that size, in the early 1960s a published guide to world air forces rated the US Air Force the largest (in numbers of aircraft) in the world – and US naval aviation a close second. The interwar US Navy bought enough carrier aircraft to be able to dictate the sort of performance it wanted. Moreover, its own R&D organisation provided it with advice on what carriers could and could not operate, which turned out to give its fighters considerably better performance than their Royal Navy equivalents enjoyed. Navy production runs were sufficient that it could sponsor crucial engine developments.

Naval War College game rules reflected the perception that carrier flight decks were extremely vulnerable; a single 500lb or 1000lb bomb would render half the deck unusable (British rules were similar). The carrier herself would be far more difficult to sink, at least under the same rules. The US Navy became interested in ways of minimising flight-deck damage. One was simply to add arresting gear at the bow,

so that a carrier with only half a flight deck could continue to recover aircraft. That is why the later pre-war US carriers and the wartime *Essex* class were designed so that they could run astern at relatively high speed on a sustained basis, for such reversed operations. The US Navy also became interested in hangar deck catapults, so that aircraft could be launched even if the flight deck was unusable (or blocked by parked aircraft).

When the game rules were first formulated, carriers had steel decks. Repairing a holed flight deck was a navy yard job taking weeks. *Ranger*, the first purpose-built US carrier, had a wooden flight deck because that minimised topweight. As the significance of flight deck hits became apparent, wood (laid over light metal plating) took on an important virtue. Unlike a steel deck, a wooden flight deck could be repaired in a few hours. A damaged carrier could keep fighting. It is not entirely clear whether this was appreciated when the next class (*Yorktowns*) was designed, but the successor *Essex* class retained light wooden flight decks specifically to simplify battle repairs. The *Midways*, completed late in the war, represented the alternative choice, to build the flight deck out of armour steel. That carried significant penalties in reduced freeboard and, therefore, wetness, particularly in the rougher seas in which the US Navy operated after the war.

The perception of carrier vulnerability was reflected in full-scale fleet exercises (the Fleet Problems). For example, after Fleet Problem X (1930) the commander of Black aircraft squadrons, who was Commander, Aircraft Squadrons, Scouting Fleet wrote that 'opposing carriers within a strategical area are like blindfolded men armed with daggers in a ring. There is apt to be sudden destruction to one or both. If the bandage over the eyes of one is removed the other is doomed'. It was widely accepted that evasive movement at high speed, not least to frustrate enemy reconnaissance, was the carrier's only real protection; a carrier tied down to a slow force (the battle line) was doomed. Carrier commanders pointed out that many non-carrier officers failed to understand as much and that they continued to require carriers to operate close to the slow Main Body. Discussing Fleet Problem XVII, Commander Aircraft, Battle Force wrote that 'once an enemy carrier is within striking distance of our fleet no security remains until it – its squadrons – or both, are destroyed'.

In the late 1930s the US Navy became interested in CAPs (see Chapter 3) and there was apparently some real hope that carriers could survive even if the enemy found them. This hope was reflected in the last pre-war US carrier design, for the *Essex*. Compared to the previous *Yorktown*, she was enlarged specifically to provide her with a fifth fighter squadron. At about the same time fleet commanders began to speculate on the advantages of using several carriers in combination, for example loading one of them mainly with fighters and scouts, others with attack aircraft. However, when war broke out US doctrine still called for carriers to operate singly. That continued into 1943.

Pre-war US naval planners generally assumed that they could not count on many major new ships even for a two or three year Pacific war,

because new ships took so long to build (one way out, abandoned pre-war, was to convert a few fast liners to auxiliary carriers). However, after France fell in June 1940, it seemed (wrongly) that the substantial French fleet would soon come under German control. The United States might face a two-ocean war, rather than the one-ocean (Pacific) war previously imagined. Congress approved a massive Two-Ocean Navy Act building programme. The head start it provided helps explain why so many new ships, including fleet carriers, were available for the great Pacific offensive of 1943–5 (wartime acceleration helped).

Virtually all of the larger ships approved in 1940 were modified versions of pre-war designs. Thus the standard wartime *Essex* class carriers completed from 1943 on were much-improved versions of the pre-war *Yorktown*, designed in 1939 to reflect the lessons of pre-war exercises and the end of treaty restrictions. They placed roughly the same restrictions on carrier aircraft design as the earlier ships; indeed, all the large US carriers were able to operate all operational naval aircraft through 1945.

Within the navy, there was resistance to a massive carrier programme. President Franklin D Roosevelt seems to have been personally involved in overcoming it. He considered large numbers of

To accelerate the carrier programme, the US Navy converted nine hulls laid down as *Cleveland* class light cruisers as *Independence* class light fleet carriers. The Bureau of Ships, responsible for design, initially rejected the idea as impractical and also argued that conversion would take as long as building a new carrier. President Roosevelt personally rejected this response and ordered a new study using much the same approach as in the new escort carriers being converted from merchant ships. This is *Cowpens*, 17 July 1944, her fighters parked forward and her strike aircraft aft.

The most radical attempt to provide additional carriers in limited time was the escort carrier, a converted merchant ship. Before the war both the Royal Navy and the US Navy had considered converting fast liners into carriers, but in each case the idea was dropped because conversion would take too long. The wartime escort carriers were far more austere and were available much more quickly. These ships are the converted tankers *Santee* and *Sangamon*, photographed from *Ranger*, 16 October 1942. The big ex-tankers were the most satisfactory of the wartime escort carriers and they were largely duplicated in the late-war *Commencement Bay* class, built as escort carriers from the keel up. These large escort carriers could operate high-performance fighters. In August 1944 the Marine Corps Commandant proposed that one division of *Commencement Bay* class carriers be assigned Marine squadrons specifically for close support of Marine assault troops. Navy escort carriers would gain and maintain air superiority. The number of Marine assault escort carriers soon grew to eight (with sixteen Marine squadrons) and then, in December 1944, to eighteen (three six-ship divisions), later changed to the four *Sangamons* and twelve *Commencement Bays*. By that time the navy wanted Marine Corsairs; replacing them with Hellcats would free 660 aircraft. The Marines were adamant that the connection between their assault troops and their aircraft be maintained. This connection survives in the operation of STOVL attack aircraft such as the AV-8B from large-deck amphibious carriers; the Marines see these aircraft as part of their artillery.

aircraft key to any Allied victory and he pressed for what seemed to be unrealistically high production targets – initially 50,000 and then 100,000 aircraft per year. These figures were actually exceeded; US production swamped that of the Axis powers (British production considerably exceeded that of the Germans). He was probably responsible for the urgency with which escort carriers were produced and also for the decision to convert nine light cruisers to austere carriers.[23]

Extemporised carriers became important because during 1942 so much of the large pre-war US carrier force was destroyed in the Pacific. By the end of the year only three of the seven pre-war carriers remained, one of them (*Ranger*) considered too weak for Pacific operations. Escort carriers were far too slow and too fragile to work with the fleet, but they turned out to be effective in supporting amphibious operations, initially in the North African landings in November 1942. It was important that at this stage of carrier development even the small flight decks of the escort carriers could support the full range of naval aircraft.

The Second World War brought an important organisational change to US naval aviation. Before the war, it was organised in separate squadrons (the British organisation was similar, but in some cases the squadrons were broken down into flights). Squadrons were mixed and matched to provide the aircraft for a given carrier. Using the squadron as the basic element of naval aviation made it possible for both the US

Navy and the Royal Navy to expand rapidly in wartime, as new squadrons were created independently of new ships. That mattered: the Imperial Japanese Navy regarded the aircraft as integral elements of a ship's armament and their aircrew and maintainers as parts of the ship's crew. Drastic losses in aircraft demanded that a ship be withdrawn from combat until the air group could be recreated, as in the case of *Zuikaku* after the battle of the Coral Sea. In the two Western navies, the squadrons would simply have been replaced.

During the war the US Navy took a further step. It made multi-squadron Carrier Air Groups (CVGs and CVEGs) its fundamental units, the theory being that they formed air task forces which had to work together. One indication of the new thinking was a new organisation in which carriers had seventy-three fighters on board – two 36-plane squadrons plus a fighter for the commander of the Carrier Air Group. Pilots continue to identify with their squadrons, but ships took full air groups aboard. Later the designation was changed to Carrier Air Wing (CVW) analogous to air force wings, which operate together from one base, allowing the Defense Department to describe its tactical air arm in unified terms.

The account of the post-war US Navy and its air component is complicated by the rise of several important subsidiary organisations. Beginning during the Second World War, the US Navy (like the Royal Navy) employed civilian operational researchers to draw conclusions from combat experience. In the US case, they were part of the wartime Office of Scientific Research and Development (OSRD), which also sponsored many other types of academic research, including radar development. After the war the Operations Research Group became the Operational Evaluation Group (OEG), which survives as part of the quasi-governmental Center for Naval Analyses (CNA). OEG supplied essential post-war advice on subjects such as the best fleet formation to resist air attack, fleet command and control in the face of air attack and optimum aircraft characteristics (BuAer's ADR conducted somewhat similar studies of fighter fleet air defence). OEG studies fed into OpNav and DCNO (Air) and thus were probably extremely influential. The post-war Operational Development Force (OpDevFor), later the Operational Test and Evaluation Force (OpTevFor), tested not only equipment but also key tactics. For this book the most important OEG studies were analyses of the performance of fleet air defence, including CICs and hence advice on future systems such as broadcast control.

After the war, BuAer also contracted with private companies for key studies. For fleet air defence, by far the most important seems to have

been the Cornell Aeronautical Laboratory (CAL) in Buffalo, New York. To some extent BuAer's relationship with CAL paralleled that between BuOrd and the Johns Hopkins University Applied Physics Laboratory (APL), except that APL became system developer for several important surface-to-air missile systems (Typhon, Aegis, Sea Sparrow and RAM) as well as an essential source of analysis. Before Typhon it had been supervising contractor for key missiles in the Bumblebee (3-T) series. CAL invented the Eagle-Missileer system but was never responsible for system configuration or development.

As with the Royal Navy, the end of the war transformed the US strategic situation. Initially the US Navy was interested more in anti-submarine warfare than in defence against land-based Soviet aircraft. Its view was that the Soviets would adopt late-war German technology, which the mass of surviving war-built anti-submarine ships would be unable to counter. The carrier contribution to future anti-submarine warfare would be attack 'at source' – dropping heavy enough bombs to destroy submarine shelters of the type the Germans had built during the war.[24] This idea, expressed before the end of the war, justified both a new carrier and a new heavy attack aircraft, the North American AJ Savage. It turned out that the early atomic bombs weighed about as much as the massive anti-shelter weapon for which the Savage had been conceived (the Savage had to be modified to deploy them, however). The AJ was designed to a specification calling for the largest bomber the existing *Essex* class carriers could operate.

The Second World War, and particularly the war in the Pacific, certainly demonstrated the value of the naval aviation the US Navy had developed. Once the atomic bombs had been dropped on Japan there was a general perception that war had changed and that by far the most important future role was nuclear attack. In contrast to the Royal Navy, the US Navy saw from the outset that it had to be able to deliver nuclear weapons. In August 1945 it extracted from President Harry S Truman the formal decision that all of the services would share the nuclear mission. By that time the navy was already interested in what became the AJ. The new bomber project is significant for this book

During the Second World War, even a very small flight deck sufficed to operate high-powered fighters. After the war, the Marines continued to provide aircraft for some of the *Commencement Bay* class escort carriers (others were modified for ASW). During the Korean War Marine Corps Corsairs flew from their dedicated close air support escort carriers such as *Kula Gulf*, shown on 1 October 1950. There was, however, no possibility of flying jet fighters from such ships and the US Navy even doubted that jet fighters could or should be flown from British light fleet carriers, no matter how modified. Other ships of this type were used for ASW and the post-war dedicated ASW aircraft (Grumman Guardian and Tracker) were designed to be able to operate from them. Typically such carriers had fighters assigned to them to deal with the snoopers which would make submarine attacks possible. One great post-war question was whether modern fighters could be developed which might support convoys without requiring large flight decks.

because it demanded far greater carrier air capacity than could have been justified for fighters. That capacity in turn later made it possible to deploy heavy fighters, particularly the F-14 Tomcat and their supporting heavy early warning and control aircraft (the E-2). Conversely, through the 1950s it was assumed that carriers were large and expensive because they had to be able to operate heavy bombers. It also happened that the need to operate heavy aircraft caused the US Navy to adopt the British innovations.[25]

Initially the nuclear mission affected fighters in two ways. One was the classic one of air defence. At the least, the carrier had to be kept alive long enough to launch a nuclear strike. For example, after an early NATO Strikeback exercise, British observers wrote that the crew of one of the US carriers concentrated on launching a simulated nuclear strike, after which they felt they had won the war. Their subsequent failures to deal with raids against their ship seemed, to them, irrelevant (although to some extent this may have been bluster, as the exercise was being reported by the media).

The US naval nuclear bomber programme was framed to provide sufficient range to strike targets deep in the Soviet Union. Range also offered stand-off, which might limit the enemy bomber threat. As a consequence, the US Navy became interested in defending against long-range bombers armed with stand-off missiles well before there was any concrete evidence that the Soviets had adopted exactly such aircraft to attack them. Initially, too, stand-off drastically limited the performance of the carrier-based nuclear bombers. The bomber project therefore included escort fighters. Long range also limited their performance, and encouraged rapid development of higher-performance bombers which might not need escorts. At the least, adopting escort fighters would reduce the number of defensive fighters a carrier could accommodate. From a fighter point of view, heavy bombers presented particular problems. They would probably be radar-guided, so all-weather fighters would ultimately have to dominate carrier decks. They would also be difficult to shoot down, which affected weapons and tactics.

For the United States, there were several early post-war shocks, each with its own consequences. The first drastic surprise was British withdrawal from supporting the Greek royalists in the Civil War. Up to that point many in the US government had assumed that the British, the other wartime Western superpower, would be able to maintain

European security. British negotiations for the vital post-war loan seem not to have shaken this perception. The shock was the British declaration in 1947 that the United Kingdom would have to withdraw its support from the pro-Western side of the Greek Civil War. Greece would be taken over by Communists unless the United States stepped in. President Truman proclaimed an interventionist doctrine.

The US Government became convinced that without massive support Western Europe would never recover economically. Without such recovery Stalin could take over much or all of Western Europe without needing any military force. In 1946–7 there were very large Communist parties active in both France and Italy and it seemed entirely possible that at some point they might take over both countries. This perception led to the Marshall Plan (European Recovery Act).

Announcement of the Marshall Plan led to the second shock. All of the European governments were invited to join. At this time Czechoslovakia had a Soviet-leaning government but was not yet under full Soviet domination. When its government announced interest in joining

Above all the post-1945 US Navy was designed to support nuclear strikes. Until the advent of the Polaris missile, that meant heavy carrier bombers and therefore large, or at least heavily modernised, carriers. For the US Navy, the point of carrier air defence was to keep the carrier alive long enough to launch that strike. This idea was turned on its head in the Maritime Strategy of the 1980s. The Soviets considered the nuclear level of war the decisive one and during the initial non-nuclear phase they intended to concentrate on gaining a nuclear advantage. That meant, among other things, wiping out all potential nuclear attack platforms – such as carriers. In the Maritime Strategy the US Navy planned to use this Soviet obsession to draw out and destroy the most potent Soviet anti-ship force, the long-range naval bombers. Here the first of the long-range naval nuclear bombers, an AJ Savage, prepares to launch from *Franklin D Roosevelt*, 11 August 1952.

the Marshall Plan, the Soviets supported a coup (February 1948). This coup in turn seemed to demonstrate Soviet hostility in a way not previously obvious (it was followed not too long afterwards by the blockade of West Berlin). President Truman sent an emergency message to Congress on 17 March and a supplemental defence appropriation was passed. The United States began to rearm, passing a peacetime draft.

At the time, the navy was operating under an autumn 1947 aviation plan which called for growth to 14,500 aircraft by 1 July 1952. The FY49 budget allowed for 10,700 aircraft, but at that time only 7850 were operational. Given the supplemental, the navy decided to build immediately to 14,500 aircraft for FY49, most of the growth coming from aircraft withdrawn from storage.

From the perspective of this book, the most important aspect of rearmament was the decision to resume production of nuclear weapons, leading to a situation of 'nuclear plenty' in the late 1950s. Re-armament included construction of a new super-carrier, *United States*, to support the navy's planned nuclear bombers.

Congress rejected deficit financing. To President Truman, the military budget, NATO and the Marshall Plan were all parts of the same national security programme. With Congress unwilling to borrow any money, the cost of the Marshall Plan had to be borne by the military budget. The limit on funding became apparent in November and December 1948; even the force level achieved on 31 December 1948 (about 8180 operating aircraft) was too high. The shift from less

expensive propeller aircraft to much more expensive jets reduced numbers bought. Thus in FY47 the navy bought 1103 aircraft, including 784 fighters. The next year it bought 708 (282 fighters). The FY49 rearmament budget boosted overall procurement to 1223 aircraft, including 683 fighters, most of them jets. The overall figure disguised even stronger growth: in FY47 the total weight of aircraft procured was 7.3 million pounds, but in FY49 it was 10.6 million, because many of

This view of *Forrestal*, on 17 May 1961, gives some idea of how much of her air wing was intended for nuclear strikes. Of the two aircraft on the bow catapults, the one on the right is a Skyhawk light bomber. The other is a Carrier-On-Board Delivery (COD) Trader. Just abaft it is one of her heavy bombers, a Skywarrior (A3D, later redesignated A-3). The requirement to launch the Skywarrior in particular forced the US Navy to adopt steam catapults. The only fighters visible – the only aircraft not intended for attack – are the four F4D Skyrays on the sponson of the angled deck and two Crusaders. Abaft the Skyrays is a Skyhawk on catapult alert, with a jet blast deflector raised behind it. The propeller-driven aircraft with folded wings are Skyraiders (ADs, soon redesignated A-1s). Their nuclear role was to fly in at such low altitude as to be invisible to radar. To learn how to do so, they often practised in the United States against the jet interceptors of the North American Air Defense Command – and they often managed to outmanoeuvre them at extremely low altitude. All of the nuclear bombers could also deliver non-nuclear weapons and a few years later all the types of aircraft shown (except for the Skyrays) would be doing exactly that in Vietnam. However, through the 1950s and early 1960s the nuclear mission was paramount and US carriers had large numbers of bombs on board, typically about 200.

The advents of the angled deck and the steam catapult made it possible to modernise smaller fleet carriers to operate the full range of aircraft, even the big, heavy jet bombers. This is *Bon Homme Richard* on 21 October 1961, with two Skyhawks on catapult alert and a third alongside the island; others are on the edge of the flight deck. She has two big Skywarriors abaft her island. The fighters are Demons and Crusaders. Modernisation included elimination of the after lift in favour of a second deck-edge lift abaft the island.

the aircraft were considerably larger. Through 30 June 1948, the navy operated thirteen attack carrier air groups and four (three in 1947) ASW carrier air groups. The 1948 mobilisation is reflected in a jump to fifteen attack carrier air groups as of 31 December 1948. After that the number of air groups had to be cut and attack carriers laid up. ASW carrier air groups were expanded, however.

Through 1949 a very painful budget-cutting exercise was conducted throughout the defence establishment. Ultimately it seemed that the only way out was to concentrate on the deterrent offered by Air Force nuclear bombers. There was considerable scepticism (including within the Air Force), but the US Government accepted the same logic as the British Joint Intelligence Committee: Stalin was not yet ready to fight. Relying largely on the deterrent was a calculated risk at a time when full rearmament seemed unaffordable. When Stalin exploded his own atomic bomb in August 1949, the deterrent argument was not abandoned, but the 'target year' for force modernisation was brought forward from 1957 to 1954 (the British did not follow suit).

Consequences of Truman's hard fiscal choice included cancellation of the *United States* and plans to lay up most of the attack carriers (other elements of the fleet were drastically scaled down). An attempt by senior naval officers to open the question of national strategy in Congressional

hearings (the 'revolt of the admirals') failed, CNO and the Assistant Secretary of the Navy for Air resigning (Arleigh Burke, who had helped organise the campaign, survived to become CNO a few years later). The deterrent emphasis meant that investment in nuclear weapon research continued. In 1945 it had seemed that only a very large bomber could deliver a nuclear bomb and the US Navy designed its nuclear bombers for just such weapons. However, by 1948 it was clear that there were ways to scale down warhead size significantly, which meant that within a few years even jet fighters might be able to lift these weapons. Among other things that meant that carriers operating those fighters could launch nuclear strikes.

The outbreak of war in Korea showed that the US bet had been misplaced: Stalin was not deterred, even though he cannot have had any bombs available. He did have spies with access to US nuclear information, almost certainly including the very small number of existing US atomic bombs. He may well have considered that he had a window of opportunity of his own, before the United States gained any real ability to devastate the Soviet Union. Moreover, it became clear that the Soviet Union had continued to arm, despite its desperate need to rebuild after the Second World War. That is less surprising in retrospect; it seems that the Soviet Union later routinely spent about half its income on its military. That was the only way an extremely poor country (sometimes derisively described during the latter part of the Cold War as 'Upper Volta with rockets') could compete militarily with the far wealthier West. From a fighter point of view, the most striking example was the rapid mass production of MiG-15 fighters, which were first seen by Westerners at the April 1948 Tushino Air Show. About forty-five of them were seen at the 1949 show.

For the US Navy, the Warm War in Korea turned out to entail carrier air strikes against tactical and strategic targets. As in the Second World War, they needed fighter cover. It was one thing to envisage flying a fast bomber over the Soviet Union at high altitude, where interception would be difficult. It was quite another for carrier attack bombers to strike at low altitude (to gain accuracy). Before war broke out, the driver for carrier fighter performance was the need to intercept fast heavy bombers before they could drop their weapons. The advent of fast Soviet bombers seemed to be several years away, so fast US carrier fighters were not urgently needed. Moreover, there were real obstacles, such as catapult limitations, in the way of the fast interceptor programme. Once war broke out and MiG-15s appeared in numbers in Korea, there was a sudden need for fighters capable of dealing with them and thus of covering tactical aircraft. The high-performance interceptor programme could not be accelerated. Instead the navy launched an urgent programme of interim high-performance carrier day fighters, the Grumman Cougar (F9F-6 and -8) and the North American Fury (FJ-2/3/4, initially a navalised F-86). The US Navy saw a new vital need for high-performance day fighters to support its attack aircraft in future wars. The Soviets and their allies would soon field higher-performance interceptors of their own. The immediate result was a 1952 competition (OS-130) which produced the F8U (F-8) Crusader, plus some interim high-performance fighters (such as the F11F Tiger).

The day fighters did not meet the perceived all-weather interceptor requirement, although they certainly could be directed by a carrier to deal with daylight attacks. Intelligence about Soviet air developments was poor to non-existent, but in 1956 the Soviets exhibited not only

Until the Soviets had nuclear submarines, fast carriers were threatened almost only by air and missile attack; diesel-electric submarines generally could not intercept them. Once the Soviets had nuclear attack submarines and particularly after early problems with the 'November' (Project 627A) class had been cured, carriers needed direct anti-submarine protection. The ASW escort carriers of the 1950s were replaced by older fast carriers which could be integrated into carrier formations (typically one ASW carrier with two or three attack carriers). The large ASW carriers could also be used for open-ocean ASW, but when operating with attack carriers they did not need their own fighters. This is *Bennington*, replenishing at sea from the ammunition ship *Mauna Kea*, 10 September 1968. Note her bow anchor, fitted because she had an SQS-23 sonar in her forefoot. The big mattress radar, fitted after she became a CVS, was a low-frequency SPS-37A, which was standard aboard US carriers at the time. The other radar is an SPS-30 heightfinder. Aircraft on deck include E-1Bs with the APS-82 AEW radar. For ASW carriers, AEW was valued mainly because it was also the best available surface-search radar, to detect small objects such as snorkels. Other fixed-wing aircraft on deck are Trackers (S2Fs).

new supersonic fighters but also new heavy jet bombers. The defence of the carrier against such aircraft gained urgency. As in the case of the escort fighter, it was not at all clear that a carrier-based all-weather interceptor would meet the strike escort requirement represented by OS-130. Alternatives included modifying the supersonic day fighters into all-weather bomber destroyers armed with air-to-air missiles and splitting off the carrier defence role with a specialised bomber destroyer (represented at the end of the 1950s by the Eagle-Missileer missile-fighter combination). The question of the proper mix of the two functions was unresolved through the 1960s.

Major US post-Korea aircraft development and production was possible because the impact of Korean War mobilisation on the United

States was very different from that on the United Kingdom. The US economy had been strengthened enormously by the Second World War. Mobilisation was not painless, but to considerable surprise the very large deficit associated with Korean War mobilisation had almost no bad economic effects. All of the weapons which seemed unaffordable in 1949 were suddenly within reach. Moreover, the war showed that carriers were by far the best way to deal with what the British called Warm War. The navy's super-carrier project was resurrected.[26]

The Korean War mobilisation programme included a massive and very expensive increase in the US Army. When he became President, Dwight D Eisenhower questioned its value. The Soviets had so many more divisions that it seemed unlikely that any affordable US ground force could win a conventional war in Europe. To Eisenhower, nuclear weapons were the only means of affordable defence. That meant concentrating on a strategic deterrent, largely wielded by the air force's

Strategic Air Command, while a US Navy built around carrier task forces handled proxy wars around the Eurasian periphery. Eisenhower declared that nuclear weapons should be treated like any other weapons, although it is not clear how far he ever intended to go. At least initially, the bulk of the defence budget went to strategic long-range bombers and most of the rest to the navy. The sheer size of the US budget guaranteed that the navy would enjoy substantial growth despite its smaller share. The army was deeply cut.

In an era of 'nuclear plenty', high-performance bombers and lightweight nuclear weapons, it was no longer obvious that carrier fighters would have to escort bombers to their targets. In 1956 the US Navy began a series of Long Range Objectives studies intended to sketch out the requirements of the future navy. The earliest such study pointed out that new long-range cruise missiles (Regulus and the abortive Triton) could replace long-range carrier bombers. A carrier which did not have to launch the heaviest high-performance naval aircraft did not have to be nearly so large and expensive as the current ships. It also seemed that vertical take-off technology had matured to the point where it could be fielded. One possibility, then, was to distribute vertical take-off fighters among the ships of the fleet, retaining only a few conventional carrier-based fighters and relying heavily on the new long-range ship-launched missiles for fleet air defence. The only remaining carrier attack aircraft would be a tactical bomber placing fewer demands on the carrier, hence making it possible to shrink carrier size and cost. This bomber eventually became the A-6 Intruder.

In Vietnam as in Korea, carrier aircraft fought a tactical war. The great value of carrier-based strike aircraft was that they could attack from unexpected directions rather than from fixed bases ashore, greatly complicating an enemy's air defence problem. Fleet air defence was not the problem: it was defeating an enemy's air defences. Fighters designed to deal with heavy bombers attacking a fleet were not well adapted to fighter-vs-fighter combat near objectives. *Constellation* is shown in the South China Sea, 2 October 1974, with Phantoms on board. Most of the aircraft are bombers: Corsair light bombers and Intruder heavy bombers, with a few Prowlers (EW) and Hawkeyes. The A-3 visible on her starboard quarter was probably a signals intelligence aircraft.

This path was blocked by reality. Despite all the talk of casual use of nuclear weapons, the navy never approached the point at which it would no longer have to deliver conventional bombs in quantity. Hence it was never able to discard tactical fighters capable of escorting the bombers. That was fortunate, since reality, in the form of the Vietnam War, certainly demanded this combination. Moreover, the VTOL air defence idea approached maturity just as the navy confronted another reality, that attacks on the fleet would be mounted by substantial numbers of large Soviet bombers launching long-range missiles. The short-legged VTOLs could not be an adequate defence. Attention turned to various combinations of longer-endurance fighters armed with missiles and ship-based long-range missiles.

The other major new factor of the 1950s was the sudden realisation that the navy could wield an essential part of the US nuclear deterrent, in the form of Polaris submarines.[27] The cost of the Polaris programme crowded out new carrier construction through the early 1960s, ending the policy of buying a new carrier every year. Other major naval programmes were cancelled.[28]

By 1965, as the carriers' future was being questioned, the United States became embroiled in a new war: Vietnam. Just as in Korea, the carriers' ability to strike land targets proved extremely valuable. It can even be argued that the US carrier programme and the associated fighter and attack aircraft programmes, were saved by the Vietnam War experience. As in Korea, carrier strikes demonstrated the need for effective fighter escorts, which meant fighters capable of dogfighting against agile lightweight Soviet-supplied interceptors. The fighters' fleet air

Off Monaco in 1981, *Dwight D Eisenhower* displays the sort of air wing with which the Outer Air Battle would have been fought. Most of the aircraft on deck are F-14s, with Corsair II light bombers (A-7s) and Intruder (A-6) heavy bombers, plus S-3 Viking ASW aircraft (by this time the separate ASW carriers were gone). The single A-3 was for signals intelligence, a vital role in the Mediterranean, where the Soviets had their own surface fleet facing the 6th Fleet.

defence role faded, although there was real concern that the North Vietnamese might try to strike back (they did attack some US ships offshore). Elsewhere the Soviet threat to the carriers remained. It grew considerably during and after Vietnam. After the 1967 war in the Middle East, the Soviets deployed a fleet in the Mediterranean, which greatly complicated the defence of the 6th Fleet – which was the main NATO Southern Flank nuclear strike force. For US naval fighters the great post-Vietnam question was how to balance the strike escort (dogfighter) role against the earlier fleet air defence mission. The F-14 Tomcat was conceived to fit both roles. Compromise demanded a very large aircraft comparable in size and demands (on catapults and arresting gear) to the earlier long-range strategic bombers.

Given the carriers' nuclear mission, the Soviets came to decide that their key naval task was to destroy the carriers before they reached their launch positions. That in turn defined the carrier air defence problem, since the most effective Soviet anti-carrier weapons were their air-launched cruise missiles. Through the mid-1970s many, including naval officers, questioned whether a carrier force could hope to beat off the sort of attacks the Soviets could mount. The Norwegian Sea strike force seemed less and less likely to be survivable. It was argued that the carriers should stand back further into the Atlantic and that they should concentrate on the submarine threat to NATO.

This story of fighters intended to defeat missile-bearing bombers was played out against a background of changing technology. Towards the end of the Second World War the US Navy, like others, began a programme of guided-missile development. Were these new weapons an extension of naval artillery (the province of BuOrd) or were they pilotless aircraft, hence the province of the naval air establishment (BuAer)? Since BuOrd produced the guns that armed naval aircraft, it was by no means clear that it would not also produce any missiles they carried. For its part BuAer sketched a series of Pilotless Aircraft (P/A), including air-to-air missiles. This was much more than a bureaucratic issue. The projected range of naval anti-aircraft missiles soon extended to tens of miles and by the mid-1950s a hundred-mile weapon (Talos) was close to fruition. How could or should such weapons be integrated with fleet air-defence fighters? There was also a financial aspect. In the late 1950s two new air-defence systems were being developed, the shipboard Typhon and the airborne Eagle-Missileer. Both would be extremely expensive; it seemed that one or the other would have to be dropped.

From a bureaucratic perspective, it seemed that work being done on weapons (by BuOrd) and on air systems (by BuAer) was beginning to merge. In 1959 the two Bureaus were officially merged as the Bureau of Naval Weapons, although there is internal evidence in contemporary documents that the merger was never particularly successful. In 1966 the Bureaus were split once more, the BuAer element becoming NAVAIR. There were still problems, because responsibility for some weapons was still split, but those problems did not affect the subject of this book.

The question of whether fleet air defence should be dominated by surface or airborne systems certainly did not die. Both Typhon and Eagle-Missileer were cancelled, but their roles survived in successor systems: the Advanced Missile System (which became Aegis) and Phoenix plus a missile fighter (the F-111B and then the F-14 Tomcat). Perhaps surprisingly, both turned out to be affordable and they became a synergistic combination late in the Cold War.

THE IMPERIAL JAPANESE NAVY

Through the interwar period, the Imperial Japanese Navy considered the US Navy its most likely future opponent.[29] It seems remarkable in retrospect that although Japan certainly planned to eject Western powers – of which Britain was the leading example – from the Far East, the Japanese navy apparently did not plan in detail against the possibility of British naval intervention. Instead, it concentrated on the United States.

Japanese naval war plans concentrated on winning a decisive fleet battle somewhere in the Western Pacific, after wearing down an approaching US fleet. There was apparently no theory to explain how a single defeat would prevent the United States from using its huge industrial power to overwhelm Japan later on. Post-1945 Japanese writers have generally explained that in her two very successful wars (Sino-Japanese, 1894–5 and Russo-Japanese, 1904–5) Japan had also faced antagonists which seemed to have overwhelming resources. Yet in each case a single devastating defeat had ended the war to Japan's advantage. There seems to have been little understanding that in the case of Russia the crucial element had been a revolution touched off by defeat in 1905 and that at the time of Tsushima the Russians had been on the point of moving their own very powerful army to Manchuria via the Trans-Siberian Railway. The unlearned lesson was that a more cohesive country might have continued the war beyond the defeat – which is exactly what happened after Pearl Harbor. A few Japanese who had actually seen the United States understood.[30] When the Japanese government decided for war in mid-1941, Admiral Yamamoto Isoroku, the architect of the

Like the US Navy, the post-1922 Imperial Japanese Navy found itself with carriers much larger than might have been justified by the current state of naval aviation. Their capacity in turn helped inspire rapid development. This is the ex-battlecruiser *Akagi* in Sukumo Bay, 27 April 1939. Like the British, the Japanese fully enclosed their hangars; at Midway that proved very dangerous, since such flight decks offered no protection to what amounted to magazines just below them. The Japanese also followed British practice in avoiding permanent deck parks. They did use temporary ones to speed air operations, but they equated carrier aircraft capacity with hangar capacity. *Akagi* and the ex-battleship *Kaga* were the largest pre-war Japanese carriers. Together they formed Carrier Division 1 of the Imperial Navy, which was one of three in the Japanese fast carrier task force (Kido Butai) which attacked Pearl Harbor and later attacked Ceylon in the Indian Ocean, sinking the British carrier *Hermes* and the heavy cruiser *Cornwall*. Both ships were sunk at Midway, burning uncontrollably after heavy dive bombs penetrated their flight decks.

Pearl Harbor attack, said that he could run wild for six months, but that peace would be dictated in the White House. When his remarks leaked out, Americans interpreted them to mean that Japan planned to conquer the United States, but Yamamoto clearly meant that Japan would be crushed. At least some Japanese exponents of war argued that after a crushing defeat the United States would settle rather than fight on. That argument was based on an erroneous evaluation of US national culture.

Despite the efforts of Japanese naval aviators, most senior Japanese naval officers seem to have assumed that the decisive engagement would be a battle-line fight. On the eve of the Second World War, considerable effort was expended to develop surface night attack forces specifically to wear down the US battle fleet by torpedo attack.[31]

Japanese belief in a decisive battle had important consequences. Although the Japanese understood that they should accumulate reserves, for example of aircraft, they could not afford to do so. Losses in a single massive operation were acceptable if it won the war. Given relative Japanese poverty, great stress was placed on qualitative superiority both in men and in materiel. In 1941 Japanese naval airmen were the best trained in the world, partly because they had accumulated considerable combat experience during the war with China, which had raged since 1937. Japan also had the highest-performance carrier aircraft in the world, particularly the Zero fighter. Some accounts indicate, moreover, that the Imperial Navy's emphasis on dogfighting capability for its fighters was intended to capitalise on the quality of its pilots. This emphasis probably encouraged the design of extremely lightweight (hence vulnerable) airframes.

Unfortunately, extremely rigorous pilot training produced relatively few pilots. Training requirements were not relaxed until the final phase of the war, so the pilots were turned out at a relatively low rate. Unlike the US Navy or the Royal Navy, the Imperial Japanese Navy did not rotate experienced pilots and aircrew back to provide their experience to new pilots. That was probably unavoidable given the limited number of pilots available. There was only a limited reserve of industrial capacity not only to make up for losses but also to produce new engines and aircraft. It took far too long to develop a successor to the Zero fighter. Lack of reserves was also manifested in the tactical practice of associating carriers permanently with their air groups (i.e. considering a carrier's aviators part of her permanent crew). Severe aircraft losses could immobilise carriers even if the ships themselves were not badly damaged.

Losses of aircraft helped delay the return to service of the large carriers *Shokaku* and *Zuikaku* after the battle of the Coral Sea. It can be argued that their absence at Midway was a factor in the Japanese defeat.

Relative Japanese poverty had a subtler consequence. The Washington Naval Treaty imposed numerical inferiority on the Japanese battle line in the form of a 5:5:3 tonnage ratio (Japan was 3, but the United States and Britain were 5). The US and British governments saw the Washington and London (1930) Naval Treaties as part of a wider movement towards peaceful resolution of international disputes, so they grossly underfunded their militaries. To the Japanese, it was vital to keep funding the navy because there was no way they could suddenly modernise by mobilisation. The immediate consequence was that during the interwar period the effective ratio between her navy and that of the United States was much better than the 67 per cent embodied in the treaties. However, the policy of maintaining steady investment made it difficult for the Japanese to respond to the sort of sudden technological development which marked the late 1930s. Although the aircraft were quite modern, Japanese electronics, such as aircraft radio, was not. Moreover, the relatively militarised Japanese economy did not provide the country with the kind of industrial muscle grown in the United States and the United Kingdom. That muscle developed largely out of the civilian applications of the new technology, particularly in the case of electronics. Another example was aircraft engines, whose design was developing very rapidly in the late 1930s. The much larger US aircraft engine industry was able to develop new engines much more rapidly and it could produce them on a much larger scale. At the outset, Japan enjoyed a lead for various reasons, including a willingness to sacrifice aircraft survivability, but also because the Imperial Navy enjoyed a much higher priority within Japan. Once the much larger US aircraft industry was oriented towards military aircraft, it could develop new ones far more quickly; the Japanese lead could not and would not last.

Within the Imperial Navy, one faction favoured the treaties as insurance against Western attack, but the 'Fleet Faction' considered the ratio an unacceptable humiliation.[32] Rejection of the ratio was coupled with belief that battleships continued to be the arbiters of naval warfare (the ratio did not affect shore-based aircraft, so if aircraft became dominant, the ratio might be meaningless). The Fleet Faction which rejected the treaties became dominant (at least in the Imperial Navy) after Japan failed to overturn the ratios at the 1930 London Conference (Japan did gain a larger cruiser ratio). In 1934 Japan announced her withdrawal from the Washington Treaty, effective in 1936. The main consequence of withdrawal was that despite her small economy, Japan could build the immense *Yamato* class battleships as well as two large fleet carriers (*Shokaku* and *Zuikaku*).

Overall, Japanese policy was to meet Western numerical superiority

with equalisers – both technological and human. Technological examples included fast midget submarines and the long-range Type 93 oxygen torpedo, often called the 'Long Lance' in the West. The Japanese sometimes relied on a mystical belief in their greater inherent human quality.

The Imperial Japanese Navy does not seem to have faced any attempt to form a single air service. Its organisation broadly mirrored that of the US Navy, with a staff (in its case, the Naval General Staff corresponding to the US Navy's OpNav) and separate technical bureaus.[33] The latter were the responsibility of the Navy Minister, who might be considered analogous to the US Secretary of the Navy or to the British First Lord. Unlike them, he was a naval officer (active or retired) who could

During the war the Imperial Japanese Navy tried desperately to build carriers to replace the four lost at Midway and to build up to a nine- (rather than six-) carrier fast task force. Given limited shipbuilding resources, the pre-war *Hiryu* class (*Hiryu* and *Soryu*, lost at Midway) was chosen as a basis for a six-ship *Unryu* class (all other war-built fleet carriers were single ships or conversions). They had a somewhat larger island, but continued the standard pattern of avoiding any obstructions on the flight deck. These ships had two rather than three lifts. As this photograph shows, the Japanese, unlike the British and the Americans, did not use catapults. *Katsuragi* is shown at Kure on 14 October 1945, her amidships lift having been blown out by bombing. This photo was taken by the seaplane tender *St. George*.

impose his own ideas on the navy. The Navy Minister dealt with the Japanese Diet (parliament), which provided funding. Among his eight bureaus was the Japanese equivalent to BuAer.

The chief of the Naval General Staff corresponded broadly to the US Chief of Naval Operations, but he had less power within the Imperial Navy. In 1941, for example, he argued against the attack on Pearl Harbor and other US possessions, on the ground that the United States would not enter the war if Japan limited her attack to European colonies. He was forced to back down when Combined Fleet commander Admiral Yamamoto Isoroku threatened to resign unless his plan to attack Pearl Harbor was approved.

Another important difference between the Japanese and US organisations was that the Japanese made very little attempt to co-ordinate their army and navy. It took the Emperor to decide between their views. For example, in 1933 the army advocated an eventual advance north into Siberia, once Manchuria had been conquered. The Imperial Navy preferred an advance to the south, to seize the resources of the European colonies and China. The opposing factions were called 'Strike North' and 'Strike South'. The Emperor favoured 'Strike South' and the Imperial Navy received additional resources on that basis. The Emperor again favoured 'Strike South' in 1936 after nationalist army officers tried to overthrow the Japanese government and this decision was repeated several times after that until in 1941 the Japanese did attack to the south. Several times the Imperial Navy found itself having to convince the army General Staff to provide the resources it needed or wanted both for the initial advance and for further operations in places like Guadalcanal and Midway. During the war there was considerable duplication of resources, to the point where the army found itself building its own escort carriers and transport submarines. Tactical co-ordination was limited at best.

France was the other Washington Treaty signatory which converted a capital ship (in this case a battleship) into a carrier, *Béarn* (the Italians did not build any carriers during the interwar period, but the Italian navy tried to obtain them). However, the interwar French Navy emphasised shore-based aircraft, because it had bases around the Mediterranean (in the Levant and North Africa as well as in France), from which its aircraft could track and attack its main enemy, the Royal Italian Navy. The difference from Italy was that the French navy controlled these aircraft, whereas in Italy shore-based aircraft, other than floatplanes, were operated by the Italian air force, which had little interest in naval operations. *Béarn* operated fighters, but they seem to have been of limited importance (fighter tactics did not figure in the 1938 summary of naval air operations used as a text by the Higher Naval School, roughly a combination of the US Naval War College and the Naval Postgraduate School). The situation changed as the Germans built a fleet capable of raiding French Atlantic trade. Carriers suddenly became much more important and the French ordered two under their 1938 programme, plus a third in April 1940. The French navy also adopted dive bombing from carriers and shore bases (its dive bombers fought in support of the French army in 1940). For this book the most important consequence of the French carrier programme was the order for eighty-one Grumman G-36As (modified F4F-3s), which the British took over when France fell; they became the first modern single-seat fighters in the Fleet Air Arm. The order was urgent because at the time the standard French carrier fighter was the parasol-winged open-cockpit Dewoitine 373/376, powered by an 848hp (metric) Gnome-Rhône engine giving a maximum speed of 340km/h (211mph) and a service ceiling of 10,000m (32,800ft). It was thus comparable to the US F3F and the British Sea Gladiator, but nothing better was in prospect.

As in the United States, aircraft were initially the responsibility of the ship designers, but an Aeronautics Bureau was hived off. Also as in the United States, it was responsible for both technology and air policy. Like the interwar BuAer, it attracted all air-minded naval officers. Perhaps the most obvious organisational difference between the two navies was that the Japanese made no effort to ensure that only officers trained in aviation could command air organisations and ships. Nor is

naval aviators had achieved a much better position relative to other naval communities than had their equivalents in the US and Royal Navies. For example, it was reported that the Bureau of Aeronautics had been elevated to a division of the Imperial Navy, its chief granted direct access to the Emperor.

The Imperial Japanese Navy emerged from the First World War still heavily affected by British practice, both tactical and technical. Although Japan laid down a carrier in 1918, the origin of Japanese carrier aviation is probably traceable to the visit of a British mission led by the Master of Semphill in 1921. It provided examples of British prototype carrier aircraft and, more importantly, an explanation of British practices. The Japanese adopted the British concept of carrier operation, in which hangar capacity equated to aircraft capacity. The contrast between Japanese and US carrier operating practices explains why, at Midway, three US carriers had about as many aircraft as four Japanese.

it clear that war gaming had anything like the same impact on non-aviation officers.

Perhaps the vital point was that in each navy the Bureau of Aeronautics attracted officers who saw aviation as the crucial factor in future naval warfare. In the United States the prophet of naval aviation was Rear Admiral William A Moffett. Moffett died in an airship crash in 1933 and his great patron, Chief of Naval Operations Admiral William S Pratt, left office the same year. The result was some decline in the priority enjoyed by US naval aviation during the run-up to the Second World War. In Japan Moffett's equivalent was Rear Admiral Yamamoto Isoroku. He headed the BuAer Technical Office in 1931–4 and then the Japanese BuAer as a whole. He rose to command the Combined Fleet by 1941. As chief of aeronautics, Yamamoto was personally responsible for developing the navy's land-based bombers. Their existence in turn determined the kind of fighter the Imperial Navy would wield in 1941. Presumably Yamamoto's aviation experience led him to envisage a decisive long-range air strike against Pearl Harbor.

There seem to have been important differences between the ways in which the two navies functioned, perhaps mirroring their parent societies. The Imperial Japanese Navy seems to have been much more conducive to forming factions unwilling or unable to communicate, such as the 'Fleet Faction' wedded to heavy-gun capital ships (and to rejection of the treaties, with their battleship ratios tipped against Japan). Similarly, Japanese naval air enthusiasts seem to have been more willing to believe that existing air technology had made all surface fleets obsolete. They certainly developed the ability to hit manoeuvring ships, claiming much higher hitting rates than were ever realised in practice. Moreover, they rejected all claims that such ships might survive their weapons, such as torpedoes with warheads substantially smaller than those of surface or submarine torpedoes. In 1941 it seems that Japanese

Four US-supplied Banshees fly above the Canadian light carrier *Bonaventure*, the visible part of a lengthy attempt by the Royal Canadian Navy to obtain modern jets to replace the Sea Furies and other piston engine aircraft it obtained with its first carrier *Magnificent* (on loan 1946–57). As *Bonaventure* was being completed and modernised, with a steam catapult and angled deck, the RCN sought Cabinet approval for jet fighters to provide it with sufficient air defence in its ASW mission. Canada approached the US Navy rather than the Royal Navy because the Canadian defence industry was being increasingly integrated with its US counterpart. Delays in approval made it impossible to obtain new-build Banshees and for a time the US Navy offered Panthers instead. The Canadians rejected them because they wanted all-weather fighters and ultimately it received thirty-nine surplus US aircraft rather than the sixty originally wanted. For its part the US Navy warned that the light carrier was too small; it offered a surplus *Essex*. While all this was going on, the Canadian naval staff sought a higher performance follow-on, the candidates being the FJ Fury and the A4D Skyhawk. The preferred candidate was an air defence version of the Skyhawk with an air intercept radar and Sidewinders, but the project was dropped and *Bonaventure* became a pure ASW carrier. The rationale was that other NATO forces could provide the necessary air defence.

CHAPTER 2

FIGHTERS

IT IS IMPOSSIBLE in a few pages to give a full summary of factors in fighter design. All aircraft designs are complicated because they must be adapted to three-dimensional air flows over their bodies and wings and control surfaces. Under some circumstances, for example, the aircraft's body may contribute lift, wanted or unwanted. The more complex the manoeuvres, the more complicated it is to develop an aircraft representing an appropriate compromise. For example, designers seek inherent stability, but in a dogfight a pilot wants to flip rapidly from one direction to another, which is anything but stability. Only in the last few decades has it been possible to provide aircraft with computer (fly-by-wire) control, so that inherently *un*stable aircraft are now flyable.

Naval fighters are affected by complications due to the ships from which they operate. Until about 1945 it was generally assumed that they would take off under their own power. The take-off run (in US practice, typically with 20 knots of wind over the deck) had to be short enough that a full deck load strike could be massed abaft the first aircraft to take off. That was necessary partly because aircraft had to warm their engines before launch. Although US carrier aircraft could warm up in their open hangars, that was not the case for the closed hangars adopted by the Royal Navy and the Imperial Japanese Navy (the US Navy much preferred to range its strikes on deck before launching them). Only late in the Second World War were flight-deck catapults routinely used. Among other objections, they launched aircraft more slowly than the same aircraft could take off under their own power.

Fighters over the fleet: Royal Australian Navy Sea Furies over *Sydney*, the first Australian aircraft carrier, 1949, in Sydney Harbour. (State Library of Victoria)

Later, particularly with jets, catapult take-offs were accepted, but in that case the aircraft had to come within the capacity of the catapult. Similarly, landing speed is limited. Until the late 1930s, fighters were relatively light and could land on short grass runways ashore, so there was no real requirement for a particular landing speed. However, with the advent of high-performance aircraft like the Zero and the Fulmar, landing speed increased and it took arrester gear to allow fighters to land on board carriers. For the US Navy, with its deck parks and barriers, this point had been reached much earlier. As with catapults, high-capacity arresting gear became essential to jet aircraft operation after the war. The take-off and landing issues were relaxed only with the advent of STOVL aircraft like the Sea Harrier and the F-35B and they remain for conventional naval fighters. Landing requires the pilot to have a particularly good view. In the US Navy and the wartime and post-war Royal Navy, landing was tightly controlled, either by an LSO or, later, by a pilot's view of a mirror (later, Fresnel lens) landing aid.

The clear height of a carrier hangar deck limits the stowed height of the aircraft. British and Japanese two-level hangars imposed particularly severe limits (the wartime *Ark Royal* class, however, had clear height equal to that used by the US Navy, so that the Royal Navy could use US-supplied aircraft). If its wings fold for better stowage, that often becomes a limit on wing span (if the wings fold up, rather than back, as in a Hellcat). Carrier lifts also limit aircraft size. The famous example, a non-fighter, was the Curtiss Helldiver (SB2C), whose length was limited by a requirement that two fit on a standard lift, for faster movement. Length affects manoeuvrability because the force exerted by a rudder is magnified by the moment arm (the distance between the rudder and the aircraft's centre of gravity, around which it turns). In the case of the Helldiver, shorter length also had unfortunate structural consequences.

Aircraft size determined how many a carrier could operate. That might mean how many could be stowed in the hangar (the key consideration for the Royal Navy and the Imperial Japanese Navy) or how many could fit in a deck park ready to fly (the US Navy). The aircraft size issue became crucial as large high-performance aircraft entered service after the Second World War. By the late 1940s it was an evident problem, to the point that in 1948 Goodyear Aircraft seriously proposed a solution in the form of an aircraft with a folding fuselage (the US Navy was not enthusiastic).

Conversely, the advent of escort carriers during the Second World War created a requirement for a generation of smaller aircraft which could operate from them. Post-war the new jets clearly could not operate from escort carriers and the US Navy sought radical alternatives in the form of vertical take-off fighters and seaplane fighters. To some extent the British STOVL aircraft (the Sea Harrier) was the only successful solution to this problem, although it can be argued that the capacity of the ships involved (in terms of numbers of Sea Harriers) was insufficient.

Probably the key factor in fighter development has been improvement in engine performance, in terms of size per unit power. More powerful engines make better aerodynamics and other changes worthwhile. Generations of fighters can be denoted in terms of generations of engines. For example, about 1926 the best fighter engine was a liquid-cooled V-12 producing about 500hp. It represented a radical improvement over the much draggier radial engines which emerged at the end of the First World War, power roughly tripling. The Hawker Nimrod, the standard Royal Navy fighter of the late 1920s and early 1930s, was built around it. Engines developed very quickly in the 1930s, so that by

1938 the best liquid-cooled V-12, the Rolls-Royce Merlin, produced about twice as much power. A minimum-size fighter wrapped around such an engine, like the Spitfire, could come close to the highest speed possible with a propeller. To do so, however, it had to sacrifice range and therefore endurance.

Within a few years, engine performance per pound had roughly doubled with engines like the US R-2800. Aerodynamic realities still limited what a propeller-driven fighter could achieve, so probably the most important change was in the weight the aircraft could lift. That went into qualities such as endurance. The Japanese Zero (A6M) fighter represented an alternative approach to gaining high performance with a 1000hp class engine. Its designer ruthlessly cut structural weight (there was no armour at all). The resulting aircraft could out-dogfight most contemporaries (although it was said that a Spitfire could turn with a Zero), but it was not survivable and it could not follow heavier contemporary Allied fighters in a dive.

Overall, the fighters of the late 1930s were generally quite small. Thin wings were adopted to reduce drag, which is why both the Spitfire and the Me-109 had narrow-track retractable undercarriages. Drag reduction also explains why the Grumman Wildcat (and its biplane predecessors) retracted its landing gear into its fuselage rather than its wings. The alternative to wrapping the smallest body around the most powerful engine was the micro-fighter, often based on a racing aircraft. Adoption of a smaller engine made it possible to pare the fuselage even further. In 1940 the US Navy evaluated and rejected such an aircraft, the Curtiss CW-21 and later it was offered (and rejected) the Bell XP-77 (F2L). Neither aircraft could have withstood the stress of arrested carrier landings, nor could it offer sufficient range or survivability.

Designers work in terms of lift-drag ratios: every bit of lift costs drag. Lift depends on how much air passes over every square foot of wing. The higher the speed, the more air and therefore the greater the lift. A faster aircraft can therefore lift itself with a smaller, less draggy wing. Conversely, the faster aircraft cannot achieve its speed unless drag is drastically reduced. As a further complication, the smaller the wing (for high maximum speed) the higher the *minimum* speed required to keep the aircraft in the air. Naval aircraft operation in particular requires the lowest possible minimum (stall) speed. To achieve it, from the 1920s on designers used simple forms of what might now be called variable geometry, changing the size and shape of the wing for low-speed flights. Examples included extendable flaps on the trailing edge of the wing and slats (moveable extensions) on the leading edge of the wing. In addition, controllable-pitch propellers could supply more thrust at low speed. Without these innovations, it would have been impossible to build naval fighters competitive with their land-based counterparts. The full range of speeds (at altitudes) over which an aircraft can operate is called its *envelope*; the object in naval aircraft design has generally been to stretch that envelope, particularly at its low-speed end.

Between the two world wars, aircraft designers learned to design thin wings which could handle much-increased loads. That is why monoplanes could replace the earlier biplanes. Without the new structural sophistication, a monoplane would have had a larger or much thicker wing, in either case contributing far too much drag.

To complicate things further, manoeuvrability is much affected by wing loading (aircraft weight per square foot of wing). The greater the loading, the less manoeuvrable the aircraft. There are of course many other factors, but wing loading explains why the transition from biplanes to monoplanes was also a transition to much less manoeuvrable aircraft less suited to dogfighting. Some air arms (Italian and Soviet) retained biplane fighters longer than others to retain dogfighting capacity. The break between the best a biplane could achieve and monoplane performance was somewhere under 300mph. Jiro Horikoshi, who designed the Zero, sought to maintain dogfighting capacity by introducing special 'combat flaps'. The British Spitfire, which was extraordinarily manoeuvrable, seems to have gained its capacity by using a specially low-drag yet large wing. In most cases high speed required pilots to adopt different tactics.

The Royal Navy may have been particularly unfortunate in this respect, because through much of the interwar period its perception that it would have to operate combat aircraft from surface-ship catapults affected its aircraft. Existing battleship and cruiser catapults offered end speeds of about 60 knots, which meant that any fighter or bomber designed to operate from them had to be able to take off at that speed. That in turn implied a large draggy wing; it explains why the Swordfish torpedo bomber was a slow biplane (it did not help that the Swordfish was designed just before piston engines suddenly became so much more powerful). It is not at all clear that the naval staff specifying British aircraft characteristics realised how important this limitation was or the extent to which it could be discarded once the treaty limit on carrier construction was lifted in 1936.

Range (or endurance) is a factor in fighter size, hence in the performance which can be wrung out of a given engine. Typically navies demanded longer range than land air forces, because they wanted stand-off and also because aircraft might have to search for their carriers on their way home. That made for some loss of performance in aircraft like the Grumman Wildcat (F4F) compared to land-based fighters using similar engines. The Japanese solution in the Zero was an engine which could be throttled down to continue to run on an unusually lean fuel-air mixture. More generally, piston engines were much better suited to throttling down than jets, whose spinning cores (compressor and turbine) are optimised for a particular rating. That was an important reason why the introduction of jets caused major operational problems.

FIGHTER TACTICS

The fighter weapon system (and the direction system in which it is embedded) may determine how important manoeuvrability or even speed is. A fighter pilot manoeuvring violently has only a very short time to fire at his target. What sort of weapon he has determines how long he needs to inflict fatal damage. His ability to manoeuvre and the nature of his gunsight, determine what he has to do to get into an effective firing position. With a few exceptions, fighters are armed with forward-firing weapons. Before the Second World War, most air arms' fighter tactics designed to place the attacker on the tail of his target, so that he could pour fire into it (how much fire depended in part on how rugged the target was). To get onto (and stay on) a target's tail (and to avoid having an enemy get on his own tail), a fighter pilot had to manoeuvre violently. The more manoeuvrable the target, the more difficult tail attack would be. That was particularly the case with Zeroes faced with Allied aircraft whose pilots initially concentrated on classic tail-attack tactics. It took time for Allied pilots to understand that they should never try to turn with a Zero, because that would generally put the Zero on their own tails. Only the Spitfire could turn with a Zero at all and then only at some altitudes. Allied pilots had to adopt tactics which would exploit their superior diving (and often climbing) speeds (at high diving speed, for example, the Zero could not manoeuvre).

Against bombers, a tail approach simplified fire control but usually endangered the attacking fighter, since it had to remain in position as the bomber's tail gunner fired back. The only other simple approach is from dead ahead and that is effective only against a fairly docile target. A fighter attacking from any direction other than dead astern or dead ahead had to make a *deflection shot*, i.e. had to lead the target, so that the bullets collided with it as it moved across the line of fire. Deflection shooting offered two different tactical approaches. One was a beam or high-side approach, the fighter maintaining the proper deflection by turning as he approached a target. It was particularly well adapted to intercepting a bomber following a straight and level course. The US Navy in particular emphasised deflection shooting from about 1921 on, using a wide variety of approaches to the target, including high attacks from the side which would make bomber defence particularly difficult. Other air arms, such as the pre-war FAA, taught by the RAF, favoured nose and tail approaches, but taught deflection shooting as a way to exploit opportunities which might arise. An incidental requirement of the US Navy's approach to deflection shooting was that the pilot needed the best possible view over the nose of his aircraft, since he would often be shooting at a target below him. This requirement coincided with the pilot's need to see over the nose when landing. Both explain the high canopies of the Grumman Wildcat and Hellcat.

In theory, tactics and gunsights should have developed in parallel, but until about 1940 the standard US naval gunsight was a telescopic sight similar to those used by other air arms since the First World War – essentially a tube through which the pilot looked (it was also the sight the US Navy used for dive bombing). This type of sight was usable only for dead-ahead or dead-astern shooting. For a deflection shot, the pilot had, in effect, to estimate how quickly the target was moving across his field of view so that he could aim at the target's future position (i.e. lead the target). What he actually saw was how quickly the angle to the target was changing. To get the appropriate lead angle, the attacking pilot needed both the rate at which target angle changed and the range.

The first approach to solving this problem was the reflector sight. The simplest version was a ring or wheel similar to the sight on an anti-aircraft gun. The pilot associated the different rings with different estimated target speeds (actually with the component of target speed across his own path), hence with different degrees of deflection he had to use. He aimed his aircraft by placing the target on the ring corresponding to estimated crossing speed. Such sights were of limited value, since the pilot's estimate depended not only on actual target speed but also on range. However, even the simplest deflection sights made it possible for a pilot to approach his target from the side.

The US Navy first adopted this kind of sight when it installed a bulletproof glass windshield in the Wildcat (F3F-4). The usual telescopic sight passed through the windshield, but now that was impossible, so a simple reflector was employed. It had the incidental advantage of simplifying deflection shooting.

A better deflection sight would actually measure the angular speed of the target and estimate range so as to compute the appropriate deflection. In the US Navy's Mk 23 sight, for example, a pilot kept the target centred in a ring of diamonds projected on the glass he saw. Adjustment of the diameter of the ring provided a range estimate, based on known target size.[1] Tracking the target for a second allowed the gyro to measure relative speed. Such sights were comparable to (and sometimes used the same mechanism as) short-range shipboard computing gunsights and even fire-control devices such as the US Mk 51.

Deflection shooting offered fighters hit-and-run tactics. Instead of seeking a stable position from which to fire, the attacker could dive

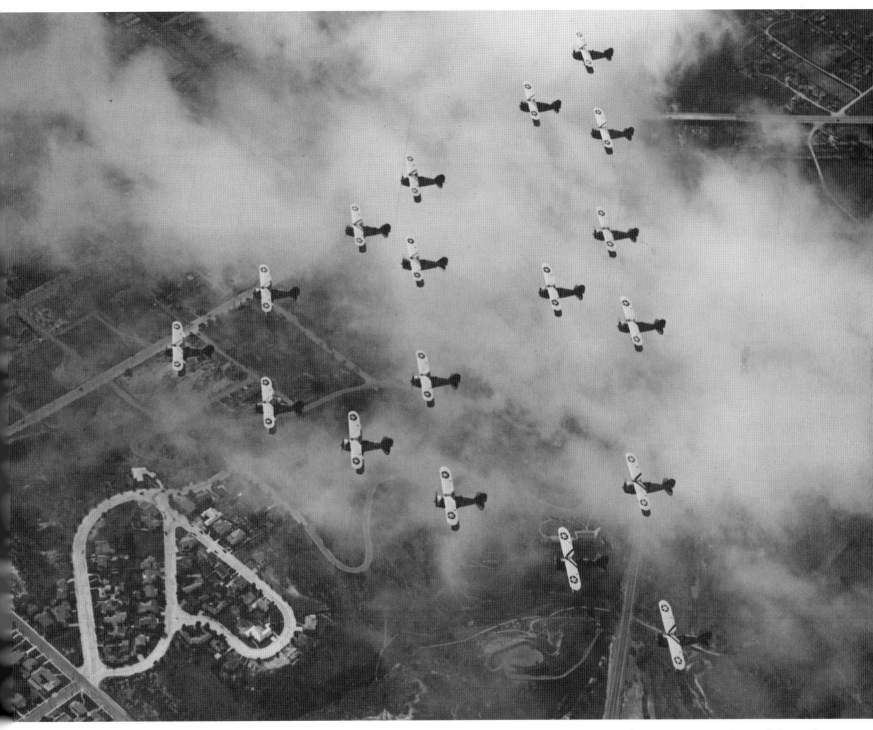

Pre-war fighter tactics were based on three-aircraft sections. Early wartime experience showed that such tactics did not work for fast fighters; the third pilot in each section had to concentrate too much attention on keeping station and not enough on covering the other two. The US Navy developed the four-plane section, using the 'Thach Weave' as a tactic. The three-plane section explains why pre-war squadrons in the major carrier navies were multiples of three aircraft. F3F-1s of VF-63 are shown on 28 March 1940.

from above past the target, using deflection to keep hitting as long as possible. Attacks would generally be from the beam or from above. Hit-and-run made it possible for faster but less manoeuvrable fighters to deal with nimble targets like the Japanese Zero (the Germans used this tactic against Spitfires during the Battle of Britain). Allied pilots learned that the Zero could not follow them in high-speed dives. At the least that made it possible for them to escape a Zero. That extended into a tactic in which the Allied fighter climbed or dived past the Zero, firing as it came within range. As long as it maintained a speed advantage, such an aircraft would be a very difficult target for the Zero. Hit-and-run also limited the time window during which the Zero could fire back at the Allied fighter attacking it.

The modern form of this idea is the energy tactic. An aircraft high above another has maximum potential energy but limited kinetic energy (speed). As it dives, it converts that potential to kinetic energy (giving it high speed). It can retain much of that speed by zooming into a rapid climb. In either case, its exposure to the enemy aircraft is limited. If it

Engines decide fighter performance. Second World War naval fighters required greater range and better landing performance than their land-based counterparts, hence were heavier and required more power. They did not become fully competitive with short-range lightweight land-based fighters until the advent of 2000hp engines. In the US Navy, the key wartime engine was the R-2800, which powered the F6F-3 Hellcat (of squadron VF-2) seen on the catapult of *Yorktown*, 6 May 1944. Note the US-type catapult bridle for a three-point take-off, which the Royal Navy adopted during the war as it employed large numbers of US fighters supplied under Lend-Lease.

can inflict sufficient damage during the climb or dive, it can destroy a much nimbler opponent. By the late 1960s such tactics were being taught to US fighter pilots facing nimbler but often slower North Vietnamese fighters.

Deflection shots offer the attacker much less time to fire at his target. Ideally his guns should be much more lethal in terms of damage inflicted per unit time. An early approach was the British adoption of eight (rather than two) 0.303in machine guns in the Spitfire and Hurricane. These guns offered volume of fire but not sufficient armour penetration. The contemporary US Navy and US Army Air Corps preferred smaller numbers of more powerful 0.50-calibre machine guns. During the Second World War, many fighters were armed with 20mm cannon. All of these weapons represented trade-offs between weight (or lethality) of shell and firing rate (how many hits per second at best) and amount of ammunition (weight: the number of bursts a fighter could fire). With the advent of jet aircraft, the available shooting time decreased dramatically and new weapons with higher rates of fire were developed. For Western navies, as the threat shifted towards large Soviet

jet bombers, guaranteeing lethality became more difficult due to the sheer size of the target.

After the Second World War, when the most important targets were large bombers, the main choices were tail attacks and collision-course attacks (i.e. deflection attacks). Generally a fighter would be directed out towards incoming bombers. A tail attack required the fighter to pass the bomber and turn towards it. That in turn required a considerable speed advantage over the bomber, as the fighter would come out of its turn well behind the bomber. The main advantage of this approach was relative simplicity, as the fighter pilot did not need any elaborate direction other than a vector towards the bomber. On the other hand, the pilot approaching from astern had to deal with the bomber's tail turret.

The alternative was a collision-course interception from roughly ahead of the bomber, the fighter being directed onto a course from which it could fire some devastating weapon. Collision-course allowed a fighter without much speed advantage to destroy a bomber. A collision-course attack was broadly equivalent to the earlier deflection shot, but on a much larger scale. To succeed, the fighter required accurate range and angle information, because the appropriate course depended on how rapidly the target was crossing the path of the fighter. Collision-course attacks and even deflection shooting at fast relatively distant targets required at the least range-only radars, which became common in US service after the war. By way of contrast, the Royal Navy did not install such radars in its early jet fighters, partly because it (and the contemporary RAF) concentrated on tail attacks.

A collision-course attack would give a fighter only a limited firing time, hence a weapon which did not need much time in which to be effective. In 1948 both the US Navy and the US Air Force were vitally interested in shooting down massive Soviet bombers and both agreed on a collision-course approach. The chosen weapon for both services was a salvo of at least twenty-four 2.75in folding-fin aircraft rockets (FFAR), a weapon inspired by wartime German attempts to destroy Allied bombers. For example, in May 1948 the US Navy issued a specification for a high-performance interceptor carrying this weapon. Some of the offers were versions of high-performance fighters offered two years earlier, but rearmed with the new rockets.

FFAR began formal development in 1952 and entered service in 1953. It turned out that the rockets were ineffective. Salvoes dispersed in flight, even over short distances. Sometimes rockets even collided with each other. The only viable alternative was an air-to-air missile. Because the US Navy wanted to use collision-course tactics, it had to be radar-guided. It also had to be large, to accommodate a sufficiently powerful warhead. The result was Sparrow, a massive, complex and expensive weapon. While it was being developed, the Naval Ordnance Test Station at China Lake proposed and developed a much simpler infra-red guided missile, Sidewinder. Unlike Sparrow, it was limited to tail chases, the advantages being that it could be fired from beyond tail-gun range and that the fighter using it did not have to loiter in the bomber's tail zone.

The British view at this time seems to have been that collision-course tactics required too much of the fighter. A tail chase did require a faster fighter, but manoeuvring was simpler and a long-range missile could obviate the problem of bomber tail fire. The British therefore concentrated on infra-red homing missiles which would be attracted by the heat of the bomber's engines. They were also interested in firing from maximum range, so their missiles incorporated small infra-red telescopes. Aiming required the aircraft fire-control system to solve a somewhat complex problem.

From the late 1930s an alternative approach to fighter combat was offered. Instead of manoeuvring the fighter, its crew could manoeuvre their weapon, guns in a powered turret. The first naval example of this idea was the Blackburn Roc, which was contemporary with the RAF's Boulton Paul Defiant. Neither was successful, but the turret idea persisted after the war in the US Navy. It was a way of providing a long-range, hence large and relatively unmanoeuvrable, aircraft with a sufficiently agile weapon. Turrets figured in abortive US attempts to develop a fighter to escort long-range turboprop bombers (the A2J) and a nose

turret was tested on board a Panther (F9F) fighter. To some extent modern wide-angle and long-range missiles are the lineal successors of the turrets.

Tactics include co-ordination between fighters. Before the Second World War air forces and naval air arms generally used three-plane sections (vees in US parlance, vics in British) as the basic tactical unit. That is why squadron (or, in the Royal Navy, flight) organisation was in multiples of three aircraft. Both the US Navy and the Imperial Japanese Navy used 18-aircraft squadrons before the war: three in a Japanese carrier, four in a US carrier on the eve of war. When US commanders complained in 1942 that they had too few fighters, the immediate solution was a 50 per cent enlargement of fighter squadrons, to twenty-seven aircraft.

However, in Spain in 1936–7 the Germans learned that the vics were ineffective, at least for fighters. The two wingmen spent too much of their time maintaining formation. The Germans found a two-fighter formation far more effective, a primary fighter protected by a wingman. The US Navy adopted this idea in 1939, based on reports from Spain, but the RAF and the Royal Navy did not. In 1941 US Navy Lieutenant Thach sought a better formation which could counter the reported high performance of the new Japanese Zero fighter. He developed a four-fighter division which practised his new 'Thach weave' tactics. Thach led successful fighters at Midway. It seems to have taken some time for his idea to be accepted within the US fleet, but by late 1942 the standard carrier fighter complement was thirty-six aircraft – nine of Thach's divisions. Later in the war the standard Combat Air Patrol unit in US carriers was the four-fighter division – the embodiment of the Thach weave.

ENGINES

Until the end of the Second World War, the greatest driver in fighter development was the evolution of piston engines. Aerodynamics limits the speed of a propeller-driven aircraft to about 450 knots. For a single propeller, the way to absorb more energy is to increase the length of the blade, which means that for a given turning rate the tip turns faster and faster. Ultimately the tip approaches supersonic speed. In physical terms the propeller blade is a wing, the force it generates being akin to lift. Near supersonic speed air flow breaks up. Contraprops (two propellers driven by the same shaft, turning in opposite directions) help (and make it possible to reduce propeller diameter), but ultimately they too are limited.

In a piston engine, such as the engine in a car, the engine compresses and thus pre-heats the air in each cylinder, adds atomised fuel and then explodes the mixture using a spark plug or its equivalent. The piston typically runs on a four-step cycle, of which the power stroke is only one.[2] Ideally air coming into the engine is as cool (dense) as possible. The greater the difference between that temperature and the exhaust temperature, the more efficient the engine and the greater its output. The greater the compression, the more air there is in which to burn fuel. The cylinder produces more power per piston stroke, but at some point heating due to compression sets off the air-fuel mixture ahead of time and the engine knocks. The Allied air forces enjoyed an important degree of superiority during the war because they were supplied with high-octane (anti-knock) fuel which made higher compression ratios possible. The cycle generates considerable heat, which has to be removed. As in contemporary cars, the fuel-air mixture might be created in a carburettor or else fuel might be injected directly into the cylinder

Through the 1930s and into the Second World War the US Navy favoured air-cooled engines, but BuAer kept investigating liquid-cooled designs to see if they offered any major advantages. That was why it bought the Bell XFL-1, which was related to the army's P-39 Airacobra. For a time it appeared that the 1941 production programme would include the XFL-1. The Bell fighter was dropped because it performed poorly compared to the winner of the 1938 fighter competition, the Corsair.

to mix with the air already there. Under some circumstances (negative g) a carburettor shuts down. On the other hand, fuel injection required a more precisely built fuel pump.

A piston engine is usually characterised by its displacement, the difference in cylinder volume between the top of the piston stroke and its bottom. For example, US piston engines were typically designated by their configuration (R for radial, V for vee, etc) and their displacement in cubic inches, as in the R-1820. Engines also had names and the British and the Japanese typically used names rather than numbers.

Engine development meant getting more out of each cubic inch and also making engines of a given displacement lighter. Among other things greater output could be achieved by providing more power strokes per minute, but that could also make for greater vibration. To get more out of each cylinder an engine had to run hotter, hence had to be cooled more efficiently (in some cases it might have a very short lifetime).

Power output can also be increased by compressing the air before it enters the engine: supercharging. That is essential at high altitude, where the air is thin, but it can also add performance at lower altitudes (hence the turbochargers in some cars). Superchargers could either be geared to the crankshaft or they could be run by a turbine driven by the engine exhaust. Typically supercharged air is cooled so that it does not add to the knocking problem at the engine. Wartime engines often also had water injection, which further cooled intake air. Water injection boosted engine power, typically above the point to which an engine could run for any great length of time, hence ratings like 'war emergency power'.

Designers sought increased power both by making each cylinder more effective and by multiplying cylinders. In theory, the more cylinders the more smoothly balanced an engine could be, but each cylinder required its own valves to bring in air and to expel exhaust and adding more cylinders added considerably more mechanism – and more chance of a breakdown. The main engine configurations were liquid-cooled vees (like car engines, the banks of cylinders at an angle) and air-cooled radials (cylinders radiating out from the crankshaft). Alternative X- and H-engines were tried but they did not enter naval service.

Designers produced two basic types of piston engines, liquid- and air-cooled. In theory a liquid-cooled engine could fit into a more stream-lined aircraft, because its cylinders could be arranged to show much less frontal area. Against that, the engine needed an external radiator which generated drag. Also, cowling, a technique invented in 1929, drastically reduced the drag penalty associated with air-cooled engines. Through much of the interwar period the British services preferred air-cooled radial engines, although some important aircraft had liquid-cooled types. In the late 1930s, however, the most important compact high-powered British engine was the liquid-cooled Merlin, which was also widely used by the Royal Navy.

The US and Japanese navies continued to use air-cooled engines because they eliminated the radiator, a single point of vulnerability which might prove particularly embarrassing during a long overwater flight.[3] Air cooling meant that air passed around each cylinder, which was finned to radiate away its heat. That offered simplicity, but it became complicated when an engine had more than one row of cylinders. Cowling made multi-row engines practical, because it could efficiently direct cooling air over more than one row of cylinders. For example, the widely-used US R-2800 was a two-row engine. The limit, probably imposed by cooling, seems to have been four rows, in engines such as the R-3350.

Jet engines were conceived before the Second World War, tested by the Germans as early as 1939 and were fielded in small numbers by both the Germans and the Allies before the end of the war. A jet is much simpler than a piston engine: air is taken in, compressed by a rotating fan and burned in combustion chambers. The resulting blast of hot air spins a turbine (which turns the compressor) and it blows out the other end of the engine. The reaction to the mass of heated air accelerated by (and ejected by) the engine pushes the aircraft forward. The only inherent aerodynamic limit is set by a shock wave generated in the air intake if the aircraft is moving fast enough. Jets were therefore the way to break the speed barrier facing piston engine aircraft. At least in theory

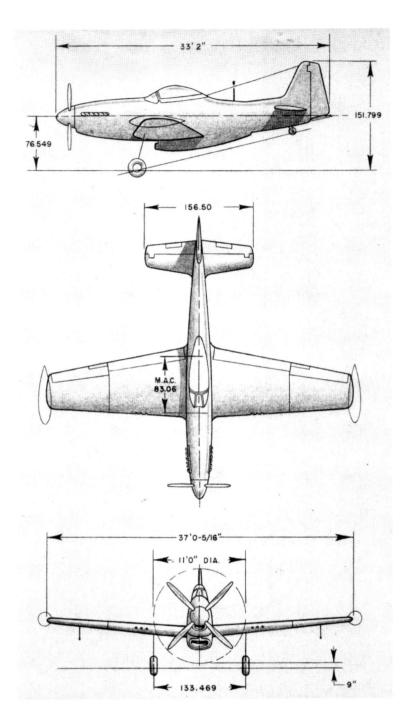

BuAer interest in liquid-cooled engines continued during the war. This is North American's proposal for a naval derivative of its P-51 Mustang; it was similar to the P-51H. Note the tip tanks, introduced because belly tanks would violate rules of deck clearance on take-off and landing. A P-51D Mustang was actually tested on board *Shangri-La* on 15 November 1944. The navy had previously accepted a P-51B in May 1943 for tests, after ADR produced a preliminary design study (D-36, Design 250) of a P-51B modified to naval requirements. It turned out 326lbs heavier than the P-51B (out of 9447lbs). Its stalling speed was reduced by 6.4mph at the cost of 15mph in maximum speed (327mph vs 344mph at sea level, 380mph vs 396mph at 14,500ft, 400mph vs 416mph at 27,500ft). ADR concluded that in general a carrier fighter could not be as fast as its land-based counterpart, although it might compare favourably in other ways. The navy required a larger and heavier aircraft with greater parasite drag. In addition, Chance Vought included liquid-cooled engines in a study of alternative fighters submitted in September 1944. It showed no outstanding advantages. Chance Vought's study included a jet, a mixed-power fighter and a turboprop. None of these was considered a design proposal.

there was no limit to the power a jet engine could generate. Jets made possible vastly larger and faster aircraft. It would be impossible to build a piston-engined 747, for example.

The force the engine produces (thrust) depends both on how much hot air it ejects (mass flow) and on how much acceleration it imparts (due to heating). The simplest way to increase mass flow is to increase engine diameter, but that also adds drag. A better way to gain power is to use the available air more efficiently, which means compressing it more highly (like piston engines, jet engines are characterised in part by their compression ratios). An alternative way to gain thrust is to draw air in outside the core of the engine, not burning it at all, but using the compressor as a fan – such an engine might be considered a very short-bladed turboprop with a duct over the blades. This is a turbofan and it is currently the main type of engine for long-endurance aircraft.

Like a piston engine, a jet engine burns compressed air: the more compressed the air, the more fuel it can burn and the more power that can be produced – and the more efficient the engine. Burning fuel more efficiently of course also makes for a hotter engine, so turbine blade metallurgy becomes a limiting factor in engine design. The compressor itself is an aerodynamic device. Most jet engines use axial compressors, consisting of stages of blades which act like small wings (the air pressure they generate over themselves, which in a wing would create lift, is what compresses the air). Like a wing, a compressor blade can stall out; a retired pilot likened the result to the sound of sand in the compressor. The description indicates that compressor problems are associated with air flow through the engine, which in turn depends on factors such as the shape of air intakes and the angle of attack of the aircraft powered by the engine. For a time the F-14 Tomcat, for example, was subject to compressor stalls, typically in one rather than both engines. The plane would go into a vicious unrecoverable spin.

Early Allied jet engines were all derived from British prototypes using centrifugal (single-stage) compressors, the same type used in superchargers. A centrifugal compressor is a single plate carrying vanes which force air out to its circumference. The larger the single plate, the greater the air flow it can handle and the greater the compression it imposes. Ultimately compressor diameter is limited because the larger the engine diameter, the greater the drag it entails. In theory such single plates can be ganged together to increase capacity, but that requires the air to go first outward, then inward, then outward again and energy and compression are lost. On the other hand, a centrifugal compressor is relatively simple. In the late 1940s, the British centrifugal engines were by far the best in the world. As the US Navy encountered engine problems, they were imported (and licence-produced) as replacements for its engines. Thus the British Nene powered production versions of the F9F Panther.

The alternative type of engine uses an axial compressor, a series of stages through which air passes. An axial engine has two great advantages. First, it does not change the direction of air flow and thus avoids energy loss in the compressor. Second, it is not limited in size, because more and more stages can be added as desired. Germans wartime jet engines (whose technology was captured by the Soviets) used axial compressors, but whatever advantages they enjoyed were largely trumped by reliability problems due to poor metallurgy. Both types of engine can be boosted by burning additional fuel in the tailpipe, a device the US calls an afterburner (the British phrase was re-heat). Afterburning was invented immediately after the war and it was often used to boost a fighter temporarily to supersonic speed. Only recently has it been possible to produce engines so powerful that they can cruise at supersonic speed. For example, the current F-35 is described as a 'supercruise' aircraft because its cruising speed is supersonic. None of the supersonic aircraft described in this book could cruise at such high speed. Instead, they typically offered less than a minute of supersonic speed. Otherwise they were about as fast as earlier sub-sonic fighters, the difference being that they could often power away from a fighter-vs-fighter problem.

Because they cannot easily change thrust rapidly, jets impose particular problems for fighters, which manoeuvre and accelerate suddenly and often violently.

British jet engines

The British developed the first Allied jet engines and they led in this technology through the 1950s and in some ways well beyond. To an important extent British engines were the insurance which made it possible for the US Navy to overcome early engine disasters, particularly the failure of the Westinghouse J40 selected for so many of its key aircraft. Although an axial-flow compressor was developed in Britain before the war by Metro-Vickers (a major turbine company), the first British jet engine to fly was Sir Frank Whittle's centrifugal-flow unit. In 1942 Rolls-Royce took over development of Whittle's engines, naming them after rivers beginning with the Welland. For the naval fighter story the significant Rolls-Royce centrifugal-flow engine was the Nene (4500lbs thrust), tested in 1944. Up-rated Nenes were licence-produced in the United States as the Pratt & Whitney J42 under US Navy sponsorship. At the time the US Navy had nothing comparable, although it was sponsoring development of the more powerful (ultimately abortive) J40. Pratt & Whitney produced an upgraded Nene (7250lbs thrust) as the J48, this engine being produced by Rolls-Royce as the Tay.

The British government sold Derwent and Nene engines (not manufacturing licences) to the Soviet Union in 1946, a development which enraged US authorities. Copied by the Soviets as RDS-45, the Nene made the MiG-15 possible and thus deeply affected US naval fighter development. Nenes powered both first-generation British naval jet fighters, the Attacker and the Sea Hawk. The Venom, which was the first British jet night fighter, was powered by a de Havilland Ghost.

Rolls-Royce was well aware that centrifugal-flow engines had a limited potential, so it shifted focus to axial-flow engines after the war, beginning with the Avon (initially 7500lbs, tested 1951). Avons powered the Supermarine Scimitar day fighter and the Sea Vixen night fighter, the two second-generation British naval jet fighters. The British version of the Phantom was powered by the next-generation Rolls-Royce Spey, a two-spool bypass engine. It was produced under licence in the United States as the TF41, replacing the TF30 in later versions of the A-7 attack bomber, but it was not used in US fighters.

Another major British jet manufacturer of the early post-war period was Armstrong Siddeley, which took over Metro-Vickers' axial-flow programme (engines named after precious stones) and produced the Sapphire (initially 7500lbs thrust). It was licence-produced in the United States as the Wright J65.

Bristol Aero Engines produced the more powerful Olympus, the first two-spool turbojet, which began as a project for a high-compression bomber engine. It was licensed to Wright as the (heavily redesigned) J67, but this engine was not produced in quantity, as it lost out to the J57.

Bristol Aero Engines merged with Armstrong Siddeley in 1959 to create Bristol Siddeley. For this book its most important engine was the

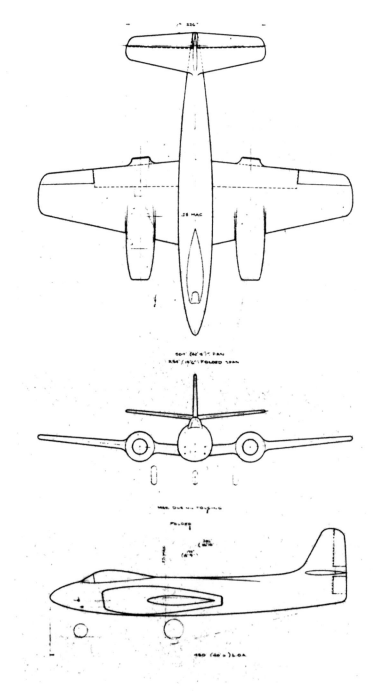

During the Second World War and for the decade after it Britain led the world in jet engine design. When BuAer asked Grumman to design a day fighter (after it dropped Grumman's F9F-1 night fighter), Grumman sketched several alternatives. Two had mixed power (propellers and jets); two had pure jets. Both pure jet designs used British engines. G-79C, with two Derwents, broadly resembled the Meteor. Grumman favoured it. Each Derwent was rated at 3905lbs thrust. On this basis the aircraft was expected to make 592mph at sea level and 559mph at 59,000ft. Estimated combat radius was 233nm. With two 150-gallon wingtip tanks that could be increased to 380nm at 25,000ft and to 499nm at 35,000ft.

Pegasus associated with the VSTOL Harrier. Development began in 1958, Hawker building a prototype aircraft (P.1127) as a private venture. The US Mutual Weapons Development Program (MWDP) provided 75 per cent of the financing for the initial engine development. In contrast to other VSTOL schemes, this one envisaged a single engine first lifting the aircraft (which would remain horizontal) and

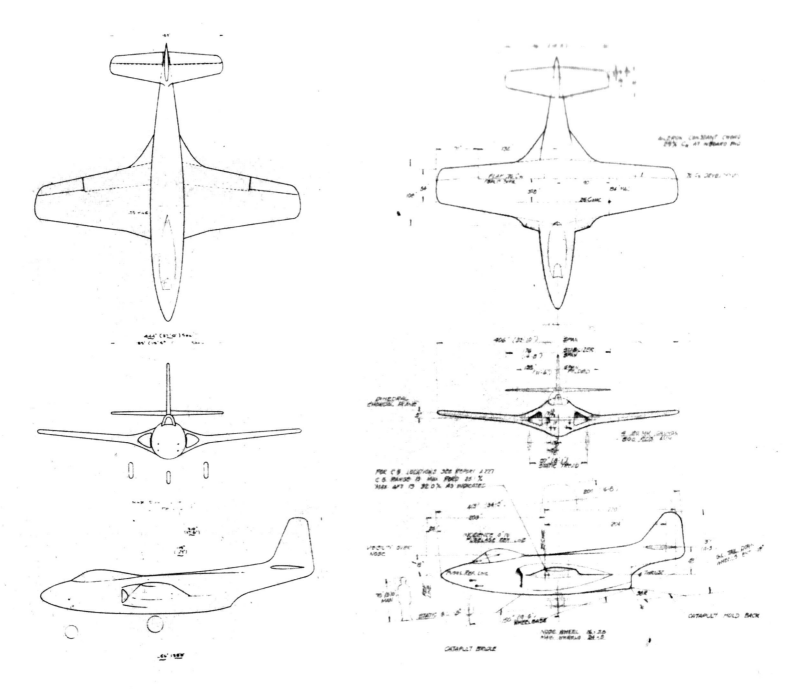

Grumman's G-79D was powered by a single British Nene engine rated at 5700lbs thrust. It evolved into the successful Panther fighter. This is the version in the comparative report. It offered a maximum speed of 590mph at sea level and 554mph at 34,000ft. A version powered by a General Electric I-40 (J33) rated at 4000lbs thrust would have been slower (525 and 535 knots) and would have needed far more deck to take off in a 25-knot wind (790ft vs 410ft). Estimated combat radius for G-79D was 230.5nm.

BuAer liked Grumman's alternative D and the company developed it further. This drawing was part of a proposal dated 6 August 1946. Although it broadly resembles the Panther (note the cut-back jet pipe), it was not quite the final design.

then transitioning to conventional flight by tilting nozzles. Stability required a 'four post' lift system, so it could not be enough to tilt the engine exhaust. The solution, in the Pegasus, was to use a turbofan to produce the two forward blasts of lift air. The two after blasts came from the normal exhaust. The prototype used the core of Bristol's Orpheus engine (designed for light fighters) to drive three stages of an Olympus LP compressor as the fan end. The inner spool of the engine drove the compressor. The spools were made to contra-rotate to avoid any insta-

bility due to gyro effects. The prototype engine produced 8000lbs of thrust, enough to prove the idea but not to lift a usable fighter. The concept having been proven, the engine grew, from 11,000lbs of thrust (P.1127, 1960) to 15,500lbs (Pegasus 5, in the Kestrel lightweight fighter) and to 21,500lbs of thrust in the Harrier (Pegasus 11).

The US Navy jet engine programme

The first hint the US government received of British interest in jet engines apparently came with the arrival of the Tizard Mission in the autumn of 1940. Until that time US engine builders concentrated on

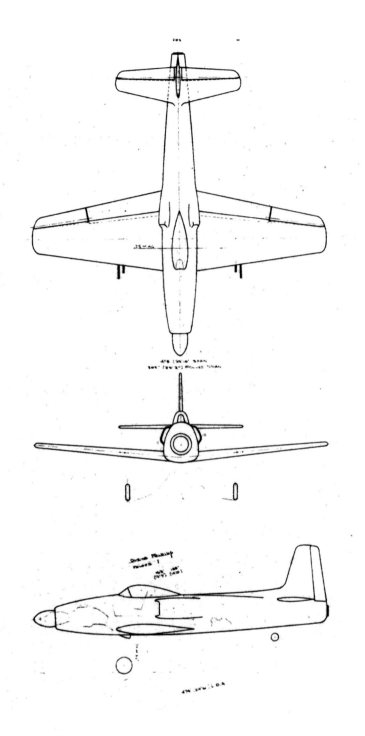

Grumman offered two mixed-power alternatives, which show that the idea was still very much alive immediately after the war. This is G-79B, powered by a TG-100 turboprop (2200hp) and a Derwent jet engine. It was expected to make 559mph at sea level and 549mph at 25,000ft. The greater fuel economy of the turboprop showed in increased combat radius, 298nm. With two 150-gallon wingtip tanks, that could increase to 694nm at 25,000ft and to 851nm at 35,000ft. Normal endurance including an hour rendezvous was 5.52 hours, compared to 3.9 for G-79C with two Derwents. G-79A had an R-2000 piston engine plus a Derwent.

highly successful piston engines. The closest US official approach to developing jet engines was a mid-1940 National Advisory Committee on Aeronautics (NACA) study of gas turbines (turboprops), which were dismissed as too heavy. General Electric was successfully developing turbo-superchargers (turbochargers), which have a great deal in common

with jet engines (they use turbines to drive compressors), but it never made the step to an engine which would provide thrust from its exhaust.

In 1941 the prototype British engine was running well enough to be viable and that March Congress passed the Lend-Lease Act: the United States would provide the British with the weapons they needed. Meanwhile, on 25 February 1941 General H H ('Hap') Arnold, then Deputy Chief of Staff for Air (later commander of the Army Air Forces) had asked Dr Vannevar Bush, who headed the new National Defense Research Committee, to form a jet propulsion group. In March a NACA committee was formed, headed by Professor Durand of MIT (who had taught Sanford Moss, the developer of US turbochargers). It included representatives of the army, the navy (BuAer), the Bureau of Standards (in effect, the government's physical research laboratory), Johns Hopkins University, MIT and the three major US turbine makers, Allis-Chalmers, GE and Westinghouse. Arnold specifically barred US piston-engine makers on the ground that jet development would distract them from the urgently-needed production of masses of piston engines, to fight the coming war. GE supercharger designer Moss later said that he was appalled to have missed the idea of interposing combustion chambers between the turbine and the compressor he typically produced.

By June 1941 all three US turbine companies had proposed engines using axial-flow compressors (rather than the centrifugal-flow units favoured by the British). The navy backed Allis-Chalmers and Westinghouse; the army contracted with GE for a turboprop it designated TG-100 (it later figured in some navy aircraft proposals; its later designation was T31). Both jet engine companies received 18-month development contracts, Allis-Chalmers being dropped afterwards. That left Westinghouse as the navy's jet engine developer, with its Type 19 series engine.

At the end of the war US military jet engines were redesignated in a J series, the number indicating where the engine was in the sequence (other letters indicated turboprops [T] and ramjets [R]). Post-war practice was for the US Navy and the US Air Force to sponsor their own engines, on the theory that each service had its own requirements, its own procurement organisation and its own production facilities (leased to companies). Navy engines were initially given even numbers, air force engines odd ones, although there was substantial crossover. The Westinghouse X19A or Type 19A (the number indicated its diameter) became J30. It powered the first US Navy jet fighter, the FH-1 Phantom.

Once the Westinghouse design was well underway, BuAer became interested in scaling the engine both down and up. Mass flow through the engine, which determines thrust, is proportional to the area of its air intake, meaning to the square of engine diameter. The first step down was to halve the diameter: a 9.5in engine (Type 9.5, J32), which could power a missile (the main applications were the Gorgon missile and target drones). BuAer soon became interested in increasing power, so in 1944 it let a contract to Westinghouse for a 3000lbs thrust engine. That required about 1.32 times the diameter (25in). Improvements in efficiency made it possible for Westinghouse to offer the desired power in a 24in package, the resulting engine being called Type 24 or X24. The BuAer history associates this engine with the Ryan FR-1 hybrid-power fighter. The 24in engine was later redesignated J34 (a scaled-up redesign, offering 4500lbs of thrust, was J46).

US development of British-style centrifugal-flow engines began in March 1941 when General Arnold visited England, where he saw British centrifugal-flow engines. He selected GE to build US versions.

This is what Grumman built, an F9F-4 Panther seen at Jacksonville, Florida, 25 September 1957. The bulge under the nose is for a TACAN (tactical air navigation) receiving antenna. The original F9F-2 was powered by a licence-built Nene, a Pratt & Whitney J42-P-8. F9F-3 was an alternative version powered by the Allison J33-A-8, which was less powerful (4600lbs vs 5000lbs thrust) but offered an alternative source of engine supply. These aircraft were soon converted into F9F-2s. The F9F-4 shown used the more powerful J33-A-27 engine (5850lbs thrust) and was lengthened by 8in to add 80 gallons of fuel. Compared to the F9F-2/3, it had a larger vertical fin to maintain directional stability. The wing was thinner (10 per cent vs 12 per cent) to increase the critical Mach number. In this version, too, the three outer wing stations were strengthened to take 500lb bombs. In service the Allison engines were replaced by Pratt & Whitney J48s. The final production version was the similarly-lengthened F9F-5, powered by a J48 (6250lbs thrust, 7000lbs with water injection). J48 was an upgraded Nene developed jointly by Rolls-Royce and Pratt & Whitney, the former calling it the Tay. The navy found the stall speed of the F9F-5 (critical for carrier landing) too high, a problem cured by the addition of a wing fence at the inboard edge of the leading edge of the flap.

Since GE already built superchargers using centrifugal-flow compressors, it used the term 'Type I supercharger' for this project. Its early engines were numbered in an I series (e.g., I-16, I-40). I-40 (J33) powered the first American production jet fighter, the P-80 (later F-80) Shooting Star. The designation indicates the intended output, 4000lbs thrust. Although an army project, the GE centrifugal-flow engines featured in some navy designs. GE's J33 (made by Allison) powered the first major US jet fighter, the F-80 Shooting Star.

GE also designed a J35 (TG-180) axial-flow engine, based on its turboprop work. Development was taken over by Allison originally to provide a second source of production. For this history J35 development had two important results. One was that Allison scaled it up to

the J71 engine (originally designated J35-A-23), which became one of the alternatives adopted after the failure of the J40, the ultimate development of the Westinghouse engines. The second was that GE continued development of the J35 as its own TG-190. The latter became the J47, a very important Cold War engine which powered, among many other aircraft, the F-86 Sabre and its naval derivative the FJ-2 Fury.

Seeking a second source of supply, in 1947 BuAer opted for a licence-made Nene (Pratt & Whitney's J42) to power the Grumman Panther (F9F-2). It paid for the licence and the tooling. Working with Rolls-Royce, Pratt & Whitney developed an improved version with 30 per cent more thrust and provision for an afterburner, the J48 (which powered later Panthers and Cougars). It was equivalent to the Rolls-Royce Tay. By this time it was clear that only axial turbojets could provide the sort of outputs needed for very high performance. Pratt & Whitney developed an entirely new axial-flow J57 engine under air force sponsorship; fortunately it was available when the Westinghouse J40 series failed.

BuAer liked the scaleable Westinghouse engines because an aircraft could be designed with different numbers of engines of alternative diameters, offering insurance against the failure of the larger-diameter units. Conversely, the rapid progress from the 19in to the 24in engine must have offered the impression that the problems of axial-flow engines had been solved and therefore that the basic engine could easily be scaled up to meet the needs of ambitious post-war fighter projects. This new cycle began with an October 1945 recommendation by the Patrol Bomber Branch calling for development of a new engine in the 8000 to 12,000lbs thrust range. It was presumably looking forward to a carrier-

based bomber which was already of great interest to the navy. In February, BuAer asked engine makers for informal proposals for a 7000lbs thrust engine. At about the same time it asked its internal design group (ADR) to estimate the optimum thrust for future fighters. In its ADR-1012 report submitted in November 1946, it pointed to a 12,000lbs thrust engine with the other characteristics of the existing 24J (J34) as optimum in a fighter (the sketch design was designated ADR-47) with the usual 300nm combat radius. Adding power would make the fighter heavier. However, a reduction to 8000lbs thrust would cost very little performance.

The BuAer programme was important because it dominated fighter design in the late 1940s, which meant the choices of fighters for the whole of the 1950s. In April, BuAer asked for proposals. Westinghouse was not included because it was already working on a turboprop (25D) derived from the J34. Of four companies invited to bid, only Allison submitted a workable proposal. Westinghouse decided to abandon the turboprop and in March 1947 it asked to bid. The project was to begin with FY47 funds, so Westinghouse had to submit its bid by 28 April. General Electric did not bid because it was already working on what became the J47, a somewhat less powerful engine than BuAer wanted. By this time the required output was 7500lbs.

Westinghouse offered the smallest diameter (40in rather than the 50in of the Pratt & Whitney JT3), the lightest weight and the best fuel economy. Limiting diameter would limit drag and better fuel economy would make for a smaller fighter. In 1947 BuAer considered Westinghouse the world's leading manufacturer of axial-flow turbojets. Allison was producing engines in much greater numbers, but it had never developed a new engine. Pratt & Whitney's only experience was in making Westinghouse-designed X19B engines. The main weakness

from which Westinghouse suffered was inexperience in mass engine production, but it seemed likely that the company's experience to date, including its work with Pratt & Whitney, had taught it how to design an engine for production. In June 1947 BuAer issued a letter of intent for prototype engines (J40-WE-2, -4 and -6).[4] The first test engine was started on 28 October 1948 and initially it generated 5600lbs of thrust. By December, it was producing 7110lbs, which was more than any other US engine. There were some delays (in April 1949 BuAer thought the programme six months behind schedule), but no major problems were apparent. As of December 1950, deliveries of the first service version, J40-WE-6, were to begin in April 1951, to mesh with production of the prototypes of the three fighters scheduled to use the engine.

BuAer now suddenly discovered that Westinghouse could not deliver engines on time. Its new high-performance fighters would be badly delayed. This must have been particularly unpleasant, since experience in Korea was showing how vital high fighter performance was.

The new fighters needed high power, so in November 1948 BuAer asked for a J40-WE-8 version with an afterburner. It expected that the basic engine could be developed to deliver 8100lbs of thrust (as J40-WE-10) and that both the 7500lb and the 8100lb thrust engines could be mated with afterburners. In April 1949 the J40-WE-8 with afterburner was expected to produce 10,900lbs of thrust. Again, that far exceeded anything else BuAer could have obtained at the time. The planned production version of the -8 engine (-8A) was later redesignated J40-WE-22. The higher-powered version (-12) added compressor stages; in 1949 Westinghouse expected it to produce 9500lbs rather than 8100lbs of thrust. The corresponding afterburner version (-10) was expected to produce 13,700lbs of thrust – again, far beyond what the navy could obtain with any other engine. Unfortunately by May 1950 Westinghouse was proposing major modifications, including a larger-diameter compressor and new combustion chambers, to the point that it seemed that an entirely new engine was being developed (Westinghouse planned to call it J50). As it encountered problems with the J40-WE-10/12, Westinghouse proposed de-rated versions (-24/26) as a way of completing engines quickly enough. Performance would still have been impressive: 9500lbs thrust for J40-WE-26 and 12,050lbs for –WE-24, as of the summer of 1952. In addition to all of these versions, in September 1949 Westinghouse proposed a growth version (J40-WE16, to produce 17,400lbs thrust with afterburner) to power the expected follow-on to the new F3H and F4D interceptors and also to power a future single-engine night-fighter to replace the Skynight (-14 was a corresponding bomber engine). As the basic J40 programme encountered worse and worse problems, any money allocated to the growth version went instead into attempts to cure the basic versions. The detail in this account is presented because BuAer abandoned the J40 (and found alternatives) in stages, referring to particular J40 versions.

BuAer began to look for alternatives not initially because the J40 failed to perform, but because Westinghouse was failing to deliver it on time. As it happened, the engine turned out to have undesirable characteristics which faster production could not have cured and it ended up as a major example of programme failure. The F3H came first, Allison's J71 being chosen as the replacement engine.[5] Replacement was badly delayed because it took two years to develop an afterburner for the new engine, so early F3H Demons were delivered with J40s. However, with the end of the Korean War in 1953, the J40 programme itself became much less urgent and BuAer less tolerant of the need to fix it. Even before the end of the war, it cancelled 400 J40s in February 1953 and another 400 in April, followed by 1000 in September. At the same time BuAer also cancelled contracts to develop the high-powered versions, leaving on order only 217 low-thrust engines (J40-WE-22s). Westinghouse delivered the first of them in November 1953, more than three years after the originally scheduled date. The whole J40 programme was cancelled in October 1955.

Meanwhile the Douglas F4D had its J40 replaced by a J57, as did the A3D Skywarrior strategic bomber. That replacement seems to have been far easier, so that when scandal surrounded the J40 programme in 1955, it referred to the F3H rather than to the F4D. The Grumman F10F was not re-engined at all.

Given problems with the J71, the navy found itself accepting F3H-1 Demons powered by the J40-WE-22, despite its problems. Of sixty aircraft ordered, thirty were delivered with -WE-22 engines, which were known to be underpowered. Unfortunately the F3H-1 had been modified as a general-purpose fighter and by the time it was being delivered weight had grown from 22,000lbs to 29,000lbs. BuAer had accepted the weight growth in view of the rated power of the originally planned -WE-10 engine, but in the interim that engine was cancelled due to compressor stall problems. The lower-powered fighter was accepted for pilot and ground crew familiarisation, but it proved unsafe; all J40-powered Demons were grounded. The navy could point out that

with a -8 engine an F4D claimed the world airspeed record and that an F3H-1 with a -22 engine made a time-to-climb record (the F3H-1 was carrier-qualified with this engine).

The J40 problem became public when Representative Frank Karsten visited McDonnell in September 1955. He saw fifty Demons parked at the plant awaiting new engines or condemned not to fly because they were considered unsafe using the -22 engine. Of the fifty, only twenty-nine could be re-engined with J71s. A Congressional investigation concluded that the J40 had been a $200 million mistake; BuAer had doubled down instead of cutting its losses earlier. That the replacement J71 could not be made to work instantly suggests that BuAer was not entirely foolhardy. Even after it was installed in Demons, it had to be derated and the aircraft was badly underpowered. Probably the most important legacy of the J40 problem was that, by ruining the F3H programme, it forced a desperate McDonnell to look for a successor design – which turned out to be the superb F4H (F-4) Phantom.

Westinghouse scaled up the J34 directly as the J46 (which was originally designated X24-10C), seeing it as the low end of a modular engine series, Severe problems with the J40 badly slowed development of the more conservative J46, which was incorporated in aircraft (such as the Cutlass and the F3D-2 Skynight) which were not intended to use the J40.

The failure of the J40 led Westinghouse to shrink its gas turbine division and ultimately to disband it in 1960. A collaboration agreement with Rolls-Royce (1955) did not solve the problem, partly because Westinghouse chose to scale down the successful Avon rather than simply to produce it under licence as an alternative to its J40.

In 1952 BuAer became interested in the British Avon (RA 14), but instead it chose Pratt & Whitney's new J57. Unlike previous axial-flow engines, the J57 had two spools, one turning a low-pressure compressor and the other turning a high-pressure compressor (the shafts for the two were concentric). Separating the two made it possible to run each spool at optimum speed. Design work on a two-spool engine (as a turboprop, XT45 [company designation PT4]) began in July 1947, the company having first considered the idea the previous year. A parallel design of a two-spool turbojet (JT3) began, the turboprop being cancelled as the sponsor, the air force, lost interest in anything but turbojets for its next-generation bomber. After initial problems the engine flew successfully in March 1951. It was the first engine to produce 10,000lbs of thrust (eventually it was developed to produce 18,000lbs) and thus outperformed the J40. The J57 was very successful and it was adopted for the first US jet airliners under the designation JT3. In commercial service its great attraction was excellent fuel economy. An improved version, the J75, powered the air force F-105 and F-106.

In 1950 Wright licensed two British engines, the Sapphire and the Olympus. As the J65, an Americanised version of the Sapphire powered the last version of the Fury fighter-bomber. The US version of the much more powerful Olympus was the J67.

From this point on the two main US producers were Pratt & Whitney and General Electric. In 1952 GE began work on an engine intended to give good fuel economy at Mach 0.9 but able to function at Mach 2, to power the coming generation of fast fighters. To do that the engine needed a variable pressure ratio. GE's solution was for the stators of the last seven of the seventeen compressor stages to vary their incidence under electronic control. This engine powered the F4H (F-4) Phantom.

In the 1950s General Electric began to offer turbofans. Instead of attaching the fan blades to the compressor at the front of the engine, it

attached them to a separate turbine at the aft end. The prototype CJ-805, a modified J79, was tested in 1957 as an airliner engine.

Pratt & Whitney won the first US military turbofan contract with its TF30, which was also the first operational afterburning turbofan (the afterburner burned both bypass air and hot air from the main engine). Like the General Electric engine, it used a turbine stage to power its three stages of fan blades, which were at the after end of the engine. This engine was chosen for the two-service F-111 (TFX), the navy version being the F-111B (GE was teamed with the losing aircraft company, Boeing). The TF30 was then specified for the abortive follow-on VFAX programme and the VFX (F-14) programmes. The version in the F-14 was notoriously underpowered and it was also subject to vicious compressor stalls.

The F-14 problem led to attempts to find (and fund) alternative engines almost as soon as the F-14 entered service. GE eventually won with its F110 engine. It also produced the low-bypass F404 (which began as the YJ101), which powered the F/A-18 Hornet. Both are bypass engines. F404 nicely illustrates how rapidly engine technology developed: it appeared about twenty years after the J79 and was intended to deliver the same thrust in half the weight.

AERODYNAMICS

Immediately after the Second World War there was misplaced optimism that with jet or rocket engines extraordinary (supersonic) performance was well within reach. German wartime research on exotic designs (swept wings and deltas) was quickly assimilated in both Britain and the United States. In the United States, for example, large numbers of captured German documents were distributed among aircraft designers, so that by 1946 proposals for swept-wing aircraft were typical. Many were described, at least by their designers, as transonic and thin wings were often associated with expected supersonic performance. However, operational aircraft capable of supersonic flight did not fly for about a decade after the war. It turned out that the material taken from the Germans had not touched on key problems such as the sudden increase in drag as an aircraft approached supersonic speed.

In 1931 BuAer began a special High Speed Flight programme, under which it bought aircraft which might not meet the usual requirements. One of them was Boeing's low-wing F7B fighter. It is shown on 1 November 1934. Reasons for rejecting low-wing monoplanes included poor visibility, buffeting and poor combat controllability and manoeuvrability. A monoplane would have to fold its wings and it seemed that would weaken the wing to the point where dive bombing would be impossible. Boeing received the order for the F7B because it was thought that the company had solved these problems. The F7B was found laterally and longitudinally unstable, it required excessive control force and a long take-off run (not acceptable on board a carrier) and it lacked manoeuvrability and structural strength. Its high speed (239mph) was not enough to qualify it even for experimental use. Another low-wing monoplane, Northrop's XFT-1, was ordered about the middle of 1933. Both monoplanes offered estimated maximum speeds of 240mph. The FT and the Curtiss XF13C, which was also tested as a monoplane (in this case with a high wing) were both powered by the new R-1510 engine, which caused problems. With an alternative R-1535, the FT was more successful, but Northrop stopped work on experimental fighters before the 1935 competition, as it was interested only in low-wing monoplanes and BuAer had not yet approved such an aircraft (BuAer thought that the real reasons were considerable army business and the company's inability to develop a satisfactory design using a proven engine). The FT-2 prototype crashed in 1936 during contractor flight tests, ending that programme. Thus the F7B did not figure in the mid-1933 fighter choice, the candidates at that time being the FT-1, a modified F2F, the Berliner-Joyce F3J-1 and the Curtiss BF2C. Of these, the FT-1 was unsatisfactory due to its high stall speed; modification was expected to take too long. The F3J promised to meet contract requirements but had been designed some years earlier and was considered obsolete. The BF2C was more bomber than fighter. That left a modified F2F.

It was known before the end of the war that at very high speeds, near the speed of sound, air suddenly became less compressible. It refused to flow smoothly over an aircraft. Diving fighters began to buffet – to shake violently – as they approached their limiting Mach numbers (fractions of the speed of sound). Sweeping a wing back could delay the onset of buffeting by smoothing air flow and aircraft companies often advertised thinner than usual wings as transonic or supersonic. However, for some time there were no supersonic wind tunnels and therefore no firm figures describing what happened as an aircraft approached Mach 1. The situation was further complicated by the

The Curtiss F13C was bought specifically to enable comparison between monoplane and biplane; it had two sets of wings, which could be interchanged. The F13C is shown in monoplane (high wing) form as the XF13C-1, 13 April 1934. It was redesignated when its wings were changed, but photos show it with the same XF13C-1 title on its tail. The XF13C was apparently initially ordered as a research aircraft (it was the Curtiss Model 70) and it received its fighter designation only after the later Model 72 had been ordered as the XF12C (this aircraft ended up as the SBC-1 dive bomber). It was thus part of the same experimental monoplane programme as the F7B and the FT. Carrier tests of the XF13C-1 proved the value of slots and flaps in a carrier aircraft and also the possible value of this aircraft for service use. Even with a new version of the R-1510 engine (the aircraft was designated XF13C-3), the F13C continued to have problems and it was not considered for the 1935 (FY36) fighter competition. Curtiss also received a contract for its version of BuAer Design 120, with a maximum speed of 215mph, but the aircraft was never completed and never received a designation. The Design 120 file dated 19 February 1932 shows a series of studies compared to a Grumman XFF-1 using the new R-1820E engine. Powerplants were the R-1535 (700hp) and a new V-770 (480hp). Weight was 3300 to 3900lbs. Details of the design are not clear from the surviving documentation.

The new jet and turboprop engines offered so much power that it must have seemed that the rules of aerodynamics would change. This is Bell's D-31 proposal for the 1945 night fighter, the contract for which was won by Douglas with what became the F3D Skynight (sometimes called Skyknight). The wingtips shown are just that, not the points at which outer wings were attached. The wings had an unusually broad chord. Span was 37ft 3in, the centres of the propellers being 32ft 6in apart; length was 45ft 8in. In its presentation, Bell pointed out that a night fighter needed an unusually wide range of speeds, since it generally had to catch the fastest targets but stay behind the slowest so as to fire from behind them. It argued that such an aircraft needed an unusually low power loading and efficient high-lift devices. Hence its insistence on an extraordinarily low aspect ratio (a broad rather than long wing) and counter-rotating propellers. A short enough wing would not have to fold. Contraprops were necessary to limit induced drag. Given a low aspect ratio wing, the effective angle of attack would be sufficient that at low speed much of the aircraft's weight would be supported by the thrust of the propellers. The aircraft could fly and glide at very high angles of attack. That might be a particular advantage in a dogfight. Power was to be provided by a pair of TG-100 turboprop engines plus a Westinghouse 24C-6 jet in the tail. Gross weight was given as 25,350lbs. Bell claimed that with all three engines running, its aircraft could make about 530mph at 50,000ft. Normally the aircraft would cruise using only its turboprops. At this time the TG-100 was rated at 2200hp and the 24C-6 jet was rated at about 3200lbs of thrust.

The exigencies of carrier operation make exotic aerodynamics attractive. For the US Navy, the most exotic was the high aspect ratio fighter proposed in 1939 by C H Zimmerman, a NACA engineer; Vought was chosen to build it as the F5U-1, often called the pancake for its shape. Vought never solved the technical problem of the transmission connecting the engines to the two articulated propellers and the F5U never flew, despite considerable investment both during and immediately after the war. The fighter is shown at the Vought plant, 21 August 1947.

At the end of the Second World War the Allies seized German records of wartime aerodynamic research, much of which concerned swept wings. They were intended to delay the onset of high transonic drag; as a German aerodynamicist put it, the shape of the wing fooled the air into thinking that it was moving more slowly than the aircraft. The British modified existing aircraft with swept wings. Although they lacked the funds to mass-produce new aircraft, they hoped that advanced research would enable them to produce modern aircraft once their economy recovered, looking towards the 'year of maximum danger' in 1957. The Supermarine 510, essentially an Attacker with swept wings, carried out deck-landing trials on board *Illustrious*. The great question was how a swept-wing aircraft would behave at low speed. The swept-wing Type 510 was an intermediate stage in the development of the Supermarine Swift jet fighter; a hooked version was considered for a time as an interim Royal Navy fighter. The corresponding US experiments were carried out in 1946 with two P-63 King Cobras fitted with swept wings and redesignated L-39-1 and -2 (proposals to use T-6 Texan trainers or Wildcats were rejected). They mated P-63A fuselages with P-63E outer wing panels modified for 35° sweep (later one of them was given a fuselage plug). These aircraft offered the advantage of having tricycle landing gear like the planned jets and its engine buried in the fuselage, like a jet's. Conversion was by Bell Aircraft, which had built the P-63s. The L-39-1 first flew on 23 April 1946. (David Hobbs)

The British also conceived the flexible flight deck and in 1945 Supermarine designed a twin-jet fighter with the sort of flat belly which seemed best adapted to it. Supermarine was ordered to modify it into a wheeled aircraft because the flexible deck seemed unlikely to supersede conventional ones immediately. The result was Type 508, shown on board *Eagle* in 1953 during deck trials. The other unusual feature was a vee (butterfly) tail. The next step was swept wings, in what became the Scimitar. The vee tail had to be discarded because at high speed it suffered from extreme forces. Type 508 had two very powerful axial-flow Avon engines, but it was not area-ruled (the idea was unknown in 1945–6) and so its swept-wing progeny was subsonic. (David Hobbs)

reality that from 1947 on US rocket-powered research aircraft did regularly break the 'sound barrier'.

In 1952 Charles Whitcomb at NACA realised that transonic flow around an aircraft was the problem. Even below the speed of sound, the flow around some parts of an aircraft could be supersonic and flow would break down. The aircraft would generate shock waves absorbing energy in what was called wave drag. Whitcomb realised that wave drag was associated with the cross-section of an aircraft rather than with details

There was also a swept-wing version of the main first-generation British naval jet fighter, the Hawker Sea Hawk: the P.1052 (VX272), which carried out deck-landing trials on board *Eagle* in May 1952. The P.1052 was, in effect, a way station towards the Hawker Hunter, which was not considered for naval use. (David Hobbs)

like the engine housings or the shape of the wings. If the cross-section changed sharply along the length of the aircraft, shock waves would be generated at very high speeds and it would take far more power to gain speed. Conversely, if the cross-section changed smoothly, wave drag would be minimised. The first naval aircraft to be designed in accord with Whitcomb's decision was the Grumman F11F Tiger. Its fuselage was pulled in around its wings, to compensate for the extra cross-sectional area represented by the wings. The result was called an area-ruled or 'coke bottle' design. The famous example of Whitcomb's work was the air force's F-102 delta-wing interceptor. As completed, it could not achieve the supersonic flight for which it had been designed. Re-designed with an area-ruled fuselage, it could, even though it had no greater engine power. Whitcomb's work explains why some aircraft, such as the F2Y Delta Dart, which were described as supersonic when designed, probably never could have made their claimed speeds. Modern fighters do not seem to be area-ruled, perhaps because they have so much power that they can overcome wave drag, but also because a design developed from the outset with area rule in mind may not show it very obviously.

Swept wings had their own drawbacks. For maximum range, it was known long before the Second World War that the ideal configuration was a long narrow wing (high aspect ratio). A shorter wing offered better manoeuvrability (particularly roll rate) and higher speed. Greater wing area (lower wing loading) offered higher manoeuvrability and also faster climb, but at a cost in drag. After the war, when it seemed that the future belonged to swept-wing aircraft, there was interest in what was later called variable geometry. The Germans had built but not flown a prototype jet whose wing could be reset at various sweep angles and after the Second World War the United States had such an aircraft built as the Bell X-5. The step beyond, in the final version of the Grumman F10F Jaguar, was a wing whose sweep could be changed in flight. Such an aircraft could cruise at a low Mach number with an efficient long straight wing, then fold it back in for high-speed combat. The F10F had a two-position wing, 13.5° sweep for take-off, landing, cruise and climb and 42.5° for combat.

Increasing wing sweep moved the centre of lift back towards the tail. It also moved the centre of gravity, but not by nearly as much. Ideally the centre of lift should coincide with the centre of gravity of the aircraft, so that lift does not tip the aircraft up or down by the nose. Grumman's engineers sought to compensate by moving the whole wing back and forth as its sweep varied. That worked, but the F10F had numerous other features, which turned out to be too complicated.

The British inventor Dr Barnes Wallis solved the problem by hinging only the outer part of the wing: the result was called a swing wing. The fixed part of the wing contributed enough lift to limit the movement of the centre of lift, so that it was no longer a great problem.

For the 1946 US Navy fighter competition (OS-105), North American offered something more exotic, a three-engine fighter with forward-swept wings (there was also a more conventional proposal using swept wings). The three-view drawing of this RD-1386A design was dated 10 April 1946. The powerplant would have been two Westinghouse 24C-4A turbojets, each rated at 3000lb thrust (military rating) at sea level (no rating was given for the afterburner). North American claimed that with afterburners it would fight at an average speed of 640mph at 20,000ft. Span of this bat-like aircraft was 43.45ft; length was 45.95ft. Gross weight was 19,830lbs. Rate of climb at sea level would be 3550ft/min with engines at normal rating, 6360ft/min at military rating and 8780ft/min with afterburners lit. RD-1386B was a more conventional swept-back design powered by three 24C-4A turbojets, one of them in the tail. Maximum speed would be slightly over 620mph. Span would have been 54.33ft, length 45.66ft and gross weight 23,784lbs. Rate of climb at sea level would have been 3750ft/sec at normal rated thrust, 6700ft/sec at military rating and 9200ft/sec with afterburners lit. Radius of action would have been 300nm. Armament would have been the usual four 20mm cannon. North American also offered NA-134, an upgraded version of the FJ-1 the navy was already buying, powered by a Nene engine.

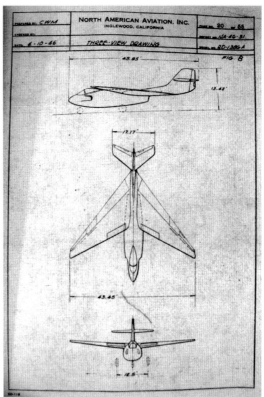

RAE proposed the swing wing as a solution for several aircraft problems, but in the late 1950s the British government was not buying many new combat aircraft designs. Key engineers brought the swing wing idea to the United States, where NACA took it up and developed it. The swing wing concept was the basis of the F-111 design and then of the F-14. It worked, but the pivot and associated structure proved a maintenance nightmare. That is why, despite the great advantages of the pivoted (swing) wing, it has disappeared from operational aircraft.

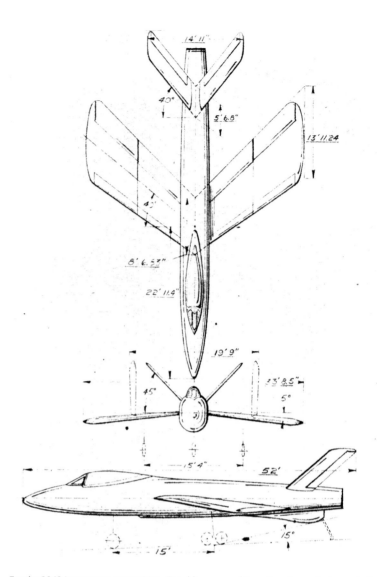

Above: BuAer chose an exotic design in 1946, the tailless Cutlass (F7U). It is shown here in 1951 with the equally exotic Douglas Skyray (F4D), which won the 1948 interceptor competition. The Skyray turned out well, the Cutlass much less so. It is not clear how much of its trouble can be attributed to its disappointing engines (at one point is was called the 'gutless Cutlass')

For the 1948 interceptor competition, Republic proposed its unique inversely-tapered wing, seen here in its single-engine NP-48 design (NP-49 was a two-engine alternative with two underwing engines). The company was then building the inverse-tapered wing XF-91 Thunderceptor for the air force; NP-48 resembled a Thunderceptor with a solid radar nose and an air intake under it. Span was 33ft 8.45in, length 52ft and gross weight 22,920lbs. The planned powerplant was a Westinghouse J40-WE-6 turbojet (7500lbs of thrust, or 10,900lbs using an afterburner) using a NACA submerged intake and a 4000lb-thrust Curtiss-Wright or Reaction Motors rocket. By this time Republic had tested its inverse-taper wing on rocket-fired test models (there were no transonic wind tunnels) and it claimed that they demonstrated that it offered low drag at high Mach numbers. Like other swept wings, this one was intended for efficiency at high speed. The inverse taper (and thickness) was intended to retard spanwise drift of air to delay the onset of wingtip stall. Inverting taper and thickness would reduce interference drag at the wing root. The company estimated that the aircraft would reach a speed of about 665 knots (765mph, about Mach 1.0) at sea level and it was willing to guarantee 650 knots (speed fell off with altitude). Unlike the XF-91, the NP-48 would have had a fixed-incidence wing.

Left: A simpler form of variable geometry was variable angle of incidence, which offered the advantage that the body of the aircraft, including the pilot, could remain at a lower angle as the fighter landed. A high angle of incidence was also useful for take-off. This idea was incorporated in the Vought F8U Crusader. An F-8E of VF-191 on board *Ticonderoga* prepared to take off, December 1968.

For the same 1948 competition, won jointly by the McDonnell Demon (its Model 58) and the Skyray, McDonnell also offered this 60° delta (its Model 60). Span would have been 30ft 4in and length 44ft 8in. McDonnell claimed that maximum speed at sea level would be 581 knots (662mph, Mach 1), 593 knots (682mph, Mach 1.03) at 35,000ft and 568 knots (653mph, Mach 0.99) at 50,000ft. The maximum rate of climb at sea level would be 30,450ft/min (9400ft/min at 35,000ft). Combat range (not radius) would be 707nm at a cruising speed of 475 knots and endurance on an interceptor mission would be 71.5 minutes. The engine was the XJ40-WE-6 also used in the Demon.

Grumman used a variable-sweep wing in its F10F Jaguar to reduce landing speed, a major problem with fast jets. The wing was moved and translated by a single hydraulic piston. Compared to an F3H Demon, which was about the same size and weight, the Jaguar had a stall speed of 78 knots rather than 96 knots. Moreover, with its wing set in the straight position the Jaguar could be flown much nearer the stall than a swept wing. The difference equated to a growth margin of about 12,000lbs against a weight penalty of only about 1500lbs for variable sweep. Initially the wing was designed to take only two angles, one for landing and one for high-speed flight, but as tested its wing could be moved to any position between 13.5° and 42.5° of sweep. The Jaguar flew well when its wings were straight, but it became directionally unstable when the wings were swept; it could be flown only in smooth air. To add directional stability 'horsal' (horizontal-dorsal) fins were added at the tail to solve the problem. However, the rudder was still too small to steer the Jaguar effectively. NACA had modified a Hellcat with variable lateral and directional stability and the Grumman test pilot, the only one who ever flew the Jaguar, flew it first with its stability adjusted to mimic that of the XF10F. He did not believe the Jaguar could be so bad, but NACA's predictions turned out to be correct. There were also other problems connected with the innovative powered tail. Variable sweep was successful, but the Jaguar had so many other problems that its project officer, who would normally have been its strongest supporter, was the one calling for cancellation. This is the Jaguar mock-up. The XF10F-1 designation was initially applied to Grumman's G-83, conceived as a swept wing (actually cropped delta) version of the Panther, on 4 March 1948, just before the aircraft was rethought as one of the 1948 interceptors, with a variable-incidence wing. The first and only flyable F10F was completed early in 1952 and first flew on 19 May 1952.

Left: The great discovery which transformed subsonic aircraft into supersonic ones was the area rule: to avoid shock waves and a steep rise in drag, an aircraft should be designed so that its cross-section varied smoothly along its length. Thus the body had to be pinched in to compensate for the added cross-section of the wings. The Grumman Tiger was the most famous early application (the Convair F-102 was another). This is the F11F-1F Super Tiger, showing its 'coke bottle' shape. Later applications were subtler. (Grumman)

Violating the area rule would prevent an aircraft from breaking through into supersonic flight. One reason the Convair Sea Dart seaplane fighter was cancelled was that, because it had been designed before the area rule, it could not reach its guaranteed maximum speed of Mach 1.25. The cost of redesign was considered excessive. (Convair)

LOCKHEED L-242 DAY FIGHTER

Flight almost without wings! For the OS-130 day air-superiority fighter competition of 1953, Lockheed submitted the design the air force was then buying as the F-104. This is Lockheed's sketch. Span would have been 22ft 1in (with a tiny 190ft² area) and length would have been 48ft 3in. Lockheed claimed that with a Wright TJ-31B3 engine (Wright's J65-W), its aircraft could make 990 knots (1000 knots at normal combat weight of 14,600lbs); with a General Electric X-24A (i.e., J79) engine it could make over 1200 knots (over 1380mph). Maximum rates of climb would have been, respectively, 36,000ft/min and 50,000ft/min. After three minutes of acceleration at 35,000ft speed would have been, respectively, 834 knots and over 1150 knots. Gross weight at take-off would have been 18,780lbs. Stall speed, a measure of carrier compatibility, would have been 116 knots (133mph).

In contrast to most proposals for the OS-130 competition, which showed swept or delta wings, McDonnell offered a short-wing (and straight-wing) Model 90/91. It argued that thickness ratio was all-important for truly supersonic speed and a thin straight wing was simpler and lighter than a thin swept wing. Drag in cruise and at high altitude was much lower than for a swept or delta wing. A graph in its proposal showed the realm of the thick straight wing extending from Mach 0.6 to Mach 0.8, the realm of the swept wing (with its sharp rise in drag) from Mach 0.8 to Mach 1.3 and the realm of the thin straight wing from Mach 1.1 up. The thin straight wing also offered advantages at take-off and landing approach speeds. The thin straight wing had been proven in low speed wind tunnel tests, in transonic and supersonic tunnel tests and in rocket model tests and flight tests – and McDonnell never used it on its later fighters. This is Model 90. Span would have been 35ft (area 305ft²) and length 48ft 3in (gross weight would have been 21,790lbs). McDonnell claimed that speed would have been 910 knots (Mach 1.58) at 38,000ft and combat ceiling 58,000ft; combat radius on internal fuel would have been 471nm. With afterburner, Model 90 was to climb to 35,000ft in 1.5 minutes. Because the engine compartment was underslung, it was relatively easy to accept a wide variety of engines: the Pratt & Whitney J57 (16,000lbs, giving a maximum speed of Mach 1.58), the Wright J67 (21,500lbs, Mach 1.94), the Allison J71 (14,500lbs, Mach 1.44), or the General Electric J73 (14,370lbs, Mach 1.075). Note the absence of the J79, which had not yet been approved and would not be for several years.

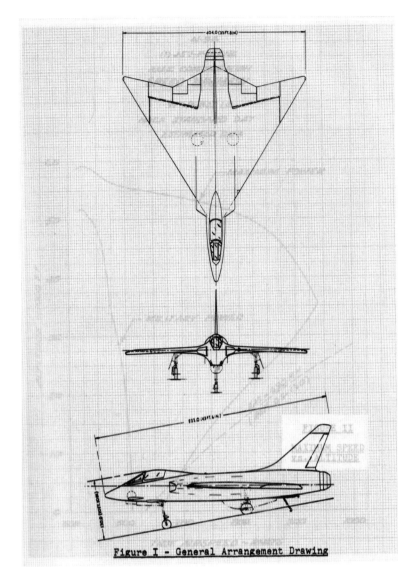

Figure I - General Arrangement Drawing

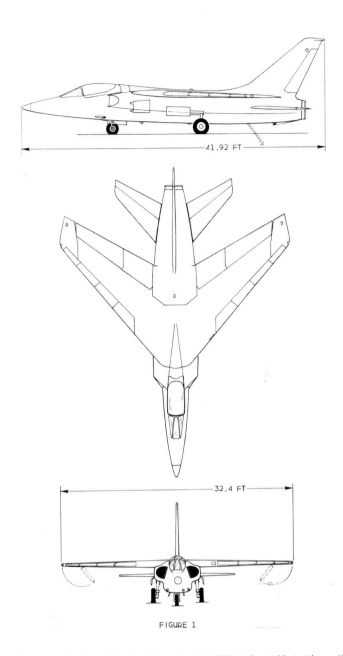

FIGURE 1

Northrop's N-94 delta was more typical of OS-130 proposals. This drawing was dated 26 January 1953. Span was 33ft 8in and length 42ft 2in. Gross weight was 19,282lbs. Alternative engines were the Pratt & Whitney J57-P-11 and the Wright J65-W (TJ31B3). The J57 offered 8000lbs of thrust (9220lbs military thrust, usable for 30 minutes) and 14,800lbs with afterburner (for five minutes). The J65 offered 11,000lbs of thrust with an afterburner Maximum speed at 35,000ft with the afterburner was Mach 1.63 (Mach 0.99 without afterburner) and combat radius with internal fuel was the required 300nm. Time to climb to 35,000ft with afterburner was 1.5 minutes.

Left: The idea that the compromises inherent in naval fighter design could be overcome by changing the aircraft's geometry for different flight regimes (combat vs carrier landing and take-off, for example) keeps coming back. Its most successful application has been the Grumman F-14 Tomcat. An F-14B of VF-32 (from *Harry S Truman*) is shown here with its wings at maximum stretch. In service the F-14 was quite successful, but the titanium joint around which the wing pivoted was a maintenance nightmare, causing it to be retired after the end of the Cold War, despite its superiority over the successor Hornet. (Grumman)

For OS-130, North American offered a fighter (its ESO 4927) with variable-incidence 45° swept wings, utterly unlike its F-100. The wing could tip up 12°. Flaps would have had boundary layer control, making it possible to deflect more steeply without causing airflow separation. The high variable-incidence wing could not accommodate landing gear, so the wheels were all in the fuselage. Span was 34.24ft and length 47.67ft (gross weight 25,510lbs). The engine was a J57-P. Guaranteed maximum speed at 35,000ft was Mach 1.51 and time to climb to 35,000ft was two minutes. Combat ceiling was 56,000ft. The nose radar was an APG-34 range-only fire-control set. The brochure showed four Sparrow missiles underwing. Since there was no space for a powerful guidance radar, required for either the beam-riding Sparrow I or the semi-active Sparrow III, they would have been the self-guided Sparrow II, using a K-band radar seeker. Developed by Douglas and Bendix, Sparrow II weighed about 420lbs. It was first air-launched in July 1952 and in August 1954 it shot down a target in a multi-target situation designed to stress its guidance. Sparrow II figured in several interceptor proposals, such as that for a missile-armed version of Grumman's F11F and later it was associated with the big Canadian CF-105 Arrow interceptor. The other armament in the brochure was a pair of packages containing eighty 1.5in NAKA rockets, successors to the then-standard 2.75in FFAR. This design was runner-up to the Vought design which became the F8U Crusader.

CHAPTER 3
FIGHTERS WITHOUT RADAR

NO NATION DEVELOPED particularly effective fighter defence during the First World War, although the British probably went furthest in their attempts to deal with German night bomber raids. Defence generally employed a standing patrol of fighters through which enemy bombers might have to pass. By 1918 the British had erected an elaborate defensive system around London, employing observers, search-lights, anti-aircraft guns and fighters. The defensive area was divided into zones (fighters or guns) to avoid a perennial problem in air defence, fighters being shot down by defending guns (later, defending missiles). The area over which the Germans might approach was too wide to cover with dense standing patrols; there had to be some way of detecting the attackers soon enough for fighters to attack them. In this case, the initial detectors were observers; even on a dark night, a Zeppelin or bomber could often be seen.

Detection was not enough. The bombers had to be tracked so that fighters could be directed against them. To do that, observer reports had to be fed into a central command post, a filter room in which data would be evaluated and then used to create a tactical picture – a picture of the evolving situation. On that basis decisions could be taken; aircraft

could be launched and directed and searchlights turned on and off. Gun batteries could be alerted. By the end of the war this system had been created, but so late that it was never really tested. Even so, it was the prototype of the system used in the Battle of Britain and then at sea, by both the Royal Navy and the US Navy.

The core of the system was the tactical picture created in the filter room. Given an effective filter room, any sort of aircraft detector could be inserted into the system – during the Battle of Britain that meant radar plus ground observers (the existing radar could not see inland) and various forms of signals intelligence. In turn, the filter room had to command fighters, which meant that it needed continuous real-time (i.e. radio) contact with them. It also had to be able to distinguish the fighters it controlled from attacking bombers, a problem even a century later.

In a pre-radar era, the naval equivalent of the British ground observers was lookouts on board ships at a distance from the fleet centre or the targets. Fighters could carry out standing patrols (CAPs in later parlance) or they could be launched on warning (Deck-Launched Interceptors).

The standard British naval fighter of the 1920s was the Fairey Flycatcher. A Flycatcher of 404 Flight (from *Argus*) is shown over Hong Kong. (David Hobbs)

The US Navy experimented with two-seat fighters. Despite its designation, the Curtiss F8C-1 was conceived as a light bomber (note the sign and the bomb visible between the wheels in this February 1928 photograph). The Scarff ring around the after cockpit holds a pair of Lewis guns. The F8C-1 was later redesignated OC-1 and was used by the Marines.

BRITISH EXPERIENCE

Through the interwar period, the Royal Navy envisaged two quite different fighter roles. One was defence of the fleet. The other was support for the vital air mission of finding and tracking an enemy fleet until it could be brought to battle. This latter mission seems to have become dominant in the 1930s. Its converse, preventing an enemy from finding and tracking the British fleet, became an essential fighter role, in 1939 more important (because more practical) than beating off air raids on the fleet. The fighters available when radar control did become possible in 1940 were shaped by this pre-war development.[1]

For the First World War Royal Navy, naval fighters were initially a way of destroying German Zeppelins, which were far more a reconnaissance than an attack threat. The German fleet evaded contact with the massed Grand Fleet on at least one occasion because its Zeppelins warned it in time; it followed that the High Seas Fleet could be trapped only if it was blinded first. Anti-Zeppelin operations were also motivated by the Germans' use of them to bomb London. From 1917 on, many ships in the Grand Fleet were fitted with flying-off platforms on their turrets or their superstructures and in 1918 British destroyers towed lighters carrying such aircraft in the North Sea. On one occasion a Camel fighter flew off such a lighter and destroyed a Zeppelin. The Germans had a few torpedo-carrying floatplanes, but they do not seem to have counted as a major threat to the Grand Fleet.

The wartime Grand Fleet also had an offensive air arm in the form of carrier-based torpedo bombers. Although floatplane torpedo bombers were deployed as early as 1914, the first truly effective fleet torpedo bombers were those launched from carrier decks. The first of them equipped the prototype carrier *Argus* just before the end of the war. The British reasoned that other navies would follow suit. In any future war their fleet would have to be defended against both ship- and land-based attackers. Moreover, by 1918 the British and other navies all saw spotting aircraft as key to the long-range gunnery of the future – the decisive weapon in a fleet-on-fleet battle. The spotters had to be protected and enemy spotters destroyed.

Given war experience, in December 1919 CinC Atlantic Fleet laid out future fleet air requirements.[2] He listed air functions as reconnaissance, spotting, torpedo attack (depth-bomb attack on submarines) and 'machine gun attack on hostile aircraft and on exposed personnel aboard

With much the performance of its land-based equivalents, the Hawker Nimrod was the standard single-seat FAA fighter of the 1930s. This one is from 408 Flight on board *Glorious*, 1931. (David Hobbs)

A Nimrod lands on *Furious*; note the arresting wire. Such gear was introduced only late in the 1930s. The Nimrod was a naval equivalent of the land-based Hawker Fury, so when it was introduced it was only slightly outperformed by the standard RAF interceptor. By the time RAF interceptor technology had made the next leap, to the Hurricane and Spitfire, it was desperately producing them because war was clearly coming; it could not spare any capacity for navalised versions. They did not appear until well after war broke out.

enemy ships and destroyers'. It was apparently assumed that carriers would be specialised, so that for example there would be reconnaissance carriers responsible for maintaining three reconnaissance aircraft airborne at all times and six more once contact had been established with the enemy. During the war each capital ship had carried a two-seater spotter, but they had proven inadequate. For the future, each division of four battleships should have its own three-seater carrier-based spotter in the air throughout an action. Ideally each division should have a carrier and eight spotters. Torpedo aircraft had not yet been tested, but CinC Atlantic Fleet suggested that in future their first duty would be to gain air superiority by sinking the enemy's carrier – a very early approach to the concept adopted later by the Royal Navy and by other carrier navies. 'All the advantages of air superiority would accrue to the side which succeeded in destroying its opponent's aircraft carriers and with them the reliefs and landing decks for any aircraft that had already flown off.' CinC Atlantic envisaged a tactical unit of twelve torpedo bombers, which would suffice to attack two or three ships and wanted at least two such units – two carriers. Fighters were clearly valuable, but it was not so easy to estimate how many might be needed. However, 'in order to provide for concentrated action at the outset, one carrier should be allocated to fighters only'.

All of this meant a substantial carrier force, even though aircraft had only limited capacities. At this time the Atlantic Fleet was expected to operate in four divisions (ten battleships, four battlecruisers). CinC Atlantic envisaged three types of carrier: the Air Reconnaissance Cruiser, the Divisional Carrier with spotters on board and Fleet Carriers for torpedo aircraft, bombers or fighters. There should be three Air Reconnaissance Cruisers, one for each three reconnaissance aircraft (presumably because they would be widely spread); four spotter carriers (with a few fighters as well as spotters); two fleet carriers with torpedo bombers on board; and one fighter carrier (twenty-five fighters). Other fighters

would be on board the capital ships and the accompanying cruisers and also on board other types of carrier. Further carriers would be needed if, for example, the Mediterranean Fleet battle squadrons joined the Atlantic Fleet.

Although the figures changed, this analysis explains why the British sought so much carrier tonnage at the 1921 Washington Conference. In July 1920 the Naval Staff met to decide how many aircraft (and how many carriers) the projected post-war fleet needed. Money was already short, so it is startling to see how large the programme was. At this time the only completed British carrier was *Argus*. The ex-Chilean *Eagle* had been partly completed for tests, but there was serious interest in converting her back into a battleship for sale to Chile (partly to justify construction of much better carriers). The cruiser-sized *Hermes* was building. *Furious* had been converted into a semi-carrier with very limited capabilities. Her two near-sisters *Courageous* and *Glorious* were in reserve, with no real battle fleet function. The Staff decided that not only should *Eagle* be completed as a carrier, but also *Hermes*; and *Furious* and one of her half-sisters should be converted into capacious carriers with double hangars.

The minimum number of aircraft would be forty-eight spotters (to keep twelve in the air simultaneously); twenty-two reconnaissance aircraft (to keep six airborne simultaneously); one flight of twelve torpedo bombers or bombers; and as many fighters as possible not only on board carriers but also on board battleships and cruisers. *Eagle* would carry twenty-two spotters for five capital-ship divisions; *Argus* would carry ten for two divisions; *Furious* would carry ten spotters for two divisions of battlecruisers (because she was as fast as those ships) plus as many torpedo bombers and fighters as possible; *Courageous* or *Glorious* would carry as many reconnaissance aircraft as possible; and *Hermes* would carry only fighters. The only later change in this programme was that both *Courageous* and *Glorious* were converted into fast fleet carriers.

This July 1920 list was later used in other contexts to explain the large British carrier requirement. The British apparently considerably underestimated carrier capability to support aircraft, hence required much more tonnage than the detailed fleet requirement would have justified.

Fighters of the 1920s

At the outset the requirement that fighters operate from turret-top flying-off platforms as well as from flight decks, drastically limited the size of any initial naval fighter. The RAF view was that because fleet fighters would be small (so that they could be fast and manoeuvrable), it would be relatively easy to adapt land-based fighters to naval use.[3] How many fighters the fleet needed would depend entirely on the opposition it was likely to meet, hence was difficult to forecast. If the fleet used the same fighter as the RAF, it could draw on RAF reserve aircraft whenever necessary. During the First World War the fleet had adopted the same Sopwith Camel used by the Royal Flying Corps. The successor Snipe, which the RAF had adopted, had not proven adaptable to shipboard operation. About 1920 the Air Ministry decided that the successor fighter would be the Nieuport Night Hawk. It offered high performance but had a defective radial engine. A few were produced for the Royal Navy as the Night Jar, powered by wartime rotary engines, but the hope of producing a common RAF–FAA fighter seems to have been abandoned. Instead Specification 7/21 was issued for a specialised fleet fighter. It produced the Fairey Flycatcher, the standard shipboard fighter of the 1920s.[4]

A competition for a new fleet fighter was held in 1926 (Specification 21/26) spurred partly because Rear Admiral F C Dreyer, Assistant Chief of the Naval Staff, pointed out in 1924 during discussion of the proposed spotter-reconnaissance aircraft (S/R) that he understood that the new French carrier fighter far outperformed the Flycatcher.[5] One of the competitors was a heavily-modified Flycatcher. Hopes that there might be a common RAF–FAA fighter were not dead. Some of the 21/26 competitors were modified versions of aircraft built for a parallel competition (9/26) for a new RAF fighter.[6] The specified Mercury IIA radial proved unreliable and the competition was rerun in 1927. By this time a new generation of low-drag liquid-cooled engines (V-12s) was appearing, beginning with the US Curtiss D-12 Conqueror, followed by the Rolls-Royce F (renamed Kestrel in 1930). Hawker offered a carrier version of a new interceptor it had designed for the RAF (to Specification F.20/27) specifically to demonstrate the superiority of such a design. As redesigned this aircraft was adopted as the Hawker Nimrod (to Specification 16/30). Uncertainty about the choice of a new fighter explains why Royal Navy documents of the late 1920s refer to the 'future fighter' rather than to the Nimrod.

There was a parallel specification for a two-seat fighter or F/R (22/26).[7] Its conception goes back several years. In 1922 the Admiralty pointed out that, given limited space on board carriers, it wanted a single aircraft to perform both spotting and reconnaissance tasks. Its logic was that reconnaissance was needed to bring the British fleet into

position to deal with an enemy fleet, after which spotting would be needed to support the fleet's gunfire. The Air Ministry, which was responsible for technical advice, pointed out that the two tasks might not be compatible. It asked the Admiralty for more details. In 1924 the Admiralty pointed to two distinct reconnaissance tasks. Fleet Reconnaissance was the search for the enemy fleet. Once the enemy fleet was found, it had to be shadowed, a role the Admiralty called Contact Reconnaissance.

The distinction mattered. An aircraft searching for the enemy fleet might break contact as soon as it spotted the fleet, hence would not need to fight for its information. However, the enemy would have every incentive to beat off any shadower; later British official publications would point out that destroying a shadower might well abort enemy air attacks. At a December 1924 meeting, Rear Admiral Dreyer called for a new type of aircraft, a reconnaissance fighter, which could fight for its information. It would not be the three-seat spotter-reconnaissance aircraft then under discussion, but it would need much higher performance. The discussion at the time was complicated by the Admiralty's wish for amphibious aircraft for both roles (the Air Ministry pointed out that for high performance they should be primarily land planes). The Air Ministry also seems to have tried to avoid developing Dreyer's reconnaissance fighter, but it had to bow to the Admiralty's wishes.

The new type of fighter appeared in the list of 1926 specifications as 22/26; it was now called a fighter-reconnaissance aircraft (F/R).[8] As indicated, it did not replace the longer-range lower performance S/R, which was not considered capable of fighting. F/R remained a vital FAA type of aircraft through the interwar period. It was never considered a means of fleet air defence; it was a means of ensuring contact with an enemy fleet so that the enemy might be attacked effectively and then so that the enemy fleet could be brought to action with the British fleet.

By this time the RAF was interested in a high-performance light day bomber with a minimum speed of 160mph – fighter speed (specification 12/26). Most firms refused to tender, on the ground that the requirements were impossible to fulfil. However, Fairey was already advertising its Fox light bomber, powered by the US Conqueror engine; in effect 12/26 called for a light bomber with similar performance. Re-engined with a British engine, the Fox could achieve 189mph, a remarkable performance at the time. Hawker won the RAF competition with its Hart. It won the parallel 22/26 competition with a navalised version, which was designated the Osprey.[9]

Tactics of fleet air defence

While these aircraft were being designed and produced, the Royal Navy analysed the requirements of fleet air defence. It had to consider two different situations, one in which the British fleet faced another fleet (by this time, presumably Japanese) and the other in which the fleet operated for a sustained period near land, on which enemy aircraft might be based. In that case it would be impossible either to provide timely warning or to maintain fighters constantly airborne, so the only viable answer to a land-based threat, it seemed, was anti-aircraft firepower. That justified a considerable effort to develop high-angle fire-control systems (HACS) and anti-aircraft guns. Although it might seem that the British fleet of the 1920s was not particularly well armed against air attack, the Royal Navy was funding development of the most advanced short-range anti-aircraft weapon in the world, the 2pdr pom-pom, as well as a variety of fire-control devices. Investment in production lagged badly, because these new weapons and systems were produced during the period covered by the 'Ten Year Rule': they could be placed in production as and when money became available because the international situation had worsened. That was much what happened in the 1930s.

It happened that British faith in shipboard anti-aircraft fire was badly misplaced. The HACS was far less effective than imagined.[10] Even when properly aimed, time-fuzed medium-calibre fire rarely destroyed aircraft, but the interwar Royal Navy never learned just how ineffective its weapons were. Although it was the first to try drone targets, unlike the contemporary US Navy it was unwilling to try to shoot them down. Thus it did not learn that even if a 4in shell burst within the supposed lethal distance of an aircraft, it was most unlikely to do fatal damage. The pre-war US Navy probably somewhat exaggerated the problem: drones were remarkably survivable. Once war began, the Royal Navy discovered that its powerful anti-aircraft batteries were mainly a way of deterring attackers but only rarely of shooting them down. Fighters turned out to be the only really effective way of destroying attacking aircraft, a conclusion the US Navy was reaching by 1939.

The British certainly continued to send fighters to sea alongside their anti-aircraft batteries, but their faith in anti-aircraft firepower probably led them to expect carriers operating with a battle line (with many such guns) would be reasonably safe from air attack. Fighters had other roles, such as protecting spotters (for fire superiority once battle was joined) and also to support torpedo attacks on an enemy fleet by strafing and thus dislocating enemy air defences.

As an indicator of early British doctrine, the official 1929 war game rules explained that the function of fleet fighters was to gain local air superiority, either over the British fleet or over the enemy's fleet (in support, for example, of spotters).[11] The first British naval fighters assigned to the new carriers were specialised aircraft (Fairey Flycatchers). However, by the late 1920s the FAA was being equipped with the Hawker Nimrod, a version of a standard day fighter showing little modification for naval use. The difference seems to have been that such unmodified aircraft were proving themselves perfectly capable of deck landing on a moving carrier at sea, whereas earlier lighter aircraft were more specialised.

It was accepted that a carrier flight deck could be destroyed by bombing, but that would not sink a carrier; it would merely render her useless as a carrier. This was much the view of the US and Japanese navies. However, the significance of flight-deck attack changed during the 1930s. Initially it seemed that even to destroy a flight deck seemed a rather difficult undertaking. In the 1920s it appeared that only horizontal (level) bombers could deliver heavy enough bombs. Anti-aircraft fire could force such bombers to high altitude (and limited accuracy)

The threat to carriers changed suddenly in the early 1930s, as the US Navy began to demonstrate that it could hit manoeuvring ships with heavy dive bombs. Suddenly a carrier flight deck was quite vulnerable. The carrier herself would probably survive fatal damage to her flight deck, but repairs to the deck would entail a lengthy period in a navy yard. Worse, dive bombers typically approached at high altitude and often could not be seen for very long before they struck. Bomber performance was improving, drastically reducing any warning time afforded by outlying fleet units.

Another important factor in British thinking was carrier capacity. Perhaps because British pilots took RAF practices to sea with them, they assumed that a flight deck had to be clear before an aircraft could land. There was no pressure, as there was in the US Navy, for very rapid

landings to get a large air group aboard. Instead, each pilot was responsible for his own landing, as he was ashore. US observers found British operation rather slow. British practice, unlike that in the US Navy, equated the capacity of a carrier to her hangar capacity. That was particularly significant for the carriers dating from the First World War, which had small hangars. As already noted, too, British landing practices made it difficult to operate large numbers of aircraft from one ship, because she might have to spend too long recovering them and thus might steam too far from the defence offered by the main body of the fleet.

About 1931 the Royal Navy became aware of the US use of barriers and deck parks. It was immediately clear that the capacity of the older carriers could be increased dramatically. At that point the separation of the RAF had a crucial effect. It could rule on carrier aircraft capacity. In 1931 British official belief in arms control and disarmament was still strong and the League of Nations was about to meet in Geneva to consider general disarmament proposals – including limits on air arms. The RAF was not about to allow the carriers, which it did not consider central, to eat further into the land-based bomber force it espoused. The conference took several years to come to nothing, but the idea of increasing capacity in the older carriers was not revived.

A barrier did figure in the design of the first new carrier in many years, Ark Royal and DNC pointed out that it made possible a deck park so large that her whole air group could be stowed on deck (as in the US Navy). The ship was built with arrester gear and a barrier, but it does not seem that the option of a deck park was fully absorbed by either the naval staff or the FAA. When the ship entered service, many pilots saw no point in using arrester gear. US observers noticed that many of them missed wires or slipped them. Certainly the ship's rated capacity was that of her hangar. That was also the case with the armoured deck (actually, armoured hangar) carriers which succeeded Ark Royal.

Limited capacity in turn affected aircraft design. The Royal Navy was certainly well aware of the range of aircraft missions it needed. Carriers were expected to provide all or most of the fleet's scouts; the Royal Navy was slower than others to install catapults on battleships and cruisers. The carriers would be the main source of any air striking force. Past British experience had emphasised the need to slow down a fleeing enemy fleet so that the main British offensive weapons, fleet guns and heavy torpedoes, could destroy it. Aircraft torpedoes could slow an enemy fleet, but given modern anti-torpedo protection, they did not carry heavy enough warheads, it was thought, to sink capital ships. The carriers also supplied the spotters which would ensure that the fleet's guns would achieve decisive results. In this list, defensive fighters came a dismal last. Some of the roles could be combined: the Swordfish was described as a TSR aircraft. Despite an attempt to frame a specification, it was impossible to combine the fighter role with the spotter role.[12] To a limited extent a fighter could be used for reconnaissance, however.

The pre-war concept of carrier support for battle line operations was demonstrated during the Bismarck operation in May 1941. After Bismarck sank Hood and drove off the cruisers and the surviving battleship Prince of Wales, she evaded detection for a time. She was found by long-range flying boats. Unless she was slowed down, she was likely to evade pursuit altogether. Aircraft from the carrier Ark Royal found her and attacked. As forecast pre-war, their torpedoes were insufficient to defeat the torpedo protection of the German battleship. They were, however, quite sufficient to damage her badly enough that other forces, which could destroy the German battleship, could catch up. In this case the fatal damage was to the battleship's steering gear.

In the Osprey, Hawker achieved near-single-seat fighter performance in a two-seater. This Osprey is shown on board *Ark Royal* in 1939. Replacement of both the Nimrod and the Osprey became urgent as aircraft were worn out during the crisis with Italy over Ethiopia in 1935–6. By that time both were completely obsolete. (David Hobbs)

As in the other carrier navies, tactical development during the 1920s was limited by aircraft performance and by the absence of large fast carriers with substantial air groups. Exercises showed that a carrier would rarely receive sufficient warning to launch fighters. Security would demand a standing fighter patrol (later called a CAP in the US Navy) whenever it was within range of an enemy air striking force. The 1928 issue of the Admiralty publication *Progress in Tactics* reported that a Bison reconnaissance aircraft from *Furious* had penetrated to a depth of 111nm and that Fairey IIIF aircraft had found and bombed *Eagle* at a range of 115nm (although her position was known within narrow limits at the time). In a 1930 exercise the maximum range of air reconnaissance was 165nm, compared to 135nm in 1929 (it is not clear that longer ranges were achieved before the Second World War).[13] These figures were not bad even by early Second World War standards, as effective strike range was determined by navigation more than by how far an aircraft could fly before running out of fuel.

In two 1928 exercises ('MU2' and 'LG'), each side maintained fighter patrols over its own battlefleet. They proved of value against simulated torpedo bomber attacks, but fighters often failed to see aircraft before observers aboard surface ships did. The 1928 issue of *Progress in Tactics* reported the 'great advantage' of having surface ships direct the fighters. The current Fairey Flycatcher had no onboard radio to make this

possible and it was already clear that visual signals could not easily be read from the air. The best the Royal Navy could do was to have an S/R aircraft, which did have radio (so that it could report from a distance and also so that it could send firing corrections to ships), in company with the fighters. Future fighters should have a radio-telephone; work on a suitable radio set began.[14] By this time, too, the Royal Navy was beginning to doubt whether its fighters could deny the air to enemy spotters. Attacks on spotters could be effective, but the fighters often failed to find them. There were also studies of proper aircraft allocation based, it seems, on gaming rather than on actual operations.[15]

By 1930, the Royal Navy was looking to outlying surface ships to warn of the approach of enemy aircraft; ships 10 miles out seemed adequate. Experiments had shown that a lookout could expect to see an aircraft at 6–8nm, although sometimes aircraft were seen as much as 20nm away; formations could be seen at slightly greater ranges.[16] Once he picked up an aircraft, a lookout could follow it slightly further. Against an aircraft flying at 60 knots or nearly 70mph (1nm per minute), the combination of stand-off and visual range might offer about 15 minutes warning. That was enough to launch fighters from deck; in a 1930 exercise ('ZC') fighters successfully intercepted enemy torpedo bombers. At this time the standard British torpedo bomber (Ripon) cruised at 70 knots, but the new two-seater was expected to cruise at 85 knots.

The main problem in operating fighters, which had the shortest endurance of the carrier aircraft, was that the carrier had to turn into the wind so frequently to launch and recover them. If the wind was unfavourable, she might easily lose touch with the fleet if she engaged in frequent air operations. The FAA learned that mass operation was possible only if returning aircraft massed, waiting their turn to land. Slow recovery was a problem: aircraft had to return to the ship with at least half an hour of fuel left.

By this time it was assumed that all of a fleet's carriers would operate together under a single Senior Officer of Carriers (soon to be Rear Admiral of Carriers in the Mediterranean Fleet), hence would contribute jointly to fleet air operations and should remain within visual signalling touch (to avoid giving themselves away by radio signals).[17] Exercises showed that two carriers could easily operate in close company, a mile apart in a steady wind (3 or 4 miles apart in 'light and fluky' wind). Three would be no more difficult; the 1932 edition of *Progress in Tactics* remarked that 'the advantages of operating in close company are manifest with regard to security from surface attack'. If one carrier turned into the wind, all had to. Typical air doctrine at this time dictated that each of the three fleet carriers send out a search of six S/R at dawn to maximum depth. Each would contribute three fighters to a joint defensive patrol. The air striking force would comprise twelve torpedo bombers supported by six single-seat fighters and one scout (an S/R).[18] No single carrier could provide sufficient S/R to handle the separate requirements for search, action observation and spotting. Three flights (eighteen aircraft) were considered a bare minimum. In a single carrier, they would have to be carried at the expense of torpedo bombers – not, note, fighters. Without sufficient S/R, it might be impossible to keep an enemy fleet under the required continuous observation. In one exercise ('CC' of 1932), an enemy fleet was unobserved for 45 minutes or more because the two fleets did not close as was usually the case.

The combination of defensive fighters and fleet anti-aircraft guns raised a difficult problem. The Admiralty view, as stated in 1931, was that the fleet could never rely on having enough fighters available; high-angle gunfire would be the main fleet defence. Fighters would operate in a kind of outer defence zone, their primary role being to attack enemy formations before they could attack, breaking them up. By doing so they would simplify the task of the high-angle guns, which would otherwise be saturated by sheer numbers of aircraft arriving together. It was clear that fighters might well fall victim to the fleet's own guns; all that could be written, in 1931 or later, was that good recognition (IFF) was vital. The problem of ensuring it was never solved and indeed remains three-quarters of a century later.

Exercises in 1931 continued to show the value of fighters distracting enemy anti-aircraft personnel to make torpedo attacks effective. The British became interested in pre-emptive attacks on enemy carriers to prevent them from launching their own strikes. They were sceptical. On the tactical table, it seemed that enemy carriers would have sufficient warning of an attack from their own advanced forces to launch their own air striking forces, as these aircraft would already be ranged on deck. Fleet exercises and tactical games were all somewhat deceptive, as they had to be staged to ensure that both fleets knew their enemy was at sea and to make sure that action was joined. The conclusion was that carriers should keep their striking forces ranged on deck to the maximum possible extent, so that they could take immediate advantage of either an enemy report or a report that an enemy attack was imminent. The three British carriers all had auxiliary (forward) flight decks intended specifically to launch fighters without interfering with the strike aircraft on the larger flight deck above, so this doctrine did not necessarily conflict with the use of fighters to defend the carriers or the fleet.

The British had been interested in using aircraft to warn of approaching air raids as early as 1927, when they had a single S/R orbit a carrier. In 1932, standard practice was to use all-round sector patrols of four to six S/R in 90–60° sectors, 10–20nm from the fleet, to warn both the fleet and defending fighters. In eight exercises, fighters achieved 67 per cent success in attacking enemy aircraft before they reached the fleet. Failures were typically due to defective communications; work was underway to solve this problem. Current instructions called for the fighters to wait above the fleet, attacking without restriction and breaking off when anti-aircraft fire became too hot. They were never to come within pom-pom range. In good visibility fighters were expected to find and attack high-level bombers, ruining their aim and reducing the threat to torpedo bombers vulnerable even to single-purpose secondary guns.

Fighter control was difficult partly because there were insufficient radio personnel to maintain a dedicated channel ('wave' in British parlance) for air defence patrol aircraft. The proposed solution was to use the Admiral's channel, which all ships of the fleet monitored.

By 1933 the fleet had fast two-seat Osprey fighter-reconnaissance aircraft, which could be used in exercises to simulate fast bombers. They demonstrated that it was difficult to detect them early enough. The Ospreys could also dive bomb with light bombs (at angles later characterised as glide bombing). They demonstrated what difficult targets dive bombers were – and how effective they could be. The best defence, apart from fighter attack, was to break up their formations by gunfire before they could get close enough to make their dives. Once they were diving, almost the only defence was the pom-pom, which was just entering large-scale production.

Methods of obtaining warning of hostile air attack were re-evaluated. The alternatives were to overfly enemy bases or carriers; to use ships stationed around the fleet; and to use aircraft stationed around the fleet. In theory, with a cloud layer, aircraft would be responsible for observation above and ships for observation below. However, the 1934 edition of *Progress in Tactics* (reporting 1934 exercises; there was no 1933 edition) warned that it was impossible to guarantee that the fleet would have any warning at all.

In an exercise ('RY'), defensive aircraft patrolled 12nm from fleet centre. Calculation showed that to be 100 per cent effective in detecting attackers, eight aircraft would have to be arranged in 45° sectors at each height patrolled. In the exercise, however, only five aircraft were available. They were placed in 72° sectors, offering coverage of about 70 per cent of incoming raids in practice (roughly agreeing with calculation). The 12nm depth was chosen because attackers were expected to sight their targets at 10–15nm, then work around on a circle to find an attacking position. Even if the whole circle was not covered, typical attacking practice would give scouts a good chance of seeing the attackers. In the exercise, high bombers were not detected. The conclusion was that the fleet needed air screens at two heights, to deal with high and low attackers or else an air screen plus a surface screen. Overall, the exercise showed that 12nm was the minimum depth for an air screen – and any greater range would have required many more aircraft.

One lesson learned from the exercise was that even a short war (in this case, 6.5 hours) imposed enormous wear on aircraft and pilots, who flew a total of 110 hours on patrol. Many exercises, including those involving RAF flying boats, demonstrated the strain entailed by day after day of reconnaissance.

In keeping with British interest in reconnaissance as a necessary prelude to any battle, the 1934 edition of *Progress in Tactics* pointed out that although it was impossible to prevent enemy reconnaissance aircraft from sighting and reporting a fleet, every effort should be made to attack them as soon as possible: 'the fact of shadowing aircraft being shot down, in itself constitutes protection against attack'.[19]

Looking back, the important observations in the 1934 edition were that warning of impending air attack was difficult at best, that dive bombing was extremely difficult to counter and that attacks could be ruined by destroying shadowers (snoopers), without which they might not materialise at all. These points must have seemed particularly important to a Mediterranean Fleet facing massed Italian land-based airpower as the crisis over Ethiopia developed. Later exercises showed that it might be difficult to deal with shadowers.[20]

The torpedo was still considered by far the most effective aerial weapon against enemy capital ships, dive bombing (of capital ships) being a useful means of disabling enemy anti-aircraft weapons to open the way for the slow torpedo bombers. Unfortunately the torpedo bombers and the new fighter dive bombers (Skuas) were poorly matched in performance, the torpedo bombers enjoying greater endurance and the Skuas (yet to enter service) much higher speed. Work on air patrols to warn of enemy aircraft continued.[21]

Exercises called the value of fighter defence into question. In a 1935 Mediterranean Fleet exercise ('SE') fighters got into range of the attacking torpedo bombers only after the attackers were within fleet gun range. Fleet gunfire was considered so much more effective that such action was unacceptable. A later exercise ('SF') showed that fleet gunfire could be saturated by well-synchronised attacks and therefore that there was an urgent need for some form of anti-aircraft co-ordination. That led to appointment of air defence officers (ADOs) on board ships, with special anti-aircraft designation arrangements. The authors of *Progress in Tactics* (1935) recognised that the ADO had to resist the tendency to focus on torpedo bombers, which the Royal Navy considered the most dangerous form of attack, to the exclusion of bombers, which foreign powers (unspecified) seemed to emphasise.

In the aftermath of the near-war with Italy over Ethiopia, the Mediterranean Fleet pondered what it could do to counter land-based Italian air power. It was clear that direct attack against any but an undefended base was too dangerous. Carrier aircraft had so short an endurance that the attacking carrier would have to remain within range not only of aircraft at the base but even fast Italian surface craft until she could recover her aircraft. Even if surprise was achieved, the slow carrier aircraft would surely be followed back by enemy shore-based aircraft and the carrier struck while recovering her aircraft. Worse, FAA bomb loads were too small to have much effect on permanent enemy defences. However, in war these risks might be acceptable if surprise could be achieved. The Mediterranean Fleet planned the Taranto Raid on this basis and incorporated it into its battle instructions as early as 1936.[22]

Progress in Tactics continued to emphasise the role of fleet anti-aircraft fire in air defence.[23] However, the focus shifted. The enemy had to locate the British fleet before attacking. Until the fleet had been found, the best formation was the most compact, to make air observation difficult. However, effective warning demanded lookouts as far from fleet centre as possible. The only way to reconcile the two was to rely not on surface lookouts but instead on air lookouts, which an enemy would not easily follow to the fleet. Until the fleet was spotted, fighters could be stood down. Deck-launched interceptors would suffice against an enemy snooper (three fighters should be flown off when one was spotted). Once attack seemed likely, a standing fighter patrol should be set up.[24] Given the priority the British placed on heavy gunnery to achieve a decisive result, *Progress in Tactics* prescribed fighter defence of

Ospreys of 800 Naval Air Squadron are shown in 1937. The squadron's other aircraft were Nimrods. (David Hobbs)

British spotting and action observation aircraft. Offensive action against enemy spotters was also emphasised, with a short discussion of what proportion of fighters should be devoted to each role.

The 1937 edition of *Progress in Tactics* pointed out that a compact formation might well evade detection altogether, even in areas within enemy air range. Operation in the Mediterranean, then, might well be less impractical than many had imagined. Even after the fleet had been spotted by enemy reconnaissance, it might be quite difficult for the enemy air striking force to make contact 'through navigational error, discrepancies in the shadower's reports, bad visibility, etc., especially when the enemy air personnel are inexperienced and distances are large. A probability of evading actual attack or a material proportion of attacks, may thus persist if the Cruising Disposition is still kept concentrated.'[25] Final transition to the dispersed air defence formation, then, in which evasion would be impossible, would probably be when fighter patrols were set up because attack would be considered likely. At that point extended warning would be essential in order to direct the fighters onto the attackers. As before, what amounted to IFF was recognised as a key problem. The Mediterranean Fleet had developed some solutions.[26]

Perhaps the most interesting remark in the discussion of fighter defence in the 1937 edition of *Progress in Tactics* was a description of the procedure to minimise the delay in reporting hostile aircraft, which had been adopted in both the Home and Mediterranean Fleets. A Controlling Ship – normally a carrier – would provide all information to the defensive fighters on patrol. On board this ship an officer would 'sift all reports of value and relay them to the leader of the fighter patrols, who detaches the necessary aircraft from his force to intercept and attack the enemy'.[27] This was not quite fighter control as understood in the Second World War, as it envisaged a separate fighter leader aloft. However, the role of sifting available information certainly foreshadowed what was done in an Action Information Centre or Combat Information Centre a few years later.

The final pre-war edition of *Progress in Tactics* was issued in June 1939. It showed considerable changes. Instead of remaining close to the battle line, carriers were now to operate in looser formation, keeping in visual touch with each other, despite the increased danger of surface attack.[28] Carrier air defence was still difficult. In an exercise, a carrier's fighters were dealing with a shadower when a striking force arrived, attacking unopposed. *Progress in Tactics* advised that when numbers were limited fighters should be confined to the area over the ship they were defending, but the previous idea of a supervising officer (who might make that possible) was not mentioned.

The most striking announcement in *Progress in Tactics 1939* was the existence of a means of air warning in the form of RDF (radar). The Portsmouth Signal School had developed the sole naval type, SA (ship-to-air, later Type 79), all other forms of RDF being Air Ministry projects. SA had been fitted to the battleship *Rodney* and the cruiser *Sheffield* during the latter part of 1938. It had already detected an aircraft at 10,000ft at a range of 40–50nm (at 1000ft, 10nm), with a range accuracy of about half a mile and a bearing accuracy of about 15°. Surface ships could be detected at ranges of 2–7nm. True to its heritage of radio silence, the Royal Navy included among disadvantages of the new sensor that an enemy could intercept its signals and D/F to find their source and that radar aerials would materially reduce flag hoisting (i.e. visual signalling) capacity. The antennas would also displace HF/DF antennas which had recently come into service and RDF signals would reduce radio range at medium frequencies, presumably due to generation of harmonics of their signals.

In addition to SA, there was AS (air-surface, later called ASV, air-to-surface vessel), which had already been demonstrated in an Anson aircraft, the type used by Coastal Command. Current range was 6nm, which was already beyond visual range in northern waters and it was hoped to extend that to 15nm. As with all airborne radars, at short range reflection off the sea ruined accuracy, so *minimum* range was about two miles. AS was to be fitted in FAA aircraft.[29]

At this stage RDF was described as a means of warning, potentially considerably better than lookouts or even airborne pickets, but there was no discussion of the use of RDF information to control fighters. That may, however, have been implicit in the earlier approach to centralising fighter control using a designated ship.

Fighters of the 1930s

Successive editions of *Progress in Tactics* described what the fleet should (or could) do with existing resources, the references to new technology being limited to developments such as new radios. For British naval air planners, the question was always how to distribute limited carrier (and

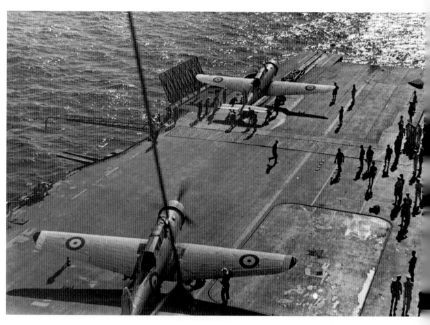

The Blackburn Skua represented a new approach to fleet air defence: to neutralise the enemy's aircraft carriers by dive bombing them. Here two of them are being launched from *Ark Royal*. Note the elaborate trolley on the port catapult, onto which the forward Skua is being loaded. (David Hobbs)

cruiser and capital ship) space to best advantage. That meant at the least combining different functions so that, when needed, the fleet would have the greatest possible striking power. Staff work on new types of aircraft began in the autumn of 1933. The Osprey was criticised because it could not contribute to fleet striking power. The British were well aware that the US Navy had been successful in developing dive bombers based on (and often designated as) fighters. Plans for air modernisation described in 1934 therefore envisaged only two types, a new F/R capable of dive bombing and a TSR (the Swordfish) which combined the torpedo bomber and S/R functions.[30] From the outset, the dive bomber weapon was specified as a 500lb bomb.

Unfortunately early Air Ministry estimates showed a speed of 193mph, which DNAD rejected as it was about the speed of existing fighters designed eight years earlier. That 'would soon leave us with virtually no Fleet fighters at all'. DNAD urged the Air Ministry to relax requirements so that designers could do better. For example, it could abandon the usual provision for conversion to floats, saving 250lbs. In August 1934 he proposed to reply to the Air Ministry that 'Their Lordships are so impressed with the importance of producing a Fighter-Dive-Bomber of really high performance for operation from carriers that they would ask the Air Council to investigate the result which might be expected to follow the acceptance of an "all-up" weight of not greater than say 7500lbs [7000lbs crossed out, replacing the earlier limit of 6000lbs] and of completely abandoning all provision for an alternative floatplane undercarriage.' He also wanted the Air Council to indicate the result of accepting a 250lb 'B' or SAP bomb instead of the 500-pounder initially requested.

Specification O.27/34 for a Dive-bomber Fighter was issued on 12 December 1934. It explained why dive-bombing capability was so important: the aircraft was 'to disable the opposing FAA by dive-bombing attacks on hostile carriers and other vessels and to undertake such other dive-bombing attacks as may be required'. Engagement of hostile aircraft was a secondary role. Reconnaissance was not mentioned;

presumably the back-seater was essential to navigate the dive bomber to its target. However, the F/R role would place the new aircraft above the enemy fleet once TSRs had found it.

The reference to the opposing FAA meant Japan, the enemy on which the Royal Navy had concentrated since the early 1920s. The wording of the specification suggests that by 1933–4 the Admiralty had concluded that the best way to deal with opposing carriers was pre-emption and that the ideal way to neutralise carriers was to dive-bomb their flight decks. That was certainly the conclusion the Japanese themselves had reached, as had the Americans and it explains why both navies spent so much effort on dive bombing. The British position was more ambiguous. *Progress in Tactics 1939* described a major fleet exercise in which aircraft from one carrier attacked the carrier on the other side with bombs; the other side attacked with torpedoes. The bombs were assessed as causing some damage (a US or Japanese view would have been that the opposing carrier's flight deck would have been destroyed); the carrier attacked with torpedoes was assessed as sunk. Readers of *Progress in Tactics* were told that torpedoes were the best aerial weapon because they made the highest percentage of hits and the greater effect of each hit as compared to a similar weight of bombs. This was certainly true of battleship targets, but on the other hand newer battleships were designed to resist heavier warheads than British aerial torpedoes could deliver.

For the moment, the Skua was the essential complement to the Swordfish TSR. The new carrier *Ark Royal*, designed in 1933–4, was to have divided its seventy-two aircraft into one-third Skuas and two-thirds multi-role aircraft (Swordfish TSRs). This was about as many dive bombers as somewhat later US carriers had on board.

From a fighter point of view, the Skua was the victim of rapidly changing policy. The specification called for two forward-firing guns and one flexible gun for the navigator/wireless operator. In April 1936 the Advisory Committee on the FAA considered production arrangements. DTD (Air Ministry) pointed out that two forward-firing Vickers guns were hardly adequate for a fighter to enter service in 1937, as the RAF was placing eight-gun fighters in service. Blackburn offered an additional gun in each wing (total four); Vickers considered it no problem to add four or even six more guns (total eight). The Skua ended up with four. It would have been desirable to add more defensive armament, but that was impracticable at so late a stage. The Skua had not yet flown, but production was urgent because the existing Nimrods and Ospreys would soon have to be retired; wastage had been above normal during the Mediterranean emergency (the near-war with Italy). Limited Skua performance, including in a dive, was considered acceptable because by this time the dive-bomber fighter was considered no more than a stop-gap until a more capable dive bomber reconnaissance (DBR) aircraft became available (see below). At this point (April 1936) the total Skua requirement was 180.

The Osprey catapult plane replacement was put off to 1935, the Air Ministry providing money in that year's Estimates for an experimental aircraft. There were three alternatives: a seaplane designed for use from ships, the objective being adequate seaworthiness; an aircraft designed primarily for reconnaissance and bombing, normally operated from carriers, but useful from other ships when converted into a seaplane; and a two-seater fighter observation aircraft designed for a wheeled undercarriage but convertible into a seaplane for use in sheltered waters, e.g. for practice flights when a carrier was not available. Of the three, the first could be explored using existing seaplanes and the second using the existing TSR. That left the third, the fighter-observation plane. Its primary role would be fighting, its secondary role spotting and obser-

vation. The fighter role would include protection of British spotters and attack on enemy spotters during and immediately before a battle. That was important given British emphasis on gunnery as the decisive factor in a fleet engagement. As a spotter, it would operate from heavy capital ship catapults, its weight as a floatplane not to exceed 8500lbs (maximum landplane weight was not given). The formal request went to the Air Ministry on 16 May 1935. At this stage armament was to be at least four forward-firing guns and twin guns for the observer-W/T operator-gunner. Maximum speed was to be as high as possible, stall speed 56 knots or less. Specification O.30/35 was issued to cover the new aircraft, with the suffix E for Experimental.

The tenders to O.30/35 were from Blackburn, Fairey and Boulton Paul, with preference in that order. Blackburn and Fairey offered much the same performance, but Blackburn offered nearly the same airframe as the Skua. If the Skua was satisfactory, its stable-mate should be, too; DNAD told the Advisory Committee in April 1936 that he wanted to order the Blackburn aircraft 'off the drawing board'.[31]

Instead of the requested combination of forward-firing and flexible rear guns, Blackburn's Roc had a Boulton Paul power turret carrying four guns, which could follow a target around the aircraft.[32] In theory that amounted to placing the performance in the weapon rather than in the aircraft itself, but in practice the guns had short range and covered only the hemisphere above the aircraft, so much of the performance to bring them to the target still had to reside in the Roc. This was not obvious until well after the outbreak of war; in 1938 the Admiralty asked for a Roc successor (specification N.6/38).[33] It also laid down a parallel requirement for a fixed-gun fleet fighter (N.5/38), which was described as a Skua replacement. These aircraft were included in the 1938 experimental naval aircraft programme. These specifications were

The Blackburn Roc was the Skua's stablemate, armed with a power turret. Both the Royal Navy and the RAF had hopes that such aircraft would be effective against the expected massed bomber formations. The Roc was also seen as a catapult fighter which could defend the fleet's vital spotters from enemy fighters. These Rocs are from 759 NAS; they are shown over RNAS Eastleigh in 1940. (David Hobbs)

both re-issued in 1939, but in 1940 the successor specification was for an F/R with forward-firing guns, the turret fighter having been abandoned.

While the Skua was being developed, the British strategic situation changed, as noted above, and the Royal Navy had to contemplate a fight against land-based air forces around Europe. The navy had already accepted that anti-aircraft guns would be its primary defence in that case. Carrier strike aircraft would still be extremely valuable, but they would have to survive enemy air attack intact. In 1936 the question was whether to build a second *Ark Royal*, a high-capacity carrier well adapted to a Pacific war. Initially construction of a second new fleet carrier was simply deferred. Then it was pointed out that carrier aircraft would be needed to protect trade on the sea lanes. That meant protection against enemy raiders, such as armed merchant ships and cruisers. A carrier could search a wide area and its strike aircraft could destroy such threats. Trade protection demanded numbers, so the new carrier had to be a lot smaller than *Ark Royal*, with fewer aircraft on board. The initial proposal was a carrier to accommodate fifteen Swordfish (or their successors). That emphasised the reconnaissance role of the Swordfish; presumably it was assumed that a single aerial torpedo could sink any raider. Initially the Skua did not figure in the project.

The trade protection carrier morphed into a fleet carrier with sufficient hangar protection that its aircraft could ride out an air attack while the fleet's anti-aircraft guns dealt with it: the *Illustrious* class. In effect the armour was bought in exchange for one of the two hangars of the *Ark Royal* and aircraft capacity was halved. In European waters all the aircraft might well be TSRs. However, the Royal Navy had to reckon with possible wars either in Europe or in the Far East, so some versions of the Staff Requirement for the new carrier showed a mixed air group including seven Skuas.

The state of Admiralty thinking in 1936 is reflected in a draft memorandum on FAA Tactics and Equipment circulated in draft form that December.[34] The authors argued that the absence of a settled policy in the past had been due as much to the lack of a clearly-defined statement of the problem (presumably of the use of naval aviation) as to lack of experience and to the use of aircraft not designed specifically for fleet work.[35] As in the case of the F/R, senior officers had often made important decisions without leaving much of a record throughout the fleet to explain what had been done. The implication that there had been no set policy in the past drew criticism; in 1934 the Board had circulated a policy on aircraft carried by cruisers. The comments on carrier aircraft were, however, new.

According to the memorandum, functions of fleet aircraft in order (presumably) of importance were listed as reconnaissance, spotting, fighting and striking. Tactics were divided into air superiority and the tactical employment of aircraft after attack on carriers. Five tactical examples were given: (enemy) carriers unlocated; attacks during the gun battle; battle soon after contact; fleet action unlikely; and mutual immobilisation of carriers. The memorandum took into account the classical FAA roles of finding and slowing the enemy battle line. However, the emphasis on attacking the enemy carriers to eliminate them and thus to gain air superiority was probably new to many readers. One of the reviewers, the head of the Military Branch of the Admiralty Secretariat, commented that the memorandum implied that a fleet without carriers could not sustain major operations against a fleet with carriers. In that case it would seem logical to explain 'how we intend to safeguard our carriers, whether we are building them virtually impregnable from the air, whether we are building Squadron or even Flotilla

carriers instead of Fleet carriers so as not to keep too many eggs in one basket and whether we rely on principle No. 1 [modern AA defence makes daylight attack on the fleet unprofitable] which would suggest that a carrier is safe *with* the Fleet'. The Naval Staff prepared a memorandum to answer this point.

Perhaps remarkably, there was no reference to the F/R function, despite the emphasis on reconnaissance (at the least, as a prerequisite to neutralising enemy carriers) and the unstated implication that the enemy fleet would have fighters assigned, like British fighters, to deal with shadowers.

According to the draft, air fighting would be essential during battle (i.e. a gunnery action) to ensure spotting and to deny it to the enemy, 'but is of little value for security against air attack except insofar as it can circumscribe the activities of enemy shadowing aircraft'. Fleet experience was said to have shown that even under the most favourable conditions, defending fighters would intercept only a small fraction of incoming enemy aircraft before they reached the gun defence zone; the Royal Navy had long emphasised fleet anti-aircraft fire as the main defence.[36] Improvements in anti-aircraft gunnery (which an enemy would also enjoy) would 'probably render daylight attacks on a fleet not in action an uneconomical operation as compared to attacks on carriers, which are more exposed to air attack and, until armoured against bombs, extremely vulnerable . . . Early and successful attack against Carriers will ensure the maximum measure of air superiority with its far reaching advantages.'[37] A later paragraph added that early attack on the enemy's battlefleet might be so unprofitable 'as not to be commensurate with the possible sacrifice of ultimate air superiority'. A later section on reconnaissance pointed out that search was vital given 'the many occasions when we should not only make the attack on the enemy's carriers the first objective of our striking forces, but make their destruction the main object of our early strategy. The fact that the enemy may also adopt this strategy only emphasises the importance of the early location and immobilisation of his Carriers and makes it imperative that we should provide the maximum number of Search Aircraft in our carriers.'

This was much the conclusion the US Navy and the Imperial Japanese Navy had reached, but with vast differences in numbers of aircraft. The British statement was consistent with intelligence information then available about Japanese carrier doctrine.[38] Much, however, was certainly not consistent with the views of those navies. A section on general policy argued that reconnaissance and strike functions, aircraft for which had to be on board carriers, were so essential that the bulk of the fighters, 'which are only required in battle' (to attack and defend spotters) 'should be carried in catapult ships, since the sacrifice in reconnaissance which would be involved in their accommodation in Carriers cannot be accepted'. This particular statement was crossed out in the draft, without explanation, but various senior officers strongly rejected the idea of relying on 'one-shot' catapult fighters.

Problems requiring investigation included dive bombing, the use of 'B' bombs and the tactics of large numbers of fighters.[39]

The evaluation of aircraft functions implied a near-term aircraft development and production programme consisting of:

• Either a general-purpose aircraft (reconnaissance and strike) or a reconnaissance/dive bomber or a dive bomber/fighter.[40]
• A two-seat Fleet Fighter suited to both catapult ships and carriers (in pencil: front gun and turret). In another section, such fighters were described as unsuited to search and heavy striking, though

As the FAA began to expand in 1938, it appeared that Blackburn could not cope with increased orders. The Fairey Fulmar, derived from a light bomber design, was accepted as an interim solution, the Skua being considered preferable despite the higher performance of the Fulmar. Unlike the Skua, the Fulmar was not conceived as a dive bomber. It was a relatively straight-forward conversion of a failed light bomber, Fairey's P4/34, but that aircraft had not been conceived as a full dive bomber and the Fulmar had no trapeze to carry a heavy bomb clear of its propeller. By 1938 that was less important than it had been, since the Royal Navy was more likely to fight in European waters in which dive bombing could not neutralise the enemy's (shore based) air power. Captain 'Winkle' Brown remembered the Fulmar fondly for its forgiving nature. It also offered a good view despite its long (liquid-cooled) nose. He recalled the controls as light and responsive, but not light enough to allow it to dogfight. It was effective against Italian bombers because it had considerable firepower in the form of eight ahead-firing guns, but it was not fast enough to get a second pass. It was also embarrassing that the rear-seater was unarmed; sometimes he was given a single Vickers 'K' gun. This Fulmar of 761 NAS was photographed above RNAS Yeovilton in 1942. (David Hobbs)

suitable for limited forms of observation and light bombing.
• A three-seat fighter spotter for catapult ships.
• A seaworthy aircraft for catapult ships.

The TSR might meet the first requirement, but in its current form it could not dive bomb.[41] The draft concluded that carriers should be equipped mainly with General Purpose (GP) aircraft, with a small pro-portion of fighters, as 'it is clearly undesirable to equip our Carriers with a larger number of fighters than can usefully be employed in driving off enemy shadowing aircraft'. Moreover, 'it appears that demands for more fighters have, in the past, been based more on an exaggerated concep-tion of their value in the defence of the Fleet against air attack than on an appreciation of their offensive value against enemy observation and fighting aircraft in battle'. That led to 'ideal' distributions of aircraft (not in fact the ones in service), such as sixty GP and twelve fighters on board the new *Ark Royal*.[42]

It was accepted that dive bombing was much more effective than level bombing; the torpedo was the most effective anti-ship weapon until the FAA had an effective dive bomber. In any case dive bombing could not supersede the torpedo, which offered the possibility of un-derwater attack in harbour and the advantage of co-ordinated attack by different means. However, dive bombing seemed to be the best way to attack enemy carriers. 'At least in the first attack which is designed to stop all flying operations, there is little doubt that dive-bombing with SAP bombs should form the main part of the attack.' That was much the conclusion the US Navy and the Imperial Japanese Navy had reached.

In February 1937 Vice Admiral (Aircraft Carriers) N F Laurence questioned the dive bombing policy implicit in the memorandum. The heaviest air weapon envisaged was the 500lb SAP, against which the new carriers were being armoured. What would happen if foreign navies followed suit? Dive bombing seemed to be justified mainly as a means of neutralising enemy carriers. The torpedo, particularly with its new magnetic pistol, seemed a superior alternative as a way of destroying enemy carriers. Moreover, the tables in the memorandum suggested that casualties to attacking aircraft would be much the same for dive and torpedo bombers. The Vice Admiral also argued that the torpedo but not the dive bomb could be used effectively at night.

The Vice Admiral agreed that there should be as few types of aircraft as possible; he wanted only TSRs and two-seater fighters. He accepted the distribution proposed in the memorandum, which meant that he agreed that there was little point in relying on fighters to intercept enemy bombers. However, he rejected the idea that fleet carriers could or should operate spotters and the fighters intended to support them (and to deny the air to enemy spotters). Fleet carriers often strayed as much as 30 or 40 miles from the fleet as they steamed into the wind to launch and recover aircraft. They were carrying out essential duties and should not be tied more closely to the fleet. Instead, two special

Squadron Carriers specialising in spotting and fighter support should be built. For them the appropriate complement would be twelve TSR and twenty-four two-seat fighters.

CinC Home Fleet Admiral Backhouse (the future First Sea Lord) disagreed. In May 1937 he pointed out that in the situation in which the enemy had no carriers but relied on shore-based aircraft – exactly what the fleet had just faced in the Mediterranean and what the Home Fleet was likely to face in the North Sea. In that case 'fighters become of greater importance as the only means of attacking enemy formations before they come within gun range'. CinC Home Fleet was also far more impressed by dive bombing than by torpedo attack, as it seemed to him (from witnessing attacks) that they were far more likely to achieve surprise.

Admiral Backhouse commented at greater length in November 1937 that the memorandum visualised only action between two battle fleets with carriers, which limited it to a war against Japan. It also assumed that both fleets were anxious to fight. He repeated the previous comment: what about a war nearer home? As soon as the attack on enemy carriers was discounted, employment of fleet aircraft against enemy bases, airfields, etc became important. Surely it should be taken into account in assessing aircraft requirements. He echoed Vice Admiral (Aircraft Carriers)'s call for specialist spotting support carriers, but also registered some scepticism as to whether aircraft spotting would actually work in battle. He likewise echoed his preference for torpedoes, but added that dive bombing appeared to be quite effective and also would probably be the most difficult form of attack to engage with gunfire, particularly when co-ordinated with a torpedo attack. 'It is also the most easy form of attack in which to train pilots.'

CinC Home Fleet noted that in the Spanish Civil War bombers were usually escorted by fighters, presumably to deal with defending fighters, 'but this condition may not exist in sea fighting'. Fighters were difficult to operate due to their low endurance, but the new carriers could launch and recover aircraft simultaneously (thanks to their arrester gear and barriers) and thus might find that easier. He would therefore continue to deploy fighters aboard the large carriers. Backhouse apparently deliberately misread the memorandum to emphasise the importance of fighters, to the point where he proposed specialist fighter carriers.

In January 1938 CinC Mediterranean Vice Admiral Dudley Pound also commented on the memorandum. He had come closest to war against a power without carriers. He liked the idea of distributing fighters around the fleet, including aboard capital ships. Their fighters would be intended specifically to deal with enemy spotters (he thought they could have little more than spotter performance to fill this role). He doubted that it would be possible to defend British spotters against enemy attack. Much of Pound's critique concentrated on the needs of trade protection cruisers.

DNAD argued in February 1938 that CinC Mediterranean misunderstood the fighter problem. To intercept attackers, fighters had either to be launched in time or be held airborne awaiting an attack. They also had to be so directed as to intercept the attackers. This was a good summary of the problem then and later, the two aircraft choices being deck-launched interception (DLI) and a CAP. To DNAD, DLI was practically impossible until detection range was materially increased (i.e. until radar became operational). CAP was rarely practicable except when attack was expected, given short fighter endurance. Fighter control was rarely possible against level or dive bombers, although it was not difficult against torpedo bombers during the last stages of their attacks

or during their final manoeuvres for position. He pointed out that the increased effectiveness of modern fighters against TSR had been more fully appreciated since the publication of the memorandum the previous year. Fighters must be used to repel torpedo bomber attacks. Otherwise, fighters could be sure of contacting enemy aircraft while defending spotters or while attacking escorted enemy bombers.

Fighters were the only valid defence for spotters because it was impossible for anti-aircraft crews to distinguish spotters from enemy fighters. Unfortunately fighters could not expect to destroy or protect spotters without fighting enemy fighters – for which purpose they had to be faster and more manoeuvrable. Such performance could not easily be combined with dive bombing, which required a low terminal velocity (so that the aircraft could pull out of its dive). It would be better to combine it with the GP role. Despite limitations in dive angle, DNAD wrote that TSRs were already better dive bombers than were the fighters (Skuas were not yet in service, however).

There was also a discussion at the Admiralty, on 7 December 1937.[43] Assistant Chief of the Naval Staff (Air) (ANCS (Air)) defended the emphasis on main fleet operations (the Japanese war) because it was still the basis of general fleet training. Backhouse pointed out that although it was unlikely that there would be a major fleet action in European waters for many years to come, in a European war the FAA would inevitably be required to attack the enemy navy in harbour and in its bases. ACNS (Air) replied that the main function of the FAA was still to assist the fleet in battle, hence that the main fleet war should be the basis of its aircraft designs. He emphasised that these aircraft could not be expected to match the performance of land-based aircraft, a constant theme in interwar FAA policy. In retrospect it is not entirely clear how heavy a penalty carrier operability should have carried. ADNAD noted that highly trained, hence irreplaceable, personnel would be lost if the FAA was wasted attacking heavily-defended enemy shore bases.[44] Backhouse saw things very differently. The Royal Navy must strike at the outset to make itself felt; if the enemy refused to come out, he must be attacked wherever he was, at whatever cost in air personnel. This was very much the attitude the Royal Navy had sought to instil in its officers through the interwar period.

It was generally agreed that FAA aircraft should not be designed largely to operate against shore objectives. Backhouse pointed out that if FAA aircraft would generally be outperformed by enemy shore-based aircraft, special stress should be laid on air-to-air training.

Assistant DNAD pointed to the advent of 'new methods of detection and keeping touch' (i.e. radar) which would make fighter protection of the fleet much more feasible than in the past. DNAD pointed out that it would be valuable to inflict casualties on enemy aircraft even after they attacked. The memorandum had advocated placing many of the fleet's fighters on board catapult ships, but CO *Glorious* strongly disagreed. Catapult ships probably would not be able to operate their fighters when needed. Once launched, they could not be recovered. Fighters carried by cruisers probably would not be able to concentrate as needed.

Backhouse doubted the value of fighter patrols, much as the memorandum had. CO *Glorious* suggested a distinction between preventing enemy aircraft from finding their objective and blocking their attacks to prevent them from being wholly successful. He thought that denying the enemy the ability to find the fleet was impossible, but that blocking might work (as stated in the minutes of the meeting, but the opposite would seem more likely). Backhouse considered aircraft offensive weapons and objected to using them on defensive patrols.

Folded Fairey Fulmars of 803 NAS are shown on board *Formidable* about 1941. Note the narrow lift further aft. British armoured carriers could not strike below fighters without folding wings, such as Sea Hurricanes and early Grumman Wildcats. (David Hobbs)

A further issue was whether to add a third type of fleet aircraft, a spotter-fighter – to beat off enemy fighters and destroy enemy spotters. The consensus was that it would much complicate fleet operation. Otherwise, with only two types (TSR and fighter), it was relatively simple to redistribute aircraft among the carriers. The new type would operate only from 'squadron carriers' attached directly to the battle line.

The memorandum was not policy and the Board approved measures contrary to it. In particular, it took fighters far more seriously. In the wake of the discussions of the memorandum, a committee under ACNS (Air) was appointed to estimate FAA requirements for war. Its report was submitted in September 1938, as the Munich crisis unfolded and war must have seemed imminent.[45] Fighter roles were driving off enemy shadowers, intercepting enemy striking forces and protecting British aircraft (particularly spotters). Numbers required would generally depend on the strength of opposing forces. By this time the British had to take into account three possible wars: against Japan, Germany and Italy. Current policy was to limit the fleet in the Far East to four carriers, in line with estimates of required naval strength, but there the enemy could operate his aircraft from considerably beyond surface range. Germany did not yet have enough capital ships to form a battle line, so a war against her would be quite different from war in the Far East. Both sides would benefit from large land-based air forces.

Against Italy the Royal Navy would gain limited assistance from British land-based aircraft against a large land-based Italian air force. The FAA would have to make up the difference.

Previous estimates of requirements had been based on the capacity of the carriers rather than on detailed aircraft requirements. The new committee agreed that carriers were a limiting factor, but numbers had to be based on the air strength of probable enemies and on the characteristics of each different war. Britain would be the first country to operate armoured carriers; 'a limited number of aircraft in a well-protected carrier are clearly comparable to a larger number in a poorly protected carrier'. On this basis the committee estimated that in March 1939 the FAA needed 238 carrier-borne aircraft, increasing to 398 in March 1942.[46] It pointed out that the totals it advocated were far less than those provided and forecast for the US Navy 'with much less need'.

The list of future aircraft types included the three-seat spotter-fighter, which would carry a heavy turret armament. The Fleet Fighter was a two-seater 'of great fighting power', to which (and to endurance) all other characteristics are subordinated'. Both front-gun and turret types were under development, the first of which 'has a limited value for reconnaissance and spotting in simple conditions such as operations between small units, but would be inadequate for long reconnaissance or for spotting and action observation in a Fleet action'. This refers to N5/38 and N6/38.

The ACNS committee revived the idea of placing fighters (in this case, spotter-fighters) aboard capital ships, due in part to the current and near-term shortage of space on board carriers. The committee argued that the existing policy of limiting carrier aircraft to TSRs and fighters had to be changed because the great increase in enemy fighter firepower demanded that spotters be armed to beat off attackers (hence the spotter-fighter). They would be on board carriers and also some catapult ships. In the event, no spotter-fighter was ever built.[47]

There was no absolute basis to set a ratio between TSR and fighters. Japan and the United States were said to maintain a 2:1 ratio.[48] 'It is evident that the modern fighter has a far greater value than was previously thought and whereas various developments may greatly increase the value of the fighter, there is little prospect of appreciably increasing the defensive power of projected TSR aircraft.' The 2:1 ratio was accepted as Admiralty policy and it was reflected in a 2 June 1939 Board note on aircraft complements. It seems most likely that the language in the committee report was a cover for a perception that radar would make fighter interception practical.[49]

Meanwhile, on 30 December 1938 the Mediterranean Fleet promulgated new instructions for air defence.[50] The basic memorandum did not even mention defensive fighters; it was concerned mainly with fleet formation and with appropriate manoeuvres under attack. An attached report, dated 9 July 1938, from the Vice Admiral commanding the battlecruisers, did include an appendix (C) on the use of fighters in fleet air defence. It was considered that at least twelve fighters would be needed to provide adequate defence against high-level bombers and then only if the attack were limited. *Courageous* and *Glorious* carried only twelve fighters each. A single carrier could maintain twelve fighters in the air for periods of two hours with three-hour intervals. Six could be in the air continuously for a short period, but only three could be in the air continuously during daylight hours. These same fighters (Skuas) would be needed for anti-submarine patrols, to dive-bomb and to attack enemy spotters. Experience already showed that warning by screening surface ships would be insufficient to allow the fighters to destroy attackers unless they were already at their operational height. On the other hand, the enemy attack would have to be preceded by shadowing, 'and it is of the utmost importance to destroy them as this may completely nullify the attack'.

The idea of air defence by dealing with a snooper proved successful during the Second World War. Once the snooper had been destroyed, the fleet could change course to evade any follow-up. Clearly snoopers were not always successfully destroyed or driven off in time, but by the time the Mediterranean Fleet faced sustained air attacks it had radar-controlled fighters.

All of this made it pointless to maintain a combat air patrol. The anti-shadowing role could be filled by keeping three fighters continuously on station or by holding three or six of them on deck alert. The airborne patrol might run low on fuel just as the shadower appeared, hence fail to destroy him. The aircraft on deck alert would, however, take at least ten more minutes to reach their objectives. Which was better could be decided only by experiment.

Reviewing the instructions on 4 February 1939, Director, Training and Staff Duties Division (DTSD) commented that 'this conclusion [to abandon fighter patrols] would no doubt have been modified had the present knowledge in regard to performance of RDF at sea been available'.[51] This was presumably a reference to the basis of the new policy which demanded far more carrier fighters than ever before.

Even before the promulgation of the 2:1 TSR:fighter ratio, the Admiralty desperately needed more fighters just to fill existing requirements. It already realised that it was betting heavily on Blackburn for both its new fighters, the Skua and the Roc. As early as October 1936 DNAD had told the Advisory Committee that the Admiralty was somewhat nervous, as it had no fall-back if both aircraft failed (the unmentioned point was that they were largely identical). By October 1937 the issue was whether Blackburn could produce the aircraft fast enough; the whole British aircraft industry was expanding, but not nearly quickly enough. Given limits on Blackburn capacity, the whole run of Roc production (135 aircraft) was sub-contracted to another firm, Boulton Paul, which was also the only maker of aircraft turrets other than Frazer Nash. Unfortunately Boulton Paul was also making its own turret fighter, the Defiant, for the RAF. The RAF later tried to convince the Admiralty to cancel the Roc (stating that it was likely to fail); the Admiralty view was that the advice was intended only to free the plant to build Defiants more quickly. DNAD observed that from a national point of view the RAF might well need fighters far more urgently than the navy, but the navy stood its ground.[52] Neither service realised that both turret fighters would prove useless once war began.

Meanwhile naval requirements grew because after 1936 there were no longer limits on total carrier tonnage. By 1939 six fleet carriers would be under construction and the first two were scheduled for completion that year (they were late). At the same time the last of the pre-London Treaty carriers, *Ark Royal*, would enter service.

In October 1937 an Admiralty representative told the Advisory Committee on the FAA that 117 fighters (forty-seven first-line) were urgently needed, due both to delays in Skua production and increased demand.[53] The Admiralty had considered ordering more Blackburn aircraft, but it told the Committee that they did not seem entirely satisfactory and that in any case they would be obsolescent by the end of 1939. They could adopt an existing RAF fighter or order a new aircraft 'off the drawing board' or continue with obsolete Nimrods and Ospreys. As the last was unacceptable, the Admiralty would accept a straightforward fighter with fixed guns (without any rear gun), as long as it could be in production by September 1939. To get a fighter

quickly enough, the Admiralty would dispense with dive bombing and even bomb capacity of any kind would be secondary. Asked whether he could accept a single-seater (a conversion of the Hurricane was offered), DNAD said that it would be better than nothing, but that two seats were very important for navigation and communication. Speed would not be as vital as for the RAF, because the new fighter would operate against other naval aircraft with much the same limitations as its own aircraft. The Admiralty preferred air-cooled engines, but would accept a liquid-cooled engine if it had to. It would also accept a wooden aircraft if it had to.

DTD (Air Ministry) pointed out that the main problem in adapting the Hurricane would be to redesign the wings to fold. The centre of gravity would move if the aircraft were modified as a two-seater. The committee chairman suggested that as a biplane the Gladiator would be easier to provide with folding wings. As in other sectors of British industry, the lack of skilled draftsmen was a major problem. Mistakes in drawings sometimes went undiscovered until parts were assembled. The navy's problem was urgent; DTD asked for three weeks to consider it. DNAD added that, should the Skua and Roc fail, the navy had no alternatives. The 'drawing board' solution failed when DTD told the committee chairman that production of an entirely new type would take a few months more than two years and, moreover, might be risky. That made conversion of an existing aircraft by far the best choice.

Admiralty representatives told the Advisory Committee in several contexts that speed was relatively unimportant, because naval aircraft would face similar aircraft built under similar limitations. That reflected a continuing Pacific mind-set, since in European waters the fleet would face land-based aircraft not subject to any naval limitations. The records of the Advisory committee do not show any recognition of this contradiction. Nor did the Admiralty generally realise that other carrier navies did not seem similarly restrained – the only reference to foreign practice in 1936/37 is to US adoption of a monoplane torpedo bomber in the form of the Douglas TBD.

The Admiralty always preferred to follow multiple parallel possibilities. The only near-term solution to the fighter shortage was to buy single-seat fighters the RAF no longer wanted. The best of them was the biplane Gloster Gladiator, which was adapted to naval use on a minimum basis. It was somewhat strengthened and it was provided with a tail hook. Despite the 1937 discussion, it was not redesigned so that its wings could fold; that in turn limited it to the larger existing carriers. Initially sixty were ordered. The November 1938 meeting of the Advisory Committee on the FAA was told informally that with the completion of three new carriers (*Ark Royal* and two *Illustrious* expected in 1939), another 100 to 120 might be wanted by the end of 1939. The Gladiator lacked the back-seater who was needed if it strayed far from the fleet and also the W/T set on board the two-seaters. It might be seen as a means of dealing with shadowers almost directly over the fleet, but no such sophisticated reasoning seems to have applied. It was a simple solution to a pressing shortage.

The new-production interim fighter was only slightly better.[54] After the November meeting of the Advisory Committee, its Technical Sub-Committee recommended a version of the light bomber Fairey had designed to specification P.4/34. It met all the requirements, with some minor concessions. As of February 1938 it was to be armed with eight forward-firing guns and was expected to attain 280mph. Specification O.8/38 was written to cover procurement. It was issued on 2 April 1938. Probably the main changes from the light bomber were provision of folding wings and of guns in those wings. The aircraft was mainly a

A Sea Gladiator is shown landing on board *Victorious*. The Sea Gladiator was acquired as a stop-gap to replace worn-out Nimrods. Its wings could not fold so could therefore be struck down only on the large lifts of the older carriers, such as *Glorious*. Navalisation was limited to catapult points, an arresting hook and a collapsible dinghy in a ventral fairing. Thirty-eight were converted RAF Gladiators, followed by sixty production aircraft. The first were delivered in February 1939, replacing both Nimrods and Ospreys; No 801 NAS embarked them on board *Courageous* in May 1939. In the Norwegian campaign they operated from *Glorious* and in August Sea Gladiators from *Eagle* covered the bombardment of Bardia in Italy. By the end of 1940 they were gone from the FAA, but the RAF famously flew a few ex-naval Sea Gladiators to defend Malta under the names Faith, Hope and Charity.

fighter, to be used in the vicinity of the fleet. A secondary requirement was shallow dive bombing (i.e. shallow glide bombing), as long as that did not compromise fighter performance (the load envisaged was two 100lb or 250lb bombs). The most important requirement was that the first aircraft be delivered in September 1939. The initial order was for the forty-seven front-line aircraft with full immediate and war reserve and wastage aircraft (the total of 117 mentioned slightly earlier). The new fighter or F/R was named Fulmar. Despite the demand in the specification, the prototype first flew on 4 January 1940. However, because

it was so similar to a successfully tested forebear, it entered service not long afterwards.

Given the continuing shortage of Skuas, once armoured deck carriers were assigned to the Mediterranean beginning in the autumn of 1940, they were equipped with Fulmars (*Ark Royal* continued to operate Skuas).

THE US NAVY[55]

As with the Royal Navy, the role of US Navy fighters was set by the expected demands of a Pacific war. Unlike the Royal Navy, the US Navy had to face a mixture of land- and sea-based aircraft as its fleet passed through the Japanese-held Mandated Islands. That precluded a doctrine in which pre-emptive destruction of enemy carriers solved the air defence problem. Like the Royal Navy, the interwar US Navy invested heavily in anti-aircraft fire control, though hardly as heavily in guns, particularly automatic ones. Given serious problems in alerting and controlling aircraft, at times the fleet seems to have relied more on guns than on fighter defence. By the mid-1930s, however, there was a widespread feeling that guns could not reach high-flying bombers, whose

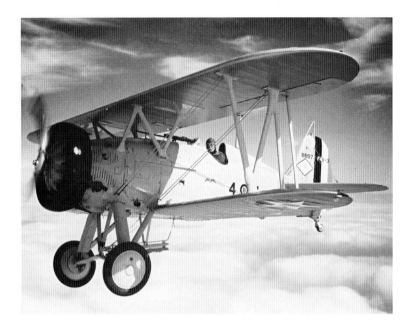

The standard US Navy fighter about 1930, when the two big carriers were fully operational, was the Boeing F4B. An F4B-3 is shown on 27 October 1933. Note the small bomb shackle between the wheels, making it possible for the fighter to deliver a light bomb, but not the 500-pounder needed to do serious damage (the F4B-1 could carry such a bomb between its wheels). The F4B had such superior performance that the Army Air Corps felt compelled to buy the same type of aircraft as its P-12. The air force did not adopt another navy fighter until the F-4 Phantom II.

performance was increasing dramatically. It seemed that the only solution to this threat was high-flying fleet fighters.

This perception had a dramatic effect on US naval fighter development. It pushed the US Navy's BuAer to seek maximum speed and altitude. By way of contrast, the contemporary Army Air Corps considered continental defence its principal legitimate mission, the army being disbarred by US politics from contemplating an overseas European campaign like the one in the First World War (the army would have been involved in a Pacific campaign, but in a subordinate role). It interpreted its mission to mean that the main role of its fighters would be to help break up enemy amphibious operations, for which it sought high speed at low and medium altitudes. That changed in 1940, but the fighters the army used when war broke out were optimised for low altitudes. The navy's were intended to fight at much greater altitudes. As war approached, the navy's view was that its guns might be effective against torpedo bombers, but that fighters were the main defence against high-altitude bombers, which meant both level bombers and dive bombers not yet diving. The priority assigned to fighters increased as the US Navy tested its anti-aircraft guns against real aircraft in the form of drones. It discovered that even when shell bursts were properly placed, they often failed to bring down the drones. Perhaps surprisingly, unlike the Royal Navy, the US Navy apparently did not see the destruction of enemy snoopers as a way of aborting major air attacks. In addition to the interceptor role, US naval fighters were seen as strike escorts, at least from the mid-1930s. That was reflected in a requirement for 1000nm range, even though the range would reduce performance.[56]

Another aspect of naval war planning also affected fighters. In 1935 the US Navy shifted from a planned direct thrust across the Pacific to a step-by-step advance, which required that the Marines seize and occupy Japanese-held islands. In such operations fleet fighters would

provide support in the form of strafing and light bombing, so all fighters had to carry bombs (typically a pair of 116lb bombs). That reversed an earlier decision to abandon bomb-carrying (for a time fighters were equipped as glide or even dive bombers, with 500lb bombs) in favour of a pure fighter role, aircraft being optimised for high performance to deal with enemy bombers.

The interwar US Navy was much affected both by the results of war gaming at the Naval War College and by full-scale exercises (Fleet Problems). The War College was at the height of its influence in 1931–2, when the last pre-war carriers, the *Yorktown*s, were being designed. They in turn were enlarged as the wartime *Essex* class, so contemporary War College judgements were extremely important in retrospect. However, the War College never found it possible to simulate air battles; they were just too complicated and would have required too many participants to act as individual fighter pilots or even group commanders. Thus detailed air tactics were developed in full-scale exercises. Tactical development seems to have begun only with the appointment of Captain Joseph M Reeves Jr as Commander, Air Squadrons, Battle Force in 1927. At that time the only US carrier was the small converted collier *Langley*, somewhat less capable than the British *Argus*. Reeves had played Blue air commander in a key game at the War College and probably on the basis of his success there had been appointed head of the Tactics Department. At about the same time Congress passed the law limiting command of air units to officers who had taken air training, generally meaning to pilots (some officers took the observer course). That made pilot training an attractive career path, which Reeves took. When he arrived in the fleet, he assembled a series of tactical and technical questions for his pilots, what he called the '1001 Questions'. The answers were the basis of the tactical doctrine he began to create. That included, but was hardly limited to, the new rapid method of recovering aircraft (using arresting gear and a barrier) which enormously increased the capacity of each US carrier.

Meanwhile the influence of the War College games was felt in carrier design and doctrine. Like the Royal Navy, the US Navy considered its battle line the ultimate arbiter of sea power in the Pacific. Even more than the Royal Navy, it placed great value on the ability to hit at extreme range, which required air spotting. As in the Royal Navy, that led to initial interest in using carrier fighters to gain control of the air over a fleet action, defending its own spotters and denying the enemy air spotting. In contrast to the Royal Navy, the US Naval War College soon concluded that this sort of control was impossible. That helped focus War College attention on the offensive role of carriers and on the extent to which an enemy's carriers could be destroyed pre-emptively.

It helped that the two capital ships the United States converted into carriers under the Washington Treaty were huge and that with Reeves' innovation they could carry – and operate – about 100 aircraft each, roughly twice as many as in the contemporary British fleet carriers.[57] On her first major fleet exercise (Fleet Problem) the carrier *Saratoga* demonstrated her striking power by launching a surprise attack against the Panama Canal. Although the army had numerous fighters defending the canal, it had no means of early warning and the strike arrived unopposed. Through the early 1930s, US carrier exercises often involved large-scale raids on land targets such as Los Angeles and Pearl Harbor. The latter were abandoned only with the advent of high-performance flying boats. It seemed that a sufficient force of such aircraft could expect to find an approaching carrier well before it reached the launch line, hence could support a pre-emptive attack.

Work on a new US carrier design began in 1931. There was sufficient tonnage for at least two new carriers. It seems to have been assumed that one would be a further fleet carrier, but that the second would be specially designed to support the battle fleet directly. That meant both achieving air superiority over the gun battle and launching and recovering (and refuelling) spotters – very much a key role for British carriers. The War College was asked to suggest characteristics. Its President, Rear Admiral Harris Laning, replied that the battle line role was pointless. In war games, battle line anti-aircraft fire had never protected a carrier in company from being neutralised or sunk. Any carrier operating with the battle line would quickly be found by opposition aircraft. Nor was there any reason to imagine that carrier fighters would generally beat off attackers. The War College made its case successfully. Both new carriers, which became *Yorktown* and *Enterprise*, were built to the same design and the battle-line carrier concept was abandoned.

Yet it was essential to seize air superiority. The only way to do that was to find and neutralise the enemy carriers first. US carriers had to operate dispersed because that was the only way to avoid detection and destruction. That is why the pre-war US Navy never developed multi-carrier tactics as did the Royal Navy and, to a lesser extent, the Imperial Japanese Navy. Dispersal was practical because individual US carriers had such large air groups, thanks to Reeves' innovation. It was abandoned only during the Second World War, when radar-controlled fighters made carrier battle survivability a much better prospect.

A major theme in interwar US naval air thinking was that the best way to deal with an enemy's carriers was to find and neutralise them before their own aircraft could find the navy's own carriers. The US navy reached this conclusion at about the same time as it developed effective dive bombers capable of delivering bombs powerful enough to destroy much of a flight deck. It was accepted that such hits would not sink an enemy carrier, but it also seemed that steel flight decks could not be repaired outside a navy yard. A carrier with two bombs in her flight deck was no longer a threat.

Conversely, the US Navy learned to build carriers which could keep operating after taking a bomb hit. By 1930 the navy was already building *Ranger*, which had a light wooden flight deck (planks laid on thin steel sheets). This arrangement had been adopted only to minimise the ship's displacement, which was limited by the total tonnage available to the United States under the Washington Treaty. However, the War College realised that this type of construction was far easier to repair (using thin steel sheets) than the more conventional heavy steel decks of the earlier US fleet carriers and also of British and Japanese carriers. A carrier with thin wooden decks could even repair them – and remain in action – during a protracted battle. The *Yorktown* class carriers designed in 1931 had *Ranger*-type wooden decks and the War College apparently pointed out this important virtue. By the time of the next major design (the *Essex* class) light wooden decks were certainly associated with quick battle repairs.[58]

Two other design innovations were specific ways of dealing with battle damage to flight decks. One was to place arrester gear at the fore end of the flight deck, so that if the carrier steamed aft, she could land aircraft over her bow. If one end of the fight deck was destroyed, the other could be used both to launch and to recover aircraft. The *Essex* class was designed with the ability to steam astern at high speed (20 knots) for a protracted period for just this reason. The double-ended flight deck was valuable even if it was undamaged. A US carrier would normally mass her aircraft at one end of the flight deck. That was standard in all navies before take-off, as piston-engined aircraft had to

The line between fighters and single-seat dive bombers was blurry. The Curtiss BF2C-1 shown here from squadron VB-5B on 18 March 1935, was descended from the company's F11C fighter. BuAer considered this aircraft as its 1933 fighter, but chose the Grumman F2F instead, because the BF2C was essentially a bomber.

be warmed up before flight and they were typically warmed up on the open flight deck. However, the US Navy was able to place more aircraft on board a carrier by always keeping a large fraction of them on the flight deck. That was no problem if the carrier launched or recovered a mass strike (landed aircraft were parked forward). It was certainly a problem if a few aircraft had to be launched while the fore end of the flight deck was full.

The other design innovation was a catapult mounted athwartships on the hangar deck. It was possible because US flight deck design left the sides of the hangar deck open; in the later Royal Navy carriers (and, for that matter, in the two *Lexington*s) the sides of the hangar deck were structural elements of the hull. Even in earlier British carriers the hangar sides were closed and magazine regulations applied to the hangar. Japanese carriers also had enclosed hangars, though they were generally not integral with the hull. Athwartships catapults first appeared in the *Yorktown* class and they were also part of the *Essex* design. They were eliminated during the Second World War because the hangar side space was wanted for light anti-aircraft guns on sponsons.

Admiral Laning was associated with CNO Admiral William V Pratt and with BuAer chief Rear Admiral Moffett. Pratt had been the main advocate of naval arms control within the navy and he was publicly associated with the smooth progress of the negotiations leading to the London Naval Treaty of 1930. Probably many within the navy thought he had been rewarded with appointment as CNO. The general hatred of arms control within the navy probably made Pratt extremely unpopular. When he returned from London, he claimed that he had extracted two major concessions. One was a clause allowing the United States to build cruisers with flight decks outside the allowed carrier tonnage – 'flight-deck cruisers'. The other was the 'sloop' clause which allowed each signatory to build slow gunboats of up to 2000 tons armed with up to 6in guns. Pratt argued that the first strongly favoured naval airpower and a US flight-deck cruiser was designed in sufficient detail for shipyards to be asked to bid on it (it might have been Cruiser

No. 39, but that ship was built instead as a conventional heavy cruiser). The sloop was considered valuable as a means of protecting wartime convoys against surface raiders, which were considered the main threat to trade at this time.

Laning's war games supported the flight-deck cruiser idea, but Laning always pointed out that the War College could not evaluate it technically. Once Pratt was gone in 1933, that was done and the idea was dropped on the ground that the projected flight deck could not be long enough for safe landings.[59]

Admiral Moffett, too, was a strong supporter of the flight-deck cruiser and indeed of any other way of increasing the number of aircraft at sea within Treaty limits. He died in the crash of the airship *Akron* the same year that Pratt left office. Admiral Laning's term at the War College also ended in 1933. It seems likely that his aggressive use of war gaming conclusions was associated in the navy with his patron Admiral Pratt, the only CNO who had previously served as President of the Naval War College. Laning did not suffer personally for his association with Pratt – his next position was at sea, commanding the battle line – but the War College certainly did. The next year it was moved from a position within the Office of the Chief of Naval Operations to the navy school system. Subsequent Presidents were often asked for their advice, for example concerning building programmes, but they never again cited war game evidence.

To some extent, then, the conclusions Laning had reached were dropped. The idea of attaching a carrier to the battle line was revived. The relatively weak *Ranger*, completed in 1934, was often seen as a prototype battle-line carrier. In 1935 the pending retirement of the slow carrier *Langley* (converted into a seaplane tender) provided enough

tonnage for one more small carrier and the resulting *Wasp* was seen to some extent also as a battle line carrier. At about the same time the idea of multiplying the US wartime carrier force by converting liners into auxiliary carriers was abandoned (the reason given was that conversion would be too lengthy). This was not, however, a full retreat from previous US interest in carrier air power. The interwar US Navy was still widely seen as the most air-minded in the world and after 1934 it invested heavily in flying boats.

An early attempt to crystallise requirements was a set of approximate aircraft characteristics issued by Chief of BuAer Admiral Moffett in January 1927.[60] Moffett listed single- and two-seat carrier fighters and a single-seat battleship fighter as well as one-, two- and multi-seat observation planes (the single-seat type was for submarines) and a multi-seat three-purpose plane (torpedo attack, bombing and scouting, a combination which was admittedly controversial). The single-seat fighter was intended primarily to attack enemy aircraft and to protect bombing and torpedo planes, with a secondary bombing role against enemy ships. The main carrier limitations were landing speed (58mph with existing arresting gear) and endurance (two hours at full throttle, six hours at economical speed with a drop tank). Moffett hoped for high performance: a maximum speed of not less than 160mph and a service ceiling of 22,000ft. He expected the carrier fighter to exceed the performance of the parallel battleship (catapult) fighter, a type which

The F8C-2 and its successors were conceived as dive bombers, named Helldivers. This F8C-4 was photographed on 13 May 1930. To show how elastic designations and roles were, its successor F8C-5 was soon redesignated in the Observation (i.e. spotting) series as the O2C-1.

soon faded out. The two-place fighter was to be used mainly for offensive patrol. It did not yet exist; it might end up identical with the two-seat observation-fighter and it might ultimately replace the single-seat fighter. Performance was to approach as closely as possible that of the single-seat fighter. In British terms, this was an F/R like the Osprey. Despite Moffett's reference to an observation-fighter type, he limited observation aircraft to battleship and cruiser catapults. This was very much unlike contemporary British naval thinking. The three-purpose aircraft was large and heavy because contemporary engines could only barely lift heavy torpedoes. Dive bombing had only just been demonstrated.

In 1927 the navy production fighters were the Curtiss Hawk (F6C-4, thirty-one delivered in 1927) and the Boeing FB-5 (twenty-seven delivered). Both were derivatives of army fighters. In each case the initial version had been powered by a liquid-cooled engine, but the navy preferred air-cooled and the F6C-4 had an R-1340 of this type. Boeing tested this engine in a modified FB and it was beginning to deliver the air-cooled follow-on fighters (F2B and F3B) which would become standard. The F2B and its predecessors (and also initial F3B-1s) had a continuous axle between their wheels, to carry the hooks needed for the lengthwise arresting gear then in use. That made it impossible for them to carry heavy bombs or drop tanks. However, the follow-on F4B, which flew in 1928, introduced a split undercarriage (also used on many production F3Bs). That transformed the situation, as the F4B could lift a 500lb bomb, which could do serious damage to a carrier flight deck if delivered in a dive.[61]

In December 1928 Moffett summarised his policies when he answered questions raised by the War Plans Division.[62] War Plans studies had shown a need for long-range strikes beyond current fighter range. Ideally new escort fighters should be developed. Moffett argued that it would be very undesirable to increase fighter range, because that would compromise performance. However, in their defensive role fighters might have to maintain a patrol over surface ships. To gain the necessary endurance at no great cost in performance, BuAer had developed droppable belly tanks. To attack surface targets BuAer was equipping existing fighters and observation aircraft (often seen as two-seat fighters) with 500lb bombs and it was pursuing two experimental designs capable of dive-bombing with 1000lb bombs. In each case what would later be called glide-bombing was envisaged, since at very steep angles a bomb dropped from an aircraft's belly would hit its propeller. Up to this time dive-bombing had been done only with light bombs (up to 25lbs) on wing racks, where the propeller was no problem; attacks with heavier bombs were still very much in the experimental stage.

When aircraft characteristics were reviewed by the General Board in 1928, it became clear that Moffett's initial characteristics were incomplete.[63] Like the Admiralty, the General Board concentrated on the ways in which aircraft could support a gun battle. It emphasised the role of fighters to protect both the heavy bomber/torpedo bomber and spotters. It also recognised that high fighter performance could be achieved only at the expense of the endurance needed for such protection. Current British doctrine was said to require that each class of aircraft be capable of self-defence. On that basis the spotter and two-seat fighter might merge. Moreover, command of the air over a battle should include dive-bombing and strafing to destroy enemy fire controls and their exposed crews. On this basis light aircraft such as fighters should predominate on board carriers. It had already proposed three light for each heavy aircraft, although that might be excessive. At most carriers should have no more than one squadron of heavy aircraft on board, VB

Grumman's two-seat FF-1, which was not conceived as a dive bomber (it had light bomb carriers under its wings), was bought because it offered unusually high performance. This one from VF-5 is shown on 25 March 1934. It introduced Grumman to the aircraft business and it featured the company's trademark retractable undercarriage.

or VT. The light aircraft class should comprise only single-seat fighters (VF) and two-seat general service aircraft (VS).[64] The latter was based on experience with the Vought O2U 'Corsair'. Although the O2U was nominally an observation (spotting) aircraft, it was also being used successfully for tactical scouting and even for light dive bombing. It also had sufficient performance to function as a defensive fighter for US spotters. Given the considerable potential of dive bombing, the Board wanted its general service plane to carry up to 500lbs of bombs in combination (not a single 500-pounder). The Board rejected the two-seat fighter on the ground that its free gun added nothing to its capability and inhibited it in dogfighting. It pointed out that the O2U-2 already had many of the characteristics of a two-seat fighter. At this time two experimental two-seat fighters were under contract, the XF8C-2 and the XF2U-2.[65] The General Board wanted one squadron of two-seat fighters built specifically for comparison with single-seat fighters. That was probably the origin of the F8C-4 Helldiver, 25 of which were built to serve with VF-1B on board the carrier *Saratoga* (the others went to the Marines and served mainly under the designation O2C-1). It starred in the movie *Hell Divers*, released in 1932, which introduced dive bombing to the general public.

The last fighter competition of this series was conducted in 1930. At this point BuAer typically circulated a draft design produced by its design section. Companies were invited to offer either a production version of the design (the 'straight' offer) or an alternative meeting about the same requirement. The 1930 competition was built around BuAer design No. 96, dated 24 January 1929.[66] It was to have had a single relatively small engine (R-975, 375hp), but it would be so light (2328lbs with normal load) that it could be quite fast (176.8mph in normal condition), with a service ceiling of 27,200ft. Initial rate of climb was 2360ft/second, far below that achieved by current aircraft with more powerful engines. Endurance in normal condition at 110mph would be 3.36 hours. The surviving data sheet does not appear to allow for a bomb load. No. 96 was an unusual approach to the fighter problem, as such aircraft had been growing heavier with larger engines (the F4B used a R-1340 of 450hp). Of the bidders, Boeing doubted the design was feasible at all. Curtiss was willing to build it. Only one bidder, Fokker, seemed to understand what BuAer was trying to do.[67]

Presumably there was a parallel competition for a two-seat fighter, which Grumman won with its FF-1 (the contract was signed 2 April 1931, just before the end of FY30). Notably it did not have any provision for a heavy bomb (it could carry two 100lb bombs underwing). In tests it was faster than any current single-seat fighter. No other manufacturer offered a satisfactory alternative. About half the FF-1s built were completed as scouts (SF-1s).[68]

There was some question as to whether aircraft capable of diving with a 500lb bomb were fighters or dive bombers. In October 1930 the commander of CarDiv ONE, Rear Admiral F J Horne (Admiral King's VCNO during the Second World War) recommended carrier aircraft characteristics. Among the types he envisaged was a high-performance carrier-borne single-seat fighter which could carry a 500lb bomb to 75nm at full throttle.[69] Moffett wanted the single-seat fighter mission expanded to include attacks on enemy surface ships. The ability to carry light bombs should be mandatory.

Thus a squadron of dive-bombing F4B-1s was designated for a time in the bomber series, as VF-1B. Curtiss produced the F11C in two versions, with fixed and retractable landing gear. Both had dive-bombing crutches, which carried the bomb clear of the propeller disc and therefore made it possible to drop the heavy bomb at near-vertical angles. Both versions were redesignated as bomber-fighters, as the BFC and BF2C. Curtiss offered a follow-up two-seat fighter as its XF12C. It was redesignated first as the XS4C-1 scout and then as the XSBC-1 dive bomber, the latter being produced in quantity as the final US Navy biplane attack bomber.[70] Grumman produced a scout-dive bomber version of its FF-1 two-seat fighter as the XSBF-1 (the F stood for Grumman, not fighter).[71]

The heavy bomb load and dive-bombing capability were apparently justified on the basis that the US carrier force was limited, so all aircraft should be multi-role. In 1931, however, a third fast carrier (*Ranger*) was being built and two more carriers were expected imminently (the *Yorktown*s ordered in 1933). By November 1931 the BuAer Plans Division was calling for a 'special' fighter not compromised by the 500lb bomb requirement.[72] BuAer and the fleet agreed that the 'special fighter' was just what a fighter should be – an aircraft designed entirely to fight other aircraft. For that it needed speed, superior performance (presumably in rate of climb and in manoeuvrability) and firepower.[73]

Grumman's F2F was derived from the FF-1. This one is shown on 7 July 1939. The F3F-1 was lengthened, with an enlarged wing and a somewhat more powerful version of the same R-1535 engine.

The F3F-2 was modified to overcome dissatisfaction with the performance of the F3F-1. This one is shown on 21 March 1938. The 'MF' on the fuselage indicates that this is a Marine Corps fighter.

BuAer conducted a special High Speed Flight programme. During the 1920s the US Navy had sponsored racing planes as a way to foster the development of higher-speed combat aircraft. The Depression made that impossible, so in August 1931 BuAer Chief Rear Admiral Moffett convened a small conference to develop a programme (in September it was further elaborated at a conference held by the Assistant Secretary of the Navy for Aeronautics). The object was to develop and demonstrate high speed comparable to that achieved by foreign countries using a minimum number of experimental aircraft as soon as possible.[74] The special programme was needed because the usual step-by-step development would not get the navy to the desired higher performance. Aircraft development was driven, it seemed, towards higher reliability and increased payloads. Performance would actually decrease, except to the extent that better engines provided more power. Aircraft designed deliberately for high speed would have to sacrifice reliability and endurance (i.e., fuel payload).

Whatever was developed was to be used where possible in service aircraft, although there was no intention of putting the experimental high-speed aircraft into service. Smaller aircraft, such as fighters, would be powered by air-cooled radial engines, but high-powered liquid-cooled engines would be developed for large aircraft, which for the navy meant seaplanes. The candidate air-cooled engines for intermediate development were the R-1535 (maximum 750hp) and the R-1830 (maximum 1000hp), of which the R-1830 was a standard Second World War engine. As an indication of what was possible in the near term, the initial FY32 programme envisaged installation of an R-1830 in a test aircraft (mainly to test cooling) and design of a special fighter with a maximum speed of 230mph. For FY33 the special fighter would have an R-1535 engine and an intermediate-speed aircraft would be developed powered by an R-1830. An intermediate speed aircraft powered by a new liquid-cooled H-2120 engine was expected to reach 300mph (1500hp), the next step being a geared 2000hp engine.[75]

Money was tight; plans for specially-designed aircraft had to be dropped. However, BuAer did buy a series of experimental fighters which seem not to have been part of its mainstream programme, including monoplanes. A December 1932 document associated them specifically with the High Speed Programme listing them in order presumably corresponding to their importance to the programme: the Boeing F7B-1 low-wing monoplane; the Berliner-Joyce F3J, the Curtiss F11C, the Boeing F6B, the Curtiss F13C, the Douglas FD and the Vought F3U (similar aircraft were listed in other categories). The F7B used an R-1340-F engine (550hp at 10,000ft, 725hp at sea level). Its output was about the same as that of larger engines used in projected fighters, such as the R-1820 (F11C-2: 600hp at 8000ft and 725hp at sea level) and the R-1535 (F6B-1: 625hp at 6000ft, 725hp at sea level).

BuAer waited until 1934 to hold a competition for a new high-performance fighter. To get that performance, BuAer was resolved to relax its rules, accepting low-wing monoplanes it had considered but rejected in the past. The Bureau wanted a range of 1000nm, which would match that of bombers it was buying: the new fighter would be both an interceptor and an escort.[76] Desired maximum speed was 233mph (stall speed 65mph). Normal gross weight should be no more than 4000lbs. Maximum span for a biplane was limited to 32ft and wing loading to 15lbs/ft^2. Although the fighter would not normally carry bombs, the BuAer paper includes references to a bomber condition, the fighter carrying bombs underwing. The contenders were Boeing, Grumman, Bellanca and Curtiss. None of the designs was new. Grumman won with its F2F-1, which had received a prototype contract in 1932 and had flown in 1933. It was a fast biplane (233mph) using the retractable landing gear introduced in the company's FF-1. Unfortunately it had been designed as a stripped-down maximum-performance aircraft and considerable equipment now had to be added, costing performance. The extra firepower now desired required a 0.50-calibre machine gun, but that would overload the F2F. However, the other alternatives were worse, so the F2F was bought. Grumman was asked to submit a modified F2F which was designated F3F.[77]

Meanwhile, in October 1933 it was proposed to split fighters into attack fighters, which would accompany strike aircraft and protective fighters intended for fleet air defence. The main requirement for the attack fighter was speed. The protective fighter needed superior manoeuvrability, climb and ceiling and a very short take-off run. The latter would make it possible to spot protective fighters ahead of all other types on board a carrier in position for immediate take-off. The idea was not approved, but manufacturers were aware of the idea and Curtiss proposed what it called an 'Alert' fighter. It would achieve high speed by eliminating many standard items, such as the radio and emergency floatation gear and even the engine cowling (an odd choice since it substantially reduced drag). The 'Alert' fighter would be powered by a new more powerful engine.[78] Within BuAer a proposal arose to develop a stripped-down 'jockey' fighter powered by a new developmental engine. Most safety equipment would be removed. Even the adjusting and trimming mechanism of the control surfaces might be eliminated. On this basis a 500hp engine, rather than the 700hp of the F3F-1, might suffice. It would probably be a liquid-cooled 'vee' rather than a radial, to minimise frontal area and therefore drag.[79] BuAer decided to run a competition for the 'jockey' fighter alongside the 1934 competition for the standard fighter. However, the project was dropped because no suitable powerplant had been sufficiently developed.

BuAer chief Rear Admiral E J King (the future CNO) tested the 'jockey' idea by proposing to the fleet that some items, which he thought would be eliminated anyway in wartime, be eliminated: floatation gear, life raft, fire extinguisher, radio (except for section or division leaders), pyrotechnics, first aid kit, emergency rations, starter crank and landing light. In addition, he pointed out that at least a quarter of a fighter's fuel was used up reaching fighting altitude. That could be relegated to a drop tank. Altogether, 300 to 600lbs could be saved. In the current standard fighter, the Boeing F4B-4, that would add 11.8mph to maximum speed (about 5 per cent), reduce take-off run about 10 per cent, increase the rate of climb at sea level and at critical

The Brewster Buffalo shown won the 1935 (FY36) fighter competition but by 1941 it was being replaced by the Grumman F4F Wildcat. Because it distrusted folding wings on monoplanes, BuAer demanded fixed wings and thus had to limit wingspan (to 30ft, with penalties for exceeding it) to allow enough aircraft to be stowed on carriers. Brewster stayed within the limit. Its inability to substitute a much larger wing (as Grumman did in the F4F-3) carried heavy penalties as weight was added. At the outset, weight was not to exceed 5000lbs and the two permissible engines were the R-1532-92 and R-1670-2. When BuAer asked for a more powerful engine, Brewster had to choose the R-1820-22 because the alternative R-1830-66 was too much heavier than the engines for which the F2A had been designed. Brewster was also asked to raise its cockpit, adding drag (Brewster estimated that it cost 3mph). Brewster did increase span from 32ft to 35ft and length from 23ft to 26ft (its original dimensions had been somewhat greater than BuAer had wanted). Design weight was 4771lbs, but as delivered the F2A-1 weighed 5307lbs. In March 1939 BuAer asked that its 950hp engine be replaced by a 1200hp supercharged version, which weighed 350lbs more but dramatically improved performance. The previous version was cancelled in favour of the new F3A-2 shown here. Early war experience showed the need for greater endurance, armour and self-sealing fuel tanks. The F2A-3 used by the US Navy at the outbreak of the Pacific War weighed about 7160lbs, nearly 50 per cent more than that of the prototype. The fighter lost so much speed and manoeuvrability that it was dropped in favour of Grumman's F4F-3, the aircraft it had defeated in the FY36 competition.

altitude by 560ft/seconds and materially improve manoeuvrability. Similar improvements were possible for other types of aircraft.

Fleet squadrons supported the idea, although they differed as to what should be eliminated. Commander Aircraft Battle Force disagreed: pilots should not be sent out in wartime without any means of saving themselves if they were forced down. Morale demanded that pilots know that every effort would be made to support them in an emergency. Devices such as rubber rafts would not be abandoned in wartime. His superior officer, the Battle Force commander, argued that in combat higher performance might save more lives than the safety devices. However, CinC US Fleet agreed with his air commander, although it might be desirable to have most of the safety devices arranged so that they could be stripped

Grumman originally offered a biplane for the 1935 fighter competition, but was permitted to substitute the monoplane XF4F-2. The F4F-3 shown was the XF4F-2 modified to solve problems displayed in initial tests. Major changes were installation of an R-1830-76 engine with a two-stage supercharger and larger new wings with squared-off rather than rounded tips. Initially the larger wing was adopted to maintain an acceptable wing loading despite the additional weight of the supercharger, intercooler and ducting. The machine gun installation in the nose was modified. During the test programme the vertical tail was enlarged. The big spinner was omitted in production aircraft. The larger wing made it possible to add considerable weight without compromising manoeuvrability. (Rudy Arnold of Craft Art Co. via US Naval Institute)

for maximum combat performance. The stripped-fighter idea was not revived until early in the Second World War.

Overall, in the mid-1930s some in the US Navy doubted that carrier fighters had a future. The same new engines which made fast dive bombers practicable also made fast bombers possible. These aircraft in turn dramatically reduced the warning time that lookouts could provide. If there was no warning and if standing patrols were effectively useless, were new fighters worth developing? In Admiral 1934 Reeves himself wrote that he saw little point in continuing fighter development merely 'to keep up with the Joneses'. This was hardly a denial of the value of carrier air power, but rather acceptance that the carriers were strong offensively but weak defensively.

Meanwhile monoplanes were gaining favour, so BuAer asked its design division to estimate the characteristics of a monoplane version of the F2F it had recently bought. The aircraft would require somewhat greater wing span and it would gain speed. However, the high-lift devices (full-span Zap flaps and NACA [up-only] ailerons) the design division assumed would be used on the monoplane wing could also be used to improve a biplane like the F2F. The monoplane wing had a shorter effective span than a biplane wing and a higher effective span loading (weight per foot of span), hence would suffer in climb, ceiling, range and endurance. The biplane was easier to balance and offered

greater torsional and flexural rigidity. Rather than specifying a biplane or monoplane for the next fighter competition, BuAer decided to allow either in the new (1935) fighter competition, announced on 31 August of that year. Proposals were due by 1 November. This time BuAer required a maximum speed of 250mph and a stall speed of 65mph on an aircraft weighing no more than 5000lbs. Optimum dimensions were 30ft span and 22ft length. Penalties for excess size were 2mph for each foot of excess span and 1mph for each foot of excess length. Folding wings were rejected as undesirable.

This was the first pre-war competition which produced fighters that were later used in combat. Grumman and Brewster were both selected for further development. Grumman's XF4F-1 was an improved F3F-1 with a more powerful engine.[80] Brewster's F2A-1 was expected to be considerably faster than the Grumman fighter, but it used experimental features the firm had already offered in its SBA-1 dive bomber. Development of the F2A-1 was delayed until that earlier aircraft had been tested.[81]

Meanwhile the fleet complained that existing fighters were too slow and too lightly armed. BuAer was forced to accept a longer take-off run and a larger and heavier aircraft. At this point fighters were still stressed to dive-bomb, albeit without crutches for heavy bombs. The Chief of BuAer considered the dive bombing requirement pointless and expensive in speed. The new F3F was no faster than its predecessor the F2F, although it did add the capacity for a pair of bombs and for one 0.50-calibre machine gun in place of one of the 0.30s of the earlier aircraft.

Pressure came from another direction. There was suddenly increased interest in defending carriers, whether or not the naval aviators continued to espouse pre-emptive strikes. In May 1935 the commander of squadron VF-5B wrote to BuAer that protection of carrier flight decks included greater emphasis on defensive fighters. He thought that during the recent Fleet Problem two-seat fighters had proven superior to single-seaters for all missions, including defence against enemy aircraft. Higher fleet echelons disagreed and re-emphasised that the single mission of the fighter was to fight enemy aircraft. The two requirements were speed (at least 10 per cent over a combat-loaded bomber) and armament superiority. The latter might mean reaching the best position to fire, firing at greater range, using a more destructive projectile or increasing volume of fire. In each respect the single-seater would be better than a two-seater. High ceiling and rate of climb would place the fighter in a better position, but they should not be traded off against speed. Existing fleet fighters were not fast enough. It was not certain that a fast-enough fighter could be developed. In that case BuAer might better concentrate on fast single-seat dive bombers. That is, defence could be either by interceptor (the fast fighter) or by pre-emption (the fast, hence less vulnerable, dive bomber).[82] One senior officer wrote that the fleet had not had a satisfactory fighter for years.

All of this contrasted with the British naval view that performance could be limited because the FAA would face only naval fighters of limited capability. At least part of the difference was that the US fleet expected to face land-based Japanese aircraft as it penetrated the chains of Mandated Islands. The British did not contemplate this kind of warfare, at least on a widespread basis, until the Second World War began and they faced, not the Japanese fleet but instead German and Italian land-based aircraft.

The problem was difficult because, although a 300mph+ fighter could certainly be designed, it would have to be stronger than a land plane, with greater range and it would need considerable combat equipment. That had been the subject of the 'jockey' discussion and of the failed tests of the Hawk 75. With the same powerplant and wing loading a single-seater would be faster than a two-seater and a two-seater faster than a bomber, but the margins of speed would be small.

BuAer pointed out that for a given powerplant an aircraft had a limiting horizontal equivalent of terminal velocity, in which drag matched power output. The greater the power, if it could be achieved with less growth in drag, the higher the limiting speed. Conversely, if the drag associated with the engine could be reduced, the limiting speed would rise. That could be done by burying an engine in the fuselage, as in the US Army's P-39 Airacobra. Alternatively, more engines could be added in low-drag installations. BuAer tried all of these approaches.

The first operational version of the Grumman Wildcat, which was the standard US Navy fighter through much of 1943, was the F4F-3. Its guns were relocated to its wings (it had four 0.50-calibre machine guns) and it had an enlarged vertical tail. Its wings did not fold, BuAer having rejected wing folding for monoplanes some years earlier. Captain 'Winkle' Brown remembered the Wildcat as a revelation after flying docile FAA fighters like the Skua and the Fulmar. The combination of about the same power as a Fulmar in a far smaller and lighter airframe offered both high speed and great acceleration; Brown's first sight of a Wildcat was of a tiny aircraft shooting up nearly vertically. He later found it had a sensational rate of climb, 3300ft/min, it was about as fast as a Hurricane at sea level (at the time it was thought to be the fastest carrier fighter in the world), very manoeuvrable, with a good rate of roll. Mock combat with RAF Hurricanes and Spitfires convinced Brown that it could hold its own, except that it was not as fast in a dive. That was more than made up for by its fast climb and excellent manoeuvrability. Other virtues were its superior view for the pilot and its heavy armament compared to that of RAF fighters. The first British aircraft had the large-diameter (because single row) Cyclone engine, but the view improved further in versions with the smaller-diameter Twin Wasp (R-1830). Brown also considered that the Martlet had the best landing characteristics of any naval aircraft he flew. One of its few peculiarities, compared to later Second World War naval fighters, was that the undercarriage was manually retracted, the pilot cranking it up. Brown later flew Martlets from the prototype escort carrier *Audacity*, shooting down two Fw-200 Condors in head-on attacks, a tactic he may have invented.

The demand for greater fighter firepower inspired, among other things, work on fire control, as at the time fighters were making only 1 per cent hits at 500 yds.[83] The army was experimenting with heavier guns, from 20mm to 3in calibre. There was also interest in air-to-air bombing, an attractive but abortive idea pursued by many air arms.

Higher speed thus demanded larger engines and larger aircraft, whose wings would have to fold to enable them to fit on board carriers. That became possible because exactly such engines were under development, largely with navy sponsorship, in the 1930s. For the moment, neither the F4F-1 nor the F2A-1 offered the desired performance. BuAer gained some performance by adopting a larger engine (R-1830) and having Grumman redesign the F4F-1 as the monoplane F4F-2. The fleet had no monoplane experience, so as an interim step BuAer bought another biplane. The F3F-1 was re-engined as the F3F-2 and ordered immediately.[84]

The F4F-2 became the Wildcat, one of the more successful fighters of the Second World War. The prototype was modified with a two-stage supercharger R-1820-22 engine. It was considered extremely producible, an important virtue, and it was attractive because it had a minimum of experimental features. Brewster's F2A-1 Buffalo was much less successful, although in Finnish hands it was quite effective against fast Soviet bombers during the 'Winter War' of 1939–40.

These fighters began their official tests in December 1937 and January 1938, respectively. The F4F was found to be suitable for carrier use, but the prototype went back to Grumman for modification into the XF4F-3. It failed the catapult requirement. The Buffalo prototype lacked stability when approaching a carrier, but it seemed that a slight increase in dihedral would solve that. Other modifications during the test programme increased its speed from 277.5mph to 295mph at 15,200ft and its stall speed was cut from a marginal 68mph to a more satisfactory 66.5mph. Weight grew from 4929lbs to 5059lbs. A first production contract was placed in June 1938.[85]

For its part the F4F-3 attained 333.5mph (guaranteed speed at that time was 330mph), the highest speed any BuAer fighter had yet attained. The aircraft was accepted for production in modified form under the same F4F-3 designation. Compared to the F3F-2 prototype, it had a two-stage supercharger, larger wings and four 0.50-calibre wing guns instead of the earlier pair of fuselage guns firing through the propeller. With the F4F, BuAer and the navy it served finally had a fighter equal to those of its land-based counterpart, the US Army Air Force.[86]

BuAer found that high speed in the Wildcat and Buffalo carried real penalties. Increases in engine size and weight had to come out of fuel capacity, so that the desired 1000-mile strike escort range could not be attained unless performance was lost. In these aircraft, adding 500lbs increased the stall speed of the XF4F-2 from 66.7mph to 69.7mph, with similar losses in maximum speed. With the overload of 130 gallons, range increased to 884 miles (1157 miles for the Buffalo). The better overload range convinced BuAer to order the Buffalo into production.

As it looked at adopting smaller fighters in the late autumn of 1939, BuAer tried to understand what had been done to add about 120mph between the F2F-1 of 1934 and the two fast fighters. The most important factor was heavier and more powerful engines. They had forced up size and the wing loading, both of which had cost manoeuvrability – at that time an increasingly important issue (see below).[87]

BuAer considered neither fighter fast enough. High-altitude bombers using multiple turbocharged engines were already approaching 300mph. The example BuAer was using was probably the new B-17. By 1938

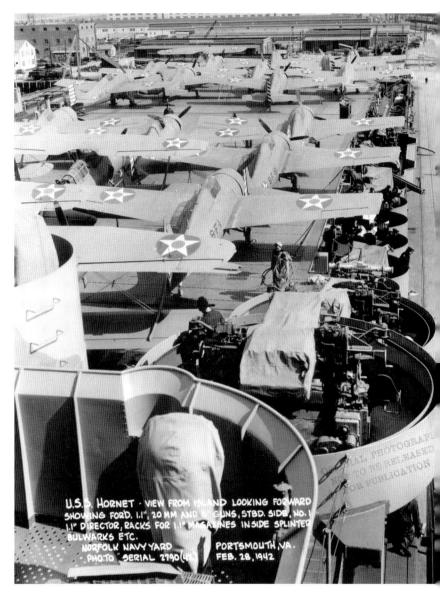

The new carrier *Hornet* shows her F4F-3 fighters at the fore end of her flight deck, in a 28 February 1942 photo. The biplanes are Curtiss SBC scout/dive bombers in their final months of service. By the time *Hornet* was in the Pacific, they had been replaced by SBD Dauntlesses.

reports of battle experience during the Spanish Civil War showed that armour protection for pilots was necessary.

The demand was still for higher speed and heavier armament. It seems to have been accepted that near-term increases in engine power would not buy enough speed, so BuAer would have to go to twin engines to get much beyond 300mph. In 1937 BuAer asked manufacturers for a twin-engine design with a range of 1000nm, 65mph stall speed, maximum possible speed and an armament of four 0.50-calibre machine guns and two 116lb bombs. Folding wings would be permitted, for the first time in a BuAer fighter competition. None of the proposals was acceptable; according to the BuAer fighter history, the requirements had been too vague. After the competition failed, BuAer asked for more internal studies. Defending fighters would be armed with two heavy (20mm, 0.50-calibre alternative) and two light (0.30-calibre) guns and 200lbs of air-to-air bombs. To gain higher maximum speed and to accommodate greater weight, BuAer was willing to increase stall (landing) speed to 70mph. It also investigated new engines

An F4F-4 on board the escort carrier *Santee*, November 1942. The bumps on top of the wings and faint lines on the wing mark this as a folding-wing F4F-4 Wildcat. Compared to the F4F-3, it had another pair of machine guns in its wings (as originally requested by the Royal Navy, to deal with heavily-armoured German aircraft such as the Fw-200 Condor) as well as more pilot armour and self-sealing tanks, all of which added weight and cost performance. Many pilots said that they much preferred the -3. F4F development reflected both US and British influence. The first British aircraft were ex-French G-36As, which the Royal Navy called Martlet I (the US Navy named it the Wildcat in 1941, the British following in 1944). They had Wright Cyclone (R-1820) engines because at the time the two-stage supercharged Twin Wasp had not been cleared for export to France (these engines had single stage two-speed superchargers). These aircraft could not fit the lifts of modern British carriers. Initially the British accepted that limitation when they ordered the G-36B (with single-stage Twin Wasps), but when they learned that Grumman was working on a folding wing they delayed delivery of the G-36Bs until they could be completed with such wings. These Martlet IIs became the first folding-wing Wildcat. Martlet III was an intermediate fixed-wing Martlet II: ten from the British contract (accepted with fixed wings due to delays in developing the folding wing) and thirty from a Greek contract. The British version of the F4F-4, the F4F-4B (Martlet IV) had a single-row R-1820-GR205A-3 Cyclone rather than the twin-row R-1830-86 Twin Wasp of the US version.

and concluded that a single-engine fighter using a very powerful, probably liquid-cooled (for low frontal area) engine might succeed. Twin air-cooled engines were still the alternative.

A new fighter competition was planned in the autumn of 1937 for either a single- or twin-engined aircraft. Proposals were due by 11 April 1938. The 70mph stall speed was now accepted. Permissible dimensions were increased; they were now limited only by the demand for a foot of clearance on a standard carrier lift (smaller dimensions, which would make it possible to handle two aircraft on the lift, were preferred). Maximum allowable weight was now 9000lbs, compared to 5000lbs for the XF4F-2.

The numbers problem

By about 1939 the navy had decided for tactical reasons (see below) that carriers had too few fighters aboard. BuAer was asked how to cram more of them onto a flight deck. When it investigated smaller fighters, it realised that drastically cutting their size would produce either slow or unacceptable designs. It turned out that high speed demanded a

monoplane layout, which in turn considerably exceeded the span of earlier biplane fighters and a massive heavy engine.

Fighter capacity on the flight deck depended on take-off run (i.e. on how much of the deck could be filled by aircraft) and on how many aircraft could be packed side to side. In the autumn of 1939 Grumman was asked to convert one F4F-3 with folding wings. Zap, who developed split flaps, was asked to apply his device to the F4F-3 to reduce its take-off run.

There was some interest, as there had been earlier, in splitting the fighters into interceptors and long-endurance pickets, the interceptors sacrificing fuel for performance. The picket would be used for a CAP. It turned out that the interceptor had to be large if it was to achieve high performance and the picket would not be an effective fighter at all. This project died, but the idea of a long-endurance patrol fighter would return in the 1950s as Missileer.

BuAer concluded that the F4F-3 was the best compromise it could get until the much higher-performing F4U entered service.[88]

Manoeuvrability and special designs

With the outbreak of war, BuAer began to receive combat reports pointing to the need for manoeuvrability – for dogfighting. Not only in the navy but throughout the air world it had been imagined that the dogfighting era was over, that pilots would be unable to sustain the G-loads associated with violently manoeuvring the very fast fighters needed to shoot down fast bombers. The fleet had placed priority on speed and firepower since at least 1936. BuAer had been concerned about manoeuvrability even before war broke out. Its concerns were apparently reinforced by early French combat reports.[89]

BuAer could not quantify manoeuvrability, but it certainly knew which characteristics contributed to it. To gain information, combat tests were conducted using the three latest US fighters, the Buffalo, the Wildcat (F4F-3) and the F3F-3 biplane.

Advocates of extreme manoeuvrability pointed towards biplanes, whose reduced span and increased wing area (reduced wing loading) offered superiority. However, the latest biplane fighter, the F3F-3, was nearly unstable longitudinally and had poor spinning characteristics. BuAer asked NACA for ways to increase manoeuvrability without sacrificing performance by reverting to a biplane. NACA suggested a small multiplane (biplane or triplane).[90] The navy became interested in a laminar-flow biplane which Douglas was developing in parallel with a laminar-flow monoplane. It would have used a pusher engine and a triplane undercarriage. The abortive army XP-48, rejected in 1940, may have been one of the Douglas designs. Ultimately BuAer had to admit that biplane performance would be unacceptably poor and it never let a contract for such an aircraft.

Pre-war US fighter interceptor tactics[91]

The US Navy roughly paralleled the Royal Navy in its approach to using fighters for fleet air defence. At the outset it seems to have relied on surface lookouts a considerable distance from the carrier. The strike aircraft of the 1920s flew at relatively low speeds; at 120 knots an aircraft travelled only two miles each minute. A lookout might spot such an attacker several miles further out, so total warning time might be as much as ten or fifteen minutes. The great change of the mid-1930s was the appearance of much faster bombers, which might fly above clouds and thus might not be spotted until they were nearly over the fleet. By the mid-1930s the view in the US Navy as a whole seems to have been that, like the Royal Navy, the fleet would rely on its anti-aircraft guns to deal with medium- and low-altitude attackers. However, it might be impossible to place bursts accurately against higher-altitude level bombers. Only fleet fighters could deal with such attackers. Whether or not high-level bombers could hit manoeuvring ships (it turned out that they could not) the high-altitude problem was important because it included shadowers and snoopers. As with the Royal Navy, the US Navy appreciated that countering an enemy's air scouts would abort his attack on vulnerable carriers and on the battle line. The interest in high-altitude aircraft explains why the pre-war US Navy was so interested in high-altitude fighters.

It is not at all clear how important defensive fighters were for the pre-war US fleet. Aviation lectures to the Naval War College emphasise both the offensive role of fleet aircraft and the role of fighters defending the spotters without whom the fleet could not fight at long range. There are generally references to the apparently secondary independent carrier roles of scouting and raiding, yet it seems obvious from contemporary war games that these activities would be the most prevalent prior to a decisive fleet engagement relatively late in the campaign.[92]

An early (1930) US Navy handbook of carrier operations envisages a multi-carrier organisation in which carriers are designated for Duty, Support or Relief within the larger battle fleet.[93] They in turn were distinguished from Battle-Line Carriers intended specifically to support the battleships (corresponding roughly to the RN carriers providing and relieving spotters and observation aircraft and also beating off enemy attempts to destroy these aircraft). All of the carriers were expected to operate together, trading off their functions so that aircraft could operate more or less continuously.

The Duty Carriers would launch an Outer Air Patrol and a CAP on signal and they would relieve these patrols continuously if required to do so. Support Carriers would be maintained in a lesser degree of readiness, prepared to launch back-up (support) scouts and fighters as required. They would relieve the Duty Carrier. Relief Carriers would be in the lowest state of readiness, concentrating on aircraft upkeep.

The Outer Air Patrol (a division of scouts [VS] from each carrier) would search for the enemy. No distinction was made between enemy warships (to be found in a search over a designated sector) or enemy aircraft. The CAP (a squadron of fighters [VF] from each carrier) would patrol over the flagship of the Carrier Divisions unless another task or station was ordered. Their targets would be enemy aircraft threatening the fleet or light vessels (remember that at this time US naval fighters were also dive bombers). Backing these continuously airborne aircraft would be support scouts (one VS division from each Support Carrier) and support fighters (one VF Squadron from each Support Carrier). Normally support aircraft would not be launched unless the Outer Air Patrol or the CAP had been sent on definite missions against a located enemy. In the event an enemy surprise air attack was likely, the Outer Air Patrol would be strengthened to consist of all available VS squadrons and the CAP would comprise all VF squadrons.

To allow Grumman to devote full energy to producing Hellcats, Wildcat production shifted to the Eastern Aircraft division created in wartime by General Motors. Its FM-1 was an F4F-4 with four rather than six wing guns (but more ammunition). Production began in 1942, but the bulk of these aircraft were produced in 1943–4. The Royal Navy designated its Lend-Lease aircraft Martlet (later Wildcat) Vs. This FM-1 is shown on board an escort carrier (as evident from the shape of the uptake on the port side of the flight deck). It is in North Atlantic camouflage, the white underside intended to blend with the sky. Note also the drop tank.

The 1930 instructions also allowed for one or more Distant Carriers stationed well clear of the fleet in the most likely direction of enemy approach. Their aircraft would search for and strike the enemy carriers. The prerequisite for such operations was that enough carriers and aircraft would remain with the main body of the fleet to offer it reasonable security against enemy air attack. Another possible air plan was to concentrate all fighters over the carriers (or, if the carriers were dispersed, the carrier flagship) as a means of defending against a major enemy air strike known to be in the air. The tactical instructions give no hint of a mechanism for controlling fighters (all US fighters had radio by this time).

The 1930 instructions emphasised the need to destroy enemy naval air power by wrecking his flight decks, but cautioned that light bombs could not do so and even that dive bombing did not impart sufficient velocity to penetrate a steel deck.[94] In the event the bearing of the enemy force was fairly well known (but not the range) it might be desirable to station fighters with the Outer Air Patrol, so that on sighting the enemy they could immediately attack his carriers. Normally that would amount to one fighter division from each designated carrier. It would accompany only the first flight of the Outer Air Patrol (from take-off to first return for refuelling) as otherwise the Combat Air Patrol would be dangerously reduced for too long.

During the 1930s the US Navy commissioned more carriers and it also embodied the results of gaming and of full-scale exercises (Fleet Problems) in its carrier doctrine. Its 1938 tactical orders (USF-10) envisaged formation of two patrols supporting a CAP. An Outer Air Patrol would give timely warning of the approach of enemy forces, mainly meaning enemy surface ships.[95] It would operate 25 miles beyond the outer screen of the fleet on the threat axis. Aerial pickets, a new development since the original doctrine had been written, would be assigned to were intended specifically to spot high-altitude air attacks. The pickets would operate singly outside the outer screen and the surface pickets, 'disposed laterally, radially and vertically according to conditions and numbers available'. CAPs would be set up over and about the unit (presumably a carrier) responsible for denying enemy air observation or air attack. USF-10 gave no indication of command responsibility for using picket information to activate the CAP, but the idea of an air command ship is suggested by the phrase about a unit responsible for air security.

Both the Outer Air Patrol and the picket stations would have been filled by floatplanes from cruisers or battleships operating with the carrier.[96] These scouts could not possibly fight their way through enemy fighters to gain information, but they offered long endurance and good cockpit visibility. Contemporary tactical handbooks also provided for patrols filled by carrier-based aircraft, presumably scout dive bombers. Visibility from the air would be far better than from the surface and these scouts could range further from the carrier than could her escorting cruisers and destroyers.

The March 1941 version of the handbook for carrier aircraft, USF-74, continued the idea of patrols, but changed the mission of the Outer Air Patrol (normally three aircraft) to one of operating well ahead of a force to offer timely warning of the approach of enemy forces – especially aircraft. It would cover an arc of a circle 25nm beyond the circular outer surface screen. An Intermediate Patrol was intended to force enemy submarines in the path of a moving force to submerge, hence to prevent them from gaining attack positions. The aerial pickets, to spot and track high-altitude targets, were retained. So was the CAP over the force.

Navy tacticians understood that fighters launched by the carrier would have to be directed towards the enemy aircraft. The theory was that a fighter control officer flying on board one of the scout planes would direct the fighters.[97] It is not clear how he was to maintain situational awareness without any way of visualising an evolving air situation, but the Outer Air Patrol, the pickets and the fighter director were the best that could be done at the time. The tactical handbooks of the time describe the concept, but it is not clear how often it was exercised. The system was tested in the 1939 full-scale exercise (Fleet Problem XX). The carrier Yorktown maintained a CAP while fulfilling other carrier functions.

The main lesson learned was that it was difficult for a single carrier to do everything required. She had too few fighters to defend herself while supporting strikes against enemy ships. The new carrier then being designed, the Essex class, was enlarged specifically to provide a second fighter squadron (total thirty-six rather than eighteen aircraft) for both offensive and defensive roles. As a more immediate solution, fighter squadrons on board carriers were strengthened by 50 per cent, so that as of August 1941 a description of standard carrier organisation showed twenty-seven fighters per carrier.

The Yorktown experiment came at a time of increasing scepticism that fleet anti-aircraft fire would solve the air defence problem for the battle line. In 1937 the US fleet began exercising with radio-controlled drones. The great surprise was that shells bursting exactly where they were intended to were not destroying such aircraft, which were both slower and considerably flimsier than real tactical aircraft. By 1939 a gunnery officer was commenting, in the official compendium of the year's gunnery exercises, that anti-aircraft fire was so ineffective that the fleet had better rely on its fighters for all of its air defence.

When it entered fleet service in 1941, air-search radar was seen as a substitute for the air patrols and the pickets. That substitution moved the fighter-direction officer from the air battle down into a space from which he could understand the situation and direct his aircraft. Initially such officers, both in the Royal Navy and in the US Navy, operated from limited spaces using improvised equipment. Yorktown had the first carrier set, reporting in March 1941 that her CAPs were quickly and reliably directed to intercept incoming raids. Her CO recommended that a radar plot be set up specifically for fighter control (the first such US plot was installed on board the carrier Hornet, then under construction). The US Navy developed its own methods of fighter control based largely on early British experience, as reported by numerous naval observers the Royal Navy welcomed.

Through the 1930s the role of carrier air defence was changing. In its 1931–2 games, the Naval War College found that attaching any carrier to the slow battle line invited attack on them and the destruction of flight decks. Carriers should operate independently, seeking out the enemy's carriers and gaining air superiority by striking them. At the same time the US Navy began to seek ways to keep its carriers operational despite battle damage to their flight decks.

Carrier tactics changed. Although tactical handbooks continued to show carriers in formation with other fleet elements, typically somewhere abaft the battleships, in Fleet Problems the carriers often operated independently, seeking out enemy carriers as a prerequisite to any other roles. This was much like British practice of the time, as reflected in the abortive 1936 Memorandum on the FAA. Until the enemy carriers had been destroyed, the battle line would not enjoy vital air support, for example fighters to deny the air over a gunnery battle to enemy spotters (and to protect its own spotters). The War College had long ago established to its own satisfaction that it was impossible

For the F4F-4 and other aircraft, Grumman devised an ingenious form of wing folding evident here on the hangar deck of the escort carrier *Charger*, 2 October 1942. The outer wing rotated before folding back. That allowed a long wing to fold back so that an aircraft could fit within a small hangar deck.

to control the air over a battle area; the only way to gain air superiority was to wipe out the enemy carriers. That was, however, a controversial idea within the fleet. Moreover, the War College freely admitted that the one aspect of naval warfare its games could not really model was air-to-air battle. It tried hard to develop rules for one-on-one air battles, but they were never particularly satisfactory. It was impossible to model the complicated tactics of air combat. Probably because the influence of the War College collapsed after 1934, interest in integrating carriers with the battle line increased.

Senior officers who had experienced large-scale action on the gaming floor were well aware of the War College's views. Nearly all US flag officers of the late interwar period had graduated from the War College; that probably explains why non-aviators like Admiral Spruance wielded carrier forces so effectively. Aviators were particularly sensitive to the

carrier's combination of extreme vulnerability and long-range striking power. In a 1938 Fleet Problem, Admiral King, who had been both Chief of BuAer and Commander of Air Squadrons Battle Fleet, commanded the carriers on one side. He operated them away from the battle line, his first priority to find and neutralise the enemy carriers. At the post-exercise conference, King was berated; the battleships badly needed air services. Why was he fighting a 'private war' with the enemy carriers? King replied that if his carriers were neutralised there would be no air services at all. Until he wiped out the enemy carriers, his own were in danger. Gaming and full-scale exercises help explain why the US Navy typically operated its carriers singly up through early 1943.

THE IMPERIAL JAPANESE NAVY

Like Admiral Reeves, the Japanese airmen of the mid-1930s saw little point in developing new shipboard fighters. Unlike the US Navy, the Imperial Navy was responsible for the defence of fixed bases and other facilities, for which it needed fighters. Before 1941 it made no distinction between carrier- and land-based defensive aircraft, so it continued

to develop shipboard fighters whether or not they seemed to contribute to carrier operations. The last entirely pre-war monoplane naval fighter (the A5M 'Claude') seems to have been envisaged more for the defence of fixed bases than for carriers.

Probably the key factor in Japanese fighter development in the immediate pre-war period was the advent of a long-range naval bomber, the Mitsubishi G3M ('Nell'). As it contemplated a possible war against the United States, the Imperial Japanese Navy needed some way of knowing when the US fleet had sortied from its base at Pearl Harbor. As chief of Japanese naval aircraft development in the early 1930s, Admiral Yamamoto was well aware of developments in aircraft engines and structure which made fast long-range aircraft practical. The major civilian case in point was probably the twin-engine Douglas DC-3. Yamamoto called for a long-range scouting aircraft capable of reaching Pearl Harbor from Japan (there were no airfields in the Mandates). In the absence of radar, a fast high-altitude scout would be almost impossible to detect, let alone intercept. Yamamoto issued contracts to Mitsubishi, which produced the G3M. The aircraft could also carry a bomb or torpedo load. In contrast to the Royal Air Force and the US Army Air Corps, the Japanese army had no particular interest in a long-range bomber.

The new aircraft technology promised attack aircraft of such performance that it seemed impossible for any opponent to intercept them. The Imperial Navy had always focused on attack, so it saw its fighters primarily as a means of protecting its attack aircraft. If bombers were fast enough, fighters might be obsolete. Some senior Japanese aviators argued that they were no longer worthwhile, a view echoed in the US Navy and in the Royal Navy of the mid-1930s.

Yamamoto's bomber entered production shortly before Japan attacked China in 1937. As the Japanese became embroiled there, they needed a way to strike deep in the rear of their enemy. The G3M was the only suitable aircraft, so the Japanese navy found itself fighting a large-scale land war, something not conceivable for the British or even for the US Navy.

The great surprise of the China War was that the G3M was not at all immune to interception. The Chinese built an early warning system based on human observers and they managed to intercept many attacks. To achieve its extraordinary range, the G3M had sacrificed armour and even structural strength and it was therefore quite vulnerable to fighter attack. The Japanese learned that it had to be escorted – a major problem given limited fighter range. Carriers could get close enough to launch the necessary fighter escorts. Fighter-vs-fighter battles became

When war broke out between Japan and China in 1937, the standard Japanese navy fighter was the A5M (Type 96) shown here (code-named 'Claude' during the war); this is the A5M4 version. It was designed to the 9-Shi requirement, competing against Nakajima. Proposals were due in February 1934. The resulting A5M became the world's first monoplane carrier fighter. It was designed by Jiro Horikoshi, who went on produce the A6M Zero. In this design he chose a fixed undercarriage to limit weight, on the assumption that careful detail design would balance the extra drag. Japanese fighter pilots emphasised dogfighting, hence manoeuvrability and there was some doubt that the new monoplane could dogfight biplanes. The great surprise was that it could, even though on initial tests it was considerably faster than expected (243 knots [279mph]). Initial examples were considered inferior in dogfighting against the current standard Japanese naval biplane fighter, the Nakajima Type 95 (A4N1), but Horikoshi introduced wash-out near the wingtips to delay stalling at a high angle of attack. Once that had been done, the A5M could out-manoeuvre the biplane. This A5M4 was photographed in 1940–1.

a fixture of the Japanese air campaign in China. When it sought a new fighter in the late 1930s, the Imperial Navy demanded an extraordinary combination of manoeuvrability and performance (for dogfighting) and range (to support long-range strikes). The result was the A6M Zero-Sen, the main Japanese fighter of the Pacific War. Its prototype flew in 1939.

The Zero shared the same generation of 1000hp class engines as the Wildcat and the Spitfire, but it achieved much higher performance (mainly manoeuvrability and level speed) by careful design and a willingness to pare structural strength and to omit protection of any kind. That was reasonable as long as superior performance and extremely experienced dogfighting pilots offered it a considerable degree of immunity. Limited Japanese industrial strength meant that in 1941 there was no generation of 2000hp class engines nearly ready for use, comparable to those which powered the US Corsair and Hellcat. Prototypes of such engines became available to the Japanese only in 1943 and then only in limited numbers.[98]

The design of the Zero was probably much affected by the bomber escort role. It had to combine very long range with exceptional manoeuvrability, as the Imperial Navy considered dogfighting essential. Long range was achieved with an engine which could be throttled down to run on an exceptionally lean fuel mixture. As a consequence, its endurance at higher speed was presumably relatively short, with operational consequences demonstrated at Midway. Manoeuvrability was gained partly by the use of innovative 'combat flaps' and partly by paring down airframe weight to hold down wing loading. Weight saving included avoiding armour but also limiting armament to two low-velocity 20mm cannon (sixty rounds each) and two 7.7mm (0.30-calibre) machine guns.

The production of the Zero, which was primarily a long-range bomber escort, was hardly a ringing endorsement of the value of fighters in fleet air defence. The Japanese shared the US view that carriers were powerful in offence but weak in defence. Their exercises showed that concentrated attack forces, launched by multiple carriers, could be extremely effective, but concentration would also endanger their own carriers. As the Japanese built fleet carriers, they seem to have concluded that a single carrier could not generate enough offensive power to be effective. They therefore created two-carrier divisions, which became the basic elements of their carrier force. The aircraft of a Carrier Division were tactically integrated and ships and aircraft were not considered interchangeable between divisions. For example, after *Zuikaku* lost many of her aircraft at Coral Sea, there was no interest in providing her with fresh aircraft and assigning her to some other division; she was withdrawn for refitting (her sister-ship *Shokaku* was withdrawn because of battle damage).

Experience in China showed that massive air strikes were needed to deal with defended land targets. A single carrier division was not enough. The solution was to form a single unified carrier strike force, built around all three fleet carrier divisions. Concentration would make it relatively simple to operate their strike aircraft together, even in radio silence. The risk that an enemy would find all the carriers concentrated together was considered acceptable. After the war it was argued that

In December 1941 the Zero was the fastest and most manoeuvrable naval fighter in the world; it could also out-manoeuvre nearly all land-based fighters, although there is some indication that the Spitfire could turn with it. Presumably the emphasis on dogfighting explains the use of what amounted to a bubble canopy. This captured example is shown under flight test, 18 February 1943.

concentrating all the carriers would also concentrate their defensive fighters, but that is questionable.[99] The same doctrine called for the carrier divisions to operate separately – dispersed – if the target were an enemy naval force. Presumably it was assumed that one carrier division would suffice to sink ships.

The Japanese formed their six fleet carriers into a six-carrier task force (Kido Butai) in April 1941, as the First Air Fleet. Japanese land-based naval bombers and fighters were formed into a parallel 11th Air Fleet. The six-carrier formation was used at Pearl Harbor, in the Indian Ocean (for the attack on Ceylon) and at Midway, which the Japanese initially saw as an attack on a land target. Midway (four carriers, because one carrier division was being repaired) certainly showed that concentrating carriers was dangerous: the US strike force hit and destroyed three of the Japanese carriers at the same time (a fourth was sunk somewhat later).

When the Imperial Navy carriers faced US attacks at Coral Sea and at Midway in 1942, they had superior aircraft operating much the way both the US Navy and the Royal Navy had imagined they would operate in the mid-1930s; by that time both had moved on. In both battles Japanese fighter defence crumbled badly. Superior aircraft were not enough. They had to be backed by fighter control and tied to it by voice radio. At most the Japanese employed an officer on the bridge as a fighter controller and there is no evidence that they had exercised such control.

There was apparently no attempt to provide airborne lookouts of the type the US Navy and the Royal Navy tried pre-war; they depended entirely on surface lookouts to spot approaching aircraft. They had inherited from the First World War Royal Navy the belief that any use of radio might well be fatal, so they seem to have relied on cruiser gunfire as the signal that aircraft were approaching a force. Experience in 1942 showed just how little surface lookouts could see in time. That first became obvious during the Indian Ocean sortie of the Japanese

carrier strike force. After the Japanese carrier task force was spotted off Ceylon it was attacked from high altitude by a flight of British bombers. As in other such attacks, no hits were scored, but the lesson was that the Imperial Navy lacked any reliable means of detecting, let alone intercepting, enemy air attacks.[100] Ironically, the Imperial Navy had already rejected an early proposal for radar inspired by Japanese observation of the RAF during the Battle of Britain. By this time the Japanese also had access to German radar.

The Japanese operated CAPs, but fighter direction, if it was exercised at all, was rudimentary. The air operations officer on the carrier bridge had responsibilities beyond fighter direction, such as controlling landings and take-offs and he had no means of building an air picture to support whatever CAP decisions he made. The air control officer was supposed to exercise control of the CAP via voice radio, but that was apparently very unsatisfactory and little used.[101] The position of air defence officer was not permanent; it was assigned to a carrier pilot who happened to be available. There was no arrangement for immediate transmission of information to the air defence officer; instead, it had to go through the air group commander.

Without real fighter direction, the concentrated defensive power of the Japanese carriers achieved very little. Once one section of the CAP pursued enemy aircraft, the other sections generally joined in, leaving the way open to any additional attack from another direction. That happened at Midway.[102] Standard practice seems to have been to keep ready fighters on deck to react to any new threat rather than try to reorient the fighters already airborne.

There had been no attempt to develop CAP doctrine or tactics. The combination of lookouts and CAP offered reasonable protection against a single attack (the British bombers in the Indian Ocean were promptly shot down) and against a sequence of attacks, but not against any sort of concerted attack from different directions. That took a much more disciplined approach to air operations and a means of building a picture of the developing air situation. The system could collapse even in the face of a single attack. During the Battle of the Coral Sea, the small Japanese carrier *Shoho* was surprised despite excellent weather.[103] She was particularly unfortunate in that she turned into the wind to launch aircraft just as the attack developed. As she did so, US dive bombers made a co-ordinated attack which overwhelmed her. The failure of CAP control showed: her fighters were all drawn off by the first attack, hence were not available when the second arrived. It happened that the attackers also lacked effective command and control: there was no senior officer to redirect attacks once it was clear that *Shoho* was doomed.

At Coral Sea, in addition to the small *Shoho* operating independently (to support a planned landing), the Japanese had a carrier division composed of their two newest fleet carriers, *Shokaku* and *Zuikaku*. A strike from *Yorktown* crippled *Shokaku*. The strike found both Japanese carriers, but the US dive bombers circled to await the arrival of the slower torpedo bombers, in order to make a co-ordinated attack. That gave *Zuikaku* time to retreat into a rain squall and so to escape attack. Once they did attack, the US aircraft managed to deal with the Japanese CAP of fifteen to eighteen fighters, apparently the standard number a two-carrier division could put up. None of the US attackers was shot down and they managed to make two hits (they claimed six and three probable hits). The follow-up torpedo attack failed, but the Zeroes failed to shoot down any of the torpedo bombers (which shot down three of them). This outcome, incidentally, suggests that the US torpedo attacks at Midway were not at all obviously suicidal. A second attack against *Shokaku* by *Lexington*'s bombers added a third bomb hit. Later experience

suggests that *Shokaku* was extremely fortunate to have survived.[104] Her sister *Zuikaku* escaped damage altogether but lost many of her aircraft.

At the time of Midway, Japanese carriers typically had eighteen fighters on board.[105] Japanese fighter tactics employed three-aircraft sections (Shotai).[106] It was probably most important that members of a Shotai trained and flew together to create mutual understanding. That lasted until the Shotais suffered losses and required replacements. In theory half the fighters of a carrier or a division would be assigned to support air strikes, for example against land targets. On board a single carrier, that would leave only nine fighters for defence. A ship would therefore maintain one three-fighter Shotai aloft, a second spotted for launch and a third in a lesser state of readiness. Within a division, one carrier would be responsible for fighter defence, so she could devote all eighteen of her fighters to that role. In theory each fighter pilot was assigned to a sector for which he was responsible and in theory other aircraft could be vectored to reinforce a threatened sector. In fact, without effective radio direction, pilots had to vector themselves. Reliance on constantly refreshed three-aircraft Shotais explains why at least some of the carriers at Midway were constantly flying off sections of fighters.

Much has been made of the offensive orientation of the Japanese navy, which precluded much attention to fighter protection. Yet at Coral Sea and at Midway the Japanese followed much the tactics that the Royal Navy or the US Navy would have followed in the pre-radar era, perhaps about 1938. They were certainly attentive to the need to shoot down snoopers and shadowers; the Indian Ocean after-action report by the carrier *Hiryu* mentions several instances. As with both Western carrier navies, the Japanese concluded before the war that the only way to seize air superiority was to destroy the enemy carriers before they could attack. To that end the Japanese emphasised strike range and in 1941 they could attack well beyond the range of US or British carrier aircraft. However, they apparently did not devote much attention to the complementary problem of finding the enemy in the first place.[107]

After Midway the Japanese concluded that the two-carrier division did not provide enough massed air power to deal with a US carrier force. Immediately after Midway, Admiral Yamamoto formed his two remaining fleet carriers *Shokaku* and *Zuikaku* into the offensive core of a new Third Fleet, supplemented by the light carrier *Zuiho*, which was responsible for fleet air defence.[108] Fighter complements of all the carriers were increased. The three-carrier division was intended as standard. A crash carrier construction programme was ordered. For example the huge battleship *Shinano* was ordered completed as a carrier. The new organisation fought at the Philippine Sea in 1944.

Without effective radar and without much attention to how radar information could be used, the Japanese seem never to have developed any effective form of fighter control. They continued to see their carriers as offensive weapons with little defensive capacity; their only tactic continued to be to find their US opponents first and then strike. As it turned out, on the one occasion this was tried, they did find the US carriers first. However, the US carrier fighters were able to destroy the Japanese strike force. This victory at the Philippine Sea and a subsequent devastating US fighter sweep of Taiwan, made it impossible for the Japanese to operate significant numbers of carrier aircraft. Beginning late in 1944, they felt compelled to rely on suicide (Kamikaze) tactics. That had profound effects on the US and Royal Navies, extending well into the post-war era.

As for aircraft, the Naval General Staff initially refused to agree to develop a successor to the Zero, having been convinced by its early successes that it was invincible.[109] Early in the war the Air Service Bureau (Japanese BuAer) and the Arsenal design staffs saw the need for a follow-on fighter, which eventually emerged as the A7M ('Sam'). Designers were thinking about it long before any such project was approved. When it was finally approved, engine development had lagged, presumably because there was no approved requirement for a much more powerful engine. When the new aircraft was ready, it turned out to be unsatisfactory; it was too slow (its wing-folding mechanism was too heavy), its deck-landing speed was excessive and it was considered too large for carrier work. The engine gave considerable trouble. The initial A7M1 was abandoned in July-August 1944 and the wing-folding gear was removed and the engine replaced. The result was successful, but it was too late. In December 1944 the factory suffered a severe earthquake, followed by damaging air attacks; the engine factory was also hard hit. The first production A7M2 was completed only at the end of the war. As a consequence, when the Japanese faced the US fleet at the Philippine Sea in June 1944, its fighters were badly outclassed. US radar fighter control might have tipped the balance in any case and by that time most of the better Japanese pilots were gone, but the lack of foresight on the part of the Naval General Staff did not help.

* * *

What emerges from this account of pre-war practices (the Japanese reflected pre-war ideas and resources well into the Second World War) is that all three carrier navies envisaged carrier vs carrier battles just like those fought in 1942, in which ships fought without ever seeing each other. Such battles were the ideal that each navy sought, not a surprise departure from everything imagined pre-war. The surprises came when carriers were suddenly faced with visible surface ships attacking them.

The great question was whether there was some way for carriers to deal with air attacks and thus to gain a measure of survivability in the face of the enemy. The Royal Navy and the US Navy developed exactly that ability in 1940–4 and they demonstrated it triumphantly, most visibly in the Mediterranean (Operation 'Pedestal' in 1942, as long as the carriers remained with the convoy) and in the Pacific at the battle of the Philippine Sea in June 1944.

Despite its great virtues, the Zero could not overcome the lack of fighter control in the Japanese fleet. In 1941–2 the Japanese fleet had no radar and no alternative means of warning itself of the approach of high-flying aircraft. Warning was provided, if at all, by lookouts in escorting ships, which could announce the approach of aircraft by firing guns (the British also used gunfire for warning, but by 1941 they had radar). The Japanese had not evolved any doctrine of fighter defence and it lacked the sort of fighter director officers trained by both the Royal Navy and the US Navy. The carrier task force was a superb offensive instrument without any means of self-defence other than a self-directed CAP poorly adapted to handle attacks from more than one direction. Here *Akagi* launches the second strike at Pearl Harbor. Her island is innocent of any electronic sensor beyond a D/F loop. Note the splinter mattresses on the bridges.

CHAPTER 4
THE SECOND WORLD WAR:
FIGHTERS UNDER RADAR CONTROL

THE FIGHTERS DEVELOPED in pre-radar days fought the Second World War, albeit in steadily improving versions. New naval fighters conceived during the war did not generally enter service until the war was nearly over and they were soon superseded by jets. Thus the most important fighter developments of the war were in control (using radar) and in air-to-air sensing at night (radar). Through the interwar period, carrier-based fighters were one among several means of fleet air defence.

RADAR

For the Royal Navy and the US Navy, radar began as a source of warning, a replacement for the air patrols envisaged before the war. The advent of radar, which the British called RDF, seems to have been responsible for the dramatic change in the importance of naval fighters just before the war broke out (it is not clear to what extent that was the case in the US Navy). The use of radar to direct fighters was a separate development. It was certainly not envisaged when the Admiralty decided that with radar naval fighters were suddenly worthwhile. Almost certainly it was assumed that an air defence officer on board a designated carrier would decide that radar and other reports indicated that a raid was coming and then pass control to a fighter flight leader aloft.

The RAF began British radar development, but the Royal Navy was intensely interested and the Admiralty Signal Establishment (ASE) soon produced a series of naval sets. The first operational set, Type 79, was installed on board some major units before the outbreak of war.[1] It was incorporated in new ship designs, such as those of the new armoured carriers, but there was no attempt to incorporate radar in the newly-completed carrier *Ark Royal*.[2] The initial British naval radar was conceived as a means of warning ships that aircraft were coming, so it was called a Warning Air (WA) set. Installation was complicated by the need for separate transmitting and receiving antennas, on two masts set well apart. Moreover, there was no semblance of the modern map-like plan-position indicator (PPI) display. An operator turned the antenna into a desired direction and looked at a display showing whether there was a target echo. The display gave the range and to some extent the size of the echo as displayed suggested the number of aircraft approaching. The only way to form a tactical picture was to plot echo positions and observe how those positions changed over time. The Admiralty was also painfully aware that in adopting radar it was breaking its long-term preference for radio silence. If a British ship equipped with radar could pick up an echo, an enemy ship with an intercept receiver could pick up the outgoing pulse and at much greater range.[3] The Royal Navy therefore began the war with a doctrine calling for no more than periodic radar sweeps, the radar being used continuously only after an attacker had been detected.

Type 79 had a very broad beam partly because it operated at a relatively low frequency (long wavelength, 7.5m). Later developments were air-search radars operating at shorter wavelengths (Type 281 at 3.5m and Types 286/291 at 1.5m). Single-mast versions were developed (for carriers with limited topside space this improvement was particularly important). Another important development was the discovery that comparison of detections at different frequencies (e.g. by Types 79 and 281) could provide an indication of the height of the incoming attacker.

Photographed at Hvalfjord (Iceland) on 4 October 1941 by a US warship, the armoured carrier *Victorious* shows her initial radar equipment. At this time the British knew how to make a single antenna share the functions of transmission and reception, but to place air-search (air-warning in their parlance) radars in service as quickly as possible, they used separate masts for the two functions. For *Victorious* that meant one mast atop her tripod, above her Type 72 aircraft beacon (in the cylinder) and another abaft her island, both shard by the same Type 79 radar. Each of the antennas consists of paired horizontal dipoles (barely visible) half a wavelength apart vertically: the vertical spacing indicates the wavelength, in this case 7.5m. Between the beacon and the antenna is the diamond-shaped antenna of an HF/DF set, a standard late pre-war fitting. The medium-calibre fire-control director atop the bridge is fitted with a Type 285 ('fishbones') range-only radar antenna. The aircraft on deck are Fulmars, the only fighters then in Royal Navy service.

In 1944, Type 79 could typically detect a twin-engined bomber flying at 15,000ft at 85nm. It was considered very reliable and its first lobe extended to 40,000ft, giving good high cover. Type 281 offered higher power and a narrower beam (40° rather than 90°, which was still excessive). It could detect the twin-engined bomber at 95nm and with a pre-amplifier it could achieve 30 to 50 per cent greater range. Unlike Type 79, it could display its output on a PPI or Skiatron (a map-like display, see below), although the broad beam created very wide blips, which were called sausages. Given their broad beams, both radars typically measured target bearing more precisely by creating lobes, between which they switched.

The most important wartime British radar development was probably the cavity magnetron, which made possible operation at much shorter wavelength (10cm). That in turn made for a very narrow beam, which could be used not only for air search but also for surface

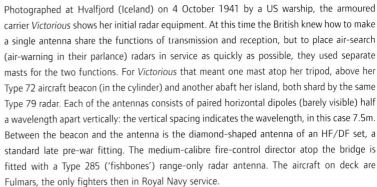

Radar-directed fighters with their own radars: F6F-5Ns line up for take-off on board an *Essex* class carrier, 2 January 1945. A carrier's CIC would coach these night fighters into position and they would use their own APS-6 radars (housed mainly in the wing nacelles shown) to complete the interception. APS-6 acquisition range was about 4nm. The 'S' indicated search; this radar was unable to lock onto a target so that the fighter could follow. Instead the pilot had to judge for himself the way the target was moving, as it was presented on his scope.

search, albeit at much shorter ranges than the metric Types 79 and 281. The cavity magnetron made it possible to package viable radars on board night fighters. It also made surface search (from the air) useful. Both roles had been tried using longer-wave radars, but neither worked very well.

Late in the war the Royal Navy was receiving the S-band (10cm) Type 277, which was both a surface-search set and a heightfinder; it could be stopped and its antenna tipped up at an angle to measure target elevation. Plans called for continuous vertical scan feeding a heightfinding display, but that was not available in wartime. Type 277 was considered capable of detecting a twin-engine bomber at 15,000ft at 25nm.

The US Naval Research Laboratory developed radars at about the same time as the British, though without the same urgency and hence more slowly. Because of the lack of urgency, it could concentrate on a higher frequency (shorter wavelength) offering better beam definition: 1.5m.[4] The first US naval prototype, XAF, went to sea aboard the battleship *New York* in January 1939. It differed from the British naval radars not only in frequency (hence beam size) but also in the fact that it incorporated a switch which allowed the same antenna to transmit and receive; the US Navy never used paired antennas as in British ships. The navy disclosed the radar concept to the two potential manufacturers, RCA and Western Electric (the manufacturing arm of the Bell Telephone System) in May 1939. RCA won the initial production contract for a series of six CXAM radars based on the Naval Research Lab's (NRL) XAF. One was installed on board the carrier *Yorktown* in 1941 (the first was installed on board the battleship *California*, the fleet flagship, in mid-1940). CXAM in turn became the basis of the standard US SK series of long-range air-search radars, a smaller version being the SC series (many ships had both).

SK had a beam width of 15–20°, hence did not need special processing if it was to use a PPI display. Its range performance matched that of the British Type 281. A British handbook (October 1944)

assessed its advantages as its good presentation and its good low and medium cover.[5] Its disadvantage was a lobe structure which made heightfinding above 7000ft extremely difficult. By 1944 the US Navy also had a larger version of SK using a dish antenna, SK-2. The US Navy also used a secondary air-search radar, SC-2, with a smaller antenna (it was the main air-search set on board destroyers). By late 1941 the Naval Research Laboratory, which developed prototypes of US shipboard radars (other than centimetric sets) was working on a radar to detect low-fliers, which the longer-wavelength CXAM and its successors could not do.

The British tested the cavity magnetron between February and August 1940. Meanwhile plans went ahead for a British scientific mission to visit the United States to reveal key technologies which the British hoped the United States would develop; by this time the United States was beginning to mobilise in the wake of the fall of France. Among the items the mission brought was a cavity magnetron – a radar signal generator both revolutionary and not yet in British service. At this time the US government was mobilising academic scientific research to support its defence programme. The Massachusetts Institute of Technology (MIT) established its Radiation Laboratory (Rad Lab) specifically to pursue microwave (magnetron: 10cm and 3cm) technology. The Rad Lab in turn developed several radars important in naval fighter control.

One was the pencil-beam heightfinder. Search radars like SK

Photographed on 10 April 1944 in Trincomalee from *Saratoga*, the fleet carrier *Illustrious* shows the combination of radars the Royal Navy adopted once it had single-antenna air-search sets in production. The antenna forward is the single aerial of a Type 79B radar, the single-aerial version of Type 79. The mast abaft the island carries the antenna of a higher-frequency (1.5m) Type 281B. On the fore side of the bridge is the pillbox radome housing the antenna of a Type 271 surface-search radar. The ship still has the Type 72 aircraft homing beacon. In the background is the aircraft maintenance ship (and, alternatively, carrier) *Unicorn*.

Refitted in the United States after action damage in the Mediterranean during the 'Pedestal' convoy, *Indomitable* shows new radars in this 25 March 1944 photograph taken by a blimp of ZP-14 out of NAS Weeksville in the United States. She has her higher-frequency radar on her foremast and the Type 72 beacon has been removed because the majority of British naval aircraft are now Lend-Lease (i.e., US) types fitted with the receivers for US beacons. A tripod mast stepped to the ship's funnel carries the necessary YE antenna (by late 1943 *Victorious* also had YE instead of her Type 72). Atop the bridge is a US SM pencil-beam heightfinder, which can also function as a surface-search radar (hence there is no separate surface-search set on the bridge structure).

produced a relatively narrow beam in bearing, but they did not provide elevation data. Height data turned out to be essential for fighter control. The broad vertical beam gave limited data, because reflection off the sea broke it into lobes. An aircraft flying at a particular height disappeared from the radar screen when it passed out of a lobe and reappeared when it entered another. Thus an operator could estimate height from the ranges of such 'fades'. However, he could obtain height much more accurately using a radar with a narrow vertical and horizontal beam, a pencil he could point at the target. The larger the antenna (in wavelengths) the narrower the beam. To make a beam narrow both horizontally and vertically required a large antenna (in wavelengths). For that to be practical, the wavelength had to be short – the signal had to be generated by a magnetron or something similar.

Rad Lab produced just such a radar, SM (SP in a lighter-weight version). SM-1 had an 8ft antenna (compared to 4ft 6in for Type 277), giving an estimated maximum range of 70–80nm, comparable to that of the SK search set. Out to the horizon it could detect targets down

to 1000ft. SP had an improved display and was light enough to be installed on board surface combatants down to specially-modified destroyers.

The great gap in radars in both navies was overhead, what was called zenith search. Late in the war the Japanese learned to exploit this gap and the US Navy deployed stop-gaps on an emergency basis. They included upward-looking night fighter radars (both APS-6 and the army's SCR-720), which were placed in the catwalks of carriers and a special zenith-search version of the standard surface-search radar (SG) using a new clamshell antenna. The Royal Navy did not deploy a zenith-search radar.

Radar cannot be separated from radar identification: identification friend or foe (IFF). The British began IFF development almost as soon as they deployed radars and in 1941 the US Atlantic Fleet was using the British Mk II system operating on search radar frequency. Adoption of common IFF was an essential part of wartime interoperability and IFF has been an inter-Allied project ever since. The main wartime type was Mk III. It and other IFF systems operate on an interrogate-respond basis: the interrogator associated with the search radar sends out coded pulses. They trigger a transponder, which sends back an identifying pulse. The response pulse is generally shown on the radar display. In the Mk III system, the interrogator was preset to a fixed frequency. The transponder swept through its frequency band every 2.5 seconds, the interrogator being tuned to a particular frequency. Coding was provided in the form of six combinations of broad and narrow response pulses. By late in the war an improved Mk V UNB (United Nations Beaconry) had been developed and was on the point of adoption.

Implacable is shown in Sydney Harbour at the end of the war, when she was part of the British Pacific Fleet. She and *Indefatigable* were the last of the six armoured fleet carriers to be completed, in 1944. She has the usual pair of long-range air-search radars, but the antenna atop her bridge is for Type 277. It was used both for surface search and for pencil-beam heightfinding. Atop the Type 72 lantern is the 'cheese' antenna for the Type 293 target-indication radar, serving the ship's 4.5in anti-aircraft battery. She shows numerous addition-al single 40mm guns, added as an anti-Kamikaze measure: five on new galleries in the island, with single Oerlikons visible below them and the cab of a power-worked 'Boffin' mounting at the fore end of the gallery. Another Boffin is visible under the quadruple pom-pom visible forward of the bridge. Two Oerlikons are visible at the bow. (Alan C Green via State Library of Victoria)

IFF was and always had been both vital and problematic. A pilot always sees his IFF transponder as both a lifeline when he is near his fleet and a menace when he is near an enemy who may be able to trigger it and thus track and identify him. The simpler the IFF code, moreover, the better the chance that an enemy may simulate it and thus appear (on radar) to be friendly. Mk III also began the long-term tendency to use lower frequency (hence a wider beam) for IFF, meaning that IFF responses might be somewhat misleading on a crowded radar display. It was never possible simply to shoot down all aircraft not showing IFF responses, because some might have suffered damage, some pilots might have switched off and not back on and a few friendly aircraft might not have IFF fitted in the first place.

From a control point of view, perhaps the most important develop-ment after shipboard radar itself was better radar displays.[6] The most important was the PPI, a map-like radar display created by a continu-ously-rotating radar, typically with a fairly narrow beam. The first PPIs were developed in Britain to support RAF fighter-control radars operating inland from the coastal radar chain, but they were not mass-produced (and did not enter naval service) until the United States,

with its vast electronics industry, entered the war. The British also developed a large-face display tube with reversed colours, so that the background was light and the blips showed as dark dots. This 'Skiatron' was mass-produced in the United States, becoming the standard fighter-direction device for both navies (to the US Navy it was a Projection PPI). Positioned horizontally, it could be used directly for fighter control.

Radar and the Imperial Japanese Navy

The Imperial Japanese Navy seems to have been reluctant to adopt radar, despite receiving reports hinting at its development before the outbreak of war.[7] A prototype air-warning radar was installed on the battleship *Ise* and a prototype surface-warning set on the battleship *Hyuga* just before both sailed for Midway.[8] There was certainly other awareness of radar. During the Indian Ocean operation by the Japanese fast carrier task force, it was bombed by British Blenheims, which approached without warning. The after-action report of the carrier *Hiryu* pointed to the need for some means of early warning, mentioning radar. After Midway, the surface warning set helped protect *Hyuga* against a collision (which nearly sank two cruisers) and her CO pressed for further development. When they took Singapore, the Japanese tried to recover the radar on board the sunken *Prince of Wales*.[9] The set tested on board *Ise* became the basis for the standard wartime air-search radar. The Imperial Navy also developed airborne radars, largely to detect surface ships for air attacks.

A post-war US evaluation placed Japanese naval radar at the end of the war about where the United States had been early in 1942.[10] There was nothing remotely comparable to a CIC and no radar plot (even though, like the Royal Navy and the US Navy, the Japanese had employed tactical plotting and indeed had better plotting facilities than other navies). There was no attempt at shipboard fighter direction using radar (late in the war there was land-based fighter direction), no anti-jam facilities on any radar, no B-scan or PPI displays (except for an experimental airborne set), no repeaters and no effective form of IFF.

However, the Japanese were well aware of US and other Allied radar. They knew and catalogued radar characteristics and their aircraft exploited weaknesses in Allied radars. For example, they chose the right altitudes, they used land shadows whenever they could and they also knew at what ranges they would be detected. A post-war evaluation placed Japanese countermeasures at about the stage the United States had reached in 1942, but added that the Imperial Navy made the most effective use of Window (chaff). There was no confirmed wartime use of a jammer (at the end of the war the navy had one

Indefatigable in Australian waters at the end of the war. (Alan C Green via State Library of Victoria)

jammer, FD-7, operating at 140 to 160 MHz). The Imperial Army had the lead in developing such equipment. Three types of intercept receivers were operational, one of which was intended for all major ships and another (W-27) for all large naval aircraft.

Japanese exploitation of increasing understanding of US radar-based tactics helped drive the development of US Navy fighter direction and tactics.

Radar fighter direction in the Royal Navy

Radar made fighter control, hence fleet air defence by fighters, practical. The pre-war problem that aircraft, particularly at altitude, could approach undetected, disappeared. Radar alone was not enough, however, The lesson the British learned in 1918 remained valid: a tactical picture had to be built, on the basis of which fighters could be vectored out. This was a kind of fire control, except that the lethal area of a fighter was vastly greater than that of, say, a shell. It was the area within which a fighter pilot could see a target and manoeuvre to deal with it. To make such control possible, the fighter controller has to track the incoming target – he needs not only its current position but also its course and speed. If he also knows the position of the defending fighter, he can calculate an interception path (if that is practicable, which is hardly always the case).

The British experience of the First World War was that a filter room could trace the tracks of incoming bombers on the basis of a series of detections. That may not seem a particularly profound point, but it was the difference between successful Allied fighter control

during the Second World War and the relative failure of German attempts at radar fighter control through much of the war. The Germans began the war with much more sophisticated radars but also with a much less sophisticated idea of how to use them. They built radars which could not only detect a target, but also track it. On land, the German approach was to pick up a bomber, set one radar to track it and then set another radar to track the fighter assigned to intercept it. A controller would command the fighter into interception position. That worked well with a single bomber in sight, but it could not handle more than one target at a time. Mass raids quickly saturated the system. There was also a subtler problem. The German radar system did not produce an overall view for a higher-level commander. It was a way of dealing with a single raid, but not with multiple or deception raids.

The original British system could only detect incoming bombers. The radars offered a broad view of the situation, but they could not focus on and track individual targets. That was the role of the filter room. Operators there associated strings of detections, by radars and also by ground observers and other sources, to track the bombers as they flew. The tracks created in the filter room were the basis of the system. Given tracks, fighters could be commanded to attack the bombers. Movies of wartime RAF operation show plotters, typically women, moving pucks (representing raids) around a large flat map. The operators are creating and reviewing tracks. Supervisors above them see the tactical picture and decide how to allocate their resources – their fighters. Phone (voice radio) operators at the table control the fighters, vectoring them into position to intercept the bombers.

The light fleet carrier *Theseus* in Australian waters just after the war, showing the then-standard combination of two air-search radars and a Type 277 heightfinder/surface-search radar atop her bridge. Note the absence of either the British Type 72 or the US YE aircraft beacon. The 'cheese' antenna barely visible atop the foremast, under the Type 281B antenna, is for Type 293 radar. Note the single-barrel 40mm guns fore and aft of the island, at least one in a 'Boffin' mounting. (Alan C Green via State Library of Victoria)

The combination of a detecting radar and a memory (the plot) makes it possible to continuously scan for new targets while tracking all known ones. This idea of tracking while scanning (TWS) is the basis of all later British and US fighter-control systems. How well the system works depends on several factors. One is the precision of the search radars feeding the system, which depends on factors such as beam width. A second is time pressure. There is a time lag (latency) between the appearance of a target on a display and the moment that information enters the plot. With a limited number of plotters entering data, the more distinct targets there are, the greater the lag between detection (when something is seen on the display) and entry into the plot. Similarly, the faster the targets, the greater the impact of any lag at all. Using the plot, for example to direct fighters, also entails a delay. Delay and imprecision in the radar (and other sources of information) all introduce errors into the plot. How serious those errors are depends on the performance of the fighters at the end of the chain.

The British system of radar, filter room, voice radio (R/T) to command fighters and the fighters themselves was dramatically successful during the Battle of Britain. The fighter-control systems used by both the Royal Navy and the US Navy during the war were in effect navalised versions of the British system. Both navies also adopted the RAF terminology for targets and for the fighter engagement itself.[11]

Bogeys were targets detected by the system. At the outset they were unidentified. Deciding which were valid targets was both a major task and a major problem, as the system could be saturated by non-targets (including friendly fighters). IFF systems developed in wartime and beyond helped and after the war the US Navy considered IFF a very important means of tracking its own aircraft. Current airliner identification systems, which respond to interrogation by ground control, are a form of IFF. Valid targets sorted out of the mass of bogeys were *bandits*.

A fighter was *assigned* to a particular bandit. This action was equivalent to target designation in shipboard fire control. Whether a fighter could be assigned depended on whether it was in position to intercept and also whether it had sufficient fuel and ammunition to make interception worthwhile. Controllers had to keep aware of these factors and their need to keep track helped limit the number of fighters a single controller could handle at any one time. Aside from these questions, fighter control broadly resembled other fire-control problems, such as torpedo control. The controller was solving a triangle whose sides represented the speeds and directions (vectors) of the target and the fighter.

When the fighter pilot saw the target and headed for it, he was said to *tallyho*, the very British hunting cry which seems to have come out of the Battle of Britain. At least in the US Navy, ideally the end result of the process was a *splash*, a destroyed target. It was vital that the probability of tallyho not be confused with the probability that a target would actually be splashed.

The type of control exercised during the Battle of Britain was later called *close control*, the fighter-direction officer taking the pilot all the way to tallyho. The more targets, the more difficult close control was and the more attractive were alternatives in which the pilot exerted more control. For the US Navy and the Royal Navy, these alternatives became vital after 1945, as possible cures for problems encountered late in the war.

There was one enormous difference between the Battle of Britain and war at sea. During the Battle of Britain, the RAF imposed serious attrition on German attackers, but it could not prevent some bombers from getting through and doing damage. It turned out that damage to cities was tolerable to an extent unimagined before war and the Germans could not tolerate bomber losses on the scale imposed. At sea, an individual ship certainly could not withstand effective air attack. On the other hand, it turned out that carrier fighters under radar control could often chase off bombers they could not shoot down. No fleet at sea was faced with the sheer volume of bombers the Luftwaffe or, for that matter, Allied air forces attacking Germany could wield.

THE BRITISH NAVAL EXPERIENCE[12]

The Royal Navy developed its fighter-control techniques independent of the RAF, but presumably it was much affected by the knowledge that the RAF was developing fighter control. The other factor in Royal Navy development was the interwar development of plotting as a means of visualising a tactical and strategic naval situation. The Royal Navy had first tried plotting during the First World War (a plot was the basis of Admiral Jellicoe's successful deployment at the beginning of the battle of Jutland). Between the wars British warships typically had separate tactical and strategic (large-scale) plots showing the current situation. In the 1930s they added a short-range air gunnery plot in a Gun Direction Room (GDR) as a way of deciding priorities for a ship's anti-aircraft battery. The natural extension was to an aircraft plot in an Aircraft Direction Room (ADR), although that did not happen instantly.

Once the Royal Navy adopted radar, it had a new source of information which affected all the plots. Moreover, information displayed on one plot often affected what might be seen on another. In 1943 the Royal Navy developed a policy of integrating its plots and its sources of information, particularly different radars, into what it called an Action Information Organisation (AIO). The AIO is often treated as a different designation for what the US Navy called a Combat Information Center (CIC), but it was quite different: it was a combination of separate but connected plots, each of them a source of what would now be called situational awareness for the command of the ship. The decentralised character of the AIO had important consequences for post-war British development of command and control in the form of the Comprehensive Display System (CDS).

The separate plots worked well as long as they were fed mainly by different radars. For example, the GDR depended mainly on short-range air-search sets (target-indication sets) and gun fire-control radars; the ADR depended mainly on long-range air-search radars. However, the summary plot for an embarked flag officer required information from several different plots, including that in the ADR and actual aircraft direction was generally conducted outside the summary air plot in the ADR. In a pre-computer era there was no obvious way to move data from one plot to another or, for that matter, from one ship to another. Ships could certainly exchange target data on a dedicated radio circuit, but once that data arrived in a plotting room it had to be entered into the ship's plot by hand.

Like their land-based equivalents, the Royal Navy's air-search (air-warning) radars generated very broad beams, although the direction to a target could be measured more precisely by comparing returns as parts of the antenna were switched back and forth. Initially the radars were not turned continuously, but instead were pointed in one direction and then turned manually to another. To further complicate matters, the Royal Navy entered the Second World War with great awareness of the role of signals intelligence in the previous war. It sought to limit radio transmissions of any kind; for example, for a time a cruiser with radar might use signal flags or a blinker light to inform the accompanying carrier that aircraft had been detected. Reluctance to use radar freely was reinforced by late pre-war trials in which one ship's radar detected signals from a similar radar at a range of 100 miles. Initial radar doctrine allowed for one scan (sweep of the radar horizon) *per hour*, the radar to be used continuously only if targets were detected.[13] That made sense if it was assumed that the fleet could operate unobserved, since radar range was less than 100 miles, but this technique was unlikely to cope with bombers approaching at 200mph or more. It appears that fortunately neither the Germans nor the Italians were listening at British radar frequencies. The Germans had already concluded before the war that the only viable frequency was about three times that used by the shorter-wave of the two British air-search sets and it is not clear that they were at all interested in airborne radar interception devices. Italian electronics was considerably less sophisticated than German.

The British air-warning radars were two-dimensional: they produced single broad beams which, in theory, covered a wide range of altitude. Effective fighter control required height information, because fighters were ideally vectored to positions above the attackers. The earliest air attackers flew at predictable heights corresponding to standard doctrine for level bombing (torpedo bombers flew much lower but, at least in the Mediterranean, they could usually be beaten off by the fleet's gunfire). The situation probably changed radically when the Germans introduced dive bombers, which would approach at higher altitude.

It turned out that reflection off the sea broke up the broad radar beams into a series of lobes at different elevation angles. The lobe structure could be predicted. As an aircraft crossed the gap between two lobes, its reflection vanished (it 'faded'). A lobe diagram (or fade diagram) made possible crude height estimation. That was clearly insufficient. By 1945 the Royal Navy was receiving specialised US heightfinding radars (SM) and it was developing its own. It was also working on narrower-beam search radars.

British fighter control began with Lieutenant Commander Charles Coke RN, who was Air Signals Officer of the carrier *Ark Royal* during the Norway campaign. She did not have any radar, but she was accompanied by a radar-equipped cruiser (*Sheffield* or *Curlew*). Coke used a small aircraft-type plotting board to turn incoming reports into tracks and on that basis he directed the ship's Skua fighters. Initially he simply transmitted the position, track and speed of an incoming aircraft, deduced from strings of reports. The Skua navigator-radio man in the back seat calculated an interception course. Coke called this technique the 'informative method'; much later it would be revived as broadcast control. In contrast to the RAF in the Battle of Britain, it placed a navigational burden on the aircrew. Also, Royal Navy aircraft all used W/T; that was practicable because the back-seater in the Skua was a skilled radio telegraphist and also because Coke could send Morse rapidly. Coke had to make do with an additional time lag, between detection by the cruiser and notification to the carrier. He also had to compensate for the difference between the cruiser's position and his own.

Coke found that he could track his own fighters by dead-reckoning, guiding them directly into the incoming raiders (he called this close control the 'directive method'). It was more complicated than informative control and it made for a slower and less effective process. Once *Ark Royal* and *Sheffield* joined Force H at Gibraltar, the cruiser often operated as fighter-control ship using the 'informative process'. The cruiser broadcasted target position in terms of her own location, so the fighters had to translate into terms of their position, which they measured from the carrier launching them. That seems not to have been a problem for the specialist navigator-radiomen aboard the Skuas. Late in 1940 *Ark Royal* had a short UK refit and half her Skuas were replaced by Fulmars. They were 40 knots faster and more heavily armed and they retained the back-seater who made the 'informative method' and W/T control practical.

Fulmars could chase off aircraft shadowing a fleet and thus could often prevent attacks, but they lacked the performance to deal with many enemy bombers. The Royal Navy became interested in higher-performance single-seaters, initially the Sea Gladiators bought before the war. They had to be R/T-controlled and the 'directive method' was unavoidable. To make it work, an air plot more elaborate than Coke's simple aircraft board was needed. R/T had significant limitations. VHF was generally line-of-sight, not a problem when there were transmitters all over southern England, but a problem for fighters flying at a distance from their carrier or control ship. The existing sets were apparently also unreliable.

To the US Navy's BuAer, British development of fighter control was simplified by making the primary carrier function fighter defence of the fleet. British practice as reported by US naval observers was to concentrate fighters over the formation in a single group, controlling them via both voice and CW (W/T) and with visual signals during periods of radio silence. All information was passed using an alphabet code. Fighters were not sent more than 30nm out. An experienced fighter director could control up to three interceptions at a time. The US Navy adopted the concept of control by a shipboard officer and also the use of raid numbers and arrows on a plot to make the situation clear.

The class of British carriers that followed *Ark Royal* all had their own radars and thus could control their own fighters directly, without the complication of translating positions from one ship to another. *Illustrious* carried her radar to the Mediterranean late in 1940 and at least initially she was extremely successful. One reason why was the nature of naval air war at the time. Before the enemy could mount a mass attack, he had to find the moving fleet. Bombers homed on the snooper (snooper position reports were often inaccurate). If the snooper (reconnaissance aircraft) was shot down or driven off, no attack could be mounted. The single snooper was a far simpler target than a mass of bombers. Also, before the Germans entered the Mediterranean air war, Italian bombers practised simple, predictable tactics, flying straight and level at a standard height. That too made interception easier. In effect early war experience in the Mediterranean made it possible for the British to develop their fighter-control skills. The crisis came when the Luftwaffe arrived, particularly its dive bombers. The dive bombers were sent in with the express assignment of sinking the carrier and thus changing the naval balance in the Mediterranean. They succeeded in scoring a hit with a 1400kg armour-piercing bomb, which penetrated the ship's armoured flight deck and exploded well below. *Illustrious* survived, but she had to be sent to Norfolk Navy Yard in the United States for repairs.

The light carrier *Venerable* and the fleet carrier *Implacable* in Australia (probably Melbourne), 3 March 1946, before going home from the Pacific. Note that they are in peacetime light grey rather than in the two-tone late wartime paint scheme. The aircraft on board the light carrier are Corsairs wearing standard Pacific markings: a roundel without a red centre and US-style bars.

Coke returned to the Admiralty in 1941 and was assigned to form a school for naval fighter directors. That meant standardising techniques so that they could be taught. By that time the United States was closely associated with the United Kingdom, supplying Lend-Lease. American observers were placed throughout the British fleet and they reported the early successes of British naval fighter direction.

Through 1941–2 Coke developed techniques for fighter direction, beginning with visualising the developing air situation. Despite radar limitations, he retained a considerable lead over his US counterparts. Coke's techniques were tested in the Malta convoy battles in the Mediterranean. For the Royal Navy, the 'Pedestal' convoy (August 1942) was the most intense air battle it experienced before Okinawa. The convoy escort faced much larger numbers of attacking aircraft than had previously appeared, but the problem was somewhat mitigated by the fact that they did not all appear simultaneously.

Parallel to Coke, in the Home Fleet James Borthwick in *Victorious* was directing fighters to intercept German Fw-200 maritime reconnaissance aircraft. Like Coke, he used a plotting table (in his case, home-made); he occupied a corner of the ship's plotting office. He controlled his fighters by R/T. Borthwick's contribution was to point to a need for a separate Main Air Display Plot (MADP) distinct from his fighter-control plot. That was much the lesson the RAF had learned as it developed its land-based system: it was essential to work from a summary of the air situation, not just to concentrate on one raid. A filter officer could evaluate information summarised on the main plot and designate raids to the fighter controller. In its initial form the 4ft diameter main plot was tipped back at a 45° angle so that the fighter controller could see it while a radar and a W/T plotter (to either side) worked on it. The single fighter-control plot was horizontal.

All three British armoured carriers were concentrated in the Indian Ocean in mid-1942. Although they did not meet the Japanese, by operating together they demonstrated what multi-carrier operations required, particularly a radio net connecting fighter directors in different ships. This net made it possible to allocate resources more efficiently. The multi-carrier concept was demonstrated during the greatest of the Malta convoy battles, Operation 'Pedestal', in August 1942.

Royal Navy Experience in the Mediterranean: 'Pedestal'[14]

To the Royal Navy, the air attacks against the August 1942 'Pedestal' convoy to Malta were both the worst it had faced to date and the proof that it had learned how to control carrier fighters. A key was that, because the convoy was moving, it was impossible for the enemy to concentrate the many aircraft he had on various airfields into a single massive strike, which might have overwhelmed the fighters. Although there were far more German and Italian aircraft than could have been concentrated on board a few carriers, a carrier force could have formed a single much more concentrated and probably more effective raid. That was the difference between the attacks mounted during 'Pedestal' and those mounted during the battle of the Philippine Sea two years later. For 'Pedestal' the close heavy escort included three carriers, the armoured-deck *Victorious* and *Indomitable* and the old *Eagle*. Of these ships, *Victorious* then had the best fighter-direction office in the fleet. The convoy also included the carrier *Furious*, but she was devoted to launching Spitfires to aid in the defence of Malta. The fighters and controllers had VHF voice radio (R/T), which the US Navy would not have in quantity for another year. It was essential because it made for far more effective control than the earlier HF radio, with its single channel. The British also had what they considered effective IFF.[15]

Fighters in the force were a mix of Sea Hurricanes, Martlet IIs and Fulmar IIs.[16] This selection offered a layered defence, the Sea Hurricanes patrolling above 20,000ft, the Martlets at medium altitude and the Fulmars at low level. The Fulmars were the latest version, with better performance than the type used in 1940–1.[17]

Before the enemy could mount any mass air attacks, *Eagle* was sunk by a U-boat which penetrated her screen. Apparently a gap had been opened when *Furious* launched her Spitfires. Fortunately for the convoy, *Eagle* had the smallest air complement of the three defending carriers. Towards dusk a raid was detected at 50nm. Four Sea Hurricanes were on patrol at the time, looking for a shadowing Ju-88, but another nineteen fighters were flown off to deal with the raid. It was beaten off, but the fighters had to be recovered in darkness and three were lost plus four more damaged. Of seventy-two fighters embarked at the outset, fifty-one remained after the loss of sixteen on board *Eagle*.

The next day about 200 bombers attacked, supported by 100 fighters. When the heavy escort turned back, no merchant ship had been sunk (one had been hit by a bomb), one destroyer had been torpedoed and sunk and *Indomitable* had been neutralised as a carrier. The convoy was very nearly wiped out after that, but that disaster does not affect the success the carriers enjoyed in the face of the sort of heavy land-based airpower which had seemed so devastating before the war. This airpower was able to strike, moreover, because it proved impossible to deny the enemy knowledge of the convoy, as at least one shadower managed to find it and another (a Ju-88 on the first day) presumably reported before being shot down.

The key factor was that the raids were not concentrated. The first, detected 65nm away, consisted of nineteen Ju-88s covered by sixteen Me-109s. Eight Sea Hurricanes at high altitude and two low-altitude Fulmars formed a combat air patrol and eleven Sea Hurricanes and four Fulmars were launched to support them. The raid was initially intercepted 25nm out; only four bombers reached the convoy and they missed their targets. The raid escort shot down only one fighter (another was lost in a low-level battle).

A second raid consisted of ninety-eight bombers and forty fighter escorts. At this time the CAP consisted of four Martlets and four Sea Hurricanes at 20,000ft and two low-altitude Fulmars. This was a massively co-ordinated attack, including torpedo bombers and Ju-88 glide bombers, as well as a radio-controlled SM 79 bomber packed with explosives and fighter-bombers assigned to drop anti-personnel bombs on the carrier decks. The convoy launched six Sea Hurricanes and four Fulmars. Raid co-ordination broke down; the entire effort resulted in a single bomb hit on a freighter. The twenty-four SM 79 torpedo bombers achieved nothing, either jettisoning their weapons or dropping them outside the screen of the convoy. The SM 79 guided bomb went out of control and crashed in Algeria.

A third attack was detected early because it formed up within radar range. It consisted of fourteen SM 79s, twenty-nine Ju-87 dive bombers and eighteen Ju-88s covered by about forty fighters. A Martlet patrol was vectored out to 30nm to make the first attack. This time the enemy attacked from two directions in eleven separate groups at altitudes of 10,000 to 25,000ft. At the outset three Martlets, twelve Sea Hurricanes and six Fulmars were airborne. More aircraft were soon launched. This attack was directed at the covering force rather than the convoy, in effect confirming how effective that force had already been. This time the enemy fighter escort was considerably more effective than in the earlier attacks. *Indomitable* was attacked by twelve German Ju-87s, which made two hits and put her out of action.[18] The destroyer *Foresight* was torpedoed. The loss of *Indomitable* as an effective carrier left the convoy with *Victorious*, which now had eight Sea Hurricanes, three Martlets and ten Fulmars aboard. Seven fighters had been lost in combat: three Sea Hurricanes, three Fulmars and a Martlet.

The British recognised that the convoy needed fighter cover after the fleet and its carriers turned back. To that end they equipped the cruisers *Cairo* and *Nigeria* as fighter-direction ships with VHF radios which would enable them to control long-range Beaufighters based on Malta. Unfortunately both cruisers were forced out of the convoy (the badly-damaged *Nigeria* turned back; *Cairo* sank). Without fighter protection, the convoy was badly damaged, although the few ships which did get through, including the famous tanker *Ohio*, were enough to sustain Malta until the battle of El Alamein and the North African landings changed the situation.

The aircraft on board the British carriers were inferior to the attackers in performance, but that was more than balanced by superior tactics based on radar fighter direction. The US Navy agreed that at this point British fighter control was superior. In July 1943, with the US carrier force badly drawn down, *Victorious* operated with *Saratoga* in the Southwest Pacific. Because her fighter-control techniques were considered superior, she was made fighter carrier, with all the fighters of both carriers on board: thirty-six Martlets and twenty-four US F4F-4s.

The British concept of fighter control after 'Pedestal' is reflected in a handbook first issued in December 1942 and then revised in October 1944.[19] The introduction of the 1942 edition emphasises that the point of fighter direction is to protect ships – which is not necessarily

Indomitable in August 1942, on the eve of Operation 'Pedestal', showing Hurricanes and a few Martlets and folded Albacores on deck. The Hurricanes could not be folded, so they were stowed on deck, outside the take-off/landing path, as indicated by the dashed lines on deck. At least some carriers stowed them with their tail wheels on outriggers, to provide a wider landing area. The folded-down barrier is visible in the foreground.

the same as shooting down enemy aircraft. The main consideration was to frustrate co-ordination of enemy attacks and break up formations, 'so that any attackers which got through would deliver unco-ordinated attacks which can readily be frustrated by ship gunfire and manoeuvre'. The 1944 edition pointed out that aircraft direction had now been successfully extended to the direction of TBR aircraft in anti-submarine warfare. Further extension was expected, so that 'Fighter Direction' was being replaced by 'Aircraft Direction'. In an offensive operation the object was to direct an attacking force into position where it could detect the target. That demanded efficient co-ordination of air and surface plotting, a recurring theme in British post-war development.

The British had begun with a single fighter director who was concerned with making sure that his fighters could reach an enemy aircraft or raid approaching the carrier. What they learned in the Mediterranean was that whatever they developed had to cope with multiple and possibly simultaneous raids from different directions. The fighter-control *organisation* had to understand the tactical situation so that it could allocate its limited resources effectively. The

limited numbers of carrier fighters achieved what they did during 'Pedestal' because they could be concentrated as needed and because some aircraft could always be held back to deal with additional raids. That implied a level of organisation above the individual controller handling limited numbers of aircraft and interceptions.

The fighter-direction space envisaged after 'Pedestal' (and presumably used during it) met these requirements by providing a large-scale plot of the air situation and two smaller plots for fighter directors in front of it. The large-scale plot (54in diameter, 3nm to the inch) showed the overall air situation out to about 80nm. Each of two fighter directors had a slightly smaller-scale shorter-range plot (35in diameter, 4nm to the inch, corresponding to a range of 70nm). In theory, the large-scale summary plot provided a picture of the developing air situation, in the form of arrows (vectors) drawn through individual radar plots (radar indications of target positions at particular times). The arrows showed where and how fast air targets were going and thus how soon they might arrive, hence how threatening they were. On that basis they could be assigned to fighter directors. The summary also showed where defending fighters were and status boards alongside the summary showed how many were available. Each fighter director was expected to handle two simultaneous interceptions, so system capacity was four.

Four may seem very few, but it referred not to four individual aircraft but to four raids. An attacker had to deal with both defending fighters and with anti-aircraft fire at the target. Any attempt to overwhelm anti-aircraft fire required numerous aircraft in a co-ordinated attack, which is why the object of fighter control was to break up raids and ruin co-ordination. Conversely, co-ordination required that many aircraft fly together towards the fleet, hence that the total number of raids be limited. Matters would become considerably worse if for some reason aircraft did not have to fly in large groups.

All of this was relatively simple, but the mechanics were not. Data were all plotted manually, so normally the front of the summary board was partly obscured by the plotters. In the 1942 version of the air plot, the summary plot was tilted back at a 30° angle to give the officers using the plot a chance of seeing enough of it. That was clearly unsatisfactory.

An average operator at a Type 279 or Type 281 radar could report the position of a single aircraft four to five times per minute or two separate but close aircraft four times a minute or two on opposite bearings three times a minute. If the radar swept continuously, an operator would report a plot a minute (in an anti-D/F sweep, that would drop to one plot every two–three minutes). The 1942 edition of the fighter-control handbook stated that three consistent plots would be enough to determine the approximate course of a target. A satisfactory estimate of the number in the enemy group could not be made until the height of the echo (on the A-scan display) was at least three times that of the noise. Time to estimate target speed would depend on target course; two minutes would be enough for a target flying directly towards a ship (constant bearing). At this time target height had to come from a fade chart; an operator using Type 279M could measure height fairly accurately in one to two minutes. At this time operators passed their data to the plotters by telephone. Typically each plot (aircraft position) was indicated by a small cross, the crosses being connected by thin lines to show target course and the times of all plots being noted on the board to within a half- or quarter-minute. Note that at 240 knots an aircraft moves four miles each minute, a mile every quarter-minute. On the master plot, raids were indicated by letters in a circle and height (in thousands of feet) by a number in a circle. Other radar information could also be entered.

In each case, the Plot Officer had to decide whether an echo was real. Clues included supplementary information from the radar operator and apparent motion of the supposed target – radars really could produce entirely false target data. The 1942 handbook cautioned that three plots were needed to establish a relative course and plots over about three minutes to establish a true course and air speed. Pooling data from several sets would help.

As a further radar complication, the major British air-search radars had considerable minimum ranges (aircraft at shorter ranges were said to be within the ground wave, invisible to radar operators). The first step in any interception was therefore for the direction officer to break R/T silence to provide fighters with an initial vector. Once they were flying along it, they could clear the ground wave and become visible. Thus an interception began with an initial 'snap' vector selected by eye before enemy course and speed could be properly assessed. The fighters were also ordered at once to the estimated height of the enemy, preferably 1000ft above to provide them with a tactical advantage (but that assumed good heightfinding). The direction officer had to be aware of cloud cover, so that he did not order fighters to fly just above clouds which would hide the enemy from them. If the enemy was in or near a cloud layer, he could order out sections of fighters to bracket the enemy.

Once the fighters had been given their initial vector, their tracks could be entered, including the estimated position at which they would reach the desired height. The fighter director could begin to plan their attack. Among other things, he had to be aware of the position of the sun, placing his aircraft up-sun except at dawn or dusk. The initial track would be corrected as soon as the fighters emerged from the ground wave. Corrections of the fighters' vector, for example to deal with a change of enemy course, should be bold; the British handbook pointed out that a series of minor course changes would congest the radio channel and would also show the pilots a lack of decision on the part of the fighter director.

The ideal attack was from ahead, but not dead ahead, because modern aircraft were heavily armed and armoured against attacks from astern. The morale effect of a head-on attack might be devastating, but such attacks were difficult (they were also the only non-deflection attacks other than tail attacks). A fighter attacking head-on would have little time even to recognise the enemy, partly because the two aircraft would be closing so quickly. If the attacker missed, he would find himself far astern of the target before he could turn back for another attack. If the enemy was attacking out of the sun, a head-on path would take the fighter pilot into the sun and he would soon be dazzled (fighter directors were cautioned to avoid vectoring fighters into the sun for long in order to set up their own attacks out of the sun). The ideal therefore was a bow or beam interception, the bow position being best. Fighters should be sent out on a course parallel to that of the enemy, closing him, so that they could turn into the enemy's bow when they spotted him.

All plotted data were approximate. The handbook cautioned that the fighters and the enemy aircraft would always be some distance ahead of their plotted positions due to time lags in plotting. Interceptions should be from ahead of the enemy aircraft, the fighters being kept between enemy and target until then. Fighters sent out on the bearing of the enemy would end up in a spiral course leading to a tail chase. If they were sent out to the point at which they would intercept if the enemy followed a straight-line course, a slight alteration of enemy course towards the fleet would place him well inside the fighters, due to the delay before that change of course was clear from the plot. Ideally, raids should be intercepted at least 25nm from the fleet to allow fighters to make several passes before they and the enemy reached fleet anti-aircraft gun range. This section of the handbook was reissued in July 1945. This time the desired interception range was 35nm, presumably to allow for higher aircraft speeds.[20]

In a carrier, the Fighter-Direction Office/Aircraft Plot Office, the Tactical Plot and the Bridge Receiving Room were all to be on the same deck (it was desirable but less important that the Air Operations Room also be on that deck). The direction officer at each of the smaller plots had an interception plotter to help him solve the triangle representing a successful interception.[21] At this time the Royal Navy was just shifting from HF to VHF radio, so the December 1942 handbook showed two HF R/T lines for naval fighter control and one VHF R/T line for RAF fighter direction, when a ship was directing shore-based RAF aircraft. The only other VHF line listed was a fighter-direction intercommunication line (also R/T). However, the shift to all-VHF was coming. So was redesign so that the Fighter-Direction Office could use signals intelligence ('Y', which in British parlance meant exploiting the fact that the enemy was transmitting various types of signals, without any sort of code-breaking) and exploitation of radar data from other services.

Indomitable refitted at Belfast after 'Pedestal'. A dockyard electrician suggested the solution to the plotting problem. His Home Guard headquarters used a vertical status board made out of two Perspex sheets sandwiched together and edge-lit. As adapted for fighter direction, this vertical plot greatly simplified the situation, because the plotters could work from behind it, writing backwards (a skill only recently discarded, because all plots are now created by computers). An officer in front of the plot would filter what was being written (in US terms, he would evaluate the plots) to turn individual plotted points (radar detections) into target tracks, on the basis of which the evolving situation could be understood. Somewhat later the fighter-direction plots were replaced by PPIs and Skiatrons, the fighter controllers using grease pencils (Chinagraph, in British parlance) on its face.[22]

In the 1944 edition of the fighter direction handbook the earlier Fighter-Direction Office was now the ADR, preferably with direct access to the Operations Room. In mid-1943 the Admiralty had decided that plotting methods should be further standardised and the plots interconnected as the AIO. Although often considered equivalent to the US Navy's CIC, the AIO was a very different entity, retaining the earlier separate plots. On board a carrier the AIO typically comprised an Operations Room, an Air (Aircraft) Direction Room (initially the Fighter-Direction Room), a separate Air Operations Room (strike control) and a Target Indication Room (for the ship's own anti-aircraft guns). The Operations Room provided the Command with a more or less current picture of the situation, in the form of both a Local Operations Plot and a General Operations Plot. The Operations Room and ADR, which ideally would be adjacent, formed the core of the Action Information Centre (the Royal Navy almost always used the term AIO). In addition, a flagship would have a Flag Plot. The ADR maintained a plot of the entire air situation including – but not limited to – fighter direction. Even more plots were envisaged by 1945, particularly a Radar Display Room (RDR) which would meld radar data into a single stream before it was plotted elsewhere. It appeared in the Pacific at the end of the war, but was not used in combat.

By this time the vertical plot had been standardised as the Main Air Display Plot, flanked by two boards, one a geographical plot and the other a height indication board. In a carrier, two Skiatrons flanked by smaller PPIs were arranged in front of the vertical plot for fighter directors. Skiatrons used a 60nm scale (5nm to the inch) plus a plain rim allowing plotting at greater ranges. Each was a remote display for a single radar, either Type 281 or Type 277. Next to each 12in Skiatron was a 9in PPI; one could be used for high cover, the other for low (Type 277 was considered an effective low-altitude search set). Each Skiatron or PPI could be provided with a dead-reckoning instrument, which was probably the intercept computer of the 1942 edition. Other ADR installations, such as an air-sea plot and status boards, were secondary.

In a carrier, the ADR was typically manned by seven flight (F) officers, one of them trained to control night fighters and fifteen ratings. The entire space was supervised by a senior Fighter-Direction Officer on a dais. Each of the three plots was manned by a Deputy Fighter-Direction Officer, with an Air Plot Officer (APO) at the main air display acting as filter man. Another Fighter-Direction Officer would be at a separate Visual Direction Position (VDP). The main plot was served by two WA plotters (air-search radar plotters), a W/T plotter (entering information from other ships), a WS or WC (surface search) plotter, a height plotter and visual and D/F (for radio or radar

direction-finding) plotters. There was also a conversion plotter taking data from the surface plot. None of the plotters actually watched radar displays. Instead, they had to be told when a blip appeared on a display. For that purpose there were what the British called tellers and the US Navy called radar talkers, using sound-powered phones.

This description emphasises the complexity of sustained plotting and also the reality that the entire system imposed delays between detection and plotting. It took moments for a radar operator to decide that something on his display was a real target – to *detect* the target, meaning to turn electronic noise into information. It took further moments for him to measure target range and bearing and to pass that information to a plotter and further time for the plotter to act. Whether those delays mattered depended on how fast the target was moving. To some extent the Skiatrons solved the delay problem, since the fighter controllers saw a raw radar display and worked directly from it.

By this time the Royal Navy had converted almost completely to VHF for ship-to-air communication, although the October 1944 edition cautioned that two medium-power HF R/T outfits were needed for the time being as the changeover proceeded.[23] There would be six medium-power VHF R/T outfits for ship-to-air communication (and two low-power emergency sets). In addition, one medium-power VHF line was reserved for inter-fighter direction communication within a force, another (range 100nm) for inter-fighter direction communication with another fleet, a fourth for intership communication (TBS). The Royal Navy also used HF for ship-to-ship R/T.

This was much the same arrangement as in contemporary US carriers. The US Navy had adopted British practices after the carrier *Victorious* brought them to the Southwest Pacific in 1943, operating with *Saratoga*.

By the spring of 1945, off Okinawa, the British Pacific Fleet had fighter-direction officers trained to handle three rather than two interceptions at a time.[24] The British carriers assigned to the British Pacific Fleet had Seafires as well as US-supplied Corsairs and Hellcats. The Seafire offered a very high rate of climb and excellent manoeuvrability at the expense of range and, as it happened, poor carrier handling (which cost many aircraft). Standard practice was to maintain a division of Seafires at low level, a second division and one of Hellcats or Corsairs at medium level and a division of Corsairs at high level, with further aircraft at readiness on deck.

THE US NAVAL EXPERIENCE[25]

US officers were sent to Lieutenant Commander Coke's naval fighter direction school. The US situation differed from the British in two important ways. US radars had much narrower beams and thus offered a better indication of the precise direction from which an attack was coming. Second, the US Navy had only single-seat fighters, so from the outset it used only the tight control technique.

At the outset, like the Royal Navy, US carriers had a series of special plots to provide situational awareness. In addition to a tactical plot showing units operating with the carrier, they had a Flag Plot (showing the large-scale situation) and an Air Plot, a feature unique to carriers. The Air Plot summarised the results of air searches (plus other data, for example from radio intelligence) and it was used to direct the carrier's air striking force. None of the plots applied to fighter control. The air sensors were lookouts' eyes (whose information was gathered in Sky One, the US equivalent of the British ADO position), the aerial

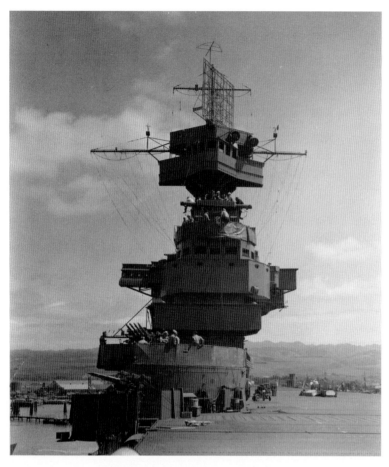

Photographed on 1 April 1942, *Enterprise* shows the antenna of the first US production air-search radar, CXAM-1, at her masthead. It was the direct predecessor of the standard wartime SK and SC series, SC using a smaller antenna. Because CXAM-1 and its derivatives operated at a higher frequency (i.e., shorter wavelength, 1.5m) than the British Type 79 (7.5m), they could have a much larger antenna (as measured in wavelengths) and so offered better definition and were better adapted to displaying their data on a map-like PPI. Even when the British adopted the higher frequency, their standard antennas offered much less definition than the US types. Above the big mattress of CXAM-1 is a curved array of dipoles for an early version of the YE aircraft homing antenna. As yet the ship had no fire-control radar for her 5in battery. She fought at Midway with this equipment.

corner of the existing Air Plot, Radar Plot employed a large vertical board on which two plotters, supervised by the evaluator, worked. He resolved issues such as track ambiguities. One Fighter-Direction Officer used the plot. The first class of such officers was trained in August 1941 by the Royal Canadian Navy, using British techniques.

At this stage the single air-search radar set was too large and generated too much heat to be installed in the plot. Instead, the plotters relied on data passed to them via sound-powered phones or a voice pipe. Later, when the first PPI displays entered service, data were often passed to the plotters in the form of tracings taken from the face of the PPI.

A 'Tentative Doctrine for Fighter Direction from Aircraft Carriers', issued in August, summarised CinCPac orders issued up to that time. Commander, Air was responsible for fighter direction and for assigning a number (designation) to each incoming raid. He would assign each radar in the force a 30° search sector (later all radars were required to search continuously). Distance was reported in nautical miles from force centre. Voice radio would be the primary means of communication between the fighter director and the aircraft. A special fighter-control vocabulary (e.g., bogey, tallyho) was set up, for clarity rather than security.

As with the Royal Navy, the pre-war US instructions envisaged both the 'informative method' and the 'direct method' of fighter control. British experience using *Sheffield* as radar ship but *Ark Royal* as controller was reflected in US instructions that direction should be from a radar ship. By late 1941 US practice was to rely on voice (R/T) rather than CW (W/T) radio as primary control medium. Instructions issued in December 1941 rejected the British practice of withholding surface anti-aircraft fire if the CAP followed enemy aircraft into the zone above the fleet.[26] By late 1941 the US Navy had definitely dropped the 'informative method' in favour of close control, the fighter director estimating the point at which his assigned CAP could meet the enemy. Accurate range and bearing were expected for targets at 50nm range. The main perceived gap in US radar performance at this stage was a lack of accurate height information – a serious matter, since ideally the CAP had to be placed above the incoming enemy aircraft.[27] The lack of an effective form of IFF was also a problem.[28]

There were further important innovations. The early radars provided displays only at the operator's position, so that any further transmission of information was by battle telephone or even by runner. During 1942 remote displays were introduced. In the same year, the advent of the map-like PPI radar display considerably simplified fighter control. An observer could mark successive blip positions directly on the face of the scope and connect these dots to show the course and speed of the incoming aircraft.

Despite pre-war emphasis on dispersed operations, in 1942 US carriers often operated in pairs, separated sufficiently that they could launch and recover aircraft without interfering with each other. Typically, also, a single fighter controller on one of the carriers handled fighters from both. That he did so made uniform operating procedures and orders extremely important – but they were not really in force during 1942, with unfortunate consequences. The single fighter controller was justified by the reality that the two carriers together were facing a single enemy air threat. However, carriers operated their strike aircraft entirely separately and even found it difficult to co-ordinate different strike squadrons, as at Midway.

US fighter control was first exercised during the 1 February 1942 raid on the Japanese-occupied Gilbert Islands by *Enterprise* and

pickets (if any) and the new radar, with its operator in a compartment separate from the plots. The Fighter-Direction Officer on *Yorktown* worked in his own space, receiving a series of radar ranges and bearings by battle telephone from the CPO operating the radar. The same circuit supplied these data to the other command positions and to the ship's conn. In her report on the radar trials, *Yorktown* called for establishment of a radar plot. Plotting the separate radar detections (ranges and bearings) would convert them into a picture of the developing air situation, on the basis of which the fighter director could work.

BuAer and OpNav agreed and with BuShips (responsible for the actual installation) they recommended creation of a specialised radar plot as the 'brain' of the air defence organisation. This project was formally approved in July 1941 and the first such plot was planned for the carrier *Hornet*, still under construction. It was to be located in the ship's island, accessible to the chart house (from which the ship was conned), Air Plot, Flag Plot and the radar operator's room. It would be manned by a Plotting Officer (to create the tactical picture), a Fighter-Direction Officer, two radiomen, talkers and recorders. Set up in a

Yorktown. CAPs were flown as the force retired after attacking, presumably because any such activity (particularly the use of radar) might have alerted the Japanese to the attack. Fighter-control radio operated at relatively low frequencies considered vulnerable to interception, so communication was held to a minimum – a real problem since there was no means of IFF. *Enterprise* detected five Japanese bombers, all of which were shot down by her CAP. Of two radar contacts detected by *Yorktown*, one was intercepted, but only over the task force. It had already dropped its bombs before being shot down. Lessons included the need to provide CAP for non-carriers; during the bombardment of the islands the heavy cruiser *Chester* was hit. On another raid, against the Japanese base at Rabaul, the carrier *Lexington* was attacked on 20 February. In mid-morning she detected two snoopers at 35nm range and her fighters shot them down more than 30nm from the force (it was not known whether they had reported). In mid-afternoon she detected a large bogey 76nm out at an estimated altitude of 8000ft (it was actually 11,000ft). CAP was not sent out for half an hour, but the fighters shot down five of the nine aircraft before they could attack. Meanwhile a second bogey was detected approaching from the opposite direction. With most of the fighters occupied by the first raid, only two were available to intercept the second. They partly disrupted the attack and the carrier avoided damage by radical manoeuvres. Cominch (Admiral King's office) commented that fighters should concentrate on protecting the surface force and not on pursuing retiring enemy aircraft. CO of *Lexington* praised his fighter controller and fighters for their effectiveness despite the lack of proper radio and IFF.

Conclusions and recommendations in the official report of the action included the comment that, apart from the F4F-3, current US aircraft lacked sufficient performance because they were overloaded. However, armour and leakproof fuel tanks were vital; VF-6 (*Enterprise*) had installed its own pilot armour, made out of ⅜in boiler plate and that had saved one pilot. There were not enough fighters, as 'fighter protection for VT is mandatory' (a lesson relearned at Midway). The fighter complement should be increased to twenty-seven (up 50 per cent) at the expensive of dive bomber/scouts.

The 20 February Japanese air raid on the *Lexington* task force east of Rabaul provided further lessons.[29] The task force successfully repelled two level bomber attacks by using a combination of radical manoeuvres, anti-aircraft fire and fighter patrols. This time the task force commander had to decide whether to persist in plans to attack Japanese shipping at Rabaul after being spotted by snoopers. The CAP beat off the first raid but its pursuit of the bombers put it out of position when the second arrived; Cominch commented that 'a good FDO can prevent this by control of all fighters'. Only two fighters remained to deal with the second group, but one of them was flown by Lieutenant E H 'Butch' O'Hare and he was effective. Although his wingman's guns jammed on the first attack, O'Hare shot down two of the bombers and damaged others, so that only four of the original nine reached their drop point. He kept attacking, shooting down two more and damaging another; the report credited him with primary responsibility for destroying five enemy aircraft. Anti-aircraft fire failed to hit the attackers, even though they approached in exactly the way against which it had been designed: straight and level for six miles. Fire was rapid but inaccurate, confirming the late pre-war perception that the only effective defence was fighters. On the other hand, the bombers were ineffective, bombing from 11,000ft. The altitude at which the shadowers worked suggested to Cominch analysts that the

Japanese were unaware that they could evade radar by flying low. The US pilots reported that the shadowers were very slow and hence comparatively easy targets. One happy surprise was that *Lexington* was able to launch four fighters and eleven scouts and recover five fighters for servicing while she manoeuvred at 30 knots with 30° rudder to evade bombs.

The system did not perform so well under heavier stress at the battle of the Coral Sea in May 1942, when *Yorktown* and *Lexington* operated together but in separate Task Forces 17 and 18, respectively.[30] On 5 May *Yorktown* launched a CAP to investigate a contact only 15nm away, shooting down a snooper. Radar contacts and a visual sighting did not result in any interceptions the next day, but on 7 May the carrier force detected three possible snoopers nearby. Only one was shot down, 15nm from the force. The Japanese had their own problems: late that evening a large group passed to the south, apparently unable to find the carrier force. It was intercepted and destroyed, but only after it had come within 18nm and was flying away. Of three snoopers, only one was shot down and that after a visual sighting (meaning it had come far too close). Later review of radar plots showed that the controller had mis-estimated the intercept point each time; by the time the defending fighters were approaching the point, the enemy aircraft was gone. He had not given a 'radical enough vector:' he had

The new carrier *Yorktown* shows improved radars in this 1 July 1943 photograph. The big antenna at her masthead is for the long-range SK-1 air-search radar. The mast abaft and above it carries the YE aircraft homing antenna. Just visible below the big SK-1 antenna is the smaller antenna of an SC-2 air-search radar. This was different from British practice: they used two air-search radars operating at different wavelengths for comparative purposes, particularly heightfinding. For the US Navy the SC-2 was a back-up radar. The 5in fire-control director (Mk 37) at the after end of the island carries a Mk 4 fire-control radar (there is another director at the fore end of the island, but it is not clearly visible here). Not at all visible are two surface-search antennas (SG radars).

aimed too close to the place at which the bogey was initially located, making insufficient allowance for enemy course and speed.

Lexington now took control of the CAP. She reported four bogeys, three close to the formation, the other 82nm away. Without IFF, CAP resources had to be used to investigate all the bogeys, the closer ones turning out to be friendlies. Nearly half an hour later a large bogey was detected approaching at 68nm range. The scattered fighters were ordered back and *Yorktown* was ordered to launch her own fighters. Seventeen fighters were orbiting the force, plus a patrol of dive bombers (SBDs) intended to deal with enemy torpedo bombers. Six minutes later the fighter controller vectored five of his fighters to intercept. Most of the fighters were at 10,000ft; later it was stated that the attackers were flying higher. The fighter director thought that some of the attackers were torpedo bombers, so he ordered two of the five CAP fighters to fly lower. He then sent out four more fighters. When the three original CAP fighters arrived at the intercept point,

they found the enemy above them and 15–20nm from the force. They could not attack at once, but did manage to make an attack before the Japanese dive bombers began their dives. There were too few fighters to deal with the threat. An after-action report pointed to the lack of IFF and also the lack of standardised fighter control procedures and even vocabulary – although that had been specified for some time. Both carrier commanders recommended that CAPs be sent out at 20,000ft, but if the fighters were too high they might not see aircraft

Essex shows her radars in this 15 April 1944 photograph, taken after a refit at San Francisco. The uppermost antenna is for the YE aircraft homing beacon. Visible at its lower edge is the antenna of one of the ship's two SG surface-search radars and below that the antenna of the SC-2 secondary air-search set is visible. It is on the same tripod mast as the YE and SG. Sponsoned out from the island is the ship's SK-1 main surface-search antenna. Visible in front of it is the antenna of a Mk 12 serving the Mk 37 director controlling the ship's 5in guns. The other Mk 12 is visible at the fore end of the island.

flying lower. Both also wanted interceptions begun at 30nm range. *Yorktown*'s CXAM had been out of action during part of the operation, so her CO proposed that all carriers should have two air-search radars (this was done for all large fleet carriers, but it could not be done for the smaller ships). CinCPac recommended increasing the fighter complement to thirty-six.

It was clear that the makeshift radar plot in the carrier's island was too small and too subject to interference from others in the Air Plot. The COs wanted it separated but contiguous to Air Plot. It should have two simultaneous plots, one (a search plot) for the air picture and the other for fighter direction. Fortunately radar repeaters were soon perfected. Now the radar picture, rather than a more or less accurate report of that picture, could be seen in Radar Plot. An operator at a repeater could concentrate on detecting targets and reporting them directly to the plotters, rather than on keeping the radar operating. He could estimate raid course and speed directly from his scope, by grease-pencilling detections on successive radar sweeps and connecting the dots. It was even possible to control an interception directly from a repeater, rather than from a plot.

At Coral Sea both carriers were damaged; *Lexington* had to be scuttled after an aviation fuel vapour explosion in her enclosed hangar, much the sort of damage the Japanese suffered at Midway. Unlike the Imperial Japanese Navy, the US Navy learned to minimise exposure to such damage by filling fuel lines with inert carbon dioxide. *Yorktown* survived to be hurriedly repaired for Midway. In the aftermath of Coral Sea, the fighter allowance for carriers was increased again, to thirty-six. That had already been done for the *Essex* class, which was under construction.

On the eve of Midway, the US carriers were organised in two task forces. Task Force 17, which had fought at Coral Sea, had lost the carrier *Lexington*, so it had a single carrier, *Yorktown*. Task Force 10 was built around the carriers *Enterprise* and *Hornet*. When encouraging formation of multi-carrier task forces in 1944, CinCPac pointed out that the two carriers of Task Force 10 had supported each other (and had shared considerable anti-aircraft support), hence had survived, whereas the single *Yorktown* had not.

Fighter direction at Midway was better than at Coral Sea, but the problems the earlier battle had revealed were not solved. For example, standard operating procedures were not followed.[31] The first large bogey was detected at 46nm range, but four fighters from *Yorktown* were not sent to investigate it until it was 25nm away. They reached the bogey 15–20 miles out, breaking up the raid. However, seven of the thirty-six Japanese aircraft got through to damage *Yorktown* seriously. A second raid was detected at 45nm. This time the reaction was prompt: four fighters sent out two minutes later, followed by another two. The first four passed over the incoming Japanese fighters and torpedo bombers without seeing them, but the other two 'tallyhoed'. *Hornet* aircraft flying at 15,000–18,000ft were far too high. The combination of the two *Yorktown* fighters and anti-aircraft guns accounted for about half the torpedo bombers before they could drop their weapons, but *Yorktown* was hit twice. Later CAP shot down a snooper. *Yorktown* was eventually abandoned. She succumbed to submarine torpedoes on the night after the battle. It had helped considerably during the battle that she was able to patch her flight deck in combat, thanks to its light wood and metal construction. An important development in this battle was the fighters' success against the Zeroes based on a combination of fighter direction and new tactics (the 'Thach weave').

Overall, the fighter communication net was badly overcrowded; it was vital to switch to higher-frequency radio which offered both greater security and multiple channels.[32] Much of CAP was distracted by non-targets, apparently due to confusion due to IFF failure. The post-battle solution to a lack of heightfinding radar was to break CAP into sections stacked in altitude.[33] That was possible because fighter squadrons had been considerably enlarged.

All of the battles showed that the Japanese were able to find and shadow US carrier forces. Just as the British had learned, shooting down a snooper or shadower could abort an entire attack. BuAer felt compelled to send a message to the fleet emphasising that the snooper might well be the first warning of an attack and that destroying it was absolutely vital. Destroying the snooper was still worthwhile even if it had transmitted a contact report, because it would home an attack on the carrier force.

The US Navy fought two more carrier battles in the Pacific during the rest of 1942, on 24 August (Cape Esperance) and 25 October (Santa Cruz) during the Solomons campaign. With little time to develop new equipment or doctrine, the weaknesses revealed at Coral Sea and Midway remained. On 24 August the fighter director and CAP managed to shoot down four snoopers, but one was only 10nm away. The main raid was detected at 119nm, but then lost and not re-detected until it was 44nm away.[34] As before, it was difficult to be sure of altitude. *Enterprise* estimated an altitude of 12,000ft based on fades, but some reports stated that the radar officer on *Saratoga* placed it at 18,000ft (a radio problem made that 8000ft). *Enterprise* again estimated 12,000ft when the bogey reappeared at 44nm. She controlled the force fighters; her fighter controller stacked his CAP at 8000ft, 10,000ft and 12,000ft. A group sent out at 12,000ft spotted the enemy 33nm from the task force but they were below it. It had to fight up through escorting Zeroes to reach the Japanese dive bombers. Only five to seven reached the bombers before they began their attacks and *Enterprise* was badly damaged. IFF performed poorly again. The fighter net was badly saturated, partly because the fighter director was controlling fighters from another carrier, whose pilots did not know him. CO of *Saratoga* (and the commander of the overall force) thought it would be better to load one carrier in a group entirely with fighters.

Fighter direction at Santa Cruz was less effective. This time the carriers were *Enterprise* and *Hornet*, with the controlling fighter director in *Enterprise*. However, the fighter director in *Hornet* had some authority over his own ship's aircraft. A snooper which reported the force on 26 October was never detected. Later a search and attack force from *Hornet* reported two large enemy groups heading for the task force; they were detected at 60nm. CAP fighters were in groups over both carriers. *Hornet*'s subordinate fighter director was the first to act, recalling two sections of his fighters from the group over *Enterprise* and then vectoring eight aircraft at 10,000ft (climbing as they flew) against the bogey. When they sighted the attackers, the Japanese dive bombers were about level with them and beginning their dives. The 'tallyho' was 25nm out, but CAP fighters high enough to intercept were not vectored into position. *Hornet* was attacked by four waves and one single aircraft and *Enterprise* by four waves during nearly seven hours. No Japanese aircraft were attacked before they deployed, although some were caught before heading into attacks. Only once were aircraft attacking *Enterprise* opposed before beginning dives and then by only two fighters.

During the battle, the two US carriers separated beyond visual range, but *Enterprise* took over all fighter direction. Those from *Hornet* attributed the loss of their ship to poor direction; it seems from the radio log that control from *Enterprise* broke down.[35] The CO of VF-62 later recommended that fighter control should have been completely split between the two ships. Commander South Pacific (Admiral Halsey) defended unified control and the idea of a fighter carrier was revived. CinCPac (Admiral Nimitz) considered the battle proof that the problem of defence against numerous enemy groups had not yet been solved. 'Enemy planes were not picked up until they were at close range, the radar screen was clogged by our own planes and voice radio discipline was poor'. The Fighter Director School had recommended, and fighter directors had adopted, the idea of orbiting CAP on a point along the projected track of the enemy rather than vectoring them out to the most distant possible interception point. That was to give them a better chance of seeing the enemy as he approached.

Fighter-control performance was disappointing, but the fleet command recognised that the basic ideas of fighter direction were valid. They had to be developed more fully. For example, it was time to enlarge the radar plot and to move it away from easy intrusion by officers from other activities. In November 1942 CinCPac redesignated Radar Plot as the Combat Operations Center (COC, November 1942). It would communicate directly with ship control, with all radars and fire control and gunnery stations and all lookouts. It would be kept informed of changes in the strategic and tactical situation and the weather. It would have radios on the Fighter Net and the Warning Net. It would initially control all of a ship's radars and it would broadcast information on bogeys and raids whenever the ship acted as Radar Guard or Fighter Director Ship. This was a considerable change from the Radar Plot; the new COC concentrated *all* available information, much of it not from radars, in one place and in one plot.

As 1942 ended, IFF equipment was still inadequate, but better models were being developed and manufactured. The existing Wildcat fighter was coping with Zeroes, but it was at a great disadvantage in rate of climb (hence the importance of stacking CAP). New fighter instructions issued in December 1942 called for the fighter director to vector out enough fighters against each attack to thwart it at maximum range, but to retain enough over the centre of his force to deal with further raids. Fighters were not to tail-chase a retiring strike, again so that they would be available to deal with the next. Pilots were to inform controllers of the composition and altitude of raids they sighted.

COC was soon renamed CIC (Combat *Information* Center), because COC implied a command function which some thought was more properly exercised from a ship's bridge.[36] Its core was the new British vertical plot, adopted after one was seen aboard *Victorious*, under repair at Norfolk Navy Yard in 1943. In turn, the Royal Navy apparently adopted US CIC arrangements for its carriers after US specifications were provided to British liaison officers at Pearl Harbor in the summer of 1943. The great difference between US and British practice was that the US Navy concentrated all available information in one place. That eliminated a major issue in British practice, which was the need to co-ordinate all those plots and make sure that all showed the same tactical picture. On the other hand, as CIC functions were added, more and more individuals needed to use the same tactical picture; CICs became crowded and noisy. By 1945 neither navy was satisfied with the form of radar integration it had developed. This was entirely aside from the major problem of plot saturation revealed by Kamikaze attacks in 1944–5.

After Santa Cruz, the air battle moved largely ashore to the Solomons, beginning with the fight for Guadalcanal.[37] With most of the heavy fleet carriers unavailable (and not worth risking in confined waters), fighters afloat could be provided by escort carriers, supplemented by land-based fighters. Since the escort carriers lacked fighter direction facilities, cruisers provided them. Radar operation was complicated by strong echoes from nearby land.[38] Mobile fighter-direction units were placed ashore. They dealt with Japanese air raids, most successfully in the spring of 1943. In a June raid, for example, over ninety of about 125 Japanese aircraft were shot down. The Japanese air effort there was executed by naval aircraft. Due to long supply lines and the Japanese unwillingness to train large numbers of pilots, their personnel were not replaced until they died.

The Solomons campaign, much more than the 1942 carrier battles, destroyed the elite Japanese aircrew which had begun the Pacific War. At the time, the impact of this destruction on the Japanese seems not to have been appreciated. It seems to have been assumed that the Japanese were well aware that a protracted naval war would destroy thousands of aircraft and pilots, so that the only way to keep fighting was to churn out new pilots at a high rate. In fact through 1943 the Imperial Navy maintained very high standards of pilot selection and training, so that it could not easily withstand massive losses, like those around Guadalcanal. Meanwhile the US Navy was training more and more pilots, while the US industrial machine mass-produced new aircraft for them. If anything, wartime training was better than the quick training of reservist pilots just before the war.

The important new development in the Solomons campaign was the use of surface ships for fighter-direction, initially cruisers and then destroyers. In June 1943, the *Fletcher* class destroyer *Jenkins* was used successfully to control CAP covering a landing on Rendova. She carried a temporary fighter-direction team (four officers, two enlisted men); the CAP in this case was land-based. Fighter-direction units then operated from other South Pacific destroyers. Later fighter control was exercised from many other types of ships and beginning in 1943 elaborate CICs were installed on board amphibious flagships.

US industrial mobilisation now produced, in effect, a new fleet to replace the ships lost in 1942, beginning with three *Essex* class fleet carriers in service by mid-1943, plus the first light fleet carriers converted from light cruisers. All of these ships had been modified while under construction to incorporate radars (two air-search sets per ship) and large specially-designed CICs, each with a large vertical plotting board showing the overall situation and two smaller plotting tables (actually Skiatrons) to control interceptions, plus remote PPIs and large status boards. These CICs were located below decks, in a fleet carrier typically in the gallery deck under the flight deck (to minimise cable losses from the radars). VHF radio was finally placed in service, providing four separate channels. Typically one was assigned to the fighter director for communication with aircraft, one for communication between CICs in a task group or task force and one between Air Plot and other patrol and strike aircraft groups. Given all of these channels, CIC personnel could practice without interfering with operations. There was still a limitation, because the inter-CIC net and the inter-plane net used the same channel, making for overcrowding. The new radios were first tested in the initial operation by the new carriers, the raids on Marcus Island and Wake in the summer of 1943. In his after-action report, the OTC pointed to overcrowding and asked for more radio channels.

Of the three new *Essex* class fleet carriers, *Lexington* had a prototype SM pencil-beam radar (designated CXBL). It would soon become

Lexington had the prototype SM (CXBL) heightfinder, its antenna visible on the platform atop her tripod foremast in a photograph taken at Puget Sound Navy Yard, 21 February 1944. Abaft it is a topmast carrying the antenna of an SG surface-search set. The big radar is her SK-1. The small mesh antenna atop the ship's funnel is a YG back-up aircraft beacon. The object atop the pole mainmast is the antenna of an SO-11 zenith-search radar, the result of experience during the ship's shakedown cruise. It proved unsuccessful, but zenith search became a very important objective once Kamikazes began to attack ships from nearly overhead late in 1944.

standard equipment. In addition to measuring target height, the pencil beam could provide better information about the composition and vertical formation of an attacking group. It could also detect and track low fliers effectively. Its only limit was against high fliers, because its pencil beam typically did not elevate high enough. In addition to new radars, the ships had the new Mk III IFF, which finally seemed satisfactory.

During the Marcus raid, the light carrier *Independence* carried twenty-four fighters and nine torpedo bombers. She acted as duty CAP carrier, in effect the special fighter carrier previously proposed. One of the commanders recommended that the light carriers have all-fighter air groups. There were now two Fighter Director Schools (the new one was at St Simon's Island, Georgia) and techniques were elaborated. New formal instructions (USF-10A) recommended orbiting fighters (typically in a figure-eight pattern) 10 or 15nm inside an enemy

strike, but the problem was that when the enemy arrived, they might be on the wrong side of the orbit, poorly placed to intercept. An alternative, possible because the new radars were so good, was to vector the fighters to a point to one side or the other of the expected interception point, then use short vectors to place them above and to one side of the enemy aircraft. That was certainly in line with the US Navy's pre-war emphasis on interception from high on one side.

The new techniques were used when the fleet attacked the Gilberts in November 1943. In effect this operation was the rehearsal for fast carrier strikes through the rest of the following year. The fighter-direction destroyer idea developed in the Solomons was taken over, destroyers directing CAPs at the objective. Other directors were in major surface ships. An innovation in the Gilberts operation was the radar picket, a ship detached from the main body of the force and assigned as a radar guard ship. As the fleet approached the Gilberts, a radar picket destroyer was stationed 30,000 yds ahead. At Kwajalein in February 1944, the fleet formed a radar screen ten miles outside the sound (sonar) screen. Plans for the Marianas operation (June 1944) included a night radar screen ten miles from fleet centre. The pickets were mainly insurance against low fliers, as at this time the fleet had few radars capable of detecting low fliers at any distance. In some cases, beginning with the Gilberts operation and the destroyer *Kimberly*, the picket and destroyer fighter-direction roles were combined. Director-pickets were used again at Saipan. These destroyers used their fire-control radars to estimate bogey altitude at about 30nm range, so they could direct night fighters.

The pickets were considered extremely valuable, so before the first US carrier air raid on Tokyo (February 1945) a patrol line of two pickets and six other destroyers was stationed forty miles ahead of the task force along the likely threat axis, the line to Tokyo. The pickets controlled a sixteen-fighter CAP, which shot down eight enemy aircraft, including four trying to follow returning US aircraft to their carriers.

Destroyer pickets were used extensively at Okinawa, where they became primary Japanese Kamikaze targets, although it was not clear after the war whether the Japanese understood their mission. The pickets had not been specially modified for their mission and they found it difficult to provide CAP aircraft with adequate altitude information. Their air-search radars were limited to fade charts and their fire-control radars, which could provide such data, had short ranges.

The battle of the Philippine Sea

The US Central Pacific operation was expected to force the Japanese into a decisive fleet engagement. In April 1944 the Japanese could see that what they considered their main line of defence was about to be attacked. They wrote an elaborate defensive plan, which unfortunately for them fell into American hands when a flying boat carrying their fleet commander crashed in the Philippines. The Japanese were painfully aware of growing US carrier air strength. They thought they had an equaliser in the form of large numbers of land-based aircraft which could be shuttled around island bases and quickly concentrated wherever the US fleet attacked. Meanwhile they had reorganised their own fleet for what they hoped would be better offensive potential. The main innovation was to form three- rather than two-carrier divisions as basic tactical units. Japan still lacked effective radar and there does not seem to have been any improvement in fighter control. The Imperial Navy still depended on the pre-war goal of finding and striking its enemy before its enemy could find it.

In mid-1943 the US fleet changed its tactical doctrine to emphasise multi-carrier group operations, which were described in a new Pacific Fleet handbook, PAC-10.[39] This new concept was reflected in adoption of British-style inter-fighter director communication, one director co-ordinating the CAP for the entire Task Force (which consisted of multiple multi-carrier Task Groups) and one co-ordinating fighters from each Task Group. The latter typically consisted of three or four carriers, often two fleet carriers and one light carrier at this time. The US Navy also adopted the British practice of using Visual Fighter Directors to control a low CAP specifically intended to deal with low fliers.[40]

Low fliers became a serious problem as the Japanese realised that fighter control and CAP had been so effective against high-flying aircraft in the Solomons. They adopted low-level torpedo attack tactics. The US fleet had no radars specially adapted to detecting low fliers. The pencil-beam heightfinders could do so, but they were used mainly to find the heights of targets already detected by broader-beam radars. Their narrow beams made them ineffective as search radars. Low-flier detection would continue to be a difficult problem post-war.

Raids were often undetected until spotted visually and by that time it was impossible to do more than alert fighters if they happened to be nearby. At most they might be given an approximate direction and height. The only available solution was a fighter-direction officer stationed topside with a plotter and talkers; at least in theory he could talk the fighters into an interception position. This practice was embodied in the fleet tactical orders (USF-10A).

A US addition to the British visual direction idea was to use the visual director to vector the standing anti-submarine patrol (inner zone patrol) against any low-flying intruder. Orders for the invasion of Hollandia (April 1944) included assignment of a fighter designated the Anti-Snooper Patrol to work with the anti-submarine patrol conducted by torpedo bombers. In this operation the anti-snooper fighter shot down two low-flying bombers (G4M 'Bettys'), one of which radar had missed. Similar patrols were used successfully for later operations, appropriate terms being introduced into the September 1944 version of the fighter control vocabulary. Radar limitations in detecting aircraft against land masses made visual control even more important when the fleet reached the Philippines in the autumn of 1944.

For the attack on Saipan the US fast carrier task force (Task Force 58) included seven fleet and eight light carriers, with a total of 446 F6F-3 Hellcats on board, as well as twenty-four F6F-3N and three F4U-2 night fighters (the latter on board Enterprise). For close support of the amphibious operation there were two four-carrier escort carrier groups equipped with FM-2 Wildcats, with five more escort carriers in reserve. The latter included large escort carriers with F6F-3s on board: a total of 114 FM-2s on board the support carriers and sixty-eight F6F-3s and another twenty-eight FM-2s on board the reserve escort carriers.

Against this force the Japanese had nine aircraft carriers and a substantial land-based air force in the Marshalls, which they thought they could shuttle from island to island: 432 carrier aircraft (including 234 Zero fighters), 484 aircraft in the Marianas and 114 in the Western Carolines. This areas was so close to Japan that aircraft from the Home Islands could be deployed to it via Iwo Jima. The Japanese also assumed that because they held the airfields on Saipan, they could afford to use their carrier aircraft at extreme range, landing them on the island to refuel.

As in previous operations, this one began with mass US sweeps over Saipan, Tinian and Guam, which destroyed about 150 Japanese aircraft. US estimates of available Japanese aircraft had been low, so it was believed that the sweeps had accounted for most of the shore-based Japanese force. However, enough was done to prevent most Japanese land-based aircraft from interfering with the operation. An unfortunate pointer to the future was that the FM-2s (modified Wildcats) from the escort carriers had little success against Japanese attackers due both to their limited performance and to the inexperience of the fighter directors on board the amphibious headquarters ships (the small Casablanca class escort carriers had only limited CICs).

The Japanese did manage to attack Task Force 58 with both carrier aircraft and land-based aircraft from Guam. Fleet commander Admiral Raymond Spruance chose not to steam towards the Japanese carriers, but instead to remain within 100 miles of Saipan to cover the amphibious operation. This choice was later controversial. Spruance had chosen not to concentrate on destroying the Japanese fleet carriers, which many in the US Navy saw as the permanent threat to further US operations (his aircraft managed only to sink the single Japanese carrier Hiyo, badly damaging the larger Zuikaku). As a consequence, when Admiral Halsey took over the fast carrier task force (renamed Task Force 38) for the invasion at Leyte Gulf, Pacific commander Admiral Nimitz specifically emphasised the need to destroy the Japanese carriers, even at the cost of some of the invasion shipping. That is the main reason why Admiral Halsey took his fast carriers north to engage what turned out to be a Japanese decoy force. His decision was controversial because there was also a Japanese surface attack force, which nearly did penetrate to the invasion shipping; it was stopped only by the heroism of an escort carrier group (and its escorts) intended to cover the invasion proper. The issue was why Halsey had taken his fast battleships with him when heading north; his orders had allowed for their possible detachment. Halsey could point to standard doctrine: if the Japanese had any big-gun ships, carriers operating alone were vulnerable to possible surface attack, for example at night in coastal waters in which radar would be ineffective. He did not want another *Glorious* sinking.

When the Japanese fleet appeared, it managed to do exactly what pre-war doctrine prescribed. Its search aircraft performed effectively, finding the US fleet long before the Japanese fleet was found by the Americans. Japanese shadowers performed effectively but suffered badly. The nine Japanese carriers were organised in three divisions, each of which struck separately.

The US fleet was so large that it was able to destroy aircraft being concentrated on Guam while a sufficient CAP was maintained over the carriers. The battleship *Alabama* detected the initial Japanese strike (from CarDiv 3) at a range of 130nm. These sixty-four attackers were met by about 200 Hellcats. The Japanese pilots were relatively inexperienced: American fighter controllers were astonished that they orbited 75 miles from the task force while their leaders distributed instructions by R/T. On the other hand, some of the new Japanese torpedo bombers (B6N 'Jill') were able to outrun Hellcats vectored for interception. This was notice that new US fighters were badly needed, but a combination of heavy anti-aircraft fire and limited Japanese pilot experience limited any threat to the fleet.

A second strike (111 aircraft from CarDiv 1) was detected at 115nm and again orbited (at 90nm) before proceeding towards the fleet, giving the US fleet valuable reaction time. This time about eighty-four of the attackers were shot down, but again a few managed to penetrate to drop bombs and torpedoes (*Enterprise* and *Princeton* had to manoeuvre to avoid torpedoes).

CarDiv 2 launched two waves as a third strike. Both were sent to the wrong place, some aircraft carrying out a search which brought them to portions of Task Force 58. They were generally unsuccessful, even when they attacked.

The US Navy called the mass destruction of Japanese aircraft the 'Turkey Shoot'. Of a total of 373 aircraft launched by Japanese carriers, 243 were shot down and thirty more returned badly damaged. Two Japanese fleet carriers were lost to US submarine torpedoes, largely because of serious design flaws: the new *Taiho* and the veteran *Shokaku*. Of the fleet carriers with which Japan had begun the war only the damaged *Zuikaku* was left. The seven carriers left in the Japanese task force had only sixty-eight fighters, three dive bombers and twenty-nine torpedo bombers left. On the other side, of 295 US fighters launched, only fourteen had been lost in the air.

The 'Turkey Shoot' of June 1944 was the triumph of US Navy fighter control, much as 'Pedestal' had been the triumph of Royal Navy fighter control. The Japanese found the US carriers long before they were found themselves. As understood before war, that should have enabled them to neutralise the US carriers. Instead, the triumph of Japanese scouting bought nothing. The Japanese mounted four major attacks. Each was tracked by US radar and in each case CAPs successfully intercepted the raids 50–60nm from the carriers.

The light carrier *Independence* shows her new SP heightfinding radar (9) in a photo showing changes after a refit at Hunters Point, 15 June 1944. Dipoles above the face of the antenna are for IFF. The SP antenna displaced an SC-2 formerly located on the foremast; the ship's main SK-1 air-search antenna was further aft, just above the flight deck and sponsoned out to one side. The antenna at the head of the topmast is for a YE aircraft homing beacon; below it is an SG surface-search antenna (7).

Moreover, the US fighters were placed with sufficient altitude advantage. For the first time in the war, the Japanese made a mass attack on a US carrier force without inflicting any damage at all on the carriers. In the aftermath, the Japanese rethought their tactics and introduced Kamikazes.

The key to US success, which probably was not fully understood at the time, was that the Japanese had to concentrate attackers in order to achieve much when they reached their targets. Also, low-level attacks, which might have evaded early detection, were themselves difficult to execute in daylight. A low flier had to approach closely just to locate a US carrier well enough to attack (if it searched at high altitude it would be detected and destroyed). Such aircraft would be picked up by the new pencil-beam radars and by destroyer pickets before they could get close enough. That is, anti-aircraft firepower shaped Japanese air tactics. Concentration limited the number of separate bogeys with which the US fleet had to contend. It happened that the US system of CICs and CAPs could handle a limited number of targets at one time. The after-action report described thirty-three separate interceptions, of which twenty-eight were successfully completed, resulting in 141 Japanese aircraft shot down.

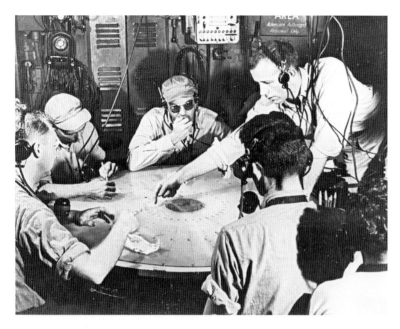

The point of all the radars was to support fleet air defence, particularly fighter direction. This is a Skiatron (black-on-white) radar display used by fighter controllers as, in effect, a plotting table, on board the carrier *Ticonderoga* off Formosa, January 1945. Skiatron was the British term; the US Navy called this a projector display (the black-on white image was projected up onto the large screen).

It helped considerably that standing CAPs (typically two divisions) were reinforced with eight more fighters as soon as one division was committed to an interception. That was possible because there were now so many carriers with so many fighters – and, moreover, fighters with such superior performance, Hellcats rather than Wildcats.

Yet there were also some troubling aspects of the victory. Over fifty Japanese aircraft got all the way through the CAP and the anti-aircraft fire to release weapons; one of them crashed the battleship *Indiana*. It did little damage, but this success demonstrated to some Japanese officers that it was still possible for a determined pilot to achieve

something worthwhile. The sheer mass of Japanese aircraft caused fighter-control problems, even though they had been bunched and thus did not present numerous separate targets. Experience against the new Japanese torpedo bomber suggested that US air superiority might be threatened, although it was probably clear that the Japanese would find mass production difficult. They had not been able to replace the Zero fighter, although there was a prototype of a follow-on.

For their part the Japanese could not be sure of what the next US objective might be; the possible targets were Taiwan and the Philippines (the US leadership debated exactly this issue). They therefore concentrated aircraft on Taiwan, which was centrally located. In October 1944 the US fast carrier task force raided the island. By this time Japan had almost no carrier pilots left, partly because it was difficult for carriers to go to sea to train them. The fast carriers had already supported the invasion of Palau, in support of which they had swept the Southern Philippines in September 1944.

The heavy carrier raids on Taiwan destroyed most of the aircraft based there. In theory more could fly in from Japan, but that would take time. The fast carriers and other US naval forces were so mobile that they could attack the Philippines almost immediately. By this time many Japanese naval leaders had concluded that US fighter control and anti-aircraft defences made attacks on the US fleet suicidal. They went one step further: if it was suicidal to make a conventional attack on the US fleet, a better alternative was suicide attacks. Such attacks were planned as the US fleet struck the Philippines in October 1944. The effect of the Taiwan raids was to reduce drastically potential

Radar, particularly short-wavelength (centimetric) radar, made it possible for a night fighter to find enemy aircraft. This is an experimental F6F-3N at the Grumman plant. The radar in the nacelle, which was standard through the Second World War, was APS-6 (AIA in an earlier designation series). It operated at X-band (3cm) and had a peak power of 40kW and used a 17in dish to produce a 5° beam. Maximum reliable range on a bomber was 5nm (4nm on a fighter). The pilot had a special type of display showing whether the target was above or below or to left or right. The 'S' in the designation indicated that the radar did not track the target, hence was not adapted to gunnery (which would have entailed a G designation). (Martin via Naval Institute)

numbers of suicide attacks at the outset. Suicide attacks became more numerous as aircraft were flown down from Japan to Taiwan to the Philippines. Thus the Lingayen Gulf landings in January 1945 were contested by many more Kamikazes, although the first Kamikazes attacked at Leyte Gulf the previous October.

By this time fighter reinforcements were available in the form of Marine squadrons which had fought through the Solomons using carrier-capable Corsairs. When the fleet retired to Ulithi in December 1944 to prepare for the invasion of Luzon the next January, two Marine Corsair squadrons (thirty-seven aircraft) joined the carrier *Essex*, which already had fifty-four Hellcats on board in one enlarged fighter squadron. To provide sufficient space, she landed her dive-bombers and reduced her torpedo bomber squadron to fifteen aircraft. She then had ninety-one fighters on board. *Wasp* was similarly equipped. These enlarged fighter groups were wanted for fighter sweeps to precede the attack on Okinawa, set for April 1945. The additions to *Essex* were, incidentally, the first Corsairs on US fleet carriers since limited carrier service had ended in 1943. Other Corsairs were soon assigned to US Navy squadrons, both as fighters (VF) and as fighter-bombers (VBF).

In February 1945 the Marines were assigned four escort carriers specifically so that they could provide close support, the first being the large *Sangamon*. She was followed by three half-sisters of the *Commencement Bay* class. Aircraft were Corsairs plus special-purpose Hellcats (night fighters and photo aircraft).

WARTIME US FIGHTER DEVELOPMENT
Night fighters and night carriers

A vital application of short-wavelength radar was to night fighters. A narrow beam was valuable because it did not reflect off the sea, swamping the small echo of a target. The British applied microwave technology to night fighters, but Rad Lab developed night fighter radars which could guide a single-seat fighter. The US Navy needed them because it could not operate large two-seat aircraft from carriers.[41] US single-seat night fighter radar was also installed on board the only wartime British carrier night fighter, a version of the Firefly.

In theory night fighter control was equivalent to day fighter control, but the fighter had to be coached much closer to the target bomber. Wartime night-fighter radars could bring a pilot into position near a target, but they were not accurate enough for gunnery. The pilot still had to make the actual attack visually and he could lose contact with the target between radar detection and the attack phase.

Through 1942–3 the Japanese learned that the combination of US radar and CAPs was effective against daylight attack. The pre-war Imperial Japanese Navy had decided that night attack was the best way to strike enemy warships. Its carrier task force never had the opportunity to exercise the tactics developed before the war, but as the US fleet began its westward advance in 1943, land-based Japanese aircraft began to attack at night. Suddenly there was an urgent need for carrier-based night fighters. During December 1943 over 90 per cent of their air attacks were conducted at night.

US work on naval night-fighter radar was delayed by the need to develop 3cm rather than 10cm radars, the latter being too large for a single-seat fighter. Work on such a system began in May 1941 and in September the navy expressed interest in a combined interception and gun-aiming radar for Corsairs. Maximum weight would be 250lbs and search range should be two miles at 2000ft or greater altitude

In 1945 the F6F-5N was the standard US Navy night fighter.

(minimum range 500ft). A night fighter development unit (Project Argus) was established at Quonset Point, Rhode Island, which was near the major radar development centre at MIT (the Radiation Laboratory). The planned initial naval night fighter was a modified Corsair, F4U-2, with a wing radar nacelle. BuAer ordered work in November 1941. Since Vought had insufficient design staff, the project was delayed; in August 1942 it was decided instead to have the Naval Aircraft Factory install a new standard night-fighter radar in production F4U-1s.[42]

It proved possible to produce a radar suited to a single-seat fighter, the display adapted to the pilot's own requirements. The radar was packaged in a wing-mounted nacelle. The initial AIA set was developed by Rad Lab and made by Sperry.[43] It was proposed in November 1941 and prototypes were ready for flight tests in the spring of 1942. Argus tests of AIA began in June 1942.[44] Production was delayed, but a pre-production version was test-flown in the spring of 1943 and then installed on board ten F4U Corsairs for service tests (installations were completed by 1 August 1943). These radars reached the fleet in time for the attack on Rabaul and production began in September 1943. A few F4U-1s were equipped with AIA radar as F4U-2s, but nearly all wartime carrier night fighters were versions of the Hellcat, the standard carrier fighter: F6F-3N and F6F-5N. The first F6F-3N squadron received these sets in December 1943, using them in the invasion of Kwajalein the following February.

AIA was a multi-purpose radar intended for the full range of night-fighter functions, including blind-fire. It could be fit into a wing nacelle because it operated at the high end of the wartime radar frequency range, X-band (3cm). AIA filled its complex role by offering three alternative display formats on its 3in screen: B-scan (range vs. azimuth), O-scan (double dot for interception) and G-scan (dot with wings for blind gun aiming).[45] The pilot selected the format he wanted. Maximum range was about 4nm (2nm for targets more than

50° off dead ahead). The O-scan gave target position in both azimuth and elevation, so that the fighter pilot could follow evasive manoeuvres. At 1000 yds the pilot operated a toggle switch to use the radar as a gunsight. Minimum range was about 500ft.

An improved APS-6A followed AIA. Installations began at NAS New York in July 1944. It reached the fleet in September 1944, followed by APS-6 early in 1945 (-6A was a simplified version of -6). It had the same display formats as AIA but added a format showing coded beacon signals, for example those emitted by carrier homing beacons. Improvements included pressurisation, which allowed it to operate above 30,000ft; increased range; automatic beacon frequency control; improved relative elevation indication; and simplified installation (it did not need the waveguide used in AIA). APS-6A was an interim version which did not incorporate pressurisation and automatic beacon frequency control. Range on aircraft increased to 5nm and large ships were detected at 50nm. At least in theory, increased range made it possible for a fighter carrying it to operate more independently of a controller, even over an enemy airfield or as a predawn strike escort.

US naval night fighting began with combinations of radar aircraft and fighters. Early night fighter radars required a separate operator working with the pilot, so the first US carrier night-fighter operations employed a radar-equipped torpedo bomber (a TBF-1C Avenger with ASB radar – an early air-to-surface type with very limited air-to-air capability) controlling two Hellcats. That might be seen as the beginning of fighter control by an airborne radar aircraft, a theme very important from 1945 on, but in 1943 it was not entirely successful. The first attempt by a carrier to use this combination was apparently by *Enterprise*, 24 November 1943. It failed. In the process the target bomber shot down Lieutenant Commander 'Butch' O'Hare, the navy's leading fighter ace and his carrier's air commander. Two nights later the team was successful, shooting down two of three attacking Japanese aircraft and breaking up a torpedo attack. The same night O'Hare was shot down a Marine controller in a shipboard CIC vectored a land-based Marine night fighter to a successful interception, showing that the basic idea of a CIC-controlled night attack would work.

Note that the TBF/fighter combination was not part of the formal

Ideally, night versions of other fighters would have been developed. Unfortunately radar installations which scaled well to big fighters were far too massive for smaller ones. The F8F-2N version of the high-performance Bearcat carried a massive pod for an APS-19 radar, the successor to the APS-6 under development at the end of the war. The size of the pod, compared to the size of the Bearcat, is really a reflection of how much smaller the Bearcat was than the Corsair or Hellcat. Performance was terrible and the type never entered service. The night fighter version of the Corsair, supplemented by some wartime night Hellcats, served instead in the immediate post-war years.

naval night fighter programme. It did include an initial phase using a heavier S-band radar and a multi-seat aircraft, but the chosen aircraft was a version of the PV-1 light patrol bomber, not the single-engine TBF. Dive bombers (SB2As and SBDs) were equipped with heavier radar for initial trials and crew training, but were not intended for operational use.

By the autumn of 1943 the single-seat night-fighter radar was entering service, the first detachments going on board *Enterprise* and *Intrepid* in January 1944. The sets had short ranges, so it was absolutely essential to provide the fighters with altitude information. *Enterprise*, which had the SM pencil-beam (heightfinding) radar, vectored a night fighter from *Yorktown* into contact with a bogey on the night of 16 February. The fighter pilot lost contact and the bogey went on to torpedo the carrier *Intrepid*. The first major successes were during the invasion of Saipan in June 1944, when ten enemy aircraft were shot down, including three by *Enterprise* in one night. For their part the Japanese were clearly aware of US night fighter-control radar; they employed Window (chaff) and deliberately flew along paths selected to draw night fighters to its echoes. There was speculation that the Japanese were able to detect the IFF signals from US night fighters.

During the summer of 1944 it was decided to form two types of night fighter units. One was a four-plane detachment on a general-purpose carrier. The other was a unit consisting entirely of night fighters and torpedo bombers on a specialised carrier (the first was the light carrier *Independence*). Inclusion of the torpedo bombers indicated a night offensive role. Night operation could be hazardous, so *Independence* typically operated well apart from the main body of the

The Corsair became the standard multi-purpose fighter of the post-1945 US Navy. Here three photo Corsairs (F4U-5Ps) accompany a Corsair night fighter (F4U-5N), 9 March 1950. The F4U-5N carried either the APS-6 radar or its post-war successor APS-19 in its wing nacelle; this radar was also on board many Tigercats. It had a slightly enlarged dish (18in) but similar power (40kW). In 1945, with development not yet complete, it was expected to detect a bomber at about 10nm, twice the range of the APS-6. In 1951 the current version was APS-19B, with a new low-noise receiver and a new acquisition scan. By this time peak power was 50kW. When the new APQ-36 was proposed in 1951, one of the major objections was that although the fleet knew how to maintain 50kW magnetrons (radar power tubes), it would find the jump to 250kW difficult. Yet it seemed that unless that step was taken, fighters would be unable to deal with jet targets.

fleet, to be free to launch and recover her aircraft. Presumably, too, separation was a way of preventing enemy aircraft from homing on the whole fleet if they spotted the night carrier. Night-fighter control was considerably more detailed than that of day fighters, whose pilots could generally see enemy aircraft. Thus a VHF channel was typically devoted to each pair of night fighters. Night operations also encouraged the use of picket destroyers; recommended practice was to station two of them 40 to 50 miles from the main body in the likely direction from which the Japanese would attack, each controlling two pairs of night fighters.

The Japanese continued to employ night attack tactics, which the Third Fleet Fighter Director Officer regarded as the worst of all air attack problems (he referred to operations off Formosa leading to the Leyte Gulf invasion). Typically large numbers of aircraft were led by one or two using running lights and flares to home the rest. Such attacks torpedoed the cruisers *Canberra* and *Houston* (a crashed plane seriously damaged the cruiser *Reno*). There were not enough night fighter units; the cruisers were hit when no CAP was present. The Japanese typically flew at dusk, so the fleet mounted an enlarged

sunset CAP: four to six divisions of fighters, including about two of night fighters.

Night attacks required specialised shadowers which had to operate in small numbers. As in the Mediterranean early in the war, shooting down a shadower could abort any attack. Thus on the night of 14 December 1944, during operations against Luzon (preparation for the landing at Lingayen Gulf in January), an *Enterprise* night fighter shot down a shadower within 17 minutes of first radar contact, before it had had any chance to report. On 24 December *Enterprise* was redesignated a night carrier with a specialised night air group. In January she and *Independence* formed a night carrier task group; *Independence* was responsible for fleet security during a night passage through Bashi Channel to the South China Sea. The task force commander (Admiral Halsey) was very favourably impressed with the dedicated night carriers; they made it possible for the other carriers to operate only during the day and their specially-trained crews were more proficient than detachments on board all-purpose carriers. The night carrier group disbanded in February 1945, *Independence* shifting to a daylight air group and *Saratoga* (which had joined the group) to close support.

Unfortunately damage to a night carrier could deny the whole fleet night fighter protection. *Enterprise*, the remaining night carrier, was out of action between 21 March and 8 April, 11 April to 6 May and 14 to 28 May 1945. The fleet therefore came to prefer the detachments and they survived after the war. Commander, Task Force 58 (the fast carrier task force) recommended that each carrier have six night fighters and six night torpedo bombers. The decision was simplified by the decline in Japanese night attacks, presumably as skilled pilots were killed off. In April, the fast carrier task force reported that night attacks were becoming smaller and were not always as well co-ordinated as before, whereas daylight attacks continued to be heavy. Night fighters on board the general-purpose carriers were effective, shooting down most enemy aircraft shot down at night.

The success of the spring 1945 night fighters reflected considerable sophistication in control. The fleet limited the number aloft to no more than four and their control often shifted from fighter director to fighter director; often control was passed to two or three before inter-

There was little question but that a separate radar operator would much improve performance, but that took a much larger aircraft with questionable carrier suitability. Grumman's F7F had been accepted in 1941 as a single-seat fighter, but by 1945 it seemed likely to serve only ashore, with the Marines. Post-war attempts to turn it into a carrier-based fighter were unsuccessful. This post-war F7F-3N prototype is flying with a Bearcat chase plane.

ception. In many cases fighter direction destroyers controlled the aircraft. This was before the era of radar-controlled carrier landing, so merely operating routinely at night with few or no lights was a major achievement. On the other hand, many interceptions had to be broken off as the fighter chased an enemy aircraft into ship and shore anti-aircraft range. This problem must have worsened as more ships were provided with blind-fire anti-aircraft control systems usable at night.[46]

Alongside APS-6 the Rad Lab developed APS-4 (ASH), a bomb-like surface-search radar with a secondary air-to-air capability. It was intended for carrier strike aircraft, but in 1944 the Royal Navy could not get APS-6, which was in great demand. Instead it placed APS-4 on board two-seat Fireflies. All existing RAF night fighters were two-seaters using search (but not gunlaying) radars to bring them to within gun range of their targets. The two-seat Firefly was not significantly worse.

In the US Navy, APS-4 equipped the night-bomber version of the improved Corsair, F4U-4E. Night bombers (intruders or hecklers) were becoming an important element of fleet air defence, as a way of destroying Kamikazes before they could be launched. Night attack survived as a vital post-war function, not least because it was difficult for an enemy to counter. The corresponding night fighter version of the Corsair, F4U-4N, was expected to replace the Hellcat (F6F-5N). At the end of the war an improved APS-19 was replacing APS-6. It was later described as the first really reliable night-fighter radar, offering detection at 6–10nm. It equipped the post-war F4U-5N Corsair.

Meanwhile a night fighter version of the Grumman Tigercat (F7F) was being developed, with a second seat for the radar operator. The initial version had the APS-6, but an alternative using the more powerful army SCR-720 was under development.

Late in the war it appeared that the Japanese would field faster aircraft. The US Navy was already developing jet fighters. In June 1945 CNO directed that a night fighter version be built of each jet.[47] The BuAer fighter division (VF) prepared a specification for a new long-range carrier-based high-performance night fighter. BuOrd was

The Royal Navy developed its own night fighters, using the US APS-4 radar (the APS-6 used in US night fighters was not available). APS-4 offered both air-to-air and air-to-surface capability. The wartime version was a jettisonable radar 'bomb'. After the war it was carried in a fixed version on board the night-fighter version of the twin-engine Sea Hornet (an NF.21 of 800 NAS is shown landing on *Vengeance* in 1951). Like APS-6, APS-4 operated at X-band. Peak power was 35kW. Air-to-air range was somewhat shorter than that of APS-6, about 4.4nm on a bomber. Unlike APS-6, which had a special pilot's display, APS-4 used a range-azimuth display. British modifications included the addition of 6nm and 2nm range scales as well as the existing 4nm scale, as targets could often be detected beyond 4nm. (*The Hook*)

beginning work on a new night fighter fire-control system and NDRC was about to begin work on a new night-fighter radar. An ADR study was produced, dated 19 May 1945.[48]

Escort carrier fighters

The main new wartime fighter development was aircraft specially adapted to the new escort carriers, with their small flight decks and low speeds. This requirement became urgent as the US Navy lost fleet carriers during 1942; large escort carriers had to fill some fleet carrier roles. A BuAer project was set up to develop a fighter specifically for light carriers.[49] No entirely new fighter could be produced in time. Instead, BuAer selected the current F4F-4 fighter for modification. Soon after the outbreak of war production of the F4F-4 was transferred to Eastern Aircraft, the new aircraft production arm of General Motors; as produced by that company it was designated FM-1. The special escort carrier version was the FM-2, designed by Grumman as the F4F-8.[50]

Development of lightweight fighters, which were ultimately intended for the small carriers, began with the fleet's shocked response to the Zero. Alternatives were drastic weight reduction and the design of an entirely new lightweight fighter equivalent to the Zero. Work on a 'nimble' fighter began in January 1942. A lighter engine would be optimised for low altitudes. Range would be cut to 600 miles. Armour and self-sealing tanks would be eliminated and radio equipment

Escort carriers presented a new fighter problem, due to their short decks and low speed. This FM-1 is on board *Kasaan Bay*, February 1944.

reduced. Armament would be two 20mm cannon and two 0.50-calibre machine guns. An F4F-3 so modified would be 370lbs lighter and another 358lbs could be saved by replacing the two-stage engine with a single-stage engine and by reducing structural strength from 9 G to 8 G. As modified the aircraft would make 323mph at 6500ft.

An alternative was to install an R-2600 in an F4F-3 with minimum redesign – in effect, to produce a grossly simplified equivalent of the F6F. Although BuAer initially rejected the idea in view of Grumman's work load, it had to take the fleet's demand into account. A BuAer study completed in August 1942 showed a 30mph improvement over the F4F-3 (40mph over the F4F-4); rate of climb at low altitude would have been better than that of the Corsair and similar to that of the Corsair at all operating altitudes. The new engine would have added about 500lbs. The idea died because by the time the study was complete the Corsair was nearing operational status and it appeared that the improved F4F would not be available to the Marines (who badly wanted it) any sooner than the F6F.

Pressure for a new lightweight fighter continued through 1942. In June the special assistant to the Assistant Secretary of the Navy for Air pressed for a stripped-down fighter to operate from escort carriers.[51] At the time, it seemed that new fleet carriers would appear only slowly, so that the bulk of naval aircraft would be operating from the extemporised flight decks. This effort, designated 'XF8F' in the initial letter describing it, seems to have led to the design of the F2M by Eastern Aircraft. The proposal to develop a US equivalent of the Japanese Zero was evaluated in September 1942.[52] It was dismissed because it could not enter production for at least two years.

Moreover, the problem of providing a fighter suitable to the escort carriers was becoming more urgent. The escort carriers offered much less wind over the deck than fleet carriers (typically they had a 14-knot service speed) and they could not normally resort to catapulting, because the firing interval of their H2 catapult was two minutes. Take-off run had to be short enough for the carrier to mass her aircraft on deck, but her flight deck overall was considerably shorter than that of a fleet carrier. The existing F4F was the most natural candidate, but other aircraft were considered, including the army's P-39 Airacobra (it was rejected for excessive take-off run). When the first BuAer (and

For the US Navy, the ultimate escort carrier fighter was the FM-2 (the production version of the F4F-8). It could be distinguished from the earlier FM-1 by its taller tail. These FM-2s from *White Plains* are escorting a strike, probably against Rota, 24 June 1944.

Grumman) study was made in February 1942, there was also a real fear that asking Grumman to develop a major new version of its F4F would derail much-needed production of the F4F-4. It seemed much better for Grumman to concentrate its engineers on the F6F and the F7F and also help General Motors augment F4F production with the FM-1, a licence-built F4F-4. The only other US carrier fighter, the Brewster Buffalo (F2A), was rejected immediately because its wings did not fold, hence it could not be stowed on board an escort carrier. The weight which would have to be added for wing folding would wipe out any possible gain in take-off run through lesser improvements. The F4F-4 already had folding wings, so weight savings would reduce its take-off run and also its stall speed. Weight could also be saved by accepting a loss in high-altitude performance (the turbocharger). To accommodate a lighter engine, the aircraft would have to be rebalanced, probably by moving the engine forward. Oil coolers would be relocated from under the wing to the engine accessory compartment and the cowling revised to match.

By July 1942 BuAer was looking at an F4F using the R-1820-56 engine instead of the R-1830-86 of the F4F-4 (i.e. a single rather than double-row engine), with redesigned wings with a lighter folding mechanism and full-span flaps (Grumman's 'Duplex' flap arrangement as used in the F4F-3 was considered satisfactory).[53] Armament would be four 0.50-calibre machine guns (to limit weight; there were strong advocates of a six-gun battery or even of 20mm guns). The combination of reduced weight and a better engine would add 15–20mph to the F4F-4 at up to 19,000ft; stall speed would be 7mph less. Take-off run would be reduced by 100ft (15 knots wind over deck) and rate of climb would be increased by a quarter. On 28 July BuAer asked Grumman to provide an informal proposal for two aircraft similar to the F4F-4, but with materially reduced take-off distance, with a material reduction in landing speed also very desirable, given the 14-knot service speed of the small carriers. The new version was designated F4F-8. Production was assigned to Eastern Aircraft, the production

version being designated FM-2. By December 1943 two squadrons had FM-2s for accelerated service tests.

By this time fleet carriers had night fighters, so in July 1944 the BuAer Military Requirements Branch proposed that, for uniformity in carrier air groups, that studies of installation of the standard APS-6 radar in the escort carrier fighters be conducted.[54] Eastern Aircraft reported on 16 October that a modified FM-2 would lose much of its longitudinal stability (and should be operated 'only by pilots who are reasonably familiar with the aircraft') due to additional inboard equipment. The radar nacelle would cause bad stall and buffeting, which had already been experienced in the much larger Avenger (TBF) with a similar nacelle. The nacelle might also cause deck clearance problems. The idea died, but the F8F night fighter survived the war to encounter fatal problems. It was given a much larger nacelle, for the newer APS-19 radar, near its centreline rather than anywhere on its wing.[55] The performance penalty was so bad that the idea had to be dropped, leaving the F4U-4/5N as the only near-term post-war US Navy night fighters. By that time there was no longer much interest in escort carrier fighters (the larger escort carriers were seen as anti-submarine ships).

As noted, Eastern Aircraft developed a follow-on F2M using a somewhat more powerful R-1820-62 engine and a bubble canopy. It was conceived as somewhat heavier than an FM-2 but lighter than the F4F-4 (7850lbs), with a turbocharger for better altitude performance. The F2M was considered promising enough for jigs and parts to be ordered before any prototype flew. Development turned out to be protracted and the project was cancelled in 1945.

In September 1943 Grumman proposed another lightweight fighter suited to escort carriers, built around the same R-2800 engine

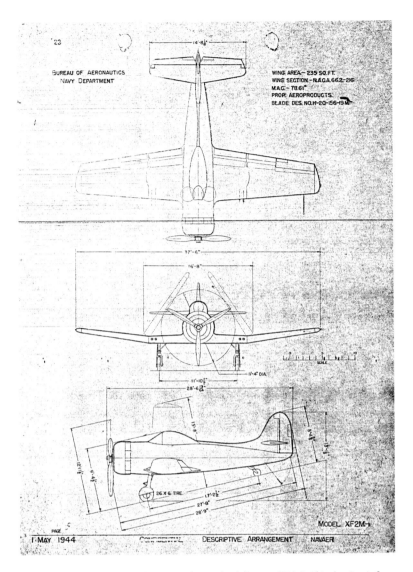

Eastern Aircraft, which made the FM-2, designed a follow-on F2M-1. This drawing is from the 1 May 1944 Aircraft Characteristics and Performance publication describing the design. It was never flown.

as the Hellcat and Corsair.[56] Grumman proposed an aircraft slightly smaller than the F4F-3, effectively a scaled-down F6F, but with a bubble canopy and wings folding up conventionally rather than back as in other Grumman aircraft. Unlike the earlier fighters, this one was conceived as a deck-launched interceptor with a high rate of climb (5600ft/min at sea level), radius of action being limited to 200 miles. To save weight, armament was cut from the usual six to four 0.50-calibre machine guns. Estimates showed that with the new C engine then planned for the F4U-4, the Grumman design (G-58 or F8F) would perform better below 19,000ft; it would climb better up to 14,000ft and was far superior to the F4U-4 below 20,000ft. At this time a further 'E' type R-2800 was planned and the new Grumman design was expected to do even better with it. The F2G, with its R-4360, would be faster but in November 1943 it was not planned for carrier use. Two prototypes were ordered in November 1943, then more prototypes and initial production tooling in July 1944. The first flight (21 August 1944) revealed few problems; a production rate of 100 per month was set for July 1945. Changes in the production version included more fuel, two more wing guns and a hardpoint

under each wing for a 1000lb bomb. The first carrier landings were made in February 1945 (there were some catapulting problems). As with the F4F, Eastern Aircraft was designated a second source, its aircraft to be designated F3M.

By mid-1944 the larger escort carriers (converted tankers of the *Sangamon* class) were operating Hellcats rather than FM-2 Wildcats and Hellcats were being tested on board smaller escort carriers. These ships, particularly the small *Casablanca* class (CVE 55s), were so large a portion of the US fleet at the end of the war that in March 1946 the BuAer Director of Military Requirements proposed a project for a new escort carrier fighter superior to the existing F8F and F4U.[57] He was told that no worthwhile improvement was possible using existing piston or turboprop engines, although turboprops under development might offer improvements. Current discussions with Vought and Grumman might result in improved fighters which could fly from escort carriers.

Nothing came of this idea, but the post-war US Navy still needed fighters which could operate from something short of a fleet carrier. The major roles the escort carriers had filled were still valid. In a convoy, an escort carrier had to be able to destroy snoopers which might home submarines on the convoy. It also took long-range bombers seriously as an anti-shipping threat. In the amphibious support role, escort carriers still had to supply enough air power to maintain air superiority until aircraft could be based ashore. The new jet engine technology seemed to offer solutions to both problems, but not in the straightforward way envisaged in 1946.

US Wartime Fleet Fighters

For the US Navy, the key development was a new generation of much more powerful engines. The 1935 fighters were powered by engines in the 1000hp class: versions of Pratt & Whitney's R-1830 Twin Wasp and Wright's R-1820 Cyclone. By 1938 Pratt & Whitney was offering the R-2800 Double Wasp (twin row) and Wright was offering the twin-row R-2600 Cyclone 14, both eventually in the 2000hp class, although initially designed for about 1500hp.[58]

Now it was finally possible to reach BuAer's speed goals. Vought's F4U won the single-engine competition. It was powered by the new R-2800 engine producing nearly twice the power of the R-1820 and -1830 powering the previous two fighters. Vought used an inverted gull wing to allow the aircraft to use the largest possible propeller (to absorb the increased power) without requiring an excessively tall undercarriage. Estimated speed was 351.5mph. Vought received a contract calling for folding wings and for an alternative engine, the R-2600. The twin-engine designs were considerably slower. Grumman's F5F was considered the best, with what were expected to be excellent vision and good handling features. However, speed was only 315.5mph.

BuAer had seen liquid-cooled engines as a way to achieve high speed by cutting drag. The only such design was Bell's naval version of the P-39 Airacobra. Initially it was expected to be too slow to be worthwhile, but during 1938 the projected output of its Allison V-1710 engine increased to 1150hp, making it competitive with the Vought fighter. A prototype was ordered in November 1938 as the XFL-1. BuAer was so interested in the possibilities offered by a liquid-cooled engine that it was willing to wait for the prototype FL-1 to be built well after the Vought fighter had flown.

The 1938 competition was the last before the war. It produced one of the two outstanding US naval fighters of the Pacific War, the F4U Corsair. The prototype flew in May 1940 and quickly demonstrated outstanding performance; it was the fastest single-seat fighter in the world. However, it also showed stability and control problems and it required substantial modification before production could be ordered.[59] As with the F4F, its pair of fuselage guns was eliminated and more guns added in its wings, for a total of six 0.50-calibre machine guns. The wing guns displaced fuel tanks. Also, BuAer wanted a 1000nm escort range, with additional capacity (using drop tanks) for overload fuel and oil for 1500 miles. The only entirely satisfactory fuel tank capacity was near the centre of gravity of the aircraft, as in the wings. With the wings unavailable, the best position was between pilot and engine. The cockpit moved back 3ft, producing a long nose which ruined the pilot's view over it. The long nose and gull wings (to provide sufficient ground clearance for the big propeller) became the characteristic features of the Corsair. To some extent the vision problem was solved by raising the pilot's seat 3in and replacing the canopy with the high bubble characteristic of the Corsair.[60]

BuAer was thus in a position to buy the most advanced fighter in the world, twice as heavy as the F3F-2 it had just ordered. Carrier handling equipment and technique had not been designed for the new type of aircraft; even the Wildcat and Buffalo were considerable jumps beyond the biplane F3F.

The Corsair was apparently difficult to produce, so once war began BuAer sought further sources. It did not want any more of Brewster's F2A Buffaloes, so it ordered Corsairs from that company as F3As. It also ordered Corsairs from Goodyear, which had never previously built naval aircraft, under the designation FG-1. Brewster encountered serious production problems and was dropped from the programme.

The 1938 competition also produced a Grumman design (its G-35) for a fighter powered by an R-2600, which was not selected. G-35 was a redesigned version of the company's Wildcat (F4F), with the same landing gear retracting into the fuselage and with two machine guns firing through the propeller disc and two more in the wings.[61] This idea was revived in 1940. It evolved into the Corsair's stablemate, the F6F Hellcat – which became the standard US Second World War carrier fighter.[62] Production Corsairs appeared at about the same time as production Hellcats.

BuAer decided that it had enough fighters under contract, so it did not need a 1939 competition. It continued to receive unsolicited proposals for unconventional fighters, most spectacularly the flying wing or pancake conceived by NACA engineer Charles Zimmerman. Conceived as a safe private plane, the Zimmerman configuration promised a maximum speed of 500mph in fighter form. Zimmerman's key idea was to reduce the usual wingtip vortices, in which air flows

With the advent of 2000hp class engines, BuAer was finally able to realise its ambition: to produce carrier-based fighters at least equal to anything ashore. The Vought XF4U-1 won the 1938 BuAer fighter competition, but it required considerable modification before it could be approved for production. The fuselage guns, standard in pre-war fighter designs, were abandoned in favour of more wing guns. Fuel stowage in the wings had to be eliminated and BuAer wanted more endurance in any case. The solution was an additional fuselage fuel tank. To keep it near the aircraft's centre of gravity (so that trim would not shift as fuel was burned), the tank was placed forward of the cockpit, producing the fighter's distinctive long nose. Vought designers adopted the gull wing to provide ground clearance for the huge propeller needed to absorb the power produced by the R-2800 engine. This type of wing also offered an advantage in that it met the fuselage at right angles, hence did not need a fillet.

from the high-pressure area under the wing to the low-pressure area above it, by using near-wingtip propellers rotating in the opposite direction. The result would be equivalent to a much longer wing of high aspect ratio, but it would not suffer from the usual drag of such a wing. The much shorter wing would offer high manoeuvrability (in one study Zimmerman compared his projected fighter to a Spitfire). BuAer was interested, but it would not hire an individual to design an aircraft. Zimmerman chose Vought to build his radical fighter. It had two R-2000 engines buried in its wing, driving the two wingtip propellers via long drive shafts. Gearing and clutches made it possible for either engine to drive both propellers. At least at first, it seemed that the aircraft could rise vertically like a helicopter, the pilot and passengers lying prone during horizontal flight. NACA wrote to the navy that, should the project work at full scale, it would be very valuable. That would not be certain until a flying scale model was built. BuAer contracted for the large-scale model (V-173). When the model was completed in the spring of 1941, Vought sought a contract for a full-performance Zimmerman fighter as the only way to keep the development team intact. Despite some scepticism as to Vought's ability to develop the high-speed hydraulic transmission required, BuAer let a contract for a fighter designated XF5U-1.

As of July 1942, Vought was proposing a fighter (VS-315) with a

The first operational Corsairs had low canopies offering neither a good view over the long nose nor a good overall view; the framed canopy was replaced by a bubble and the pilot's seat raised. This is the original version, as flown by the first Corsair squadron to operate from a carrier, VF-17 (it moved ashore when its carrier, *Bunker Hill*, reached the Solomons). The numbers on the lead fighter indicate the squadron (VF 17) and the position within it; by this time the standard US Navy fighter squadron was thirty-six aircraft.

23.3ft span. As an indication of what that meant, wing area was 427ft^2, which compared to 450ft^2 for an F7F Tigercat with a 51.5ft span. That made for a wing loading of 35.2lbs/ft^2, comparable to that of a Corsair (35.4lbs/ft^2). Vought estimated that speed at 33,500ft would be 491mph (BuAer estimated 481mph), which compared to 399mph for an F4U Corsair at 25,300ft. The big wing would dramatically reduce stall speed with power. Vought estimated it at 38mph (a more sceptical BuAer thought 65.8mph). A development contract was delayed because Vought had two much more urgent projects, the Corsair and the TBU torpedo bomber (which ultimately was built only in small numbers and never placed in service). As built, the XF5U-1 was powered by two R-2000 engines rated at 1350hp each for take-off (1100hp under normal conditions). With war emergency power, it was expected to make 413 knots (480.7mph) at 28,000ft at a weight of 16,722lbs. Estimated stall speed was 67.7 knots (77.86mph). There was no longer much expectation of near-VTOL performance, as the final characteristics sheet showed a take-off distance of 541ft with 25 knots of wind over the deck – nothing extraordinary. Wing loading was now 39.2lbs/ft^2. A sketch showed the huge propellers whose arcs almost touched. By this time severe problems with the propellers had been overcome by giving them articulated joints like the rotors of a helicopter. However, it was never possible for Vought to solve the worst problem, which was the hydraulic transmission connecting both engines to both propellers. Without such a connection, any problem in one engine would instantly flip the aircraft over, making it unflyable. The XF5U-1 was never flown, because it was considered far too dangerous. It remains the great might-have-been of US Second World War aircraft.[63]

The navy also became interested in other exotic designs, such as

Through 1944 Corsairs were assigned to shore stations, flown by Marines in places like the Solomons. During 1944, however, it was decided to move them back into the carriers, initially the projected large *Midway*s but then the other fleet carriers as well. This Corsair is flying over invasion shipping off Okinawa, 10 April 1945.

lightweight fighters. A Douglas lightweight was offered for naval use, but it was soon clear that adapting it to carrier operation would add so much weight that it would be useless. Its most interesting feature was probably its laminar-flow wing (the type used on the later P-51 Mustang); Douglas was also working on a laminar-flow biplane.

In August 1940 BuAer asked manufacturers to state their interest in entering a new design competition for both single- and twin-engine fighters. It sent out a request for proposals that December.[64] The basic specification was for a single-engine fighter, tricycle landing gear being a definite requirement. However, the Bureau planned to award contracts for both single- and twin-engine fighters. It welcomed designs with unconventional engines, although they might require step-by-step contracts for design and testing. Standard requirements were somewhat relaxed: take-off run at 25 knots wind over deck could be up to 250ft and stall speed could be up to 75mph. The take-off distance was greater than the Bureau had initially wanted, but it seemed likely that by the time the aircraft entered service it could be reduced by the use of high-lift devices such as the new two-speed engine gears and full-span flaps (designs should use the proven partial-span flaps). The successful bidder would have to be careful not to allow the take-off requirement to compromise maximum speed. Range at economical speed was to be the normal 1000 miles (the escort require-ment), with 1500 miles at overload condition and desired service ceiling was 35,000ft. Specified armament was six 0.50-calibre guns, with four 20mm cannon as an alternative (if that was impossible, BuAer would consider two 20mm and two 0.50-calibre). Designs and informal proposals were due on 10 March 1941.

None of the submissions was considered satisfactory, but Grumman's twin-engine fighter was considered worthy of further development. It went even further than previous fighters towards heavy weight, in this case 17,000lbs, nearly twice as much as the Corsair. At this time the carrier design operating limit was 14,000lbs, but that could be increased. Grumman received a development contract for what became the F7F Tigercat. Note that it was not, as is often written, conceived for the new *Midway* class carriers – which had not yet been designed or even authorised. However, the F7F did require far more hangar space than a single-engine fighter, so adopting it would have reduced carrier fighter strength drastically. It was not at all clear what would have happened had the war not intervened. Once the United States entered the war, projects for entirely new fighters were drastically curtailed, to the point that the F7F could not enter operational service until 1945.[65] Initially the first 200 and then all F7Fs were ordered completed as night fighters, the radar operator replacing some internal tankage (in daytime additional tanks could replace the radar operator). As evaluated by May 1945, the F7F-2N was found to be superior to the F6F-5N, at that time the standard carrier night fighter, both in overall performance and in that the radar operator was able to reduce interception time substantially.

Both Brewster and McDonnell submitted attractive proposals. A BuAer staffer suggested that it would be simpler to modernise the F4U – which was not yet in service – with a more powerful engine (R-3350) and tricycle undercarriage. That would probably be quicker and less expensive. All of the proposals fell short of the 38,000ft ceiling the British were then achieving with Spitfires and all were heavier partly because they incorporated protection and heavier armament.

More importantly, the United States was already mobilising. Even before that, the British and the French had ordered large numbers of American aircraft, taking up most existing capacity not only for production but also for design.[66] The iron law of such mobilisation is that the only way to obtain large numbers is to limit production to what is already in production. For aircraft, the most critical component was probably the engine and the production engines were the 1000hp class R-1820 and R-1830 and the 2000hp class R-2600 and R-2800. The only available high-performance fighters were the F4U (R-2800) and a much-modified Wildcat adapted to the 2000hp class engine (it became the F6F Hellcat). The winner of the 1940 competition would be developed, but necessarily slowly. Even development work suffered because there were insufficient aircraft; they could not be spared from more urgent roles, including training the vast number of pilots required for the new aircraft.

As proposed in January 1941, BuAer's fighter programme envisaged three production aircraft, the F4U, the F6F-1 and a development of Bell's buried-engine FL-1. All were expected to be ready for production by March 1942.[67] The Bell fighter never materialised. Its Allison engine was undependable and its centre of gravity was poorly located and could not be moved. However, it interested BuAer because many in the organisation saw the success of the Spitfire in the recent Battle of Britain as proof of the superiority of the liquid-cooled engine over the air-cooled radials favoured by the navy. BuAer went further in an attempt to see whether liquid-cooled engines were worthwhile.[68]

Initial tests of the F6F-3 and the production F4U-1 convinced BuAer that the two aircraft were very nearly interchangeable as far as performance was concerned. A BuAer comment on a January 1943 report by Vought test pilot Boone T Guyton on a flight in a Hellcat was that 'carrier captains will probably like the shorter take-off of the F4U-1 (40ft) and the fighter pilots will like the nice ground handling characteristics of the F6F – if performance becomes closely competitive the pilots might like the higher speed and rate of climb of the F4U in preference to the F6F ground handling characteristics'. Guyton liked the roomy well-arranged cockpit of the F6F and he was impressed by its ground vision, ground control and ease of ground manoeuvring. Taxiing was no problem due to the somewhat flat attitude of the aircraft on the ground. The aircraft yawed less on take-off. Vision was somewhat better than that in the F4U, but Guyton argued that the main issue was the large nose and wide fuselage required by the big R-2800 the two fighters shared. 'The writer has always contended that, within reason, moving a pilot aft in respect to wing position does not create the most serious impairment to vision . . . [but] due to the fact that the pilot is closer to the leading edge of the wing in the F6F, he obviously can see more down past each side of the fuselage over the wing.' Guyton defended his own aircraft, claiming that the modified Corsair with the raised seat was about as good. Generally the F6F offered good pilot control because its control forces in all three directions were well co-ordinated, but Guyton claimed that it did not have the solid feeling in respect to lateral, directional and longitudinal stability and control of the Corsair. The rate of roll seemed slower. Not surprisingly, Guyton ended by saying that he would prefer to fly the Corsair in combat. The BuAer route sheet includes the comment that by itself this report was useless; it should be set alongside a report by a Grumman test pilot trying a Corsair.

In November 1942 the chief of BuAer pointed out that 'in marked contrast to the F4U' the F6F 'possesses flying and handling qualities which are almost ideal in an aircraft of this type and is simpler and easier to fly than any remotely comparable aircraft. The handling characteristics and vision are such that this aircraft will probably prove to be a superior gun platform to the F4U. The transition from the F4F type to the F6F, even for inexperienced pilots, will be practically no step at all – in fact in some respects will result in considerable reduction in hazard to material. This is again in marked contrast to the same procedure with F4Us . . . it is the general opinion . . . that the overall handling characteristics of the F6F are such that the confidence and morale of service pilots will be boosted to a striking degree if substituted for other available fighters. This alone would so increase its effectiveness as to justify reconsideration at this time of the whole fighter programme and the most drastic measures are believed justified if greater production can be obtained thereby.'[69] To some extent this was intended as a threat to force Vought to accelerate its own Corsair programme; if it failed to do so the Corsair could be cancelled outright. Coupled with the demand for acceleration was a demand for systematic development of the F4U to cure its operating and production problems.

In December 1941 expected delivery dates for initial production aircraft were April 1942 for the F4U and October for the F6F, the latter remarkable for an aircraft which would not fly until June. The first production F4U-1s were delivered in October 1942 (the first carrier squadron was VF-17, aboard the *Essex* class carrier *Bunker Hill*). The first production F6Fs were delivered early in 1943. The Hellcat was somewhat easier to fly and apparently much easier to produce and to maintain, than the Corsair. Logistics dictated that one fighter or the other be chosen to equip the fast carriers. In August 1943 the US Navy standardised on the Hellcat for carriers, assigning Corsairs to Marine units ashore and making them available to the Royal Navy.[70] This decision was taken before the first Corsair squadron went on board *Bunker Hill*. When the carrier reached New Georgia, VF-17 was sent ashore. No Corsairs went aboard US carriers for more than a year. However, a shift back to placing them on carriers began as early as the spring of 1944, when they were first included in the planned air groups of the new *Midway* class carriers and then in replacement air groups planned for *Essex* class carriers.

In August 1942 BuAer decided to use the same R-2800B engine in production F6Fs as in production Corsairs. It considered that with the same engine the two aircraft would have comparable performance. The following spring BuAer wanted to replace the B engine with the more powerful R-2800C, which was still experimental. Grumman wanted to test the new engine in a prototype; Vought was willing to install it in production aircraft without testing it first. The Grumman version was designated F6F-6 and as of August 1944 production was to shift from the -5 to the -6 in July 1945. The Vought version was the F4U-4, production of which was to begin in January 1945 (Goodyear's FG-4 was to begin production in November 1945). With the 'C' engine still experimental, BuAer wanted to continue production of aircraft powered by the existing 'B' engine as insurance. It also hoped to begin installations of a further two-stage supercharged version of the 'C' engine. In September 1944 it therefore chose to retain the F6F-5 in production as insurance (the F6F-6 was cancelled) until the F4U-4 was definitely satisfactory or until the follow-on F8F Bearcat had been fully evaluated. There was also provision to switch the F6F to the 'C' engine, depending on the outcome of F4U-4 evaluation.

At this time, late in 1944, plans called for replacing the F6F with either Grumman's F8F Bearcat or the mixed-power Ryan FR-1 Fireball, but neither would be ready before late 1945. By that time many F6F-6s could be produced, the conversion from the 'B' to the 'C' engine being relatively simple. The F6F-5 was only marginally better than some of the newer Japanese fighters, but its margin could be restored with the new engine.[71] Moreover, Grumman was considerably out-producing Vought. Late in 1944 the F4U programme was less than half the size of the F6F programme.

The F4U-1, F6F-3 and the army's P-47C Thunderbolt, all of which used the R-2800 engine, were tested at Anacostia in December 1942. Both navy fighters had better rates of climb and the F6F had the best turn rate, although both navy fighters out-turned the P-47C. In sustained speed the Corsair came first, the P-47C second and the Hellcat third (with the supercharger engaged, the P-47C came first). In acceleration the Corsair came first, followed closely by the Hellcat, with the P-47C a distant third. Below their critical altitude both navy fighters were superior, the superiority being very great with neutral blower and almost negligible in high auxiliary stage. The P-47C had less drag than the navy fighters, but had inadequate engine cooling. Another conclusion was that the turbocharger offered improved performance which more than offset its relatively slow acceleration to full power. A formal demonstration of army and navy fighters was held at Eglin Air Field in May 1943 (the follow-up was at Patuxent River in 1944). Naval representatives were impressed by glide bombing demonstrations, which seemed to be adaptable to their aircraft and by rocket-firing by a P-38 and a P-47. The navy adopted both innovations. Perhaps the clearest indication of just how much power the new R-2800 engine offered was that it was now possible for a fighter to deliver not only heavy bombs but even a torpedo.[72]

BuAer seems to have considered the Hellcat a better carrier fighter than the Corsair. It was much easier to maintain.[73] Both Corsairs and Hellcats entered carrier service. In the autumn of 1943, reviewing the situation, BuAer observed that many more Hellcats were aboard carriers, presumably because they were far more producible. To simplify logistics, fleet carriers standardised on a single type – the Hellcat. Corsairs were given to the Marines and to the Royal Navy. However, by April 1944 Corsairs were being assigned to new carrier air groups as they were formed and BuAer was accelerating production to match.[74]

These aircraft were all initially armed with 0.50-calibre machine guns, which the pre-war BuAer considered sufficient. However, the BuAer armament division argued strongly that all current and future fighters should be capable of converting to 20mm guns, not because bombers would be particularly well protected, but because the cannon would be more effective against surface targets.[75]

By 1943 a new fighter engine was in prospect: the Wasp Major (R-4360). Pratt & Whitney fitted one to an F4U and late in November 1943 BuAer ordered its station at Patuxent River to test it with a view to using it as a navy or Marine Corps fighter. Development of this fighter was turned over to Goodyear under the designation F2G.[76] The Goodyear fighter incorporated the bubble canopy tested on a Corsair but rejected because it would interrupt production. Presumably it was acceptable in the F2G because enough other changes were already needed to accommodate its massive engine.[77]

The basic Corsair was given a more modest production upgrade as the F4U-4: it had the 'C' version of the R-2800 (R-2800-18; the F4U-1 used the 'B' version). BuAer wanted the new engine in both its fighters, but Grumman did not want to convert production to the new engine, which it thought would have numerous problems. Like the F4U-1, it was also built in a night fighter version (F4U-4N) with an APS-6 pod in one wing. It had 20mm guns; BuAer also wanted a study of possible installation of the 0.60-calibre gun it was developing. At the end of the war a further F4U-4E version, with night bombing equipment (APS-4 radar), was under test and scheduled for production.

A Fighter Conference held at Eglin Field in May 1943 compared operational US fighters. Among the fighters present were the navy's F6F Hellcat and F4U Corsair and the army's P-38J Lightning, P-47D Thunderbolt and P-51B Mustang. All pilots present were encouraged to fly all the aircraft so that they could make valid comparisons. No official comparison tests were conducted, although the pilots made some informal competitive runs. The only aircraft with water injection were the Corsair and the Thunderbolt. The F4U was flown by a Vought pilot, who reported that with water injection he could make about 415mph at 21,000ft, which was definitely faster than both the P-51 and the P-38 at that altitude. At 30,000ft the F4U (close to 405mph) was somewhat slower than the P-38 and P-51. The F4U outclimbed the P-51 from sea level to 21,000ft and it was very close to the P-38 at 21,000ft. Without water injection, the two navy fighters were equal in everything but speed. Army and company pilots considered the awkward stick position, stiff ailerons (on the F6F) and heavy stick forces and poor visibility on the F4U (much improved with the bubble canopy) the main undesirable features of the navy fighters.

Although all present considered the Corsair the outstanding navy fighter because of its speed, the cockpit arrangement of the Hellcat was well liked, as was its ease of operation both on the ground and in the air. The Mustang was admired by all because of its speed, manoeuvrability and simplicity of cockpit design. The P-47D, particularly with water injection, was the fastest of all above 30,000ft. The speed, rate of climb and single-engine performance of the P-38 were considered noteworthy.

Another report of the trials reported competition between the F6F-3 and an army P-51A flown by a navy pilot at the best altitude for the Mustang (15,000ft). The Mustang had about a 30mph speed advantage at 5000ft and about 15mph at 15,000ft, but neither was enough to be decisive and the F6F-3 outclimbed the Mustang both straightaway and in a tight turn; the navy pilot preferred the Hellcat. He considered both the Hellcat cockpit arrangement and its cockpit visibility by far the best.

Even so, the Mustang was impressive, because it combined long range, heavy armament and high performance with very light weight (8400lbs). British Group Captain Summers claimed that the British had found no difference in reliability between air-cooled and liquid-cooled engines, opening the possibility that the US Navy might adopt a liquid-cooled engine fighter. That made the Mustang an interesting potential naval aircraft.

The British, who were using the Corsair in European waters, evaluated it against a captured German Fw-190 in February 1944.[78] At 11,000ft both aircraft were about as fast, but the German fighter was 20mph faster at 17,000ft. By 21,000ft both aircraft were again at parity and above 21,000ft the Corsair gained spead until at 30,000ft it was about 35mph faster. In climb there was little to choose up to 5000ft, the German fighter being slightly superior; between 5000 and 15,000ft it was 30 seconds faster and up to 25,000ft it was 1 minute 40 seconds faster. The Corsair could turn within the Fw-190 with ease;

The Corsair became the main British carrier fighter in 1943–5, operating from even the small escort carriers. This is an FG-1D, a Corsair built by Goodyear because Vought production was limited; it was designated Corsair IV by the Royal Navy. Corsairs were also built by Brewster (as F3A-1s), but that company was unable to produce enough and it went out of business in 1943. The Royal Navy clipped the tips from the wings of its Corsairs so that they could fit hangar decks with less clearance than those of the US Navy. 'FT' on the nose of this aircraft indicates that it was used for flight test at Patuxent River. Captain 'Winkle' Brown recalled serious handling problems, manifested even at the prototype stage, particularly at low speed (as in landing). He mentioned a bad torque stall and serious directional instability immediately after touchdown. He recalled a feeling of great solidity (as compared, say, with a Seafire) in flight, but also poorly-harmonised controls. However, the Corsair could be rolled at maximum rate even when diving at high speed. Because the Zero had poor roll control at high speed, Marines could generally shake it off in a dive. Brown also recalled dramatic acceleration to very high speed. In Brown's view, the US Navy had wisely consigned the Corsair to shore operations while solving its deck-landing problems, whereas the Royal Navy had felt compelled to accept it as a carrier fighter. 'I knew that, by consensus, it had been pronounced a brute' (by the FAA).

when the Fw-190 started on the tail of the Corsair the positions were reversed in just over one and a half complete turns. However, the Fw-190 rolled considerably faster and could therefore reverse a turn so quickly that the Corsair could not follow it. There was little to choose between the two in a dive, the Corsair being slightly faster. However, at the height involved the Corsair was using three-quarters power and the FW half-power. The report concluded that apart from superiority in a turning dog fight (in which enemy pilots would seldom if ever engage), the only real advantage enjoyed by the Corsair (except at high altitude) was its outstandingly good climb after a dive. A Corsair encountering an Fw-190 should therefore make every effort to attack

from above and to maintain height superiority by zooming after the attack. If jumped, the Corsair would have to evade by turning as tightly as possible and it would have very little chance of seizing the initiative from the Fw-190.

Probably impressed by the Mustang, in March 1944 DCNO(Air) asked whether it was still worth using air-cooled radial engines in naval fighters. Every large increase in power had required a larger engine with more frontal area and therefore more drag. Perhaps it was time to look again at a liquid-cooled engine. The BuAer Engineering Division argued that the radial was still the only acceptable naval engine. It was more reliable and less vulnerable than a liquid-cooled elevators engine (since it did not have a radiator, a single point of failure); it made for a shorter, less draggy airframe; and neither ADR nor the contractors had been able to design a superior aircraft with a liquid-cooled engine. As proof, a P-51B was tested against an F4U at Patuxent River. Up to 25,000ft both had about the same speed. Although the P-51 was faster above that, the F4U-1 was superior in all other areas except diving speed. It also carried a heavier armament and was a better gun platform.[79] Proponents of the liquid-cooled engine pointed to the possibility of building a smaller, lighter fighter, even though, horsepower per horsepower, the liquid-fuelled engine was heavier. Neither the British nor the Germans had found liquid-cooled engines unreliable and the Army Air Force found such engines entirely acceptable. Shrinking aircraft size would increase the number which could be carried and if such aircraft consumed less fuel, a carrier could mount more strikes between replenishments.

It appeared that the Mustang could not make a rolling take-off from a carrier within the space set by the aircraft spotted on deck. DCNO(Air) seems to have considered it so superior that the navy needed an aircraft

in its class. BuAer concluded that future fighters would have to be catapult-launched, so that the only performance requirement would be that they land safely (which meant a stall speed of no more than 90mph). It developed a specification for a future carrier fighter: it should attain at least 475mph at a critical altitude of 25,000ft and at least 425mph at sea level, both superior to Mustang performance.[80] It had to climb to 30,000ft in five minutes. Combat radius should be 300nm for the escort mission and 75nm for an interceptor mission. Endurance would be six hours. The envisaged threat, which was probably derived from the German guided bomb attacks at Salerno and Anzio, was an enemy force approaching at 400 knots using homing missiles; the force would be detected at extreme radar range. Instead of the multi-role fighter, the fleet would need a single-role interceptor. To make it as small as possible, BuAer assumed that it would be powered by a liquid-cooled engine or perhaps by a combination of such an engine and a jet. Armament would be four 0.50-calibre machine guns, a bare minimum. Contractors could use either US or British engines.

BuAer asked manufacturers for comprehensive fighter studies, including aircraft with jet engines and with combinations of power-plants. Vought offered the comprehensive study (including jet engines) and North American offered a modified version of its P-51. The Vought study showed no outstanding advantage for the liquid-cooled engine. BuAer decided not to do further studies until North American had submitted its design and a P-51 had been tested on board a carrier.

North American, whose Mustang had inspired the project in the

The Corsair's stablemate was the Grumman Hellcat (F6F). This photo was released on 23 November 1943; it probably shows the aircraft during a carrier shake-down cruise (note that no one on the island is wearing a helmet). The Hellcat equipped the great bulk of US fleet carrier squadrons in 1944–5 and it was credited with 75 per cent of all US naval air-to-air victories of the Second World War . The Hellcat had the largest wing of any US wartime production single-seat fighter. It was mounted at a minimum angle of incidence to limit drag in flight, but that in turn required that the Hellcat take off at a pronounced up-angle, limiting pilot visibility. It took a pronounced tail-down attitude in flight, the engine having been given a negative thrust line to give the required large angle of attack needed for take-off. Compared to the Zero, the Hellcat had twice the power but also twice the weight, so that it could easily out-dive the Japanese fighter, but could not outmanoeuvre it below 200 knots. At higher speeds the more robust structure of the Hellcat allowed it to pull more Gs. The controls of the Zero were heavier and the difference in turn rate was considerably reduced. Once on the tail of a Zero, a Hellcat could usually stay there through 70–80° of a turn, which was often enough time for a fatal burst from its heavy machine guns. Above 10,000ft the Hellcat could nearly match the Zero in climb and it could generally dive away. As an indication of the sheer size of the Hellcat, Brown pointed out that its empty weight was 15 per cent more than the fully-loaded weight of a Sea Hurricane IIC.

first place, demurred at first, citing a heavy work load, but ultimately it offered a slightly modified P-51, the main change being the use of tip tanks rather than drop tanks to increase range; this may have been the first US proposal for such a configuration. BuAer was concerned that the tanks would cause flutter or lower the flutter speed and also that the piping taking fuel from the tanks would make the aircraft more vulnerable.

By the time the North American proposal had been evaluated and the P-51 tested aboard *Shangri-La* in October 1944, interest in liquid-cooled engines was gone. BuAer had decided that any entirely new fighter would have to be jet-powered. It was most unlikely that any new piston-engined fighter would be available before the war was over. North American was offered a contract for the XFJ-1 jet fighter it had submitted in a different design competition.

Concentrating on (and gradually improving) existing aircraft did not preclude the development of small numbers of more advanced types. In 1943 Hellcats and Corsairs enjoyed dramatic superiority over the aircraft with which the Japanese had begun the war. By 1944 much better Japanese aircraft were entering service, albeit in very small numbers. Suddenly it seemed likely that the war-winning fighters on which the US fleet was relying might be outclassed. For example, it was reported that a new Japanese twin-engine aircraft could outrun the F6F at sea level and at altitude and also that a 'Judy' dive bomber escaped an F6F at low level while the F6F was indicating 269 knots. Other Japanese aircraft were expected to achieve higher speeds. At the same time it seemed likely that the overwhelming US superiority in daylight would cause the Japanese to operate more and more at night, so that a new night fighter with day fighter performance was needed. It should be convertible into a day fighter.[81] It was impossible to provide the required performance quickly enough. The only current fighter which qualified was the F2G, a modified Corsair powered by the R-4360 engine; but the engine would not be mature until late 1945. The new jets offered the desired speed, but not the required range.

Even the jets might not be good enough, because in the near future an enemy might field heavily-armoured bombers. In March 1945 the BuAer Military Requirements branch suggested that by 1947 a viable bomber destroyer might have to use heavy rockets rather than cannon. It suggested an armament of at least twenty fin-stabilised 5in rockets with proximity fuzes fired by two automatically-reloaded projectors. They would be fired using a radar ranging computing sight. The future fighter would also be able to carry two heavy Tiny Tim rockets either internally or in faired jettisonable containers. Performance should be comparable to that of the XFJ-1, which had just won the

An F6F-5 being launched to attack Tokyo, 26 March 1945. Note the drop tank.

1944 jet fighter competition. Nothing came of this proposal, but it seems to have been the ancestor of the idea that interceptors should be armed with multiple rockets. The idea may have been inspired by the German use of air-to-air rockets against US bombers.[82]

BRITISH WARTIME FIGHTERS

Radar changed the role and character of fighters in the Royal Navy: it made performance far more important and it made interception a practical proposition – which it had not really been earlier. The wartime story really begins with the Skua and Roc replacements conceived in 1938, because they ended up as the wartime Firefly. As in the United States, the wartime story is also largely about the increased potential offered by a new generation of 2000hp rather than 1000hp engines: the Bristol Centaurus, Napier Sabre and the Rolls-Royce Griffon.[83] As in the US Navy, because there was an ultimate limit on the speed a propeller-driven aircraft could attain, at this point more power translated into a combination of speed competitive with land-based aircraft and required naval characteristics, including long range.

The Skua/Roc replacement would be powered by the new Griffon engine, in effect the larger relative of the Merlin then powering the Royal Air Force's new interceptors. The new aircraft were included in the 1938 programme for experimental aircraft: N.5/38 and N.6/38. The Skua successor was to be capable of dive-bombing, like the Skua. The two-seat turret fighter (N.6/38) seems to have been contingent on successful development of a remote-controlled power turret, which in 1937 was also wanted for a projected twin-engine TSR (S.30/37). For the Admiralty, a manned turret (as in the Roc) was unattractive because when he occupied it the operator could not use the wireless, which was so important in naval operations. When the N.6/38 idea first came up in October 1936, the idea seemed entirely practical because Frazer-Nash, one of the two gun-turret makers, expected to have a prototype in something more than a year. The 1938 specifications were cancelled because it was impossible to buy the two new fighter prototypes this year; the project was bumped to 1939 (as N.8/39 and N.9/39). Both in turn were superseded by N.5/40, which was a front-gun fighter. It is not entirely clear when the Royal Navy (and, for that matter, the RAF) decided that no powered turret could make a fighter effective.[84] Before that happened, the Royal Navy was

interested in a turreted version of the Barracuda TBR to fill its requirement for a spotter escort (and, incidentally, for a TBR escort). The aircraft designed to Specification N.5/40 eventually emerged as the Fairey Firefly F/R. It entered fleet service only late in the war.

Late in 1939 the Director of Air Materiel (DAM) initiated work on a second fleet fighter. By this time, as noted below, it was clear that the fleet needed maximum performance.[85] By this time various firms had offered proposals for N.8/39 and N.9/39. The Admiralty found them unsatisfactory, so in December the specification was modified to ask for alternative one- and two-seat designs. The single-seater was to have a maximum speed of no less than 330 knots (385mph) at 15,000ft (the comparable figure for the two-seater was 300 knots). By this time many naval officers associated the usual two-seat requirement with poor performance. DAM doubted that the second seat was the problem, but he was willing to pare down the usual navigation and W/T facilities to give something close to a single-seater but with a second seat enabling a navigator to operate a Morse key and do elementary navigation. He saw the single-seater as a sop to critics. He hoped that the tenders would show how little his austere second seat would cost. Another factor was stalling speed, which limited maximum speed: DAM was most unwilling to increase it. He wrote that war experience had shown that often there was less, not more, wind available. Yet exhaustive discussion had shown that stalling speed was the overriding factor controlling designs. Even so, those attending the 5 January 1940 tender conference (on N.8/39 and N.9/39) were told that it marked a change in policy, presumably towards maximum performance.

DAM liked Fairey's tender best; it was the most acceptable and least speculative. It also showed little advantage gained by eliminating the second seat. Fairey's two-seater became the Firefly.[86] There was some interest in modifying an existing single-seater, one candidate being the RAF's projected future fighter, the Sabre-powered Hawker Tornado. For the moment, the Air Ministry (DAM's technical advisors) rejected any Sabre-powered aircraft as too heavy.

Although he ordered the Fairey design, modified with a Griffon engine, DAM found Blackburn's proposed design worth pursuing. It included a high-lift wing flap which might make it possible to reduce

At the outbreak of war the Royal Navy sought a higher-performance fighter, which became the Fairey Firefly. Like earlier British fleet fighters, it had a back-seater, a wireless operator/navigator/observer. Fireflies are shown on the deck of *Implacable* during one of the 1944 strikes against the Norwegian coast. The aircraft in the background are Barracuda torpedo/dive bombers. The unusual feature of the Firefly was a Youngman flap which could be extended in flight to increase wing area – a feature Captain 'Winkle' Brown saw as an early example of variable geometry, like a swing wing. In this case the effect was a sudden decrease in wing loading, hence an increase in manoeuvrability at low speed. Thus, according to Brown, with the flaps extended at take-off setting the Firefly could turn with the best single-seat fighters near the stall and could turn inside most of them. Increased lift also improved endurance, a particularly important feature in a naval aircraft. The flaps could be extended at near zero incidence beneath the trailing edge to increase wing area, or they could be extended normally for landing. Brown recalled good handling characteristics, although the controls, particularly the ailerons, became heavy at speed. In diving it became tail-heavy. (*The Hook*)

A Sea Hurricane traps on the training carrier *Argus*, August 1943. It first became evident that the Hurricane was carrier-capable during the 1940 Norwegian campaign. The carrier *Glorious* flew RAF Hurricanes off to support the army in Norway. When the British withdrew, she recovered them. That convinced CinC Home Fleet, who was less than pleased that 'everything in the air' outperformed his aircraft, that the difficulty of carrier take-off and landing had been grossly exaggerated. For the time being the RAF desperately needed all the high-performance fighters it could get to fight the Battle of Britain and the assignment of Hurricanes to the Royal Navy was held in abeyance. As with the Gladiator, navalisation was limited to catapult spools and an arrester hook (catapult fighters, which remained in RAF custody, had only the spools). Aircraft received local strengthening to cope with loads such as those from arrested landings and RAF radios were replaced by naval ones. The first 300 were modified as Sea Hurricane IBs in 1941. They were followed by Mk IC, which had the Hurricane IIC wing with four 20mm cannon and then by the Mk IIC with a more powerful Merlin XX engine. Originally Mk IICs were to have been specially built, but instead it was a conversion of a land Hurricane. Captain 'Winkle' Brown, who had previously flown Martlets (Wildcats), considered the latter a much better carrier fighter, with greater endurance, a better cockpit view (particularly for landing), better low-speed characteristics and a more robust undercarriage. It also climbed faster, but it was heavier to manoeuvre. It also had much better ditching characteristics. However, Brown remembered the Sea Hurricane as an excellent dogfighter and a pleasure to fly. Its most famous action was the defence of the 'Pedestal' convoy to Malta in 1942. (*The Hook*)

wing area substantially and so to reduce the structural weight needed to gain a particular performance. This idea had reached the point where it had to be tested on a full-scale aircraft. In March 1940 DAM decided to order twenty-five test aircraft. If they were successful, he would place a full-scale production order. The Blackburn fighter would also be insurance against the failure of the favoured Fairey fighter. By July 1940 the Blackburn fighter prototype was important enough to replace the planned second prototype of the Fairey fighter (by then being designed to the revised N.5/40 specification).

The specification for the new fighter came out of the Admiralty and it seems to have called for a single-seat front-gun fighter rather than for DAM's favoured two-seater. This new N.11/40 specification was approved by the Ministry of Aircraft Production (MAP) on 24 August 1940. Despite Air Ministry opposition, it called for a Sabre engine (in a 'power egg' installation). This was a very large fighter by Royal Navy standards; the specification allowed for an all-up-weight not to exceed 12,500lbs. As a single-seater it would depend on R/T rather than on the usual naval Morse installation. Maximum speed at an operational height between 15,000ft and 20,000ft was not to be less than 350 knots (403mph), stall speed not more than 68 knots and take-off run 350ft against a 20-knot wind. Endurance was to be four hours at 120 knots at 15,000ft plus 10 minutes for take-off. The aircraft would have additional tankage for another two hours. Armament would be four fixed forward-firing 20mm cannon. The endurance placed the new single-seater in the same category as the Fairey two-seater, but with considerably better performance. Blackburn's fighter was later named the Firebrand. It had a much less happy life than the Firefly, despite having much the same parentage.

When war broke out in 1939, the only potential near-term source of other fighters was production for the RAF, which had concentrated on relatively short-range high-performance interceptors, the Spitfire and the Hurricane. Of the two, the Hurricane was available in greater numbers, which is why it was offered to the navy (and then withdrawn) in 1938. Both aircraft were optimised for high-altitude combat. Short range was acceptable because they were intended to defend the United Kingdom against incoming bombers, but it made naval use problematic. In the case of the Spitfire, optimisation for high-speed combat had included the use of an unusually thin wing, which in turn made for a narrow-track undercarriage and difficult ground-handling characteristics, hardly attractive if it was used on board a carrier.

The Royal Navy sought Spitfires. When war broke out, it provided Skuas and Rocs to defend the fleet base at Scapa Flow and also the Orkneys. These aircraft soon encountered fast German shore-based bombers, which they could hardly intercept. The defence of the fleet base seemed to set up a new FAA function, actually an RAF responsibility, but beyond RAF capability due to its heavy responsibilities. By December 1939 the Royal Navy wanted fifty Spitfires with folding wings, both to defend shore bases (including but not limited to Scapa) and for special carrier operations.[87] The rub was that the RAF had to agree to allow the Royal Navy to take over the defence of the bases at home and abroad; the issue had to go through the Air Council, the RAF equivalent of the Admiralty. It was all the more delicate because the Royal Navy wanted to take RAF aircraft to do this job. The RAF resisted; it needed every Spitfire it could get for home defence. Its winning case was that the fifty navalised Spitfires would cost many more conventional Spitfires (the original number was seventy-five, but the winning argument claimed 200). The RAF representative at the production meeting talked up (he admitted, deceptively) the virtues of the Fulmar, particularly its potential when it was provided with an improved Merlin XXX engine.

The Admiralty was not fooled. It used rejection of the naval Spitfire as leverage to demand production of the higher-performance N8/39 without waiting for the usual prototype procedure; at a tender design conference at the Air Ministry the Fairey design had been pronounced good enough to be ordered 'off the drawing board'. The Admiralty wanted 200 as an initial order. This aircraft, which became the Firefly, offered a maximum speed of 310 knots compared to the 230 knots of the Fulmar. The Admiralty also still wanted higher-performance fighters: Spitfires with arresting hooks but without folding wings, which would be stowed on a flight deck. No special development effort (for the folding wing) would be needed; surely a few could be made available by July 1940. That did not happen.

This 885 NAS Seafire Mk IIC is shown on board *Formidable* in the Mediterranean in 1944. The navalised Spitfire (Seafire) initially had fixed wings because of problems folding its very thin wings. The first Seafire IBs were reworked Spitfire VBs, the Mk IIC was essentially the same apart from having a universal ('C') wing carrying a pair of 20mm cannon. It also added catapult spools. There was some strengthening. Captain 'Winkle' Brown recalled the Seafire LIIC as the most exciting aircraft he had flown up to that time, with magnificent initial climb and acceleration. Clipped-wing versions rolled more rapidly and were about 4 knots faster, albeit at a cost in take-off run and service ceiling. However, it demanded careful handling. Seafires deployed on board escort carriers to support the landings in Sicily ('Avalanche') suffered a very high rate of deck-landing accidents, availability falling by about 38 per cent on the first day. The Royal Navy later attributed the high accident rate partly to the use of very inexperienced pilots taken from the RAF. In preparation for the use of Seafires to support the 'Dragoon' landing in Southern France, Jeffrey Quill, the most experienced Spitfire pilot (and an RNVR Lieutenant Commander) carried out special trials. He concluded that the Seafire had inherently poor low-speed controllability and was not robust enough for carrier landings, although changing from the A-frame hook to a sting hook might help. Brown himself became chief naval test pilot at RAE because his predecessor was killed landing a Seafire on a carrier early in 1944. The serious accident rate continued in the Eastern Fleet and in the British Pacific Fleet, problems including the relatively weak undercarriage. At the end of the war the Seafire XVII introduced a more robust under-carriage with long-travel oleo legs, which would have helped keep Seafires from bouncing over wires as they landed. (*The Hook*)

Meanwhile overall Royal Navy fighter policy was rethought at a February 1940 meeting, with Fifth Sea Lord in the chair.[88] Basic priorities were set: (1) destroy shadowers, (2) intercept enemy strike forces, (3) destroy enemy spotters and protect our own, and (4) escort our own strike forces to their objectives. Priority (1) was consistent with the late pre-war thinking of the Mediterranean Fleet: it might not be possible to intercept a strike, but the strike could be aborted altogether if the shadower homing it on the fleet was destroyed. Minutes of the meeting included crossed-out notes by DNAD: 'despite increased weight and loss of speed, which is not however very great, it was agreed to keep to the previous policy of developing two-seat VF' because (a) flying over the sea outside visual range of parent ship involves in many circumstances more navigation than can be undertaken by the pilot alone; (2) in the cases of functions 1 and 2 above, FAA fighters have to be directed to their objectives and for technical reasons these directions can only be given by W/T. It was however agreed that provision for the back-seater should be kept to a minimum (an attached paper stated that the new radio beacon [Type 72] solved the navigational problem). Another crossed-out note argued that the escort role probably required a turret fighter, as RAF and French war experience suggested that hostile fighters would attack at such high speed that front-gun fighters could not cope.

Probably the most important agreed conclusion was that war experience had shown that FAA fighters had to be fast enough to deal with German aircraft likely to attack the fleet in the North Sea: shore-based bombers such as the Ju-88 (maximum speed in level flight given as 285mph); and long-range fighters which might escort them (the newest Me-110 of this type was reported to have a maximum speed of 350mph). The only major German type the FAA was not required to fight was the short-range Me-109 fighter. This was the formal end of pretensions that FAA fighters could have inferior performance because they would face only low-performing enemy carrier aircraft. Moreover, any British carrier fighter designed in 1940 would not enter service for two or three years (which turned out to be optimistic), by which time the enemy might well have 300mph bombers and 400mph fighters. DAM pointed to the claimed 380mph speed of the new FAA two-seater. By this time he had felt compelled to ask firms for single-seat fighter designs, but he pointed out that the penalty incurred by the second seat in the new Griffon fighter was only 2–25mph. With a larger Sabre engine, the new two-seater might reach 400mph. It was agreed that DAM should discuss the tender designs with the Air Ministry and that he would raise the possibility of fitting the Sabre instead of the planned Griffon engine.

For the short term, the navy was committed to the Fulmar, but unfortunately it was three months behind in production (it was now scheduled to appear in April 1940) and it could not be accelerated.[89] DNAD made the best of a mediocre deal: with its high endurance, powerful armament and speed of 260–270mph, it should prove valuable. It could be used for reconnaissance and to maintain patrols at sea which would give it opportunities of attacking faster aircraft.

The meeting reiterated the need for a few fast modern single-seaters. Their prospective role was shifting. Although their primary mission would be as a mobile shore defence force, an added role was fleet air defence, supplementing Fulmars: the single-seaters could be flown off to attack incoming enemy aircraft when attack was imminent (the Fulmars would carry out patrols). Without W/T, the single-seaters could not be directed once airborne and they could not navigate. They would have to fend for themselves, spotting enemy aircraft approaching the fleet. DNAD agreed that within these limitations their high speed would enable them to force combat on a proportion of attackers and they would have sufficient fuel for a short pursuit. A re-written version of the minutes pointed out that near-term wireless developments such as homing beacons and R/T sets might eventually give single-seaters sufficient capability, in which case their superior performance might make them preferable to two-seaters; but that point had not yet been reached.[90] The meeting agreed that the single-seat fighter project should be pursued urgently.

The only alternative source of single-seaters was the United States. DNAD produced a table of characteristics of US aircraft, including the obsolescent F3F-1, pronouncing all of them except the experimental twin-engined F5F undergunned. The existing version of the F4F did not fold its wings, hence could not be struck below by any British carrier except the old *Furious*.[91] It is not clear to what extent the table and the argument were actually moves in the ongoing argument over whether the navy could get Spitfires.

After the Norwegian operation in the spring of 1940 Home Fleet commander Admiral of the Fleet Forbes complained that everything in the air outclassed his naval aircraft.[92] The problem of flying on and off a carrier had been used to excuse low performance, but during the Norway operation RAF pilots in Gladiators and Hurricanes had found no difficulty in flying onto a carrier. Forbes' Vice Admiral of Carriers presented notes from CO of 804 Squadron Lieutenant Commander J C Cockburn, written on 2 May 1940 on board *Glorious*: his Gladiators had insufficient performance to chase and hold enemy aircraft. There was very little time between a pilot's sighting of the enemy and the time when he dropped bombs, so to ruin his attack the fighter needed concentrated fire – eight guns, as in the new RAF fighters. To avoid losing too much time turning into the wind to launch them, fighters needed a reasonable endurance, say five hours. The Spitfire could provide the speed and the guns, but US fighters such as the Buffalo the RAF was then buying could provide speed, guns and endurance (DNAD considered the Buffalo obsolescent at best).

DNAD pointed out that, given its very small numbers, the FAA had to buy multi-purpose aircraft which were difficult to design. Their necessarily long gestation made it likely that they would be obsolescent before they entered service – a particular problem in a period of rapid technological change. The FAA also suffered from low priority, which further delayed its aircraft. Nor, under the agreement returning control to the navy, was it permitted to buy aircraft which could not operate from carriers. DNAD also blamed poor performance on special characteristics imposed by carrier operation. Typically, speed had to be surrendered (and lower speed meant shorter range for the same endurance). He considered deck-landing a relatively small influence compared to the demands for navigability (meaning a back-seater), wing folding and (where applicable) dive bombing and torpedo attack.[93] Not surprisingly, DNAD particularly resented the emphasis on speed as a criterion for comparing his aircraft to their land-based rivals. 'Yet the same people will simultaneously condemn the "inefficiency" of a Force armed with high-speed aircraft for being incapable of Naval air reconnaissance or dive bombing etc, not seeing that the high-speed features preclude the others required.' The surviving copy has a pencilled question mark opposite this remark.

DNAD defended himself with a table showing that in the great majority of truly comparable characteristics British FAA aircraft excelled their contemporaries.[94] He somewhat ruined his argument by saying that if the FAA were master in its own house, it would do better still. If it had formal (statutory) responsibility for shore-based operation, it would know what to specify. If it had any national status, it would get its aircraft in half the time it currently did.

In theory the only available US aircraft were the obsolescent F3F-2 and F2A-1 Buffalo, but with the fall of France eighty-one Grumman F4F-3s were offered. DNAD reported that the F4F, the current US Navy fighter, had been thoroughly inspected and flown in the United States by a very experienced FAA pilot and that it was later seen by a member of the Naval Staff who spent a week on board *Saratoga*. They concluded that 'while it is a good aeroplane of its class, it is not designed to meet the far more stringent seagoing requirements of the FAA (which include wing-folding and navigability) and is inferior for shore-based interceptor duty to current RAF types'. The home-grown Fulmar was better, as it offered first-class navigability and communications as well as long endurance and it was fast enough to attack all contemporary German bombers and shadowers. CinC Home Fleet doubted this: the 230-knot Fulmar could not bring down a 260-knot Ju-88 (a pencil note pointed out that the best level speed of the Ju-88 was 285mph – 240 knots – and that the Fulmar was expected to gain 10 to 15 knots as its engine improved).

After all this self-justification, it must have been surprising that Fifth Sea Lord was informed on 5 July that arrangements had been made to acquire 181 Grumman F4Fs (including the former French ones) from the United States, a portion of which would have folding wings. These aircraft formed the initial force of high-performance single-seat fighters envisaged earlier in 1940 (Air Branch wanted their employment settled as soon as possible).[95] The British soon ordered folding-wing F4F-4s, which they called Martlets.[96] They were adaptable to British carriers because the British had adopted arrester gear (and barriers) beginning with the *Ark Royal* just before the war. By mid-1941, the air groups of British carriers typically included twelve single-seat fighters operating alongside two-seat Fulmars.[97] Meanwhile CinC Home Fleet pointed out that with the fall of Norway the North Sea was no longer tenable for carriers. Operations from Hatston, which was functioning as a temporary carrier substitute, had demonstrated that existing FAA aircraft had grossly inadequate range.[98]

After the Battle of Britain, the RAF was willing to release Hurricane Is. The first to go to sea were RAF aircraft assigned to emergency catapult-equipped merchant ships (CAMs) conceived as a stop-gap solution to the threat of German long-range maritime reconnaissance aircraft (Fw-200 Condors). The Condors were both a direct threat to ships and a larger threat in that they could home U-boats on a convoy which might otherwise evade them; at this time evasion was the main defence of lightly-protected convoys. Thus, at least in British eyes, fighter protection of a convoy was very much an ASW function (only later did it become clear that the Condors provided very little support to U-boats). This reality explains why ASW carriers generally had some fighters on board, even after the war, when submarines were unlikely to fight it out with ASW aircraft on the surface. The fighters are often described as a form of air defence, but they were much more a means of blinding the enemy and thus aborting possible submarine attacks – submarines themselves had and have only a limited ability to find distant surface ships. Conversely, relatively low-performance fighters would suffice for this role because the snooper or shadower needed very long endurance, hence had limited performance.[99]

Experience in the Mediterranean showed that Forbes was right: the Fulmars were too slow.[100] With the Battle of Britain over, Churchill

was willing to release high-performance fighters. In January 1941, responding to the Mediterranean Fleet, he minuted that 'it is absolutely necessary to have a comparatively small number of really fast fighter aircraft on our carriers'. This minute may have released 200 Hurricanes for conversion to carrier operation as Sea Hurricanes (Churchill was unhappy that they were all conversions of Hurricane Is).[101] Almost all had been completed by June 1942. Conversion was relatively simple because there was no attempt to provide folding wings. As neither the initial Martlets nor the Sea Hurricanes could be struck below, they had to be kept on deck, their tail wheels swung outboard on special outriggers. The outriggers in turn made it possible to navalise Spitfires without designing folding wings for them.

It took time for fast fighters to materialise, so when Churchill visited *Indomitable* in September 1941 he was unhappy that her best fighters were reconditioned Hurricane Is; 'I trust it may be arranged that only the finest aeroplanes that can do the work go into all carriers . . . the aircraft carriers should have supreme priority in quality and character of suitable types.' In December 1941 the Defence Committee (Supply) under his chairmanship agreed to give the highest priority to fighters to equip and maintain the armoured carriers (representing initial equipment of 225 fighters plus twenty per month to replace expected wastage). The Chiefs of Staff decided that navalised Spitfires (Seafires) would replace the Sea Hurricanes, with an initial order for 250. The current version had fixed wings, although work would proceed urgently on a folding-wing design.[102]

At this point Admiralty opinion was still divided as to the virtues of single- vs two-seat fighters. Both were being developed, the single-seater as the Blackburn Firebrand and the two-seater as the Fairey Firefly. The Sabre engine planned for the Firebrand was also used by the new RAF Typhoon fighter, but in 1942 the Firebrand had a higher priority and was not being delayed by lack of engines. All Griffon production was earmarked for the Firefly, which was being pushed ahead with high priority.[103]

Unfortunately the Firebrand was unlikely either to materialise very quickly or to be very satisfactory. It was heavy and large and lacked the manoeuvrability needed in a fighter. It was comparable to the Sabre-powered Typhoon, which the RAF acknowledged was inferior to the Spitfire it had been conceived to replace, except possibly as a specialised bomber destroyer. The Firebrand was similarly inferior to the extemporised Seafire. By mid-1942 it was seen more as a possible future fighter-bomber or dive bomber or torpedo bomber. The maximum speed of the prototype was 345mph, 40mph slower than expected and 15mph slower than a Seafire. That was aside from aerodynamic problems which would take many months to cure. The Firefly seemed more satisfactory, but it was too large and heavy to be a pure day fighter. It seemed more likely to be effective as a fast reconnaissance or night fighter and also as a possible dive bomber. As of mid-1942 the first twenty-five production Fireflies were being built by hand and a total of 1100 were on order.[104]

During 1941 the Board of Admiralty reviewed the naval air programme and approved Staff Requirements for a single-seat day fleet defence fighter (Fleet Fighter, FF); a two-seat night fighter suited to day reconnaissance and also for action observation and to escort a strike force (Night Observation-Reconnaissance or NFOR); and a long-range TBR.[105] The basis for the FF was the need for really high performance for fleet defence. The Admiralty accepted that it had to abandon navigational facilities and also considerably reduce endurance. The night fighter requirement seemed increasingly urgent, as radar aids to enemy night shadowing were being developed. It was understood that a night fighter had to be a two-seater. Aircraft already under development matched both requirements: the Seafire was the obvious choice for the FF and the developmental Firefly was the obvious candidate for the NFOR. As an interim measure, Fulmars would be equipped with AI (Air Interception) Mk VI radars (100 would be converted if trials were successful). The dual role seen for the NFOR required that the Firefly have a radar offering both AI and ASV (air-to-surface vessel, i.e. sea search) capabilities.

Within a few months the Japanese were demonstrating that they had first-class naval fighters, so that high performance was needed not only for interceptors defending the fleet but also for strike escorts. In mid-1942 the Admiralty felt compelled to adopt development of the Seafire and Firefly as a short-term policy but to seek completely new aircraft on a longer-term basis.[106] Unfortunately no solution had been found to the problem of mating the high performance of the interceptor with the endurance needed by the escort fighter. The Firebrand had been conceived as a single-seat fighter with the sort of endurance normally provided for two-seaters like the Firefly, but it was a failure as a fighter. For the time being the Firefly remained the preferred night fighter, although the British were interested in matching the US development of a single-seat night fighter. A 1943 attempt to extend the Firefly as a torpedo bomber as well as a fighter failed. However, the Firebrand, having dropped out as a fighter, was being developed as a fast torpedo bomber, its centre section extended to provide enough lift. It was broadly analogous to the single-seat attack bombers, most notably the Skyraider, that the US Navy was then developing.

In February 1943 the Admiralty position on fighters was to adopt the Seafire as the standard British short-range naval fighter and to develop a folding-wing version. The immediate Seafire III replacement was a Griffon-engined version which became the Seafire XV and entered production in 1944. The only available solution to the long-range escort problem was to adopt US fighters.[107] In this way the Admiralty could take maximum advantage of RAF fighter development, which was generally intended to provide maximum performance but short range.

It was now time to develop entirely new fighter designs.[108] By this time it was well understood that an interceptor needed sufficient performance to compete with shore-based enemy fighters, so endurance was cut from the usual 2.25 hours to 1.75 hours at maximum economical cruising speed. To some extent the range problem could be solved by providing extra tankage (not to be filled when the aircraft was used as an interceptor) and drop tanks. Ammunition capacity was also cut. Formal proposals for a next-generation fighter were offered by Fairey, Hawker, Folland, Boulton Paul, Westland and by aircraft designer Youngman (sponsored by Fairey). The project was urgent enough that the navy wanted an aircraft which could be bought 'off the drawing board'. That eliminated all the radical proposals, leaving only Folland and Hawker. Both adapted designs for new RAF fighters (the Hawker design was based on what became the Fury). Folland's was somewhat better and it was preferred by the Chief Naval Representative to the MAP. However, Folland had no production capacity. An attempt to link it to English Electric failed, so the project collapsed. The Hawker design was adopted instead. The naval version had the same wings and Centaurus engine as the RAF interceptor, but with a redesigned fuselage. It entered service as the Sea Fury.

A less conventional design offered promise; there was interest in a fighter (like the US FR-1 Fireball) with a piston cruise engine backed

The competition which produced the Firefly allowed for an alternative single-seat fighter, despite the strong preference of the Naval Air Department for two seats. Blackburn received a small order for its single-seater because it incorporated an innovative flap design. Development was badly delayed and the Firebrand did not offer much advantage over the far nimbler Seafire. Moreover, the RAF enjoyed priority for the Sabre engine for its Typhoon and Tempest. The Firebrand was therefore redesigned with the air-cooled Centaurus engine and re-tasked as a single-seat torpedo bomber ('torpedo fighter'). The Firebrand IV is shown in this role, carrying a torpedo (the production version was Firebrand TF.5). (*The Hook*).

by a jet for take-off, climb and combat. It might also be worth looking at a fighter with an excellent forward view offered by a buried or pusher powerplant. Variable-incidence wings and tricycle landing gear were also under consideration. The Future Building Committee reviewing the aircraft programme thought that at least one unconventional fighter should be developed in prototype form, but that did not happen at the time. Instead, a jet fighter was ordered in 1944 (it became the Sea Attacker). Perhaps to the Royal Navy's surprise, the RAF produced a prototype long-range escort fighter in the form of the de Havilland Hornet, a sort of miniature Mosquito. Its advent must have seemed fortunate, because by 1944 the end of the war and therefore the end of US aircraft supplies, was in sight. The aircraft was navalised as the Sea Hornet.

The great failure of the late-war programme was the night fighter Firefly using a British AI Mk X radar in a wing radome. The British felt compelled to adopt a US radar. They would have preferred the APS-6 which equipped US carrier night fighters, but it was in short supply. Instead they got APS-4, which offered both air-to-air and air-to-surface capability. In the British view, although the US Navy was successfully operating single-seat night fighters, it was far better to have a separate radar operator.

Assault escort carriers and the Royal Navy

Because it spent the entire war badly short of fleet carriers, the Royal Navy used its escort carriers far more heavily than the US Navy, for which ASW was the primary escort carrier mission. For the Royal Navy, the striking 1942 development was the successful use of relatively high-performance Sea Hurricane IIs on board escort carriers. In September 1942 Convoy PQ-18 became the first Russian convoy to have a carrier in close support, in this case *Avenger* with twelve Sea Hurricane IBs and three Swordfish and another six Sea Hurricanes in her hangar with their wings unshipped. The convoy was almost continuously shadowed from 12 September onwards, as the fighters were seldom able to get within range of even the low-performance shadowers (the first was a Bv-138 seaplane) before they escaped into clouds. The main lesson learned was that attempts to deal with the shadowers dissipated fighter resources needed when the enemy mounted a mass attack on the afternoon of 13 September. Radar detected a large group 62nm away and two fighters were flown off to supplement four already airborne to deal with a shadower. These fighters were engaged by a diversionary attack by Ju-88 bombers and He-111 torpedo bombers, expending their ammunition without shooting down any aircraft. The main attack (torpedo bombers) appeared five minutes later, sinking eight merchant ships. Further attacks proved ineffective, but in exchange for damaging one Bv-138, one Sea Hurricane was shot down. In all, eighteen fighter sorties were flown that day, a large number for a small escort carrier.

The next day the convoy husbanded aircraft resources, fighters being held in readiness on deck and shadowers ignored; in any case the convoy was continuously shadowed by U-boats. Apparently it lacked the resources to force them down, although it did fly continuous ASW patrols. This time the Germans concentrated on the carrier. Groups sighted approaching from ahead at low altitude at 12.33 proved to be twenty-two He-111s and a few Ju-88 dive bombers. Sea Hurricanes were flown off and *Avenger*, in the van of the convoy, managed to evade the torpedoes dropped by the He-111s. This attack was followed by shallow dive bombing from clouds at 4000–6000ft by Ju-88s and then by another torpedo attack by twenty-five He-111s, attacking simultaneously from two bearings. They managed to hit one ship in the convoy, which blew up. *Avenger* managed to fly off two fighter sections at 13.00 and three more at 13.40, with a total of sixteen Hurricane sorties between 12.35 and 15.20. Assessed fighter successes were five shot down, three probables, fourteen damaged. There was good evidence that a higher percentage of enemy torpedo bombers failed to return, but it was impossible to distinguish between fighters and AA.

Enemy air attacks continued on the next day between 12.20 and 16.40, but this time bombing was haphazard and ineffective. *Avenger* launched twenty-one fighter sorties, but this time the enemy retired into cloud as soon as he was threatened. The Sea Hurricanes claimed three enemy aircraft damaged and the assessment was that the enemy 'had gained considerable respect for the defence of the convoy'. *Avenger* and the sea escorts left the convoy on 15 September, the last day of the attacks, to join homeward-bound Convoy QP 14.

Once it was clear that an escort carrier operating in rough seas could operate Sea Hurricanes, they could be used to supplement aircraft on board fleet carriers supporting major amphibious operations. The 'Torch' landings in North Africa relied entirely on carrier fighter support, because no Allied air bases were anywhere near the operational area. Support for the 'Torch' landings in November was provided by much of the existing British carrier force, including the armoured fleet carriers *Victorious* and *Formidable* and the elderly *Furious* and *Argus*. They were supplemented by escort carriers: *Biter* and *Dasher* in the Central Task Force and *Avenger* alongside *Argus* in the Eastern Task Force. An additional escort carrier, *Archer*, operated with the US task force. Seafires were deployed on board *Formidable* and *Furious*, while Sea Hurricanes operated successfully from *Biter*, *Dasher* and *Avenger*.

The success of the Sea Hurricane on board escort carriers in 1942 encouraged the Admiralty to place the much higher-performance Seafire on board these ships in 1943: Seafires provided essential air support to the Sicily landings ('Husky') in August 1943, again because they were mounted too far from any Allied air base for land-based support. Sea Hurricanes were scheduled for complete retirement, even from escort carriers, by the end of 1943.

Escort carriers were again used to support the Salerno landing in Italy in September 1943.[109] The British carrier force was divided into Force V (fleet carriers) and Force H (four escort carriers plus *Unicorn*), the latter with the cruiser *Euryalus* as flagship. She proved very successful, inspiring the Royal Navy to use cruiser flagships for escort carrier assault groups. The cruiser was used because the escort carriers themselves had very limited control facilities. She had good fighter-direction facilities and two more R/T sets than any other ships. She sent off fighters and then turned them over to the fighter-control ship *Palomares*, which was closer to the beach. The carriers were closely grouped (a mile apart, so that their aircraft would not interfere with each other) for protection by a circular destroyer screen. Flag conditions on the cruiser were far better than on a carrier, as there was no aircraft noise and no distraction caused by accidents etc. This was an ASW screen, as British destroyers had very limited anti-aircraft firepower. The Royal Navy considered submarines a much more serious threat than did the US Navy. The group tried to arrive about 20nm off the coast an hour before sunrise to provide air cover for the operation from half an hour before sunrise to half an hour after sunset or nautical twilight – the maximum period during which flying was practicable. The force then had to leave the coast. Lack of wind and lack of visibility caused considerable anxiety. Fortunately enemy air opposition over the beaches was limited to hit-and-run raids by fighter-bombers. The British interception patrol never saw enemy aircraft at all. One lesson was that it was impossible to keep up a sustained air effort by the carriers for more than 48 to 72 hours. If no landing strip could be seized immediately, there would have to be two carrier groups operating in rotation.[110] At Salerno, groups of four to six Seafires provided high cover and groups of sixteen aircraft provided medium high cover (sixteen was found to be too many). During the work-up at Gibraltar before the operation, groups of four aircraft from each escort carrier learned to work together as a team, hence the use of sixteen aircraft together. Seafires suffered many deck-landing accidents, typically coming to rest nose-down with their propellers badly damaged. This problem was largely allayed by cropping the propellers by about 4in. More generally, it was clear that landing procedures had not been sufficiently standardised. The accident rate dropped rapidly the longer a squadron operated from a particular carrier, as the pilots and the LSOs became familiar with each other.

The Royal Navy decided to create permanent Assault Escort Carrier Squadrons specifically to support amphibious operations; the first was formed in December 1943 when Rear Admiral (Escort Carriers) hoisted his flag in the cruiser *Royalist*. A second was to be formed around the cruiser *Scylla*. Although in theory escort carriers could shift between their two roles of trade protection and assault support, the British view was that they had to specialise in one or the other.

The British assault escort carriers fought again during the invasion of the south of France in August 1944 ('Dragoon'). They were organised this time as Task Groups 88.1 and 88.2. TG 88.1 consisted

Firefly production and development continued after the war; this is an RAN Firefly Mk IV in 1950. The great problem for the British in 1944–5 was that they did not really need new conventional military aircraft after the war, given the vast numbers they had received under Lend-Lease. Yet none of their aircraft companies was likely to survive a completely dry period until the new generation of jets envisaged to meet the 1957 'year of maximum danger' entered production. As early as 1944, a study conducted by the Ministry of Aircraft Production envisaged discarding all Lend-Lease aircraft as soon as the war was over. This was quite aside from the usual justification, that after the war the United States would charge scarce dollars for spares. Firefly IV was a standard post-war long-range fighter and fighter-bomber, one of the two nacelles on its wing housing a radar and the other additional fuel. The wartime chin radiator was replaced by two wing radiators. Later the Firefly was adapted for ASW, production continuing (even though the final ASW version was unsatisfactory) in order to keep Fairey in business while it developed the Gannet ASW aircraft. (State Library of Victoria)

of the cruiser *Royalist* (flag), the carriers *Attacker*, *Emperor*, *Khedive*, *Searcher* and *Pursuer*, each with one squadron; and the anti-aircraft cruiser *Dehli* plus seven destroyers. TG 88.2 consisted of two US escort carriers, *Tulagi* (flag) and *Kasaan Bay*, the British *Hunter* and *Stalker*, the British cruisers *Caledon* and *Colombo* and six destroyers. There were a total of 240 aircraft: 105 Seafire LIIC and LIIIs, eighty-five Hellcats (sixty with rockets) and fifty Wildcat V and VIs.

There was little air opposition during the day and the carriers withdrew at night. After a time the two task groups had to rotate

(*Khedive* was shifted to TG 88.2). The force was used mainly to provide bombardment spotting and also close air support under the control of the ground commander responsible for close air support. Air losses were limited, in contrast to the heavy if largely accidental losses at Salerno. TG 88.1 had six aircraft ditched due to action damage, eight shot down over enemy territory, three ditched from other causes and twenty-four deck-landing accidents. TG 88.2 lost four aircraft to enemy action.

In 1945 British assault escort carriers were being refitted to support expected landings in South East Asia. *Trouncer* was refitted as flagship for the Assault Carrier Force, with SK and SG radars; she was to be fitted with the British Type 277 heightfinder and with an ADR enlarged, as far as possible, to fleet carrier standards. The US radars were being specially modified so that their output could be displayed on a British Skiatron. Communications and staff were being greatly increased.

The US Navy first used an escort carrier in the amphibious support role in the Aleutians. The famous example of their operation was the desperate but successful fight between 'Taffy Six', a group of escort carriers assigned to support the Leyte Gulf landings (and their heroic escorts) and the Japanese battle fleet in the battle off Samar. By the end of the war the US Navy, like the Royal Navy, was learning to fly high-performance fighters from its small escort carriers.

CHAPTER 5
THE COLLAPSE OF RADAR CONTROL: OKINAWA

I F THE PHILIPPINE Sea was the triumph of CIC-controlled naval fighters, the next major air-sea battle off Okinawa was the opposite. It turned out that the capacity of a CIC was quite limited. At the Philippine Sea it was good enough, because Japanese raids were concentrated. Although the Japanese might launch numerous aircraft, they tried to stay together so that they could overcome anti-aircraft fire once they reached their targets. Everything that each navy had learned before and during the war favoured exactly such concentrated attacks.

No single aircraft could be sure of making an effective hit, but many aircraft attacking together had a good chance of doing so.

The Japanese learned the lesson of the Philippine Sea: conventional air attacks were unlikely to succeed against an increasingly powerful US fleet. A Japanese officer later said that his country had adopted suicide tactics because conventional tactics were inherently suicidal. US analysis showed that, to impose a given level of damage, the Japanese actually lost fewer pilots when they adopted these tactics.[1] A

Kamikaze inflicted far more damage than conventional attackers because, no matter how brave, a pilot facing intense anti-aircraft fire is likely to flinch; his aim suffers. Attackers can turn away. A pilot determined to die steers for the most intense fire. During the Second World War, anti-aircraft fire was most often a deterrent rather than a means of destroying incoming aircraft. At least in theory, the only way to deal with a Kamikaze was to destroy the aircraft before it could get close enough. If it did get too close, its momentum might well carry it into a ship, even with a dead pilot at the controls.

The devastating reality was that a single Japanese aircraft crashing a ship would typically cause serious damage. There was much less need for attackers to bunch together. That was acceptable to the Japanese: few of the their pilots left alive late in 1944 could have flown in co-ordinated formations. Suicide attackers were necessarily dispersed. It is not clear whether the Japanese understood that dispersion would attack the CIC organisation by saturating it. By this time the Japanese were well aware of the nature and limitations of US naval radar. They realised that the two best approaches to US ships were at low altitude and from almost directly overhead.

An unremarked factor was that because they were supplying so much of the air support to the landing force and the troops ashore – particularly fighter support – the fast carriers could not exploit their speed and mobility. They could not force the Japanese into protracted scouting by long-range aircraft which might have been particularly vulnerable to their fighters, however the scouting was followed up. Instead the Japanese knew roughly where the carriers were. Even so, they generally needed more experienced pilots to lead and escort massed Kamikaze groups.

Kamikaze attacks began during the campaign in the Philippines, particularly during the January 1945 landings at Lingayen Gulf. Really massive Kamikaze attacks were first mounted during the April–May 1945 battle for Okinawa. At that time an invasion of Japan itself was expected for November 1945 and it seemed clear that Okinawa was in effect a rehearsal for what the fleet would encounter off Kyushu.

The first suicide attacks had been planned for the October 1944 landings at Leyte Gulf, but only small numbers were carried out. They had largely been frustrated by the sweeps against Formosa earlier that month. These sweeps demonstrated that the best countermeasure to Kamikazes was to destroy them on the ground before they could be used. Hence the massive fighter sweeps conducted during the Okinawa campaign and then against airfields in Japan in preparation for the projected invasion of Kyushu in November 1945 (Operation 'Olympic'). For example, the main role of the British Pacific Fleet carriers during the Okinawa operation was these neutralising sweeps.

It is difficult to say how effective airfield attack was or could have been. Because Kamikaze warfare did not demand a high level of pilot

skill, ultimately what counted was the number of aircraft which were still serviceable. That turned out to be far more than Allied intelligence estimated. No one has been able to estimate the degree of damage that Kamikazes might have inflicted on a fleet invading Japan; after Okinawa the Japanese simply husbanded their aircraft and their fuel, awaiting the invasion.

The anti-Kamikaze attack campaign probably explains why the US Navy revised its carrier air group composition in June 1945, replacing torpedo bombers (TBM Avengers) with dive bombers (SB2C Helldivers) despite the far better reputation of the TBM. Arrangements were made to increase Helldiver production to match the new organisation.

The suddenness of the Kamikaze onslaught and the tight schedule for the invasion of Japan limited what could be done. In April 1945, at Okinawa, the only possibilities were to change fleet tactics and the proportion of fighters in the fleet. To the extent that CAP could not handle the dispersed Kamikazes, there were only two solutions. Either the Kamikazes could be destroyed on the ground ('at source') or the fleet could be given so much more anti-aircraft firepower that it could deal with whatever leaked past the fighters. The latter accounts for the most prominent near-term programme, massive up-gunning, particularly of destroyers (they could exchange torpedo tubes for added 40mm guns, the smallest considered effective against Kamikazes). New close-in fire-control systems were pushed towards production and work proceeded on an automatic 3in/50 gun (the smallest whose shell could carry a proximity fuze).

Even after the war ended, the Kamikaze campaign and possible countermeasures were hardly of merely academic interest. No one expected mass suicide attacks in the future, but the Germans had already introduced guided missiles which were something like Kamikazes: the Hs-293 and FX-1400 (the latter a guided bomb). Like a Kamikaze pilot, an unmanned missile would hardly be deterred by shells bursting around it; it had to be hit and hit hard enough and far enough away to be prevented from hitting a ship. It seemed inevitable that the Soviets would adapt the new German missile technology, which they had captured. We now know that they placed the wartime German weapons in production soon after the end of the war, although Western intelligence apparently did not detect this development. In addition, nuclear bombs could be tossed from a considerable distance to attack a fleet. In either case, even a single attacker could inflict considerable damage. Attackers would probably be dispersed like the Kamikazes, to impose maximum stress on fighter defence.

KAMIKAZE TACTICS AND THE CIC–CAP SYSTEM

Kamikazes often attacked in large numbers, but not in a concentrated mass (at least not when they approached their target area). Instead they broke up to attack singly or in small groups from different directions, each of which required its own section or division of CAP fighters. The Japanese had long intercepted US R/T circuits (which were poorly disciplined), so they were aware that a fast task force used just two channels to control up to twenty fighter divisions. The greater the number of separately-attacking groups, the greater the stress on the entire fighter-control system. To the fast task force command, the enemy showed clever execution and enormous determination. As aircraft approached, they made radical changes of course and altitude, dispersing when intercepted and using cloud cover effectively. They tried to follow US aircraft home from their strikes, they used decoy

The great lesson of Okinawa was that radar control had to be decentralised. Twenty-four destroyers were hurriedly modified as specialist radar pickets, with heightfinding radar. Other unmodified destroyers were assigned to picket duty between the fleet and Japanese air bases. They were assigned CAP sections which they could control. The Japanese realised that they had to destroy the pickets before they could reach the carriers and many destroyers suffered devastating damage. The newly-modified *Chevalier* is shown off Hampton Roads. Earlier converted destroyers retained their after set of torpedo tubes. The new tripod mainmast carries, top to bottom, a YE aircraft homing beacon, an SP heightfinder and a TDY radar jammer. The radome on the foremast is a DBM radar direction-finder, part of a countermeasures system.

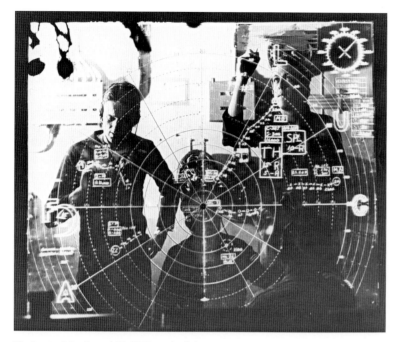

The heart of the Second World War radar fighter-control system was a vertical plot showing the evolving situation. The one shown, on board the carrier *Randolph* in 1956, was little changed from the type used during the war. How quickly the plot could change to reflect an evolving situation depended on how quickly the plotters shown could receive and use reports of radar contacts. The officer in front of the plot evaluates the situation displayed by the two plotters, writing backwards.

aircraft to draw CAPs and they came in high and low. The Kamikaze campaign demonstrated all the limitations of existing equipment, most of which the Japanese seemed to understand. At this time they were developing their own form of fighter control to defend against US bomber attacks on Japan and it seems likely that their experience contributed to Kamikaze tactics.

The vertical plot and fighter-control plots all operated on the tacit assumption that an approaching aircraft would stay roughly on course at a steady speed. Otherwise it was impossible to predict his movements simply by connecting the dots representing a series of radar detections. It was the practice of connecting those dots – dead-reckoning the movement of an incoming aircraft – which made possible the vital leap from a search radar (like SK) to a track-while-scan (search) *system* consisting of the radar plus the plot. Without that ability to predict, targets could not be assigned to CAP fighters and interceptions could not readily be arranged. The alternative would have been to assign a dedicated tracking radar to each target and to employ much faster CAP fighters. By frequently radically changing course, speed and altitude, the Japanese could frustrate the system. At the very least, they could force the fleet to adopt faster-scanning radars which would detect the incoming aircraft more frequently (assuming that more frequent detections could be plotted). That in turn would reduce the probability of detection.[2]

All of this was apart from the subtler problem of plot saturation. The operation of a vertical plot entailed time lags (the ones the British recognised when they told controllers to consider targets and fighters somewhat further along their paths than the plots indicated). There was an inevitable delay between the moment an operator decided that a blip on a scope was a real target and when he reported a range and bearing to a plotter. The plotter imposed a further delay and so did the

CIC evaluator who drew a line through a series of plots to create a basis for decision, contributing to the tactical picture represented by the vertical plot. The supervisor in CIC had to juggle the targets on the plot, deciding which was most threatening, before assigning one to a fighter director at a Skiatron or PPI. The latter showed target and fighter in something closer to real time.

The time lags involved in plotting and using information built up as more and more separate raids appeared. Those in CIC had no way of knowing how accurate their picture was, but at some point the picture would be so far off that it could no longer be an effective basis for directing fighters. For example, at some point it would become impossible to disentangle a mass of turning, twisting aircraft well enough to place CAP fighters in their path. Through 1945 the US Navy desperately sought some means of regaining the advantage. Some ships assigned officers topside who simply reported what they saw in a clock code to assign targets to guns (as in 'target at six o'clock', meaning dead astern).

Cominch (Admiral King) ordered a series of anti-aircraft studies of the problem by the Operations Research Group (later the OEG). In July 1945 it examined how well the fast carriers had done. This study mattered after the war because it gave some idea of how vulnerable a fast carrier task force would be in the face of guided missiles.[3] During the period through 21 March 1945 (i.e. before Okinawa), fourteen ships of the fast carrier task force, all but two of them carriers, were damaged by Kamikazes, but only five of the carriers and both destroyers were force to leave the force for repairs. This damage was done by an estimated forty-three Kamikazes (this figure included aircraft shot down before their intention to make suicide attacks was known; it was assumed that the ratio of suicides to non-suicides was the same as that for known suicides to non-suicides). At the same time all ships operating off the Philippines encountered 364 Kamikazes. Of the Kamikazes which targeted the fast carrier task force, 30 per cent hit and another 9 per cent came close enough to cause damage. The ratio of hits to total numbers was much that experienced overall, but the fast carriers experienced fewer near misses. The analysts noted that it might have been expected that the fast carriers would have done better because they were more heavily armed with anti-aircraft guns, but the carriers themselves, with the least anti-aircraft firepower, were the main enemy targets within the fast carrier task force.

A study of anti-aircraft action off Okinawa pointed out that, having discovered that Kamikaze tactics were successful in the Philippines, the percentage of such attacks was higher there.[4] Both suicide and non-suicide attacks were less successful at Okinawa, pointing to a decreasing level of Japanese training – but also to the greater skill with which US anti-aircraft guns were used, probably as a result of recent experience, particularly in the Philippines. Overall, there were more anti-aircraft actions in April 1945 (off Okinawa) than in any other month of the war. The sheer scale of the Japanese attacks was indicated by the fact that the number of enemy aircraft fired at (by ships) off Okinawa was 49 per cent more than in the Philippines. The percentage of suicide attackers rose from 26 to 39 per cent.

After the war OEG studied CAP performance during the same period.[5] No raid by a single group of aircraft succeeded in putting any aircraft over a carrier group in position to make a suicide dive. However, all raids consisting of two or more separated groups approaching nearly simultaneously managed to place at least some aircraft in position for suicide dives. Overall, the range at which Kamikazes were first detected was considerably less than maximum air search (SK) radar range, even counting the best performance by any ship in the task group. Maximum detection range was attained for bogeys at 10,000–15,000ft; range fell off sharply for higher and lower fliers. Medium raids (three to seven aircraft) were generally detected about 12nm further out than small raids (one or two aircraft) and large raids were detected about 24nm further out.

In OEG's view, the massed Japanese raids mounted at the beginning of the Philippine operation challenged the combat strength of the defending fighters rather than CIC performance. After all-out raids against the landings at Leyte Gulf were repeatedly beaten off by US fighters, the Japanese shifted to planned Kamikaze attacks attempting to avoid CAP rather than overwhelming it; they also gradually developed deceptive methods of approach. That increased the burden on CICs.

OEG divided the period into three phases: I (15–24 October 1944), the final use of mass bombing formations; II (25 October 1944 – 21 February 1945), the introduction of Kamikazes; and III, reduction to small groups and single aircraft and also the partial reversion to bombing attacks (February–May 1945). The Phase I raids consisted of as many as sixty aircraft, including fighter escorts, following a stereotyped approach pattern, closing directly at moderate speed (180 knots) and a constant altitude (average 15,000–20,000ft) with little or no attempt to use clouds or deceptive measures such as window (chaff). Aircraft were typically stacked in altitude (typically with a 5000ft spread). Numerically-inferior CAP teams defeated the attacks because, in OEG's view, they failed to keep formation and fight as a team. Their fighter cover typically deserted the bombers and either scattered or adopted a defensive formation such as a Lufberry circle (to prevent an enemy fighter from getting on any Japanese fighter's tail). The bombers usually turned back when their fighter cover left; aircraft which continued were cut down by the CAP.

Despite being heavily outnumbered, the US fighters exacted a heavily favourable exchange rate. It seems likely that the failure of these raids was due to a combination of very poor training and a sense among Japanese pilots that their aircraft were badly outclassed.

In Phase II, in each penetrating group, typically one or more tried suicide dives. Their tactics were designed to avoid CAP and to reach the targets as quickly as possible. In twelve of sixteen cases, these aircraft flew directly towards the ships from the nearest land mass, 75nm from the task group. All raids were made by Japanese naval aircraft. In successful raids, a single large group would generally split up 80–100nm from the target into a smaller group of three to six aircraft and a larger one of six to fifteen. Both groups would then manoeuvre to separate in altitude, bearing and range, the larger group following the smaller 10 to 20 minutes behind. In most cases both groups would maintain altitude until 60nm from the target ships, then begin a shallow glide. They would fly at relatively high speed (170–210 knots) despite flying into the prevailing wind (they generally flew west to east). One or both would use cloud cover if it was available. Raiders would push over into a steeper glide as they neared the target and once there they would make final dives without hesitation. On interception, groups would break up, individual aircraft avoiding combat and trying to escape either by diving close to the water or flying into cloud. To OEG, such tactics showed considerable skill. Although there were relatively few raids of this successful type, they were effective in terms of damage inflicted. They were the only successful raids.

Phase III raids were numerous because the enemy continued to divide his forces. He also increasingly used deception. During this phase the Japanese learned to trail returning US strikes and also to fly erratic courses, use even thin cloud cover for concealment and sometimes make extensive use of window. The greatest proportion flew at low altitude. Several carriers were severely damaged. Post-war analysis was complicated by the absence of complete CIC information – the Japanese tactics effectively countered CIC capabilities. For example, CIC tracked incoming aircraft by assuming that they maintained steady course and speed. An aircraft flying erratically countered

The advent of the Kamikazes coincided with the development of a new generation of naval fighters, which had not been conceived with the Kamikazes in mind. Grumman had proposed its Bearcat (F8F) in 1943 as a high-performance fighter small enough to operate from escort carriers. This is a new F8F-1B. After the war the Bearcat became the stablemate of the Corsair.

that method. It was clear to OEG that fleet CICs had been saturated.[6]

To understand what had happened, OEG plotted the interval between detection and tallyho. Its analysis of Phase II attacks showed that on average groups of multiple raids got considerably further between detection and tallyho. Three groups were never tallyhoed at all, even though they were detected reasonably early. Increasing urgency and effectiveness in CICs showed in quicker tallyhoes in Phase II than in Phase I.

A fighter director had to place fighters in positions where their pilots could see the incoming enemy and follow through. OEG concluded that CAP had to be placed at about the same altitude as the enemy, which made accurate heightfinding vital. Pilots apparently often failed to scan the sky vertically. The loss in sightings due to a difference in altitude was greater than expected. Given these conclusions, the fleet's heightfinding radars (SM and SP) were tested. At 40nm range with a bogey at 6000ft, the standard deviation of altitude measurements was 1500–2000ft, which was not acceptable.

This Bearcat is shown on board *Valley Forge* during a 27 April 1949 demonstration for the American Ordnance Association (hence the numerous visitors). The carrier shows the large antenna of the new combination search and heightfinding SX radar atop her tripod mast (the search element is to the right).

The Japanese tactic of fleeing as soon as CAP appeared placed the burden of interception on the first fighters to arrive. How well they did depended on the ratio of strength. Even when outnumbered 2 to 1, CAP shot down 61 per cent of enemy aircraft (about 70 per cent when strength was equal). Any further strengthening of CAP yielded little improvement. A fourfold strengthening of the CAP bought only a 50 per cent increase in the proportion of attackers shot down. CAP losses were practically zero, because the Japanese wanted to concentrate on their targets.

Only some of the Japanese aircraft had ASV radar, with a range of about 30nm. If they could escape CAP interception, they could find targets. The others found that much more difficult.

By late 1943 it seemed that new Japanese aircraft might outclass the standard Hellcat and Corsair, so BuAer let a contract to Goodyear to mate the powerful new R-4360 engine to the Corsair it was already building under license. Vought was ordered to work on improving the Corsair using new versions of the existing R-2800 engine. Initially the super-Corsair was conceived as a follow-on Marine Corps land-based fighter and it was ordered in quantity for that purpose. Then, as the island war in the Solomons wound down, the Marines decided that all their future fighters should be carrier-capable. The original land-based version was the F2G-1, the project carrier version being the F2G-2. A large order for the land-based version was cancelled due to the change in Marine air policy and by the end of the war the carrier version had not yet completed development. As a result, only five of each version were completed. This is an F2G-2, with an F4U-4 in the background. (*The Hook*)

FIGHTERS

CAPs were strengthened substantially by changing the proportion of fighters. In 1942 the fighter complement had been increased from eighteen to twenty-seven and then to thirty-six aircraft. In 1944 it was doubled to 72 (two squadrons plus a fighter group leader, one of the squadrons typically designated a fighter-bomber [VBF] unit) at the expense of strike aircraft (typically fifteen dive bombers and fifteen torpedo bombers). That was acceptable because the large fighters could function effectively as fighter-bombers. Indeed, they might be preferable when attacking heavily-defended airfields. This organisation was still standard in April 1945. At that time the standard escort carrier air group consisted of one eighteen-plane fighter squadron and one twelve-plane torpedo bomber squadron. The fighters could glide-bomb for precision and they could fire 5in rockets. For the February 1945 strikes against Japanese airfields prior to the invasion of Okinawa, each of the carriers *Wasp* and *Essex* temporarily had ninety-one fighters aboard (and only fifteen torpedo bombers) on board. In mid-1945 plans called for additional fighters and fewer strike aircraft, with dive bombers (Helldivers) favoured over torpedo bombers. The vast numbers of fighters available to the fast carrier task force at the end of the war were sometimes described as the 'big blue blanket' over the fleet.

In the aftermath of Okinawa, carrier air groups were redesigned on the basis that the projected campaign against Japan would require more bombing.[7] That had already been foreseen, so production of the heavies available carrier bomber, the SB2C Helldiver, had been main-

tained above what was required. In June 1945 BuAer was ordered to increase production of this aircraft from 215 to 300 per month by 1 January 1946; SB2Cs would replace torpedo bombers in all groups.

Carrier air groups would immediately be changed, reducing the fighter complements to buy more bombers:

	OLD	NEW
CVB	97 VF, 48 VSB	73 VF, 64 VSB
CV	73 VF, 15 VSB, 15 VTB	55 VF, 32 VSB, 12 VTB
CVL	24 VF, 9 VTB	36 VF

The torpedo bombers would be discarded. After 1 October 1946 the standard *Essex* class carrier air group would be fifty-five fighters and forty-five dive bombers.

Air groups as described by BuAer on 31 October 1945 reflect the shift back towards attack aircraft:

CVBG:	65 F4U, 4 F4U(P), 4 F4U(N), 64 SB2C[i]
CVG (*Essex* class):	8 groups: 49 F8F, 4 F8FP, 4F8FN, 24 SB2C, 20 TBM
	4 groups: 49 F4U, 4 F4U(P), 4 F4U(N), 24 SB2C, 20 TBM
CVGN (night carriers):	1 F8F(P), 36 F8FN, 18 TBM
CVEG	16 F8F, 2 F8F(P), 12 TBM[ii]
AEW	4 TBM
Marine CVEG	16 F4U, 2 F4U(P), 12 TBM[iii]

i   F6F P/N/F8FN substituted for F4UP until available.
ii Limit VF of one post-war CVEG to get FR.
iii Substitute F6FP for F4UP until latter is available.

BuAer's January 1947 mobilisation plan showed projected wartime groups: the air group aboard a fleet carrier was set at forty-nine F8F-2 interceptors, four F8F-2N night fighters (soon to be proven unacceptable), four F8F-2P photo-reconnaissance aircraft, thirty-six (later thirty-two) AD-2 day attack bombers, four AD-2Q electronic countermeasures (ECM) aircraft and later four AD-2W airborne early warning (AEW) aircraft (F4Us might be substituted for the F8F Bearcats). The parallel group for a *Midway* class large fleet carrier (CVB) was sixty-five F4U-5 plus the same additional night (F4U-5N) and photo (F4U-5P)

During the war BuAer became interested in another way to boost fighter performance: mixed power. This is the first US Navy mixed-power fighter and the only one built in any quantity: the Ryan FR-1 Fireball, which was considered suitable for light and escort carriers.

fighters, but in this case forty-four (later forty) of the larger AM-1 Mauler bombers and, in place of four of them, four AEW aircraft. However, there were alternative all-fighter groups including the new jets: forty jet fighters (at that time FJ-1 or F6U-1 or F2D-1 Banshee) backed by sixty-two (later fifty-two) F8F-2 interceptors and the usual eight special-purpose fighters. Reducing the number of propeller fighters would allow for four AEW aircraft and four ECM aircraft (AD-2Q). Yet another fighter alternative was forty F7F Tigercats plus four AEW aircraft. It shows how much larger the twin-engine F7F was than the usual single-seat fighters. The fighters came back during the Korean War.

In 1945 two new high-performance fighters, the Grumman F8F and the Goodyear F2G, were nearly ready to enter service. They had not been conceived with the Kamikazes in mind, but their increased performance would certainly have helped had the war continued past August 1945 to a hotly-contested invasion of Kyushu and then of Hokkaido. The very high rate of climb of the Bearcat offered considerable advantages. For example, it could be held on deck to complement CAP sections already airborne. It was also considerably smaller than existing fleet fighters, hence could be carried in larger numbers. The F2G, a modified Corsair with a much more powerful R-4360 engine, offered much higher low-altitude speed (hence was favoured post-war by racing pilots). Only the F8F entered production, to become a major post-war US naval fighter.

Existing fighters were modified. New VHF radios offered more channels. A new Mk IV IFF was ready for trials, with Mk V under development (Mk III was considered compromised).

There were also CIC improvements. A new precision PPI offered a maximum range of 50nm. Doctrine requiring the fighter director to follow particular methods of control was abandoned.

RADAR PICKETS

Before Okinawa the fleet had learned to use destroyer radar pickets to detect low-fliers before they reached the carriers and during the protracted battle off Okinawa these ships suffered badly. Typically they were assigned CAP sections both for self-protection and as a way of reducing the threat before it arrived at the carriers and other major ships. Again, it is not clear to what extent the Japanese realised that destroying the pickets would open the carriers to more effective attack, but they certainly concentrated on pickets not too far offshore. For the US Navy, a lesson of the operation was that destroyer pickets were invaluable but also that they had to be better able to direct assigned fighters. Twenty-four new *Gearing* class destroyers were modified with a tripod radar mast in place of their after torpedo tubes. The mast carried a lightweight heightfinding radar (SP), a TDY jammer and an aircraft homing beacon, the latter to ensure that the ship's assigned CAP could find her. Seven smaller destroyer escorts were also converted. They would presumably have been integrated with transport groups, the destroyers working with fast carriers.

Another possibility was to hide the picket when a mass of Kamikazes approached. The Pacific Fleet planned to convert submarines into pickets using their existing, albeit not particularly high-powered, air-search radars and turning their wardrooms into miniature CICs. This work was ongoing at Pearl Harbor when the war ended. Both the destroyer and the submarine pickets had important post-war roles. The pickets had another virtue. They decentralised fleet CAP and air control, absorbing enough attackers to relieve some of the pressure on the carriers and their own fighters and CICs.

Curtiss produced a mixed-power fighter with a more powerful R-2800 engine, the XF15C. It was tested in both the configuration shown and with a T-tail.

Even after BuAer was buying pure jet fighters, interest in mixed power persisted. Convair's 10 July 1945 proposal, probably unsolicited, combined a TG-100 turboprop and a GE I-40 jet engine. Convair claimed that it would make 545mph at 15,000ft, or 567mph with water injection (130 per cent power); maximum rate of climb at sea level would be 8200 (10,550)ft/min. Stall speed would be 90mph and combat radius would be the typically required 300nm. Span would be 43ft, length 41ft 4in and gross weight 15,000lbs.

OPERATIONAL EXPERIMENTS

A special experimental Task Force 69 was formed on 1 July 1945 specifically to find an effective defence. It was backed by a special unit of the Readiness organisation within OpNav. A 16 July 1945 note from CinCus to CinCPac reported anti-Kamikaze development projects undertaken by TF 69:

- Anti-aircraft rockets to be fired by rocket bombardment ships (LSMRs).
- Rapid target indication, acquisition and designation.
- Rapid-scan search radar.
- The 3in machine gun (i.e. the 3in/50 to replace the 40mm, because it could fire proximity-fuzed shells).
- Increased radar range gained using AEW.
- Increased night fighter efficiency by installing searchlights in the fighters.
- Field changes to the SG-1 surface-search radar to provide zenith search.
- Use of guided missiles (but that could not be done immediately).
- IFF in the 5in/38 fire-control system (Mk 37), so a fire-control crew did not have to go through CIC to get permission to fire.
- A self-destruct feature in proximity fuzes.

- Submarines modified as fighter directors.
- Use of G-band IFF with SM, SP and SC search radars.
- Provision of two types of anti-aircraft ammunition, smokeless with bright tracer for day use and flashless with dim tracer or no tracer for night.
- PPIs for radar directors, which could then be used as low-level search radars (switching instantly to fire control).
- MTI (moving target indication) to detect aircraft through clutter.

An early experiment was to place an army air-search radar (SCR-270) on board a landing ship (*LSM 446*) to provide Kamikaze defence en route to the beach and immediately after landing – i.e. to meld existing ships and equipment in new ways. The LSM-borne radar, which used MTI (moving target indication) and pulse-Doppler processing, was intended to help solve a serious amphibious assault problem, targets moving over land. The normal naval radars offshore would find that difficult. The army radar proved effective, although it could not determine altitude and had no PPI. With its A-scope, it could track one or two targets, even over land. It could effectively supplement the usual warning net. Once troops were ashore, the radar could be dismantled and disembarked within 6 to 12 hours, then erected in a similar period ashore (that was not simulated). In tests near Mount Desert Island, Maine, on 13 July 1945, the radar easily detected aircraft approaching over Mount Cadillac (1532ft) when they came over (pilots were flying 20–50ft above the mountains). The radar also easily tracked targets through Window, which the Japanese were using effectively.

Other equipment was less successful. The emergency response to Japanese attacks from nearly directly overhead was zenith-search radar, such as a modified version of the standard surface-search SG using a 'clamshell' antenna. TF 69 found it disappointing, both in its ability to pick up overhead targets with its narrow vertical beam and also in its ability to support CAP. The air-search element of the new SX radar (which combined air search and heightfinding, using two antennas) was also tested. It was tested on an SP pedestal, meaning that it could be tilted up to detect higher flying aircraft. It did not work. These failures pointed to airborne radar (see below) as the only viable solution to detecting and tracking high-altitude aircraft.

TF 69 survived the end of the war to become the Operational Development Force (OpDevFor) and then the Operational Test and Evaluation Force (OpTevFor) charged with developing tactics and evaluating weapons. It made important contributions to later US Navy development, some of them described in later chapters.

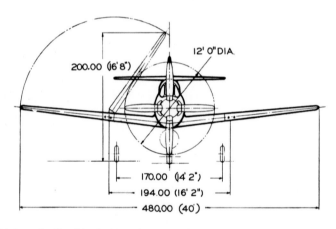

MODEL 17A

NORMAL GROSS WEIGHT 10,253 LBS
WING AREA (TOTAL THEORETICAL INCLUDING
AILERONS): 250 FT.²
ASPECT RATIO: 6.4
INCIDENCE: 1° AT ROOT; -1° AT TIP
DIHEDRAL: 6°
SWEEPBACK: 5° 33' 25"
WING AIRFOIL SECTION: ROOT 66,2-415 TIP 66,2-413
HORIZONTAL TAIL SURFACE AREA (TOTAL): 50 FT.²
ELEVATOR AREA (AFT OF HINGE): 17.22 FT.²
VERTICAL TAIL SURFACE AREA (TOTAL): 24.8 FT.²
RUDDER AREA (AFT OF HINGE): 9.53 FT.²
AILERON AREA (EACH SIDE AFT OF HINGE): 8.16 FT.²

ENGINE:
ONE GENERAL ELECTRIC TG-100 GAS TURBINE
WITH EXTENSION SHAFT, RATED AT 2430 STATIC
EQUIVALENT SHAFT HORSE POWER AT SEA LEVEL

FUEL CAPACITY: 450 GALS. TOTAL
(INTERNAL 250 GALS.
EXTERNAL 200 GALS.)

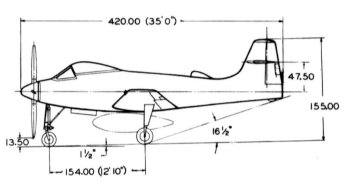

McDonnell offered both this turboprop Model 17A and a mixed-power Model 18J. This drawing of Model 17A was dated 2 September 1944. The engine was General Electric's TG-100 buried in the fuselage abaft the pilot, producing power both via its propeller and via its jet pipe emerging under the vertical tail (the air intake visible just forward of the tail seems to have been intended as supplemental, the primary engine air supply coming through the nose, in ducts on either side of the propeller spinner). McDonnell claimed that its aircraft would reach 505mph with fuel injection (in the tail pipe, i.e., afterburning) at military rating and 485mph without, based on a take-off rating of 2140hp and a military rating of about 2800hp. Rate of climb at sea level would be about 4900ft/min. Stall speed would be 82mph. Span was 40ft and length 35ft and gross weight was 10,253lbs.

AIRBORNE EARLY WARNING[8]

At the time of Okinawa the US Navy was already sponsoring a programme for an AEW radar which would provide data directly to a carrier or another major ship. This type of radar had been conceived in 1942 as a way of extending a ship's horizon, under the project name Cadillac, supposedly for the highest mountain in Maine, which was used for early radar relay experiments. Given the cost of the programme, the name might also be associated with what was then the

most expensive type of US car. Cadillac began with a spring 1942 (shortly before Midway) conversation between Dr Vannevar Bush, who headed the wartime US National Defense Research Council (NDRC), responsible for scientific research outside the military and CNO Admiral E J King. King wanted some means of using radar beyond the horizon. Bush told King's co-ordinator of research and development that a ship's radar range could be increased four-fold by having several patrol bombers equipped with British air-to-surface vessel radar linked to the command ship.[9] As many as three alternative methods were considered, the third (which was selected) being a means of radar relay, so that an officer on board the ship would see the aircraft's radar picture directly. A formal project was established on 25 June 1942, assigned to the Rad Lab.[10] To the Rad Lab, this meant providing an airborne radar (capable of detecting surface ships) with a radar relay which would drive a display on board a surface ship. The new part of the project was the radar relay, which proved rather difficult to develop. At first it worked effectively, supporting the Rad Lab's claim that the project was entirely feasible. However, by the spring of 1943 it was clear that installation in an aircraft and interference from other aircraft equipment were serious problems. A planned demonstration

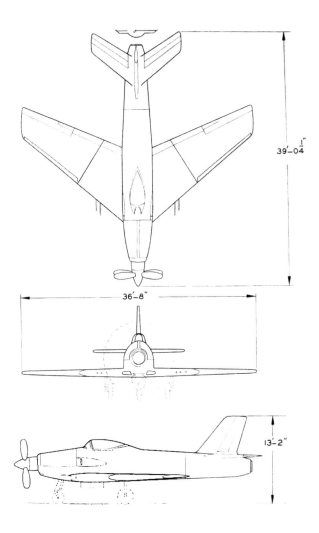

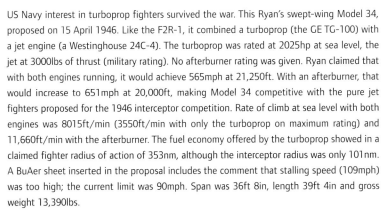

US Navy interest in turboprop fighters survived the war. This Ryan's swept-wing Model 34, proposed on 15 April 1946. Like the F2R-1, it combined a turboprop (the GE TG-100) with a jet engine (a Westinghouse 24C-4). The turboprop was rated at 2025hp at sea level, the jet at 3000lbs of thrust (military rating). No afterburner rating was given. Ryan claimed that with both engines running, it would achieve 565mph at 21,250ft. With an afterburner, that would increase to 651mph at 20,000ft, making Model 34 competitive with the pure jet fighters proposed for the 1946 interceptor competition. Rate of climb at sea level with both engines was 8015ft/min (3550ft/min with only the turboprop on maximum rating) and 11,660ft/min with the afterburner. The fuel economy offered by the turboprop showed in a claimed fighter radius of action of 353nm, although the interceptor radius was only 101nm. A BuAer sheet inserted in the proposal includes the comment that stalling speed (109mph) was too high; the current limit was 90mph. Span was 36ft 8in, length 39ft 4in and gross weight 13,390lbs.

During the war both Boeing and Curtiss offered multiple unsolicited proposals for conventionally-powered fighters. This is Curtiss' April 1943 Proposal 3 for a fighter powered by a Wasp Major engine. Adoption of this huge engine resulted in an interesting design approach. The engine was so long that it pushed the pilot far back into the fuselage, ruining his vision. Curtiss' approach was to place the pilot over the engine, an arrangement it called a 'cab over engine'). Curtiss estimated that the engine would produce 3360hp at take-off (BuAer considered 3000hp more realistic). On that basis, at a gross weight of 16,600lbs, Curtiss estimated that maximum speed at 27,000ft would be 440mph (BuAer thought 423mph more realistic). Stall speed without power would be 80mph. With a two-speed gear ratio, speed at 27,000ft might be as much as 445mph (428mph, according to BuAer). Span would have been 49ft 6in and length 39ft 7in. Curtiss had already offered a more conventional design, with the pilot abaft the engine, in January 1943. Dimensions would have been the same. Both designs showed contraprops to absorb the huge power of the R-4360 engine with a two-stage supercharger. This proposal seems to have been evaluated against the Goodyear F2G version of the Corsair, which had the same engine. The surviving copy of the proposal bears a handwritten note listing other aircraft with the 3000hp engine: the Boeing F8B, the COE (not described), the Vought V-322 (not described) and the F2G (which also had an alternative 3600hp engine). The previous year Curtiss had proposed a navalised version of its army Ascender (XP-55) fighter, which had twin booms and a pusher engine. Boeing proposed a series of conventional fighters and then the huge F8B, which was more a single-seat attack bomber than a fighter. There is some indication that BuAer bought the prototype F8B under external pressure.

for Cominch had to be deferred. For example, electrical noise could ruin synchronisation between a PPI in an aircraft and the corresponding shipboard PPI.

However, Cominch (Admiral King's office), CNO, BuAer, BuShips and DCNO (Air) discussed the feasibility of the project in January 1944. In a 14 March 1944 letter to NDRC BuAer formalised the requirement.[11] It called for an airborne early warning radar specifically to extend warning range against aircraft, particularly low-fliers, to meet an urgent requirement revealed by recent task force operations. The radar aircraft would operate at 5000–25,000ft near the task force, using a relay link 'of the type already developed to a shipboard repeat

indicator tied to the CIC'. NDRC was asked to produce about forty complete systems as soon as possible; BuAer seems not to have had any idea of how complicated that would be. Admiral King soon approved

The US Navy's first pure-jet fighter, the McDonnell FD-1 Phantom (later redesignated FH-1) was contemporary with the mixed-power aircraft. Here it takes off from a *Midway* class carrier, 10 May 1948.

the project – for the relay. It must have gained considerable importance once the Japanese began to exploit the limitations of shipboard air-search radars with Kamikaze attacks in October 1944. A 23 October 1944 conference among Cominch, CNO, BuAer and BuShips decided on crash production of forty systems and conversion of thirty-one TBMs after successful engineering tests at Bedford Field. By December 1944 it had been named Cadillac and in a 19 December note to the Rad Lab industrial manager BuAer called it the most urgent programme it had.

BuAer issued formal specifications on 8 November, including a requirement that the radar detect single low-flying aircraft over an area of not less than 15,000 square miles (equating to a range of about 68nm) and not less than 40,000 square miles for groups of six or more (about 114nm), but the corresponding reliable ranges were given as 65nm and 125nm. Single surface ships should be detected and tracked at 200nm. To get those ranges took enormous power. APS-20A would

operate in S-band (2880 MHz) at 1 MW with two-microsecond pulses (300 pulses/second). Very high power limited radar tube life and ensured reliability problems at the outset, but there was no other way to obtain useful ranges. According to the post-war NDRC radar history, the total weight of the airborne part of the system was about 3300lbs.

Cadillac employed three interlocked elements: the APS-20 radar in an aircraft (with its relay), the shipboard receiver and an integrated IFF system. Rad Lab trials involved two experimental airborne devices and three alternative shipboard sets. Navy trials at Brigantine, New Jersey, began in January 1945. Of the possible carrier aircraft to carry the big radar, the only choice seems to have been the Avenger (TBM-3) torpedo bomber, which had a large bomb bay and substantial ground clearance.[12] A radar operator position replaced the former turret gun structures and the turret and rear canopy were replaced by a fairing covering the radar modulator. Twin auxiliary fins were added to maintain stability despite the additional side area of the radome. The catapult hook had to be relocated. The Avenger was adapted by the Naval Air Modification Unit (NAMU) at Johnstown, Pennsylvania. The first aircraft was delivered to NAMU on 9 May. Aerodynamic tests began on 25 and 26 July and on 4 August the two prototypes were delivered to Bedford Field at Bedford, Massachusetts for Rad Lab tests. A project order to convert twenty-seven aircraft as a crash programme was issued on 7 November 1944 (the first specifications were dated 3 August). The first were to be ready for installation of electronics by 1 January 1945. A 15 January 1945 memo from CNO emphasised that the programme had the highest priority: 'the introduction of this material to the Fleet at the earliest possible moment is a matter of urgent operational requirement'. At this point the initial requirement was set at thirty-four aircraft, including three pre-production. Of the production aircraft, three would be used for tactical evaluation, operational training, etc, the other twenty-eight being formed into four

In 1943, about when the Bearcat was being proposed, the Royal Navy formulated a comprehensive aircraft-development programme. Given the limitations of the British aircraft industry, it had to seek fighters acceptable to the RAF. The Hawker Sea Fury was closely related to Hawker fighters then being developed for the RAF. It became the standard postwar Royal Navy fighter and it was also the initial carrier fighter used by the RAN and RCN. These Sea Furies are shown above *Sydney* about 1949.

units of seven planes. Three pre-production and forty production shipboard units were to be produced, beginning with three in March, two in April, then four per month, for installation on board CV, CVB and BB flagships, shore bases and schools. The four carrier units would presumably go on board the four Task Group flagships of the fast carrier task force.

The first navy tests were conducted at the CIC Group Training Center at Brigantine, New Jersey, between February and April 1945, the aircraft flying from Atlantic City. This was when the ship-centred form of the display was chosen as standard (the alternative was to centre the display on the aircraft). An aircraft flying at 5000ft detected ships 175nm away. One at 10,000ft detected low-flying aircraft at 55nm and high fliers out to 71nm. Even though the radar beam was narrow and the antenna could be tilted to keep it off the sea, at long range it hit the water and aircraft echoes were swamped by sea returns (a permanent problem for AEW over water). The initial Rad Lab report stated that only in 40 to 60 per cent of flights did the radar achieve ranges greater than 40–45nm, but even that was a lot better than what a surface radar could do.[13]

Originally the system was to have been tested on board *Saratoga*, but she was not available, so the smaller *Ranger* was chosen. Trials began on 10 May 1945, including one- and two-plane formations attacking the ship at low altitude, like Kamikazes. Fighter directors in CIC were able to use the relayed radar data to arrange interceptions well beyond the range of the ship's own radar. The display in CIC was a new specialised remote PPI. In addition to proving the value of the radar, the trials showed that it and the associated electronics could

The Royal Navy was able to take advantage of RAF development of the long-range Hornet fighter. A side benefit was that tests with the larger Mosquito, to see whether a twin-engine aircraft was compatible with carriers, showed that it was, opening the possibility of operating Mosquitoes from carriers (initially for long-range reconnaissance). This Sea Hornet F20 of 806 NAS is shown flying over Tronoto Island in 1948. The porthole is for a reconnaissance camera. (*The Hook*)

withstand the shocks of repeated carrier landings and take-offs. A key point was that airborne early warning radar aircraft would not introduce any new problems into carrier operations. The ship had a special YQ (Black Maria) beacon which responded to the IFF interrogator on board the aircraft to indicate that the ship had the necessary receiving equipment. The system employed both a special receiver and a special voice radio. In effect the airborne radar was another one of the ship's own radars, except that it was several thousand feet in the air. Its operator had much the same functions as a shipboard operator, but in this case the remote radar display (in the CIC) was connected not by a wire but by a radio link.

Some time early in 1945 the idea of a 'flying CIC' integrating the radar with operators and evaluators was proposed; it was later designated Cadillac II. Cadillac II was later described as a supplement to destroyer pickets.[14] The chosen aircraft was the army's B-17G bomber, using the same APS-20 radar as the modified TBM. Quite aside from its protection, the converted bomber overcame chronic problems with the data link used by the TBM. Data were fuzzy and not entirely reliable and radar transmission entailed a security problem: the stream of radar data might reveal the position of the aircraft to an enemy intercepting it.

At the end of the war some TBMs had been converted but no dedicated squadron or detachment had been formed. Plans called for equipping four fleet carriers to operate Cadillac I, including the radar relay receiver. The first was *Bunker Hill* (tested in October 1945), followed by *Hornet* and *Shangri-La*. Ideally AEW radar data would have been provided to other types of ship. Unfortunately the YQ beacon was too heavy (3000lbs) to fit on board radar picket destroyers, even though, according to a January 1945 Ship Characteristics Board bulletin, 'AEW is presently recognised as the only satisfactory long range search radar and it [has] possible future application to the guidance and/or detection of guided missiles . . .' However, YQ and the rest of the AEW outfit were fitted to amphibious flagships, which functioned as fighter-control ships near a beach. The first was *Adirondack*, approved in 1946.

At the end of the war the Pacific Fleet sponsored a series of reports on materiel lessons learned. The one on radar pressed for continued work on AEW and the airborne CIC, but found overland performance

inadequate (a continuing problem well into the future); range over land should be more than 100nm. A statement that 'the remote control and television aspects of AEW are of very dubious value' suggests that the Pacific Fleet much favoured combining all aspects of AEW in a single flying CIC package. The report also saw no future for AEW unless sea returns could be eliminated.

A squadron of sixteen Cadillac II aircraft (VPB-101) was formed on 2 July 1945.[15] The aircraft were designated PB-1W (P for patrol, B for Boeing, W for Airborne Early Warning). The formal squadron designation suggests that it might have been operational in time for a November 1945 invasion of Kyushu (aircraft were delivered much later, but that was after wartime priorities had lapsed). The first PB-1Ws had at least some defensive guns (upper deck turret and ball turret, but not nose turret) left over from their time as B-17s, although they were omitted after the war to reduce operating cost and to simplify movement within the aircraft. An APS-53 radar was installed under the nose, where a B-17G had a turret.

The airborne CIC concept had already been tried by the RAF in more primitive form, as a counter to German bombers launching V-1 missiles early in 1945. An ASV radar was installed on board a Wellington bomber. The system worked, but by the time it was tried the Germans had already abandoned the air-launched V-1 campaign.[16] British experiments continued immediately after the war using a Liberator bomber carrying a bombing radar.

Both the remote radar and the airborne CIC survived into the postwar world. Only a few TBMs were converted as TBM-3Ws. Instead of further conversions, AEW versions of the post-war Skyraider attack bomber were produced as AD-3W, -4W and -5W (W indicated warning). They served on board carriers until carrier-borne CICs were produced in the late 1950s, beginning with the Grumman WF-2 described in a later chapter. In addition, AD-4Ws were transferred to the Royal Navy under the post-war Mutual Defense Assistance Program (MDAP). In contrast to the US Navy, the British used their radar operator positions for fighter control. All of these aircraft used versions of the APS-20A radar, its peak power increasing over time.

The PB-1W airborne CIC was clearly experimental, but the navy sought a long-range aircraft of this type post-war, planning to fly it out to operate with task forces. It chose the Lockheed Constellation airliner, initially designated PO-1W (O for Lockheed, soon replaced by V when the separate name Vega was dropped). The WV series served through the 1960s. Eventually these aircraft were best known for their contribution to North American air defence, but they had an important fleet role and they are described in a later chapter.

The APS-20 radar itself turned out to be a useful means of detecting small objects such as snorkels and as such it became an important post-war ASW sensor. Many aircraft, such as the P2V, were equipped with it not as a means of AEW but primarily for ASW; it is not clear to what extent they also had AEW (not CIC) capability.

EVALUATION, 1945

In 1945, then, it seemed that fighter defence had succeeded brilliantly against conventional attacks but had been saturated by what amounted to missile attacks. Looking back immediately after the war, the Pacific Fleet listed important gaps in the wartime systems. They could not reliably detect aircraft beyond 100nm and they could not detect aircraft flying below the horizon or aircraft at high altitudes. The beams of the big air-search sets all showed gaps (nulls) in their areas of coverage. Although the nulls made it possible to estimate target altitude, they were also openings for attackers. Aircraft could not be detected reliably near land or in heavy cloud (which radar would detect as objects) or within clouds of 'Window' (aluminium foil or 'chaff').

CICs were slow and information display was complicated and inadequate, making it difficult for a supervisor to grasp the full situation either rapidly or correctly. He could handle only a few raids at a time. Communication both within ships and between ships seemed weak. Airborne interception equipment was considered inadequate. The existing IFF system failed to distinguish positively between friend and foe; it also could not distinguish between different 'friendlies'.

The only prospect for immediate improvement was to use pickets (see the discussion of airborne pickets below). However, OpNav looked to a future solution using a new generation of longer-range radars. In October 1945 the stated future requirement was for a shipboard radar which could detect both aircraft and guided missiles (i.e. much smaller objects) at 300nm and up to an altitude of 50 miles (300,000ft). The future airborne early warning radar should offer 100nm range and other airborne radars should suffice to guide a fighter against a target 20nm away. Radar should be able to determine altitude of a target up to 150nm away with an error of no more than 40–60 minutes of arc (i.e. at that range, an error of 1.7–2.6nm vertically, 10,000 to 15,000ft). Aircraft should be detectable despite land masses, weather or 'Window'.

Radar information should be presented automatically, instantaneously and in such a way that an observer would instantly form a coherent usable picture of the situation. IFF should positively identify particular 'friendlies'.

A British analysis of US Kamikaze reports reached much the same conclusions.[17] It emphasised the success the Japanese achieved by

When the Kamikazes struck, the US Navy was already developing an AEW radar under the Cadillac programme. However, the advent of Kamikazes made Cadillac urgent, as it seemed that only an airborne radar could provide effective distant warning of low-flying attackers. This TBM-3W was carrier-based. It transmitted its radar picture down to a carrier, the airborne data contributing to the overall plot and helping in fighter control. The big radome housed an APS-20 radar, which for many years was the standard AEW set. The difference between this radar and the air-to-air radars on fighters is suggested by the difference in power: 1MW vs the 40kW of an APS-6, a factor of 25. The XA tail code indicates the experimental squadron to which the aircraft was assigned.

breaking up their raids into a large number of small units and also of using land cover. The small number of attackers then had to be identified among a large number of friendly aircraft, both defending fighters and strikes. By this time the British were looking ahead to a long-term post-war programme intended to bring dividends in ten to fifteen years (they had not yet adopted the formal 'year of maximum danger' of 1957, but were clearly moving in that direction). This view was expressed at the time by the Director of Radio Equipment (DRE), writing immediately after the war (27 October 1945). He was responsible for radars and associated systems.

For DRE, the situation was already grim, because the new radars under test (Types 960 and 980/981 for long-range detection and heightfinding) would completely swamp an existing AIO with their mass of information. A new display system was already envisaged. He pointed out that so far Kamikazes had not attacked at night and to only a limited extent at dusk, so that the shortcomings of the current blind gunnery (target indication, a short-range system) had not yet been demonstrated. If the war continued and the Kamikazes used effective ASV radar, that would change dramatically. The Royal Navy was about to introduce blind-fire control for both long- and short-range anti-aircraft weapons, which would rely on the target indication system for target designation.

The faster the aircraft, the worse the impact on the CIC–CAP system. A British summary of US data (August 1945) indicated that increasing the speed of the Kamikaze about doubled its chance of success. Fleet radars were relatively ineffective near land, particularly near mountains. Army aircraft protecting the fleet near land shot down only about 35 per cent of Kamikazes, compared to 60 per cent for CAP in the open sea. This lesson was relearned expensively in the Falklands nearly four decades later. To a considerable extent these observations laid out the path the US and Royal Navies would follow over the next two decades.

THE CIC PROBLEM

To understand what they had to do, both the US Navy and the Royal Navy badly needed some way of measuring the capacity of their control systems. Both conducted depressing experiments with existing plots to estimate the point at which they would saturate. Tests on board the carrier *Illustrious* showed that a conventional vertical plot could handle no more than twelve raids per hour. At a 1949 CIC conference, a British naval officer credited each intercept officer with the ability to control four interceptions, rather than the two or three assumed in wartime. With twelve tracks the vertical plot performed poorly and with twenty 'the whole thing is practically useless'. The problem was time lags: the delay between a reporter at a radar set beginning to make his report and the filtered plot appearing on the front of the plot written in by the air plot officer was about 20 seconds. A 360-knot aircraft would move 2nm in that 20 seconds, but the vertical plot would only show where it had been. Accuracy was lost. With twelve targets, errors of 4–5nm were common and some tracks were omitted altogether. Worse, those running the plot were unaware of saturation.

Later US experiments showed that with ten targets on a PPI, eight were plotted satisfactorily and the median time to detect a new target was two minutes. With sixteen on the PPI, only twelve were plotted satisfactorily. With fourteen targets, median detection time was three minutes; with twenty targets, it was more than five minutes. The CIC evaluator chose the most threatening raids. In the experiment the criterion was how soon they would arrive within 25nm of the ship. With thirteen raids, the evaluator was 70 per cent correct. That fell to 55 per cent with eighteen raids and to 35 per cent with twenty-two. NRL concluded that a CIC tracker/plotter team could handle four or five targets per PPI/plotter, so a two-PPI system should be able to handle eight to ten targets; a three-PPI system tested at NRL handled nearly fifteen.[18]

The situation would worsen as jets entered service, because the problem was essentially one of time – of how long it took a plotted tactical picture to lose validity. The faster the incoming aircraft, the greater the impact of plotting errors. For example, if the wartime Royal Navy could envisage a one-mile error in handling aircraft flying at 200–250 knots, then doubling speed (i.e. jets) would double the error. Errors would be acceptable as long as pilots were still able to find assigned targets and manoeuvre into firing positions. At some point that would no longer be possible. At high speeds, moreover, tight manoeuvres would become impossible because they would impose unacceptable G-loads on pilots (not to mention airframes).

Both navies began work on solutions, in effect, to the disastrous problems demonstrated at Okinawa. By 1949 they were exchanging ideas. British ideas as to how to collate information and how to direct fighters were more advanced than US ideas. Although the British were also more advanced in radar design and development, the US Navy was far better placed to put its own advanced concepts into production and to deploy them on board ships.

Broadcast control

For the moment, the British considered abandoning close control altogether and reverting to the 'informative method' they had used briefly in 1940. This time it was called broadcast control. Late in the war the Germans had felt compelled to abandon their own version of close control (without filter rooms) in favour of simply broadcasting the

rough positions of the bombers, particularly when they were over cities. In theory a fighter pilot who knew where the bombers were could navigate himself into position to attack them.

A British lecture on future fighter policy at the US CIC Conference (June–July 1949) gives some idea of thinking at that time. The three main problems were plot saturation, an inability to distinguish tracks; control saturation, an inability to decide which targets to assign; and interceptor saturation. Control saturation seemed to have been overlooked. The British considered it essential to concentrate air control in a single ship rather than to decentralise by sectors – which could, after all, saturate. However, it would be possible to decentralise aircraft direction among as many ships as possible.

Ultimately any system had to compute an intercept, either on board a ship (close control) or on board the aircraft (broadcast). The Royal Navy was resisting broadcast control because it required a computer on board every aircraft rather than at every intercept position in the AIO. The airborne computer could, moreover, break down where it could not be serviced. At this time the British assumed that a two-man crew was needed for the necessary navigation, a perception which helps to explain the demand for two-seat fighters.

The Royal Navy still assumed that fighters would attack from the bomber's tail. However, they would approach the bomber from dead ahead, turning in to make their passes while the bomber flew about 20nm closer to its target. After that the fighter would have to catch up with the bomber; that might take another 2.75nm. Appreciation time (time to determine to initiate interception, including evaluation of the tactical situation) also had to be taken into account (four minutes). It could be assumed that the fighter would be orbiting directly over the fleet. Even so, it had to fly to the right altitude and accelerate to full speed. The Royal Navy saw the future threat as a bomber armed with an air-to-surface missile, at this time credited with 30nm range from 50,000ft or 20nm from 35,000ft (10nm from sea level). All of this meant that a bomber at sea level had to be tracked by an intercept radar (90 per cent probability of paint by the radar) 52nm out. That increased to 70nm for a bomber at 45,000ft and to 82nm for a bomber at 55,000ft. The intercept radar would be cued by a search radar, as otherwise its narrow beam would never find a target. To put the interception (fighter control) radar on target, the search radar had to find the target at 97nm at sea level, 100nm at 20,000ft and 135nm at 50,000ft. A 6 seconds data rate (radar scanning at 10rpm) was assumed. If the enemy used a gravity bomb rather than a guided missile, the intercept range could be reduced about 10nm and the warning range about 15nm.

How manoeuvrable the fighter was also affected requirements. That depended on wing loading. Doubling wing loading from 20lbs/ft^2 to 40lbs/ft^2 would push the range out about 10nm at 50,000ft, but very little at sea level. Reducing the catch-up distance to 1.75nm (which many considered reasonable) would reduce interception range by about 10nm and warning range by about 15nm. On the other hand, a faster bomber (Mach 0.85 vs Mach 0.8) would push intercept range out by about 30nm at sea level and 25nm at 55,000ft; warning range would increase by about 70nm at sea level and about 60nm at 55,000ft.

These figures justified the current Royal Navy programme, which amounted to the automated (if analog) CDS combat system supported by the big Type 984 radar and by long-range AI radar on board fighters. In the navy's view, the fighter would carry the high-data rate high-precision radar to where it was needed, where the final turn by

The step beyond carrier-based early warning was an aircraft which could combine the new radar with an airborne CIC. Early experiments with this technique (Cadillac II) employed converted B-17 bombers. Tests included placing the big APS-20 radome above rather than below the fuselage.

the fighter began. No shipboard radar could be precise enough.

Broadcast control seemed attractive because it eliminated the fighter controllers. However, data transmission was much slower than the radar data rate. Also, the relative positions of two aircraft, which was all that close control required, could be simply and accurately derived from radar using a Skiatron or PPI. Broadcast control required that the sum of two positions, in absolute terms, be transmitted. Existing British naval aircraft lacked the necessary navigational system and none was expected in the near future. Computation was far easier in an air-conditioned space on board a ship than on board a fighter. Also, broadcast would become more complex as fighters were given data on nearby targets. In a mass raid, controllers would want to direct fighters against either the centre or the perimeter of the raid. The British officer added that manpower was a serious problem; the AIO in the new carrier *Ark Royal*, then under construction, would require sixty officers and ratings.

A US officer challenged British rejection of forward-hemisphere attacks, but all the available figures were depressing. A fighter needed a minimum of 2000 yds to break away after firing. He assumed a 500-knot bomber and a 550-knot fighter capable of 2G turns (radius about two miles). Assessment time might be 10 seconds and decision time (for the fighter pilot) 20 seconds. He further assumed that control would place two-thirds of fighters within 3000 yds of where it thought they were. The best current US AI radar was APS-21, with a range of 3.5nm for a full scan and up to 8nm for a more restricted scan. Whether that was good enough depended on how accurately the fighter had been vectored. With a control accuracy of about 500 yds and a 10-second delay, the fighter needed a 9.5nm range radar. For something worse (3000 yds, 20-second delay) that would grow to about 15nm. To use a 1nm AI radar with 1500 yds vector error delay time would have to be cut to about 3.5 seconds.

The British broadcast control concept intrigued the US Navy, so OEG was assigned to assess it.[19] OEG estimated that in the face of a mass attack, when there were enough interceptors, broadcast control could handle about twice as many targets. The alternative automatic close control system could not be evaluated because the necessary equipment did not yet exist. OEG estimated that close control could be implemented before the desired automatic close control. In the one-vs-one case, broadcast control was 90 to 98 per cent as effective as close control – given sufficient data, a pilot could solve the interception problem very nearly as well as a fighter-direction officer. The RAF had adopted broadcast control as a way of dealing with high-density stream attacks which would saturate any close-control system. OEG did not say as much, but the Germans had adopted what amounted to broadcast control during the Second World War because their own close-control system (one director working with a tracking radar and a fighter-tracking radar) could not possibly handle mass raids. The US and British wartime systems had been able to deal with massed aircraft, up to a point, because their CICs and AIOs could track multiple targets before assigning them to fighter controllers. By 1949, when it studied broadcast control, OEG had already analysed the breakdown of the CIC system at Okinawa and it had warned that future fast bombers would worsen the situation. It had not yet carried studies of actual fleet exercises in the early 1950s, which would show just how bad the situation already was.

The key fact, which OEG analysis confirmed, was the British estimate that a close controller could handle two interceptions at a time, whereas he could broadcast information allowing him to handle at least four. Against a stream attack, interceptors would be vectored to attack points along the stream. Once there, they would find their own targets.[20] What broadcast could *not* do was solve saturation in the fighter-control picture.

Broadcast control required that fighters be able to navigate to the broadcast position. It had to know its position and it had to be able to carry out simple navigational calculations. The RAF was generally arguing at this time that the navigational part of the problem demanded a second crewman. OEG cited some simple solutions. A simple civilian navigational device (DME, Distance Measuring Equipment) already existed in prototype form. A dead-reckoning navigator was expected to be available within about six months.

Given DME and the navigational computer, OEG agreed with the RAF that broadcast control required a two-seat interceptor. Probably the key reason was that the fighter crew had to keep track of its heading relative to the carrier. BuAer solved that problem by adopting a different type of navigational beacon: TACAN (Tactical Air Navigation). Unlike DME, TACAN provided a pilot with his position relative to the carrier. Like DME, it used a beacon communicating with an airborne transponder. The shipboard element (the first was URN-3) was a transmitter-receiver. It received distance-measuring interrogating pulses from the aircraft, transmitting its replies. It also continuously transmitted bearing information signals, a set of parasitic reflectors rotating continuously about a centrally fed radiating element. The pilot received his bearing information on a compass-like display and distance from the beacon as a digital read-out. To an extent TACAN replaced the earlier aircraft homing beacons, but it was much more important as a means of supporting air navigation within line-of-sight of a carrier or other warship equipped with it. TACAN began to enter service in 1956. That was fortunate, because by that time the US Navy no longer had a two-seat interceptor, because the F3D Skynight was considered unsuitable for carrier operation. The navy did have numerous single-seat interceptors, many of them with onboard radars.

CHAPTER 6
THE JET AGE BEGINS

THE FIRST JET aircraft flew (in Germany) in August 1939 and by the end of the Second World War both the British and the Americans had small numbers of operational jet fighters. Jets imposed such problems on carrier operations that there was some question, immediately after the war, as to whether they could replace propeller-driven naval fighters. Whether that was acceptable depended on what the naval fighters had to face. If the threat was long-range propeller-driven bombers, propeller-driven interceptors might still be viable. If it was enemy interceptors threatening the carrier's own strike aircraft, the situation was very different.

The new jet fighters turned out to cost far more than their wartime predecessors and to require far more maintenance. In 1949, for example, a new Panther (F9F) fighter, probably the least expensive of the new US Navy jets, cost more than twice as much as its piston predecessor, the Grumman Bearcat (F8F-2). A really high-performance aircraft, a Cutlass (F7U-3), cost more than ten times as much as a wartime Hellcat. To make matters even worse, post-war technology, both for the attacker and the defender, was changing so rapidly that aircraft became obsolete well before they wore out.

Half-way into the jet age, *Franklin D Roosevelt* shows both Banshee (F2H-2) jet fighters and, abaft them, propeller-driven Corsairs. This photograph was taken during Operation 'Longstop', a NATO Mediterranean exercise, 4 November 1952.

EARLY BRITISH NAVAL JET FIGHTERS

Overall naval aircraft policy, which led to the post-war projects, was developed by the Board of Admiralty, as it was advised by Fifth Sea Lord. He in turn chaired a Naval Aircraft Design Sub-Committee of the Future Building Committee, which operated between 1943 and 1954 (the Future Building Committee itself was concerned with ships, including carriers).[1] For convenience this organisation is described here simply as the committee. The committee was hardly the sole originator of new projects, but its proceedings give a good idea of developing policy.

The British developed aircraft during the early post-war period on two simultaneous levels. One was immediate or interim projects designed initially to gain jet operating experience and then to meet the day fighter requirement. A second was longer-term projects using more powerful engines under development rather than production and also the new aerodynamic concepts taken from the Germans in 1945. The Attacker and Sea Hawk fit the first category, the Sea Vixen the second. The Scimitar straddles both categories.

The committee's files include a memo from the British representative to the US Navy Bureau of Aeronautics listing current projects as of 15 October 1943, including both the first US naval jet fighter (the McDonnell FD) and the mixed-power Ryan FR-1.[2] This is the earliest mention of jet aircraft in the committee file. At this point BuAer

described the mixed-power FR as its most promising interceptor project; the FD depended on the success of the Westinghouse jet engine. It was a 'second string' to the FR (alternatively it might be seen as a logical follow-up). The British representative urged the Admiralty to seek FRs under Lend-Lease. It employed a British jet engine, which removed much of the uncertainty the Admiralty might feel; otherwise it was a purely conventional design. This was 'the horse we should back'. At a 1 December meeting of the committee, it was decided to bid for up to twelve FRs 'for technical development and experience in the operation of a jet cum conventional engine carrier aircraft'. No action was to be taken on the pure-jet FD.

Westland offered a mixed-power fighter when the Royal Navy asked for fighter designs in 1943, to Specification N.7/43 (later replaced by F.19/43). It would have had a Griffon piston engine and a Halford H.1 turbojet. This choice was rejected in favour of Folland and Hawker designs, the latter becoming the Sea Fury.

At the Committee's 19 February 1944 meeting ACNS(A) pointed out that the war against Japan was estimated to last through 1947 (for planning purposes). On that basis it was necessary to consider beginning a new naval fighter project at once, rather than an adapted land-based type. However, strike aircraft were a higher priority. By the autumn of 1944 the European war seemed to be nearly over and the Admiralty could look ahead. It supported the MAP when the latter called for a 'bold programme' of new aircraft development (both military and civil) to 'ensure a strong and virile aircraft industry in the immediate post war years'. The committee would be responsible for setting requirements.

The Supermarine Attacker was conceived as an experimental naval fighter, but it was bought in quantity due to Korean War mobilisation. *Eagle* shows Attackers as well as Skyraiders (AEW aircraft) and Avengers (for ASW) in the mid-1950s. (*The Hook*)

The 8 September 1944 meeting took up the question of whether the next naval fighter should be a jet interceptor. An interceptor was the one type missing from the current naval development programme, the question being whether it should be a jet. Chief of Naval Requirements (CNR) pointed to increased speed and nearly constant performance from sea level up, whereas piston aircraft performance fell off with altitude. On the other hand, there were drawbacks for carrier operation; ACNS(A) asked whether a turboprop would be better. That would have been something like the later Wyvern. Director, Air Warfare and Training (DAWT) said that the Aeronautical Research Committee had concluded that the turboprop was better for long range, but that the jet was better for performance.

CNR asked whether the interceptor would operate within 30–50nm of a ship, so that it could carry much of its fuel in drop tanks (more than the usual 50 per cent). ACNS(A) thought that interceptions might be further out and he also asked whether the usual four 20mm cannon were enough. The decision was to seek a design to see how it might fit Staff Requirements. Alongside the interceptor the committee planned a new long-range day fighter. In December, the committee sketched the design programme for 1944–7. It included a mixed-power day fighter or fighter-bomber to replace the Sea Fury (which was then entering service) and an experimental interceptor. By this time the all-jet idea had been dropped in favour of a combination of a gas turbine driving a propeller or ducted fan and a jet engine, as first priority for early development. Supermarine would be asked for a design. Preliminary work would begin in 1945.

At this time Supermarine was developing a Spitfire offshoot with a laminar-flow wing (as in the US Mustang fighter) called the Spiteful (a naval version was named Seafang). In response to the navy request, it offered a jet version, minimising changes by using the same wing and some other components. While considering the Supermarine project, the committee also asked RAE to compare all possible power-plant combinations – pure jet, ducted fan, conventional plus jet boost, turboprop, turboprop plus jet boost and pure conventional. RAE concluded that anything other than a pure jet would have inferior performance. To adopt a pure jet the navy would have to modify its usual requirements for take-off, military load, endurance and landing speed. The alternatives to pure jets were so inferior that RAE did not even list

A production Attacker FB Mk 2, August 1952. The initial British naval jet fighters were powered by the same Nene engine which the US Navy adopted in the late 1940s for the Grumman Panther and Cougar. (*The Hook*)

them in its report. Instead, it compared its own sketch design (designated TJ 6) with the jet Spiteful and two US jet proposals (FJ-1 and F6U-1) accepted by the US Navy (as a result of the 1944 design competition described below). All offered very similar performance. This report was discussed at the 9 April 1945 committee meeting.

MAP had already ordered three jet Spiteful prototypes the previous September (to Specification E.10/44) and one was now to be navalised. A draft specification for the fully- and partly-navalised jet Spiteful was to be written (it was E.10/45). British jet experience and the use of existing Spiteful components, made it possible to fly the first prototype on 27 July 1946, before the US F6U-1 (2 October 1946) and FJ-1 (27 November 1946). As a production aircraft, Supermarine's fighter was named Attacker.[3]

The projected standard first-generation British naval jet fighter was the Hawker Sea Hawk. An FB Mk 3 is shown landing on board *Eagle*. This fighter also equipped the Royal Australian Navy, the Royal Netherlands Navy and the Indian Navy, in each case flying from modernised light fleet carriers.

RAE's comment about relaxing requirements was an initial hint of problems to come. Fifth Sea Lord did not want a rash of deck crashes to damn jet fighters from the outset. He asked whether there was a snag in time to work up power, not realising that the problem was the way in which a jet fighter was pushed along a deck. He also wanted the jet Spiteful to have a tricycle undercarriage. CNR saw no insuperable difficulties due to sluggish power response: jets would have to be catapulted as a matter of course. The sooner the navy had a prototype jet fighter, the sooner it would understand how to use jets. As a first step, an RAF Meteor was to be tested on board the large escort carrier (trials and training ship) *Pretoria Castle*. It would be used to investigate deck-handling and taxying but not landing and take-off, for which the Meteor was considered unsuitable.

By this time Churchill had directed that all effort was to be devoted to jet propulsion, definitely killing off the piston fighter alternatives. Plans now called for MAP to buy twenty-four Jet Spitefuls, eighteen of them being semi- or completely navalised. This pre-pro-

The Royal Navy developed its second generation jets while the first generation was being produced. This Scimitar was cross-decked on the US carrier *Forrestal* during the Riptide III exercise, 14 August 1962. Captain 'Winkle' Brown recalled it as an excellent low- and medium-altitude aircraft but useless above 25,000ft. It was supersonic in a shallow dive, but despite its great power not in level flight, because it was not area-ruled. At 10,000ft it had sensitive controls and was very manoeuvrable. The power-operated controls were well-balanced and harmonised and the aircraft had a high rate of roll. Stability was excessive for a fighter but well suited to the strike role the Scimitar eventually assumed. The Scimitar was the first Royal Navy nuclear strike aircraft, carrying a 3kT (i.e. low-yield) bomb selected to attack surface ships. Like US naval nuclear strike aircraft, it was eventually fitted with the LABS system for low-level over-the-shoulder delivery. In service the Scimitar suffered from a heavy maintenance load due to small but persistent leaks in its fuel and hydraulic systems.

duction run would enable the navy to solve jet problems before it placed such aircraft in large-scale service. It was accepted that, as it stood, the Jet Spiteful embodied many compromises and thus might leave much to be desired, but it would be available sooner than anything else. Supermarine was already beginning work on a follow-on jet interceptor, which might prove preferable. Large-scale jet production was probably two years off (1947). Reviewing the situation in August 1945, DAWT wrote that the Jet Spiteful was the most suitable available type, but by no means certain to be carrier suitable. It was considerably larger than earlier British carrier aircraft: it was too wide for either lift in an *Illustrious* class fleet carrier and it could be stowed only in the upper hangar of *Indomitable* and *Implacable* classes.

It was already understood that a jet engine could not simply be throttled down when the LSO (DLCO) signalled a 'cut', so the E.1/45 specification for the navalised Jet Spiteful envisaged a 'thrust spoiler' inside the jet pipe, sufficient to cut cruising thrust in no more than half a second when triggered. No specific requirements for take-off run or landing speed were levied.

The Royal Navy needed some immediate experience with jets in order to decide how to operate them. It could not wait two years for Jet Spitefuls, but the existing RAF fighters had been conceived as short-range interceptors and were unsuited to naval use. To gain experience, the navy bought de Havilland Vampires and installed arrester hooks.[4] Flying the second Sea Vampire prototype, Eric 'Winkle' Brown made the world's first jet carrier take-off and landing on 3 December 1945. Both feats were notable, given the dramatic difference between piston and jet engine characteristics. Very short range made the Vampire entirely unsuitable for carrier operation, but the Royal Navy did buy some as Sea Vampire trainers (T.22 version).

The end of the war did not end British interest in jet fighters.

The Scimitar ended up as a tanker, its high power allowing it to carry a considerable fuel load in external tanks. Here one tanker Scimitar from *Ark Royal* refuels another in NATO Exercise 'Straight-Laced' in the Norwegian Sea. (David Hobbs)

Hawker, Supermarine's wartime rival, designed its own jet fighter as a private venture alternative to E.10/44. Submitted to the MAP on behalf of the services, it was dropped by the RAF because it did not offer fast enough climb (they wanted it to reach 40,000ft in three minutes, as a pure interceptor). As reported in May 1946, the navy was more interested, as the aircraft was likely to be small and to be within the required overall weight. It seemed likely to offer good approach and landing speed, although range and endurance might be limited. It could fit on board the three *Illustrious* class carriers. Its Nene engine (also in the Supermarine fighter) was the most advanced then available.

Controller (Air) pointed out that the navy doubted it could execute deck-launched interception; it would have to use the existing CAP technique, so it did not need an extraordinary rate of climb. Maximum speed was more important. Like the Jet Spiteful, Hawker's fighter had laminar-flow wings, but in its case they were unusually thin. A memo in the files of the committee pointed out that any jet fighter would require a very different tactical policy from that developed during the war. The main problem was endurance. Although top speed was little different between sea level and very high altitude, endurance changed radically: at 1000ft combat radius would be about a quarter of that at optimum altitude and patrol endurance about half that at 15,000ft. DAW agreed that this could be accepted. Low-altitude endurance would be a particular problem only in the strike escort role. A CAP would have to orbit at high altitude (for endurance), then dive to deal with attackers; the question was how high it could operate without missing interceptions.

The Royal Navy decided to ask for a navalised version of the new Hawker fighter, which was to meet Specification N.7/46.[5] As in the case of the Jet Spiteful, ultimately it was attractive as a means of gaining jet experience. It was expected to be somewhat faster than the

Jet Spiteful (600 to 620mph at sea level, 560 to 580mph at 40,000ft). Patrol endurance at 15,000ft with tanks full would be 2.8 hours, about half as much as a conventional fighter. The Hawker fighter flew for the first time on 2 September 1947. Its navalised version was named Sea Hawk (there was no Hawk).

DAW raised some questions as to carrier suitability of the new fighter (discussed at a 1 October 1946 committee meeting): high stall speed, difficulty in deck-landing by an average pilot (landing speed was 15 knots higher than that of any existing naval aircraft) and limited combat radius.[6] Vice Controller (Air) rejected the argument: carriers should suit their aircraft, not the other way around. Some of the problems lay in the fact that the carriers were two years behind the aircraft. A suitable catapult (130 knots end speed) had been mooted two years earlier, but was still in the project stage. Presumably this was the steam catapult. Improved arresting gear was needed. As for endurance, the N.7 was better than its US counterparts. For example, the Americans demanded 100nm radius at sea level plus five minutes combat or a climb to 25,000ft plus three hours endurance to dry tanks. N.7 was much better – and it was understood that the US requirement was not being met. BuAer was reportedly so badly frustrated that it was considering abandoning piloted aircraft for short-range interception and adopting guided missiles instead. It might be possible, moreover, to increase effective endurance by cutting combat time from the current 15 minutes. The RAF was accepting much less. Vice Controller (Air) likened a decision to abandon N.7/46 to the 1939 decision not to adapt the Spitfire to carrier operation because of its limitations, which he said had set back adoption of a proper carrier

A de Havilland Sea Vixen (XN699) of 890 NAS is shown on board *Ark Royal* with a Firestreak missile underwing (it is recognisable by its pointed nose, under the protective cover). The R on the tail indicates the ship, whose flight deck bore the same letter. Note the off-centre canopy: the radar operator sat alongside and below the pilot. Like the Scimitar, the Sea Vixen was powered by a pair of Avons. The Firestreak seeker was inspired by the German Kiel-Gerät IR sensor seized in 1945, designed to detect bombers (from a Ju-88G fighter) up to 4 miles away. Blue Jay Mk 2 would have used an alternative seeker. Mk 3 was a version for super-sonic fighters like the SR 177. Of different versions of Blue Jay, only Mk 1 and Mk 4 (Red Top) entered service. This photograph was taken about 1963. (*The Hook*)

version by three years. The navy should consider itself fortunate that Hawker had developed the design on its own.

All of this raised the possibility that the navy should look for insurance in the form of a long-range piston-engine fighter. Alternatives raised were the Seafire 47 (a Griffon-engined Seafire), the Sea Fury and the twin-engine Sea Hornet. The navy looked to N.7/46 as a replacement for the Seafire 47 and the Sea Fury, to enter service in 1948 or 1949. At the time the navy was also developing the turboprop strike fighter which became the Westland Wyvern; N.7/46 might possibly be an alternative. However, the day interception role was by far the most important.

By this time RAE was pushing its idea that jets could achieve high performance by dispensing with undercarriages.[7] Supermarine received this development contract. As of October 1946 MAP was deferring the undercarriageless aircraft. It reassigned the project as a conventional naval fighter on the basis of the N.7/46 specification. It seemed possible that the Supermarine fighter might be better than Hawker's N.7/46. Unlike both the Hawker fighter and the Jet Spiteful, this aircraft had two engines offering an exceptional rate of climb, actually greater than what the navy needed. The main problem was endurance. It seemed unlikely that shutting down one engine to

loiter would offer much, but that had to be investigated. As of March 1947, DAW saw the Supermarine fighter as insurance against the failure of the Hawker fighter (which had not yet flown). He also pointed out that if the Royal Navy obtained some form of AEW, a very fast-climbing deck-launched interceptor would become attractive. Development of a prototype was approved, with the understanding that operation from modernised *Majestic* class carriers would have to be examined. This project was covered by Specification N.9/47 (N.113).[8] The aircraft was Supermarine's Type 508, powered by two Avons, Rolls-Royce's first axial-flow turbojets. It did not fly until 1951. Eventually it developed into the Scimitar, in effect the Royal Navy's second-generation jet day fighter.

All-up weight of the N.9/47 fighter (18,000–18,500lbs) substan-tially exceeded the 11,852lbs of the N.7/46 (the Staff Requirement limited weight to 18,000lbs). The Supermarine aircraft was much faster (575 knots vs 537 knots at sea level) and climbed far faster and it would take off in a much shorter distance (375ft vs 772ft in 27 knots of wind over deck). Endurance at sea level was much shorter, only 45 minutes vs 1.4 hours, but with drop tanks it was not too much less (3 hours vs 3.3 hours). These figures were slightly altered as the design was reported in June 1947. Changes included greater wing area, which reduced approach speed to a more reasonable 94 knots. This and other improvements led Fifth Sea Lord to recommend on 6 June 1947 that MAP order prototypes.

By early 1948 both the Attacker and Sea Hawk were nearly ready for production. The Naval Aircraft Design Sub-Committee met on 3 March to compare the two and to decide how many Attackers should be ordered instead of Sea Furies, if the Attacker was considered suitable pending availability of the Hawker fighter. The Attacker could be catapulted from the coming *Ark Royal* and *Hermes* classes if their BH 5 catapults could be modified to give an 80-knot rather than

A Sea Vixen FAW Mk 2 from *Victorious* is serviced on board the US carrier *Oriskany*, September 1966. The missile is a Red Top. An alternative under consideration as early as 1956, was a radar-guided version of Blue Jay/Red Top. A CW version (Blue Jay Mk 5) was dropped due to problems with adaptation of the Sea Vixen's AI 18 radar, but was revived in November 1957 under the new name Blue Dolphin.

75-knot end speed (by 1949, BH 5 was giving 85 knots and it was expected to give 95 knots in the near future). Both could recover it, though *Hermes* would require some improvement in her arrester gear. It could not operate from the light fleet carriers, however. A limited number of Attackers would be bought, followed by larger numbers of Sea Hawks, so there might be logistical problems. It would help considerably that both fighters used the same Nene engine.

Another possible stopgap was the Sea Vampire, which had already operated from a trials carrier. It was rejected because it could not be catapulted or folded, hence could not be used in combat. Nor had it sufficient endurance for realistic evaluation trials at sea. Also, de Havilland lacked sufficient capacity to make any more. An argument in favour of the Attacker was that it was considered desirable to keep Supermarine interested in naval aircraft after the end of Seafire 47 production.

Director of Air Equipment (DAE) wanted sixty Attackers for tests. If production began in 18 months, the first thirty would probably become available in the latter part of the 1949–50 fiscal year. The committee decided unanimously to push for final tests of the Attacker at Boscombe Down, which were expected to take at least three months. It and the N.7 should cost about the same and their performance was comparable (the Attacker had a somewhat shorter range, but that was a comparison between proven Attacker performance and estimates for N.7). In any case the Attacker was insurance against failure of the more sophisticated N.7 (Sea Hawk). Controller (Air) approved the order for Attackers. Both Attacker (Specification 19/48) and Sea Hawk were ordered into production the same year (Specification 25/48). The

contract to Hawker was dated 4 November 1949, the first production aircraft flying on 14 November 1951.

By early 1948, then, the Royal Navy was well on the way to buying its first jet day fighters, with a second aircraft close to the production stage. However, none of its carriers could operate them. The first jet-suitable carriers would be *Ark Royal* and *Eagle*, which were still under construction (*Eagle* would be completed in October 1951, *Ark Royal* not until 1955). The new jets could also be operated by the *Hermes* class large light fleet carriers, the first of which, *Centaur*, would not be completed until September 1953. A fleet modernisation plan called for reconstruction of all six wartime fleet carriers, but only *Victorious* was ever taken in hand and she was not to be completed until 1957. Thus the experience the Royal Navy hoped to gain from interim jet fighters was likely to be limited at best.

As it had during the Second World War, the Royal Navy needed a companion jet night fighter. The Royal Navy never accepted the US idea that a single-seater could fill this role. In 1946 the Ministry of Supply issued Specification N.40/46 (this aircraft does not appear in committee records until the 20 July 1948 meeting). It called for a twin-engine fighter for night CAP and for night intrusion. De Havilland offered the twin-boom DH 110.[9] At the 1948 meeting, the questions were whether to accept a Ministry of Supply recommendation to order a prototype from de Havilland and also whether to seek an alternative design from another company, such as Fairey, as insurance against inability of de Havilland to produce enough aircraft in an emergency. The possibility of just such an emergency had just arisen in Europe with events such as the Czech coup and the Berlin blockade.

The sheer size of the proposed fighter created qualms, but DAW explained that it was necessary to accommodate the envisaged massive air intercept (AI) radar using a 35in dish (initially a 40in dish had been required). He said that thought was now turning to a two-seat night fighter, a role for which the DH 110 would be suited. The committee accepted the project, but expressed fears that it would not be available for trade protection, as it could not be operated by anything but a fleet carrier. Given nervousness about a second supplier, Fairey was asked for an alternative design, not the one previously submitted (it was considered suitable not only because its design was promising but also because it needed work).

DAW wanted to reduce the number of separate aircraft types. To that end he wanted the strike role to be met by adapting an aircraft bought primarily for another role. He apparently saw the N40/46 as both the next-generation day fighter and the next-generation jet night fighter (a replacement for the current propeller-driven Sea Hornet). At this point there were requirements for both a single-seat strike fighter (initially conceived as an adaptation of the big Supermarine N9/47) and a two-seat strike fighter. DAW saw versions of the DH 110 in both roles. All of this made the aircraft so important that a back-up

was vital. An emergency would be like the Second World War, with priority going to the RAF.

The committee agreed that N.40/46 should meet the two-seat strike requirement, but if two seats were not needed bomber versions of the N.7/46 and N.9/47 could be produced, again reducing the number of separate types. The committee agreed that the N.9/47 should be investigated in the single-seat strike role. If it failed, N.40/46 would be adapted. Specification N.40/46 was then cancelled and N.14/49 substituted, but it was only a revision of N.40/46 and the same DH 110 was envisaged. It eventually entered service as the Sea Vixen.

The 1948 political shocks in Europe showed that modernisation might be more urgent than had been imagined. The committee met on 19 May 1950 (an earlier meeting had been postponed) to consider an interim night fighter based on the de Havilland Venom, essentially a modified Vampire using the more powerful Ghost engine and a thin (higher-speed) wing. Developed as a private venture, it first flew on 2 September 1949. Range, badly inadequate in the original Vampire, could be increased using tip tanks. De Havilland marketed both a single-seat fighter-bomber version and a two-seat (side by side) night fighter. DAW considered the two-seat Venom ripe for consideration by the committee both as a replacement for the Sea Hornet and also because it could operate from smaller carriers intended for trade protection, particularly the *Hermes* class and the Australian *Melbourne*. Introduction would provide the fleet with initial experience using a high-capacity AI radar.[10] In the event the navy could not buy enough quality night fighters (N.14/49, ex N.40/46), the night fighter Venom would be a cheaper (but inferior) alternative. Without a jet night fighter, ships would need special barriers to handle the Sea Hornet.

Like the other jets, the Venom would have a high approach speed, 115 knots in the worst case and 107 knots in the best. Trials in *Warrior* and later in *Illustrious* had provided more experience and perspective,

Delays in Sea Vixen development led the Royal Navy to buy an interim night fighter, the Sea Venom. It was also sold to the RAN. Australian Sea Venoms were later replaced by Skyhawks (which lacked their all-weather capability) and the Gannets by Grumman S-2 Trackers. This Sea Venom is in the RAN's FAA Museum at Nowra.

encouraging the staff to accept such speeds. The undercarriage of the land-based Venom would have to be strengthened. It was not clear whether the complication of wing folding was needed. To be worthwhile as an interim aircraft, the Venom night fighter had to be available at least two and a half years earlier than the DH 110 built to N.14/49.

The Venom could hardly match the DH 110. All-up weight (12,980lbs) would be about half that of the DH 110 and its thrust was 5000lbs compared to two 6500lb Avons (as understood in 1949). Maximum speed at sea level would be 493 knots rather than 537 knots; endurance (without tip tanks) at 30,000ft would be only 1.12 hours rather than two hours (with minimum fuel in the case of the DH 110). Given its parentage, the Sea Venom did not meet current requirements. It could not accommodate ejection seats, its strength factor for arresting gear was 1.5 rather than the current 2.0 in the Sea Hawk and its catapulting strength (4.2G) was barely enough for an 85-knot BH 5 catapult and not for the 95-knot version envisaged.

When the committee met in May 1950, it faced two problems. The estimated unit cost of the Venom night fighter had risen by about a third (on a run of fifty aircraft) and estimated development cost was high (the cost increase would be reduced to about 17 per cent on a longer production run of 150 to 200 aircraft). At the least, a navalised night fighter Venom would cost nearly twice as much as a Sea Hornet night fighter. On the other hand, the Ministry of Supply now expected to deliver the first DH 110 night fighters in 1956–7 rather than 1953, as it had expected in April 1949. As of May 1950 production of navalised Venom night fighters was expected in 1952. Also, the RAF had decided to buy the land-based version as its own interim night fighter pending appearance of the Gloster Javelin, its equivalent to the navy's DH 110.

DAW added that the navalised Venom would be adaptable to trade protection carriers as a replacement for the existing Sea Fury. That would make it a long-term day/night fighter, not only a short-term gap-filler for the big DH 110. References to suitability for the Australian *Melbourne* were significant in this respect; she was a modernised light fleet carrier (she would enter service as such in 1955). The day/night role helped justify the aircraft even though in the past DAW had sold a policy of reducing the number of different carrier aircraft types to a bare minimum. At the meeting, Fifth Sea Lord added another consideration, the desire of Dominion navies (Australian and Canadian), which had bought British light fleet carriers, to operate modern fighters to replace their Sea Furies.

The committee decision was circulated on 15 June 1950: the Royal Navy would press hard for the navalised Venom night fighter and it would have folding wings. The aircraft entered service as the Sea Venom F(AW) 20, the AW (all-weather) designation reflecting the day/night fighter concept. This was the last decision taken by the committee before war broke out in Korea and the British naval situation changed radically.

Work proceeded on the more acceptable higher-performance night fighter, so at a 14 July 1952 meeting the committee produced a final Staff Requirement, NA 38, for submission to the Ministry of Supply.[11] A fresh design competition to a revised version of the NA 14 (F.19/49) requirement was held in 1951, but no choice was made at the time. One question raised in 1952 was whether a new competition should be held to the new Staff Requirement. The committee decided to keep faith with the aircraft industry by writing the requirement in such a way as to favour the firms which had competed the previous year.[12]

At this point a prototype was expected in mid-1956, deliveries beginning in 1958 if orders were placed early enough. DAW's idea of a single day/night fighter survived: the new aircraft was called an all-weather fighter, its roles being day and night CAP and night fighter intrusion. Armament was to be four 20mm cannon or two 30mm Aden or two 30mm Hispano 825s, but consideration was to be given to carrying guided missiles. The specified radar was AI Mk 17 (i.e. the successor to the Mk 16 planned for DH 110) or the US APS-21, available under the mutual aid programme (when it was discussed in 1953, the radar was AI Mk 18). The aircraft would normally orbit at high fuel-efficient altitude (40,000ft), but if an enemy attacked at low altitude it had to be able to dive vertically from 40,000ft to 8000ft in the shortest possible time (with two-thirds fuel) without exceeding its limiting Mach number.

De Havilland won again with a modified DH 110, the choice reviewed at the committee meeting held on 14 July 1953. By that time the Royal Navy planned the Red Angel missile to attack ships. The committee was assured that this question had been under study for some months and that the fighter could carry it (the project was soon abandoned). The main change to the original design was a heavily redesigned tailplane; RAE (Lewis Boddington) assured the committee that this would not ruin its deck-landing characteristics. At this stage the aircraft still had to be navalised. The committee was concerned with overcoming objections to ordering an unflown aircraft, but against that the day/night fighter had a very high priority and was unlikely to be cut from the naval budget.

EARLY US NAVAL JET FIGHTERS

At the outset, BuAer took two parallel approaches. One was a mixed-power fighter with a piston engine and a supplementary turbojet. In theory, a hybrid offered substantial advantages in carrier handling and in endurance thanks to its piston engine. The jet offered increased performance. There were two projects for such a fighter, one sized for fleet carriers, the other for escort carriers. The other was a pure jet.

The clearest indication of BuAer interest in mixed-power fighters was a design study series produced by its Aircraft Design Research Branch under the designation D-18 (it was part of the DR series which succeeded its earlier numbered designs). The earliest part of the series was a set of graphs dated 6 July 1942 indicating various aspects of jet engine boost to a mixed-power fighter (rockets were also considered). Curves showed the required piston engine power to reach various speeds when jet or rocket engines were added, the maximum speed being 400mph. The initial study (D-18B) used a 575hp XV-770-7 engine. This lightweight fighter (6984lbs gross) would make 304.7mph on its piston engine alone, but with a rocket it would make 381.4mph, enough of a boost to make the idea interesting.[13] D-18B combined the V-770 engine with a Westinghouse 'A' engine (1000lbs thrust). An alternative D-18C was not far from the FR-1, combining an R-1830 with the same Westinghouse 'A' engine (the actual FR-1 used a GE J31-GE-3 [I-16]). Others in the series had two Westinghouse engines underwing or, in D-18F, a much more powerful (3000lbs thrust) Halford H-1 (later renamed the de Havilland Goblin). Several, including the D-18F, had R-2800 engines. An initial summary of D-18F performance was dated 17 November 1942. A performance summary sheet dated 22 March 1943 showed that with an R-2800 rated at 2320hp using water injection and the turbojet, the D-18F would make 464mph at its critical altitude (388mph without the jet). D-18C was credited with 389mph at 21,600ft.

The US Navy held a design competition in 1944 for a jet fighter. The winners were the North American FJ-1 (shown here) and the Vought F6U Pirate. This Fury is making a free (non-catapult) take-off from *Boxer*, 30 April 1948.

Presumably BuAer used the ADR study as a yardstick to evaluate proposals for mixed-power fighters. Unfortunately surviving BuAer correspondence does not include any indication that the manufacturers were canvassed, although the BuAer proposal file certainly includes several mixed-power designs in addition to the two actually built, the Ryan FR-1 and the Curtiss F15C.

The Ryan FR-1 Fireball was intended for escort carriers. This project began about December 1942, Ryan submitting its informal proposal in March 1943, about when it received a letter of intent.[14] The Fireball combined the R-1820-56 engine of the FM-2 escort carrier fighter with GE's I-16 jet engine.[15] It was attractive because it offered the speed of a Corsair with a light-enough weight (8000lbs) and low-enough stall speed for escort carrier operation. The FR-1 flew, without the jet engine, on 25 June 1944. With the jet, it offered outstanding

performance, estimated maximum speed being 430mph at 22,000ft (and possibly more) and a maximum rate of climb at sea level of better than 5000ft/min. It was expected to take off in 120ft (25 knots wind over deck) with the jet engine or in 200ft without it. A pilot production order was placed before the FR-1 flew and it was expected to enter service early in 1945. First carrier trials were conducted on board the escort carrier *Charger* in January 1945, the aircraft showing excellent landing and deck-handling characteristics.[16]

To the extent that there was a formal or informal requirement for a mixed-power fleet fighter, it was filled by Curtiss' F15C, powered by an R-2800 and a Halford (Allis-Chalmers) centrifugal-flow jet.[17] Estimated maximum speed was 480mph. Armament was the standard four 20mm cannon. During 1943 Curtiss had tried unsuccessfully to interest BuAer in a conventional fighter powered by the big Double Wasp engine. This fighter never went into production.

Grumman offered its own mixed-power G-57 fighter (R-2800 plus turbojet), as did McDonnell (Model 18J, R-2800 plus I-40, apparently a version of an aircraft offered to the army). Grumman also offered

FJ-1s were soon relegated to reserve duties. These aircraft from NAS Oakland are shown on 26 August 1950.

the G-67, a Tigercat with a jet engine in each nacelle. Goodyear wanted to develop a mixed-power fighter and was told to develop the F2G instead. There may have been further proposals. The BuAer proposal file includes abortive turboprop fighters from Convair, Goodyear and McDonnell.[18] There were also hybrid projects for other purposes. The Mercator (P4M) patrol bomber had jet engines in its nacelles, behind its piston engine. The Grumman TB3F torpedo bomber was designed with a jet engine in its tail, although when it was redesigned as an anti-submarine aircraft (the AF Guardian), the jet was eliminated.

Early in 1944 the BuAer fighter division considered the two mixed-power aircraft the most attractive way to use jet power. They covered both important fighter sub-classes, for escort and for fleet carriers. In March, therefore, the VF branch asked the BuAer power-plant branch to develop appropriate jet engines.[19]

The first pure jet US naval fighter was the McDonnell FD-1 Phantom (McDonnell's Model 10, later redesignated FH-1, because D was being used for Douglas). According to the BuAer history, initially mixed power was favoured, the pure jet described as 'useful for special [unspecified] Naval missions'. At the outset it was understood that high jet fuel consumption would limit the aircraft to interceptor missions, for which it was armed with four 0.50-calibre machine guns.

McDonnell apparently began studies in 1942, probably at BuAer request. There was no initial competition, at least in any formal sense. The BuAer proposal file (RG 72 Entry 1044-F at NARA II) includes two pages of undated requirements, presumably those levied by BuAer. The aircraft is described as a carrier interceptor armed with four 0.50-calibre guns with 250 rounds each (and space for another

150). Take-off distance should be no more than 250ft with internal overload fuel on board and stall speed was specified as 82mph, both grossly optimistic for jets. There was to be no provision for barrier crash, since there was no propeller for the barrier wire to wrap itself around. McDonnell considered two alternative powerplants, two 19in (19C or J30) or eight 9.5in (J32) engines. Another alternative was six 9.5in engines (take-off weight 6000lbs vs 7760lbs). BuAer wanted alternative designs for two and more engines, but McDonnell submitted only the two-engine design. From its point of view shutting down some engines did not offer sufficient improvement in fuel consumption to make more complicated engine controls worthwhile.

In March 1943, when McDonnell submitted its proposal, it estimated that its fighter would make 468mph at 15,000ft with military thrust (given as 1370lbs for each 19in engine, but as yet quite uncertain); BuAer thought 441mph more plausible. McDonnell based its design on the assumption that thrust could be augmented by as much as 60 per cent by injecting liquid air. Alternatively, it wanted to use jet-assisted take-off (JATO) boosters. Since then, it had turned out that in high humidity (as in the Pacific) ammonia boost would not work, but JATO had proven itself. With an eye to Pacific operations, one of the BuAer analysts pointed out that jet performance depended on the difference between inlet and exhaust temperatures; an engine would lose 13 per cent if air temperature changed from 59°F to 87°F. In a later calculation, increasing temperature to 100°F would increase take-off run from 420ft to 500ft. However by using two JATO units (1000lbs thrust each), that could be reduced to 242ft at 59°F and 285ft at 100°F.

With the future of jet engines uncertain, McDonnell opted to place one or more Westinghouse engines in each wing root. When the design was being completed, the design of the Westinghouse 19A engine had not yet been frozen. Without definite dimensions or weights, design progress was difficult. For example, in May 1943 the length of the engine was increased by 19.5in to 87.7in. Since so little was known about problems like jet inlet design, this project included much more than the usual amount of large-scale wind tunnel work. Much of the work was done at the NACA Ames facility, which had tested other models of jet aircraft. A McDonnell request for information about the Rolls-Royce B-37 (Derwent) and B-38 engines, which the company was presumably being considered as alternatives to the Westinghouse engine, was rejected on security grounds. Somewhat later BuAer asked McDonnell whether it would consider using an alternative 3000lbs thrust Westinghouse 23C engine, which the company was then proposing as an auxiliary engine in a mixed-power

The F6U-1 Pirate was underpowered; it interested BuAer mainly because it had an early afterburner. That failed and only thirty were bought. This is the XF6U-1.

The only fully successful product of the 1944 competition was the most conventional: McDonnell's Banshee was a scaled-up Phantom using more powerful engines. This F2H-2 from *Essex* is shown returning from a Korean mission, August 1951.

fighter. This was probably the engine which emerged later as the company's 24C (J34) and which powered the follow-on F2H Banshee.

McDonnell's reaction to the possibility of using the more powerful engine in its existing design shows just how wildly optimistic jet aircraft design then was. It wrote that with two 23C engines its light-weight fighter would have twice the rate of climb and that in level flight its speed would be 'supersonic except for the effects of compressibility'. Take-off would be so improved that no catapult would be needed. The only drawback would be much higher fuel consumption. McDonnell did point out that extensive experiments, many of them impossible in wind tunnels, would be needed.[20]

Ivan H Driggs of Aircraft Design Research thought that the design did not give 'the impression of skilful or finished technique. Considering the help given here and the length of time taken in working up the data the Bureau rightly should expect a considerably better study. It is possible that the number of experienced personnel were not available that were, as first stated, to be put to work on this design.' The outstanding feature was the massive fillet connecting wings to fuselage, in which an engine was mounted on each side. Driggs thought it was probably OK as a means of suppressing compressibility shock next to the fuselage and it might even reduce overall drag, but there was some doubt that given the size and shape of the air intake opening on the fore side of the fillet that air flow would be satisfactory. Any breakdown would greatly increase drag. The big fillet would also tend to promote tip stall. Driggs found the nose extremely long, offering more drag than necessary. Another BuAer engineer pointed out that McDonnell had not counted the fillet in calculating wing area, which would overstate effective aspect ratio (span to chord) and understate induced drag. Driggs found the wing loading low for a high-performance fighter and the aspect ratio rather high.

BuAer estimated characteristics of the new fighter before it flew. It was expected to have a combat radius of only 117nm, but that depended on the problem (flight profile) used. Jets were more efficient (in distance terms) at higher altitude, so modifying the standard profile so that the fighter returned at 15,000ft rather than 1500ft gained radius. Reserve fuel retained throughout could be cut from 60 minutes to 30 minutes. One engine could be shut down for low-power cruise. That increased combat radius to 228nm (McDonnell estimated 262nm). A low-drag design made for high stall speed (83mph), so it was estimated that the Phantom would need an unacceptable 770ft for a free take-off (310ft with three JATO units). The Phantom did have enough rate of climb in hand at approach speed (90mph, 7mph above stall) for a wave-off.

The first flight of the XFD-1 was considerably delayed by slow progress with its jet engine; taxi tests with a single engine were completed on 2 January 1945.[21] The Phantom first flew on 25 January, a letter of intent for 100 production aircraft (cut to eighty-seven at the end of the war) following on 7 March. Compared to the prototype, production aircraft would have more fuel and higher-rated engines. The Phantom made its first carrier take-off from *Franklin D Roosevelt* on 21 July 1946. The first was assigned to a squadron on 23 July 1947. The first full squadron to complete carrier qualification did so on 5 May 1948.

By the time the prototype Phantom was nearing completion, BuAer had already gone the next step, to a competition for a more advanced jet fighter. As it reviewed the situation in mid-1944, BuAer had nothing in the 550–560mph class which jet fighters were likely to attain.[22] BuAer engineers were divided as to whether a hybrid could achieve this sort of performance or whether it had to be a pure jet.[23] It was not clear whether a propeller would function above 500mph. On the other hand, a jet could not take off in the short distance required for carrier operation. It would have to use some form of assistance (rockets or else a more powerful catapult) or the carrier would have to generate greater wind over her deck and perhaps have a longer deck.

BuAer considered catapults the most promising possibility and work began on a new catapult design.[24]

On 14 October 1944 McDonnell submitted proposals to modify the FD-1. Modification A would lengthen the fuselage 18in (with a section abaft the pilot) to provide enough fuel for the desired 300nm combat radius. The 19B engines of the original design would be replaced by more powerful (1600lbs thrust) 19XBs and span would be reduced from the original 42ft to 30ft to cut drag. The vertical tail would be enlarged. Maximum speed would increase to 527mph at sea level (509mph at 20,000ft). That compared with current estimates offering 473mph at sea level and 508mph at 25,000ft. Endurance would be four hours at 20,000ft (but the brochure for the production version of FD-1 showed 6.5 hours) and the rate of climb would be 5560ft/min at sea level. McDonnell called this XFD-1A. An Alternate I retained the original wing. The brochure describing the production version of the FD-1 (written before it flew, as its illustrations were drawings rather than photographs) mentioned a direct development using the Westinghouse 23C engine (soon to be redesignated 24C, the J34).

McDonnell proposed this upgraded Model 24 on 18 October 1944. As proposed somewhat earlier, it was lengthened by 18in to provide more fuel to meet the standard 300nm combat radius requirement. The projected clipped wing was abandoned, but the new aircraft had a thinner low-drag wing. As forecast in the slightly earlier brochure, it used the more powerful 24C (J34) engine. Compared to the earlier Phantom, Model 24 also had much more ammunition: 400 rather than 250 rounds per 0.50-calibre machine gun. Estimated speed at sea level was 595mph (520mph at 20,000ft); combat radius was 303nm. Given the extra fuel, McDonnell estimated that endurance at 20,000ft would be 4.6 hours. This proposal was apparently not connected with the single-engine fighter competition BuAer opened in September 1944. Model 24 was attractive because it built on what would soon be a proven design. Detail design work began in March 1945, the FD-1 having flown in January. To some extent the new design may have been attractive as insurance against the failure of the single-engine fighters, as it was a more conservative design. Model 24 went into production as the F2D, later F2H, Banshee.

In 1944, when it began buying jet fighters, BuAer estimated that 450mph at sea level and 525mph at upper critical altitude was the best that a conventional aircraft could do without incurring serious size penalties. In three years, when aircraft conceived in 1944 entered service, 500mph would be less impressive than 400mph already was. BuAer's immediate goal was 550mph, which meant a pure jet.

Not everyone agreed that jets would be carrier-capable. Ivan Driggs contributed a handwritten comment on the review. He pointed out that jets might be so thirsty as to be unusable, in which case it might be better to reconsider the assumptions than to rebuild carriers and their catapults. The jet problem of poor fuel efficiency at low speeds was a consequence of physical realities and therefore could not be solved. The key problem was that the jet had a very limited cross-section (hence a limited air mass moved through it). That mass had to be accelerated to very high speed to produce sufficient thrust. By way of contrast, a variable-pitch propeller driven by a geared gas turbine (turboprop) offered excellent static thrust and fuel economy, because it needed so much less air to be accelerated inside the engine to accelerate air outside for thrust.

Driggs' organisation had already studied the army's P-80A Shooting Star fighter as a carrier problem, assuming the standard navy combat problem (flight profile). At the assumed gross weight of 16,600lbs, it would stall at 122mph, far above what was considered acceptable for carrier landing. At 10mph above the stall, there would be about 1010lbs of excess thrust. If a pilot were waved off at this point, he would probably stall and spin, since there would be little slipstream to reduce his stall speed. It seemed that he would have to accelerate gradually at a constant angle of attack, to turn the added lift (due to slow acceleration) into vertical acceleration. The aircraft could land on a carrier, but only with a very expert pilot. Very small mistakes would be fatal. As an illustration, Driggs provided a second-by-second table of the pilot's position and his excruciatingly low rate of climb. The new FD-1, which did not meet the navy's standard combat problem, would climb somewhat more quickly, but it was not clear whether it was climbing fast enough (Driggs wanted calculations made for comparison using an aircraft 'that is barely OK'). If the FD-1 was given enough fuel to meet the combat problem requirement, it would be in about the same position as the P-80A.

Driggs doubted that any jet aircraft would do much better. If wing area was increased to provide more lift, it would also increase drag, so the aircraft would need a more powerful engine. The larger engine would need more fuel, so the aircraft would continue to grow. At the least the navy had to specify minimum allowable climbing angle under a wave-off condition. Driggs' comments explain why no one was sure that early jet aircraft could operate from carriers. It was not merely a question of whether higher landing speeds could be tolerated.

On 1 September 1944 BuAer announced a competition for a single-engine jet fighter. It was the Bureau's first fighter competition since 1940. Any of the existing jet engines could be used: the General Electric I-16, I-20 and I-40 and the Westinghouse 19XD and 23C (soon to be redesignated 24C). As with other carrier fighters, size would be limited by carrier lift dimensions. Armament would be four or six 0.50-calibre machine guns. Combat radius would be 300nm and power-off stall speed with full ammunition and fuel was not to exceed 110mph. Landing speed with quarter-fuel was not to exceed 90mph. The wave-off requirement was that, with full fuel and ammunition and flaps and landing gear down, the aircraft had to climb at no less than 500ft/min when flying at 10mph above power-off stalling speed.[25]

The supporting Design Research sketch design (reported 24 January 1945) described a fighter powered by the General Electric TG-180 engine. It had a nose air intake and a butterfly tail. ADR reported that the usual fighter combat radius of 300nm could not be met; it had to be reduced to 250.[26]

BuAer was also interested in a rocket fighter; the German Me-163 Komet was arousing considerable interest as it outflew existing Allied fighters (one report had it shooting down sixteen of twenty-four P-51s it encountered).[27] The sponsor was a small group in the Bureau which had begun with the JATO programme and then progressed to other types of rockets. BuAer had just awarded a contract to Reaction Motors for a 3000lbs thrust rocket motor (four 750lbs thrust units in a cluster) burning gasoline and liquid nitrogen. Grumman engineers visiting BuAer in January 1945 were given details of the Me-163; they left with the impression that BuAer wanted to gain some experience with this technology. Those backing it said that the only way to get money at once was to sell the rocket as the only powerplant with which an aircraft could reach high Mach numbers. It seemed that BuAer was considering the rocket interceptor as an anti-Kamikaze weapon, but in their memo the engineers pointed out that it would not have to

The long-nose Banshee was produced in both night fighter (general-purpose fighter) and photographic versions, the -3 and -4 models of the night fighter differing only in the radar installed and thus externally indistinguishable. This RCN night Banshee was armed with Sidewinder missiles (which were not carried by US Banshees). (Royal Canadian Navy)

operate above 20,000ft and that a better interceptor could be built around the 24C jet engine. It could be about half the size of the Me-163. The engineers suggested that it might be best to use a rocket for auxiliary power, a choice the navy would explore during the 1950s. The war ended before BuAer could state any formal requirement for a rocket fighter.

Eight contractors expressed interest in the 1944 competition, but only Grumman, McDonnell, Chance Vought and North American submitted proposals. BuAer rejected Grumman's G-71 proposal because its promised performance was less than that of the parallel Design Research study.[28] It accepted the best proposal offered by each of the others.

North American offered its NA-134; the proposal for the version powered by a 24C engine was dated 14 October 1944. It became the FJ-1 Fury (NA-141). NA-134 was proposed in parallel with an air force fighter designated P-86, but the air force aircraft was never built and the P-86A Sabre was very different, with the air force's first swept wing.[29] NA-141 drawings showed tip tanks and wing dive brakes. Initially North American offered a fighter designed around the Westinghouse 24C (J34) with brief additional studies using the General Electric TG-180 (J35, taken over post-war by Allison) and I-40 (J33).[30] BuAer policy was to use all available engines, making

North American the choice for the TG-180. In North American's October 1944 brochure, the TG-180 variant was credited with a maximum speed of 550mph at sea level, compared to 537mph for the lower-power 24C (555mph at 12,000ft vs 540mph at 6000ft). TG-180 was then credited with 4000lbs of thrust, compared to 3000lbs for the 24C. With an I-40 (3400lbs thrust) the aircraft was expected to make 536mph at sea level and 546mph at 14,000ft.

The FJ-1 was the first US fighter to use a straight ram duct connecting its engine with a nose intake. It was the fastest tactical fighter in the world in 1947, with a speed in level flight of 480 knots (552mph) and a speed of Mach 0.87 in a dive. It offered better take-off, climb and high Mach performance than the contemporary air force F-80C and F-84. The first squadron operation was on 10 March 1948. The Fury was the first navy fighter to operate from a carrier in squadron strength, but the thirty-three delivered to the navy were used only for jet indoctrination and carrier qualification.

Chance Vought's Pirate (its V-340) was powered by a single Westinghouse J34-WE-30A turbojet (the Banshee initially had two J34-WE-22, the later engine offering 3200lbs rather than 3000lbs of thrust). Its unusual feature was the first afterburner in a US Navy fighter; with afterburner lit, thrust increased by nearly a third, to 4100lbs. Another unusual feature was the material used, metalite (two thin aluminium sheets bonded to a balsa wood core). Although estimated performance justified the BuAer choice, once delivered Pirate performance was considerably worse than that of existing propeller fighters. The afterburner proved extremely unreliable (typically it had to be replaced after eight minutes). Plans to place the

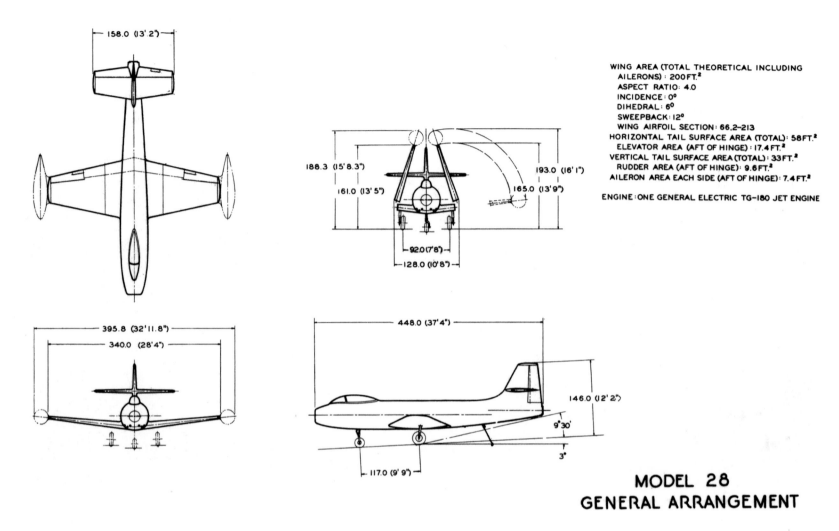

WING AREA (TOTAL THEORETICAL INCLUDING
  AILERONS) : 200FT.²
ASPECT RATIO : 4.0
INCIDENCE : 0°
DIHEDRAL : 6°
SWEEPBACK : 12°
WING AIRFOIL SECTION : 66.2-213
HORIZONTAL TAIL SURFACE AREA (TOTAL) : 58FT.²
  ELEVATOR AREA (AFT OF HINGE) : 17.4FT.²
VERTICAL TAIL SURFACE AREA (TOTAL) : 33FT.²
  RUDDER AREA (AFT OF HINGE) : 9.6FT.²
  AILERON AREA EACH SIDE (AFT OF HINGE) : 7.4FT.²

ENGINE : ONE GENERAL ELECTRIC TG-180 JET ENGINE

MODEL 28
GENERAL ARRANGEMENT

aircraft in mass production were dropped in 1948 and the thirty delivered were never in operational squadrons. Given underpowering, BuAer cautioned that it 'not be used for any purpose involving flight unless the pilot is experienced and the conditions favourable'.

McDonnell offered a single-engine Model 28 (submitted 24 October 1944), powered by one General Electric TG-180 (J35). It had a conventional nose intake and a sketch showed tip tanks (possibly the first on a US Navy jet fighter). McDonnell claimed it would make 556mph at sea level or 541mph at 20,000ft and that it would have a 302nm combat radius. Endurance would be 4.1 hours at 20,000ft. These figures made it somewhat inferior to the two-engine Model 24, so it is not difficult to see why the earlier twin-engine Model 24 (F2H Banshee) was ordered instead. Although it was considerably heavier and more expensive than either of the winning single-engine designs, it was the only one of the three 1944–5 fighters to be produced in quantity.

In the summer of 1946 Grumman suspected that its F9F-1 night fighter, one of the winners of a 1945 competition, was unworkable (see the night fighter discussion below). Under the designation G-79 it examined four alternative day fighter sketch designs using the available powerplants: G-79A (R-2800 and Derwent VI), G-79B (one TG-100 or TG-110 turboprop and one Derwent VI or one 24C), G-79C (two Derwent VIs) and G-79D (one Nene). The object was to exceed the combat performance of current naval jet fighters while

McDonnell offered a fresh single-engine design (one GE TG-180, later designated J35, giving 4000lbs of thrust) alongside its scaled-up Phantom: Model 28, the proposal for which was dated 24 October 1944. Maximum speed at sea level was given as 556mph (541mph at 20,000ft); rate of climb was 6440ft/min at sea level. Combat radius was 302nm. Span was 28ft 4in (32ft 11.8in over wingtip tanks) and length was 37ft 4in, with a gross weight of 10,318lbs.

retaining the take-off and low-speed performance of the Hellcat. The two mixed-power aircraft had tailwheel landing gear and offered considerably better performance than the Bearcat. Given the definite trend towards jets and the feeling that a jet could probably outperform any composite aircraft, the Grumman engineers studied the two pure jet types. They began with series of designs using one, two, three or four Westinghouse 24Cs, one, two and three Derwent Vis and one, two or three Nenes. Curves could be drawn relating thrust loading (weight divided by thrust) to the number of engines for any of the three engines. Thrust loading improved rapidly going from one engine to two and more slowly above that. Lower thrust loading made for a shorter take-off. The Nene gave the best figures, the Derwent the next best and the 24C the worst. A further factor was overall length, which had to be no more than 40ft. Shorter aircraft would have shorter wings with higher wing loading. The only practicable alternatives, which were studied further, were G-79C and G-79D. They were carried to the point of estimating weights, balance, performance and arrange-

The failure of the two-seat Tigercat night fighter as a carrier aircraft led to an order to develop night fighter versions of the new jet fighters, using the APS-19 radar developed at the end of the war. The only such project to proceed was the F2H-2N, shown here. It was never operational, being superseded by the F2H-3/4 (which were indistinguishable).

ments. Grumman favoured the twin Derwent (G-79C) on the ground of safety and easier maintenance. A sketch showed large wing nacelles in an arrangement something like that of the British Meteor. The Nene-powered G-79D showed wing root air intakes and a rooster tail, which minimised tail pipe length (and losses).

BuAer chose the Nene and modified the night fighter contract so that Grumman developed a Nene-powered day fighter as the F9F-2 Panther. Grumman submitted an outline specification for its G-79D design on 28 August 1946 (there was also a 6 August version). It offered a maximum sea level speed of 608mph at the 5750lbs thrust rating of the Nene (600mph at the 5000lb rating) and a sea level rate of climb of 12,070ft/min (5750lbs) or 9720ft/min (5000lbs). Given the high thrust rating, it could climb to 25,000ft in 2.7 minutes. High performance was possible partly because G-79D was likely to be a lightweight aircraft, with a combat weight of only 10,350lbs. Grumman estimated that with 25 knots of wind it could take off in 440ft (5750lbs thrust). Combat radius with the 5750lbs thrust engine was 300nm (with 5000lbs, 342nm).

It was not immediately obvious that jets would be the best carrier fighters, so in July 1946 BuAer asked ADR to see what a turboprop might offer.[31] It asked both for a fighter designed around the most promising current turboprop, to obtain characteristics as close as possible to those of the F2H Banshee, but capable of operating from a large escort carrier (*Commencement Bay* class). The Allison 500 (T40) was selected and the combat radius set at 300nm (ADR-46A). The other project was a turboprop of Hellcat size, weight and range. ADR added a mixed-power fighter (ADR-46B) powered by an Alison 501 (T-38) and a Westinghouse 24C jet (J34). ADR reported in January 1947 that its turboprop ADR-46A was faster than the Banshee at 35,000ft, though slower at sea level. ADR-46B lay between the two at both altitudes. ADR-46A climbed considerably faster than the pure jet fighter and it would take off in a much shorter distance. ADR pointed to its potential as an interceptor. All three aircraft offered essentially the same combat radius.

For the Hellcat-sized fighter ADR chose a de Laval type turboprop, presumably meaning the GE T31 developed by its steam turbine division. It offered superior fuel economy and could fit within the envelope defined by the Hellcat. If it were rated at 91 per cent nominal output (3400hp), it would increase speed from 378mph at 18,000ft to 440mph at 20,000ft. That might not seem impressive, but rate of climb at sea level would increase from 2980ft/sec to 5800ft/sec. That is, given the inherent drag of the aircraft it would gain little from another 70 per cent of horsepower.

In 1946, then, the navy had a total of ninety jet fighters on order, the FD-1s and the FJ-1s (the F6U had not yet been ordered). Deliveries of production Phantoms were to begin in the autumn of 1946, with squadron operation beginning the next year. The FJ-1 would be about a year behind.[32] That year a test dogfight between the hottest existing naval piston-engine fighter, the F8F-1 Bearcat, and an air force P-80 Shooting Star brought out the need to convert to jets. Given its vastly superior speed, diving speed and zoom-climb, the F-80 could easily defeat the Bearcat. It offered the Bearcat only fleeting firing opportunities, but could have fired long bursts into the Bearcat. There was also political pressure to adopt jets on a large scale. The 1947 air force programme called for nearly all jet fighters, although a few propeller-driven F-82s (twin Mustangs) were still being bought as night fighters. The navy's situation was further aggravated by a strike at Westinghouse which badly delayed the 24J (J34) engine planned for most of its fighters. In May 1946 BuAer wrote to OpNav that an additional jet fighter should be in production in 1948. BuAer still saw jet fighters it was buying as developmental; it was currently running a competition for a high-performance jet interceptor. Given the problem at Westinghouse, it was anxious to develop a second source of jet engines.[33] The Nene was manufactured under licence by Pratt & Whitney as the J42. It was attractive partly because it was interchangeable with General Electric's I-40 (which became the Allison J33).

The question was whether, despite the potential for radical advances in aerodynamics, BuAer should buy another conventional fighter. BuAer held an internal conference on 2 July 1946.[34] Head of fighter design Commander A B Metzger argued that the programme for conventional straight-wing jet fighters was adequate, but there was no tailed swept-wing fighter, a configuration which had been of considerable interest for about a year. Sweepback would make it possible to push maximum speed up about 50–70mph, to about 670mph; a straight-wing fighter was limited to about 600mph. It would offer a similar advantage in diving and a swept-wing fighter would also suffer less from buffeting in accelerated turns due to its higher critical Mach number. Experiments with the L-39 (a P-39 Airacobra with swept wings) had already shown that carrier approaches and landings with a 35° sweep were entirely practical. Within about a year the D-558-II Skyrocket project would begin to produce data on high-speed swept-wing flight. The tailless swept-wing Chance Vought F7U Cutlass was already being evaluated as part of the 1946 interceptor contest.

Grumman's relatively small jet fighter was also attractive because there were hopes that it could operate from smaller carriers (CVLs). That never happened; it took a large carrier to launch jet fighters. Grumman was offering a much less experimental aircraft and it had proven very successful in developing earlier fighters. It would also soon end production of its Bearcat. Given its record, BuAer wanted to maintain the company in fighter production.[35] The BuAer conference recommended that Grumman should build the single-Nene fighter it had proposed. The first two of them should be straight-wing prototypes which might be the basis of an interim fighter. The third should be a swept-wing version as a prototype for a high-performance interceptor, in effect a fall-back against possible failure of the tailless F7U. On 30 August Grumman submitted a formal proposal to build three straight-wing F9F-2 fighters and also to provide design data for the swept-wing aircraft. It is not clear when the conference recommendation changed, but it seems likely that BuAer wanted to use FY46 money to buy the F9F-2 and the three straight-wing F9F-2s plus the design study cost the same as the three F9F-1 night fighters originally planned. The projected swept-wing fighter became the separate F10F, procurement of which began early in 1948. BuAer may have wanted to avoid overloading Grumman's engineering staff and it did not have concrete data on swept-wing designs until they were developed as part of the D558-II Skyrocket research aircraft project (1947).

Grumman's Panther quickly became more than a prototype,

because by 1948 the navy badly wanted large numbers of high-performance jet fighters. The Bearcat vs F-80 trial was followed by others, always with the same results. In December 1949 Chief of BuAer Rear Admiral A W Pride summarised what had been learned (which he described as opinions) in a letter to CNO.[36] Piston-engine fighters could not stand up to jets, either offensively or defensively. They could not successfully attack jet bombers. Nor could they successfully protect propeller-driven attack aircraft – the only type the navy had – against attacks by jets. They were of dubious value against piston-engined attackers escorted by jets. Turboprop fighters were not worth building, at least for the present. However, the cruising performance of turboprop attack aircraft was close enough to that of jet fighters that jets should be able to escort them effectively. Enough jet fighters should be bought to fill all fighter roles, including night fighters and photo-reconnaissance. Piston-engine fighters and attack aircraft should be retained for ground attack.

Large-scale jet fighter production had begun the previous year. With its single engine, Grumman's F9F-2 Panther was less expensive than the twin-engine Banshee and probably also easier to build. The FY49 aircraft programme (as listed by BuAer in April 1948) showed 178 F2H-1s (and fifteen F2H-1Ns) but 344 F9F-2s. Monthly Panther production was estimated as twenty-three in July 1949, rising to thirty for November 1949 through June 1950.[37] By way of contrast, the expected peak Banshee production rate was eighteen per month between April and June 1950.

The important issue was how to handle the rapidly-developing F2H and F9F families. For the F2H, the dramatic development was the F2H-2, which was lengthened by 12in forward (for extra tankage, 177 gallons) and could take special 200-gallon tip tanks, giving it a combat radius of 600nm. That made it a suitable escort fighter for the first-generation AJ-1 Savage strategic bomber. However, it could take off safely only from the *Midways* and the modernised *Oriskany*, the first US jet carrier.

Development of longer-range versions continued; the F2H-3 was further extended forward for more tankage, inserted amidships (the nose extended forward). It was conceived from the outset as an all-weather fighter (see below). The final F2H-4 version was a slight further improvement.

In the case of the F9F, the important new development was the use of alternative engines: the US-built Nene (J42) in the F9F-2 and versions of the J33 in the F9F-3 and -4, the engine in the -4 offering substantially better thrust. Unfortunately the engines were not interchangeable. A carrier could operate F9F-2s or -3s and -4s, but not both.

Comparison was difficult but unavoidable. A Banshee cost about twice as much as a Panther: in a November 1948 table, $847,000 for an F2H-2 vs $463,000 for an F9F-4 or -5. It offered much greater radius of action, 655nm rather than 582 or 540 for the -4 or -5 (using manufacturer's figures). However, it was slower, 464 knots at 35,000ft rather than 472 or 473 knots. It also climbed more slowly at sea level, 7350ft/min compared to 8390 or 9100ft/min. That was no surprise: the twin-engine Banshee was also considerably heavier: 19,817lbs compared to 15,768ft for the F9F-4 and 15,968ft for the F9F-5. A FY51 change to the more powerful J34-WE-32 engine (instead of the current -34) was expected to boost the next version of the F2H to the same performance as the F9Fs without costing its edge in combat radius.

By November 1948, US naval tactical thought was turning once more towards fighter-heavy carrier air groups, at least for the initial

An F2H-4. As an exchange test pilot at Patuxent River, Captain 'Winkle' Brown flew the F2H-2 and -3 Banshee. He found it amiable but mediocre, inferior in almost every way to the much earlier Gloster Meteor IV. 'It was, however, immensely popular with US Navy pilots, as it gave them a fairly carefree introduction into the use of carrier-borne jet aircraft.' In addition to the radar and the extra fuel, the F2H-3 introduced irreversible hydraulic controls with artificial feel. Compared to the F2H-2, as regards stability and control it was a great improvement and it also flew much better at high Mach numbers. Its safe flight Mach limit was 0.97, but the tactical limit was 0.85 and it began to buffet at Mach 0.84, reaching a peak at Mach 0.91 and then decreasing. 'Personally I enjoyed flying this amiable aircraft, which conveyed a feeling of docility combined with nippiness, making it a pleasure to handle.' (McDonnell)

stages of any war. As in the Second World War, the extra fighters might be provided by Marine (VMF) units and that reasoning in turn justified placing jets in Marine Corps service. The other important source of additional aircraft and pilots was the Reserves, which in 1948 were flying wartime propeller aircraft, largely Hellcats. The new policy of pressing forward with jets required that the Reserve pilots receive jet training, so the initial jets should be transferred to them.

In November 1948, too, the budget was tightening, so looking towards FY50 BuAer had to consider cutting some of the fighter models it was buying. Six were in or near production: three general-purpose fighters (F9F, F2H and the newer F7U Cutlass) and three night fighters (the existing Corsair [F4U-5N] and the projected jet F2H-2N and F3D-1). The budget squeeze shows in projected cuts. Of the day fighters, 234 F2H, 418 F9F and nineteen F7U were on order, split among various sub-types. For 1950 plans called for 140 F2H, 242 F9F and ninety-six F7U.

BuAer saw strong pilot preference for twin-engine reliability; 'until the jet engine is well proved in the fleet'. If the F7U could not be dropped from the programme (it was the only fighter to offer anti-bomber performance), the only way to save money in FY50 would be drop the expensive F2H in favour of an equal number of much less

expensive F9Fs. However, the F2H was much closer to carrier suitability. BuAer was also reluctant to eliminate a live source of fighter production. The Chief of BuAer therefore opted to keep both fighters in production. Proposals to cut night fighter production were also dropped. It appears that BuAer planners found another way to cut their costs during FY50, drastically slowing production, hence delaying re-equipment of the fleet with jet fighters.

However, in December 1949 the Chief of BuAer pointed out to DCNO (Air) that modernisation with jets was vital.[38] Operational tests had recently shown that piston-engine fighters had no chance of successfully fighting jets, either offensively or defensively, nor could they successfully escort attack aircraft in the face of jet opposition. They were of dubious value against enemy piston-engine bombers or attack aircraft escorted by jets, unless they enjoyed so much numerical superiority that they could prevail despite heavy losses. They would be effective against unescorted enemy piston-engined bombers. Turboprop fighters did not offer enough performance (compared to jets) to be worth developing further. Piston-engine attack aircraft like the Skyraider (AD) were viable only with jet escorts. This was the policy in force when the United States went to war in Korea about seven months later.

A new kind of armament?

As it looked ahead in 1945, BuAer had to wonder whether the coming generation of fast fighters could manoeuvre tightly enough to hold fixed guns on targets long enough to destroy enemy aircraft. This was much the argument many had made before 1939, when it seemed that the fast new piston-engined aircraft could not possibly dogfight. The Germans had taken it so seriously that they had concentrated on deflection and zoom tactics in training Me-109 pilots. Now it seemed to BuAer that there might not even be enough time for a jet zooming

FIGHTERS OVER THE FLEET

past another jet to do much damage. Manoeuvring would be difficult at best. Furthermore, to destroy a heavily armoured (and armed) bomber a fighter would need longer-range firepower. None of this was very far from the logic which had led the British to the abortive turret fighters of the late pre-war period, such as the Blackburn Roc. However, there is no evidence that BuAer was deterred by that experience. Instead, in December 1945 it projected development of remote-controlled turrets, both optically and radar-controlled.[39] Even without the fighter application, it would have developed such turrets to protect long-range bombers and patrol aircraft, although the details of a fighter turret were different.

Development of remote-controlled turrets for fighters continued, with waning support, at least through 1954. Conventional turrets traversed and elevated to track targets. The new turrets BuAer wanted rolled around the axis of the fuselage while traversing. Just as the British had imagined before the war, such a turret could be used by a fighter flying outside a bomber's cone of defensive fire. There were problems. Guns protruding into the slipstream around a fighter's nose or wing (the two favoured positions) created drag. Typically the guns could traverse (for example, elevate) through 90°; to fire at targets below the aircraft, the turret rotated (rolled) around its centreline. To track a fast crossing target, the entire turret had to accelerate very rapidly. BuAer let a contract to Emerson Electric, which made many of its turrets, in June 1949 for what became its X17A, carrying four 0.50-calibre machine guns.[40] It was intended to test the concept in a Grumman Panther (F9F) fighter. Ground tested in May 1950, it was installed (without guns or radar) in an F9F-3 in September. Initial flight tests were successful and the four guns were installed, but the radar and fire-control system proved problematical. By the time the project died early in 1954, the future of fighter weapons clearly belonged to guided missiles.

The first formal study of what it would take for a carrier fighter to intercept a fast jet bomber seems to have been undertaken by OEG in 1946.[41] It drew on wartime fighter studies, including a September 1944 study of slow fighters – i.e. fighters with little or no speed advantage over their bomber targets. The 1946 study envisaged bombers flying at 400–500 knots, which were the accepted targets for the late 1940s and early 1950s. Existing weapons were lethal out to 5000–7000 yds, but accuracy limited effective range to about 800 yds. All existing fighter tactics were based on a pursuit course, the fighter following the bomber on a course which, if extended, would end in a collision. Any sustained burst of fire had to come from astern and the G-load the pilot could sustain limited how far off the bomber's tail the attack could begin. At sonic speed, against a bomber of near-sonic speed, a fighter would have to begin inside 25° from the bomber's tail at 1000 yds (50° at 1500 yds). Quite aside from effects on the pilot, a fighter flying some tight paths would suffer from buffeting severe enough to ruin its aim. Regions of severe buffeting made it difficult for a fighter to close within a thousand yards of a bomber (on some courses, 1500 yds), except from astern. If the fighter was flying at roughly bomber speed, it had to attack from ahead, because it could not turn sharply enough and get within gunnery range. If it began substantially off the bomber's nose, it would never get within firing range. In any attack from ahead, the range would close so quickly that the fighter would fire very few shots. However, a fighter attacking from astern would spend longer in the arc of fire from the bomber's tail gun than it would spend in a shooting position of its own. OEG concluded

that any future fighter fire-control system (and the associated weapon) had to support attacks from any direction.

A later analysis showed that increases in speed or altitude increased the area around the bomber which the fighter could not penetrate. Firing time would decrease. The problem was worst in ahead or beam attacks, which would always have to be made from long range. Firing time could be increased only by attacking from astern, but in that case the fighter would be flying into a very narrow area around the tail of the bomber, what was called 'being sucked into the tail cone'. That would place the fighter in the fire of the tail gun carried by virtually all bombers. For this reason bomber designers generally gained performance at the expense of all but tail guns.

When it looked at the interception problem in 1947, the BuAer Fighter Branch went further. It assumed that nearly all attacks would have to be made from ahead, because fighters would not be too much faster than bombers. Attacks from astern would be impossible because of the way that fighters were typically directed by a carrier. The fighter director would vector them towards an incoming bomber. To carry out a stern attack, a fighter would have to fly past the bomber and then turn back towards it. It would have to be fast enough to catch up, which would probably mean flying through fire from the bomber's tail gun until it got within range. During the war US CAP fighters typically first saw their targets approaching from ahead and post-war practice envisaged attacks from roughly ahead (the forward hemisphere).

To BuAer, the question was how to make the limited available firing (and decision) time count. A 500-knot fighter would close on a 450-knot bomber at 950 knots and higher speeds for both were coming. Even if the bomber was detected at 200nm, the fighter would have very little time to engage it. Earlier fighter tactics were impossible. The fighter could always be directed towards an incoming bomber. Although it could make a long tail chase (into the bomber's tail gun), more likely it would attack from ahead. In a head-on attack at a closing speed of 950–1150 knots, a pilot would get only one opportunity and he would have only 15 seconds between first seeing the target and opening fire, which was hardly enough.[42] A small error would ruin the single firing run, so the pilot had to begin any correction as far away as possible. At very high altitudes, where turning radius was large, the problem would be even greater.

Past fighters had followed pursuit courses, because if a pilot could see his target he could point his aircraft at it. The question was how tightly he would have to turn. If he was making a deflection shot, he would point ahead of the target, but he would still follow a curving pursuit-type course as he approached. BuAer conceived an alternative: a collision course. The pilot would be directed onto a nearly straight line pointing at the point at which, if he did not pull away, he would collide with the approaching bomber. He would not be following a curve and he would not be pulling a high G-load. The pilot might have to pull maximum Gs to get onto the final straight-line path, but not once he was on it. At least in theory, a collision course could approach a target from any angle, rather than limit attack to nose or tail aspects. The main disadvantage of a collision-course attack was that the weapon had to be used at only one place along the path. However, that was not too different from a pursuit course giving a pilot one or two seconds of firing time.

A pilot had no intuitive way to fly such a course. He needed assistance. In a way he needed a much more powerful equivalent of a computing gunsight. BuAer developed it in the form of its Interceptor

184

Armament and Control System (IACS) Aero XIA.[43] Its new APS-25 tracking radar measured both range and target movement across the path of the interceptor. IACS indicated the proper path in a pilot indicator. If future interceptors were intended primarily to deal with fast bombers, it followed that all needed radar. Thus future fighters should be night or all-weather fighters; there was no point in building day interceptors. They also needed more lethal armament; in 1947 one proposal was to use an air-to-air version of the existing high-velocity aircraft rocket (HVAR) with a proximity fuze.

The BuAer Armament Division began work on this problem late in 1946, beginning with a simulated attack on a fast bomber using a Corsair as a bomber stand-in. Tests at Aberdeen Proving Ground showed that the surest and quickest method of destroying a large bomber was to explode a small TNT charge (1–3lbs) inside the bomber. The size of the charge ruled out a heavy-calibre gun. The Armament Division and the Armament Laboratory at NAMU began studying rockets in February 1947. To obtain the desired radar, BuAer let a contract with Fairchild Camera and another with the Avion Instrument Company to modify the existing APS-19 night-fighter radar as a pointer to a future system. Despite its limitations, APS-19 most closely fit the requirements. The final radar would use a stabilised antenna and two small integrating gyros to measure target motion. The division hoped that the coming APS-25, which had been conceived for single-seat night fighters, could be developed for the purpose.[44]

The US Air Force was reaching a similar conclusion as it faced possible future attacks by the Soviet version of the US B-29, the Tu-4. There was extensive wartime experience showing that B-29s were difficult to shoot down. Both services joined to adopt the new 2.75in FFAR, which had been under navy study since 1945. By the mid-1950s, unfortunately, these rockets turned out to be ineffective. In tests, rockets often collided with each other and the desired shotgun effect was ruined. For the moment, the navy continued to rely on cannon, albeit faster-firing than their Second World War predecessors. The requirement for explosive power and quick effect remained through the Cold War, the main change being that the bomber had to be intercepted further and further from the carrier. Both BuAer and its air force counterpart were soon looking beyond unguided rockets to guided missiles.

As an interim measure, BuAer pursued the development of 5in high-velocity aircraft rockets (HVAR) with proximity fuzes. While the rockets were being developed, new data suggested that at high altitudes bombers might be less susceptible to fire damage than had previously been imagined. In the past, fire had been a major damage mechanism. In 1949–50 experiments suggested that at high altitudes automatic inerting techniques might make it difficult to start a fire aboard a large bomber. Guns in particular might be much less effective than had been imagined. The emphasis shifted to weapons capable of smashing an enemy's airframe, either by blast or by chopping it up (continuous-rod warheads).

The single pass with automatic control raised the question of radar: every interceptor would need a powerful radar, so every interceptor would become a limited night fighter, whether or not (as noted below) the only really effective night fighter would have a dedicated radar operator. Initial analysis suggested that no US fighter radar was good enough. Some in BuAer wanted to adopt new British AI radars, remembering how effective their wartime sets had been. The new British sets offered a range of 9–10nm, which was not really enough for a head-on shot. However, it turned out that the APS-21 already under development for the F3D interceptor offered much what was needed.[45] It could detect a small aircraft at a range of at least 12nm. It was probably also the best that could be done. Radar range could be increased either by enlarging the radar dish or by increasing power. It seemed that APS-21 had gone about as far as possible in both directions, with a 30in dish (in a new interceptor that might have to be reduced to 24in or less) and the most powerful available X-band power tube (magnetron). Estimated range against a 15,000lb fighter was 15nm. The requirement was coverage to at least 45° to either side, but APS-21 already covered 180°. In elevation the new radar should cover 30° above and below the centreline, but APS-21 already covered 60° above and 30° below. The only requirement not yet met (and not met by any other radar) was the day scope – unlike the F3D, the interceptor would have to use its radar all the time. As for integration with a fire-control system, it was already integrated with one in the APG-26 system of the F3D fighter.

The value of the FFAR was called into question by an OEG report on *Future Requirements for Air Interception in Fleet Air Defense* (OEG 91). To reach that conclusion, OEG did not take into account efforts to develop an effective director for collision-course interception and it also attributed a relatively high kill probability for the fighter's 20mm gun against fighters. In February 1950 the Director of the BuAer Military Requirements Division pointed out that a fire-fighting system might make a bomber relatively immune to 20mm fire.[46] The two new interceptors (XF3H and XF4D) were both armed only with FFARs. An interceptor might find itself fighting enemy escort fighters or continuing to fight after exhausting its FFARs. The Director considered it advantageous to provide the new interceptors with 20mm guns or with VT-fuzed 5in rockets to supplement the FFARs. He asked that the study include the Sparrow air-to-air missile then being developed and that it include the new Grumman XF10F because as a general-purpose fighter it might find itself fighting both bombers and fighters as well as carrying out strike sweeps.

At least through 1950 there was also US Navy interest in toss bombing as an air-to-air weapon. In the autumn of 1944 the army had considered it as a means of attacking bomber formations and later the RAF was interested in toss bombing (using small nuclear weapons) as an alternative to air-to-air missiles. In July 1949 BuOrd was asked to report on the concept. It considered the method effective, pointing out that its new Mk 8 fire-control system would be flexible enough to support such attacks (toss bombing required more than a collision-course computer, because the bomb slowed down in the air). Toss bombs never became operational, but the idea of a large explosive with a proximity fuze certainly continued to interest the air force. It employed an unguided nuclear rocket (Genie, also called Ding-Dong) in the late 1950s, in effect as a successor to the FFAR.

It took time for the fleet to shift to radar-equipped interceptors and even then it retained day air-superiority fighters into the 1960s. The day fighters could not make collision-course attacks. They had to fly past any incoming bomber and turn to attack its rear hemisphere. The day fighters of the late 1950s were armed with Sidewinder, a rear-hemisphere missile.

While weapons were being developed, a practical test of fighter interception was nearly carried out. It is interesting because it gives a pilot's-eye view of the problem. In August 1949 the Joint Chiefs of Staff assigned evaluation of the strategic air offensive plan, including the capability of the B-36 bomber, to the new Weapons System Evaluation Group (WSEG).[47] By this time the navy was increasingly embroiled in a debate over whether the sort of protracted war it expected to fight (for which seapower was needed) was likely in view of the ability of the air force's huge B-36 bomber to drop atomic bombs on the Soviet Union. The navy view was that the immunity of the B-36 was an illusion. Just because the Japanese had failed to intercept the two atomic bombers of 1945 did not mean that such aircraft were at all immune. CNO ordered both fleets to draw up preliminary plans to demonstrate that a B-36 was indeed vulnerable by intercepting it. The Atlantic Fleet chose the F2H Banshee; the Pacific, the F9F Panther. The very high altitude tests envisaged by the Atlantic Fleet were not carried out, but Pacific Fleet Panthers did intercept B-36s on at least two occasions.

CNO was encouraged by a memo written by one of the Patuxent River test pilots, Commander V J Widhelm, which analysed the possibilities enjoyed by the Banshee. He pointed out that, because of the low wing loading needed to gain acceptable carrier landing characteristics, navy fighters enjoyed much better climb and high-altitude performance than their air force counterparts. The air force had sacrificed climbing performance for higher speed in aircraft such as the F-86 Sabre. Widhelm did not say so, but he implied that such sacrifices might have made it seem that a very high-altitude bomber was actually immune. Wildelm's analysis gave an idea of just how a radar-directed Banshee would have attacked a high-altitude bomber. Although he did not say so, this was much the problem fleet air defence had to solve.

Forwarding Widhelm's paper, the CO at Patuxent River (Captain F M Trapwell) wrote that since the delivery of the Banshee his pilots had had far more experience than the air force in really high-altitude fighter operation; he thought the air force was disappointed, or at least surprised, by the poor performance of their own fighters at altitude. He added that the air force's choice of the B-36 was illogical: the air force had posed a relatively easy problem when the real problem the navy had been attacking was how to knock down a very fast bomber. The huge size and propellers of the B-36 made it an ideal radar and visual target and its low speed gave the interceptor the invaluable advantage of increased attack time. At this time the navy was developing an interceptor designed to operate at or above about Mach 1, an 'extraordinarily difficult and expensive' objective. If the B-36 was the only threat, the navy could make do with much less. The Russians' problem would also be much simplified, since the B-36 could not possibly be escorted all the way to the target.

Current navy fighters suffered from short radar range and short gun range, but the B-36 took less advantage of radar limitation than any other possible aircraft. Coming rockets and missiles would greatly improve the fighters, but the B-36 was armed with fighter guns and could not be given anything more potent.

Altitude would not affect the fighter pilot's vision, although he would suffer a loss of manoeuvrability: his radius of turn and rate of turn would increase by a factor of about 2.5 at 40,000ft. At 45,000ft the fighter would be limited to nose and tail attacks. That would make the fighter more vulnerable, but the bomber would present a much larger target. The bomber would be particularly vulnerable to group attacks, given the necessary limits of its fire-control system. A large group of B-36s might be mutually supporting, but mutual support would be limited by gun range. Overall, Banshees should be able to stop the Mach 0.65 B-36 but not a Mach 0.8 jet bomber. However, as

long as it claimed to be able to mount a nuclear offensive from the United States (hence not to need foreign bases or the sea routes to them), the air force had no use for a fast jet bomber with a range of 1000–1500nm. However, the more ruthless Russians might find exactly such a bomber acceptable on the basis of one-way attacks. In fact the air force soon bought the B-47, which was roughly what Trapwell thought would work, basing it in Europe, North Africa and Japan.

For the fighter pilot, the main question was whether surface radar could bring him close enough to the target. That was the CIC fighter assignment problem; the Banshee had to be brought within 4nm of the target. That was questionable with current shipboard radars. On the other hand, at very high altitude bombing would be so inaccurate that even a nuclear bomb would not be effective, so the B-36 would probably have to fly considerably lower and more vulnerably. Even at 30,000ft a well-trained crew missed the aim point during the Bikini tests, under ideal conditions, by half a mile.

In 1949 the Banshee was the only fighter in US service which could climb to 40,000ft, the maximum altitude for a B-36, in 9.5 minutes. While climbing it would cover about 70nm. Operating in pairs at normal rated power, sections of Banshees could arrive at 40,000ft in 17 to 18 minutes (about 105nm). If the B-36 was detected 200nm out, the fighters would meet it 105nm from their ship. Air-to-air exercises had shown that fighters could attack a 400–450mph target at this altitude every three minutes, counting manoeuvring time in that rarified air. They would be able to make five runs on the B-36 before it reached its target. Every 20-mile reduction in initial detection range would cost one run. Based on experience attacking the smaller B-29, a B-36 should be visible in daylight at 30 to 35 miles if was leaving contrails and 12 to 18 miles if not. However, detection range might also vary considerably depending on the colour of the aircraft (an unpainted aircraft seemed best) and whether it was level with the fighters or above or below them. Experience showed that the fighters could generally expect to make their initial run before being seen. That reinforced the argument for more lethal fighter weapons such as the FFAR (Widhelm did not refer to them). Once the fighters saw the target, they would consider the tactical situation before choosing their tactics. Below 35,000ft there would be no problem at all with a bomber flying even at maximum B-36 speed, 395mph (343 knots). Above that the problem was more difficult, but the Banshee would continue to be effective up to 42,000ft. Above that the only option would be a stern attack. Widhelm thought that two Banshees would suffice up to 35,000ft, four being required above that. Banshees could reach 45,000ft, but at such altitudes more would be needed – perhaps six to eight. Widhelm based his estimates on numerous dummy attacks he and other Banshee pilots had made against aircraft flying at 40,000ft at true airspeeds up to 480mph (Mach 0.73), far faster than a B-36.

Much depended on how far the bomber was from its target. A head-on attack would be effective, but after completing it fighters would need considerable time for another pass. Other manoeuvres offered more time for repeated attacks, hence for a better chance of killing the bomber. In effect Widhelm was pointing to the need, which BuAer certainly recognised, for weapons which would be lethal on the first head-on pass. At or below 35,000ft the Banshee would have complete freedom of manoeuvre, so it could make any type of firing pass: overhead, high side, flat side, low side, head-on and runs from beneath. At 40,000ft it could no longer make overhead runs because it would have compressibility problems during the vertical dive after it passed the target. At 45,000ft it would be limited to head-on and tail-on runs. Widhelm wanted at least 2 to 1 odds against a B-36, but in his covering letter the CO of Patuxent River wrote that he would be satisfied with even or worse odds.

The navy lost this battle; Secretary of Defense Louis Johnson had adopted the B-36 solution to national security because his funds were too tight for anything more and he was not going to reverse course because the navy demonstrated that the bomber could be shot down. However, he did allow the navy to continue developing its own nuclear bombers and it appears that any cuts in naval aircraft procurement were quite limited. The more lasting impact of Widhelm's letter was to reinforce the idea that very high altitude interception required a better air-to-air radar and more lethal fighter weapons, initially in the form of FFARs.

After the fight was over, DCNO(Air) pointed out that the B-36 interception project had given overriding priority to high-altitude interception training, accelerating the development of fleet air defence tactics, uncovering important deficiencies and also accelerating the development of jet tactics. It had been extremely valuable. After it was dropped, fleet air defence continued to be the highest priority in operational development.[48]

Beyond the FFAR was the air-to-air guided missile. The speed with which such weapons were introduced in the 1950s testifies to the failure of the FFAR. Initially there was competition for both surface-to-air and air-to-air missile between BuAer and BuOrd, the former arguing that they were pilotless aircraft (P/A). In 1945 BuAer was developing a beam-riding radar guidance system for an ultimately abortive surface-to-air missile called Lark. Soon after the war its P/A programme included three categories of air-to-air missiles: short (interim) range, intermediate range (17nm) and long range (35nm). It turned out that the interim missile was the only one developed. It began as Project 'Hot Shot' to produce a beam-riding guidance system for the 5in high-velocity aircraft rocket which fighters already carried (a parallel British programme was called 'Long Shot'). BuAer recognised that electronics came first, so it contracted with Sperry, an important radar firm. Sperry in turn sub-contracted the airframe to Douglas. In May 1946 Sperry was asked to submit a formal proposal for a missile with a maximum range not less than 2000 yds (1nm) and a minimum of no more than 1000ft, capable of intercepting a Mach 1 target. At this stage the target-tracking and beam-generating functions were expected to be separate.

Sperry reported about March 1947 that the 5in rocket was not large enough to carry the necessary electronics, nor could it fully exploit the range a radar could achieve. BuAer accepted an 8in airframe as the basis for future development. A weapon contract was let in May 1947, the missile being named Sparrow in July. Point Mugu Naval Air Missile Test Center was created specifically to support this programme, the first unpowered test flights being made in August 1948. Production began in 1951 as part of the Korean War mobilisation; the first successful interception, of a Hellcat drone by an F3D, was made on 3 December 1952.

By that time BuAer had split the programme into three alternative elements. Sparrow I was the original beam-rider, the attacking fighter keeping a radar beam on target throughout the missile's flight. Sparrow II was an alternative using an active radar, a fire-and-forget missile. Sparrow III was guided semi-actively, homing on radar energy reflected from the target aircraft. Compared to Sparrow I, it could

work with a simpler airborne radar, but it did not place nearly so much of a burden on the missile seeker as did the fully-active Sparrow II. On the other hand, Sparrow II figured heavily in fighter studies of the mid-1950s because it demanded so little of the firing aircraft.

All three systems were well-suited to interception from ahead of the target. Sparrows of this initial generation were boost-glide missiles, their short-burning boosters accelerating them to maximum speed. That offered high speed, but it limited manoeuvring power near the target. Any particular required manoeuvring power set effective range. Typically a missile was launched at Mach 2.4, decelerating to Mach 0.9. That sort of limitation was acceptable because the missile was intended to deal with relatively docile bombers rather than with violently-manoeuvring fighters. Combat in Vietnam pitted these missiles against agile fighters, with predictably poor results.

Sparrow I was initially designated AAM-N-2 in a tri-service system introduced about 1949, then redesignated as AIM-7A in a tri-service system introduced in 1962 alongside the revised aircraft designation system. Sparrow II was AAM-N-3 (AIM-7B in the tri-service system, even though by 1962 it was gone) and Sparrow III was AAM-N-6 (the initial version was later designated AIM-7C).

Sparrow I was designed for a range of 11,000 yds (5.5nm) against a target at 15,000ft or 14,000 yds against a 50,000ft (maximum altitude) target, reaching an initial speed of Mach 2.7. It was 12ft long and weighed 315lbs. Test versions of Sparrow I rode a beam controlled by the fighter's optical gunsight. It equipped Squadron VX-4, established at Point Mugu in September 1952 to operate sixteen Sparrow-configured F3D-2 test aircraft. To hit a target, a fighter had to be within its 30° tail cone. The lethal range of the warhead was 30ft.[49] The radar system was designated APQ-51.

Later aircraft were intended to have the APQ-36 radar, which automatically tracked the target and moved its guidance beam to match. That made collision-course attacks possible and the fighter could pull away while still focusing its beam on the approaching target. This technique could deal with a degree of evasion by the target. As of 1953, plans called for adding Sparrow I to one fighter squadron and one interceptor squadron in each existing air group and to one VMF in each Fleet Marine Air Wing beginning in August 1954. Sparrow II entered fleet service in 1956 on board Demon (F3H-2M) and Cutlass (F7U-3M) fighters. They generally carried four missiles underwing. The missile-guidance radar (APG-51A) was a standard night-fighter gunnery radar (APG-51) modified to generate a guidance beam. It was slaved to an optical sight, which required visual identification. As a consequence, it was not an all-weather missile. APG-51 was modified into APQ-51 to provide all-weather capability for the Sparrow I fighters. Beam-riding was abandoned for Sparrow for much the same reason as for the surface-to-air Terrier: its low-altitude performance was unacceptable, at a time when low-fliers were considered the most serious threats to the fleet.

Sparrow II was a Douglas active-radar missile using a K-band radar. As of 1953, expected range was 7.3nm at 50,000ft. Compared to Sparrow I or III (below) it made much less demand on the fighter firing it, because it was a fire-and-forget weapon. It featured in numerous fighter projects of the 1950s, but never entered service. Sparrow II is probably best known as the projected weapon of the abortive Canadian Arrow (CF-105) fighter. Douglas offered Sparrow II on board its lightweight F5D Skylancer. BuAer dropped this project in 1956 and the missile was cancelled in 1958.

Sparrow III was Raytheon's semi-active version of the missile, homing on radar energy reflected by the target. It was adopted for the F4H Phantom fighter, the guidance radar initially being the massive APQ-50 (APQ-72 added target illumination for semi-active operation). Raytheon took over production after completion of Sparrow I deliveries in 1956; Sparrow III deliveries began in January 1958 and deployment in August. Initially Sparrow III was carried by Demons whose radars had been modified to incorporate Continuous Wave (CW) injection (as APG-51Bs).[50]

The modified AAM-N-6a (AIM-6D) was designed for supersonic launch (i.e. by a Phantom) used a storable liquid-fuel rocket which increased its effective range by a third and its ceiling by 10 per cent to 30,000ft. It and -7C had 65lb continuous-rod warheads creating a 56ft circle and then separating, to cut into a large aircraft as much as 125ft from the missile when it detonated. Fuzing was contact or proximity.

AIM-7E, which entered production in 1963, had an even more powerful solid-fuel motor, which increased effective range by about 75 per cent, actual figures depending on launch speed. It had the same continuous-rod warhead as AIM-7D. Raytheon called this missile Sparrow IIIB. In 1963 it credited it with an effective intercept range of 16nm (when launched at Mach 2) against a 5m² target (a bomber) at 50,000ft. Under some circumstances effective range might be closer to 20nm. About five years later AIM-7E was credited with a maximum range of 13nm against a high-altitude fighter head-on (3nm in a tail attack). Typical minimum ranges were 5000ft for a stern attack and 12,000ft head-on.

In 1963 Raytheon proposed 'Advanced Sparrow III' as an alternative to the Phoenix missile then in the early development stage to arm the F-111B and later the F-14. Effective range was limited by the requirement that the missile lock onto energy reflected from the target before it could be launched. If the missile could be commanded to fly out until it was closer to the target, it could receive its minimum energy at greater overall range (much the same idea was later applied to the Standard Missile in its New Threat Upgrade configuration and Aegis uses the same idea). In this case Raytheon envisaged a programmed fly-out and increased range provided by a new dual-thrust (boost-sustain) rocket motor. The missile might fly for as much as 75 seconds, to reach a range of 52nm. Typically AIM-7E range would be doubled to about 30nm. More compact electronics would make it possible to increase warhead weight from 65lbs to 90lbs. For such a missile the effective range limit would be set by the power of the illuminating radar. Instead of relying on CW illumination, 'Advanced Sparrow' could exploit reflected energy produced by a pulse-Doppler fighter radar. Many of the features Raytheon offered in 1963 appeared about a decade later in the next version of the missile, AIM-7F. Before that happened, AIM-7D and -7E were deployed to Vietnam; the experience there is described in Chapter 10.

BuOrd was also interested in air-to-air weapons. Its Naval Ordnance Test Station (NOTS) at China Lake had been set up to test the many rocket weapons developed during the Second World War. After the war it became interested in new possibilities and on its own initiative it began work on an air-to-air missile with infra-red guidance. At this stage such a weapon could be fired only towards the tail of a target, so it was hardly compatible with the collision-course tactics being developed. NOTS argued for its one major advantage, simplicity. It was also a fire-and-forget missile, unlike Sparrow I or Sparrow III. In 1949 the US defence budget was badly stretched and special efforts were made to rationalise the missile programme. NOTS' weapon narrowly escaped cancellation. It became Sidewinder.

Sidewinder I was designated AAM-N-7 (later AIM-9). The original Sidewinder I was a prototype only, the first operational version being Sidewinder IA (AIM-9B). Where Sparrow had been conceived as a guided 5in rocket, that is exactly what Sidewinder was.

The first Sidewinder was fired successfully on 11 September 1953 and it entered fleet service in May 1956. It required far less of a fighter than Sparrow, so it was quickly deployed on board the air-superiority fighters bought during the Korean War emergency: Furies (FJ-3M and -4M) and Cougars (F9F-8s). In each case all that was required was wiring connecting the pilot's headphones with the missile and its seeker, plus a firing circuit. The pilot heard a tone when the seeker locked onto a target and then fired. He did not need any kind of fire-control system.

In September 1958 Sidewinder became the first guided missile to shoot down an aircraft in combat; Chinese Nationalist pilots used it successfully during the Formosa Straits crisis. Reportedly one of the Chinese Communist MiGs brought home a missile which had failed to explode and the Soviets were able to copy it. Sidewinder design was deliberately extremely simple. Its IR telescope was caged (fixed) to the missile body until the pilot pressed the trigger. As soon as the missile dropped free, its seeker began to track the target. The 25lb blast-fragmentation warhead was lethal up to 30ft, using either a proximity or contact fuze. Maximum range at high altitude was about 2.6nm, the solid-fuel rocket accelerating the missile to Mach 1.7. Minimum launch range was about 3000ft and at low-altitude range was reduced to about 4000ft.

The navy wanted longer range and all-weather and all-aspect homing. A new motor tripled mission range to 60 seconds and increased range to as much as 11.5nm, the missile growing slightly. Sidewinder IB (AIM-9C) was given a semi-active warhead. The parallel IR version was Sidewinder IC (AIM-9D). It was credited with limited head-on capability using a liquid nitrogen-cooled seeker and it could attack with greater deflection than could Sidewinder IA. For a time during the Vietnam War, the standard Crusader missile load was three AIM-9D and one AIM-9C; no -9Cs were credited with kills. Like Sparrow, this missile was intended primarily to attack bombers. Tests against manoeuvring targets were not apparently undertaken until 1964. At that point the seeker maker, Philco, suggested a Low Altitude Performance (LAP) improvement retrofit, which produced the short-range AIM-9E, with a narrow field of view (to exclude other hot spots), a wider look angle and faster tracking. The navy bought a similarly improved AIM-9G.

Part of the problem when fighting fighters in Vietnam was that the missile seeker would not lock onto a fast-moving target. A new SEAM (Sidewinder Expanded Acquisition Mode) slaved the seeker to the fighter's radar as it scanned.

The British also developed air-to-air missiles.[51] They began with Blue Sky (Fireflash), a beam-rider like Sparrow I, but with a shorter range (3500 yds).[52] The code name Blue Sky was assigned in 1949 and it was ready in 1958, slightly after Sparrow I. In 1955 it was decided that it would be used only for training, production being limited to 250 missiles.

The preferred air-to-air solution was infra-red guidance, which (at least in theory) placed less burden on the launching aircraft. Blue Jay Mk 1 (Firestreak) was under test by 1960 and a limited number were placed in service. Initial platforms included three Royal Navy Sea Venom Mk 21 night fighters, but later Firestreak armed Sea Vixen Mk 1 fighters on four wing pylons. Range was extended to 6000 yds

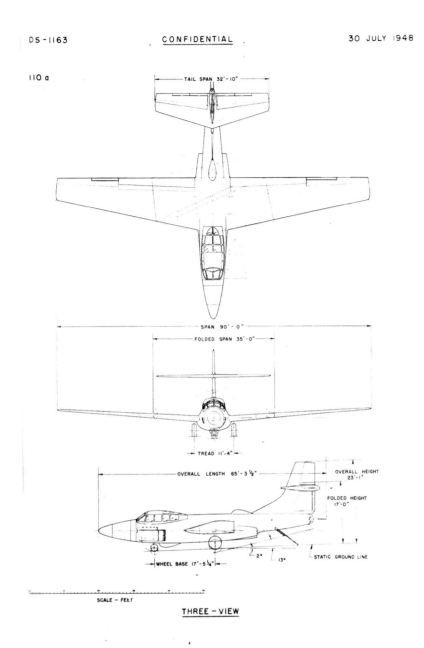

110 a

TAIL SPAN 32'-10"

SPAN 90'-0"
FOLDED SPAN 35'-0"

TREAD 11'-4"

OVERALL LENGTH 65'-3½"

OVERALL HEIGHT 23'-1"

FOLDED HEIGHT 17'-0"

WHEEL BASE 17'-5¼"

2°   13°   STATIC GROUND LINE

SCALE - FEET

THREE - VIEW

Douglas Santa Monica won the 1948 strategic fighter competition with this DS-1163 design. The proposal was dated 30 July 1948. Estimated maximum speed at 40,000ft was 465 knots (535mph), the figure required in the Specification (OS-112); similarly, estimated combat radius was the required 1200nm. Speed was for military thrust at maximum gross weight less 40 per cent of fuel (gross weight would then be 44,380lbs), with radomes extended. Power-off stall speed at normal landing weight was given as 76.6 knots, compared to the required maximum of 83.3 knots. Rate of climb at sea level was given as 4850ft/min. The nose and tail contained power-operated twin 20mm gun turrets carrying T-34 guns (the nose turret is not shown; it may have been similar to that later tested on board an F9F-3). Engines were three J46-WE-3s each rated at 4200lbs thrust at take-off, mounted alongside each other, the centre engine exhausting under the tail. Span was 90ft and length 65ft 3.5in. Note that the wings had to be skewed to fold to within the desired space, 35ft wide (which was still considerable). Take-off weight was 52,000lbs (combat weight, with much of the fuel burned, was 41,818lbs). No prototype was ever ordered. Funds were short by this time, but when the OS-112 competition was announced the escort fighter was an urgent project. A few months later it must have seemed much less so, since the navy was developing a higher-performance strategic bomber (which became the A-3 Skywarrior) which could, at least in theory, operate unescorted.

and the missile could be launched at speeds of Mach 0.7 to Mach 1.3; it could fly to 55,000ft. It carried a 43.5lb warhead. The first guided rounds were fired in 1954, a Venom firing a pre-production Firestreak the following year. The Royal Navy received its first Firestreaks in 1958 for Sea Venoms of 893 NAS.

The production missile, which armed Royal Navy Sea Vixens, was Blue Jay Mk 4 (Red Top).[53] It had to be modified so that it could exploit its new nearly all-aspect capability (it could not home in the 40° wide cone ahead of a manoeuvring target). The earlier Mk 1 simply flew up the tail of the target, manoeuvring as required but expending little energy in the process. It pointed itself directly at the target. If Red Top did the same while flying from anything except dead aft, it would expend its energy too quickly. Instead, it had to lead the target – to find a collision course, which meant deflection shooting on a much larger scale. That required a computer associated with the AI Mk 18 radar.[54] The IR sensor in the nose of the missile could pivot to point at the target when the missile was pointing beyond it. The telescope could also point up, giving Red Top the snap-up capability demanded after the SR 177 interceptor was cancelled. Red Top could be distinguished from Fireflash by its nose; Fireflash had sharply angled facets, but Red Top had a simple rounded nose. It was, however, longer than Fireflash, 138in vs 125.25in, with the same diameter (8.75in, compared to 8in for Sparrow) and somewhat heavier (369lbs vs 306lbs, with a 65lb vs 43.5lb warhead). Both missiles used cordite motors, rated range of Red Top being 8500 yds. It could be launched by a Mach 2 fighter and could fly as high as 65,000ft, giving it the desired 'snap-up' capability.

Red Top offered sufficient space for a radar guidance system instead of its IR seeker and by about 1961 RAE was advocating a semi-active version based on the AI 18 and AI 23 radars of the Sea Vixen and Lightning. If the missile could not be modified to home on pulsed radar, then the AI 18 of the Sea Vixen could be modified with CW injection (as in US naval air-to-air radars), although the Lightning's AI 23 could not.

Red Top armed Lightning interceptors as well as the Sea Vixens. It entered service in 1964 (in 1960 the projected in-service date was 1963). A new missile planned for the abortive Sea Vixen successor (P.1054) never materialised.[55]

Strategic bombers and escorts

With the end of the war, the US Navy shifted emphasis dramatically to long-range attack. In April 1945, well before the end of the war and the advent of atomic bombs, DCNO (Air) assembled a special Informal Advisory Board to discuss characteristics for a follow-on to the *Essex* class, which was conceived as a 35,000-ton carrier.[56] By that time the navy was already interested in using carrier aircraft for strategic strikes against land targets, a capability demonstrated to some extent by a January 1945 mass strike against Tokyo. This attack revealed both the limited bomb loads of the aircraft (compared to the air force's B-29s then bombing Tokyo) and other problems, but it was a pointer to a future in which the United States would face a land rather than a maritime enemy.

Any such study was linked to consideration of new carrier aircraft, both jets and new attack aircraft. By the summer of 1945 the main conclusion seems to have been that the future role of US naval aircraft would be to strike land targets. Revelation of German wartime submarine advances suggested that in a future war a primary means of countering submarines would be to destroy their bases; the Germans

For the 1948 escort fighter competition the Curtiss Columbus division offered this long-range escort fighter in both jet and turboprop form (turboprops would replace the jet nacelles shown here). It had power turrets in both nose and tail. Two radar-operator/gunners would have sat at consoles behind the pilot and co-pilot and the antennas of the APS-29 radars would have been in the wingtip tanks, taking them clear of interference from other parts of the aircraft. With four Westinghouse X24C10 engines (military rating 4080lbs thrust, or 6100lbs with afterburner), claimed maximum speed at 40,000ft was 506 knots (stall speed at normal landing weight with power off was 84.4 knots). Range was 1118nm. Span was 87ft 6in and length 67ft 9in; gross weight was 68,500lbs. The alternative turboprop design had two Allison XT40s driving contraprops, rated at 7070hp and 1075lbs of thrust at take-off. In 1947 Curtiss had proposed what it called VF-31, VF-32 and VF-33, designed to escort the AJ-1 Savage bomber (the 1948 escorts were designed with the longer-range A2J in mind). BuAer contracted for these designs to decide whether the project was feasible. Curtiss doubted that any aircraft which could defend both itself and the bomber and could also meet the desired range and speed requirement, would be far too large and heavy for carrier use. It therefore offered three compromise designs. VF-31 could meet the desired 500 knots at 30,000ft, with the maximum possible radius and an automatic 20mm turret aft. It was powered by a single Pratt & Whitney PT2D (T34), augmented by an afterburning Nene exhausting under the fuselage, leaving a kind of rooster-tail rear section. The single turboprop gave it a combat radius of 704nm and the Nene and afterburner gave it a maximum speed of 504 knots. With a turboprop in the nose, it was limited to two fixed forward-firing 20mm guns plus an automatic twin 20mm turret in the tail. Span was 50.5ft and length 56.2ft, with a gross weight of 33,020lbs. Rate of climb at sea level with afterburner was 9450ft/min. VF-32 was a twin-engine airplane offering the optimum armament configuration, probably the aircraft Curtiss offered in 1948. VF-33 was an attempt to reach higher speed by coupling the two turbojets together, with the same Nene aft as in VF-31. In this case, however, Curtiss provided two forward-firing turrets in wing nacelles, which also housed landing gear. With all engines, claimed maximum speed at 30,000ft was 476.5 knots (487 knots with afterburner; 504 knots at 15,000ft). Rate of climb at sea level was 6580ft/min (7780ft/min with afterburner). Stall speed was 78.2 knots. Combat radius was 1200nm. Span was 86.14ft and length was 63.92ft. Normal gross weight was 58,530lbs.

had shown just how effectively such bases could be buried under concrete. The Kamikaze campaign suggested that future fleet air defence would rely more and more on attacks 'at source'. The advent of nuclear weapons reinforced any such thinking.

At most, Second World War carrier strike aircraft could carry 2000lb bombs to a radius of about 400nm. BuAer pointed out that analysis of the bombing campaign against Germany showed that lethal damage often required 4000lb bombs and sometimes 12,000lb ones. Maximum striking range offered maximum stand-off and the greatest immunity to enemy air attack. In December 1945, BuAer formally pointed out that its preliminary studies had shown that turboprops offered extended range and bomb load beyond what either piston or jet engines offered.[57] Future carrier bombers could be divided into three categories. One could operate from the existing *Midway* class heavy carriers (CVBs). A second could operate in a restricted manner from a *Midway*, e.g. they could not be struck below, but they could take off fully loaded and could land when in light condition. A third would require a new class of carrier, with a larger flight deck and higher-capacity catapults and arresting gear. Initial studies by the Aircraft Design Research (ADR) branch offered the characteristics of turboprop bombers in each category.[58]

If strikes against land targets were the primary future role of US carriers, BuAer's 1945 estimates defined not only the bombers and the new carrier but also the most important characteristics of future fighters. A carrier would attack from maximum range, to limit the enemy's ability both to find her and to strike her. It must have seemed

unlikely that the big turboprops BuAer envisaged would enjoy such high performance over the target as to be immune to enemy jet interceptors. If anything, war experience had shown that bombers needed escorts. If the bombers were BuAer's highest priority, the highest priority among fighters went to their escorts.

CNO formally approved the BuAer heavy bomber programme just over two weeks after it had been proposed, on 28 December 1945. In a follow-up, DCNO (Air) noted BuAer's comment that the ultimate carrier bomber, the 100,000lb aircraft with a radius of 2700nm, would require a wholly new carrier. It should operate sixteen to twenty-four such aircraft, with capacity for a total of about 100 sorties.[59] These numbers in turn defined the new carrier, design of which began in 1946. It was the ship authorised in 1948 as *United States* (CVA 58). A detailed design study of the heavy bomber was approved on 7 February, the project so urgent that a progress report was to be submitted by 15 June (it was submitted on 31 May).[60]

The earliest descriptions of the special bomber carrier included no fighters at all. The new carrier would operate in a task group with conventional carriers which would supply fighters both for group defence and to escort the bombers. That placed important limits on any fighters developed specifically to support the bombers.

CNO established a three-phase bomber programme, beginning with a bomber which could deliver nuclear weapons yet operate from a slightly modified *Essex* class carrier. In December 1945 CNO described the Phase I bomber, a mixed reciprocating- and turbojet-engine aircraft capable of carrying 8000lbs of bombs to a maximum of

300nm at 500mph (435 knots) at 35,000ft. The next stage would be a turboprop carrying the same bomb to 1000nm at 500mph at 35,000ft. These characteristics were then redrawn, so that the Phase II turboprop was to reach 1200nm, followed by a Phase III high-performance jet.

The jet could overcome enemy interceptors by itself (ultimately it was limited to a tail turret), but the turboprop almost certainly could not. It needed an escort. In November 1946 the BuAer Fighter Division issued a list of requirements, of which the escort fighter had the highest priority – because strategic strike was the most important role in naval aviation. At that point the escort was required to fly 300nm missions (escorting the initial strategic bomber), but 'under special conditions' it might fly 1200nm. The fighter division soon clarified: the initial version of the escort fighter should be able to escort the initial AJ-1 strategic bomber to a distance of 600–700nm. The longer-range requirement was separate and would be filled later.[61]

This was an extremely difficult problem for jet aircraft, which had to operate from carriers (hence had to be relatively small) but had very thirsty engines. The air force soon established its own escort fighter programme, but its F-88 and F-90 were far too large for carrier operation. In December 1946 the fighter branch offered two possibilities based on its most economical fighters, the mixed-power Ryan F2R (turboprop plus jet) and the twin-jet F2D Banshee (later redesignated F2H).[62] The branch asked both contractors to estimate how much further their aircraft could fly with drop tanks. The F2R escort fighter would fly at 280mph at 25,000ft until it was 100 miles from the target, at which point it would climb to 30,000ft and accelerate to 500mph. At the objective the F2R would descend to 25,000ft; it had fuel for five minutes of combat. After that it would fly back at that altitude. Its combat radius could be increased from 600nm to 1186nm. The Banshee could fight for 15 minutes at 30,000ft and return to base at 25,000. Its combat radius could be increased to 600nm, just the lowest of the desired ranges. It seemed likely that the Banshee could be given longer range by increasing fuel, but in that case it might exceed catapult launch conditions. Reducing combat to five minutes would increase its combat radius to 660 miles. The shorter combat time seemed compatible with the limited ammunition load, 150 rounds per gun. All of the figures were estimates, as neither aircraft had yet flown. However, since that would happen in 1947, they would be available when the AJ-1 entered service. The planned F9F-2 Panther offered a combat radius of 342nm, but with drop tanks it would probably fly about as far as the Banshee.

It seemed, then, that the initial problem of escorting the AJ-1 Savage had already been solved. The real problem was its 1200nm successor, the A2J, which was incorporated in a formal requirement set in May 1947 by CNO.[63] Both the strategic bomber and its escort figured in the 1949 Master Development Programme approved in October 1947. BuAer expected both to operate from the projected flush-deck carrier.

Despite the problems, in April 1948 BuAer announced a design competition for an escort fighter (OS-112). Bidding closed on 3 August 1948. By that time, of thirteen invited firms, Curtiss-Wright and Douglas Santa Monica had submitted three designs.[64] Both of the Curtiss designs had straight wings with tip nacelles for their radar dishes. One was powered by two T40 turboprops, the other by four J46 turbojets with afterburners. Douglas also offered a straight wing, but its radar dishes were in fairings atop and under its fuselage. It used three J46 engines. The Curtiss designs were eliminated because they

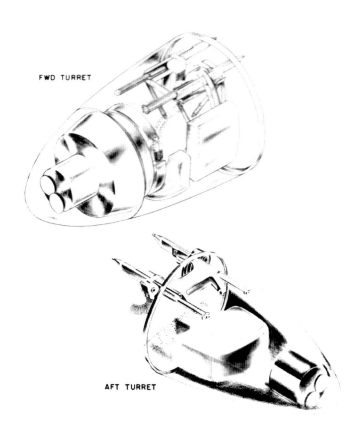

Turret Arrangement

FWD TURRET

AFT TURRET

The 1948 Curtiss escort design incorporated nose and tail turrets, each with two 20mm cannon.

failed to meet the stall speed requirement; they could be arrested only with surface wind, even without any fuel on board. Douglas' design was considered capable of escorting the A2J for 1200nm, even though the BuAer estimate of its range in the given flight profile was only 1110nm (the A2J flight profile had since been changed to a more favourable altitude). It failed to meet the CVB (*Midway* class) catapulting requirement by 5 knots, but that could be accepted more easily than the arresting gear problem with the Curtiss design: a ship could accelerate more easily when launching aircraft. The new *Oriskany* could operate the Douglas aircraft without any restrictions. The aircraft was faster than current operational bombers, but about equal to some experimental bombers (presumably the AJ Savage).

That was not enough. The Douglas fighter would be expensive and money was tight; if the project went ahead, others would have to be cancelled. A series of November 1948 meetings decided to try a less expensive alternative, an armed version of the A2J bomber itself. The FY50 budget was so tight that, despite the high priority accorded the escort, it had to be cut out. BuAer decided in March not to award any contract.

Although no one said as much, by this time the Soviets had demonstrated the MiG-15 fighter. The A2J programme continued, but it seems likely that there was some scepticism as to whether it could survive in the face of such opposition. In the autumn of 1948 BuAer conducted a competition for the Phase III strategic bomber, a high-performance jet which would not need any escorting fighter. It was won by the A3D Skywarrior (later the A-3) which, despite its much smaller size, was in effect the navy's equivalent to the air force's B-47 high-performance jet strategic bomber.

Jet night fighters

In June 1945, before the 1944 fighters flew, BuAer announced a competition for a high-performance carrier night fighter powered by either a turboprop or by jet engines. Aircraft Design Research compared an aircraft powered by two or four 24C turbojets, the most powerful then available from Westinghouse, to one powered by two TG-100 turbo-props.[65] It concluded that the aircraft powered by four 24Cs would be best, but that given its size its carrier characteristics would be marginal. This study indicated that with the desired 500nm combat radius speed would vary between 440mph and 494mph. An Outline Specification for the night fighter was issued on 1 June 1945, although manufacturers received some preliminary information in mid-May. The specification included a requirement for side-by-side seating, a combat radius of at least 350nm (six hours' endurance) and a speed of at least 475mph at sea level. The APQ-35 radar (see below) was specified.

Closing date originally set as 1 September 1945, was extended to 1 October. Of twelve companies invited to submit designs and cost estimates, five dropped out, one because it was not interested in night fighters, the others due to press of other work.[66] Once it received proposals, BuAer realised that its original estimates (for example, for the combat problem) had been unrealistic, so at the evaluation stage it revised the combat problem, re-evaluating the alternatives.[67] BuAer decided that at least in the initial phase of a future war the night fighter role would be most important, with high speed and climb plus

the ability to intercept targets out to 100nm. Offensive sweeps and night intruder operation would be secondary. With relatively minor changes, the Grumman design promised outstanding interceptor performance. The Douglas jet could be modified into a suitable night intruder. BuAer therefore decided to buy both aircraft for complementary roles.[68] BuAer rejected the turboprops offered by Bell and Curtiss.

Progress with the Grumman design was slow; at the end of May 1946 BuAer's project officer reported that the company planned to propose major modifications in view of problems encountered operating the large F7F Tigercat from carriers (the planned F9F was comparable in size and weight).[69] Despite seven series of field tests and three series of carrier tests, the F7F still had not been approved for carrier operations. After an F7F broke in half during February 1946 tests on board *Shangri-La*, OpNav suspended production until deficiencies had been corrected and carrier suitability demonstrated. Planned Marine Corps F7F squadrons were cut from five to three. On 20 June 1946 Grumman was formally notified that the F9F project was in abeyance (formal notification within BuAer that the requirement was cancelled was made only in a 9 October memo). Grumman seems to have realised that the night fighter project was dying, so it submitted an informal proposal comparing several different possible day fighter designs using various engines. BuAer chose one with a single Nene engine and let a development contract to Grumman.[70]

After the competition, McDonnell offered a less expensive night fighter in the form of a two-seat Banshee, the seats being in tandem. It did not attract BuAer interest. Later McDonnell would win contracts for a Banshee night fighter, but with a single seat.

Alongside the Skynight, BuAer maintained the wartime policy of developing night versions of the new jet fighters, using the latest

Douglas won the 1945 night fighter competition with the F3D Skynight. An F3D-2 of VC-3 is shown over San Francisco, 9 March 1951.

An F3D-2 of the experimental squadron VX-4 makes a free take-off from *Hancock*, 22 June 1954.

single-seat night fighter radar, the APS-19. In June 1945 CNO directed BuAer to prototype a night fighter version of each of its new jets. Of the four jets in production or development in February 1947, BuAer had just committed to production of a night version of the F6U-1 Pirate and a change request to modify the F2H-1 Banshee was being processed. It appeared that a night fighter version of the FJ-1 Fury would be impractical and the contractor's bid to modify the FH-1 Phantom was dismissed as too expensive (with too few – sixty – produced).[71] Work on such aircraft alongside the new Skynight was justified on the ground that the fleet was still using and would probably continue to use, the 'night fighter unit' system, which practically required that a carrier's night fighters be of the same basic type as her day fighters. At this point there was interest in using an aircraft's tip tanks for night-fighter electronics, preserving lateral balance (the after part of each tank could still be used for fuel). Radar tip tanks might be replaced by normal tip tanks to turn an aircraft into a day fighter. This idea did not work out and within a year the F6U programme was entirely dead. The Banshee went on to become a standard single-seat all-weather (including night) fighter.

BuAer reviewed the night fighter programme in March 1948.[72] The only available fighter radar was the wartime APS-19, which did not seem adequate for a fast jet. The weight of a radar determined its performance, so that about 400lbs was needed to achieve the desired range of 10–15nm. The F2H Banshee was the only really good bet. By this time McDonnell had lengthened its nose and it was not suffering any substantial loss of performance with an APS-19 installed. There was some problem with the generators in the jet engines. The APS-19 itself was considered inadequate.[73] The F3D was expected to be a far better night fighter than any single-seater, both due to the dedicated radar operator and to the much larger (750lb) radar. That in turn boosted its take-off weight from about 14,000lbs to 21,000lbs (it could be 18,000–18,500lbs without the second man, but it would not gain much in performance). There was some hope that by 1950 the Westinghouse 24C engine in the F3D would gain about 50 per cent in power in its 24C-10 version (J46); the up-engined version was designated F3D-2.[74] The new engine was not ready in time, so the F3D-2 was powered by a 3400lb (rather than 3000lb) thrust version of the J34 (J34-WE-36).

The 1948 meeting concluded that there was no longer a need for night fighters as such, but rather for all fighters to be equipped for high-speed interception requiring radar. The single-seaters were so

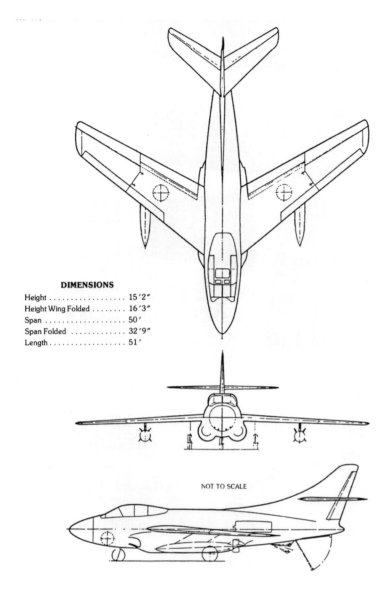

DIMENSIONS

Height	15'2"
Height Wing Folded	16'3"
Span	50'
Span Folded	32'9"
Length	51'

NOT TO SCALE

In 1950 the great hope for a high-performance night fighter was this swept-wing F3D-3 version of the Skynight. Within two years a contract for 102 had been let and then quickly cancelled because the single-seat fighters were so effective under close control. That was acceptable if it was assumed that no enemy would mount a mass night attack. This drawing has been adapted from an official performance summary, a Standard Aircraft Characteristics Chart produced by Douglas. The powerplant was two Westinghouse J46-WE-4 engines. Maximum speed at 14,000ft would have been 529 knots (608mph) and sea-level rate of climb would have been 4670ft/min. Combat radius would have been 347nm, extendable to 600nm with full internal fuel and two 150-gallon drop tanks. The reprinted version of the chart does not include the assumed thrust of the engines, an issue since the J46 failed to meet expectations. Span would have been 50ft and length 51ft. Gross weight in normal condition was 25,550lbs. (Courtesy Steve Ginter, from his book *Naval Fighters No. 4: Douglas F3D Skyknight*)

clearly inadequate against fast jet bombers – the threat of the near future – that they should all be abandoned.

Reviewing the conference record, DCNO (Air) decided to keep the F2H-N programme alive both as insurance against any problems with the F3D and also to make possible continued investigation of the value of single vs two-seat night fighters. A successor to the late-war APS-19 radar was also kept alive, under the designation APS-25, on the

theory that even if the F3D became the standard carrier night fighter, single-seaters would remain in service for the next four or five years. It was also seen as the natural radar for a future general-purpose fighter, the candidate in 1948 being the Grumman F10F. It was a combination search/fire-control radar with an additional air-to-surface capability. The contractor was Farnsworth (later RCA). Estimated weight in 1948 was 350lbs compared to the 750lbs of the F3D radar combination. The prototype was scheduled for delivery in December 1949. Meanwhile production of APS-19 continued for use in propeller night fighters and it was being tested with larger dish antennas (18in, 22in, 26in or 30in).

The 1948 night fighter meeting looked forward to a new high-performance night fighter to deal with the much faster bombers to be expected in the near future. This project was discussed in the autumn of 1949, just after the Soviets exploded their first atomic bomb. In September 1949 Commander T F Caldwell, at Patuxent River, looked ahead in a memo for the head of the BuAer fighter division.[75] Caldwell pointed to the new air-to-air missiles as the fighter weapons of the future, so potent that they might make large moderate-performance bombers obsolete. Future enemy bombers might be designed to operate at extreme altitude, perhaps 55,000–65,000ft. Instead of increasing the ceiling of a fighter, it might make more sense to design its missiles to snap up, climbing perhaps 10,000ft. That would require much more sophisticated fire control than in the past. He also pointed out that any bomber carrying an atomic bomb would surely be accompanied by jamming aircraft. Such aircraft had worked with bombers in Europe during the Second World War and Soviet jammers became an important feature of stand-off missile tactics during the Cold War. At the least, the new fighter must be able to switch from active radar to homing on the enemy's jammers. An attached estimate suggested that the new fighter might need about twice the weight of electronics as the already-massive F3D, yet there was also a new stated requirement that it achieve 600kts at 40,000ft. Caldwell offered a smaller-radar alternative, in which an AEW plane acquired the target and passed radar information directly to the fighter. This, too, was prophetic: it is the way an E-2 and an F-14 worked.

The result of the night fighter meeting was a project for a new two-seat night fighter. April 1949 list of BuAer's desired prototype projects listed a replacement for the F3D, designated XVF(N), as its first priority. Like the F3D, it was to have a crew of two, but BuAer wanted much better performance: Mach 0.95 to 1.0, with a ceiling of at least 50,000ft and a combat radius of about 600nm. Compared to the F3D, it would be about 100 knots faster and its ceiling would be about 10,000ft greater. The improved performance was justified on the basis of increased bomber performance. Relevant studies included ADR's DR-63 design study for what became the day interceptor just bought, plus several other studies.[76] In a 1950 BuAer list, XVF(N-1) was expected to be ready in 1954.

This aircraft was intended to meet the same threat as the day interceptor of 1948. Alternatives were a supersonic deck-launched interceptor and a CAP interceptor. A study by the Aircraft Design Research division (ADR-1166, the aircraft sketched being ADR-82) showed that CAP was consistently better than deck-launched interception, the latter being the technique implicit in the 1948 interceptor specification. The ADR study gives an idea of the issues as they were understood at this time.

Required radar early warning range depended not only on fighter twenty-four FFAR plus four 20mm, as both would be needed if the fighter had to combine head-on and tail attacks.

Of three sketch designs ADR investigated, two were deltas and one had swept wings. Only the swept-wing fighter could be catapulted by a carrier (H4-1 or H-8 catapult) with the usual 25 knots wind over deck; the others needed 35 to 40 knots or JATO boost.

This may have fed into an interceptor design competition BuAer was then planning, for an aircraft capable of 640 knots at sea level and Mach 0.95 at 50,000ft, climbing at 19,000ft/min to reach 50,000ft in 6.75 minutes. Like the earlier interceptor, it would be armed with twenty-four FFAR rockets.

In 1951 Douglas received a contract for a swept-wing version designated F3D-3. Its perceived importance is indicated by the size of the contract, 287 aircraft compared to total F3D production of 237. However, its value was soon called into question and BuAer held a conference to decide the issue.[77] The main question was whether a two-seat night fighter was better than a single-seater and, if so, whether it was so much better as to justify the heavy aircraft penalties involved. The projected F3D-3 had insufficient endurance with either the J46 or its potential replacement the J65 to fly normal night CAP. With the J65 it might function as a deck-launched interceptor, but that was attractive only if the single-seater, as exemplified by the F2H-3, could not be used. However, the single-seater could fly night CAP while operating under close control. The F3D-3 could operate effectively except against a high-performance bomber.

The two-seater offered about 20 per cent better intercept range, half of it attributable to increased dish size (range was proportional to dish diameter). The other half was due to the greater efficiency of the dedicated radar operator. In theory, the two-man team also offered an ability to search while the radar locked onto one target. However, in

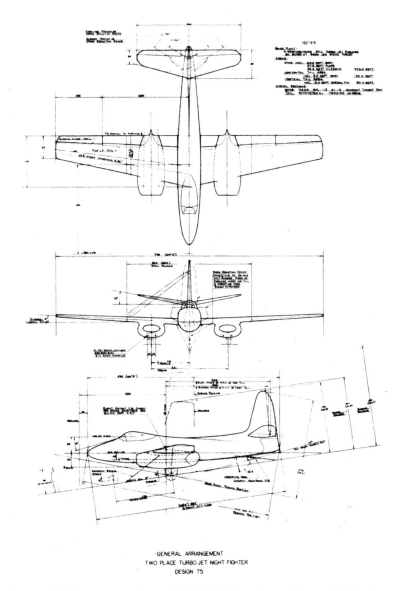

GENERAL ARRANGEMENT
TWO PLACE TURBOJET NIGHT FIGHTER
DESIGN 75

Grumman's G-75 won a contract alongside that for the Douglas night fighter, but BuAer terminated it in favour of a Grumman day fighter powered by a Nene engine. It would have been powered by four Westinghouse 24C engines, each rated at 3000lbs static thrust. Estimated sea level speed was 608mph (584mph at 20,000ft), stall speed being 87.5mph. The rate of climb at sea level at combat weight was 11,400ft/min. Combat radius was 388nm. Span would have been 64ft 2in and length 46ft; gross weight would have been 26,964lbs.

speed but also on whether it was deck-launched. A supersonic fighter on CAP over a carrier needed 100–125nm warning. A subsonic CAP fighter needed 200–220nm. A deck-launched supersonic interceptor needed 150–170nm, but a deck-launched subsonic interceptor needed 300nm of warning, an impossible figure. However, very high supersonic speed was not very useful, because it took so long to accelerate from subsonic speed. Thus the highest speed any of the ADR aircraft used was Mach 1.15. To accelerate from Mach 0.9 to Mach 1.4 at 50,000ft, the chosen operating altitude, would take 11.5 minutes – and an hour's endurance fuel.

The turning radius at 50,000ft was so large that only a collision-course attack was practicable. To make one, the fighter needed 6nm (subsonic) or 10–12nm (supersonic) radar range plus an airborne computer for the final approach. Armament would be the usual

Convair offered this Model VF-4505 jet design for the 1945 night fighter competition. Details are dated 28 September 1945. The powerplant was three Westinghouse 24C jet engines (3000lbs thrust). With all three burning, at combat weight, speed would be 551mph at 10,000ft (561mph at sea level). Rate of climb at sea level would be 7260ft/min; stall speed would be 85mph with most of the fuel burned. Span would have been 49ft and length 44ft 5in; gross weight would have been 25,500lbs at take-off. Radar would have been in the nose and in the single wing-tip nacelle. The required APQ-35 had three elements, in this case a search radar in the nose, a separate gunlaying radar in the nacelle and a tail warning radar. In the F3D and other fighters with similar sets, the gunlaying (target-tracking) antenna was mounted ahead of the big search dish, the loss of antenna area being accepted.

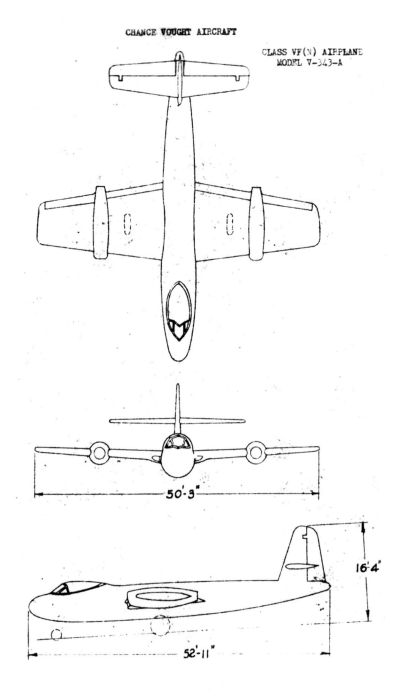

CHANCE VOUGHT AIRCRAFT

CLASS VF(N) AIRPLANE
MODEL V-343-A

50'-3"

16'-4"

52'-11"

Vought offered both a turboprop and a jet in the 1945 night fighter competition. This is the jet, V-343-A. It would have been powered by three Westinghouse 24C-4 engines (3000lb thrust each), two in the wings and one in the fuselage (using the two wing root intakes barely visible here). Maximum speed at sea level was 586mph, where rate of climb was 4000ft/min. Combat radius was 350nm. Span was 50ft 3in and length was 52ft 11in. Gross weight was 26,960lbs.

fact the C-scan which showed target altitude (in the search role) was usable only at the range at which a target was locked-on. Range and bearing without altitude were considered of questionable value. Also, the radar operator would concentrate on the target during the final stages of an attack and would not be searching elsewhere. Nor would the operator help if the enemy jammed the radar: the pilot would know that immediately and he could lock-on again. Under ideal conditions, the APQ-35 could lock onto a target at 7000 yds (it was

designed for 4000 yds); in a single-seater, the radar could lock onto the target as soon as it was acquired. The pilot could immediately correct for difference in altitude (from the target) and he would probably do better than the two-seater.

If the questionable advantage of search while locked-on could be discounted, the two-man APQ-35 would become very similar to the APQ-41 (in an F2H-3) or a similar radar. As it was, in the APQ-35 the fire-control element caused a hole in the search pattern. The BuAer conference on the question agreed unanimously that the higher performance of a single-seater more than offset any advantage enjoyed by the two-seater when operating under close control. When under broadcast control both aircraft would have similar capabilities, provided each had a navigation system. The two-seater would have some advantage if there were no navigation system. There would be no significant difference in dealing with low-fliers except that if visual contact was required the two-seater would enjoy an advantage.

The BuAer conference concluded that the F3D-3 had insufficient endurance, armament and protection for the night interdiction or intruder role. Its gains in performance over the F3D-2 were insignificant for this mission and the loss in endurance made it less useful.

Overall, the F3D-3 offered too little and it was probably not worth keeping. The conference did recommend studies of tandem two-seat versions of suitable general-purpose fighters, which meant the F10F-1 and the F3H-1. The only surprise in the story is that the strong recommendation to cancel the F3D-3 took until January 1952 to take effect.

The standard F3D-2 turned out to have an additional drawback. When the Korean War broke out, the new F3D night fighter was at the service trial stage. The only fleet night fighter was a version of the propeller-driven Corsair (the F4U-5N), which was clearly obsolescent. F3Ds were deployed on board the carrier *Lake Champlain* in June 1953. As with other jets, F3Ds had to be catapulted into the air. Unfortunately that proved difficult. Due to a tendency to nose-down on taking off, an F3D badly damaged the ship's catapult. The F3Ds were moved ashore after six days of operations (the catapult took ten days to repair). There they performed effectively supporting the Marines and escorted air force heavy bombers in night missions. Of the three elements making up the Westinghouse APQ-35 radar, the search radar and the tail warning radar worked well (the latter was considered a lifesaver in Korea), but the lock-on/track radar rarely worked. Radar maintenance was also difficult.

The navy report evaluating Korean operations pointed out that the Skynights were unique in the US Navy and in the US Air Force, but were vulnerable to anti-aircraft fire due to their low speed, low rate of climb and the extreme visibility of their exhaust. Although the F3D was deployed on board carriers after the war, it seems to have been clearly understood that the aircraft had to be replaced. It was in only two carrier fighter squadrons, VF-11 and -14, which deployed briefly on board the largest available carriers, such as the new *Forrestal*, in 1955.

Fighters and radars[78]

In 1946, when the jet night fighter was ordered, the distinction between radars for day and night fighters was clear. A day fighter needed a range-only radar to feed a range into an otherwise optical computing gunsight.[79] A night fighter needed a combination radar which would detect the target and then measure its movement to feed into a fire-control system. The first such radar in US service was

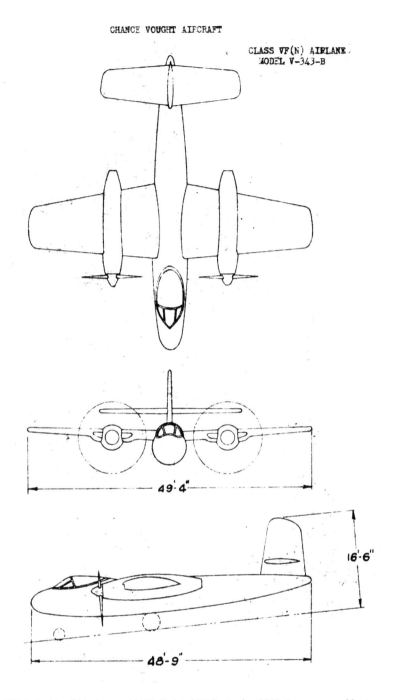

This is the Vought turboprop, V-343-B, dated 25 September 1945. It was powered by two TG-100s (V-343-B-3 had two 'future gas turbines' instead). Maximum speed at sea level was 429mph (452mph at 20,000ft) and rate of climb at sea level was 5390ft/min. Radius of action was 365nm. Span was 49ft 4in and length was 48ft 9in. Gross weight was 22,940lbs.

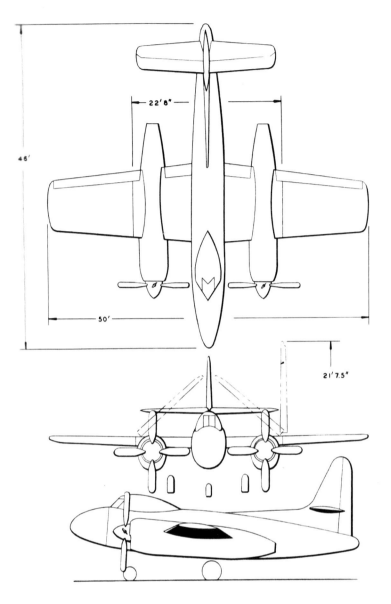

Curtiss Columbus offered a piston/jet design for the 1945 night fighter competition. Its proposal VF(N) I is shown. Each nacelle contained an R-2800-30W in front and a Westinghouse 24C4 jet engine in its rear (an alternative was to replace the R-2800s with TG-100 turboprops). Maximum speed was 544mph at 5700ft and rate of climb at sea level was 6065ft/min. Combat radius was 350nm. Span was 50ft and length 46ft. Gross weight was not given.

Westinghouse's APQ-35, which equipped the F3D Skynight. It comprised an APS-21 search radar, an APG-26 for gun aiming and an APS-28 for tail warning. Night gun aiming required a radar to track a target, so that the aircraft could fire deflection shots. The system could detect a target at 18–25nm and lock-on at 4nm, the operator shifting from one radar element to the other. As in other radars of this era, it tracked its targets using a conical-scan dish. The dish spun a beam slightly off-centre. If the target was directly on axis, target strength (as observed by the radar) did not change as the beam spun. If it moved off-centre, the beam would periodically return a stronger or weaker echo. The change in strength could drive a tracking mechanism. Unfortunately an enemy could simulate movement, strengthening the returning pulse at times to make it seem that he was off-centre in a preferred direction. Also, depending on how rapidly the beam spun, it could miss manoeuvres by a very agile target.[80]

The earlier night-fighter radars lacked the conical-scan tracking element; they did not lock onto their targets. In 1946 the current night fighter radar was APS-19, which was in effect a modernised equivalent to the wartime APS-6. Unlike APQ-35, it was intended as a pilot-operated set, hence was used in single-seat night fighters.

Given BuAer thinking about the interception problem and collision-course attacks, aircraft in the 1948 interceptor competition were required to carry APS-25 intercept and fire-control radars. This system was designed to search for and acquire targets and to track them automatically. It was designed for collision-course interception using FFARs, but it also incorporated a 20mm fire-control system. The first prototype was delivered in December 1950. In 1951 the order for APS-25 was reduced to twenty-five because the F4D was the only remaining interceptor, hence the only aircraft which was expected to use it. APS-25 was being developed by Farnsworth, which was taken over by RCA. That company dropped out of the BuAer interceptor market; APS-25 was never installed. Instead the F4D entered service with the far more sophisticated APQ-50, which came out of a series of night-fighter radars conceived from 1951 onwards.

In March 1951 the fleet night fighter situation was critical, as only seven carrier-capable night fighters existed – F2H-2Ns – and they were deficient in radar performance.[81] The Skynight was already showing many deficiencies, leaving the F2H-3 Banshee as the only near-term solution. By this time the Banshee was clearly deficient as a fighter, but 514 were ordered because it was likely to be an excellent CAP aircraft, day or night and thus might fill the gap in the night fighter programme.

The F2H-3 was built only in a radar version, hence did not receive a separate N designation. With extra fuel tanks amidships, it had a much longer nose and the fleet called it the 'Big Banjo'. The main issue in its development was the radar. The APS-19 of the first F2H-2Ns had proven unacceptable. The navy decided to try the Hughes APG-36, then being made for the air force, on the remaining forty F2H-2Ns. In the spring of 1951 one such radar was already flying in a modified F2H-2N and showing outstanding performance, both electronically and in its need for maintenance. The radar was therefore chosen for the follow-on F2H-3 and it was mocked-up and approved by the official F2H-3 mock-up board. Since F2H-3s would be delivered within a few months of the F2H-2Ns, OpNav decided to cancel the forty less-satisfactory F2H-2Ns to accelerate delivery of the longer-range -3s.[82]

The APG-36 had been designed for the air force, which wanted a pure air-to-air radar. It therefore did not incorporate the surface-search and beacon features the navy wanted for a fighter which might be needed for close air support. The BuAer Electronics Division proposed as a superior alternative the much more powerful (250kW vs 50kW) APQ-41 based on the APQ-35 of the Skynight, which was already in production. It argued that so much of the radar came from the earlier programme that the choice could be made even though no prototype yet existed. Only the APQ-41 offered enough range to enable the F2H-3 to manoeuvre into attacking position. Conversely, unless a controller placed the fighter either in the target's tail cone or on a parallel course pointed at the target, the system built around the APG-36 would not manoeuvre it into attacking position. The Armament Control Director (Aero 1A) integral with the APQ-41 would provide continuous target position to a computer so that guns could be fired at a range as great as 3000 yds with a lead angle up to 25°, offering much wider possibilities than the other systems. Against all of that, the BuAer maintenance division argued that the fleet could not maintain the relatively delicate 250kW magnetron powering the new radar, although it was certainly capable of maintaining the 50kW magnetron in an APG-36.

After considerable debate over the wisdom of installing an entirely untested radar or a radar without key capabilities, another possibility was raised: the Hughes APG-37, then being developed for the air

Goodyear, which had entered the aircraft business during the war to produce Corsairs, tried to continue after the war. For the 1945 night fighter competition it offered this GA-13 design with two nacelles, each combining an R-1820-74 piston engine with a Westinghouse 24C jet. Maximum speed was 523mph (550mph with afterburning). Sea level rate of climb was 7000ft/min. Combat radius was the required 350nm. Span would have been 58ft and length 44ft 9in; gross weight was 22,800lbs.

force. It had the desired search and beacon facilities and seemed about equal to the APQ-41, except that the APQ-41 was being made at a navy facility. That was an important point, because with its much larger budget the air force might well squeeze the navy out of production at one of its own plants. The Chief of BuAer decided that the first 100 F2H-3s should have APQ-41. The remaining 414 would have either it or APG-37.[83] This evaluation was to be based on trials on board two F2H-2Ns. However, Hughes decided that it could not install the radar in a Banshee; the navy accepted its proposal to evaluate it on board an air force fighter.

Then it became clear that the APQ-41 was unlikely to meet the schedule for installation. In that event the first 100 F2H-3s would have APG-36s. APQ-41s on order would be installed in later aircraft, while the test against the APG-37 would be run to see whether it would replace the APQ-41. The BuAer Armament Division protested that APG-36 was no more than an interim system and that the fire control computer associated with APG-37 was designed only to fire FFARs, whereas the Banshee was armed with guns. However, the computer designed to work with the APQ-41 could be substituted (originally Hughes had offered the APQ-44 version with gun fire control, but it had then withdrawn that offer).

In an attempt to win the navy contract, in August 1951 Hughes produced a brochure describing the 'Hughes Fire-control System for Navy Interceptors' embodying its radar. It claimed that development was essentially complete because its systems were all modular. The proposed system employed the APG-36 display already tested in a Banshee with the RF and other parts of the APG-37 currently being manufactured for the air force. Hughes claimed that it could already meet navy requirements for surface-search and beaconry and for a space-stabilised (against roll and pitch) search pattern which was of particular interest to the navy. Hughes pointed out that its experiments showed the importance of space stabilisation: without it, targets well off-boresight would be lost when the interceptor went into a turn, since the search pattern would 'roll away' from the target. There was a special 'bright display' which the navy wanted because its single

Grumman's day fighter was the F9F Panther. This F9F-4 was photographed on board *Franklin D Roosevelt*. As a British test pilot on detached duty at Patuxent River, Captain 'Winkle' Brown flew the F9F-5 in 1951 as Project Officer. It was already in squadron service in limited numbers; his role was to fill in gaps so that it could be fully operational. He found it enormous by British standards. Take-off was unimpressive; Brown had the impression that the Panther was underpowered. His flight experience convinced him that the Panther 'was essentially lacking in the indispensable requirements of a fighter, namely gun-platform stability, manoeuvrability and harmony of control'. It snaked badly, it required too much stick force, its elevators were heavy and its ailerons light. Poor lateral control made instrument flying difficult. Maximum rate of roll was too low by then-current standards. It was easy to deck-land, with a very good view. Brown added that in the ground-attack role in Korea, the Panther benefitted from its high sea-level speed and good endurance; it was better as a bomber than as a fighter. Unfortunately Brown never evaluated the follow-on Cougar. (J W Hawkins collection via John Gourley)

operator (the pilot) could not use a hood. A unique attack display provided a pilot with easily-understood cues to steer and attack. Maximum tracking range was 30,000 yds (15nm). Hughes also claimed that work already underway, to be completed in 1952, would result in what Hughes called a Universal Fire-control System capable of firing guns and rockets, using either radar or optical sighting.

Despite the difference in designations, both APG-37 and APQ-41 had similar search and fire-control functions and both could also be used against ground targets. APG-37 was the radar of the air force E-4 system, then being installed in the F-86D single-seat fighter (modified versions equipped the two-seat air force interceptors of the time, the F-94C and F-89D). Like APQ-41, APG-37 used a 250kW magnetron. A prototype was flying in November 1950.

After all of this, the APQ-41 was finally tested. In September 1951

F9F-5s from VF-154 (*Yorktown*), 1954. (Fahey Collection, US Naval Institute)

it was evaluated as not suitable for service use; it would take one to two years to solve its problems. That brought back the possibility of some emergency substitute, even the range-only APG-30 then being installed on board day fighters. The Military Requirements Division proposed buying the Hughes radar at once, provided it proved satisfactory, leaving the APQ-41 to the next interceptor, the Demon (F3H-1). Meanwhile a combination of the APS-19A and APG-30 might be tested as a stop-gap. The stop-gap was so bad that the Military Requirements Division soon proposed immediately ordering 200 APG-37s and retaining the order, as it then stood, for 344 APQ-41s. Since no APG-37s had yet been delivered to the air force, this was even worse that staying with the APQ-41, which could be brought to acceptable condition.

BuAer was already developing a wide range of fighter radars. Its Electronics Division argued against taking on an entirely different radar in the form of Hughes' APG-37. It certainly would not do so until the Hughes radar had demonstrated a marked improvement over the APQ-41 in which it had already invested heavily. The Electronics Division also pointed that the large number of existing night fighters (a total of 665 as of December 1951) was operating completely adequately; the new radars were needed to deal with anticipated threats. For its part, the R&D division pointed out that APQ-41 was unsuitable not only because it had maintenance problems, but also for operational reasons such as a poor display, poor lock-on and lack of stabilisation in search. Westinghouse was working on cures. APG-37 might well show various bugs on extensive testing, but it was operationally suitable right now, as it already had the desired features except a computer, which neither radar would have for at least a year. Production APG-37s could be available in January 1952 and production APQ-41s in February; in each case McDonnell would need two months to install and check out the radar. The navy decided to order about 150 APG-37s and also to find a second source for APQ-41. An important point brought out at this time was the Hughes had already delivered some APG-37s and that the radar had been under develop-

ment for longer than APQ-41 and was tied to a larger programme (which would provide much more support).

In the end, production was cut somewhat short. Instead of 514 aircraft, BuAer bought 250 F2H-3s with the APQ-41 radar and then 150 F2H-3s with the Hughes radar.[84] The shift to the Hughes radar proved fortunate, as Westinghouse never did provide the desired stabilisation and APQ-41 was considered unreliable in general. The Hughes radar and the associated fire-control system were considered quite reliable and the company's form of space stabilisation worked. It offered the first reliable ability to lock on at long range (12–15nm). Detection range was 18–25nm.

In effect the F2H-3 and -4 were the first of a new category of general-purpose all-weather fighters, not as good as a two-seater at night, but good enough. In January 1951, well before problems emerged with the Skynight, BuAer decided to modify one of its two 1948 interceptors, McDonnell's F3H (see the interceptor competition described below), as a general-purpose all-weather fighter superseding the Grumman F10F previously projected for that role. At this point the F10F programme was lagging to the point where it could not meet the general-purpose fighter requirement and the F4D was considered the best of the two interceptors. Moreover, the F3H could carry a heavier weight, including a large radar. By 1953, when the all-weather Banshees were just entering service, their production run was cut short (by 114 aircraft) in favour of the Demon.[85]

The success of Hughes' APG-37/E-10 in the Banshee general-purpose fighter caused BuAer to fit the F3H Demon with a version of the same radar designated APG-50. When a beam generator was added to guide a Sparrow I missile in the F3H-2M, the radar became APQ-51.

However, the Hughes radar did not equip the F4D interceptor. Instead it was fitted with the Westinghouse APQ-50. It was the first airborne radar designed to fit inside a cylindrical module for simplified installation and servicing. APQ-50 was described as the first radar using a complex airborne computer system to detect targets at ranges as great as 25–40nm (it could lock on at up to 14.2nm). It could assist a pilot in conducting blind attacks in conjunction with the Aero-5B fire-control system. APQ-50 had a 24in dish antenna. In 1959 it was described as the most advanced current US air intercept system. APQ-64 was a modified version for the F5D Skylancer, which would have been armed with Sparrow II missiles using the Aero X-24A system. It could search out to 25nm and lock on at up to 24nm. The radar in the Phantom (F4H) was APQ-72, an APQ-50 modified to guide Sparrow III missiles.

At this time the F3D was just being withdrawn from carrier operations off Korea. The commander of Task Force 77 (the carriers) wrote

The exotic Cutlass won the 1946 US Navy jet fighter competition. This is the F7U-1 version, which never entered fleet service. By the time he arrived at Patuxent River as an exchange test pilot, Captain 'Winkle' Brown had already flown the tailless DH 108 (he may have been the only pilot it did not kill) and was most anxious to learn of US experience with such aircraft. He found the F7U-1 underpowered and over-complicated. Its high rate of roll could not really be used in combat. Buffeting at high speed (Mach 0.82) was a serious problem. Brown found longitudinal stability unsatisfactory at high speed and at high altitude and longitudinal control too sensitive for formation flying. He found the follow-on F7U-3 underpowered, although it climbed rapidly once afterburners were cut in. It still had a high roll rate, but it also had major new problems. For example, if Brown changed speed he had to re-trim the aircraft in all three axes. Directional stability was worse than in the F7U-1. Brown's final word was that neither version was particularly pleasant to fly: the aircraft 'looked ugly, flew badly and was a menace anywhere near a carrier deck'. However, Brown was particularly concerned with the irreversible hydraulic system powering the elevons on the trailing edge of the wing. Since power, which many designers favoured for transonic fighters (due to the very high forces on the control surfaces), denied the pilot any sense of the forces on the elevons, the system incorporated artificial 'feel.' Brown argued that artificial 'feel' masked serious problems. When the hydraulics failed, as they often did, the F7U-1 revealed its really bad characteristics. He considered them particularly dangerous because at the time US fighters were designed to what he considered low limits. The F7U-3 had a more reliable dual hydraulic control system.

at the time that as aircraft the Banshees were equal or better, but he cautioned against abandoning the two-seat night fighter. That was why the question of one vs two seats was still very much alive when the two-seat Phantom (F4H) competed with the super-Crusader (F8U-3) in 1955–8.

All of these fighter radars used dish antennas with single feeds and conical scanning. The AWG-9 radar of the F-14 Tomcat had a very different antenna, a slotted plate. The slots formed a single beam, the plate scanning like the previous dish. The flat plate configuration was also compatible with monopulse tracking, although in the F-14 and the later F/A-18 (in the APG-65 radar) it was typically used for track-while-scan operation. The beam was typically raster-scanned (like a television picture in an analogue set) in what was usually described as a series of 'bars.' Like the radars of the earlier F-4, the F-14 and F/A-18 radars incorporated CW injection to guide Sparrow missiles. As a measure of the power of the AWG-9, it could guide Sparrow missiles at 38nm, compared to 24nm for the AWG-10 in the F-4J. Reportedly it achieved 2.5 times the range of the smaller radar. The F-14D had the APG-71 radar. The significance of the radar rather than weapon system (W) designation was that, where the radar of the original F-14 was integrated with the computer tracking targets, in the F-14D the tracker was part of the central combat system computer.

The step beyond such radars is an active electronically-scanned array (AESA), typically a fixed array of individual transmit-receive (Tx-Rx) elements which together form any desired radar beam. Among the advantages of an AESA are that it can form a beam shaped to null out a jammer. It is also inherently stealthier than a conventional radar, because it does not require a reflector to collect its signals. The F/A-18 has been upgraded with an AESA APG-79 (F/A-18C/D had the APG-73, an upgraded version of the original APG-65). It was first installed in July 2003. The F-35 Joint Strike Fighter has another AESA, APG-81.

The British developed their own fighter radars. As noted elsewhere, at the end of the war the RAF sets were too massive to be installed on

board FAA fighters. They made do with the US APS-4 radar 'bomb,' which offered both AI (Air Interception) and ASV (air-to-surface vessel) capability. Modifications made by the Royal Navy improved its displays somewhat. This radar equipped the night fighter versions of the Firefly and of the twin-engine Sea Hornet. It was sometimes referred to under its wartime designation of ASH.

Just as the US Navy found its wartime radars inadequate after the war, the Royal Navy needed something better. Its first post-war night fighters were Sea Venoms. The initial FAW 20 had the RAF AI 10 radar (the US SCR-720 used in some Tigercats), but the main production version, the FAW 21 (and the equivalent Mk 53 for Australia), had the US APQ-43 radar, a variant of the APQ-35 in the F3D Skynight. In British service it was designated AI 21. Another version of this radar served as AI 22 in RAF Javelins.

The Sea Venom and its radar were bought as stop-gaps so that the fleet would have an all-weather fighter available while the Sea Vixen and its AI 18 radar were developed. AI 18 was broadly comparable to the US radars, with a 29in dish conically-scanned antenna and a peak power of 180kW at X-band. It could lock on at 25nm and it was credited with the ability to detect a B-47 sized target (like a 'Badger') at a range of 38nm. It also had a surface-attack mode.

Jet interceptors in the US Navy

When the Second World War ended, the Allies (including the Soviets) captured German aerodynamic research. The Germans had tested swept-wing and delta-wing designs in their wind tunnels and they had flown examples of both configurations. Translations of German aero-

dynamics documents were quickly disseminated by BuAer and by its Air Force equivalent. BuAer asked firms to incorporate the new aerodynamics in entries in a January 1946 fighter competition. These high-performance fighters were described as interceptors, but the term seems to have been dropped, to the point where the 1948 interceptor described below was treated as the first of its class. The high-performance fighter competition apparently was conceived during an April 1945 conference reviewing the projected competition for a high-performance night fighter.[86] Outline Specification OS-105 for a single-seat multi-engine aircraft was issued on 28 December 1945.

Vought, which won the competition, offered four designs: V-346A, -346B, -346C and -346D in brochures dated 12 April 1946. All were powered by Westinghouse 24C turbojets (J34s), the same powerplant used by the McDonnell F2H bought in 1945. V-363A was a twin engine tailless swept-wing aircraft. Vought claimed a considerable weight advantage, due not only to eliminating the horizontal tail (and part of the fuselage normally supporting it) but also to a low aspect ratio which considerably reduced structural weight per unit wing area. This version won the competition to become the F7U Cutlass. V-363B was a conventional swept-wing fighter, its engines mounted side by

The much-modified F7U-3 is shown on board *Coral Sea* for trials, November 1952. Not evident here was the relocation of the guns to a position above the air intake. The small radome on the side of the funnel is for a SPN-8 landing-control radar, a standard fitting by this time (operational evaluation of this radar was completed on board this ship in October 1951). The dish antenna to the right is for a wartime-type SK-2, a long-wavelength radar adopted as an emergency measure when shorter-wavelength types such as the SPS-6 on the mast to the left proved ineffective.

The Cutlass shows its exotic configuration: this is an F7U-3 of Aircraft Development Squadron 3, 9 May 1953.

side buried in its fuselage (it had wing root intakes). Vought credited it with a maximum speed of 616mph at 20,000ft with combat power and a service ceiling (with similar power) of 53,100ft. V-363C was another tailless swept-wing fighter, powered by three rather than two 24C engines. Vought credited it with a maximum speed of 670mph at sea level on combat rating and a corresponding rate of climb of 12,320ft/min; service ceiling would be 53,500ft. V-363D was a swept-wing fighter using twin widely-spaced nacelles plus a third engine buried in its body, using wing root intakes. No estimated performance was given.

McDonnell offered a swept-wing twin-jet Model 40A (brochure dated 1 April 1946) with a nose intake and a prominent rooster tail, which it claimed could achieve 654mph at sea level using its after-burners (631mph without), with a combat radius of 328nm. The engines would have been Westinghouse 24C-6s with a normal rating of 2430lbs of thrust at sea level. That would rise to a 3000lb military rating and to 3750lbs with an afterburner.

North American offered RD-1386A (brochure dated 8 April 1946), with forward-swept wings and a conventionally swept rooster tail. The two 24C-4A afterburning engines were fed by cheek intakes. Estimated speed at sea level was 672mph with afterburning; at 20,000ft (with military power) it was 617mph. With afterburning, the calculated rate of climb at sea level was 8780ft/seconds. Combat radius was given as 300nm. An alternative RD-1386B would have had three 24C turbojets, two forward and one aft, the latter using a flush inlet in the underside of the fuselage. The two forward engines would exhaust at the trailing edge of the wing (their intakes would be closer to the wing roots); the third engine would exhaust under the conventional swept tail. Unlike 1386A, this design showed conventionally swept wings as well as tail surfaces.

Three prototypes of Vought's V-346A, powered by afterburning J34-WE-32 engines, were ordered on 25 June 1946. Although the 1946 fighter was described at the time as an interceptor, when BuAer was planning to buy it as the Vought F7U Cutlass, it was characterised as a general-purpose fighter. Compared to the others, the Cutlass offered much higher performance: 542 knots at 35,000ft, with a 464nm combat radius (with extra fuel) and an initial climb rate of 16,500ft/min. However, it was much heavier (23,638lbs) and much more expensive ($1.081 million each). In November 1948 the F7U seemed to be the first navy fighter adequate to fight jet bombers. No less expensive alternative was in prospect. The F7U-2 was a somewhat improved version powered by the J34-WE-42. In fact the F7U-1 proved sufficiently unsatisfactory that all aircraft were assigned to training units. The F7U-2 was cancelled because performance of the J34-WE-42 engine was deficient.

Parallel to the 1946 competition, as noted, Grumman received a contract for the conventional F9F-2 and a study contract for a swept-wing version, which developed into an entirely different aircraft, the F10F Jaguar. In March 1947 Grumman tested a ⅙-scale model it called G-83 in the wind tunnel at MIT. It resembled the later F9F-6 Cougar, but without the massive fillets of the later aircraft (and the Panther). It had a T-tail (alternative tails were tested). Its conventional wings were swept back at an angle of 35°. The model test was an early stage of development leading to an informal proposal submitted in September 1947.

A formal outline specification submitted on 25 November 1947 showed a conventional arrangement with a somewhat cropped-delta wing and a T-tail, the horizontal tail with much the same configuration as the wing. Like the Panther, it had wing-root air intakes and the vertical tail extended back beyond the end of the jet pipe. Grumman planned to use the same Nene I engine as in the Panther. The new aircraft would be considerably heavier (it would take off at 18,729lbs and combat weight was 15,825lbs), but the new wing and a reshaped

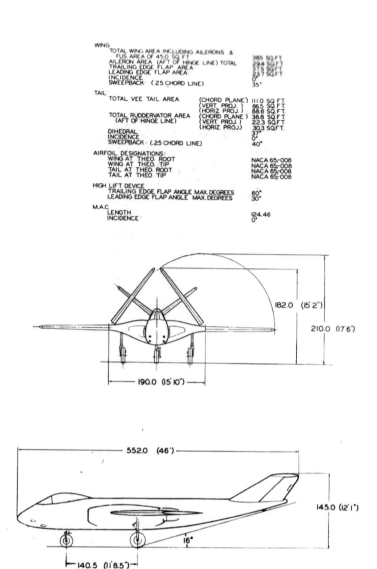

GENERAL ARRANGEMENT
MODEL 40 WITH VEE TAIL
Figure 6A

fuselage would offer better performance. At combat weight and combat engine rating, speed at sea level would be 596 knots (685mph). The corresponding speed at 20,000ft would be 552 knots (635mph). Combat radius was 438nm. Extra weight would reduce the rate of climb, which at sea level with combat rating would be 10,100ft/min. The aircraft would climb to 20,000ft in 2.35 minutes. Armament would be the four 20mm cannon which had become standard.

There was no immediate interest in a high-performance general-purpose fighter other than the Cutlass, which in 1948 was already under contract. However, BuAer was moving towards buying one or more interceptors. The Grumman G-83 file includes the formal BuAer outline specification dated 14 May 1948 for the interceptor competition (see below). Grumman responded with a new proposal it designated G-86, dated 20 September 1948. It substituted the most powerful available engine, a J40, for the Nene of the G-83 design. It added a liquid-fuel rocket engine (plus fuel) in a prominent keel under the fuselage. The J40 was rated at 7310lbs of thrust (10,900 with afterburner) and the rocket, whose nozzle pointed down, at 5000lbs. The cropped-delta mid-wing was replaced by a variable-incidence shoulder wing, which could tilt up during landing so that the pilot would

McDonnell's Model 40 was 'designed for a higher speed than any aircraft has yet flown.' The proposal was dated 1 April 1946 and was presumably aimed at the OS-105 interceptor competition. Guaranteed speed with afterburning was 660mph at sea level (634mph without afterburning) and combat radius was 300nm. Sea-level rate of climb with afterburners was 10,300ft/min with combat fuel on board. As in the Banshee, the engines were two Westinghouse 24Cs. Span of the 35° swept wing was 38ft 6in and length was 46ft. Gross weight was 17,226lbs. Another version of Model 40 had a conventional tail.

retain a better view. This idea was later taken up by Chance Vought in its successful bid for the Crusader. On military power with an afterburner, Grumman expected G-86 to make 658mph (572 knots) at sea level (but maximum speed was given as Mach 0.975, 646 knots, at sea level). With the rocket, it could climb at 30,000ft/min at sea level. Grumman claimed that it could reach 50,000ft in two minutes (2.5 minutes if it retained some rocket fuel for combat). On this basis G-86 was an interceptor on a par with the new F7U; it was intended to deal with bombers at 50,000ft, firing FFARs. It had the APS-25 radar required for the single-seat interceptors of the 1948 competition. BuAer compared it to the other entries.

In the autumn of 1947 McDonnell proposed a swept-wing version of its existing Banshee. By then BuAer accepted that swept wings and

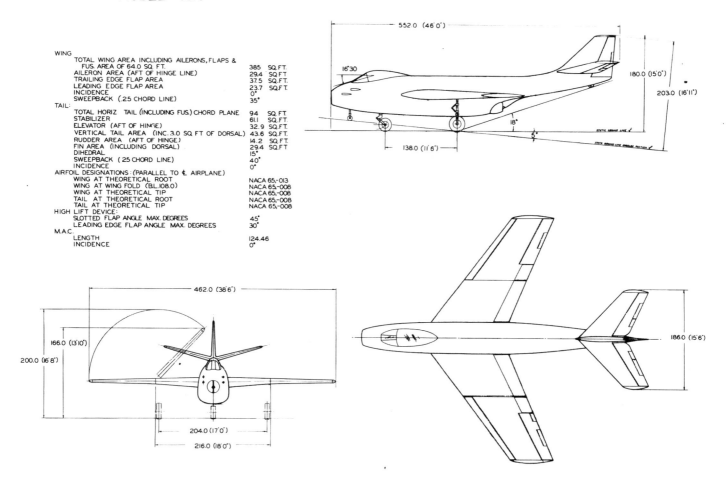

GENERAL ARRANGEMENT
MODEL 40A

WING
TOTAL WING AREA INCLUDING AILERONS, FLAPS &
FUS. AREA OF 64.0 SQ. FT.   385 SQ.FT.
AILERON AREA (AFT OF HINGE LINE)   29.4 SQ.FT.
TRAILING EDGE FLAP AREA   37.5 SQ.FT.
LEADING EDGE FLAP AREA   23.7 SQ.FT.
INCIDENCE   0°
SWEEPBACK (.25 CHORD LINE)   35°
TAIL:
TOTAL HORIZ. TAIL (INCLUDING FUS.) CHORD PLANE   94 SQ.FT.
STABILIZER   61.1 SQ.FT.
ELEVATOR (AFT OF HINGE)   32.9 SQ.FT.
VERTICAL TAIL AREA (INC. 3.0 SQ. FT OF DORSAL)   43.6 SQ.FT.
RUDDER AREA (AFT OF HINGE)   14.2 SQ.FT.
FIN AREA (INCLUDING DORSAL)   29.4 SQ.FT
DIHEDRAL   15°
SWEEPBACK (.25 CHORD LINE)   40°
INCIDENCE   0°
AIRFOIL DESIGNATIONS: (PARALLEL TO ₵ AIRPLANE)
WING AT THEORETICAL ROOT   NACA 65,-013
WING AT WING FOLD (B.L.108.0)   NACA 65,-008
WING AT THEORETICAL TIP   NACA 65,-008
TAIL AT THEORETICAL ROOT   NACA 65,-008
TAIL AT THEORETICAL TIP   NACA 65,-008
HIGH LIFT DEVICE:
SLOTTED FLAP ANGLE MAX. DEGREES   45°
LEADING EDGE FLAP ANGLE MAX. DEGREES   30°
M.A.C.
LENGTH   124.46
INCIDENCE   0°

McDonnell's Model 40A differed from Model 40 in having a nose intake instead of wing root intakes. Dimensions were the same. Maximum speed at sea level was slightly different, 664mph.

deltas were the next step in fighter development, but they were a rather large step involving many unknowns.[87] The head of the BuAer Piloted Aircraft Division saw the swept-wing F2H as an inexpensive way to begin; it would be available a year before any of the other experimental jets. That was important, because without additional funding (already tight), the navy could not afford to support more than two fighter programmes. Anything which could help decide which ones would be worthwhile.[88] At this time the navy was still using funds left over from the wartime FY45 budget; they might pay for the swept-wing design. Grumman was already on track to design a swept-wing version of the F9F Panther (not the later Cougar, but rather the F10F Jaguar). It is not clear why the swept-wing F2H died.

US interest in all-wing and delta-wing aircraft began before the end of the war, encouraged by the success of the Me-163 rocket fighter. Two Douglas aerodynamicists travelled to Paris as part of the US Naval Technical Mission to Europe.[89] There they found a mass of German technical documents, including studies by Alexander Lippisch, who

had designed the Me-163. Lippisch had been caught and was being held in Paris, where he gave a seminar on flying-wing interceptors. Douglas had been interested in tailless aircraft since the 1930s. Now BuAer became interested in what it called the 'Lippisch Principle'. In September 1946 one of the two aerodynamicists wrote a memo advocating a delta-wing aircraft – a flying wing – of very low aspect ratio, using boundary layer control to reduce drag (a low aspect ratio model had just been tested). Douglas began building four scale wing models in October 1946, using 50° sweepback. They proved very promising in wind tunnel tests. By this time BuAer was becoming interested in a high-performance interceptor. A December 1946 study showed that with two 24C engines the interceptor could climb to 40,000ft in 3.35 minutes to attack a 550mph bomber.

Curtiss (Columbus, Ohio division) offered its own delta-wing interceptor proposal (VF-11) in November 1946. Its wing and tail fin were so large that it was as much flying wing as pure delta. It may have been a private proposal issued after the 1946 interceptor had been chosen. Curtiss envisaged a deck-launched interceptor to counter a 450mph bomber detected at 100nm at 40,000ft. It claimed that its interceptor could reach 40,000ft in 3.7 minutes, locating the bomber using its own radar during climb-out and destroying it with its six

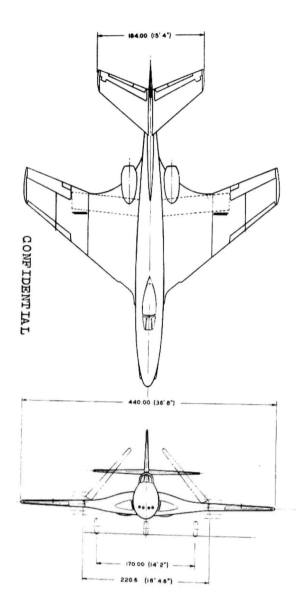

CONFIDENTIAL

184.00 (15' 4")

440.00 (36' 8")

170.00 (14' 2")

220.6 (18' 4.6")

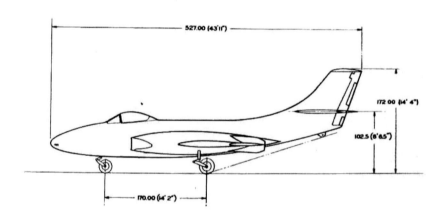

TOTAL WING AREA INCLUDING AILERONS,	
FLAPS & FUSELAGE AREA	343 SQ. FT.
AILERON AREA (AFT OF HINGE LINE), TOTAL	20 SQ. FT.
INCIDENCE (OUTER WING)	0 DEGREES
SWEEPBACK — AT 25 % CHORD	35 DEGREES
WING FLAP AREA, AFT OF HINGE LINE, TOTAL	43.0 SQ. FT.

TAIL AREAS:

TOTAL HORIZ. TAIL AREA (INCLUDING FUSELAGE)	70.92 SQ. FT.
DIHEDRAL, HORIZ. TAIL	0 DEGREES
STABILIZER, TOTAL	55.06 SQ. FT.
ELEVATOR, AFT OF HINGE LINE	15.86 SQ. FT
INCIDENCE, HORIZ. TAIL	0 DEGREES
TOTAL VERTICAL TAIL AREA (INCL. 7.6 SQ. FT. OF DORSAL)	49.66 SQ. FT.
FIN TO RUDDER HINGE LINE (INCL. 7.6 SQ. FT. OF DORSAL)	40.16 SQ. FT.
RUDDER, AFT OF HINGE LINE	9.52 SQ. FT.

AIRFOIL DESIGNATION (PARALLEL TO ₵)

WING AT WING FOLD STATION	NACA 64-111 MODIFIED
WING AT THEORETICAL TIP	NACA 64-109 MODIFIED
HORIZ. TAIL	NACA 65-009 MODIFIED
VERTICAL TAIL	NACA 65-009 MODIFIED

GEOMETRIC ASPECT RATIO

WING	4.3

HIGH LIFT DEVICES

LEADING EDGE FLAP	30 DEGREES
FLAP ANGLE, MAXIMUM	60 DEGREES

M. A. C.

LENGTH	110.00 INCHES
INCIDENCE	0 DEGREES

527.00 (43'11")

172.00 (14' 4")

102.5 (8' 8.5")

170.00 (14' 2")

proximity-fuzed spin-stabilised 5in rockets. Endurance would be 68.7 minutes on normal fuel. The powerplant consisted of two 24C engines with afterburners plus a 1000lbs thrust rocket with two minutes of fuel; Curtiss claimed that it chose the 24C engine because it was so well developed and already so reliable. Maximum speed without rocket boost was given as 572 knots (657mph) at sea level and stalling speed was 78.2 knots (90mph). Climb rate using only the turbojets at combat thrust was 16,150ft/min. In justifying its all-rocket armament, Curtiss may have been the first to point to the need to destroy an approaching bomber at a single stroke, a position the navy adopted in 1947. The proposed radar was APG-22, a type not adopted for navy fighters. At about the same time Curtiss was proposing supersonic research aircraft to meet the requirement met by the Douglas Skyrocket (D-558-II).

In January 1947 it became clear that the navy would be interested in a new interceptor. Douglas began formal design studies under the designation D-571. The initial configuration was a 50° flying wing, the fuselage confined to a ridge running down the back of the wing and culminating in a swept tail. Like the 1946 Curtiss interceptor, it was powered by two afterburning 24C engines. The armament was the

This is McDonnell's 6 October 1947 proposal for a swept-wing Banshee with or without an afterburner; BuAer almost bought it to gain experience with swept wings. The wing would be swept back at 35° and provided with leading-edge flaps and stall plates, with a span of 36ft 8in (length with the swept tail would be 43ft 11in). McDonnell offered three alternatives. F2H-2 and -3 had afterburning J34-WE-22 engines (for another 37 per cent of thrust) and different amounts of fuel. F2H-4 had non-afterburning engines but extra fuel; it would have made 560 knots at sea level, with a rate of climb of 7480ft/min. Radius of action would have been 310nm. At the other end of the scale, F9F-2 (591 gallons rather than 967 gallons) would make 602 knots at sea level with a rate of climb of 21,300ft/min.

same as that envisaged earlier, four 20mm cannon. As the design evolved, the wing shrank and a larger and larger nose protruded from it. Thus the D-571-4 (March 1948) had a wing area reduced from the original 700ft² to 676ft² and the F4D-1 had a 557ft² wing. The D-571-4 may have been the first in the design series to be powered by a single engine, in this case the most powerful in prospect, the Westinghouse J40. To sell the design to BuAer, Douglas engineers had to overcome fear that a flying wing without any balancing tail would tumble uncontrollably. At about the same time that Douglas was offering its delta, Northrop's flying-wing bombers were exhibiting fatal instability. Fortunately the wide (low aspect ratio) delta wing was inherently more stable longitudinally than Northrop's high aspect ratio flying wings.

The first formal US Navy directive requiring a jet interceptor was included in a 19 May 1947 CNO directive outlining developments planned for FY49. In June, Douglas received a contract for preliminary investigation of a delta-wing interceptor based on its D-571, including a mock-up. Note that this preceded the 1948 design competition described below. A BuAer list of background interceptor studies included the VTOL interceptor (ADR completed its DR-57 design study in May 1947) and a study contract awarded to Grumman in June 1947 for a short take-off fighter conceived as a supplement to VTOL studies.[90] Of these only the Douglas design was what would later be called a high-performance interceptor.

The Fighter Branch pointed to the high-performance Douglas delta-wing D-571 (which eventually emerged as the F4D Skyray) as a natural candidate for the new interceptor radar and armament which came out of the interceptor analysis described above. It proposed that Douglas should be asked to reserve space and weight for new as yet unspecified weapons, for an APS-25 radar (or equivalent) and for a manoeuvring autopilot. The cockpit should be arranged so that the pilot could rapidly shift from radar to visual contact with the target. The Military Requirements Branch agreed that any new fighter should reflect the new ideas and in October 1947 it planned a series of conferences to find a way to provide the fleet with a truly effective interceptor.[91]

On 9 December the BuAer Fighter Design Branch held a conference to develop specifications for the next fighter, a competition for which would be held the following year.[92] The conference envisaged a single-seat fighter capable of 600 knots (Mach 1.04) at 50,000ft and the same speed at sea level (Mach 0.91). It would warm up for half a minute, take off in a minute, take five minutes to climb to fighting altitude (50,000ft), fight for five minutes there, loiter for 40 minutes at 40,000ft and for 15 minutes at 15,000ft. Landing would include circling the carrier for 15 minutes with wheels and flaps down.

The two jet engines expected to be available in 1950 were the J40 (7500lbs thrust) and the J47 (6000lbs), possibly supplemented by a rocket. An afterburner might also be available in 1950. The intercep-

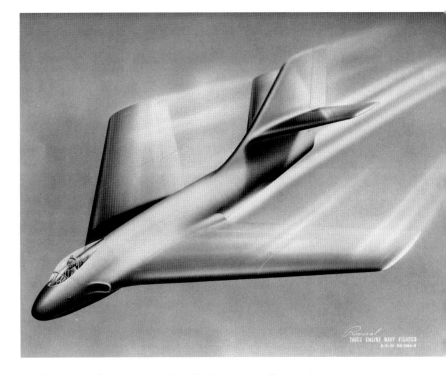

In addition to its forward-swept design, North American offered a three-jet swept-wing fighter in the 1946 competition, its RD-1386B (RD-1386A is in Chapter 2).

tor would be armed either with FFARs or Sperry's AAM-6 missile (the beam-riding version of the Sparrow, expected to be ground-fired in October 1948).[93] The conference decided to try alternative versions of the designs in competition. In order of preference initial alternatives were fifty small fin-stabilised rockets, available for service use in July 1951, followed by spin-stabilised rockets and then fast-firing (10,000 rounds/min) 20mm cannon. The least favoured choice was a turret carrying four 0.50-calibre machine guns or two 20mm cannon. Following the Electronics Division recommendation, the radar would be a modified APS-21, which would be available for a prototype aircraft in January 1951. The conference concluded with a request that ADR conduct a design study. It reported a DR-63 series

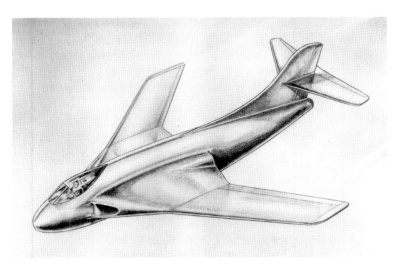

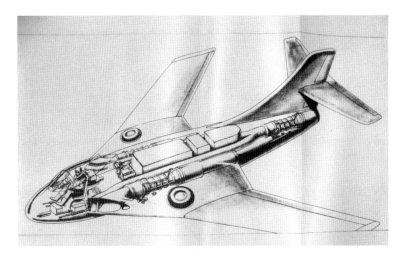

Curtiss Columbus offered this three-jet VF-1 proposal in the 1946 competition. It offered 640mph at sea level (climb rate 13,360ft/min) and a combat radius of 300nm, with an endurance of 2.6 hours at 30,000ft. Interceptor radius was 100nm. The powerplant was three Westinghouse 24C-4B jet engines, to provide sufficient power. Span was 44ft 2in and length was 42ft 8.4in. Gross weight was 22,500lbs. The VF-1 proposal was submitted in December 1945.

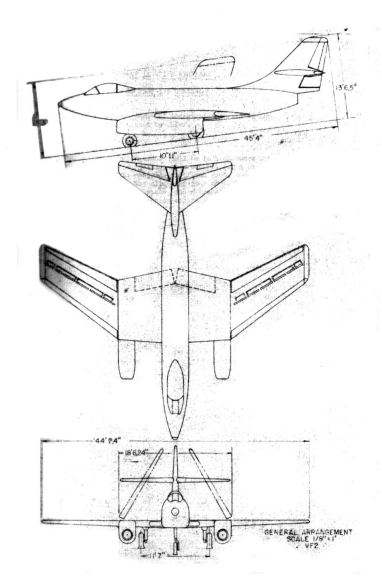

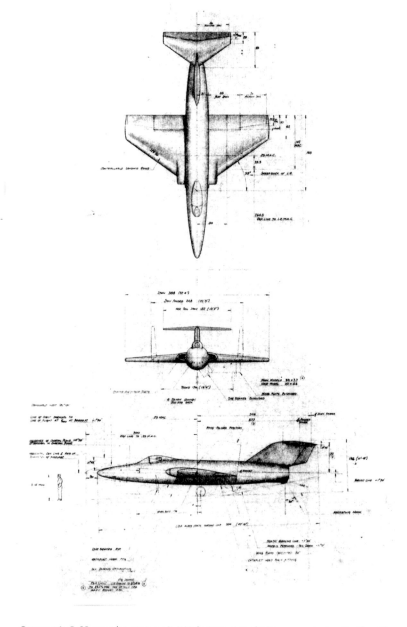

Curtiss' VF-2 alternative OS-105 proposal (April 1946) had two podded 24C-4B engines under its wings and a third in the tail. With afterburning, maximum speed at sea level was 644mph and rate of climb at sea level was 12,580ft/min. Span was 44ft 2in and length was 44ft 7.2in. Gross weight was 22,950lbs. After the competition closed, in November 1946 Curtiss Columbus division proposed a very different interceptor, a delta it called VF-11, powered by two afterburning 24C-4B/2 jets plus a 1000lb thrust rocket (two minutes of fuel). Estimated speed was 572 knots (658mph) at sea level without the boost rocket; sea level rate of climb would be 16,150ft/min. This was conceived as a deck-launched interceptor, its key advantage being a very fast climb (to 40,000 ft in 3.7 minutes); it would use its onboard radar to find its targets, then kill them using six 5in spin-stabilised rockets. Span would be 31.5ft, length 29ft 10in and gross weight would be 11,872lbs. Alternatives were VF-11A powered by one Nene and the rocket motor, offering 587 knots at sea level (climb rate 20,450ft/min); and a more conventional swept wing VF-11B with a vee tail, powered by a Nene and a rocket motor (562 knots without the rocket, climb rate 16,800ft/min).

Right: For the 1946 competition, Martin offered a twin-engine fighter somewhat reminiscent of its much larger air force XB-51. In this case it had one rather than two podded engines under its fuselage near its cockpit, with a second in the tail fed by a flush dorsal air intake forward of the vertical tail (it is barely visible in this drawing). Maximum speed at sea level would be 680mph, compared to the required 650mph; maximum rate of climb was 13,100ft/min compared to the required 10,000ft/min. Combat radius as a fighter was the required 300nm. The engines were Westinghouse 24C-4Bs. Span was 36ft 10in and length 45ft 4in. Gross weight was 14,800lbs.

Grumman's G-83 was the company's initial attempt to design a swept-wing Panther. The powerplant was a single Nene (XJ42-TT-2) producing 5000lbs of thrust dry plus an afterburner which would increase dry thrust to 6950lb and wet thrust to 8000lbs. According to a 25 November 1947 design summary, maximum speed at sea level was 596 knots (685mph) and sea level rate of climb was 10,100ft/min. Combat radius flying at 30,000ft was 438nm. Span was 32ft 4in and length was 49ft 6in. Gross weight was 15,825lbs.

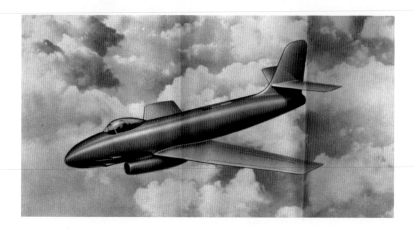

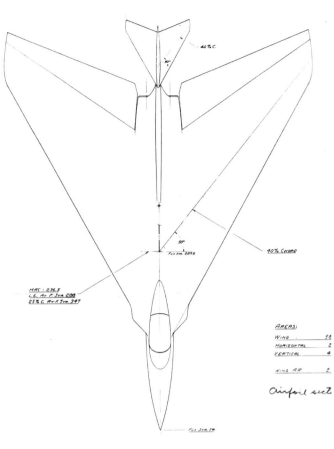

Outside the competition, Lockheed showed this delta-wing concept as its L-169. Its proposal, sent to the BuAer representative at its Burbank plant, was dated 20 December 1946. The initial powerplant was to be a pair of Westinghouse 24Cs, but Lockheed planned to replace them with an L-1000 engine it had developed, which was being built by Menasco. It was intended to operate at particularly high temperature and pressure, for greater efficiency, using a variable-speed compressor ahead of the first low-pressure stage, an intercooler between low and high-pressure stages and intermediate fuel injection before the last turbine stage and other exotic features. Lockheed claimed that at 17,000lb combat weight, sea level speed with the 24Cs would be 535mph with normal power, but 682mph with military power and 738mph with war emergency (afterburner) power. Sea level rate of climb with war emergency power was 11,900ft/min. Lockheed claimed that the L-1000 would perform much better than conventional engines at altitude and would also reduce fuel consumption at all altitudes. It gave figures for the engine burning either kerosene or gasoline. Lockheed had submitted the L-1000 design to the Army Air Corps in 1942 and in 1943 the company received a contract for long-term development under the designation XJ37; Lockheed wanted to develop an L-133 fighter design around it. Instead, it was ordered to develop the XP-80, powered by the de Havilland Goblin, which was built by Allis-Chalmers. In October 1945 Lockheed licensed its turbojet design to Menasco; it built a prototype XJ37 but was unable to continue development. Wright took over the project, but ultimately abandoned it. Presumably L-169 was partly an attempt to revive the project. Span was 35ft; length was 44ft 6in.

in April 1948, its sketch resembling the F3H Demon (the report was ADR-1056).

Meanwhile there was a call for a VTOL interceptor completely separate from the turboprop programme on which BuAer was already engaged.[94] It cited ongoing British work. The argument for a VTOL interceptor, which recurred later, was that a carrier lost crucial time, about five minutes, turning into the wind to launch. That was aside from the advantage of being able to fly from a small platform such as a submarine. Ryan had already received a contract in April 1947 to investigate the possibility of using jet thrust for directional control, mainly to stabilise a vertical take-off aircraft. A further step, not necessarily by Ryan, would use a horizontal J33 engine to achieve a degree of control. The step beyond might be a piloted VTOL aircraft, which could fly in FY54. Reactions from the BuAer staff included proposals for temporary vertical launchers something like the ones used in V-2 rocket tests.

BuAer issued an Outline Specification (OS-113) for an interceptor on 14 May 1948. The target was a 500-knot bomber flying at 50,000ft, which had to be intercepted at least 20nm from the carrier. BuAer asked for a speed of at least Mach 0.95 at 50,000ft with 60 per cent fuel (drop tanks jettisoned). Maximum sea level speed was to be 600 knots or more. Time from take-off to 50,000ft should be no more than six minutes, excluding take-off and acceleration. The problem (flight profile) envisaged half a minute of warm-up, a minute of take-off and acceleration to climbing speed, six minutes' climb, five minutes of combat at maximum power at 50,000ft, 40 minutes of loiter at optimum speed and altitude for fuel economy and then 20

minutes' loiter at sea level at maximum endurance speed. The need to land on a carrier limited stall speed to no more than 105 knots (if gross weight – take-off less fuel to reach 50,000ft and five minutes of combat there – was more than 23,000lbs, it could not exceed 101 knots). If any contractor could exceed the required performance, first priority should go to reducing size, then to increasing endurance.

Permissible engines were the J33 (5850lbs thrust or 6500lbs with afterburner in one version, 5600lbs/7500lbs in another), J40 (7500lbs/10,500lbs thrust), J46 (4200lbs without afterburner, 4080lbs/6100lbs with afterburner), J47 (5750lbs/7500lbs) and the J48 (6250lbs/7000lbs), of which the J48 was a version of the Rolls-Royce Tay developed under licence (further versions of the J40 and J47 were later added). The J40 was both the most powerful of all the engines and also the largest. Three alternative rocket engines were also listed, one offering 20,000lbs of thrust. The fighter would use a modified APS-25 to find and track a target and direct fire by twenty-four FFARs (the only armament).

The problem (flight profile) as understood in December 1948 assumed that the target was a 500-knot bomber flying at 50,000ft, identified 100nm from the carrier. It had to be intercepted while still 20nm away. This distance was defined by the assumed threat, that the high-flying bomber would toss a nuclear bomb. That gave the fighter 9.6 minutes from deck to attack. It would take four minutes for the carrier to launch a fighter in Readiness I condition (aircraft on catapult, pilot aboard, four minutes to turn into the wind) followed by a six-minute climb to 50,000ft based on existing engines (studies were based on a five-minute climb using a future engine). That would leave

The elegant Douglas F4D was intermediate between the 1946 and 1948 competitions. In 1948 it was already under navy contract as a research project; afterwards it was under development as an operational interceptor. Captain 'Winkle' Brown flew it at the Douglas plant while serving as an exchange test pilot at Patuxent River. When he arrived, it was being hailed as the answer to the MiG-15s in Korea. When he arrived at El Segundo in May 1952, he had already been told that it had problems. Take-off acceleration was good, but Brown found the climb rate disappointing and in need of an afterburner (he also found level speed without afterburner disappointing). Presumably these were symptoms of the failure of the J40 which then powered the aircraft. Brown was impressed by how fast the aircraft could fly before it began to buffet near Mach 1, but he considered it too stable laterally, particularly for landing. Overall, his feeling was that the Skyray promised far more than it could deliver.

An F4D-1 of VF-162.

only 0.6 minutes for manoeuvres and a firing run. Fuel capacity should allow for warm-up, take-off and climb, five minutes of combat, 40 minutes at altitude and 20 minutes at sea level.

The proposed problem was criticised on the ground that the British were struggling to develop a bomber capable of 500 knots at 50,000ft; the existing US B-45 made 432 knots at 35,000ft and the Soviets were apparently flying a comparable aircraft. The current navy specification for a heavy attack bomber called for Mach 0.9 (518 knots) at 40,000ft. It was also argued that the 20nm range was too conservative; a bomber would probably drop its weapon at 7nm range. BuAer was aware that if the Soviets deployed stand-off missiles the situation might change radically, but it observed that no missile-bomber combination was under development in the United States capable of meeting the 20nm requirement from 50,000ft. It seemed unlikely that the Soviets were doing better.

Competitors

The competing designs deemed acceptable were the Chance Vought V-362, Douglas D-571 and -571A, Grumman G-86, Lockheed 183 and the McDonnell 58 and 60.

Vought's V-362 was based on the Cutlass already being bought. It was an F7U-1 with a new fuselage (with more voluminous nose) to accommodate the desired interceptor APS-25 radar and FFAR armament as well as more powerful Westinghouse J46-WE-2 engines (the 24C-10 follow-on to the 24C [J34] engine) with afterburners. The wing was slightly modified with new constant-chord slats. The lower fin stub was made somewhat thinner. Vought claimed a gross take-off weight of 18,463lbs. Maximum speed at 50,000ft would be 556 knots.

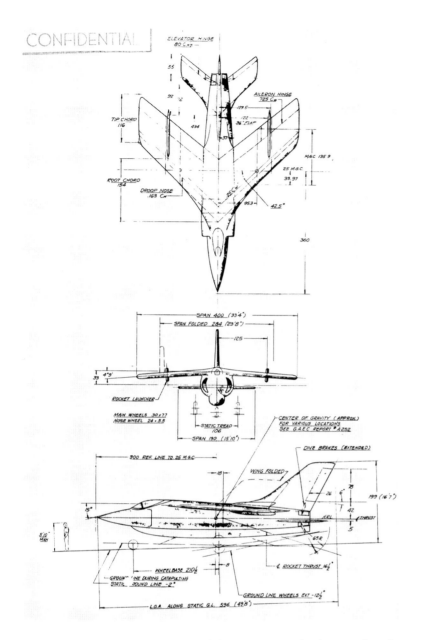

CONFIDENTIAL

Grumman's G-86 was entered in the 1948 fighter competition. This drawing is from the proposal dated 20 September 1948. The keel shown under the body is for the rocket motor and its fuel. Adoption of a variable-incidence shoulder wing forced the main wheels into the fuselage. With the afterburner, maximum speed at sea level was 645 knots and sea level rate of climb was 18,300ft/min. With the rocket, the rate of climb was 31,000ft/min. Span was 33ft 4in and length was 49ft 8in. Gross weight was 22,311lbs.

Douglas' D-571 was its Skyray delta, which became the F4D-1. Douglas' F4D-1 brochure was produced just after the competition (it was dated 31 December 1948). Douglas claimed, it turned out correctly, that wind tunnel tests showed that with higher-power engines probably available during its lifetime, the aircraft would be supersonic (but it attributed low drag rise only to the thinness of the wing, as the area rule had not yet been enunciated, at least in the United States). The current engine was the 7500lbs thrust version of the J40; the future engine would produce 10,500lbs of static thrust (using an afterburner). In 1948 the future engine was already under development and it was expected in the near future (as it was, this engine did not enter service, but other high-powered engines did). In

The McDonnell F3H was one of two winners of the 1948 interceptor competition. These are F3H-2Ns.

the brochure, Douglas contrasted the F4D with a swept-wing D-592/592A and a shorter-nose delta D-591. D-592 had cheek intakes like the Grumman G-86 and a high tail something like that of a Panther. All of the alternatives were powered by versions of the J40. The F4D would take off at 16,700lbs, which made it one of the lighter alternatives. Douglas claimed that it would make 586 knots at sea level and climb at 6290ft/min there. An alternative version with 20mm cannon instead of rockets offered slightly better performance despite its somewhat greater weight (17,060lbs). The was probably because Douglas planned to place the rockets in underwing pods, which added drag. D-592/592A were rejected as unsatisfactory.

Grumman's G-86 has already been discussed. Gross weight at take-off would be 22,311lbs. In take-off condition, speed at sea level would be 645 knots; in combat condition, speed at 50,000ft would be 549 knots. With the booster rocket, it would make 865 knots (Mach 1.5) at 50,000ft. All speeds, but probably particularly the last, probably would not have been achieved, due to compressibility problems of the sort which plagued contemporary fighters.

Lockheed's 183 had swept wings and wing root intakes, its most unusual feature being variable-sweep wings. They were chosen to hold down the size the aircraft without violating the OS-113 requirements. In its proposal, Lockheed argued that no swept wing fighter of normal type could meet the specification. Its solution was variable sweep, apparently with two positions (zero sweep and 47°). When wing sweep changed, so did the angle of the vertical tail, which meant also the angle of incidence of the horizontal tail. Presumably that was intended to solve the usual variable-sweep problem, that the centre of lift moved away from the centre of gravity when wings were swept back. To

211

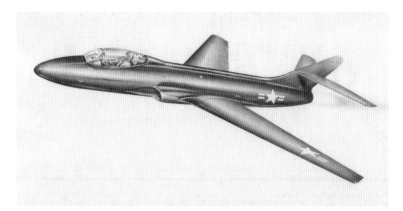

Lockheed offered its L-183 in the 1948 interceptor competition (OS-113). It had a variable-sweep wing, perhaps the first offered to the US Navy (Bell was then testing the variable-sweep X-5, based on a wartime German project in which the sweep could be varied on the ground to test alternatives). The main engine was a Westinghouse 24C10 with afterburner, supplemented by two liquid-fuelled rockets (500lbs thrust each at 35,000ft), one on each side of the fuselage below the engine. Estimated maximum speed at sea level was 659 knots (Mach 0.99) and 591 knots at 35,000ft (Mach 1.03); speed in a dive was Mach 1.30. Sea level rate of climb was 14,070ft/min without the rockets. None of these figures was likely to be at all realistic, since the L-183 was not area-ruled. Sweep could be varied between 0° (for the wing trailing edge) and 47° (quarter-chord line of the wing). The pivot of the wing was fixed, so the incidence of the horizontal tail had to change to compensate. Span varied from 28ft 4in to 38ft 7in; length was 47ft 3in; gross weight was 15,400lbs.

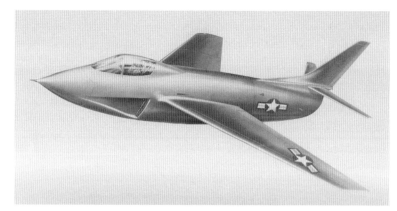

North American entered this RD-1544 design, dated 15 September 1948, for the interceptor competition (OS-113). It resembled the F-86C (soon redesignated F-93A), a heavily-modified version of the Sabre with NACA-type flush inlets. The power plant was a Westinghouse J40-WE-8 turbojet engine with afterburner (6560/10,900lbs thrust) plus a 1500lb thrust Reaction Motors boost rocket (for the climb from 35,000ft to 50,000ft). At a gross weight of 23,000lbs, estimated maximum sea level speed was 656 knots (Mach 0.993); at operational altitude (50,000ft) it was 549 knots (Mach 0.954). Sea level rate of climb was 20,800ft/min. Span was 40ft 6in and length 51ft 6in.

provide sufficient space for the sweep mechanism, the pilot was seated well forward of the wing. In addition to making low-speed flight more practicable, Lockheed claimed that variable sweep would provide greatly superior manoeuvrability, particularly at high altitude. Lockheed proposed the least powerful engine among the acceptable entries: a single 24C-10 (J34). It chose the J34 in preference to the next larger engine, the Nene; its analysis showed that the larger aircraft with the larger engine would have about the same performance and would require the same degree of rocket boost. To help its interceptor climb fast enough to 50,000ft, it would have two 500lb thrust booster rockets exhausting just under the tail pipe. The small engines helped hold down weight to only 11,243lbs empty and 15,400lbs loaded, presumably showing that a really lightweight aircraft could achieve remarkable performance without a large engine. Lockheed claimed a maximum speed of 659 knots (757.9mph) at sea level (Mach 0.99) and 564 knots (Mach 0.98, 648.6mph) at 50,000ft and maximum speed of Mach 1.3 in a dive. In its proposal, Lockheed referred to a somewhat similar swept-wing fighter it was currently building, the long-range air force F-90 (the repot illustrated a drag comparison it had conducted during that programme). The duct air intakes, near the wing roots, were similar to those of the F-80 Shooting Star. Lockheed argued that it offered very high ram recoveries (air flow into the engine) with minimum drag. Unlike a nose intake, these side intakes left the full volume of the nose available for the desired radar. Placing the cockpit immediately abaft the radar offered the pilot maximum visibility. The file on the Lockheed design does not include the BuAer critique, but this was the only one of the four acceptable designs which made it no further.

McDonnell offered two similar aircraft, both powered by single afterburning J40 engines. Its Model 58 had conventional swept wings; it became the F3H Demon. Model 60 had a similar radar nose and cheek intakes, but instead of swept wings it had a large 60° delta wing

with two vertical tails somewhat similar to those of a Cutlass. For comparison with Lockheed's proposal, Model 58 weighed 13,190lbs empty and 18,200lbs at take-off. McDonnell claimed a maximum speed of 560 knots (Mach 0.97) at 50,000ft and 642 knots (Mach 0.97) at sea level. At take-off the rate of climb would be 3900ft/seconds. The wings were swept back 45°. For Model 60, McDonnell claimed a take-off weight of 17,182lbs. It claimed a maximum speed of 568 knots (Mach 0.98) at 50,000ft and 662 knots (Mach 1) at sea level; BuAer had specified 600 knots at sea level and Mach 0.99 at 50,000ft.

For its interceptors, BuAer selected the Douglas F4D Skyray and the McDonnell F3H. BuAer considered the delta configuration so promising that a delta had to be included in any programme. Of the four acceptable designs, the F4D offered the best interceptor performance, in terms of level speed and climb. McDonnell's Model 60 was rejected, despite claims that it had undergone substantial wind tunnel tests which proved its supersonic potential. McDonnell's Model 58 (which became the F3H Demon), was preferred, even though it barely met the worst-case requirement. It offered greater handiness and was smaller and lighter. Low take-off speed made for a roll-off (rather than catapult) take-off.[95] It seemed to offer fewer development problems than the alternatives. As for marginal performance, current bombers were not considered as threatening as the specification implied. In March 1949 BuAer expected it to take off at 18,220lbs and to reach 50,000ft in 5.5 minutes; sea level speed was 638 knots. It was described as the Very High Performance Interceptor Fighter, previously the XVF (INT-1). BuAer records do not include the evaluation of Lockheed's Model 183, but the figures it provided seem grossly overoptimistic.

Of the totally rejected interceptor proposals, North American's RD 1544/1544A was based on the F-93 (F-86C) fighter it was then developing for the air force, a drastically-modified Sabre with cheek air intakes leaving the nose free to accommodate a radar. Like the F10F and the Lockheed design, it incorporated a boost rocket. It was much heavier than a Sabre, taking off at 23,000lbs. Sea level speed was given as 656 knots (Mach 0.993).

Republic offered something more exotic. At the time, it was developing the XF-91 Thunderceptor for the air force, using unique

In the late 1940s no one knew quite how to deal with the much faster speeds at which jet fighters would approach jet bombers. One approach was to mount the fighter's guns in a turret, so that the turret rather than the fighter could be manoeuvred. This is the experimental installation in an F9F-3 Panther fighter, flying over Long Island. (J W Hawkins Collection via John Gourley)

inverse-taper wings (broader and thicker at the tips than at the roots). Its NP-48 resembled the XF-91, but had a solid nose and an under-nose intake. The alternative NP-49 used such wings and an inverse-taper butterfly tail, but instead of a powerplant in the fuselage, as in all of the others, it carried its two J46 engines in underwing nacelles with side inlets. A 4,000lb thrust rocket engine occupied the tail cone. Weight fully loaded was 22,902lbs. Guaranteed sea level speed was 650 knots (560 knots at 50,000ft) and time to climb to 50,000ft was 4.25 minutes not including take-off and acceleration time.

General-purpose fighters

Grumman's proposal offered a higher rate of climb than the F3H (2.1 minutes vs 5.5 minutes to reach 50,000ft), but only by using a rocket. However, BuAer was interested in developing the Grumman aircraft as a general-purpose all-weather fighter. It was of such interest that in March 1949 BuAer decided to transfer part of the $2 million of FY49 money earmarked for the armed escort version of the A2J attack bomber to the Grumman programme (now designated F10F) to advance its first flight by six months. At this point take-off weight was 26,705lbs, sea level speed was 625 knots and the fighter was expected to climb at 15,600ft/min at sea level. Grumman replaced the high variable-incidence wing with a mid-mounted variable sweep wing, the change in sweep on approach improving landing characteristics.

BuAer did not want the Cutlass interceptor, but it was interested in a version enlarged into a general-purpose fighter. It therefore funded a further series of Vought studies designated V-366D and -366E.[96] Issues raised by BuAer included insufficient vision over the nose and undesirable catapult characteristics. BuAer also wanted either cannon or FFARs as alternatives, because by 1949 it saw the developed Cutlass as a potential general-purpose fighter. Vought enlarged the vertical

tails (which BuAer found essential for satisfactory handling qualities) as well as the chord of the ailevators (combined ailerons and elevators). In one of the Vought studies the two J46 engines were replaced by a single J40-WE-10, at that time the most powerful engine BuAer envisaged (given its later problems, the Cutlass was lucky that it was not adopted). With its afterburner, the single engine would produce 13,700lbs of thrust (as then estimated), compared to 12,200lbs for the two J46 engines. With the single engine, speed at sea level increased from 570 knots to 574 knots.

BuAer liked the V-366D design and through early 1950 Vought developed it further into the F7U-3 (V-366F), the production version of the Cutlass. Like the interceptor, it was powered by considerably more powerful J46-WE-2 engines.[97] Its expected performance was much better than that of the Grumman F10F, which it was expected to supersede as an all-weather general-purpose fighter. Given the additional power, the new fighter could accommodate a GE APQ-42 search and fire-control radar (250kW) which could control 20mm guns and FFARs; it also had provision to control the new Sparrow I missile. The new fighter offered considerably more fuel and therefore combat radius. It had been extensively redesigned based on experience with the F7U-1. Limited production (twenty-eight aircraft) was approved on 21 August 1950.

The project then collapsed. It grew heavy enough that it could not normally be launched from the most powerful existing catapult (H-8) and its new engines were considerably less powerful than expected, with worse fuel consumption. It was expected to present serious control problems. Meanwhile two alternative general-purpose fighters had appeared, the FJ-2 Fury and the F3H-1 Demon (note that the Cougar was not mentioned). Because general-purpose fighters were needed so badly, on 10 February 1951 BuAer mailed a letter of intent notifying Vought that purchase of 212 more F7U-3s had been approved. In a later memo, the Aircraft Division wrote that this was far beyond anything it had expected when approving limited production.

When a BuAer team visited Chance Vought in April 1951, the company's representatives agreed that there was a serious problem. Possibilities for reducing weight included redesign of fuel tank protection, re-evaluation of existing strength requirements (which BuAer

The favoured solution to the air-to-air problem was the guided missile. This F7U-3M Cutlass has four Sparrow Is under its wings.

admitted might well be excessive) and a drastic reduction in military load (radar, advanced fire control, heavy air-to-ground armament, provisions for Sparrow and perhaps the FFARs except as an overload). The current fire-control system and 20mm cannon would be substituted. Saving this much weight would somewhat improve rate of climb, ceiling, combat radius and stall speed. At a take-off weight of 30,100lbs, the fighter needed 10 knots too much wind over the deck. Chance Vought's proposed solution to the catapult problem was to use four to six JATO rockets. BuAer calculated that nothing short of saving about 2500lbs would solve the problem.

The worst problem was failure of the J46-WE-2 engine to meet its guarantees. The best solution would be for the engine to reach its full thrust. As a backstop, the only available engine was the Allison J35, for which a simple afterburner could be developed. No other engine would fit the twin-engine space. A single J47, J40-10 or J47-21 could be installed, but only with difficulty.

Even after all the weight had been saved, the aircraft would not compare well with other fighters under development unless the original thrust could be provided. The BuAer group which visited Chance Vought wanted the 212-aircraft programme held in abeyance, although the original twenty-eight fighters could be delivered.

The most attractive replacement was the FJ-2 Fury, a modified F-86 Sabre bought as an emergency high-performance fighter after the outbreak of war in Korea (see Chapter 7). The alternatives were worse. The F4D was an interceptor not suited to the general-purpose fighter role. The other two high-performance fighters under development, the F3H-1 Demon and the Grumman F10F, were still too experimental to mass-produce. The only other high-performance fighter, the F9F-6 Cougar, was still highly experimental, it offered worse performance (except range) and Grumman's engineering staff was badly overloaded.

Any increased work on the Cougar would impose a cost on other important programmes, such as the F10F and the S2F ASW aircraft. As for the FJ-2, the only unattractive aspect was that production would not begin until September 1952. That raised the possibility that Vought should be asked to produce FJ-2s at its plant, instead of F7U-3s.

All of this made the F7U-3 still potentially more attractive than any alternative aircraft available in the short term. In May, BuAer certified that, as modified, the F7U-3 would be a satisfactory day fighter. DCNO (Air) reinstated it in the FY52 budget. As modified, the Cutlass was armed with 20mm cannon but not with FFARs. However, in December BuAer evaluated it as 'parent aircraft' for the optically-guided version of the Sparrow I missile. Its representatives went on to consider installing the whole radar beam-riding system, with a 250kW APQ-36 or -41 radar and a 24in dish – essentially what had been dropped during the savage weight-cutting earlier in the year (the alternative was a simpler radar, also with a 24in dish, but with much lower power). Ideally four missiles would be carried, meaning a total of 1656lbs – about 10 per cent of the aircraft's empty weight – for the APQ-36 version (the superior APQ-41 would add another 120lbs). Vought offered to perform a feasibility study at no cost.

Remarkably, Chance Vought built 290 F7U-3s, including ninety-eight F7U-3Ms armed with Sparrow missiles. By the time BuAer was looking for a way to salvage the F7U-3, it was also developing the McDonnell F3H as a general-purpose fighter; on 24 January 1951 DCNO (Air) wrote the Chief of BuAer that 'there is evidence to indicate that the XF3H-1 interceptor aircraft possesses an attractive

General Purpose Fighter potential'. If BuAer agreed, he wanted a minimum of four of the twelve aircraft in the 1951 third supplemental appropriation and 1952 procurement to be prototype general purpose fighters. That made sense because the F4D was clearly a superior interceptor.

The engine mess

BuAer's interceptor programme demanded the most powerful jet engines available. In 1947–8 that meant the afterburning version of the Westinghouse J40, so it powered three of the four high-performance fighters BuAer was developing: the F3H, F4D and F10F (the Vought Cutlass had two lower-powered Westinghouse engines). BuAer saw Westinghouse as its principal jet engine builder.[98] In 1950 all three single-engine fighters were scheduled to use the J40-WE-10. In December, it seemed that the engine would be available in time for production F4D and F3H fighters, although not for the F10F. The follow-on J40-WE-22 (11,600lbs thrust with afterburner) was chosen for the F10F. Production of the J40 slipped, so in 1951 it was clear that it would not be available in time for early F4Ds and F3Hs, so the J40-WE-22 was chosen instead for the first twelve F4Ds and the first 250 F3H-1s. Although the originally planned J40-WE-10 performance could not be achieved, a future J40-WE-24 was expected to approach the performance expected of the -10 version. BuAer studied alternative engines offering the same performance, but as of June, the Aircraft Division could find no other engine which it could recommend to replace the J40 altogether. J40 development kept slipping, so that as of November more F4Ds would have to be powered by the -22 engine, at a cost in performance.

BuAer began to look again for alternatives. Allison proposed its J71, which could fit any airframe designed for the J40 and was superior to the -24 and comparable to the forthcoming J40-WE-26. The Aircraft Division was clearly reluctant to abandon the J40 programme altogether, but it proposed using the J71 mainly in the F3H, F4Ds continuing to use the J40 for the time being. An alternative was to adopt a British engine; the 9500lb thrust RA-14 Avon seemed to be as advanced as the J40, with superior weight, thrust and fuel economy. In the event the Avon was not bought, but BuAer ended up with the Pratt & Whitney J57, the company's first entirely original design, using a new twin-spool configuration. It ended up as the powerplant of the F4D.

At this stage BuAer thought that the J40 could be salvaged. It was using large numbers of Westinghouse engines and Westinghouse had established a good production record. The J40 seems to have been a step too far, given limited Westinghouse development capacity. The problem became public only in 1955, well after BuAer had decided to switch engines, when a Congressman visiting McDonnell saw F3H-1s outside the plant waiting for their J71 engines – for the replacements already chosen for the J40. An investigation showed that the J40 programme had cost the navy $200 million.

Further interceptors

In 1948–50 BuAer periodically listed long-term aircraft projects as a kind of wish list. The April 1949 wish list included XVF (Interceptor) to replace the F4D and F3H. It would appear in 1956.

The list also included a replacement for the F10F (and, later, the Cutlass) to be ready in 1953: XVF (GP-1). It would be the first super-

sonic general-purpose fighter, with a 5000–10,000ft ceiling advantage over existing general-purpose fighters. It should have low supersonic speed, a ceiling of 50,000–60,000ft and a combat radius of 600nm. The primary armament would be FFARs. Its search radar would offer a 15nm range against fighters and lock, follow and fire capability.

The attached justification pointed to the need for higher speed, ceiling and manoeuvrability in future interceptors. The GP fighter was conceived both as an interceptor and as a strike escort, which would need similar capabilities. BuAer pointed out that an aircraft with such qualities would be an excellent all-round general-purpose fighter for the time period it had in mind.

About 1950, probably before the outbreak of war in Korea, BuAer had prospective projects in hand for a low-supersonic (Mach 1 plus) single-seat fighter with a radius of 500–700nm and also for a Mach 2 fighter with this radius. It was still interested in escort fighters, including conversions of day fighters. None of these projects seems to have gone anywhere.

New possibilities

Quite aside from the problems they entailed, jets offered exciting new possibilities unlike those offered by the earlier piston engines. Because they were so much lighter (on a pounds per power produced basis) than piston engines, it was almost immediately obvious that they might be the basis for vertical take-off aircraft competitive with more conventional types. To the US Navy, that promised a solution to a new problem. During the Second World War, escort carriers had provided vital for convoys. Now the air threat to convoys seemed to be growing, but it was impossible to imagine mass-producing jet carriers. In 1947 the Aircraft Research Design branch conducted a study of a VTOL fighter to operate from merchant ships or even submarines (in one account of BuAer thinking, the submarine role was primary): DR-57. The May 1947 report outlined a means of carrying and operating three such aircraft from a standard fleet submarine. The available powerplant was the 5100hp Allison Model 500 (actually two linked engines). ADR planned to use an eight-blade contraprop. At zero speed the 5100hp engine offered 16,200lbs of thrust, meaning that it could just lift a 16,000lb aircraft. The result was unsatisfactory; combat radius was only 100nm. DR-57 promised a maximum speed of 458 knots (527mph) at 35,000ft and a high rate of climb, 11,650ft/min at sea level.

By July 1948 the rating of the engine, now designated XT-40, had increased to 7070hp, engine weight increasing from 2500lbs to 2960lbs. ADR conducted a new study, producing a new DR-72 sketch design, reported in 1948. It maintained the same thrust to weight ratio of 1.5, but much more power offered a lot more performance: a combat radius of 384nm, maximum speed of 543 knots (624mph) at 35,000ft and a climb rate of 13,770ft/min at sea level (time to 35,000ft would be 3.85 minutes rather than 4.8 minutes). Useful load was much greater. ADR suggested adding effectiveness by using an APS-25 radar and a Mk 6 fire-control system and also be adding more fuel. Armament would be twenty-four FFAR in two wingtip pods.[99]

On this basis BuAer held a competition for a vertical take-off 'Convoy Fighter' to counter a 400-knot bomber. A formal Operational Requirement (OS-122) was issued in May 1950.[100] Each manufacturer was asked to design both a full-scale fighter and a 0.766 scale version (OS-121).[101] BuAer planned to award contracts for the scale models to test the feasibility of the concept before awarding contracts

for full-scale fighters. However, all the manufacturers preferred to offer full-scale aircraft, stripped to reduce weight, powered by T40-A-6 engines modified for vertical operation. Both Northrop and Martin estimated savings if the scale model stage was foregone. BuAer's own analysis showed that would save $2 to $5 million and 1 to 2½ years.[102]

The aircraft was described as a means of defending convoys when land planes or carrier aircraft were not available. Required speed was 540 knots up to 35,000ft, the aircraft climbing to 35,000ft in five minutes. At 45,000ft the convoy fighter would have to be capable of 2G turns and a climb rate of 500ft/min. Envisaged missions were CAP (two-hour endurance at 30,000ft) and high-speed reconnaissance to 350nm. The convoy fighter should be operational by FY54.

After a design competition, Lockheed and Convair received prototype contracts. Their aircraft were called 'pogosticks', after a popular spring-powered toy with which a child could bounce vertically off the ground. Convair's XFY-1 performed a full programme of vertical take-offs. Lockheed's XFV-1 was completed with a temporary undercarriage so that it could be tested in conventional flight and it never did fly vertically.

The VTOL interceptor came to be seen as more than a specialised means of convoy defence. In a 1953 BuAer study a 525-knot VTOL interceptor outperformed an advanced (600-knot) carrier-based jet interceptor, largely because it could be launched far more quickly and in greater numbers.[103] This time the criterion was whether the defence could impose unacceptable damage on the enemy, rather than one how many bombers penetrated to the carriers, based on a calculat-

The Convair XFV-1 was the only successful fruit of the initial naval VTOL programme (the rival XFY-1 never flew vertically).

ed exchange rate. The unacceptable level of damage to the bombers was an average of 75 per cent per raid. For both types of interceptor, the same radars would detect the incoming raid, typically one SPS-2 at the force centre and SPS-6Bs on eight radar picket destroyers on an 80nm circle. A carrier could support ten to sixty conventional fighters or fourteen to eighty VTOLs. Two catapults could launch four conventional fighters per minute, but VTOLs could launch at a rate of twelve per minute. In each case interceptors would be vectored onto a course towards the bomber course but 10nm to one side, the interceptor being vectored onto a beam track for radar search, tracking and attack. Their weapons would be forty-eight FFAR or four Sparrows.

The incoming bombers were the same B-47 equivalents for which the new conventional interceptors were being designed, capable of 500 knots at 200–45,000ft. The threat was a boost-glide missile (55nm range from 45,000ft, 10nm from sea level) or a longer-range missile (75nm/30nm from these altitudes) carrying either a nuclear or conventional warhead.

The bombers were expected to be widely dispersed to avoid destruction by single defensive nuclear missile warheads. Dispersion greatly favoured larger numbers of interceptors, hence VTOLs. Somewhat lower interceptor speed was tolerable if the carrier could vector fighters into the forward hemisphere of the bombers and if its weapons were likely to be effective either at long range (Sparrow) or in a very short engagement (FFAR).

Apparently the 1953 study was unconvincing. When the turboprop VTOL project was dropped in 1956, the explanation was that these aircraft had been designed to deal with 400-knot bombers flying at 40,000ft; the current bomber threat was a 500-knot aircraft at 50,000ft. It may be that altitude rather than speed was the key, as the turboprops had a limited ceiling.

For the US Navy, the other major post-war problem was the need to support amphibious operations, again a wartime escort carrier role which could not be carried out by jet fighters. It is not clear whether or to what extent, VTOL was seen as a solution. BuAer's favoured solution was apparently a jet seaplane fighter. During the Second World War the Japanese had used floatplane fighters, most of them modified versions of the Zero, to defend islands. Both the United States and the United Kingdom tested floatplane versions of standard landplane fighters (Spitfire and Wildcat), but never put them into production. In 1945 EDO (the name is the initials of the owners, not an acronym), a manufacturer of floatplane floats, proposed a jet seaplane fighter to BuAer. EDO's proposal was unsolicited, but it attracted considerable interest (and uncertainty). DCNO (Air) plans division considered that a limited future requirement might arise, so BuAer accepted an EDO proposal to conduct further studies. However, in April 1946 the BuAer Fighter Branch commented that it could not see how such a fighter, which would necessarily have inferior performance, was to be used; logistics favoured superior fighters operating from escort carriers. The branch doubted that EDO had the capacity to develop a high speed aircraft and suggested that Curtiss be contacted instead. Ultimately BuAer dropped the EDO study because the likely performance of its proposed fighter was far too low.[104]

However, the idea of a jet seaplane fighter survived. In August 1947 the head of the BuAer Fighter Design Branch reported details of the British Saunders-Roe SR-A1 seaplane fighter. He added that during evaluation of the EDO design the BuAer Military Requirements Branch had concluded that although the usefulness of such an aircraft seemed extremely doubtful, such a proposal was worth evaluating; the branch recommended desirable performance, armament and operational characteristics.[105] EDO was then seeking support from the army, which was interested in its flying boat for operation from snow and ice.

By this time BuAer had turned to Convair to study a blended hull-wing seaplane configuration called 'Skate'.[106] Under BuAer contract, before the end of the war the company developed a means of evaluating seaplane hull forms using small radio-controlled free-flight models as well as towed models. In 1946 BuAer issued Convair a contract for systematic evaluation of water-based aircraft; Convair was to develop a flying-boat configuration with performance comparable to that of a land-based aircraft. It evaluated a radical blended hull form it called 'Skates'. When at rest the aircraft would ride so low in the water that its wings would help keep it afloat. Convair's programme was to develop a satisfactory hydrodynamic configuration and then develop it into a high-performance aircraft. The company was been given military requirements and was expected to report by about December 1947.

At the same time NACA began with a high-speed aircraft and sought to provide it with satisfactory hydrodynamics. The programme included fitting a model of the navy's transonic Skyrocket research aircraft (D-558-II) with hydro-skis. A report issued late in 1947 indicated that the skis would climb to the surface of the water as the aircraft accelerated. At high speed, then, the aircraft hull would not have to withstand the stress of contact with the water, so it could be

Convair's Skate is shown in model form. Note the offset single canopy covering the pilot. The radar operator would have been inside the hull alongside him, much as in the British Sea Vixen. The engines would have been two J40-WE-10s. Maximum speed at 35,000ft would have been Mach 0.955 (549 knots) compared to a required Mach 0.95 (546 knots); combat radius would have been the required 400nm. Sea level rate of climb would have been 16,800ft/min. Skate would have had a 62ft 6in span and overall length would have been 83ft 8in. Gross weight would have been 41,907lbs.

designed primarily for high-speed flight. EDO began full-scale experiments with a hydro-ski.[107]

Early in 1948, then, BuAer could see two paths to a jet seaplane fighter, the blended Convair hull and the hydro-ski. BuAer recommended that an airframe be developed. BuAer reported preliminary studies in April 1948 and DCNO(Air) directed that further work proceed using FY49 money with a relative priority of two – not the most important, but hardly the least. The reason for the relatively high priority seems to have been an expectation that the fighter could be used as a scale model of a much more important aircraft – a seaplane bomber exploiting wartime and post-war research into new kinds of seaplane hull forms which offered both excellent in-water performance and low drag. BuAer was already calling for new long-range seaplanes, but they did not offer the sort of performance needed to penetrate enemy land defences. The large fast jet seaplane materialised as the P6M Seamaster a few years later. Some parts of the projected specification were rewritten specifically to enlarge the fighter so that it would be a better model for the long-range bomber. That seems to have been the reason for making it a night fighter with a two-man crew (side by side, but with the radar operator staggered back slightly) and a heavy radar (APQ-35, as in the F3D Skynight). On the other hand it was given the lightest possible armament, the twenty-four FFARs of the contemporary interceptors.

In May 1948 DCNO (Air) asked that development be carried beyond preliminary studies and that a design competition be held

Seen from below, Skate shows its seaplane-type hull.

instead of simply negotiating with Convair. There was some expectation that the fighter would be valuable not only in itself, but also as a means of testing the aerodynamics and hydrodynamics of projected larger fast seaplanes.[108] A note written in August 1948 (attached to a memo describing the project) pointed out that in view of the complexity of scaling laws it was unlikely that the seaplane fighter could provide more than very general information concerning an attack seaplane two or three times its size and about three years later. 'If there is a prospective need for an attack seaplane, the cheapest and fastest method would be a design programme pointed specifically at the model required.' Thus any justification for the special-purpose seaplane fighter depended on its ability to fill an operational requirement in competition with opposing aircraft which might be in service in three to five years. BuAer did not have enough money for such a project, particularly given the high cost of the attack aircraft then being developed for the supercarrier *United States*.

BuAer did not give up. In July 1948 it issued a requirement for what it called a model (i.e. experimental) seaplane fighter (OS-114).[109] As usual, ADR conducted a parallel sketch design project, in this case designated DR-67. The initial design, reported in June 1948, was a single-seater. A redesigned DR-67A added the second crewman and also provided space for 'special equipment' to be dropped clear of the step (presumably FFARs). The speed requirement was reduced, so sweep-back was reduced from 45° to 35°. The reduction was expected to reduce an expected problem of low speed stability and thus reduce structural weight. This version, reported on 6 July 1948, would have a maximum speed of 566 knots (Mach 0.9) at 15,000ft or 520 knots (Mach 0.9) at 40,000ft and its combat radius, as defined by OS-114, would be the usual 300nm.[110]

The draft of OS-114 was apparently not entirely satisfactory, so in September BuAer tried again. Now it estimated that within the current state of the art a Mach 0.95 fighter could be built which would be able to operate in 5ft waves in sheltered water (amounting to 99 per cent availability). As in other fighter specifications of the time, the aircraft would loiter for two hours at 35,000ft. In this case it was expected to cruise out 100nm at military power, fight for 2.5 minutes and cruise back. Estimated gross weight was 30,000–35,000lbs and armament was the usual four 20mm cannon.[111] This aircraft was conceived as a night fighter, with a pilot alongside a radar operator (the seats might be staggered). A possible nose turret was ruled out as too massive and FFARs (good for only one or two attacks) were ruled out because a night fighter might have to make repeated attacks.

A design competition was announced on 1 October 1948, the rewritten specification being OS-116. NACA conducted a special seaplane conference in November 1948 specifically to provide potential contractors with the latest developments in high-speed seaplane design, much of the information not having been made available up to that time. It was considered particularly valuable not only to the contractors but also to BuAer personnel who would have to evaluate their efforts. Much of this work had been done by NACA's Langley Aeronautical Laboratory, the object being to reduce the aerodynamic penalties usually associated with seaplane hydrodynamics.

Two designs were submitted, Convair's for the blended hull and an alternative hydro-ski design. The blended hull was considered superior. A formal Operational Requirement (CA-05501) was issued on 30 November 1949 for a seaplane fighter to defend advanced bases under all weather conditions, operating in waves up to 5ft high. This was an all-weather fighter with a radar operator as well as a pilot. It was to make not less than 600mph at sea level and climb to 45,000ft in less than 10 minutes. A CAP mission would require two hours' endurance. Another mission was reconnaissance 500nm from a base. This requirement was supported by a CNO letter to BuAer stating that as a matter of policy BuAer should maintain leadership in the seaplane field by vigorously pursuing studies to insure the navy's position.

Only Convair and Curtiss offered proposals; fourteen other manufacturers decided not to compete.[112] Convair offered a Skate design powered by two afterburning J40-10 engines protected by retractable spray dams and with a retractable step. It had an all-moving horizontal tail and powered controls with artificial feel. Curtiss offered a single-engine hydro-ski design (one J40-10 afterburning engine). A question not yet answered was whether the ski would cause lateral control problems at low speed, once the aircraft was up on the ski with its wingtip floats clear of the water. That would be a particular problem in the Curtiss design, which had a take-off speed of 154.5 knots. Curtiss had a broader fuselage than Convair, as its two aircrew sat side by side rather than in staggered positions. Its design had very high wing loading and thrust loading, which made its altitude performance so poor as to be unacceptable and its take-off performance marginal. Its major advantages over the Convair design were smaller size, weight and cost and possibly better rough water performance, but none of these could balance its problems or the superiority of the Convair design. Unfortunately money was too tight. The estimated cost of two prototypes and one static test airframe was $17.7 million, but funds allocated between FY49 and FY53 amounted to only $12.8 million. If the programme were stretched out to solve the problem, it would become even more expensive. Worse, Skate was competitive with current carrier fighters, but hardly with those likely to be in service in five years (when development would be complete) and not even with some current experimental aircraft. All BuAer could do was obey the order to proceed by negotiating a Phase I (design study) contract with Convair. It decided not to go any further.

This model shows the Curtiss seaplane fighter, which was much smaller than Skate. According to the 11 January 1948 proposal, maximum speed at sea level would have been 627 knots (Mach 0.948). Rate of climb at sea level would have been 15,910ft/min. The engine was a single J40-WE-10 producing 7920lbs of thrust without an afterburner and 11,750lbs with the afterburner operating. Span was 42ft 6in and length was 64ft 2.31in. Normal gross weight was 28,900lbs.

Skate was hardly a nimble fighter – no surprise given the requirement to make it larger so that it would approximate the future heavy attack aircraft (gross weight was 45,000lbs). It was also considered deficient in rough-water handling.[113] By May 1950 model tests had demonstrated various deficiencies. The programme was redefined with the object of designing a 1955 fighter with acceptable water performance. To do that Convair had to abandon its blended hull in favour of an aircraft in which aerodynamics would not be affected very much by hydrodynamics – a hydro-ski. A hydro-ski fighter would inevitably be much smaller than a Skate, simply because nearly all of its hydrodynamic performance was provided by its retractable ski. By the time the new design had been selected, a model Skate had already been tested with hydro-skis, which promised to improve rough water take-off and landing and to reduce landing impact loads. However, necessary compromises were made and Convair concluded that the Skate configuration was basically incompatible with hydro-skis.

By February 1950 Convair already had a contract to study high-speed seaplanes employing hydro-skis. It was proposing a delta-wing design (Betta) and a swept wing attack plane (Cudda).[114] Convair also had a contract to investigate incorporating a hydrofoil type landing gear in a high speed seaplane. NACA had agreed to conduct tank tests of ADR's DR-77, a fast attack seaplane using skis. It was also making wind-tunnel tests of DR-56, a planning tail-type attack seaplane. Full-scale ski tests were proceeding using a small amphibian (JRF). In addition, ADR was making a design study of an FJ-1 fighter modified to incorporate hydro-skis, the idea being that skis would turn a conventional aircraft into a seaplane (this experiment was apparently never done).

Convair's new design was called Y2-2, a delta with two hydro-skis which was aerodynamically similar to the company's F-102 fighter.[115] Convair offered a maximum speed of Mach 1.5 and a sea-level rate of climb of 30,000ft/min. The company received a contract for two aircraft on 19 January 1951. The two engines were to be J46-2s, with J34-32s to be used until the J46 was available. The Y2-2 was conceived as a pure test aircraft with sufficient space and weight available for conversion into a night fighter.

The Y2-2 was bought as an experimental aircraft to provide a basis for future seaplane fighter design. However, it offered fighter performance and thus became the basis for various proposals. One was beachhead defence. An amphibious force deploying seaplane fighters would not tie down fast carriers and there was no question that existing escort carriers could operate very high performance jets. Moreover, it was known that a distant carrier could not possibly supply a viable CAP over a beachhead; that had to be done from close inshore. A small escort carrier (*Casablanca* class) could be refitted with a catapult powerful enough to launch the aircraft and it could land on the sea and return to the carrier hangar deck via a ramp. Preliminary studies of such a conversion were carried out and the stern ramp tested in scale form. There was also interest in basing the aircraft on a submarine; it would take off and land on the sea. A DCNO (Air) officer later stated that the hydro-ski fighter was the most adaptable aircraft yet designed for submarine use. It could conduct reconnaissance, guide cruise missiles or deliver nuclear weapons. Model tests had shown that a hydro-ski aircraft could operate from snow and ice.[116] The Y2-2 was therefore redesignated XF2Y in August 1951. It was now the prototype of a possible production fighter, envisaged as a high-performance single-seat all-weather interceptor.[117]

As of August 1952 BuAer had agreed to buy twelve aircraft for delivery in mid-1954. This schedule proved over-optimistic, but as of March 1953 a total of eighteen aircraft were on order, plus one static test airframe.[118]

Initial water tests disclosed a new problem, 'ski-pounding': at and above 60mph the skis vibrated badly and that vibration was transmitted into the aircraft structure, threatening to damage it. The J46-WE-2 engine planned for the F2Y was not producing its expected thrust. The F2Y, like the original version of the air force's F-102, was not area-ruled and that further reduced its performance. The specification for production aircraft required a speed of Mach 1.25 (and Convair expected Mach 1.5), but it seemed unlikely that the aircraft would exceed Mach 0.99. In September 1953 Convair offered to restore performance by redesign (as in the F-102) involving a different wing; and also by replacing the two J46 engines with a single J57-P-4. Additional redesign was needed to solve the ski problem (in January 1954 Convair proposed a single ski to replace the original twin skis). By this time BuAer was short of R&D money. On 14 October 1953 one of the two XF2Y-1s was cancelled. A month later ten of the production aircraft were terminated, the recovered money going into the much more urgent F8U-1 Crusader programme. Since considerable money would be needed to solve the problems of the F2Y, in March 1954 the remaining two production aircraft and the static test airframe were cancelled, leaving a total of five aircraft on order – one XF2Y-1 and four YF2Y-1s.

The programme survived as considerable work was done to solve the hydro-ski vibration problem. One YF2Y-1 disintegrated on 4 November 1954 during a public demonstration when the pilot exceeded flight limits. The preliminary evaluation was therefore postponed until May 1955. It established that a single-ski configuration was better than the original twin-ski type. At the time it seemed that a year would be needed to solve remaining problems before the aircraft could be placed in production. By this time the F2Y was obsolescent due to its low performance. In January 1956 DCNO (Air) recommended no production be undertaken and the Operational Requirement was soon cancelled. Further hydro-ski tests established that skis about a fifth the size of those originally installed would have been successful.

ADAPTING CARRIERS TO JETS

The steam catapult

From a carrier point of view, jets presented a difficult new problem on take-off. A propeller generates lift by creating air flow over an aircraft's wing. At take-off that air is moving far faster than the aircraft, so it generates substantial lift. A jet simply pushes the aircraft along, so that air flows over its wing no faster than over any other part of the aircraft. Since lift is generated by the speed of the airflow, a jet needs a higher take-off speed, even if its wings are not much different from those of a propeller aircraft. Early jets did demonstrate rolling take-offs from carriers, but they needed the full length of a flight deck to do so. That would have precluded deck parking of any kind. To take off within any reasonable distance, a jet had to be catapulted or otherwise

accelerated (the only non-catapult option was JATO take-off rockets, which were not attractive on a sustained basis).

In 1945, when operational naval jets were being tested, catapults were beginning to be used operationally on a regular basis. They were not nearly powerful enough for jet aircraft then in prospect. At this time the standard type of catapult in both the Royal Navy and the US Navy was hydraulic. It was powered by a ram under pressure from oil in its cylinder, the oil being pumped into the cylinder. Wire ropes and pulleys multiplied the stroke of the ram to pull an aircraft along the flight deck. The same multiplication process moved the shuttle of the catapult much faster than the ram.

The British seem to have become aware of the inherent limits on catapult performance during the war and they investigated alternatives. One was a flywheel catapult, in which energy was stored by running up a heavy flywheel using an electric motor. It was tested at Farnborough, but it did not offer enough power to launch a heavy jet aircraft. A second alternative, which did work, was developed by C C Mitchell, a wartime Farnborough staff officer. He had been interested in what he called a 'pop-gun' catapult before the war, in which a powder charge pushed a piston along a cylinder. In 1944 Mitchell examined German gas catapults used to launch V-1 missiles against Britain and he realised that he could adapt their mechanism to a carrier catapult. Instead of steam generated by decomposing high test peroxide (HTP) he would use steam from a carrier's boilers. The Admiralty recognised the potential of Mitchell's invention and it was pursued post-war despite very limited British finances. Work began in 1947.

The project was not highly classified. For example, it was described in detail in the 1947 edition of the official summary of British naval research projects. It is not certain that this edition was given to the US Navy, but the steam catapult was mentioned in the 1948 edition, which was. The BuAer file on the British steam catapult includes an 8 August 1950 cover letter for plans of the Type C (B.S. 4) version of the British catapult, to be provided to BuAer 'in accordance with verbal instructions . . . This procedure will be continued unless instructions to the contrary are received'. The prototype steam catapult (BXS-1) was installed in the aircraft repair ship (ex-carrier) Perseus, which was reactivated in 1948 specifically for these tests. For simplicity, all catapult machinery was installed on her flight deck, which was covered by a false deck.

At least initially, the US Navy seems to have considered the catapult the key problem in operating jets; there was no apparent concern with landing problems, apart from the need to absorb much more energy when a faster, heavier aircraft landed. The ship installations part of a February 1947 classified BuAer technical symposium was limited to catapults, arresting gear and barriers.[119] Much the same emphasis emerged from work on converting the suspended Essex class carrier to a jet carrier.

The jet catapult programme started in December 1944, roughly in tandem with the BuAer design competition for a carrier-based jet fighter. A specification was issued for a new catapult called for accel-

The US Navy modified its carriers to operate jets. Oriskany was the first. She is shown at Yokosuka, 17 March 1954, with Skyraider attack bombers forward and jet fighters (Banshees and Cougars) aft. Modifications included clearing the flight deck of gun mounts and installing the most powerful hydraulic catapults available (H-8s). Atop the remodelled island was an SX search/heightfinding radar. Just visible up the mast is the clamshell reflector of a zenith-search radar.

The problem: launching huge jets, particularly the A3D Skywarrior (later redesignated A-3). The US Navy felt compelled to adopt the British-developed steam catapult after its own internal-combustion design faltered (it never entered service). This A3D is launching from *Ranger*, July 1959. The ropes on the deck beneath the aircraft are the catapult bridle, which connected it to the steam catapult. The catapult problem became urgent as the A3D approached service; in 1950 plans called for the three *Midways* to be rebuilt to operate it.

eration of a 5000lb load to 250mph (not knots, as later specified) or a 20,000lb load to 125mph with a maximum acceleration of 3.5G.[120] The programme was justified by the trend towards heavier aircraft with greater take-off speeds. In January 1945 the BuAer Military Requirements Division pointed out that aircraft development would stop *unless* more powerful catapults became available. BuAer seems to have assumed that its catapult developers could solve the problem, because it kept buying aircraft which current carriers could not launch.

Between 1945 and 1948 catapult requirements exploded, largely because the US Navy was becoming intensely interested in carrier-based strategic bombers. As understood in 1945, bombs weighed 10,000lbs, so it would take a massive bomber to deliver them. The navy also wanted long range, both to penetrate deep into the Soviet land mass and to allow the carrier plenty of sea room to evade counter-attack – it remembered Okinawa. Although an aircraft suited to an *Essex* class carrier (with an improved catapult) could deliver the bomb, it would take a great deal more to deliver it at the desired range. OpNav assembled a three-phase nuclear bomber programme, beginning with the shorter-range aircraft (the North American AJ Savage), proceeding to a longer-range turboprop (the A2J, which never entered service) and culminating in a high-performance long-range jet. The desired high performance explains why BuAer soon came to ask for catapults capable of launching 100,000lb aircraft. Jet fighters were incidental to all of this, because in theory a carrier would launch its long-range bombers so far from the target that the carrier would face little or no opposition.

There was actually an alternative way to launch heavy bombers, but not on a protracted basis: JATO, solid-fuel take-off rockets, were another alternative, developed during the Second World War. For missiles, they in effect superseded catapults, to become the boosters which are now so familiar. Apparently JATO was considerably less acceptable for carrier aircraft, although it had been used in wartime. In 1949, when it wanted to demonstrate the potential of heavy carrier bombers but had no suitable catapults, the Navy used JATO to launch three Neptune bombers from *Midway* class carriers. These aircraft became the core of an

interim navy nuclear attack capability. As such they would have been launched from the same type of carrier in wartime, in the same way. BuAer interest in solid propellants for catapults could be seen as a way of domesticating JATO, to suit it to regular carrier use.

In 1944–5 BuAer was contemplating 15,000lb jet fighters to an end speed of 120mph. In 1946 BuAer became interested in 100,000lb bombers. To provide enough energy, in January BuAer changed the requirement to a 45,000lb aircraft at the same speed. Its catapult designers estimated that a much more massive hydraulic catapult would be needed.[121] In November 1947 CNO approved the Characteristics (design requirements) for a new carrier which would operate 100,000lb bombers and 50,000lb fighters. That December BuAer reported that it had completed a design study of a catapult capable of launching 100,000lb aircraft at 100-knot airspeed (counting 25 knots wind over deck due to the motion of the ship). This far exceeded the performance of any earlier or developmental catapult. In January 1948 BuAer further increased desired performance, to 100,000lbs at 90 knots (about 103mph) and a maximum speed of 105 knots (the former maximum was 120mph) with a 73,500lb aircraft. BuAer decided in April 1948 that with H9 the limits of hydraulic catapults had been reached, All future effort should go into slotted cylinders. C1 as specified now seemed too small for future aircraft but too large for experimental work. It was therefore redefined as a test catapult, suited to but not intended for shipboard installation, with a capacity of 18,000lbs and an end speed of 100 knots (maximum acceleration 3.5G). For the future, lessons learned its design would be applied to a catapult capable of launching a 200,000lb aircraft at 150 knots. Somewhat later there were references to 300,000lb aircraft.

BuAer tried three alternatives. One was to push existing hydraulic technology further. A second was a direct-acting catapult, a piston driven down a cylinder slotted on top, with the aircraft hooked to the piston (as in the new British catapult). A third was an electric catapult. BuAer realised that hydraulics was at about the end of its potential, so it saw a new hydraulic catapult as insurance against the failure of the other types. The electric catapult was apparently a linear motor similar to the current electric type; there was also a flywheel similar to that the British had tried during the war and there was a linear turbine project. The slotted catapult was considered the most promising of all, partly because it offered the greatest promise. The larger the cylinder, the more powerful the catapult, apparently without limit. In November 1945 BuAer's designers were authorised to go ahead with a slotted cylinder designated XC-1 and a preliminary study was approved the following month. Development of slotted cylinders was promoted by BuAer interest in guided missiles.[122]

C-1 was seen as the basis for a larger catapult, scaleable as needed – which was the great attraction of the slotted cylinder. By January 1948 BuAer expected to complete the C-1 design on 1 April 1948 and a final shipboard design by 1 April 1949, in time for the new carrier

United States designed specifically to handle the projected strategic bombers.

The issue in designing a slotted-cylinder catapult was the source of power. BuAer considered internal combustion (as in a car engine or a diesel), hydrogen peroxide (as in the German V-1 catapult) and explosives. It had already used gunpowder to launch floatplanes from battleships and cruisers, but now it needed far more energy. In 1947 it saw liquid fuel as a back-up, characterising both it and explosives as pressure generators. Presumably their gas products would have been vented into the catapult cylinder. Steam was not on the list, although one of the small slotted cylinders was tested using steam from a small boiler. BuAer catapult developers later argued that it was impractical to take steam from a ship's boiler. The ship would be slowed unacceptably, presumably because so much steam would be required (due to losses as it escaped through the slot). They also argued that the interval between launches would be excessive. By 1948 BuAer had chosen powder and it ordered a powder chamber from the Naval Gun Factory at the Washington Navy Yard.

Despite its importance for the BuAer aircraft programme, catapult work seems to have been underfunded, particularly after deep Defense Department budget cuts were mandated in 1949. The decision to limit C1 to a prototype made sense as part of a protracted development plan, but not if slotted-tubes of various sizes were to equip the carrier *United States*, scheduled for laying down in 1949. Since sketch designs

Two A3Ds on *Forrestal*, September 1956, give some idea of their great size. Note how their vertical tails have to fold down to fit most hangar decks then in service, with their 17ft 6in headroom (*Forrestal* and later carriers had 25ft).

The post-war US Navy became interested in flush-deck carriers because it expected to operate huge heavy bombers. This configuration was adopted for the abortive attack carrier *United States* and for her somewhat scaled-down successor, *Forrestal*, shown here in official sketch form. Although the big sponsons shown could have been used as angled landing decks, that was never contemplated. This configuration raised serious design problems. It was difficult to imagine how to eliminate smoke from the massive powerplant and it was also difficult to provide powerful long-range radars. This 1951 sketch shows no solution to either problem, as it omits both uptakes and air-search radar (plans called for antennas on both sides of the ship feeding a common set of displays).

of the ship showed slotted tubes, it is not clear what would have been done had the project proceeded. The big carrier was cancelled on 23 April 1949 as part of the budget cuts. The Douglas A3D, which had won the design contest for the heavy carrier bomber, was ordered modified so that it could be launched by a suitably modified *Midway* class carrier. Allowable weight was reduced to 70,000lbs, which was still a great deal.[123]

The catapult programme was still essential. The deadline did not really change very much, because the United States would have been completed about the same time a modernised *Midway* would have emerged. Required catapult performance was cut to 80,000lbs at 125 knots, which was about the best a proposed hydraulic catapult (H9D) could do. Unfortunately it would be far too massive for the rebuilt carrier. The only viable alternative was a slotted cylinder, which was tentatively designated C-7. To meet the estimated completion date of the modernised *Midway*, all tests on a prototype had to be completed by 30 June 1953. CNO assigned the project the highest priority, planning to use the new catapult not only in the big *Midway*s but also in converted *Essex* class carriers 'in order to permit unrestricted operation of certain aircraft currently programmed and in order to remove limitations which are seriously restricting new developments and advances in aircraft design'.[124] The new A3D Skywarrior heavy (twin jet, swept wing) attack bomber was the important aircraft which could not be launched *without* a C7 catapult. In 1950 it was expected

to enter service within a few years (A3D was given particularly high priority). In August 1950 work began on a smaller (shorter) C-10 slotted-cylinder, with half the performance, specifically for modernised *Essex* class carriers.[125]

BuAer's catapult developers at the Naval Aircraft Factory kept claiming that they could meet the deadlines CNO had set, but C-1 development proved difficult and protracted, even after the project received top priority in 1951.[126] By that time the pre-Korean War budget cuts had been reversed, so the navy was modernising as many carriers as it could and preparing to build a large new carrier, a slightly scaled-down *United States* (*Forrestal*, CVA 59).

Meanwhile all BuAer could offer was the H-8 hydraulic catapult, which was at the practical limit for such devices. It was limited by the ultimate strength of the wire ropes. Very high power also made for great energy expended in the hydraulic cylinders. Two US carriers later suffered large catapult fires when hydraulic fluid burned. The first catapults were installed on board *Oriskany*, the first *Essex* to be modernised. The first four production sets of H-8s were going aboard the next four carriers in the *Essex* class modernisation programme (*Kearsage*, *Lake Champlain*, *Essex* and *Wasp*). Unlike C-1, the H-8 programme was running on schedule, but this catapult was not powerful enough to launch the new strategic bomber. Without that bomber, the US Navy would not be able to deliver on its claim that it was a strategic force co-equal to the US Air Force.

Through 1951 BuAer continued to promise DCNO (Air) that the catapult programme was viable and that it could deliver the smaller XC-10 by June 1952, if the project were given maximum priority and

The solution to the radar problem was to move the radar and probably also fighter control, off the carrier to a command ship. *Northampton* was the prototype command ship, carrying a massive diamond-shaped SPS-2 air-search radar atop her tower mast. At this time her after tower mast was occupied by a lower-frequency (long-range) SPS-37. The only other ship fitted with the massive SPS-2 was the missile cruiser *Galveston*.

other Bureaus (Ordnance and Ships) were ordered to give it the same priority. The split between BuAer, which designed the catapult and DCNO (Air), who needed it to meet navy strategic needs, was important. The catapult developers at the Naval Aircraft Factory were part of BuAer and it took them at their word that they would soon have a viable catapult. DCNO (Air) did not really care what sort of catapult was produced or by whom. He cared enormously that the nuclear bomber programme would stay on schedule. H-8 could launch current jet fighters, but they were a very secondary consideration; it would take C-7 or its like to launch the new bomber.[127]

BuAer had to offer further alternatives to DCNO (Air). About February 1951 he included the British steam catapult for the first time as 'the only other high capacity catapult development', capable of launching a 30,000lb aircraft at 126 knots, using 340lbs of low-pressure steam per shot. 'From available data' it was about 25 per cent heavier than its higher-pressure US counterpart. 'Due to the low pressures used . . . its size is sufficiently large to impose a difficult installation problem. Latest information indicates that an aircraft will be launched from the catapult during March 1951 and that consideration

is being given to equipping a sister-ship of *Ark Royal* with catapults of this type. In any event, the excessive steam consumption, which has been roughly calculated to require a steam rate of 40,000lbs per hour, deserves special study before this catapult can be seriously considered. A previous study of the advisability of using steam for slotted tube catapults made by personnel of the Bureau of Ships and of this Bureau [BuAer] led to the conclusion that the use of powder has many important advantages over the use of steam.' BuAer's defensive tone suggests that DCNO (Air), unhappy with delays in the programme, had cited the British steam catapult as a possible alternative. The unclassified BuAer catapult file for 1950 thus includes a cover letter from the British Joint Services Mission in Washington dated 8 August 1950 enclosing 'Notes on British Steam Catapults' and eight classified Brown Bros. (manufacturing) drawings.

An attached note describes the BuAer letter as 'an attempt to inject a note of realism' into the programme to replace H8s with C10s. BuAer suggested replacing one rather than two H8s in near-term *Essex* conversions, but the earliest C10 could not be tested before the eighth modernised carrier was completed in June 1953. The issue was so serious, because of the nuclear bomber implication, that CNO was asked to decide.[128]

It seems to have been crucial that US Naval Attaché in London Rear Admiral Apollo Soucek was a naval aviator well aware of how important catapults were. His reports went to OpNav, not just to BuAer, which could pigeonhole them. It seems that DCNO (Air) decided to press the case. In May 1951 BuAer offered 'an extensive detailed investigation of the relative merits of all the various types of slotted cylinder catapults' before switching to steam, the study to be completed during the coming fiscal year. OpNav would have none of that; in May 1951 it ordered the study expedited. In response, the Chief of BuAer asked OpNav to have the Naval Attaché in London keep in close touch with the British programme. BuAer refused to admit that it was stymied; it kept claiming that its preferred catapult was promising. However, it admitted that early British tests had been encouraging. Reality forced it to set up a steam catapult design programme in June 1951, the stated rationale being that the sheer number of explosive charges needed for a powder catapult would be unaffordable. The steam catapult was assigned Priority 3, the powder catapult retaining Priority 1 and the H8 Priority 2.

At Admiralty invitation, two US officers, Captain H S Clarke and Captain F H Horn, visited *Perseus* in Belfast Lough to watch catapulting. By the time of their report, another ten steam catapults were on order for specific British ships, with another ten for future installation. The prototype had fired 727 times, including thirty-two manned launchings. On 27 June 1951 the Admiralty offered to send the ship to the United States the following November for two months of demonstrations. The two captains and Naval Attaché Rear Admiral Soucek warmly recommended acceptance, as 'it is the opinion of this office that the steam catapult has great possibilities'.[129] On 14 July CNO offered an invitation. The Naval Attaché in London worked out arrangements such as payments for fuel (the British supply of dollars was very limited). The test programme used dead weights of 15,000lbs, 21,000lbs and 28,000lbs. In October 1951 CNO circulated an announcement that *Perseus* was coming; she arrived at Philadelphia Naval Shipyard in January 1952. During the trials, British steam catapult inventor C C Mitchell made the startling claim that it could stand up to American steam conditions (550 psi). Using such higher-pressure steam it could match planned C10 performance. *Perseus* was

held in the United States for high-pressure steam trials, launching deadweights of up to 55,000lbs.[130] The trials having succeeded, Admiral Soucek forwarded Admiralty catapult drawings.[131]

By this time BuAer was pulling back so that it could accept steam catapults, at least for the time being, never admitting that unless it did so the strategic bomber programme would have been derailed. In January 1952 Captain Sheldon W Brown, who headed the BuAer Ships Installations division, circulated a 'brief comparison' between the British and US catapults. He cautioned that a determined British effort to sell the steam catapult might be motivated by a desire for dollars as much as by a willingness to be helpful. He attached a table showing that in its existing form the BXS-1 catapult aboard *Perseus* did not meet US requirements. It had a 203ft power stroke, launching a 30,000lb aircraft at 123 knots. By way of comparison, C10 could launch 40,000lbs at 125 knots and C7 could launch 80,000lbs at that speed. Both had 184ft power strokes. The projected production version of the British catapult, BS-1, was rated at only 30,000lbs at 105 knots using a 144ft stroke. Mitchell's proposal to use high-pressure steam solved this problem. BuAer did mount a last-ditch attack, arguing that by draining steam from a ship's powerplant a steam catapult would affect ship performance. It estimated that firing every 30 seconds (to provide C10 capability) it would need about an eighth of the full steam capacity of an *Essex* class carrier. Firing 150 times a day it would need 10 per cent of the ship's water capacity. Captain Brown saw the British catapult should be seen as a back-up for his own superior product.

A final argument against the steam catapult was that it entailed both a heavy weight near flight-deck level and a long cut in the flight deck, which in a new carrier would be the strength deck. By this time BuAer was pressing for an indirect-drive catapult, which would drive an aircraft using a cable passing up through the flight deck and then along a trough rather than a slot (the Mitchell catapult used direct drive, the piston connected directly to the aircraft). The Naval Aircraft Factory even sketched an indirect-drive steam catapult. BuShips quashed this last argument, pointing out in addition that BuAer's preferred catapult needed a much heavier structure to handle the lateral loads it imposed.

Overall, it was amazing that the operational side of the navy, led by DCNO (Air), managed to overcome what seems in retrospect stiff BuAer opposition to a catapult 'not invented here'. The US Navy of the 1950s was able to operate the heavy bombers it so badly wanted only because Admiral Soucek in London made sure that DCNO (Air) knew that there was a real alternative to the endlessly delayed BuAer powder catapults. Once the navy had catapults capable of launching heavy aircraft, it could also develop others, such as the A-6 Intruder and, eventually, the F-14 Tomcat. The F-14 in turn helped make US fleet air defence effective in the face of massive Soviet naval air forces. But the big decks and the big catapults all came out of the urgent need to maintain the US Navy as a nuclear striking force. Ironically, by the time the steam catapults were being installed, nuclear bombs had shrunk to the point where fighters could deliver them.

The US steam catapult was tested successfully on board *Essex* class carriers. The C-7 and C-10 designations were taken over for British-style steam catapults. However, the 'not invented here' issue survived; the BuAer catapult developers never considered the steam catapult altogether acceptable. In 1959 the BuAer catapult division reported that it was about to complete work on a new internal-combustion C-14 catapult specifically for the nuclear carrier *Enterprise*. Like the powder catapults of 1950, it never went to sea. Until the recent advent

As long as it planned carrier task forces built around flush-deck carriers, the US Navy also planned to convert large surface combatants into command ships equipped with the SPS-2 radar. This model shows the abortive design planned for the large cruiser (CB) *Hawaii*. The big radar aft is an SPS-8 heightfinder; the radar atop the after tower mast is SPS-3, a short-range three-dimensional (range and bearing plus elevation) target-indication radar for the ship's guns.

of electric catapults, all US carriers have had steam catapults descended from Mitchell's BXS-1 prototype rather than from the intense BuAer effort of the late 1940s and early 1950s.

The catapult saga seems to have had an interesting effect: it overcame the 'not invented here' problem at a crucial time. Catapults, barriers and arresting gear were hardly the only barriers to successful jet carrier operation. It seems likely that the prestige generated by the British catapult success extended to two other vital innovations, the angled deck and the mirror landing sight, without which jet operation would have been far more hazardous than it has been.[132] In effect the steam catapult was the beginning of a brief era of British-invented innovations being adopted by a grateful US Navy. Beside carrier improvements, they included the far less well-known method of rafting to silence a nuclear submarine – a technique adopted in the face of Admiral Rickover's considerable preference for electric drive, a method with which he was personally involved.

The steam catapult made a short carrier flight deck equivalent (for take-off) to the thousands of feet of concrete of a runway ashore. The combination of the angled deck and the mirror sight had the same effect for landing. Together, the two made it possible for carriers of the 1950s to operate aircraft fully competitive with anything ashore. That had been the case with the advanced propeller fighters in service from about 1943 on, but for a time post-war it must have seemed that carrier aircraft would ultimately be outclassed, as supersonic jets entered service. By 1954 it was clear that no such problem would arise.

New flight deck configurations: the flexible flight deck and the angled deck

Another British carrier innovation was the flexible flight deck. It began at Farnborough in the autumn of 1944, with reports of the German Me-163B rocket fighter.[133] This aircraft took off from a trolley and landed on a skid. A jet or rocket aircraft did not need conventional landing gear. It did need some means of absorbing the shock of landing. Eliminating landing gear altogether would save considerable weight, hence add performance. Naval aircraft were the obvious candidates for undercarriageless operation, because carriers already had catapults capable of launching them. The question was how to absorb the shock. The two candidates were a 'sprung' deck and an inflatable deck. The sprung deck would entail a considerably more elaborate structure, so Farnborough concentrated on an inflated flexible deck supported by rubber tubing (the British called the deck a carpet). Its main proponent was Lewis Boddington, head of the Farnborough naval section. In the spring of 1945 he sketched a development programme culminating in full-scale landings by adapted jet fighters.[134] Boddington estimated that by eliminating landing gear an aircraft designer could save 10 to 15 per cent of overall weight.

Farnborough let a contract to Supermarine to estimate the weight saving. This work convinced Supermarine to give its prototype Vickers 508 jet fighter, which eventually developed into the Scimitar, a flat belly specifically to enable it to land on a flexible deck. Supermarine was working on an undercarriage-less aircraft by August 1945. With the end of the war it was clear that far less money would be available for naval aviation and the flexible deck project was scaled down to a research effort to determine how future aircraft might benefit. Type 508 was developed as a conventional wheeled aircraft because it was very unlikely that the whole existing British carrier fleet would be converted for flexible deck operation.

After initial tests using unmanned surplus Hotspur gliders, the light carrier *Warrior* was fitted with an inflatable deck in 1947. British test pilot Eric 'Winkle' Brown successfully landed a Sea Vampire on board.[135] There was already a sense that landing jets on carriers could be difficult. When he landed a Vampire on *Ocean* (the first British naval jet landing), Brown had to stall the aircraft onto the deck, a technique Farnborough said was 'dependent on very fine judgement by the pilot'. The British were soon well aware of the main drawback to the scheme, the need to pull a landed aircraft off the flexdeck so that it could be serviced and launched. Unless that could be done quickly,

The jet problem included limitations of the existing crash barriers. They were intended to wrap themselves around the propeller of any aircraft bolting over the wires of the arresting gear, as this Firefly has done. The pilot would not be injured. However, if the landing aircraft also shed its propeller blades, as Seafires often did, the wires would ride up the nose of the aircraft and could decapitate the pilot. (State Library of Victoria)

use of the deck would preclude rapid landings and would thus drastically limit a carrier's capacity. It turned out that the solution to this problem was the key fruit of Boddington's idea. It led to the angled deck.[136]

A 7 August 1951 meeting on the future of the flexible deck was chaired by Captain D R F Campbell, at that time Director of Naval Aircraft Development and Production (and thus Deputy Chief Naval Representative to the Ministry of Supply) and also prospective CO of the new carrier *Ark Royal*. That no formal Staff Requirement had been put forward for a flexible deck was slowing development, so RAE Farnborough, the main proponent of the flexible deck, asked for a meeting to consider outstanding questions. Did the flexible deck require a basic change in approach technique (if not, was one desirable)? Was the deck park to be retained and if so, was a barrier still essential? Should there be only one wire, as in current experiments or more, as in a carrier? What LSO requirements were needed? How could aircraft be handled and parked? Campbell saw the meeting as a preliminary to giving DAW sufficient background to frame a formal staff requirement. At the same time he wanted to know what kind of aircraft a flexible-deck carrier would operate: pure undercarriageless, adapted flying boat or a conventional aircraft with wheels retracted. Instead of discussing possible advantages in aircraft performance, which had previously sold the flexible deck idea, he wanted to concentrate on to extent to which the flexible deck could improve deck operation: a lower damage rate and a higher degree of rough-weather operation.[137] Among other things, Campbell asked whether landing should still be controlled by an LSO (DLCO in British parlance) or

whether a 'stabilised siting [a typo for sighting] system' should be introduced.

This was about the fundamental method of jet aircraft operation as much as about how to make the flexible deck work. Given increasing approach speeds, an LSO (DLCO) could only make a visual check to make sure that all gear was down and possibly give the 'cut' (if used) – the meeting did not take into account that the 'cut' (throttle off) was of only limited value to a jet. Its conclusions included the comment that some alternative means of 'mechanical sighting' would be needed to control the approach. This referred to the mirror landing sight introduced three years later. Given the impossibility of throttling down a jet engine quickly enough, there was increased interest in an alternative 'going round again' technique. Instead of cutting his engine to hit the deck, a pilot could maintain high engine power, enough so that if he missed all the wires he could still fly off and come around for another try. This technique was attractive, but it was impossible if the carrier had a conventional crash barrier immediately in front of the landing area. Campbell had to admit that there was no way to eliminate the barrier, whether or not there was a deck park, because aircraft might attempt to land with a damaged hook or when out of fuel. Multiple arrester wires would be better than one.

The meeting agreed that the rate and severity of barrier crashes would doubtless rise as aircraft performance increased. Neither tricycle undercarriages (not yet in use) nor the flexible deck would solve that problem. Boddington later wrote that he was convinced that a 'stagnation point' had been reached in naval aircraft development, but that it would be recognised only after 'bitter experience with the unnecessary loss of valuable lives and material'.

The meeting agreed that aircraft stowage and operating capacity must not be reduced. The meeting reported that upon landing aircraft might be moved immediately sideways to one of the side lifts to be struck below, the deck park being maintained on a separate lower take-off and parking deck.[138] If this arrangement was adopted as the only possible application of the flexible deck, no flexible deck could enter service until a radically different carrier was designed and built. Campbell later wrote that he conceived the angled-deck arrangement when looking at a model of *Illustrious*. He immediately sketched it on the back of a paper showing alternative flexible-deck arrangements already drawn up.[139] He showed it at the meeting.

At the same time Campbell was concerned that it might be difficult to recover the new fast jets, such as the Scimitar (N.113), which might land at speeds of up to 100 knots. A month after the

flexible-deck meeting he circulated a paper summarising the problem, including the long pull-out needed to stop so fast an aircraft without excessive deceleration. He pointed out that in the largest current fleet carrier (*Ark Royal*), which was 750ft long, the foremost 250ft was taken up by catapults and parking. The pull-out should be 200–230ft. Current aircraft typically touched down 200ft up the deck, but the faster the aircraft, the further up the deck it would touch down Any attempt to land such aircraft further back, at the present position, would subject their undercarriages to excessive loads.

Campbell made the leap from the flexible-deck discussion to the current problem, recalling that a barrier was a problem with a flexible deck. He remembered that the flexible-deck meeting had considered a variety of different deck configurations, including a lower flying-off deck which allowed for a landing area out of alignment with the catapult-parking area. It seemed that nothing could be done until entirely new carriers were built, as all solutions involved radical redesign. He also recalled that he suggested simply offsetting the flexible deck to port. That would do away with the deck barrier without requiring radical redesign of the ship. Lewis Boddington of RAE came independently to the conclusion that the jet-landing problem and the flexible-deck problem were linked. Boddington proposed an angled deck for *Ark Royal*, sketching an 8° deck. This idea was discussed at Bath (DNC) on 5 September. It was generally agreed that it showed great promise and that it would not entail radical change to pilot technique. The trials carrier *Illustrious* had an angled

The solution for jets was the nylon Davis Barrier shown here, but that still did not make it safe to land a jet on a carrier with a straight flight deck. This A4D Skyhawk was crashing on *Hancock*, 7 October 1969. (US Navy photo by PH3 Cephas S D Buck)

deck painted on her for trials. *Ark Royal* herself was not modified, DNC having pointed to immediate problems.[140] Initially the Royal Navy limited itself to a slightly angled (4°) deck, because they did not require ships to be rebuilt.

As it happened, the angled deck did not eliminate the barrier altogether, for exactly the reasons Brown cited. However, it dramatically changed standard operating procedure, the barrier being kept down unless it was needed to deal with a damaged aircraft (the LSO/DLCO decided to raise it as necessary). The angled deck enormously simplified landings. The landing area was lengthened without costing parking space forward. A pilot no longer faced a crash if he bolted over the arresting gear wires. The barrier was no longer so important. Moreover, the angled deck was perfectly adapted to the kind of power-on landing which was more natural for a jet than for a propeller aircraft. A US article describing the angled deck added that flight deck arrangement was easier, as the angled part of the deck left more room for longer (hence more powerful) catapults in the bow.

This advantage was connected with the new problems of landing jets on board carriers. The controlled landing technique developed by the US Navy between wars required the LSO to signal the pilot to cut his engine when he was in the appropriate position. Cutting the throttle stopped the engine more or less instantly and the aircraft stalled out for the last few feet from the deck. This type of landing was therefore often called a controlled crash. The pre-war Royal Navy used a more controlled landing with power on, but it had to adopt US procedure during wartime in order to operate at a higher tempo.[141]

Jet aircraft could not operate in this way. A jet engine could not simply be shut down instantly. No matter what the throttle setting, the engine remained hot, so it continued to accelerate gas out its nozzle. The pilot needed much more reaction time and the delay between what the LSO saw and what the pilot realised he had to do was unacceptable. That is one reason early jets suffered so high a landing accident rate. It appears that initially BuAer did not think that the LSO concept had to be re-thought.[142] Rather, it seems to have considered a somewhat higher accident rate acceptable, at least for the

A pilot's view of the problem: an F2H-2P approaches *Oriskany*, 8 February 1955. The high Davis Barrier protecting the aircraft parked forward is visible.

The solution: a Sea Vixen approaches the angled deck of *Ark Royal*. The ship's prospective commanding officer invented the angled deck. No barrier was needed, because aircraft could all be parked to one side of the landing deck.

moment. Surely with experience jets would not be too much more difficult to operate than their predecessors. The requirements levied on aircraft designers included the usual landing limits, such as stall or landing speed – but not sink rate, which might have been a factor in making jets more difficult to control on approach. A high accident rate became far less acceptable as individual jet costs escalated and production runs contracted in the late 1950s.[143]

The angled deck helped solve this problem, because the approaching aircraft was no longer headed towards a barrier with parked aircraft beyond. Instead, it faced a clear landing deck, with a parking area to one side and also forward, away from the axis of the angled deck. The pilot could maintain power as he approached, because if he failed to contact the arresting wires (bolted), he could simply accelerate, remain airborne and come around again.

For the US Navy, jet operating experience during the Korean War dramatised the jet-landing problems some had expected. With the LSO cycle drastically shortened, the accident rate shot up. Initially that meant more bolters and, because barriers were not really effective,

more flight deck accidents. Initial effort therefore went into developing a nylon-mesh barrier which could stop a bolter without badly damaging it. However, that was clearly not enough.

At the end of January 1956 the British Ministry of Supply finally deleted the flexible deck project from the naval aircraft research programme; the RAE was instructed to dismantle its flexible deck site.[144] The fruit of the programme, the angled deck, survived to make later carrier designs viable.

The British disclosed the angled deck to a US naval delegation at a meeting held by Vice Controller (Air) on 7 September 1951.[145] The British envisaged a 4° deck, but the US Navy went immediately to an 8° deck, which offered much greater advantages. When the Americans considered increasing the angle to 8 degrees, the idea became far more interesting. For initial tests, the flight decks of the carriers *Wasp* and *Midway* were marked to simulate 8° decks, a mark 340ft from the stern indicating the point at which the pilot should apply full throttle if he had not engaged a wire. Two days of sea tests (2 March and 27 May 1952) were so successful that NATC Flight Test Division recommended that a full angled deck be tested at once. Thus the first full US angled deck was installed on board the *Essex*-class carrier *Antietam* and tested at sea between 29 December 1952 and 1 July 1953. Fifteen types of aircraft were tried on board. The test was so successful that within months the decision had been made to replace the flush deck then planned for the carrier *Forrestal* with an angled deck.[146]

In retrospect it is remarkable that the US Navy did not stumble on the angled-deck idea. The deck layouts for both the abortive *United States* and the *Forrestal* embodied very large sponsons intended to carry catapults, the idea being that the ship should be able to launch her heavy bombers (over the bow) while also launching fighters (from the sponsons). With arresting gear relocated, the sponsons would have been the terminations of angled decks going both to port and to starboard. Instead, the ships had arresting gear in the usual position on the centreline. The two new carriers were designed specifically to operate very large aircraft with long wings. To land up the centreline of the deck, they needed considerable clearance and therefore the carriers were designed with flush decks, their masts retracting into spaces at the starboard side of the flight deck. All flush-decked carriers had experienced significant difficulty disposing of smoke and the two new US carriers would have had substantially more powerful machinery than their predecessors. It is not at all clear that they would have been particularly successful as ships.

The angled deck made such carriers practicable, because the big aircraft would land well clear of a conventional island. That disposed of the smoke problem. It also solved a major radar problem. Although the *United States* would have had air-search radar, it was accepted that it would be relatively ineffective. Plans called for a 'pilot fish' ship to work with the carrier, providing radar and controlling aircraft. The 'pilot fish' was little emphasised because the big carrier was conceived primarily as a nuclear strike platform, working with other carriers providing fighter defence. However, a prototype 'pilot fish' was built as the task force command ship *Northampton*, a converted cruiser with the most powerful available air-search radar on board. A second such ship was to have been converted from the 'large cruiser' *Hawaii* and work began to strip her for this role. It does not seem coincidental that this project was cancelled at about the same time that the angled deck made it possible to fit a large strike carrier with massive radars.

The US Navy flexible flight deck project, which BuAer associated with the angled deck from the outset, began in March 1952. BuAer personnel visited the Admiralty on 1 July 1952 to learn about both the flexible deck and the angled deck. When the US delegation visited the United Kingdom, the British had studied the angled deck but as yet had made no definite plans to use it. The British had tested the flexible deck but had not proceeded further because they wanted to maintain their policy of standardisation with the US Navy: they expected to use US aircraft in an emergency. Any flexible deck programme would have to be mutual. The US representatives pointed to the advantages of combining the flexible deck and the angled deck and, according to their report, the British became deeply interested. Although at first deeply dubious, they asked to participate in any further development. The meeting concluded that the combined arrangement was advantageous because it allowed for an additional catapult and because interceptors could be launched without respotting the deck (a catapult would always be available). The next day the US party visited RAE Farnborough, watching an undercarriageless Sea Hawk being catapulted. A carriageless Vampire made three landings, the deck being cleared in 40 seconds using a winch to tow the aircraft about 100ft directly ahead. The British said that an angled deck and proper equipment could cut that to 30 seconds. They also discussed a 'hybrid' deck which could handle both undercarriageless and conventional aircraft.

For the US Navy, the close connection between the flexible-deck idea and the much more significant angled deck is shown by the presence in the US flexible deck file of a 21 May 1952 report on canted (angled) decks for US carriers. However, the initial US memoranda on the operation of a flexible deck were written *after* various angled-deck configurations had been sketched (it is dated 14 July 1952). In US discussions, the flexible deck was generally associated with an angled-deck layout, the landing mattress being placed on the angled part of the deck. A plan for a proposed development programme was dated 14 August 1952. It envisaged tests using one day fighter and one general-purpose attack aircraft. It also referred to a modified version of the F2Y Seadart seaplane fighter, the only US naval fighter which actually lacked an undercarriage, for use from modified carriers (including escort carriers) and expeditionary (Marine) shore bases. At this stage

the whole programme, running from FY53 through FY60, was expected to cost $35 million. At this point the goal was to place undercarriageless aircraft in extensive service by 1960. BuAer sponsored a January 1953 visit by Boddington, at that time no longer on the Farnborough staff.[147]

The main flexible-deck proponent seems to have been Captain Sheldon W Brown, head of the BuAer Ship Installations (SI) division. He sponsored initial studies by various companies of the advantages to be gained in flexdeck versions of their aircraft. For example, Grumman submitted a graph showing that their current interceptor (G-98L), which weighed 22,000lbs at take-off, would weigh 18,000lbs in flexdeck form; it would be able to fly about 5000ft higher and it would be Mach 0.1 faster. The BuAer Research Division made two comparisons of flexdeck vs conventional aircraft. One showed a saving of 5500lbs (the flexdeck design would use the lighter and less powerful J48 instead of a J57 engine) and a dramatic reduction in wing span, allowing for stowage of eight more aircraft (compared to fourteen) in a particular space. Another estimate compared an aircraft with two J46 engines to one with one J65, the difference in span being 4ft and in weight 6000lbs. Combat radius would increase from 270 miles to 273 miles.[148]

Aircraft companies were asked to estimate how much better their aircraft would be in undercarriageless form. A quick study by North American of a modified FJ-3 Fury showed a saving of about 1700lbs without loss of performance. Chance Vought thought that size and weight could be cut as much as 25 to 30 per cent if engine size were cut as the aircraft shrank. Maximum speed might increase 5 to 10 per cent if size was reduced by 10 to 15 per cent. Northrop received a contract for a more elaborate study of a flexdeck version of its N-94, an unsuccessful competitor for the OS-130 day fighter contest which Chance Vought had won with its F8U Crusader. The aircraft could

In Buckner Bay, Okinawa, 12 June 1962, *Ark Royal* shows how aircraft forward of the island could be parked outside the landing lane defined by the angled deck (the lane is indicated by lines running down the deck). The jets shown are Scimitar attack bombers and Sea Vixen all-weather fighters. The turboprops are Gannet ASW aircraft.

save 226lbs of fuel for the same speed and combat radius. With the same fuel load, radius would increase from 300nm to 340nm. Alternatively, with the same combat radius speed could be increased from Mach 1.38 to 1.54. Fuel could be carried in the space otherwise occupied by the landing gear, in which case the aircraft could make Mach 1.63 with the 300nm radius.

Both the air force and the navy became interested. In 1952 the air force was placing the new smaller atomic bombs on board fighter-bombers in Western Europe. It wanted to operate them without fixed air bases, a virtue later claimed for the STOVL Harrier. In this case launch was simple. The ramp launcher designed for the Martin Matador cruise missile and the associated large solid-fuel booster, were combined to make a 'zero-length launch' possible. Some readers may remember photos of F-100s and F-104s blasting off such ramps during the 1950s and early 1960s. Landing was more difficult, as there would never be enough prepared bases. It seemed that the flexible deck, which could be envisaged as an inflatable mat, would be a solution. The air force erected a flexible deck (mat) at Edwards Air Force Base and landed an F-84G Thunderjet on it, the main modifications being a guard to protect the aircraft's air intake and an arresting gear hook. The main lesson seems to have been that the aircraft bounced so violently on landing that the pilot risked a broken neck. The programme was called ZELMAL (Zero-Length Launch Mattress Landing).

The navy took slightly longer to test its own flexible deck, profiting from air force experience. It set up the deck at Patuxent River, BuAer's test base and Grumman received a contract to modify a Cougar fighter for tests.[149] Given the air force experience, Grumman installed a special restraint for its pilot, who survived ten landings. Navy pilots made a few more and in 1955 there was some expectation that the navy would be buying a whole generation of flexdeck aircraft. At this time BuAer was also buying Convair's Seadart (F2Y) seaplane fighter, which conveniently already lacked a conventional undercarriage. Convair received a contract to design a fairing which would make the Seadart fighter (F2Y) suitable for flexdeck operation.[150]

By late 1955 it seems to have been clear that the original goal was over-ambitious; it had to be reoriented.[151] The cost was too high to be worthwhile, but Ships Installations conceived a new application, extending US national air defence to seaward using small carriers (CVE and CVL) otherwise not considered suitable for jets. Relatively few shore establishments would have to accommodate such aircraft. This was the project which justified the tests with the Cougar fighter. A contract was let to Convair to study the idea of using the small carriers as an advanced part of the seaward defence line. At this time the navy was providing significant barrier elements in the form of picket ships (converted destroyer escorts and also Liberty ships [YAGRs]) and AEW picket aircraft. Convair argued that a flexible deck plus a high-performance catapult would provide such small ships with valuable fighter capability. The example Convair chose was the seaward extension of the radar early warning line developed to protect North America from Soviet bombers. Its idea was that fighters launched from the carrier could trail enemy formations as they approached the US coast, keeping track of the raid and also reporting types and quantities of aircraft, something the radars themselves could not do.

The US flexible deck file shows a small war-built *Casablanca* class escort carrier modified to operate undercarriageless aircraft. Much of its flight deck is taken up by the landing mattress, with its single arresting wire. Alongside it to port is a long catapult, onto which the

aircraft can be transferred. The drawing is undated, but it seems to have originated with BuAer rather than with a contractor.

The BuAer Aircraft Design Research branch revisited the flexible-deck fighter issue in December 1955, sketching a fighter powered by two J79 engines like the new F4H Phantom (but carrying two rather than four Sparrow missiles, both internally) and capable of Mach 2 at 60,000ft, with a gross weight of 34,500lbs. The military load was 2375lbs. The basic aircraft could remain on CAP station for 55 minutes, but the flexdeck version could manage 86, yet it would be lighter empty (19,380 rather than 21,060lbs). It would carry more fuel. Wing area would be slightly reduced. The flexdeck version could gain considerably by putting the 1760lbs gained back as fuel and tankage (280 gallons of JP-4). This was not enough to save the flexible deck.

The US project collapsed in 1956, the BuAer representative at Grumman complaining that the company had lost interest in it.[152] Apparently, too, the departure of Captain Brown eliminated the main sponsor; his replacement circulated a letter on 16 June 1956 allowing the release of information because 'the advantages offered by a flexible deck undercarriageless aircraft system are of insufficient magnitude to warrant further testing and evaluation . . .'.

The mirror sight

There was still the problem of pilot reaction time, which was part of a cycle of LSO observation, reaction and pilot reaction. As jets appeared with greater landing speeds, any such cycle became too lengthy. By mid-1951, as evidenced by the discussions leading to the angled deck, RAE (Farnborough) and the Royal Navy were already interested in a stabilised landing sight which a pilot could use to decide how to approach his carrier. A 1952 RAE report described a simplified technique which eliminated the last-minute corrections supplied by an LSO and thus might be a suitable first step towards automated landing.[153] It was already clear that the time lags between the LSO's observations and the pilot's reactions were too long. With a fast-approaching aircraft, all the LSO could do was signal the 'cut' or wave off the approaching aircraft. RAE concluded that the pilot needed some automatic aid, either radio or optical. The pilot should fly a straight course at a speed of descent which could be handled by his undercarriage when he touched down, the path giving adequate clearance over the round-down and a reasonable touch-down point among the arresting gear wires. There should be no last-minute cor-rection ('flare'). Trials showed that the 'cut' could be eliminated and indeed that it was easier to land with power on (as long as the aircraft was descending). In 1952 *Illustrious* tested the 'no-cut', 'no-flare' method without a DLCO (LSO) using Vampires, which landed at high speed.

This seems to have been the first sea trial of the mirror landing aid. A large slightly curved mirror (8ft x 4ft) was mounted 160ft from the round-down facing aft, illuminated by a bar of light from lamps shielded from the pilot's view. When viewed from the required flight path, the bar in the mirror was centred. Otherwise the apparent position of the bar showed the pilot that he was above or below the proper path. The mirror was not stabilised, but it was clear that a sta-bilised mirror would work in a seaway. The idea was apparently tested initially using a lipstick and a secretary's pocket mirror. Both the Royal Navy and the US Navy adopted the mirror landing sight, which was the third crucial innovation making it possible to operate fast jets reliably from carriers. Eventually the mirrors were replaced by Fresnel lenses, but the idea has not changed since it was introduced in 1954.

The mirror sight and the angled deck certainly made it much safer to operate jets from carriers, but at least the US Navy had to deal with a high crash rate through the 1950s and well into the 1960s. It might not have been much higher than for propeller aircraft, but jets were far more expensive and they were built in far smaller numbers. The navy was also producing far fewer pilots than in the past. The accident rate brought into question the viability of the jet navy, at a time when it was under considerable pressure from the US Air Force. The eventual solution included not only the new hardware but also a much more detailed and rigid approach to aircraft operation, as reflected in the far more voluminous air operating manuals (NATOPS) of the late 1960s and beyond. That in turn reflected the much less forgiving character of jets landing at high speeds. The situation would have been far worse had it not been for the simultaneous introduction of much larger carriers which offered not only larger decks but also much less motion in a seaway.

A mirror sight is shown on board *Saratoga*, May 1959. The sight made it possible for an approaching pilot to gauge his own approach rather than react only to instructions from an LSO. Modern carriers use Fresnel lenses instead, but the principle is the same.

Carrier-controlled approach and automatic landing

Work on a means to help carrier aircraft land despite bad weather began in the Royal Navy during the Second World War. Its trade-protection escort carriers were operating in the filthiest weather, particularly on the Russian convoy route, but their aircraft, particularly their torpedo bombers fighting submarines, still had to operate. Also, weather which limited or precluded air operations sometimes did not affect enemy land-based torpedo bombers. The initial solution was a narrow-beam radar beacon producing a signal a pilot could hear using the same equipment used to receive the beacon signal from the standard carrier landing beacons (YE and YG).[154] It was tested on board an escort carrier in 1944. A more sophisticated approach, which both the Royal Navy and the US Navy tried after the war, was to bring an approaching aircraft close enough to the carrier for the pilot to see signals from the LSO/DLCO. It used much the same idea as fighter control: a controller on the ship using a short-range precision radar would track the incoming aircraft and talk the pilot down. That was not the ideal, which would have been some form of totally blind landing aid, but it was far simpler. The British Type 961 talk-down radar was a standard air-to-surface radar, which the Royal Navy already used, with its antenna inverted, to look up from the deck instead of down from the aircraft.[155] It fed a PPI with expanded display, to provide the landing officer with maximum precision. Royal Navy priorities show in its planned installation. This idea was tested on board the escort carrier *Vindex*, using an ASV Mk XI with its antenna inverted to point up instead of down. Escort carriers came first, followed by *Ocean*, a light fleet carrier scheduled to be the first British night carrier. The post-war production successor was Type 963.

The US Navy began its own programme of Carrier Controlled Approach (CCA) after the war. In contrast to the wartime theatre, the Central and South Pacific, its future operating area in the north Atlantic and Pacific would confront it with the sort of weather the British had encountered on the North Russia run. A carrier all-weather flying programme was established in June 1949 and the Operational Development Force (OpDevFor) ran initial tests in January and April 1950.[156] It showed that jet aircraft could operate with a 500ft ceiling and with three-mile visibility (1.5 miles for conventional aircraft). The object was to operate large groups of aircraft whose pilots were not spe-

cialists in instrument flying. The carrier had the usual sector-coded YE homing beacon as well as a non-directional radio beacon and VHF homing equipment (URD-2). Jets and AD-4Q attack aircraft had airborne radio direction-finders plus the usual IFF Mk V transponder (APX-6). This effort corresponded broadly to the initial phase of British CCA development, using a beacon on board the carrier. It was assumed that surface conditions were good enough for normal visual launch and recovery, the problem being to operate through an overcast. Under these circumstances carrier aircraft could sustain a 30-second landing interval and maintain the desired three-dimensional separation as they landed (the average was up to 20 seconds greater than the usual interval).

BuShips was running a more elaborate positive-control CCA programme. It employed a longer-range Traffic Control Radar (SPN-6) to bring returning aircraft into a landing battery (later equivalents were called Marshall Radars; all were medium-range air-search sets). Once they were in the pattern, aircraft could be handed over to a controller using the SPN-8 Final Approach Control (precision) radar. The two prototype radar systems were installed in 1949–50 on board the carriers *Philippine Sea* and *Valley Forge*, with SPN-8 (but not -6) installed somewhat later on board *Coral Sea*. By March 1950 CCA was on the approved allowance for all carriers.

Like the wartime British Type 961, SPN-8 was intended to help a controller talk a pilot down to within visual range (in this case 500 yds) of a landing signal officer. It provided precise bearing, but neither height nor closure rate, both of which were needed for any satisfactory system. The ultimate (ten-year) goal of the carrier approach programme, as stated in April 1950, was to provide fully automatic equipment enabling carrier aircraft to land at an average rate of two per minute, with a minimum interval of 20 seconds. Given limited funds, the ten-year goal seemed impossible. However, it was possible to develop an intermediate system, a single three-dimensional landing radar. By the 1960s, US carriers typically had a CCA system comprising a medium-range marshalling radar (SPN-6) to help controllers talk aircraft into the landing pattern, backed by a single-pedestal SPN-35 carrying both a short-range heightfinder and a short-range search radar. This was not enough for automatic control, because none

A Cougar approaches to land on *Saratoga* using the mirror sight in the foreground. This photo was taken some time before February 1957.

of these radars directly measured aircraft velocity, yet any fully automatic system had to make decisions based on predicted aircraft motion. Hence the need for a new set of radars specifically for the automatic function. They measured velocity using the Doppler effect, transmitting a CW signal and detecting a change in frequency on reception (the other radars gave aircraft position well enough).

After the Korean War broke out, funding increased enormously, because all-weather operation was so vital. Development began in 1950, based on a landing control central, which meant a landing control system, SPN-10. It needed a link to the approaching aircraft through which a device on the surface could control the approaching aircraft via its autopilot. Bell Labs began development of the USC-2 link system, which was also part of the ongoing attempt to link CICs. It included a surface element (SSW-1) and an air element (ASW-13). These were digital links, although the devices at each end were analog,

because digital methods would overcome noise (the Royal Navy later adopted a digital link for its analog CDS combat system for the same reason). ITT was developing a navigational system, the surface element of which was URN-2 and the airborne element ARN-26. In 1952 OpNav issued an operational requirement for an air navigation, traffic control and landing system. This was the origin of TACAN and the TACAN data link as well as ACLS.

Feasibility study contracts for both the Honeywell and Bell versions of the landing central were let in 1954 and both were tested at Patuxent River. Neither met the requirement to keep the approaching aircraft within 20ft: Bell had adequate radar performance but an inadequate means of controlling the aircraft and Honeywell the opposite problems. A new specification combined the Ka-band radar of the Bell system and the tighter flight control system of the Honeywell system. By this time the US Air Force was developing the SAGE (Semi-Automatic Ground Environment) system to control interceptors over North America. The navy participated, not only by providing airborne radars but also by providing some interceptors. The data link envisaged for landing control might also be used to command interceptors. The navy chose a Bell Labs link because it was preferred by the air force for use in the SAGE system.[157]

An experimental version of SPN-10 was installed in trailers which were placed aboard the carrier *Antietam* in 1957. The system was not stabilised, so it was tested only in a calm sea. It made thirty-five successful automatic landings in September 1957, proving that the concept was workable: Bell Aircraft received a contract for twelve shipboard systems plus two shore trainers. The first production SPN-10, which was stabilised, was installed on board the carrier *Midway* in 1963. It ran into problems. Pilots could be talked down, but the major elements of the system were not reliable enough. Stabilisation did not take the ship's yaw into account. A reliability improvement programme was begun and a new Specific Operational Requirement issued in 1964. The project was important enough that a special Project Office was created in June 1964.

By this time the analog technology of the SPN-10 had been superseded by more reliable digital computer technology and solid-state radar technology, so a new SPN-42 system was started (existing SPN-10s were converted to -42s). A back-up system was added so that the pilot could be warned of any problem as he approached. The new associated airborne element was the ASW-25 link receiver. SPN-42 was approved for service use in 1967. When *America* deployed in April 1968, it had the first capability to couple the autopilot of an approaching aircraft to the ACLS data link, using the analog SPN-10. Typically the data link was decoupled 12.5 seconds before touchdown, due to limits to the analogue system.[158] All sorts of other details had to be resolved. For example, the ACLS depended on shipboard radars, but the precision radars could be ineffective in heavy rain – in exactly the situation in which ACLS was needed. That was solved by modifying the existing radar bombing beacon in aircraft. The first operational test aircraft were twelve F-4G Phantoms fitted with one-way data links. They had flight command indicators (for text or numerical messages) and a flight path indicator for the pilot (the data link was controlled from the back seat). The first fully operational ACLS aircraft were a squadron of F-4J Phantoms deployed to *Saratoga* in 1969. During their deployment they made over 100 automatic landings, most of them at night and in low visibility.[159]

The only unfortunate feature of the carrier landing system was that its radars were so clearly characteristic of an aircraft carrier, hence would frustrate any attempt to conceal the carrier. During the 1970s, for example, the US Navy standardised radars so that all ships in a battle group would show the same emissions (hence the widespread use of the SPS-49 radar).[160] SPN-6 was certainly characteristic of a carrier and as a medium-range air-search set it could be detected at a distance. At the end of the Cold War the US Navy became interested in a stealthier form of air traffic control and automatic landing, based in part on substituting GPS for SPN-6 (aircraft could receive geographic data information via a satellite network).

ZIP AND OTHER JET FUEL

Jets drank fuel far more quickly than their propeller-driven predecessors. That had consequences for both tactics and for ships operating jets. Even if a jet engine was inefficient, a multi-jet aircraft might shut one engine down to increase endurance. About 1950 the US Navy had two roughly equivalent jet fighters, the single-jet Panther (F9F) and the twin-jet Banshee (F2H). The Panther was simpler and considerably

less expensive, but the Banshee had much greater endurance on CAP because it could shut down one of its engines. Operators therefore preferred it, but the budget could not provide it in numbers comparable to those of the Panther.

At the outset there was no simple way to increase carrier capacity for aviation fuel. The avgas that drove piston-engined aircraft was dangerous enough that it was typically stowed under armour, with special arrangements to prevent flight and hangar-deck fires from spreading into fuel lines. Fuel vapour explosions destroyed several carriers.

Jets could burn a wider variety of fuels than their predecessors, but there was some question as to whether refineries could produce enough of them During the Second World War the United States defined and dropped JP-1 and -2 because existing refineries would be unable to produce enough of them.[161] The first tentative specification for JP-3 was issued in December 1947. It was opposed as too volatile: an aircraft would boil off too much of its fuel as it flew. On the other hand, a less volatile fuel would present problems in starting, in cold-weather performance and in the danger of tank explosions. A modified JP-3 with compromise volatility was adopted as JP-4, which became the standard replacement for avgas. US Navy evaluations of aircraft endurance show that JP-4 offered more energy than avgas, at least as it was burned in jet engines and therefore somewhat longer range. The two could not simply be interchanged, because a jet engine could handle only a certain energy flow and therefore temperature.

The navy adopted a modified version as JP-5, which resembled a kerosene with a high flash point. Initial problems (the JP-5 flame was unstable, hence it was used only in blended form) were solved. JP-5 was sometimes called High Energy Aircraft Fuel (HEAF).

Unlike gasoline, kerosene could be stowed like normal fuel oil, in unarmoured spaces; in nuclear carriers it formed part of the torpedo protection in place of the usual ship fuel. From a carrier point of view, unless some way could be found to stow fuel outside protected spaces (which had limited volume), it would be impossible to operate jets on a sustained basis. The first US carriers converted to jet operation (*Oriskany* and other SCB 27 conversions) had special mixing pumps to turn gasoline and kerosene (stowed outboard) into a fuel mixture for jets. The British disliked this solution because if the ship had to de-fuel, the blended fuel was still explosive enough that it had to go into a special tank.

Once special jet fuels were adopted, the US Navy found that its boilers could be adapted to burn it, so that ships could carry a single type of fuel. That is presumably the case with the current British gas-turbine carriers, since gas turbines are related to the jet engines in the aircraft.

For the Royal Navy, the problem was refinery production and availability.[162] In 1945 the Royal Navy wanted a jet fuel with 150°F flash point rather than the 100°F of avgas, based on experience of bomber losses to vapour gas explosions. Unfortunately at the time at most a barrel of crude oil would yield only 10 per cent kerosene and the additional restrictions the navy wanted would cut that to 3 per cent. That might not be a problem in peacetime, but it would certainly count in wartime. In 1946 the RAF therefore chose a wide-range (i.e. 25 per cent yield) distillate, a mixture of kerosene and low-grade gasoline called 'wide cut'. At this time the United States was using a different 'wide cut' fuel more like low-grade gasoline, but with about three times the vapour pressure. Low vapour pressure was disliked not only because a tank would form more dangerous gas, but also because the

Jet aircraft drank fuel to an extent which horrified commanders trying to maintain CAPs or to support the numbers of sorties common during the Second World War. The only saving grace was that the jets did not need to use volatile fuel like avgas, so it could be stowed outside armour. For the US Navy, this education began when jet fighter squadrons made their first full-scale deployments in the late 1940s. The first East Coast cruise was on board *Boxer* in September 1949. Here two F9F-2s are about to be catapulted off. Two more await their turn. The forward 5in mount has been turned away to provide as much flight deck space as possible.

fuel in a tank could boil while the aircraft climbed, cutting range by up to 25 per cent.

The British services held a joint meeting with the US services at the height of the post-war British oil crisis (March 1947). They learned that the US oil industry, which was tooled up to produce gasoline for cars, was unwilling to switch. At this time the US Navy thought it could carry enough avgas in protected tanks, relying on tankers to keep topped up.

In 1949 the British Chiefs of Staff decided that the British would have to use avgas in their jets because the United States was using it, hence would be able to provide it in sufficient quantity in wartime – even though it was considered very unsuitable for shipboard use. A carrier could stow only high flash point fuel (such as kerosene) in unprotected tanks. This was not a happy choice, so the Chiefs of Staff sought talks with the United States and agreed to adopt AVTAG (essentially JP-4) in 1951. It became the NATO standard ashore, but it was unsuited to the Royal Navy.

By 1952 the US Navy was developing a better fuel (flash point 140°F) specifically for carriers: JP-5. Because it would be available in quantity in wartime (due to US Navy purchases), the Royal Navy no longer had to accept JP-4. On her autumn cruise in 1952 *Eagle* carried a small quantity of JP-5, but it was found too acid for British turbojets. The Ministry of Supply drew up a new specification for a JP-5-like fuel. Designated AVTUR, it could be considered JP-5½. The quantities involved even in a global war would be small enough that supply was no problem.[163] The Royal Navy received the first AVTUR in August 1953. This left the RN no longer using the same fuel as the RAF, but with the advantage of commonality with the US Navy.

That still left the problem of insufficient range or endurance on the fuel a high-performance jet could carry. During the 1950s the US Navy sought a solution in the form of a new high-energy ('ZIP') fuel, a boron compound. Higher energy could not translate into more thrust, because the engine itself could not run at higher temperature. It could translate into longer range for a given weight of fuel, because the engine could reach the same temperature by burning less fuel. Hence the interest in high energy.

The alternative solution, to provide strike aircraft with sufficient range, was refuelling, either using a 'buddy' pack or a specialist tanker. For a time ZIP fuel seemed to be a much better solution, as a carrier using it did not have to dedicate attack aircraft or aircraft slots to tanking. ZIP fuel was conceived about 1952 and by 1959 the US Navy was financing a special plant to make it. The US Air Force was also involved (its programme was split off in 1956 as HEF, High Energy Fuel).

A November 1955 study by the BuAer ADR branch showed that in a strike operation ZIP fuel would roughly double range on a weight for weight basis.[164] The heat content of ZIP fuel was 1.46 times that of JP. At this time the navy was buying the supersonic A3J (later A-5) attack bomber. Its combat radius was 680nm, burning JP-4. With ZIP fuel that would expand to 1325nm. Most attractively, adopting ZIP fuel would eliminate the need for buddy tanking, so more of a carrier's air group could strike targets. ADR based its calculations on a three-carrier group, making ten strike days per month. To get the same performance without ZIP fuel would require a tanker group with four carriers and converted A3D bombers operating as tankers (one tanker per A3J or F4H fighter).[165] ADR did not count reduced attrition as an advantage.

About 1959 the ZIP project suddenly died, perhaps partly because of the sheer cost of the fuel. Also, ZIP fuel was extremely toxic and if it dried in place it left an extremely hard residue which was almost impossible to remove.[166]

ZIP fuel was attractive because it could provide more energy per pound, so that aircraft might not have to be refuelled to extend their range and endurance. Otherwise the carrier had to support tankers, such as this former strategic bomber (an AJ-2), shown fuelling two FJ-3M fighters from *Essex*, 15 June 1958.

CHAPTER 7
THE KOREAN WAR AND AIR SUPERIORITY

THE KOREAN WAR helped save US carrier aviation, which was under dire threat just beforehand. It demonstrated that nuclear deterrence was not enough; the ability to fight a much more conventional war was essential. The active carrier force was rapidly built up by recommissioning fleet carriers from reserve and aircraft were bought in much-increased numbers to fill out their air wings. The navy found itself delivering close air support on a large scale and also striking many fixed North Korean targets. That mission justified general-purpose carriers and it also demonstrated a vital need for carrier fighters to be able to face not only relatively docile long-range bombers (as envisaged before the war in the strategic context) but also to deal with short-range enemy interceptors, particularly the MiG-15.

Furthermore, the overall US defence budget exploded, because it seemed that Korea was most likely the opening move of a larger global war. The new funding paid for the new supercarriers and for new aircraft, missiles and other systems. The sense of emergency justified rapid fielding of weapons which might otherwise have been considered too immature, particularly guided missiles. That applied both to air-to-air and to surface-to-air weapons.

The immediate post-1945 period of developing new technology against a somewhat abstract enemy ended in June 1950 with the North Korean invasion of South Korea. The US Navy had a mixed

fighter force of the best Second World War piston-engine fighters (F4U Corsairs) and first-generation jets (Panthers and Banshees). They were quite adequate to the mission envisaged before the war, which was to protect the carrier from long-range attacks (by necessarily low-performance bombers) while she mounted long-range strategic nuclear attacks on the Soviet Union. The outbreak of war demonstrated that even in a nuclear age carriers might well have to concentrate on much more conventional tasks, such as close air support and non-nuclear bombing. Their aircraft would not enjoy the filter of distance to limit enemy air performance. Instead, they would face the enemy's best interceptors.

The US Navy was certainly aware of the MiG-15, a prototype of which had been displayed at the 1948 Tushino Air Show over Moscow. The following year forty-five MiG-15s flew overhead as an announcement that the fighter was in mass production. Initially the only opposition to US naval aircraft was limited numbers of North Korean piston-engine fighters, Soviet Second World War types. However, the perception that the Soviets were behind the war made it impossible to doubt that the MiG-15 would soon appear. It first overflew Korea on

1 November, when the Chinese entered the war (later it would be clear that many of the Chinese and Korean MiGs were actually Soviet aircraft flown by Soviet pilots). Thus a lasting effect of the war was an urgent requirement for high-performance carrier day fighters to deal with opposition over tactical targets.

Tactical strikes were very different from the deckload strikes standard in the Second World War and carrier operating practices had to change. The earlier system was to launch and recover all of a carrier's aircraft in one operation, leaving a dead spot aft when the aircraft were launched. Now only some of the ship's aircraft were launched at any one time, leaving many others on deck hampering the process of preparing them for launch. Servicing prior to the next launch required at least one re-spot. Propeller aircraft not scheduled to fly at a particular launch period had to be pulled aft, then moved back forward to permit recovery.

Off Korea the fleet learned to keep some aircraft airborne at all times to limit dead spots on launch and to facilitate rapid turn-around. It was possible to distribute aircraft more evenly in flight during the day, leaving fewer aircraft aboard. The critical time factor was rearming; the carrier crew could barely meet the requirement (set by aircraft endurance) of 1.5 hours for jets and three hours for propeller aircraft. Commander of Task Force 77 wrote in 1953 that his ships probably could not have met the sortie rates of the late-war period without adopting the new schedule. The comments about flight deck scheduling fed into the shift to angled decks, although the idea seems not to have been considered off Korea.

The two jet fighters in service through the war were the F9F Panther and the F2H Banshee, of which the fleet much preferred the Banshee. A late-war evaluation report characterised the Panther as ruggedly dependable, but with relatively low performance and short endurance.

JET OPERATIONS

The war tested the navy's ability to sustain jet operations using the new fighters. The latest of them, the Panther and the Banshee, had only recently entered service. Now fleet carriers, none of them specially modified for jet operations, were supporting whole 36-aircraft squadrons of them. All of the problems suspected since 1944 were now seen on a daily basis. Moreover, many of the aircraft developed in the late 1940s already presented problems.

In the autumn of 1951, for example, the Atlantic Fleet had seven carrier air groups. Its carriers were mainly unconverted *Essex*es and *Midway*s.[1] For the moment, they were successfully operating the F9F-2 version of the Panther and the F2H-2 version of the Banshee. By July 1952 three of the groups were scheduled to have the heavier if higher-powered F9F-5. Successful launch of an F9F-5 required 45 knots of wind over the deck in an *Essex* or 35 knots in a *Midway* or 27 knots even in the *Oriskany* with her new H-8 catapults. The F2H-3 was even worse (52 knots for an *Essex*, 38 knots for a *Midway*, 33 knots for an *Oriskany*). Half of the Atlantic Fleet fighters would be unable to operate safely and consistently from any of the Atlantic carriers except perhaps the rebuilt *Oriskany*. The situation would improve as more carriers were rebuilt, so that by December 1952 six Atlantic carriers

Bon Homme Richard prepares the jet part of an air strike, 27 November 1952. The propeller-driven aircraft in this photograph are Skyraiders, the most powerful tactical naval attack aircraft available.

would be able to operate the F9F-5, but even then some would be limited and very marginal using the F2H-3.

Fuel was also a major problem. By March 1953 CVG 7 would have three squadrons of the new Cougar (F9F-6), one of F9F-5 and one of A2D Skysharks (which was not, in the event, placed in service). A large carrier (presumably the coming *Forrestal*) would have on board eighty jet fighters and twenty-seven turboprop attack aircraft, consuming 65,000 gallons per hour. That was about the rate at which aviation fuel could be transferred at sea. Paper figures, as reflected in standard aircraft charts, were misleading; the Atlantic Fleet was finding that in strike operations the figure was 1.3 to 2.0 times expectation. On this basis the *Coral Sea* group had only 18 hours of aviation fuel on board. They were fuelling after two simulated strike days. Under such assumptions CVG 7 had only 0.7 to one strike days of fuel on board its carriers.

Compared to the F9F-2, the F9F-5 was faster, but thirstier. It burned 20 per cent more fuel, it had 10 per cent less range and its stall speed (which determined how safe it was to land) was 11 knots higher. It was 3000lbs heavier and it could not be handled nearly as safely as the F9F-2. The contrast between F2H-2 and -3 was even worse. The only virtue of the -3 was that it could carry a reasonable bomb load – if it could be operated at all. The coming jets (F10F, F3D-1, F3D-3, F2H-3 and F7U-3) were all outside the 25-knot ship speed catapult envelope for the most powerful current catapult, presumably the H-8. At this time BuAer was still pressing its powder catapult as the solution; ComAirLant saw it as 'no bargain. Aside from the fact that this adds the equivalent of an 8in gun in magazines, handling rooms,

For the US Navy, the Korean air war was a mixed jet and piston-engine affair. Here is the propeller-driven aspect of the Korean naval air war: *Bon Homme Richard* prepares her F4U-5 Corsairs and some Skyraiders. Typically these aircraft were launched well before the jets intended to support them over their targets, since they would take much longer to get there (and had far greater endurance). The foremost Corsair is immediately abaft the folded-down crash barrier.

hoists etc there are a number of unrelated problems still to be solved.'

For one operation (BEEHIVE), 340 sorties had been scheduled for two jet fighter squadrons, VF 11 and VF 12. They had only 48,000 gallons (41,000 gallons usable) from 355,000 gallons available left after 187 sorties. A full 340 sorties by thirty-six aircraft in four days would be only 4.6 hours/day (2.3 hours per flight). In the Second World War the average on strike days was nine hours per aircraft per day.

The existing F2H-2 could not land into arrester gear at over 15,600 knots, which meant that when it landed it could not exceed 3300lbs of fuel. On the average it consumed 6000lbs (1000 gallons) of fuel per flight, so 340,000 gallons would be 340 sorties. The capacity of a large carrier left only another 15,000 gallons (of which would be unusable) for conventional aircraft over the four days of an exercise like BEEHIVE.

ComAirLant was already concerned that his air groups were too fighter-heavy and that fighter range was far too short for support of attack aircraft. He doubted that jets were effective in combat, sourly quoting a newspaper report: of 'biggest jet battle in history, one aircraft damaged'.

The Korean War was played out against the expectation, at least in the West, that it might well lead to a world war, or at the least to a war in Central Europe. The US Navy maintained its nuclear deterrent in European waters and considered its nuclear attack capability a central priority. Its three largest and most capable carriers, the *Midways*, spent the war (and many years afterwards) in the Mediterranean because they could launch even interim nuclear bombers like modified Neptunes. Here *Midway* rides out a gale off Sicily, 4 February 1949. This photograph (taken from her companion carrier *Philippine Sea*) emphasises the ship's limited freeboard (in terms of her length), a consequence of adopting a heavy armoured flight deck. British observers of early NATO North Sea exercises commented that the US Navy found its practice of keeping aircraft permanently on deck, as here, unfortunate in this kind of weather. As the photograph shows, at this time the ship had no heavy attack aircraft permanently on board.

Perhaps it was time to turn back and adopt a turboprop fighter. The Douglas A2D Skyshark, essentially a jet bomber, was sometimes credited with the ability to carry out fighter missions. It could take off without a catapult, it had better climb, range and endurance than a pure jet fighter and it was almost at fast. It had far better landing characteristics. ComAirLant preferred it to the new F3D Skynight night fighter and he even wanted to drop the F7U Cutlass in favour of the existing Corsair.

Nothing like that could be done, at least partly because early experience in Korea showed that it would take fast jets to deal with fast North Korean and Chinese MiG-15 interceptors. Even before the war, opinion had supported fighter-heavy carrier air groups. In 1952 standard air groups were:[2]

	CVBG	CVG
VF	74	66
VF(N)	8	4
VF(P)	4	4
VA(day)	18	16
VA(N)	11	11
VA(W)	6	6
VA(H)	6	3
Total	127	110

From 1948 on, night fighters had been assigned to ASW carrier groups (CVSG) because these ships operated on a 24-hour basis and snoopers might be expected to operate at night.

In 1953 the new jet night fighters were not yet in service, so off

Korea the only night fighters were Corsairs (F4U-5N). Nearly all the fleet carriers operating off Korea had two sixteen-fighter jet squadrons and one sixteen-fighter Corsair (F4U-4) squadron, the exception being *Boxer* with two squadrons of F9F-2 and one of F9F-5. *Kearsage* had one of F9F-2 and one of F2H-2; *Lake Champlain* had two of F2H-2s. All-jet groups were considered unacceptable because propeller fighters were needed to escort strikes by propeller attack aircraft (Skyraiders).

FLEET AIR DEFENCE

It might seem in retrospect that the fleet enjoyed a sanctuary off Korea (as it later did off Vietnam), so that air defence might be considered almost moot. However, the perceived context of the Korean War, which was fought so close to Chinese and Soviet borders, made a sudden bomber attack a real issue. On 4 September 1950 a pair of Soviet Tu-2 bombers was detected approaching the fleet off Inchon, before the landing there. A section of Corsairs intercepted them and one fled at once. The other began a dive towards friendly territory, but its rear gunner fired at the Corsairs. They requested permission to engage and they shot the aircraft down.[3]

A second occasion came late in the war. On 18 November 1952 *Oriskany* detected about eight MiG-15s closing on the fleet at a range of 83nm. There was a real fear that MiGs would surprise the fleet, overwhelm its lower-performance fighters and open air defences for an

attack by bombers, perhaps the jet Il-28s now based in Manchuria (but not in action over Korea). *Oriskany* sent out a four-Panther division. The MiGs' course indicated that they had come from Vladivostok; the ship's radio intercept sets detected Russian-language chatter. The MiGs overflew the Panthers and then turned back towards them, indicating that they were looking not so much for a fight with the fleet as with the fighters protecting it. The Panthers saw seven MiGs flying well above them. In the dogfight, despite the clear superiority of the MiGs' performance, the Panthers managed to shoot down five or six of them.[4] The lesson was that although for the moment the superior training of US naval aviators might tell, the navy badly needed the new jet fighters already under development to match the MiGs.

MOBILISATION AND THE F3H DEMON

The F3H Demon was caught up in the Korean War mobilisation. Korea was seen, not as a localised problem, but as the possible beginning of a much larger war. Early in 1951 the US Navy sketched out a programme to produce a thousand aircraft per month – nothing like the Second World War, but far more than the pre-war figures.[5] BuAer therefore sought alternative sources of production, as during the war. For example, in February 1951 it considered farming out production of either the F2H-4 Banshee or the F3H-1 Demon to Goodyear, which had produced Corsairs during the war as the FG and F2G. The F2H-4 was insufficiently advanced, but the F3H was considered attractive, particularly given its high estimated performance.

Moreover, in 1951 the Demon was designated a general-purpose fighter. Its only stablemate was the Banshee, which was clearly inferior. It was therefore ordered in large numbers: 250 each in FY52 and FY53. As of mid-1952 plans for the FY54 programme called for 1000 more plus 100 photo versions (F3H-1P). However, McDonnell could not produce enough aircraft, particularly since it was also

Existing jet carrier fighters, like this Panther, had sufficient performance in 1950–3 to deal with any Soviet long-range bombers which might attack US carriers well out to sea and the planned introduction of higher-performance interceptors like the Demon would have been completed well before the Soviets fielded their own high-performance jet bombers. However, in Korea the same navy jets found themselves fighting Soviet-built high-performance interceptors: MiG-15s. They were badly outclassed. This Panther is hunting targets of opportunity over Korea near Hungnam, 9 June 1951.

The US Navy urgently needed an air-superiority fighter. It could either buy a navalised version of an existing aircraft, like this FJ-2 Fury (a modified F-86 Sabre) or a modified version of an existing naval fighter (the Cougar). This test aircraft is being positioned on board *Coral Sea*, November 1952.

building large fighters (F-101s) for the air force. BuAer had to convene an ad hoc board on the F3H-1 programme.[6] In September the projected FY54 programme was cut to 552 Demons, which was still a large number – production would total 1052 aircraft, for delivery through 31 December 1955. Temco was brought in as a second source.

In September, DCNO (Air) pointed out that the 1052 fighters on order exceeded the total needed for all-weather squadrons, hence included aircraft which would be operated by day fighter squadrons. DCNO (Air) therefore asked BuAer to produce the Demon in both its planned all-weather form and also in a stripped-down day fighter version.[7] This was hardly an efficient way to obtain a good day fighter, since the F3H had been designed for the all-weather requirement. However, the navy would have no day fighter in its performance class during the procurement period and the stripped F3H would be a more efficient day fighter than the all-weather version. The requirement would be for 502 all-weather Demons and 550 'stripped' day fighters. Since the all-weather requirement was paramount, DCNO (Air) wanted those aircraft delivered first. The day fighter version was tentatively designated F3H-2.[8]

The BuAer Electronics Division was sceptical that a fully stripped-down day fighter was worthwhile. The pilot using a range-only radar

and a simple fire-control system depended on visual sighting, identification and firing and would have little assistance from ground control. A full air intercept system would probably be too difficult to maintain, even if the day fighter could afford the penalty, but a combination search – ranging set would much increase the overall performance and utility of day fighters. Ultimately this argument was accepted by DCNO (Air) and it led to installation of such a set in Crusader fighters (F8U-1E version) a few years later.[9]

The BuAer Guided Missiles Division pointed out in late October that in January DCNO (Air) had requested that the Sparrow I optical beam-rider missile system be installed in 166 F3H-1s, increased to 238 in July, with the additional proviso that all-weather installations would be preferred and that they should be substituted if they could be completed about as quickly as the optical system. BuAer had gone further: late in September it called for all F3H-1 systems to be of the full all-weather type (built around the APG-50 radar) *so long as the missions of this type of aircraft were those of a general purpose fighter* (emphasis in the Division's 27 October memo). DCNO (Air) was holding conferences on missile installation and the idea of fitting a block of Demons with the optical system was being considered. The Guided Missile division recognised that, as defined, the 'stripped down' F3H-2 would not be armed with missiles; but if it was wrong, it wanted to be involved. In any case, it argued that no future day fighter 'should be configured without full consideration of the use of guided missiles in executing its primary mission'.

The F3H programme was heavily revised in December 1954, the

The FJ-2 turned out to be badly underpowered, so North American replaced its J47 engine with a licence-built version of the Rolls-Royce Sapphire, the J65. The carrier launch photo was taken on board *Forrestal*; another FJ-3 has just been launched from one of the two waist catapults.

stripped day fighter being abandoned.[10] Instead, attention focused on the problems of the J40 engine. The F3H-2 designation was shifted to a version of the general-purpose fighter powered by the J71. Some F3H-1s were re-engined with J71s. Interest in an operational version of the optically-guided Sparrow I disappeared. The missile-firing F3H-2M (later redesignated MF-3C) had the all-weather version in which the radar tracking the target generated a moving beam the

missile rode. The modified radar was designated APQ-51; effective guidance range was 13nm.

In theory the only competitor to the F3H as a general-purpose fighter was Grumman's F10F. In September 1952 it was still very much alive, albeit on not nearly the scale of the Demon: plans called for twelve in FY51, fifty in FY52 and fifty in the FY53 programme, with deliveries beginning in February 1954. At this point the planned engine was still the afterburning J40-WE-22/10 and all aircraft were scheduled to go to the Atlantic Fleet. The problem seems to have been that the F10F was full of innovations, quite aside from its variable-sweep wings (which were apparently successful). One of the test pilots remarked that, because so much had to be tried, each flight was in effect a first flight. The prototype flew on 19 May 1953, but it was impossible to deal with the multiple entirely new systems and the project was cancelled.

NEW US FIGHTERS

In 1950 the US Navy was already developing very high-performance naval interceptors which had been conceived to meet requirements stated in 1946 and in 1948. These programmes had not been urgent because it seemed unlikely that war against the Soviets was at all imminent. Rather suddenly the earlier-generation jet fighters were faced with the best the Soviets had, the MiG-15. The US Navy urgently needed an interim high-performance jet fighter to compete with this new threat. On a longer-term basis, the navy realised that it needed high-performance day fighters to compete with the next-generation Soviet bloc interceptor. These day fighters could of course add to a carrier's defence at times, but they were not really part of the story of direct fleet air defence. They were, however, very much part of any concept of reducing the air threat to carriers by attacking the enemy air force at source.

BuAer seems not to have issued any formal request for emergency high-performance designs, but the aircraft companies were certainly alert to what was happening in Korea and there was probably an informal request for proposals.

The immediate result of the MiG-15 threat was two contracts, one for a navalised version of the successful air force F-86 Sabre, the other for the Cougar, a swept-wing version of the existing Grumman Panther.

The navalised F-86E became the FJ-2 Fury, the FJ-1 having been a straight-wing fighter which evolved into the original swept-wing F-86.[11] North American submitted its proposal for the navalised F-86 on 29 December 1950, presenting it at BuAer at a 3 January 1951 conference. Navalisation was simplified by the basic structural similarity between the F-86 and the earlier North American FJ-1. Immediately after the conference, the Assistant Chief of BuAer for R&D wrote that the FJ-2 had a definite place in the navy fighter programme – if it could be delivered quickly enough. It was far superior to the Banshee as a fighter and it was adaptable to engines still growing in performance, possibly by as much as 50 per cent over the next three years. Better, they were outside the limited number of engine types the navy was already using and on which it depended so heavily – which meant the J40.

Predicted Fury performance was lower than that of some aircraft which might soon be available, but on the other hand it was based on a real rather than a paper aircraft. It was also 5000–10,000lbs lighter than any alternative. It was also very short-legged, having been conceived as a point interceptor rather than a long-endurance CAP fighter. It had only a short radius of action (396nm) which could not really be increased, because more than half its fuel was already in two drop tanks. Only minor modifications were proposed, mainly an enlarged intake to feed the much more powerful engine. During production, the leading-edge slats were replaced by extended (dog-tooth) outer leading edges and fences, as in the F9F-8 version of the Cougar.

Fury performance was considered marginal, so in July 1951 North American proposed replacing its J47 engine with the much more powerful J65, a British Sapphire licence-built by Wright.[12] In December 1951 the BuAer Production Division was considering the project, the only question being whether the air force (which sponsored the J65) would make it available (the manufacturer, Wright, appeared 'most anxious' to provide them to the navy). At this point the Sapphire Fury was one of three air-superiority fighters under consideration, the other two being the swept-wing Panther and the Cutlass (F7U-3).

The Sapphire FJ-2 would be designated FJ-3. It was expected to benefit materially from the more powerful engine, particularly at high altitude and in combat radius (the weakest points of the FJ-2).[13] The FJ-2 had been designed from the outset with an additional 50in^2 of duct area so that it could be re-engined when the Sapphire became

The other emergency air-superiority fighter was the Grumman Cougar, a minimally-modified Panther. Initially it seemed that so little additional work was involved that Cougars could be built on the same assembly lines and even converted from Panthers at naval air rework facilities. Two Cougars (F9F-6) are shown on board *Midway*, 13 August 1952, next to an F7U-3 Cutlass, conceived as an air-superiority fighter but not ready in time.

available. The existing F-86, the basis of the FJ-2, had performed very effectively; in December 1951 the Director of the BuAer Aircraft Division wrote that 'probably every pilot who has flown the F-86 has taken it above Mach 1. Its stability and control have been reported as ideal by NATC [Patuxent River] and it is considered as being a standard against which to measure other aircraft. In creating the FJ-2, great care has been taken to preserve the aerodynamic qualities of the F-86 in spite of the great number of internal, structural and equipment changes required. The extra weight . . . is more than offset performance-wise by the additional thrust.' BuAer noted that the proven irreversible control system of the FJ-2/3 was not matched by the control system of the modified Panther.

Grumman presented its proposal for a swept-wing Panther (its design G-93) on 15 December 1950, tentatively identifying it as the F9F-6.[14] The fuselage, vertical stabiliser, cockpit, engine and landing gear would be the same; the air duct entrances, outer wing panels and horizontal stabiliser would differ. To maintain about the same fuel capacity, the 120-gallon tip tanks would be replaced by 100-gallon wing tanks. Grumman claimed that at sea level the modified Panther would reach 579 knots (Mach 0.877) compared to 532 knots (Mach 0.807) for a Panther. At 35,000ft the new version would reach 516 knots (Mach 0.9) vs 467 knots (Mach 0.812). Cruising speed would be 450 knots rather than 408 knots. Landing (stall) speed would be somewhat less, 96.5 knots vs 103.5 knots. Because it would be somewhat heavier (by 121lbs) the new aircraft would climb somewhat more slowly (6800ft/min vs 6950ft/min at sea level). With somewhat less fuel, it would lose some combat radius (525nm vs 532nm).

An F9F-6 Cougar shows the modified planform Grumman adopted. This aircraft is carrying Sidewinders, which were well-adapted to day fighters because they required virtually no special wiring nor computer. The pilot turned on the missile seeker and listened for a tone indicating that the seeker had locked onto its target. He could then fire it. Experience in Vietnam showed that the situation was rather more complex, because the missile might be unable to follow a target once launched; the pilot needed a computer to tell him whether the target was inside the missile's envelope. Early Sidewinders could home within only a relatively small cone around the target's jet pipe, so a violently manoeuvring target (like a small agile fighter) could evade. The bulge under the fighter's nose is a Tacan receiver. Tacan made British-type broadcast control possible, but it was also valued because it offered much more than the earlier YE.

Grumman proposed to modify three F9F-5s at once. Its modified Panther would be relatively inexpensive yet available almost immediately; production aircraft could be built on the existing F9F-5 assembly line. The power plant was already in production. It seemed likely that existing Panthers could be upgraded at an overhaul facility. Against that, Grumman engineering talent was already fully committed. The programme most likely to suffer was the Rigel cruise missile, which would be slowed by five or six months (it turned out that Rigel never entered service). That seemed acceptable. There was also some question as to whether the swept wing would cause a problem in a carrier landing approach, since it would increase the angle of attack. Grumman doubted this would be much of a problem.

Grumman's proposal was quickly approved; the swept-wing Panther became the F9F-6 Cougar. Early modifications during flight tests were a larger horizontal tail and leading-edge slats instead of the earlier droop nose wing. The Cougar inherited some deficiencies from the Panther: a tendency to dutch roll (simultaneous yawing and rolling, a particular problem in early swept-wing aircraft), poor longitudinal stability and control at both high and low speeds and inadequate ground clearance under its tail. In pressing for FJ-3 production, the Director of the BuAer Aircraft Division warned that the shift to a swept-back wing might accentuate the problems and that Grumman had had no experience with such an aircraft. Flight tests were showing very poor lateral control at high Mach numbers and at approach speeds and the adequacy of the new large tail had not yet been established.

BuAer bought the Cougar because it would be the first US Navy swept-wing fighter with performance equal to or better than the MiG-15; its mission would be straight day air superiority rather than (as in the Panther) a combination of air-to-air and air-to-ground combat. Within BuAer there was some opposition to the idea: past US naval aircraft had succeeded, it was said, because they were versatile. The rejoinder was simple: those aircraft had 2000hp engines and fought enemy aircraft with 1200hp or 1400hp engines. The MiG was very different: it had the same Nene engine (or a derivative thereof). Adding bombs and rockets would reduce Cougar performance to that of the Panther (Grumman's chief engineer agreed).

BuAer was considering one other alternative, an improved Cutlass designated F7U-3 (not the F7U-3 actually produced). For air superiority BuAer wanted minimum size and weight, simplicity and minimum equipment, to gain performance. Relatively large numbers of such small aircraft could be embarked to defend against daylight raids. The F7U-3 had moved into this class by being stripped of radar and other equipment, but was not in the size and weight class of the other two. Tests had shown that it enjoyed only slight superiority in most performance categories except rate of climb and that it was seriously short-legged. About 50 per cent more Cougars or Furies could be spotted aboard ships; 'in a day fighter, numbers of planes is almost as important as performance in determining the outcome of a battle'. Weight and cost made it obvious that the Cutlass was far more complex than either alternative. The Director of the Aircraft Division recommended buying only FJ-3s in FY53, but BuAer also bought the Grumman Cougar that year.

In 1952 both companies proposed new versions of their fighters based on the Sapphire for the FY55 programme (production aircraft to be ordered about May 1954, for which a prototype would be ordered during 1953). At this point the Sapphire was rated at 7600lbs thrust, although it was about the same size as the earlier J42/48 and J47, which produced less than 6000lbs.[15] Although the two proposed aircraft were presented as developed versions of the aircraft already in production, in fact both were entirely new designs. North American called its project FJ-4; Grumman initially called its aircraft the Sapphire Cougar and then the F9F-9 (it was Grumman's design G-98).[16]

North American conceived the FJ-4 as a fully-redesigned version offering 50 per cent more fuel, with a thinner (7 per cent) wing and tail surfaces. The wing root was modified to effectively increase sweep and decrease thickness (as a percentage of chord). The horizontal tail was lowered to the bottom of the fuselage, in line with the low wing.

Adding internal fuel capacity made it possible to abandon the use of drop tanks, which had presented problems in barrier crashes. Moreover, the FJ-2 could not make its required radius without the tanks, but it could not meet the claimed climb and speed figures until it had dropped them. Except for the wing, all aerodynamic changes were tested on board F-86 aircraft and could therefore be considered proven before any FJ-4 flew. The new design was expected to embody considerable weight saving (as of December 1952 estimated gross weight was 17,815lbs compared to 19,361 for the FJ-3 and 18,882 for the FJ-4). FJ-3 generally did not figure in comparisons between the various options, the Furies listed being the FJ-2 and FJ-4.

The two were evaluated in January 1953 (Grumman submitted the G-98 proposal in December 1952). Both aircraft could be justified as growth versions of the earlier aircraft. Although the changes to the F9F were more dramatic, both were actually entirely new designs. If it could not have both, which should BuAer choose? North American submitted first, but its engineering proposal was incomplete, so as of January 1953 BuAer decided to defer any decision until Grumman could present its alternative G-98 in detail. An important factor in any choice was BuAer's plan to compete the next day fighter. Neither Sapphire fighter was worthwhile unless it could be built relatively quickly, before the winner of the 1952 day fighter completion (OS-130) could enter production.

The Sapphire fighter programme was developed against the back-

ground of poor carrier fighter performance. The programme was evaluated in January 1953, just as the Sapphire fighters were being considered. By this time the F10F programme was dead and the Cutlass was failing. The only three high-performance fighters were the F3H-1 Demon, the F9F-6 Cougar and the F4D Skyray. Of the three, the Cougar was considered marginal to unsatisfactory in the day fighter category (apparently its rival the FJ-2/3 was not considered at all). The heavy (30,000lb class) Demon burned about 800 gallons per hour, the highest of any of the fighters. With the J40-WE-22 engine it was unsatisfactory in overall performance and marginal in radius. With the –WE-24, it was marginally satisfactory as a fighter, but lacked satisfactory radius. It seemed that with the J71 engine and high-energy JP-4 fuel, it would be a satisfactory fighter with sufficient combat radius.[17]

The F4D had the potential of being the best manoeuvring aircraft of those considered. As a day fighter, it was satisfactory with all three available engines: J40-WE-22, J71-A-7 and J57-P-7, but only with the J57 (and JP-4) did it offer satisfactory combat radius. As an interceptor, it was marginal with the J40-WE-22, but satisfactory with the other engines and its combat radius was satisfactory only with the J57 and JP-4 fuel.

This evaluation justified cutting the J40 programme to just enough engines to tide over the F3H and F4D programmes until the F3H could get the J71 and the F4D the J57. The F3H-1 was cancelled altogether as a day fighter, only the all-weather general-purpose role remaining. As a day fighter, it was replaced by the F4D with the J57 engine. To get enough J57s, Ford was approved as a second source, its contract to make J40s dropped.

This evaluation favoured the G-98 over the FJ-4, pending

Cougars (F9F-6) of VF-24 on board *Yorktown* are shown on 19 November 1953. The propeller-driven aircraft further aft are Skyraiders. The aircraft to the left is a photo-reconnaissance Banshee. A carrier was in effect a self-contained strike system, relying on its own aircraft both to find targets and to evaluate strike damage.

The F9F-6 could not turn with a MiG-15 without buffeting. To improve high-speed manoeuvrability, the F9F-8 had a redesigned and somewhat enlarged wing with an extended trailing edge and a fixed extended and cambered leading edge (inward to the wing fence) instead of slats. Extending the big wing root fairing all the way back to the tail pipe made the wing effectively thinner (in terms of actual thickness as a percentage of chord). The modified wing improved pitch-up in normal and accelerated stalls, offered better transonic behaviour (faster acceleration) and better high-speed manoeuvrability (the aircraft could turn more tightly without buffeting). Both versions used flaperons (hydraulically-powered spoilers) rather than conventional ailerons. The fence (enlarged in the -8) was used to help cure the pitch-up problem common in swept-wing aircraft. The -8 also had an all-flying tail, the tailplane moving in conjunction with the elevators. The follow-on Tiger (F11F) used the modified control system planned for the F9F-8 and tested in a modified -6. (Grumman)

complete engineering work on both, because the G-98 offered much greater potential due to its advanced aerodynamic design (meaning the area-ruled fuselage). It also offered versatility, since afterburner and non-afterburner engines could be interchanged. However, it was worth buying only if it could be produced at least 18 months before any aircraft resulting from the OS-130 competition (for a supersonic day fighter) then being held.

Grumman began work in 1951. It was aware that the new air force F-100 day fighter (which flew in 1953) was intended to be supersonic and supersonic performance in level flight became Grumman's internal goal. There was also a conscious determination to cut weight, particularly compared to the F10F, which was then already in considerable trouble. An early sketch shows an aircraft with the same distinctive tail as a Panther or Cougar, much of the tail fin extending beyond the end of the jet pipe.[18] The big intake fillets of the earlier aircraft were eliminated as an obvious source of transonic shocks. Experience flying (diving) the Cougar at Mach 1.05 revealed an unacceptable pitch-up in an accelerated stall. Grumman planned to solve that problem by moving the tail plane down, extending the tail of its fuselage to do so. There was also an early decision to move the wing up to mid-body, presumably to simplify the connection between wing and body, otherwise filled by those massive fillets. To improve transonic performance, Grumman selected the same technique others did, thinning the wing (in this case, from 10 per cent to 5 per cent of chord). Because the wings provided insufficient depth for landing gear, the wheels retracted into the fuselage; the resulting narrow track was one of the few stated drawbacks of the design. BuAer considered the new design close enough to the Cougar that primary control system features proven on that aircraft for longitudinal control (the flying tail), as well as the

general flaperon arrangement and a yaw damper showed that the new design would have satisfactory control.

While Grumman was working on the Sapphire Cougar, NACA announced the area rule. Grumman's seems to have been the first fighter to embody it, in the form of a pinched waist at the wings. Evaluating the design on paper, BuAer was not sure how much good the 'coke bottle' would do. Apparently neither was Grumman. With the Sapphire, the aircraft was just subsonic. Grumman looked forward to a more powerful engine, perhaps an afterburning Sapphire, to boost its fighter beyond Mach 1. It envisaged a G-98L powered by an afterburning J65-W-12 engine (12,000lbs thrust on take-off). Beyond that was a somewhat redesigned G-98D using the much more powerful J79 (at this time 14,350lbs thrust with afterburner, 9300lbs without) and a 45° rather than 35° wing. As it turned out, the J65 was derated at about the same time the new Grumman fighter flew, so it was never more than barely supersonic.[19] The J79 version (F11F-1F) certainly was supersonic, but it lacked fuel and therefore endurance.

This F9F-8 shows the refuelling probe eventually adopted, extending from its nose. Grumman tested specially-shaped drop tanks, but they did not enter service. This photograph was taken at NAS Jacksonville on 7 November 1957. The aircraft served with an attack squadron (VA-44) rather than a fighter squadron, implying that it had been modified as a light nuclear bomber.

When it offered the G-98, Grumman expected it to take off at 15,807lbs and to achieve a maximum speed of 631 knots (Mach 0.955) at sea level and 551 knots (Mach 0.958) at 35,000ft, using a 7800lbs thrust J65-W-7 engine. BuAer speed estimates were somewhat more pessimistic, e.g. 616 knots (Mach 0.932) at sea level. BuAer expected G-98 to climb to 40,000ft in 5.8 minutes (to 35,000ft in 3.5 minutes), both slightly longer than Grumman estimates. The BuAer estimates did not take into account Grumman's use of the area rule, which BuAer initially thought might increase speed by about Mach 0.2 to Mach 0.3.

By the time G-98 was ready for production, it had gained considerable weight, so that at take-off it was expected to weigh 19,442lbs. Against that, its J65-W-6 engine was expected to offer 11,000lbs of thrust using an afterburner (the FJ-4 could not be fitted with an afterburner). Given its drag-rise characteristics, the FJ-4 was not expected to benefit much even it could be fitted with an afterburner.

At this time North American credited the FJ-4 with 620 knots at sea level and 557 knots at 35,000ft (BuAer estimates were 627 knots and 561 knots, respectively). The FJ-2 could make 596 knots at sea level and 521 knots at 35,000ft; comparable figures for the Cougar were 561 and 506 knots. Cougar combat radius was 320nm and that was the design figure for G-98 (BuAer estimated that it would be 294nm). The FJ-2 combat radius was 305nm and for the FJ-4 BuAer estimated 308nm. With the J40, the F4D combat radius was 240nm and with the J71 it was 165nm; but with the J57 it was credited with 405nm and the longest endurance of any of the day fighters, 1.9 hours. With the J40, the thirsty F3H was credited with a 280nm radius and with the replacement J71, 270nm. The standard requirement was 300nm, which explains why the F3H was not considered an acceptable day fighter.

Comparing G-98 to the FJ-4, BuAer commented that G-98 offered better climb, but FJ-4 was faster, except that 'if coke bottle pays off speeds will be the same'. However, if Grumman could get rid of its slat, it would have the edge in both speed and climb. The

FJ-4 offered better radius, 312nm vs 296nm as an interceptor (compared to 270–325nm for the F3H and 295nm for the F4D) and would do still better if it were using the new JP-4 fuel. Grumman offered better carrier suitability, but neither really suffered badly in that respect. With little apparent difference, the FJ-4 would be easier to justify as a straightforward production improvement of the FJ-3, which was already in production. However, G-98 offered far more growth potential and with an afterburner and more fuel it would outperform even the spectacular F4D. The weight saved to make the FJ-4 design more efficient had been paid for by reduced strength (6G standard). Grumman was likely to offer slightly better flying qualities, but its control system had not yet been proven, whereas the FJ-4's had been.

After BuAer evaluation, Grumman modified the design by adding fuel (the original bladder tanks had not completely filled their spaces).[20] That amounted to 100 gallons. Additional data on the advantage of the 'coke bottle' design had become available. With the additional fuel and using the new data, Grumman estimated that at 35,000ft the aircraft would be supersonic (613 knots, Mach 1.06

In 1953 both North American and Grumman offered the navy what they described as redesigned versions of their interim air-superiority fighters. North American's was the FJ-4 shown here. Despite its family resemblance to the FJ-3, it was an almost entirely new aircraft.

The FJ-4 could not match the performance of either its rival the Grumman Tiger or its immediate successor the Crusader, but it could carry a heavy load and it was modified as a light bomber, the FJ-4B. An FJ-4B from VA-63 (*Midway*) is shown on 8 September 1960 carrying a pair of stores. These shapes probably corresponded to a version of the Mk 105 'Hotpoint' nuclear bomb. The long probe is for refuelling. Note that the aircraft was from an attack rather than a fighter squadron.

instead of the originally estimated 553 knots). At sea level it was now credited with 675 knots (776mph) rather than the original 630 knots. The projected 8500lbs thrust J65 would add some additional speed: at 35,000ft the aircraft would make Mach 1.08 (620 knots). However, with an afterburner Grumman expected much more: 714 knots (821mph) at 8500ft, 750 knots (Mach 1.3) at 35,000ft and 673 knots (Mach 1.17) at 50,000ft. That would cost endurance, down from 400nm (gained by adding the fuel to the 295nm aircraft) to only 181nm. With two specially-designed external tanks (150 gallons each) radius would be more than restored (to 444nm) but performance would not suffer very much (748 knots at 35,000ft).

BuAer ordered the G-98 on 27 April 1953 (it ordered the FJ-4 prototypes that October). The initial order described the aircraft as the F9F-8, because the two existing versions of the Cougar were the F9F-6 and -7 (with different engines). What became the F9F-8 version of the Cougar was already under development, so the new aircraft was soon redesignated F9F-9. Production was ordered under the FY55 programme, with deliveries to begin in March 1956: initially 193 fighters and eighty-nine photo-reconnaissance aircraft. In September 1954 DCNO (Air) ordered sixty of the photo aircraft reordered as fighters. In late April BuAer decided to redesignate the aircraft F11F-1, because it was an entirely new design. It was named the Tiger.

When the prototype was completed in July 1954, the afterburning J65 was not yet ready; the aircraft reached Mach 0.96. The first afterburner flight was completed in January 1955. However, the Tiger was not far enough ahead of the OS-130 fighters: the Crusader flew in March 1955. Although a prototype was flying with an afterburning J65, that engine was not yet fully satisfactory.

Concerned that the J65 afterburner might fail altogether, Grumman turned to alternative engines. It also wanted to overcome the competition presented by the Crusader. In April 1954 it proposed a modified aircraft with 45° wings and a J79 afterburner engine (alter-

natively it could take the J73 or the afterburning J65-W-12).[21] With the J79, Grumman expected the fighter to attain 1000 knots (Mach 1.73) at 36,500ft and 688 knots (Mach 1.04) at sea level, with a rate of climb of 34,200ft/min at sea level. Combat radius would be 586nm (cycle time 2.64 hours) with two drop tanks. Each wing would have two hardpoints sufficient for 1200lb nuclear weapons. With minor modifications the aircraft could be modified as an all-weather fighter or a Sparrow fighter. The navy accepted the Grumman proposal to install J79-GE-3s in two aircraft. Grumman guaranteed a speed of Mach 1.65 at 35,000ft and a combat ceiling of 53,000ft, at a weight of 18,230lbs. Internal Grumman papers designated the new version the F11F-2, but the two test aircraft were designated F11F-1F.

The J79 version presented its own problems. Given the production schedule of the new J79, the Super Tiger could not beat out the OS-130 fighter, by this time the Vought Crusader. It would be attractive only if it offered much better performance. An initial navy evaluation report credited it with outstanding performance, except for insufficient fuel and hence too little endurance – a serious problem.

By this time the Tiger itself was in trouble. It could not meet the guaranteed low supersonic speed, which was its main advantage over the FJ-4. Worse, the J65 was derated (as J65-W-18). The photo version was cancelled altogether and production cut to a total of 201 aircraft including the two Super Tigers. Tests showed, moreover, that fuel consumption was greater than expected. On paper the Tiger could outrange the Crusader, but in reality it could not. Grumman had to fill

An FJ-4B is shown with its successor, the A4D (later A-4) Skyhawk light bomber. Both aircraft are armed with Bullpup air-to-surface missiles, the first tactical stand-off ground attack weapons to enter service.

the tail fin and space around the jet intake ducts with fuel, a change approved in November 1956. A new long nose housed a radar. Delays due to modification put the Tiger, conceived as an interim fighter, behind the Crusader in fleet introduction. Few aircraft reached the fleet, the most prominent employment of the Tiger being with the Blue Angels aerobatic team (in November 1958 the net to last batch of Tigers were assigned). The others became operational trainers.

Grumman sketched numerous versions of the G-98 and it also worked the export market.[22] It submitted its G-98D for the general-purpose fighter competition which grew out of the OS-130 competition described below. The company described G-98D as the logical step beyond the F9F-9 (F11F-1 Tiger) with a thinner wing of greater area, a longer fuselage and additional fuel. The wing might employ boundary layer control. The engine was the J79.

The less promising FJ-4 presented fewer developmental problems and it entered service much earlier. Once the higher-performing Crusader had passed its tests, DCNO (Air) directed that the last 221 of a total of 371 FJ-4s should be reconfigured as attack aircraft, meaning light nuclear bombers to replace the lower-performance bomber version of the Banshee (F2H-2B).[23] The change was attractive because modifying an existing aircraft, albeit one conceived for high-altitude combat, was much faster than developing a new attack bomber (at this time the A4D Skyhawk was being developed for the light nuclear attack mission).[24]

The key change was installation of an Aero 18C Low-Altitude Bombing System (LABS) to enable the fighter to execute a special manoeuvre (loft or 'over the shoulder') so that it could release the bomb and escape its explosion. Other major changes were additional speed brakes, spoilers for better control during the radical pop-up loft manoeuvre, an improved longitudinal control system and a boosted rudder.

The less numerous companion special attack fighter was the F9F-8B version of the Cougar. It used the same LABS system as the FJ-4B, but apparently did not incorporate the other modifications, so no first flight was recorded indicating that it was a special type of fighter. For

Instead of modifying the Cougar, Grumman chose to design a new fighter capable of transonic speed: the Tiger. Initially BuAer accepted Grumman's argument that it was a lineal descendant of the Cougar and designated it F9F-8 (before the improved Cougar was the F9F-8) and then F9F-9, before choosing an entirely new F11F-1 designation. A Tiger is shown on board *Forrestal* for tests, 4 April 1956.

example, the BuAer scrapbook of aircraft reports for 1957 lists the F9F-8, -8P and -8T, the latter a two-seat training version produced in large numbers as the standard advanced trainer (after 1962 it was designated TA-9J). The -8B designation was established effective 12 April 1956, applying to 191 aircraft.

Air superiority: OS-130 and the Crusader

The longer-term effect of the MiG-15 experience was a 1952 design contest for a new high-performance day fighter under the designation OS-130. It began with an 8 January 1951 letter from the Director, Piloted Aircraft Division, to the Research Division asking for a feasibility study of a new general-purpose fighter to be procured after a competition early in FY52.[25] The request deliberately did not set detailed requirements, apart from a requirement that the new fighter be able to fly 300nm, fight enemy interceptors and return to a carrier.

DESIGN BRIEF

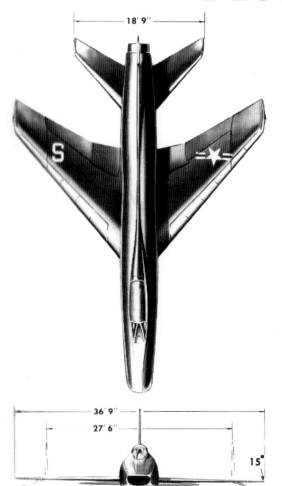

- Take-off Weight . . . . 28,130 lb
- Design Weight . . . . 24,560 lb
- Landing Weight . . . . 21,000 lb
- Max Speed (Max Power at 35,000 Ft) . . . . MACH 1.63
- Time to Accelerate (Max Mil Speed to Mach 1.2) . . . . 0.72 min
- Combat Ceiling (Max Power) . . . . 53,800 FT
- Combat Radius (MIL-C-5011A) (Internal Fuel) . . . . 425 N MI
- Deck Spotting . . . . 22 airplanes
- Fuel—Basic Internal . . . . 1370 Gal
- Availability After Go-ahead . . . . 20 Months
- Performance Potential With Altitude Potential
  J57 Engine . . . . MACH 1.80

AERODYNAMIC CONFIGURATION

Wing—45-degree Sweep, 5% Thickness, Boundary Layer
Control Flaps, Leading Edge Slats, Wing Tip Droop
Fuselage—High Fineness Ratio, Area Variation Control
Engine—J57-P-(JT3N) 16,000 lb SL Static Thrust

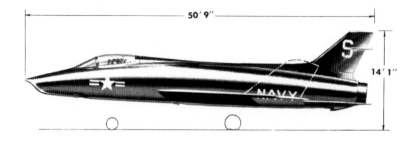

It had to be able to operate from *Oriskany* class carriers and it should be as small as possible.

The 1951 ADR study has not surfaced and the competition was not run until 1952 (the OS-130 specification was still being revised in December 1952). To support BuAer in writing the specification, in August 1952 ADR sketched four possible air-superiority fighters (DR-122) using available powerplants: two J46 or one J57 or J65.[26] All were intended to reach Mach 1.6 at 35,000ft (ceiling 52,000ft). They give a fair idea of what sorts of proposals BuAer hoped to receive. Estimated weights ranged from 16,500lbs for the lightest powerplant (two J46) to 20,000lbs (J57P-1). All would be subsonic at sea level, the J57 aircraft limited to 450 knots due to their engines, the others rated at about 635 knots. They would make about Mach 1 at 35,000ft, well below BuAer's requirement (the heaviest, DR-122B, would be just subsonic, Mach 0.97). Desired combat radius was 300nm, which was exceeded by the two J57 designs; the others were far worse, only 136nm for DR-122C powered by the J65. All would be catapult-launched at 140 knots, landing at 139–144 knots. The twin-engine

After the OS-130 competition closed, North American offered this version of the F-100B, which it called the Super Fury (the F-100B morphed into the rather different F-107). The brochure was dated 15 November 1953. BuAer considered a later modified version in 1954 as a general-purpose fighter. The Super Fury had the 45° sweep 5 per cent wing of the F-100 Super Sabre, using boundary layer control flaps, leading edge slats and wing tip droop (the wingtips could be drooped 15° to improve low-speed lateral stability). The fuselage was area-ruled. Maximum speed was Mach 1.63 at 35,000ft, but North American claimed that given the altitude potential of the J57 engine (17,200lbs thrust, to be available January 1956 and in production a year later) that could increase to Mach 1.8. Combat radius on internal fuel was 425nm. The engine was a 16,000lb thrust J57-P (JT3N). Span was 36ft 9in and length was 50ft 9in. Gross weight was 28,130lbs. A small APG-30A range-only radar was in the nose. North American offered its NASARR search and ranging radar, which would automatically search and detect targets over a 90° x 35° sector, with a detection range of 6nm on a fighter and 10–12nm on a bomber – far too short to be useful for an interceptor. Radar information would be presented on a B-scope (range vs bearing) and a warning light would tell the pilot that a target had been detected.

The Korean War experience led the navy to issue a specification for a new air-superiority fighter, OS-130. Vought won the OS-130 competition with its F8U-1 Crusader. This F8U-1 of VF-32 is shown on board *Intrepid*. The large dielectric area on its nose identifies it as an F8U-1E with a search radar (APS-67) rather than a range-only radar (APG-30).

DR-122A might benefit from reduction in its engine weights (for example by using more titanium) and it could gain combat radius by shutting down one engine. ADR pointed out that these aircraft might be made smaller yet by using drop tanks to provide the required combat radius. ADR liked the J57-powered DR-122B best. It might be developed to make Mach 1.2 at 35,000ft.

Before the competition was run, Douglas offered a modified Skyray as an interim approach to the OS-130 requirement. It does not seem to have been associated in any way with the two Sapphire fighters. The aircraft originally designated F4D-2, was later recognised as a fresh design in much the way that the F9F-9 became the F11F-1. It was therefore redesignated F5D-1 and named Skylancer. It would be powered by an uprated J57 (16,000lbs thrust) and it would have a thinner wing, a longer fuselage and more internal fuel. A tentative 1957 aircraft programme (dated 9 July 1954) showed twenty-four delivered that year, the first two being scheduled for delivery in April and July 1956.

OS-130 initially called for a maximum speed of Mach 1 at 35,000ft, a combat ceiling of 52,000ft and a combat radius of 300nm.[27] Combat was to consist of a ten-minute period at maximum speed at the combat ceiling, plus five minutes at maximum speed at 15,000ft. Size was set by a requirement to spot twenty-five aircraft in a 200ft x 96ft area.[28] The original Operational Requirement issued in July 1952 (CA-05503A) called for a non-afterburning engine and a combat ceiling of 52,000ft.[29]

The day fighter mission limited radar weight, as only a range-only set was needed, feeding a fire-control system as a deflection rangefinder. Previous fighters had used the APG-30; the Douglas submission showed the more powerful APG-34. OS-130 called for either four 20mm guns, three T-160 guns or 2in FFARs (later the BuAer armament division changed this to 20mm cannon or 2in or 2.75in FFARs). At this time the only high-powered engines which had been 150-hour were the J65-W-2, J57-P-1 and J73-GE-3, of which the latter would be cancelled once the J79 proved successful. Contractors could use engines expected to be 150-hour qualified by 31 December 1953 only to show possible improvements: later versions of the J57 and J71 and the afterburning J40-WE-24. The formal Request for Proposal was issued on 12 September 1952.

At this point the emphasis was on simplicity and minimum weight. Then OS-130 was revised to emphasise performance, increasing the minimum acceptable speed to Mach 1.2 and permitting an afterburning engine. Of the bidders, Lockheed and Temco both pointed to the dramatic change. In Lockheed's case the aircraft grew considerably, to the point where the company chose to offer a version of its current air force interceptor. Temco undertook to improve performance at a minimum cost in growth.

Eleven alternatives were submitted and evaluated: the Douglas D-652 (F4D-2, later redesignated F5D-1 Skylancer), Grumman G-97, Lockheed L-242, McDonnell Model 90, North American Super Fury

An F8U-1 shows the small dielectric nose section, indicating a small, simple range-only radar, of initial production Crusaders.

(with J57 and J65 engines), Northrop N-94 and -94A, Temco 31 and Vought's V-383 and V-384.[30] Vought won with its V-383, three examples of which were ordered in May 1953.

Douglas probably offered a higher-powered version of the F4D some time in 1951 as an interim day fighter. It formally offered what it called the D-652 or F4D-2 for OS-130 in February 1953, when the other companies submitted their proposals. Unlike the F4D-1 Skyray, this was a pure day fighter whose only radar was the range-only APG-34. The engine was a version of the J57 producing 16,000lbs of thrust using an afterburner, compared to 14,800lbs in the version in the F4D-1. The brochure guaranteed 810 knots (Mach 1.41) at 35,000ft with afterburner (580 knots without) at a take-off weight of 23,000lbs (combat weight 20,150lbs – take-off less 40 per cent of fuel). Compared to the F4D-1 Skyray, this aircraft had a thinner wing and a longer fuselage with more space for fuel. The new design culminated a process of evolution from the F4D-1. First the heavy Aero 13-D radar fire-control system was replaced by the simple Mk 16-3. Provision was made for external fuel for increased range. The Avon engine (never licensed in the United States) was considered as an alternative to the J57. Douglas called this simplest departure from the F4D-1 its D-652-2. The alternative D-652-1 had the wing fillet lines refined to increase the critical Mach number, the cockpit was moved forward 10in (the aircraft was 24in longer) and the space available used to help add a 265-gallon tank, increasing combat radius with the J57-P-JTN engine to the desired 300nm. With an afterburning J57, this version would meet or exceed all OS-130 requirements, except that it had 100 rather than the desired 125 rounds per gun (the original F4D-1 had 70). In D-652 the thickness of the wing was reduced from 7 to 5 per

cent at the root and 4.5 to 3.2 per cent at the tip. The fuselage was lengthened (by 86in) to increase fineness ration, hence reduce supersonic drag. This version had the refined fillet lines and it could accommodate 125 rounds per gun, as desired. This was the design Douglas actually submitted. Douglas pointed out that although the Avon-14 was not on the approved list, it offered considerable promise due to its light weight and efficiency. An aircraft powered by it would achieve the same performance as with the J57 but it would weigh 4500lbs less (D-652 weighed 23,000lbs on take-off). Douglas' D-652-A was D-652 with the Avon, based on Rolls-Royce performance figures. In effect it was a shrunken version of D-652.

At least initially the F5D seems to have been seen as insurance against problems with the Vought fighter bought to meet the OS-130 requirement. Thus the July 1954 tentative programme for FY56 procurement showed twenty-four aircraft to be delivered in 1957, the first two being delivered in April and July 1956 (in fact only four F5Ds were delivered). By early 1957 the F5D was the only planned US Navy programme using the self-guided Sparrow II and its Aero X24A fire-control system. Nineteen production aircraft were ordered during 1956, but in November the last eight were cancelled. By March 1957 the NACA Ames Laboratory wanted two of the four completed aircraft and BuAer was considering alternative uses for seven partly-completed airframes, including underwater escape (from a crashed aircraft), wing fatigue, catapult/barrier and vulnerability tests. All other incomplete airframes were scrapped. Meanwhile Douglas continued to work on the design; a reduced inlet duct angle offered so much better engine performance that it was willing to guarantee Mach 1.63 at 35,000ft with the P-14 engine.

Grumman's G-97 generally resembled its earlier (despite a later number) G-98 Tiger, with four underwing positions for Sparrow II missiles and a shorter nose. Using this version of the Sparrow considerably simplified guidance and reduced the necessary radar load. In addition, the aircraft had the usual four 20mm nose cannon. The most obvious change from the Tiger was the powerplant: the J57 engine used by the Skyray. At this time (1953) the navy was actively interested in using a flexible deck, so in its brochure Grumman argued that the mid-wing configuration it proposed was well adapted to such operation.

The Grumman G-97 folder in its archive carries a note saying that news of the OS-130 competition reached Grumman in the summer of 1952; the design team began work without any formal specification. The design book covers the period between July 1952 to March 1953, by which time the final version of the design had been set. According to the note on the cover, Grumman won the competition by a considerable point margin (according to a BuAer source), but BuAer considered it unwise to award the contract to Grumman since it had just received the Tiger contract for the interim day fighter. Some of the innovative Grumman wing features appeared on the F8U (it is not clear from the formal proposal what they were). It is not clear from the note whether they were in the initial Vought proposal or whether BuAer elected to show them to Vought after it had been selected.

Lockheed's L-242 (proposal dated 26 February 1953) was a carrier version of its F-104 Starfighter, with the same diminutive wings (span 27ft 1in, area 191ft^2) and high T-tail. According to Lockheed, initially it pursued parallel studies of an OS-130 fighter and an air force day

The F8U-2 could be identified by its large ventral fins. It had the AWG-3 armament control system built around the APS-67 search radar and the EX-16 aircraft fire-control system. (Chance Vought)

fighter, but changes to the navy requirement paralleled air force requirements, hence the decision to adapt the air force interceptor design. Initially Lockheed had tried something more radical, a non-afterburning (J65) fighter capable of Mach 1 with a combat radius of 300nm; among weight-saving measures was elimination of the undercarriage on the assumption that it would use a flexible deck. This design was pursued until November 1952 even though Lockheed considered its performance mediocre. Its designers were proud that the supersonic aircraft was little larger and that the only additional complication was the afterburner (take-off weight grew from 13,000lbs to 16,000lbs [without undercarriage]). Lockheed offered two alternative engines, the Wright J65B3 and the General Electric X-24 (J79), neither of which was included in the original OS-130. The aircraft was quite small, so such powerful engines promised spectacular performance, a maximum speed (with the J67) of more than 1000 knots (Mach 1.74), far beyond the desired Mach 1.2. With the J79, it might reach Mach 2.0 at 35,000ft and it might also have a combat radius of 550nm based on a combat speed of Mach 1.2 and tip tanks. The small wing made for a high stall speed of 139 knots (160mph). The desired landing speed (10 per cent above stall speed) embodied in OS-130 was 130 knots and several companies offered lower speeds.

McDonnell's Model 90/91 was a straight-wing aircraft with its air intake under its cockpit and a rooster tail. McDonnell's and Lockheed's were the only designs using straight wings. McDonnell argued that the most important factor in supersonic speed was thinness and that a thin straight wing was simpler and lighter than a swept or delta wing. It presented a drag coefficient curve which showed that swept wings were superior only between about Mach 0.8 and Mach 1.3. A straight wing also offered superior take-off and landing (for example, it needed a much lower angle of attack as it approached a carrier). McDonnell claimed that the thin straight wing had been proven be low speed, transonic and supersonic wind tunnel tests, by rocket model tests and by full-scale flight tests by the X-1 and X-3 research aircraft. Nonetheless, its far more successful Phantom had a cropped-delta

wing. The underslung engine installation offered flexibility; McDonnell offered the J57 (16,000lbs thrust), J67 (21,500lbs thrust), J71 (Allison: 14,500lbs thrust) and J73 (14,370lbs thrust) as alternatives. Of these, the J67 offered the highest speed, Mach 1.94. As it turned out, of the four alternative engines, only the J57 survived. Maximum speed with an afterburning J57 was 910 knots (Mach 1.58) at 38,000ft; without afterburner, it was almost supersonic (Mach 0.98). Combat ceiling was 58,700ft and combat radius was 471nm (it was 235nm with the J67). Overall, McDonnell claimed twice the performance of its earlier Banshee in the same size and weight. Model 91 was a lighter-weight alternative which met the OS-130 specification but had considerably inferior performance due to its less powerful engine (maximum speed on afterburner was Mach 1.23).

Northrop offered a 58° modified delta powered by a J57-P-11(14,800lbs thrust with afterburner) or a J65-W-B3 (11,000lbs thrust with afterburner) as N-94 and N-94A. N-94B offered increased wing area. N-94C deviated from the basic blended wing-body shape. The design was submitted in February 1953 and Northrop claimed that it culminated nearly two years of work on a compact high-performance navy fighter. It argued that its configuration was ideal for long-term growth with minimum change and hence minimum production impact. It estimated that N-94 would attain Mach 1.63 at 35,000ft, with a rate of climb at that altitude of 16,200ft/min. N-94A would be slower: Mach 1.33 at 35,000ft, with a climb rate of 12,200ft/min, but it would weigh less (14,865lbs). The lower weight would give it a higher rate of climb at sea level, 32,900ft/min rather than 30,300ft/min and a lower stall speed, hence better carrier landing characteristics. The argument for growth potential was that the basic design would retain its good transonic drag characteristics at greater speeds attainable with more powerful engines. Both versions exceeded

the required 300nm combat radius (326nm for N-94 at specified speed, 300nm at Mach 1.38). In addition to the usual cannon and 2in FFARs, either aircraft could carry four Sparrow II missiles underwing. The basic design had a trailing edge which was angled in at roughly mid-wing. In N-94B, the trailing edge was straight, wing area increasing from 457.8ft^2 to 550ft^2. Compared to N-94, which had the same engine, -94B was slower (Mach 1.42 at 35,000ft) but could fly higher. It would climb more slowly at sea level (28,200ft/min). The larger wing did reduce its stall speed, hence make it more carrier-suitable. In N-94C the wing was raised to shoulder level, so that the aircraft could no longer be characterised as a blended wing-body design. The wing was much that used in -94B.

In February North American offered ESO 4927 as its OS-130 entry, with a solid nose and side intakes and a shoulder-mounted variable-incidence swept wing. It was powered by a J57 rated at 16,000lbs thrust with afterburner. Maximum speed at 35,000ft would be Mach 1.51 and time to climb from sea level to 35,000ft was given as two minutes. BuAer evaluators considered the North American entry second best after Vought's, but rejected it because it began as a much heavier aircraft (about 30,000lbs vs 20,000lbs). Although the evaluators considered Vought's weights somewhat unrealistic, it could never be as heavy, at least at the outset.[31]

In November 1953 North American offered a very different day fighter it called the Super Fury, essentially an air force F-100B (which eventually became the F-107, an aircraft with little obvious resem-

An F8U-2N on the catapult of *Forrestal*, armed with a 2000lb bomb underwing. The pods carry Zuni ground-attack rockets. Note the FT (Flight Test) letters under the cockpit and the absence of any air group letters on the tail. The tail device was used for Chance Vought test aircraft. The wing is raised to the high-incidence position for take-off.

An F-8E (F8U-2NE) of VF-191 waiting to take off from *Ticonderoga*, December 1968, carrying a Sidewinder. This type of Crusader was adapted to carry not only infra-red Sidewinders but also the semi-active radar-guided AIM-9D version, called SARAH. It was intended to provide an all-aspect capability, but it was unpopular and was not used in combat.

blance to the F-100). Through 1953 North American offered equivalents of the F-100B as the Super Fury. This early one had an extended upper air intake lip carrying the required APG-30A range-only radar. F-100B features included the thinned integral fuel wing, variable-geometry inlet and shaped (area-ruled) fuselage. For low-speed performance, it had boundary-layer control flaps, automatic full-span slats and wing tip droop provision. With the J57 (16,000lbs thrust) engine, it could achieve Mach 1.63 at 35,000ft. North American estimated that it could be in production 20 months after a go-ahead, an important issue in the OS-130 competition. It offered an alternative NASARR (North American Search and Range Radar) which would extend detection range. This radar automatically searched, detected and ranged in an area 90° x 35°; detection range on a fighter would be 6nm (10–12nm for a bomber). The pilot would be alerted to a detection by a warning light. Presumably the OS-130 competition had already been decided. This design was the starting point for a general-purpose fighter North American offered in February 1954 as part of a new but informal competition described below.

Temco was a new company, its only military product a jet trainer

(it had qualified as second source for the Demon). Later it merged with Vought and the Ling steel company to form LTV and in this sense it was involved in the design of the later A-7. Its Model 31 was a delta with a rooster T-tail. Temco guaranteed a speed of Mach 1.25 at 35,000ft (720 knots) and a rate of climb at sea level of 20,000ft/min. It argued that its minimum size offered maximum manoeuvrability and easy shipboard handling. Minimum size was connected to a minimum engine, in its case a JT-3-M without an afterburner, offering 10,500lbs thrust.

Vought offered two designs, V-383 and V-384. Both were shoulder-wing designs with air intakes under their noses. Both had variable-incidence wings. Vought saw two alternative design paths: to design the smallest possible aircraft around the OS-130 requirement or to wrap the smallest possible aircraft around the most powerful possible engine. Goals were to achieve Mach 1 at 35,000ft without afterburner; to achieve Mach 1.3 to 1.5 that altitude with afterburner; and to offer the potential for Mach 1.5 to Mach 1.7 at 35,000ft. The aircraft had to climb to 35,000ft in less than two minutes and normal combat radius had to be 300nm on internal fuel (overload radius on such fuel 500nm or four-hour CAP endurance). Manoeuvrability requirements were to be able to exceed 4.5G at 35,000ft and to accelerate at 0.1 G in level flight at Mach 1.2 at 35,000ft. Approach speed had to be no more than 130 knots and size was limited by the requirement that twenty-five be spotted in 200ft of deck. The design had to be adaptable to future flight decks, both angled and flexible (i.e. the aircraft should have a flat bottom). The design had to be flexible to benefit from engine and other improvements.

V-383 was designed around the most powerful available engine, the J57. V-384 was the minimum-size approach using the J65, weighing 17,950lbs rather than 22,600lbs at take-off. Given the difference in engines, speeds at 35,000ft with afterburner were, respectively, Mach 1.5 and Mach 1.25 (without the afterburner, Mach 1.0 and Mach 0.98). Vought estimated that with an 18,000lbs thrust future version of the J57, V-383 could attain Mach 1.7. The variable-incidence wing had two fixed positions, one (+7°) for take-off or landing and the other (-1°) for normal flight. High wing incidence for landing or take-off increased lift without the drag associated with a nose-up position. It gave the pilot a better view without requiring a high cockpit which would add drag, gaining about Mach 0.17 (100 knots at 35,000ft). The aircraft sat as close as possible to, and parallel with, the deck, so that it could have the shortest possible landing gear. Vought pointed to the small angle between aircraft and deck on landing as a considerable advantage with a flexdeck. Mounting the wing atop the fuselage made it possible to use a continuous centre section and a simple three-point attachment to the fuselage. It was also possible to set the horizontal tail well below the wing, a position wind tunnel tests had shown to be favourable, particularly to avoid pitch-up in the transonic range (many of the other designs offered for OS-130 had shoulder wings for this reason).

BuAer bought the V-383 design as the F8U-1 Crusader. Vought offered not only an attractive design but also considerable production capacity freed by the death of the Cutlass programme. Conversely, a later study of BuAer procurement pointed to the desperation Vought clearly felt as the Cutlass programme failed, which led it to try an unusually innovative approach.

The new fighter proved extremely successful, to the point where in May 1957 an internal BuAer memo called it 'the finest fighter aircraft in the world *in squadron use*. Little publicity has been given to the fact that we are now back in the fighter business with a *first-line* aircraft. We are missing a public information opportunity that we have not had for some years. It is interesting to contrast the lack of public information releases on the F8U-1 with the many releases from the Air Force on the F-102 and F-104. The F-102 is inferior in performance to the F8U and the F-104 is not in operational use.' The navy began to demonstrate its fighter on record runs, beginning with a 16 July transcontinental flight by an F8U-1P (NAS Los Angeles to NAS Floyd Bennett) in 3 hours 23 minutes. In August 1956 an F8U established a US national speed record of 1015.4mph over China Lake. Almost in parallel with the Crusader, BuAer was developing the supersonic A3J Vigilante bomber. The air force became interested in using it as a long-endurance missile fighter for North American air defence. In 1958-9 BuAer found itself in the weird position of resisting air force interest in the aircraft for fear that Congress would see the Vigilante as a fighter and ask why the navy needed two new supersonic fighters (the Phantom was not yet in production). North American did end up offering a three-engine version of the Vigilante to the air force, but it was not adopted. Production began in FY55.

In September 1954 Vought offered a follow-up day air-superiority fighter it called F8U-2 (later designated F-8C) carrying a pair of Sidewinder missiles under its mid-section, on stubs under and just forward of the wings. Another two would be carried internally. The brochure showed a maximum speed at 35,000ft of 886 knots (Mach 1.59). The engine (not shown in the brochure) was the J57-P-16 (16,900lbs thrust). Problems arose with the internal Sidewinder stowage and it was abandoned.

In 1955 DCNO (Air) decided that even day fighters needed radar assistance, a position similar to that the British were now taking. OpNav decided that the last 130 F8U-1s should have a new APS-67 search/ranging radar (with a 14.5in dish antenna) instead of the range-only gun fire-control radar (APG-30) of the original version. They were redesignated F8U-1Es (F-8Bs in the post-1962 system). The first F8U-1E flew on 3 September 1958.

At the same time the APS-67 radar was ordered for the follow-on F8U-2 (F-8C) with the new engine. In this version it was integrated with the EX-16 aircraft fire-control system in the AWG-3 armament control system. Procurement began in the FY57 programme (directed 31 October 1957) alongside the last F8U-1s. The FY58 programme included both F8U-2s and a limited all-weather F8U-2N (F-8D). The last of 1217 aircraft was delivered in October 1964, production reviving briefly to produce forty-two F-8Es for the French navy (June 1964 through January 1965, at a peak rate of eight per month).

In Vietnam the Crusader gained a reputation as the only true air-superiority fighter the navy had; certainly it was rather different from its stablemate the Phantom. Early air combat showed that Phantoms and other navy bombers on strike missions needed escorts, just as they had in Korea. In September 1965 the navy requested a programme to remanufacture existing F-8C/D/E aircraft and in December the Office of the Secretary of Defense (OSD) approved a total of 225 of them (limited to F-8D/E). The remanufactured F-8D became an F-8H; the remanufactured F-8E became an F-8H (a remanufactured reconnaissance aircraft {RF-8A} became an RF-8G). Envisaged changes were a 4000-hour wing, Direct Lift Control, MAGDARR radar (F-8E: Magnavox APQ-124, a modified APQ-94 with a Doppler mode) and other items.[32] Another 150 earlier Crusaders (F-8A/B/C) were added in September 1966: the upgraded F-8C became an F-8K (eighty-seven aircraft) and the upgraded F-8B became an F-8L (sixty-one aircraft). Modifications included adding wing hardpoints to fifty-six F-8Cs (originally seventy-five had been planned; the reduction was due to the shortage of these aircraft in the fleet). In addition, seventy-three RF-8As were modified as RF-8Gs. The DF-8F was a drone director conversion of the F-8A (F8U-1).

The general-purpose fighter

In mid-1954 the BuAer evaluators reported on a follow-on comparison of alternative designs to choose a new general purpose-fighter to replace the Demon. There was apparently no formal competition, but some companies were asked for designs. BuAer wanted to include the new fighter in the 1955 and 1956 programmes, presumably because it was urgent to replace the defective Demon. To ADR that meant that whatever design was chosen had to be suitable for immediate development around engines matching its airframe capability. BuAer also had to have sufficient confidence in the contractor's ability to produce an aircraft which would not require lengthy development.

The great difference between OS-130 and the August 1954 designs was the much heavier radar required for the general-purpose, which meant all-weather, role. ADR issued its first report in July 1954. Grumman submitted its design in May 1954 and North American in May and June. By this time ADR had also completed its study of a possible future single fighter (ADR-1603), which affected the evaluation. It also took into account McDonnell's unsolicited proposals for what became the Phantom.

DESIGN BRIEF

- Take-off Weight . . . . 29,055 lb
- Design Weight. . . . . 25,493 lb
- Landing Weight . . . . 21,931 lb
- Max Speed (Max Power at 35,000 Ft) . . . . MACH 1.60
- Time to Accelerate (Max Mil Speed to Mach 1.2) . . . . 0.82 min
- Combat Ceiling (Max Power) . . . . 53,200 FT
- Combat Radius (MIL-C-5011A) (Internal Fuel) . . . . . . 407 N MI
- Deck Spotting . . . . 22 airplanes
- Fuel—Basic Internal . . . . 1370 Gal
- Availability After Go-ahead . . . . 20 Months
- Performance Capability With Advanced J57 Engine . . MACH 1.73
- Performance Capabiltiy With J67 Engine. . . . . MACH 2.0

AERODYNAMIC CONFIGURATION

Wing—45-degree Sweep, 5% Thickness, Boundary Layer
Control Flap-Aileron Leading Edge Slats, Wing Tip Droop
Fuselage—High Fineness Ratio, Area Variation Control
Engine—J57-P-(JT3N) 16,000 lb SL Static Thrust

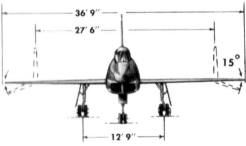

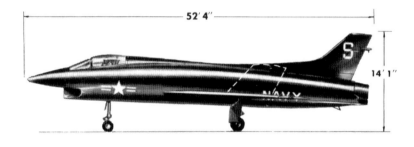

This modified Super Fury was among the possibilities BuAer considered in 1954 as a general-purpose fighter; the brochure was dated 4 June 1954. Compared to the previous year's submission, this one added the Aero 11B fire-control system which could be used to control guns, rockets and missiles. It employed an APQ-50 radar (as in the Skyray) to acquire and track targets. Missile alternatives were four Sparrow II (there was no CW injection) or eight Sidewinders (on four pylons). Another new feature was the variable-geometry inlet under the radar nose to control the oblique shock at the duct. With a J57, this Super Fury would make Mach 1.6 at 35,000ft. That would increase to Mach 1.73 with the advanced J57 and to Mach 2.0 with the J67. Estimated rate of climb at 35,000ft was 11,300ft/min (no sea-level figures were given in the brochure). Radius of action was 407nm. Span was 36ft 9in, length was 52ft 4in and gross weight was 29,055lbs.

ADR had just compared existing and near-term jet engines. The engines of the OS-130 fighters, the J57 and J65, were best suited to a maximum speed of Mach 1.5. The newer J67 and J79 were more suitable for Mach 2.0. Neither had been included in the OS-130 fighters, but to ADR they represented such an advance in quality that it would be appropriate to rerun the competition allowing them. The

navy was already buying Douglas' F4D-2, a much-modified F4D which was soon redesignated F5D-1 (Skylancer). It was used as a baseline for the 1954 general purpose fighter evaluation

This time Grumman submitted not G-97 but instead a modified Tiger it designated G-98D, powered by a more powerful J79 rather than the J57 of the OS-130 competition. Its fuselage was lengthened and its wing thinned, with increased area and more sharply swept (at 45° rather than 35°). It carried more fuel and it had four wing hardpoints. It offered a boundary control system tested in the F9F-4. ADR considered G-98D premature. Its engine was not yet available and the basic G-98 was just reaching flight test status (BuAer did not yet know that development would be protracted).

North American offered a Super Fury based on its much-modified F-100B version of the air force F-100, with a thinner wing and a substantially redesigned fuselage. A sketch showed that the air intake had been relocated aft to a position under the cockpit so that the aircraft could have a massive radar nose. In its brochure North American claimed that the Super Fury could enter production (as then planned)

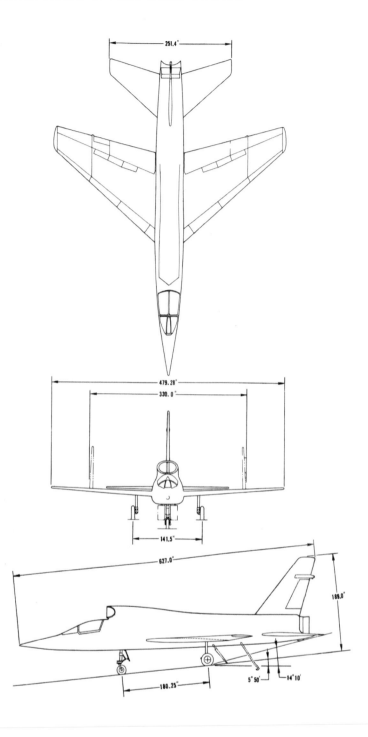

North American called this version of its air force F-107 the FJ-5, although it is unlikely that designation would have been adopted by the navy. As proof of the FJ-4 lineage, North American offered to build one prototype from a production-type fuselage and empennage and an FJ-4 wing and main landing gear. This drawing was dated 6 July 1955, well after the various competitions had ended. This aircraft combined the previous wing with a more powerful J79-GE-X207 or J79-GE-2 engine. The radar would be either North American's NASARR or a government-supplied Magnavox set (as in a Crusader). Armament would have been either two Sidewinders or sixty-eight small-diameter 'Gimlet' rockets carried internally. With a J79-GE-2, estimated speed at 10,000ft would be 663 knots (Mach 1.04); at 35,000ft it would be 828 knots (Mach 1.44). By 1957–8 the engine would be developing greater thrust, so that speed at 35,000ft would be 909 knots (Mach 1.58). With the -GE-2, the aircraft would be able to turn at 1.65G without changing altitude at 50,000ft and it would climb at 31,800ft/min at 10,000ft. Combat radius would be 226nm.

by 1957 because most of its features were now being incorporated in the production F-100B for the air force: the thinned wing with integral fuel tanks, variable-geometry inlet, shaped (area-ruled) fuselage and a new boundary-layer control flap and aileron combination. The fuselage had been reshaped to improve the pilot's view over the nose for landing. Fuel sufficed for a 407nm combat radius. The basic engine was the J57-P (16,000lbs thrust with afterburner), but a 17,200lbs thrust version would be available in 1956–7. The aircraft could accommodate the projected J67. It had four wing hardpoints. North American estimated that with two drop tanks it would have a 991nm area intercept capability and that it could deliver a Super 7 nuclear weapon 874nm away. Speed would be 922 knots (Mach 1.6) at 35,000ft (592 knots without afterburner); rate of climb at 35,000ft would be 11,300ft/min. To emphasise its Fury parentage, North American called this aircraft the FJ-5. The brochure was dated June 1954. Note that the company had previously proposed a Super Fury to meet the OS-130 requirement.

Vought provided some data on a modified Crusader, but it was too late for an August 1954 comparison. To ADR, the F8U was also premature, because the prototype would not fly until the spring of 1955. It was also 'considered too experimental in some quarters to satisfy both the day fighter and general purpose requirements'.

ADR included the new McDonnell designs (F3H-G and –H, which are described in greater detail under the 'single fighter' project below).

In its evaluation, ADR pointed to the need for structural strength both for air-combat manoeuvring and for nuclear delivery (the various loft-bombing manoeuvres). It called for a load factor of 7.5, which only McDonnell was then offering. Both Grumman and North American offered 6.0 and Douglas offered 7.0 in its F4D-2. However, the F3H-G was not fast enough at low altitude. All of the designs showed substantial capacity to carry weapons (typically four hardpoints underwing); all could carry the standard light attack load of one nuclear bomb and one drop tank. ADR commented that this showed that they were conceived more as attack bombers than as general-purpose fighters. McDonnell in particular offered store stations resembling those of past attack bombers (presumably meaning the Skyraider). ADR did not consider that a particular advantage, but it did like the centreline store station, which made possible symmetrical loading instead of the usual combination of a drop tank and a nuclear weapon. At this time a specification for an attack aircraft was being written, presumably around the A4D.

All of the proposed aircraft had the APQ-50 radar then being carried by the F4D interceptor. It was the best available radar, but ADR considered it unsuited to the high speeds the proposed aircraft could attain, the logic being that they would close so quickly with targets that they had to detect them much further away. ADR had just argued in its ADR-1603 report that a future fighter would need an integrated electronic system with far better performance if it was to make full use of its performance. Otherwise its value would be limited by its fire-control system. If all the aircraft had the same radar, with the same size dish, the smaller ones would have an advantage because they would be less detectable by enemy aircraft. That favoured the G-98D, the smallest of all, with the Super Fury coming next. The very large McDonnell aircraft were the worst in this respect. All were superior to the F4D-2 in load-carrying ability and performance.

To ADR a general-purpose fighter was primarily for air-to-air combat, with some attack capability. On that basis the North

Grumman submitted this unsolicited G-118 proposal in December 1955 for the expected BuAer all-weather fighter requirement; BuAer ordered two XF12F-1s but soon cancelled them in favour of the Phantom II. Like the Phantom, it would have had a modified APQ-50 with CW injection, but it would have carried two rather than four Sparrow IIIs supplemented by three Sidewinders, or else two unguided Ding Dong (Genie) nuclear rockets. Two J79-GE-3 engines (as in a Phantom: 10,000lbs thrust, 15,000lbs with afterburner) would have been supplemented by a 5000lb thrust throttleable rocket using hydrogen peroxide. Speed with afterburner would have been Mach 2.0 above 35,000ft and sea-level rate of climb would have been 37,800ft/min (service ceiling 55,600ft). With all missiles on board, the rate of climb at 35,000ft would be 24,150ft/min. Span was 43ft 11.69in and length was 58ft 6in. Take-off weight with two 300-gallon drop tanks was 51,216lbs (combat weight was 37,366lbs). (Grumman)

American GP Super Fury was best for speeds of Mach 1.5 to 1.6, albeit with some reservation as to its strength. Since higher speed (Mach 1.8 to 2.0) was more desirable, it would be best to go back to industry for new designs.

With the G-98D and the modified Crusader out of the running, ADR was left with the Super Fury and the McDonnell proposals. It considered evaluation difficult because the existing J57 and J65 engines had to be matched against the future J67 and J79. Thus a complete picture would have to include a Super Fury and F4D powered by the J67.

All contractor weight estimates except McDonnell's were considered reasonable; McDonnell was about twice as optimistic as any of the others. The twin-engine McDonnell designs offered outstanding speed and climb, speed being limited only by the engine limits below 45,000ft. G-98D offered the high climb rate of the future designs, but it had relatively low thrust and hence low speed and acceleration. Overall, the McDonnell F3H-G and the Super Fury were about equal in speed and climb and slightly superior to the F4D-2. ADR spent considerable effort evaluating manoeuvrability, comparing time to turn 90° and 180°. Such turns would, for example, be required of a fighter attacking an incoming bomber without having a collision-course weapon. In supersonic manoeuvrability the F3H-G and Super Fury were about equal and substantially better than the F4D-2; sub-sonically the F4D-2 was better than the Super Fury, which was better than the F3H-G.

Given current engines, the F3H-G was not good enough to be worthwhile. However, the future F3H-H, powered by the J79, offered outstanding performance. So did a single-engine J67 fighter, either another version of the McDonnell design or a modified Super Fury, at an appreciable weight saving. Yet another factor was the status of the McDonnell plant if the F3H-G was not bought. To ADR, planned continuation of F3H-2 production (as indicated by inclusion of 250 in some 1956 shopping lists) would keep McDonnell healthy enough to work on the ideal F3H-H.

ADR therefore offered four possibilities. One was to defer all action pending establishment of a new operational requirement. A new competition could be held in 1955 allowing the use of the coming J67, J75 and J79 engines. This was the soundest approach from a business relations point of view, but it would be the slowest way to buy aircraft. A second was to select the Super Fury, which offered the highest current performance, in the knowledge that its fuselage could be redesigned to take a J67 or J75, although other chances might be desirable. Alternatively McDonnell's single-engine proposal, F3H-E2, could be selected as the lightest fighter designed around a future engine. If the J67 failed to live up to expectation, it could be powered by a J75 (the J57 would be used in the initial prototypes). Finally, the F3H-G could be selected for its excellent attack capability, twin engine reliability and growth potential, the latter depending entirely on the success of the J79. ADR recommended buying the F3H-G designed for later installation of the J79 as soon as that engine became available. ADR's advice was not followed, except that for the long-term BuAer looked to the F3H-G.

In September 1954, not long after ADR submitted its report, Vought submitted a proposal for what it called a VFA (fighter/attack). In place of the range-only radar and simple gunsight of the day fighter, Vought offered the APG-50 and E-10 fire-control system of the general-purpose Demon, enlarging the radome in the nose to accommodate a 22in dish.[33] For Vought the attack mission was the usual nuclear strike, a fighter delivering a single weapon (store). Normally fighters such as the FJ-4B had at least one other hardpoint, so that they could carry a drop tank on the opposite side. In the case of the Crusader, it was difficult to hang anything heavy from the variable-incidence wing. Vought's solution was to semi-bury the bomb under the fuselage near the centre of gravity (and lift) and to eliminate the need for a drop tank by adding about 300 gallons (equivalent to two drop tanks) to fuselage stowage. The lengths of the landing gear legs would be increased slightly to maintain ground clearance with the bomb in place. Electrical generator and air-conditioning capacity would be increased to cater for the more powerful (hence hotter) electronics. To maintain performance, this heavier aircraft would use a more powerful version of the J79 and the air intake enlarged to match.

Vought saw semi-submerged weapon capacity as a major advantage, since it would not create much drag; it estimated that its proposed aircraft would achieve Mach 1.44 carrying the weapon and Mach 1.46 without it. The extra fuel would greatly expand its radius of action, to 750nm while carrying the bomb or 640nm as a fighter. In fighter configuration, presumably carrying less fuel, the aircraft should be able to achieve Mach 1.51. BuAer did not bite; it was not interested in a Crusader night fighter.

By 1955 the aircraft companies expected BuAer to hold a new competition for an all-weather fighter, an extension of the general purpose fighter concept. Vought and Grumman both submitted proposals, Vought's V-401 (F8U-3) and Grumman's G-118. Meanwhile BuAer

was financing development of the McDonnell F3H-H, the single (unified) fighter which it actually bought in quantity.

Vought described its projected missile-only F8U-3 fighter (V-401) in an October 1955 brochure. It would be armed with three Sparrow III semi-active missiles, two semi-buried in the sides of the fuselage and one underneath. Obvious differences from previous Crusaders were a new intake with a protruding lower lip and two large ventral fins, but the J75 was also considerably larger than its predecessor, so the Crusader III needed a longer fuselage. A much more powerful engine, the 25,000lbs thrust J75-P (JT4B), would increase maximum speed from the Mach 1.6 of the F8U series to Mach 2.2 at 35,000ft (Mach 2.18 at 40,000ft). A data table included a somewhat unusual entry giving the speed attained after accelerating for three minutes from cruising speed at 35,000ft (Mach 2.0). Like the general-purpose fighters offered in 1954, this one would use the APQ-50 radar. Nothing more powerful was immediately available. Although the designed battery was the three Sparrows, Vought offered as alternatives a pair of fixed-fin Sidewinders plus two Sparrows, four fixed-wing Sidewinders and four folding-fin Sidewinders in a submerged launcher which would swing out to fire.

In February 1956 Vought offered a day fighter version armed with the four folding-fin Sidewinders in the submerged pack. Using a modified version of the all-weather airframe, it would be slightly faster (Mach 2.25 rather than 2.0 at 35,000ft). A day fighter using an optimised airframe would be even faster, Mach 2.30. Both would be lighter than the all-weather fighter, hence the speed advantage. This idea went nowhere, because by this time BuAer was no longer interested in a day fighter.

Grumman's parallel project was the G-118, a proposal for which was submitted in December 1955. As in the Super Crusader, the radar was the APQ-50 modified (as already planned, with CW injection) to

Vought's approach to the likely all-weather requirement was the XF8U-3 shown. The company also offered a heavily-modified F8U-2. (*The Hook*)

guide Sparrow missiles. Projected armament was two semi-submerged Sparrows plus three internal Sidewinders (which could be replaced by a third Sparrow). G-118 was a pure all-weather fighter powered, like the Phantom, by two J79-GE-3 engines. In this case they were augmented by a 5000lb rocket burning JP-4 with hydrogen peroxide. The engine had a limiting Mach number of 2.0, which the aircraft could attain. A more advanced version of the engine promised a higher limiting speed. The rocket was apparently included to boost combat ceiling, which would be 75,500ft at Mach 2 (but 56,900ft without the rocket). G-118 would have had swept wings, so broad at the root that they were not too far from a delta. Grumman envisaged a crew of two, including a separate radar operator.

In its proposal, Grumman emphasised its modelling of a task force, which had led it to choose rocket boost, the separate radar operator, mixed armament and enough fuel for an increased CAP cycle time. Its survey of known current projects led it to split possible threats into five categories. The first was long-range subsonic bombers with 100nm stand-off missiles, corresponding to the developing 'Badger'/AS-2 threat (AS-2 was unknown at the time and 'Badgers' were only beginning to enter service). These aircraft had to be intercepted at 55,000ft. A second threat was specialised medium-range subsonic bombers, which would be intercepted at 65,000ft. A third was conventional supersonic-dash medium-range bombers (Mach 1.4 to 1.6, 45,000ft) typified by the B-58 Hustler. A fourth was high performance fighter-bombers (Mach 2, 60,000ft). Finally there were supersonic surface to surface and air-to-surface missiles (Mach 2.5, 75,000ft). The list must have been typical of the time. In practice the important Soviet threat of the 1960s was the first and the supersonic anti-ship missile threat was largely at much lower altitudes. For Grumman the important point was that by 1960 G-118 could not rely entirely on forward-quarter or beam attacks, but instead had to be able to match the speed and altitude of mot potential attackers and also have the ability to turn, climb and accelerate to position itself to attack.

Fighters had to be able to kill targets before they penetrated to within 100nm of task force centre. At this time Grumman was about to offer what became the WF Tracer, which it expected would extend the task force horizon to about 250nm or more from sea level to 80,000ft. Grumman estimated that generally an attacker would be identified by the time it reached a range of 200nm and that plus the 100nm keep-out range defined what was needed. Grumman also argued that it would be impossible to launch interceptors quickly enough on warning, so task force defence would depend on CAP fighters orbiting far from the task force . That in turn demanded substantial endurance, which Grumman set at two hours 'clean' or three with drop tanks. To keep fighters on CAP stations, Grumman pointed to the advantage of air-to-air refuelling, a point a BuAer reader marked as 'very interesting'. This was close enough to generally-understood tactics that it is worth setting down. It appears that the point of Grumman's lengthy discussion was to prove to BuAer that it understood the problem on BuAer's terms. Of the available missiles (Sparrows and Sidewinders), Grumman singled out the semi-active Sparrow III as the only one which allowed beam attacks at long enough range to allow the fighter to re-attack at once on a pursuit course. Sidewinder was valued for its reliability and simplicity; it would be extremely useful for tail attacks. Mixed armament would also defeat countermeasures.

BuAer ordered two prototypes of each design, G-118 being desig-

nated F12F-1; the Super Crusader was designated F8U-3. The two F12F-1 prototypes were, however, soon cancelled, presumably because they were inferior to what became the F4H Phantom. Work on the F8U-3 continued.

There was still a need for all-weather interceptors smaller and less expensive than the Super Crusader. In May 1957 Vought submitted a proposal for an all-weather version of the current production version of the Crusader, the F8U (its V-413 design). It was described as a fighter for the 1959–61 period, available before the Super Crusader. Armament would be two Sparrow III and four Sidewinders, the aircraft being fitted with an APG-51B with CW injection. This was the radar currently carried by the Demon, except that it added CW injection for Sparrow missile guidance. Vought's argument for such an aircraft was that although prospective enemies currently had only limited all-weather capability, in the 1959–61 time period that would change. The enemy would be fielding an all-weather bomber with a 50-mile air-to-surface missile. An interim AEW aircraft could push the early warning envelope out to about 300nm, making it possible for all-weather interceptors and CAP to augment surface-to-air missile defence. Vought assumed that the enemy at this time would be a bomber capable of a Mach 1.3 dash, flying at up to 50,000 to 60,000ft.

Vought's proposed aircraft was an F8U-2 with the same P-16 engine and retaining the internal Sidewinder stowage. It would have a larger nose cone to accommodate the larger radar and a 30-gallon tank was added just forward of the engine feed fuel tank to extend time on station. Careful design limited the effect of added weight, so that the proposed aircraft would weigh only 28,782lbs compared to 28,176lbs for the F8U-2.

The aircraft actually built as the F8U-2N (later F-8D) was armed with two or four Sidewinders, but no Sparrows. Its guns and missiles were controlled by an AWG-4 armament control group built around a Magnavox APQ-83 angle-tracking radar and the same EX-16 fire-control system as the F8U-2 (forming the AWG-4 weapons control system). Compared to the earlier APS-67, the new radar used the same size dish but offered greater power (160kW) and it enjoyed about a 25 per cent range improvement. Most importantly, it would track a target in angle as well as in range, hence could be used for blind fire and all-weather attack. Estimated range on a 1m² target was 20nm. By this time there was a semi-active radar version of the Sidewinder, which could be used to attack from angles at which the target would not be hot enough to create an IR target for a conventional Sidewinder. A new autopilot provided a three-axis attitude hold. The new version of the Crusader had the more powerful (18,000lbs thrust) J57-P-20 engine, which was to give it a maximum speed of Mach 1.57 while carrying four missiles (Mach 1.68 with two missiles). Extra fuel tankage amounted to 75 gallons rather than 30 gallons.

The follow-on F8U-2NE (later F-8E) had the same armament control system. Compared to the F8U-2N it had an improved radar (APQ-94), still part of the same AWG-4 system. APQ-94 was essentially an APQ-83 with a new 20in dish producing a narrower beam. It added auxiliary track on jam and IR slave modes. It retained CW injection for the semi-active Sidewinder. Unlike previous Crusaders, this version had provision to carry ordnance on tandem multiple ejectors, one pair under each wing. Each could carry either a Bullpup (one each side) or three (total twelve) Mk 81 or two (total eight) Mk 82 or one Mk 83 or Mk 84 bomb on each side. Zunis or Sidewinders could be carried on fuselage stub mountings. Bullpup electronics was in a guidance equipment fairing on the wing in the dorsal spine. In addition, it had an AAS-15 IR head on the top centreline of the fuselage immediately forward of the windscreen. Remanufactured aircraft (e.g. F-8H) had further radar improvements to the AWG-4 control system. The F8U-2NE first flew in June 1961 and was first delivered to the fleet in February 1962.

THE SINGLE FIGHTER

DCNO (Air) and BuAer had been rethinking the nature of the fighter. They were buying both fighters and nuclear attack bombers. The new nuclear bombs weighed about as much as four Sparrows, not counting the radar. As always, it would be a great advantage to reduce the number of types of aircraft on board a carrier. In October 1953 DCNO (Air) (Op-05W) asked BuAer to study the question and the Aircraft Design Research branch offered a study called Fighter with Bomber Capabilities (DR 1603: submitted 8 July 1954 but dated June 1954). ADR envisaged a twin-engine aircraft powered by the new J79 engine, the most powerful then available, carrying its armament internally.

ADR argued that guided air-to-air missiles would be far superior to unguided weapons for any fighter of fixed performance, as long as they achieved a certain level of reliability. To support its case, it compared Sparrow and unguided FFAR in an imaginary fight, two groups approaching at Mach 1.5.[34] Using an advanced radar (as then understood), they would detect each other at 10nm, turning towards each other to fire (an attempt to escape would be suicidal). In 12 seconds they would close to 4nm Sparrow range. Missile-armed fighters would fire and evade, the missiles hitting or missing six seconds later. If Sparrow was any good, not too many FFAR fighters would be left to fire back. Under optimistic assumptions, ADR estimated an exchange rate of 4.7 to 1.[35]

The choice of missiles rather than FFARs required the future fighter to carry a weight not far from that of a nuclear bomb, which was the key point (ADR assumed that either would be carried internally and it went so far as to sketch the characteristics of a nuclear stand-off weapon [DR-129]). If the future fighter carried a heavy internal missile load and future fighter and attack aircraft had the same maximum speed, then a series of design studies showed that the difference in configuration, size and weight between the two tended to disappear. If the fighter was given a radius of 400nm (for the fighter combat problem), the radius of the corresponding attack bomber would be about 700nm for the standard low-altitude attack problem and 800nm for the standard high-altitude problem. In the ADR studies, the combat ceiling was nearly 55,000ft. The key to higher combat ability seemed to be lighter engines (lower specific weight, meaning pounds of engine per pound of thrust) with equivalent or better specific fuel consumption.

ADR backed its comments with an elaborate engagement model showing that faster strike aircraft were more likely to survive over enemy territory, hence that it really did make sense to adopt fighter-like attack aircraft. Like the new F4H Phantom, then in the conceptual stage, the assumed fighter was powered by twin J79 engines. That was coincidental; in 1954 the J79 was the coming high-powered jet engine and thus the natural powerplant for a sketched fighter.

It happened that McDonnell offered an unsolicited candidate. By 1953 the Demon programme was clearly in serious trouble, so McDonnell began a series of internal design studies in a series beginning with F3H-A. Despite the designation, they were unrelated to the Demon design. F3H-A through –F were single-engine aircraft;

F3H-G and –H had twin engines. In September 1953 McDonnell showed the F3H-G and -H to BuAer. Both were large twin-engine aircraft designed to be powered initially by J65 engines but later to use the more powerful J79. At this time the J65 was expected to be qualified in the spring of 1955, the J79 following by mid-1957. Both showed general-purpose fighter electronics as in the F3H itself, but both also offered much greater external stores capacity: one underbody station and eight underwing stations. At this time other fighter designs showed as many as four underwing stations. The horizontal tail was relatively high, as in the company's F-101 Voodoo. The all-moving tail and the ailerons were all powered. Boundary layer control would be exerted through suction in the flap leading edges. The company proposed alternative interchangeable forward fuselage sections for alternative configurations including photo and a two-place tandem cockpit. ADR reported on these designs in November 1953 and April 1954.

At the end of May 1954 McDonnell offered a further single-engine (J67) F3H-E2. At this point the J67 was expected to be available earlier than the J79. With minor changes the Pratt & Whitney J75 could be substituted. Other features matched those of the F3H-G and –H.

When ADR evaluated the proposals for general-purpose fighters, it found F3H-G and –H very attractive, but these designs did not really respond to any particular stated or developing requirement. McDonnell may have guessed that while considerable money was being spent on dedicated fighters, something with more of attack flavour had a better chance of securing a contract.[36]

With the existing J65-W-6 engine, McDonnell promised that the F3H-G could fly at 875 knots (Mach 1.52) at 35,000ft, with a combat radius of 400nm and a combat ceiling of 55,500ft. Take-off weight was 34,692lbs, heavy for a contemporary carrier fighter. With the prospective J79, take-off weight would be reduced to 33,932lbs. Performance would be much better: 1133 knots (Mach 1.97) at 35,000ft and a combat ceiling of 59,200ft, but radius would be only 210nm, unacceptable even for a day fighter. McDonnell offered three prototypes for $30 million.[37] BuAer evaluated the proposal in October-November 1953, concluding that McDonnell's performance estimates were optimistic (it estimated the speed of the J65 version at Mach 1.35) and its weight estimate was low by about 1700lbs. It would have stability and control problems: the horizontal tail would be a problem and limitations in the control design would restrict supersonic manoeuvrability. The related hydraulic system was considered unacceptable. Finally, the proposed radar would be unlikely to find a target, presumably on the surface. Given the comparable performance of the F8U and F4D (presumably F4D-2), BuAer saw little point in buying the aircraft.

However, the McDonnell proposals were included in the list of all-weather fighters considered informally in June 1954. This time DCNO (Air) wanted a twin-engine design and McDonnell's J79 version was the best of the designs considered. Further wind tunnel tests showed that the J79 version would make Mach 2.0 and the J65 version Mach 1.44, but the estimated combat radius of the J79 version was now down to only 150nm, half the usual day fighter figure. BuAer rejected what it called McDonnell's structural design philosophy of negative margins of safety and considered its structural limit speed too low. Many other structural features were unacceptable. The fire-control proposal was vague, the fuel system was too complex and vague and the J79 engine was not expected to qualify for fleet service until June 1957. McDonnell's weight estimates were still considered 1500lbs too low, before any structural redesign.

However, the design was so promising that on 3 September 1954 the chief of BuAer ordered two aircraft, designated in the attack class (AH-1) for delivery in March and May 1957. McDonnell received a letter of intent and asked to rewrite his original detail specification. When that arrived at BuAer in November 1954, it revealed that McDonnell still assumed numerous deviations from standard practice. Its aircraft was not designed to fight at Mach 2. The J65 engine required special modifications to fit the aircraft (the –W-12 was substituted).

By this time Wright, the engine builder, was in trouble; in early April its planned delivery date slipped seven months. Now it estimated that its J65-W-12 would pass its 50-hour test in March 1956 and would be 150-hour qualified in February 1957 (BuAer thought it would be June 1957). Meanwhile General Electric's J79 programme was moving faster. It estimated that the much more powerful J79-GE-3 would be 50-hour qualified in October 1955 and 150-hour qualified a year later. The J79-GE-2 planned for the new fighter would be 150-hour qualified 22 months after the navy contracted for it. BuAer's estimates were somewhat more pessimistic, but in fact the J79-GE-1 was 50-hour qualified in October 1955 and the J79-GE-3 in December 1956.

Meanwhile detail redesign and the heavier –W-6 engine had added

By 1955 DCNO (Air) and BuAer were interested in a single fighter which could function both as a fleet interceptor and as a nuclear bomber. McDonnell's twin-engine fighter, which had been conceived as an attack aircraft, fitted this requirement. The F4H-1 Phantom II prototype was identifiable by its small radome covering its APQ-50 radar. The object underneath is an IR sensor. The combination of high speed, a powerful radar and semi-actively guided missiles made forward-hemisphere attacks practicable, because targets could be detected early enough to be engaged. The air intake shape was revised in production aircraft.

3662lbs to the AH-1 (with J65-W-12 engines). The only compensating weight reduction was 488lbs saved mainly by reducing store stations to five. Additional weight included the LABS over-the-shoulder bombing system required for the primary attack role, nuclear strike.

Because the McDonnell design had not been conceived to meet any particular military requirement, in effect one had to be written around it. In October 1954 BuAer sent its proposed design criteria and military requirements to DCNO (Air), who signed off on it in November. However, there were still issues. In December 1954 DCNO (Air) specifically withdrew a requirement for a two-seat version. The entire programme was reviewed at a Pentagon conference on 31 March 1955.[38] Issues were whether to continue the programme at all, the military capability of the aircraft, its performance, size, weight and expected dates of delivery to the fleet. The programme was kept alive with the proviso that BuAer review performance, weight and configurations. By this time BuAer and McDonnell finally agreed on weights and BuAer accepted McDonnell's performance estimates. However, as of early April the detail specification was not yet ready for signature because no military requirement had yet been written, BuAer had not yet decided which engine to use and there were still substantial disagreements between it and McDonnell. In mid-April BuAer finally decided to replace the J65 with the more powerful J79 engine. On 31 May an OpNav directive finally specified the desired features, including the decision (which BuAer had opposed) to arm the new aircraft only with missiles and a nuclear bomb.[39]

Only at this point did DCNO (Air) formally decided that the McDonnell aircraft would be an all-weather fighter rather than an attack-fighter; it was redesignated F4H-1. Beside the J79 engine, DCNO (Air) specified

- A minimum of four Sparrow III missiles.
- A radar with Sparrow III capability and detection performance equivalent to APQ-50.
- A simple lightweight semi-automatic navigational device.
- A three-hour cycle time. When DCNO (Air) circulated characteristics in February 1956, the fighter was credited with a 2.9-hour cycle time using drop tanks.
- Visual delivery capability for special (i.e. nuclear) weapons. At this stage the aircraft was to be able to carry the older Mk 7, the new Mk 28 (a powerful thermonuclear weapon also used by the air force) and the navy Mk 91 on its flush-mounted centreline rack. In July 1956 the Mk 7 and Mk 91 requirements were both deleted. An important point was that the original hope of using the aircraft for all-weather nuclear attack was abandoned (at a December 1954 conference in DCNO (Air)). At that time it seemed that all-weather attack would require a separate large antenna and a separate large computer; no existing equipment would meet this requirement and no true blind-bombing device (aside from the ASB-1 of the heavy AJ and A3D bombers) was likely to be available before 1960. The nose of the aircraft would not accommodate the ASB-1 or the radar without complete redesign. The alternative of inertial navigational and/or bombing equipment would not be ready before 1960. The APQ-50 offered limited blind-bombing capability via its ground-mapping feature. It seemed, moreover, that enlarging the nose radar dish beyond 24in diameter would probably require redesign of the rest of the aircraft if it were to retain supersonic capability. The standard Aero 21 visual bombing system provided the necessary low-level (LABS) visual nuclear delivery capability. The 1955 correspondence suggests that the special weapons capability was retained because it cost virtually nothing in aircraft weight or performance and when DCNO (Air) listed characteristics in February 1956 special weapons capability was an option to be used if the current attack programme, probably meaning the A3J (A-5) Vigilante, encountered problems.
- Counter-countermeasures against enemy communications and radar jamming.

At this point McDonnell expected to carry the four Sparrows on wing pylons, but BuAer wanted something offering less drag. That was the origin of the semi-submerged arrangement the Phantom had (which was considered good for an increase in speed of Mach 0.35). McDonnell now offered both one- and two-seat versions. The DCNO (Air) Air Warfare Division firmed characteristics during early July 1955. On this basis a 19 July 1955 DCNO (Air) letter added further details:

- As a back-up for Sparrow III, the aircraft would be designed with space and weight for Sparrow II and unguided rockets. In July 1956 the backup armament was specified as at least two Sparrow II and two Sidewinders. The unguided rocket requirement was dropped. The Sparrow II problem was solved by carrying them (if desired) on wing pylons.
- The CW injection equipment (for Sparrow III) would be inter-changeable with a computer need to aim unguided air-to-air rockets.
- As a means of overcoming radar jamming, an IR detection and tracking device; if that could not be provided, visual control of the radar illuminator used by the Sparrow III missile. At this time an alternative infra-red guided Sparrow III was being discussed; it never materialised.

- Jump up (and down) missile firing for a 15,000ft altitude difference, the fighter flying level.
- Minimum performance using JP-5 fuel were Mach 2 with missiles on board and a combat ceiling of 55,000ft.
- A two-man crew (pilot and radar operator).
- Semi-submerged missiles.

McDonnell signed the revised detail specification on 20 July. The aircraft company was not responsible for the fire-control system, so at this point BuAer began work on that. This was the first navy all-missile fighter, so responsibility for fire control went to the BuAer Guided Missile Division rather than, as was usual, to the Armament Division; the system was the Airborne Missile Control System (AMCS) Aero X1A. It consisted of the Westinghouse APQ-50 radar, Raytheon CW injection (to guide the Sparrow III missile) and the Mk 16 Mod 0 optical sighthead. As a space and weight backup to use unguided rockets and the self-guided Sparrow II, Raytheon developed an alternative system using a North American computer.

Raytheon received the lead contract for the fire-control system. There was no system integrator as such. In this situation the formal specification describing the fire-control system was badly needed so that all parties could understand what they were doing. It was seriously delayed; in August 1956 it had not yet been received by BuAer. The delay suggests that the weapon system was the most difficult part of the programme, with the greatest potential to delay or derail it. It did not help that Sparrow III was a new weapon, which had not been on board any previous fighter (it was very different from the beam-riding Sparrow I already in service). Sparrow II was listed as a back-up because it made much less demand on the system on board the fighter. Unfortunately the two missiles differed in length, wing location and even in the location of the umbilical plug.

When BuAer was told that any all-weather nuclear attack system would require an antenna so large as to impair fighter performance, it chose to develop the new aircraft as a fighter with a visual nuclear attack role. At least initially this was much the aircraft ADR had described in ADR-1603 about a year earlier. Once the fighter role had been made primary, the visual special weapons capability was reduced to a secondary mission using only the Mk 28 bomb.[40] However, BuAer still valued the new aircraft's unequalled sea-level speed not only for overmatching other fighters and bombers, but also in the nuclear role.

The choice could have gone the other way. The BuAer Fighter Branch correspondence on the early history of the F4H-1 includes a 6 July 1956 memo pointing out that the contemporary Vigilante (A3J, later A-5) strategic bomber could be turned into a fighter by replacing its bombing radar (APS-60) with an air-to-air radar (APQ-50 or APQ-47) and modifying the lower fuselage for semi-submerged Sparrows. The question was revived in January 1960. This time the answer was that neither aircraft was an efficient replacement for the other. The F4H was smaller and cheaper and had higher performance; it was cheaper to buy a mix of both.[41] The A3J actually was proposed as a North American Air Defense fighter.

From a fighter perspective, perhaps the most important development during 1954–6 was transformation from a very short-range aircraft to a long-endurance CAP fighter, thanks to the long cycle time. By early 1956 the F4H-1 was expected to operate on station 150–300nm from base, giving it a three-hour cycle time. It was expected to achieve Mach 2 speed (1150 knots) from 35,000ft to

An F-4B (F4H-1) of VX-4, 16 April 1963, shows not only the standard four Sparrows but also four Sidewinders and two bomb-sized drop tanks. Compared to the prototype, the production F-4B had an enlarged radome for its APQ-72 radar, with a new AAA-4 IR sensor underneath it. It had a retractable refuelling probe on the starboard side of the nose and enlarged cooling inlets on both sides for the more powerful radar. The intake ramps were enlarged and the intakes themselves were revised, the canopy line was raised and a window added between the two seats. Of two pitots visible on the leading edge of the vertical tail fin, one was a sensor for the stabilator feel system (the controls were powered, hence did not offer any feel). There was a ram air intake at the base of the fin. Late production F-4Bs had a ventral bump on the AAA-4 IR sensor for an APR-30 radar-warning and homing receiver, with another APR-30 atop the tail (the forward one was not always fitted). A UHF blade antenna was added atop the spine of the aircraft (another was already under the nose). The inboard leading edge of the wing was fixed and the mid- and outer wing leading edge flaps were blown. Some aircraft were later given slotted stabiliators. The nose oleo could be extended to increase the angle of attack on take-off. Aircraft received essentially this configuration from the nineteenth on, the B series (F4H-1F) formally beginning with Block 6.

48,000ft and a sea level speed of 747 knots (strength for flight limited it to 800 knots). The limit on speed was engine inlet temperature rather than drag, so it could not go any faster until engines could withstand higher inlet temperatures. On a CAP mission the aircraft would normally carry a belly tank, using that fuel until it approached combat. At supersonic speed at 35,000ft, it would burn 3400–5000lbs of fuel in five minutes, so it needed all the reserves it could get at that point.

The mock-up conference, the step before a prototype was built, was held on 17–23 November 1955. As of April 1956, the first flight was expected on 31 October 1957 (the prototype actually flew on 27 May 1958). The projected schedule did not compare well with the recorded performance of other programmes: it amounted to 36 months from go-ahead to first flight and 27 months from detailed specification to first flight. That was by far the longest of any current fighter. The F8U-1 went from contractual go-ahead (June 1953) to first flight (March 1955) in 21 months and the Grumman F11F-1 Tiger took only 15 months from go-ahead (May 1953) to first flight (July 1954). The shortest time was for the FJ-4 Fury, 12 months from go-ahead (October 1953) to first flight (October 1954).

Even so, by 1956 the F4H programme was operating on a rush basis, McDonnell working 46-hour weeks. Those involved wrote afterwards that they had barely put the programme together and that they were amazed that it worked so well. The F4H became the most successful of the navy's jet fighters, the Phantom II (Phantom I was the much earlier FH-1). A few prototype F4H-1s were followed by the production F4H-2, the main difference being replacement of the small-dish APQ-50 by a larger-dish (36in) APQ-72, which incorporated the desired CW injection. As desired, it had the AAS-4 infra-red detector under its nose in a prominent fairing. Contrary to initial intent, it could deliver a range of nuclear bombs, Mk 28, Mk 45 and Mk 57, and it could carry a wide variety of conventional bombs and rockets on its pylons.

When all naval aircraft were redesignated in 1962, the Phantom II became the F-4, the initial version being the F-4A and the main naval

production version the F-4B (the air force got the F-4C, -4D and -4E).

The one important feature which could not be incorporated in the F4H-1 was a data link. Fighter control via data link was an important feature envisaged in the Naval Tactical Data System/Air Tactical Data System (NTDS/ATDS) fleet digital system. In 1956 Collins, which was developing Link 11, asked BuAer whether the new fighter would incorporate a surface-to-air or air-to-air link. It was told that the link was desirable, but that BuAer would not use it until it had been thoroughly tested – an impossibility given how embryonic the whole NTDS/ATDS system then was. The F4H did have space provided for a link and twelve aircraft, designated F-4G, were fitted with ASW-21 Link 4 receivers for service tests. They were operational over Vietnam beginning in 1965. These aircraft reverted to F-4Bs after the tests, the F-4G designation being used for 'Wild Weasel' anti-radar F-4s.[42]

The F-4J was the second major naval production version, incorporating a coherent pulse-Doppler radar (APG-59 in the AWG-10 system). Pulse-Doppler operation gave the radar the first US naval look-down capability. AWG-10 was the first radar in US naval service to use a computer-generated waveform and therefore it was a true multi-mode radar. It was less powerful than the AWG-9 then being developed for the F-111B (and placed in service on board the F-14 Tomcat), with an average power of 1kW, but it could still detect another F-4 at 100nm and lock-on at 40nm (when briefing the British Phantom mission in January 1964, BuWeps estimated that against a $10m^2$ target the radar would have an 85 per cent of detection at 47nm with wide scan and 47nm with narrow scan). Estimated 85 per cent range against a 'Blinder' (Tu-22) with wide scan (narrow scan would increase range by about 20 per cent) was 43nm head-on, with target and fighter both at 35,000ft and the fighter flying at Mach 1.8, the

The power designed to lift numerous air-to-air missiles could also lift bombs. Maximum bomb load was about 16,000lbs. For example, an F-4B could carry up to eight 1000lb bombs. Alternatively, it could carry considerable extra fuel: the centreline hardpoint was plumbed for a 600-gallon fuel tank and the two outer pylons for 370-gallon ones. These F-4Bs of VF-213 were photographed en route to North Vietnam from *Kitty Hawk*, 23 January 1968.

target at Mach 1.5. With the bomber at right angles to the fighter, the range would increase to 100–110nm. The really important improvement was against a low flier. Against a bomber at 500ft, with the fighter also at 500ft and flying at Mach 0.95, the target at Mach 0.8, the bomber could still be detected head-on at 45nm and beam-on at 100–110nm, a performance absolutely inconceivable in the past. The pure pulse-Doppler mode could be switched to a pulse mode for air-to-air ranging. There were also pulse air-to-ground modes: mapping (including pulse compression for a range of 200nm and a high-contrast mode), terrain-following and Doppler navigation (i.e. Doppler-derived ground speed and drift angle, provided to the ASN-39 navigation computer). In addition, there was a 200 Watt CW injection to provide illumination for the Sparrow missile. Unlike the contemporary AWG-9 in the F-14, AWG-10 had no track while scan capability, because it was not connected to a digital computer (the F-4J had an analog fire-control system).

A two-way ASW-21 data link was used to vector the interceptor. It provided the fighter-control system on board a carrier or an E-2 with fuel and weapon status. In return it provided data overlaid on the radar display showing target identification, optimum target to attack and command steering information for the pilot. It also connected the fighter to the automatic carrier landing system.

The F-4J also had a new bombing system (AJB-10 vs -3). AWG-

10 was designed to be compatible with the Walleye television-guided missile. This version of the Phantom also had a more powerful - GE-10 (rather than -2 or -2A) engine and heavier undercarriage to permit greater landing weight.

The choice

By 1956, when the F4H was being developed on a rush basis, two fighters were at the development stage, the other being the F8U-3 Super Crusader. The two were often described as alternatives, not really direct competitors, but both were long-range all-weather fighters. As early as March 1958 it seemed likely that the navy could buy only one and CNO Admiral Arleigh Burke and others favoured the F4H for its superior all-weather capability. However, until late in the year no decision was necessary.

An F-4J of VF-161 (*Midway*) is shown on the catapult, en route to an attack on North Vietnam. Its AWG-10 pulse-Doppler radar was credited with the ability to lock-on to a 5m² target at the same altitude (35,000ft) at 38nm head-on and 52nm tail-on. That compared with 23nm head-on and 28nm tail-on for the APQ-72 of the earlier F-4B, which had the same size radar dish. The APQ-72 had essentially no high-altitude look-down capability (taken as looking down from 35,000ft to sea level or from 5000ft to sea level). From 35,000ft the AWG-10 could lock-on at 42nm head-on or 39nm tail-on; the figures for 5000ft were 44nm and 16nm. At low altitude the APQ-72 could lock onto a target at the same altitude. At 5000ft the figures for AWG-10 were 38nm head-on and 14nm tail-on (because the target would generate less Doppler because it was moving at a speed closer to that of the fighter). Because the APQ-72 was unaffected by this change in relative speed, it could lock on to a head-on target at 20nm and to a tail-on target at 25nm. Its performance deteriorated at lower altitude; at 200–500ft, it could lock on to a head-on target at 12nm and to a tail-on target at 15nm, but AWG-10 could lock onto a head-on target at 38nm (but onto a tail-on one at only 6nm).

The decision was forced by the House Armed Services Committee, which approved fighter production money in the FY59 budget but only on condition that the navy choose one or the other. Even without a forced choice, buying both aircraft in smaller numbers would probably make each about 17 per cent costlier. Until that point both aircraft had been developed concurrently. Both had essential the same fire-control system, except that the F4H had a dedicated radar operator.

The Navy Air Board met on 1 December, choosing the F4H. Experiments showed that a dedicated radar operator would detect targets at about 50 per cent greater range because, staring at the radar scope, they would often see the first echo. A pilot concentrating on flying would glance periodically at his radar scope. The second-seater radar intercept officer (RIO) ensured a higher probability of target acquisition and lock-on and greater assurance that lock-on would be maintained (or of regaining it if it were lost). Moreover, the F4H had greater weapon-system growth potential, because it could accommodate a larger radar dish without interfering with its air intakes. Too, the F4H carried four Sparrow air-to-air missiles against the Super Crusader's three.

The F4H was already fitted to carry bombs, but the Super Crusader wing could not be fitted with the necessary hardpoints short of major redesign (this point was not raised in other explanations of the choice). The pilot could concentrate on flying, which would give him a better chance not to fly into the water or the ground. Similarly, he would be better able to overcome enemy countermeasures by using his rudder while the RIO handled his radar controls. A single pilot could not easily do both.

Two engines would buy reliability and reduce the accident rate. At this time the accident rate (per 10,000 hours) for twin-engine fighters was 4.6, compared to 6.7 for single-engine fighters. The accident rate

due to engine problems was only 0.47 for twin-engine fighters, but 1.7 – more than three times as much – for single engines. The Air Board report noted that the air force's twin-engine F-101 had flown over 28,000 hours without any engine-caused accident, although it had been forced to make numerous one-engine landings. At this time it had the lowest accident rate among the air force's 'Century Series' supersonic fighters, 1.48. The worst was 6.73 for the single-engine F-104.

The F4H would also be easier to maintain and to handle on deck, because it was smaller than the Super Crusader and its engine was short enough to fit existing storerooms. Its engines and fire-control system were more accessible.

AN AFFORDABLE NAVAL AIR FORCE: THE LATE 1950S

Through 1958 the navy budget tightened, partly because of the rising cost of the Polaris programme and the surface-to-air missiles (and ships). DCNO (Air) deleted seventy-six F3H-2 Demons from the FY58 budget, together with 122 A4D-2E Skyhawks. On 27 February 1958 BuAer suggested killing production of the big (and very expensive) A3J Vigilante.

Looking to the 1960–70 period covered by the Long Range Objectives studies, DCNO (Air) had to admit in May 1958 that he could not afford the best aircraft in sufficient numbers to fill out the carrier air groups within the fixed aircraft budget, then taken as $2 billion per year. He wanted to maintain sixteen attack carrier air groups, ten ASW air groups, thirty patrol plane squadrons and three Marine wings. An early possibility was to eliminate all Naval Reserve fighters and attack aircraft and to reduce Reserve ASW aircraft. Although some advanced aircraft (Phantom/Super Crusader) could be bought, much of the fleet would have to operate for at least part of the period using aircraft (such as the F8U-2N) which might be considered modern in 1959 but somewhat dated in 1965.

At this time the active fleet at any one time was to include a strike force (two attack carriers) in each of the four numbered fleets (2nd off

This VF-213 F-4J was photographed on board *Kitty Hawk*, early 1976. By that time F-14 Tomcats were replacing the F-4 in service. Distinguishing features were the absence of the earlier IR sensor under the nose, a bulged inner wing root to take larger wheels, a TACAN antenna on the spine about half way back and a new APR-32 radar homing and warning (RHAW) system with antennas both under the after end of the radome and under the juncture of wing leading edge and fuselage.

the Atlantic Coast, 3rd off the Pacific Coast, 6th in the Mediterranean, 7th in the Far East).

Thus the affordable fleet, as envisaged in 1958, would have half of its air groups modernised by 1965, meaning twenty-eight of the best fighters (Phantoms or Super Crusaders) backed by four AEW (NTDS) aircraft (Hawkeyes) and four photo-reconnaissance fighters (F8U-2P Crusaders). That might be overly optimistic; another study of fleet air defence for this period pointed out that in 1965 NTDS would not yet be in many ships and the analog WF-2 would still be the main AEW aircraft. The other forty-eight aircraft would be strike types: twelve Intruders, twenty-four Skyhawks (A4D-2N) and twelve heavy attack Vigilantes (A3J, later redesignated A-5). Thus all of the attack aircraft would be capable of night operation, when enemy air opposition would be minimised.

The other half of the carrier air groups would have F8U-2N fighters with limited all-weather capability, controlled by analog AEW aircraft (WF-2s). Instead of modern Intruders and Vigilantes, their attack aircraft would be twelve of the older heavy attack bombers (A3D-2 Skywarriors) and the rest would be light attack bombers (A4D-2Ns). The attack aircraft would be unable to fly into enemy territory at high speed at low altitude and thus they would be more susceptible to enemy fighters and anti-aircraft missiles.

Note the implicit assumption that the Crusaders would be phased out in favour of gunless Phantoms. The mix of Phantoms and Crusaders turned out to be a useful one once war broke out in Vietnam. Although the Crusader had a limited air-to-surface capability, it was primarily an air-superiority fighter with the navy's last fighter guns on board. The 1958 study (and other contemporary studies focused on fleet air defence) generally did not contemplate a Korea-like situation in which US naval attack aircraft would have to break through an enemy fighter defence. Nor did it envisage the IFF problem encountered in Vietnam, which badly hobbled an all-missile fighter and made guns far more important. In this environment the air force, which had no equivalent of the fleet air defence mission, was more than willing to adopt a version of the F-4 with a smaller radar and an inboard gun.

The navy had a more serious problem, because it could not play down fleet air defence. Guns would have been useless against big Soviet missile bombers with their stand-off weapons. Even the Sparrow might be considered too short-legged. There was apparently no interest in continued Crusader production, although existing ones were upgraded during the war.

THE BRITISH EMERGENCY FIGHTER PROGRAMME

For the Royal Navy in Korea, the situation was worse; jets were coming, but the carriers which fought the war were equipped with the propeller fighters entering service just after the war: Sea Furies, Fireflies and Seafires (the light carriers involved were too small to operate Sea Hornets). Adequate jet fighters were further off (in 1950 the British defence programme was still oriented towards a 'year of maximum danger' of 1957). There was some interest in an interim naval jet comparable to the Fury or the Cougar, but it seemed unlikely that it would be ready much before aircraft already under development. For the time being, the Royal Navy would make do with two early-generation jet fighters, the Supermarine Attacker and the Hawker Sea Hawk.

When war broke out in Korea, the Royal Navy had Attacker and Sea Hawk about to enter limited service and projects underway for the higher-performance Supermarine N.113 and the swept-wing DH 110 day/night fighter, of which the Supermarine fighter had been conceived as insurance against the failure of the earlier Sea Hawk. On the other hand, its very powerful engines offered much greater performance.

Like the US Navy, the Royal Navy became interested in interim high-performance fighters. Unlike the US Navy, it had been interested since the Second World War in developing such aircraft, but it had been thwarted by limited funds. In 1950 the two obvious candidate interim fighters were the two new RAF swept-wing aircraft, the Hawker Hunter and the Supermarine Swift. In 1952 a Staff Requirement (NA 34) was issued for twenty hooked Swifts as interim high-performance day fighters pending availability of the Supermarine N.113, which had been under development since 1947.[43] These aircraft were not intended as naval fighters, but rather as a means of familiarising pilots with the problems of operating a high-performance swept-wing fighter (Fifth Sea Lord did not, however, rule out limited operational use). A fully navalised Swift would be insurance against either the failure of the N.113 project or a further emergency occurring before the N.113 could enter service. One problem was high approach speed, which would impose high landing forces. They would be acceptable for a batch of twenty special training aircraft, but not for any operational version. Thus navalisation of the twenty hooked Swifts would be limited to arrangements for catapulting and arresting, the weight with drop tank not to exceed 19,000lbs (which required a reduction from four to two Aden cannon). The aircraft was expected to launch without using an afterburner (re-heat) from the 150ft BS 4

catapult with 15 knots wind over deck and from the 138.5ft version with 21 knots wind over deck (i.e. it could be launched from a carrier in a calm). With JATO (RATOG) in overload condition its take-off run was not to exceed 500ft with 35 knots of wind over the deck. Time to reach 45,000ft was not to exceed seven minutes using the afterburner, far less than what N.113 promised. Maximum speed at 45,000ft was to be at least 530 knots (609.5mph). These performance figures, which presumably mirrored actual Swift performance, were far less impressive than those claimed for either of the two new longer-term naval fighters.

THE RADAR PROBLEM

Before the Korean War broke out there were already concerns that existing radars were ineffective against jets. A jet carrying drop tanks or bombs was relatively easy to detect, but it moved about twice as fast as Second World War carrier bombers. A jet aircraft in clean condition was much more difficult to detect. This was probably the first experience of what became the stealth problem: the streamlined shape of the aircraft reflected incoming radar pulses away from the radar which produced them. The longer the wavelength, the less aircraft shape counted. The faster the incoming aircraft, the fewer scans a radar of a given range would make before the aircraft reached some critical range (for example, 20nm in the 1948 interceptor problem).

At the end of the Second World War the US Navy began to deploy higher-frequency air-search radars operating in the L-band (about 1200 MHz, 25cm wavelength) rather than the P-band (1.5m, 200 MHz) beginning with a new radar designated SR. The advantages of the higher frequency were supposed to be fewer fades for better coverage and a smaller antenna for the same beam width. Initial antenna problems were solved, the post-war versions being the widely-deployed SPS-6 and -12. In 1948 a US officer told a CIC symposium that these radars had solved the fading problem, but their antenna design was poor – there was 'not enough antenna'. Ranges were no more than 20–30nm, which was unacceptable. The antennas of the L-band radars were redesigned, the standard versions with better antennas being SPS-6A and -6B. The somewhat later SPS-12, which was also important in the 1950s, was a redesigned SPS-6.

As of 1948, SPS-6 was considered effective against jets up to 20,000ft, but poor above 25,000ft; the improved -6A and -6B could, it was hoped, detect much higher fliers. An SPS-6B detected two F2H Banshees at 80nm at 43,000ft, with no fading within 70nm. They were closing at 450 knots. Earlier radars seldom gave half as much. In other tests, SPS-6 detected two propeller-driven fighters at 30,000ft at 60nm, but range against a Phantom jet fighter (FH) was only two-thirds of that. SPS-6B was able to detect a B-29, the stand-in for Soviet heavy bombers, flying at about 31,000ft at a range of 145nm, which was the sort of performance needed for effective interception. For the first time in US experience, these radars were affected by the sort of sea clutter that airborne early warning sets experienced.

In exercises off Korea (ADEPT) SPS-6 typically detected a flight of four jets closing from 125nm at 350 knots at assigned altitude at a range of 63nm, which was not enough to intercept them The other radars did worse: the late-war SRa detected the jets at 30.2nm and the wartime SC-2 at 39nm. A few times the jets were detected at 120nm, but 17 per cent of the time they were never detected at all.

Radars sometimes did perform well. The destroyer *Radford* achieved the best reliability with her SPS-6B. She could detect a B-29

271

at 20,000ft 180nm away – and the main Soviet threat at this time was a B-29 copy, the Tu-4. A seaplane (PBM Mariner) could be detected at 105nm and twelve or more propeller-driven carrier aircraft at 15,000ft could be detected at 185nm. A group of twelve or more jets at 25,000ft could be detected at 140nm, but a single jet at 12,000ft could be detected only at 55nm and a group of four (at 20,000ft) at 95nm. Probability of detection of the single jet was 50 per cent (75 per cent at 35nm). Similarly, the twelve jets could be detected with 75 per cent probability of detection at 100nm. The fleet considered the SPS-6B its best air-search radar, but according to a navy evaluation report, 'no radar presently installed can be depended upon to detect and track consistently small numbers of approaching jet fighters at ranges beyond 30 to 40 miles'.

The figures were worrisome because a target had to be detected at long range to scramble fighters. So many of them were needed for strike missions that by 1953 fleet air defence used deck-launched interceptors. Because Korea was a limited war, interception required that the fighter pilot inspect the incoming aircraft and communicate with CIC before receiving permission to make a pass. That pushed the desired interception range from 20nm to 25nm. Any air action had to break off 10nm from the carrier to allow the destroyers to use their anti-aircraft guns, interference between fighters and surface guns being a perennial problem.

To deal with a 300-knot Tu-4 flying at 30,000ft, Panthers required that it be detected 78nm out (Corsairs needed 84nm). That was barely possible, but under the same rules a MiG or a modern 500-knot bomber had to be detected 146nm out (for Panther interception; Corsairs could not deal with such targets). Each minute of delay brought a 300-knot bomber 5nm closer, a 400-knot bomber 6.7nm closer. In fifteen days of exercises, Task Force 77 improved its performance to the point at which maximum detection range was 100nm and more than half the time targets were detected beyond 53nm.

Time lines included three minutes of decision time by the CIC before launching a fighter. Launching would take four minutes, including the carrier's turn into the wind, alerting the catapult crew and the launch crew, giving final instructions to the pilot and getting him into his aircraft. That did not include time to altitude. If the ship was running downwind, launch time might be as long as seven minutes.

The two-dimensional air-search radars worked with heightfinders. Carriers off Korea had SX, which in effect integrated an early version of SPS-6 with an S-band heightfinder. Unlike wartime heightfinders which tilted the antenna up and down to find a target, it (and its successors) rapidly scanned a narrow beam up and down, typically over an arc of 8° or 11°, using a special Robinson scanner. It turned out that SX had an average maximum range of only 32nm and it got altitude only 18 per cent of the time. The Second World War SP had an average maximum range of 28nm, but it got altitude on 40 per cent of raids.

The main early post-war heightfinder was SPS-8, with a 5ft x 15ft orange-peel shaped antenna. It was stabilised in roll and pitch. SPS-8B substituted a higher-gain nearly circular antenna (12 x 15ft). When the new antenna was combined with a much more powerful radar tube, the radar became SPS-30. SPS-8 and -30 were the standard heightfinders of US carriers through the mid-1960s. A combination of S-band and little dwell time limited range: SPS-8 was considered effective out to only 65nm against a typical fighter target (1m²). In Korean War tests it detected the jets at an average of 68nm, but it obtained altitude information on only 70.8 per cent of runs. However, SPS-30 was con-

sidered good to 250nm or 395nm if it did not scan in elevation.

The heightfinders could be directed to look in a set direction, the feed nodding the beam up and down up to twenty times each minute or they could scan in azimuth as well. Typically a carrier had a long-range air-search set and a heightfinder, their data co-ordinated in her CIC. That introduced another problem. If the picture in CIC was becoming saturated, CIC could not be sure that both of the carrier's radars were pointing at the same air target. Although the search and heightfinding antennas of the late-war SX radar were located on the same massive pedestal, it did not solve this control problem: the two radars did not rotate together.

Moreover, IFF had not been modernised on board all US aircraft since the Soviets had received Mk III systems as wartime allies. That denied CICs a vital means of disentangling what air targets they did detect; a Mk III 'friendly' might well be anything but. Some more modern aircraft had the current Mk V and Mk X systems.

Given the limitations of its shipboard radars, Task Force 77 asked for land-based AEW aircraft, which were still the late-war Cadillac 2s. AEW Ron (Squadron) 1 sent three of its PB-1Ws to Atsugi in Japan for about six weeks (early February 1953 through 25 March 1953). They formed a 50nm barrier centred 30–40nm from the task force, athwart the threat axis. They were better than shipboard radars, but they could not determine the height of a target. On average they could detect low fliers 32nm out, giving shipboard interceptors time to get to them. Results were limited by land but were still considered impressive. The carriers had their own AEW aircraft (Skyraiders [AD-3W]) but they were used for submarine (snorkel) detection rather than AEW. A 1953 evaluation pointed out that the standard carrier formation, unchanged since the Second World War, was too tight if an enemy used nuclear weapons.

The first US Navy response to the jets was a much longer-range search radar, which would have more opportunities to detect an incoming jet: the huge diamond-shaped S-band SPS-2. It was far too large for a carrier, but when it was conceived the navy planned flush decks and only small radar antennas for future carriers. SPS-2 appeared only on board the task force command ship *Northampton* and the missile cruiser *Galveston*. Even after carriers were redesigned with islands, SPS-2 was far too massive for them.

SPS-2 was conceived primarily to gain range, with accuracy a side benefit. It began as a radar to detect long-range high-altitude targets like the German V-2 ballistic missile and then became a central warning radar with some air-control possibilities. The designers used fixed stacked beams to achieve a degree of heightfinding. The designers admitted that any such radar would confuse the heights of two targets on the same bearing, but considered that acceptable – surely it was unlikely that two high-speed targets would stay together for one or two scans. All earlier heightfinders had swept narrow beams up and down to find the elevation angle of an aircraft. They might offer the desired precision, but sweeping up and down drastically limited the time the beam would dwell on any place in the air, hence the probability of detecting any aircraft.

At this time it was becoming clear just how badly CIC saturation affected the survivability of the fleet. Ideally the navy would solve the problem by rethinking the CIC itself (as it did with the introduction of computers in the form of NTDS), but the most immediate solution was to extend the time line for air defence by extending detection range. The NRL pointed out that this was a matter of the chosen radar frequency as much as anything else. The wavelengths used in wartime for long-range air search might make for massive antennas, but echoes at those frequencies were little affected by the shape of the aircraft. That is why in the mid-1950s the *Midway* class showed wartime SK-2s on special flight deck masts abaft their islands.

An entirely new series of long-range low-frequency radars was developed, beginning with SPS-17 (used on board radar picket ships [YAGR]). It was credited with the ability to detect a bomber (with 90 per cent probability) at 180nm. However, even with a large 17.5ft antenna it lost precision compared to the much smaller and lighter L-band radars: its beam was 18.5° wide. It also used a long pulse (which

This F-4N was a rebuilt F-4B. The APQ-72 and AAA-4 remained (the latter gained an amplifier behind the sensor head), but the data link of the F-4J was installed, together with a dogfight computer (to tell the pilot whether he could launch his Sidewinder missile). The new AIMS IFF and air-to-air IFF were added, the latter a response to the IFF problem revealed by the Vietnam War. This version had the ALQ-126B deceptive ECM system, employing an antenna under the fuselage at the leading edge of the wing and others under the wing at about the point at which dihedral began. An elongated ALQ-126B cable duct could be seen just abaft the cockpit. This version also had fixed inboard leading-edge flaps. The corresponding rebuilt F-4J was F-4S, its radar upgraded to the digital AWG-10B. An additional ALQ-126B antenna was located on the side of the aircraft near a long duct (which might appear to be a refuelling probe, retracted). In addition, ALR-46 radar warning and homing (RHAW) antennas were added at the wingtips. The TACAN antenna was relocated under the nose. The wings were slatted (with two-position leading edge manoeuvre slats) and they were given long fences at about the point where the dihedral began. The slats were credited with providing a 50 per cent improvement in combat turning ability and operated automatically as a function of angle of attack. 'Smokeless' J79-GE-10B engines were installed. Low-voltage formation-keeping lights were added on the sides of the nose, mid-fuselage and tail fin. Both versions were strengthened.

limited range precision) to pour enough power onto the target to detect it at very long range. An experimental version detected an F9F fighter 200nm away. With a larger antenna, it was expected to detect the fighter at 300nm. With a 25ft antenna a developed version of the L-band SPS-12 was expected to produce a far narrower beam – 2.2°. However, its rated range was only 100–135nm. SPS-28, which was intended for destroyers, used much the same antenna as SPS-17, as did the more widely-used SPS-29. Later radars in this series (SPS-37 and -43) had much larger antennas in their carrier versions, but even the 1956 figures give a good idea of what they could achieve.

The post-war Royal Navy continued to use wartime radars and their offshoots, so for it the jet detection problem was somewhat deferred. Its initial generation of carrier-related radars was Type 960 (using the same wavelength as the wartime Type 281, hence with the same sort of broad beam) and a pair of S-band interception-control radars, Type 982 and Type 983. Type 982 offered a narrow beam for fighter control and Type 983 was a heightfinder. The combination could be accommodated by existing carriers, but the scanning heightfinder suffered from the limited dwell time of the wartime US SP and SM. By the time these radars were in service, the Royal Navy had introduced Radar Display Rooms specifically to ensure that different radars could focus on the same target, so that Type 983 would be looking at the same target which Type 982 was tracking. The Royal Navy considered the UHF Type 960 too susceptible to jamming, although it had some counter-countermeasures features.

All of these radars were considered interim types. In 1947 the ASE began developing the huge S-band Type 984, whose antenna was a big stabilised rotating nacelle carrying a microwave lens to focus its five simultaneously-scanning pencil beams, supplemented by a sixth low-

elevation long-range search beam. It was conceived to provide a high data rate and continuous heightfinding. The massive nacelle was pitch, roll and radar sight line stabilised. It rotated at 4.6 or 6 revolutions per minute. Type 984 operated at S-band despite the limitation of additional clutter. That probably gave it better performance against streamlined jets. Its design goal was accuracy to within half a mile or better and to within 1500ft in altitude. In service range discrimination and accuracy were 500 yds, which was half the goal. Bearing accuracy was half a degree (discrimination was 1.8°). Height could be measured to within 1000ft at 60nm and to within 2000ft at 100nm. Cover was solid from the horizon to 40,000ft, out to the instrumented range of 180nm. The development model was set up at ASE in August 1955 (it was started up in 1956). In contrast to the US SPS-2, Type 984 was used only on board carriers: *Victorious*, *Eagle* and *Hermes*. Planned installation on board a missile cruiser died with the ship itself in the 1957 defence cuts. *Victorious* first took it to sea when she was commissioned in January 1958.

In effect Type 984 was the more successful British equivalent of the US SPS-2, which operated at lower frequency (L-band). Describing the design philosophy of Type 984, the British freely admitted that L-band offered greater range and better immunity to weather effects such as cloud clutter, but an L-band version of the sort of scanning radar they had in mind would have been prohibitively massive. In 1948 they expected to mount two on a carrier or large cruiser, but as the radar grew the standard installation was only one.

LOOKING AHEAD: THE LONG RANGE OBJECTIVES GROUP

In the aftermath of Korea the US Navy had enough money to build a new generation of carriers and other warships, but it needed a coherent plan covering all of its major programmes. Carriers and aircraft had to be integrated because aircraft procurement in itself was comparable in cost to shipbuilding. A special Ad Hoc Committee on the Long-Range Shipbuilding Programme was formed in 1954. Its 20 December 1955 report was the starting point for the series of reports produced by the Long Range Objectives Group (LROG) (Op-93) created in 1956. It and its successors reported to the Chief of Naval Operations. Their reports were not statements of declared policy, but they are unique guides to what the navy was doing and where it was likely to go.

Although all the long-range studies were conducted after the Korean War, those of the 1950s them took into account both the increased funding provided by Korean War mobilisation and the future need to be able to fight limited as well as central wars. In that sense the LROG was the child of Korea and is worth discussing here.

The Ad Hoc Committee report looked towards abandonment of massive nuclear attack as a way of dealing with anything short of massive aggression (it suggested that the United States would probably seek a tacit or overt agreement limiting the use of nuclear weapons). The East-West conflict would move towards limited war. This was much what the Admiralty was then arguing as it made its case that Warm War was the most important contingency for the near future. The 1955 report looked ahead fifteen years to 1970.

The most important new technology was the ship-launched missile, both surface-to-surface and surface-to-air. Long-range surface-to-surface missiles might replace long-range carrier strike aircraft. The US Navy was then deploying Regulus I and developing Regulus II and the entirely abortive Triton. They would be carried by submarines and by converted battleships (BBG). These weapons could transform naval

aviation by ending the need for long-range carrier-based strategic bombers.[44] Before 1950, the advent of such weapons would have justified eliminating all carrier strike capability and the advent of anti-aircraft missiles (whose capability was wildly overrated) might have justified eliminating the carriers altogether. After Korea the situation was very different. It mattered enormously that the fleet could wield numerous light attack aircraft – which could operate from smaller, less expensive carriers. The committee envisaged a new class of attack aircraft which could operate from ASW carriers, designed to attack at low altitude and therefore reasonably immune to radar. This was probably the origin of the A-6 Intruder.[45] If the new attack aircraft was the offensive weapon wielded by carriers, the only justification for large decks and powerful catapults would be fleet air-defence fighters and radar aircraft.

To deter major war the US Navy would field three kinds of striking force: five carrier task forces, a submarine missile striking force and a seaplane striking force. The shipbuilding committee limited itself to available ships, with limited discussion of the aircraft on board. The carrier force it envisaged consisted of fifteen attack carriers and five ASW support carriers, working with missile-armed battleships (BBG).[46] At this time a nuclear carrier was included in the FY58 programme (*Enterprise*); the committee assumed that by 1970 there would be six such carriers. With the six large *Forrestal* class carriers (either completed or under construction) and three modernised *Midway* class carriers, that would make a total of fifteen, three per task force. Five *Essex* class carriers (SCB 27C) would still be viable, to provide ASW cover. Each task force would work with the usual surface ships plus two submarine radar pickets. To keep up with the force, ideally they would be nuclear-powered (the prototype was *Triton*). In 1970 eight such submarines would be in service, plus two existing diesel picket submarines (SS 572 class). Projected surface escorts for each task force were four missile cruisers, three large missile destroyers (DLG) and six smaller missile destroyers (DDG).[47]

The most interesting fighter development the committee envisaged was a VTOL fighters capable of high-altitude interception using heat-seeking missiles. They could operate from limited carrier deck areas or even from heavy support ships. VTOL fighters aboard cruisers would fill outer air defence stations. VTOL generally offered the important advantage that they could be launched instantly; whatever ship carried them did not have to turn into the wind to launch. VTOLs were therefore particularly interesting as a way of defeating low-flying attackers, which might be detected at relatively short ranges near the task force. These aircraft were expected to be available about 1962. BuAer was soon trying to develop just these aircraft, as described below.

The report listed a future attack carrier air group headed by sixteen to thirty-two fighters and four to six VTOLs. The conventional fighters would be interceptors operating mainly in an inner low-altitude defence zone. The attack part of the air wing would comprise four to six photo-reconnaissance aircraft, six to twelve all-altitude strike aircraft (i.e. heavy strike aircraft) and twenty to thirty-two of the new low-flying attack aircraft. The carrier would also operate four AEW aircraft, but the committee wrote that they might be helicopters. The smaller support carriers would not be able to operate either the conventional fighters or the high-altitude strike bombers. They would operate four to six VTOLs and sixteen of the new low-altitude bombers, plus twenty-four ASW helicopters and four AEW aircraft. The missile cruisers (CAG) might operate their own VTOL fighters.

The US Navy was then contributing to the seaward barriers of the North American Air Defense system. The 1955 plan included new types of ships for that purpose, a helicopter-missile carrier (CVHG) and a large radar/missile ship (PBG). Neither was built.

By this time there was interest in what became Eagle-Missileer, a heavy aircraft with a large radar carrying long-range missiles. The report predicted that such missiles (20–50nm range, with low-yield nuclear warheads) would be operable from large AEW aircraft by 1965. Otherwise, fighters would be armed with improved (jump-up) Sparrows and Sidewinders (with double the range, decreased vulnerability and internal stowage, available by 1960).

Any enemy air attack should be completely destroyed before the attackers reached the bomb or missile release line. To do that, the fleet of the future needed defence in depth. As a first and key step, it had to deny an enemy adequate intelligence by maintaining electronic silence in the main body. This became an important element of US fleet air defence, but not until the late 1960s. Surveillance, fighter and missile zones had to be spread out so that snoopers could be destroyed before they detected the main body. Electronic deception would help.

New air-search radars promised ranges as great as 200nm and heightfinding at 150nm. The committee therefore envisaged locating two ships, 75–100nm apart, on the 50–100nm circle athwart the likely threat axis. They would establish extended surveillance and defence zones. They would work with AEW aircraft with 100nm search radar and they would control fighters. If possible, the cruisers would have their own VTOL interceptors to supplement their 100nm missiles (Talos). Each would provide integrated control of all fighters and missile defence in its 90° sector from the 75nm circle outward, including the carrier-based CAP on the 150nm circle.

Defence in depth against high-altitude attackers or snoopers would begin with interception by CAP fighters in two layers, a forward layer 150–250nm from force centre and a rear layer 100–150nm from force centre, with the defence closer in provided by missile ships (the missile cruisers could reach out to 200nm from force centre).

It would be impossible for the missile ships to engage low fliers at very long range, because they would be below the radar horizon. Defence against such aircraft would begin with fighters cued by AEW aircraft. Closer in, it would be provided by VTOL aircraft both from the sector defence ships (75–150nm forward of force centre) and from carriers (25–75nm in all directions), with back up by missiles from the inner screen ships (at up to 25nm range). As a consequence, all mass attacks would be under continuous missile fire for 200nm. Any attacker trying to approach at low altitude would still have to locate the task force in the first place. To do that he would have to pop up somewhere within the 200nm outer defensive zone. This vision of task force air defence presumably reflects other authoritative studies made at the time.

The next year the vision of a future navy reported by the new LROG was largely that of the Ad Hoc Committee. It retained the five task forces of the Ad Hoc Committee and their BBGs, although it allowed for a smaller future carrier building programme (the task forces might include two rather than three attack carriers). The carriers would operate a total of 700 to 800 light attack aircraft and 300 to 400 all-weather fighters plus a total of 120 to 160 AEW aircraft. The jet attack aircraft would not need fighter escorts, so the future fleet included no day or air-superiority fighters. The fleet would include 150 to 200 VTOL fighters to achieve medium range against low-flying attackers. These aircraft would normally be dispersed around the fleet, some of them on board missile cruisers far from fleet centre. There was already interest in the heavy missile-armed radar aircraft which became the Eagle-Missileer described below. Both the AEW aircraft and the carrier fighters might be replaced by a total of 250 to 300 such aircraft.

The 1956 report did not take costs into account. The next report by the LROG (January 1957) showed what alternative fleet objectives might be affordable within various budgets. At this time it appeared that the basic navy annual budget for shipbuilding and modernisation (SCN, for Ship Construction, Navy) would be about $1.5 billion. To get a balanced force the LROG suggested that some 'glamor' items such as nuclear-powered warships could be eliminated. Carriers were the most expensive item. The previous report had assumed that one nuclear carrier would be bought each year between FY58 and FY63, for the desired total of six. Sharp increases in aircraft costs made it difficult to justify expensive new carriers. On the other hand, if the long-range strike aircraft were no longer needed, the big carriers also might become less important. It seemed that by 1965 or even sooner, half the fleet aircraft would be fully operable from modernised *Essex* class carriers or their equivalents: AEW, ASW (VS), light jet attack aircraft and turboprop attack aircraft. Too, carriers already funded (six *Forrestal*s, three modernised *Midway*s, six modernised *Essex*) contrasted with the far less modern state of other ships in the strike forces, such as Talos missile cruisers, underway replenishment ships and other escorts.

The current policy of building six nuclear task groups around the six nuclear carriers by 1970 was unaffordable at less than $2 billion per year and there were more pressing needs. By 1964 the cost of nuclear propulsion might fall dramatically. Meanwhile more tankers were a less expensive way to gain greater endurance.[48] Current policy (from the Ad Hoc Committee) also called for a total of twelve radar picket submarines (by this time only four of them nuclear), but AEW aircraft were improving rapidly, with carrier-launched airborne CICs close to fruition. The LROG pointed out correctly that the need for the nuclear submarine pickets would disappear before any new ones could be completed. Standard nuclear attack submarines could be provided with an alternative capability adequate for radar intelligence and/or distant early warning in support of other naval forces.

Construction of missile cruisers was directly related to the number of fighters the fleet needed. What counted was fleet offensive power, meaning strike aircraft and the only way to provide enough strike aircraft within the carrier fleet limited by the budget was to limit the number of fighters. To do that the navy had to build enough missile cruisers. The minimum number of long-range missile launchers (Talos cruisers) which would justify substantial cuts in carrier fighters was six (the optimum seemed to be eight, at least while the shorter-range Terrier missile cruisers remained).

Overall, the navy had to take into account the reality that some ships obsolesced slowly and that in recent years carriers (and minecraft) had been bought at a high level. Some other ships, such as destroyers, could be given interim modernisations. In some areas technology was promising but not yet mature, so investment could be deferred (the example given was long-range escort sonar). Other areas deserved early emphasis.[49]

The committee offered high and low figures for aircraft totals in 1966 and 1971, the low numbers being the minimum to justify its proposed carrier strength (twenty-four in 1966, twenty-two in 1971). The high figure was optimal, but would be the air equivalent to a $2 billion SCN. Both were contrasted with the 1958 programme. The

STOL attack aircraft listed for 1971 was the low-flier which emerged as the A-6. VAH were heavy jet attack bombers (A-3 and A-5).

	1966		1971	1958
	High	Low	Change	
VF	288	480	Decrease 15–20 per cent	714
VA (STOL1971)	216	360	Increase 30–50 per cent	880 total
				jet/piston
VA (turboprop)	216	360		
VAH (jet)	135	180		72

In 1966 typical air groups for the carriers would be:

	CVA 59	CVA 41	CVA 19
VF	24	24	–
VA (jet)	36	36	–
VA (turboprop)			
VAH	12	9	–
Photo	4	4	–
VW	–	–	24
VS/HS	–	–	36

Minimum fleet air strength would be one deckload for each carrier, but optimum was two. Note that within a task force the ASW carrier (the modernised *Essex* [CVA 19]) would supply all the AEW aircraft (VW).

At this time a jet VTOL fighter was expected to enter fleet service in FY63, but it was not incorporated in the long-range plan. Work was also beginning on a jet-rocket fighter to gain climb rate for high-altitude interception. The test platform was an FJ-4, using hydrogen peroxide and jet fuel (JP-5), like the contemporary British SR-53 and SR 177. At this time US plans called for using rockets both in the new F4H Phantom interceptor and the A3J (A-5) Vigilante heavy bomber, if the tests were successful.

A further LRO-59 (24 February 1959) was described as more austere and more realistic than its predecessors. It pointed more toward a navy role in limited war. Long-range cruise missiles (the 1500nm Regulus II) would be useful, because they could be precise enough to use low-yield nuclear warheads. By the late 1960s they might be the only way to break through modern air defences (US intelligence was aware of Soviet surface-to-air missiles).

Although a quarter to a third of attack aircraft would be electronically sophisticated, with high performance, to penetrate and disrupt enemy air defences, the fleet would still need some air-superiority fighters controlled by AEW-CIC aircraft. The high-performance attack aircraft would be armed with offensive ECM and with anti-radar missiles (the navy was then developing such a weapon, Corvus) and they would attack at minimum altitude. This report dismissed the VTOL fighter as not worthwhile given budget limits; it was little more than a manned surface-to-air missile. BuAer backed away from it.

Task force air defence would be primarily by long-endurance CAP aircraft carrying long-range (50–75nm) missiles – the Eagle-Missileer combination which would soon begin development. They would orbit 150–200nm from task force centre, directed by AEW aircraft on the same circle. They might be augmented by high-performance fighters, which would be intended primarily for offensive action. Inside 100nm the task force would be defended by Talos or the coming Super Talos (soon renamed Typhon) using nuclear warheads. Inner zone defence would be by Super Tartar (later Typhon MR), Terrier and Tartar

surface-to-air missiles. The task force would also rely on countermeasures including deceptive formations and jammers.

For the present, the US national deterrent relied heavily on soft (vulnerable) land-based ICBMs, so through 1963 carriers with long-range bombers would be a valuable balance. A special strike group with maximum attack bomber load might be dispersed and continually stationed in the Eastern Atlantic specifically to provide the deterrent (this was not done). By about 1969 the carriers would be primarily a limited-war asset, optimised for limited-range strikes (defined as 600–1000nm, very long ranges by later standards).

The very long range outlooks essentially ended in April 1960 when Long Range Requirements for 1970–5 (LRR-60) were approved. Further LROG studies were considered long range guidance for short-term planning. LRR-60 itself was more austere than its 1959 predecessor and it had a shorter cut-off date, 1972. By this time the navy was deeply engaged in the Polaris programme, which had cost it the annual carriers and the jet seaplane striking force. LRR-60 made some slight cuts in the Polaris programme (forty-one rather than forty-five SSBN). In accord with increased interested in limited war, it expanded the amphibious force. Numbers of AEW aircraft and fighters were cut, as were the safety margin against attrition and Naval Reserve aircraft. The active carrier force objective of past plans, equivalent to maintaining twelve active carriers with one air group each, survived despite considerable cuts in other forces.

Limited war demanded more attack aircraft, the objective now being forty-three per carrier, of which at least a third should be all-weather aircraft with large payloads and long range (i.e. A-6 Intruders). That implied a deep cut in carrier fighter strength, which could be justified only by relying more heavily on shipboard missiles. Fighters would be used mainly against snoopers and small raids and to grind down larger raids before they approached the surface-to-air missile zone. They would concentrate on missile-carrying bombers, raid leaders and low altitude attackers beyond 150nm. Deck-launched fighters would be useful mainly to extend or augment low-level defence. The task force surveillance zone would be extended to 300nm or beyond by using AEW aircraft at least 150nm from task force centre. Tactics would emphasise timely destruction of enemy reconnaissance aircraft, the use of ECM and deception. A typical carrier fighter force would be twenty-four aircraft backed by three AEW aircraft, many of them being long-range fighters with multiple missiles (Missileer or its equivalent).

Supersonic fighters were still needed in limited numbers for CAP and Cold War interception, because in the latter case intruders might have to be identified visually. Since in later reality fleet air defence was tested only in a Cold War context, what must have seemed a secondary point in 1960 became extremely important.

BuAer long-term planning reflected the realities embodied in the LROg papers. Just before BuAer was merged with BuOrd to form the Bureau of Naval Weapons in 1959, it produced its own weapon system plan. In accord with the LRO studies, it saw no point in any near-term development of a completely new fighter to replace the Crusader (F8U) supersonic day fighter. At this time a limited all-weather version of the F8U was coming as the F8U-2N. The F4H Phantom was just entering service. In 1963 a new version would be available with a much better radar offering twice the range of the existing APQ-72 and significantly better low-altitude search and track capacity. The new radar was the pulse-Doppler AWG-10, which appeared somewhat later on board the F-4J. It would have a new version of the Sparrow missile with 70 per cent greater range. The new fighter was the projected Missileer, devel-

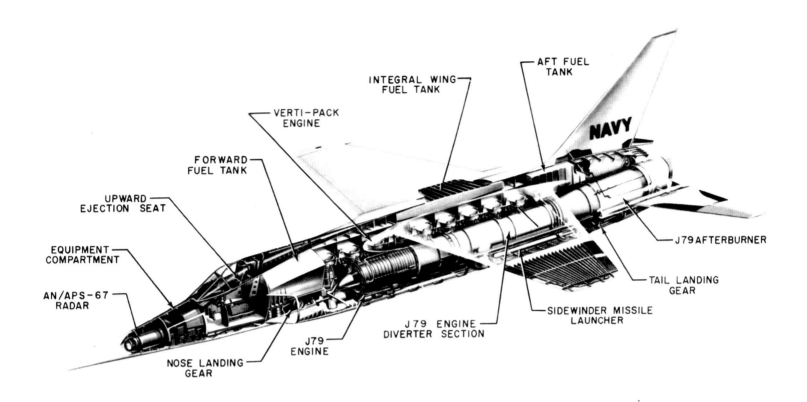

INTEGRAL WING FUEL TANK

AFT FUEL TANK

VERTI–PACK ENGINE

FORWARD FUEL TANK

NAVY

UPWARD EJECTION SEAT

J79 AFTERBURNER

EQUIPMENT COMPARTMENT

TAIL LANDING GEAR

AN/APS–67 RADAR

SIDEWINDER MISSILE LAUNCHER

J79 ENGINE DIVERTER SECTION

J79 ENGINE

NOSE LANDING GEAR

Bell dominated the 1956 VTOL competition. This is its initial D-188 proposal, incorporating a pair of J79s and no fewer than eleven lift engines. Bell's 1 November 1956 proposal showed an aircraft with a span of 33ft 4in and a length of 61ft 6in with a take-off weight of 34,000lbs. The brochure did not show the usual detailed predictions for performance.

opment of which was to begin in FY60, with fleet introduction expected about 1965. It would offer five-hour endurance and it would be able to attack six enemy aircraft simultaneously at ranges of 70–100nm. Alongside the new fighter, BuAer expected to introduce Forward Pass: AEW aircraft on station would provide missiles with mid-course and terminal guidance.

BuAer offered as a further possibility, a 30,000lb Mach 3.5 VTOL fighter, which might begin development in 1963 if the state of the powerplant art was exploited. Development would be worthwhile only if a requirement developed for a small-platform or small-field capability. This was much more a pointer to future possibilities than a proposal and it went nowhere.

For the moment, attack carriers were still fighter-heavy, with three fourteen-plane squadrons. Typically one was supersonic day fighters (F8U Crusaders), one was all-weather fighters (F4D Skyray and F3H Demon) and one was actually light nuclear bombers (FJ-4s, giving way to A4D Skyhawks). They were backed by a medium attack squadron (Skyraiders) and, in carriers other than modernised *Essexes*, a nine- or twelve-plane heavy attack squadron (A3D Skywarriors).

In 1961–2 the Demon would entirely displace the Skyray. The Skyhawk would replace not only the FJ-4 but also the propeller-driven Skyraider, to give the carriers two fourteen-plane attack squadrons. In 1963–4 the F4H Phantom would begin to enter service in enlarged sixteen-plane squadrons, supplementing the Crusader and replacing

the Demon. One of the Skyhawk squadrons would give way to Intruders, both attack squadrons being reduced to twelve planes each. The supersonic Vigilante (A3J, later A-5) would replace the subsonic A-3 on a one-for-one basis. In 1965 the long-endurance Eagle-Missileer combination would enter service in eight-plane squadrons. The two other fighter squadrons would remain, but they would be reduced to twelve aircraft each: one of Phantoms and one of Phantoms or Crusaders. In fact by 1965 the situation was radically different. Because so much changed after 1960, further accounts of US long-term thinking are deferred to a later chapter.

VTOL REBORN (AND RE-KILLED)

BuAer held a design competition for a high-performance VTOL fighter (TS-140). It invited bids on 6 June 1956 and received proposals on 1 October, but the supporting R&D funds were nearly halved to move money into the much more urgent project to adapt the army Jupiter missile to a submarine (this programme soon became the Polaris project). Only Bell and Ryan submitted formal proposals and in a brief discussion of the project in October 1956 BuAer commented that due to the lack of interest among major contractors the programme might revert to system studies and test-bed work.[50] BuAer wanted a speed of Mach 2 at 35,000 and 60,000ft, the aircraft climbing at 40,000ft to 60,000ft/min at sea level with maximum power (it should reach 50,000ft in two minutes). Ceiling would be 60,000–62,000ft. Combat radius would be 100nm: this was a test platform for a deck-launched interceptor armed with FFARs or with four internal Sidewinders. The engines could be J79, J75 or J72 and two aircraft were envisaged in the FY59 programme.[51]

Ryan had been advocating tail-sitting jets since 1947, on the theory that this configuration was the simplest possibility.[52] For the 1956 contest it submitted its Model 112, for which it claimed extreme high altitude and high speed at a minimum of weight and complexity. Aircraft weight was set by engine thrust, as Ryan guaranteed that thrust would exceed weight by 10 per cent on a tropical day as defined by the navy. That much excess power offered high speed; Ryan claimed Mach 2. Model 112 was a small twin-engine delta (two J79s) with sawtooth leading edges. Limited weight (up to 26,727lbs) limited range: Ryan claimed that its aircraft could intercept a target at 60,000ft 137nm away. The main problem with this configuration, as with the two pogos of the earlier VTOL programme, is that the pilot is poorly placed during the vertical part of the flight. Ryan never received a navy contract for an aircraft, but it did build the X-13 tail-sitter under an air force contract with some navy support.

The alternative was Bell's: an aircraft with lift jets distributed down the length of its fuselage. Unlike Ryan, Bell preferred to keep its aircraft horizontal as it lifted, eliminating the pilot-position problem. Bell had been involved in jet VTOL work since 1950 and it had built a test vehicle with two swivelling J44 engines plus a compressor supplying air to a reaction control system for low-speed control. It made its first tethered flight in January 1954. Bell then built the X-14 test aircraft for the air force, using two Viper engines whose exhaust could be turned downwards (this was the way a Harrier flew,

except for the lack of bleed air to balance the two jet exhausts). In April 1952 Bell conducted a feasibility study of a VTOL interceptor for the air force, which convinced it that the best fighter configuration used thrust diversion for low-speed and vertical flight (this was much the basis of the Harrier). Bell's initial D-188 proposal showed a combination of vertically-mounted lift jets down the length of its fuselage and diverter valves for its two J79 cruise engines to add vertical lift on take-off and landing.[53]

BuAer recommended against both Ryan and Bell. The Ryan tail-sitter was rejected due to the disadvantages of the vertical attitude VTOL and the logistical and operational problems of a special launch-recovery rig, lack of a horizontal tail and unconventional stainless-steel structure. Bell was rejected for the complexity of the eleven-engine configuration, the volume lost to auxiliary lift engines, excessive weight and less than specified performance. When the problems were discussed with the two manufacturers, Bell offered a modified D-188A using small high-thrust jet engines (J85 or J83) which showed great promise. In the modified design, all the engines contributed to both lift and forward flight.[54]

Bell's D-188A employed only J85 lift engines, including four in tilting wingtip nacelles. It won the 1956 competition. Although the US Navy never bought it (it would have been the F3L), it did co-sponsor tests of a prototype built in Germany as the VAK 191. As drawn in 1957, D-188A had a span of 23ft 8in and a length of 54ft 11in (these figures later varied slightly). Gross weight was 22,670lbs.

Ultimately the modified D-188A had swivelling pairs of afterburning J85 turbojets at its wingtips plus four lift J85s in its fuselage: two mounted vertically in the forward fuselage, used only for vertical flight and two more mounted horizontally aft with a means of diverting non-afterburning thrust for vertical flight. They could use their afterburners for forward flight. The two J79s of the original design were gone.[55] Bell estimated that D-188A had enough power to make Mach 2.78, but engine limitations would hold it to Mach 2 at 35,000ft and to Mach 1 at sea level. The result vaguely resembled the Lockheed F-104 and it was credited with supersonic performance, albeit over a short distance. Bell offered a similar configuration in the competition which produced the A-6.

VTOL did not have a high enough priority to bring the D-188A to fruition, although one of the Bell brochures in the navy proposal file was marked XF3L-1, which would have been its navy designation (F2L was an abortive wartime navalised version of Bell's lightweight P-77 fighter). In June 1957 signature of the initial contract was held up due to a spending ceiling and it appeared that it might be pushed back to FY58. However, a contract was signed on 28 June 1957, using FY57 R&D funds. By August Bell had abandoned the six-jet configuration in favour of the eight-jet one 'in order to increase mission capabilities'.

Given the severe budget problem, the air force was invited to join the programme. The air force agreed to split costs 50–50; as of October 1957 plans called for a mock-up by 31 July 1958, a first flight in March 1960 and one squadron each for the navy and air force by January 1963. By this time other more urgent projects were squeezing funding, so in October 1957 the two services agreed to buy three test aircraft in FY59, deferring any production decision. That still allowed for first deliveries in early 1963. Then delays in funding the J85 engine caused the projected first flight date to slip from September 1960 to May 1961, somewhat easing the navy's funding problem for FY59. By this time the navy had decided to withdraw funding once the mock-up was complete; the air force saw a solid requirement for this type of aircraft for its Tactical Air Command (TAC) and the aircraft received the tentative designation F-109. By January 1959 the air force planned two flyable prototypes, without any weapons or electronics. The air force asked the navy what it intended beyond the Phase I mock-up. To further complicate matters, although the air force wanted a VTOL for TAC, it also wanted to hold a competition. BuAer recommended that the navy protect its end of the partnership and the Bell programme by continuing to fund it. DCNO (Air) decided that he could not do so; money was just too tight. However, the Marines officially reaffirmed their own interest in the Bell VTOL.

In July 1958 the anonymous BuAer commentator who prepared weekly accounts of items of interest argued that despite tight money, 'there are certain development paths, such as represented by the jet VTOL, which are badly in need of detailed exploration and they should be travelled all the way to full-scale flight experience. On matters of technical development of this sort and in the constant endeavour to keep pace, if not to lead, time is of the essence . . . we already have a foot firmly in the jet VTOL door; a hand as well would help to open it even wider and much more quickly. The jet VTOL will fill a special gap in the current pattern of offensive/defensive weapons . . . Our technical capability in this area would permit us to achieve a tactical first instead of a Sputnik second.'

Nothing came of this plea. Ultimately the navy entered into a co-operative agreement with VAK in Germany, which built and tested a prototype designated VAK 191. The Bell fighter was desirable but not vital; in 1958 the idea of killing off most of the carrier attack aircraft in favour of long-range nuclear cruise missiles was dead, because the navy was developing the Polaris ballistic missile. It seems certain that the funding problem which killed the D-188A for the navy was the Polaris programme.

The potential of VTOL also found advocates in the United Kingdom. By 1949 Farnborough was investigating the possibility of jet VTOL operation. When the Royal Navy developed staff requirements for a new carrier in 1952, there was a suggestion from the British naval air staff that a much smaller and less expensive ship should be designed with future VTOL aircraft in mind. Probably because the underlying technology was hardly mature enough, nothing came of this idea and VTOL does not seem to have figured in discussions leading up to the abortive carrier (CVA 01) of the 1960s.

Avro Canada proposed this VTOL using tilting engines at the tips of its canard and wings. Maximum speed was 635 knots at sea level and 1146 knots at 60,000ft. Combat ceiling was 62,000ft. Rate of climb at sea level was 55,600ft/min (13,200ft/min at 45,000ft and Mach 1.75). Span was 25.25ft (18.25ft over the canards) and length was 50ft. Gross weight was 16,250lbs.

CHAPTER 8
A NEW KIND OF THREAT

MUCH OF THE development of Western fleet air defences used through the later stages of the Cold War was carried out during the period up to 1960, which was also the period of nearly complete ignorance of what the Soviets were actually doing. The assumed threat therefore drove development, both of fighters and of the equipment designed to support them. Reality began to assert itself only after 1960. In particular, from the late 1950s to nearly the end of the Cold War, most of the Soviet naval air force consisted of subsonic 'Badger' (Tu-16) bombers carrying increasingly sophisticated stand-off missiles and jammers. Only in the 1980s did a supersonic successor, 'Backfire' (Tu-22m3) enter naval service. However, in the 1950s Westerners could only assume that the Soviets were developing much the same kinds of aircraft that they were. By 1956, then, the assumed future (1970s) Soviet naval bomber threat was supersonic. This assumed threat in turn helped shape the fighters developed for the US Navy and the Royal Navy.

SOVIET ANTI-SHIP MISSILES

Like the pre-war Japanese, the post-war Soviets maintained excellent security. For more than a decade, the US Navy and the Royal Navy had to develop fleet air defence based not on what the Soviets were actually doing but on what they thought they might be developing. The main glimpse of Soviet aircraft development was at the fly-pasts of the annual Tushino air shows, which is where the MiG-15 was first seen (mis-identified as the MiG-14). In 1952 the Soviets began sending home German engineers they had dragooned into working in the Soviet Union and interviews with these men revealed something of the ongoing Soviet missile programme. These interviews (called Dragon Returns) were probably the first Western glimpse of the programme to develop a stand-off anti-ship missile the Soviets called Komet (AS-1 'Kennel' in NATO parlance; the Soviet designation was KS).[1]

The Western allies assumed that the Soviets would exploit the new technology developed by the Germans, which included a stand-off

The Soviet naval air arm was the single greatest threat to US and British carriers from about 1960 on. 'Bear D's (Tu-95RTs) like this one conducted maritime reconnaissance which could, in theory, defeat the radio silence US and British carriers used to evade attack. The big radar could link its picture down to missile-firing ships and submarines operating beyond the horizon. This F-4J of VF-213 (*Kitty Hawk*) is escorting a 'Bear D' away from a carrier formation, 6 December 1973.

anti-ship missile (Hs-293) and a guided anti-ship bomb (FX-1400). Both had proven effective during the Second World War; both could be delivered outside anti-aircraft range.[2] US analysts went further, assuming that the Soviets would use atomic bombs against carriers whose aircraft could deliver just such weapons. Because it did not have to be aimed precisely, a nuclear bomb could be tossed from a distance: it too was effectively a stand-off weapon. Alongside such exotica were standard anti-ship weapons such as torpedoes, which might be delivered at low altitudes.

The Soviets displayed their first post-war heavy bomber, the Tu-4, in 1947. It was a copied B-29 Superfortress, whose performance was well understood by the Western navies which might face it. No one outside the Soviet Union could say how the Soviets might combine such aircraft (if at all) with the light bombers which then equipped their shore-based naval air units. Fleet air defence exercises therefore combined high- and low-altitude attackers, often demonstrating that low-altitude aircraft were by far the most difficult targets. Unknown to the Western navies, the Soviets emphasised stand-off tactics and attacks delivered from high altitude, perhaps not least because at higher altitude their aircraft stood a better chance of seeing their targets. In contrast to Western torpedo attack tactics, the Soviets developed co-ordinated massed attacks using torpedoes dropped from high altitude (US observers were surprised that, once they had achieved sufficient accuracy at one altitude, the Soviet torpedo bombers tried attacks from higher altitudes). The chosen weapon, unknown to Westerners, was a rocket torpedo (RAT-52) which could be dropped from considerable altitude.

The Soviets developed heavy jet bombers, the first important one being the Tu-16 (NATO 'Badger'). Initially 'Badgers' supplied to Soviet Naval Aviation were armed with torpedoes and air-dropped mines, but in 1956 the Soviets displayed them equipped with AS-1 stand-off anti-ship missiles. A few Tu-4s had been equipped with the new stand-off missile, but a 'Badger' was a very different proposition. Soviet Naval Aviation received its first thirty missile-carrying 'Badgers' in mid-1956, but it was reported to have almost 300 by mid-1960. At that time the US Navy characterised the missile-firing 'Badger' as the most serious of all threats to its carriers. If anything, the threat was emphasised by a shift that year in which all anti-ship 'Badgers' were transferred to Soviet Naval Aviation. The naval torpedo bombers were declared surplus and all naval fighters (which had defended naval bases) were transferred to the Soviet air defence force (PVO). For the remainder of the Cold War, the air threat to major Western warships consisted of heavy missile-armed bombers, initially 'Badgers' and much later 'Backfires'.

A missile bomber changed the air defence problem because it had to be destroyed much further away from its target. Otherwise fleet air defence would have to concentrate on numerous relatively small missile targets rather than large bombers. The air-to-air missiles

developed specifically to destroy the bombers were likely to be far less effective against small, fast incoming missiles. By 1956 the two projected Sparrow warheads were blast-fragmentation and continuous-rod. Both would be triggered by proximity fuzes. The fuze would detect a target flying more or less directly towards the missile and it had to embody a sufficient delay so that the explosion or the rods reached the target rather than passing ahead of it (or behind it, if the delay was too great). Delay timing depended on the size of the target. At the same passing speed, the right delay to cut a bomber in half would leave the rods or blast far behind a smaller missile.

Both the US Navy and the Royal Navy were already demanding that incoming bombers be destroyed beyond 20nm range, a figure presumably set by the threat of a bomber tossing a nuclear weapon or using a somewhat improved version of the German wartime missiles. AS-1 roughly doubled that range, although the missile attack would still be aborted if the bomber were destroyed while it guided the missile.

A follow-on supersonic AS-2 (K-10S) missile appeared in 1960.[3] It was a far more serious threat: much faster and with a far greater range, about 100nm. It used an active terminal seeker, so the bomber could turn away well before it reached its target. Prior to the terminal phase, AS-2 was guided by radio command by the launching bomber. Looking back at what we now know about AS-1, it was a less drastic threat than was imagined at the time. AS-2 was substantially worse, although its short active radar homing range made it profitable to destroy a 'Badger' well after it had launched the missile (this seems not to have been known at the time). Worse was coming.

From the Soviet point of view, the only major drawback of the new missile was that it was so much heavier than KS that a 'Badger' could carry only one of them. In 1957 the Soviet air force set a requirement for a direct replacement for KS which could be launched at greater altitude and speed, with a new guidance system making salvo-launching possible. The barrier to altitude and speed was the turbojet

KS-1 (NATO AS-1 'Kennel') was developed under a 13 May 1946 directive. The entire programme was to have been completed during 1948, but it lagged badly. KS-1 rode a beam towards the ship (hence the tail antenna), switching to semi-active homing 15–20km from the target (using the nose radome) because the beam was too wide by that time. The missile began a terminal dive when 500–700m from the target. This technique obliged the Tu-4 to continue to fly towards the target after launching (the attack could be disrupted by shooting down the bomber). To stay outside anti-aircraft range of a task force (defined as 40km), the bomber would slow to 360–320km/h (223–198mph). Missile airframe design was assigned to the MiG design bureau, which is why it looks like a scaled-down MiG-15 (with more sharply swept wings) with an adapted copied Derwent (rather than Nene) engine (an earlier failed design would have resembled a scaled-down MiG-9). The system was declared operational in 1953, Tu-4K missile bombers serving in two naval air regiments (Black Sea and Northern Fleets) and in two long-range air army (DA) regiments. The first, 124 TBAP (Heavy Bomber Air Regiment, later the 124th Long Range Mine-Torpedo Regiment) was formed under a 30 August 1955 directive from the Main Navy Staff, with twelve Tu-4Ks and other aircraft. Later in the 1950s these units converted to Tu-16 'Badgers' designated Tu-16KS and their Tu-4s were mostly converted to Tu-4D transports. The first Tu-16KS were delivered to the 124 TBAP in June 1957. The Tu-4K was apparently never seen by Westerners, so their first glimpse of the KS-1 and its carrier (by this time the Tu-16KS 'Badger B') came when a Tu-16KS was seen in August 1961 at a Tushino air show. By that time the system was already known, to the point that the US Pacific Fleet was describing it as the greatest current threat to carriers. The first large-scale simulated Tu-16 missile exercise known to the US Navy was conducted in September 1958. The January 1956 edition of the British Joint Intelligence Committee review of Soviet capabilities, which presumably reflected both British and American intelligence, correctly dated the programme as having begun in 1947 and been completed in 1953, but was more tentative about deployment and gave the range as 80nm rather than the 55nm of the completed version. The Tu-16KS was designated 'Badger B' by NATO, the Kobalt-M (NATO 'Crown Drum') guidance device being in a retractable faired radome at the fore end of the former bomb bay, with a pressurised cabin for the operator. The target acquisition radar, under the nose of the aircraft, was Rubin or Rubidy (NATO 'Mushroom'). The missile had a span of 4.722m (15ft 6in), a length of 8.29m (27ft 2in) and a diameter of 1.145m (3ft 9in); at launch it weighed 2735kg (6030lbs). Its warhead weighed 800kg (1760lbs). (Steve Zaloga)

The supersonic turbojet-powered K-10S (NATO AS-2 'Kipper', guidance system K-10) was the first really effective Soviet anti-ship missile. The Tu-16K-10 ('Badger C') carried a single K-10S, which was 50 percent heavier than KS-1, on its centreline, but the two Tu-16K-10-26 bombers shown could also carry a KSR-5 (AS-6) under each wing. Like KS, K-10S was developed by the MiG design bureau, which also developed a shipboard version, P-40. It died when Khrushchev cancelled most of the Soviet surface combatant programme, including the modified *Sverdlov* class cruisers which would have carried it. In contrast to KS-1, K-10S had an active radar seeker. The launch aircraft designated the target and tracked the outgoing missile, locking it on 15–20km from the target (the command link used a small antenna above the bomber's cockpit). To do that it needed the big under-nose YeN (NATO 'Puff Ball') target acquisition and tracking radar, which could detect a target at 220nm; the bomber launched at 100nm and broke away at 90nm. Missiles could be fired at much higher altitude than KS (10,000m) and at much higher bomber speed (400–430 knots). During system development, minimum launch altitude was reduced from 5000m to 1500m and minimum missile flight altitude from 1200m to 600m. A longer-range version (dalnyy, K-10SD) completed in 1966 had its launch range increased to 300–350km; it was followed by 1971 by K-10SDV. YeN radar performance was improved accordingly. The warhead was twice as heavy as that of the KS. As with KS, the jet engine was a modified fighter engine, in this case that of the MiG-19. The programme was nearly cancelled due to problems revealed in tests, but it survived because the ninety existing Tu-16KS bombers were considered obsolescent. By 1962 K-10S was in service in seven regiments and it had been modified for acceptable reliability. K-10S dimensions were length 9.5–10.0m (31ft 2in–32ft 10in), span 4.6–4.9m (15ft 1in–16ft 1in) (launch weight 4533kg (9995lbs)). Beginning in the late 1960s Tu-16K-10 bombers were converted into Tu-16RM-1 reconnaissance aircraft. Development of a jammer version, K-10SP 'Azalea,' was completed in 1979 and it participated in the May 1981 Northern Fleet exercise.

In the early 1960s the Admiralty justified the sophistication of its new fighters and its new carrier largely on the basis that even in Warm War it would face the most modern weapons, such as the 'Badger'/AS-1 system. In the summer of 1962 the Soviets transferred to Indonesia twelve Tu-16 ('Badger A') and twelve Tu-16KS ('Badger B'), together with KS-1 missiles, presumably as part of an attempt to keep the Indonesians from favouring the Chinese. The bombers came from air force (DA) rather than navy stocks. Initially they might have been used had war broken out over the Indonesian claim to Dutch New Guinea. There was public speculation that the presence of the missile bombers convinced the Dutch not to fight (it was said that six KS-1 hits would have sunk their carrier *Karel Doorman*), but there is little evidence for that in archives. The decisive factor was probably that the United States government refused to back the Dutch, in what turned out to be mistaken hopes that by backing the Indonesians it could gain their favour (the Dutch were angry enough not to support the United States in Vietnam a few years later). At this time the bombers had not yet fired their missiles and Soviet aircrew would have flow them. After the crisis subsided, the Soviets trained Indonesian aircrew, who test-fired at least one KS-1 on Arakan Island in 1964 or 1965 against a fixed steel platform target. The Soviets broke relations with Indonesia in 1965, cutting off the supply of spares. Six Tu-16KS and their missiles were exported to Egypt, but they were destroyed during the Six-Day War. Afterwards they were replaced by decidedly less capable Tu-16T torpedo bombers from Black Sea Fleet stocks. This AS-1 missile is shown under the wing of a Tu-16 at the Indonesian Air Force Museum, Yogjakarta.

which powered KS. At this time the Berezhniak design bureau was developing a small rocket-powered missile (K-15) which became well-known as 'Styx' (SS-N-2). It substituted the rocket for the turbojet in a KS, adding a new autopilot and an active seeker. The result was designated KSR.[4] The delay in Western knowledge is reflected in its NATO designation, AS-5 rather than AS-4.

A typical 'Badger'/K-10S attack, as practised in the mid-1960s, involved a regiment of bombers in two waves, each of six to eight aircraft (several regiments might attack together). The regiment would be preceded by two pathfinders and accompanied by 'Badger' jammers and chaff layers. The pathfinders were intended to confirm target position. The Soviets were well aware that US carrier formations could be deceptive; they wanted to know where in the formation the carriers were. Radar was not enough, because by the 1960s the US Navy was deploying blip enhancers on board destroyers, to make them appear (on radar) to be carriers. The Black Sea Tu-22 'Blinder' regiment was probably typical. One of its two pathfinders would fly into the US formation at low altitude to spot the carrier, a mission which was considered nearly suicidal. The other was the high-altitude communications link back to the regiment leader. The visual mission was sometimes practised in peacetime; it is probably why a 'Badger' suddenly cartwheeled into the sea after making a low pass over *Essex* in 1968. For surface attack units, the equivalent to the pathfinder was the

'tattletale' ship, which always tried to stay with a carrier group. It does not appear that this concept was understood by Western navies, who tended to view tattletales as a means of keeping track of formations, not of examining them to see where the high-value target was. The air pathfinder tactic would have been dismissed as absurdly risky, but it was revealed after the Cold War in an account of the single Black Sea 'Blinder' anti-ship unit.

While these missiles were being developed, a follow-on supersonic bomber was being developed as the Tu-16 successor. This development had been expected in the West and the supersonic threat motivated British work on the mixed-power SR 177 interceptor. This Tu-22 was in the late development stage in 1956, as Khrushchev was declaring that all future bombers should be missile carriers. Naturally a new missile had to be developed to match the new aircraft: Kh-22 (NATO AS-4). Development of the missile and its fire-control system were approved on 17 April 1958. The new bomber was spectacular enough to be worth displaying at Tushino in 1961 and naturally a dummy version of the new missile was carried beneath it. KSR received no such publicity, so NATO assigned a lower number (AS-4) to this next-generation weapon.[5]

Having been conceived well before Khrushchev's missile decree, the new Tu-22 was ill-equipped to carry a big external missile. The system's big radome did not help performance. After disappointing tests, produc-

KSR-2 (NATO AS-5 'Kelt', K-16 guidance system) was intended to replace AS-1 without requiring a new guidance system aboard the bomber. Its airframe was developed by a sub-bureau (OKB-155-2, later the Raduga organisation) of the MiG design bureau, which had already developed the P-15 (SS-N-2 'Styx') anti-ship missile. Modified Tu-16 bombers had a new chin radar, Ruby-1K (K-PM, NATO 'Short Horn') and the entire system was Rubikon-1K. Typically Ruby-1K could detect a large warship at 200km. Missiles were launched at 700–800km/h at an altitude of 4000–10,000m. KSR-2 and K-10S entered Soviet service at about the same time. KSR-2 cruised at 1500–10,000m and reached Mach 1.18 at high altitude. By way of comparison, K-10S cruised at Mach 1.2 and reached Mach 1.8 in a dive; it had slightly longer range (325km vs 180–230km at high altitude). Because KSR-2 performance was so inferior to that of K-10S, it did not last as long in Soviet service. A 'Badger' armed with KSR-2 was designated Tu-16K-16 or Tu-16KSR ('Badger G'); it retained its glass nose and the new radar fit much the same chin radome as 'Mushroom'. The missile was accepted for service on 30 December 1961 and the formal decision to modify the Tu-16KS was made the following February. Development of an anti-radar version of the KSR system, K-11, was approved on 20 July 1957, the missile being designated KSR-2P or KSR-11. 'Badgers' which could carry the anti-radar version and the anti-ship version were designated Tu-16KSR-2-5-11. KSR-2 dimensions were: 8.6m (28ft 3in), span 4.6m (15ft 1in), weight 3000kg (6609lbs) (compared to 2735kg [6030lbs] for KS-1). Egypt bought about twenty Tu-16K-11-16 after the Six-Day War; when the next war broke out in 1973, they had eighteen in service. They launched twenty-five KSR-2 and KSR-11. Twenty were shot down by Israeli fighters. The other five destroyed two radars and a supply depot Iraq also obtained 'Badgers' carrying KSR-2s, as well as Chinese H-6 versions carrying C-601 missiles based on the Soviet 'Styx'. They took part in the closing stages of the Iran-Iraq War, attacking Iranian cities with both bombs and missiles. All the Iraqi Tu-16s and H-6s were destroyed during the 1991 Gulf War.

The Tu-16 'Badger' formed the core of the Soviet anti-carrier bomber force until it was super-seded by the supersonic Tu-22m 'Backfire'. As of early 1974, US intelligence credited the Soviet Navy with 290 missile attack 'Badgers', of which 190 were armed with AS-2. They were backed by another ninety bomb strike aircraft ('Badgers' and 'Blinders') and by 120 recon-naissance/photo/ELINT aircraft ('Bear D', 'Blinder' and 'Badger') and by eighty 'Badger' tankers. The number of strike reconnaissance aircraft testifies to the vital importance of finding targets for the missile aircraft. This pathfinder 'Badger' (Tu-16RM-1) was pho-tographed in 1989. It has the same 'Puff Ball' nose radar as the 'Badger C' which carried AS-2 missiles, but it also has a radome visible under its engine. It and another radome further aft served the SRS-1 electronic reconnaissance system, with a single radome between them for SRS-4. In these aircraft the YeN radar was modified as the YeN-R. The Tu-16RM-2 version was quite different, converted from a Tu-16R with a Rubin-1K radar in place of their RBP-4 or -6 chin radar. Antennas of the SPS-4 system, both directional and omni-directional, were installed under the former bomb-bay, which carried additional fuel.

tion of the bomber version of the Tu-22 'Blinder' was cancelled, only a single Black Sea regiment receiving it. However, the new missile was substantially more threatening than its predecessors, because it offered true fire-and-forget performance. Using its large search radar, the bomber picked up the target and set the missile autopilot; the missile locked itself on between 70–80nm from the target. The combination of very high altitude flight and a steep terminal dive made interception by surface-launched missiles particularly difficult; AS-4 was the new threat which prompted the 'New Threat Upgrade' programme for the Standard Missile. The missile was accepted for service use in 1964, but the entire system (on board 'Blinders') was not operational until 1970. Because Kh-22 was too heavy for a 'Badger', a smaller equivalent was developed: KSR-5 (NATO AS-6). It was accepted for service on 4 December 1969.[6] 'Badgers' sometimes carried a K-10S on the centreline and two KSR-5s underwing. With the advent of a true fire-and-forget missile, the Soviets pushed the required bomber destruction range back to at least 300nm (for a high-flying 'Backfire'). It was also generally assumed, until the end of the Cold War, that the Soviets wanted, but did not yet have, anti-ship missiles which could be targeted (locked-on) after they were launched. This was a crucial point. A bomber which locked on its missiles before launching them had to be above the radar horizon of its target. If, however, it could lock on afterwards it could use some form of over-the-horizon information to locate its target, at least approximately. Its missile could rely on its own search radar, using a link back to the launch aircraft for initial target location. The first Soviet bomber with this capa-bility was the 'Backfire' (Tu-22M). Its designation suggested a relation-

A KSR-5 (NATO AS-6 'Kingfish') is shown on a 'Badger' at the Monino Central Air Museum. It was a completely new supersonic missile developed by the same OKB-155-2 bureau which had designed KSR. KSR-5 was conceived as an alternative to Kh-22 which could be carried underwing by a 'Badger'. Development was ordered in August 1962 (development of the anti-radar KSR-5P was ordered in February 1964). The associated fire-control system was K-26, so 'Badgers' modified to fire either KSR-2 or KSR-5 became Tu-16K-10-26 ('Badger G'). Those equipped only to fire KSR-5 were Tu-16K-26.The associated radar was YeN-D. K-26 was accepted for service on 4 December 1969. As the Cold War continued, the West built up considerable understanding not only of Soviet missile tactics, but also of the limitations of the weapons. For example, the launching bomber had to lock the missile on before coming to within a set distance of its target. Lock-on was necessary to ensure that the missile attacked a high-value target such as a carrier rather than some other warship. The bomb-aimer could hope to decide which was which by observing the whole formation, but he could be frustrated by deceptive tactics and by blip enhancers. Hence the need for tattletales, both airborne and seaborne. By the time this photograph was taken in 1983, US perception of this limitation had led to, among other things, the idea of operating carriers in fjords ringed by mountains which would make it difficult for the 'Badger' to lock on outside minimum range.

This 'Badger' shows an AS-6 (KSR-5) supersonic missile under one wing. KSR-5 could be substituted directly for the much less capable KSR-2, but the range of the missile's active seeker exceeded that of the Rubin-1K radar under the bomber's nose. One Baltic Fleet squadron solved the problem by fitting Berkut radars normally carried by Il-38 'May' ASW aircraft, but in most aircraft the Rubin and its radome were removed and a more powerful Rubin-1M fitted in a large belly radome. As altered the aircraft were not specially designated. When 'Badger Mod C' appeared with both K-10S and KSR-5, one interpretation was that it was an attempt to optimise KSR-5 performance by mating it with a better search radar.

ship with the failed 'Blinder', but in fact it had been chosen to ease the authorisation process (Tupolev had enormous political pull). The corresponding missile was a version of Kh-22 designated Kh-22M. Its video data link back to the bomber provided its operator with the missile's radar picture.[7] It was also believed that many or all of these missiles had nuclear warheads, so that from about 1956 on an important consideration in fleet air defence was that carriers had to spread out, so that a large nuclear burst on one of them would not destroy others in the formation.

The Soviet economy was tilted heavily towards military production, so it created a surplus of new equipment which could be given to friendly governments. When the Royal Navy, for example, contemplated Warm War operations in the Third World, it had to reckon with the possibility that it would be facing reasonably modern Soviet weapons, such as anti-ship missiles. As if to demonstrate this point, in 1962 Khrushchev sought to ingratiate himself with the Indonesian dictator Sukarno by transferring naval materiel, including submarines, a cruiser and 'Badgers' with their AS-1 anti-ship missiles. At the time Sukarno was trying to oust the Dutch from their colony in New Guinea. It is difficult to say how impressed the Dutch were with the missile-bearing bombers, but the Russians later told themselves that the presence of these aircraft had been significant. A few years later the Royal Navy found itself in waters near Indonesia during the 'Confrontation'. Again, it is not clear whether or to what extent the presence of the 'Badgers' affected British operations. The Royal Navy certainly argued that the Indonesian arms programme showed that a fleet optimised for 'Warm War' had to be capable of facing the most

modern naval weapons. That would not have been argued a decade earlier, when the concept was first mooted.

SNOOPERS

Quite aside from the bombers themselves, snoopers might be expected to guide submarines to attack convoys and other surface units. The Germans had made very limited use of such aircraft during the Second World War, mainly because co-ordination between land-based reconnaissance aircraft (of the Luftwaffe) and the German navy was so poor. That could not be expected to continue; the Soviet navy always had a large air component. By 1948 US ASW carriers had fighters aboard specifically to deal with snoopers and this requirement probably explains why ASW carriers later had jet attack aircraft (A-4s) on board. These aircraft were generally described as a means of air defence, but that must have meant the anti-snooper mission. Later the Royal Navy bought an air-to-air capability for its Sea Harrier specifically for anti-snooper operation; it did not envisage a true fleet air-defence mission for that aircraft until after the Falklands War.

The most important Soviet snooper was probably the huge turboprop 'Bear D' (Tu-95RTs), with a massive under-body radar; the ASW version of this aircraft (Tu-142) presumably also had a snooper mission. The radar was in effect a more massive equivalent of the APS-20 that the US Navy used both for airborne early warning and for surface search from the air. The Tu-95RTs was conceived as part of an aircraft-submarine combination, providing submarines with a picture

Kh-22 (NATO AS-4 'Kitchen', K-22 fire-control system) was the impressive weapon which, among other things, caused the US Navy to upgrade its anti-aircraft missiles in the 1980s under the New Threat Upgrade programme. Conceived as the weapon of the Tu-22 bomber, it was delayed by that aircraft's failure (only one Black Sea regiment received the missile bomber version). For a time it seemed to be a strategic weapon; its appearance on board Tu-22M naval bombers was an unwelcome surprise. The associated radar was PN (NATO 'Down Beat'). The missile used an autopilot for mid-course guidance plus a J-band terminal seeker. Kh-22 was normally launched at an altitude of 10–14km (33,000–46,000ft) climbing to a cruise altitude of 22.5km (about 75,000ft). Time of flight from a typical operational range of 150nm was 9.4 minutes. The terminal seeker was activated about 80nm from the expected target position and the missile began a 3° terminal dive when the seeker registered an appropriate depression angle. Minimum range was 70nm; the missile was ineffective if it could not distinguish its target in the 10nm between seeker turn-on to minimum range. The Tu-22M incorporates a video down-link similar to that used in the SS-N-3 and other long-range anti-ship missiles. Using it, the launching aircraft received the radar picture seen by the missile, so that the missile could be launched from below the horizon and locked-on by the bomber. This capability was apparently unsuspected in the West before the collapse of the Soviet Union. It still required the launch bomber to gain an effective radar picture of its own before firing, so it is not clear how decisive it might have proven. The data link version could also be launched from beyond the horizon from low altitude, climbing to 12,000m and then approaching its target in a shallow supersonic (Mach 1.2) dive towards an attack altitude of 500m. Kh-22 was too large to be carried by 'Badgers': 11.65m (38.2ft) long, with a span of 3m (9ft 10in) and a diameter of 0.92m (3ft); it weighed 5780kg (12,739lbs) and reported warhead weight was about 1000kg (2200lbs). Development of the successor anti-ship version of the Kh-16 aeroballistic missile (comparable to the US SRAM) was stopped by the collapse of the Soviet Union, so Kh-22 remains in service. This Kh-22 is shown on board a Tu-22M 'Backfire', which can carry three: one under its belly and two on wing pylons. (Steve

The huge Kh-20 missile (NATO AS-3 'Kangaroo,' K-20 fire-control system) was carried only by Tu-95K-20 'Bears' of Soviet Long-Range Aviation (DA), which had a secondary anti-ship role (all anti-ship 'Badgers' were turned over to the navy under a 1960 decree). It was developed by the MiG bureau. There was no seeker, the bomber commanding the missile into position. The radar was YeN-D in a chin radome (NATO Puff Ball, because it had the same emissions as YeN). At an altitude of about 10,000m it could detect large surface ships at ranges of 300–400km (up to 220nm [Western estimates were somewhat lower, about 175nm]). The Kh-20M version of the missile could fly 650km (about 350nm) at Mach 1.8 (or 350km at Mach 2). Trials showed that with its large thermonuclear warhead (reportedly 1MT) it could be effective against large moving ships. Development was authorised on 11 March 1954, trials began on 6 June 1957 and the system was declared operational on 9 September 1960, forty-nine aircraft being built. Total weight was 11,000kg (24,500lbs), about twice that of Kh-22 and the warhead weighed 2500kg (5568lbs). Tu-95KDs (the air-refueled version of Tu-95K-20) often used their big search radars to guide Tu-95MRs to Western warships; the Tu-95MR would overfly the ships and take photographs. In the 1970s and 1980s the Tu-95MRs generally operated alone, which suggests that they were cued by other systems, most likely by satellite ocean reconnaissance.

of the target formation before they fired their SS-N-3 missiles (they matched a radar picture provided by the missile with that provided by the aircraft). However, 'Bears' were also used for more basic ocean reconnaissance. During the Cold War, a US saying was 'Bears in the morning, missiles in the afternoon', a play on sayings about the way the colour of the sky would predict coming weather.

POST-WAR AEW

The US Navy ended the war with Cadillac I and Cadillac II. Both were developed after the war. The much larger Cadillac II and its offshoots offered more space and weight and therefore led to further radar development, which in turn was later applied to the carrier-based aircraft. In 1950 it tested a modernised APS-20B radar with twice the output of APS-20 (and 20A), a more sensitive receiver, automatic sector scan and the ability to receive an S-band beacon.

Land-based naval AEW

The converted Flying Fortress was never more than an interim land-based AEW aircraft. It proved that an airborne CIC was well worth having, so the navy sought a better platform. The navy acquired two Lockheed Model 749 Constellations in 1949, converting them to AEW aircraft under the designation PO-1W (P for Patrol, O for Lockheed – soon changed to V) and W for early warning. Later a new class of AEW aircraft was created with the type letter W. The two prototype Constellations became WV-1s. Once they proved the feasibility of the concept, the navy standardised on the L-1049 Super Constellation, which offered more internal space. It became the WV-2 Warning Star. This project was so urgent that by the time the mock-up board (for the CIC section) met in February 1952, the navy had already bought twelve WV-2s plus another sixteen planned for FY53. In addition it was converting ten Air Force C-121Cs into interim AEW aircraft for the Air Force designated RC-121Cs and was buying another fifteen WV-2s (as EC-121Ds) for the Air Force. At the design gross weight of 120,000lbs, a WV-2 was expected to be able to remain on station, 1000nm from its base, for 2.3 hours at sea level (1.4 hours at 20,000ft). However, the aircraft could take off at an overload of 145,000lbs, giving it enough fuel to remain on station for 12.8 hours at sea level or 8.9 hours at 20,000ft. Overload condition included the two 600-gallon wingtip tanks and a 1000-gallon aft fuselage tank, plus full wing fuel, approximately doubling standard fuel capacity.

Fighters from *Kitty Hawk* intercepted this naval reconnaissance 'Badger F' (Tu-16R) over the Sea of Japan in January 1963. In this and similar incidents the reconnaissance aircraft wasted no time searching: the Soviets had a long-range carrier detector, which turned out to be their network of large HF/DF arrays (Krug). The US Navy and the Royal Navy learned to evade detection by going silent. The two underwing pods of the SRS-3 system identify this aircraft as an interim pathfinder for bombers carrying K-10S missiles. The vertical blade antennas above and below the fuselage were for the SRS-2 system. The successor pathfinder intended to support AS-2 strikes was Tu-16RM-1, which had the same YeN radar as a Tu-16K-10 (it could be distinguished from a missile bomber by the three radomes on its faired-in belly). Tu-16RM-2, intended to support KSR-2 regiments, had their Rubin-A radar. 'Badger' regiments also had specialist jammers, beginning in 1961 with conversions of obsolete Tu-16A nuclear bombers and Tu-16KS missile bombers. There were complementary jammers and chaff layers, total production of which was 135 (second-generation jammers were converted from first-generation chaff layers). The second-generation jammer ('Badger J') could be recognised by its Buket (Bouquet) system employing antennas in a 5.5m (18ft) canoe, NATO 'Chip Long', under its former bomb bay, as well as flat-plate and jamming antennas at its wingtips. These aircraft first appeared in 1961, roughly contemporary with K-10S. Reportedly, a typical anti-ship regiment of the early 1980s consisted of two strike squadrons (nine to twelve missile bombers each), supported by a third squadron consisting of two to four chaff-layers ('Badger H' or Tu-16P Yelka), one or two Tu-16P Buket ('Badger J') and three to six 'Badger' tankers.

These aircraft had APS-20s with enlarged antennas (17ft x 4ft compared to the 8ft x 3ft of a carrier-based AD-5W) in belly radomes and dorsal fin radomes carrying APS-45 heightfinders (with a 7.5ft x 2ft antenna). Unlike the heightfinding radars on board ship, APS-45 could not turn into the direction of a detected target (it could turn to only a very limited extent inside its radome). Instead, the entire aircraft had to turn. That said, APS-45 was credited with a 75nm range on a 2m^2 target. The WV-2 had sufficient internal space for five

Air Control Officers (ACOs) handling interceptions, backed by separate radar (APS-20B), heightfinding (APS-45) and ECM (passive) operators and a ship-type DRT table for navigation.[8] The intercept officers were supervised by a CIC officer (CICO). The WV-2 had tip tanks for increased endurance and its vertical fins were enlarged to compensate for the added side area of the radomes. At BuAer request, the Douglas DC-7C was considered (and rejected) in October 1954 as an alternative AEW-CIC platform, carrying both antennas above its body because it lacked ground clearance.

The story of these aircraft as fleet assets is complicated by the fact that the navy contributed them to help form the seaward extensions of the North American radar barrier. The air force bought aircraft of the same type as EC-121s. However, land-based WV-2s continued to operate in direct support of the fleet until carriers began to operate their own AEW-CIC aircraft beginning in the late 1950s.

By 1956 it was clear that the S-band APS-20 was too limited. As on board ships, it seemed that the future AEW radar ought to operate at UHF frequency. Although that eventually materialised on board the Grumman E-2 Hawkeye, the idea was first raised in connection with the big land-based aircraft, which could most easily accommodate a large antenna. A UHF APS-70 radar was first tested on board a single WV-2E.[9] It was housed in a rotodome and it seems to have been conceived as an operational radar to replace the existing types.[10] Unlike APS-20, it was housed above the body of the aircraft. At that time it was estimated that at 5000ft the APS-70 had twice the range of an APS-20E (on board an AEW Super Constellation) at 3000ft. If both radars were at 20,000ft, the APS-70 not only had twice the range, but could detect targets a tenth the size at the same range. In 1956 APS-70 was expected to be at the breadboard stage within a year.

Above: A Tu-22M2 'Backfire' shows its two wing pylons and its bomb bay, with attachments for an under-body Kh-22 missile in a 1989 photograph. This aircraft entered production at Kazan in 1971, the initial Tu-22M1 being intended for the Soviet navy. It apparently encountered problems; it was not officially accepted for service until 1976, apparently after modification to its flight control (presumably fly-by-wire) system. This production version was Tu-22M2, 211 being made between 1972 and 1983. The standard payload was a single Kh-22, although two or three could be carried at the expense of range. This version was issued to both the navy and the long-range air force (DA). Its complexity led to serious maintenance problems. The current version, the Tu-22M3, had more powerful NK-25 engines and it could be distinguished by its raked inlets. It also had a strengthened wing for low-level operation (the Tu-22M2 encountered problems at low altitude). Reportedly the Soviets saw the aircraft's ability to carry multiple missiles as a way for a single regiment to saturate battle group defences. Twelve examples of a reconnaissance or pathfinder version, Tu-22M(R), were also built. Attempts to build a companion jammer seem to have been complicated by interference with the fly-by-wire system and a satisfactory jammer was completed only at the end of the Cold War.

Below: Tu-95RTs ('Bear D') was both an essential element in Soviet anti-ship attacks, relaying a radar picture down to surface ships and submarines and a standard Soviet maritime reconnaissance aircraft. The targeting system, of which the 'Bear D' was an element, was Oospekh-1A (Success-1A), the big search radar (NATO 'Big Bulge') being named Oospekh. The downlink was Arfa (Harp). Oospekh might be likened to the US APS-20 and Arfa to its Bellhop downlink. Arfa occupied the deep chin fairing which in a standard Tu-95 contained a Rubidiy-MM ground-mapping radar. Completion of trials was delayed by electrical interference within the system. Production at Kuibyshev amounted to fifty-three aircraft: two in 1963, five in 1964, an average of ten per year in 1965–8 and then the last five in 1969. Production aircraft like this one added the SRS-5 Vishnya (Cherry) COMINT system and a Romb-4 (Diamond) SIGINT system. Aircraft were later fitted with an ogival tailcone housing an additional jammer. Some of these aircraft may have been operational as early as 1963, but official acceptance for service came on 30 May 1966. This photograph of a 'Bear D' was released in May 1975.

Fleet air defence could not be separated from defence against submarines. A submerged submarine sees targets within only a limited area. The faster the target, the louder, but to intercept the submarine must run at high speed, which blinds its sonars. Effective submarine warfare therefore requires some means of ocean surveillance. In the Second World War that usually meant code-breaking, but maritime reconnaissance aircraft could overcome gaps in it. The lesson was that codes had to be handled much more carefully, so it was assumed that enemy maritime reconnaissance aircraft – snoopers and shadowers would be more essential than ever. Even when other long-range alternatives were present, such as land-based HF/DF,

satellites and code-breaking, aircraft were needed to gain sufficient precision to back submarine attacks. Snoopers therefore became a focus in ASW, justifying fighters like the Sea Harrier aboard ships otherwise dedicated to ASW. Here an F-14 from VF-114 (on board *America*) intercept a Soviet Il-38 maritime patrol aircraft, presumably playing snooper. This photograph was released in September 1981. Note that the F-14 was unarmed except for its cannon and was carrying extra fuel. Later in the 1980s all such aircraft always flew with missiles on board, in accord with a rising sense of US response to Soviet aggressiveness.

Because snoopers were essential for submarine attacks, the US Navy formed ASW fighter squadrons (VSFs), detachments from which could be assigned to ASW carriers (CVS). Their aircraft were what amounted to light jet fighters: Skyhawks armed with 20mm cannon, with range-only radars (which were also useful for ground attack). These Marine A-4s from VMA-223 Detachment T share the flight deck of the ASW carrier *Yorktown* with the ship's S-2E Tracker ASW aircraft. Ahead of the two Skyhawks is an AD-5W AEW Skyraider. These Skyhawks were considered subsonic day fighters. The British Sea Harrier originally had much the same role, the idea being that snoopers would be subsonic long-endurance aircraft they (like Skyhawks) could deal with. (*The Hook*)

Because the VSFs were formed just before the United States entered the Vietnam War, they were generally used as attack units. That is why this VSF-1 Skyhawk (A-4C), trapping in 1968, was assigned not to an ASW carrier but to the attack carrier *Independence*. Its port 20mm cannon muzzle is just visible at its wing root. (*The Hook*)

A low-frequency radar could simultaneously measure height and range. One method was lobe counting, much as shipboard UHF radars had measured height during the Second World War, but benefitting from the greater height of the AEW radar. Another was the one finally used by the E-2, time difference. The pulse going from the aircraft to the target and coming back can follow alternative paths, either direct or reflected (once or twice) off the water. If the height of the radar is known, as it is, the time difference between the paths gives the height of the target. The method works only above the sea, which reflects radar signals, but it does away with the need for a separate heightfinding radar. Even in 1956 it seemed that errors would be no more than 5 per cent and presumably the system works better now.

By that time Lockheed had designed what it thought would be the ultimate land-based naval AEW aircraft, its CL 257-29, which had been developed over the past two years. Compared to the existing WV-2, it had an enlarged wing and instead of piston engines it would have four T56-A-7 turboprops, supplemented by wingtip J34-WE-36 turbojets for use at high altitude. Heightfinding techniques not yet having been perfected, the big rotodome for the APS-70 would sit atop a pylon holding the APS-45 heightfinder. As of 1956, this aircraft was expected to enter service in 1959. Given so short a time, the radars could not be fitted for digital signal processing, but Lockheed (which was responsible for overall system design) hoped that the current analog displays could be integrated with a digital computer to assist operators in tracking, data storage and interceptor computation – an airborne equivalent of an early NTDS. If that succeeded, the aircraft could handle fifty tracks and twelve interceptions – not very impressive compared to what the E-2 could do a few years later, but far better than past capability. At this time the ATDS specification was a capacity for 256 tracks and ten simultaneous interceptions.

In 1957 BuAer planned a WV-2 upgrade programme, which might have included installation of the APS-70 radar. At about the same time the CL 257-29 design was accepted as the follow-on W2V-1, which would incorporate high-speed air-to-air and air-to-ground

The post-war successor to the PB-1W Flying Fortress (Cadillac II) was a much-modified Super Constellation airliner, the WV-2, shown here as part of the barrier force supporting North American Air Defense. This one was from VW-15 and it was photographed in March 1957 above another element of the seaward barrier, a converted destroyer escort (*Sellstrom*) of Destroyer Escort Squadron 18. The belly radome housed the antenna of an APS-20 search radar (much larger than that of APS-20s on board carrier aircraft) and the dorsal radome housed the antenna of an APS-45 heightfinder. The number of small dipole antennas testifies to the massive communication capability of the aircraft, with its own CIC. WV-2s were also used to gather signals intelligence, using their radar antennas as high-gain receivers.

A CIC officer is shown supervising one of his fighter directors on board a WV-2 in June 1957. The DRT (dead-reckoning tracer) table, a navigational plot, is on the left. There was also a CIC-type vertical plot, not visible here.

As on surface ships, airborne radar developers realised that they could achieve greater ranges by shifting to lower frequency, which required a much larger antenna. The first such airborne radar was APS-70, which was tested on board a modified Super Constellation designated WV-2E (E for electronic, not for the fifth member of the WV-2 series). Note the absence of the usual tip tanks. Despite its considerable advantages, this radar was not fitted to operational WV-2s. However, the development of APS-70 was an important factor in the design of the next generation of carrier-based AEW aircraft.

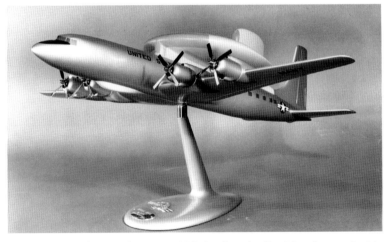

BuAer sought an alternative long-range AEW aircraft, so it offered Douglas a contract to design an AEW version of its DC-7C airliner. This model shows the result. The big flat radome would have housed the new APS-70 low-frequency radar, with the heightfinder above it. This photograph was dated 5 October 1954.

Under a navy contract, Lockheed developed an improved WV-2 with the new radar and with jet engines instead of tip tanks. The internal designation was CL257-8, in the CL257 series of radar Constellations. The APS-45 would have been in the pedestal supporting the APS-70 rotodome. Had it been built, this would have been the WV-3. It is not clear why support for such improvements collapsed.

communications equipment (not described, however, as data links).[11] A draft of the detail specification was signed on 22 March 1957 and contract negotiation begun. The mock-up and long-lead contract was signed. However, the contract was partially terminated in June 1957, leaving the CIC compartment mock-up complete. As it represented the latest thinking in AEW-CIC development and arrangement, it was considered worthwhile. The W2V never flew. Nor did any more WV-2s with the new radar, although existing aircraft remained in service on barrier patrols through 1965. By 1957 money was so tight that fifteen of the thirty-three planned WV-2s in the FY57 budget had to be cancelled to free cash for maintenance of the existing fleet. As far as the carriers were concerned, the E-1B and then the E-2 provided AEW CICs on a much more satisfactory basis.

In addition to aircraft, airships were fitted with large AEW radars. They could accommodate really large antennas inside their envelopes, but they lacked the mobility of aircraft. It appears that the big AEW airships were intended exclusively for barrier duties, so they are not discussed further here.

Carrier-based AEW

Production of Cadillac I ended with the end of the Second World War; the decision was soon made to use variants of the much more massive Skyraider (AD) for the purpose. However, the APS-20 radar was soon in considerable demand for anti-submarine warfare, since it could detect small surface targets such as submarine snorkels. Many Avengers

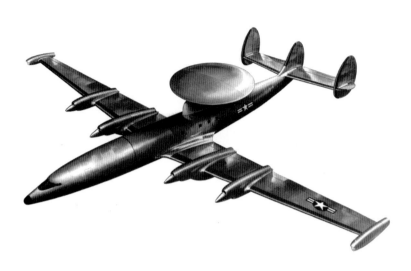

Lockheed's ultimate improved WV-2 was this turboprop CL257-29. Development began under the designation W2V-1, but it stopped in 1956.

With the development of the Naval Tactical Data System (and its airborne node, the Airborne Tactical Data System) underway in 1956, BuAer sought bids for an interim carrier-based AEW-CIC aircraft. Grumman won. Its WF-2 (E-1B) is shown landing on *Bennington*, 28 February 1969.

(TBM) were converted after war to TBM-3W2s not for AEW but instead to detect submarines. Compared to Cadillac I, they had an improved radar (APS-20A) and the after crew space was rearranged. More importantly, they did not have the VHF radar relay of an AEW aircraft. Instead, because they were expected to fly beyond the horizon of an ASW carrier, they had HF radio, which lacked the capacity to relay a radar picture. Normally they had a crew of three, including an air controller/evaluator who would control the companion ASW attack aircraft (a TBM-3E). These aircraft were superseded in US service by a radar version of the Grumman Guardian (AF) anti-submarine aircraft, the AF-2W. The companion AF-2S carried a smaller radar and a homing torpedo. The two were intended to work together as a hunter-killer team, but by 1949 BuAer wanted a 'single package' ASW aircraft. That had nothing direct to do with carrier AEW, but it was about the size needed for a carrier-based CIC aircraft. ASW involved a crew some of whom would carry out what amounted to CIC duties.

There was increasing interest in developing a carrier version of the flying CIC (Cadillac II). The idea seems to have been proposed by DNCO (Air) even before the end of the war and it was repeated in May 1946.[12] A study by the BuAer Aircraft Design Research branch showed that such an aircraft was feasible, although it would have no heightfinder (no such airborne radar then existed). The great question BuAer raised was whether it might be best to obtain such an aircraft simply by modifying an existing type, the candidate being the AJ-1 Savage bomber. OpNav was interested, although it saw no point in arming the aircraft, which would be operating with fighters.

As of April 1949, the planned carrier CIC-AEW aircraft was a modified version of the new long-range A2J attack bomber, but among the nine prototypes BuAer wanted, it had only the seventh priority, hence was not bought given limited funds (in this list the first priority was XVF(N), a replacement for the F3D).

After 1945 the converted TBM was used for experiments (a TBM with an APS-20 radar was used extensively for ASW) and instead the big new Skyraider was modified into a carrier-based AEW aircraft. This is an AD-4W. Fifty aircraft of this type were transferred to the Royal Navy under MDAP. (Douglas via Naval Institute)

Two AD-5Ws from VAW-12 are shown over *Forrestal*, 25 April 1960. This version had a wider body allowing side by side seating for the radar operators.

BuAer saw the single-package ASW aircraft as the obvious candidate for the extension of carrier AEW to a full airborne CIC. Grumman won the ASW competition (OS-117) in 1950 with its S2F Tracker. Vought then proposed an AEW version of its failed competitor, which was apparently initially selected under the designation S2U-1W.[13] However, Grumman offered an AEW version of its S2F, which must have been attractive for its commonality with the anti-submarine aircraft. To minimise changes, Grumman placed the APS-20 radome above the cockpit, rather than in the belly position used in the past. By placing it so far forward, Grumman could avoid changing the unusual form of angled wing-folding it had used to allow it to employ an unusually long wing (which had won it the ASW competition). Neither the S2U-1 nor the WF-1 was built, although a report on the WF-1 mock-up survives.[14]

Nothing was done until the late 1950s. The initial post-war production carrier AEW aircraft was the Douglas AD-2W, a version of the Skyraider attack bomber with the massive radome of the wartime Cadillac I. Two radar operators sat side by side in the fuselage below a fairing running back from the cockpit and the aircraft could carry two drop tanks underwing. As of 1948, thirty-one of these aircraft were planned, to replace the Cadillac I aircraft. Later versions were AD-3W, -4W and -5W of which fifty AD-4Ws were supplied to the Royal Navy under MDAP.[15] In British service, their radar operators acted as fighter controllers, so the British aircraft may have been the first carrier-launched airborne CICs.[16]

A 1956 report of AD-5W performance (from VC-11) using data gathered over an eight-month period gives some idea of AEW capability at that time. Results were better than in the past. On 21 March selected crews were able to detect low-flying jets (a section of two) at an average of 82nm and a maximum of 100nm. About a month later normal crews were able to complete fourteen of seventeen attempted interceptions against jets (whose altitude was known) at an average of 80nm, in a canned exercise. In July, when the squadron was evaluated, high-flying jets (section of two) were detected on average at 60nm (maximum 130nm); high propeller aircraft (section of two) were detected on average at 90nm (maximum 130nm). Low propeller-driven aircraft, the worst threat in most exercises, were detected on average at 70nm (maximum 80nm).

At this time an AEW aircraft was typically stationed 150nm from task force centre. A barrier of three AD-5W created an impassable barrier, although a great deal depended on the altitude of the aircraft. It seemed reasonable at this time to expect to detect a low altitude fighter section or single bomber 70nm from the aircraft (maximum 130nm). The same target at high altitude would be detected on average at a range of 50nm (maximum 130nm). The great limit on minimum range was sea returns, which depended on AEW altitude: the higher the aircraft, the worse the problem, but high-altitude AEW was valued as the only way to detect low-fliers in time to intercept them.

It appears that what finally made the carrier AEW-CIC happen was the development of NTDS (see Chapter 10), which included an airborne node.

Left: Both Lockheed and Vought saw the interim requirement as a much closer step to the desired final AEW aircraft, so both offered APS-70 radars and computer combat systems. Presumably both saw their proposals mainly as somewhat simplified versions of the final fully-computerised AEW-CIC aircraft. This is the Lockheed CL-327 proposal, May 1956. Its rotodome was similar to that adopted for the E-2C. Span would have been 82ft 6in and length 52ft 11in.

Below: This is one of Vought's proposed designs, V-404B. Vought's proposal for the full AEW-CIC aircraft, which was probably very similar, initially won the competition on technical grounds, but it lost on industrial grounds, which presumably meant that it was less producible than the Grumman design which won. Span was 84ft 10.8in and length was 56ft; gross weight would have been 39,024lbs. The engines were T56-A-1s producing 3750 equivalent horsepower each (presumably including the effect of jet thrust).

GENERAL ARRANGEMENT —

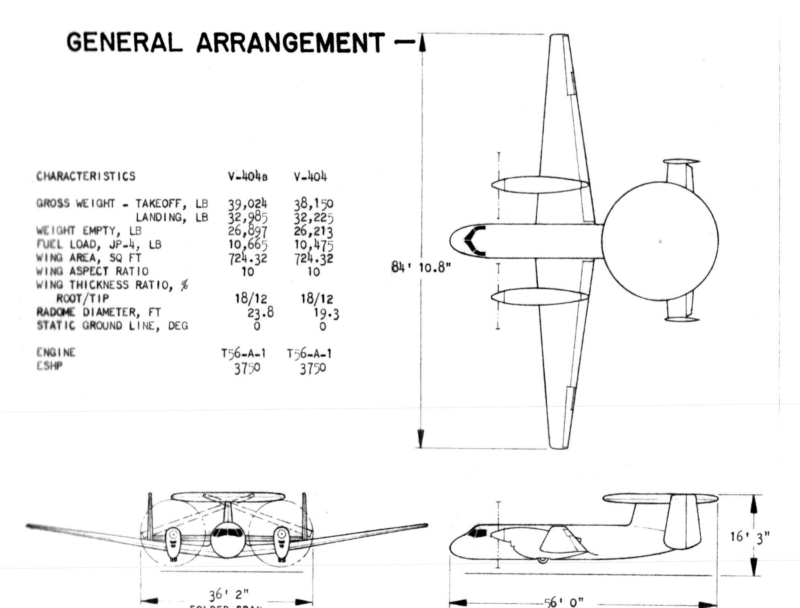

CHARACTERISTICS	V-404B	V-404
GROSS WEIGHT - TAKEOFF, LB	39,024	38,150
LANDING, LB	32,985	32,225
WEIGHT EMPTY, LB	26,897	26,213
FUEL LOAD, JP-4, LB	10,665	10,475
WING AREA, SQ FT	724.32	724.32
WING ASPECT RATIO	10	10
WING THICKNESS RATIO, % ROOT/TIP	18/12	18/12
RADOME DIAMETER, FT	23.8	19.3
STATIC GROUND LINE, DEG	0	0
ENGINE	T56-A-1	T56-A-1
ESHP	3750	3750

84' 10.8"

36' 2"
FOLDED SPAN

16' 3"

56' 0"

The ultimate winner of the AEW-CIC aircraft to fit within the NTDS/ATDS system was Grumman's E-2 (originally W2F) Hawkeye, which remains in production in much-modified form sixty years later. The original design was a gull-winged aircraft with an APS-70 rotodome, but the APS-70 was replaced by a more powerful General Electric radar (APS-96) and the gull wing replaced by the high wing shown here. That in turn opened necessary space in the fuselage.

Even after the Grumman design won the carrier AEW-CIC competition, Douglas proposed an AEW-CIC version of its multi-role carrier transport, powered by four Lycoming turboprops. This its 1957 sketch of the AEW version of its Douglas 1906. It was not bought in any form.

The Royal Navy adapted its standard ASW aircraft, the Gannet, for AEW using the existing APS-20 radar. These AEW Gannets (note the belly radomes) and Scimitars were cross-decked from *Hermes* and *Centaur* to *Forrestal*, 14 August 1962. Although it had only one contraprop, the Gannet was twin-engined, with two turboprops in its body. The AEW Gannet might be considered equivalent to Grumman's WF-1 project, a Tracker (S2F) with an APS-20 in a radome above its nose. Like the S2F, the Gannet was an AEW-CIC aircraft, the two men buried in its fuselage being fighter controllers rather than radar operators. A further version of the Gannet carrying the APS-82 radar of the WF-2 (E-1B) was considered by the Royal Navy but not built.

CHAPTER 9

A CRISIS IN FLEET AIR DEFENCE

POST-WAR US fleet air defence was formally defined by a policy first stated in 1948, which reflected wartime practice.[1] Guns would be responsible for targets out to a slant range of 10,000 yds, beyond which the fighters were responsible. A clause which would cause trouble later explained that any guided-missile zone would overlap both the gun and the fighter zones. The stated underlying assumption was that enemy aircraft were the primary threat to US naval forces whose 'immediate and primary mission' was to seize and maintain the tactical advantage of offensive action. In order of priority, the primary means of fleet air defence was to destroy the enemy air force on the ground, which tied fleet air defence to the navy's projected nuclear capability. The second priority was interception in the air. Recent progress in air weapons 'and the possibility of sudden airborne threats' demanded radical improvement in fleet air defence. The policy paper recognised that a radar-equipped enemy might be able to attack in any weather, so all-weather carrier operation became an essential element in fleet air

defence. It also recognised the need for much better co-ordination among ships of a task force, for longer-range radars and for much better IFF.

Priorities were formally set in November 1949.[2] Long-range radar (SPS-2 and follow-ons) came first, followed by the Sparrow air-to-air missile and then by continued tests of carrier-based interceptors (including those capable of operation as night fighters) and fourth by 'an adequate system for the display, evaluation and use of information for air defence purposes'.

In April 1949 the Operational Development Force (OpDevFor) was assigned to develop procedures to deal with fast high-altitude aircraft.[3] It did so by conducting an exercise early in May 1949. The set-up gives an idea of contemporary guesses as to the threat and also the character of the likely response. In this case low-fliers were not included, due to the original assignment. Plans clearly called for defence in depth. That depth would be provided by surface and air pickets. Conditions were

controlled: the approximate time of attack and the altitude of a raid were known to the defenders. Altitude had to be given because available radars did not give satisfactory altitude information, a very serious deficiency. The light carrier *Saipan* (with the plane guard destroyer *Kraus*) represented the fleet. She had Mk V IFF and SRa, SR-2 and SP radars (the SRs were a preliminary form of SPS-6). The radar picket destroyers *Zellars* and *Massey* were deployed at maximum reliable Mk V IFF range of the carrier, with the experimental radar picket destroyer *Winslow* closer in. An AEW aircraft near the carrier provided surface coverage. Another operated on the 60-mile circle around the two picket destroyers, that being the average maximum control range for jet aircraft without either Mk V IFF or an electronic beacon. Average detection range on a multi-engine bomber using the SPS-6B destroyer radar was 120nm. B-29s were detected both inside and outside that range. Each destroyer had a minimum effective radar range inside which sea clutter precluded effective radar operation.

A major question in fleet air defence was how to specify the location of an incoming aircraft which one ship detected and then handed over to another. Pickets strung out far from the centre of a task force would not be controlling the fighters which intercepted the attackers they detected, particularly not high-altitude attackers they might detect at extreme radar range. The solution adopted in the exercise was to provide all the pickets with a gridded chart which they could use to indicate positions. As long as all ships understood the same gridded references, they could pass air contact information back and forth. This was understood to be the step before the fleet adopted a grid based not on land features (this exercise was run off the Virginia Capes), but centred on the fleet itself. For the 1949 exercise, the grid was divided into 5nm squares. Information placing a contact within a square was considered sufficiently precise.

Without a mutually-understood grid, reporting by the pickets could be useless or, worse, misleading; two pickets seeing the same incoming attacker could easily report it in positions different enough to indicate two separate attackers to the controlling ship, typically the carrier. The problem was difficult because the pickets were most valuable if they were stationed well over the horizon, as in this exercise. That left them no simple line-of-sight means of determining their locations relative to the control ship. Once computer systems entered service, they too needed a means of maintaining a consistent grid. The computer system continued the previous practice of defining what ships saw in terms of a rectangular grid. It turned out to be quite difficult to ensure that the grid a picket used was the same as the grid used by the carrier and the aircraft. In the computer era this problem was called 'gridlock'. It was not really solved until the 1980s, with the advent of fast computers which could compare positions on a ship's own grid and on another ship's grid. Even then results were sometimes poor, to the point where it seems that only GPS ended the gridlock problem.

Plans called for a later phase in which a picket destroyer would be placed 180nm south of the carrier; its 120nm SPS-6B would give the carrier 300nm warning (that could not be done). It turned out that the AEW aircraft, a PB-1W, could have been stationed further south. As

Through the 1950s, BuAer invested heavily in new fighters, but its exercises showed that they were not enough. Bombers would get through and undoubtedly they would be armed with thermonuclear bombs. Something better was needed. Here one of the new supersonic Crusaders (an F8U-1 of VF-32) occupies the starboard catapult of *Saratoga*, 23 May 1958, while an F3H-2N Demon of VF-31 occupies the other bow catapult.

it was, it was 50nm from the outer picket, which allowed it to detect a B-29 at a range of about 75nm. Although the SPS-6B radars used performed better than other fleet radars against high-altitude targets, stormy weather created enough clutter on their screens that they could not track through it. The clutter area was usually 24–30nm in diameter. The radar adjustment (STC) which reduced clutter also suppressed target echoes.

Saipan flew off two Banshees which tried to counter an attack by two other Banshees at 40,000ft. They began their approach beyond picket radar range. When they were detected, *Saipan* scrambled a Banshee (she had only one suitable catapult). Seven minutes later the second jet was launched to join the first over the ship. Eleven minutes were then lost because it took that long for the section leader to realise that his compass was reading 90° off. Even so, they managed to tallyho 70nm from the carrier, within the clutter area of the ship controlling them (*Winslow*). The controller could not see the fighters, so he dead-reckoned them into position. There was enough time to switch control

to the pickets 60nm south, who had a clearer picture. Control errors precluded a successful interception. Flying at 40,000ft, the attackers clearly saw contrails from the interceptors at 43,000ft, 10 miles away. The interceptors, however, found it difficult to see the attackers' contrails against the gray atmosphere below. Interceptors should, the report said, be placed about 1500ft below the target. At this point it was not yet policy that all interceptors should have air-to-air radar.

When B-29s served as targets, the interceptors were sections (four aircraft) of F4U-5 Corsairs. One section was stationed about 30 miles south of the outer picket station orbiting at 35,000ft. The rest of the

Supersonic Tiger fighters line the landing ramp of *Intrepid* during LantFleet Ex 2-58. The most difficult air defence threat is abaft them: low-flying Skyraiders. Any satisfactory fleet air-defence system had to handle both high- and low-flying threats. Until the 1960s there was insufficient intelligence to show that the Soviets had never developed an effective low-altitude anti-carrier threat, perhaps because simply locating a moving target from a low-flying aircraft was so difficult.

available Corsairs – two of them – were stationed about 40nm from *Winslow* as a back-up. The B-29, flying at 30,000ft at its maximum sustained cruising speed of 300 knots, began its run outside the radar range of the outer pickets. It was detected at 145nm and the outer picket section sent in. At the same time two Banshees were scrambled from the nearby Naval Air Station at Oceana, 40nm from the carrier and vectored to her. The Corsairs intercepted the B-29 when 80nm south of the outer pickets and the two back-up Corsairs made their interception near the *Winslow*. The Banshees were vectored so that *Winslow* could control them. However, of her two controllers, one was not qualified to make the intercept. The other was busy with the two Corsairs, so the Banshees had to be sent back to the area of the carrier without trying to intercept.

Without good intelligence to describe Soviet aircraft, US air defence developers worked in terms of aircraft they knew, such as the air force's B-47 and the A3D Skywarrior, shown here on board *Saratoga*. The fighter being launched from the port bow catapult is a Demon.

The report concluded that under reasonably realistic conditions the two attacking Banshees had been intercepted despite their high speed (475 knots) and altitude (40,000ft). It appeared that no existing bomber could make that speed. The Banshees had, moreover, achieved their interception even though they were not aided by either a beacon or Mk V IFF. The B-29 was intercepted 200nm from the carrier, having been detected at a range of 265nm.

Everything had worked, but the exercise had uncovered the basic limitations of the system. Communication was an obvious weak point. Performance in the exercise was above current fleet standards but average by Second World War standards. As a whole it was inadequate to fight a fast-moving air battle. A widely dispersed picket force would have to rely on MHF radio until a reliable VHF or VHF relay system was developed. Current receivers and transmitters were inadequate.

The new SPS-6A and -6B radars worked well, but the older SR-2 on board the *Saipan* did not and the SP heightfinders were unsatisfactory. The Mk V IFF in *Saipan* worked well but the ship's CIC did not

exploit it as it should have. CIC performance improved noticeably each day. Even with a skilled controller from the Operational Development Force in each CIC, they were short-handed.

The exercise showed how important it was to keep track of friendly aircraft; current CICs offered only a low level of what the report called accountability. Ideally each PPI scope operator should be able to display the identification of each blip. At the least aircraft needed beacons until the current Mk V IFF could be installed in the fleet. To reduce the burden on CICs, aircraft needed some form of automatic navigational system.

OpDevFor kept testing and its June 1950 report was encouraging.[4] This report described tactics the force had developed, which the fleet presumably was encouraged to adopt over the next few years. As it had suggested earlier, if the fleet could track its own fighters using radar beacons, pickets could provide a defence in depth, making it possible to destroy attackers before they came within missile-launch range. As in 1949, the force continued to simulate a whole carrier task force with a single carrier. In effect it was a Second World War system expanded by adding a second line of destroyer pickets and a third (outer) line of submarine pickets. There were also AEW aircraft. Any picket system had to detect both high-speed high-altitude aircraft (as in the 1949 tests) as well as raids at medium and low altitudes. Radar cover had to overlap so that the force could track attackers continuously and it and communications had to maintain reliable fighter control well beyond the horizon of the carrier or any other ship. It was assumed that the situation would allow a commander to estimate the likely direction from which an enemy attack might originate. The report did not say

Photographed about 1950, *Franklin D Roosevelt* shows radars developed at the end of the Second World War. The SR-3 on the foremast (a long narrow reflector with a separate IFF interrogator) operated at L-band (20cm rather than the wartime 1.5m). It was so ineffective that on 25 April 1948 CNO ordered replacement of SK-series sets stopped. Existing SR-3s were refitted with the new parabolic reflectors of the SPS-6 series, SR-3B using an SPS-6B antenna. The rotation rate of 2.5 or 5rpm was considered far too low to deal with jets (SK rotated at 4.5rpm). Modern search radars typically rotate at 15rpm. The rotation rate determines how quickly the radar returns to an place in the sky; the faster it scans, the better it can follow a fast-moving target. However, the faster the radar scans, the less time it spends staring at any one place: the probability that it detects a target depends on how much energy it pours onto it, which depends on how long it stares. The SR-2 aft operated at 50cm wavelength. The pilot model was tested in April 1945; eighteen of the planned 300 were made. SR-2 was dropped due to inferior performance and replaced by the post-war SPS-6 operating at 20cm. Just visible is the base of the SX combined search and heightfinding radar, both elements operating at S-band (10cm).

so, but that would be most difficult in the Eastern Mediterranean, as a fleet there would face Soviet and satellite air bases spread over a considerable area. The 1950 exercise simulated that problem by assuming a 180° threat sector.

Based on a total of fifty-three raids, OpDevFor concluded that 89 per cent of all actual raids (as opposed to friendly or neutral aircraft) would be detected. Of these, 67 per cent were sighted by defending fighters and 58 per cent of all raids were attacked at least once. The force managed to detect half of all raids 190nm out and to attack half before they came within 65nm. These successes were offset by the fact that most raids were by single multi-engine aircraft such as Neptunes,

Privateers and B-17s at medium altitudes, but some were by two-fighter sections (Corsairs and jet Banshees).

In the exercise, submarine pickets and two AEW aircraft operated in the van of the force across the likely threat axis. Each submarine could detect incoming aircraft up to 40nm away (if they flew high enough). Each of the AEW aircraft flew a racetrack (barrier) patrol, its

Photographed on 8 June 1955, *Coral Sea* shows an initial step towards adopting lower-frequency radars: her SR-3 has been replaced by a wartime-type SK-2 operating at much longer wavelength. The radar atop the foremast is an SPN-6 for air traffic control. It is somewhat awkwardly located, since aircraft are marshalled into a landing circuit coming from aft. Above it is the ubiquitous SPS-6B L-band air-search radar. Above that is an SPS-8 heightfinder, which replaces the dual-antenna SX. About level with the SPS-8 is a YE aircraft homing beacon, in an unusual low position. The antenna barely visible further up is a clamshell attached to a dual-purpose surface- and zenith-search radar, probably SPS-4. The arms visible above it support the short vertical dipoles of the newly introduced UHF ship-to-air radio system, which superseded VHF. Below the clamshell is a set of three ECM (actually receiving) antennas, spinners inside radomes to determine the direction of an enemy signal. The small radome at the very top of the mast is for HF/DF (URD-4). Also visible is one of the two Mk 25 fire-control radars used with the ship's Mk 37 anti-aircraft directors. Finally, the thimble radome alongside the funnel is for an SPN-8 carrier-controlled approach radar, the beginning of US efforts to develop automatic carrier landing. The aircraft are long-nose Banshees (F2H-3 or -4).

maximum detection range being 60nm. Overlapping the inner side of this barrier was radar coverage by two (of a total of four) destroyer pickets. Each could detect a target 100nm away, but could not control fighters (without beacons) beyond 60nm. The destroyers were spread around a command ship, with the main force further back, as far from the threat as possible. If the threat axis could not be predicted at all, about four times as many pickets would be needed. All ranges were characterised as maximum reliable figures, often exceeded in practice. Initially the force would have no more than two CAP sections in the air, over the command ship rather than the carrier (as would have been the case in the Second World War). Once a picket had recognised a contact as hostile, it could take over control of the CAP assigned to it. If the CAP was not sufficient, further aircraft could be scrambled. CAP control would be passed from ship to ship until a raider was shot down.

In the exercise, the light carrier *Saipan* was both command ship and a source of CAP fighters (jets operated from ashore). That looked forward to specialised command ships, beginning with the prototype *Northampton*, then being built. The heavy cruiser *Newport News* was tried as a simulated tactical flagship controlling air defence and co-ordinating anti-aircraft defence, communicating with three surface pickets 60nm away.

In the initial stages of the exercise all aircraft operated from shore to provide both targets and CAP. Later all defending aircraft were ship-

Photographed early in 1953 about to catapult a Panther, with an AD-4N Skyraider flying off her angled deck (not catapulted), *Antietam* shows the standard radar antennas of the early post-war period. The big radar atop her tripod mast is the SX developed at the end of the war. On the left is the big dish of SK-2, the successor to the SK-1 mattress. On the right is an SPS-6B air-search radar sponsored out from the island. The radome above SX is for electronic countermeasures. Atop the mast, not visible here, was a YE aircraft homing beacon. It was not yet understood that the low frequency of the SK series offered much greater potential, particularly against streamlined aircraft, than the higher frequencies of SPS-6 and SX. Existing SK series radars did not generally realise this potential because they scanned too slowly. However, a few years later they were installed on board ships as stop-gaps to make up for the limited capability of the more modern sets.

based, the carrier *Saipan* operating Corsairs and Bearcats and the larger *Philippine Sea* operating Banshees and day and night Corsairs. The Banshees normally remained airborne for an hour and three quarters (actual time averaged one hour 35 minutes) to keep 1500lbs of fuel on board when landing. The longest time airborne was an hour and 53 minutes, the aircraft landing with 550lbs of fuel on board. In comparison, a Corsair with full drop tanks could typically remain airborne for about 2.75 hours, landing with 70–80 gallons of fuel. Pilots considered the Corsair excellent up to 35,000ft and less effective above that, although in the exercise they were operated extensively up to 40,000ft. At the upper end of the altitude scale pilots had to be unusually attentive, because the aircraft would stall at relatively high speed in the thin air, not too far below its limiting Mach number. The pilots also suffered from inadequate heating and a lack of pressurisation, problems the Banshee did not have.

Late in the exercise, the Banshees were used almost exclusively as scrambled interceptors. That worked because the pickets offered such

long warning ranges. The best time for scrambling two Banshees was five minutes five seconds from the order to scramble. However, the worst times were far worse, up to 33 minutes (possibly for a propeller fighter). Some of the problem was due to lags in transmission, from the Task Force CIC to the carrier CIC and thence to Primary Fly (Pri-Fly) and bridge and finally to the flight deck. *Philippine Sea* solved this problem by cutting out intermediate stages. CIC bypassed Air Operations and sent the order directly to Pri-Fly and bridge. Pri-Fly ordered a scramble using a bullhorn without referring back to the ship's commanding officer.

Because their low-altitude fuel consumption was so great, the Banshees normally flew at 25,000 to 45,000ft. They could easily deal with anything but another Banshee. In an emergency, a Banshee could reach 40,000ft in 15 to 20 minutes (about 25 minutes if there were no emergency). The Operational Development Force pointed out that this time lag, plus time lost in scrambling and control by a fighter director, made the scrambled Banshee only marginally effective against a medium-speed high-altitude target and unsatisfactory against a high-performance target. The navy really did need the high-performance interceptors BuAer was then developing. OpDevFor recommended that to conserve fuel and extend their endurance, Banshees should be allowed to shut one engine down whenever possible below 30,000ft (pilots needed up to a minute to restart). That technique was later common. In the exercise, Banshee pilots preferred a 25,000ft holding altitude, as at that height they had the best fuel economy and they could quickly restart an engine. Short endurance would make it difficult for a Banshee to make repeated wave-offs while waiting for a carrier deck to be steady enough for landing. That would make heavy sea/high wind operations problematic. Existing Banshees had a weak landing gear support structure which caused problems serious enough that the squadron commanders considered the aircraft unusable in anything but the smoothest seas. *Philippine Sea* managed a landing interval of about 50 seconds, which was slightly longer than normal, as pilots took slightly longer to avoid wave-offs.

The Bearcat was effective below 25,000ft, but could not be considered useful above that. Their performance was much reduced and they suffered too many materiel failures. The altitude limit seems reasonable since the Bearcat was conceived to counter lower-altitude aircraft.

On the *Philippine Sea*, the short endurance of the Banshee and the relatively short endurance of the Corsair at high altitude greatly increased the load on the air department personnel. Incompatibility between the two aircraft forced the carrier to respot almost continuously. Had the exercise forced the Banshees to operate at lower altitudes, their fuel consumption would have increased enormously, much complicating the carrier's operations. Fuelling time was too long: on average a Banshee required another 600 gallons after landing, but typically each hose delivered only 40 gallons per minute. Banshee readiness was 'only tentative. Even after complete pre-flight checks and sometimes even pre-flight turn-up, the percentage of last-minute duds was high.' Duds ruined scramble performance, because given the problem the aircraft could not be spotted on catapults before starting. Pilots had to be in aircraft fully ready with starting jeeps manned and plugged in. Even so time to start two jets averaged two minutes 10 seconds and time to load two catapults to launch them averaged two and a half minutes. The ship could easily turn into the wind while all this was being done, but typically it was cruising at low speed before the scramble. Deck operations were slowed by the duds; it would have been better if the ship had been able to start two jets at a time. Typical launch interval was two minutes; OpDevFor thought it could be halved by experienced crews.

As yet there were no jet blast deflectors; the report pointed to the need for an excessive clear area behind catapults, which made spotting even more difficult. As it was, a Banshee required considerable wind over deck to launch, so the carrier had to cruise at high speed when these aircraft were being held in readiness to scramble.[5] The carrier had to maintain speed because it accelerated slowly. Even though the catapults were not used at maximum pressure (capacity), they leaked and their valves sometimes stuck.

As in the Second World War, a good air controller on board a picket could handle two interceptions at the same time on the same channel. He could deal with two raids at the same time. This must have been one of the earliest exercises involving submarine pickets. Despite their limited facilities, they were generally the first to detect attackers, reporting until a destroyer picked them up. When they were provided with CAPs, they controlled them effectively. For outer air patrols, the submarines were intended as reference points for AEW aircraft (in the exercise, PB-1W airborne CICs). Without identifying beacons, the aircraft found it difficult to distinguish the submarines within the mass of shipping (this exercise was conducted off the US East Coast). These aircraft could have controlled CAP of their own, but they were too far from the carrier furnishing the aircraft; even the Corsairs lacked sufficient endurance. CAP could have been stationed over the submarines and under control of the AEW aircraft if it could remain on station for four hours (twice Corsair or Bearcat endurance at this distance) below 10,000ft or 15,000ft. Jets would of course have been in an even worse situation, given their short endurance.

The same ideas of defence in depth would permit a wider extension of task force defence if fighters had identifying beacons, so that effective air control range of the destroyer pickets (DDR) was 100nm. This formation envisaged CAP aircraft linking their data down to the DDRs and the command ship. The fleet might include a dedicated light carrier (CVL) operating mainly AEW aircraft and RAPCAP fighters for the radar picket stations.[6]

OpDevFor found in practice the same problem BuAer analysts were predicting in jet vs fast bomber interception: a fighter closing at 800 knots (a 'head-on intercept') could not tolerate much of an error in the time at which it turned to attack the bomber. Existing radars had a relatively low data rate, typically rotating at 5rpm (offering at most a plot every 12 seconds). Many of them suffered fading from time to time. Operators had to dead-reckon (connect the dots of indicated target positions) on the face of the PPI instead of passing individual target positions to the plotters working the vertical plot. OpDevFor suggested that some kind of automatic intercept computer-plotter was needed, to display fighter and raid plots, show course and speed of a

The immediate post-war generation of air-search radars had difficulty detecting streamlined jets at long range. *Randolph* is shown at the Jamestown Review, 1957. Her pole mast shows, at top the new Tacan aircraft navigation beacon, with a surface search antenna below it on the front of the mast. Below that is an L-band SPS-6. On the after side of the mast is the ship's SPN-6 carrier aircraft control (marshal) radar, used to control aircraft in the landing pattern. Atop the island, just forward of the uptake, is the ship's SPS-8 heightfinder, which was slewed in the direction of a contact. Aircraft visible on deck are Savage long-range bombers (and tankers), Fury day fighters, Banshee general-purpose fighters and Skyraider propeller-driven bombers.

Part of the solution was better long-range radar, operating at low frequency. *America* displays her radars about 1973. On the left, atop the lattice mast, is an SPS-30 heightfinder, which operated at high frequency. Atop the barbette is an SPG-51 used to guide the ship's Tartar self-defence missiles. The pole mast is topped by a TACAN antenna. Below it are ESM radomes and below them is the antenna of an SPS-10 surface-search radar. To the left, below that, is an SPN-43 for air traffic control (marshalling). It brought aircraft into a landing pattern. Automatic control required more precision, provided in part by the two small SPN-10 or -42 dishes, on the after part of the island. Other elements of the precision landing system are not visible. The cones are UHF radio antennas. The fore side of the pole mast shows a three-dimensional pencil-beam SPS-39 antenna. It swung its beam up and down rapidly, using electronic scanning, while it rotated. Like SPS-30, it operated at high frequency (S-band). The fore part of the island shows the ship's low-frequency long-range air-search radar, an SPS-43A. (Giorgio Arra)

raid and compute interception courses. This type of device was produced within a few years.

Low data rates made for poor radar information in the late stages of an interception; OpDevFor recommended that pilots be informed that data was poor so that they could search for their targets over a wider area. Jet pilots wanted to be placed so that the target was slightly above and forward of the beam. It was not the best attack position, but it was best for sighting a target not producing contrails. If the target did produce a contrail during the day, there was almost no final (tallyho) positioning problem, because the fighter pilot would see it at extreme range. The controller only had to vector the fighter for the earliest possible interception. As in the past, the controller had to be careful to position pilots favourably with regard to the sun; several intercepts failed because the fighter pilots were looking into the sun. Night interception sometimes failed, the reason generally being that the target was below the fighter. OpDevFor recommended dropping altitude in 4000ft increments until the fighter found the target on its radar. For the fighter radars then under development, the larger lesson was that they had to search a considerable cone in height as well as in bearing.

All ships would report radar contacts on a single net common to the whole force, using a simple grid system so that all could understand the positions of attackers and pickets (the report acknowledged the gridlock problem as a source of double counting of incoming raids). In the exercise, it turned out that AEW aircraft could pass out grid positions of the surface ships. CICs were co-ordinated over a voice net combining the usual roles of a Combat Information Net and an Air Control Net; it was successful after a period of training as an integrated force. In the raids simulated by OpDevFor, saturation of the radio net was not a serious problem; the net managed to handle all of the traffic. However, OpDevFor acknowledged that saturation could be a problem: the amount and type of traffic that could be passed on the net was in direct proportion to net discipline and to radio reliability. Most ships were so limited in the 1950 exercise that they had to use a single net not only for radar reporting and air control, but also for target and AEW control, to report carrier deck conditions (as in, whether a carrier could accept aircraft), to prepare and order scrambles and to change picket stations. A teletype net could have done as well, but the idea of using it was not favoured until late in the test.

The crucial voice net could clearly be jammed; ships in the exercise often inadvertently did so when tuning their transmitters or when a key was stuck. Some other means of communication than the MF voice net was needed. The net in the exercise had to operate at MF because the usual higher-frequency voice channels (VHF) were horizon-limited and HF, which was not, could not transmit rapidly enough. MF voice was recognised as insecure, unreliable and subject to jamming. The force needed a separate radio channel to handle assignment of tactical control of scrambled CAP fighters and similar control functions. In addition, each picket needed at least two radio channels to control CAP.

In later exercises, saturation of the reporting net itself became a problem, as ships struggled to report despite other ships' reports. That became a worse problem as aircraft speeds increased, because ships were picking up attackers at a higher rate. About 1956 a possible solution was proposed: net control by having ships report in round-robin fashion, in fixed time slots. This solution carried over to the

automated NTDS system (and its equivalents) which were under development at that time.

OpDevFor considered its proposed tactic effective despite its obvious (and solvable) complications. Most of the other problems which the tests brought out could be solved relatively quickly and at a reasonable cost. The worst was a lack of suitable navigational aids allowing a defending fighter to position itself. This was the key requirement for the emerging technique of broadcast control and it would be solved within a few years with the advent of TACAN. Aircraft lacked beaconry which would allow them to be tracked even if a radar did not pick up their echo. This too was a limited problem. Ships lacked effective radio direction-finders, again largely to track their own aircraft. There were no adequate heightfinding radars, but some were close to entering service. A more difficult problem was deficient communication.

OpDevFor was concerned with high and medium altitude targets. After OEG made its own study of fleet air defence requirements, OpNav assembled a review group.[7] Its April 1950 report pointed to a major gap. Since the end of the Second World War, attention had been focused almost entirely on high-flying bombers due to the development of jet engines (most efficient at high altitude), the atomic bomb (typically dropped from high altitude to spare the attacker), the guided missile and the temporary inability to detect high-altitude aircraft at reasonable ranges, due to the beam shapes and ranges of existing radars. The reality was that low

Launching a pair of Skyraiders on 4 June 1965, *Bon Homme Richard* shows both her big low-frequency air-search radar (SPS-43A) and her SPS-30 pencil-beam heightfinder. The radar above the SPS-30 is an SPN-6 marshalling radar (other elements of the air traffic control system are not visible). The small antenna visible to the left of and below the SPN-6 is the IFF interrogator associated with the SPS-30.

At San Francisco Navy Yard on 25 January 1965, *Hornet* shows her radars. The most important are her long-range SPS-43A air-search radar (81) with its IFF interrogator (82), her long-range SPS-30A heightfinder (80) and her SPN-6 marshalling radar (87). Other elements of her air traffic control system are the small dish of her SPN-12 radar (68) and the coupled heightfinder and horizontal scanner of her SPN-35 (67, the number barely visible, but directly under 68). Of these radars, SPN-35 antennas were normally housed in a large radome abaft the island. Aircraft entering the automatic landing system were initially picked up by SPN-35 and then transferred to the precision-tracking SPN-10 (SPN-12 measured their approach speed). UHF surface-to-air antennas are (72), on the starboard side of the island. The TACAN dome at the masthead is (99). The level below carries ESM antennas in radomes (91, 92 and 94). Antenna 93 is an HF/DF (URD-4) antenna using an internal spinner. This type of annotated antenna photo was produced after refits for reference purposes.

flyers were much more difficult targets: 'by such tactics in 1945 a second rate air force was doing terrific damage to our ships at relatively little cost. With the exception of airborne early warning and some advance in shipborne fire-control radar, we are as vulnerable to attack as we were five years ago and perhaps more so, due to the increased speed of aircraft.' Inadequate warning made it essential to minimise dead time, which for a low-flier meant that some form of CAP had to be provided at low altitude. 'The Working Group shares with OEG the uneasy feeling that our interceptor design planning for future low altitude defence requires careful and profound examination.'

The Working Group and OEG thought the solution for low

altitude was turboprop fighters with supersonic propellers, which offered high subsonic speeds. No such aircraft materialised, but low fliers were certainly an important (and difficult) element of the big fleet air defence exercises of the 1950s. The near-impossibility of finding and intercepting such aircraft doubtless helped encourage the navy to rely heavily on low-flying deep strike aircraft, such as Skyraiders, through the 1950s. It is also possible that work on the turboprop VTOL fighters was pressed because they offered a solution to the low-flier problem: a combination of quick launch and good low-altitude performance at high speeds.

As an indication of what was expected at this time, DCNO (Air) laid out mobilisation requirements in Aviation Planning Study 3-49.[8] A key point was that the number of defensive teams needed by a task group did not depend on the number of carriers in it, so it was best to operate several carriers together. It was assumed that in the early days of a war enemy night or low-visibility attacks would be limited to small numbers of aircraft (but there was a caveat that this might already be wrong). To deal with them, the force would need round the clock AEW and all-weather fighter cover. Two AEW aircraft would have to be kept overhead at all times. Given their 67 per cent availability, a third would have to be maintained nearly ready. Under current conditions, four airborne and four deck-ready all-weather fighters were needed at all times, again with 67 per cent availability. As for day fighters, 'if we can meet foreseeable conditions in the Mediterranean, other areas fall within our capabilities'. Each Mediterranean task group had to be able to meet attacks with sixty day fighters, all-weather fighters augmenting the day CAP as needed. Availability would be 75 per cent, meaning that to maintain sixty day fighters the force would need a total of eighty day fighters. Conversely, it was expected that a day strike in the Mediterranean would be met by sixty enemy fighters rising at one time. The strike needed a 3:1 superiority of escorts to enemy fighters to keep losses acceptable, which meant a total of 180 day fighters for strike escort. These calculations explain why US carrier air groups were so fighter-heavy at the time of the Korean War. They also explain why the US Navy strongly favoured multi-carrier task groups. Sometimes the aircraft on board a carrier were described as an air task group (ATG) rather than a carrier air group (CVG).

Through the 1950s, the US fleet held full-scale air defence exercises. They were generally extremely depressing and their results spurred the development of new systems, generally based on computers. The OEG analysed the exercises and proposed improvements.[9] Its first reports were issued in 1952–3, with a supplementary report on countermeasures to low-fliers. The reported exercises were conducted by the 6th Fleet in the Mediterranean, but exercises elsewhere (2nd Fleet in the Atlantic and 7th in the Pacific) showed similar problems.[10] In 1951, the average range for 50 per cent detection of bandits was 40nm. That rose to 60nm in the middle of 1951/2, then to 80nm in 1953/4. This improvement was due mainly to the use of radar picket destroyers to provide the sort of detection in depth tested by OpDevFor in 1949.

Low fliers were the worst problem.[11] One of OEG's major contributions was to point out that airborne radar aircraft were the best and almost the only way to push low-flier detection range well out from fleet centre. By about 1953 new long-range shipboard radars were coming, but none of them could see beyond the radar horizon to low-flying aircraft. AEW aircraft flying overhead could. Where initially they had been seen mainly as a way of extending detection range against high fliers (as in the 1949 OpDevFor exercise) now they were increasingly seen as primarily a defence against low-flying aircraft. That meant deploying them at greater altitudes, because the greater the altitude, the longer their low-altitude reach. Earlier practice had been to deploy AEW at lower altitudes set by the radar horizon for medium-altitude aircraft. It is not clear to what extent Cadillac was seen in 1945 mainly as a way of tracking low-flying Kamikazes, but that is not how it was viewed in the early post-war period.

OEG pointed out that the exercises favoured the defence: reality would be worse. Analysis of poor performance often mentioned that CIC and radar personnel were not up to Second World War standards of training – they had not had several years of war to learn their trade and incidentally to impress on them that their effectiveness was a matter of life or death. This time war would probably begin with a surprise attack on their task force. The main note of optimism from OEG in 1955 was that in the last quarter of 1955, the 6th Fleet steadily improved the probability of assigning CAP to bandits (ultimately to 90 per cent).

Exercises conducted in 1953 tested both CAP and DLIs, with air control exercised mostly by AEW aircraft (flying CICs) but sometimes also from radar picket destroyers. The big land-based AEW aircraft carried out synchronised patrols to create a barrier 50–70nm from the centre of the formation. CAP fighters orbited over the carrier. The targets were mainly Skyraiders flying at 200ft from 150nm out (to evade task force radar, which might have picked them up if they flew higher at long range). There were a few high-altitude raids. In all, of 182 raids, AEW detected 139 and directed interception of eighty-nine (AEW and pickets arranged a total of 104 interceptions). In all, 150 of the raids were detected (82.4 per cent), which meant that thirty-two raids arrived entirely undetected. Of 161 low-altitude raids, 124 (77 per cent) were detected at an average of 98nm (average interception range was 47nm). In all seventy-eight of the raids were not intercepted at all. There was some feeling that the tests were biased against the task force. Each AEW aircraft was assigned a 45° sector.

In these tests, sea returns were a major AEW radar problem; tests showed that their intensity was proportional to the square root of the aircraft's altitude. The higher the aircraft flew, the worse it was, because its radar saw a much greater area of the sea surface. The problem at 10,000ft was twice as bad as it was at 2500ft, but by flying low the AEW aircraft lost line-of-sight contact with the task force (which was used, for example, for voice radio). In this exercise AEW aircraft reported via a relay link (Autocat) on board an aircraft orbiting 10,000ft over the task force. CAP missions were flown by Banshee fighters with one engine shut down to give them longer endurance. The lesson was that AEW radars had to be modified to limit sea returns.

Two years later OEG's most sobering observation was the reality that in 1955, 75 per cent of all raids arrived at the force completely unopposed by fighters. Whether ships survived would depend entirely on their own anti-aircraft guns, which were less and less effective against fast bombers. This sort of figure explains why shipboard missile systems were considered so important. The 75 per cent figure reflected the failure of CIC operation. However, 20 per cent of raiders were never detected at all; it did not matter whether CICs were perfected.

One problem was mis-assignment of CAP fighters, which often just could not get to the incoming aircraft in time. Control facilities

The low-frequency radars gave long range but they were also so distinctive that an enemy could identify carriers and some high-value missile ships using them. During the 1980s the US Navy shifted to the higher-frequency SPS-49 air-search radar to make it far more difficult for an enemy to distinguish its ships. That sacrificed range, but by this time the carriers were operating E-2 Hawkeyes offering back that range. Compared to SPS-43A, SPS-49 also offered a narrower beam and better resistance to jamming. *John F Kennedy* showed the new radars installed in the 1980s when she fuelled at sea from the fast combat replenishment ship *Seattle*, 22 April 2002. The radar atop her bridge is SPS-49. The large flat array on the lattice mast is SPS-48, a multi-beam three-dimensional radar (the multiple beams offered a better chance of detecting a target). Visible abaft her uptake are the two SPN-42 precision approach radars, with SPN-35 in the radome on the lattice mast. The bar-like antenna on the pole mast is TAS Mk 23, the radar used with her NATO Sea Sparrow self-defence missile system. Although this photograph was taken long after the major shift in radar types in the late 1980s, it reflects the radar choices made at that time.

were limited, data was transferred too slowly and there were no height data. The separation between search and heightfinding radar led to the worst problem: the heightfinder pointing at the wrong target. If such errors were excluded, the mean error was 2600ft, which should have been tolerable in daylight. OEG therefore pressed for installation of an existing device which could transfer target co-ordination between a PPI serving a search radar and a height scope.

Adopting broadcast control would eliminate impossible CAP assignments, since the fighters themselves would be computing their interception courses. OEG thought that step alone would bring the probability of tallyho against high fliers to 50 per cent. The broadcast technique, using TACAN, would start interceptions sooner, it would permit more efficient transfer of control and it would reduce saturation. It might be possible to tallyho 90 per cent of raids. If two CAP sections were assigned to each raid, 90 per cent of those could be splashed if two firing runs were made in each case.

In the fleet exercises, the 80 per cent of bogeys (radar targets) detected at long range were assigned numbers as bandits (raiders). It turned out that 69 per cent were typically friendly aircraft or transients (IFF was a problem); it was vital not to waste air defence resources on them. Much of the CIC effort was devoted to sifting real bandits among the bogeys. CIC managed to assign CAP to 75 per cent of the real bandits, but it assigned nearly as much CAP to mis-identified friendlies.

Half of the bandits closed to within 17nm or even less before they were detected and CAP was assigned. That was barely acceptable if the

enemy was using unguided bombs and torpedoes, but not if he had air-to-surface missiles and nuclear weapons.

Until new radars entered service, the only way to extend the radar horizon of a carrier task force was to use pickets, both destroyers and AEW. As in standard US tactics of the time, OEG used circles centred on the carriers to arrange forces (in this case, on 20nm circles). AEW on the 40nm circle would detect at least 20 per cent of bandits. Picket destroyers on this circle could detect incoming bogeys at a median range of 50nm (they would detect half of all raids).

Overall, the main body of the task force would detect half of bogeys at 80nm and 65 per cent beyond 55nm. Overall, the task group could expect to detect 80 per cent of raids flying at 500 to 40,000ft. The best 10 per cent of units could do better: the main body could pick up 75 per cent of bogeys at a median range of 53nm and all but high-flying jets at some range. However, 10 per cent of jets, flying at extreme altitude, would not be detected at all. The best radar picket destroyers could detect 75 per cent of bogeys at a median range of 53nm. With carrier-based AEW pushed somewhat beyond the 40nm circle, they could detect over half of incomers at 50nm from their stations. An airborne CIC (WV-2) could loiter over the main body.

In the exercises, 60 per cent of attackers were high-flying jets, the other 40 per cent being propeller-driven attack planes (most under 1000ft). Since low-fliers would be detected later than other attackers, OEG proposed stationing a special LOCAP directly over the main body. To gain time to deal with other aircraft detected further out, it proposed CAP stations 10nm, 20nm or 30nm from the main body. On average seven would be maintained and the fighters would be available

In the Arabian Sea in January 2012, *Abraham Lincoln* and *John C Stennis* show the current standard US carrier radar outfit. The antenna on the lattice mast is for SPS-49(V)5, the current standard two-dimensional air-search set. The big flat array is for SPS-48E, a three-dimensional air-search radar operating at a higher frequency. The antenna on the fore side of the pole mast is TAS Mk 23, for the defensive NATO Sea Sparrow system. On the after side of the mast is the SPN-43 air traffic control radar. The double antenna just below SPS-43E is for the Mk 91 Sea Sparrow guidance radar. The TACAN antenna is the small flat one on the topmast. The massive spherical masthead radome is for a WSC-6 SHF satellite link to the DSCS satellite. The small 'thimbles' are for the Global Broadcast satellite system. Other satellite antennas are on the fore side of each ship's island. *Stennis* shows the antenna of her SPQ-9B, which replaces TAS Mk 23, on the after side of her pole mast, on the upper platform. The new carrier class, beginning with *Gerald R Ford*, has a multi-role phased-array radar instead of this radar combination.

65 per cent of the time. Such numbers were possible because the typical carrier task force of the time included three or four carriers, not the single carriers used later.

Poor ID flooded plots with extraneous data. The US Navy was introducing the TACAN beacon. If all aircraft had TACAN receivers, they could accurately and frequently report their positions, hence were less likely to be confused with bandits. A ship in the main body could be assigned responsibility for tracking and monitoring friendlies, with no other air defence responsibility. The task force could establish an Air Defense Identification Zone. Aircraft would all have to file flight plans with a traffic control centre. That clearly applied more to strike aircraft than to defending fighters, but the fighters might be compelled to fly out and back through the zone on set paths.

Delays in assigning CAP to bandits wasted a quarter to a third of average detection range. Delay was a function of detection range. When detected at 50nm, the average CAP assignment was made after bandit had closed another 13nm; with detection at 75nm, delay cost 20nm penetration; at 100nm, 32nm.

OEG's solution was to decentralise CAP, assigning sector air defence ships. The force flagship would relieve a sector ship if it was

saturated. Delays would be even shorter if all air control ships assigned their CAPs immediately to any bogey they detected. The OEG analysis highlighted the CIC problem. Many of its solutions required constant transfers of data from ship to ship. Each such transfer took time and imposed errors through delays – the faster the aircraft, the worse the range error associated with a given delay. In effect OEG's solution could work only once CICs had been automated. Until that happened, the only way out of the problem was to gain time by extending detection range. To do that the fleet needed new radars. In 1956 the coming lower-frequency (UHF) SPS-17 radar promised to detect 85 per cent of all targets 20–40nm after they crossed its 200nm horizon.

The Sidewinder-armed FJ-3 Fury was a typical new air-defence fighter. OEG analysed its performance against a Mach 0.9 bomber such as a 'Badger'. If bandits were to be splashed 20nm from force centre (which would soon be considered grossly inadequate, given Soviet missiles), existing stationing practices would make it possible to convert no more than two-thirds of detections to splashes. OEG thought that its proposals might raise that to 89 per cent, with pickets

British post-war light carriers had a much simpler radar suit, as exemplified here by HMAS *Sydney*, approaching a pier in Melbourne after a Korean War tour. Her foremast carries an antenna for Type 960, successor to the wartime Type 281 and the 'cheese' of Type 293 alongside and below it. The 'egg timer' atop the topmast is the associated IFF transponder. The long dipoles on the yards are for VHF rather than UHF radio, the RAN (and RN) not yet having switched to UHF. The YE aircraft-homing beacon is on a separate mast. Atop the bridge is a version of the Type 277 surface-search and heightfinding radar with the larger post-war reflector, giving higher gain and a narrower beam. The small mast right forward carries a UHF D/F array for aircraft homing. Aircraft visible on deck are Fireflies. (Alan C Green via State Library of Victoria)

50nm from the main body an CAP 20–30nm from the main body. If existing radars were used more efficiently, CAP might be stationed as much as 40nm out. That would become necessary once missile ships took over the zone closer to the carriers.

OEG argued that a combination of TACAN and decentralised control would make it possible to move the radar picket destroyers and CAP closer to the main body. Its analysis showed that moving CAP in did not much affect interception range. A CAP stationed at 20nm would tallyho 96 per cent of contacts at an average range of 49nm. A CAP 60nm out would splash 79 per cent of contacts a radar picket destroyer could make with its SPS-6 radar (range 50nm) – at an average tallyho range of 53nm. Current performance was that 88 per cent of raids assigned CAP were tallyhoed by the best 10 per cent of units, the figure being much lower in others. When several CAP stations were assigned to the same bogey, the success or failure of one of them did not affect that of the others. Using TACAN, the radar picket destroyers could support broadcast control. If virtually all friendlies and bandits were recognised as such, 85 per cent of bogeys would have CAP assigned. Bogeys could close only 5–10nm before CAP was assigned. OEG proposed a combination of a RAPCAP beyond the pickets and other CAP closer to the main body. This combination might offer as much as a 90 per cent tallyho rate (meaning that 10 per cent of bandits would arrive unopposed).

OEG both showed a way ahead and warned that none of the possible solutions using fighters was leakproof. That must have encouraged investment in the new anti-aircraft missiles as, at the least, a backstop to the fighters. Whether the missiles were the primary defence of the carriers or a backstop against leakers depended on expectations as to how well they would perform. It does seem to have been clear through the 1950s that neither weapon by itself could guarantee the survival of a carrier task force. Each of the two systems was often evaluated as though the other did not exist at all. Before the advent of the missiles, the only backstop was fleet anti-aircraft gunnery and the fleet had only very limited gun armament compared to the Second World War.

Although OEG saw AEW as an important part of any solution to the fleet air defence problem, in 1955 it was only coming into its own.[12] In ADEX Ten (16 April 1955), of eleven bogeys originating with AEW in the interceptor net, six were single-plot contacts offering no indication of course or speed, hence useless. Their relay was delayed six to eight minutes. The problem was adjudged the fault of the reporting picket, which had received the AEW report.

In another exercise (5 May 1955), the single AEW bogey reported to the controlling air defence ship as a single plot and opening was actually a raid. The fault lay again with the picket passing on the information; the AEW aircraft gave six positions, but they were not passed on. In a full-scale air defence exercise (23 June 1955), no detections at all were credited to AEW; that was blamed on lack of teamwork. On the other hand, a 25–29 July 1955 exercise employed both a land-based AEW aircraft and radar picket submarines (SSRs). The land-based aircraft was on the 200nm circle, the SSRs on the 120nm circle, all on a net controlled by the air defence ship. To avoid confusion, the net used a round-robin technique and simple code, with geographical grid co-ordinates. It proved slow but reliable. A raid detected by a picket's SPS-6 radar at 90nm was already being tracked by the net with a plot showing at 100nm. Co-operation of AEW and submarines was good and the SSR commander offered to move out to 150nm or 175nm. In another exercise (a Carrier Strike Exercise, 12–18 May

1955) land-based AEW aircraft formed a barrier 180nm from force centre. During the last two days of this exercise, all raids detected by AEW were tallyhoed and five of six were splashed. The radar picket destroyers performed particularly well, on several occasions taking over responsibility for a bogey as soon as they made radar contact on it. They successfully intercepted three of four raids and were involved in fourteen of the twenty raids detected.

OEG reported on CAP in carrier task force air defence in April 1956, looking at the effect of the nuclear threat. New tactics moved the carriers of a task force apart, so that a megaton hit on one of them would not destroy the other two or three. That greatly expanded the area CAP had to cover. Unfortunately, existing fighters had short endurance. OEG speculated that a combination of better early warning and a good surface-to-air missile would make it possible to dispense with CAP in favour of deck-launched interception, which might be the only tactic compatible with short-endurance high-performance jets. Alternatively fighters on CAP duty could be tanked to keep them in the air, but in that case tankers flying back and forth through the fleet air defence zone had to be tracked and distinguished from possible attackers. It took time to ready a CAP fighter for flight and in many cases it seemed that fighter endurance would be less than time on station. The situation was bad enough for fighters orbiting directly over the fleet, but now they might have to orbit 100nm or even 200nm away. Maximum endurance for a typical fleet air-defence fighter, an F3H-2M Demon with four Sparrow missiles at 35,000ft, was 103 minutes. However, at 100nm it would loiter for only 87 minutes and at 200nm it would loiter for only 54 minutes. The longest-endurance fighter was the obsolescent Banshee (F2H-3N: 3.4 hours directly overhead, translating to 187 minutes on CAP, but only 177 minutes at 100nm and 145 minutes at 200nm, at a low CAP speed of 308 knots).[13]

A December 1959 OEG report on fleet air defence (OEG 81) showed that not much had changed. It examined the results of many full-scale exercises and estimated the impact of fifty dispersed attacks (raid density of seven aircraft per hour, each raid consisting of one to four aircraft at up to 45,000ft). Of fifty attackers, typically ten would be completely unopposed. Of the forty detected, no fighters would be assigned to seven of them. Of the thirty-three to which fighters were assigned, they would never tallyho fourteen of them. Of the nineteen tallyho'ed, no firing runs would be made on six. Of the thirteen firing runs, three aircraft would not be splashed. In the end, only ten aircraft out of the fifty would be splashed. Of the thirty acquired but not engaged, anti-aircraft fire would never acquire ten, so twenty attacking aircraft would be entirely free to inflict damage.

In a pre-nuclear world, without anti-ship missiles, each aircraft might be expected to carry four 500lb bombs or two torpedoes – say a total of eighty bombs and forty torpedoes aboard the twenty attacking aircraft. Second World War data suggested that twelve of the eighty bombs would hit manoeuvring carriers, plus twelve torpedoes. It was very unlikely that one of the two carriers would continue offensive operations. Of course if each aircraft carried a nuclear bomb, there would be no survival at all. Even a ten-aircraft raid would likely have five survivors in condition to hit the carriers.

The ultimate probability of success was low because each active air-defence measure depended on the one before it: a bogey had to be detected, then assigned, then tallyhoed, then attacked by a fighter. Even high probabilities of success could add up to a low net probability. For example, an 80 per cent chance of detection, a similar probability of assignment to detected targets (bogeys) and the same proba-bility of success in a firing run might seem impressive. With a 70 per cent chance of converting assignment into a tallyho (i.e. placing a fighter in the right place to intercept), the net probability of success was only 0.36 – much less than half – as the probabilities multiplied out.

By this time the Soviets had deployed their first anti-ship missile, Komet. It was understood that fighters would be assigned to the enemy bombers, the anti-aircraft missile systems dealing with the missiles launched by the attacking bombers. However, long-range Talos missiles would be able to hit some bombers before they dropped their 55nm missiles. OEG applied probabilities both to the success of the missiles and to the success of Komet. If the fighters killed only ten of fifty attackers, the other forty would enter the SAM zone. Talos would kill three of them, leaving thirty-seven to launch their missiles. Terrier

Initially HMAS *Melbourne* had much the same radar fit, but when she was modernised the Type 960 was replaced by the big antenna of a Dutch (Signaal) LW-01 (at the same time Dutch radars, including the smaller LW-02, were installed on board Australian destroyers and frigates). *Melbourne* retained her Type 277 heightfinder, presumably because the Dutch alternative VI-01 would have been too heavy. The radome at the masthead is for TACAN and the radomes below are for ECM, as in contemporary US carriers. As modernised the ship had a lengthened steam catapult with a US-style bridle-catcher at the bow, to serve her new Skyhawk fighter-bombers.

missiles might destroy nine of the missiles, leaving seventy-four, which OEG credited with twenty-nine hits – which was far too many.

Overall, the problems OEG found could be described as failures to transfer data promptly and accurately within the massive fleet air-defence system. Detection happened at a PPI, but it did not count until the radar plot had been placed on the vertical plot, which entailed data transfer from PPI to the plotter. Evaluation of bogeys depended largely on their apparent motion, as indicated by repeated positions indicated on the vertical plot – repeated data transfers. There would always be friendly aircraft present, at the least CAP fighters flying back and forth to the carriers. Distinguishing bandits from friendlies was a data transfer issue, involving a combination of delays and precision. The positions (and fuel status) of the fighters deter-mined whether they could properly be assigned to given bandits. Failures of CAP assignment (raids which were unchallenged) were due to limited ability to handle fighters and also to limited knowledge of where the fighters were. Subsequent failures to tallyho translated into failures to assign fighters to bandits they had a fair chance of finding. Failed firing runs could be interpreted as failures by fighter control to place fighters in effective positions (even though their pilots thought they could intercept).

The data transfer problem explains why broadcast control was both attractive and insufficient. It simplified data use on board the carrier or other fighter-control ship, but it placed a considerable burden on

pilots. They had to estimate whether they were in position to assign themselves to given bandits. Broadcast control also discarded a vital advantage of central control, that a command aware of the full air picture could prioritise threats and apportion its fighter resources accordingly.

All of this made development of some replacement for the wartime fighter-control system urgent. A formal Operational Requirement (AD-04401) was stated in September 1949.[14] It was to fully integrate pilots, controllers and operators into an air-defence system employing both aircraft and missiles. There would be adequate means of integrating the interception-control system with target-designation and assignment systems and with independent tracking systems. Interception control would be semi- or fully automatic. Contributing elements included the BuShips/BuAer Automatic Aircraft Intercept Control System, due for completion in 1953, the BuShips Intercept Evaluator (1951), the SPS-2 radar (1954), the SPS-8 radar (1950) and a long list of missile systems and system components, including analog computers. In 1948 it must have seemed that whatever was being developed for the long-range Talos anti-aircraft missile would contribute to aircraft interception at similar ranges.

The expected dates for the interception devices were not met, but the existence of the 1949 project shows that the US Navy of the time recognised the problem it faced. That is also evident from the minutes of joint US-British CIC conferences in 1948–50.

DEALING WITH MASS MISSILE ATTACKS: EAGLE-MISSILEER VS TYPHON

In the mid-1950s both BuAer and BuOrd sought solutions to the coming problem of saturation raids by missile-bearing bombers supported by decoys and jammers. BuAer studies began somewhat earlier, leading to the Eagle-Missileer project of the late 1950s. The corresponding BuOrd project was the Typhon missile system. Both fell victim to the McNamara Defense Department. Cancellation seems justifiable in retrospect, but it is not clear how much was understood at the time.

At this time Bell Labs was the premier US technology developer. It was deeply involved in the air defence problem, initially mainly in the context of North American air defence. In 1953–5 Bell Labs conducted a Naval Interception Programme Study. It recommended a pulse-Doppler interception radar, which would not suffer from low-altitude clutter. The Defense Department LAMPLIGHT (NORAD) study made the same recommendation in 1956. BuAer let the initial contract for the new radar (APQ-81) to Westinghouse in March 1957. Although concerned mainly with high-performance fighters, the study mentioned that on a cursory look a subsonic fighter armed with high-performance missiles might have advantages.

A pulse-Doppler radar measures not the range of a target but instead its speed. To do that it puts out pulses at a much higher rate than normal. With so many pulses, the radar can measure the change of frequency (Doppler) caused by the target's movement. It cannot measure range accurately, because the pulses are bunched so closely together that an echo from a target will come back after the next pulse (or one much later) has gone out. In a conventional radar such a 'second time around echo' is a problem because the echo seems to come from somewhere closer to, rather than further from, the radar. The faster the target, the greater the Doppler shift. The great advantage of pulse-Doppler is that it can detect a fast-moving target against a highly

reflective but more or less static background, such as a mountain ashore or the sea below an aircraft. Pulse-Doppler is also attractive because it pours so much energy onto an air target, giving it a high probability of detection even though each pulse may have only moderate power. Just as a conventional radar suffers from range ambiguity, a pulse-Doppler radar is affected by speed ambiguity – it has blind speeds corresponding to multiples of its pulse rate. The higher the pulse rate, the higher the first blind speed. The first pulse-Doppler radars were tested during the Second World War.

BuAer's main air defence think tank was the CAL. It delivered a fighter study on 15 January 1957. By this time it was assumed that any Soviet attack on US carriers would be delivered using megaton weapons. To survive, the carriers had to be spread out. There was no longer any point in keeping CAP fighters over the carriers, particularly since missile ships working with the carriers would soon cover the area out to as much as 100nm. CAL therefore envisaged AEW aircraft working further and further out. Fighters would orbit there.

The assumed threat was a combination of high- and medium- and low-altitude bombers. The high-altitude bombers (similar to the new US Mach 2 B-58 Hustler) would launch 100nm Mach 2 missiles. Lower-altitude 'Badgers' and other Soviet subsonic bombers would launch the missile and at low altitudes they would toss bombs. A key point was that each bomber could carry two to eight decoys. Studies of US continental air defence were then showing that if the Soviets used long-range decoys they could saturate the system. The bombers would also use jammers and CAL evaluated various ways in which radars could be designed to counter them. Counting decoys, a raid would consist of 100 objects.

CAL's assumed threat somewhat exceeded the navy's. The navy assumed that a heavy Mach 1.2 bomber (combat radius 650nm, altitude 52,000ft) and a medium bomber (Mach 1.2, otherwise similar to Badger) would materialise during this period.

CAL assumed that the carriers in the task force would be distributed around a 10nm circle to limit nuclear damage. At the centre of the circle would be a command ship. A long-range (Talos) missile cruiser would be on the 13nm circle and Terrier cruisers would be on the 20nm circle. At this time Talos was credited with an ultimate 100nm range and the advanced version of Terrier with 20nm. The Talos cruisers would be able to engage aircraft in the area which in the past had been reserved to fleet fighters. In order to fight outside the missile zone defined by Talos, the fighters would have to orbit much further from task force centre. In the CAL model, AEW aircraft were deployed on the 300nm circle, offering warning out to 425nm. The outer perimeter defence of the task force might be 310nm deep, the 100nm Talos defining an inner surface-to-air missile zone.

Roughly parallel with the CAL study, ADR followed up on the Bell study with 'Piloted Fighter Weapons System Providing Outer Perimeter Fleet Air Defense' (OPFAD), which was completed in September 1956. It compared a subsonic fighter with a long-range pulse-Doppler radar with a Mach 2.5 fighter (slightly faster than a Phantom). The subsonic fighter had long-range air-breathing semi-active missiles, the supersonic fighter missiles slightly better than the Sparrow III planned for the Phantom. In the study, the subsonic fighter was two to four times as effective as the supersonic fighter against high altitude Mach 2 raids, Mach 0.9 medium-altitude raids and Mach 1 low-altitude raids. A subsonic fighter also offered other advantages, including better battle control (because its missiles were longer-ranged).

The BuAer solution to mass bomber attacks was Missileer, a long-endurance fighter armed with long-range missiles. The competition was won by the Douglas F6D-1 shown, in a painting by Douglas configuration engineer R G Smith, who became a famous aviation artist. (*The Hook*)

In its more elaborate study, CAL compared four fighters, a fast one, a VTOL and two slow (400-knot) fighters, all carrying missiles. The Mach 2 fighter would carry four Sparrow X missiles (10nm range), as would the VTOL. One of the slow fighters would carry six 100nm missiles (proposed by the Naval Air Development Center [i.e. ADR]), the other sixteen 30nm missiles. Both would offer much longer endurance than either of the fast fighters, which would be limited to 2.4 hours for the conventional Mach 2 aircraft and only 0.35 hours for a Mach 2 VTOL. The six-missile aircraft would have six hours' endurance, the sixteen-missile aircraft 4.8 hours. Both fast fighters could operate as deck-launched interceptors; the conventional fast interceptor could also fly CAP.

Both slow aircraft were turboprops. The smaller one had a long-range radar scanning a narrow forward sector; it was cued by the task force CIC system or by AEW aircraft. The thirty-missile aircraft was envisaged with a big 360° radar like that of an AEW aircraft. It could be seen as not so much a fighter as an armed AEW aircraft. With only six missiles its endurance would be seven hours. CAL called it 'Bogey Buster'. Grumman received a contract to study an armed version of its new W2F (E-2A) carrier AEW aircraft and in March 1956 it reported that it would be best to keep the two functions separate. This study may have been Grumman's analysis of 'Bogey Buster', which concluded that the combined aircraft would weigh 75,000lbs and that the required AEW/fire-control radar was not feasible.

CAL looked at both conventional and nuclear missiles (both were being considered at the time). Nuclear air-to-air warheads were attractive because by their existence they could force the attackers to disperse and thus reduce saturation. CAL did not, however, take into account the fireball effects of nuclear air bursts, which would block shipboard and airborne radars (they may not have been well understood at the time).

In its analysis, CAL assumed that successful fighter defence would mean that all attacking bombes would be destroyed before they reached the 100nm surface-to-air missile (SAGM) zone. It took into account dead time before an aircraft became effective: two minutes from initial detection for a CAP fighter, which had to fly around the SAGM zone to get into position; five minutes for a deck-launched fighter the carrier would catapult (four minutes for a VTOL fighter). CAL also took into account recycle time for AEW aircraft and fighters.

It assumed that two-thirds of CAP and AEW aircraft would be available when needed, compared to five-sixths of deck-launched intercepting fighters.

This model did not take jamming into account, but CAL assumed that it would affect small fast fighters more severely (they could devote much less weight to anti-jamming measures in their radars). Long-range missiles could shoot up at higher-altitude attackers, but not the shorter-range ones. The fast fighters could fire their four missiles in two minutes. The big slow fighters with very long range missiles would typically fire a salvo and observe its effect before firing again: the first six missiles in 5.5 minutes. The medium-range missiles would all be fired in 3.75 minutes. To simplify its analysis, CAL assumed that all the missiles offered the same single-shot kill probability (SSPK).

The slow missile fighter enjoyed advantages. For example, it needed less manoeuvring to get into missile range. Its longer-range missiles would be larger, hence could carry heavier warheads and more sophisticated seekers. They could be locked-on further from the approaching bombers and they could use multiple modes of terminal homing.

Calculations showed that it would take dramatically fewer slow missile fighters on CAP than fast fighters. The study also examined the possibility that individual fighters could see the whole raid. A battle controller could lay out lanes along which fighters could fly out to get alongside the incoming bombers, peeling off to make their attacks.

This study also proposed another way of using an airborne radar. Instead of placing the missiles on board the AEW aircraft, they could be carried on board surface ships but controlled by the aircraft after they were launched. This concept, which was revived several times through the 1980s, was called Forward Pass.[15] Later it was called SLAT (surface launched, air targeted).

CAL went further in another study completed in June 1957, Project TAFAD (Fighter System Requirements 1962–7). The version of 'Bogey Buster' in this study had twelve 30nm missiles. It added a track-while-scan capability to its basic radar, so that 'Bogey Buster' could handle multiple targets in quick succession. The alternative ADR fighter used a basic air intercept (AI) radar whose dish antenna would lock onto one target at a time. CAL's 'Bogey Buster' could therefore handle saturation raids (against thirty bombers or fewer, the single-target tracker would be good enough).

BuAer designated the long-range missile/subsonic fighter system AWS-404A and about October 1957 it let contracts to Chance Vought and to North American to sketch subsonic missile fighters. This was much the feasibility study function previously performed by ADR. Results were submitted in mid-December.

The question went back to ADR, which completed a further study (Research Analysis of Fleet Air Defense, RAFAD) in July 1958. By this time a big pulse-Doppler radar (APQ-81) was under contract. All 14 RAFAD alternatives had fire-control systems using it. Their speeds went from subsonic to Mach 2.2 and gross weights were 39,000 to 85,000lbs. RAFAD again showed that a subsonic fighter carrying a high-performance long-range missile was best.

BuAer now knew what it wanted. It chose a big subsonic Missileer fighter armed with six missiles (as in the ADR study) but equipped with a big nose radar using a huge 60in radar dish antenna. The Westinghouse APQ-81 was a multi-mode radar using a digital (for flexibility) computer to synthesise its wave form and also to maintain tracks in a track-while-scan mode.[16] Computer control of the waveform made it possible to vary the pulse rate so that the radar could intersperse range and velocity measurements. The radar could switch to a target illumination mode. It would control a long-range Eagle missile. By 1959, APQ-81 was credited with the ability to detect the usual 5m^2 target at 120nm and to track sixteen such targets simultaneously at 80nm. It was assumed that the radar would normally have to fight intense jamming, so it was designed from the outset with anti-jam features. They began with a narrow beam (3°) and a narrow bandwidth (24 kHz), both intended to avoid most jamming signals. The antenna was massive. In 1958 existing fighter radars had what were considered large 24in dishes, but APQ-81 would use a 60in (5ft) dish.[17]

Given that radar, BuAer chose to buy first the missile system (not just the missile) and then an airframe capable of carrying it. BuAer would be system integrator, as it had been for earlier aircraft fire-control/missile systems. A Bendix/Grumman team won the Eagle missile system competition in 1958, the development contract being awarded in May 1959 (Grumman was responsible for the missile airframe). This contract included the system computer, which would track the targets (dead-reckoning between detections) the radar detected. A BuAer summary of relevant contractor experience included the computer systems of the Intruder (A2F, later A-6) and of the E-2 Hawkeye.[18]

The Eagle system comprised a homing guidance system, the missile itself, a tactical computer which could receive data from any of several radars (or from a data link), a three-scope display (based on that Litton was then developing for the W2F, which became the E-2 Hawkeye) and a separate missile tracking system.[19] The missile tracker was necessary because the system would command missiles to engage multiple targets; it had to know where its missiles were. The system computer was a modified version of the Litton computer already adopted for the E-2 Hawkeye. In its solicitation BuAer left to the contractor the missile environment (i.e. the kind and degree of jamming the system had to overcome), range, guidance and propulsion. It was assumed that the fighter would be a node in the Link 11 (USC-2 radio) net, connected to both other Eagle fighters and to computer AEW aircraft (the emerging Grumman W2F/E-2 Hawkeye).

Based on their own analysis of likely enemy countermeasures, Bendix and Grumman designed the system to operate against an enemy force using powerful jammers distributed among the attacking bombers to deny the defence the ability to pick out individual targets (the alternative was to assume that the bomber would carry its own jammer). That was roughly what the Soviets were then developing, in the form of specialised escort jamming aircraft, although US intelligence is unlikely to have been aware of it. It could be assumed that the AI (air intercept) radar would be subject to strobe or sector jamming, which would deny it range and velocity information but not angle and angle rate. The aircraft-to-missile link would be attacked and any homing seeker (active or semi-active) would be jammed to deny it coherent target information.

The system was designed to exploit jamming. Thus if it was assumed that the enemy would jam the C-band system radar, the missile had to be able to home on a C-band jammer. The same receiver would cover the command link to the radar, which would operate at a frequency close to that of the radar. The link was considered less susceptible than the radar to jamming. In a clear environment, the Eagle system would use command mid-course guidance via the C-band link. It would have a terminal guidance system, using a pulse-Doppler seeker (at a different frequency). The missile also had a memory circuit

it could use to reject jammers whose apparent movement was physically impossible.

Missile range was set by the likeliest environment, the heavy-jamming situation. In this case average maximum useful range might exceed that of the supporting AI radar, because the missile would be homing on a jammer. Bendix estimated that in this case range might be as great as 100nm. By way of contrast, in a clear environment the aircraft's AI radar would have to detect and track the target, so useful missile range would be slightly less than AI range, about 60nm.

This view of the situation differed from that which shaped the contemporary Typhon surface-to-air system. The countermeasures environment envisaged for Typhon emphasised the use of decoys to saturate the air-defence system. However, both Typhon and the emerging Eagle system were intended to deal with numerous attackers, well beyond the capacity of earlier systems There was a vast difference, for example, between an air defence using semi-active Sparrows (one target at a time, from firing to destruction) and one using Eagle missiles (six targets at a time).

Bendix and Grumman chose a rocket over a ramjet because the ramjet would require a large booster to accelerate it quickly enough to deal with a close-in target. Instead they chose a boost-glide-boost rocket combination. To achieve maximum range, the missile could be lobbed: first it would rise almost vertically, gaining energy which it could turn into kinetic energy on the way back down. The final boost would give it enough energy to outmanoeuvre a distant target. Thus the booster would accelerate the missile to Mach 3.5, providing steering in the form of four thrust vector nozzles. After a glide the sustainer (end-game booster) would accelerate it further to Mach 4.5. This combination required a massive missile. The Phoenix which replaced the Eagle in the F-111B and the F-14 Tomcat was more compact because it incorporated the initial booster and eliminated the terminal or end-game rocket. It could therefore be carried by a higher-performance aircraft, but it was much less capable against a high-performance target, like the Soviet 'Backfire' bomber. Both missiles could follow either lob (up and over) or direct (ray) trajectories, the latter for shorter-range targets.

From a guidance point of view, the up-and-over trajectory was possible because the missile did not have to lock onto the target when it was fired. Instead it could follow the most energy-efficient path, attaining the greatest possible range. The guidance system tracked the target and computed a path for the missile, commanding it into that path (the Aegis surface-to-air system operates in this way, which is why it roughly doubled the range of its missile without any change in the missile motor). The missile was launched with a preset path, which could be updated in flight via the data link back to the firing aircraft. The system in turn tracked and monitored the missile using a beacon on the missile. Maximum Eagle range was 80nm and maximum altitude was 100,000ft. The missile was considered effective from sea level to 100,000ft, against targets with speeds of up to Mach 4.

Guidance depended on the degree of jamming. If the AI radar was jammed heavily enough, the missile had a home-on-jam mode. In a clear environment it would follow the commanded and updated trajectory ordered by the system computer, using its own active seeker for terminal homing. Because the system on board one fighter would be data-linked to other fighters and to AEW aircraft, it might well be able to triangulate enemy jammers even if its own AI radar was jammed (the Bendix proposal showed this possibility).

Eagle had a separate booster (an alternative rocket-ramjet was

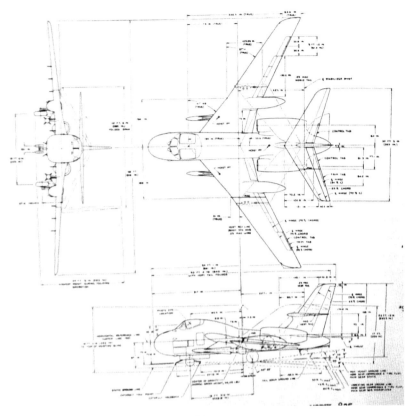

Boeing's proposed Missileer was this Model 835.

rejected). As of 1959, it was expected to weigh 1284lbs (almost as much as a ship-launched Tartar), with a 110lb warhead; the missile-booster combination was 16ft long with a diameter of 14in (16in booster); span was 34in (50in over the booster fins).

Because the system was built around a powerful airborne computer, the Eagle-Missileer combination naturally fitted into the evolving computer-based fleet air-defence system. Grumman and Litton were packaging a computer into the E-2 Hawkeye, the airborne node of the new fleet digital system (NTDS). BuAer could reject CAL's idea of providing 'Bogey Buster' with a big long-range radar (as in the E-2) because a data link from the E-2 would provide it with just such coverage.

Including its six missiles and the big Westinghouse radar, Bendix estimated that the total weight of an Eagle system would be 10,765lbs. That was slightly less than BuAer had estimated when it had asked for proposals, but it was still huge compared to the weight of the four-Sparrow system on board an F-4. Bendix and Grumman sketched a 50,000lb twin-turboprop long-endurance (eight-hour) carrier aircraft which would carry its six Eagles internally in a kind of bomb bay. As an alternative, Bendix and Grumman offered an Eagle version of Grumman's A2F (A-6) Intruder, then under development, with an APQ-75 radar and five missiles (four underwing and one under the belly). Another alternative was a version of Grumman's G-118 fighter, offered and rejected two years earlier. It could carry two missiles underwing and two semi-submerged under its fuselage. The APQ-72 associated with the G-118 would be replaced by an APQ-75 in a slightly larger nose. These alternatives were described to prove that the Bendix-Grumman system was entirely feasible. It is not clear to what extent Grumman hoped that BuAer would buy any of them.

Aircraft characteristics were discussed at a 31 March 1959 conference chaired by Deputy DCNO (Air) and attended by DCNO (Air) Admiral Pirie. He pressed for adaptation of an existing aircraft and was told that it would be as expensive as a new one, with too little commonality to be worthwhile. BuWeps (successor to BuAer) therefore wanted to open a design competition. The aircraft would be operated not only by the fleet but also by the Marines, who questioned the value of an aircraft which might not be able to survive in the face of enemy surface-to-air missiles. The conference decided that the aircraft might carry a jamming pod on one of its missile stations; the navy was also developing the Corvus stand-off missile specifically to destroy enemy surface-to-air missile sites.

BuWeps sent out a circular describing a separate design competition (TS-151) for the aircraft to be wrapped around the Bendix-Grumman system and the separately-developed Westinghouse APQ-81 radar on 13 October 1959 and the competition was formally announced on 10 December.[20] OpNav had already circulated Operational Requirement AD-10501-5, for the aircraft on 13 May 1959. Targets envisaged were Mach 1 aircraft at sea level, Mach 2 at 35,000ft, Mach 3 at 60,000ft and Mach 4 at 90,000ft. The fighters would orbit on station 150–200nm (later changed to 100nm) from task force centre, working with both AEW aircraft and shipboard CICs, outside the surface-to-air missile zone of the task force. System requirements were 90 per cent probability of detecting a B-47 size ($5m^2$) target at 100nm between sea level and 80,000ft (a lesser range against a target at up to 90,000ft was acceptable), 75 per cent system availability and 90 per cent SSPK using a nuclear warhead (50 per cent with a conventional warhead). As of October 1958 the APQ-81 radar was expected to detect the B-47 target at 120nm and track it at 80nm (it would track a $10m^2$ target at 100nm). The missile control system had to be able to engage at least three and preferably six targets simultaneously. The Operational Requirement also envisaged the use of the system by the North American Air Defense Command. The system was to enter service in 1965.

When the proposal was circulated, BuWeps included a secondary mission of maintaining air superiority in an objective area, shipping lane or air corridor. Airspeed was not a controlling factor, although the highest possible airspeed without weight penalty was desirable. What mattered more was loiter time on station: at least five hours at 35,000ft, the aircraft cruising out to its station at that altitude at maximum economical speed. Acceptable engines were the J52 (then being used in the A-6); the T34, T56, T61 and T64 turboprops; and a notional turbofan. None of the competitors chose turboprops and nearly all used engines off the approved list. Each company offered a design using the Pratt & Whitney TF30 turbofan, development of which was then under consideration. DoD had ordered development deferred pending the outcome of the competition, so BuAer considered the six TF30 designs first.

Douglas won with an aircraft broadly resembling its earlier F3D Skynight, though very different in fact.[21] It was designated the F6D Missileer. Its APQ-81 radar was so powerful that Missileer could be a substitute AEW aircraft, albeit much less effectively than the new E-2 Hawkeye (and albeit limited to the sector its radar swept out).

Clearly the low-performance Missileer could not gain air superiority over a contested area, so it had to be bought in combination with a more conventional fighter. That would be the F4H. As of 1959 the assumed 1965 carrier air wing included eight Missileer fighters armed with Eagle plus twenty-four conventional fighters, compared to thirty-two conventional fighters (typically sixteen heavy F-4 and sixteen lighter fighters [F-8 Crusaders]) in 1963.

Eagle-Missileer promised to be a large and expensive programme. It coincided with a new shipboard missile programme, Typhon, which was premised on much the same threat and developed by the Johns Hopkins APL, which until then had been concerned with shipboard anti-aircraft missiles but not the underlying systems. APL won the Typhon competition with a particularly penetrating analysis of the fleet air defence problem, including the threat of decoys and jammers.

Another study, conducted in 1960, gave an idea of the synergism between Typhon and Eagle-Missileer by comparing the situation in 1965 and 1970. The 1965 fleet (pre-Typhon and pre-Eagle-Missileer) would have the usual layered defence, but because the surface-to-air missiles were so limited it would depend almost completely on fighters. Thus for 1965 the study envisaged a layered defence in which high-altitude attackers would be intercepted 100–150nm from task group centre, the fighters being controlled by ships with advanced three-dimensional radars (presumably the big phased-array radars on the carrier *Enterprise* and the cruiser *Long Beach* were meant). Fighters under AEW control would intercept low-altitude penetrators about 25–60nm from the vital area. Surface-to-air missiles would provide point defence against low-altitude attackers. Without really effective surface-to-air missiles, fleet air defence rested heavily on fleet fighters, possibly beyond their abilities. Certainly there were not enough fighters to mount an offensive air defence – using fighters beyond the fleet or in fighter sweeps. Limited shipboard and AEW radar range made it difficult or impossible to destroy snoopers. Radar range and reaction time might even make it impossible to destroy missile-launching bombers before they could launch.

The major weaknesses revealed in nearly a decade of exercises had not yet been overcome. Without an automated data system, fleet reaction time was too long. Existing radars were too jammable. The saturation level was too low, particularly if an enemy used decoys. None of the existing systems was considered effective against enemy missiles.

The situation would, it was hoped, change radically by 1970, when NTDS and other digital systems would be in service, including Eagle-Missileer. Surface ships would be armed with the Typhon system, whose long-range missile would have a range of 200nm out to a maximum altitude of 100,000ft. Instead of relying heavily on its fighters, a carrier task force might rely much more heavily on its missiles. The combination of missiles and fighters would deny to an enemy an area out to about 150nm and to an altitude of 100,000ft. Missileers on the periphery of that zone would be able to defend out to another 100nm. Fighters would deny an area out to 200nm or 250nm to snoopers, missile-armed bombers, cruise missiles, ECM aircraft and (using Eagle) low-altitude attackers. Even severe ECM would only about halve effective range. Also, the new digital AEW aircraft (the W2F, later redesignated E-2 Hawkeye) could control fighters for offensive anti-air operations. In effect the radically-improved surface-to-air missiles would free fleet fighters for roles they alone could fill. This hope was realised in the Outer Air Battle of the 1980s.

The authors of this study urged that Typhon and Eagle-Missileer be taken together as a Single Force AAW system. Killing Eagle-Missileer would at the least severely limit peripheral task force defence against snoopers and missile launchers. All that would be left would be Phantoms, whose performance could be improved somewhat by extending their endurance through better tanking and also by close co-ordination with AEW. Overall, it would take two or more Phantoms

to do the job of one Missileer. It was impossible, moreover, to cure the defects of the current surface missile systems. CNO Admiral Burke considered offensive power absolutely essential. It was unacceptable to buy only the AAW system, but it was also unacceptable to substitute the Phantom, the offensive fighter, for Eagle-Missileer.

An OEG study of 'Total Fleet Air Defense Through 1961' (OEG Report 81, 11 December 1959) gave an idea of just how bad the situation was. OEG considered a fleet at three different times: 1961, 1965 and 1970, in two different formations, concentrated and widely dispersed. By this time dispersion and deception seemed to be the best means of diluting an enemy air attack, given the limits of existing surface-to-air systems. Thus OEG considered two alternative formations, a close 'Active AAW' and a dispersed 'Total AAW' using decoys and deception devices. In the close-in formation, the carriers would occupy the inner 10nm circle, the missile ships the outer one. In the dispersed formation, the two carriers would be 50nm apart, with a missile cruiser half-way between them and other ships and decoys spread around them. Three shorter-range missile ships would surround each carrier. The advantage of the dispersed formation was that any enemy had to spread out simply to find the targets; given radar sweep widths, only a percentage of all approaching bombers would even get to attack. OEG had been advocating dispersal for some time and by 1959 the fleet was experimenting with it. Some of the tactics were called 'Haystack', because the idea was to make Soviet bombers search for a needle in a haystack. 7th Fleet was also interested in using land areas such as Japan as cover while it launched strikes; enemy attackers would have to confront land-based fighters en route to the carriers.

OEG considered two different threats. Threat one was a Mach 2 bomber flying at 60,000ft carrying a Mach 3 missile (100nm range). Threat two was a low-flier penetrating at 75ft altitude and launching a weapon 5nm out. It assumed a concentrated raid. In this and other studies, saturation meant a 95 per cent probability that at least five bombers or weapons would penetrate defences.

In 1961 a carrier would have two 28-fighter squadrons, one all-weather (Demons or Skyrays) and one day only (Crusaders). Note that by this time DCNO (Air) was accepting that by 1965 there would be only one fighter squadron per carrier. Defending missile ships would be the current ones: a Talos cruiser (100nm missile) and three Terrier ships (20nm). The threat at high altitude would be a Mach 0.9 bomber ('Badger') with a 55nm Mach 0.9 missile (AS-1). It would take twenty-nine bombers to saturate the close-in formation. When the formation was dispersed, it took fewer bombers (twenty-six) to saturate defences. However, to get those twenty-six bombers into position an enemy would have to approach the area with sixty-five aircraft. In the 1961 fleet, the fighters wasted half their kills on non-threat targets. OEG assumed that computer systems in the 1966 and 1970 fleets (NTDS and ATDS) would solve that problem and provide target evaluation and intercept co-ordination.

In 1966 the all-weather fighters would be replaced by twenty-four Missileers and the day fighters by twenty-eight all-weather Phantoms. Current building programmes would provide more Terrier ships and also Tartar destroyers with a 15nm missile. The envisaged threat was a Mach 2 bomber with a 100nm Mach 3 missile (a threat which did not materialise for a long time). The much greater number of surface-to-air missiles would kill 60 per cent more targets (sixteen in the tight formation). All would be air-to-surface missiles, given the range of the defending missiles. The 1966 close formation would be saturated by thirty-four high-flying bombers. However, to saturate the dispersed

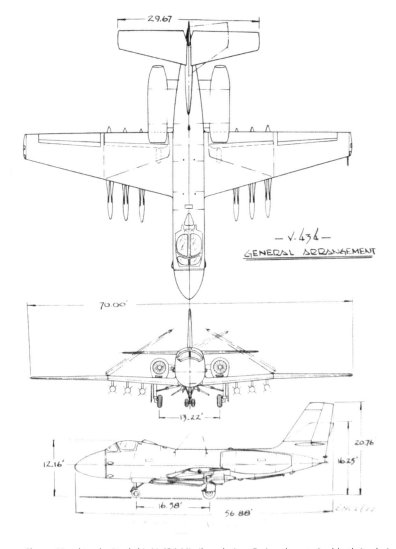

Chance Vought submitted this V-434 Missileer design. BuAer characterised both its design and Boeing's as 'Caravelle' types, their engines mounted externally aft, as in the French Caravelle airliner.

formation, sixty-five bombers had to get close enough to their targets and to do that a total of 160 bombers had to attack the formation.

For 1970 OEG envisaged the same fighters but a Typhon fleet with 200nm long-range and 40nm medium-range missiles; surviving Terrier ships would have been upgraded to 35nm range. The threat would be the same as in 1966. Replacing the early surface-to-air systems with Typhon would increase the number of high-level bombers needed to saturate to about seventy-five. Effective decoys and deception devices plus a dispersed formation would increase the number required to saturate by a factor of 3 to 5. In a pre-Typhon task force, about a third of all fighter kills would be at high altitude. Fighters operating with Typhon ships would kill fewer enemy aircraft, partly because they had to stay out of the considerable Typhon envelope (it could hit targets as much as 200nm away), but they helped Typhon by thinning out incoming raids, reducing saturation. Whatever fighter system was used, OEG considered fighters invaluable as a way of countering enemy snoopers (or pathfinders) which might be able to evade surface-to-air missiles. With its much longer range, Typhon could fire twenty-five salvoes at bombers before they could fire and it could also kill four of their missiles beyond 40nm.

The close-in 1970 fleet would kill a total of sixty-four targets, nine of them by fighters and the rest by surface-to-air missiles. In the spread-out case, the missiles would destroy eighty targets and the fighters fifteen. OEG calculated that it would take seventy-seven high-fliers to saturate the defence of a close-in 1970 formation. It would take 107 aircraft getting close enough to saturate the dispersed formation, but to do that an enemy would need 268 aircraft.

Against a low-flier performance, of the 1966 and 1970 fleets was similar. Typhon made little difference because it was horizon-limited to a range of about 23nm. Low-fliers would find it even more difficult simply to find their targets. OEG cautioned that its study probably understated the effect of tactical deception, which might be to avoid attack altogether.

Typhon and Eagle-Missileer were both likely to be extremely expensive. In 1960 the navy planned to maintain six operational two-carrier task forces. For those ships the Eagle system would cost about $2730 million. Total Typhon cost for the same task forces would be $5970 million. Through 1960 CNO Admiral Burke wrestled with the question of how to balance the two new systems, which had comparable costs and capabilities. In May 1960 the Assistant Secretary of the Navy for R&D wrote that one or the other might have to be cancelled. Limited funds had already forced the navy to stop buying the A3J (A-5) strategic bomber and to stretch the A2F (Intruder) and W2F (Hawkeye) pro-grammes, reducing production to uneconomical rates. Missileer could be considered a supplement to the existing fighter systems, particularly if the navy could not avoid buying high-performance fighters. Typhon was the required replacement for the existing surface missile systems. One measure of effectiveness was the annual system cost per timely enemy missile launch averted. On that basis, in the worst case for Typhon (a wave attack at 200ft altitude), Typhon cost a third as much – on the basis of estimates for two systems, neither of which was anywhere near the point of production.

When the navy leadership tried to decide which way to turn, it took into account some unique capabilities Missileer offered. It stretched outward the area in which attackers could be destroyed, making it possible to destroy either the bomber (before it launched) or the missile. It might break up raid co-ordination, timing and leader-ship, thus making surface-to-air missiles more effective (by reducing saturation). It could destroy remote jammers and deal with feint attacks. Most importantly, only a fighter could destroy a snooper and thus abort an attack altogether.

There was also a considerable advantage in the very different characteristics of Typhon and Eagle-Missileer, which would complicate enemy raid planning and tactics. Also, developing two different systems offered insurance against a technical breakthrough or a tactical surprise, not to mention outages in either system.

Eagle-Missileer seems to have been closer than Typhon to the point of production, although in 1960 the navy expected to begin ordering very expensive Typhon ships quite soon. In 1960 new President John F Kennedy was elected. The outgoing Secretary of Defense chose not to sign the contract for the Missileer aircraft so as to leave the next Administration free to decide whether to proceed with it. Soon after entering office, President Kennedy's new Secretary of Defense Robert S McNamara decided to cancel Eagle-Missileer in favour of the alter-native F-111B with a new Phoenix/AWG-9 system. The main decision seems to have been cancellation of Missileer in favour of a navy version of the joint F-111, Eagle following because the new aircraft could not have carried it.

CHAPTER 10
THE COMPUTER AGE IN FLEET AIR DEFENCE

IN 1945 THE Kamikazes demonstrated that the wartime fighter-control system could be saturated. Ultimately saturation was a time problem: it took too long for each detection (of a raid) to be turned into fighter control. The problem is reflected in the time line from initial detection to assignment of a CAP fighter to engagement (tallyho) to destruction (splash). The faster the incomer, the less time the system had to react. To make matters worse, it turned out that existing radars detected jets at shorter ranges than propeller aircraft, due to the jets' streamlining (an early example of the way in which the

shape of an object affects radar, something like modern stealth). By the mid-1950s better radars were available, but they did not solve the underlying saturation problem.

The core problem was saturation of the tactical picture underlying any form of fighter control. Those maintaining the picture could never tell how close it was to reality. Up to a point, even an erroneous picture (plot) could be used to direct a fighter, the pilot's eyes and his aircraft's performance making up for errors in direction. Beyond a point, errors in the plot would preclude effective fighter control altogether. This

picture was compiled (produced) on the basis of incoming radar data. Time lags, for example between seeing a blip on a screen and entering target data on a plot, limited the system's ability to handle really fast targets or even very numerous ones. The problem was suspected late in the war and revealed in all its horrors a few years later, when controlled tests were run both by the Royal Navy and the US Navy.

THE BRITISH APPROACH: CDS

The two major carrier navies handled their data in somewhat different ways and these differences led to different post-war solutions to the saturation problem. The pre-war Royal Navy was substantially more sophisticated in its approach to tactical data. On board a flagship, for example, it maintained both large-scale and tactical plots intended to convey the situation to the ship's command. In many ships a viewing tube on the open bridge provided access to the tactical plot for those in command. There might also be a flag plot. In the 1930s the Royal Navy added a Gun Direction Room (GDR) in which (at least in theory) a small-scale plot was created so that anti-aircraft targets could be prioritised. When radar was introduced, the natural result was a radar plot. Fighter control required an Aircraft Direction Room (ADR). About 1943 all of these separate spaces were amalgamated into the Action Information Organisation (AIO). All of them shared radar data, but there was no way of automatically transcribing a plot produced in one of them so that the others could share it. The best that could be done was a window looking down onto one plot so that those operating another (for example a flag plot) could see what was being done. That was hardly likely to work during an intense air raid.

For the British, the obvious problem was that all the users of plots did not have easy access to the same information. Dr Ralph Benjamin, a scientist at the Admiralty Signals Establishment (responsible for radars), suggested an answer, which he developed from about 1947 on.[1] Benjamin's invention was called the Combat Data System (CDS). It was associated with a massive three-dimensional radar, Type 984, which was also invented by Benjamin. Because Type 984 could not be installed on board British missile destroyers, a digital data link called Digital Plot Transmission (DTP) was devised to provide them with the CDS picture, including target height.[2] The CDS/Type 984 combination was first installed on board the carrier *Victorious*, which visited the United States in 1958, soon after being rebuilt.

Benjamin adopted an analog approach because it was the only available method. It was possible to build an analog memory which would carry an aircraft track, projecting ahead (dead-reckoning) aircraft position. A stack of such memories would represent the air situation. Because each track was carried in a separate memory, the size of a CDS installation set track capacity, up to ninety-six tracks on board a carrier (surface ships might carry twenty-four or forty-eight tracks). Each target required six separate memories, for three co-ordinates (including height), track number, height/raid size and a reference number indicating the tracker group.[3] An operator at a terminal could retrieve information by 'hooking' a track number using a joystick. The production version provided forty-eight tracks but

Dr Ralph Benjamin sought to solve the multiple-plot problem by a degree of automation, creating an analogue memory to hold data on up to forty-eight or ninety-six separate air tracks. He integrated this memory and multiple plots, with a single Type 984 three-dimensional radar. It was first installed on board *Victorious*, shown here. The accompanying CDS could handle forty-eight tracks. Although US naval fighters outperformed their British counterparts, the combination of Benjamin's CDS (Combat Direction System) and its Type 984 radar offered them a decisive advantage in the Riptide exercise held on 15–20 July 1959 after *Victorious* crossed the Atlantic. This advantage might be likened to that enjoyed by US fighters defending carriers at Midway against superior Japanese aircraft, a decisive factor being radar fighter control (plus 'Thach weave' tactics). The island of *Victorious*, with its huge Type 984, is shown on 3 August 1959. The ship could not accommodate any back-up two-dimensional radar, only the 'cheese' of a short-range Type 992 intended as target indicator for her 3in gun armament. The cylinder at the top of the mast is a TACAN antenna. The only other British carrier to have CDS was *Hermes*, which had a 32-track version.

could be scaled up to ninety-six or down to twenty-four or sixteen in a 'utility' version.[4] The system wrote alphanumeric data onto the screens in addition to radar video they displayed. It could not, however, display a combined picture summing up the forty-eight targets it was handling. To the extent that such a summary was available, it was provided by an alphanumeric tote which an officer could scan to decide how to handle a situation.

Data were entered by radar operators (detectors), who could see radar video on their screens. Separate trackers assembled separate

A computer-era carrier: *America* in the early 1970s, with a Hawkeye on her port bow catapult. The Hawkeye was conceived as an airborne node within the Naval Tactical Data System. The other aircraft is an A-3 Skywarrior, probably used for signals intelligence. The fighters are Phantoms. Other aircraft are A-7 light bombers, a few A-6 Intruders and RA-5C Vigilante reconnaissance aircraft (conceived as supersonic strategic bombers, but not used as such).

Victorious shows part of her air group of Scimitars and Sea Vixens and her heavily-angled deck. Note too the US-style bridle catcher at the end of the port (but not starboard) catapult.

target reports into rate-aided tracks, checking displays periodically to make sure that aircraft were still following the assumed tracks. In both CDS and its digital US equivalent, NTDS, detectors at radars entered plots into the system by 'hooking' them and moving cursors across their screens using joysticks. A tracker entered target course and speed by informing the system that a second plot was the same aircraft detected slightly later. The system fed back a marker at the calculated current target position, both to keep trackers from re-entering the same target and to make it possible to check whether the target was still on its assumed path at the calculated speed. In British tests, operators entered a plot in two seconds (the radar data rate was six seconds, meaning three plots per scan). Tests conducted in 1949 showed that an operator could handle as many as eight targets. Separate analysis (filtering) operators could review the targets. They had A- and B-scopes and precision height displays enabling them to examine target echo characteristics in detail.[5] Using buttons on his joystick, an operator could query the corresponding track memory.

The detectors fed data to the trackers, who fed data to the analyser; both trackers and analysers fed their data into the central system memory. From that memory data went to intercept operators (who had direct access to radar video), to tactical operators and to the operator of the semi-automatic tote/status board which was, in effect, a summary of the tactical situation.

Any operator on board ship could consult the overall picture; there was no longer any need to copy data from one plot to another, with the resulting lag time and inaccuracy. To some extent, moreover, fighter control could now be automated.

New and rebuilt British carriers had a two-level Action Information Center designed to overcome the sort of confusion the US Navy was then experiencing with its CICs. The lower level consisted of adjacent radar display room (in which operators entered data) and aircraft control room (IFF and fighter control). Its IFF operators had a special track correlator display, so that they could see both tracks and IFF. The supervising officer had a triple console with tracking and correlator displays. The fighter control room had a vertical semi-automatic tote board. Above the fighter control room was a force function and staff room for battle management, with an open well through which the tote board could be seen. The tactical picture was compiled by operators in this room. CDS provided them and the fighter controllers with a picture using the data input by the radar operators in the radar display room below.

When the CDS system entered service in *Victorious*, the Royal Navy had no long-range heightfinding radar suitable for a smaller ship, yet the new Sea Slug surface-to-air missile system in the 'County' class guided-missile destroyers required height information. The British

Ark Royal was refitted in 1967–70 to support Phantoms and Buccaneers after the decision had been taken to cancel CVA 01 but also after the decision had been taken to keep her in service as long as possible. Initially she was to have matched *Eagle*, using a 'spare' developmental Type 984 radar, but to limit costs the refit focused on aviation capability, for example installation of a more powerful catapult. She had the analogue CDS system rather than the digital ADA. *Ark Royal* emerged with a second Type 965 and a Type 983 heightfinder where *Eagle* had her Type 984 (a second Type 983 is shown aft). One of her Phantoms is visible forward of her island. The view from forward dates from November 1970; the view from aft, from September 1970. The view from aft appears to show the Type 982 precision air-search radar.

solution was for the carrier to provide it (and long-range target data) to the accompanying destroyers via a special digital data link (digital to limit corruption by noise) called DPT (Digital Plot Transmission). DPT in turn tied the first four 'Countys' to the CDS system on board the carriers they were intended to escort (*Victorious* and *Hermes*). That explains why these ships were disposed of when their carriers were either discarded or lost their long-range heightfinding Type 984s. DPT was also projected for other purposes, particularly to co-ordinate ASW action, but it was overshadowed by fully-digital command systems and other digital links. To the Royal Navy, DPT was Link I; the NTDS link (see below) became Link II. When NATO standardised links using Arabic numerals, it was simplest to turn Link II into Link 11 (eleven).

The great difference between CDS and its digital successors, the British ADA/ADAWS and the US NTDS, was that each track was handled completely separately. There was no way of comparing tracks to decide which target was most threatening or which could or could not be intercepted using available resources. In CDS the evaluation and comparison function fell to a supervising officer at a display showing all the tracks in the system.

CDS/984 made a huge impression when *Victorious* visited the United States. Although the British Sea Vixen fighters were inferior to their US counterparts, the combination of CDS and fighters grossly outperformed US naval fighters during exercises.[6] By this time the US Air Force had come close to adopting CDS for the North American Air Defense (NORAD) system. The RAF had adopted CDS for British national air defence, albeit without the Type 984 radar.

THE US APPROACH TO COMBAT AUTOMATION: NTDS

The US Navy also plotted data before the war, but not on so sophisticated a scale. When it adopted radar, it created radar plots. Ultimately the radar plot became the core of a CIC which also integrated other

data and data passed from other ships via a dedicated radio circuit. The key difference from the Royal Navy was that all users shared a single common plot. By 1945 that made for considerable congestion and even for confusion, as all users wanted to refer to that single vertical plotting board. There was, however, no problem of instantly transferring data from one plot to another. British observers reported that by 1945 the US Navy was interested in decentralising its CIC operation (like the British), whereas the Royal Navy was more interested in centralising to reduce errors and time lags in re-plotting.

Initially the US Navy tried an analog approach using equipment developed by the Naval Electronic Laboratory (NEL) in San Diego. Soon after he took command there, Lieutenant Commander Irvin L McNally ordered development of what he called Co-ordinated Display Equipment, inspired by an existing NEL radar simulator. It was analogous to CDS, but the NEL engineers opted for digital rather than analog tracking, only to avoid the wear (which would cost accuracy) on analog scanning switches. NEL's Semi-Automatic Digital Analyzer and Computer (SADZAC) used a magnetic drum memory. It did not go the further crucial step to handling all its data digitally and thus comparing tracks automatically. Instead, data from operators was converted into digital form, placed in memory and then converted back into analog form for display. Even so, BuShips, which was responsible for shipboard radars and their auxiliary equipment, found SADZAC promising enough to let a contract to a small computer firm, the Teleregister Company, for a development it called the Semi-Automatic Air Intercept Control System (SAAICS), an automated plotting and vector computing aid for fighter interception. It was never completed, but the experience convinced McNally that an automated air-defence computer was practicable. He took that knowledge with him to the tri-service LAMPLIGHT symposium in 1954.

Roughly in parallel to NEL, NRL developed its own Electronic Display System (EDS). Work began in 1951, using data collected for

The scope of the refit to *Ark Royal* is evident from this pre-refit photograph. The ship has a single-bedstead Type 965 forward and a Type 960 low-frequency air-search radar aft, with a precision air-search radar (Type 982) abaft that. The Type 983 forward is barely visible. Aircraft on deck are Scimitars, Sea Vixens and Gannets. Note the absence of the bridle-catcher later fitted to the lengthened (more powerful) port catapult. The ship's port forward pair of 4.5in guns had been removed to make space for the angled deck.

a BuShips–Bell Laboratories study of the interception problem (Project COSMOS, which continued through 1956). Like CDS, EDS used separate electric dead-reckoning memories, but the output was much cruder: a conventional vertical plot on which automated pens moved. Capacity was twenty-four targets. Tests showed that EDS could handle data much faster than manual CICs (whose net saturated at eight to eleven targets).[7]

LAMPLIGHT was not a naval conference. It was called by the scientists and engineers who were then developing a digital computer system for the NORAD system. They in turn had been inspired by the Whirlwind computer developed for the navy. It began life in 1944 as a flight simulator, a training tool. Working at MIT, project manager

Jay Forrester chose a digital rather than analog computer to provide the flexibility he needed. Its unique feature (in 1949) was its ability to accept inputs while running; it was the first time-shared computer. All other digital computers then in existence handled fixed problems in batch mode; they followed fixed programmes using data entered at the beginning. That is why they were assigned simple but brutally repetitive jobs such as solving German codes or calculating gun ballistics. Unsurprisingly, the futuristic Whirlwind proved very expensive to develop and in 1949 its sponsor the Office of Naval Research (ONR) ran out of money. That may have been a consequence of the larger defence budget disaster of the time.

However, there was money for continental air defence, clearly a very high priority. In 1949 the problem seemed hopeless. It was understood officially that the only valid function of early warning radars was to give the Strategic Air Command time to launch its aircraft before Soviet bombers could destroy all of them.

In January 1950 the US Air Force set up a Government Air Defense System Engineering Committee, chaired by MIT physicist George E Valley – who met Forrester. He understood that Whirlwind

The CIC problem. The CIC of *Randolph* as an attack carrier, from the plotters' side, with radar consoles in the foreground. Radar operators reported contacts which the plotters visible on the left plotted by writing backwards on the vertical plot and the status boards. Men at the phones entered data from other sources, also passing it to the plotters. Both the US Navy and the Royal Navy employed similar vertical plots, but they used them very differently. The Royal Navy split up functions to limit noise and confusion in any one plotting space – but that required multiple plots, which might not entirely match. The US Navy preferred the single plot shown, but that required multiple users to make sense of the single vertical plot. Both navies suffered from time lags as information was passed verbally to plotters and then entered into plot and status board ('tote' in British parlance).

could be the basis for a successful air-defence system. Computers would collect radar data, evaluate threats, assign interceptors, even guide the interceptors to their targets. In effect Forrester had already solved the worst technical problem Valley faced. In March 1950 the air force contracted MIT for a prototype air-defence system. Its computer was operating by March 1951 and by April it was receiving data from a prototype Microwave Early Warning (MEW) radar. On 20 April 1951 it demonstrated that it could vector a fighter into a collision intercept course. Quite suddenly North American air defence seemed to be a solvable problem. Given a clear computer-generated picture of an incoming attack, an air defence commander could assign interceptors to the incoming bombers and the computer could handle everything else. The air force soon decided to develop fully-automated interceptors, in which the pilot would be no more than a system supervisor, taking off and landing and then allowing the computer to do the rest. This rather futuristic vision took years to realise and the huge computers NORAD bought always had problems. However, the air defence problem the air force faced was little difference from the navy's and inevitably its new system inspired a naval equivalent.[8]

Initially SAGE used radars in Canada to block the easiest bomber route to the United States, over the pole. However, there were other possibilities; Soviet bombers could fly around the Canadian barrier and approach over the coasts. That perception brought the US Navy into

NORAD, mainly to provide surface and airborne radar pickets, which did not feed the SAGE computers directly. However, participation in NORAD justified inclusion of a naval officer in the major 1954 conference, LAMPLIGHT, which the NORAD system developers held.

The officer was McNally, who was already well aware of the need for automation via his experience at NEL. Perhaps prodded by McNally, the conference recommended that the navy automate its CICs so that ships at sea could connect with SAGE. Navy pickets offshore could have their radars modified so that, like digitised radars ashore, they could enter data directly into SAGE computers. That entailed digital data handling on board the ships and a digital link from ship to shore.[9] The conference recommended deploying EDS as an interim measure, followed by a fully-digital system. Any analog alternative was rejected: expanding something like EDS to handle hundreds of targets would be astronomically expensive. As a first step, the conference proposed that the navy buy six sets of the Canadian digital system (DATAR) then under development.

During the conference McNally began to think through what the navy needed, not to supplement North American air defence but to solve its own air-defence problem. He envisaged a scalable system on board many kinds of ships, its computers exchanging data automatically. Airborne early warning aircraft would participate in this net (as they would in the offshore net LAMPLIGHT envisaged). If ships were no more than about 20 miles apart, they might use the new line-of-sight UHF radios then being introduced for ship-to-air communication. They offered the high data rates McNally knew he would need. Given new radars looking out 250nm or even 300nm, McNally estimated that each ship might have to handle up to 1000 tracks (including ships and submarines, friendly and enemy), which might be derived not only from radar data but also from alternatives such as IFF trackers, EW sensors and sonars.[10]

McNally could not possibly use the IBM big vacuum-tube computers just entering production for SAGE; his vision demanded a new kind of computer using transistors. They barely existed in

Radar operators in a US manual CIC, February 1958. The supervisor standing behind the radar scopes transmitted radar detections to the plotters outside this picture (having the operators report independently would have overloaded the plotters).

prototype form: Dr Jerrold Zacharias, the senior MIT member of the air defence committee, told him that his idea was a fantasy. However, an IBM representative was more encouraging. He told McNally to write a formal proposal for his naval system. McNally submitted it to the ONR. An ONR Committee endorsed it in the summer of 1955 and CNO tentatively approved it that autumn. It was considered so important that it was assigned a short five-year schedule.

As navy delegate to LAMPLIGHT, McNally had the opportunity to speak early in 1955 at the headquarters of the Atlantic destroyer force linked with SAGE (the first pickets were converted destroyer escorts).[11] This force was closely associated with radical ongoing changes such as arming destroyers with anti-aircraft missiles. It would soon urge the navy to build nuclear-powered destroyers even though large nuclear cruisers seemed barely practical. In the audience was Admiral Arleigh A Burke, who would become CNO that August. A former gunnery officer and a survivor of Kamikaze attacks, he had headed the July-August 1945 anti-Kamikaze experiments in Casco Bay, Maine. Kamikazes produced the sort of saturation NTDS was intended to overcome. Burke was willing to take technological gambles like adopting the Fleet Ballistic Missile (Polaris) and an all-nuclear submarine fleet. His enthusiastic support for McNally's ideas proved crucial. McNally's Tentative Operational Requirement was

formally approved on 24 April 1956. It envisaged automated data systems aboard ships, aboard an airborne CIC aircraft (ultimately the Hawkeye) and for Marine Corps air defence. The NEL was made prime contractor, partly to ensure fleet involvement with the technology. An NTDS Project Office was formed within BuShips. Having set the project in motion, McNally retired in June 1956.

McNally's system consisted of the shipboard computerised NTDS, the associated ATDS, the latter on board an airborne radar plane, and a Marine Tactical Data System (MTDS). In what follows, NTDS stands for all three. To provide growth potential, the systems used general-purpose rather than special-purpose (i.e. hard-wired or fixed-programme) computers, even though at the time it seemed that only the latter would be fast enough. Different types of ships would have different numbers of standard computers and consoles. The minimum was two computers, to provide a fall-back in the event of computer failure. In larger versions separate computers would perform different functions, exchanging data on a memory-to-memory basis. In 1955 these concepts were radical (the distributed architecture was not implemented).

No US company had yet built the required compact transistorised computer. Univac won the contract. Its computer designer, Seymour Cray, later famous for supercomputers, conceived the time-sharing architecture. The computer shifted programmes in and out of memory, storing intermediate data in special stacks so that it could later resume the earlier task. Time-sharing made possible a modular programme, only some modules of which were loaded at any one time. Cray wanted to use the same 32-bit words as SAGE, but found that transistors limited him to thirty. Initially the navy team planned to use 20,000 words of memory in each of the two minimum-version computers, opting for 24,000 to allow for growth. Cray argued that memory was becoming cheaper, so he chose 32,000. McNally had to scale down his requirements to some extent. Instead of 1000 tracks, the large-ship version could handle 256 and the small-ship version, 128.

Much as in EDS or CDS, radar operators entered data by moving cursors at their consoles. They automatically measured target range and bearing by 'hooking' its blip. Hooking the same target on three successive radar scans entered it (with three successive positions) into the computer's track file. Much as in CDS, the computer automatically deduced target course and speed and then dead-reckoned (and displayed updated target positions) until the operator decided that the target had changed course or speed. Because he could enter a target quickly, an operator could shift attention to other targets. Unlike CDS, NTDS carried all its tracks in the same memory. They could be compared, for example to decide which targets should be engaged most urgently. The computer could decide whether a given target could be engaged and it could choose which weapon should be assigned (paired with) which target. To do that with airborne interceptors, it had to keep track of their changing fuel and weapon status (at least on an estimated basis). It also had to keep track of special points (such as Formation Center), fixed or slaved to another point or track or moving at a speed set by an operator.

NTDS was conceived as a picture-keeper which could pass targets to a separate weapon system. It was the province of BuShips, which made search radars; in effect it was the memory which turned a ship's radars into a track-while-search system. Weapons and their controls came under the separate BuOrd. By this time BuOrd was developing Weapon Direction Systems (WDS), which functioned as small-scale analog picture-keepers (something like small equivalents to CDS).

As a way station to NTDS, the US Navy developed a modular CIC in which different functions were separated, yet retained access to at least a television picture of the common plot. This is the 'Decision and Display Area' of a carrier's modular CIC. Note the classical vertical plot and also the way in which this module is separated from others, to eliminate the usual congestion inside a CIC.

They stored target data so that a missile system could switch rapidly from target to target.[12]

NTDS might be considered much less sophisticated than CDS and its digital follow-on, in that it was only loosely connected with a ship's radars and other sensors. That was deliberate: given wartime experience, McNally and his sponsors were very sensitive to the possibility of battle damage. Ships had to be able to keep fighting even if their computers were wiped out.

In addition to automating a ship's CIC picture, NTDS enabled a ship to share other ships' data. Once all of the air-defence ships in a group had NTDS, they shared data via a digital Link 11. It operated by sending computer commands, including data, directly to the

computers on board NTDS ships (and, later, its NATO equivalents). This link used HF rather than higher-frequency radio, despite problems that entailed, to make it possible for an NTDS task force to disperse in the face of nuclear threats.[13] The use of multiple HF channels (and encryption) in turn greatly complicated the use of Link 11, so that during the 1960s Link 11 imposed a considerable financial burden on NATO navies. Several of them adopted a high-low mix in which a Link 11 'gateway' ship communicated with other ships via a less elaborate Link, typically Link 10.

In an NTDS net, a designated master ship called the roll, the others (called the pickets) responding with their information. When a ship first detected a target it assigned a track number. A second ship assigned its own track number. To avoid flooding the group with data, the system constantly compared new tracks with ones already in memory (correlation: cancellation of double-counted tracks).[14] That was possible because all tracks were in the same digital memory. Starting from an empty picture, the ships in a net all built up their pictures in parallel. Any ship might miss the occasional message.

However, ships constantly reported what they were detecting. Data would be redundant enough to ensure that pictures would match. Each ship's data terminal carried all addresses in the net. If the master ship were sunk or disabled, another ship in the net could replace her.

The great problem in an NTDS net was navigation. Ships out of sight of each other had to report targets in terms of a common fleet grid. The system tried to cancel out multiple reports of the same target, to avoid saturation; but if two ships were mis-positioned relative to each other, they would report the same target as two separate targets. To maintain position, NTDS ships had the new Ships Inertial Navigation System (SINS), but it was not nearly enough. The positioning problem was called 'gridlock'. When much more powerful NTDS computers were introduced, a partial solution was achieved by having ships compare the relative positions of other ships, trying alternative sets of grid references until they matched. This was not enough; the gridlock problem was ultimately solved only with the advent of GPS.

NTDS was born in an era of great computer optimism. The new solid-state machines would be entirely reliable and their power seemed unlimited. A classified brochure, produced about 1960, describing the advantages of NTDS, referred to its vast computer capacity of over a million bits – we now calculate capacity in bytes (8 bits each) and we are not impressed by figures less than several billion of them. A typical NTDS system of the 1960s could handle 256 target tracks at one time, which was certainly a vast improvement over earlier systems.

In 1959, well before the system had been tested, OpNav decided to install NTDS on board all combatants large enough to take it: all carriers, all missile cruisers, all heavy cruisers (presumably because they were used as flagships), all missile 'frigates' (DLG/DLGN, later reclassified as cruisers and missile destroyers) and all missile destroyers (DDG).[15] Later amphibious flagships, existing and planned, were added. Through FY62 the programme included the carriers *Enterprise* and *America*, the nuclear cruiser *Long Beach*, the three *Chicago* class missile cruisers (CG 10–12), the two nuclear-powered 'frigates' *Bainbridge* and *Truxtun* and the *Belknap* class 'frigates' (DLG 26–34).

Enterprise and *Long Beach* were given NTDS because their electronically-scanned radars already required so much digital computer processing. The FY61 budget paid for the conversion of the 'frigates' (large missile destroyers; only the US Navy used this term for such ships at the time) *King* and *Mahan* for a service test with the carrier *Oriskany* (her conversion was paid for by RDT&E funds). After successful evaluation, in July 1964 OpNav stated that NTDS was definitely worth its cost, as it had finally provided effective fleet air defence. Too, in current terms it was no more expensive than a Second World War CIC: about 1.5 per cent of total carrier task force cost vs about 1 per cent for conventional CICs.

As of July 1964, half the NTDS funding was in place, for a programme to be completed in 1972. Then costs escalated and funds dried up, probably largely because of the war in Vietnam. All of the large carriers received NTDS, although by 1962 planned conversions of smaller *Essex*-class ships had already been abandoned. The programme was reviewed in 1967. By this time Secretary of Defense McNamara planned a new class of destroyers (DX/DXG, built as the *Spruance* class), which could be completed as either ASW or missile ships. He used the prospect of these ships to justify killing NTDS on board the two remaining *Cleveland* class missile cruisers. Of the other three missile cruisers, *Albany* was already being converted. Conversion of the other two, planned for FY67 and FY69, was

rescheduled to FY70 and FY73, cost per ship having risen from $27 million to $96 million. The last ship, *Columbus*, was dropped. As a measure of what was involved, with NTDS *Albany* could handle 128 local and 128 remote tracks.[16] An unmodified ship handled only twenty-four. DLG (large missile destroyer) conversions survived because they offered more AAW firepower six years earlier than the projected DXG (which materialised only in the form of four *Kidd* class ships begun for Iran). Installation in the *Leahy* and *Belknap* classes (in a new deckhouse) was apparently quite tight: as much as six years after completion there was still talk of how difficult the project had been. By this time it was clear that installation planned for *Adams* class missile destroyers was impractical, but the advent of the new UYK-7 computer made that possible (only six ships of the twenty-three were ever fitted).

NTDS was a time-shared central-computer system, which meant that it switched among the multiple tasks it had to carry out, saving its data in a special stack when it switched. All of its modules thus had access to the same data embodying its tactical picture. Initially memory was tight enough that not all modules could be loaded at the same time and some of the functions envisaged at first, such as an electronic warfare function, were not available in the earliest version. The consoles initially had no computing capacity at all; the central computer even generated the symbols they displayed (later consoles could generate their own symbols, somewhat reducing the load on the central computer). Because operation was time-shared, with the central computer switching among tasks and also among the consoles, when the central computer was particularly heavily loaded, there was sometimes a noticeable time lag between pressing a button and seeing the associated response on the screen. That is, the computer had to switch to the programme module in which it detected that a button on a console had been pushed and if it was very heavily loaded the time lag in switching from module to module was noticeable. The situation was exacerbated because as deployed NTDS allowed a ship's programmers to add modules to the basic programmes issued to the ship. By 1970 there was an urgent 'get well' programme which included new computers (UYK-7 and then UYK-43, supplemented by UYK-20 and UYK-44 mini-computers) and much tighter control of a ship's own programming.

THE US INTERIM SYSTEM

In 1956 it was clear that some solution to the CIC mess was urgent, but it was also clear that the necessary computers would take time to develop. CNO Admiral Burke ordered development of an interim manual system which could give way naturally to NTDS once the computers and other elements were ready. On board ship this was the Modular CIC. By this time existing CICs had become more and more crowded as functions were added. All users needed access to a single summary (vertical) plot. The space around it was crowded with operators trailing the lines of their sound-powered phones, all trying to make sense of what they were hearing over the noise of loudspeakers overhead. If OpNav could not immediately solve the problem by automation, it could split up CIC functions into spaces all of which would be able to see the vertical plot. That was done by focusing a television camera on the summary plot in a central Display-Decision Area, around which were the other CIC areas. The dual designation indicated that central decisions were made here, on the basis of what was seen on the vertical plot. As might be imagined, one of them was

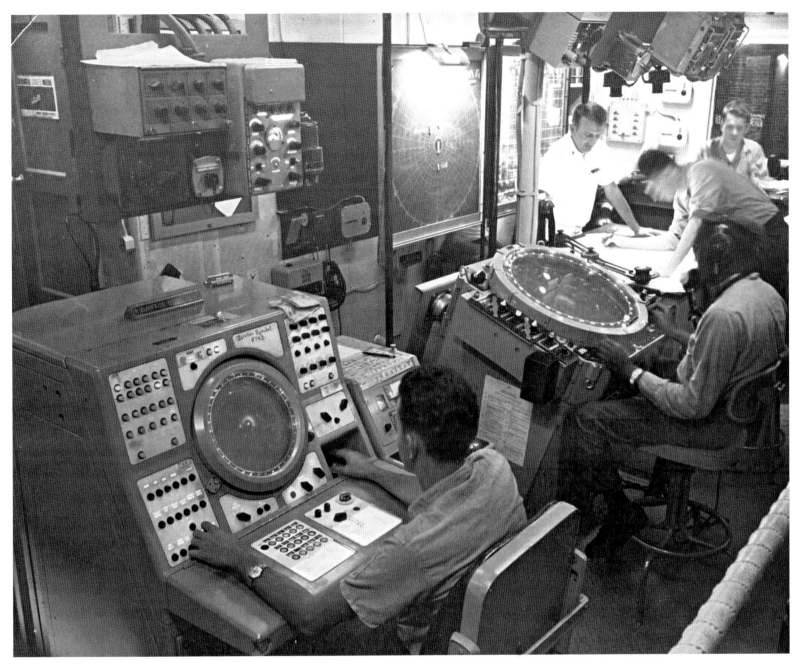

Part of an automated CIC, on board *Enterprise*, March 1967. The screens shown are output consoles displaying the tactical picture held in the system. Radar operators in the NTDS system entered target positions using pantographs which they could manoeuvre across the face of their screens. Entering a target position three times entered it and its course and speed into the system. Manual elements, like the plotting board at right, survived. The important difference between NTDS and the British ADA was that the US system was loosely coupled. It never used a dedicated radar (although *Enterprise* herself had electronically-scanned air-search radars, SPS-32 and -33) and it deliberately avoided automatic data entry. Much later it turned out that automatic plotting and tracking were invaluable, but the NTDS developers doubted that the technology available in the early 1960s could have supported such functions.

an input area feeding data to plotters working behind the vertical plots visible in the central area. Other areas had their own 24in television monitors showing the air summary plot built up in the input area: an Air Operations Area, a CCA area, an Air Warfare control area, an Ordnance Control Area (including the carrier's gun target assignment system, a Target Designation System Mk 6), a Surface Operations Area and an ECM Area. Between the ECM and Surface Operations Area was a table with an area chart to be used for long-range plotting, intelligence plotting and ECM triangulation. The surface area kept its picture on a DRT (there was no feedback of this picture to the display-decision area). All of this was a substantial improvement over the earlier CIC arrangement, but it was hardly ideal. For example, the means of indicating decisions to the modular areas was sound-powered telephone, with the delay and possible errors that implied. Nor was there any way of automatically feeding back what was done in the various areas of CIC into the main plot, e.g. noting CAP assignments.

This CIC was modular by function. OpNav saw it as Phase 0 of a three-phase automation programme, in which Phase I would be the interim EDS system and Phase II the ultimate digital system (which became NTDS). The Integrated Modular CIC was approved by OpNav in October 1956 and the first such CIC was installed on board the carrier *Oriskany* (completed April 1959). By late 1960 a total of fifty-five such installations was underway.

The programme was intended in large part to smooth the way towards the ultimate digital system. Since that system would have an airborne node (the ATDS on board an AEW aircraft), the modular CIC was paralleled by an interim airborne system. The airborne CIC was finally urgent enough to be funded.

ATDS

From the outset, the NTDS project envisaged an integrated airborne CIC with its own computer, controlling fighters. The final pre-NTDS Operational Requirement for a carrier-based CIC aircraft was issued on 27 July 1954. When NTDS was conceived, the navy was on the point of bringing carrier-based airborne CICs into service. On 2 November 1955 a formal Operational Requirement (AD-06501[Rev]) was issued for a computerised AEW aircraft as part of the emerging NTDS system. It was intended as the basis for a formal design competition. BuAer followed with a Type Specification on 23 November (OS-139). In February 1956 BuAer circulated an invitation to bid for a carrier-based AEW/CIC aircraft it called VW(X). Proposals were received on 22 May and evaluations were submitted in August 1956, with a decision due before 1 November. The first two aircraft were to be bought as part of the FY58 programme.

Before that could happen, in February 1956 BuAer pointed out that the fruit of the competition would not be available before mid-1962. It argued that the need was so urgent that an interim AEW aircraft should be bought at once, as it could provide a greatly-improved AEW capability by July 1959.[17] The interim aircraft may have been included in the AEW-CIC Type Specification from the outset.

The question for potential bidders was whether to offer a scaled-down version of the aircraft they hoped would win the real prize, the ATDS aircraft. Of four known proposals, Fairchild offered a version of its C-123B equipped with a nose radome for an APS-45 heightfinder and a dorsal radome for an APS-20. It was an attempt to approximate the WV-2 in a carrier-capable package and it seems out of place, given the navy's interest in a future computer aircraft carrying a new low-frequency radar. Alone among the bidders, Fairchild apparently had no interest in an automated mission system.

Both Lockheed and Vought offered scaled-back versions of their planned ATDS aircraft, the difference being that they had a much less capable, though automated, system on board. Both had APS-70 radars in rotodomes, Vought having developed a retarded-wave radar which was particularly thin.

Grumman seems to have realised that the key to winning the contract for the interim aircraft would be to use immediately-available equipment. Like Lockheed and Vought, it offered an automated intercept system. Unlike them, it used an existing airframe (the TF-1 Trader carrier onboard delivery aircraft, which offered more internal space than the S2F of its earlier WF-1 project). It also used a radar which minimised developmental problems: the S-band APS-82 which could be seen as a much-enlarged APS-20. Grumman had sensed early that an interim aircraft would be welcome and it had begun work in the early summer of 1955, before any formal requirement had been issued. July 1955 wind tunnel tests showed that a modified TF-1 could carry a 20ft x 30ft radome, large enough to enclose a 17.5ft x 4ft antenna, far larger than the 8ft antenna in earlier carrier AEW aircraft,

without seriously compromising flying qualities (the new radar was the S-band APS-82). The aircraft also had an airborne direction finder (ALD-2) which it could use to locate an enemy aircraft by its radar emissions, a new feature in carrier AEW.

In September Grumman and the Hazeltine electronics company began work on a formal proposal, which they submitted in January 1956. Hazeltine was responsible for the lightweight AEW radar and the tracking and plotting displays. It offered a memory device (with a capacity of four targets and four interceptors) feeding information to the control indicator (display). There were secure digital links to both individual interceptors and a surface CIC. The proposed crew would be a tracker and a single fighter controller. The co-pilot could occupy a folding seat between the two operators to act as tactical director. BuAer accepted the new longer-range radar but apparently rejected the automated system Hazeltine offered. The tracker became a second fighter controller and BuAer manual intercept computers (integrated with the radar displays) replaced the electronic system Grumman and Hazeltine proposed. There were no data links to fighters. The new aircraft used the same Bellhop radar video link (to a carrier CIC) as earlier AEW aircraft.

Hazeltine and Grumman also offered a new heightfinding capability provided by two receive-only horns. As the radar antenna was tilted up and down, these horns could indicate vertical target position. BuAer doubted that the technique would work, so the specification was rewritten; progress in heightfinding would not be allowed to interfere with the design of the radar (the aircraft was provided with a central gyro as a vertical reference for any heightfinder which could be installed).

Grumman alone had understood what 'interim' meant: a carrier AEW-CIC aircraft with an effective radar which could be produced almost instantly. BuAer ordered the computerised combat system deleted, probably because it would not have been compatible with NTDS/ATDS once that became available. It bought the Grumman G-117 design, designating it WF-2. Under the post-1962 system it was redesignated E-1B.

All three companies competed for the full ATDS contract. Vought and Lockheed almost certainly offered versions of their interim aircraft with a full ATDS system instead of the earlier limited mission systems. Vought's proposal won the technical competition and it appears that two aircraft were ordered under the designation WU. Grumman offered a low-wing turboprop with a bulkier antenna. It was awarded the ATDS CIC contract on industrial grounds. That may have meant continuity with the WF-2; BuAer also wanted to keep Grumman alive so that it could produce the new A2F (later A-6) Intruder bomber. At this time Grumman was selling only to the navy and its fighter production was ending.[18] After the competition, Grumman revised its design. It adopted a high wing, which added internal space and apparently it adopted the thin radome. It replaced the APS-70 with a more powerful General Electric APS-96 radar, the basis of several generations of airborne early warning. The Grumman ATDS aircraft was bought as the W2F-1, now familiar as the E-2 Hawkeye. Grumman received a contract for the E-2 on 5 March 1957. The E-2A flew in October 1960 (the first fully-equipped aircraft flew in April 1961).

The keys to adequate performance against massive raids were a lower-frequency radar (comparable to the APS-70 developed for the larger land-based AEW aircraft, with a 17ft antenna) and a high degree of automation.[19] The APS-96 of the original E-2 and all its successors detect targets automatically. The computer with its data links (to aircraft and down to ships) forms a node in an NTDS net. In 1960 it was estimated that an E-2A (not yet in service) could maintain 250 tracks and control thirty interceptions (via automatic data link), compared to four to six tracks and two interceptions for the manual E-1B it was replacing. Ideally the E-2 was always intended to control fighters via a data link (Link 4), but initially carrier fighters lacked the necessary receiver (it entered service temporarily in the F-4G and then became a standard item in the F-4J; the Crusader never had a data link receiver).

When it was tested in October 1964, the reliability and maintainability of the E-2A were so poor that the aircraft was impossible to evaluate. Planned FY65 purchases were cancelled. A 'get-well' programme ensured a successful first deployment in November 1965. The basic problem was serious enough that in August 1966 the navy verbally suggested to OSD that the FY66 purchase of further aircraft be deferred. All E-2As would be backfitted and an E-2B developed. The plan approved in November included replacing the existing APS-96 radar with a new APS-111 'overland' type offering better performance. APS-111 offered much better overland performance and somewhat better overwater performance and it could control strike aircraft (1.5nm Circular Error Probable [CEP]). Integration of the carrier air inertial navigation system greatly improved its positional accuracy (drift was halved to 1.25nm/hr). Reliability rose from 9.6 hours to 50 hours between failure. The new version offered automatic jamming alert. The E-2A/APS-111 programme was formally approved on 18 April 1968. The new radar was later described as the breadboard version of the APS-125 in the initial E-2C, whose rated range was 125nm.[20]

The 'get-well' programme succeeded well enough that OSD approved FY66 purchases and development of an improved E-2B. By that time the US Navy was operating in Vietnam and radar operation near land required urgent changes called Mod Ax. The original hard-wired computer was replaced by a programmable unit. Vietnam experience showed a need for new capabilities, such as detecting aircraft over land. Capacity fell to thirty tracks (all of which could be designated for interception). The requirement had been 256 tracks (as in NTDS) and support of ten simultaneous interceptions. The modernised E-2A was redesignated E-2B and a new version with a new computer and a new radar was developed into the current E-2C. The impact of Moore's Law shows in growth from capacity projected about 1968 (150 targets [seventy-five interceptions]) to 650 tracks (300 from own sensors, 350 from external sources) in 1974. Given the computer, other sensors could be integrated with the radar: a passive detection system (ESM) and the ALQ-108 Extended ECM system to track Soviet targets by triggering their two standard IFF transponders, Type 2 (ships and most aircraft) and the newer Type 9 (aircraft only). ALQ-108 exploited tight Soviet control policy using IFF (ALQ-108 was so important that its use was barred except in wartime).[21]

Reportedly an E-2C could control three or four F-14s (i.e. in theory, up to twenty-four interceptions) via Link 4. Unlike previous carrier aircraft, the F-14 had two-way ASW-27 communications and thus could exchange data with AEW aircraft. Reportedly about 2000 an E-2C equipped with the current version of the L-304 computer could track over 600 targets and control over forty airborne intercepts. Further modernisation has produced the E-2D, which has an electronically-steered radar and a far more powerful computer using Link 16 (JTIDS).

During both the Kosovo (1999) and Afghan (2001) Wars, the E-2C was primarily a battle-management platform, directing strikes and managing air traffic. The perceived advantage of a crew in the air over the battle area was that it could resolve problems in real time. In Afghanistan, land-based AWACS were the primarily air controllers, because their S-band radars were more effective over land. E-2s in effect filled a control gap between the time aircraft left a carrier and the time they came under AWACS control.

THE BRITISH DIGITAL SYSTEM: ADA/ADAWS

Benjamin and his team were certainly aware of the potential of digital computers. Their follow-on to CDS was ADA (Action Data Automation). In concept it was more sophisticated (i.e. integrated) than NTDS, in that targets were automatically detected and entered into the system memory. The computer system then monitored targets to measure their course and speed and to indicate whether they deviated from it (automatic detection proved problematic). The US view had been that NTDS should impose the least possible change on existing equipment; it was much easier to arrange for a radar operator to enter a target position manually than to develop automatic detection. Automatic detection proved difficult to implement. Plans for ADA apparently initially included an electronically-scanned Type 985 radar, but that was never developed. Instead, ADA used the Type 984 which had been associated with the earlier CDS. The step beyond ADA was to add weapon control, initially for the Sea Slug guided missile; in this guise ADA became ADAWS, the ADA Weapon System version.

Work on ADA began in 1959, using a new Ferranti Poseidon computer running software written by the Admiralty Surface Weapons Establishment (ASWE), which was responsible for British surface ship radars.[22] The fleet carrier *Eagle* had the first ADA system, integrated with her Type 984 radar. She had three Poseidon computers, the radar having its own detection computer with automatic detection.[23]

Eagle's sister *Ark Royal*, which was never equipped with Type 984, was fitted with ADA when given limited modernisation. The projected next-carrier system (ADAWS 3) was designed for the abortive CVA 01.[24] She would have had a Dutch three-dimensional radar which the British designated Type 988 (BROOMSTICK); it would also have been fitted to the Type 82 class guided-missile destroyer (only one of which was built, as *Bristol*, with ADAWS 2). The combined weapon direction and action data automation version of ADA equipped the three *Invincible* class light carriers.

Perhaps ironically, neither CDS nor ADA nor NTDS required a radically different form of fighter control like broadcast control; instead, they made close control effective.

SR 177

In June 1954 the Admiralty created a Working Party on Fleet Air Defence to develop a unified fleet air-defence policy for the 1957–70 period.[25] It laid out the weapons which would work with the new computer fleet command system, a key part being a new supersonic fleet fighter: SR 177. The envisaged threat was a combination of supersonic light bombers and subsonic medium bombers, the latter flying at very high altitude. The Soviets might have short-range stand-off missiles. The Working Party apparently saw only limited value in fleet air-defence fighters; its interim report (20 July 1955) advocated

Dr Benjamin went on to envisage a fully digital equivalent of his analogue CDS called ADA, Action Data Automation. Like CDS it was tightly coupled to the Type 984 radar (an electronically-scanned Type 985 never materialised). The only carrier installation was in *Eagle* (during her 1959–64 refit). The system was designed so that radar contacts were automatically entered into the computer and automatically tracked. As delivered the system incorporated a Threat Evaluation and Weapon Assessment (TEWA) module intended to present the command with prioritised recommendations. Fighter controllers would be given automatic vectoring messages. Despite extensive pre-deployment testing, TEWA failed catastrophically in the face of echoes from shore and anomalous propagation. It also proved extremely difficult to extract data automatically from a radar with multiple stacked beams. Human operators were needed to deal with the resulting confusion. ADA was modified so that tracks were initiated manually rather than automatically; it became in effect a digital version of CDS. Software had to be rewritten and memory capacity doubled. That in turn precluded planned integration of Link 11 and ECM triangulation (*Eagle* had the same DPT data link as the two CDS carriers). In *Eagle* ADA had 100-track capacity, compared to 48 tracks in the CDS in *Victorious*.

Roughly contemporary with CDS was the project for a high-performance SR 177 interceptor, shown here (inset) in model form with its two wingtip air-to-air missiles. (David Hobbs) acquisition of the US long-range (100nm) Talos missile. In response the Naval Staff raised the priority of the medium-range (17nm) Sea Slug missile and directed the Staff Divisions to frame a Staff Target for a long-range guided weapon. The latter was soon conceived as an adaptation of the evolving land-based Stage 1¾ missile code-named Blue Envoy.

Until Blue Envoy was ready, the only way to deal with a supersonic high-altitude bomber would be a fleet fighter. This would not be a Sea Vixen replacement, but rather a specialised high-performance interceptor, envisaged at the outset as a Mach 2 rocket or turbojet aircraft.[26] If it was assumed (as per the Working Party) that the high-performance guided missile would enter service in 1970, the high-performance specialised fighter, which was not too different from a missile, would be needed between 1962, when it was assumed that the Soviets would introduce supersonic anti-ship bombers, and about 1970. The fighter requirement was defined by a May 1955 study by the Director of Navigation and Direction. By this time there was already a draft staff requirement for a high-altitude supersonic naval fighter.[27] More importantly, by this time there was already a tentative solution, in the form of a mixed-power aircraft, using a powerful rocket to achieve high performance or to accelerate the aircraft to supersonic speeds and a relatively small afterburning turbojet to provide sustained power. Saunders-Roe was already building a proof-of-concept aircraft, the SR 53, which flew in 1957.

The assumed British force was three fleet carriers, all with Type 984 radars. Two-fifths of the aircraft aboard each carrier would be high-altitude fighters (twenty aircraft), of which two-thirds (twelve) would be ready at any one time. Two different threats were envisaged.[28] One was forty light bombers approaching at Mach 1.3 and closing to within Sea Slug range to drop free-fall bombs. The other was forty medium bombers (Badgers) flying at Mach 0.95 and closing to just outside Sea Slug range to fire air-to-surface missiles. Both types of bombers were assumed (incorrectly) to approach at 60,000ft, though admittedly that was unlikely until late in the study period. In either case, the three carriers could launch about one fighter per bomber. The study did not address low-flying attackers, except to say that the main radar coverage against them would be by pickets. AEW performance was not yet considered at all adequate.

The Director of Navigation study in effect validated the mixed-power idea. It pointed out that against a mass raid (forty aircraft) a few fighters on CAP would have little impact. With its relatively short-range weapon, each fighter would have only enough time to attack one bomber in a group, so many would have to be launched from the carriers' decks. The deck-launched interception role demanded a rocket motor for a quick climb. The study considered both collision-course and pursuit-course attacks, but in fact in 1955 the British were developing only pursuit-course (IR) air-to-air missiles.

To be effective, a fighter had to climb to 60,000ft in no more than four minutes, then turn onto the interception course in a 2.2G or preferably 3G turn and then cruise at Mach 2 at 60,000ft without rocket power. It would be very desirable for it to be able to accelerate to Mach 2.5. After attacking the bomber the fighter would return to base at subsonic speed for maximum endurance (typically returning 100–135nm at Mach 0.8). The entire sortie would last 50 minutes, including five minutes on rocket power. The fighters could have either collision-course or pursuit-course weapons, but the defence would find it simpler to use collision-course fighters. On the other hand, to support a collision-course attack the fighter radar would need a range

of 22nm, to give the pilot time to attack. A pursuit-course attack would require only 17nm range. The pursuit-course case required somewhat longer rocket burn because the fighter had to pass its target and turn back onto the pursuit course; it needed extra power to maintain its speed in the turn.

The maximum raid density of six per minute was associated with the inherent limits of CDS; the 'control delay' from the moment of detection to the moment that defensive action could be taken, was two minutes.[29] On this basis, deck-launched fighters could make collision-course attacks to destroy subsonic bombers at ranges between 60nm and 100nm. If they used pursuit-course interception, they would attack the bombers at 20nm to 60nm range. In either case considerable control errors were allowable. Against supersonic bombers, the fighters would have to be controlled far more precisely (they would be more flexible if they could manage a Mach 2.5 burst). Bombers would be destroyed at 60nm range in the collision case and 20nm in the pursuit case. These figures explain why the contemporary US Navy saw no alternative to collision-course interception. The analysis also explains why the Royal Navy wanted a mixed-power fighter. A pure turbojet Mach 2 fighter could intercept a subsonic bomber at 50,000ft, but at 60,000ft it might not be able to turn for long enough to fire its weapon. It would be unable to intercept a supersonic bomber. This study did not cover interception of snoopers or of high-density raids (more than six aircraft per minute) or the effects of enemy electronic warfare.

The RAF joined the Royal Navy in seeking a mixed-power interceptor. Having sponsored the SR 53, in May 1955 the Ministry of Supply authorised Saunders-Roe to undertake a design study of an aircraft to meet the joint RN/RAF requirement.[30] Saunders-Roe offered a larger and more powerful interceptor than the SR 53 and the F 177 specification seems to have been written around its initial proposal. This design was designated P 177D. Saunders-Roe issued interim brochures for the navy P.177N in August 1955 and for the air force P.177RAF in October 1955. Initial development work was authorised in September 1955 and a year later (September 1956) Saunders-Roe received a contract for the first nine of a development batch of twenty-seven aircraft and also authority to order long-lead items for the rest. The aircraft is often called the SR 177.

For the Royal Navy the project was covered by Naval Staff Requirement NA 47, for a single-seat mixed-power (jet and rocket) fighter, a draft of which was dated 7 July 1955.[31] The mission profile was a climb to 60,000ft in six minutes, followed by three minutes of cruise at that altitude at Mach 1.4. This was the vector out towards the incoming bomber. The fighter then made a 180° turn (2G) to place itself on a pursuit course, which it would fly for three minutes (at Mach 1.4). The return to the carrier would be at 40,000ft at economical speed for 15 minutes, followed by a descent to sea level for five minutes, then loiter (in the carrier landing circuit), one overshoot and landing (20 minutes total).[32] The fighter had to take off using a BS.4 catapult with 10 knots of wind over the deck. It had to reach 60,000ft at Mach 1.4 in no more than four minutes and although it would operate mainly at Mach 1.4 at 60,000ft, it had to be able to attain Mach 2.0 at that altitude. It had to be able to maintain a height of 75,000ft for at least a minute. Armament was to be two Blue Jay missiles (unguided rockets as an alternative) with an AI 20 (to be replaced by AI 23) radar.[33]

This fighter was to be in service by mid-1959. Although the Staff Requirement did not specify an engine, apparently the Bristol

Orpheus, rated at 8000lbs thrust (in future about 9000) was intended (it was soon replaced by a more powerful Gyron Junior with afterburner). It was the rocket, fuelled by avgas and hydrogen peroxide, which provided so much burst power that it could offer a very high rate of climb and acceleration to Mach 1.4 or beyond. Given the commonality between Royal Navy and RAF requirements, in April 1956 the Ministry of Supply framed a joint Specification F.177D for the Saunders-Roe mixed-power interceptor. It was issued in July 1956.

The project was soon in trouble. Like other advanced projects of the 1950s, this one was expensive. In the autumn of 1956 the Defence Research Policy Committee (DRPC) produced a paper listing research cuts to keep the Ministry of Supply Defence Research and Development Programme within a £175 million ceiling. Major projects proposed for cancellation were the P 177 and a naval version of the projected long-range surface-to-air missile, Blue Envoy (the Stage 1¾ guided weapon).[34] The Admiralty managed to have consideration of this paper deferred until the completion of the ongoing Defence Review. The review immediately killed the RAF version as part of Minister of Defence Duncan Sandys' general massacre of RAF interceptor projects; it was cancelled in March 1957.

The naval requirement barely survived for the moment. At an 8 March 1957 meeting, with Sandys in the chair, First Sea Lord asked that no precipitate action be taken to cancel the aircraft, as there was a clear operational requirement and a good chance of US financial assistance. Minister of Supply pointed to German interest, as already evinced by a military mission. However, a Ministry of Defence participant observed that the Germans were really interested in a high-altitude quick-climbing defensive weapon, which might better be a guided missile. It might make more sense to interest them the current British Stage 1 and Stage 1½ land-based surface-to-air missiles. Sandys summed up: if the aircraft were being developed only for the navy there was no room for it in the defence budget. It would survive only if within a short time the British could be reasonably sure that there was a way to develop it without paying for it themselves. That meant either the Germans or US support via NATO.

Sandys is said to have pointed out that he could not wipe out the RAF fighter programme without killing at least one navy project. However, in the file on the cancellation Sandys wrote that he could not justify providing the Royal Navy with better protection than the national deterrent – which was still the V-bombers. Other factors were the likely cost escalation if the RAF component of the SR 177 programme was killed (as it was) and the substantial problems of providing worldwide storage for the HTP (high-test peroxide) the SR 177 used for the rocket component of its power plant. Sandys was also sceptical of the navy's justification for this very high performance aircraft. SR 177 was intended to destroy very high-flying bombers. Sandys argued that in order to hit a ship, such a bomber would have to use a guided missile, which could be jammed or shot down by a shorter-range system such as a ship-launched missile. That left high-altitude snoopers. To deal with them, Sandys was prepared to finance a snap-up missile for the navy's Sea Vixen fighter. Sandys later reportedly admitted that cancellation of the SR 177 had been unwise, presumably when he learned just how limited the performance of ship-launched air-defence missiles proved to be.

The Ministry of Supply looked to the United States, which was then funding some NATO development and production under MDAP and MWDP. It was already funding the SR 53 and it had helped in the development of the NA 39 Buccaneer. The standard justification for such support was that a programme met an urgent operational requirement but was unaffordable without US aid.[35] There was some question as to whether by this time the SR 177 was a weapons development programme or a production programme. At the time, P 177 was the largest single project for which US support had been requested. The situation was further complicated in that the request was received very late in FY57 (which would end at the end of April of that year). Ultimately aid was not forthcoming. Apparently the potential US sponsor, the air force, feared that the British were not planning to buy the SR 177 at all for themselves; it was not interested in supporting a British export project.

Sandys did agree that a German export order would provide crucial support, so he postponed cancellation of the Royal Navy programme while it seemed that the Germans might buy the P 177 (there was also Australian and Canadian interest, but not on the German scale). The Germans were never willing to make up their minds, so the programme was killed.

The P 177 project survived for a time after formal cancellation; by October 1957 the Ministry of Supply was considering a reduced programme involving five prototypes. A final stop work order was issued on 1 January 1958.

Looking back, it would appear that the P 177 was designed to meet an unrealistic threat: the range of the Soviet stand off weapons was far greater than that envisaged in the mission profile. By 1960 the Soviets had a 100nm stand off weapon, AS-2. At Mach 1.4 the SR 177 would fly about 15nm each minute, i.e. 45nm during its Mach 1.4 dash. It would fly somewhat further during its climb to 60,000ft, but it would also lose some distance as it turned and began its tail chase of the bomber. The RAF had solved the problem to some extent by proposing drop tanks for increased endurance, but despite its very short endurance the SR 177 without drop tanks was already close to the carrier weight limit of about 30,000lbs. In this sense the SR 177 was a much more transitory project than it appeared at the time. It was really limited to dealing with very high altitude high speed snoopers (shadowers) – but the Soviets did not deploy them; instead they used the much slower 'Bear D' (Tu-95RTs).

Aftermath

The Working Party wrote its final report in the autumn of 1956, looking ahead to the 1965–75 period.[36] It defined a near-term 1957 air-defence system and a target 1970 system. The painful part of the report was the demonstration of just how much adequate fleet air defence against the expected 1970 threat would cost. The Working Party suggested that the technical complexity and financial implications to provide a modern fleet of even moderate size were very great. According to the introduction to the Working Party report, its studies 'may be just one more indication that, for financial and industrial reasons, we must make a radical change in national policy by accepting that the Royal Navy can fulfil its role even in major limited wars only in co-operation with the USN'.[37]

The 'major limited war' problem was becoming paramount, because the Royal Navy's approach to the ongoing Defence Review was that the most important future wars would be Warm Wars in the Third World. In 1956 the Soviets had just supplied Nasser's Egypt with modern weaponry, just as they had supplied North Korea with the latest MiG-15 fighters a few years earlier. Warm War therefore would have to be fought against modern Soviet equipment. That was

The Royal Navy was presented with a possible Sea Vixen successor well before it needed one: the Hawker P.1154 supersonic VSTOL. The Royal Navy AWS 406 specification required the fighter to be able to destroy a Mach 2.5 attacker flying at 65,000ft, as well as low-fliers. Maximum continuous sea level speed was set at Mach 0.92 with supersonic dash and Mach 2.0 at the tropopause. Although initially it would be armed with Red Tops, ultimately it would use a new missile to Specification GDA.103. The desired strike load was 8000lbs on six stations and it could include the lightweight WE 177 nuclear bomb. All-up weight without stores was not to exceed 40,000lbs, which turned out to be the killer. Royal Navy documents cite the Vickers Type 584 as a preferable Sea Vixen replacement, but they probably actually refer to the swing-wing Type 583. It was a large twin-engine aircraft (40,000lbs) using lift engines; an early sketch shows two of them mounted to either side of the necked-in air intakes and thrust vectoring for the two main engines. Type 583V (proposed about August 1963) used two vectored-thrust engines side by side. BAC (Vickers) claimed that it could be in service by 1971, but the Royal Navy wanted an aircraft by 1971 and the RAF wanted it by 1968. A bizarre feature of the Type 583V proposal was that it might also be used for AEW. (David Hobbs)

not a bad assessment. The major Warm War the Royal Navy fought during the next decade was the Confrontation against Indonesia – which had been supplied with Soviet 'Badger B' bombers and AS-1 stand-off missiles.

The 1957 system included both Sea Slug and P 177.[38] With both and provided the British could operate where necessary in company with the US Navy, it would be effective through 1962, except for the air defence of Atlantic convoys in a global war. The convoy exception was due to reliance on AEW and pickets for sufficient early warning, as these systems would not usually be available to a convoy. Thus a convoy within 700nm of a Soviet base would probably be unable to defend itself. After 1962 the Russians were expected to introduce Mach 2 bombers, making the 1957 fighters inadequate and after 1965 they would have stand-off weapons outranging Sea Slug. As it was understood by the Working Group, the most serious stand-off threat was a 150nm missile. Since the bomber (generally assumed to be a turboprop 'Bear' [Tu-95]) would be outside surface-to-air missile range, it could afford to trade performance for capacity.

The 1970 system was built around the long-range Blue Envoy missile. Other elements were much-improved radio warfare equipment (to confuse the enemy, also with better ECCM and with the ability to locate and track jamming aircraft), a long-endurance fighter to engage targets outside the long-range missile envelope, improved radars (for ECCM and for better performance against low fliers), AEW working with the long-endurance fighter, a small-ship guided weapon, a ship-to-ship data link and a ground-to-air fighter control data link.

The Working Group understood that the long-range missile was an alternative to a fighter with a long-range active/passive radar and an advanced collision-course weapon. 'Development of such a fighter and its equipment would be as great an undertaking as that of the long-range guided weapon and it would compete for the same resources.'

In reality the Soviets did not deploy supersonic anti-ship bombers in any numbers until the 1980s, with the advent of 'Backfires' (Tu-22m3s). On the other hand, even in 1956 they had the 55nm AS-1 (which seems to have been known to Western intelligence), which considerably outranged Sea Slug. It is not clear how the 1962 date for the Soviet Mach 2 bomber originated. Such aircraft did not appear in public until the early 1960s.

By the time the report was submitted to the Board of Admiralty, the Defence Review was killing off many of the envisaged weapons, including both the long-range missile and the P 177, it had considered essential. Without the P 177, there was no immediate counter to a high-flying (above 50,000ft) bomber or to a supersonic bomber. The review also killed the 100nm missile, a choice inherent in in the cancellation of the large missile cruiser the Royal Navy planned. Design alternatives for this ship had included the US Talos (100nm range) as well as Blue Envoy. Without a large cruiser, no such options were available.[39]

The immediate solutions proposed were a collision-course jump-up missile for Sea Vixen and improvements to Sea Slug (longer range and better low-altitude capability) and to AEW aircraft and radar. In fact there was no way to turn Sea Slug into even a 50nm missile (Sea Slug II range was only 20nm). For the longer term there would have to be a long-endurance fighter on CAP, controlled by AEW aircraft.[40] It was too early to raise a Staff Requirement for such a fighter, but not too early to consider what was needed.

THE SEA VIXEN REPLACEMENT

With both the SR 177 and the long-range missile gone, almost the whole burden of fleet air defence would fall on carrier fighters. The Admiralty became interested in much the same solution the US Navy was then investigating, a relatively low-performance fighter armed with very capable missiles. Initially the Admiralty seems to have been only vaguely aware of the details of the US Eagle-Missileer programme. Like the US Navy of the mid-1950s, the Admiralty recognised that missile loads were not too different in weight from useful bomb loads, although in its case it emphasised non-nuclear bombs, for example for close air support. The Naval Staff became interested in a single aircraft which could quickly be switched between fighter and strike roles.

That raised an additional problem, since it would be difficult to replace the radar itself. As the project started, RAE, which conducted the initial study for the new aircraft, asked the Royal Radar Establishment whether it would be possible to produce a convertible radar. It would function in both air-to-air and terrain clearance or contour flying modes.

Once this idea was accepted by the staff in November 1958 Director of Air Warfare (DAW) asked the Ministry of Supply (meaning the Naval Aircraft Division of RAE) for a study to show what sort of aircraft would be wanted, of what sort of air-to-air system it would need, of how many weapons and of what sort of weapon control system it should have. As a basis, DAW suggested two alternative cases, two or four aircraft on CAP 150nm from the fleet, covering a 180° sector with associated AEW aircraft. By this time digital computers were sufficiently mature that DND could propose that each aircraft carry an intercept computer with discrete addressing software.

The threat was Soviet bombers of increasing speed and capability:

Mach 0.9 and 45,000ft in 1960 ('Badgers'), Mach 1.3 and 55,000ft in 1963 and Mach 2 and 65,000ft in 1966. It was further assumed that Soviet client states would have such aircraft two to three years after the Soviets. The current Sea Vixen with AI 18 radar should be able to deal with a Mach 0.8 target at 45,000ft in 1960 and with a Mach 1.3 target at 55,000ft in 1963, subject to the availability of the Red Top IR missile or something comparable. The threat statement pointed out that, apart from stand-off missile carriers, enemy aircraft would probably attack at either extreme or very low altitude, hence that the fighter had to deal with anything between sea level and 70,000ft. The threat statement presumably reflects current very limited intelligence and the assumption that the Soviets could and would match whatever the United States produced (the US Mach 2 bomber often cited was the B-58 Hustler). In 1958 the Soviet naval air arm still contained large numbers of light bombers intended mainly for torpedo attack, as well as fighters defending naval bases. There were only a few 'Badgers' carrying AS-1 stand-off missiles. Two years later the character of the threat was far clearer, as all aircraft except the 'Badgers' were transferred out of the Soviet naval air arm or discarded, torpedo attack being abandoned altogether. It also must have become apparent that the Soviets were not moving nearly as quickly as had been imagined towards supersonic bombers.

On the assumed basis after 1966 the fleet would be unable to defend against air attacks even in limited war and even if the enemy used conventional rather than nuclear weapons. The outstanding limitations of the Sea Vixen system were an inability to deal with attackers above Mach 1.3 and 55,000ft and in all weather conditions (because Red Top was IR-guided) as well as insufficient endurance. The desired successor should deal with attackers at up to Mach 2 (with stretch to Mach 2.5) and at altitudes up to 70,000ft in all weather, with increased endurance.

The formal request to RAE laid out two alternatives: the performance could be concentrated in the missile (as in the US Eagle-Missileer) or shared between aircraft and missile. Because of the high cost and the weight penalty of high fighter performance, the Naval Staff favoured the subsonic fighter approach. In either case the aircraft would provide defence in depth outside the range of fleet surface-to-air missiles, which with the cancellation of Blue Envoy was no more than 20nm. To do that the fighter would have to patrol well away from the carrier. As there would be few such fighters, they would need high subsonic performance so that they could concentrate quickly towards the threatened sector. Desired endurance on a CAP station 100–200nm from the fleet was four hours.

The RAE Naval Air Department formed a special Working Party.[41] Because the initial date to place the new fighter in service was 1965, it had to be a modified version of an existing carrier aircraft: the Buccaneer, Sea Vixen or Scimitar. For 1970 or later an entirely new aircraft could be developed. It might be the high performance type envisaged as an alternative. This possibility was soon translated into a certainty that a supersonic fighter (possibly Mach 2.5) would be needed after 1970, either using variable geometry or VSTOL to manage carrier landing without sacrificing very high speed. Vickers received a study contract. This possibility was tied to the additional capability of the 50,000-ton carrier (CVA 01) then being planned. The key point was that these ships would be able to handle much heavier aircraft: 50,000lb fighters and possibly somewhat heavier ones if they were VTOLs.

By this time the firms making the existing naval aircraft were already offering follow-ons, which in effect were candidates for the new fighter. De Havilland and Vickers offered classic fighters, for which the key issue was performance. This time the navy (hence the naval section of RAE) was much more interested in the interceptor system built around radar and missiles, rather than the platform characteristics which had been decisive in the past. Both proposals were developed versions of the existing naval fighters. De Havilland's developed Sea Vixen carried the Red Top missile but had insufficient endurance. Vickers' supersonic version of its Scimitar was too heavy at 53,000lbs and also had insufficient endurance. Neither firm had done sufficient work on interception.

Blackburn, however, understood just what was wanted. In the Buccaneer it had a high-performance aircraft with sufficient carrying capacity and endurance. Replacing the engine and adding fuel could give it the desired four hours at 100nm; the aircraft would weigh 48,000lbs (approach weight was an acceptable 32,000lbs). In March 1959 the firm was halfway through work on a developed Buccaneer which might carry the US Eagle missile. At this time the US Navy had not yet chosen an aircraft to carry the Eagle missile and one alternative was the Intruder, which might be analogised to the Buccaneer.

The Eagle was credited with a 150nm propulsive range and a 75nm systems range. However, a radar small enough to fit the Buccaneer, such as a developed version of the AI 18 in the Sea Vixen, could not lock onto a target beyond perhaps 50nm; no modified Buccaneer could accommodate the 60in dish of the US APQ-81.[42] The fighter would generally have to close to 30nm to fire. With the Eagle missile with 30nm closing range, one aircraft per 120° sector could just stop a Mach 2 target at 100nm. It was assumed that the fighters would be supported by a developed AEW aircraft 200nm from task force centre, with a 150nm radar and automatic data processing.

The Working Party focused on the interaction between radar and target. The target would detect the lock-on (the onset of steady tracking) and immediately begin to evade. The target might be able to deny accurate range information by jamming, which might reduce fighter radar range well below the 30nm closing range of the Eagle, rendering its long range useless. As to the number of weapons, the Working Party was aware of US studies with six and twelve missiles by CAL and ADR. DAW formed a team to visit the United States to learn more about the Eagle-Missileer system.

It seemed that the Eagle might not be available in 1965, the required in-service date of the new fighter. Blackburn's studies showed that the missile would need at least 30nm range. The most practical option seemed to be to extend the range of an existing British missile such as Red Top by using a boost-sustain (two-pulse) motor.

The Working Party suggested assisting Blackburn in its analysis of the interception problem. RAE had recently made a study showing that a Mach 0.9 fighter on a 40nm CAP radius would have a good chance of intercepting a Mach 1.3 bomber using a conceptual Blue Dolphin missile. By this time proposals for an improved AI 18 (as used in the Sea Vixen) were offering a 50nm lock-on range.

During the autumn of 1959 the near-term analysis project was abandoned, but as of February 1960 the Admiralty was seriously considering buying a Buccaneer Mk II fighter for service in 1965. The Working Group was asked to determine the best radar for the purpose which could fit the existing nose and radome shape. The alternative, which was adopted instead, was Sea Vixen Mk II. Presumably the nose/radome problem doomed the idea of a single fighter/strike aircraft. Plans called for the upgraded Sea Vixen to enter service in

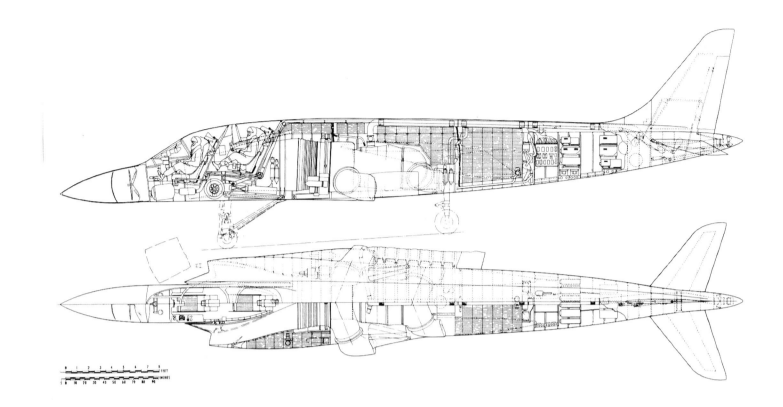

Hawker's sketch shows the proposed naval version of the P.1154, with two seats and a large nose antenna (dish). Parallel to its AWS.406 fighter specification was GDA.103 (OR 1193) for a new longer-range radar-guided (hence collision-course) air-to-air missile. Companies proposed air-to-air versions of current surface-to-air missiles, apparently mainly weapons proposed for the Royal Navy SIGS (Small Ships Integrated Guided weapon System), which would produce the Sea Dart. The two main contenders were apparently Bristol Guided Weapons (by this time part of BAE) with its SIGS-16 solid-fuel missile (range 14 miles) and a Sea Dart without a booster (range about 45 miles), Sea Dart having won the SIGS competition. It would have fit the navy's view that the future lay in something like Eagle-Missileer, but it is not clear to what if any extent a corresponding radar/fire-control system was being developed. The project for an air-launched version of CF 299 was dropped about March 1963. Sparrow III was already being considered as a preferable alternative and it was bought when the P.1154 project died in favour of buying Phantoms. (David Hobbs)

1964 with a slightly modified AI 18 radar and the Red Top IR missile. It would have 2.25 hours endurance at high altitude. In 1965 the Sea Vixen would be re-engined to give improved rate of climb and an endurance approaching four hours. It would have the same radar and the same missile. In 1966 the re-engined Sea Vixen would be given a better radar, identified about 1962 as AI 25, with a range of 90–120nm. About 1970 it would be given the long-range air-to-air missile planned for the 1970 fighter. As of 1960, Sea Vixen was expected to remain in service through 1976, when the last of the new carriers entered service and therefore when all fleet carriers would be able to operate the 1970 fighter. In fact the Sea Vixen FAW.2 was developed, a prototype flying on 1 June 1962. Compared to the original Mk 1, it had extra fuel in prominent forward extensions of its tail booms and four Red Top missiles instead of the earlier Firestreaks. The projected further upgrades were never carried out.

The Working Party was now to focus on the 1970 problem. To make it possible to reach some conclusion in the short available time, the assumed 1970 threat was simplified (actually heavily revised) early in June. Now it was a group of ten Mach 2 (Mach 1.3 at 50,000ft) missile carriers in open formation at 80,000ft (soon reduced to 60,000ft), spaced 5nm apart, each carrying a 100nm Mach 2 missile – in effect, an AS-2. The low-level threat was the same bombers flying at Mach 1 below 1000ft. The aircraft had to be destroyed before they could launch, which set the minimum destruction distance and the

study was not to consider attacks on any missiles which were launched. This was taken as a minimum; if any fighter seemed promising enough it could be evaluated against a more severe threat.

At this point the alternatives for 1970 were slow (400-knot) deck-launched and CAP fighters; subsonic (Mach 0.95) deck-launched and CAP fighters; supersonic (Mach 2) deck-launched and supersonic fighters; variable-geometry (swing-wing) fighters; VTOL; and Forward Pass, of which discussion of Forward Pass was deferred and VTOL not to be discussed for the present (later it was rejected: catapults had not yet reached the end of their potential). For purposes of comparison, all of the fighter alternatives would have all-up weights of 50,000lbs, all would devote the same weight to AI radar and all were assumed capable of fighting at 150nm from base. The slower the fighter, the heavier its missile payload: 10,000lbs for the 400-knot fighter, 9000lbs for Mach 0.95, 7000lbs for Mach 2. Each fighter could carry varying loads of 20nm, 50nm and 100nm missiles and the rule was that the target had to be killed 100nm from fleet centre. When the analysis was discussed, three more alternatives were added: a higher-performance fighter, with emphasis on higher acceleration to maximum speed; a small Mach 2 fighter (presumably with fewer than four missiles); and a combined AEW/fighter (a conventional fighter whose radar could be used in the search role, not CAL's 'Bogey Buster').

As of late July the Mach 2 fighter with 20nm Mach 3 missile was the most promising possibility, which was directly opposite to the US conclusions which had led to Eagle-Missileer. However, a revised report produced in October added a turboprop fighter (370 knots) carrying six 100nm Mach 3 missiles. The Mach 2 fighter (four missiles) could be used either on CAP or as a deck-launched interceptor; the turboprop would be for CAP only. Both fighters were at the 50,000lb limit. Another alternative was a smaller Mach 2 fighter (31,700lbs) carrying two 20nm missiles. Although a carrier could accommodate more of the smaller fighters, they would deploy fewer missiles. The light fighter would also be much less satisfactory in the strike role. As for the question of CAP vs deck-launched interception, with 300nm warning (AEW aircraft at a distance from the carrier), either would work with the Mach 2 fighter, but two or three times as many fighters would be available if they were deck-launched. Analysis confirmed that the Mach 2 fighter was better than the turboprop on CAP. Further analysis indicated that the Mach 0.95 fighter with 50nm missiles (the modified Buccaneer) was considerably inferior to the Mach 2 fighter with 20nm missiles in the deck-launched interceptor role. If the Mach 0.95 fighter had 20nm missiles, the advantage of the Mach 2 fighter would be even greater. There was little advantage in increasing interceptor speed beyond Mach 2.

By November the Working Party had the US Navy studies which had led to the Eagle-Missileer project and it was able to show that its own studies were consistent with them. The US Navy had discarded deck-launched interception because the necessary AEW screen was vulnerable. However, the AEW aircraft might be stationed over the fleet to give effective warning out to 400nm in conjunction with shipboard radars, in which case it would not be vulnerable. The US Navy also assumed more than twice the time to launch the first off-the-deck interceptor (seven minutes vs three minutes) and a longer launching interval (60 seconds vs 40 seconds) for later ones. The US force was also much larger, capable of maintaining twenty to twenty-five aircraft on CAP, but the threat force was assumed similar to that used by the Working Group. Also, the US Navy was assuming that the Mach 2 interceptors carried only two missiles each. The group considered and rejected long-range shipboard missiles as an alternative to fighters.

By this time Vickers was pursuing a variable-geometry fighter design in collaboration with the US government (NASA), financed in part by the same MWDP programme which had not been able to fund the SR 177.[43] It used a tailless configuration with a narrow wing and the gloves which proved important in the US F-111 programme (invented by Barnes Wallis, they limited the usual movement of the centre of lift in a swing-wing aircraft).[44] The threat was that previously considered, except that it was expected to make Mach 3 at 80,000ft (a low-flier was also considered). A 'jump-up' capability would be built into the aircraft rather than the weapon, which would be a 30nm semi-actively guided missile. Vickers differed from the Working Group in arguing that the higher speed (Mach 2.5 or better) that its design could achieve would be of great value, based on a Mach 3 rather than Mach 2 threat.

A Joint Staff Target for a variable-geometry aircraft was agreed with the RAF and the Chiefs of Staff agreed that it was a vital requirement for 1970. This was OR 345/346, the latter for the navy. Until about 1970 the navy would make do with Sea Vixen Mk II as its interceptor and with Buccaneer as its strike bomber, the navy view being that by about 1970 the Sea Vixen would become marginal. The air force withdrew from the 1970 requirement and stretched it to 1975 as OR 355.

The RAF wanted the target date for the supersonic aircraft pushed back because 1975 was the projected date for a replacement for the new TSR.2 strike bomber (which was itself cancelled in 1964). The Royal Navy saw little point in deferring the desired supersonic fighter-bomber and argued that by placing it in service a few years before the RAF, it would de-bug it for them. It pointed to the current US bi-service TFX programme as an analogy. As for the NMBR (NATO Military Basic Requirement) 3 aircraft, it had no attraction at all for the navy. The main naval interest was that the RAF should buy an aircraft which could operate from a carrier, the expectation being that this capability would bind the RAF to the carrier project. The Chiefs of Staff had already agreed that turning the supersonic swing-wing aircraft into a fully joint project was the 'most important step' in the current British aircraft development programme.

The Royal Navy sold its projected new carrier to the Defence Ministry partly by claiming that it could accommodate the projected RAF VTOL strike aircraft, intended as a successor to the Hunter fighter-bomber. VSTOL was a prerequisite for such operation because RAF aircraft had neither catapult fittings nor arrester hooks. The RAF grasped an opportunity to spread the development cost of the new aircraft, so in January 1962 it proposed that the joint supersonic fighter project be deferred to 1975. Instead it wanted the navy to agree to a Joint Staff Target for a supersonic single-seat VSTOL fighter-bomber, P.1154.[45] The RAF aircraft was intended to meet a NATO specification (NMBR 3) for a VTOL fighter-bomber, the hope being that it would attract large export orders.[46] Apparently the RAF had fastened on the NATO requirement in order to sell the desired Hunter replacement and in later negotiations the navy was anxious not to be seen to be sabotaging that deal. The navy was also aware that the projected supersonic swing-wing might not be an effective strike aircraft, so that at some future date it might have to come back to the RAF programme. Note that none of the documents envisaged a rolling take-off, so these were not understood as VSTOL aircraft.

The navy already had better capabilities in the form of the Buccaneer and Sea Vixen and the only step which was worth taking was the big supersonic swing-wing projected for the 1970s. Director of Naval Air Division wrote that DCAS (Deputy Chief of Air Staff) 'knows as well as we do that we could not possibly rely for 7 years into the 1970s on a single pilot-operated AI set of the size of a soup plate for the defence of the fleet. The RAF themselves have called for a two-seat aircraft with a 100 mile observer-operated AI set and four hour endurance as their fighter for the 1970s.'

Chief of Air Staff replied that the variable-geometry aircraft would not be available in 1970; it had taken 14 years to make the simpler V-bombers operational. He portrayed the P.1154 as a superb interceptor, superior in some ways to both the Sea Vixen and the Buccaneer; if the navy persisted in rejecting it, it would face a 'hideous' gap in the first half of the 1970s, relying on outmoded Sea Vixens and non-existent Buccaneer IIIs. The P.1154 offered a high rate of climb, rapid acceleration, good manoeuvrability, high ceiling and high top speed; sustained ceiling would be 60,000ft and zoom ceiling would be 90,000ft. Maximum speed with four missiles on board would be Mach 2.2 (combat speed about Mach 1.6). The Air Ministry brushed aside the 'soup plate' antenna argument: it would be capable of carrying an AI radar coupled to an auto-pilot (so that a pilot could operate the radar) and thus should be effective against targets flying at up to Mach 2.5 at up to 65,000ft. In the strike role the hi-lo-hi radius when taking off vertically would be 600nm with a 2000lb load. This would be no worse than the Buccaneer II. The Chief of Air Staff suggested that the navy 'cut its losses' by abandoning the Buccaneer in favour of the P.1154.

In return, the navy pointed out that the RAF was delaying its version of the swing-wing aircraft for fear that if it materialised too quickly the order for TSR 2s would be questioned. It did not buy the strike argument, as the navy's own estimates showed that at low altitude the P.1154 would have a far shorter radius of action and that at the same range the Buccaneer could deliver four times as much ordnance. That had probably not been a major problem for NATO and the RAF, whose 2000lb payload translated to one nuclear weapon; but by 1962 the Royal Navy was mainly interested in the requirements of limited war, which was almost by definition non-nuclear. That limited Royal Navy interest to the interceptor version of the P.1154 and it brought up the same issue the US Navy had faced a few years earlier in deciding to buy the Phantom instead of the single-seat Super Crusader: the value of a dedicated radar operator. In making this point the navy cited US experience.

As for the speed of the interceptor, given improvements in shipboard anti-aircraft missiles (Sea Dart was now early in its development), the most difficult problem was a low-level attacker and until at least 1970 it would be subsonic. The Sea Vixen was good enough and the P.1154 would not be much faster at low level. A draft paper for the First Lord argued that the single-seat limitation more than offset the higher speed of the P.1154. As for ceiling, Red Top had a 15,000ft snap-up capability, hence was fully adequate against the NMBR 3 high-altitude threat (Mach 2.5 at 65,000ft). Moreover, the second-seater in the Sea Vixen would give it a considerable advantage against an enemy employing ECM. It was understood that the navy requirements of a 30in dish and a second seat could not be provided without a sacrifice of other capabilities, particularly VTOL.

By April, the Admiralty staff in Washington was reporting that the US TFX programme, which might be analogised to the projected joint British programme, would lead to two different aircraft, at the least because to fit aircraft carrier lifts the navy version could be no more than 56ft long, whereas the air force would accept 73ft to improve performance. At this point the navy version would weigh 55,000lbs, the air force version 60,000lbs. Under what must have been considerable pressure to stay in a joint programme, the naval staff proposed a compromise: the joint VTOL might be acceptable if, like TFX, the aircraft had alternative navy and air force versions, the navy version being a two-seater. The initial suggestion was that this could be achieved by eliminating VTOL performance in the navy version. There was no question that this would be a very good solution, as the RAF had already cautioned that the P.1154 might have only marginal transonic manoeuvrability – i.e. it would perform poorly in the most important naval fighter defence role, at low level and high speed. Since, unlike most VTOLs of the time, P.1154 had no separate lift engines, it is not clear how the naval staff thought that VTOL could be traded off against the second seat and a larger AI radar.

By this time the Ministry of Aviation was deeply engaged in an attempt to secure a large export order from the Germans, who had the largest air force of any European NATO country. VTOL was generally favoured as a way of dispersing vital NATO tactical aircraft to protect them against a Soviet first strike. As of June 1962 the French had decided to produce the Mirage IIIV and if it went into production it would gain an important advantage over the P.1154. A joint RAF-Royal Navy programme for P.1154 thus gained considerable value from the Ministry of Aviation point of view. Once there was a joint programme, the P.1154 would have the same status as Mirage IIIV.[47] The government planned to emphasise its case for P.1154 by stating to

NATO that it had no other aircraft under development. To some extent that undermined the longer-term swing-wing programme.

Minister of Aviation Harold Watkinson wrote in June that from the outset he had not been willing to entertain anything except joint proposals for next-generation tactical aircraft and that he had therefore joined the Sea Vixen and Hunter replacement programmes together. He saw this as the test of his basic policy. He pointed out that the driving factor was the need to replace the Hunter with a supersonic aircraft by 1968, a requirement so urgent that it would justify cuts in other research and development programmes to finance it. Although normally the project would go through the DRPC before going to the Cabinet Defence Committee for approval, the imminent NATO competition with the Mirage IIIV might justify short-circuiting the process. At a May 1962 NATO meeting in Athens, it was decided that the NMBR 3 winner would be chosen by 1 December 1962; however, critical meetings would be held by the end of June and again in mid-July. The NATO governments would be required to state their interest as regards type and timing and if possible some approximate numbers desired. The Germans and Americans were already involved in the earlier Hawker P.1127 programme, but unfortunately the P.1154 used an entirely different engine (there was still a chance that an operational version of the P.1127 would emerge – it became the Harrier). 'If we are to play a leading part in military research and development within NATO, by far the most promising line for us seems to be in the VTOL field, in which we at present have a clear lead over our competitors and in particular in pressing on with the family of deflected thrust engines being developed by Bristol Siddeley.'

The navy's objections had no chance of overcoming this logic, particularly since the Chiefs of Staff had already decided that the two services would have to buy a single aircraft. Not long afterwards, the main reason for buying the single VTOL collapsed, as at the late June meeting the Germans stated that they were no longer interested in NMBR 3 as such.[48] By this time the Buccaneer replacement requirement was designated AW 346 and the Sea Vixen replacement was AW 406. The Royal Navy gave way on AW 346 in favour of AW 406 because the Buccaneer did not have to be replaced until 1974; AW 406 would meet the required replacement date for Sea Vixen. The RAF agreed that it would support a joint Buccaneer/TSR 2 replacement based on AW 346 and its OR 355, to enter service in 1974–6.[49] To support that project, both services would sponsor an experimental variable-sweep aircraft. Naval Air Division was less than satisfied. On entirely non-military grounds it had been manoeuvred into accepting an inferior aircraft, which had already been pared down 'to a last-ditch minimum in an effort to reach a compromise with the RAF for a joint aircraft'.

In September the situation worsened, as the Air Ministry admitted that the RAF could not support a variable-sweep experimental aircraft as a lead-in to AW 406/OR 355, as they were not convinced that they needed any successor to the TSR 2 in 1975. At about the same time the Chairman of the Aerodynamics Executive Committee stated that the experimental variable-sweep aircraft was in jeopardy because of the cost of P.1154 development; it could no longer be supported as the lead-in aircraft for a military programme. It seemed that the Minister of Aviation had opened the possibility of killing the programme when he had demanded that the navy commit itself to the P.1154 before the Admiralty Board had approved the Joint Staff Requirement.

To further twist the situation, by September the Mirage IIIV was in a far better position, as a version with a Pratt & Whitney cruise engine and Rolls-Royce lift engines was attracting considerable support. Minister of Defence Peter Thorneycroft asked for an evaluation of the consequences if on grounds of economics the British felt compelled to buy the Mirage IIIV. The reply was that the Mirage was superior in speed, acceleration and rate of climb and slightly inferior in range and endurance. It would be ready 2–3 years sooner. English Electric was offering a naval version which would be superior in all parameters to the P.1154, but had no VTOL capability (which was not needed). Moreover, because the Mirage had Rolls-Royce lift engines, it could be presented as an Anglo-French project. On the other hand, the French nuclear deterrent project was straining their R&D resources, so the Mirage IIIV would probably be dropped. On that basis the Ministry of Aviation wanted to pursue the P.1154.

No country bought an NMBR 3 fighter or a production Mirage IIIV, despite the appearance of a prototype Mirage IIIV. However, the Ministry of Aviation won the day and the navy was yoked to the P.1154 project, despite having to pay a considerable VTOL penalty. The overriding factor in the P.1154 programme was the need for an RAF Hunter replacement by 1968. In January 1963 the Naval Staff produced an analysis of what the navy needed in its Sea Vixen replacement. It agreed that there was a need for long-range shipboard missiles and that whatever could be afforded would determine fighter characteristics. A related question was the likely effectiveness of radar picket ships and of AEW (the Royal Navy was considering licence production of the US Hawkeye). It was expected that by 1973 adequate medium-range shipboard missile capability would be in service (meaning Sea Dart), after which the fleet might be able to afford considerably less carrier fighter capability. Even then it would be essential to deny the enemy unrestricted use of the air outside the surface-to-air missile envelope and it would be particularly important to destroy snoopers. Fighters would also be needed to identify aircraft near the fleet in a period of tension or early in a limited war. They would provide the army with air cover during the early phase of an operation. They might also be needed in a jamming environment. Taken together, these tasks would justify continuing investment in fighters.

CAP would be less important than in the past, but a carrier would have to maintain at least two fighters aloft. Each could engage up to four targets, since Red Top was a fire-and-forget missile, but fighters would typically fire two-missile salvoes. Given the limited endurance of the Sea Vixen on station (1.5 hours) and allowing for some back-up deck-launched interceptors, a carrier would need at least twelve fighters to maintain a CAP for an extended period, say four days. AW 406 extended time on station to 2.5 hours and thus reduced the requirement by two or three aircraft. In either case diverting 30 per cent of a carrier's aircraft from its primary strike and close support role was a major cost.

The current Red Top missile could intercept bombers up to 65,000ft; aircraft flying higher than that probably could not mount effective attacks. However, Red Top was a pursuit-course weapon and it might not even be effective against a bomber capable of supersonic speed without using its afterburner. It was unlikely to home on a propeller-driven aircraft and it could not lock onto a target through any substantial amount of cloud. Whatever missile the next-generation fighter carried, it would be unlikely to carry more than four.

To make matters worse, a 'potential limited war adversary' (Indonesia) had just obtained Soviet 'Badgers' armed with a stand-off missile (AS-1). These missiles could be launched in cloud, since targeting and guidance were all by radar. The 2in unguided rocket was being retained specifically to deal with this threat and also to attack slow propeller aircraft. In both cases, the Sea Vixen was fast enough to approach an aircraft its radar could detect and track.

In approaching the AW 406 project, the navy pressed for two seats, a good AI radar and good high altitude manoeuvrability. It also argued for folding wings and/or nose and carrier catapulting and recovery using arresting gear (vertical landing was an option, not a requirement, but if the aircraft could land very slowly, the arrester hook and the supporting structure could be made much lighter). There would have to be a new all-weather air-to-air missile. The previous four-hour loiter on CAP was reduced to 2.5 hours 100nm from the carrier. The Air Staff supported these requirements, which indicated that no single bi-service aircraft could be developed. However, there could be a considerable degree of commonality, perhaps enough to satisfy the Ministry of Aviation. The two aircraft would share the same engine and some of the same airframe. RRE at Malvern offered the possibility of a true dual-purpose radar, which might be available by January 1970.

In February 1963 the joint paper was submitted to the Defence Research Policy Committee, whose most important decision was to authorise the air intercept radar the navy needed. The Committee authorised a project study of the complete P.1154 weapon system and initial work on the BS.100 engine which would power it. The latter was essential, since to make supersonic speed the P.1154 needed a new kind of VTOL engine with Plenum Chamber Burning (PCB), in effect a kind of afterburning. Interim contracts which would run through the autumn of 1963 were already financing work on the airframe and engine. Without the Committee's approval, the project could not go ahead. Admitting that the RAF and RN versions of the P.1154 would be radically different, the Committee nonetheless endorsed the project, arguing that the common engine and a common design team were sufficient advantages.

The export market was still a powerful factor in any decision. The French were still developing the Mirage IIIV, despite the Ministry of Aviation forecast that it would be abandoned. The Germans were still working on the VJ101D (derived from the earlier US Bell D-188A, left over from the VSTOL competition of the late 1950s). The P.1154 and the Mirage IIIV still led the field – if there was a field at all. The DPRC report included an extensive analysis of export possibilities. Belgium still had a requirement for seventy-five NMBR 3s and they had expressed a preference for the P.1154. Canada had no requirement, but was prepared to contribute to an agreed NATO programme. France had a requirement for 300 NMBR 3s, which would be Mirage IIIVs; the French might buy the P.1154 if they cancelled the Mirage IIIV. Germany and Italy had agreed in principle to jointly develop a successor to their G.91 light attack aircraft, but they had not yet chosen a design. The result might be almost as large and heavy as NMBR 3 and up to 400 aircraft might be involved. Germany and perhaps Italy might also be in the market for an F-104G successor, for which the P.1154 might also be suitable, particularly if the G.91 successor was very lightweight. The Netherlands would need an F-104G successor about 1968–70. The United States had no stated requirement at all. Outside NATO, Hawker had been marketing the P.1154 to Australia, Israel, India, Japan, New Zealand, South Africa, Sweden and Switzerland; the degree of interest varied considerably. According to the final NMBR 3 report, only the P.1154 had a useful low-level radius of action, although the Mirage IIIV offered better growth potential, as it had greater capacity and was heavier. However, the P.1154 concentrated on lightness and simplicity and had acceptable equipment. Both aircraft could be in service by 1967.

The Ministry of Aviation said that it backed the P.1154 on the ground that the Mirage IIIV was more complex and more difficult to maintain (because it had multiple engines), it had inferior range performance, it was 25 per cent more expensive to make, it might be more liable to engine failure due to ingestion of foreign bodies in its fixed lift engines and it might be difficult to control in the event of engine failure and it could not be modified for carrier operation without radical redesign with a swivelling nozzle.

The naval staff saw an alternative in the BAC Vickers 584, a variable-sweep fighter about the size of the P.1154 and probably about a year behind it. It had been judged the best of the ten NMBR 3 candidates, but ruled out because it would not be ready in time. Based on Vickers figures it would meet the original naval staff requirement, but because it was not a VSTOL, it could not meet the RAF requirement. However, it would be a reasonable replacement for the Lightning interceptor and so it could be the basis for a bi-service project if the RAF were willing to bring forward the projected date of the Lightning replacement. In that case, the navy suggested, the RAF could either continue alone with the P.1154 or buy a developed version of the P.1127 (which became the Harrier).

It was too late for such ideas. The Minister of Defence had accepted the joint P.1154 and any shift at this point would be far too embarrassing. That it had also been accepted that the naval P.1154 would use catapults and arresting gear and therefore did not need the PCB engine seems to have been forgotten, yet the engine was by far the riskiest part of the project. To the navy, the fight against the P.1154 had to be abandoned because the new carrier project was now being considered by the Ministry of Defence. However, by May 1963 it seemed that the naval P.1154 was becoming too heavy to operate successfully from a carrier, in much the way that the contemporary US F-111B was failing. In February the Prime Minister had approved cancellation of the Buccaneer successor (to provide more money for the carrier replacement), adding to the importance of the project. In May 1963 Deputy Chief of Naval Staff (DCNS) wrote that he could not recommend the P.1154 to the Board of Admiralty, despite the political decisions already taken. When the Chiefs of Staff reviewed the British aircraft programme in June for the Prime Minister, it was clear that the naval P.1154 was of dubious value, its weight having risen from 30,000lbs to 42,000lbs. The engine was not powerful enough to lift it, so it would have no VTOL capability at all and limited range. The Chiefs of Staff decided not to forward the embarrassing summary of the problem to the Minister of Defence and instead to offer three alternatives. One was for the Royal Navy to accept the RAF P.1154 as is. A second would be for the Royal Navy to buy another, possibly foreign, aircraft, which might also replace the RAF's Lightning. A third was to buy another supersonic close-support aircraft for the RAF and then to seek to combine the Lighting and Sea Vixen replacement requirements. Some decision was urgently needed, because the firms developing the P.1154 had to know by June whether the project would continue. It did not help that the estimated cost of the P.1154 had risen considerably.

The immediate Admiralty reaction was that the RAF P.1154 was unacceptable as a Sea Vixen replacement, a conclusion which had been obvious for some time. The only possible foreign replacements for the Sea Vixen were the Phantom and the TFX. The Phantom met the requirement, but for the moment it was turned down on the grounds that with neither the J79 or the possible replacement Rolls-Royce Spey could existing carriers launch it at all-up-weight corresponding

to the desired CAP endurance. With its weight reduced to what a British carrier could launch, it appeared that it would have an endurance of only about an hour, rather than the required 2.5 hours. It would be seriously limited in ferry range and it would lack rough field and VSTOL capability (none of which really mattered). TFX was worse, since its weight exceeded the strength of British carrier decks and even if folded it was too large for their lifts. It could meet Air Staff requirements for a Lightning successor, but it lacked VSTOL capability. Mirage IIIV was also unsuitable, partly because it was not designed to operate from a rough field (it would ingest too much into its lift engines). By this time it must have seemed unlikely that the P.1154 would attract any foreign sales and the full cost of an all-British programme was daunting. Buying the Mirage IIIV would concede leadership in VTOL to France, the British abandoning the only aircraft field in which they currently decisively led the world and in which so much had been invested. The Ministry of Aviation warned of the catastrophic effects on British industry. It would be possible to develop a more affordable (because more modest) new supersonic VTOL, which might be a shared project with the Germans. The Naval Staff thought that the best way forward would be to combine the Lightning replacement (not yet a formal project) with the Sea Vixen replacement. The Air Staff killed this possibility by pointing out that there might be no point at all in replacing the Lightning; its role might be taken over by a future surface-to-air missile.

That left the Hunter replacement for the RAF, the possibilities being the Mirage IIIV and a developed P.1127 or some P.1154 derivative. While these options were playing out, the Profumo Case broke, leaving the Cabinet very jittery. Hawker Siddeley was expected to exert considerable influence to keep the P.1154 alive. The Cabinet would not kill the project unless the Chiefs of Staff unanimously agreed that neither version made any military sense. Chief of Defence Staff Lord Mountbatten, a former First Sea Lord, told First Sea Lord that he had 'to be tougher than you have ever felt able to before with CAS [Chief of Air Staff]. That you should take the line that he (CAS) must try to look at the whole problem nationally – and, if that fails, that you suggest that you may have to open an all-out attack on the RAF on every front – TSR 2, antipathy to any sensible scheme of rationalisation, etc. CAS has asked to see you for half an hour at 1130 tomorrow.'[50]

The P.1154 died. Defence Minister Peter Thorneycroft repeated that any aircraft must meet the requirements of both services. The two versions of the P.1154 were already so different that they were different aircraft and so failed this test. He was prepared to stretch both the Hunter and the Sea Vixen until something satisfactory could be found. Studies of a possible joint VTOL fighter continued into July 1963, but the P.1154 really died in mid-June. The Royal Navy still needed a Sea Vixen replacement, whether or not the 50,000-ton carrier project went ahead – at this point it did not seem that the British Government would abandon carrier aviation altogether. The RAF Hunter replacement was the Harrier, which turned out to be very important for the Royal Navy a decade later.[51]

The only real alternative, however flawed, was the US Navy's standard fighter, the Phantom. The British sent two fact-finding missions to the United States in January 1964. A joint study by the Ministry of Aviation and the Admiralty staff concluded that the initial Phantom version, the F-4B, was not suitable, as it could not be launched from the existing short British catapult with any useful capability. The Admiralty and the Ministry of Defence therefore focused on the improved F-4J, which would meet British requirements.[52] Initially the Ministry of Aviation also rejected the new production version, the F-4J, probably because it hoped to salvage the naval P.1154 it had championed. It claimed that the naval P.1154 outperformed the Phantom, but that was true only of CAP endurance under tropical conditions and landing performance (no surprise, given that the P1154 was conceived as a VTOL aircraft). The Phantom offered a better rate of climb, acceleration, maximum speed and weapon system. The Ministry of Aviation had made its case by assuming the worst possible combination of wind, temperature, payload and maximum arrester gear safety limits; only a marginal change in any one of them would reduce the necessary wind over deck to a figure the ship could produce by its own speed. Under tropical conditions the Phantom would need its afterburner to take off from *Eagle* and *Hermes*, but a P.1154 would need plenum chamber burning (a form of afterburning) to take off every time.

The key change to meet British requirements was substitution of an afterburning version of the civil Spey engine for the US J79, specifically to improve endurance for a given weight of fuel. Unlike the J79, it was a two-spool engine (separate HP and LP compressors), hence substantially more efficient. CAP endurance was set by the weight (meaning the weight of fuel) which could be catapulted. McDonnell had been trying to sell it to the Royal Navy for some time. They had not included the AWG-10 radar because that would have lengthened the aircraft by 18in and have caused stowage problems, but relocation of the ASW-21 data link had solved that problem. For the Royal Navy both the radome and the antenna inside would fold for stowage. The US Navy suggested that the Royal Navy might dispense with the expensive data link and gain 85 gallons of fuel which it displaced. The afterburning Spey itself had been proposed for the TFX. To accommodate it the aircraft needed a new intake with its control system and a modified engine bay to accept an engine 6in greater in diameter. Compared to the current J79-GE-8, the projected version of the Spey would be somewhat lighter (3478lbs vs 3608lbs). It would offer about the same thrust (10,840lbs/18,285lbs [dry/afterburning] vs 10,800lbs/17,000lbs), but its airflow would be greater (209lbs/sec vs 169lbs/sec) and its specific fuel consumption better (1.28 vs 1.027 at sea level, 2.56 vs 2.35 afterburning at maximum power at 45,000ft). At cruising speed, fuel economy would be about 20 per cent better.

CAP endurance using the US J79 engine on the main 199ft catapult of *Eagle* would be two hours; the lower weight limit of the main 176ft catapult of *Hermes* would reduce that to one hour. With the afterburning Spey, endurance would be 2.3 hours and 1.8 hours, respectively. Each carrier had a lower-capacity 151ft standby catapult, offering 0.6 hours' endurance with the J79, but 1.3 hours with the Spey. These figures were for the least favourable tropical conditions; the aircraft would do appreciably better West of Suez. They allowed for only the wind over deck which the carrier could generate at a sustained speed of 28 knots for *Eagle* and 25 knots for *Hermes*. In the F-4J the US Navy introduced automatic engine thrust control at low speed for better control of landing speed, a change the British considered essential. Maximum speed above 36,000ft would be Mach 2.25 (the AW 406 requirement had been better than Mach 2).

A quick decision on the Spey was essential in order for the British to gain the advantage of shared production with the US Navy. A go-ahead had to be given by June 1964 to ensure that the project was included in the US FY65 (July 1964 to June 1965) programme. That factor short-circuited the normally lengthy British decision process. As

of early 1964 plans called for the first four aircraft in 1967–8, followed by sixty-six in 1968–9 and then seventy in 1969–70, a rate higher than the British would have liked but still acceptable. The programme could be spread further only if the TFX programme failed (as it did) and Phantom production continued longer than expected. The Spey was more expensive than a J79 and extra R&D would have to be paid for. In 1964 it was expected that 140 Phantoms with J79s would cost £116 million, compared to £179 million for the Spey version.

The Phantom was primarily an interceptor with a secondary strike capability. Even so its navigation/attack system was no worse than that of the Sea Vixen. Its AWG-10 was considered roughly equivalent to the pulse-Doppler radar then under development in the United Kingdom, capable of detecting a 5m^2 target at 50nm at all altitudes. It would provide the desired full low-altitude capability.[53] Its all-weather Sparrow – finally providing the Royal Navy with a collision-course missile – was much better than Red Top and it was lighter and half as expensive as Red Top. Red Top had higher terminal lethality, but Sparrow was more likely to engage a target at high altitude and more rapid engagement of a target with a low IR signature; it would also be effective in cloud. A radar version of Red Top had been considered, but Sparrow was considered superior, particularly at high altitude. It might be possible to develop a longer-range Sparrow successor, using the same weapon system, in the United Kingdom (that project produced the Skyflash missile). The Phantom could also carry the IR-guided Sidewinder. The other important item was the two-way ASW-21 data link.

In the strike role the Phantom's navigation/attack system would be comparable to that of the Sea Vixen and its load-carrying capability considerably better. The US Navy was contemplating two further improvements: drooped ailerons (for use as flaps to permit lower take-off and landing speeds) and an extended nose wheel strut (to give the aircraft a greater up-angle on take-off, so that the engine pushed it up as well as ahead). Both would give just the improved landing and take-off performance the British needed. When the second British fact-finding mission visited the United States late in January 1964, only the drooped ailerons (essential for the Royal Navy) had not yet been cleared by trials (some early problems were being resolved). As for size, the Phantom could replace the Sea Vixen on a one-for-one basis on board *Hermes* and *Eagle*, although one or two aircraft might have to be sacrificed on board the new carrier.[54] The British version would share the stronger landing gear of the F-4J, cleared for 36,000lbs.

The main barrier to the purchase was the expectation that the British aircraft industry was likely to protest that the navy requirements had been relaxed for an American aircraft and not for any British company (as in the P.1154 disaster). That would ignore the reality that the Phantom was far less expensive than any prospective British aircraft – and that it would be available much more quickly. The only requirement actually relaxed was maximum stowed width – 22ft for the P.1154, 27ft for the Phantom, but that presented no problems.

The Royal Navy Phantom was designated F-4K by the US Government. Ironically, in the Phantom the British actually did get the bi-service aircraft which the P.1154 was intended to be. The RAF bought the very similar F-4M.

On 29 April 1964 the letter of intent to buy it was signed by Minister of Defence Thorneycroft; Secretary of Defense McNamara had signed on the 25th.[55] There was a possibility that it would be manufactured in Canada rather than the United States.

As for the RAF, whose obsession with its TSR 2 had led to the entire

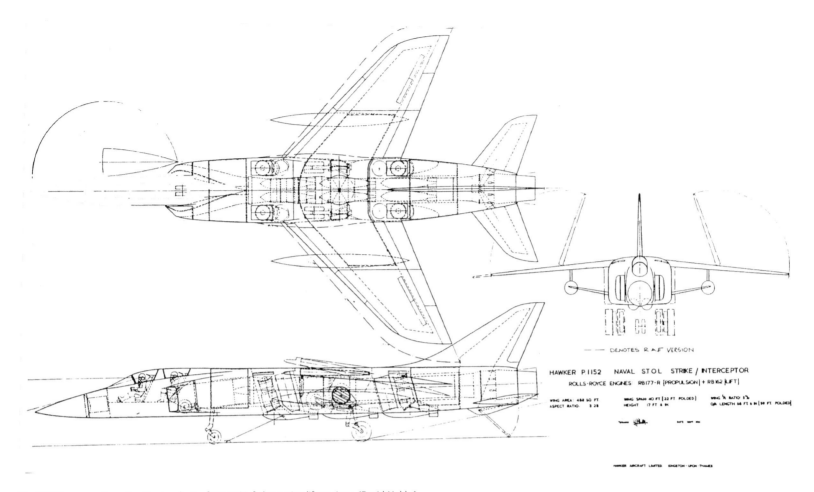

The P.1152 was an alternative Hawker design for a STOL fighter using lift engines. (David Hobbs)

P.1154 disaster, it lost that war when the British government killed it in favour of a longer-range swing-wing aircraft, a projected version of the US TFX called the F-111K – which was not, in the event, bought at all. Before the F-111K was killed, its supposed range was used to argue that the new British carrier was not really needed, because F-111Ks could cover all national requirements from island bases in the Far East. That was the notorious episode in which the Air Staff presented maps in which these bases were moved hundreds of miles to buttress its point. However, it seems more likely that the carrier project collapsed because of the high cost of the British Polaris programme and also the escalating cost of the army in Germany. The fight over future aircraft cannot have helped. Nor did it help that, in making its case for the carrier, the Admiralty generally used analysis to show that nothing short of the 50,000-tonner would be worthwhile. During the early stages of the CVA 01 project, the Civil Lord of the Admiralty perhaps prophetically told the Board that it could probably sell a 40,000-tonner but not the larger carrier it wanted. When the carrier was cancelled, the Board was unable to provide a rationale other than the need for naval forces East of Suez, which was not nearly good enough to convince a Government which badly needed to cut defence spending.

Overall, the moral of the story is that 'the best is the enemy of good enough'. The more analysis was done to buttress decisions, the less anyone would tolerate anything less than the best possible fighter. Since the assumed threats were always overstated, the Royal Navy could have done well with something not nearly as good – and in the end the Phantom, which did not meet the most extreme requirements, was a lot better than anything else the Royal Navy could have had. To be fair, the analysis was done to defend navy requirements in a hostile atmosphere and once a 1965 or 1970 threat had been agreed in MoD, it might have been dangerous for the navy to pull back. The whole process of elaborate formal analysis, which was intended to prevent the services from seeking over-capable and over-expensive aircraft and weapons, had the opposite effect.

CHAPTER 11
THE VIETNAM ERA

MCNAMARA AND TFX

President Eisenhower's national strategy was based on a massive nuclear deterrent backed by mobile naval forces designed to deter any local Soviet aggression by threatening nuclear attack. That strategy shaped the US Navy of the time, including its fighters, with their nuclear attack capability. Eisenhower paid for strategic and naval forces partly by gutting the US Army, reversing its rapid Korean War growth. Critics of Eisenhower's policies argued that there would be circumstances in which the United States might want to apply some lesser degree of force. When John F Kennedy ran for President in 1960, among his close advisors was retired army General Maxwell Taylor. Kennedy decided to build the army back up to the point where it could be effective. Initially the army's justification was that the United States and NATO should be able to fight a limited war in Europe, but soon after President Kennedy's inauguration Khrushchev gave a speech about 'wars of national liberation'. Operations in the

Third World could end-run NATO and its European nuclear deterrent. Kennedy was deeply impressed, although Eisenhower told him that the speech was nothing new. Reconstruction of the army became much more important because Kennedy now imagined that he would have to fight just such wars.

Modern armies are expensive, because they are highly mechanised, with large numbers of sophisticated weapons. To rebuild the army (and also to redirect it to the new role) the new Administration needed money, but it could not afford any great increase in defence spending. New Secretary of Defense Robert S McNamara entered office with a mandate to find the necessary money. He sought it by what he described as a more rational approach to defence, which meant avoiding inter-service duplication. There was already considerable Congressional pressure to do exactly that. The merit of this approach was that it avoided a public declaration of a change in direction towards limited war in the Third World, which soon came to mean

The F-4 Phantom II was the first example of Secretary McNamara's attempt to force the services to end duplication; he compelled the air force to adopt the aircraft. This VF-114 F-4B from *Kitty Hawk* is shown over North Vietnam in March 1968.

war in South East Asia. It also avoided making publicly obvious the deep cuts which had to be made in the air force budget, which under Eisenhower had greatly exceeded that of the other services.

Another factor in 1961 was that the high-technology programmes of the previous decade were generally reaching maturity and the need for large production investment. Through the 1950s, military technology developed at a frantic pace, the most visible items being compact nuclear weapons, missiles and supersonic jets. It was almost impossible to predict the costs of building weapons based on technologies which had never before been in production. By the late 1950s, cost overruns were so severe that the navy found itself cancelling major programmes, such as many planned missile cruiser conversions. The logic of navy cancellations at the time is not entirely clear, because in some cases, probably including the Seamaster attack seaplane, money had to be shifted to the vital Polaris missile/submarine programme. The cost overruns of the late 1950s also fuelled a demand for better defence management, although in retrospect it is difficult to see how the problem could have been averted. The great enduring monument to McNamara's regime was the PPBS (Planning Programming Budget System) which imposed a series of programme reviews ('milestones') between the start of a programme and release for production. Critics of the defence procurement system have pointed out that these apparent safeguards so delay programmes that their cost explodes, but that they appear not to kill programmes which deserve to die. Moreover, the layers of review make it too easy for those outside the programmes, with no stake in them, to add new requirements (gold-plating). McNamara seems to have seen PPBS as a way of delaying spending as long as possible, so that money would be freed for the urgent reconstruction of the army (which was never a stated Defense Department objective, but is obvious from tables of US force structure).

McNamara was far more powerful than his predecessors, thanks to a 1958 Reorganisation Act. It had had no impact at the time, because in effect Eisenhower had been his own Secretary of Defense. It was left to McNamara to create the modern Defense Department out of its much weaker predecessor, with what amounted to his own staff (beginning with his System Analysis 'whiz kids') as an alternative to the service staffs. The logic of the new administration was that it was time to force true integration on the separate services and that only with such integration could they operate efficiently. McNamara in turn inspired creation of the powerful British Ministry of Defence capable of taking over crucial decisions such as the continued existence of the British carrier force. In effect such decisions rose to the Defence Ministerial or Defense Secretarial level because the ships and aircraft involved were now so expensive.

McNamara's real problem, which is obvious from the experiences of later Secretaries of Defense, was to gain control of his department. He could do so only by showing absolute resolution and by killing existing programmes (to show that he could overrule the services). Moreover, to get the money he needed, he had to kill a few large programmes rather than trim many smaller ones; he lacked the staff to review the whole defence budget in detail. In 1961 there were not many huge programmes. One was the air force's Skybolt missile, which was associated with further production of B-52 bombers. Another was a projected air force light bomber (misleadingly labelled a fighter), not yet in production (TFX). The navy had the two programmes Admiral Burke had agonised over, Eagle-Missileer and Typhon. McNamara's public position was that the new administration would replace Eisenhower's reliance on nuclear weapons at every level with a much more graduated form of deterrence, including the ability to fight non-nuclear wars. Since the major programmes had all been conceived under the previous administration, most of them had a distinct nuclear flavour. For example, air force tactical aircraft were intended mainly to drop nuclear weapons in Eastern Europe at the start of a war, hopefully slowing a Soviet advance. Although many of them were called fighters, they were actually light bombers. Any air-to-air fighting they might do would be to brush aside enemy interceptors. The latest of the light bombers, the F-105 Thunderchief, was intended to avoid interception by making its final approach at low level. The navy espoused a similar approach and by 1961 it was no more interested in air superiority than the air force. Its newest strike aircraft, the Grumman A2F (A-6) Intruder, was designed to fly towards the target at minimum altitude, albeit somewhat more slowly than the F-105.

In the late 1950s the Soviets began to deploy medium-range ballistic missiles, placing NATO airfields at risk. The air force had long been aware of the vulnerability associated with large fixed air bases and in the mid-1950s, as already described, it envisaged a solution in the form of zero-length launchers for nuclear fighter-bombers. That proved to be a limited solution. By 1960 the solution espoused by the air force Tactical Air Command (TAC) was a high-performance fighter which could operate from a short field. As it happened, the navy's A-6, which was already in procurement, could already do just that, but it never figured in the subsequent debate; it does not even turn up in books critical of the entire TFX project. TAC coupled the short-field requirement (take-off in about a third the distance required by the F-105) with a requirement that the aircraft be deployable across the Atlantic without refuelling. In theory, such deployment would make it possible for the new light bomber to fly immediately to any of the numerous short runways in Western Europe

and then to fight at once. That in turn made sense only if the aircraft deployed complete with its nuclear payload and the unpredictable airfield idea (like the idea of using VTOL aircraft) did not take into account the need to provide considerable back-up on the spot, such as fuel, spare parts and maintenance personnel. The long runway was the least of the problem.

All of this mattered because once McNamara got into action the requirements TAC was levying could be twisted to approximate what the navy wanted for its Missileer. Transatlantic deployability translated into long endurance on a CAP station. A short-field capability could translate into carrier suitability, although in reality current carrier aircraft were perfectly adequate but could not have operated from short runways. The only really exotic demand TAC made was supersonic speed during the 400-mile low-altitude dash the aircraft would make from a base in Western Europe to a target in Eastern Europe. That alone substantially pushed up the size and cost of the aircraft. TAC seems to have chosen supersonic rather than high subsonic dash speed to make the project more attractive within the air force; there is reason to doubt that it made much difference in surviv-ability (the navy sponsors of the A-6 certainly thought not).

A subtler factor was the air force's designation of its light nuclear bomber as a fighter, which implicitly justified supersonic speed at high altitude. There was no particular reason for such performance, since the aircraft was intended to descend to low altitude before entering enemy territory and then to make its high-speed dash. It was unlikely that it would have to deal with enemy fighters over its home territory. On that basis it is difficult to explain the need for either the new aircraft or its predecessor F-105 to be supersonic at high altitude. The navy did demand supersonic speed for its F-4 Phantom, but that was mainly to enable it to function as a fleet interceptor and general-purpose fighter, possibly tangling with enemy fighters.

McNamara appears to have used the new need to fight a non-nuclear war as a club to beat down the air force. First he demanded that the existing light bomber, the F-105, be modified to carry a heavy non-nuclear bomb load. That was not a major problem, since he was not demanding that the aircraft be given a tactical system better adapted to non-nuclear attack. A nuclear weapon could wipe out a large target area, so when using such weapons there was only a limited need for precision. Non-nuclear weapons had to be dropped very nearly directly on their targets, as anything more than a few hundred yards away would not be effective (in 1961 precision weapons, which really did guarantee such results, were very much in their infancy; wartime experience would show that anything except such weapons could not be dropped nearly precisely enough).

McNamara's next step was to claim that the navy had effective ability to deliver conventional weapons and that the air force should adopt its aircraft. The crudity of his office's analysis shows in its con-centration not on the navy's attack aircraft programme (the A-4 and A-6 certainly qualified) but rather on its own high-performance fighter, the F-4 Phantom. Advertising the F-4 as a better limited-war bomber than the F-105, McNamara cancelled F-105 production. The entirely unrecognised reality was that superior Marine close air support had been achieved by developing such crucial equipment as radar control centres which could vector fighters to targets designated by Marine controllers. Forcing the air force to buy the F-4 was very much in line with McNamara's claim that duplication should and could be squeezed out of the services. He had already decreed that both services should buy versions of the same long-range fighter (actually a

light bomber) derived from the air force's new tactical nuclear bomber. Other attempts to force commonality failed: McNamara tried and failed to force the air force to buy the navy's RA-5 Vigilante as its next reconnaissance aircraft.

The air force was already interested in the Phantom; a few years earlier its officers had readily told a visiting British delegation that the Phantom was the best fighter in the world. McNamara's edict had a somewhat bizarre outcome. The air force was already testing the Phantom under the designation F-110, in its 'century' series of super-sonic fighters. The navy F-4H designation was in an entirely different system. McNamara apparently did not realise that the F-110 and the Phantom were the same aircraft. He became embarrassed when he found that they were and he demanded that the service designations be unified. Perhaps the underlying reason was that he wanted to unify aircraft procurement altogether. The Phantom became the F-4 in a new fighter series.

McNamara deliberately chose system analysts without ties to the services, which meant that they disdained military judgement – and often had very little idea of the situations they were addressing or of the pitfalls in current technology. A service's decision often reflected considerable experience across a wide range of possible situations as well as painful experience of how weapons worked in reality rather than on paper. Such a judgement could not easily be quantified or explained as an alternative to what might otherwise seem to be a rational choice. Typically the new McNamara choices were explained briefly in 'Draft Presidential Memoranda' replete with estimates of effectiveness (necessarily in a single scenario) and cost estimates, to show how much better the System Analysis choice was than the service alternatives. Many of the memoranda reflect remarkable ignorance. That suggests that they were rationales concocted after decisions had already been made, largely off the cuff.

McNamara's team was also entirely unaware of service cultural factors affecting new aircraft. The design of the F-111, which became McNamara's signature programme, was much affected by a require-ment that it achieve low supersonic speed at low altitude (its predeces-sor F-105 achieved high subsonic speed at low altitude). The change from high subsonic to low supersonic made very little difference to the aircraft's survivability, but it enormously affected cost and complexity, not to mention required structural strength (hence weight). There is every reason to think that the new requirement was stated only because the original customer, the air force's TAC, wanted to justify replacing the F-105.[1] Unlike the navy, apparently the air force did not routinely develop feasibility designs (as ADR did) before stating requirements, hence had no way of knowing the cost of the small increase in speed TAC wanted. The absence of such studies may explain why the air force was more beset than the navy by gross cost inflation in the aircraft it adopted in the 1950s. That McNamara's cost-control analysts apparent-ly did not appreciate the value of feasibility studies, hence could not estimate the cost of particular choices embedded in aircraft specifica-tions, suggests how superficial their approach to cost analysis was.

When McNamara entered office, the air force was pursuing the light tactical bomber which became the F-111 and the navy was pursuing the Missileer long-endurance missile fighter. Although designs had been selected for both the Eagle missile and the Missileer, the outgoing Eisenhower Administration had deliberately not signed the order for the Missileer fighter because it wanted the next adminis-tration to have the freedom to decide whether to buy it. No design had been chosen for the TAC bomber. Apparently the idea that the design for the bomber could be adapted to meet the Missileer requirement originated in the Directorate for Defense Research and Engineering (DDR&E), possibly before McNamara entered office. It was certainly soon offered to McNamara and DDR&E rather than the system analysts dominated the programme as it was run from inside McNamara's office.

Whoever had the idea, McNamara made it his own; the merged aircraft became his signature programme, announced soon after McNamara entered office.[2] It combined two new technologies, the swing-wing and an afterburning turbofan engine. They combined to offer unprecedented endurance and the reasoning may well have been that the navy loiter requirement would be no more than an application of the long range the air force already wanted. DDR&E seems to have been unaware that any naval aircraft would have to meet exacting standards of size, landing weight and approach speed which might be quite as daunting as the long endurance and high maximum speed the air force wanted. It is also possible that DDR&E had been involved in the earlier air force choice of speed and range requirements.

During the struggle over a joint requirement, navy negotiators pointed out that if the low-level dash speed was cut to Mach 0.9, a joint design would be feasible. They never pointed out a crucial reality: there already was a single aircraft capable of both the low-level attack and missile options: the Grumman Intruder, which the navy classified as an attack bomber.[3] A version of the Intruder had been rejected in the 1959 Missileer competition, but it was certainly acceptable. Unlike the air force light bomber, it carried all its weapons externally – but it had a very large capacity for conventional weapons and a high-precision delivery system. McNamara does not seem to have considered it (and it does not appear in accounts of the F-111 disaster), perhaps because he never realised that fighters and attack aircraft were really two parts of much the same group of aircraft and that what the air force called fighters were aircraft the navy would have classed as bombers. The navy may have avoided mentioning the Intruder for fear that it would be cancelled in favour of some adapted air force aircraft, perhaps even a further version of the joint aircraft. However, it is remarkable that the question has not been raised by later historians, who certainly could have been aware of the character of tactical aircraft at this time. McNamara's decision to merge navy and air force requirements seems to have predated considerably his demand that the air force buy the navy's F-4H Phantom, so he cannot have made his decision based on unwillingness to force two navy tactical aircraft in succession down the air force's throat.

The new joint programme, which both services resisted, was designated TFX (Tactical Fighter Experimental). A June 1961 Secretary of Defense memo approved both the TFX and a new attack aircraft called VAX. For the moment it was a rubber aircraft. In January 1962 BuWeps issued System Characteristics to define VAX and in June 1963 an OpNav Sea Based Strike Forces Study was completed for the Secretary of Defense. It split VAX into a new light attack aircraft (VAL, which became the A-7) and a multi-mission aircraft. The multi-mission VAX was described as a complement to the ongoing TFX. That October a Tentative Specific Operational Requirement (SOR W11-06T) for a High Performance General Purpose Attack Aircraft was issued.[4] It became VFAX, a combination fighter/attack aircraft after BuWeps issued An Evaluation of Attack and Attack/Fighter Aircraft for the 1970s in January 1965. That October SOR 11-06 was titled High Performance Multimission Fighter/Attack Aircraft (VFAX). Ultimately it edged the TFX out of the navy and led to the F-14 Tomcat.

TFX became the F-111, the navy version being the F-111B. The TFX decision has often been attacked on the ground that the needs of the two services were so very different. It seems likeliest that McNamara badly needed an example of how he could cut costs by forcing commonality, as well as an early proof of his determination. Through the summer and early autumn of 1961 representatives of the two services tried and failed to develop common requirements. In the end the air force specification, with navy additions, was issued to industry and companies were asked to find some way to produce an aircraft in two versions with maximum commonality. In the end, they used the air force requirements with important differences for the navy aircraft, particularly in length (to fit lifts) and in landing weight. Even so, the navy had serious misgivings, not least because air force leadership meant that its concerns, connected with both carrier operation and the fleet air defence role, would have little impact. The only two acceptable bids were from Boeing and General Dynamics (Convair), of which Boeing had not built a production fighter since the early 1930s. Convair had built the air force's F-102 and F-106. A joint air force-navy selection board favoured Boeing; McNamara chose General Dynamics.[5] There was widespread belief that the choice had been made on political grounds. General Dynamics was in Texas, Vice President Lyndon B Johnson's home state and a major source of political donations to the Administration. Boeing promised lower cost; McNamara claimed that General Dynamics' costing was more realistic. Boeing offered better performance, but McNamara always claimed that the services asked for more than they really needed. General Dynamics offered much more commonality. Since the F-111 never met its performance goals and since it suffered spectacular cost overruns, it is impossible to evaluate McNamara's position. Substantial efforts by Congressional investigators failed to prove political manipulation of the contract. They certainly left key Senators permanently hostile to the programme, hence favourably inclined to kill it when they could.[6]

As for Admiral Burke's dilemma, McNamara cancelled the surface ship Typhon system outright, before it or its radical new radar had been tested. His argument was that none of the existing naval air defence missile systems was reliable enough and that the navy should not field anything new until the problem had been resolved. A small amount of money was provided for pilot studies of what was then called the Advanced Surface Missile System (ASMS). Experience with the prototype Typhon radar suggests that McNamara was right to cancel the system, though he probably had no idea of the problems involved. ASMS was fortunate, because its studies coincided with the rise of really reliable solid-state radars. It gave birth to the very successful Aegis programme. Most remarkably of all, it turned out that the US Navy could indeed afford both the new surface missile system and the new airborne system, which formed a very potent combination in the 1980s. The new airborne system entered service first, in 1974.

The air force was lead developer of the TFX; naval input was limited. The formal decision to unify the services' heavy fighter under one programme was accompanied by (or quickly followed by) a decision that the two services would develop their own tactical fighters, the F-4 follow-ons: the navy's VFAX and the air force's FX. It seems likely that the process of grinding the two services together in the TFX programme had proven so bruising that McNamara was not willing to repeat the process. The 'A' in VFAX indicated an attack role the air force did not want, although there was air force interest in an alternative FAX.

McNamara, or more likely his Director of Defense Research and Engineering Dr Harold Brown (later Secretary of the Air Force), seems to have been very favourably impressed by the air force's single-package approach to high-technology projects. Unlike BuAer, the air force made no attempt to integrate weapon systems. Instead, it relied on sophisticated contractors to take responsibility for entire systems. In the case of Missileer, BuAer had planned to integrate the Westinghouse pulse-Doppler radar with the Bendix Eagle missile. No contractor would be responsible for the complex fire-control system connecting the two.

AWG-9 AND PHOENIX

At this time only one US contractor was developing integrated systems of the sort Brown needed: Hughes Aircraft. It was responsible for the weapon systems of the air force interceptors developed for the North American Air Defense Command, including their Falcon missiles. During the 1950s Hughes had developed a system specifically for the next-generation NORAD fighter, the North American F-108 Rapier; the missile was designated AIM-47. It offered the sort of long range envisaged for Missileer, but the air force did not ask for a multi-target system. After the Rapier was cancelled, the Hughes project for its ASG-18 fire-control system was kept alive. Brown saw it as the basis for the system on board the navy version of the TFX. In 1962 Hughes received the contract for a new AWG-9 system, the W indicating a weapon system and the G fire control. The existing AIM-47 missile lacked the desired range, so Hughes began work on a longer-range development designated AIM-54 (Phoenix).

Both missile and radar had to be squeezed down to fit a high-performance fighter. The 60in dish of the Missileer radar was far too large, so Hughes opted for much higher power and a smaller antenna. The associated radar was of the new multi-mode type, using a computer to generate its waveform. That made it possible to intersperse a ranging mode, for example, with a pure pulse-Doppler air-to-air mode and also to provide air-to-ground modes.

The new missile was considerably smaller than the Eagle planned for the Eagle-Missileer combination. Instead of a massive booster plus a sustainer motor in the missile, it had a single internal motor. Like many contemporary air-to-air missiles, Phoenix had a boost-glide trajectory, the booster accelerating the missile to high speed. Guidance made a considerable difference. A missile like most Sparrows was fired directly towards the bomber target. To some extent it could follow a more energy-efficient path pointing at a collision point rather than directly at the target, but that added relatively little range. That type of operation was inevitable in a system whose radar tracked the target directly. A track-while-scan system could project ahead an aim point. An associated computer could calculate an energy-efficient path to get there. A missile with an autopilot could be commanded to follow that path, even though it might spend much of its time with the target out of sight. This type of operation was key to both the AWG-9/Aegis system and the roughly contemporary Aegis/SM-2 surface missile system. In the shipboard case, commanding the missile to follow an energy efficient path nearly doubled range with the same missile and the same rocket motor. Moreover, if the missile did not have to home on the target until it came close, it did not need a very powerful illuminating radar for terminal homing late in its trajectory (conversely, the same illuminating radar would be effective at much greater range). Some form of terminal homing was necessary because the radar on

board the guiding fighter could not be accurate enough to command the missile all the way to the target.

In the case of Phoenix, the missile gained range by using its motor to take it to very high altitude, thereby gaining kinetic energy. It used that energy to dive down towards its target. The result was a very long-range yet reasonably compact missile. Phoenix initially followed a trajectory programmed into its autopilot. To deal with possible target motion, the autopilot was data-linked back to the controlling fighter and thus could be updated during flight. Closer to the target the missile switched to semi-active guidance. That was not enough. The system was required to engage multiple targets simultaneously. To do that, the fighter had to switch its illumination among the targets, the missile continuing on course between bursts of illumination. Once it was close to the target, the missile switched guidance modes again, to its own active seeker.

The result was very impressive; in tests Phoenix shot down drones at ranges of over 100nm. However, there was a cost. A Phoenix rising to maximum altitude created a visible column of smoke. A pilot in an approaching bomber could see it. If he understood what was happening, he could try to evade. The gliding missile had only limited energy, particularly when it tried to manoeuvre across its line of sight. The faster and more energetic the bomber, the worse the very long-range problem. The initial solution was a low-smoke motor, to minimise warning, but it still did not solve the problem of a fast crossing target at long range. Phoenix might be effective against a relatively docile target at long range, but it would be much less effective against a manoeuvrable fighter. That was why F-14s were armed with Sparrows rather than the more impressive (on paper) Phoenix when they faced enemy fighters over Libya and Iraq. The special character of the Phoenix missile also explains why its replacement by the much lighter-weight AMRAAM, which also uses command mid-course guidance (hence can benefit from trajectory-shaping) is not as much of a retrograde step as it may appear.

THE F-111B

Grumman was General Dynamics' partner to develop the F-111B naval version of the joint-service TFX. Compared to the air force F-111, it was shortened to fit lifts and it had an entirely different weapon system built around the Hughes AWG-9 and the Phoenix missile. The main design issue was landing weight, the navy having barely accepted a maximum of 55,000lbs. The legacy of the original air force design requirements, such as supersonic low-altitude dash, was a much heavier aircraft than was required for the fleet air defence mission. Grumman's main task was to pare enough weight from the F-111B to make it carrier-capable. To this end it mounted a series of Weight Improvement Programmes (WIPs) and Super Weight Improvement Programmes (SWIPs).[7] In the end, when the F-111B was declared not suitable, excessive weight was the stated problem. However, other problems contributed to excessive weight. For example, the TF30 engine turned out not to be as economical as expected, so to meet the key loiter requirement the F-111B needed more fuel (eventually 6800lbs), which meant more weight even when it was nearly empty. When the F-111B design was accepted, General Dynamics gave its empty weight as 38,804lbs. In December 1963 General Dynamics estimated a weight of 45,259lbs including a projected saving of 3226lbs that had not been formally accepted by the government.[8]

McNamara's more dramatic attempt to force the services together was considerably less successful: the F-111B. This prototype is shown in February 1965.

Early navy protests failed because the joint programme was far too important to McNamara and his associates in the Defense Department; it was the signature programme for efficient management. When the navy protested that no modification of the F-111 could produce an effective aircraft, the Defense Department position was that surely some acceptable aircraft could be built. This was much the position that the British Minister of Defence took at much the same time over the attempt to merge Royal Navy and RAF projects in the failed P.1154. In each case, it represented the hoped-for triumph of political will over what seemed to be intractable engineering reality. The political argument was that any F-111B which was more cost-effective than previous navy fighters would be acceptable; the navy argument was that the carrier suitability problem was a hard engineering limit that could not be overcome. Navy test pilots uniformly condemned the F-111B. Despite the SWIPs, the F-111B would have been the heaviest operational navy aircraft of its time.[9]

The navy was certainly nervous. In June 1965 it awarded a nine-month contract to Grumman to investigate possible design changes in the F-111B, but also to consider possible installation of the Phoenix system in the A-6 Intruder; a version of the Intruder had been one alternative in the Missileer competition.[10] Initially Grumman concentrated on estimating the performance of the SWIP version of the F-111B and on a possible modification using a different engine, the JTF10A-27. It was a growth version of the TF 30 recently proposed by Pratt & Whitney, offering 10,680lbs of thrust (without afterburner) compared to 9900lbs for the TF-30 (at sea level, at Mach 0.2). The new engine would be somewhat heavier. The after fuselage would have to be redesigned to accept larger-diameter afterburners and the air inlets enlarged. The weight would be about the same as that of the SWIP aircraft, estimated at the time as 77,030lbs at take-off. Given the navy's requirement that the aircraft weigh no more than 55,000lbs on

landing, it was unacceptable (the SWIP landing weight was then estimated as 57,788lbs). Further studies showed that if the aircraft could be pared down to 69,500lbs at take-off (54,100lbs on landing) it could meet the carrier requirement, expressed in terms of wind over deck for landing. Further reduction of subsonic drag would buy more combat time available at Mach 2, another problem for the F-111B. The weapons bay would be eliminated and all six Phoenix missiles carried semi-externally (the weapons-bay volume could be used for additional fuel). All of this amounted to saying that a largely redesigned aircraft – recognisably not a version of the F-111 – could meet the navy's needs. The study supported the navy's view that the joint aircraft could not work. The pared-down weights could not be met, because Grumman was already doing everything it could in the SWIP programme.

As for the A-6, unsurprisingly, initial studies showed that it could be integrated with Phoenix, which was considerably lighter than the Eagle missile originally planned. More work was needed to develop the idea in detail, but the point was that there was already an affordable navy alternative to the F-111B. As prime contractor for the AWG-9/Phoenix system, Hughes received a sub-contract to study a possible A-6 version.

Grumman submitted its final report in April 1966. Revised calculations and wind tunnel tests showed that the SWIP aircraft was worse than had been imagined. It could only spend a fifth of the desired time in Mach 2 combat, 1.9 minutes and acceleration time was increased from 8.321 minutes to 10.01 minutes. Lengthening the aircraft by 24in would reduce supersonic drag – but it would also make it less suitable for a carrier. Parts of the missile-control system could be relocated, freeing volume for additional fuel. New engines could help; Grumman cited the General Electric GE1/F12B and the Pratt & Whitney ST F250C-30. GE offered better cruise and loiter, but less supersonic thrust. Pratt & Whitney's afterburner had too large a diameter, though it could be reduced. As part of its navy project, on 11 April 1966 Grumman offered a formal development plan for what it called Phase III, an entirely new aircraft using the best currently planned engine, the GE1/F12B and carrying the Phoenix weapon system of the F-111B. All that would have remained of the F-111B project was the designation. The drawings Grumman presented retained the side-by-side cockpit of the F-111B and the aircraft generally resembled the F-111B.

In August 1966 Grumman circulated a series of slides describing a further new aircraft, which it called the F-111CS (the set of slides is marked 'not for GD'). Unlike an F-111, this aircraft would have a fighter-style tandem cockpit. Take-off weight would be cut to 56,138lbs (empty weight would be 33,643lbs). The powerplant would be a pair of GE 1/105-152B engines producing 19,000lbs of thrust compared to 20,350lbs for a TF-30-P-12. The aircraft looks like an F-14 and the project was probably the beginning of the F-14 project. A graph showed that it was better area-ruled than an F-111B, hence would have better transonic performance. Loiter time would be 3.5 hours at 35,000ft (as desired, rather than the 30,000ft offered by the F-111B). The aircraft would accelerate from Mach 0.7 to Mach 2 in 4.5 minutes, compared to 6.1 minutes for the F-111B. Cruising ceiling would be 36,000ft rather than 33,000ft. Instead of needing at least 5 knots of wind over deck to catapult, the new aircraft would be able to take off with the wind blowing 18 knots the wrong way (it would similarly be able to land on with the wind blowing 7 knots the wrong way). These vu-graphs seem to have been the beginning of the F-14, because they showed that, at least based on early estimates, there really was a way to build an effective fleet fighter armed with the Phoenix missile. It didn't have to be something heavy and unwieldy like the F-111B. That Grumman called it an F-111CS was beside the point; the designation might save face.

A slightly later set of Grumman slides (8 August 1966) summarised the current situation. It compared the F-111 (1079) with a swing-wing F-4 which would cost $3.6 million rather than $5.8 million for each of 300 aircraft. The F-4 offered 3.6 hours of loiter time against the original – now frustrated – hope that the F-111 could loiter for 4.98 hours. Grumman also showed a range of possible simplifications which might cut the cost and weight of the F-111B. The Phoenix system could be replaced by the AWG-10 and Sparrows of the F-4J. The escape module could be replaced by side-by-side ejection seats. The fanjets could be replaced by J79s. At another remove, the two seats could be placed in tandem and the complicated 3-D inlets replaced by 2-D inlets. The engines might even be podded. The package included a drawing of the tandem-seat fighter, the F-111CS of the other vu-graphs.

The navy formally moved to cancel the F-111B in November 1967. The previous month Grumman had offered an unsolicited proposal for a complete redesign (in effect an alternative aircraft).[11] The timing was set by the imminent formal production commitment. Also, by this time Secretary McNamara had been broken by the Vietnam War, so his power to defend his signature procurement programme was rapidly ebbing. He would resign as Secretary of Defense effective February 1968. In March 1968 the Defense Department offered a face-saving proposal to quietly cancel the F-111B after the 1968 Presidential election. By this time the navy was already working on a successor and the agreement included terminating the F-111B at the eighth (production version) prototype and shifting resources to the successor, which became the F-14. The Department approached the Senate Armed Services Committee, which wanted nothing of face-saving and only wanted to know whether the navy could afford a further delay in

the fleet air-defence fighter it needed. To the committee, in proposing cancellation the navy was also stating that it could afford the delay. That was enough; the committee formally recommended cancellation and the Defense Department announced it on 10 July 1968. By that time the navy was evaluating alternatives for what became the F-14 Tomcat.

General Dynamics did not surrender easily; the navy file on the F-111B includes a set of its vu-graphs dated 14 March 1968, describing the virtues of the F-111B in limited war.[12] They summarised remaining room for growth and described successful carrier trials. The main topic was a navy-funded GD/Hughes study of the limited war mission, which entailed strike, escort, barrier CAP (to sanitise an area) and forward area strike and fighter control, the latter having been explored by GD the previous year.

Neither the air force F-111A nor the navy F-111B could be described as fighters. The air force aircraft was a fast light bomber, the navy aircraft a fast missile carrier. The F-111B could barely be made into a carrier-capable aircraft, but it would have no significant growth potential. It was an extremely expensive way to meet part of the navy fighter requirement. Its high cost and visibility threatened to make it the navy's sole fighter. As the cost of the F-111B mounted, the Office of the Secretary of Defense (OSD) pressed for a carrier air wing whose only fighter would be the F-111B; the other main aircraft would be the inexpensive A-7B light day bomber. Both versions of the F-111 were known to have poor fighter performance, but in late 1967 the official OSD position was that the aircraft could be cured by replacing its underpowered engine. Asked whether that would solve the problem, at a Senate hearing DCNO (Air) Rear Admiral Thomas F Connally said bluntly that 'all the power in Christendom' would not make the F-111B into a real fighter.

By that time the navy was working hard on a VFAX multi-mission fighter to supplement the F-111B, but the existence of this alternative fighter programme had received no publicity at all. OSD was probably all too aware that once Congress was aware that there was a fighter alternative, it would kill the F-111B. Conversely, once the F-111B had been killed, the VFAX programme quickly grew into the alternative VFX programme which in turn produced the F-14 Tomcat. Without VFAX, the road to an entirely new naval fighter would have been far longer. The navy therefore became intensely interested in a supplementary VFAX programme, which at times was described as a fighter, using the same swing-wing technology but half the size and cost. The single overwhelming advantage of the F-14 which was bought instead of the F-111 was that it was agile enough to function both as a loitering fleet air-defence fighter and as an air-superiority fighter: carriers could operate with F-14s alone.

VFAX

VFAX was envisaged as the F-4 successor, to operate alongside the TFX/F-111B. TFX would defend the fleet, but VFAX would carry the offensive air-to-air fight to the enemy (by this time it was obvious that unescorted strike aircraft would run into enemy defensive fighters). In theory, during the early phase of an operation, when air superiority had yet to be achieved, the VFAX would back F-111Bs defending the fleet directly. At some point the F-111Bs would suffice and the VFAX could either escort bombers or bomb themselves in adverse weather (the new A-7B bomber was usable only under visual conditions). Although the strike mission had clearly been very secondary for the F-4,

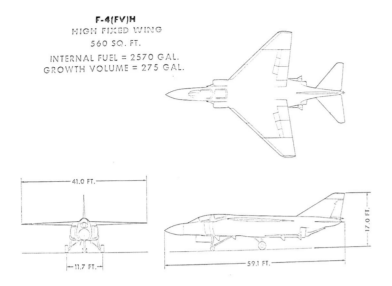

F-4(FV)H
HIGH FIXED WING
560 SQ. FT.
INTERNAL FUEL = 2570 GAL.
GROWTH VOLUME = 275 GAL.

41.0 FT.

11.7 FT.   59.1 FT.   17.0 FT.

McDonnell's sketch of an F-4X with a high rather than the earlier low wing, from a set of vu-graphs produced for the navy.

VFAX would have something closer to a precision bombing capability.

By the time the navy was developing VFAX, aircraft development was considerably more bureaucratic than it had been, Secretary McNamara having introduced a system of staging which considerably slowed development. McNamara's technique also made much more specific demands on the design of the aircraft as part of a large system. In the past BuAer and its successor BuWeps had generally specified performance, including the loads the aircraft had to carry, but avionics had been a separate matter and maintainability and availability had generally not been specified at all. Once aircraft were in service, they certainly counted and by the early 1960s there was considerable experience with the complexity of jet fighters. Now desired levels were specified, which is not at all the same as saying that they were met or even that it was possible to predict them. The list of even the earliest VFAX requirements was far more detailed than anything used previously, to the point that aircraft sketched under such rules are almost indistinguishable except on a detailed level. Conversely, in the 1960s it seemed that such proposals could be evaluated entirely on paper, without any competing prototypes at all. Much later the fly-off of the lightweight fighters was a direct reaction to such practices.

VFAX began formally with Tentative Specific Operational Requirement (TSOR) W11-06T dated 15 October 1963, which called for a high-performance attack plane rather than a fighter; it became a fighter for much the same reason that, about a decade earlier, ADR had posited a single fighter for both the missile fighter and nuclear strike roles; from an aircraft point of view the two missions were compatible because the loads involved were similar (a somewhat similar vision of compatibility led to the TFX disaster). Early studies culminated in a January 1965 BuWeps report which indicated that it was both feasible and desirable to have a relatively small high-performance aircraft that could replace the F-4 in the fighter role and be at least as good as the A-7A in the attack role. Hence the VFAX designation.

The McNamara Defense Department demanded a very formal process beginning with mission requirements rather than with a choice of overall aircraft performance; aircraft performance could (in theory) be traded off against weapon performance. Once the TSOR had

been written, BuWeps undertook two years of broad design studies, including subsonic and supersonic aircraft, VTOLs and variable-sweep aircraft. Given the recent use of variable sweep in the F-111 and the degree to which the F-111 was identified with the Secretary of Defense, it is no surprise that a supersonic variable-sweep type was chosen. Before McNamara, that choice would have taken a few days and a lot less paper.

The initial effort associated with the TSOR included single-purpose and multi-purpose aircraft, as well as conventional and VSTOL configurations. BuWep conducted some studies itself, but it contracted out work to three aircraft companies and to one engine company.[13] The aircraft companies developed preliminary designs. This work was conducted between March and November 1963. All of the system studies favoured a multi-mission STOL aircraft (STOL applied to a short-field capability). They were reported by BuWeps in January 1965. This report was reviewed between February and September 1965 and BuWeps conducted further effectiveness and cost comparison studies.

The result of all the studies was Specific Operational Requirement (SOR) for VFAX issued by DCNO (Air) on 8 October 1965. Development was assigned to BuWeps on 26 October. A formal Technical Development Plan (TDP) followed in February 1966 (it was approved in May 1966). The Chief of Naval Materiel approved the VFAX advanced procurement plan in August 1966.[14] By this time BuWeps, which had begun the VAX/VFAX project, had been superseded by the Naval Air Systems Command (NAVAIR), which fell under the jurisdiction of the Naval Materiel Command. VFAX was described as 'a high performance, multi-mission fighter/attack aircraft of superior flexibility'. All of this was to be achieved within a moderate weight by exploiting variable geometry (the swing wing) and expected lightweight engines and micro-miniaturised and highly reliable avionics – the computer revolution.

In January 1967 OpNav completed an F-111B Requirements Study which confirmed the need for VFAX to complement the larger aircraft, particularly in fighter roles other than fleet air defence. It pointed out

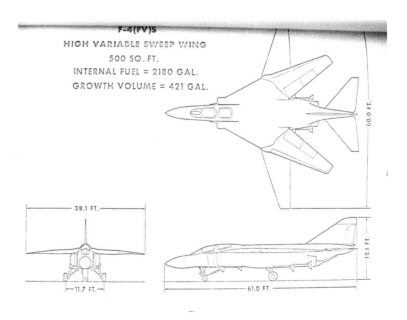

F-4(FV)S
HIGH VARIABLE SWEEP WING
500 SQ. FT.
INTERNAL FUEL = 2180 GAL.
GROWTH VOLUME = 421 GAL.

60.0 FT.

38.1 FT.

11.7 FT.   61.0 FT.   19.1 FT.

McDonnell's proposal for a swing-wing version of the F-4 Phantom, from a McDonnell vu-graph.

that because the F-111B straddled air force and navy requirements, it was larger and less manoeuvrable than the navy had wanted. Due to its size and specialised character, it would be bought in relatively small numbers. The projected number per carrier was cut from twelve to six to eight per carrier. VFAX would make up the numbers. Until it was ready, the F-4J would complement the F-111B. VFAX would also replace some A-7As and possibly some A-6As, since it would have an advanced multi-function radar and digital fire-control system giving it enhanced all-weather attack capacity. Based on past studies, OpNav envisaged two squadrons (twenty-four aircraft) per carrier, replacing twelve F-4J and ten A-7A. By this time OpNav had the study by Grumman and Hughes showing that the AWG-9/Phoenix combination could be installed in a growth version of VFAX, offering the possibility that this version would ultimately replace the F-111B.[15]

The TDP envisaged a CAP mission: three hours' loiter 150nm from the carrier at 35,000ft (compared to 2.1 hours at 33,000ft for the F-4J), plus four minutes of combat. Armament would include two (four desired) internal 20mm guns and at least four air-to-air radar-guided (Sparrow) or IR-guided missiles. The four minutes of combat would consist of acceleration to Mach 1.5 and manoeuvring at that speed. The demand for internal guns was due to early unhappy experiences with gunless F-4s facing North Vietnamese fighters. Combat capability included buffet-free manoeuvring at 2G at Mach 0.85 at 35,000ft (a possible requirement for 2.5G was rejected because it would require a much larger wing which would compromise other characteristics). The 2G loiter capability was expected to require leading or trailing edge lift devices (slats or flaps, for example). There was also a point intercept mission, in which VFAX would have to climb and dash to 125nm at 45,000ft while carrying the same load as in the CAP mission. For close air support it would carry nine Mk 82 bombs (500lbs). The long-range strike mission was nuclear attack with a Mk 61 bomb (other nuclear weapons might be substituted).

The TDP specified a maximum speed of Mach 2.2 (acceleration from Mach 0.8 to Mach 1.8 within 3.3 minutes, compared to 2.82 minutes for the F-4J), a combat ceiling of 58,500ft in the air-to-air mission (49,950ft for the F-4J), a manoeuvrability of 2G and a ferry range of 3000nm (2160nm for the F-4J on internal fuel). Take-off weight would be 45,000lbs, compared to a maximum of 56,129lbs at take-off for an F-4J Phantom (and 77,566lbs for an F-111B carrying six Phoenix missiles). Mission success probability was set at 80 per cent (90 per cent desired). Utilisation rate per month would be 50 hours in peacetime and 100 hours in wartime. Connected with that was a desired reduction in maintenance man-hours per flight hour to about 16.4. The desired spotting factor was about 1.25, compared to 1.65 for the F-4J or 2.1 for the F-111B, where 1.0 was the A-4C.[16] A crew of two, as in an F-4, was planned. The aircraft would operate from even the smaller *Oriskany* class strike carriers with their C-11 catapults and the desired landing speed was 100 knots.

As was usual in such documents, VFAX was justified by expected dramatic improvements in technology. The computer revolution was certainly happening and it certainly did affect fighters like VFAX and its successor the F-14. VFAX would be a digital aircraft with a central tactical computer and the radar would be multi-mode because its waveform would be computer-generated, then amplified, as in the AWG-9 and -10 (the TDP listed the desired radar modes, but the reference to detection of low fliers implied a pulse-Doppler mode which would only be available to a radar with such a waveform) Specifying a central tactical computer implied that for air-to-air

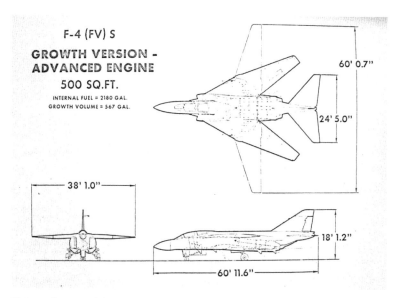

McDonnell's proposal for an advanced swing-wing F-4 with new engines, from a McDonnell vu-graph.

combat the fighter would enjoy track-while-scan (multi-target) capability.

Any hope for holding down weight while improving performance lay mainly in new engine technology. The TDP called for two turbofan engines (8500lbs/14,500lbs thrust) offering a combination of better fuel economy and lighter weight. They were to be the type the air force (with navy support) was then developing in a Lift-Cruise Engine programme.[17] This was certainly not the TF 30 later associated with VFAX. It was supposed to offer a major weight improvement through dramatic advances in compressor and fan design and in high-temperature turbine technology. The number of compressor blades would be roughly halved by increasing the loading per blade. New forced air film/convection cooling technology would boost operating temperature by about 400°F. In 1966, the navy was contrasting the large heavy TF30-P-6 engine of the F-111 with the much shorter JTF16-B it hoped to use. Although the newer engine weighed only about half as much (2250lbs vs 4070lbs) it was expected to produce more thrust (11,500lbs/21,500lbs vs 10,750lbs/18,500lbs) with the same air flow (235lbs/seconds) but a much higher pressure ratio (25 vs 17.8). Higher efficiency would come partly by much higher temperature: 2400°F at the turbine inlet vs 2100°F.

Before the TDP was issued, BuWeps did an in-house feasibility study comparable to the old ADR efforts; the TDP included a representative VFAX design. It had a multi-mission radar (MMR) with a 32in dish, the dish diameter making it possible to limit fuselage cross-section. That and a tandem crew arrangement offered a low-drag lightweight configuration. The aircraft would sustain Mach 2.2 at 36,000ft and Mach 0.85 or more at sea level. Service life would be 6000 hours. This sketch design showed a wing which extended at 20° sweep for cruise (span 53–55ft) and swept back at 70° for supersonic flight, with an area of 350–400ft². It weighed 28,000lbs empty (13,000lbs of fuel).

By this time the North Vietnamese were beginning to attack US strike aircraft using their equivalent of the Sidewinder missile. The text of the TDP called for IR signature suppression (and countermeasures). The aircraft (crew and vitals) was also to be protected against ground fire, which by early 1966 was a major problem.

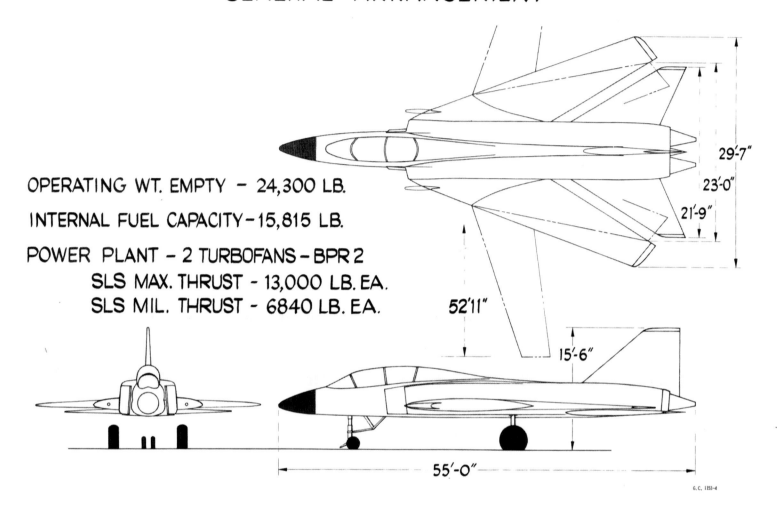

BOEING MODEL 959-001
GENERAL ARRANGEMENT

OPERATING WT. EMPTY – 24,300 LB.

INTERNAL FUEL CAPACITY – 15,815 LB.

POWER PLANT – 2 TURBOFANS – BPR 2
SLS MAX. THRUST – 13,000 LB. EA.
SLS MIL. THRUST – 6840 LB. EA.

29'-7"

23'-0"

21'-9"

52'11"

15'-6"

55'-0"

G.C. 1153-4

Boeing's VFAX design.

The multiple missions were those the F-4 was already fulfilling: CAP, point interception (from the deck), close air support, interdiction and long-range strike. VFAX had to carry enough internal fuel for at least 300nm in clean configuration; this was the old 300nm combat radius. The aircraft had to be suitable for buddy refuelling.

McNamara had introduced a single-package form of procurement in which a concept was formulated and then a contract was defined (CF/CD): a single contractor was responsible for all aspects of an aircraft project, including avionics. A schedule attached to the outline requirements showed airframe studies alongside avionics and propulsion. Airframe studies were to extend from the beginning of FY66 (June 1965) through the third quarter of FY67, leading to contract definition in FY68 and design in FY69, with flight testing expected in FY71. The aircraft would enter service about January 1972. In the paper version of reality, the avionics would be built in breadboard form in FY68–69, production of a prototype beginning about January 1970. Full-scale engine development would extend from late FY67 (about May) through about January 1970.

Evaluation of alternatives would be based partly on how they played in a five-day task force attack model described in a January 1965 BuWeps report. It considered several levels of enemy attack on the task force and measured the ability of the force to strike while devoting sufficient fighters to defence. Overall, fighter and attack aircraft would use 65 per cent of flight deck space, a figure aligned to the planned 1972 air group. Each attack carrier would have one squadron of F-111Bs (twelve aircraft), with additional defence provided either by F-4Js or by VFAX. The model made it possible to play off levels of strike capability against levels of fighter defence within a fixed total of fighter and attack aircraft. Ultimately it estimated the level of task force capacity to destroy particular targets and thus took into account aircraft system accuracy and weapon lethality.

At the outset the task force would try to gain air supremacy by a combination of attacks on enemy aircraft and airfields and direct fleet air defence (the model did not take into account the restrictions on such attacks at source which had been imposed on the US fleet off Vietnam). Given how effective fighter defence of the fleet was, at some

GENERAL ARRANGEMENT
MODEL 199-302

DATA

1. **TOGW** .... 46,100 LB.
2. **ENGINES** .... (2) GEI/10S092B
3. **TOTAL** THRUST .... 39,800 LB.
4. **WING** AREA .... 400 SQ. FT.
5. **WING** LOADING(COMBAT) ...... 99 LB/SQ.FT.
6. **FUEL** (INTERNAL) .... 15,500 LB
7. **AVIONICS** (BLACK BOX) .... 1925 LB
8. **SPOTTING** 1.31

ARMAMENT

9. **GUN** (600 RD.) .... (1) M-61
10. **MISSILES** .... (4) AIM 7F.

34' 7"

57'5"

C1129 (18 JANUARY 1967)
MCDONNELL

CONFIDENTIAL/PROPRIETARY

McDonnell's VFAX (its Model 199-302) broadly resembled an F-4 with variable-sweep wings.

point fighters could be taken from that role and used instead for strikes. The model suggested that the desirable VFAX force was two to three squadrons (twenty-four to thirty-six aircraft). Representative threats were forty enemy bombers, 250 enemy fighters and forty or eighty enemy bombers with stand-off weapons. The five-day model was used to show that over a wide range of enemy threats, mixes containing VFAX were substantially more effective than those consisting of F-4Js and A-7 day bombers.

At this point the planned carrier complement (as listed in the SOR) was twelve F-111Bs and fifty-eight A-7Bs, but most navy analyses had F-4Js operating alongside the F-111s. The optimum listed in the SOR seems to have been one squadron of F-111Bs, two of VFAX (twenty-four aircraft) and thirty-four A-7Bs. A briefing slide showed relative costs and effectiveness in the face of a strong enemy defence. If the F-111B/A-7 air wing had a relative effectiveness of 1.0, a VFAX/A-7 air wing had an effectiveness of about 2 and an F-111B/VFAX/A-7 air wing 3.0. The VFAX/A-7 air wing would cost about as much as the F-111B/VFAX/A-7 air wing, in each case about 20 per cent more than the F-111B/A-7 air wing.

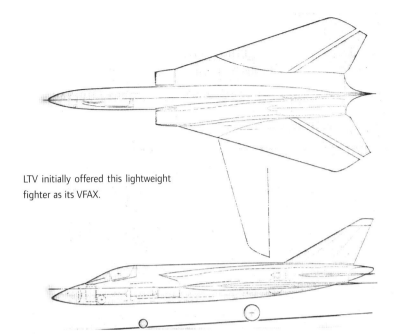

LTV initially offered this lightweight fighter as its VFAX.

The TDP, which was laid out in a large loose-leaf book, reflected a serious effort to make the VFAX the best possible multi-role fighter.[18] It is not obvious that it was worth the trouble. Nothing remotely like this effort had been needed to make the Phantom the best fighter in the world, with very useful flexibility. For the historian, the TDP is a wonderful summation of the state of the aircraft art in 1966 and its likely future. That suggests that the entire process was designed to appeal to the staff of the OSD, whose members were chosen for their analytical ability but not for their familiarity with current technology or with the basis for requirements. BuAer did much better with a lot less paper because its officers had an excellent intuitive feel for possibilities and trade-offs, based on professional experience. The hallmark of the McNamara administration was its deep distrust for such judgement.

In October 1966 Grumman and Hughes submitted a study of the feasibility of a Phoenix-Carrying VFAX under navy contract (it is impossible to say whether this originated as the companies' proposal).[19] This study was the true origin of the F-14, because it showed that something considerably smaller and more fighter-like could accommodate the key fleet air-defence system.

Four potential contractors (Grumman, McDonnell, Boeing and

VFAX STUDY

CAP TOGW: 44,664 LB

WT EMPTY: 26,695 LB

FUEL WT: 13,900 LB

MIL THRUST: 8950 LB ea

MAX THRUST: 16,000 LB ea

W/S: 118 PSF

T/W: 0.715

MAX X-SECT: 41 FT^2

FINENESS RATIO: 8.6:1

$C_{L\,MAX}$: 3.0

STRUCT WT: 33.7%

MISSION LD: 18.6%

PROPUL SYST: 11.6%

FUEL + FUEL SYST: 33.5%

97.3

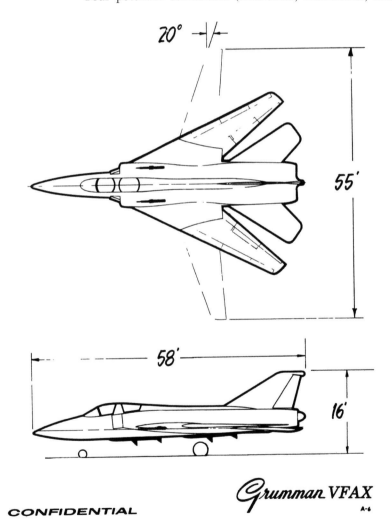

20°

55'

58'

16'

CONFIDENTIAL

Grumman VFAX

A-6

Grumman's initial VFAX was a Sparrow-armed fighter like the others. However, as the failure of the F-111B became more obvious, Grumman also offered a version armed with Phoenix. This is the Sparrow version; a NAVAIR evaluator has asked why the weights don't quite add up. Grumman guaranteed a maximum speed of at least Mach 2.2 (with the TF30 engine), acceleration from Mach 08 to Mach 1.8 at 35,000ft in no more than two minutes, a combat ceiling of 60,000ft and a cruise ceiling of 35,000ft. Manoeuvrability buffet-free at Mach 0.85 and 35,000ft was to be no less than 2.0G. These categories indicate the ones the navy cared about at the time. Other requirements included a ferry range of 3000nm.

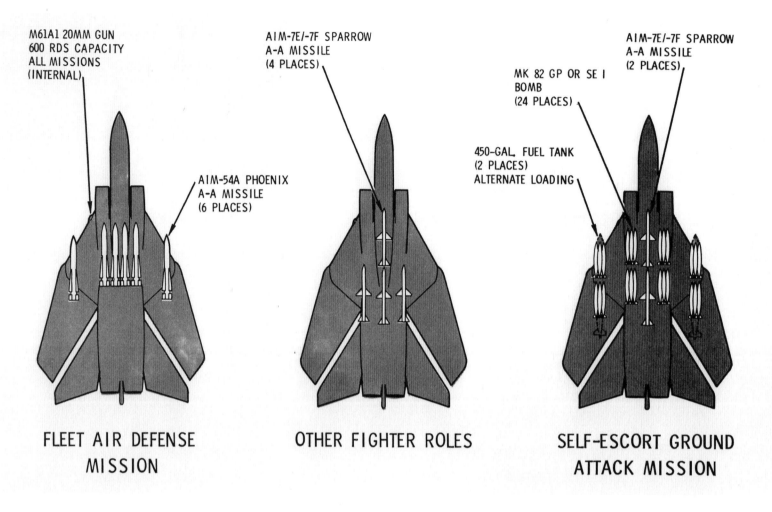

M61A1 20MM GUN
600 RDS CAPACITY
ALL MISSIONS
(INTERNAL)

AIM-54A PHOENIX
A-A MISSILE
(6 PLACES)

AIM-7EI-7F SPARROW
A-A MISSILE
(4 PLACES)

AIM-7EI-7F SPARROW
A-A MISSILE
(2 PLACES)

MK 82 GP OR SE I
BOMB
(24 PLACES)

450-GAL. FUEL TANK
(2 PLACES)
ALTERNATE LOADING

**FLEET AIR DEFENSE
MISSION**

OTHER FIGHTER ROLES

**SELF-ESCORT GROUND
ATTACK MISSION**

North American Columbus) submitted Improved VFAX Fighter Design Trade-Off studies in February 1967. Each was asked to show how fighter and attack capability could be traded off without abandoning the desired multi-purpose capability.

Once the VFAX programme documents had been completed, OSD asked that this planned fighter be compared with the air force FX to see whether a single programme might be set up. That was difficult because the FX had not yet been defined. OSD therefore asked that the air force present an FX concept and requirement by October 1966. That date kept slipping and there was apparently never a formal comparison – both services had learned from the TFX fiasco to avoid a forced joint programme. Meanwhile the air force was directed to continue engine development suited to both aircraft; the navy was responsible for the avionics. Of the two, the engine programme was better funded and threatened to outrun navy resources. OpNav decided that to keep VFAX alive it had to create a VFAX Task Group to recommend further policy.

PHANTOM UPGRADES

While initial VFAX studies were proceeding, BuWeps let a contract to McDonnell to explore major improvements to the best current fighter, its Phantom. These studies offered an alternative to the fresh VFAX designs and also an indication of what sort of improved performance NAVAIR could hope to achieve. In August 1966 McDonnell Douglas proposed a swing-wing version of the Phantom.

All the potential fighter builders realised that the F-111B would soon die, so they morphed their VFAX proposals into much heavier and more powerful fighters. LTV produced this armament comparison for its V-505.

In January 1967 McDonnell reported what it called the F-4X. Objectives were to improve both fleet air defence and air-to-surface capabilities. For fleet air defence the needs were increased CAP time without using up too much of the fuel needed for combat and perhaps a new weapon system. Air-to-surface requirements were better payload at a given radius, greater overall range and a better bombing system. Overall, carrier capability had to be improved and cost minimised.

For the airframe, McDonnell could offer a minimally revised F-4J+; an F-4(FV)L with increased wing area; a high-wing F-4(FV)H; and a swing-wing F-4(FV)S. In each case the design criteria were two-hour endurance on CAP and an approach speed of no more than 125 knots. Weapon system improvements could be an improved AWG-10 (track while scan, for simultaneous multiple shots), a modified version of the AWG-9 then planned for the F-111B (and adopted for the F-14), an improved Sparrow missile (AIM-7F); and a Phoenix missile (as on the F-111B). A more powerful J79-GE-10 engine could be adopted or else some advanced technology engine.

The basic AWG-10 was a single-target radar guiding the AIM-7F Sparrow. The most basic upgrade would be to add a track-while-scan computer, so that the system could track multiple targets. The next step up was a multishot AWG-10 with a new antenna (32in x 26in rather than the previous 32in dish). With that radar AWG-10 could

SPAN (WINGS SPREAD)	61 FT 9 IN.
SPAN (SPOTTING FOLD)	27 FT 6 IN.
OVERALL LENGTH	60 FT 0 IN.
INITIAL ENGINES	
DESIGNATION	TF30-P-12 (2)
S.L. STATIC THRUST	20,290 LB
ADVANCED ENGINES	
DESIGNATION	STF-297 (2)
S.L. STATIC THRUST	27,450 LB

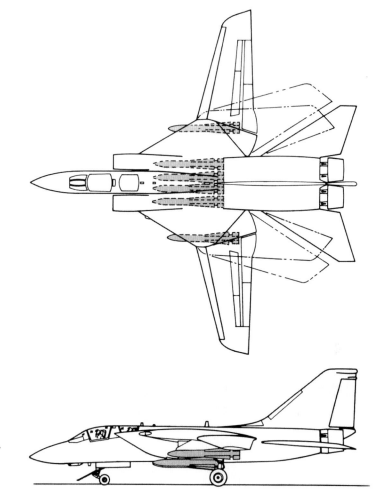

LTV's V-505, shown carrying Phoenix missiles.

be upgraded to multi-shot capability, guiding Phoenix as well as Sparrow missiles, but still short of the AWG-9 in the F-111B (and, as it happened, in the future F-14). Compared to AWG-10, AWG-9 had a 34in dish and triple the power (3kW vs 1kW), but it weighed 1692lbs compared to the 1107lbs of the original AWG-10 and 1408lbs for even the multi-shot AWG-10. A single-shot AWG-10 was expected to detect a nose-on target at 43.5nm (0.85 probability of detection) or at 53nm on the beam and 37.8nm tail-on. By way of comparison, at this time the comparable AWG-9 ranges were 111.3nm, 129nm and 88.5nm. Because its antenna was smaller in the vertical dimension, the multi-shot AWG-10 had somewhat lower gain and somewhat shorter range. All of the targets were $5m^2$ aircraft at 40,000ft at a closing rate of Mach 1.5.

F-4J+ was a minimum upgrade using a modified wing, an extendable nose strut for better catapult operation (and the new nose tow rather than a bridle for the catapult), a multi-shot AWG-10 radar and the advanced Sparrow. A fuel capacity of 2463 gallons compared to 1998 gallons in an F-4J. The F-4J and -4J+ could also carry 1340 gallons externally, which was how they achieved their CAP times of 2.7 hours and 3.17 hours, respectively. Without this fuel, CAP time on station was only 1.32 hours and 1.64 hours, respectively. Radius for a nuclear strike mission (one Mk 28, 740 gallons externally) was

387nm and 496nm, respectively, assuming a hi-lo-lo-hi profile (approach at altitude, then a dash on the deck, a lobbed attack, escape also on the deck and then cruise away at high altitude).

The new-wing version offered an increased fuel capacity (2535 gallons) with enough internal volume to add another 222 gallons. The new wing offered a better lift/drag ratio (10.4 rather than 10.25). It was in the same low position as the standard fixed wing, but had reduced area ($595ft^2$ vs $640ft^2$) and better high-lift devices (altered flap and flaperon area, leading edge slats and trailing edge blowing), which McDonnell saw as a better trade-off between carrier suitability, range and weight. The added fuel increased CAP time (without drop tanks) to 1.88 hours (3.94 hours with 1800 gallons of external fuel). Because this version could carry a larger drop tank (1200 gallons), nuclear attack radius increased to 658nm. The larger drop tanks featured in all the other versions.

The high-wing version offered a thinner wing (reduced by 0.7 per cent) and more internal volume for growth. Internal fuel capacity increased to 2570 gallons, with a potential growth volume of 275 gallons. In this version the landing gear had to be relocated to the fuselage and the track considerably narrowed. More fuel meant proportionately longer CAP endurance (1.97 hours without and four hours with drop tanks) and a longer nuclear range, 696nm.

McDonnell had been studying a swing-wing F-4 for some time, so its 1967 slides showed a version with increased wing area ($500ft^2$ vs

420ft²), trailing edge boundary layer control on the flaps and a larger tail (the enlarged horizontal tail for better low-speed trim, the enlarged vertical tail for improved directional stability). The wing was dry, so internal fuel volume was reduced to 2180 gallons, with a growth volume of 421 gallons. Because it made for much more efficient cruise, the swing-wing version offered slightly greater CAP endurance on considerably less fuel. Adding the drop tank, which was proportionately more of the total fuel than in the other versions, extended CAP endurance to five hours.

Another possibility was an advanced engine plus a swing wing. By this time the Spey version for the Royal Navy (F-4K) had been designed with a new inlet. The engine envisaged was a new GE-1 with much better fuel economy. With the same 2180 gallons of internal fuel as the first swing-wing version, this one could remain on CAP for a spectacular 3.09 hours without drop tanks and 6.82 hours with, and its nuclear strike range was 942nm. With drop tanks, its ferry range was 3482nm, enough to get it across the Atlantic. This performance, incidentally, put the swing-wing F-4 in the same range category as the new F-111.

Where a standard F-4J needed 1 knot of wind over deck to be launched by a C-7 catapult, all the improved aircraft could do so with wind blowing the wrong way, the swing wings being most extreme: -28 knots for the swing-wing plus the advanced engine. Approach speed was reduced from 136 knots to 122 knots. The fixed-wing alternatives did not exceed the maximum speed of the F-4J (Mach 2.25), but the advanced swing-wing aircraft was expected to achieve Mach 2.51 (Mach 2.27 for the more basic swing wing, because it had a smaller less draggy wing). None of the improved versions much beat the acceleration achieved by the F-4J: from Mach 0.8 to Mach 1.8 at 36,089ft in 2.46 seconds (the advanced engine was best at 2.40 seconds, the increased wing area version worst at 3.04 seconds).

A handwritten note (by a NAVAIR officer) on the cover of the report supported the swing-wing alternative, with the improved systems then being installed in the F-4J. It would provide urgently-needed service experience showing the real advantages and disadvantages of the swing-wing configuration represented by the F-111B and the permissible VFAX design. It also offered maximum airframe improvement with minimum powerplant and system changes.

VFX: THE F-14 TOMCAT

Grumman was well aware that the F-111B programme was failing, so in October 1967 it submitted an unsolicited proposal for an alternative fighter using the engine (TF30) and the weapon system (AWG-9/Phoenix) of the F-111B. DCNO (Air) responded by asking the OpNav analysis division (Op-96) to begin a fighter study to determine the feasibility, advantages and disadvantages of the Grumman proposal, which was its Design 303. Other companies became aware of the Grumman proposal through press publicity and they offered their own designs; they were told that they would be considered if submitted by 31 December 1967. Because they had already developed VFAX designs this was not difficult: they were McDonnell (Design 225), North American Columbus (NA 323) and LTV (V-505). All were considered by the Fighter Group originally formed to study the Grumman proposal; the new fighter was designated VFX. The Fighter Group conclusion (1 April 1968) was that VFX would be most effective and should be developed. By this time General Dynamics was also interested and it was included in the Contract Definition phase of

the project. The Secretary of Defense signed the Development Concept Paper (DCP), the first formal stage in developing a new system. It authorised release of formal Requests for Proposals from the five companies. All were asked to submit engineering development proposals with production options by 1 October 1968. The time scale gives some sense of the urgency of the programme, given the collapse of the long-running F-111B project. The programme moved very quickly. Grumman flew the first prototype on 20 December 1970.

The F-14 was the first US naval fighter to have a full computer-controlled combat system connected to the nodes of the NTDS fleet data system (on board ship and on board an E-2C Hawkeye) via data link (Link 4A). The link could vector the F-14 to a target or designate multiple targets. It could carry the F-14's target data back to an E-2C. The system could handle up to twenty-four targets at a time in track-while-scan mode and it could simultaneously engage a separate target with each of its six Phoenix missiles. Via the link it could receive data on (or report) up to eight targets simultaneously, which its central tactical system would integrate with its tactical picture. In addition to receiving target and vectoring information, the link carried own-ship altitude, speed, heading, fuel quantity, TACAN bearing, remaining liquid oxygen and remaining weapon status, all of which were needed for effective fighter control. On the flight deck the link carried inertial navigation alignment data as well as up to seven navigational waypoints. In the attack role, Link 4A could update waypoints while the F-14 was in the air. In effect the F-14 system was analogous to the roughly contemporary Aegis: it was a tactical (situational awareness) system grown out of a fire-control system. The system was derived from that developed for the F-111B.

By the time the F-14 was being developed, the navy well understood the Vietnam War lesson that visual identification would often be required before any weapon could be fired. The F-14A therefore had a television sight unit in its nose, alongside the pod carrying an IR sensor. In its original form it was credited with the ability to identify

Grumman won the competition for the F-111B follow-on with its design. There was no fly-off; all the competing designs were considered candidates for the eventual F-14 production fighter. All were externally similar. This F-14 shows its load of six Phoenix long-range air-to-air missiles. The fighter was underpowered, so it rarely carried more than four of them.

a MiG-21 at 6nm. Production of a television camera sight (TCS) began in 1981 and by 1988 all F-14s had it. When F-14s engaged Libyan MiG-23s in January 1989, TCS showed that they were carrying missiles (which normally they did not) and therefore could be considered to have hostile intent; the F-14s shot them down.

As part of the Outer Air Battle project, the F-14 was digitised as the F-14D, which meant that in place of separate digital and analog elements, it had all-digital radar, weapon system and air data computer connected with each other and with other elements such as a jammer by a data bus. That made it relatively easy to add further upgrades. Instead of the AWG-9, which combined a radar with a dedicated weapon system computer, the new version had a pair of central computers which, among other things, handled radar data. The change was indicated by the designation of the radar: APG-71, instead of being integral with a weapon system (AWG). Other new elements were a new data link (JTIDS: Link 16), an IRST and a new defensive jammer (ALQ-165). Further upgrades made before the first F-14Ds deployed included a fighter-to-fighter data link (as on the F/A-18), improved radar ECCM, GPS navigation and AMRAAM capability. This sort of modification would have been painful in the original analog system, because each new box would have needed its own connections to others. In a fully digital F-14D, the connections were made through the digital bus and software, much as a computer can be upgraded through plug-ins. Later adaptation to add GPS and to adapt the aircraft to drop GPS-guided JDAMS smart bombs were also relatively simple (GPS was also installed in the pre-digital F-14A and -14B). JDAMS capability was provided largely by a software modification, beginning with those on board the carrier *Theodore Roosevelt* in January 2003 (the weapon was first operationally used on 1 March 2003: an F-14 could carry four 2000lb JDAMs).[20]

As built, the F-14 had the same TF30 engine as the F-111B and hence was badly underpowered (particularly when not on afterburner). The navy bought the F-14 partly in the expectation that its engine would be replaced in the 68th aircraft, giving it not only the desired loiter capability but also a dogfighting capability entirely absent from the F-111B. Initial plans called for building sixty-seven F-14As with the TF30 engine, followed by F-14Bs with a new Pratt & Whitney engine then under development by the air force. That would have given not only more thrust but also better fuel economy. The next step would have been a new avionic suite giving good all-weather capability, so that the aircraft could fill the A-6 role without any major increase in complexity. That would have been the F-14C. It was soon dropped, perhaps because the 'tunnel' under the F-14 tended to suck bombs back up after they had been released. The F-14C designation was later applied to an aircraft powered by a projected Advanced Technology Engine (ATE) with a 51 per cent better thrust-to-weight ratio (either the General Electric F400 or the Pratt & Whitney F401). This was an enormous leap. The navy was compelled to cancel procurement of the ATE while continuing work on a new engine. Money was also a problem. Only later was it possible to re-engine F-14s with an adequate engine. Until then, F-14s were limited in acceleration and speed, noticeably so when they faced Libyan Foxbats (MiG-25s). Underpowering also showed in a necessarily reduced missile load: the F-14 was designed to carry six Phoenix missiles, but in service it often carried four, or else carried Sparrows instead. When F-14s fought Libyan aircraft over the Gulf of Sirte in 1981, they fired Sparrows, not Phoenix and they also used Sparrows during the 1991 war against Iraq.

The F-14 was considered effective, but it suffered from compressor stalls (a problem in the F-111, too). With engines well off the centre-line, a stall could send the aircraft into a fatal spin. As in the F-111, the problem was the interaction between the inlet and the engine itself. In a conventional turbojet, the afterburner is isolated from the inlet to the engine, because the engine itself takes up all the space between them. In a turbofan with its fan at the after end (as in the TF 30), some air bypasses the engine proper and goes into the afterburner via the fan blades outside the core engine. Hot air (with its higher pressure) from the afterburner can sometimes pass back into the inlet and then into the compressor at the front of the engine. Backflow would be caused if for any reason the flow of air into the front of the engine was disturbed and it in turn could cause the compressor to stall. The inlets of the F-111 had to be redesigned twice and even then the aircraft was not entirely satisfactory (one of the redesigns added considerable drag). It is not clear whether the F-14 suffered inlet problems or whether the engine itself was at fault. At the least the compressor problem limited the flight envelope of the F-14. Once there was money for a replacement engine, Pratt & Whitney suffered from bad feeling about the original TF30.

Through the 1970s and 1980s the navy tried to find an engine to replace the TF30. Two prototype F-14Bs had GE F401-GE-400 engines.[21] The first flew on 12 September 1973, but the second was not completed. The F-14C with F-401-P-414A engines was also stopped, but the engine was flown once (in March 1974) on board the single F-14B. Both upgraded Tomcats would have had improved avionics. At the time the favoured engine was apparently the F401. As indications of improved performance, with the F401 the F-14B climbed from 8000ft to 32,000ft in 200 seconds and from 8000ft to 40,000ft in 340 seconds. It took an F-14A 310 seconds to get to 32,000ft. With the new engine, the F-14B could accelerate from 225 knots to Mach 0.9 in 85 seconds; it took an F-14A 150 seconds to get from Mach 0.69 to Mach 0.9. There was also a significant improvement in level flight turning performance. All of this was without using an afterburner, in some cases in which an F-14A pilot would have to use his afterburner. F-14B afterburner performance was judged better than that of the F-14A.

Both engines were substantially smaller than the TF30. The F401 derived its improved performance through a higher compression ratio, variable-incidence compressor stators, a hotter turbine and a smaller, lighter afterburner, all made possible by using new materials and new means of assembly. Limited funds made it impossible to produce either engine during the 1970s, but in 1981 Grumman successfully tested an F-14A powered by the GE F101-DFE (Derivative Fighter Engine) derived from that in the F-16. Money finally became available due to the Reagan Administration naval revival. The first step was a modified F-14A (Plus), work on which began in 1984. It used GE F110-GE-400 engines. The first F-14A (Plus) fighters flew on 14 November 1987. This version was later redesignated F-14B. In all, thirty-eight F-14Bs were built as such and another forty-seven F-14As were rebuilt to -14B status (originally thirty-two, but Congress added money for fifteen more in 1992–3), for a total of eighty-five.

The longer-term objective was a fully digital F-14D with a satisfactory engine, the GE F110 (which was also chosen for the F-15E and for some F-16s). The first flew on 24 November 1987. The programme was cancelled in 1989 in favour of concentration on the less expensive F/A-18 as the Cold War wound down. It was revived in 1990, cancelled again in February 1991 and then partially restored in April 1991. The last of thirty-seven new-build F-14Ds was completed in

February 1995 and the last of eighteen F-14Ds converted from -14As was delivered in May 1995. As of April 1996, the active F-14 force comprised 199 F-14As, eighty F-14Bs and fifty F-14Ds. As of May 1995, the planned year 2000 force was 118 F-14As, eighty-two F-14Bs and fifty-one F-14Ds. Another 234 F-14As were to be placed in storage or scrapped. The US Navy retired the Phoenix missile in 2004; surviving aircraft were armed with Sparrow and with Sidewinder. The last F-14s were retired in 2006.

The F-14 was retired not because it was obsolete – digitising it had given it an enormous growth potential, which Grumman advertised quite effectively – but because it was too expensive to maintain and to operate in a post-Cold War world in which its impressive performance and its long-range weapon were no longer nearly as important. The key maintenance problem seems to have been the swing wing, which had been so important during its development. The titanium joint became a focus for corrosion, but it was also difficult to reach for repairs. The big engines which gave this heavy fighter excellent performance (in the B and D versions) drank far more fuel than the smaller engine of the lightweight F/A-18 Hornet.

An F-14 from VF-154 banks away from *Kitty Hawk*, 21 April 2002. By this time the aircraft was more often used as a bomber than as a long-range fighter; there were no longer big Soviet bombers to oppose. Note the two large drop tanks.

NAVAL PLANNING IN AN ERA OF LIMITED WAR

By 1965 the US focus was shifting towards limited war, which soon came to mean Vietnam. That year's Long Range Objectives report pointed out that it would take six attack carriers (CVA) to project power effectively. In addition five to six would be needed to gain air superiority (with two carrier air wings to sustain it). In an assault, the air-superiority carriers would also carry out deep strikes to isolate the objective area. Another three carrier air wings would be used to support an opposed landing. These figures were presumably for sustained operations. Under normal carrier overhaul schedules, five or six carriers would generally be available, carrying 375 combat aircraft (seventy-five per carrier on average). Each could sustain 100 sorties per day (ninety for a *Midway*), with a peak capability of 150 (135 for a *Midway*) for 48 hours. This effort could support four US divisions under relatively static conditions or interdict and support one ground division under heavy attack or during a rapid advance. At this time the planning factor for amphibious lift was one division in each ocean.

Note that to the US Navy at this time, at the beginning of engagement in Vietnam, limited war did not include major air threats to the carriers, only the air threat raised by an enemy over his own country. The one-division standard justified a minimum of six carriers in each ocean. In peacetime one of three would be forward-deployed, meaning two of six carriers in each ocean. At least those two would be needed for mutual support. At this time nine carriers were assigned to the Pacific and they were barely enough. Two had to be maintained off South East Asia and another for other contingencies. A planned presence in the Indian Ocean had to be deferred for lack of Pacific Fleet attack carriers. However, with the advent of the Polaris missile, the previous policy of buying an attack carrier each year had been abandoned, among other sacrifices.

For long-range planners, the great nightmare of Vietnam was that it was consuming nearly all defence resources, including those needed for research and development, while the Soviets kept up their own investment. Increasingly US R&D was focused on the needs of the Vietnam War. Meanwhile the Soviet fleet was growing more effective. Its threat was dramatised by the appearance of a Soviet fleet in the Mediterranean after the 1967 Middle East War.

Through the 1960s the Soviets deployed growing numbers of nuclear attack submarines; in 1968 one of them managed to trail the nuclear carrier *Enterprise* as she deployed across the Pacific. The only saving grace was that the submarines were so noisy that they could be detected and tracked at long range, for example by the fixed SOSUS (sound surveillance) system. The nightmare was that at some point the Soviets would manage to silence their submarines. Although obviously not an air-defence system, SOSUS and its success or failure had important implications for fleet air defence. As long as SOSUS was effective, it could vector limited numbers of long-range aircraft (mainly P-3 Orions) against submarines. Although it and the Orions could not be considered inexpensive, they were far less costly than the alternative, which would be some form of convoy protection for the fleet and for vital shipping. Since total navy funding was unlikely to increase in that event, Soviet silencing might well make a strong carrier strike fleet unaffordable. At the least, it might preclude modernisation to match increasing Soviet anti-carrier strike capabilities.

This possibility animated the last Long Range Objectives report (LRO-81 of August 1969). Without SOSUS, ships would have to be supported directly by large numbers of helicopters, many of them deploying sonars far from the noise of the surface ships. The report envisaged helicopter-carrying escort carriers (CVHE) and helicopter-carrying destroyers (DHK). The report envisaged a 1981 fleet including twelve DHK, described as 12,000–14,000-ton 30-knot carriers accommodating twelve advanced ASW helicopters. Fifteen slower CVHE would carry similar helicopters to support amphibious assaults, underway replenishment groups and military convoys. Each DHK or CVHE would replace two or three destroyers, based on its capacity to maintain two helicopters in screen stations. They would not be simple substitutes, because the destroyers would act as a secondary forward screen, as pouncers. They would also cover rear sectors using passive towed arrays to detect submarines overtaking a force at high speed.

It was probably crucial that the study was led by Rear Admiral Elmo Zumwalt, Jr, a surface officer rather than an aviator. Later in his career he made it clear that he felt that too much was being spent on carriers and too little on the surface fleet. He was much impressed with the appearance of Soviet warships in the Mediterranean armed with anti-ship missiles and probably considerably understated the degree of ocean surveillance needed to make those weapons effective.[22] It seemed that the Soviets were managing to deploy real seapower without investing in carriers and their strike aircraft. Thus the LRO-81 report called for over-the-horizon missiles to arm all strike forces and submarines as well as most destroyers and patrol ships, but it did not address the critical ocean surveillance issue.

The critical judgement was that existing anti-air warfare capability was essentially sound – the crises which had led to the expensive carrier-based fighter missile systems had been, it seemed, overrated. The study envisaged continued evolution away from a fighter-heavy carrier air wing, but it still had to take Vietnam War experience into account. There would be no fighters intended primarily for fleet air defence. Very high performance all-weather fighters (Phantoms) would account for 20–30 per cent of carrier aircraft, backed by high-performance but low-cost fighter-bombers (45–55 per cent). They could be limited to minimal avionics, because their smart weapons would do much of the work. The report called these aircraft VFA, probably because they would have inherent day fighter (VF) capability. The remaining 20–30 per cent of offensive carrier aircraft would be high-performance all-weather bombers, presumably Intruders.

LRO-81 mattered because its author became CNO in 1972, after a term as commander of naval forces in Vietnam. Money was, if anything, even tighter than before. In LRO-81 the DHKs were intended partly to replace ASW carriers (CVS), which were wearing out. Now that the CVS were actually worn out, Zumwalt had to find a way of maintaining the long-range ASW capability they had provided. His solution was to change the attack carriers (CVA) into general-purpose carriers (CV), the ASW aircraft being integrated into their air wings. They were also given ASW command and control facilities.

This change had consequences for fleet air defence. At the very least, carrier flying schedules were complicated by the presence of fixed-wing ASW aircraft (S-3 Vikings not long after the change) and ASW helicopters. Within the available space, something had to be eliminated, meaning either strike aircraft or fighters or both. No matter how it was modified, the S-3 could not contribute directly to detecting or destroying incoming enemy aircraft, although it could be modified to attack enemy surface ships and it eventually served as a communications relay.

As for the special helicopter ships, Zumwalt wanted to build twelve Sea Control Ships (SCS), which could operate helicopters and VTOL aircraft. The helicopter assault ship *Guam* operated as an experimental Sea Control Ship, conduction anti-submarine operations. Given Zumwalt's hostility towards the large carriers, it was generally believed that the SCS programme would be the beginning of an attempt to do away with strike carriers altogether. At the least, it encouraged those who found the high cost of carriers unaffordable to imagine a new world in which naval aircraft could operate in smaller numbers from much less expensive ships.

In Zumwalt's view, anti-ship missiles had doomed all large expensive warships, including large-deck carriers. There is little or no evidence that he understood that in the absence of reconnaissance aircraft, anti-ship missiles were not particularly effective, hence that some sort of high-performance carrier aircraft were needed to support strikes. Nor does he appear to have realised how uneconomical it was to put the striking power of the fleet into surface ships of limited capacity.

Before entering office, Zumwalt was promised by President Nixon that he could pay for badly-needed fleet modernisation by scrapping the mass of older ships which were expensive to operate and to maintain. For example, gas turbines would be far less expensive than steam plants. Zumwalt therefore planned a large fleet of low-end surface combatants (*Perry* class frigates and missile hydrofoils). He found that the money saved by mass scrapping simply evaporated. In order to dramatise the problem, he took to saying publicly that his simulations showed that the US fleet had less than a 50 per cent chance of surviving against the modernised Soviet threat – which meant a combination of surface ships armed with anti-ship missiles and submarines armed mainly with torpedoes. Whether or not that was anything more than a ploy, Zumwalt's public stance had unfortunate results for the Defense Department view of what the fleet could or should do in wartime.

Zumwalt was well aware of the limitations of existing fleet air-defence systems and he seems to have doubted that they could be overcome. The proposed affordable alternative of jamming and decoying had recently foundered on the reality that too little was known about the detailed character of Soviet missile guidance systems; without that knowledge effective jamming would be difficult or impossible. As CNO, Zumwalt took the position that the only effective counter to such weapons was to develop the ability to sink the Soviet surface shooters before they could attack. At the least, the US Navy had to be so numerous that however the Soviets began the war they could not end it in a single battle. The Admiral's pessimistic calculation may have been based on little more than a comparison of the number of forward-deployed US warships with the number of missiles in the deployed Soviet fleet. The question of how the Soviets would manage to target their missiles did not figure in the calculation – why would they deploy missiles they could not usefully deploy?

For Zumwalt it was pointless to keep building the big carriers; for that matter the *Spruance* class destroyers, whose contract he had signed on entering office, were far too expensive. If large size did not make for survivability, the only way to create survivable seapower was much larger numbers – which seemed to be the Soviets' solution. To gain the numbers, in his view, ships had to become much less expensive. Hence his signature ship programmes, the small carrier, the *Perry* class frigate and the missile hydrofoil to dominate narrow waters. In this vision, the carriers and their long-range strike aircraft were more a continuing burden than a major asset, particularly if their striking power was important only in wars like Vietnam. Surely they were unlikely to recur. The appropriate target was the Soviet fleet and its growing surface component.

Zumwalt was therefore interested in what would now be called disruptive technologies, the first of which was the anti-ship missile. When he entered office, NAVAIR was developing the air-launched Tomahawk, and he ordered it adapted to surface ships and then to submarines. He created an office to find and develop the technologies he hoped would make it possible to build his much more numerous and much less expensive fleet, headed by Rear Admiral Tom Davies. Davies naturally became interested in VTOL fighters, ideally with the sort of performance otherwise associated with large-deck carrier jets (he also sponsored an alternative to the Aegis system based on the Phoenix missile and the AWG-9 radar/control system). Making Davies' office rather than NAVAIR responsible for the projected VTOL fighter may have been seen as a way of preventing what Zumwalt saw as the hidebound naval air establishment from scuppering his technological revolution. It may also have led Davies to bet on more radical technology than he should have.

Davies asked the major aerospace companies to propose high-performance VTOL fighters. The desire for performance ruled out the technology already employed by the forerunners of the British Harrier. Zumwalt's successor, Admiral James Holloway III, was an experienced naval aviator. What he took from Zumwalt was the sense that the carriers were too vulnerable. Naval aviation should be spread though much more of the fleet. That kept Davies' programme alive.

AIR WAR OVER VIETNAM

The US Navy entered the Vietnam War just as its futuristic NTDS system and its new F4H fighter seemed to mature. As in Korea, naval aircraft attacked ground targets, including strategic ones, which were defended by the current crop of Soviet interceptors. A new feature was large numbers of anti-aircraft missiles. To a greater extent than in Korea, US air attackers were restricted in what they could attack; on the other hand, there was no North Vietnamese fighter sanctuary in China, as there had been for the North Koreans and their Russian and Chinese allies during the Korean War. The US government might decide not to attack North Vietnamese airfields, but the North Vietnamese were always painfully aware that restrictions could be lifted as desired.

With attack-at-source denied, US naval aircraft found themselves fighting North Vietnamese MiG-17s and MiG-21s. As in Korea, these were small, manoeuvrable aircraft exploiting close ground control to direct them at their aerial targets. All of the US naval aircraft were larger because they had all been designed to fight at greater ranges. The heavy Phantom was poorly adapted to dogfighting and tactics had to be devised to make maximum use of its strengths, such as its high speed. In a sense, the fight between Phantoms and their North Vietnamese enemies might be likened to the contest between relatively heavy US naval fighters and Zeroes during the Second World War. Crusaders, which had been designed for air-superiority missions, were seen as more effective MiG-killers, at least initially. Overall, the early dogfighting experience led the US Navy to rethink its fighter tactics and to concentrate on energy-manoeuvrability as a criterion, rather than on previous standards such as the number of Gs an aircraft could pull under particular circumstances (as in the VFAX requirements documents).

Of the two US naval fighters, the Phantom had no guns at all, because it had been conceived as a fleet air-defence fighter to engage huge Soviet bombers with missiles; it was not at all clear that guns would have been effective against such a target. The missiles in turn had been designed to destroy relatively docile targets. Initially they gained a very poor reputation because they achieved very little. Worse, they had been designed to engage aircraft beyond visual range – it was vital to destroy a missile-carrying bomber as far from the carrier as possible. That was perfectly acceptable in fleet air defence, when most aircraft a fighter encountered were hostile and when a controlling CIC could indicate target identity. Over Vietnam most aircraft were friendly, so errors would most likely cause the destruction of friendly aircraft. After some embarrassments, rules were introduced in which fighters had to identify their targets visually – generally by coming up alongside – before falling back (to minimum effective missile range) and firing. Few North Vietnamese fighters co-operated and the fleet gained the unfortunate feeling that missiles were worthless. Air force missile fighters fared even worse, as their principal weapon (Hughes' Falcon) required even more time to be set up.

In 1967 General Dynamics (GD), which was still working on the F-111B, summarised lessons learned in the air war over Vietnam.[23] It concentrated on the air force, but the lessons applied to the navy (the vu-graphs of the lecture were in the VFAX file). North Vietnamese fighters were ground-controlled, as had been the MiG-15s in Korea. Yet, according to General Dynamics, such vectoring was a surprise. It brought MiGs into position to attack from below and behind and it also allowed them to concentrate on their strike aircraft targets while avoiding escorts.

North Vietnamese fighters engaged about 0.5 per cent of US missions into North Vietnam. MiGs generally tried to attack the bombers and to evade escorting US fighters. Thus 59 per cent of the engagements were against US aircraft on air-to-ground missions. MiGs initiated 72 per cent of the engagements and 91 per cent of the US aircraft involved were F-105s – which amounted to only 27 per cent of the attack force. Conversely, US aircraft initiated 91 per cent of engagements with escorting fighters. Of these engagements, 80 per cent of the US aircraft were F-4Cs, although they amounted to only 16 per cent of the CAP/escort force.

In air battles between 1 January and 31 May 1967, the outcome in defensive engagements was even: six MiGs for six US aircraft. These amounted to 54 per cent of engagements. The other 46 per cent were offensive, US fighters seeking out MiGs. These engagements cost three US fighters – and forty-six MiGs. This was despite the supposed advantages of the MiGs, such as small size and agility and it was well before the US Air Force began special air-combat training.[24] Attacking aircraft could have an enormous advantage. Most engagements were initiated at low altitude, with 73 per cent below 8000ft.

The environment was controlled by the North Vietnamese, their fighters controlled from the ground. The MiGs generally fought near Hanoi, near their bases and far from US bases. Fighter controllers were able to coach them into tail attacks and the small MiGs often were not detected until they were ready to fire. US aircraft generally got onto a MiG's tail when the MiG was occupied chasing another US aircraft. Both sides generally fired from within 4000ft. In the US case that could be explained by rules of engagement, but in the North Vietnamese case it was a free tactical choice. Both guns and missiles could be frustrated by target manoeuvres. Most engagements lasted less than five minutes and up to 6Gs were often pulled offensively and defensively.

Pilots wanted better air-to-air capability in terms of manoeuvrability, ordnance and ancillary equipment. They wanted better manoeuvrability at low altitude and air speed; five-minute combat capability; and in-flight refuelling so that they could afford to expend fuel in combat. They wanted a larger missile launch envelope, with increased azimuth and reduced minimum range; the ability to launch and track at high G; low altitude and rear launch capability (to hit an aircraft closing in from behind); and minimum drag so that missiles did not interfere with dogfighting. They wanted multiple cannon (the air force was providing just one gun in the F-4E), extended gun range, an increased rate of fire and greater impact energy (i.e. greater lethality per hit). GD saw a great need for an all-aspect missile and for a shorter (minimum) range IR missile.

Of the weapons the MiGs fired, 96 per cent were fired from the 5 to 7 o'clock position and 91 per cent were fired from 4000 yds or closer. MiGs launched missiles 41 per cent of the time and used cannon 59 per cent of the time. They made 17 per cent hits. Cannon did much better than missiles: 26 per cent hits vs 5 per cent for missiles. As far as it was known, MiGs generally held cannon fire until they were within 1000ft of their targets (but that was only four instances). If they were firing only missiles, they typically fired from 24,000ft (4nm).

Given the rules of engagement, better detection and identification were valued. On average, target aircraft were identified at a range of 1.3nm (about 2600 yds). Of the MiGs sighted, 54 per cent were in the 5–7 o'clock sector and 83 per cent were not seen until they were close enough to be identified as MiGs. Cockpits should be redesigned to give better visibility to the rear (5 to 7 o'clock). Since pilots were not permitted to fire until they could visually identify their targets, they wanted a zoom lens for this purpose (the navy bought zoom-lens television cameras after the war). Air-to-air radar coverage should be extended to all altitudes and azimuths, which really meant better low-flier performance.

Because dogfights were so sudden and violent, pilots wanted heads-up displays with a lead-computing optical sight for gunnery and minimum switching necessary to change to combat mode. Fighters flying in groups needed two radios rather than one, so that they could communicate with the strike force and also within the formation. Not surprisingly, pilots wanted better electronic countermeasures to deal with surface-to-air missiles.

The ultimate conclusion was simple. The US fighters had to gain the initiative. They had to have their own means of vectoring, based on long-range detection and tracking of all air activity anywhere near North Vietnam. Given sufficiently long-range detection, the US fighters could be directed to attack the North Vietnamese before they reached the US bombers. That might be impossible deep in enemy territory, but North Vietnam was a narrow country bordered by the sea. In 1967 General Dynamics offered a solution in the form of F-111Bs using their sophisticated radar to control US fighters.

In fact the United States enjoyed an effective sanctuary off North Vietnam. To some extent ships in the Tonkin Gulf could detect and track MiGs preparing to intercept US strikes. So could AEW aircraft based in South Vietnam, their radars looking down into North Vietnam. During the Vietnam War, both the US Navy and the US Air Force learned to provide air striking forces with the desired cover, the best-known effort arising out of the PIRAZ project.

PIRAZ

When the United States entered the Vietnam War, fleet air defence must not have seemed very essential. The North Vietnamese lacked any strike aircraft capable of reaching the carriers in the Tonkin Gulf. There were periodic scares due to reports that the North Vietnamese had surface-launched anti-ship missiles, but none materialised. On a few occasions North Vietnamese MiGs bombed US ships offshore, but in these cases carrier air defence was not involved. Thus at the outset it must have seemed that the massive investment in NTDS was irrelevant. That proved not to be the case.

The war revealed a need for several forms of air control growing out of its limited character. IFF had always been a major concern, generally in the sense of allowing an air control centre to concentrate on the proper air targets. There was no attempt to devise any form of air-to-air IFF; aircraft carried transponders which enabled them to identify themselves to surface radars. The essential airborne IFF function would be carried out by control centres watching all parties on their radars. Aircraft over enemy territory beyond the horizon of surface radars (and

An F-14 from VF-103 lands on *George Washington*, 2 September 2002.

controllers) would fend for themselves. In the Second World War, air combat was mostly in daylight and identification was usually visual. In Korea, where high speeds might make visual identification difficult, the combat zone was small enough that it was largely covered by controlling radars. The number of aircraft was small enough that controllers could keep reasonable track of who was who.

North Vietnam seems to have been a far more difficult place. Because nearly all the aircraft in the sky were American, random identification errors would fall mainly on US aircraft. In this limited war, cases of US aircraft shot down by other US aircraft would have disproportionately bad consequences at home. This reality explains why long-range air-to-air missiles performed so poorly in Vietnam. After some early blue-on-blue embarrassments, it became obvious that no long-range attack could be approved unless the attacker was personally sure of target identification. The IFF problem made guns the preferred air-to-air weapons, because they could be used at the very short ranges at which targets were certain to be identified and also because they could be used (again at very short ranges) by violently manoeuvring fighters. The question ever since has been whether the Vietnam experience of air-to-air combat remains meaningful.

The IFF issue extended beyond the usual air-to-air combat. Airliners regularly flew over the Tonkin Gulf en route between major Asian capitals. Clearly such aircraft were not to be shot down, but they did not announce their identities via the US IFF system. It was entirely possible for a North Vietnamese plane to use a standard airline route to arrive over the carriers in the Tonkin Gulf. Raw radar video certainly did not make it obvious which was which.

Moreover, as the fleet moved north to launch strikes against North Vietnam, it moved closer to possible air attack. The fleet required sufficiently early warning that it could react effectively to any attack, without having to maintain large numbers of interceptors on station (hence not contributing to the war against the North Vietnamese). Given that most of the aircraft over the Gulf of Tonkin at any one time were friendly, it became vital to disentangle the air picture. To a considerable extent, this issue was the same as that of the non-target airliner.

US government policy dictated strict limits on air operations. For example, it was considered essential that China not be brought into the war. That translated into keep-out zones for US aircraft. Aircraft navigational capabilities were limited, whereas a ship offshore, tracking US aircraft, could certainly keep them out of such zones.

The solution was to maintain an air picture good enough that a ship could sort out hostile aircraft. This was a classic radar picket role.

After mulling the problem from April 1966 on, on 16 July 1966 Pacific Fleet set up a Positive Identification Radar Advisory Zone (PIRAZ) operation in the Tonkin Gulf, centred on a picket ship with the call sign Red Crown (by which the operation was often known). PIRAZ was also a geographical reference point (indicated by a radar buoy) in the Tonkin Gulf. From 7 November all US aircraft operating over the Gulf were subject to PIRAZ procedures, the ship defining a zone in which aircraft would be positively identified and, to an extent, controlled ('radar advisory zone'). Given the experience of pickets off Okinawa, the picket had to have adequate anti-aircraft armament, which meant surface-to-air missiles.

Each of the three Task Force 77 carriers flew air strikes separately, each passing over the PIRAZ ship. The ship identified each aircraft in the strike, assigned it a track number and tracked it out to the target and back. That in itself overcame the possibility that, like the Japanese in 1945, the North Vietnamese would follow a returning formation back to its carrier. Once a questionable contact had been identified, the ship could vector a carrier-based fighter to examine it visually and either to engage it or to leave engagement to the ship's missiles. Too, because she was tracking each aircraft separately, the PIRAZ ship was also aware of the position at which it might have ditched; she could vector rescue helicopters as necessary.

Previous practice had often been to station a ship between a carrier and a shore target to detect any enemy aircraft trying to follow the strike home, a role called Tomcat. When heavy air attacks against North Vietnam began in the autumn of 1965, a destroyer was typically stationed in the Gulf. As might have been imagined, her CIC was quickly saturated. The new kind of operation required much more than checking to see whether the right aircraft were going home. In effect NTDS had been built for just this purpose, as it alone offered the capacity to disentangle really complicated air situations. Although at the outset NTDS was not made a precondition for PIRAZ assignment, non-NTDS ships occupied the PIRAZ station for only 16 days, all in July 1966. After that PIRAZ was always an NTDS ship.

That was initially a problem, since there were only two NTDS ships in the 7th Fleet, the cruiser *Chicago* and the missile 'frigate' (large destroyer, DLG) *King*. *Chicago* became the first PIRAZ ship. NTDS crews learned that they could keep track of friendly traffic largely by using pre-filed flight plans and IFF beaconry. Given its complete air picture, the PIRAZ ship was naturally assigned control of the CAP (two to five sections) between the targets in North Vietnam and the fleet. PIRAZ missions naturally included the earlier mission of de-lousing returning strikes, control of search and rescue and arrangements for tanking for returning strikes. Reviewing an article on PIRAZ submitted to the official *Combat Readiness* magazine, a reviewer in OpNav (Op-353F), Commander P K Collins, pointed out that 'for the first time the Cruiser-Destroyer force is actively contributing to Air Warfare as well as performing their classical Anti-Air Warfare role. The PIRAZ flight-following concept and services that can be provided to aircraft of all Services over the Tonkin Gulf and the target area, in effect enable the PIRAZ ship to provide the interface between sea strike forces and land targets.'

Air-search radar on a ship in the Gulf of Tonkin would see deep into North Vietnam. For example, it could track North Vietnamese fighters trying to intercept American bombers. Because NTDS had been conceived for fighter control, the NTDS system could vector US fighters to deal with the North Vietnamese. The first success came on 9 October 1966, when *King* vectored an F-8E from *Oriskany* to shoot

F-14s move into position to launch from *Enterprise*, 9 November 2001. As the carrier's air wing was then constituted, the F/A-18s on the left were the ship's light attack bombers (the F-14s were in effect medium bombers) and could also function as short-range fighters. This was the ship's last deployment with the F-14. Note that the wings of the foremost aircraft are in high-speed (fully swept) position. She would be launched with the wings spread further out for maximum low-speed lift.

down a MiG-21, the first such aircraft shot down by a US Navy fighter. One enlisted air controller aboard *Chicago*, Senior Chief Radarman Larry B Novell, was credited with twelve 'kills' he had arranged in this way. He received a DSM.

The PIRAZ ships had missiles of their own. *Long Beach* shot down two MiGs with her Talos missiles while on radar picket duty in the Gulf. These successes came despite a reluctance to risk compromising missile-system technology by firing weapons over North Vietnam. There was also a real fear that the tactical picture used by the missile shooters was unreliable; they might well shoot down US aircraft, particularly if most aircraft in the air at any one time were friendly. At least part of the problem was poor training, making for poor communication both within ships and between ships.

By 1972 the combination of long-range radar, computers and missiles was considered so reliable that *Chicago* had the primary role in protecting carrier aircraft mining Haiphong Harbor from North Vietnamese MiGs trying to stop them. This meant far more than weapon system reliability; it meant that the ship's tactical picture was considered reliable enough that she was most unlikely to shoot down any of the friendly aircraft laying the mines.

PIRAZ demonstrated an important weakness in NTDS. Operators entered radar target data manually. The operator then checked periodically to confirm that the target was proceeding as predicted, which might well not be the case. Early experience in Vietnam showed that an operator could handle no more than five tracks at a time, so a typical frigate (DLG) with four input consoles was limited to twenty tracks. That was far below the computer's capacity of 256. The ultimate solution was automatic radar detection, which Moore's Law ultimately made quite practicable; the Royal Australian Navy installed the first US Radar Video Processor (RVP) in 1975. A decade earlier, the SPS-48 radar was barely demonstrating this sort of capability, at a very high cost in dollars and maintenance.

PIRAZ itself made it obvious that more ships needed NTDS installations, the most obvious case being the large missile destroyers (DLGs) which had not received NTDS when they were completed. Installation was challenging, because they had so little spare internal space. Typically NTDS was fitted in a deckhouse, the presence of which shows that the ship had been converted to the system.

To simplify tracking friendly aircraft the interim solution was to install a Beacon Video Processor (BVP) based on their IFF signals. The BVP was requested in the summer of 1966 by PIRAZ commanders; it would allow their CIC teams to concentrate on unidentified aircraft and on aircraft emitting IFF distress mode signals. In October 1966 CNO made the BVP a high-priority project; all prospective PIRAZ ships deploying after July 1967 were to have it. Hughes delivered a prototype in 1967 and the engineering development version was very successfully tested on board *Belknap* in the Tonkin Gulf that autumn. It was service approved in November 1968. As an example of what PIRAZ offered, when the North Vietnamese sharply increased air activity in mid-April 1967, the PIRAZ ship found herself handling thirty-five MiG warnings (to US strike aircraft) each week.

It was still vital to reduce the load on the ship's NTDS system. With more NTDS ships in 7th Fleet, it was possible to double up on the PIRAZ station. As PIRAZ, *Long Beach* tested operation with a second NTDS ship designated Strike Support Ship (SSS). She would provide warning and control services and would control tankers joining US Navy aircraft. That would free the PIRAZ ship for surveillance and early warning and also for services required by the Air Force. Typically the SSS ship operated well to the north of the PIRAZ ship. The idea was tested from June through September 1967 and made permanent on 10 October. As a measure of the value of these ships, in November 1967 CinCPacFleet asked CNO to provide enough ships with BVP and expanded communications capacity to maintain four PIRAZ/SSS-capable ships in the Western Pacific at all times.

Through 1967 the potential offered by the PIRAZ ship came to be appreciated more and more and additional services were requested. For example, Seventh Air Force wanted the ship to take control of tankers over the Gulf. 7th Fleet had to refuse, because the ships' CICs were already heavily loaded. By February 1967 merely controlling air traffic over an increasingly congested Gulf was becoming a serious problem. The only way to increase capacity was to net the PIRAZ ship with the Air Force's own airborne control aircraft (Big Eye) via a voice circuit (Big Eye was not computerised). The Marines set up their own air control facility at Monkey Mountain, Danang, and on 12 July 1967 they joined the Tonkin Gulf Link 11 net.

The larger lesson of PIRAZ was that it was possible to create a single computer net covering the whole area of operations. Among other things, that would enormously cut IFF errors and perhaps make it possible to change the rules for air-to-air combat. The effect of the new net is not obvious because it was brought into operation not long before attacks on North Vietnam were suspended. A JCS team which visited Vietnam in 1967 realised the possibility. The three services' nets would be connected by the standard Link 11, because that was already used by the navy and the Marines. The crash element of the programme was creation of a buffer which translated the air force data into Link 11 form. However, the ships offshore were still limited by the capacity of their early NTDS systems, which could handle only ninety-six local and ninety-six remote (i.e. reported via data link) tracks. The PIRAZ experience was reflected in a redesign of NTDS to expand its capacity; the new Model 3 became operational in 7th Fleet on 12 November 1967. Within a year the PIRAZ load had nearly vanished, because offensive air operations against North Vietnam were stopped on 1 November 1968.

When the United States resumed large-scale air raids against the North in April 1972, the PIRAZ ships were far better prepared than they had been in 1967–8 and they proved quite successful. Their air-control role included warning of MiG attacks (PIRAZ was responsible for more than half the thirty-four air force MiG kills in April–September 1972), controlling CAP and joining escorts to strikes as required. PIRAZ also supported air force B-52 strikes.

When the Vietnam War wound down, PIRAZ was proof both of the value of computerised air defence and also of the weakness of existing computers. PIRAZ worked despite the limits of NTDS because so many of the tracks were friendly, hence predictable and automatically registered using a BVP. In 1979 the fleet in the Indian Ocean found that its systems were quickly saturated by large numbers of neutral air contacts, while potential enemies were present in larger numbers (particularly after Iran became hostile). It became obvious that something much more powerful than the existing NTDS was needed. That is why the NTDS successor, ACDS, was an integral part of the 1980s project to develop the capacity to fight the Outer Air Battle – against many more aircraft, with many more friendly aircraft possibly present.

OUTCOME: THE F/A-18 HORNET

From a fighter perspective, the immediate effect of the Vietnam experience, like that of Korea, was to emphasise the need for high-performance air-superiority fighters capable of dealing with the lightweight interceptors the Soviets were building and distributing among their client states. That applied particularly to the air force, in which advocates of minimalist air-superiority fighters (by no means a dominant faction) argued forcibly.[25] The navy, which still saw the importance of fleet air defence, was less convinced. In effect the air force had drawn the conclusion the navy had after the Korean War, when the navy had bought the stripped-down Crusader.

The F-111 and also the F-14 were both ordered on the basis of analysis of proposed designs. Prototypes were built after the designs had been selected; there was no fly-off, as in the past.[26] Both services

An F/A-18C of VFA-86 launching from *Enterprise*, 28 June 2004. The basic versions of the Hornet, F/A-18A and -18C, were nearly indistinguishable.

argued in the early 1970s that it was time to go back to prototyping to test really radical ideas for future aircraft.[27] Air force projects included a full-scale test of the stealthy airframe which had been tested statically on radar ranges and also a competitive test of the lightweight fighter so strongly advocated within its fighter community. By this time it was obvious that the F-14 would be extremely expensive, as would be the parallel air force F-15 fighter, the outcome of that service's F-X programme. However, the lightweight fighter prototypes were initially explained as tests of relevant technology rather than as production prototypes. That may have been OSD's attempt to evade expected service hostility, even from the air force.

At this time both services wanted new fighters. The air force was seeking an Air Combat Fighter based on its lightweight prototype to supplement its expensive F-15s.[28] It envisaged a high-low mix of F-15s and the new lightweight fighter. It envisaged an aircraft optimised for dogfighting, which would have a significant advantage over threat fighters fielded in 1980–90. Adoption of a low-end (in cost) fighter might be the only way to maintain the overall size of the air force fighter force, now that Vietnam-era F-4 Phantoms had to be replaced.

The navy had a similar numbers problem and its low-end project was variously designated VFX and VFAX.[29] It was intended to replace both the F-4 and the A-7 and to gain its air-to-ground capability by using the new precision weapons (smart bombs). The object was an impressive fighter costing half as much as an F-14. A VFAX Operational Requirement was issued on 28 August 1974.[30] When the chairman of the House Appropriations Committee asked whether the air force and navy requirements could be merged into a single F-4

replacement, he was told that this would be impossible. The whole point of the Air Combat Fighter project was to hold down size and cost and the aircraft would have to surrender significant performance to make it carrier-capable. The range and attack requirement would drive size and cost above what the air force considered acceptable. In the spring of 1974 it was expected that the air force competitors would be scaled up to compete for the navy contract. Prototyping was justified by the need to investigate advanced technology (presumably mainly fly-by-wire in a dogfighter) and new aerodynamic concepts (presumably now practicable thanks to improved computer design and evaluation techniques). Fly-by-wire made it possible to build an inherently unstable aircraft, which would be smaller than any conventional design, relying on a computer to maintain it in stable flight. Inherent instability would make the fighter unusually manoeuvrable, exactly what was wanted in a dogfighter. Given computer control, the pilot could use a sidestick, which he could manipulate effectively even at high Gs. A new lightweight engine would provide a much better thrust to weight ratio.

A lightweight fighter programme was started in FY72, the Fiscal Year beginning in June 1971. Two contractors were to be chosen to build prototypes of a low-cost lightweight visual fighter incorporating new design concepts. The same programme started work on a new advanced technology engine. A Request for Proposals was released on 6 January 1972 and a bidders' briefing held on 26 January. Five

An F/A-18C of VFA-86 lands on *Enterprise*, 29 June 2004.

companies submitted proposals on 18 February 1972 and evaluation was completed about 1 April – a very quick schedule for a fighter.[31] The emphasis was on aerodynamics rather than avionics, but fly-by-wire was a major advance and a new gunsight system was wanted to provide a snap-shoot gun firing solution. Stated design goals were a weight of about 20,000lbs, aerodynamics optimised for manoeuvrability at Mach 0.8 to Mach 1.6, sufficient internal fuel for a stated combat radius (with a 20-minute reserve), an emphasis on superior handling qualities and outstanding cockpit visibility. Contractors were told that sustained turn rate at Mach 1.2 at 30,000ft was important. The mission profile was an air superiority operation using a drop tank on the outward leg. The new designs were intended to eliminate the out-of-control and spin-susceptibility problems of previous high-performance fighters.

General Dynamics and Northrop were chosen for a fly-off. The first of the prototypes, General Dynamics' YF-16, was rolled out in December 1973 and flew on 2 February 1974. Northrop's YF-17 flew on 9 June 1974. Both aircraft incorporated fly-by-wire electronics and both had blended wing-body shapes for better manoeuvrability. They were fitted with the sort of austere range-only radar used in the dogfighters of the 1950s, but it was expected that production versions would have something more sophisticated. The YF-16 was powered by a single Pratt & Whitney F100 turbofan (as in the F-15), the YF-17 by two GE YJ101 turbofans. Of the two companies, Northrop had developed the F-5 Freedom Fighter, the only lightweight US fighter of its generation, for export to US allies.[32] The specification was deliberately vague, but it called for an aircraft weighing about 20,000lbs (half the weight of an F-15), armed with a cannon and two Sidewinders (the YF-16 was about the desired weight, the YF-17 being 4000lbs heavier). Small size was considered a virtue in itself, as enemy fighters were often initially picked up visually. At an early Congressional Hearing the F-16 was described as comparable to the MiG-21 which had caused so much trouble in Vietnam and which was the standard fighter of the Soviet Union and its clients. The design life goal for the prototypes was 4000 hours, the target for operational versions being twice that. It equated to about 15 years of service (10 years of peacetime at 30 hours per month, five years of wartime at 50 hours per month). This was typical of current fighters.[33] Because the prototypes

were optimised for air combat, the contractors could not rely on drop tanks, so they had to provide considerable internal fuel. The air force told Congress in March 1974 that the YF-16, the only prototype which had already flown, had demonstrated twice the combat radius of its F-4E (presumably without the usual drop tanks).

Plans initially called for 12-month tests and an award in April 1975, but earlier flight tests with the YF-16 made it possible to announce General Dynamics the winner of the contest on 13 January 1975.

In July 1974 Secretary of Defense James Schlesinger ordered the navy to follow the air force initiative, a McNamara-style edict forcing together the two programmes his own DDR&E had stated were incompatible. Probably the central problem was that the navy definition of combat radius included considerable more loiter time than the air force, so that an aircraft acceptable to the air force (as both lightweight prototypes had to be) would be too short-legged from a naval point of view. That is why, for all its important virtues, the navy's F/A-18 Hornet which emerged from the lightweight fighter programme was derided as the 'lawn dart', with no reach – and also with little CAP capability.

The new five-year defence plan included increased procurement funding for the new fighter in FY79. Both services would buy the new lightweight fighter as the low end of an affordable high-low mix.[34] Given the navy's need for a multi-function fighter, demanding that it revert to a visual-only dogfighter was unrealistic at best. Each lead company was teamed with a naval partner, just as General Dynamics had been teamed with Grumman for the F-111B. In this case LTV was teamed with General Dynamics and McDonnell Douglas with Northrop.

The navy was not entirely convinced that it wanted an ultra-austere fighter. It had tried such aircraft in the past and had generally had to add considerable avionics over their lifetime. Any new fighter would have to contribute to fleet air defence and it would also have to contribute to carrier air attack. The navy became interested in an enhanced version of the F-17, which had considerable advantages from a carrier compatibility viewpoint. Northrop and McDonnell Douglas, which had far more experience in naval fighter design, developed a new F-18 fighter based on the F-17. Under the agreement, McDonnell would be primarily responsible for the naval version; Northrop would market a land-based derivative.[35] Even in its enhanced version, the new fighter was far less expensive than an F-14 and also far less expensive to operate and to maintain, albeit much shorter-legged.

The FY76 budget submission, which was made without benefit of engineering studies, called for the navy to buy a 'minimum modification' of the aircraft the air force selected if attainable. However, in January 1975 the Secretary of Defense announced that the navy would select whichever lightweight fighter was most appropriate from its standpoint: he did not want another F-111 disaster.[36] It was enough that the navy would be buying a substantially simpler and less expensive fighter than the F-14. The chairmen of the relevant House and Senate committees made it clear that they would support whichever lightweight fighter the navy chose. Again, light weight was much more important than commonality. On 2 May 1975 the navy announced its choice: a derivative of Northrop's F-17 which was designated F-18 (because it had been heavily modified). As naval partner in the project, McDonnell received a sustaining engineering contract.

Not surprisingly, LTV protested that surely the navy had been intended to follow the air force selection. The navy argued successfully that this had never been intended. Moreover, the F-16 was funda-

An F/A-18C shows its impressive stores capacity: two Harpoons, four bombs, a FLIR pod below the port air intake and four Sidewinders. The same aircraft could carry two Sidewinders and two Sparrows for air-to-air combat. The drop tank is on the hardpoint opposite that for the FLIR.

mentally unsuitable. F-16 derivatives the navy might have considered suitable entailed considerable modifications, beyond what the budget language envisaged.[37] Among the advantages the navy claimed for the F-18 were a mechanical backup for its fly-by-wire control system; the F-16 had no such backup. If the system crashed for some reason, the aircraft, which was inherently unstable (to make it violently manoeuvrable), would be entirely uncontrollable. The system was quadruply redundant, but the four systems came together at five separate points, so that enemy fire could wipe the system out, as could an electrical failure. The navy pointed to special sources of such problems at sea: high humidity and salt spray causing corrosion and electrical problems, as well as the effect of the repeated stress of carrier take-off and landing and the effect of strong shipboard electromagnetic fields from, for example, radars. These were real problems; many years later the air force suffered a rash of F-16 crashes due to electric wiring failures. Fly-by-wire was not the key reason for rejecting the LTV design, but it was an important contributing factor.[38]

The most obvious differences between the F-17 and F-18 were extra fuselage width, which roughly doubled internal tankage (from 5500lbs to 10,800lbs) and a consequent increase in wing span and area (350ft^2 to 400ft^2, now with a fold and a dog-tooth), heavier landing gear and an enlarged nose carrying a 28in radar antenna. More subtle changes were provision for the Sparrow air-to-air missile (as well as the short-range Sidewinder), all-weather avionics, a strengthened fuselage and more internal fuel. The developed version of the F404 turbofan engine offered greater thrust to balance off increased weight. A decade of development gave it the same thrust as the J79 of the current F-4 in half the weight and three-quarters of the length. It was expected to

be more reliable because it was much simpler, with 14,300 parts instead of the 22,000 of the J79. Other parts of the aircraft, such as the radar, were similarly simplified. Where current aircraft averaged less than one flight hour between failures, the design objective for the F-18 was 6.18 hours between failures. Because designed weight increased from 25,250lbs to 33,720lbs (by 1977 it was 35,000lbs), the thrust-to-weight ratio, which determined manoeuvrability to some extent, was reduced from 1.27 to 1.14. At subsonic speed, the two aircraft performed about equally. At supersonic speed, the F404 offered better thrust variation with Mach number, hence offered significantly better performance. For example, the YF-17 had a slight edge in a sustained turn at 10,000ft at Mach 0.7 to 0.8, but the F-18 was better supersonically. The supersonic advantage of the F-18 was more marked at higher altitudes.

In 1977, selling the F-18 to Congress, NAVAIR claimed that in fighter escort range it was 31 per cent better than an F-4J carrying four Sparrows; in excess power it was 40 per cent better, in acceleration time it was 30 per cent better and in sustained Gs it was 70 per cent better. Congress was asking pointed questions because it appeared that the projected programme cost was escalating. The navy pointed to rampant inflation: the development cost listed in the FY78 budget was $1.5 billion in FY75 dollars, but $1.97 billion in then-year dollars, meaning inflated dollars each year. The navy argued that in

An F/A-18C of VFA-146 on the deck of *Nimitz*, 17 August 2013.

Two F/A-18Ds fly over *Harry S Truman*. The navy had no real interest in a two-seat version of the F/A-18, but the Marines wanted it for close air support.

constant dollars (i.e. not counting inflation) production costs in FY78 would actually be lower than those projected the previous year. At this time the first production aircraft were to be nine F-18s in FY79. Issues raised in the Congressional committees included the radar (why not use that of the F-16?) and the computer (the F-18 used the navy's standard AYK-14 rather than the specialised computer bought for the F-16). The Carter Administration was squeezing the navy budget and there were press reports that the navy was willing to sacrifice the F-18 to make up for shortfalls in the F-14 programme (the Senate Armed Services Committee cut the planned FY78 F-14 purchase from forty-four to thirty-six; the navy had wanted sixty). Reportedly the navy was willing to accept a year's slippage in the F-18 and to cancel the planned purchase of P-3C maritime patrol aircraft in FY79, but some in Congress went further and claimed that the navy would be willing to abandon the F-18 altogether. In an official letter report inserted into the *Congressional Record*, Commander J M Smith, CO of the Navy Fighter Weapons School (Topgun), described March 1977 mock dogfights pitting the YF-17 against the F-4 and the smaller F-5; he had previously evaluated the F-14 and the F-4J. The YF-17 matched the F-5 from 250 knots to 500 knots, which the CO found impressive. It easily forced the F-5 into a defensive position. As a dogfighter, the YF-17 was clearly superior to the F-14A – it was not underpowered and it was extremely manoeuvrable. The YF-17 was not a small light-weight aircraft – until it was compared to the F-14. There was no

The F/A-18E/F was a considerably enlarged and revised Hornet, conceived by McDonnell Douglas as a replacement for the ageing A-6, just as the earlier versions of the F/A-18 replaced the A-7. The navy resisted the project because it preferred to wait for the stealthy A-12 Avenger. When the A-12 project died, the enlarged F/A-18 became far more attractive. This single-seat F/A-18E of VFA-147 is on board *Ronald Reagan*, August 2011. These aircraft are easily distinguishable by their canted rectangular air intakes, adopted to reduce their radar cross-section from ahead.

doubt that an F-17 would defeat an F-14 in a one-on-one dogfight. Although the F-14 had a second crew member, hence should have had better situational awareness, due to its size it had never survived a one against many dogfight at Topgun (many F-4B/J had survived). Current 'loose deuce' tactics seemed to give a single-seat aircraft a good chance of survival in a one-vs-many dogfight.

On a more basic level, the F-18 programme could be opposed as the favoured alternative to a VSTOL fighter programme which Admiral Zumwalt had seen as the key to transforming the air navy. After he retired, his idea that it was vital to proliferate carriers by switching to VSTOLs found supporters in Congress. Thus NAVAIR's file on Congressional action on the F-18 in 1977 includes a statement by Senator Gary Hart, the most vocal of the VSTOL supporters, arguing that the lower performance of VSTOL aircraft could not be allowed to stop deployment of VSTOL carriers. The navy disagreed. The navy five-year shipbuilding programme was consistently cutting the number of projected VSTOL carriers, from seven in 1976 to one in 1977 to zero in 1978. Hart had no lasting impact, but as a sop to the VSTOL lobby the next large-deck amphibious ship, the LHD, was given an alternative role as a VSTOL carrier – and the Marines actually deployed their Harriers on board such ships (albeit for close air support rather than any fighter role).

In the autumn of 1977 NAVAIR was running two parallel programmes using essentially the same airframe, the F-18 as the low-end fighter and the A-18 as the A-7E replacement.[39] The estimated F-18 requirement was six navy, twelve marine corps, four naval reserve and two marine reserve squadrons, a total of twenty-four to supplement the eighteen navy F-14 squadrons. The A-18 would replace all of the light (i.e. day-only) attack aircraft: twenty-four navy squadrons and six naval reserve squadrons. Compared to the F-4, the F-18 offered better performance at three-quarters of the weight and also better fire control using a more modern digital radar. Compared to the A-7E it would replace, the A-18 offered better performance, higher survivability and a better bombing system. Both would have the same basic structure and sub-systems. Each would have a one-man cockpit – no great change for the A-7, but a revolutionary change for the F-18 vs the F-4.

Comparison of the two one-man cockpits showed surprisingly few differences. Both had a heads-up display and up-front communica-

tions/navigation/identification (CNI). Each had a large electronic display under the CNI: an electronic horizontal situation indicator for the fighter, a horizontal situation display for the bomber. The fighter had a master monitor display, the bomber a multi-function display which could show a map. Other differences were in the radar, optimised for either air-to-air or air-to-ground functions, armament (two Sparrows and two Sidewinders plus a gun in the F-18, six Sidewinders and a gun in the A-18), the hardpoints of the A-18 (one on the centreline, four under the wings, three of them wet, for fuel) and the FLIR and laser spot tracker (LST) in the A-18.

Those explaining the programme often said that the difference between the two versions was a few radios and displays. Some time, probably in the late spring of 1978, someone in NAVAIR realised that since the displays were all run by software and since the multi-mode radar used a computer to create its waveforms, there might really be no difference at all between the F-18 and the A-18. The F-18 could be given the two additional wing pylons planned for the A-18 and the Sparrow position planned for the FLIR pod and laser spot tracker could be wired so that either a missile or a pod could be carried.

The two projects were merged as the F/A-18. Its truly revolutionary aspect was that it was the first fully-digital aircraft built for the US Navy, with a pair of AYK-14 central computers (tactical and navigational), digital avionics (1553) and weapons (1760) buses, a 'glass cockpit' (according to one account, it had the first truly modern cockpit), a full quad-redundant digital fly-by-wire system (using a special computer unique to the F/A-18) and a digital radar. The tactical computer is responsible for all sensor and weapon control and for the displays. The navigational computer keeps track of aircraft position, using the aircraft's inertial and other systems. It calculates aircraft velocity. It also takes into account any flight plan fed into the fighter, for example by the carrier's mission planning system. The

A two-seat F/A-18F of VFA-22 lands on *Ronald Reagan*, July 2009. This aircraft is acting as a buddy tanker; note the small propeller (turbine) which powers the pump in the centreline tank (fuel is also fed through the other four tanks).

separate fly-by-wire system communicates with the two AYK-14s via a data bus, for example to supply data for the displays.

Because all the controls send their messages through the same data bus, they do not need separate cables and so can be placed very close together, located for maximum pilot convenience. All are therefore above knee level, with the most vital controls, including those for sensors and weapons, clustered on throttle and stick (for HOTAS, hand on throttle and stick, operation). The pilot need never look down to change switch settings, hence can always keep his eyes on the scene outside.

As in the F-14, the central computer system provides track-while-scan radar performance. That is not too important to an aircraft firing Sparrows, since the radar must continuously illuminate the target. However, AMRAAM is a fire-and-forget missile, broadly analogous to Phoenix, though with a shorter range. An F/A-18 armed with AMRAAMs can track multiple targets while conducting multiple engagements, just as an F-14 can, albeit at shorter range. The F/A-18A was credited with the ability to track ten aircraft simultaneously, the central computer displaying the eight most important targets (on the theory that a pilot could not readily deal with more than eight).

All of this had two consequences. First, the systems on board were extraordinarily flexible, hence the F/A designation, never previously used. Second, the aircraft was far easier to upgrade than its predecessors. For example, the computer could easily be replaced by a product-improved version (in the F/A-18C/D) and the capacity to fire the AMRAAM missile added. More different types of surface weapons could be carried, because the stores management system and the software bomb fire-control system could both be upgraded.

Multi-function capacity had real consequences. When the F/A-18 was adopted, it replaced the light attack (A-7E) squadron aboard carriers, supplementing the usual fighter squadron of F-14s. In theory the F/A-18s could thus 'swing' to the fighter role in what became the vital Outer Air Battle mission of the 1980s – with the important limitation of short radius.

In combat a pilot could switch quickly between radar and operational modes. During the 1991 Gulf War two Hornets encountered Iraqi fighters while on an attack mission. Past attack aircraft would have been compelled to jettison their bombs in hopes of evading the enemy fighters. In this case the pilots switched to air-to-air mode and

shot down the Iraqis using radar-guided Sparrow missiles. Then they switched back and completed their original missions.

The prototype F/A-18 Hornet was rolled out in September 1978 and it flew on 18 November.[40] This flight had previously been scheduled for July 1978. The first production aircraft flew in April 1980. During the 1980s, there was intermittent navy interest in buying a two-seat F/A-18 to replace the ageing A-6. At that time the navy decided to forego this interim aircraft in favour of a new A-12 attack bomber incorporating stealth technology, while modifying the A-6 to extend its useful lifetime. Then the A-12 programme collapsed and the A-6F was abandoned as funding tightened. That left the F/A-18 as not merely the successor to the A-7 light bomber, but also, probably, to the long-range heavy A-6. The Marines bought the two-seat F/A-18B and there was a two-seat F/A-18D version of its F/A-18C successor.

The main failing of the new aircraft was in range. Its proponents never pointed to its endurance on a CAP station and as a bomber it had significantly less radius than the A-7E.[41] At the end of the Cold War some in the navy argued that short strike range was acceptable. Most of the targets would surely be in littoral areas not too far inland (and carriers could operate much close to shore than during the Cold War). Deep targets could be left to Tomahawk missiles, if indeed they should be the navy's responsibility. The one fighter mission which demanded long endurance, CAP, seemed less important.

These arguments seem not to have won the day. At the end of the Cold War the navy was developing the stealthy deep-strike A-12. The programme ran into serious trouble and it was the main victim of a post-Cold War review of new development programmes by Secretary of Defense Dick Cheney. It was cancelled in January 1991. Whatever the arguments favouring shallow strikes, at least some in NAVAIR and in DCNO (Air) wanted to retain a deeper strike capability. Their obvious option was an enlarged F/A-18, a much larger airframe using much the same avionics as the F/A-18C/D, built around a new mission computer.[42] The hope was that by avoiding major avionics costs and by using much the same aerodynamics (albeit scaled up) development could be quick and relatively inexpensive. The navy announced the Super Hornet (F/A-18E/F) as a relatively simple derivative of the earlier Hornets. The aerodynamics turned out to be considerably more complex than expected, but the prototype flew in November 1995 and

Digital flexibility made it possible to adapt the F/A-18F as jamming aircraft. This is an EA-18G Growler of VAQ-133 on board *John C Stennis*, June 2016. A jamming pod is visible underwing and the usual wingtip Sidewinder positions are occupied by other pods. The most powerful jammer aboard the aircraft is its electronically-scanned radar, which can be used in jamming mode.

low-rate production was approved in March 1997. The aircraft completed operational evaluation in November 1999. In addition to features taken over from earlier Hornets, it incorporates a degree of stealth, which makes it a competitor to the far more expensive F-35 series.

OUTCOME: THE REVIVAL (AND RE-DEATH) OF VTOL

The navy issued a solicitation for a VTOL fighter on 15 November 1971, emphasising 'imaginative ideas which were not constrained by detail specifications'. The navy letter connected the new VTOL to the Sea Control Ship, then expected to displace 10,000 tons or less; it would usually counter smaller threats where carriers were not capable. The Sea Control Ship would, however, have to deal with the submarines, surface ships and anti-ship missiles as well as enemy aircraft. It therefore needed both a long-endurance sensor platform (which might also attack low-resistance targets such as submarines and fast patrol boats) and a fighter-attack aircraft to deal with both enemy aircraft and larger enemy ships. The fighter therefore had to be able to lift a substantial weapon weight. No hard performance figures were given.

The VTOL became the navy's main item in the new Defense Department prototyping programme. Prototypes were intended to demonstrate new concepts rather than necessarily to meet full engineering requirements. To this end the solicitation was only a page and a half long and proposals were limited to no more than twenty pages and to be submitted within forty-five days so that advanced development could begin in 1972. Companies whose offers were deemed promising received Phase I contracts to elaborate them. In the course of the Phase I work, NAVAIR indicated that the aircraft had to be supersonic. That ruled out McDonnell's Harrier proposal; in any case, the Harrier was already being bought for the Marines, so that it became a fall-back for the programme. Because the programme was initially run through Admiral Davies' special advanced development office rather than NAVAIR, the latter's records apparently do not describe the alternative designs. Company records show that at least two of them other than Rockwell (which won the competition) received Phase I contracts: Convair (Model 200) and Grumman (G-607). Both were essentially full-up fighters with the same armament as the later F-18: two Sparrows and two Sidewinders (as in the F-18, on its wingtips).[43] Convair later entered a non-VTOL version of its design in the VFAX competition.

Most of the competitors used lift-plus-lift/cruise engines, the lift engines (except for Grumman's) being Allison's XJ99 (a licence-built version of a Rolls-Royce RB-162 engine rated at about 5580lbs thrust).[44] The power of the two or three lift engines limited the take-off weight of the aircraft. They also had to balance the lift power of the lift/cruise engine. Because it envisaged a heavier aircraft, Grumman specified a new GLE-607A engine rated at 11,526lbs thrust. As its designation suggests, this engine did not yet exist; its characteristics were keyed to a NAVAIR solicitation and were considered achievable in an engine which would be in service in 1981. At this time a US-German strike fighter project, presumably related to the NATO NBMR 3 competition, envisaged a lift-plus-lift/cruise configuration in which the two lift engines swung out and were pushed forward before swivelling down, to balance the swivelled nozzle of the lift/cruise engine further aft. Grumman pointed to the simplicity of its design, to its lower drag during transition and to higher reliability, as

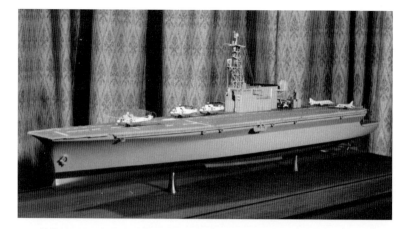

This official model shows the Sea Control Ship, Admiral Zumwalt's initiative which justified a new generation of VSTOL aircraft. Note the two Harriers aft.

failure of one of the side-by-side lift engines of the alternative design would destabilise the aircraft both longitudinally and transversely.

Boeing alone offered a tail-sitter, its Model 908-535. It would have been powered by a pair of YJ101 turbojets, with tiltable nozzles to tip the aircraft into horizontal flight. The problem in such an aircraft was that as the aircraft rose vertically the pilot would have an extremely poor view. Boeing's solution was a 'nutcracker' configuration whose nose (including the cockpit) would fold, so that the pilot was always horizontal. The configuration was a blended delta wing with very small canards for additional control. It does not appear that Boeing received a Phase I contract.

North American Rockwell offered the most radical configuration of all, a single engine creating lift by entraining air flowing over its canards and wing. As in a Harrier, air bled from a turbofan would be directed down, in this case via openings in the canards. Hot gas from the single engine would flow through openings in the wings. The great difference from other VTOLs was that both canards and wings had openings on top, through which air was supposed to flow into a low-pressure area created by the blown air and gas. Calculations suggested that so much air would be entrained in this way that the aircraft could lift. Compared to a lift-plus-lift/cruise design, Rockwell's offered the enormous advantage of simplicity (one rather than three or four engines) and reliability (the failure of any of the multiple engines would doom a lift-plus-lift-cruise aircraft). Unlike a Harrier, it did not suffer from the drag of the lift nozzles and it did not need any exotic technique like plenum chamber burning to give it high speed.

Although it had not developed the original requirement, NAVAIR was asked to evaluate the alternatives.[45] It rejected the Rockwell project because it considered their weight estimates over-optimistic and its lift concept speculative (albeit worthy of further investigation). NAVAIR much preferred a lift-plus-lift/cruise configuration, ranking Convair (and possibly Grumman) first, followed by Fairchild Republic and Vought (V-517). Convair was preferred for its combination of low risk and significantly increased capability. NAVAIR did consider a swing-out lift configuration (as in Vought's V-520) a worthwhile possibility for prototyping as a back-up to the simpler arrangement offered by Convair (and Grumman).

NAVAIR, however, was not in charge of the programme. Admiral Davies preferred the most radical technology and on 29 March 1972 Admiral Zumwalt announced the choice of the Rockwell design (work

The VTOL that wouldn't: Rockwell's FV-12A prototype, which refused to fly. It is shown on rollout in August 1977. The tail plug would have been opened for level flight; otherwise it helped direct jet engine gas through the wings and canards.

on the Convair design would continue for a time with limited funding). NAVAIR continued to argue that the aircraft would be far heavier than expected and that its development was far too risky. However, on 18 October 1972 two prototypes were ordered, plans calling for an initial conventional flight in November 1974 and a first VTOL flight in February 1975. The programme was somewhat delayed by the lack of money in the FY73 programme. Once Zumwalt (and Davies) retired, it lost momentum and the prototype was not rolled out until 26 August 1977.

What happened certainly justified prototyping. Rockwell had relied on calculations indicating that the air flow through the canards and wings would entrain 50 per cent more air. In captive tests at Langley, the augmentation was actually 6 per cent from the canards and 19 per cent from the wing; the aircraft could not lift itself. The XFV-12A never left the hangar used for initial tests. The project was closed down in 1981 with the sad comment by some of those involved that the design of the thrust-augmented wing (TAW) was still promising, but that the version in the FV-12A had been rushed ahead too quickly. By that time Zumwalt was long gone and the US naval leadership was no longer interested in small carriers (although there was still Congressional pressure to build them).[46]

BuAer much favoured Convair's more conventional lift-plus-lift/cruise configuration. This drawing was released on 26 February 1973. Convair later offered a version without lift engines for the VFAX competition terminated in favour of joining the air force's light fighter contest.

CHAPTER 12
THE FALKLANDS WAR

In 1982 THE Argentines seized the Falkland Islands, one of the last British dependencies. They were able to do so because once the last British large-deck carriers had been retired, it was no longer possible (at least in theory) for the Royal Navy to operate freely against serious air opposition anywhere out of land-based fighter cover. After the carrier cancellation, the Royal Navy practised extensively with RAF fighters based in Northern Scotland, AEW services being provided by land-based Shackletons. These exercises showed that, despite considerable effort on the part of the RAF, it was often impossible for them to intercept patrolling 'Bear Ds'. The time to fly out to an intercept point was often too great for the fighter to cover within its normal endurance. That was aside from the problem often demonstrated in the past, that weather often prevented land-based aircraft from taking off to support sea-based forces when weather at sea certainly permitted an enemy to strike.

In this sense the Falklands War really began with the 1966 decision to cancel the projected new British carrier and to allow the existing carrier force to run down. That left *Ark Royal* as the last operational British full-deck carrier; she decommissioned in 1973. The only other British full-deck carrier then operational was the smaller *Hermes*. She was converted into a commando (amphibious) carrier operating troop-carrying helicopters.

THE SEA HARRIER

When the government of the day decided not to build the new carrier, the Royal Navy staff produced a paper describing a carrier-less fleet. It still had to deal with Soviet missile-firing warships which could attack from several hundred miles away. A carrier would have dealt with them by launching Buccaneer bombers. They would have searched for the enemy ships and then struck. Without the carrier, the only possible anti-ship weapon with comparable range would be a large new missile. It could certainly be developed and it might well be affordable. The paper pointed out that the missile was hardly enough; something had to replace the search capability represented by the carrier. The authors of the paper suggested that the only viable replacement for the sea search function would be a small carrier operating a few aircraft (VSTOL technology was already on the horizon, promising that such a ship would be viable). The then First Sea Lord had interpreted the government decision as a veto of anything even vaguely resembling a carrier. He rejected the paper and its authors. However, they were right: not too long afterwards the Royal Navy was pressing for a small air-capable ship it initially called a 'through-deck cruiser' and it was making a case to buy a fast VSTOL aircraft, which became the Sea Harrier.

The Harrier was the first really practical VSTOL combat aircraft. Unlike all other jet VTOLs, it used a single engine rather than a combination of lift engines and a cruise engine. The key was to divert both fan air (from the front of the engine, at the compressor) and exhaust gas through nozzles which could be rotated from a cruise (horizontal) position to a vertical (lift position). The combination of four separate downward-thrusting air blasts offered considerable stability when the aircraft was rising more or less vertically and it also had a reaction-control jet under its tail for pitch control. Because the engine had to be powerful enough to lift the aircraft, it had an unusually high thrust-to-weight ratio. The nozzles, moreover, could be vectored to turn the aircraft in ways not available to a conventional fighter manoeuvring using its control surfaces. That would make it a good dogfighter, though this sort of manoeuvrability would not be enough to protect against long-range air-to-air or surface-to-air missiles. The Pegasus engine produced enough fan air and thrust to lift a moderate-size aircraft and in turn the aircraft did not pay the usual weight penalty due to separate lift engines.

The US Marine Corps was involved because it saw its close-support aircraft as artillery and a Harrier could operate closer to the action than any conventional aircraft. In 1971 the US Marines became interested in what they called the Advanced Harrier or AV-8C, a near-term upgrade (they bought the AV-8B version instead). The aircraft was significant because it was being proposed for the small carrier US CNO Admiral Zumwalt was then advocating. This was definitely a shipboard aircraft: the brochure listed trials aboard many ships including *Ark Royal* (in February 1963 with the P.1127 Kestrel and also in March 1970 and April 1971), on board *Eagle* in March 1970, on board the US carrier *Independence* (April 1966), on board the helicopter (commando) carrier *Bulwark* (June 1968 and September 1969), on board the US helicopter carrier *Guadalcanal* in March 1971 (fifty-six flights) and, ironically in view of what was to come, on board the Argentine carrier *25 de Mayo* in September 1969. A Harrier had also flown from the Italian helicopter cruiser *Andrea Doria* (in October 1967) and the Italians were said to be very interested in operating such aircraft. One improvement was substitution of a Pegasus 15 engine for the original Pegasus 10 to increase the useful load on either vertical or short take-off. Given the additional power, the modified aircraft could accommodate an air-to-air and air-to-surface radar with a 20in dish and a useful navigation/attack system including a secure data link. The aircraft would have carried two 30mm Aden cannon. The wing would be enlarged (from 201ft^2 to 229ft^2) with a super-critical section and advanced structure. That would substantially improve the lift-to-drag

The hero of the Falklands War: Sea Harriers on board *Invincible* for a NATO exercise, August 1991. Sea Harriers were credited with shooting down twenty-four Argentine aircraft (one was finished off by Argentine gunners in the Falklands who did not recognise it), with no loss to themselves. Two were lost to Argentine ground fire and four more to operational accidents. A major advantage of the Sea Harrier was its clean, nearly smokeless engine, which made it far less likely to be seen by opposing pilots. The Argentines were aware of just how limited Sea Harrier range was. Their radars in the Falklands tracked Sea Harriers flying out to their stations over the islands. Assuming that they were flying directly from their carriers and knowing Sea Harrier range, the Argentines could estimate the positions of the British carriers quite accurately. That made possible a series of attacks mounted on 1 May, when the British raided the islands, the 4 May attack which sank *Sheffield* (acting as radar picket for *Hermes*), the attack on the task force which sank the container ship *Atlantic Conveyer*, an abortive attack by Skyhawks against *Invincible* and also probably a later abortive submarine attack against *Hermes*.

The Harrier was conceived not as a fighter but as a long-range anti-ship attacker, in effect a manned alternative to an over-the-horizon cruise missile. Its air-to-air capacity was intended to defeat Soviet snoopers, which were essential to support either submarine or over-the-horizon anti-ship missile attacks. This Sea Harrier is shown with its Sea Eagle anti-ship missile. The aircraft's radar was optimised for anti-ship attack. (BAE)

ratio, hence range performance. The Pegasus 15 engine offered more thrust (24,500lbs vs 20,500lbs for the production Pegasus 10) and better specific fuel consumption (economy: 0.64 vs 0.72). Potential near-term developments could improve it further.[1] Useful vertical take-off load would have increased from to 4850lbs to 7200lbs and useful short take-off load from 11,250lbs to 13,700lbs. With a 100ft deck run, this Harrier could dash out at Mach 0.9 to a combat radius of 300nm carrying four missiles to intercept a target at 35,000ft with sufficient fuel for 10 minutes of combat. With two Sidewinders (or a successor then called Agile) it could spend 2.58 hours on CAP 100nm from a carrier (with two 120-US gallon tanks it could spend two hours on CAP 220nm away). In 1971 McDonnell hoped that if the programme were started at once the AV-8C could be in service on board a Sea Control Ship in 1976.

In December 1973 NAVAIR (acting for the Marines) joined the Ministry of Defence in a joint programme for an Advanced Harrier, tentatively designated AV-16A.[2] It would have been essentially the AV-8C proposed two years earlier. That programme lapsed and the Marines and the RAF jointly developed a more austere AV-8B Harrier II, which had the supercritical wing but not the Pegasus 15; instead it had an improved Pegasus 11. The projected radar was omitted, because both sponsors were interested in close air support rather than in air-to-air combat; that possibility returned only when the Royal Navy bought the Sea Harrier. The RAF dropped out of the programme in 1980. The Harrier II was bought by other NATO navies: Italy and Spain, both of which were interested in the full range of naval missions. Ultimately their Harriers were fitted with the same APG-66 radar which equipped the F/A-18 Hornet fighter.

From 1974 on the Marines sometimes deployed their Harriers (AV-8As) from amphibious ships, although not on a regular basis and not against naval targets. The Soviets developed their own VTOL jet fighter, the Yak-38, and did deploy it from 1974 on. Unlike the Harrier, it had separate lift engines and it was severely limited by the weight they consumed.

For the Royal Navy, the revival of fixed-wing naval airpower was tied to the project for a command cruiser, which was one of three surface warship types approved by the Cabinet in July 1967 (the others were the austere Type 42 missile destroyer and the Type 22 frigate, with the Type 21 as interim). The new fleet configuration was intended to respond to the new emphasis on the defence of NATO sea communications in the Eastern North Atlantic, the Government of the day having dropped the earlier emphasis on maintaining security East of Suez, hence on power projection. The Royal Navy now conceived a Maritime Contingency Force (MARCONFOR) as the core of the future British naval contribution to NATO. It would offer a combination of anti-submarine, anti-air and anti-surface capabilities. In theory a MARCONFOR could dominate a selected sea area, conduct offensive anti-air and anti-submarine operations, offer seaward support for amphibious operations (sealing off the beach from enemy seaborne attack) and could offer distant and close support of sea lines of reinforcement/supply to the UK and to Western Europe.

Each such force would require command facilities far too extensive to fit in the austere frigates then envisaged; hence the command cruiser. In effect it would provide the command and control capability otherwise residing in the carriers now being given up.

ASW would require Sea King helicopters, far too large to be operated by a frigate. The command ship thus became a command helicopter cruiser (CCH). Each of two or three such forces would consist of a CCH, ten surface combatants and nuclear submarines. In addition to whatever ships might be operating with the command ship, she would control co-operating land-based aircraft (as the Royal Navy had been doing for many years). This was particularly important (at the least in justifying the character of the ship) because part of the rationale for giving up carriers in the new NATO context was that the mission of their air groups in maritime warfare could be taken over by land-based aircraft. This sort of command and control required, above all, elaborate computer systems with large numbers of operators – hence considerable internal volume in a ship.

By 1969, with the Type 42 and Type 22/21 programmes well underway, it was time to define the command cruiser and to approve the three-ship programme. The first jump above the original idea of a command ship operating only helicopters was to add the Sea Dart anti-aircraft missile, as the ship would be too important to rely on other ships for her defence. Adding Sea Dart was also attractive because it reduced the number of relatively expensive Type 42 destroyers required. When it approved this single-package concept, the Ministry of Defence Operational Requirements Committee asked for three parallel design studies. The austere Study 21 offered six Sea Kings; Study 22 increased that to nine; and Study 23 added provision for a massive bottom-bounce sonar on a 'for but not with' basis, as this sonar might become available at half-life in the late 1980s (this version was soon abandoned). These studies showed that for anything more than about six helicopters it was most economical to use a flat deck with a hangar below it. Study 21 was killed because US Navy experience showed that it took two big helicopters to contain and track (and attack) a single nuclear attack submarine. To maintain two on task for ten days required at least seven helicopters. With seven helicopters as a bare minimum, larger numbers made sense; the naval staff took twelve as a reasonable compromise. The through deck was also attractive because it offered the greatest potential for accepting helicopter growth over the lengthy (25-year) life of the ships. The through deck made it practical to operate VSTOL aircraft, although the Soviets had managed to do so on board ships with only stern flight decks (*Moskva* class). The 'command cruiser' morphed into the light carrier *Invincible*, whose large superstructure suggested disproportionately large command spaces (actually they were mostly buried in her hull).

While the command cruiser study proceeded, navy discussions with the RAF and discussions within the Ministry of Defence Sea Air Warfare Committee were identifying roles for a limited number of embarked VSTOL aircraft: probe, identification (e.g. of surface ships),

limited air defence and organic strike. At times it might be desirable to carry VSTOL aircraft instead of some helicopters. In July 1969 the Navy Staff produced a paper on the extent to which the through-deck cruiser could improve organic naval strike capability. Just how tentatively the Harrier was included shows in the fact that options other than Harrier were helicopter-launched anti-ship missiles and submarine- and ship-launched anti-ship missiles (the Royal Navy bought Exocet).[3]

The Naval Staff saw VSTOL aircraft offering, in addition to a capability against snoopers, a probe function (tactical reconnaissance), limited fighter air defence and surface strike capability, although these functions would all be limited for the current Harrier. The staff justified an organic strike capability on the ground that the deployed naval force needed an ability to respond instantly to a pop-up threat. This has been the classic justification for sea-based defensive or reactive air power: it takes too long for anything based far away to come to the aid of a seaborne force. That was quite aside from a possible future situation in which the fleet would be far from British land bases, because the decision to withdraw from East of Suez seemed to have closed that possibility. The Naval Staff pointed to possible export sales of the navalised Harrier as an important argument favouring it; at this stage Chief of Naval Staff wrote that he had no real doubts about the value of VSTOL for maritime operations.[4] The MoD Operational Analysis unit was conducting a study of maritime strike, including the possible role of VSTOL aircraft, under joint RN and RAF sponsorship. The Naval Staff characterised it as the first time that formulation of a naval weapon concept of this magnitude had been approached in this way.[5]

For its part the RAF had always required that the Harrier be carrier-capable, in the sense of being about to take off from a carrier and land back on, because it had planned to use the carriers to ferry this relatively short-range aircraft. Initial carrier trials scheduled for *Bulwark* in December 1969 had to be postponed to March 1970 and moved to *Eagle* (*Bulwark* was unavailable). In the RAF view the main problem to be solved was alignment of the aircraft's inertial navigational system on board the moving ship (the ship's velocity had to be fed in). In December 1969 RAF policy was that it would be prudent to build VSTOL capability into the new cruiser at minimum cost, but major improvements to the Harrier would entail considerable extra money. Vice Chief of the Air Staff had repeatedly stated that any embarked fixed-wing VSTOLs would be flown by the RAF, a position the navy had to undermine.[6] As might be expected, much of the RAF reaction to the cruiser project amounted to obliged support for the ship, but a claim that long-standing studies had shown that long-range shore-based aircraft provided more efficient support. Navy references to the loss of planned shore-based support generally referred to the cancellation of the F-111 programme, which itself had been a major justification for the withdrawal of the carriers.

The joint (RAF/RN) Sea/Air Warfare Committee was asked for a study of the application of VSTOL to maritime operations.[7] Reporting in September 1969, it identified three roles: anti-snooper (including enemy aircraft co-operating with enemy missile-firing units), probe and reconnaissance of surface contacts and quick-reaction surface strike. Wider fleet air defence was not included. Naval staff studies had shown that the reconnaissance-probe role required a range of about 350nm as the minimum required to permit shore-based strikes against an enemy missile shooter closing at a speed of 60 knots (own plus enemy speed), based on maximum enemy weapon range (170nm) and the response time for shore-based aircraft at a maximum range of 1300nm. The required equipment was a wide-band homer for passive reconnaissance and to assist in locating targets plus a simple X-band radar. Assuming that shadowers and aircraft supporting enemy missile shooters would continue to be subsonic (the Soviets used the 'Bear D' throughout the Cold War), the anti-snooper fighter could manage with the high subsonic speed offered by the Harrier. The aircraft would need a lightweight fighter sight, an air-to-air missile (e.g., Sidewinder) and a radar with limited AI capability. For strike, the aircraft would have to attack enemy missile shooters beyond their attack range (at least 170nm, but the Committee preferred 230nm to allow for an hour at a closing speed of 60 knots). The VSTOL aircraft would carry two air-to-surface missiles and it would fly a hi-lo-lo-hi profile. It would need a lightweight radar, a wide-band homer (to approach silently, below the radar) and a missile such as the existing Martel or a development (which is what was produced as Sea Eagle).

The existing Harrier had none of this equipment, so it would have to be modified extensively. Unfortunately the cost of the modifications would be spread over a very limited number of naval aircraft. The Sea/Air Committee pointed out that by 1976, when the first cruiser would be entering service (it actually entered service in 1979), the RAF Harriers would have been in front-line service for seven years and it would be time to look at a successor (front-line aircraft were given a ten-year service life). If the choice were deferred to a Harrier successor, then the cost of the special naval features might be spread over a much larger dual-service purchase. This choice might also meet the navy's argument about exports.

The major US Marine Corps investment in the Harrier seems to have saved the naval programme, because it would spread at least some of the required features over a much longer production run. Although the new strike and air-to-air avionics would be a major departure from the existing RAF Harrier, it would be more or less off-the-shelf items. It helped that the RAF badly wanted to avoid agreeing to a next-generation Harrier. Although the available documents do not include any indication of just how the RAF objections were overcome by the navy, it seems likely that in the RAF view it was better to surrender control of the aircraft to the navy than to commit to continuing development of a Harrier follow-on. Britain withdrew from the joint (UK-US) Harrier II programme, which produced the US AV-8B, though later it returned as junior partner.

Late in 1969 the cruiser project had to be justified in detail to the Treasury, since the navy wanted to order the first ship in 1972 and it would have to begin detailed design work in 1970. Some VSTOL policy had to be set out.[8] The Secretary of State for Defence wrote that although no provision for VSTOL had been envisaged at the outset, now it was included because in some circumstances 'an embarked force of VSTOL aircraft could undoubtedly prove to be a very worthwhile supplement to shore based air support and that, in a ship of the size of the cruiser, it would be imprudent not to provide a capability for operating aircraft of this type at some stage during the ship's life, which will last until the end of the century'. The Secretary of State hedged by writing that he was not prejudging whether the current RAF Harrier should be embarked, with or without modification. However, given the unsuitability of an unmodified Harrier, this was very close to approving the Sea Harrier programme.

Formal design work on the Sea Harrier began only in 1975, as the 'through deck cruisers' took shape.[9] Each was intended to embark up to six Sea Harriers alongside its Sea King ASW helicopters (the normal complement was five Sea Harriers and nine Sea Kings).[10] There was no form of organic AEW, because the ship's main air-search radar was quite sufficient to detect a high-flying snooper (typically a 'Bear D').[11] It seems to have been assumed, moreover, that the ASW task group including the carrier would be operating close enough to northern Scotland to make use of long-range land-based AEW aircraft. Before the first of the 'through deck cruisers' had been completed, it was modified with a 'ski jump' at the forward end of its flight deck. The Sea Harriers had generally been expected to make rolling take-offs and to land vertically. By launching them at a considerable up-angle, the ski-jump greatly increased their load capacity.

The airframe was modified from that of the RAF Harrier GR.3 with better corrosion resistance. The most important difference was provision of a Blue Fox radar intended mainly for surface search. As a conventional pulse radar, it had little look-down capability. In common with nearly all radars of its generation, it was powered by a magnetron, hence could not be given multiple alternative operating modes. The radar was intended primarily to support the reconnaissance and stand-off anti-ship missile attack roles, the missile being the new Sea Eagle. By the time the Sea Harrier was approaching service, the Royal Navy had an important role in the defence of Norway. It was the reinforcing strike force (and also support for Royal Marines abroad). To that end the Sea Harrier had provision to deliver the WE 177 nuclear weapon. It was therefore designated the Sea Harrier FRS.1, the R standing for reconnaissance and the S for strike.

A modest upgrade planned for both the Sea Harrier and the RAF Harrier would not have affected fighter performance. It amounted to a new 'Kingston Big Wing' of increased area with wingtip rails for Sidewinders, more underwing hardpoints and leading edge extensions (LERX) for better turning performance, plus added tankage. The RAF upgrade was cancelled in 1980 and no corresponding Sea Harrier programme emerged.

Sea Harrier air-to-air capacity lay in provision to carry a pair of Sidewinders, which imposed no requirements on the aircraft system. There was no associated special hardware (other than the link between missile and headphone) and no computer associated with a particular

The ski-jump made it possible for the Sea Harrier to carry enough fuel and missiles to deal with incoming Argentine aircraft at a useful range. This is the first Sea Harrier ski-jump take-off from *Invincible*, 30 October 1980.

type of Sidewinder. At most there was a sight indicating when the missile could actually hit a target once locked on. That turned out to be very significant. In 1982, when the Falklands War broke out, the RAF and the Royal Navy were both using a first-generation version of the missile. The current US version, AIM-9L, was a radical improvement. First-generation missiles could home only on hot engine nozzles. AIM-9L could home from any direction, probably because it could see the cooler plume of hot gas surrounding the jet exhaust. All-aspect homing turned out to be a critical combat advantage.

While the Sea Harrier was being developed, the Air Staff issued a requirement for a supersonic attack aircraft (AST 403). BAe Kingston (formerly Hawker Siddeley), which had developed the Harrier in the first place, proposed an aircraft (HS 1205-5) to meet it.[12] It was descended from the earlier P.1154 and HS 1150 studies. Like the Sea Harrier, it was a single-seater. Each wing carried three hardpoints and a wing tip station, the inner hardpoint carrying two air-to-air missiles and the wing tip a 300lb air-to-air missile (the middle hardpoint was stressed for 3000lbs and the outer one for 1000lbs).

RAE studied the projected aircraft not in the strike role envisaged for the original Sea Harrier, but in a classic fleet air defence role, the assumed threat being a regimental (eighteen to twenty-four aircraft) 'Backfire' attack in the 1990s, each of the 'Backfires' carrying two air-to-surface missiles and firing outside the range of the surface-to-air missiles. The assumed Soviet weapon was an improved AS-4 which could be launched 180nm from the task group, the bomber flying at Mach 1.5 (rather than the current Mach 1.3) and 40,000ft, both somewhat beyond 1978 capabilities. The assumed fighter weapon was the same Sidewinder that armed the Sea Harrier.[13] The scenario showed that even at supersonic speed a fighter launched from the deck could not reach an incoming bomber quickly enough; at its own supersonic speed the bomber would close too much while the fighter flew out. For example, it would take 18 minutes to reach the bomber launch line at 180nm. During that time a Mach 1.5 bomber would have flown 260nm, meaning that for a deck-launched interceptor to be effective the bomber would have to be detected 440nm from the carrier. That was manifestly impossible using the carrier's radar. On the other hand, if the bomber were unable to launch beyond 100nm, the carrier's radar coverage would be good enough. Overall, the analysis showed that the aircraft (and any comparable VSTOL fleet air-defence fighter) would have to fly CAP missions. Without any organic form of AEW, it might have to use its own radar for that purpose and the independent CAP mission might even define radar requirements.

Although the RAE study is unlikely to have affected Royal Navy policy, its calculations give a fair idea of what the Royal Navy was doing at the time and then later, when the Falklands War showed that the Sea Harrier could be (and should be) a fleet air-defence fighter. The key requirement was to force the Soviet bombers to come far closer before they launched weapons. The Royal Navy deployed what it called a counter-targeting countermeasure specifically to attack the radars on board the approaching bombers. The navy also had to extend the range at which any defensive fighter would fire without reducing the fighter's ability to handle multiple targets. Hence the choice of the AMRAAM missile for the later Sea Harrier FA.2. Any other long-range radar-guided missile the Sea Harrier might have carried would have limited the fighter to a single engagement at a time, because such missiles were semi-actively guided.

What the navy could not do was extend aircraft endurance on CAP

The three Harrier carriers were primarily anti-submarine ships designed to defend themselves against air attack using the same Sea Dart system as British Type 42 air-defence destroyers. In this photo the launcher occupies much of the bow of the ship, limiting the size and length of her ski-jump. After the Falklands War, the ships were modified to optimise their aircraft capability. The missile system was removed, its magazine replaced by additional fuel tankage and the ski jump was extended. This photograph of *Invincible* (identified by her flight deck letter, N) was dated 29 September 1986.

missions, as the US Navy extended its CAPs by in-flight tanking. Sea Harriers did have the necessary plumbing for a detachable refuelling probe, but with so few aircraft on board a light carrier, there was no question of wasting any of them as buddy tankers.

RAE's 1978 study gives a fair idea of what was being discussed just before the Nott defence cuts. At the same time the Royal Navy was also considering buying larger missile ships and the RAE study suggests that it expected to have to defend its new carrier task group against heavy Soviet attacks. Such ideas were abandoned due to the cuts, but they probably explain that post-Falklands Sea Harrier upgrade. The high subsonic speed of the post-Falklands Sea Harrier, as compared to the supersonic speed of the abortive AST 403, could be justified if the Soviets could be drawn a lot closer to the task force (thanks to anti-targeting ECM) and also if the fighter could strike back at a far greater range (thanks to a new radar supporting the AMRAAM missile).

The Royal Navy always preferred to stow its aircraft below decks. That became particularly attractive once it operated primarily in northern waters, where waves could break over even a high flight deck, as here with Sea Harriers. (BAE)

THE WAR

Margaret Thatcher decided to take the Falklands back. She ordered the Royal Navy to form a task force for the purpose and to send it to the South Atlantic. The task force was built around two carriers, *Hermes* (which had been converted into a commando carrier) and the new *Invincible*. The availability of the latter ship was a stroke of considerable irony. Defence Secretary Nott had already decided that the vestigial British fixed-wing air arm was too expensive to retain and Australia had agreed to buy *Invincible* as the core of her own revived naval air arm. British amphibious ships were scheduled for disposal. Many writers have pointed out that, had the Argentines waited only a few months, the Royal Navy might well have been unable to reconquer the islands, because it would have lacked organic air power.

Hermes and *Invincible* were relatively small and they lacked catapults and arresting gear. To the extent that they could support high-performance aircraft, they were limited to the VSTOL Sea Harrier. It had been bought not as an air-superiority fighter but to support NATO operations in the north. Harriers could attack Soviet surface ships using a new Sea Eagle missile and they could support marines ashore in Norway with bombs, including nuclear ones. The Royal Navy was oriented towards anti-submarine warfare, which entailed the destruction of snoopers supporting submarine attacks. To that end the Sea Harrier could be armed with Sidewinder air-to-air missiles. However, its radar was optimised for air-to-surface operation in support of its surface attack role.

The Royal Navy relied mainly on its shipboard anti-aircraft missiles to deal with air threats. The most important of these was the ramjet Sea Dart, on board not only missile destroyers but also *Invincible*. Probably because the Sea Harrier was not considered an important element of fleet air defence, the British had not made much effort to develop a doctrine allowing them to operate fighters near their missile ships. Such a doctrine would probably have entailed considerable communication. The pre-Falklands Royal Navy, however, was much concerned to maintain radio silence so as to avoid detection. Perhaps the clearest symbol of that doctrine was that the Tacan beacon atop the mast of *Hermes* was cut down on the way to the South Atlantic. Without the beacon, aircraft could not home effectively on the carrier; two Sea Harriers were lost in the air en route.

Once British troops were ashore, a second missile problem would become evident. The British army set up its own defensive missiles,

Hermes, departing for the South Atlantic on 5 April 1982, shows three Harriers on the ski-jump.

The enemy in the Falklands: an Argentine navy Super Etendard, shown here taking off from *Ronald Reagan*. When war broke out the Argentines had five of fourteen ordered, plus five Exocets (they hoped to obtain more through Peru). Argentine tactics were to operate the aircraft in pairs, supported by stand-off targeting aircraft (S-2 Trackers in pre-war exercises, an SP-2E Neptune in combat). Although the Argentines had other strike aircraft, only the Super Etendard had the radar and combat system required to fire Exocet. The first attack was ordered on 4 May, after the Argentine cruiser *Belgrano* was sunk. Two missiles were fired, one of which hit *Sheffield*. A second strike was ordered for 23 May, the position of the Task Force being estimated based on the observed path of Sea Harriers flying over the Falklands: it hit the container ship *Atlantic Conveyor*. That left only a single missile. On 29 May *Invincible* was located 100nm from Port Stanley and an attack was ordered. A second Super Etendard would fly with the missile aircraft. Four air force Skyhawks accompanied them (two were shot down). The Argentines claimed that they attacked and possibly damaged the carrier, but the British denied that they did so and the carrier showed no sign of damage on her return to the United Kingdom. The post-war British summary records two A-4s splashed by Sea Darts and an Exocet seeker head detected. It notes a possible hit on the Exocet by either a Sea Dart from *Exeter* or 4.5in Mk 8 fire from *Avenger*. (*The Hook*)

but it had no way of co-ordinating their use with the defensive aircraft operated by the fleet. That would have been a serious problem had the British been operating in Norway, supported by Sea Harriers from offshore.

Ironically, Argentina had been the only export customer of the Sea Dart missile. The missile did not prove very effective against Argentine aircraft, but its presence seems to have had one very important consequence. The Argentines were aware that it had a minimum effective altitude (as do other shipboard air defence missiles) and their attack pilots often flew very low. That made bombing difficult, because bombs had to be fused with sufficient delay to allow the aircraft to escape before they burst. Several Argentine aircraft were destroyed by their own bomb bursts and in a sense these losses can be attributed to Sea Dart.

The large-deck FAA had operated airborne early warning and control aircraft, but they were not considered essential for the limited role of the Sea Harrier carriers. Thus a proposed radar version of the standard Sea King helicopter was not funded before the war. Once the Royal Navy was in action against Argentine aircraft, a crash programme was launched, but radar Sea Kings did not figure in the war.

The naval side of the Falklands War had a major air component

because the main weapon the Argentines could wield against the British fleet and its amphibious force was aircraft (there were also Argentine submarines). Argentina had one aircraft carrier, *25 de Mayo*, but she never launched her aircraft against the British force, reportedly due to insufficient wind over her deck (due to her limited speed and the weather). Instead, the Argentines relied on land-based strike aircraft, flying to about the limit of their endurance. They were armed mainly with bombs, but the Argentines also had a few air-launched Exocet anti-ship missiles. They had been supplied by France and the French provided the British with some details of their guidance systems (however, jamming did not apparently work).

In effect the naval side of the Falklands War was not too different from the way the US Navy envisaged a war in the Norwegian Sea (in 1982 a major preoccupation), albeit on a much smaller scale. That made it of far more than academic interest.

After brief hesitation, the US government backed the British fully. From an air defence point of view, the most important form of support was the supply of the latest AIM-9L version of the Sidewinder missile. Unlike the Sidewinders already in British service, AIM-9L could be fired from dead ahead, as it was able to home on the exhaust plume of an oncoming aircraft.

The air war opened with a surprise. The British had assumed that they could get to the islands unopposed, on the theory that the Argentines had no ocean surveillance system comparable, say, to the Soviet system which NATO faced. However, the Argentines found a crucial vulnerability in the British use of satellite communications. Satellite communication was attractive because the up-link from a ship is a narrow beam, difficult to intercept. In theory a ship could commu-

The war revealed both the extraordinary capability of the all-aspect AIM-9L Sidewinder and a disturbing reliability problem; US analysts estimated that the British had lost several sure kills due to missile problems. In several cases Sea Harriers shot down Argentine aircraft using their cannon, a weapon which by 1982 was widely denigrated. The reliability issue helps explain why the Sea Harriers were modified after the war to carry four missiles each. The original two-missile outfit, however, is also explainable in terms of their pre-war mission, which was to deal with single snooper/shadowers. (BAE)

In the wake of the Falklands War, the Sea Harrier was modified to become an all-weather fighter armed with the longer-range AMRAAM missile. This Sea Harrier FRS.2 was photographed at an air show at Eglin Air Force Base, 24 April 1993. It could be distinguished from the earlier Sea Harrier by its enlarged radome.

nicate freely in this way, never risking being located by the sort of HF/DF the Soviets had used. The satellite link used by the British (and indeed all others then in service) operated simply by repeating the up-linked signal and sending it back to earth in a broad beam, so that moving recipients could receive it. What the Argentines realised was that whatever incidental information the up-linked beam contained would survive in the down-link. In particular, the satellite was moving, so that whatever it received incorporated some Doppler due to its motion. How much Doppler depended on where the transmitting ship was. This was a new application of an existing idea. Soon after the Soviets launched their first satellite, Sputnik, several Western laboratories had pointed out that the Doppler due to the satellite's motion could be used for precise navigation. The US Navy had even launched Transit satellites for just this purpose. It was not a great leap for the Argentines to reverse the process.

The Doppler tracking process could not provide precise target location, but it was good enough to guide an Argentine Boeing 707 airliner impressed for ocean reconnaissance – a snooper. The Task Force failed to shoot it down. It seems that the force was relying mainly on its shipboard anti-aircraft missiles and they did not do the job. It is not clear why Harriers were not launched to deal with the snooper, since that would have been their role in the Norwegian Sea. In any case, soon after the airliner appeared, so did Argentine aircraft. They were unsuccessful and several were shot down, but the task force clearly did not expect the attack at all.

Once the British fleet arrived at the Falklands, Argentine air attacks intensified, because now they were well aware of where the British were. The first major attack was an Exocet strike on the destroyer *Sheffield*, which was escorting the carrier *Hermes*. The carrier was maintaining radio silence, *Sheffield* transmitting by satellite to London. It happened that the satellite link was on a radar frequency (satellite dishes are about the size of radar antennas), so the ships passive electronic intercept set was shut down. She had no warning whatever of the impending missile attack. The question ever since has been whether other elements of the Task Force, particularly its aircraft, could have prevented the attack and thus saved the ship.

The Argentines had Neptune maritime patrol aircraft equipped with the same APS-20 radar which the British had used for airborne early warning, albeit in an earlier incarnation. They were well aware that an attacking aircraft searching for a target would give away its presence and probably would be shot down. Instead, they teamed the attacker, a Super Etendard, with a Neptune. The Neptune acted as snooper, spotting the target from well outside anti-aircraft range and coaching in the Super Etendard. The latter bounced up and down, intermittently contacting the target until it came within Exocet range.

Other ships in the Task Force detected the emissions of the Neptune and Super Etendard radars; the Royal Navy had some of the best radar intercept equipment in the world. However, by itself this data was useless. It had to be translated into an attack warning or into directions for a Sea Harrier to intercept the Super Etendard. It appears that fighter interception, which had never been the intended role of the Sea Harrier, was not attempted.[14] Information did go out over the Task Force data link, but it seems in retrospect that the responsible officer on board *Sheffield* did not consider his data link an essential source of tactical information: with his radar and ESM down so that the ship could transmit by satellite, he considered all of his sources of information suspended. It is not clear how much he could have done, but it is clear that the first sign of the Exocet strike was the hit.

The *Sheffield* experience and a later Exocet attack on the container ship *Atlantic Conveyor* (which had many of the expedition's helicopters on board), seem to have convinced the British command that it was essential to keep Sea Harriers aloft to deal with Argentine air attacks. With so few aircraft and with short VSTOL endurances, that required warning. It was supplied by British submarines off the Argentine coast; the British could estimate how long it would take strike aircraft to arrive over the islands. The US-supplied Sidewinders proved quite effective, although reliability problems aborted some attacks.

Much of the air battle was fought over Falkland Sound, the waters between the two islands, where the British amphibious force was landing men and equipment. The British tried to set up aircraft traps in hopes Argentine aircraft could be lured into missile range. They also teamed ships with long-range Sea Dart and with the quick-reaction Seawolf point-defence missile, the idea being that Seawolf could deal with Exocets if it was close enough to their target. Co-ordination between ships and Sea Harriers was not always effective and it may explain the loss of the missile destroyer *Coventry*. *Coventry* was working with a Seawolf ship and also with Harriers. She detected incoming Argentine aircraft, but it was difficult to shoot as long as the Sea Harriers were within range and might be hit by her own weapons. Other problems included very short warning time, as the Argentines popped up over hills (the British Type 965 air-search radar had no moving target indication function, hence could not distinguish aircraft flying overland). *Coventry* took three large bomb hits as well as strafing damage at her waterline; she could not possibly have survived.

Despite their considerable limitations, the Sea Harriers shot down more Argentine attackers than any other form of British fleet air defence. At the time some British commentators pointed out that shorter-range shipboard weapons might well be able to abort attacks, but that it took fleet fighters to destroy the attackers and thus to end the threat of further attacks. The British government took this lesson to heart. It completed the two *Invincible* class carriers then under construction and it substantially increased their Sea Harrier complements. In the case of the *Invincible*s, one symbol of the increased importance accorded the Sea Harrier was the removal of the Sea Dart system to provide more space, for example for fuel. Work on a full AEW version of the Sea King was approved and a new version of the Sea Harrier, optimised for air defence, was developed. Existing Sea Harriers were modernised to this new configuration.

A Sea Harrier FRS.2 of 899 Squadron. (BAE)

THE FLEET AIR DEFENCE UPGRADES

The great surprise of the Falklands War was that the Sea Harrier fighter had proven so essential to the fleet. Surface-launched missiles, the great air defence hope of the Royal Navy, had proven far less effective. Sea Harriers were credited with twenty-two aircraft and a helicopter shot down. None was shot down by enemy aircraft; two were lost to ground fire. In the wake of the war, the navy chose to emphasise the fighter (and, incidentally, strike) role and also to increase the number of Sea Harriers on board the carriers.

Feasibility studies for an upgrade began in 1983.[15] They envisaged a longer-range air-to-air capability, better navigation and additional fuel. The key technology was the same computer-generated radar waveform capacity which was already making the F/A-18 Hornet into a true dual-purpose fighter. Ferranti had announced just such a radar in 1980: a generic lightweight fighter set it called Blue Falcon. The Sea Harrier had been cited as a primary application, but the project died in the defence cuts which included the planned disposal of the British light carriers.

While this work was proceeding, existing Sea Harriers were subject

to a Phase I Update, completed in 1987. The existing single Sidewinder launch rails were replaced by double rails, the drop tanks were enlarged (to 190 imp gallons) and the nozzles modified so that they could be turned at small angles. Aircraft were fitted with a blind-landing aid, MADGE (Microwave Aircraft Digital Guidance Equipment), which provides indications in the pilot's display guiding him to a landing.

BAe and Marconi received a project definition contract for a more extensive Phase II upgrade in February 1985. The centrepiece was a software-powered radar, this time designated Blue Vixen, but apparently derived from the earlier Blue Falcon (with liquid rather than air cooling, presumably indicating greater power). Like Blue Falcon, it was a true multi-purpose radar (reportedly eleven modes) with low and medium pulse rates for long-range and pulse-Doppler operation. This was a track-while-scan system, hence had to use a fire-and-forget missile. The only such weapon then in service was the Raytheon AMRAAM, a Sparrow-size missile with an active seeker and a data link from the firing aircraft. The computer system reportedly prioritisesd the targets the radar detected. The new radar was evident in a bulged nose. Overall, the aircraft was digitised, with a computer-centred combat system. The earlier analog displays were largely replaced by a pair of multi-function displays (one for the radar). The pilot had a heads-up display using synthetic video from the combat system computer. Digitisation made it possible to integrate the AMRAAM air-to-air missile with the radar combat system. With all important avionics on the same dual 1553B bus, the pilot's multi-function display (and head-up display) could show not only the raw radar video of the past, but also processed (synthetic) video and even data from the radar-warning receiver. In addition to the usual IFF transponder, the aircraft had an airborne IFF interrogator. The projected integrated GPS was abandoned in favour of a stand-alone receiver. A slightly more powerful version of the Pegasus engine was installed. Some time after 2000 the aircraft was redesignated FA.2.

When the project was completed in 1996, the British described this version of the Sea Harrier as the most sophisticated fighter in Europe. Unfortunately the war in which the British found themselves after 2003 did not favour an underpowered air-to-air fighter. Sea Harriers could not execute strikes effectively (they were eventually designated FA.2 instead of FRS.2). They performed poorly compared

to RAF ground-attack Harriers in the hot-and-high conditions of Afghanistan and they were retired in 2006. That left the Royal Navy with a gap in fleet air defence. Even the F-35Bs being bought for the new carriers are not primarily air defence aircraft, but essentially light bombers.

The Falklands War demonstrated the need for some form of airborne early warning. A radar version of the Sea King helicopter had been proposed even before the war and during the war some Sea Kings were modified on a crash basis. The programme continued after the war. Helicopters were fitted with Searchwater radars optimised for air-to-air detection. As with earlier British carrier AEW aircraft, the two system operators acted as fighter controllers using data links, ultimately JTIDS.

The Harrier carriers were modified to emphasise their air function. Here the three steam together, 29 August 1990, with *Ark Royal* in the foreground and *Invincible* in the distance. *Ark Royal* shows a steeper ski jump and a Phalanx CIWS forward of it. Although the Sea Dart missile launcher and magazine had been removed, all three ships retained its Type 909 guidance radar, in the radomes at the ends of the island (*Invincible* shows the antennas but not the radomes, a common practice when the radar had to be repaired). (Fleet Photo Unit Portsmouth)

CHAPTER 13

THE OUTER AIR BATTLE

IN THE 1980s the US Navy looked at its carriers and their fighters in a new way, as part of an offensive-oriented strategy. Ultimately the projected offensive to seize command of the sea was linked to offensives against shore targets which the navy argued would materially change the outcome of a NATO war in Europe, the war US and NATO forces were designed to fight. The combination of a naval campaign to seize sea control, largely from Soviet naval bomber forces, with attacks to change the course of a land campaign ashore, was called the Maritime Strategy. When the Cold War ended, it was a matter of considerable contention, the army and air force arguing instead for a conventional strategy designed to stop or reverse a Soviet ground offensive on the Central Front, meaning the inter-German border. That the Reagan Administration and Congress bought what the navy said it needed to execute the Maritime Strategy suggests that it was accepted at the highest levels.

The idea that naval strike forces could affect the course of a European war was not new. When he became Supreme Commander of Allied Forces in Europe in 1950, Eisenhower likened Western Europe to a peninsula thrust from Eurasia, surrounded on three sides by water. He pointed to the North Sea and the Mediterranean as flanking opportunities. His own wartime experiences in large-scale amphibious operations culminating in D-Day probably helped him visualise the situation from a maritime standpoint. His views contrasted sharply with those expressed by the army and the air force a few years earlier during the unification debate, when they vociferously rejected the navy's arguments in favour of a mobile seaborne US force, including troops.

In retrospect the Maritime Strategy of the 1980s expressed a classic naval approach to land warfare, which can be found in Mahan's writings. The reason it seemed so new in 1982, when it was first publicised, was that the navy had never before publicly explained its favoured approach to a European war. This time its activist Secretary John H Lehman Jr argued that he could not expect Congress to authorise the considerable expansion he considered necessary unless he could explain what it would gain the country. For that reason the Maritime Strategy became a very public lesson in seapower. Since it was a strategy of power projection, the attack carriers were central. For power projection from the sea to work, the carriers' main enemy, the Soviet naval bomber force, had to be destroyed. Thus the Outer Air Battle against the bombers became a prerequisite for the larger maritime strategy.

ORIGINS

In the aftermath of the Vietnam War, US naval attention was concentrated on the Soviet naval threat. Even during Vietnam, the fleet in the Atlantic and particularly in the Mediterranean had faced powerful Soviet anti-carrier strike forces, but funds for new anti-air initiatives had been limited. To a considerable extent as a way of encouraging the Nixon and Ford Administrations to provide increased resources, CNO Admiral Zumwalt famously stated that his fleet had less than an even chance of surviving Soviet attacks. He seemed to accept that at the beginning of a war, the 6th Fleet would have to withdraw altogether

Bait: an A-6 bomber on board *Saratoga* in the Mediterranean.

The target: a 'Badger' missile bomber intercepted by an F-14 during NATO Operation 'Teamwork', 1976.

from the Mediterranean, even though at the time it was the main reserve of NATO nuclear firepower in the area. The Soviets wrote about the 'battle of the first salvo', in which they would mass firepower at the outset to wipe out hostile naval forces, particularly carriers. By the late 1970s many US naval officers seemed to be willing to concentrate simply on surviving such an onslaught. A senior naval officer wrote that the usual exercise demonstrating strike operations in the Norwegian Sea was no more than the 'ritual dance of death'. It seemed that there was little interest in winning the first battle or in using any such success to gain anything more in a NATO war. The new Carter Administration which entered office in 1977 assumed that in any future major war the navy would be limited to the protection of NATO transatlantic shipping against Soviet submarine attacks (the ships would be routed far enough south to avoid air attack). Carter saw carriers entirely as a means of projecting power into the Third World in limited wars (like Vietnam) which he was determined not to fight.

Called upon to describe how it would carry out its future major war responsibility, the navy countered with its own study of its future, Seaplan 2000. Those conducting the study, including future Secretary of the Navy Dr John Lehman, Jr, saw possible dramatic promise in the advent of powerful and reliable new computer technology. The computer-driven systems included the F-14/Phoenix combination and the new Aegis surface anti-air weapon system. Just entering service, the F-14/Phoenix might be used to gain what was now called maritime air superiority because it could deal with much more numerous attackers than before. That recalled the outcome of the battle of the Philippine Sea about thirty years earlier. It might be possible to wipe out the regiments of Soviet naval bombers sent to destroy carriers. Unlike the situation after the 'Turkey Shoot', there would be no question but that such destruction would eliminate the threat of the Soviet naval air force for the rest of any war. There were only about 300 large bombers. New ones were produced at too low a rate (which could not easily be accelerated) and their pilots were too highly trained for either to be replaced during the course of a war. The Japanese really had faced that problem, but in 1944 the US Navy did not understand just what it had done in terms of eliminating most of the Japanese air problem.

The other new technologies would help. Fighters had always been far more effective against bombers than against the much smaller missiles they launched. Surface-to-air missiles, however, were intended mainly to destroy exactly those missiles. In the coming Aegis system the navy would gain a means of destroying the missiles leaking past defending fighters. In the past, the rule had been that once the Soviet

bombers launched their weapons, defending fighters would switch their attention to the missiles. Bombers which had launched were free to return home for future attacks. If the fighters did not have to switch, they could concentrate on the bombers, whether or not they had launched. It might be possible for the fighters to destroy the Soviet long-range attack capacity, rather than simply help the US carriers survive to keep fighting.

A carrier force operating in the face of the Soviet naval air arm would face other kinds of attacks, most importantly by submarines. In the 1970s the new computer technology promised to help in various ways, most notably by offering much greater detection range with towed arrays (using digital signal processing). Seaplan 2000 noted specifically the potential of the new software-controlled Mk 48 torpedo as a way of exploiting long-range detection by US attack submarines.

Given new technologies which suggested that the carriers could do more than merely survive, senior naval commanders became interested in using them to shape the course of a war. In 1979 the Carter Defense Department assumed that the only contribution the Pacific Fleet could make to a major war would be by 'swinging' to the Atlantic. After all, the focus of any such war would be NATO and the inter-German border. Pacific Fleet commander Admiral Thomas Hayward disagreed. It would take so long to 'swing' his big carriers, via the route around Africa, that they would probably arrive in Europe after the war had ended.

Hayward could do a lot more if he stayed in the Far East. If the Soviets were forced to take his carriers seriously, they could not deploy powerful air and submarine forces to Europe. About a quarter of Soviet troops were currently on the Sino-Soviet border, thanks to continuing friction between the two main Communist powers. Troops in Asia cost far more, on a man-for-man basis, than those closer to the Soviet industrial heartland in Europe. Keeping them and their supporting aircraft in the East would make a major contribution to the survival of NATO armies at the opposite end of the Soviet Union, in Europe. The threat of strikes by Hayward's carriers would be invaluable, particularly if the paranoid Soviets feared that they would be supporting a Chinese offensive. The Soviets were well aware that the Chinese considered much of their occupation of Siberia illegitimate, this territory having been seized via unequal treaties the Russians had imposed on the weaker China of the nineteenth century. Hayward seems to have been the first in many years to see carrier strikes as a vital part of a larger NATO strategy, contributing directly to NATO success on land. Such strikes made sense only if the Soviet anti-carrier threat could be faced down – and the new technology promised exactly that.

Airborne hunter: an F-14 of VF-143 launches from *John F Kennedy*, 13 July 2002.

THE MARITIME STRATEGY

Other fleet commanders had their own ideas about how their fleets should be used if war broke out. When he became Secretary of the Navy in 1981, Dr Lehman asked his fleet commanders to integrate their war plans into an overall plan for the naval role in a possible global war. Such a plan would highlight naval needs. It would also make the navy's case to Congress and the new Reagan Administration. The global plan certainly showed how valuable carrier-based strike could be, not only in the Far East but also on the NATO flanks.

Overall, there was a dramatic shift towards offensive operations, which would become possible given the new technology to beat off Soviet attacks. The 1970s focus on open-ocean operations changed towards a vision of operations closer to the Eurasian land mass, which meant co-operation with the other services and with allies. At the same time the Soviets were becoming interested in using fighters to escort their anti-carrier strike bombers and they were also expected to use tactical aircraft if the fleet came close enough to land.

That the fleet commanders' ideas fitted together into a coherent strategy reflected the reality that all of them had much the same understanding of the potential sea power offered – not only protecting ocean-going traffic but also projecting power. In 1981 the US Navy was almost unique in NATO in this view, which it held because it had long operated the main means of power projection from the sea, the large-deck carriers and also Marine Corps amphibious ships (including large helicopter carriers). The French navy had much the same vision as the US Navy, but its air component was far smaller. The other NATO navies, including the Royal Navy, largely equated their sea control mission with anti-submarine operations (the British and the Dutch had some interest in amphibious operations to support the Norwegians on the NATO Northern Flank).

Each of the US fleets evolved a new operating vision. The Atlantic Fleet had planned to keep its carriers south of the Greenland-Iceland-UK (GIUK) Gap at the outset, moving north only after a prolonged ASW campaign had cleared the way. For example, there was interest in using the Irish Sea as an ASW sanctuary for carriers, because its northern and southern entrances could be made into ASW choke points. Any fleet waiting to clear Soviet submarines could not affect the opening phase of a war. The new concept called for the carriers to deploy into the Norwegian coastal area during the expected period of rising tension before war actually broke out. That made sense because any major Soviet ground offensive into Europe would require extensive preparation, which would be detectable.

The 6th Fleet in the Mediterranean had debated how far to withdraw its carriers before the outbreak of war, again because it seemed that Soviet submarines and anti-ship surface ships had to be cleared out of the key operating area in the Eastern Mediterranean. The usual question before the early 1980s was where Zulu Zulu – task force centre – should be placed at the outset. Given their long combat radius, Soviet naval bombers based on the Black Sea could reach into southern Spain. The typical choice was either the central or western Mediterranean. Now the question was whether the eastern Mediterranean or the Aegean was a better starting point for the carriers. This more active view was espoused by the commander of the 6th Fleet and by his superior officer, the CinC of US Naval Forces in Europe (CinCNAVUSEUR). Both became interested in radar shadowing as protection against early anti-ship missile strikes. It explored 'safe havens' such as Aegean islands. As in the north, it became interested in co-operating with friendly air forces past which

Soviet anti-carrier bombers would have to fly. By 1985, forward presence and early offensive operations were a fixed principle in the Mediterranean.

The Pacific Fleet planned an early offensive operation in the North Pacific. It had the advantage of geography. If it operated in the Kurile 'wedge', it might be able to attack while forcing Soviet submarines to pass through choke points where they could be detected and destroyed.

When the new administration thought about the vital role of safe-guarding Atlantic shipping reinforcing NATO, it realised that the Soviet missile bombers were not only the best Soviet anti-carrier weapon, but also the best Soviet anti-shipping weapon. Each bomber might carry only a few weapons at a time, but unless it was destroyed it could come back again and again. No NATO force except the carriers had much chance of destroying bombers which could strike from a long distance. The large role that naval aviation already played in the US Navy made it far more sensitive to this reality than were European navies, including the Royal Navy, for which ASW was the central role.

Moreover, once the Soviet bombers were gone and the submarines contained or destroyed, the strike carriers offered invaluable firepower on the NATO flanks. They could undertake risky operations which would probably reduce the forces the Soviets could deploy on the Central Front in Germany. For example, the Marines bought amphibious craft specifically so that they could land on the flanks of a Soviet advance in Denmark – or even on the Soviet Baltic coast. Whether or not such operations would really have been mounted, a Soviet leadership aware that they were possible would have to hold back forces to counter them. This possible threat and the threat in the Far East, were examples of 'virtual attrition' of Soviet ground forces facing NATO. The more attrition the strike fleets could impose, the less attractive the odds the Soviets might calculate.

The strategy review made the Outer Air Battle – the battle beyond surface-to-air range – crucial. Only in the Outer Air Battle could the Soviet naval air fleet – in effect its battle fleet – be destroyed. The Outer Air Battle term had been used since the mid-1970s, but only after 1981 was its possible significance as an offensive fight understood.

It was well understood that the Soviets regarded the carriers as prime targets, mainly because they were the means of delivering

The intermediate step: an F-14A Tomcat and its stablemate, the E-2C Hawkeye, 1974. The Tomcat is carrying only two of its Phoenix missiles, with drop tanks on two of its hardpoints.

nuclear strikes. In Soviet doctrine, the initial non-nuclear phase of a war had to be devoted to action such as strikes against carriers and attacks on strategic submarines, which would tip the nuclear balance of power and thus decide the outcome of any later phase (if the balance was tipped sufficiently, there might not be a follow-on phase, only surrender). During the early 1980s US naval intelligence discovered another reason the Soviets would badly want to attack the carriers. They had only one naval asset they really valued: their strategic submarines. During the initial phase of the war, their strategy demanded not only that they attack Western strategic forces, but also that they protect their own. They therefore planned to keep their strategic submarines in bastions, such as the White Sea, which their navy would defend. Defence included Soviet attack submarines and also surface and air ASW forces intended to keep Western attack submarines from operating in the bastions. This thinking had been suspected for years, but early in the 1980s credible sources, which have never been identified, confirmed it. The US Navy publicly discussed the way in which its attack submarines would fight Soviet strategic submarines early in a future war. That had long been understood.

The Soviet strategic concept made the carriers doubly important, because the Soviets expected that their aircraft could attack any Soviet surface units trying to keep Western attack submarines out of the bastions. Quite aside from the nuclear threat US carriers represented, this expected role made the carriers vital strategic targets early in a war.

At about the same time the navy's own studies pointed to the critical role of Norway in the defence of the Atlantic (and to its vulnerability to Soviet attack). The situation recalled that of the Second World War, in which the German U-boat force gained enormous impact as soon as it was based on the Norwegian and French Atlantic coasts and no longer had to make the long dangerous trip around Scotland to reach the Atlantic. In this case, if the Soviets could seize the Norwegian coast, NATO would no longer be able to exploit the choke point of the GIUK Gap, through which Soviet submarines based in the Soviet north, had to pass to get to their hunting grounds in the Atlantic

Given the new thinking about a 'Turkey Shoot', all of this was good rather than devastatingly bad news. Now the carriers could be seen as the lethal bait which, it was hoped, would destroy the Soviet air striking force. The object was now to force the Soviets to fight on the worst possible terms, so that their battle fleet – their anti-ship bombers – could be destroyed. This reality was expressed as 'kill the archer, not the arrow', meaning that the priority was now to destroy the incoming bombers.

For example, US tacticians became interested in operating carriers in fjords on the Norwegian coast. They were aware that the main Soviet anti-carrier missile, AS-4, had to lock onto its target at a considerable distance. The mountains around a fjord created enormous radar clutter, which would make it very difficult for a bomber to lock its missile onto the target. Yet they could also offer enough sea room for the carrier to operate her own aircraft and the Royal Norwegian Air Force could contribute to a battle against attacking Soviet bombers. The fjord also had advantages from the point of view of defence against submarines, because any attacking submarine had to pass through the chokepoint of its mouth. The idea of land masking as an air defence measure was apparently first raised in a 1983 review of the evolving maritime strategy. At the least it would force enemy bombers to fly higher in order to detect their targets, making them more vulnerable.

As part of the Outer Air Battle project, an effort was launched to digitise the F-14 and also to provide it with sufficient power. The F-14D was the result. This one from VF-31 is landing on *Abraham Lincoln*, 26 January 2001.

DEFENDING THE FLEET

It was always clear that effective air defence required the earliest possible warning of an approaching enemy, a problem which worsened when the Soviets put the supersonic 'Backfire' into service. This issue had two separate aspects. One was to detect a Soviet bomber strike as early as possible and certainly as far from a carrier group as possible. The second was to force the Soviets to engage carriers as far as possible from their own bases. The second became even more important when the Soviets began to use long-range fighters as bomber escorts. These fighters could not be allowed to get close enough to the carrier battle group to engage the F-14s and other carrier aircraft involved in the Outer Air Battle. To convince the Soviets that they had to deal with US carriers beyond escort fighter range, the US Navy demonstrated that A-6 Intruder attack aircraft could strike at ranges of over a thousand miles, refuelling in flight.

At this time the expected strength of a Soviet attack was two regiments (forty to fifty bombers). Each would carry up to three missiles. The post-launch situation might have worsened later. At the end of the Cold War the Soviets were working on a small semi-ballistic missile, the inertially-guided version of which was entering strategic bomber service. A 'Backfire' could carry six of them internally in its rotary launcher. The projected Kh-15S naval version was never developed and it is not clear whether its projected millimetre-wave guidance system was practicable.

The Soviets were known to favour combined-arms tactics, so they would try to combine bomber attacks with submarine missile and torpedo attacks and also, if possible, with attacks by surface missile shooters. They also favoured electronic warfare, which they called 'radio-electronic combat' and which was generally said to be more inclusive than its Western equivalent. Thus any Outer Air Battle plan to fight incoming bombers had to include ASW and possibly anti-ship elements. In addition, through the 1980s it was thought that the Soviets might use nuclear-armed missiles. At the least that would favour dispersal of US carriers and other warships.

Formal Outer Air Battle studies considerably predated the

Maritime Strategy. By the 1970s, the primary navy advisor on fleet air defence was the Applied Physics Lab (APL) of Johns Hopkins University, which had conceived Typhon and had helped launch Aegis. In the 1970s the navy studied a variety of possible force mixes under different conditions; APL studied the Outer Air Battle using an Air Battle Analyzer to calculate the outcomes. In its final December 1976 study it envisaged two carriers facing fifty-two Soviet bombers, forty-two of them missile shooters (the rest were jammers). The carriers were defended by eleven F-14s, which managed to shoot down 35 per cent of the bombers before they could launch their missiles. If the bombers managed to jam the link between the fighters and the E-2 radar aircraft, their score was halved: they could not pass back information they collected. If the bombers spread out, they also did better (the F-14 score fell 40 per cent). APL concluded that the great value of the F-14 was to probe the attack, giving the task force commander the time to decide how to commit his force.

A summary of further studies through 1982, including some by DARPA (DoD's Advanced Research Projects Agency), showed that the effectiveness of CAP and deck-launched fighters was limited by current systems and tactics. Effectiveness was sensitive to jamming and the possible use of nuclear weapons. Early warning was crucial. The fleet needed more fighter firepower, which meant lighter and more numerous air-to-air missiles. The fleet could disrupt an attack by counter-targeting: by jamming the big radars the Soviets used to find their targets (the EA-6B Prowler was given the necessary capability). A really long-range surface missile (Forward Pass) could augment the CAP fighters, helping destroy the bombers and the jammers. These studies, not all of which were done by the navy, also showed that generally the fleet would have to fight its own battle; land-based aircraft were unlikely to get to the battle in time.

A study made at this time by TRW, a major defence contractor, showed just how early warning should be: it estimated that a carrier group had to stand down all of its fighters and AEW aircraft for 48 hours to prepare for a large raid. In effect it was showing that no such preparation was possible, unless intelligence information was far better than could be assumed.

Elements of Outer Air Battle development were naturally spread among different navy commands and their laboratories. A November 1983 list of items relevant to the Outer Air Battle included an F-14 upgrade, an A-6F upgrade, VFX (which became the F/A-18 Hornet), Forward Pass (concept development), an Outer Air Battle surface-to-air missile (which could be distinguished from an Advanced Surface-to-air Missile in the proposal stage) and Space Based Radar (SBR). At this time the 1990–2000 threat included the stealthier (0.1 rather than 10m^2 radar cross-section) 'Blackjack' heavy bomber carrying four anti-ship missiles locked on after launch, using multi-mode (hence less jammable) guidance. Lock-on after launch would extend missile launch range to 200–300nm. As in the past, the raid would consist of fifty to sixty aircraft. A carrier might place two to four F-14s on CAP out to 600nm, using tankers.

This was an unco-ordinated list of everything which might help fight the battle, not a focused list showing what was most likely to work and most likely to be affordable. Secretary of the Navy John Lehman was a great advocate of focus based on a total system approach. He was very much aware that the Reagan Administration was willing to spend money, but also that if he wasted too much money (or time), the tap would be shut off. In 1983 he therefore opted for a study of all alternative approaches, with fleet operators supplying tactical guidance. One major split was between a surface missile community which wanted to develop a new surface-to-air missile (then called SM-3, capable of engaging high altitude targets at long range) and an air community focusing on a follow-on to the Phoenix missile (AAAM). Another possibility was to adopt a very high performance ship-launched missile controlled by an aircraft (Forward Pass, an earlier idea). Candidates for such control were the E-2 and a modernised A-6 with a new radar.

Probably from the outset it was clear that there was a direct relation between fighters and surface defensive missiles. At some point the bombers would launch their missiles. If the fleet's own anti-air missiles were effective enough, few if any of those missiles would be effective. The US fighters could concentrate on the bombers, whether or not they had launched their weapons. Heavy investment not only in the new Aegis system but also in a dramatic upgrade of existing surface missile systems (the New Threat Upgrade) enormously increased the fleet's ability to destroy any missiles the Soviet bombers might launch. Although that might not be considered part of the Outer Air Battle programme, it made the Outer Air Battle a viable proposition – if the air part of the carriers' defence could be sufficiently improved.

The programme also focused on forcing the attackers to come closer to the fleet before any missiles were launched. The closer the Soviet bombers had to come, the more opportunities to shoot them down. The US Navy had long been interested in deception devices which would force bombers to approach their targets in order to distinguish them, one of the earliest being blip enhancers on escorts (making them appear to be much larger radar targets). The programme of the 1980s added further deception devices, including chaff bombs which aircraft could drop far from a carrier group to bloom into something which would seem similar to a bomber radar.

The US Navy had already made enormous efforts to limit or eliminate electronic emission, particularly of characteristic signals, by a carrier. That had been motivated by early experience, in which Soviet bombers were able to fly directly towards carriers without searching for them, guided by long-range land-based HF radio direction-finders. By about 1970 US carriers were managing to disappear from Soviet view (as evidenced by strenuous efforts to locate them) by turning off their radios and characteristic radars. By that time the Soviets were already developing ocean-surveillance satellites, including a radar satellite which could, in theory, have overcome emission control (however, it needed some way of identifying particular blips with particular types of ships, for which purpose there was a companion electronic intelligence satellite). As it happened, the active-radar satellite programme was dropped, apparently because the Soviets were embarrassed when one of them crashed to earth, carrying with it the small nuclear reactor which powered it. That left the Soviets still vulnerable to emission control by the carriers and to decoying by anything simulating carrier emissions. The navy became interested in substituting alternatives, for example using the E-2 to control carrier air traffic.

Submarines might substitute for snoopers and satellites to locate and even track carriers. The US Navy developed acoustic deception devices which would enable a destroyer to simulate a carrier. The existence of these devices was heavily publicised, to reduce any confidence the Soviets might have in submarine tracking. The appearance of the devices on board ships was kept very secret, so that the Soviets would never know which ships were potential deception platforms.

In the Pacific on 6 April 1981, *Constellation* shows the typical air wing of the 1980s: Tomcat fighters, Corsair II (A-7) and Intruder bombers and Hawkeyes, plus S-3 Vikings for ASW. There were also ASW helicopters for close-defence. One major challenge was to set up the flight deck so that the ship could keep launching and recovering the fighters which would fight the Outer Air Battle. They would be backed by Prowler (EA-6B) EW aircraft which would, if possible, jam the targeting radars of the incoming Soviet bombers. The big empty sponson on the ship's port quarter originally held a Terrier missile launcher. By this time US carriers were being armed with short-range Sea Sparrow defensive missiles, but the longer-range Terrier and its Standard Missile successor were not considered worthwhile. No Sea Sparrow launcher is visible here. The large circular hole just forward of the stern was an exhaust from a jet engine test cell.

Initial detection

The other element of the problem was how to detect the bombers as far forward as possible. Solutions put forward at this time included a constellation of radar satellites and unmanned aircraft (UAVs). The Naval Materiel Command (which included NAVAIR and NAVORD) prepared a request for industry proposals for an end-to-end systems analysis, from initial indications and warning through to engagement. It was ordered to examine commonality between air and surface elements, communications and electronic warfare. This work was somewhat slowed by cuts in funding in FY84. By 1985 it seemed possible that concept definition for an Outer Air Battle system would be completed in 1986, with the usual demonstration/validation phase following in 1987 and full scale engineering development (FSED) following (these were standard designations for different phases of a project).

Probably the earliest warning of a Soviet bomber attack would come from the radio chatter of bomber pilots preparing for take-off. According to Russian accounts, NSA satellites detected exactly such chatter during the Soviet build-up in the Far East. Given a take-off warning, the arrival of the bombers near the fleet could be predicted to within a few hours. 'Badgers' would probably have to fly straight towards the carrier, but 'Backfires' had the range to turn so as to approach from the flanks.

Initial detection came first. Satellites offered solid reliable detection, but only from fairly low altitude. No single satellite could be within range of the bomber path (from bases in the Kola Peninsula down the Norwegian Sea) for long, so this solution would have required large numbers of expensive satellites. Secretary Lehman personally killed it as unaffordable. He decided that the Outer Air Battle study should focus on the alternative of an over-the-horizon (OTH) radar covering a sector pointed towards the Soviet bases. As developed, this radar was relocatable (it was called ROTHR); its antenna was wires strung from a line of telephone poles. Plans called for erecting the ROTHR in Scotland, facing up the Norwegian Sea. It was not nearly as good as a constellation of satellites. It was limited not only to a sector, but also to a particular range band. It could also be affected by auroras, since it relied on HF radio signals. However, it was good enough, because it was affordable. The ROTHR prototype became operational at Amchitka in the Aleutians in 1985, facing the direction from which Soviet Pacific Fleet bombers would likely come towards US carriers. An incidental advantage of ROTHR was that its low-frequency signals would not be much affected if the Soviets managed to build stealthy aircraft. Relocatability was valued because the radar could be moved to match changing strategic circumstances. After the end of the Cold War, that made it possible to use a ROTHR emplaced in the United States to monitor Caribbean drug traffic.

The need to detect Soviet bombers flying south made naval officers look at other possibilities. It turned out that the existing DSP satellites, which had been built to detect missile launches, could spot high-flying aircraft using afterburners – such as 'Backfires'. After eight years of fruitless attempts to interest the air force in this capability, Aerojet-General (which built the satellites) turned to the navy about 1982. Almost at once the navy sent a contingent to the Nurrungar (Australia) DSP ground station. Jets were called Slow Walkers, because they seemed to crawl across the vast area monitored by each satellite (satellites, visible by the glint of sunlight they reflected, were Fast Walkers). The Navy briefed the commander of the Air Force Space Command on its bomber-tracking Project Slow Walker on 3 May 1983. The first formal US Navy Operational Requirement for what became the Slow Walker Reporting System was drafted in 1984.

In the 1980s the United States was already developing an Ocean Surveillance Information System (OSIS) intended mainly to track Soviet warships so that, among other things, they could be attacked by long range (over-the-horizon) Tomahawk missiles. OSIS worked by predicting a ship's position based on her course and speed, assuming that she did not change either (ships were periodically monitored to see whether this was true). The ship's speed did not matter to the system, so it could handle aircraft as though they were thousand-knot ships. After Slow Walker was demonstrated in the Ocean Venture Fleet exercise, the fleet commander wrote that he had never before received such timely data. Off Southern California in the 1980s Slow Walker and OSIS were combined so that F-14s could be cued to intercept fast jets.

Tactics

Offence was always better than defence. If the raid could be tracked far enough out, it would be possible to send out F-14s to attack it before it got within range to launch its own weapons. This was a STRIKECAP and given F-14 range it might be effective as much as 500nm from a carrier. If the planned enemy strike axis could be determined, F-14s could fly down it to disrupt its formation and co-ordination and inflict losses before the attackers reached the CAP.

Overall, once the bombers were the target for offensive AAW, the fleet had to expand the battle space, engaging Soviet bombers as far forward as the F-14s could fly (and as far as their missiles could fly beyond them). Since air defence depended heavily on reliable communication and since UHF was the main means, fighters 500nm from the battle group needed relays. A special automatic relay pod (AUTOCAT) was developed, to be carried mainly by S-3 tankers.

Given the long ranges at which Soviet anti-ship missiles could be fired, it was essential to intercept the attacking bombers as far forward as possible. The F-14 Tomcats intended to kill those archers had to take up CAP stations as far forward as possible. That requirement inspired the development of special tanker procedures called 'Chainsaw', which maintained the maximum possible number of F-14s in the forward positions by cycling F-14s between the flight deck and the layered CAP defence. Some of the forward F-14s would be out of line-of-sight communication range with their carriers and even with their controlling E-2s, so the tankers (generally S-3s otherwise used for ASW) became communications links.

Previous tactics had envisaged separate defensive zones, the fighter zone being 200nm or more from the carrier. The E-2 Hawkeye would be the main source of information. By 1980 the Soviet emphasis on electronic warfare was bringing this type of operation into question. In particular, fleet air defence relied heavily on communications – which the Soviets might jam. Successful jamming of both communications and fleet radars would reduce warning, detection and engagement ranges and make it difficult or impossible to maintain centralised control over a rapidly-moving air battle – particularly since an F-14 200nm from the carrier was at the outer limit of UHF radio range.

Tactics were based on the expectation that external sources of information would indicate the general direction of an attack within a

45–60° sector, so fighters could be concentrated in that sort of sector. Within the sector, fighters occupied CAP positions on a grid defined by sectors of circles and radials. CAP was split into a Long Range CAP (LRCAP or LRC) and a Mid-Range CAP (MRC), both backed by deck-launched interceptors. The latter would fill stations vacated in response to a threat or to reinforce against a major attack. Typically it took 60 to 90 minutes to set up ('stabilise') the grid. The long range that CAP operations demanded emphasised the tanking to keep the grid populated with fighters.

The Soviets were expected to jam US communications. The simpler the messages, the better the chance of overcoming such jamming. Outer Air Battle studies therefore encouraged development of a simplified system specifying fighter position in the CAP grid and commanding it. This technique was called 'vector logic'. It used short, formatted calls to pass crucial information and initiate automatic reactions without the need for further communication.

Vector logic had another virtue. In 1980 US carriers usually operated singly, but the early Outer Air Battle studies made it obvious that multi-carrier operations offered a much better chance of dealing with heavy Soviet attacks. As in the Second World War, multi-carrier operations required standardised procedures and position reporting: in this case, vector logic.

At the same time the navy sought to replace the existing digital data links with a new Link 16 (JTIDS), which would pass more precise information and also be far more difficult to jam. Link 16 was associated with a new-generation tactical data system (the Advanced Combat Data System [ACDS]) using a much more powerful computer. Link 16 has since proven very successful. Developments after the Cold War, particularly the integration of intelligence data with tactical data, proved too much for the single-computer ACDS system and it has since been dropped in favour of a distributed combat direction system. In the 1980s, however, it was exactly what was needed.

The E-2 was key, because the carriers would maintain electronic silence. Unfortunately its UHF radar (APS-125 or -138) was considered so susceptible to jamming that by the mid-1980s its relegation to 'preraid grid management' was being discussed. The E-2C was also the key battle management node for the fighters in the Outer Air Battle, including vectoring deck-launched interceptors and CAP fighters. The deck-launched interceptors were critical because they would replace fighters drawn from their CAP stations to respond to incoming bogeys. Simulations and exercises showed that the reserve of deck-launched interceptors was critical to kill large numbers of aircraft in a mass raid, but they were difficult to deploy. For example, to get them to 200nm range, they had to be committed when the raid was still 500nm away – which meant that the battle group had to rely heavily on information it obtained from external sources.

Given the new concept, priority targets for the F-14s were, in order, bombers still carrying their missiles, jammers shielding them, bombers which had already launched and the missiles themselves in last place. For surface missile ships, bombers with missiles on board were also first priority, but the missiles came second. Since such ships would rarely find themselves far enough out to deal with the bombers, missiles were really their first priority.

Defence included jamming by the carrier group and its aircraft. The EA-6B Prowler was expected to fly towards the Soviet bombers and jam their targeting radars, just as the bombers would be accompanied by their own jammers. At this time the West apparently did not know that the Soviets were labouring under the considerable disadvantage that they had been unable to develop a jammer version of their supersonic 'Backfire'. They had to retain 'Badger' jammers, so any raid by the newer aircraft was hamstrung by the need to co-ordinate with the subsonic jammers. The problem was probably interference with crucial 'Backfire' systems such as fly-by-wire. It was solved only at the end of the Cold War.

There were real problems. It took hours – probably much more than 'Backfire' flight time – to prepare a flight deck for an Outer Air Battle, for example by moving tanker S-3s into position and striking inessential strike aircraft below. One question was therefore whether the strike aircraft could contribute directly to the Outer Air Battle. That was out of the question for light attack aircraft (A-7s). However, new technology offered the possibility that the standard medium attack bomber, the A-6 Intruder, could change roles.

Fixing the F-14

Given its long-range weapon system, the F-14 Tomcat was clearly the key fighter in any Outer Air Battle. It had long been plagued by engine problems; in 1984 the Pratt & Whitney TF30 was considered responsible for 32 per cent of all accidents. It suffered compressor stall, particularly in high-altitude interceptions of simulated anti-ship cruise missiles and in high angle of attack manoeuvres. Engine and afterburner

The Outer Air Battle concept focused attention on tactics which would upset any advantages the Soviet bomber force might enjoy. One idea was to operate a carrier from within a fjord. The steep walls of the fjord would greatly complicate the bombers' radar picture, forcing them to fly closer so that they could target the carrier (perhaps too close to launch missiles). The carrier could benefit from the presence of friendly land-based aircraft. An important principle of the Maritime Strategy was to use land-based fighters to destroy Soviet missile bombers which had to fly within their range. Here *Forrestal* operates inside a Norwegian fjord during Ocean Safari 1987. In this case the land-based fighters would have been Norwegian F-16s. To get to a carrier in the Norwegian Sea, Soviet bombers would have had to fly past Iceland, within range of air force F-15s based there. As part of the Outer Air Battle effort, the US Navy persuaded the US Air Force to maintain the F-15 force in Iceland rather than commit it to the Central Front in Europe. The Soviets became interested in using long-range fighters to escort their bombers. Had they succeeded, the task of the F-14s defending the carriers would have been considerably more difficult. One reason to force the Soviets to attack at maximum range was to strip away any such escorts. Fighter escort may have been the primary intended role of the carrier *Kuznetzov*, although the Soviets certainly became interested in the full spectrum of carrier aircraft.

operation was considered unreliable during catapult launch. Engines stalled following missile firing in a simulated hostile environment. Given the TF30, the F-14 was considered inferior in air-combat manoeuvring due to its inferior dash speed. It could not disengage from foreign aircraft, hence always had to fight. That had been demonstrated when F-14s from *Nimitz* engaged Libyan 'Foxbats' in September 1981. The Libyans routinely used their speed advantage as their primary tactic.

Underpowering limited the load an F-14 could carry effectively. Although it was fitted to carry six Phoenix missiles, an F-14 typically carried four, because it had to carry additional fuel and because with six missiles it was too close to maximum take-off weight. Most F-14s flew with much lighter Sparrows and Sidewinders. The loss of missiles was unacceptable if the fleet was counting on F-14s and their Phoenixes to destroy large numbers of attacking bombers. Only the Phoenix could be launched simultaneously at any great range against multiple attackers. An F-14 carrying a larger number of Sparrows would have to fire them at one target at a time, not switching targets until the previous salvo had hit or missed. It could hardly deal with a mass raid.

A replacement engine had long been planned, but there had never been enough money. Congress appropriated funds in 1979, prior to the Outer Air Battle effort, to develop alternative competitive engines for the F-14 and F-16 and CNO and the Air Force Chief of Staff signed a Memorandum of Understanding in February 1979, effective through 1981. Each service was to manage its own near-term programme. The near term programme made the air force lead developer for a fighter derivative of the General Electric F101 designated F110-GE-100, which successfully flew in both an F-14 and an F-16. It was selected for the F-14 in favour of Pratt & Whitney's F100.

Overall, the F-14 needed reworking. Although it had a digital radar, overall it was an analog aircraft. Whatever was developed to fight the Outer Air Battle would have to be integrated into it by adding new avionics. It was also grossly overweight and the problem was worsening because each avionics box added needed its own analog-digital interfaces. A fully digital aircraft would be built around a data bus. It would be far easier to keep upgrading. In the 1980s the navy view was that the F-14 and A-6 would be needed beyond 2000. Grumman won the digital upgrade programmes for both aircraft; the navy version was the F-14D. One attraction of a fully-digital system was that the central computers could be replaced relatively easily. In the late 1990s this possibility was realised in a submarine programme called ARCI (Acoustic Rapid COTS Insertion, COTS being commercial off-the-shelf technology). ARCI is built around a high-capacity digital bus plus servers whose processors (chips) can be changed periodically. Improved chip capacity gives the whole system new capabilities because the more powerful chips can run new software. There is an aircraft equivalent. In the early 1980s, the F-14 and A-6 were the last analog combat aircraft in the US Navy inventory.

The F-14 also had to adapt other related technology. In the 1980s GPS was under development. It had revolutionary implications for the Outer Air Battle. If a bomber could be tracked by any one system and its position established, a missile with GPS guidance could be despatched to that place to connect with the bomber. There might no longer be much need to keep the attacker under observation by the fighter launching the missile or at least the missile might not need active or semi-active guidance until it neared the bomber, when the GPS position was no longer accurate enough. To exploit any such possibility, the fighter had to be able to integrate GPS location data with fire control. Doing that in an analog system would be a nightmare.

Operating in a fjord, a carrier would have enjoyed the services not only of her own fighters but also of those of the Royal Norwegian Air Force. Here a Norwegian F-16 intercepts a 'Backfire' carrying its AS-4 (Kh-22) missile semi-recessed under its belly. (Norwegian Ministry of Defence)

Other outer air battle aircraft

The A-6 had been designed in the era of analog radars, whose signals were shaped by the power tubes inside. By the time the F-14 was being designed, there was an alternative. The radar waveform could be created by software and emitted at low power through a wide-band amplifier such as a klystron or a travelling wave tube. In the F-14, that potential translated into a true multi-role radar offering both pulse-Doppler performance for air-to-air detection and tracking and surface-to-air operation. In air-to-air mode, moreover, the high pulse rate (for Doppler) feature could be turned on and off in such a way that the range to a target could be measured, something a pure pulse-Doppler could not do. A new version of the Intruder was proposed. It would have a new wing offering both better performance and greater strength, so that it could manage greater take-off weight. More importantly, this A-6F would have a Norden APQ-173 multi-role radar. Among its modes would be air-to-air modes offering it the ability to control long-range missiles like the Phoenix and its successors.[1] This project came directly out of Outer Air Battle studies.

Another factor was the emergence of the new F/A-18 Hornet light-weight fighter, which could replace the single-purpose A-7 light attack bomber to provide a carrier with another 'swing' capability, albeit with only limited range. Several alternative carrier air wings were considered during the 1980s. The carrier *John F Kennedy* experimented with an 'all-Grumman' air wing built around twenty-four F-14s and twenty-four A-6 bombers, plus the fixed ASW force of ten S-3 Vikings and six SH-3H close-in defence helicopters. It included five KA-6 tankers. A proposed new (1984) alternative air wing sacrificed four F-14s and four A-6 Intruders to add eighteen F/A-18s. This air wing included no dedicated KA-6 tankers and it had more ASW helicopters and also more AEW aircraft (five rather than four E-2Cs) and jammers (five rather than four EA-6Bs). This latter air wing was approved as the basis for further aircraft procurement. The new notional air wing was predicated on the planned A-6 upgrade giving it air-to-air capability. The air wing without any light attack was dropped because tests showed that it lacked flexibility.[2]

Air-to-air missiles

Thus the only entirely new weapon associated with the Outer Air

Battle was an Advanced Air-to-Air Missile (AAAM, provisionally designated AIM-152). A Tentative Operational Requirement was issued on 13 April 1984. It required compatibility with the F-14, the A-6 and the new F/A-18 Hornet, to gain the greatest possible number of missile platforms. Phoenix was too heavy and not nearly manoeuvrable enough to deal with supersonic bombers. Weight currently limited the unmodified F-14 to four Phoenix missiles and the F-14 was certain to gain further weight and so to lose even more Phoenix capacity. At this time plans called for providing the A-6E with a multi-mode (including air-to-air) radar in 1990. The upgraded A-6F was to be able to lift four AMRAAM (AIM-120) missiles and three 400-gallon tanks, for a maximum endurance of 3.5 hours. AAAM would be no heavier than AMRAAM.

The AAAM in turn required a new (adaptable) weapon-control system on board the F-14 and thus became another reason to digitise that aircraft. The original F-14 could not land with more than four Phoenix missiles on board. The new missile would be the size of a Sparrow or AMRAAM, so an F-14 would be able to land with eight on board. The navy reportedly specified a maximum diameter of 9in and a weight of 650lbs, with a unit cost less than $750,000, to attack crossing and violently manoeuvring targets at a range of 100nm. Maximum system weight was given as 5303lbs.

Proposals were submitted in May 1987. Each of the two chosen competing teams, Hughes/Raytheon and General Dynamics/Westinghouse, was awarded a demonstration/validation contract running from FY88 through FY90, the winning team to receive a development contract in FY91. By the time the contracts had been completed, the Cold War was winding down and the Outer Air Battle no longer seemed urgent. Without a massive threat presented by regiments of 'Backfires', the AMRAAM air-to-air missile, successor to the Sparrow, seemed good enough. AAAM never reached the contract stage.

Hughes offered an integrated rocket-ramjet, General Dynamics a smaller rocket with selectable burn (so that it could reserve energy for a terminal engagement) it had begun developing in the 1970s as a private venture. It was so small that the company estimated that an F-14 could carry as many as fifteen, though normally it would have six to nine on board. General Dynamics published a graph showing that its missile would have a far larger envelope than Phoenix, with about twice the range and greater altitude capability. The axes were not labelled and it is not clear what sort of target was involved. However, the graph suggests that it was offering 200nm capability.

The great question was how a small missile far from a controlling fighter would engage bombers despite heavy jamming and, probably, decoys. Hughes' solution was a combination IR and active radar seeker, the IR element being used to avoid radar jammers.

With the demise of the AAAM programme, the navy was left with Sparrow and the follow-on AMRAAM (AIM-120). Unlike Sparrow, AMRAAM has an active radar seeker and a data link back to the firing aircraft. As a true fire-and-forget missile, it provides any aircraft carrying it with the sort of multiple-target capability associated with the F-14, albeit at shorter range. To the extent that Phoenix really lacked long range against a manoeuvring target, AMRAAMs aboard an F/A-18 are not much worse and may even be better. There have been persistent reports that the long-range AMRAAM programme includes a rocket-ramjet or ramjet version, which would restore very long range and might approximate Phoenix or even AAAM performance.

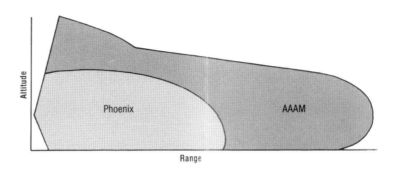

The most visible element of the Outer Air Battle project was a new air-to-air missile, AAAM. It was intended to replace Phoenix, to be far lighter but also to offer enough end-game energy to deal with an agile target such as a 'Backfire'. This is the rocket missile offered by General Dynamics Pomona and Westinghouse. It was the same length as a Sparrow, but only two-thirds the weight and it could be carried by the F-14, F/A-18 and A-6. It had a booster plus an onboard rocket engine to give it end-game energy. This model was displayed at a Navy League show. Note the vanes in the booster exhaust. The missile was described as multi-purpose, so presumably General Dynamics and Westinghouse also saw it as a possible replacement for Sea Sparrow. The project was cancelled at the end of the Cold War.

The claimed superiority of the General Dynamics/Westinghouse missile in the form of comparative operating envelopes. The rival Raytheon/Hughes team merely claimed that its missile had up to four times the range of a Phoenix. Neither comparison was entirely meaningful, because actual missile range depended on an enemy's evasive manoeuvrability.

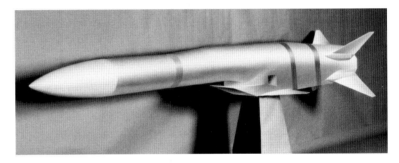

The rival Raytheon/Hughes rocket-ramjet missile in mock-up form.

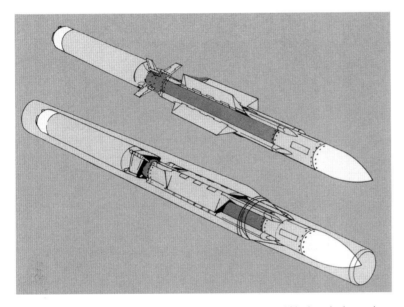

The General Dynamics/Westinghouse missile in its canister. It would be launched towards an expected engagement 'basket', using mid-course inertial (autopilot) guidance with data linked updates as needed. In the terminal phase, the missiles would switch to interrupted CW semi-active homing, but would also have backup infra-red seekers. The specification of interrupted CW was important because a single fighter could then engage multiple targets.

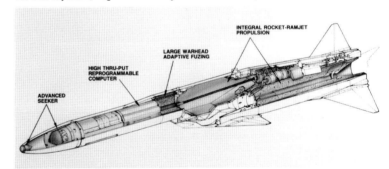

The Raytheon/Hughes AAAM candidate.

WOULD IT HAVE WORKED?

By about 1986 the Outer Air Battle project had created new tactics, including chainsaw and vector logic, which would have given a carrier battle group a considerably better chance of beating off a Soviet bomber attack. Aegis and New Threat Upgrade ships were coming into service, but not yet in sufficient numbers to backstop the fighters. On the other hand, the 'Backfire' force had no viable jammer to operate with it and a force of approaching 'Backfires' could have been jumped by F-14s before it joined up with its jamming 'Badgers' (alternatively, the 'Backfires' could have flown at 'Badger' speed, but with the disadvantages that implied). F-14 performance would still have been limited. Phoenix would have been effective against 'Badgers' but much less so against higher-performance 'Backfires'.

By this time the US fleet had adopted very dispersed operating formations and the Soviets might have had to come a lot closer to the carriers than they would have wished. That would have given the F-14s far more opportunities to hit them with their missiles still onboard. There is no way of knowing how well Soviet jamming would have worked against the E-2s and the communications holding the fleet air-defence system together.

By this time, too, US naval tacticians had given enormous thought to the creative use of nearby land and the Soviets might have found their task extremely difficult.

By the end of the Cold War, the balance seemed to be tipping in favour of the US Navy, not least because much-improved surface missile ships offered an effective backstop against missiles which bombers might be able to launch before the F-14s engaged them. Whether or not the F-14s managed to destroy most of the attacking bombers, the carriers would likely survive to fight another battle. It would not take many battles to neutralise the bombers and achieve the object of the Outer Air Battle.

EPILOGUE

It is a quarter-century since the end of the Cold War. The period since 1989 has seen a great deal of carrier operation, but it has been unopposed. Attention has turned to strikes from the sea. The F-35 which the US Navy and the Royal Navy are buying was conceived not really as a fighter, but rather as a stealthy light bomber which would evade rather than engage enemy air defences, including enemy fighters. In this sense it is broadly analogous to the Cold War A-6

Future fighter defence: the carrier-based F-35C Lightning II. It was conceived as a fast, stealthy light bomber, its main advance being the ability to cruise at supersonic speed, rather than cruise sub-sonically and fly only briefly at supersonic speed using an afterburner. Development emphasised electronic systems to make up for sacrifices in speed and stealth. That made the F-35 extraordinarily expensive because the cost of individual software items could not really be predicted, hence could not be evaluated compared to what they would offer. The F-35 is likely to be quite effective in fleet air defence, not least because its stealth will make it difficult for attacking aircraft to detect. On the other hand the fleet air defence net as a whole is likely to detect incoming stealth aircraft. Even the stealthiest aircraft occasionally returns a usable echo to a radar. One radar does not see it often enough to track it, but multiple radars pooling their data can form usable tracks as a basis for defence. The key factor in defence would probably be the quality of their air-to-air missiles, taking netting and data links into account. This would be the Eagle-Missileer situation; dogfighting would not come into it. Offensively, the US Navy sees the F-35 C as its 'day one attack bomber', much as it once saw the A-6 Intruder, an aircraft capable of penetrating without escort. Certainly the F-35 was never conceived as an air-superiority fighter. F-35C prototype CF-2 is shown with AIM-9X Sidewinder missiles on its wingtip pylons.

Intruder, though it is much faster and it carries a much lighter load of precision weapons. During its development it was given a high-capability radar and it can carry air-to-air missiles. In this way it is broadly analogous to the projected digitally upgraded A-6 of the Outer Air Battle era.

Perhaps the most important change since the Cold War has been the explosive growth of digital technology. In the 1980s the most important new US development was the Co-operative Engagement Capability, an extension of the Aegis missile system to embrace multiple ships. That took longer to develop than had been hoped, but by the mid-1990s it worked. Further integration within the fleet has produced a co-operative command and control system which is intended to integrate all of a fleet's weapons, probably including those in the air.

This is an enormous increase in fleet defensive firepower, but not in the sort of offensive air-to-air capability envisaged in the Outer Air Battle. That makes sense: the main threat to Western fleets since the end of the Cold War has been relatively short-range anti-ship missiles, usually shore-based. However, with the rise of antagonism between the People's Republic of China and the West and also with the growth of a Chinese anti-carrier bomber force reminiscent of the force raised by the Soviets, that may be changing. The Outer Air Battle and the

The F-35 programme includes a VTOL variant, which will equip both US Marine Corps squadrons (which operate from large-deck amphibious ships) and the Royal Navy. This F-35B test aircraft is shown on board *Wasp*, 12 August 2016. The F-35 uses a variation on the Sea Harrier theme of a single lift and cruise engine. Instead of vectored thrust forward of the engine it uses the engine to drive a fan via an extension shaft. The fan provides the forward component of lift while the main engine thrust is vectored to provide the other leg. Compared to a multi-engine VTOL, this is probably considerably more reliable, because the aircraft cannot be brought down by the failure of one of its engines: as long as the main engine runs, the aircraft can rise vertically. The argument for greater reliability with two engines fails because the failure of one of them during lift will crash the aircraft.

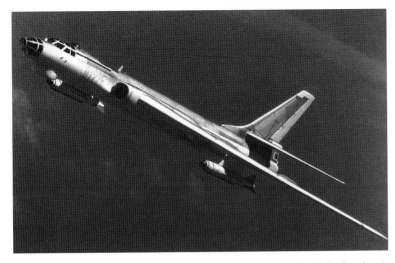

This Chinese-built 'Badger' carries the standard Chinese long-range anti-ship missile, the subsonic YJ-6L based on their copy of the ship-launched Soviet 'Styx' (SS-N-2). The bomber resulted from a manufacturing agreement signed early in 1956; assembled from Soviet components, the first flew on 27 September 1959 with the Chinese designation H-6. Production from Chinese components continued after the Sino-Soviet split, the first all-Chinese airframe flying on 24 December 1968. About 120 had been built before production ended in 1987; it later resumed. Development of the anti-ship H-6D, began in 1975; it first flew on 29 August 1981. Its missile fire-control system employs a Type 245 search and target acquisition radar in an enlarged chin radome. Its claimed performance (detection of a 7500m^2 surface ship from 9000m at a range of 150km matches that of the YJ-6(Y) (export version C-601), whose range is 100km. The first firings of inert missiles were conducted in December 1981, followed by live firings at the end of 1983; the H-6D and its YJ-6 missile formally entered naval service in December 1985, having been exhibited at the Paris Air Show the previous May. H-6 production was resumed in the late 1990s, initially to provide the Chinese air force with a new strategic strike aircraft, H-6H. A further H-6G (also known as H-6M) has a new internal system and four weapon pylons. It was announced with a video at the 2002 Zhuhai air show. In 2014, the Chinese naval air arm was credited with thirty H-6 heavy bombers, thirty H-5 light bombers (copies of the old Soviet Il-28 'Beagle') and fifty-four JH-7s, as well as thirty-five older Q-5 attack bombers and numerous fighters.

This H-6G shows its YJ-12 launch rails. YJ-12 has also been shown under the wing of a J-15 fighter-bomber. An H-6G can carry four YJ-12 missiles, but thus far usually only two are shown.

A Chinese YJ-6 on display at the Chinese Naval Museum, Qingdao. The missile behind it is a ship-launched 'Silkworm', which is much the same missile. YJ-6 has a range of 100km; the later YJ-6(L) has a range of 200km. YJ-6 entered service in 1987; YJ-6(L) followed in the mid-1990s. Also visible are the JL-1 submarine-launched ballistic missile and the booster of an SA-2 (HY-2) land-based anti-aircraft missile. YJ-6 length is 7.36m (24ft 1in), diameter is 0.76m (2ft 6in) and weight is 2440kg (1106lbs) with a 510kg (231lb) warhead. Speed is Mach 0.9.

The YJ-6L is now being superseded by the supersonic rocket-ramjet YJ-12, shown on board this H-6G. YJ-12 was first shown publicly at the 3 September 2015 parade marking the fiftieth anniversary of the end of the Pacific War. Photos had previously appeared. YJ-12 is a rocket-ramjet like the Russian Kh-31 (AS-17) previously bought by China, but it is considerably larger. Approximate length is 7.5m (24ft 7in) and diameter is probably 0.5m (1ft 7in). Range is probably 300km and the warhead is likely to weigh about 250kg (551lbs). Speed is likely to be Mach 2.5 to 3.0.

A Chinese naval JH-7A fighter-bomber shows two YJ-83K training rounds underwing; it can carry up to four. As its designation suggests, this is a dual-purpose (fighter [J] and bomber [H]) aircraft. It was adopted by the Chinese navy after the Falklands War seemed to demonstrate the value of such aircraft against surface ships. The nose holds a new JL-10A Shan Ying J-band pulse-Doppler radar with a detection range of 80km and a tracking range of 40km in look-up mode, or 54/32km in look-down mode (air-to-surface range is not given). Compared to the original JH-7, it has composite structures and an improved fly-by-wire control system. YJ-83K is the air-launched version of the YJ-8 anti-ship missile, which seems to have started life as a derivative of the Exocet. It has a range of 200–250km and a speed of Mach 0.8 to Mach 0.9. Length is 5.14m (16ft 10in) and diameter is 0.36m (1ft 2in); the missile weighs 595kg (1311lbs) and carries a 165kg (363lb) warhead.

philosophy of offensive rather than purely defensive fleet air defence may once again be relevant. To the extent that an F-35 is truly stealthy, it may be able to get much closer to approaching bombers than the F-14s of the 1980s and in that case the limited range of its AMRAAM missile may not be a significant issue.

The other great development since the end of the Cold War has been the continuing rise of carrier fleets in navies which have not his-torically operated carriers against serious opposition, particularly in the Chinese and Indian navies. On the other hand, the Russian carrier force, which in the 1980s was a fascinating and serious future issue, is less likely to be significant in the future, as Russia continues to suffer considerable economic problems. There is insufficient information to be able to say how each of these navies sees the role of carriers, let alone the tactics and technology of fleet air defence.

NOTES

INTRODUCTION

1. For a more elaborate discussion of anti-ship tactics up to the end of the Second World War, see my *Naval Anti-Aircraft Guns and Gunnery* (Barnsley: Seaforth and Annapolis: Naval Institute Press, 2013).
2. In the Mediterranean, the Royal Navy could decrypt Italian air reconnaissance reports. If they were far enough off in position (which was not uncommon), fleet policy was to avoid shooting the snoopers down, on the theory that they were harmless. I am grateful to Alan Raven for this insight, gleaned during his own research on British cruiser operations for a forthcoming book.

1. THE CARRIER NAVIES

1. For its part the Air Ministry evaluated the staff requirements for feasibility. Initially such evaluation was informal (it is reflected in discussions of the S/R and F/R in 1922–4), but in 1927 the Air Ministry set up an Advisory Committee on Aircraft for the FAA. For the historian, the great value of the Advisory Committee is that the Admiralty had to explain its requirements. Otherwise much of what it wanted would have fallen into the category of 'know to all, hence unstated', a bane of any historian. The initial Advisory Committee file, beginning with the second meeting, is AIR5/872, opened 22 September 1926. It includes discussions of important aircraft equipment, such as W/T fitted to Fleet Fighters. The Committee also figures in many files on aircraft specifications.
2. These command arrangements were complicated by the fact that there was no single British fleet during the interwar period. The two major fleets were the Home Fleet (originally the Atlantic Fleet) and the Mediterranean Fleet. In wartime the Mediterranean Fleet would form the core of the War Fleet which would steam east to meet the Japanese fleet. It therefore included, for much of the interwar period, the three largest British carriers, *Furious*, *Courageous* and *Glorious* and the (ship-based) air commander in the Mediterranean was, for most of the afloat. As senior air officer, he was also the major source of operational thinking to balance the more technical ideas of the Naval Staff. Note that even after the FAA was restored to the Royal Navy, Coastal Command was not, so there was no direct line of command between, say, an embarked fleet commander and the long-range flying boats which might provide him with initial reconnaissance.
3. On this basis the tentative 1924 building programme included a new carrier, but it and the programme died after the 1924 General Election.
4. The holiday may have been intended by its US sponsors to cripple naval industry and thus to preclude any future naval arms race; in its original form it covered all warships, not only the big-gun capital ships limited by the Washington Naval Treaty. The British records of treaty discussions suggest that the building holiday was proposed for its political impact and that the US delegates soon regretted it. The British strenuously opposed it on the ground that it would destroy the British naval arms industry. To a very limited extent they received a sop in the form of permission to build two more battleships (*Nelson* and *Rodney*), but the deep industrial damage done by the treaty and the 'holiday' extension shows in difficulties encountered during naval rearmament in the 1930s. To some extent the United States evaded the problem because much of its heavy building capacity resided in navy yards not wiped out by the curtailment of construction (major private yards, most notably Cramp, were not so fortunate).
5. The Washington Treaty allowed an additional 3000 tons for each existing ship to add protection against new weapons (bombs and underwater weapons), as encouragement not to build new capital ships. The US Navy interpreted this clause as allowing the addition of the 3000 tons to the converted battlecruisers, which were therefore designed to displace 36,000 tons (a figure never used publically). The displacements of the two ex-battlecruisers were always given as 33,000 tons with an asterisk, the note indicating that they had additional (unspecified) provision for protection against bombs and underwater weapons. The somewhat loose reasoning involved prompted a Secretary of the Navy to ask, while the ships were being redesigned, whether the extra 3000 tons could be foregone; that was impossible.
6. The Royal Navy found it in the Locarno Treaty, by which Britain, among others, guaranteed German post-war borders. In theory, then, Britain might have to fight France if France attacked Germany. Admiralty papers

include studies of the effects of blockade on France and Italy, written at this time.

7. The interwar issues of the official (more or less annual) *Progress in Tactics* included an intelligence section, part of which reported US and French agreement that battleships remained the core of sea power because only they could reliably sink other battleships. Japanese agreement was implied by a 1937 report that Japanese carrier doctrine concentrated on anti-carrier strikes to the exclusion of attacks on other types of warships (this was hardly entirely true, but Japanese security was excellent).
8. Modern analysis of the sinking suggests that the tactics employed by the ship were at fault. Her commander relied on his medium-calibre high-angle guns (5.25in) rather than on evasive manoeuvres. He did not realise how ineffective they were. He waited until too late to comb the torpedo tracks and as a result the ship was hit well aft. That was extremely unfortunate, because it was the one place in which the ship's torpedo protection was ineffective. The first hit, near where a propeller shaft emerged from the hull, was fatal. See my *British Battleships 1906–1946* for this analysis. Part of the argument was that a manoeuvring capital ship at sea was a very difficult torpedo target. At Taranto (1940) and at Pearl Harbor (1941) aerial torpedoes were used effectively, but against static capital ships in harbour.
9. The comment that carriers could be sunk by surface warships appears frequently in the interwar issues of *Progress in Tactics*. It was not a particularly unique observation; among the comments on a US Navy Fleet Problem (a full-scale fleet exercise) is that this one repeated the well-known lesson that carriers had to have heavy cruiser escorts. The comments in *Progress in Tactics* make it particularly notable that during her run back from Norway to Scapa *Glorious* did not maintain scouting aircraft aloft. It is possible that she was too low on aviation fuel, but no records of her fuel state survived her sinking. She did try to place strike aircraft in position to launch, but early damage by the German battleships precluded that.
10. Hence the great attention the Royal Navy paid to the aerodynamics of its carriers, reflected in airfoil-shaped islands on board the Second World War armoured-deck carriers and also in the rounded after ends of their flight decks. These features were tested in wind tunnels. The US technique allowed not only for much less attention to carrier air flow but also for higher landing speeds, which could translate into better overall performance.
11. This particular conclusion was mentioned in connection with the failure to provide sufficient 'depth' in the code used by convoys. Required cipher 'depth' is determined by how many messages are envisaged; pre-war estimates were wildly low. The consequence was that the Germans broke and exploited the codes to set up ambushes by wolf packs of U-boats.
12. *Progress in Tactics* for 1928 (ADM 186/144) reported that it had been possible to bring an aircraft back to a ship from 45nm away.
13. The idea of using a VHF beacon in the carrier and a specialised homing device in the aircraft is first mentioned in the 1931 edition of *Progress in Tactics* (published in June 1932). Typically carrier pilots were informed of the carrier's intended movements before they took off (the US Navy called this the 'point option' method). However, in a 1932 exercise ('CC') the carriers found it difficult to reach the planned rendezvous, because they found themselves making unexpected manoeuvres. The carrier had to break radio silence, which was clearly dangerous. The best solution suggested at the time was that the carrier launch an aircraft specifically to broadcast her change of course (in code), but that proved impossible during the exercise due to 'limitations of materiel'. Hence the importance of the beacon. The prototype VHF beacon was installed on board *Courageous* in 1935. Type 72 had been accepted as a success by 1939 and was considered accurate at 50nm and approximately accurate (in bearing) at 100nm. Aircraft generally had to fly above 7000ft to use it and, according to Progress in Tactics 1939, 'a high degree of training is necessary for an observer to obtain consistently accurate bearings'.
14. At this time policy was established by Fifth Sea Lord and the staff and aircraft procurement functions were under the Director of the Naval Air Division. Naval aircraft and related equipment was bought by the Director of Air Materiel, who might be likened to DNC. The post of Fifth Sea Lord lapsed briefly in July 1942 (replaced by Chief of Naval Air Services) but was restored by the end of 1942. Fifth Sea Lord was double-hatted as Chief

of Naval Air Equipment. A new post of ACNS (Air) was introduced. The Naval Air Division, which might be considered the British equivalent of the US BuAer, was replaced by two separate organisations, the Naval Air Organisation Division (responsible for the day-to-day work of the FAA) and a Naval Air Warfare and Flying Training Division, responsible for Staff Requirements, Air Tactics and Training. During 1943 the Department of Air Materiel was split into an Air Equipment Department (which stated quantitative requirements for aircraft, engines, etc and allocated, also dealing with technology) and an Airfield and Carrier Requirements Department, which laid out airfields and equipment for aircraft in carriers and catapult ships and also had technical sections dealing with airborne radio and radar and photography. The proliferation of departments reflects the explosive wartime growth of the FAA.

15. I have omitted discussion of wartime and post-war experience using land-based fighters to protect seaborne forces, particularly convoys. That was important both near Malta and around Britain. This experience was reflected after the war in the construction of Type 61 aircraft-direction frigates (they were not fast enough to function as fleet radar pickets). The closest US equivalent was the destroyer escort converted into a radar picket, but it had a very different role: it was intended to support the seaward extension of the radar system protecting the continental United States from bomber attack.

16. A transcript of a 1952 speech survives (in Hungarian archives) in which Stalin told some key East European government officials that they should prepare for a new world war. Stalin was sufficiently paranoid that by 1952 he could have interpreted Western defensive mobilisation (in response to the outbreak of the Korean War) as preparation to attack him. Unfortunately the mass of material which became available to Western historians after the fall of the Soviet Union did not include relevant war planning documents.

17. Initially the United States supplied NATO states with surplus equipment, including naval aircraft, intended to help them build up their own forces to deter the Soviets. However, there was no Supreme Commander of NATO forces in Europe (SACEUR) and no Alliance-wide war plan to be activated if the Soviets moved West.

18. The need to defend sterling was evident to anyone travelling out of the United Kingdom through the mid-1970s: the amount of sterling which could be exported (e.g. in one's pockets) was strictly limited.

19. Contemporary British observers sometimes made the mistake of seeing the General Board as equivalent to the Board of Admiralty. It had been created largely as a war planning body, the quasi-staff requirement role being added in 1908 on the theory that it represented the views of the seagoing navy. After 1919 the General Board lost its war planning role to OpNav. Historians have benefitted heavily from the excellent state of the General Board's papers, including transcripts of its numerous hearings. There is some question as to whether the state of these papers leads to overestimation of the significance of the General Board.

20. The President's Aircraft Board (Morrow Board) reported on 30 November 1925. Its report is in GB 449 file 1924–5. The Secretaries of War and the Navy had jointly asked for a board to examine US air policy and it was appointed by a letter from President Coolidge signed 12 September 1925. Chairman Dwight W. Morrow was a lawyer and banker. One member was William F Durand, who later chaired the committee which arranged initial US gas turbine (jet engine) contracts in 1941. In 1925 he was President of the American Society of Mechanical Engineers and a member of the National Advisory Committee on Aeronautics (NACA), the forerunner of the current NASA. The board held four weeks of hearings (ninety-nine witnesses). Many were airmen, chosen because there was a widespread opinion among fliers that their views were not being heard. Key conclusions were that US civil and military aviation should remain entirely distinct; that the proposed Department of National Defense (amalgamation of the services) should not be created; and that there should not be a separate Air Department distinct from the services (an independent air force). The committee was well aware that since creation of the RAF there had been considerable controversy over the future of the FAA, to the point where a special subcommittee of the Committee on Imperial Defence had been appointed in 1923. Its evidence had not been made public, but it seemed clear that the problem continued to be acute, the Admiralty considering it 'intolerable' that it should be responsible for the success of the Battle Fleet without controlling the supporting air force. The committee further pointed out that, unlike the army, the US Navy integrated its aircraft into the fleet. Its air personnel expressed dissatisfaction over their poor chances of promotion and of high command, because they could not meet all the requirements levied on other officers. The command of flying men by non-flying officers was objected to by the fliers. The navy had no aviators in its upper ranks. The committee recommended appointment of an Assistant Secretary of the Navy for Air and, as importantly, that 'selection for command or for general line duty on aircraft carries and tenders or for command of flying schools or for other important duties

requiring immediate command of flying activities should be confined to those officers who, while otherwise qualified, are also naval aviators . . .'. Congress passed the necessary legislation.

21. In 1934 the War College was moved into the naval school system and its strategic influence declined sharply. That seems to have been a consequence of the retirement of Chief of Naval Operations Admiral William V Pratt in 1933. Pratt, who had previously been President of the War College, seems to have been associated with its President in 1930–3, Admiral Harris Laning, who was particularly outspoken in using gaming experience to suggest how carriers and their aircraft would function in future wars. Pratt was widely disliked within the navy for his advocacy of naval arms control (his appointment as CNO was probably seen as a reward for helping make the 1930 London Naval Conference a success). Laning did not suffer for his association with Pratt, but it is noteworthy that after he left no War College President cited war gaming experience when asked for advice on, for example, building programmes. Without the backing of War College gaming, US naval aviation seems to have lost some of its drive; the building programmes planned in the late 1930s and as late as 1939 showed very few new carriers. It appears that much of the impetus for the large carrier component of the 1940 'Two-Ocean Navy' programme can be traced to President Franklin D Roosevelt.

22. By this time there was also considerable scepticism as to whether any part of the Philippines would still be under US control by the time the fleet arrived.

23. A 1941 study showed that the result would be an expensive but unsatisfactory carrier. President Roosevelt personally rejected the conclusion and demanded something more like an escort carrier. The result was the Independence class light carrier.

24. Other exotic measures, such as specialised ASW submarines, were also envisaged and were later developed, but they had nothing to do with carrier and fleet air defence.

25. As the premier carrier force in the world, the early post-war US Navy and it showed little or no interest in foreign innovations. The British-developed steam catapult was adopted because the failure of US projects for high-capacity catapults led to a crisis: US carriers would be unable to operate the new nuclear bombers (particularly the A3D Skywarrior) when they became available in 1953.

26. To avoid embarrassment the new *Forrestal* was somewhat smaller than her cancelled predecessor and she was described as a general-purpose rather than a nuclear strike carrier. However, nuclear capability was at the core of the new design.

27. The key development seems to have been a study of nuclear war planning ordered in 1957 by President Eisenhower. The air force asked him to approve a substantial increase in the nuclear stockpile. Eisenhower approved but asked for a review of the Strategic Air Command (SAC) war plan – by the other services (the navy's review was conducted by China Lake). The review showed that SAC did not need anything like the number of weapons it planned to deliver. If it delivered its planned strike, fallout would kill many in countries allied with the United States. A limited nuclear force – which could be provided by Polaris submarines – would suffice.

28. The best-known outright cancellation was the seaplane striking force built around the new P6M Seamaster jet. The programme for a new high-energy aircraft fuel (ZIP fuel) seems to have been another victim of the Polaris decision. It is also possible that the financial problem led to the requirement that either the F8U-3 Crusader III or the Phantom (F4H, later F-4) be cancelled. The situation was exacerbated by the unexpected cost escalation of various naval programmes, such as missile cruiser conversions. The hiatus in carrier construction made it possible for sceptics outside the navy to ask whether carriers were still worthwhile.

29. The Japanese government maintained a list of likely enemies in order of probability, as ratified at Imperial Councils. In 1907 and again in 1914 the list was Russia, the United States and China, in that order (China had replaced France in third place in 1907). At that time the United Kingdom was a Japanese ally. In February 1923 the defence policy was modified to specify the United States, Russia and China in order of probability, but the United Kingdom was listed as a potential enemy. After the failure of the 1927 Geneva conference a new Japanese naval policy (August 1928) made the United States (with the United Kingdom) the primary possible naval enemy. By 1933 the Japanese army and navy were debating future expansionist policies, the army offering 'Strike North' (into Siberia) and the navy 'Strike South' (into China and beyond to the Dutch East Indies). The 'Strike South' option was formally approved in 1936, leading to the attack on China the following year. These decisions justified naval expansion to meet both US and British threats, since the 'Strike South' concept included expansion into Malaya, a British possession. A new formal defence policy approved in June 1936 listed as potential enemies, in order of probability, the United States, Russia, China and the United Kingdom. After the success of the German blitzkrieg in Europe the Japanese government

decided that only the United States could oppose the Japanese determination to set up a 'new order' in Asia (i.e. hegemony, supplanting the European colonies).

30. The Japanese created a Total War Institute specifically to estimate US war potential. It reported at the crucial June 1941 Imperial Council meeting which decided on war. The Institute's estimate was substantially more optimistic (for the United States) than US estimates of the time, because it assumed correctly that barriers to mobilisation would be overcome. It forecast a three-year war ending in total defeat. The United States had just imposed an oil embargo (Japan imported all her oil and at the time the United States was the world's greatest producer). After the Institute representative left, a Japanese naval officer summed up: Japan had enough oil for eighteen months at peacetime rates or for twelve months at wartime rates. The Japanese could 'live like slaves or die like men' – the sort of choice which should be extremely sobering to any believer in deterrence or economic coercion. The meeting decided that the Japanese should 'die like men'.

31. US analysts suspected correctly that Japanese interest in a battle-line engagement would lead them to withhold their own battleships while mounting air attacks. Integration between Japanese carrier forces and battleships was extremely limited before 1944. Only the four expendable *Kongo* class fast battleships were deployed to support the carriers at, for example, Midway. US expectations that the Japanese would not risk their battle line probably made the destruction of the US battle line at Pearl Harbor less devastating for the United States, enabling the navy to risk carriers in raids on Japanese islands as early as February 1942.

32. Western proponents of the treaties argued that a fleet crossing the Pacific or the Indian Ocean to confront Japan would lose strength for every mile it steamed from its base, so the 5:3 ratio actually offered Japan sufficient strength to beat off either of the larger fleets. This argument seems not to have enjoyed any support in Japan; the ratio was seen simply as a humiliation. Some Japanese pressed for a 70 per cent rather than 60 per cent ratio, without much analytic support.

33. The Naval General Staff had four bureaus: naval affairs (personnel), war plans, mobilisation (including shipping protection) and intelligence. It apparently prepared the equivalent of British Staff Requirements, which were filled by the technical bureaus. It does not appear that there was a large formal Naval Staff on the British post-1917 model, although the Japanese were certainly aware of what the British were doing. All staff organisations were very lightly manned by US or British standards.

2. FIGHTERS

1. Pilots sometimes complained that this sight required an extra measure of target recognition; it was no longer enough to be sure that the target was an enemy aircraft. Now the pilot had to know which type it was. Some US fighter pilots preferred the earlier reflector sights.

2. The engine draws in air on the first down-stroke, then fuel is injected into the cylinder. On the up stroke it compresses the air-fuel mixture, which is ignited at the top of the stroke. The next stroke is the power stroke, the expanding mass of hot gas forcing the piston down. The final stroke of the cycle is the second up stroke, the ascending piston forcing the mass of burned air out of the cylinder. Typically poppet valves in the cylinder head are co-ordinated with the strokes, to admit air or allow the expulsion of exhaust gas. Their action is typically controlled by cams on auxiliary shafts driven by the engine. Valves and controlling rods make engine design more and more complex as cylinders are added.

3. Radials have their own problems, such as vibration in a very short crankshaft. When the Air Ministry began developing British naval aircraft in the 1920s, it clearly preferred the new generation of air-cooled radials, but initially it pointed out that they were less reliable than the Napier Lion, a liquid-cooled engine. Successive versions of the Lion were apparently competitive with radials in torpedo bombers and multi-seat aircraft and the streamlining associated with an in-line engine helped provide the Fairey IIIF with unusually high maximum speed in the late 1920s. The two principal radials between about 1922 and 1930 were the Bristol Jupiter and the Armstrong Jaguar. By the late 1920s Rolls-Royce was competing effectively with a new generation of lighter-weight in-line engines, the Falcon and its derivative the Kestrel and the Kestrel powered the fighters ordered at that time for the FAA (the RAF continued to use air-cooled fighter engines).

4. Paul J Christianson, *Westinghouse J40 Axial Turbojet Family* (Bleeg Publishing, 2015), p 5. ADR scaled engine weights to thrust, based on the earlier Westinghouse series. Thus the 12,000lbs thrust engine required a 27,000lbs fighter (maximum speed 686mph). Scaling back to 8000lbs thrust reduced overall fighter weight to 19,000lbs and that reduction compensated for the loss of power: maximum speed was 670mph.

5. The situation is explained in a 19 November 1952 memo from the Director, Power Plant Division and the Director, Aircraft Division in the BuAer Confidential VF3H1 file for 1952. At this time the F3H was

scheduled to use the J40-WE-22 until the desired -24 became available. Because the output of the -22 was considered marginal to unsatisfactory, BuAer and McDonnell had been looking at alternatives during 1952. They concluded that without major modifications, which no engine manufacturer was willing to undertake, only the J40 could fit the F3H without major redesign. If the -24 did not materialise quickly enough, the navy would have to accept underpowered aircraft for some time. The situation changed when Allison declared its willingness to redesign its J71, making it nearly interchangeable with the J40; it would also become available at about the same time as the J40 (under the optimistic schedule then envisaged). At the least, Allison was offering valuable insurance against the failure of the J40, which by then must have seemed entirely possible. At the end of October 1952 Allison submitted a formal proposal for the necessary redesign. McDonnell indicated that it could produce an F3H which could use either engine at a weight penalty of 40lbs and that it might become available before July 1954. Estimated performance with the J71 was 5 to 8 per cent better than with the J40. As an explanation of the problem, the memo pointed out that the -22 engine had about the same thrust as the engine in a Cougar, which was far lighter than a Demon. The J71 was even more attractive because, since it could fit an essentially unmodified Demon, it could also fit the other two J40 fighters, the F4D Skyray and the F10F Jaguar (ultimately it was used in neither). The J71 was also expected to be substantially less expensive than the J40. The memo recommended a 50–50 split between J40 and J71 engines.

3. FIGHTERS WITHOUT RADAR

1. It is of course impossible to say how much the interwar Royal Navy concentrated on fighter defence or indeed on fighters of any kind. Writers, both official and unofficial, later claimed that fighter defence of the fleet had enjoyed no great priority during the interwar period. However, the official publication *Progress in Tactics* described considerable efforts to develop a pre-radar form of warning and fighter control. The fighter control technique described in 1936 seems to have been a direct precursor of that employed in 1940.

2. ADM 1/8576/341, which includes remarks by DNC and the conclusions of a 15 July 1920 staff meeting on policy.

3. ADM 1/8602/52, *Review of Progress in Naval Aviation*, March 1921, as submitted by the Naval Air Section of the Naval Staff. This is a draft typescript. *Progress in Naval Aviation* was later issued on an annual basis.

4. The fleet fighter was required to operate as a landplane (deck take-off), as a floatplane and as an amphibian; the same requirements would hold through the interwar period. Competitive prototypes were ordered the next year under specification 6/22 and Fairey won the production contract (to Specification 6/24: forty-two in August 1924 and another sixty-four in 1925) with its Flycatcher. By this time there was a satisfactory radial fighter engine. Although air-cooled radials were very much the navy's preference, the choice for such an engine was made because there was no alternative modern liquid-cooled engine. Nor had cowling been invented, so the radial created considerably more drag than a liquid-cooled in-line engine would have.

5. Unfortunately no papers justifying the 21/26 specification appear to have surfaced (the Air Ministry file on this aircraft describes experiments with radial rather than the original liquid-cooled engine and it also lists the weights the aircraft had to carry). Dreyer's remarks are in the S/R material.

6. Although no file on the 21/26 competition has survived, files survive concerning the attempt to develop a dual-purpose spotter-reconnaissance aircraft (S/R). At a December 1924 meeting Rear Admiral F C Dreyer, the ACNS, asked the Air Ministry to develop a new fleet fighter because he had seen reports that the new French fleet fighter would make 150mph with a ceiling of 27,000ft. His remarks seem to have been part of the impetus for the 21/26 specification. The time lapse between Dreyer's request and the issue of the specification would not have been unusual for the time, as the projected 1926 programme would have been under discussion in the spring of 1925.

7. A specification for an experimental shipboard fighter (17/25) had been issued the previous year, calling for an all-metal aircraft with a lower-powered (230hp Lynx IV) engine. K J Meekcoms and E B Morgan, *The British Aircraft Specifications File: British Military and Commercial Aircraft Specifications 1920–1949* (Tonbridge: Air Britain, 1994). The rationale for choosing a substantially lower-powered engine is not clear, unless it was to increase endurance. Air Ministry files do not appear to include a discussion of this project. Avro offered the biplane Avocet and Vickers the monoplane Type 125 Vireo. The Vireo performed deck-landing trials on board *Furious*. The 1926 fighter specification required the 450hp Bristol Mercury IIA.

8. The copy of the specification in AIR 2/825 dated 15 October 1926 reads 'two seater Fleet Fighter Reconnaissance Ship-Plane'. Main requirements, in order as listed, were good angles of vision for Fleet Reconnaissance work, close co-operation of crew, high performance, capacity for self-defence, suitability for catapult launch and deck-landing (as either landplane or

seaplane) and seaworthiness (as seaplane). Conversion from seaplane to landplane (or the reverse) was to take no more than 30 minutes. Specified powerplant was either the Bristol Mercury radial (585hp maximum, 550hp normal) or the Rolls Royce Falcon X (510/480hp, but much lower-drag). Falcon X was later redesignated P.XI(S) and then Kestrel. The specified load included two-way W/T (100lbs) and one forward-firing and one flexible gun. The aircraft would also have bomb carriers for eight 20lb bombs. Minimum acceptable speed (landplane) was 120 knots (138mph) at 15,000ft, which the Hart/Osprey easily exceeded. Catapult end-speed was given as 55mph (not knots); the aircraft was to be suitable for catapulting in both seaplane and landplane configurations. Provisions for shipboard operation included a requirement that folded span not exceed 37ft.

9. The three finalists in the 22/26 competition all received prototype contracts, their aircraft forming a formal Flight which carried out deck-landing trials in 1930. Apparently the crucial advantage of the Hart was in resistance to corrosion. Of the three alternatives, the Fairey Fleetwing was well-liked but suffered from corrosion. The third alternative was the Blackburn Nautilus. The Osprey production specification was 19/30.

10. For just how bad, see my *Naval Anti-Aircraft Guns and Gunnery*.

11. ADM 186/78, CB.3011, issued April 1929. These rules probably give a fair idea of current expectations. A single aircraft could be spotted from a ship at 5nm, a formation at 7nm. An aircraft could be seen from another aircraft at 3nm (a formation at 5nm). W/T and R/T ranges were given. Torpedo bombers, which were single-seaters, had R/T. A ship could contact them at 10nm, an aircraft at 0.5nm. S/R had W/T (Morse code): ranges were given as 180nm between ship and air and 50nm air-to-air. Floatplanes and flying boats were assumed to have the same W/T ranges as S/R. Under these rules, the existing fighter (Flycatcher) cruised at 94 knots (maximum 108 knots) and had an endurance of two hours, compared to 2.5 hours for the 85-knot (maximum 97 knots) torpedo bomber and four hours for the 100-knot (130 knots maximum) S/R. The new F/R (Osprey) was credited with a maximum speed of 140 knots and an endurance of 3.5 hours and the new fighter (Nimrod) with a maximum speed of 146 knots (cruising 130 knots) and the same endurance. Plans called for new S/R and torpedo bombers to have increased radius using either temporary tanks or enlarged fuel tanks. Of these aircraft, the Flycatcher alone had no radio of any kind. The Nimrod and the torpedo bomber were both credited with radio telephones (R/T); the two-seaters all had W/T (Morse code) radios. To launch or recover aircraft, a carrier needed 20 to 35 knots of wind over her deck. Aircraft could be flown off with an average interval of 20 seconds and recovered at an interval of three minutes (a two-minute landing interval was sometimes cited). The rules included an estimate of the risk of landing-on: one in fifty landings would be a crash requiring 12 hours of repair and 1 in 200 would be a write-off. In Sea State 7 (20 knots or more wind), 25 per cent would be crashes on a large deck and 50 per cent on a small deck (as in *Hermes* and *Argus*); half of these crashes would be write-offs. It was assumed that in 100 flights there would be one engine failure at the end of one hour and one at the end of three hours, requiring a return to the carrier. Carriers with two decks (*Furious*, *Courageous* and *Glorious*) could fly off up to six fighters while landing-on in the intervals while the recovering aircraft were struck below. In addition to time taken to place aircraft on deck, warming-up time was given as two minutes for radial (air-cooled) engine and five minutes for a liquid-cooled engine. *Furious* normally carried six fighters, her two near-sisters nine each. Each also had six F/R and twelve S/R; *Furious* had twelve and each of the others twenty-four torpedo bombers. Capital ships normally carried one fighter or F/R and one S/R. Lists of how many aircraft could be ranged (spotted) on carrier flight decks gave twelve large or eighteen fighter and F/R for the three big British carriers. 'It is assumed that *Lexington* and *Saratoga* can range aircraft on the forward end of the flight deck and still use the remainder of the deck for landing on', which indicates understanding of US operating procedures at this time. Game rules included topics such as the number of fighters required to prevent attack by bombers or torpedo bombers (the assumption was that 50 per cent losses would cause the attackers to turn back, although that was uncertain). As 'experience shows that the fighting value of a good formation of bombers is higher than that of the same number of single-seat fighters' the fighting value of bombers was assessed as 2:1 vs fighters. Likely effects of bombing carriers included bombs passing through the flight deck to burst in the hangar and destroy aircraft there. In contrast to US war game rules, there seems to have been no interest in the effect of bombs tearing up flight decks (there certainly was interest in light bombs destroying aircraft on deck).

12. In an August 1939 letter to the Treasury, which had reserved decision on the Spotter Fighter in the Air Ministry prototype programme, the Admiralty explained that this aircraft was conceived mainly to spot in the face of enemy fighters, rather than to carry out the usual fighter duties. It was being renamed the 'Spotter Observation Aircraft' and placed in the TBR rather than fighter class. ADM1/10747. In this 1939 paper the new aircraft was to be as similar as possible to a planned Barracuda (TBR)

replacement, with an economical cruising speed of not less than 185 knots at 10,000ft and an endurance of 5.5 hours at maximum cruising rpm plus five minutes at take-off power at sea level. Armament would be a turret with four 0.303in or two 0.5in (written in) guns, not occupied in combat by the gunner (who was also the W/T operator). There would be a crew of three: pilot, observer and air gunner/radio operator. There was a special requirement that the observer be able to pass (and receive) messages in flight and to be able to tune the radio. In earlier discussions the Roc was nominated as a spotter defence fighter.

13. According to the 1930 edition of *Progress in Tactics*, after an hour on patrol, the average error in enemy position (relative to the carrier) was 6nm. The 1931 edition of *Progress in Tactics* gave an average error of 4.5nm after an hour of flight. Errors in enemy course reports were 8° from 'rough' observations and 2° from 'accurate' observations. The typical error in enemy speed was 3 knots. In peacetime, the depth of a search was limited to the range at which the call signs could be reasonably distinguished. In wartime, that could be increased 70 per cent by using linking aircraft. Alternatively, aircraft could be sent out in pairs, one returning to communication range. Range was therefore linked to atmospherics. By 1938–9 carriers were using their D/F gear to check aircraft reports, errors as great as 10nm being corrected.

14. In 1927 it was decided by the Air Ministry that the new fleet fighter should not have a radio telephone (R/T), but that *Hermes* had put up a very good case for it (CinC Mediterranean agreed). The Admiralty referred the question to the Advisory Committee (AIR 5/872). In a September 1926 exercise, a Bison (which had radio) guided a flight of Flycatchers to attack an enemy carrier 25 miles away and then to guide them back to *Hermes*. CO *Hermes* argued further that in any future war fighter formations would be opposed by enemy fighter formations to gain air superiority. Tactical manoeuvrability would be as important in the air as at sea. At sea efficient tactical communication existed, but not in the air; inter-communication would surely be as important in the air as at sea. Moreover, the RAF had already recognised the importance of R/T as a means of rapid communication in its 'Provisional Manual of Air Drill'. CO *Hermes* gave an example, a torpedo attack which might break into sub-flights. Only a radio would allow the commander of the defending fighters to allocate them effectively to break up the attack. He thought the issue had not yet arisen because peacetime exercises had not yet included air fights between flights of fighters. The Air Ministry tested an alternative, an upward-looking signal lamp which the pilot could control to send Morse. In a test, a pilot indicated that he was ready to receive by rocking his wings. Range was short, whereas in RAF experiments R/T had been received by fighters at a range of 25 to 30 miles from a ground station and three miles air-to-air. The set weighed about 100lbs, which was a great deal for an aircraft which might weigh about 3000lbs. The RAF estimated that the set would cost 2mph at 10,000ft and 1500ft in ceiling. R/T was considered at the February 1927 meeting. DCAS agreed that R/T was desirable, but fleet fighters already carried a considerably greater load than their land equivalents; the addition of more weight (R/T) would compromise manoeuvrability. That raised the question of what weights could be eliminated; one of the naval representatives went so far as to suggest eliminating the parachute (DCAS agreed that floatation gear could be sacrificed in wartime). A potential compromise, fitting two-way R/T only to the flight leader, was rejected. Ultimately the meeting agreed that R/T should be carried, its weight balanced by elimination of other features such as floatation bags (in wartime). Development seems to have been slow, so that the 1930 edition of *Progress in Tactics* reported that a new set, to be fitted in the new Nimrod fighter, would be capable of transmitting by R/T between aircraft and of receiving Morse code (interrupted CW) from ships. The 1932 edition reported that aircraft were now being supplied with two types of radio: S/R, F/R (two-seat fighters) and T/B all received a combined high- and medium-frequency set with radio telephone (i.e. voice) capability (it did not yet exist). Single-seat fighters would all have high-frequency radio telephones. High frequency (HF) radio was that it offered much greater reliable range. S/R could change over to medium-frequency for reconnaissance and use high-frequency, as now, for spotting. Sea trials of the full set including the radio telephone (for all aircraft other than single-seat fighters) began in 1934. The 1935 edition of *Progress in Tactics* reported that, 'owing to the increasing scope of FAA activities', all large carriers would be fitted with two transmitters capable of operating as radio-telephones or –telegraphs (CW and Interrupted CW) to communicate with their bombing, fighter and torpedo-bomber forces. Deliveries of the new general-purpose aircraft sets were to begin at the end of 1935, the first aircraft to be the new TSR (Swordfish). In 1935 the Royal Navy began to test a VHF set (Type 7DX), which offered greater short-range reliability, but it was intended for ship-to-ship use, not for ship-to-air (the twelve ships selected for initial fitting were six battleships, five cruisers and one carrier). Range was 3nm and the great stated advantage of VHF was that it operated at frequencies which made radio direction-finding impossible.

There is no indication that anyone realised that it also made for far clearer voice transmission than the high-frequency radio then in use. In 1939 the Royal Navy was testing a short-range manoeuvring (bridge to bridge) Type 73X, offering a maximum reliable range of about 7nm and a normal maximum receiving range of 30nm (but under some circumstances it could be heard at 300–1200nm). A further UHF set was under development. By 1938 all TSR had the new General Purpose set (transmitter and receiver respectively T.1083 and R.1082) and a replacement set (TX.53, RX.62) was being tested. In 1939 Progress in Tactics reported increased reliance on aircraft-to-aircraft W/T (Morse). It was now possible to launch an air striking force early in the approach to the enemy, correcting its course on the basis of reports from reconnaissance aircraft. It does not appear that the Royal Navy was concerned that the enemy would use radio intercepts and D/F to track its own strike aircraft as they approached.

15. *Progress in Tactics* 1928 (ADM 186/144) described Tactical Investigation 1, in which both sides had approximately equal surface forces, but Red had 18 torpedo bombers and 118 fighters out of a total of 181 aircraft. Blue had ninety bombers and forty-six fighters out of the same total (the Royal Navy could not have operated the number on either side at this time). Blue launched seven torpedo attacks against Red, one every 12 minutes or so from the time the fleets were 45nm apart, the final attack coming when the main fleet action began. Red concentrated his fighters over his battle fleet, except for a few which attacked the later waves of torpedo bombers as the Blue carriers launched them. The total of eighty-eight Blue torpedo bombers which survived to attack was allowed eight hits; fifty-four of the aircraft were destroyed, but one Red battleship had her speed reduced to 11 knots. The game seemed to show that mass torpedo attacks against a much-superior fighter force were unlikely to achieve commensurate results. To be successful they needed large numbers of supporting fighters to dispute command of the air, both over their own carriers and over the objective. However, at this time the torpedo bombers were single-seaters, because their engines were not powerful enough to lift both a torpedo and a gunner. It seemed likely that the situation would be somewhat different once two-seaters were in service. There were also full-scale experiments. The only existing fast carrier, *Furious*, could launch up to thirty torpedo bombers. A mass attack was tried. Although the results were proportionately greater than those of the usual one or two six-aircraft flights, considerable time was lost as the extra flights had to be brought up to the flight deck and warmed up (*Furious* had a relatively short flight deck). Also, the time taken to recover so many aircraft, in addition to fighters and S/R which might be waiting, precluded a second strike. On the other hand, the effect of an attack by twelve torpedo bombers 'is so small as to hardly appear worth the effort. At the most, however, only two carriers have been allowed to a fleet; with more carriers the cumulative effect would be serious'. Some of the experiments were intended to test the current policy of holding back torpedo attacks until the two opposing fleets were engaging. That limited the torpedo bombers to a single attack, given the time needed to refuel and rearm. Games on the tactical table showed that results were better when aircraft struck at long range, giving them time to return and rearm and attack again before the action was over.

16. Figures given in *Progress in Tactics* 1928 (ADM 186/144).

17. This seems to have been assumed by the author of the carrier doctrine published in the 1930 edition of *Progress in Tactics*.

18. As laid out in the 1930 edition of *Progress in Tactics*, in connection with carrier operation. The same edition pointed to problems in reconnaissance because there were not enough aircraft to be sent out in pairs; if one missed the carrier on her return, her information would be lost. That apparently assumed that typically the aircraft would not break radio silence in the air, but various editions of *Progress in Tactics* devoted substantial space to appropriate use of radio by reconnaissance aircraft..

19. *Progress in Tactics* 1934, p 38, para 144. In exercises, fighters had sometimes been directed onto shadowing aircraft by taking D/F bearings of their transmissions.

20. *Progress in Tactics* 1938, p 27 described three exercises in which eleven fighters in four sub-flights were assigned to deal with a total of six shadowers, one in each sector. The carrier *Glorious* passed lookouts' sighting reports to the fighters. Half the shadowers were found and attacked. The conclusion was that even in clear weather an aircraft shadowing from not less than 12,000ft and 12nm away could escape detection by both look-outs and fighters. However, in cloudy weather a snooper would nearly always be silhouetted against clouds (but might use them to evade fighters).

21. *Progress in Tactics* 1935 included Home Fleet Cruising Disposition No. 7, in which eight air patrols were arranged around the main body. Cruisers in a Surface Warning Zone were expected to spot incoming enemy aircraft and indicate their approach by firing at them, the approved technique to be used in wartime. Firing was considered better than any visual signals and radio signalling was not acceptable even after the enemy had found a force. Exercises had shown that early indication of the course of hostile aircraft

was vital, as without it estimation of the likely direction of attack would be difficult; it might even be uncertain whether an enemy formation was approaching the fleet or flying away from it. This disposition was intended particularly for use when the fleet had already been located and attack by shore-based aircraft was expected. It was tested in Exercise 'EF'. Until the fleet had been located, a more compact formation was preferred on the theory that it might be more difficult for a search aircraft to spot.

22. *Progress in Tactics* 1939, p 17, reported a February 1938 exercise off Singapore in which a carrier attacked a shore position and withdrew without having been found by shore-based aircraft, but cautioned that this was still a very dangerous thing to do. The exercise suggested that the danger of counter-attack due to shadowing aircraft was greater than that due to aircraft following a strike back to the carrier, hence that time should not be wasted by returning aircraft attempting to conceal the carrier's position by following indirect routes back.

23. Based on *Progress in Tactics* 1937, there having been no 1936 issue due to the crisis in the Mediterranean. The section on the use of fighters and air patrols begins on p 58.

24. *Progress in Tactics* added that whether air attack was likely depended on the time at which the fleet was located, either by an enemy aircraft or by submarine or surface craft and the position of the enemy's carriers or air bases.

25. *Progress in Tactics* 1937, p 63, para 227.

26. All formations would approach ships below 1000ft, leaders firing a combination of Very lights and smoke puffs as recognition signals. Fighters on patrol would remain high and it was impractical for them to carry the required two pistols (yellow smoke puffs and Very lights). They would carry single pistols for white smoke puffs. Single aircraft returning from reconnaissance or anti-submarine patrols would not fire any recognition signals unless fired upon. The main implication of these techniques was that the recognition problem was not entirely insoluble. Another possibility was for the fleet commander to indicate the bearing on which aircraft should approach a carrier. A surface ship on that bearing might be detailed to establish aircraft identity, perhaps on the basis of visual or radio signals. All of these ideas had much later equivalents, the problem always being that electronic forms of identification could fail or be damaged in combat. *Progress in Tactics* pointed out that none of the solutions would save spotting aircraft, which had to operate close to the battle line, from being fired upon. *Progress in Tactics* 1939 admitted that the two-star (two-flare) method of identification had not proven successful, partly because flare colours were difficult to distinguish. Three-colour fixed identification lights had been designed but had not yet been installed as of June 1939.

27. *Progress in Tactics* 1937, p 59, para 212.

28. *Progress in Tactics* 1939, p 13, paras 35–38. It was understood that carriers operating this way would need separate protection, but apparently that was accepted. However, a later discussion (p 37) of carrier defence against air and submarine attack described the practice in both Home and Mediterranean Fleets of operating a carrier in a column of battleships or cruisers, screened by a flotilla of destroyers. One problem was that the path of water swept by the destroyers' Asdics (sonars) was too narrow to allow the carrier to manoeuvre to launch or recover aircraft for even the shortest period. One solution was to station additional destroyers outside the screen in the bow-to-wind direction.

29. RDF meant Radio Direction Finding, a cover name for what was later called Radar (a US word). It was deliberately meaningless, as the Royal Navy already used radio direction-finding (which it called D/F) very extensively. *Progress in Tactics* listed radar functions in priority order: long-range air warning with rough indication of direction (met by SA); short-range warning of ships for use in low visibility and at night (to be met by adapting SA); location of ships by aircraft over a wide range of flying heights (AS); ranging of aircraft from ships for anti-aircraft fire; ranging of ships by ships; and continuous location of aircraft by bearing and range with sufficient accuracy to direct searchlights and, later, high-angle guns. Of these, Type 79 met the first requirement. The later Type 281 was intended to add a useful degree of surface warning by using shorter-wave-length signals (surface warning was not really successful until the advent of microwave radar, not envisaged in 1939). For gunnery ranging a new series of radars with much shorter wavelengths (50cm rather than 1.5m or 7.5m in Type 79) was soon developed, beginning with Type 282 for pom-poms (which had no associated rangefinders), followed by Type 283 for medium-calibre guns and then Type 284 for surface guns. The accurate bearing and range sets did not appear until later, with the success of microwave radar.

30. ADM 1/10103 describes FAA policy at this time, but it does not document the decision to amalgamate the torpedo bomber and S/R roles. It is concerned mainly with the decision to develop the Skua as a fighter-dive bomber. A 14 February 1934 Minute by DNAD in this file states it has already been decided that future FAA expansion is to be based on a reduction to only two types: a TSR and an F/R capable of dive-bombing with a 500lb bomb. In these papers a distinction is drawn between

terminal velocity (T/V) bombing and diving bombing. The former was the near-vertical attack later called dive bombing. DNAD wrote that the US Navy had greatly developed this form of attack and that at least one other foreign power (Italy) was experimenting in that direction. Dive bombing was at a smaller angle and would later be called glide bombing. Much of the file is concerned with an attempt to develop a single type of aircraft suitable for dive bombing both in wheeled (landplane) and float form. At this time Hawker was developing a dive bomber for the Air Ministry and it was asked whether this combination was practical. The company replied that floats would so shift the centre of gravity and centre of pressure of the floatplane version that it would be incapable of steep dive bombing. It would be far better to develop an alternative type intended primarily as a floatplane (with bombing capacity) with auxiliary landplane capability. The cruiser bomber concept was abandoned a few years later. For the moment, about May 1934, the Admiralty wanted the new fighter so badly that it was acceptable to drop a weight limit associated with existing cruiser catapults; this would be primarily a carrier aircraft. The file opens with a 6 November 1933 letter from DNAD stating that enough experience had been gained with the Osprey on which to base a specification for its replacement. That was urgent given the several years likely to elapse before the replacement could become operational.

31. The only questions raised concerned the engine and bomb stowage. The proposed aircraft was powered by a Taurus engine (double Aquila), which did not yet exist. It was replaced by the Perseus which powered the Skua. The design showed internal rather than external (wing) bomb stowage, but DNAD said that the bomb requirement was secondary. There was also an alternative Vickers design, Its mid-wing configuration offered better performance and also a better view for reconnaissance, described as a subsidiary role for the dive bomber fighter (recalling the F/R concept). It also promised higher performance. The project was delayed because Vickers was too fully occupied with a medium bomber (B 9/32, the basis of the later Wellington). Given the urgency of replacing the obsolete Nimrods and Ospreys, selection of the Skua became inevitable.

32. The requirement to provide movable front and rear guns could be met by installing a single power turret, as was done. The Air Ministry file on this type of fighter ('with moveable front and rear guns', Specification F.22/33) is AIR 2/681. There was also a specification (F.5/33) for a fighter with a front gun station but no rear gun; in July 1934 DTD (Director Technical Department) suggested that it and F.22/33 be considered together as a single type, which would save considerable money. Both would have had twin engines. For the RAF this type of fighter was conceived for home defence, meaning to deal with enemy bombers (however, the initial draft specification placed the priority on use overseas). The main object, as stated in 1933, was to produce a fighter which could fly and fight in formation, something no existing fighter could do. It was intended to break up enemy formations, then destroy them in detail, but it would also be capable of fighter vs fighter combat. Flexible guns made broadside attacks possible. The argument advanced in favour of a turret fighter was that the tactical alternatives were sporadic close-in attack and sustained 'lie-off' attack. The close-in attack would be delivered by single-seat fighters, combining firepower 'with an element of moral force'. However, it could not produce the necessary concentration of fire. The stand-off attack offered, it seemed, the necessary concentration of sustained fire, the single-seat fighters being retained to shatter already-damaged bomber formations. In March 1933 DCAS wrote that RAF tactics envisaged two-seat fighters drawing ahead of enemy bomber formations to attack them with their rear guns, but the existing single Lewis guns were feeble at best. Meanwhile the single-seat fighters would fire at ranges from 500 yds down. DCAS looked forward to development of six- rather than four-gun single-seat fighters and to some type of turret fighter, hence the new specifications soon issued. The hope was originally that by limiting the aircraft to two forward-firing guns its size could be held down. Estimates showed that the big nose position cost so much speed that the multi-gun fighter would be significantly slower than new light bombers, whose predicted speed was 275mph. By the spring of 1935 DCAS was arguing that the nose turret fighter could never have sufficient performance; better to ask for a single-engine fighter with a midships turret (F.9/35, the Defiant). DCAS did not see limited ahead fire (the turret could fire only at 15° and greater elevation) as a serious problem. The Fairey F.22/33 contract was cancelled, leaving the firm free to concentrate on what it considered more promising projects, the single-engine light bomber (P.4/34) and the P.27/32 medium bomber. That was not a bad assessment: P.27/32 became the Fairey Battle and P.4/34 became the Fulmar F/R.

33. AIR 2/3473. This file encloses a copy of N.9/39, the renumbered version of the specification. Fairey and Hawker submitted proposals to N.6/38, but for N.9/39 they were joined by Blackburn, Gloster, Supermarine and Westland. The only difference between N.6/38 and N.9/39 was that the latter specified the turret armament as four Browning 0.303in guns with 4000 rounds of ammunition. At least in draft form, the Admiralty wanted

the turret fighter designed so that its machine-gun turret could be replaced by a hypothetical cannon turret. In contrast to past practice, the ability to convert to a floatplane was not required. All-up weight (as a landplane) was not to exceed 10,000lbs (9,000lbs if possible). As usual, speed was to be as high as possible, but it was hoped that it could achieve about 275 knots (316mph) at 15,000ft, the operational altitude. The Admiralty sought a minimum speed of 300 knots (345mph) in the original N.6/38, the Air Ministry complaining that this was more than could be achieved (on paper) with even the most powerful existing engine, the Hercules (the alternative was a somewhat smaller fighter powered by a Merlin, Taurus or Exe engine). At this point the estimated speed of a Hercules powered N6/38 was 280 knots (N5/38 could do 290 knots because it would not have to contend with the weight and drag of a turret). It seemed entirely possible, moreover, that a Hercules-engined fighter would exceed the absolute limit set by Fifth Sea Lord, 10,500lbs. On that basis the Air Ministry estimator suggested offering a Merlin/Taurus/Exe aircraft with a stated target speed of 278 knots without the turret and 268 with; the Fulmar was rated at 254 knots (292mph). A take-off run of 200ft with 20 knots wind over the deck was also specified. In addition to the primary role of air combat, a secondary role of maintaining W/T communication (as an airborne link) was stated.

34. ADM 116/4030 contains the draft and fleet and staff comments. Initially the draft was somewhat confusing, as it mixed the current situation with projected developments. These two parts were then split, Part I being limited to current carrier equipment. Part II covered catapult ships and future aircraft.

35. The letter of submission, which made this argument, was signed by DNAD, D of TD (Director of Tactical Division) and by DTSD (Director, Training and Studies Division), on 13 March 1936. Director of Operations Division (DOD) immediately argued the need to concentrate fighters designed for deck-landing on carriers. One of the comments mentioned that on 20 February 1934 CinCs were asked for their opinions as to the proper proportion of TSR and fighters to be carried in capital ships and carriers. The letter assumed that capital ships must carry at least one TSR for spotting and that the main function of fighters was defence of the fleet against air attack – not at all what the 1936 memorandum said. CinCs and Rear Admiral (A) proposed 60 per cent TSR and 40 per cent fighters, compared to 67 per cent and 33 per cent proposed by the Naval Staff. Third Sea Lord (Admiral Henderson, formerly RA(A)) wrote on 12 August that he did not agree with everything in the memorandum and that it would be better not circulated. 'My general view is that you can have too many policies, which fluctuate and at this particular period I feel it would be better for the Admiralty not to issue this, at any rate in the form of policy'. Henderson was then inventing the armoured-deck carrier. In October First Sea Lord Admiral Chatfield wrote that he agreed, as it might be read to indicate that the Naval Staff was proposing how CinCs afloat should use their weapons, which was not their duty. Their job was to keep in touch with CinCs and with weapons development so as to advise the Admiralty as to what was required. Policy must be based on the opinions of those in command at sea; Chatfield though that the memorandum could be rewritten and then circulated. That was done in January 1937 with the December version cited here. In December 1937 it formed the basis of a high-level discussion from which no conclusion emerged. DNAD wrote on 26 April 1939 that Board decisions on FAA policy based on the report of ACNS' Committee on Air Requirements (M.06313/38) and summarised in Appendix I of 'FAA Requirements' (A.035/38) did not altogether follow its proposals. At the same time war game rules were revised to tally with notes on the effectiveness of various forms of air attack and defence summarised in the memorandum.

36. The draft memorandum went into detail. Even were it possible to intercept large striking forces with as many as 50 per cent of their number of fighters at a distance of 20nm from the fleet, the result would 'be of little practical value'. Current assessment supported by the RAF's exercises ashore was that only 1.5 per cent of attacking aircraft would be shot down before they reached the gun defence zone, at the cost of a quarter of the fleet's fighters. To attain fighting equality with the attackers, the defenders would need 50 per cent more fighters. Even then the destruction of the bombers would take time, in any case no more than 2.5 per cent per minute. It followed that fighter defence was impractical, even allowing for the morale effect on the enemy and the increased firepower of projected fighters (this was written as the first RAF eight-gun fighters were being built).

37. Once in action, a fleet would be more vulnerable, since it might be unable to use its anti-aircraft guns freely. For example, the blast effect of main-battery guns would limit the use of open mountings. Other navies understood as much, which is why the Japanese provided blast shields for light anti-aircraft guns in their *Yamato* class.

38. The 1937 edition of the official British *Progress in Tactics* (December 1937, pp 144–5) included a particularly detailed account of what the British understood of Japanese naval aviation. The most interesting comment was that the only important target of the carriers' air striking forces was enemy

carriers, not (as in the Royal Navy) enemy battleships. Only after destroying the enemy carriers would the aircraft turn to attacking enemy ships' control positions. The Japanese were said to understand the extreme vulnerability of carriers – to gunfire. That had led them to position their carriers well to the rear of their battle line. Japanese carriers were said to be armed with fighters and torpedo bombers, all spotters being on board surface combatants (in direct contrast to British practice). Japanese opinion, moreover, was said to be turning against fighters and towards concentration on torpedo bombers. The British seem to have been unaware of any specialised Japanese dive bombers, although they reported successful exercises using 220lb bombs, presumably dropped by the torpedo bombers (the 1939 edition correctly reported that the Japanese were carrying much heavier bombs on board their carriers – 250kg, 500kg and 800kg, of which the 250kg (551lb) was said to be most common). The 1937 report not include any reference to shore-based aircraft, including the new long-range bombers. As with other intelligence reports, this one mixed reality with fiction. At this time Japanese naval air opinion seems to have held that carriers could defeat all types of ships, including battleships. However, as in the US Navy, the carriers could not operate safely until they had destroyed the opposing carriers. It also appears that before the outbreak of war in China, Japanese naval air opinion did favour the elimination of fighters, but by late 1937 the situation was changing. The 1938 edition of *Progress in Tactics* (December 1938) mentioned the use of naval aircraft in China, including the frequent use of fighters to escort the bombers and added that 'reports indicate that the naval air arm. standard of efficiency is a great deal higher than the Army Air Force'. This edition also mentioned naval shore-based aircraft, of which there were said to be twenty-five squadrons in June 1937. The heavy land-based bombers were 'probably used for long-distance reconnaissance'.

39. The 'B' (buoyant) bomb was to be dropped alongside a target. It would rise and explode under or nearly under the target's bottom. Both the RAF and the Royal Navy devoted considerable attention to this weapon from about 1924 through the outbreak of war and British warships were designed to survive its shock effect. It seems not to have been used in combat and all stocks were destroyed in 1946 as too dangerous for service use.

40. The July 1937 Advisory Committee meeting (in AIR 2/1793) discussed new bombers for the FAA, beginning with a dive bomber reconnaissance (DBR) included in the 1936 programme of experimental aircraft along with a replacement TSR. Specification O.8/36 was issued for the DBR and M.7/36 for the replacement TSR (the Fairey Albacore). The Admiralty was anxious to get the DBR into service as quickly as possible and suggested that only Fairey should be asked to bid, with the expectation of a production order. Fairey was slow and eventually offered a biplane, which the company considered safer than a monoplane. It could also fulfil the TSR requirement, so it was decided to combine the two (as 41/36). Fairey later produced a satisfactory low-wing monoplane and at a meeting of the Technical Sub-Committee DNAD was asked to revert to the monoplane (and to a single type of aircraft) and agree to a production order. At this point the Admiralty envisaged buying 600 aircraft in 1940–2. The Admiralty agreed. DTD (Air Ministry) cited the US order for 114 Douglas low-wing monoplane torpedo bombers (TBD Devastators) as proof that the monoplane would be satisfactory. Reportedly the US Navy had accommodated them by extending flight decks and perhaps by using accelerators (catapults); in any case the FAA would now be two years behind the Americans in introducing larger monoplanes into naval service. The most difficult parts of the TSR requirement were the good view for spotting and reconnaissance, coupled with ease of deck handling. The Admiralty now suggested ordering at least three prototypes each (to speed evaluation) of high-, mid- and low-wing designs. However, that would lose more time. He suggested that the Air Staff and DNAD should get together and write a specification which would not stipulate wing position. DNAD said that the Fairey biplane DBR had been accepted because it was safer. The monoplane did not meet the requirements of take-off and view and it was more of a gamble. DNAD cited the Blackburn fighter dive bomber. He thought the delay was due to difficulties in producing so radical an aircraft; there was no proof that the problems had been overcome when the Admiralty chose the biplane. The biplane would be slower, but speed was not as important to the FAA as to the RAF. Apparently the greatest problem in providing FAA aircraft was in meeting the 200ft take-off requirement with 20 knots wind over deck. The solution might be a better accelerator. Trials with Coastal Command's low-wing Anson convinced the Admiralty that it needed the unobstructed view which only a high wing could provide. Without it, the aircraft would need a bottom observation blister which would make it impossible to stow a torpedo internally (in the end, that was impossible anyway).

41. The Swordfish successor, the Albacore, could dive bomb, as could the later Barracuda, which was the longer-term successor. Immediately available types were the Shark and Swordfish TSR, suited to these duties but not to dive bombing. Existing single- and two-seat fighters (Nimrods and

Ospreys) were obsolete. The Fighter Dive Bomber (FDB) Skua was 'being developed to examine the problem of Dive Bombing' and to replace the obsolete fighters. It had been designed to deliver 250 or 500lb bombs, but a heavier dive bombing capable of delivering a 1000lb bomb was under development. It was described as the Dive Bomber Reconnaissance (DBR) and differentiated from the TSR. It was described as a three-seat high-wing monoplane with an auto-pilot, with a maximum speed of 200 knots (a note in the memorandum stated that a TSR monoplane probably could not be developed on the required 50ft wing span). This aircraft would have one front gun and a twin power turret. Economical speed would be 125 knots Despite the reference to a 1000lb bomb, the bomb load of the DBR was given as two 500lb or four 250lb. Presumably this project developed into the Barracuda, which could lift a torpedo. The Fleet Fighter was the Osprey; its armament was given as a four-gun power turret. Unlike the Skua, it could be carried on catapults. It could carry two 250lb bombs, but bombing (shallow dive, meaning glide-bombing) was an entirely secondary function. Both it and the FDB were credited with a maximum speed of 230 knots, the highest of any of the projected types. The Fighter Dive Bomber (Skua) was credited with four front and one rear guns. The table of new aircraft included a GP aircraft to replace the current Swordfish TSR. It would be capable of dive-bombing and would have somewhat higher speed (180 knots vs 135 knots) and longer endurance at the same cruising speed of 120 knots (10 hours for reconnaissance compared to eight–ten hours, six hours vs four hours with a full bomb load). Bomb load would match that of the TSR, but it would have a twin power-operated turret instead of the single flexible gun of the Swordfish. It appears that this was an early approach to what became the Albacore.

42. The three large existing carriers would have sixty fighters each, plus forty-two (*Courageous* and *Glorious*) or 30 (*Furious*) GP aircraft. *Eagle* and *Hermes* would have no fighters at all, only eighteen and twelve GP respectively.

43. It was chaired by ACNS (Air) Rear Admiral J H D Cunningham. The Home Fleet was represented by its CinC Admiral Backhouse, his Rear Admiral (A) G CC Boyle and by other officers including the Rear Admiral commanding 2nd Cruiser Squadron (Rear Admiral T F P Calvert). The Admiralty staff was represented by officers from ACNS (Captain L E Holland), DNAD (Captain C M Graham), D of TD, DDNAD (Captain R H Portal), ADNAD (Captain G M B Langley), NAD (Cdr R M Ellis) and Plans Division (Cdr A W Buzzard).

44. ACNS (Air) cited Japanese losses to Chinese fighters when they attacked Nanking, but the cruiser admiral suggested that the casualties and poor results might be traceable more to Japanese inefficiency and the lack of escorts. No one realised that the Japanese were even then solving the escort problem and designing the Zero fighter primarily as a strike escort.

45. This report is in ADM 116/4038, most of which is concerned with training facilities and war reserves. ACNS(A) referred to the recent emergency, meaning the Mediterranean emergency due to the Italian invasion of Ethiopia. Much of the report concerned questions such as the value of mobile base ships to support flying boats for fleet reconnaissance, the relative values of a small carrier and a cruiser for trade protection and the necessity for FAA depot ships.

46. The 1942 figures assumed that the five armoured carriers then building would have been completed. The report gave a hypothetical distribution. In peacetime and in war, all three *Victorious* class carriers would be in home waters, where they faced the greatest danger of enemy air attack. *Ark Royal* and one of the armoured carriers (*Indomitable*) would be in the Mediterranean. Her sister *Implacable* would be on the China Station, replacing the earlier small carriers there. *Courageous* would be training carrier, her two sisters in reserve. *Hermes* would be in the West Indies. In wartime, four carriers would be in the Far East and three on the trade routes (which ships were not specified). The committee acknowledged a case for further construction beyond the 1938 carrier (*Indefatigable*). In general carrier capacity did not match requirements based on likely enemy strength. Nor did it take into account future Japanese and German carrier construction.

47. Specification S.9/36 envisaged a three-man turreted aircraft (the four-gun turret would have been remote-controlled) with a speed of at least 200 knots at 10,000ft, with an endurance of at least 2.75 hours at that altitude at ⅔ power. It would be operable as an amphibian or as a carrier plane, in the latter case having a landing speed of no more than 56 knots. Carrier performance would have included a take-off distance of 200ft with 24 knots wind over deck. For the Admiralty the spotter fighter was later linked with the new TBR (not TSR) to S.24/37, which specification produced the Barracuda. Plans called for ordering prototypes from each of Fairey, Hawker and Westland, although only Fairey prototypes of the spotter fighter was ordered. At the November 1937 meeting of the Advisory Board it was decided to cancel the two Fairey prototypes and to try to adapt the new TBR, when it became available, to the spotter fighter role. DNAD pointed out that there would be few orders for the spotter fighter, whereas if it could be combined with the new TBR the numbers

would be greater and the project therefore more attractive to the firms. The order for the mock-up of the S.9/36 would not be cancelled, however, as it seemed that much might be learned from it. At a 9 November 1938 meeting of the Advisory Committee (AIR 2/1793) Admiralty representatives explained that although the Fairey prototypes were well advanced, Hawker and Westland should be allowed to incorporate new developments, particularly operation with assisted take-off gear (catapults on flight decks), a folded width of 15ft 9in and high-lift improvements. At the same time the Admiralty wanted to order an experimental TBR with 13ft 6in folded width, variable-incidence wings, high-lift devices, a tricycle undercarriage and any other new devices which might become available in time for the 1939 programme. The committee approved the Admiralty request to cancel S.9/36 (which was now considered unsatisfactory) in favour of a new Staff Requirement. The Advisory Committee meeting held on 9 November 1938 (AIR 2/1793) included a discussion of cancelling S.9/36 in favour of a new spotter fighter to new Staff Requirements.

48. It is not clear where this arose, as the actual ratios were quite different. The new US carriers had four squadrons aboard, only one of which was fighters. *Progress in Tactics* had recently claimed that the Japanese were eliminating carrier fighters altogether.

49. This note is in the file on the memorandum; the 1936 memorandum was now 'obsolescent'. For some reason ships in a class were not standardised. Thus, of the three initial armoured carriers, *Victorious* and *Formidable* would have twenty-four TSR and nine fighters, but *Illustrious* would have twenty-one TSR and twelve fighters. *Indomitable* and *Implacable*, with extra hangar space, would each have fifteen fighters and, respectively, thirty and thirty-three TSR. *Ark Royal* would have forty-two TSR and eighteen Fleet Fighters. *Courageous* would have eighteen fighters to her thirty TSR. As a small trade-route carrier, *Hermes* would have no fighters at all (twelve TSR). *Glorious*, *Eagle* and *Furious* would all be in reserve, allocated a total of forty-eight TSR and no fighters.

50. ADM 1/10131, enclosing a copy of Mediterranean Fleet Tactical Training Memorandum No. 37 and providing Admiralty comments. This file was dated 5 January 1939. The fleet commander characterised torpedo attack as the greatest threat. Most of the material in the file concerns action, including evasive manoeuvres, by surface ships. The bulk of the file is a memorandum produced by a Mediterranean Fleet committee.

51. DNAD also reviewed the new instructions and offered detailed comments on how evasive action might work, but did not comment on the use of fighters.

52. In preparation for the November 1938 meeting of the Advisory Committee on the FAA, the Air Council wrote the Admiralty asking whether future naval fighters would be carried on board catapult ships and whether, if not, the Admiralty would consider cancelling the Roc. In the event of cancellation, would that mean larger orders for the Gladiator and Fulmar, the two interim fighters? The Admiralty answer was that fighters sometimes would be carried by catapult ships and that they were unwilling to cancel the Roc; at the least it would provide useful experience with turret fighters.

53. AIR 2/1793.

54. The Fulmar specification is AIR2/3251, for an 'Interim Two-Seater Fighter for FAA', opened 11 February 1938. It was a revised version of an Admiralty draft specification dated 20 January. The specification required a maximum speed of at least 230 knots (264.5mph) at an operational altitude of 10,000ft, with maximum manoeuvrability. Stall speed was not to exceed 56 knots with engine off at full load (i.e. landing on deck). Take-off was to be within 225ft with 20 knots of wind over deck, but this figure could be relaxed if necessary (DTD estimated that the best take-off distance would be 240ft). Required endurance (for fighter patrol) was six hours at operational height at not less than 120 knots plus a quarter hour at maximum power at sea level (combat) or at least 2.75 hours at maximum economical cruising speed at 10,000ft plus the quarter-hour at maximum power at sea level. The specified engine was the Merlin 'H' with moderate supercharging. The specification file includes a note indicating that the Hawker Henley was an alternative to the adapted P.4/34. Whichever was chosen, Fairey would have to produce it because it had the capacity; the Technical Sub-Committee considered capacity the telling argument favouring the adapted P.4/34.

55. Sources of information for this section differ from those used for the Royal Navy. The US Navy did not test its tactics in small-scale exercises and there was no US equivalent of *Progress in Tactics*. On the other hand, the US Navy apparently made much greater use of gaming (at the Naval War College) to develop strategy and large-scale tactics. Gaming was not, however, applicable to air-to-air combat, despite substantial effort to do so on the part of the War College. Air-to-air tactics were developed in full-scale exercises, including the full-scale Fleet Problems. On the other hand, the record describing interwar aircraft development is far richer for the US Navy than for the FAA.

56. The BuAer fighter history couples the range requirement with the strike escort mission. Its origins are not entirely clear. According to the BuAer fighter history in the Confidential Bulletin, which is based on the longer typescript, about 1934 strike escort was the primary fighter mission. Yet that is not reflected in the comments in the typescript about the need for maximum performance and the willingness to accept a stripped-down fighter at about this time. The 1000nm requirement is mentioned only later, in connection with attempts to develop a maximum-performance fighter in 1937–8.

57. Even before Reeves, these ships were assumed capable of operating large numbers of aircraft. A May 1922 table of air requirements prepared for the General Board (in General Board file 449 for 1922) showed seventy-two aircraft in each ship: thirty-six fighters and thirty-six torpedo bombers in one and thirty-six fighters plus eighteen torpedo bombers and eighteen three-seat observation aircraft (VO) in the other. The small converted *Langley* was assigned nine fighters. The proportion of fighters was far beyond that advocated by the Royal Navy. A 9 November 1925 memo from Admiral Moffett, BuAer chief, to the Secretary of the Navy (in GB 449 file for 1924–5) lists the capacities of the new carriers (as yet uncompleted) as forty-eight torpedo bombers (VT), fifty-four fighters (VF) and nine or eighteen observation aircraft (VO), but this allowance included a 50 per cent reserve against wastage. *Saratoga* was allotted more VO because she was intended to operate with the Battle Fleet, carrying replacements for their spotters. *Lexington* was allotted to the Scouting Fleet, which had six rather than twelve battleships. In FY29 *Saratoga* was assigned four squadrons plus four utility aircraft. The squadrons were: VF-1B (eighteen fighters), VB-2B ex VF-6B (eighteen dive bombers), VS-2B (twelve scouts VS.) and VT-2B (eighteen torpedo bombers). The four-squadron organisation was standard through the 1930s.

58. As indicated in a 1941 General Board Hearing discussing the British armoured-deck carriers, prompted by US observation of *Illustrious* under repair at Norfolk Navy Yard after battle damage in the Mediterranean. US naval officers were much impressed by the armoured deck, which was incorporated in the last US Second World War fleet carriers, the much enlarged *Midway* class. They were told that the light (but repairable) wooden decks of US carriers had been adopted to suit a protracted Pacific campaign, as they allowed a ship to operate a much larger air group. At the hearing, the British armoured deck was associated with a Mediterranean campaign fought out in the face of heavy land-based air power.

59. As pointed out by Admiral Reeves, certainly no enemy of naval air power or of limited-length landings into arresting gear. In retrospect it is surprising that no advocate of the flight-deck cruiser thought of extending the flight deck by angling it outboard. The Japanese also considered exploiting this clause and they too designed a flight-deck cruiser before rejecting it, as part of the run-up to the *Hiryu* design. The US flight-deck cruiser episode, including its demise once its CNO sponsor was gone, seems reminiscent of more recent episodes such as Admiral Zumwalt's Sea Control Ship (with its VSTOL aircraft) and Admiral Boorda's Arsenal Ship.

60. Aer-P-1-ERG VV, dated 11 January, in 'Aircraft Design Planning and Production Pre-WW II' file, Aviation History, NHHC. I have begun with these Characteristics because they roughly coincided with the development of carrier aircraft tactics. General Board files show earlier submissions by BuAer, such as a 19 May 1923 summary (in GB 449 file 1923) calling for a maximum weight of 2000lbs and a maximum speed, as a land plane, of 135mph (endurance 2.5 hours at full throttle). At this time BuAer hoped to provide the maximum number of fighters to the fleet by placing them on board battleships and probably also the fleet train, whose numbers were not affected by the Washington Treaty. Such aircraft, on board tankers, figured prominently in the war game in which then-Captain Reeves successfully defended his carrier. Moffett's 1927 memorandum was supported by a 31 January 1927 memo from the head of the BuAer Design Section Commander E B Wilson on the design programme (in GB 449 file 1926-29). Looking back to 1925, he pointed to a gradual movement from single-seat fighters adaptable to operation on wheels or floats (as in the Royal Navy, but he did not say so) to four classes: single-seat and two-seat fighters for land or seaplane use, but not both. At this time the single-seat fighter with an air-cooled engine was considered satisfactory. A design competition expected to choose a catapult equivalent. There was no two-seat fighter, although the Vought O2U might be used as a makeshift. The design chief argued that development of a specialised two-seat fighter should be pursued vigorously in view of 'the growing appreciation of the value of high-speed aircraft with light bomb equipment for bomb straffing [i.e., dive or glide bombing] purposes.' If the two-seater was fast enough, it could be used for other purposes once it had dropped its bombs, something not possible for heavy bombers. He had made a brief study (i.e., a preliminary design) of a two-seat fighter powered by the new Pratt & Whitney Hornet (R-1690) or the Wright R-1750 engine. It should be developed as a carrier land plane (the F8C-4 used the less powerful R-1340). The design chief acknowledged that the fleet disliked the battleship fighter, but he thought that was because the one in service was the antiquated Naval Aircraft Factory TS, the navy's first specially-built fighter. If a battleship catapult fighter could be built with performance superior to enemy

landplane fighters, it would be well worthwhile. That never happened. The concept of the battleship fighter, as expressed in 1927, was much like later British arguments that catapult ships should carry their own fighters to protect their spotters. Wilson listed an experimental aircraft programme in which one item was a two-seat air-cooled fighter with provision for bomb straffing and a carrier observation-two seat fighter-light bomber using a large air-cooled engine. He also wanted to test a very light single-seat fighter offered by Ward Hall. It is not clear to what extent these recommendations were followed. In April 1927 the Secretary of the Navy convened a Board to Consider the Naval Aeronautic Policy; it reported on 11 May 1927 (its report is in GB 449 file 1926-29). Its senior member was Rear Admiral M M Taylor, and Moffett was a member, as was Reeves. Wilson was a witness. The Board was impressed by the need for a battle-line carrier, both to provide fighters for its protection and to service and refuel its spotters. The other carriers would be left free for scouting and for offensive operations. Note that this was before either of the big carriers was in service. On fighters, the Board preferred single types suited to carriers and to catapult use. The only two-seater should be the combined fighter-light bomber. The questionnaire submitted to the Board described foreign practice: the tendency was towards a split into a 'jockey' type sacrificing armament for manoeuvrability and speed and an 'interceptor' carrying heavy armament at the expense of manoeuvrability and speed; the army had an 'attack' type emphasising armament at the expense of speed and manoeuvrability, presumably in that order.

61. A set of aircraft armament characteristics dated 15 March 1931 in GB 449 file 1931-32 shows the F4B-1 as the only fighter capable of carrying a 500-pounder. The Curtiss O2C-2 (aka F8C-4 Helldiver) was credited with two 100lb and five 30lb bombs. The F4B-2 and -3 were limited to four or two (respectively) 100lb bombs plus 30lb bombs (a 1936 armament sheet showed that the F4B-2 carried two of its bombs under its fuselage in displacement gear and the other two under its wings). Other fighters were limited to 30lb bombs. According to the table, the F4B-1 would carry the 500lb bomb only on displacing gear (a crutch), unless it was to drop it horizontally. It was, therefore, a true dive bomber. The F4B-1 squadron on board *Lexington* was initially designated VB-1B, i.e., it was a dive bomber squadron (it was later redesignated VF-5B). The later versions of the airplane had continuous axles and were apparently set up to carry drop tanks under their bellies, both changes explaining why they could not carry the single 500lb bomb. At this time it took a large slow torpedo bomber (T3M or T4M) to carry the 1000lb bomb.

62. GB 449 file 1928–9 discusses an October 1928 submission by the War Plans Division on aircraft roles, with Moffett's 4 December 1928 comments.

63. GB 449 (Serial 1388) of 22 December 1928, with Moffett's comments, in 'Aircraft Design Planning and Production Pre-WW II file', Aviation History, NHHC. This paper is also in GB 449 File 1928–9.

64. In US Navy parlance, the V indicates heavier-than-air. It and similar letters for helicopters (H) and airships (Z) were applied to squadrons, so that a squadron of fighters would be a VF but a type of fighter would have a designation prefixed by F (airships were the exception, Z being used in their individual designations). The same meaning explains why US carriers were designated in a CV series. Torpedo bombers were VTs, but the Douglas Devastator was designated TBD, indicating a bombing role (but not dive-bombing). Similarly the wartime Avenger was a TBF or TBM. In each case the last letter of an aircraft designation indicated the manufacturer, e.g. D for Douglas and F for Grumman. Aircraft were numbered in a separate series for each mission and manufacturer, so that Grumman fighters were FF, F2F, F3F, F4F, etc (the number 1 was not used). A suffix number indicated a modification of the basic aircraft, as in F4F-4 and F-4F-5 for different types of Wildcat. Suffix letters after the number indicated special modifications, such as E for electronic or N for night-capable (as in F6F-5N, for the night-fighter version of the F6F-5 Hellcat). For this book the important manufacturers were Curtiss (C), Douglas (D), Grumman (F), McDonnell (H originally D but changed to avoid confusion with Douglas), Bell (L), Vought (U, because it began as part of United Aircraft) and Convair (V, because it began as Consolidated Vultee). Aircraft built under license during the Second World War had separate manufacturer's designations: A for Brewster (which had built its own aircraft before and early in the war), G for Goodyear (which continued to develop aircraft after the war), M for Eastern Aircraft (a General Motors operation) and W for Canadian Car and Foundry. In 1962 the navy system was dropped and naval aircraft redesignated in the system already used by the air force, consisting simply of a mission letter (F for fighter) and a sequence number, as in F4 (formerly F4H, the Phantom II) and the F-14 Tomcat.

65. The Board compared the actual performance of the Boeing F4B, two prototypes of which existed, with the estimated performance of the F8C-2. Maximum speeds were, respectively, 168.8mph and 149mph; service ceilings were 26,900ft and 20,700ft; time to climb to 10,000ft was 5.3 minutes and 7 minutes (initial rates of climb 2930 and 2070ft/seconds).

The table did not show relative endurance.

66. Data from RG 72 Entry P7, a proposal file which includes the pre-1944 Design Division designs from No. 35 up. There were two other sketch fighter designs, No. 94 (two-seater, 6 November 1929) and No. 95(5 Dec 1929). No. 94 would have been powered by a supercharged liquid-cooled 625hp V-1570 engine and would have weighed 4296lbs. Estimated maximum speed was 179.2mph and initial climb rate 1570ft/seconds. Endurance at cruising range would have been 5.98 hours (505 miles). No. 95 was a fighter powered by the new mechanically-supercharged Wasp engine producing 500hp at 2200ft. It would have weighed 2710lbs in normal condition. Calculated maximum speed was 180.8mph and initial climb rate was 2760ft/seconds. Endurance at cruising speed was 4.69 hours (382 miles). The design file does not provide dimensions for any of these designs. BuAer used such designs partly to gauge whether submitted designs were feasible. The figures for No. 94 give some idea of why the Grumman FF-1, with about 100 more horsepower, was so impressive; it made 207mph at 4000ft and had a range of 921 miles. It is not clear from the record whether No. 94 was involved in the choice to buy the FF-1.

67. BuAer Confidential Correspondence files, NARA II, VF Vol 1. At this time the BuAer Plans Division expected to recommend an experimental contract to Boeing (FY31) for either an improved F5B monoplane, an improved F4B (the current service fighter) with monocoque wings or an improved all-metal F4B type biplane. It was considered particularly desirable to give Curtiss a contract to keep two experimental fighter builders in the field. The Boeing aircraft was the XF6B.

68. According to the BuAer fighter history many of the proposals offered as alternatives to the FF-1 were unsatisfactory because they incorporated experimental features such as folding monoplane wings, slots and flaps (referencing a 12 November Plans Division memo). Slots and flaps had previously been proposed for scouts and folding wings were rejected for fear that they would fatally weaken the structure of a dive bomber, although in general they were considered valuable. Monoplanes generally needed folding wings because their wingspans were so much greater than those of biplanes (which limited manoeuvrability, because it added to the aircraft's moment of inertia, which resisted turns and rolls). Low-wing monoplanes were disliked because they had limited visibility (a particular problem for a scout), were expected to cause buffeting and offered poor combat controllability and manoeuvrability. According to the BuAer history, late in 1932 it was believed that Boeing had solved the problems with its XF7B. The next year Northrop delivered the XFT-1, another low-wing monoplane. Curtiss produced the XF13C, which had interchangeable monoplane (parasol) and biplane wings, so that it could be used to compare the two configurations. None of these aircraft entered service. According to the BuAer fighter history, p 5, none of the experimental aircraft was a satisfactory fighter. With extensive adaptation, the FT-1 or a modified F2F or the Berliner-Joyce XF3J-1 might be acceptable. A fourth alternative, the Curtiss BF2C bomber, was dropped. Tests of the F13C later established the value of slots and flaps in a carrier aircraft. The BuAer fighter history cites a 19 March 1934 Plans Division memo on 'Fighting Planes' and other references going back to a 27 October 1933 memo from Class Desk 'A' to the Materiel Division on 'Single-Seat Fighters – Trend of Development of'. The files containing these papers seem not to have survived. RG 72 Entry P7 includes papers on the 1934 competition.

69. GB 449 file 1931–2.

70. The XF12C-1 was a parasol monoplane. After a test failure a new biplane prototype XSBC-2 was built and accepted. Like the earlier fighter-bombers, it could deliver a 500lb bomb. The up-engined SBC-4, which was still in service in 1941, could deliver a 1000lb bomb, by then the standard for US Navy dive bombers.

71. The XSBF-1 had a crutch and a 500lb bomb hung from its engine mount. This aircraft was delivered in 1936, hence was part of the larger programme of adapting two-seat fighters as scout dive bombers. Grumman counted the XSBF-1 as a new design, its G-14. Data from Grumman archive file on the FF-1. This file does not include any indication of the navy requirement to which the aircraft was built.

72. BuAer history of fighter plane development, unsigned but almost certainly by Lee M Pearson, the BuAer historian; it was probably the basis of his articles in the BuAer *Confidential Bulletin*. Notes are from the copy in the files of the Aviation History section, NHHC. Pearson quotes extensively from the BuAer fighter file, which is apparently *not* the surviving corresponding file at NARA II. It is not clear whether the November 1931 paper by the Plans Division was the beginning of the 'special' fighter project or instead a reaction to an earlier request by the Bureau chief, Admiral Moffett. At this time two fighters capable of delivering 500lb bombs were under development, the XFM-1 and the XF6B-1. The XFM-1 (Martin) seems not to have been built; the XF6B was redesignated XBFB in 1935.

73. The design competition was announced on 28 June 1934; development contracts would be let by 10 August. Of the alternatives, the XFT-1

monoplane was both not fast enough and had too high a landing (stall) speed, the latter a critical factor for carrier operation. It would take too long to modify and then re-test, so it was dropped. The Berliner-Joyce aircraft was considered obsolete, as it had been designed too long ago and too many requirements had changed meanwhile. The BF2C had, according to the BuAer history, been designed as a bomber, hence had poor fighter characteristics (it had actually been designed as a dual-purpose fighter-bomber, in the same class as other aircraft of its generation). Despite its drawbacks, the F2F was the best of the lot. It exceeded contract performance guarantees for full speed, stalling speed, service ceiling and rate of climb.

74. Papers setting up the programme are in BuAer file A1-1(1) in the Confidential 1922-1944 RG 72 series. This file includes a 10 December 1931 letter from Bureau Chief Rear Admiral Moffett to the Assistant Secretary of the Navy for Aeronautics referring to the Foundation Shriner High Speed. It laid out cost estimates for development of an aircraft and engine capable of making about 500mph. Alternatives were two aircraft from one source and two from each additional source; 'two planes are considered necessary for each step in the programme in order to prevent sudden interruption of development work should one plane crash and be destroyed.' As a step towards the 500mph aircraft, it would be necessary to build intermediate planes capable of 350mph and 400mph. The entire process was envisaged as a five-year programme. As formulated in November 1931, the programme included special high-speed aircraft powered by the 3000hp H-4240 engine and by a 1200hp air-cooled radial (a developed R-1830). Ultimately neither was affordable, the H-4240 being abandoned altogether and the R-1830 tested in the existing XT3D torpedo bomber.

75. At this time BuAer was sponsoring several engines for potential high-speed use. The highest power was expected from an H-engine. BuAer's H-2120 was intended to develop 1000hp, but it was in the 1000–1500hp class. By 1932 there was a strong preference for air-cooled radials, so a project to develop the H-2120 into a 3000hp H-4240 was abandoned. The H-2120 was attractive because it weighed only 1200lbs, compared to 1100lbs for the R-1830 (Twin Wasp), which was in the 850–1000hp class, hence lacked the potential of the liquid-cooled H-engine. The Twin Wasp went on to be a very important Second World War engine. For 1933, the other engines to be intensively developed under the High Speed Engine programme were the R-1510 and R-1535 two-row radials (900lbs, 700–850hp class); the R-1690 and R-1820 (900lbs, 700–850hp class); the R-1340 (700lbs, 650–700hp class); and the R-1178 (two rows, 700lbs, 550–700hp class). Of these engines, the R-1820 rose into the 1000hp class and was widely used during the Second World War as an equivalent to the R-1830. The R-1535 was the previous-generation high-powered engine, used in the Grumman F2F fighter and in the TBD Devastator torpedo bomber.

76. Note that according to a short BuAer fighter history written post-war, in 1934 the main fighter role was strike escort. That does not jibe with the BuAer manuscript fighter history. The strike escort claim is in 'Fighter Development: The Prewar Years', by BuAer historian Lee M Pearson, in BuAer *Confidential Bulletin*, October 1948. Pearson was then writing a longer history of US naval fighters through 1945.

77. Changes were general improvements including better streamlining, provision of a 0.50-calibre gun, provision for two bombs (116lbs), increased wing area (260ft^2 rather than 230ft^2) to hold down take-off and landing speed, slightly increased tail length (for stability), redesigned retractable landing gear and reduced interference between upper wing and fuselage. The two main alternatives to the F3F were the Curtiss XF13C-1 (the monoplane version) and the Northrop XFT-1. The Curtiss design was dropped because it incorporated many experimental features and it was expected to require 18 months of further development. It also incorporated the relatively undeveloped R-1510 engine. According to the BuAer manuscript fighter history, the initial recommendation for procurement, dated 16 August 1934, rejected both the XFT-1 and the XF13C-1, but BuAer opinion as a whole was more favourable to them.

78. BuAer manuscript fighter history, p 12. According to the history, the existing Wright single-row R-1820-F would have met Curtiss' requirement.

79. A single-row radial was considered too large hence too draggy; a two-row radial would be too complicated due to its exhaust and the baffling inside the cowl for cooling.

80. Span was 23ft and length 22ft, making the new design slightly smaller than the F3F-1. Alternative engines were the Pratt & Whitney XR-1535 and the Wright XR-1670-02. Grumman claimed that maximum speed would be 258 to 264mph.

81. A Curtiss proposal, a version of the company's army Y1P-36 Hawk 75, was considered a fall-back in case the SBA-1 proved unsuccessful. Although BuAer selected the Grumman and Brewster designs, Curtiss asked it to test the Hawk 75 to see whether it could be modified for carrier use. Tests revealed many minor problems, including excessive stall speed (68mph)

and lack of stability; and it was no faster than the latest experimental fighters. It would have required folding wings, to which BuAer was still strongly opposed. BuAer also suspected that actually adapting the Hawk 75 to carrier operation would reveal many further problems.

82. The BuAer history cites a 9 May 1936 letter from CinC US Fleet. No fast single-seat dive bomber was developed before 1941. The biplane F4F-1 in particular seemed unlikely to retain its speed in production form.

83. According to the air armament section of the BuAer Ten-Year R&D history, the ring and post sights and telescopic sights in use in 1935 were not superseded until the Second World War. BuAer became interested in reflector sights in 1940, using concepts originally developed by the French and adapted for anti-aircraft weapons by both the army and the navy. It entered limited production in 1941. BuOrd began work on a lead-computing sight, which first appeared early in 1943. Bendix adapted a British lead-computing sight later in the war.

84. The proposal was suggested in June 1936 and approved by the Bureau Chief on 8 July. Both aircraft would use the Pratt & Whitney R-1830-C with two-stage supercharger and would be armed with two 0.50-calibre guns, with provision for two 20mm and one 500lb bomb. Grumman had already proposed installation of an R-1820-65 in the F3F-1, adding 200hp at the cost of 200lbs of engine, increasing maximum speed from 226mph to about 260mph. At this time, too, Grumman proposed changing the F4F to a monoplane based on wind tunnel tests which showed that the monoplane was superior aerodynamically and could achieve a higher speed. The redesigned aircraft incorporated an R-1830-C engine but was considered suitable for other powerplants. BuAer chose an R-1830-66 with single-stage supercharger, which was rated at 900hp and 9000ft and 1000hp for take-off. That placed it in the power category of the Merlin then being chosen for the new British interceptors, the Spitfire and the Hurricane. Wing span was limited to 35ft. Brewster was offered both the R-1830-66 and the R-1820-22, the former proving impracticable. In its case the cockpit had to be raised, at a cost in drag. As re-engined, the F4F-2 offered a guaranteed maximum speed of 290mph and the Brewster 280mph. The re-engined F3F-2 offered 255mph (stall speed 66.2mph). The production version had a maximum speed of 256mph. The BuAer fighter history describes these choices as very successful. Within a few months BuAer had moved maximum speed up by as much as 30mph while protecting itself against any surprises inherent in monoplanes by continuing to buy the F3F. The cost was increased size, mainly in wing span: an increase of three feet for the F2A and seven feet for the F4F, as well as increases in length to maintain balance with the heavier new engines.

85. The BuAer fighter history states that two Buffaloes were later converted to F3A-1s, but that version did not enter production. No details were given. The F3A-1 designation was later used for Brewster-produced Corsairs.

86. In June 1942 the Naval Air Station at Anacostia test-flew an army P-40F for comparative purposes; the report compared to an F4F-4, which was a somewhat worse performer than the F4F-3. The report is in RG 72 confidential correspondence for 1922–1944, VF Vol 6. The P-40F was powered by a Packard Merlin V-1650-1 engine rather than the usual V-1710. Its military rating of 1120mph (for five minutes) was comparable to that of the R-1830 which powered the F4F. It was armed with the six 0.50-calibre machine guns of the F4F-4. Both aircraft had about the same fuel. In normal condition the P-40F required 350ft to take off with 25 knots of wind over the deck, which would have been acceptable in a naval fighter (and is why *Ranger* was able to launch P-40Fs during the North African invasion the following November). Stall speed with full flaps was 81.5 mph (at rated power with full flaps, 78mph). However, the stall was abrupt with little or no warning and that seemed to seriously hinder the combat manoeuvring characteristics of the P-40F. A comparison with the F4F-4 showed that below about 20,000ft the army fighter climbed faster, but above the F4F-4 climbed faster. At normal rated power the army fighter was faster below 20,000ft, although its advantage was less than in climbing. At indicated air speeds below 150 knots the F4F-4 was a faster climber at all altitudes. Above 24,000ft the F4F-4 had a marked speed and climb advantage. It also had a smaller turning radius at all altitudes. The P-40F could dive away from the F4F-4 at all altitudes. The F4F-4 could be operated from smaller take-off and landing areas than the P-40F. BuAer's interest in higher altitudes showed in the superior performance of the F4F-4 engine above 16,000ft. The F4F-4 enjoyed markedly better visibility because its pilot sat higher and particularly because it had a shorter nose; 'in the area directly over the nose on the centreline, where vision is critical for deflection shooting, the P-40F is very deficient.' The hydraulic gun chargers on the P-40F were rated far superior to the manual chargers of the F4F-4 in rapidity and ease of operation. However, the gunsight of the P-40F was entirely inadequate. Its reticule provided only a linear mil scale, without the deflection circles or radial lines the navy considered essential. Moreover, the F4F-4 was considered a far superior gun platform due to gross deficiencies of the P-40F: poor visibility over the nose; high rudder forces and large changes in directional trim with speed and power, causing

considerable difficulty in making accurate gunnery and bombing runs; and an abrupt high speed stall with lack of stick movement, making accurate close-range deflection shooting extremely difficult. The P-40F cockpit was quieter than that of the F4F-4 and had much better-controlled temperature and ventilation, but it was also quite cramped. The P-40F offered a higher rate of roll and in pushover dives it did not lose oil pressure (in the F4F-4 that dropped to as low as 6 psi; in a P-40F the recommended *minimum* pressure for flight operation was 60 psi). Overall, the P-40F offered a more comprehensive and precise degree of power control. The P-40F engine produced an annoying 'beat.' The Anacostia report ended with the comment that it would be difficult to choose between the F4F-4 and the P-40F as a combat fighter, but 'for all-purpose use it is believed the F4F-3 could safely be chosen as the superior fighter.

87. According to the BuAer history, p 57, the other major factors making for higher speed, listed in order of importance, were the adoption of a monoplane wing with high-lift devices (40 per cent), increased operating altitude (30 per cent), increased minimum (stall) speed (8 per cent) and an improved power/weight ratio (7 per cent). The limited effect of increased stall speed suggested that it would not be too difficult to increase maximum speed further without sacrificing too much in the way of carrier landing characteristics.

88. According to the BuAer fighter history, p 60, BuAer concluded that the F4F-3 was the best all-round fighter in the world at the time, but that seems excessive. It did realise that once it had been given pilot armour and self-sealing tanks it would sacrifice enough performance that it would be marginal. Stall speed increased to 74.6mph (72mph with power), the greater load would reduce manoeuvrability and take-off run increased from an already-long 257ft to 284ft. BuAer proposed a redesign using the R-1830-D engine (larger cylinders), which would reduce wing loading and also the take-off run (to 231ft, even less if high-lift devices were used). This 'Design S' would weigh 7917lbs gross compared to 6200lbs for the F4F-3. Stall speed would be 69.4mph (68.8mph for F4F-3) and maximum speed would be 348mph (rather than 350mph) at 20,500ft (rather than 21,000ft). Ceiling would be about the same, 33,100ft (vs 33,400ft), range would be slightly greater (1007 miles vs 954 miles). However, the new take-off run would be far longer than the 192ft of the earlier aircraft. Grumman was unenthusiastic.

89. BuAer fighter history, p 57. Presumably the US Navy had particularly good access to French data because the French were buying US naval aircraft, both Wildcats and dive bombers.

90. According to the BuAer fighter history, the biplane and the Zimmerman ('pancake') fighter (see the next chapter) were the first instances of close co-operation with NACA, both of them in 1939. At this time NACA had just completed a study of its wartime role as an adjunct of the services' Aeronautical Board.

91. Perhaps the earliest surviving discussion of US naval air tactical development is a file in the archives of the Naval War College, Aircraft Tactics – Development Of, issued in San Diego on 3 February 1927 and corrected to 20 July 1927 (Intelligence and Research files RG 8, coded UANT/1927-147). It is Reeves' account of experiments by and conclusions reached by, his Battle Fleet aircraft. He provides considerable advice on air-to-air fighter tactics, but there is no evidence of patrols or means of directing fighters against the main threats of the time, enemy torpedo bombers and enemy fighters threatening the fleet's spotters. Instead, there are references to what a pilot should do after being ordered to intercept enemy aircraft and to how fighters should form escorting formations to protect spotters. The file opens with Reeves' initial questions, presumably an early version of his '1001 Questions' to the airmen he commanded. Reeve's recommendations included the urgent need for a small lightweight radio for fighters, since without it pilots would be limited to instructions issued before take-off. Alternatively a special radio liaison aircraft could accompany fighters, but it would probably lack their performance.

92. Interpretation is more difficult because the role of the lectures can easily be exaggerated. The pre-war War College students played numerous lengthy games (typically eight or more, including a month-long campaign, the 'big game') and game experience in itself was probably more important than what they heard in lectures. However, the lectures are much more accessible and they can be interpreted as the navy's views. Lecturers may also have been reluctant to challenge conventional wisdom that surface forces would determine the outcome of a naval war. Thus the December 1936 aviation version of 'The Employment of Aviation in Naval Warfare', prepared by the Operations Department (Naval War College RG 4, Box 71, folder 5, item 1929) pointed out that it would take 156 torpedo bombers to carry as many torpedoes as one destroyer squadron and 1200 aircraft to carry as many large bombs as a single battleship carried shells. Against this, aircraft could rapidly concentrate and overcome target defences. This pamphlet also pointed out that 'it is difficult for an enemy to intercept and destroy aircraft in the air even when superior. So long as their bases are secure, aviation forces quite inferior to the enemy can seldom be prevented from accom-plishing many important missions.' According to this paper, 'if bombing attacks upon a fleet appear imminent, an outer aircraft picket line might be established and an escort of fighters combat air patrol kept overhead to engage the bombers before they come within range of anti-aircraft batteries. Unless some system is employed that will insure some advanced warning, the bombers are likely to get home their attack. Even in this case, they should be engaged by our fighters as soon as the again pass beyond anti-aircraft range, in order to reduce the power of subsequent attacks.' Much the same ideas were presented in the September 1937 version of the pamphlet. The 21 January 1939 version (a Staff Presentation by Lieutenant Commander T H Robbins Jr) refers to the bomber as the fighter's main target and points to a requirement for a one-third speed advantage (Robbins notes that the cost of such performance is drastically reduced range, so that fighters can no longer escort the carrier's own strike aircraft). The reference to air pickets and a CAP repeat those of earlier editions. The 11 September 1940 Staff Presentation (by Commander Henry S Kendall) omits all discussion of aircraft in fleet air defence, but emphasises that aircraft are an essentially offensive rather than defensive arm; 'Command of the Air' 'can practically never be attained through direct action against aircraft in the air, but is only possible through the destruction of aircraft bases'. That meant pre-emption against the enemy's carriers. This was written while the British were demonstrating effective air defence against the Germans, but that may not yet have been apparent. The final pre-war lecture in the series was delivered on 19 August 1941 (by Captain H W Crosby, the College Chief of Staff), after the Battle of Britain and also after the US Navy had its first operational air-search radars (and was closely collaborating with the Royal Navy). Crosby did not discuss defensive fighter topics, but only noted that 'the development of RDF radar will doubtless profoundly influence present tactics, dispositions and search. The ability of the aircraft to effect surprise in attack will be greatly curtailed; correspondingly, the defence will gain in strength'. He seems to have been the first in the series to point out that even when operating in company, carriers had to be widely separated to avoid interference between their air groups. At this time the standard carrier air group was one eighteen-plane VT squadron, two eighteen-plane VSB squadrons (in effect, one to scout, the other to strike) and one fighter squadron – now of twenty-seven rather than eighteen aircraft. Comments in the text refer to the importance of beating off enemy air attacks, but methods are not discussed.

93. *Carrier Divisions, US Fleet: Aircraft Tactical Instructions Vol II: Major Aircraft Tactics*. This was a tentative handbook (Vol I was the air fighting tactics) dated 17 December 1930. It is in RG 38, NARA II; their copy is Register No. 164. The handbook was signed by Rear Admiral J M Reeves, who was then Commander, Carrier Divisions, US Fleet; his closest British counterpart was Rear Admiral (Aircraft). Most references are to *Lexington* and *Saratoga*, which had recently been completed. A distinction was made between a Carrier Division, which was one or more carriers with their aircraft and a Carrier Group, which was typically one carrier plus escorting cruisers and destroyers. The style of US command handbooks, then and later, makes it somewhat difficult to extract doctrine from them; they were written to give a commander a sense of alternatives and crucial considerations, not to provide specific advice. The US Navy had no equivalent of the British Progress in Tactics, which described tactical experiments intended to answer particular tactical questions. *Current Tactical Orders* (USF-10) for 1934 and 1938 included prescribed fleet cruising formations, in which the carriers were concentrated abaft the battleships, but it is not clear how seriously they were taken. Aircraft squadrons were divided into divisions (as their basic tactical units), each of which consisted of two or three three-plane sections. To further complicate interpretation, although the pre-war US Navy operated its carriers on a dispersed basis, its carrier tactical publication (USF-77) envisaged multi-carrier formations, the ships being separated by three miles when launching aircraft.

94. To further complicate understanding, Change No. 1 (12 June 1931) declared that the role of carrier fighters was 'to destroy all enemy aircraft in the battle area, particularly the enemy spotters' and 'to destroy enemy aircraft threatening own spotters and battle line'. The fourth among four roles was to support own strikes (torpedo bombers). None of the four items was to defend the carriers or the wider fleet. This edition points out that foreign navies (both British and Japanese, though that was not said) 'not only normally stow their aircraft in two hangars but also some foreign carriers apparently are equipped with double flight decks, the upper deck being for landing and the lower for taking off. Attacks upon carriers should therefore be made with bombs of sufficient weight to penetrate the upper flight decks'. In fact the double flight decks of British and Japanese carriers were both used for launching (the lower one for fighters with short take-off runs). The 1931 changes were embodied in a new October 1931 edition, which is also in NARA II. It was printed rather than mimeographed, but it was still marked 'tentative'.

95. NARA II RG 38. The same language was used in the 1940 edition. The

1934 edition, which was apparently the earliest, was only partial and did not include information about air defence. Unfortunately RG 38 does not include early editions of USF-74, *Current Tactical Orders and Doctrine, US Fleet Aircraft: Volume I, Carrier Aircraft*, the successor to the handbook Reeves produced in 1930–1. It does include the revised edition dated March 1941. In the 1941 edition, aerial pickets would be stationed at 8000ft altitude, which would enable them to spot aircraft between that altitude and the surface. However, 'it is desirable that the vertical spacing of pickets extend upward to the highest altitude at which the approach of enemy aircraft may be expected. The vertical spacing between adjacent pickets should not exceed approximately 6000ft'. The CAP was to operate at 12,000 to 20,000ft and above the level of broken clouds, in order to deal with enemy strike forces. If they faced only snoopers or shadowers (patrol or scout planes) they would operate at 7000 to 10,000ft.

96. The section on scouting in USF-75, *Current Tactical Orders and Doctrine, US Fleet Aircraft, Vol II: Battleship and Cruiser Aircraft* issued 16 August 1938 mentions both the outer air patrol and the pickets and requires that they operate in sections of at least two floatplanes each. The current floatplane was the Curtiss SOC. Note that the corresponding but later handbook for carrier aircraft (USF-74 of March 1941) also mentions the outer air patrol and the pickets. In its case the outer air patrol operates with three aircraft. In this handbook the pickets operate single, so that the pilot can give his entire attention to lookout, without having to fly in formation with a wingman. This handbook states that 'aerial pickets, if comprising aircraft of adequate performance and armament, should be prepared to attack enemy aircraft scouts immediately upon sighting them without waiting for the arrival of the combat patrol. Any delay might permit information to be transmitted to the enemy. However, disproportionate losses of aerial pickets should be guarded against'. Unfortunately no earlier edition of USF-74 has surfaced (the 1941 edition is the revised version).

97. The official Confidential *CIC* magazine carried the text of a BuAer fighter control history beginning in its April 1946 issue. This history refers to the elaborate series of air patrols to be flown by a carrier task force operating within range of enemy aircraft, but points out that the outer patrol could never provide warning until the enemy was little more than 25nm from task group centre. Initially the CAP was intended to orbit over task group centre and it would have barely enough time to mount a counter-attack. Later the CAP was spread in sectors ten to fifteen miles from task group centre so that it could meet the enemy further out; however, only some of the fighters could respond to an attack from any one direction. The history notes further that the fighter controller had to be airborne to see how to direct that counter-attack, but he might find it difficult to direct a battle if her were in the midst of it. According to the history, the defence of ground objectives was handled similarly. The history refers to USF-74 (instructions for carrier aircraft), which directed that the CAP always be given an altitude advantage over the attackers and that attacks should never be unopposed.

98. According to interviews conducted by US officers at the First Naval Air Technical Arsenal, which performed BuAer technical functions, including setting requirements. RG 72 Entry UD-117, Air Technical Intelligence Group reports and correspondence, 1945. Late in the war engine workmanship was so bad that the Air Arsenal had to inspect the standard high-powered engine (Homare) minutely before passing it for use; only about 5 to 10 per cent of engines were approved. They went into 'George' (N1K1) fighters. Presumably the problem was that in order to increase production it was necessary to farm it out to inexperienced firms.

99. As pointed out by Commander Genda Minoru, who planned the air component of the Midway operation, in his short history of pre-war Japanese carrier tactics. He claimed credit for the concept of the six-carrier task force, which he wrote that he had conceived after seeing a newsreel of four US carriers steaming together. Genda wrote of the pilots' view that the carrier was both supremely vulnerable and supremely effective offensively. Aside from the reference to a concentrated CAP, he did not mention defensive operations at all. Copy of the Genda history in author's collection.

100. The after-action report of the carrier *Hiryu* stated that it was difficult to sight targets at an altitude over 5000m (16,400ft). Task forces in AA warning cruising disposition were dispersed over a wide area and an enemy breaking into the centre of the formation from aft could not be sighted. 'On the *Akagi* there have been many times when the first warning was the splash of the bombs. Moreover, it is said that on the *Akagi* there have been times when they first started evasive action after several bombs had been dropped without firing a single round, sighting of the target being so tardy that they were not ready for "blitzkrieg firing".' The report advocated immediate installation of AA search radar (as expressed in the original) or sound equipment. In anti-aircraft action, the first ship sighting the enemy, at whatever range, should report to all the other ships and to the fighter striking units (presumably CAP) and at the same time should open fire to indicate the approximate direction of the target. US translation, document courtesy of Jon Parshall.

101. It is not entirely clear whether the Japanese Zeroes had voice radio in 1941–2. Japanese officers describing defensive tactics at Midway in 1945 referred to fighter control using it (with W/T reserved for long ranges). The immediate post-war Japanese account is questionable because one of the same officers incorrectly claimed that at Midway the carrier *Hiryu* had radar; they may have been conflating pre- and post-Midway practices. Jonathan Parshall and Anthony Tully, *Shattered Sword* (Washington: Potomac Books, 2005), p 136 describe Japanese airborne radio in 1942 as substandard, noting that there was only a single frequency for communication with all aircraft aloft, including reconnaissance and strike forces. That suggests the use of Morse rather than voice radio, as the single frequency had to support long-range communication. They add that Japanese fighter pilots rarely relied on their radios: once they were aloft, they were on their own. According to Mark R Peattie, *Sunburst: The Rise of Japanese Naval Air Power 1909-1941* (Annapolis: Naval Institute Press, 2001), p 137, a Type 96 radio telephone was developed in 1936 but not installed on board naval aircraft until early in the war and even then it suffered badly from interference and static. Fighter pilots typically relied on visual signals such as wing-wagging and flares (and clearly could not rely on ship-to-air communication). Fighter pilots not previously trained in W/T had to master Morse before the Pearl Harbor operation because only W/T was effective at the 250–300nm range involved.

102. Parshall and Tully, *Shattered Sword*, p 215.

103. This account is based on Admiralty *Battle Summary* No. 45, *Battle of Coral Sea, 4–8 May 1942*, compiled in 1951 (issued 31 December 1952), using all available sources, including the post-war interviews with Japanese naval officers compiled as *Campaigns of the Pacific War* by the US Strategic Bombing Survey. For Midway I have relied on the more recent account by Parshall and Tully, *Shattered Sword*.

104. The pre-war US expectation was that major bomb hits would ruin a large carrier's air capacity and send her back to a shipyard for repairs, but were unlikely to sink her; in this sense *Shokaku* met expectations. The surprise was the destruction of the carriers at Midway due to hangar fires and explosions.

105. Peattie, *Sunburst*, p 156. Immediately after the war, two senior Japanese officers described standard CAP tactics at the time of Midway somewhat differently: typically one two-carrier division maintained an eighteen-fighter CAP while the other divisions held another eighteen aircraft in readiness, nine per carrier (this omitted fighters to cover the strike aircraft). CAP duration was two hours, aircraft being relieved on station. At Midway, the initial CAP stations were stacked over the Japanese task force, nine fighters at 2000m and another nine at 4000m. Air Technical Intelligence Group report, Japanese Carrier Operations Part I, 4 and 5 October 1945, in RG 72 Entry UD-117. It was based partly on testimony by Captain Kawaguchi Susumu, who had been Air Officer on board the carrier *Hiryu* at Midway. Part II (5 and 6 October 1945) was an interrogation of Captain Amagai Takahise, who had been Air Officer of the *Hiryu* from August 1941 to April 1942 and was Air Officer of *Akagi* at Midway. Captain Amagai recalled that the CAP at Midway had consisted of aircraft from all four carriers: eight each from *Akagi* and *Kaga*, six each from the smaller *Hiryu* and *Soryu*, with another twenty-six aircraft on deck as reliefs, launched when the US attack developed.

106. Peattie, *Sunburst*, p 135.

107. Peattie, *Sunburst* p 74.

108. Peattie, *Sunburst*, p 175.

109. Based on interviews conducted by US officers at the First Naval Air Technical Arsenal, which performed BuAer technical functions, including setting requirements. RG 72 Entry UD-117, Air Technical Intelligence Group reports and correspondence, 1945. The Japanese said that development of the carrier-based A7M was further delayed when a landplane version of the Kawanishi seaplane fighter (N1K1 Shiden, 'George') was adopted as a stop-gap (but it was never a carrier fighter).

4. THE SECOND WORLD WAR: FIGHTERS UNDER RADAR CONTROL

1. The Royal Navy set up its own radar development organisation, citing differences between the shipboard and land environments. Both the RAF and the navy initially used television technology; the initial BBC television system operated at about 43 MHz (7m). The prototype Type 79Y was tested at sea in 1938, achieving a range of 30–50nm on aircraft. The first British warships fitted were the cruiser *Sheffield* (August 1938) and the battleship *Rodney* (October 1938). Forty improved versions (with higher power) were ordered in August 1939.

2. *Ark Royal* was scheduled for radar installation when she was sunk in November 1941.

3. The power of a radar signal falls off as the square of the range, which determines the range at which an enemy can intercept it. The echo, which is made by a signal already weaker by the square of the range, suffers a further square of range weakening on its way back to the ship. Not counting losses in reflection at the target, an enemy receives the same signal strength at

100 miles as a ship detects in an echo at 10 miles. The British were unaware that the pre-war Germans thought that radar was usable only at shorter wavelengths (50cm), hence were unlikely to detect their search radar. The British did adopt 50cm for fire-control radars, which are not relevant to this story.

4. The term 'radar' as an acronym for Radio Direction And Ranging was invented by the US Navy; it was officially adopted in November 1940 as an acceptable cover term, analogous to the British use of RDF.

5. This is the British fighter direction handbook. I have used British figures because they make comparison between British and US sets easiest. At this time the British were using all standard US naval radars.

6. The original radar display, the 'A' scan, showed blip strength against time, which equated to range. The trace did not fade instantly, so that repeated detections at a given range would create a stronger and more easily-seen blip indicating the range. Initial radar practice was to turn the beam in a given direction, look for a blip, then turn to another direction to see whether a target was present. A variety of displays was developed for rangefinding and gunnery radars, one object being to display both the target and any nearby splashes. For fighter control and air defence, the more important development was the PPI, because it continuously showed the whole situation, not just what lay in a particular direction. It might be imagined as a collection of A scans seen from above, the brightness of a blip corresponding to its strength. In British terms a Height Position Indicator (HPI) was a PPI turned on its side to show target elevation angle (not altitude directly). An HPI was inscribed with 'constant height curves' indicating elevation angle at various ranges for an aircraft at a particular height. According to the British October 1944 fighter direction handbook, a good operator could read height to within 1000ft out to 25–30nm (an angular accuracy within 30 minutes of arc). An alternative display showed angle of sight vs range. At this time the Royal Navy was just about to receive US SM or SP heightfinders and it relied mainly on fade charts for heightfinding, exploiting the difference in fades between its two main series of air-search radars, Types 79 and 281. In addition, the Royal Navy was deploying an S-band Type 277 surface-search set whose antenna could be tipped up to measure height directly.

7. Yasuzo Nakagawa, *Japanese Radar and Related Weapons* (Laguna Hills: Aegean Park Press, 1997). Mr Nakagawa had previously published an account of the Japanese Navy's Technical Research Department, which was responsible for naval radars, in 1987 and also an account of technology development at NEC (1992). In 1935 a second-generation American of Japanese descent offered to sell an apparatus he was developing for radio detection of aircraft at about 100km. Nothing was done because the report was not believed. A Japanese delegate to the International Consultative Committee in Radio Communications in Bucharest (1937) learned from his former German teacher that 'it would appear that the German Navy has been successful in the development of a wireless distance-measuring device that would permit range to be determined during hours of darkness'. This was an accurate description of initial German radar development. He also heard from the famous Italian radio inventor Guglielmo Marconi that work was proceeding on a new weapon based on radio, but that report was more ambiguous. When the heavy cruiser *Ashigara* visited England for the Coronation Review of May 1937, she passed through the Dover Strait; the British were exercising with aircraft. The Japanese noticed that multiple searchlights seemed rather quick to pick up aircraft and an officer on board interpreted that as an indication that radar was being used. However, that cannot have been the case, as there was not yet any British naval radar. An ordnance officer had already proposed an electronic device to detect an enemy, but it had been rejected because radio silence was considered more important. During a tour of Britain in May 1938, the head of the NEC vacuum tube section noticed that a passing aircraft disturbed television transmission. He repeated the observation when monitoring reception from an experimental Japanese television transmitter. These observations were very much like the ones (involving radio rather than the higher-frequency television) which had already led the US Naval Research Laboratory to develop US naval radars. In Japan, this observation led to army funding for a bistatic radar. The navy showed slight interest in a surface-search set for submarines. The Japanese navy did develop a method of estimating the range of an HF transmitter from HF multipath data, exploiting the time delay between different versions of the same signal. In 1940 this method made it possible to monitor movements in and out of Hawaii and on one occasion to follow warships between Pearl Harbor and the Philippines; Nakagawa (pp 19–20) claims that the Pearl Harbor attack was timed for a Sunday based on such observations, but the Japanese could also have known the pattern of US fleet movements by many other means. About the same time the Japanese developed a cavity magnetron. In 1941 a Japanese military delegation to Germany was shown German radars, including land-based air-search and fire-control sets. A prototype Japanese air-warning radar was set up on the grounds of the Naval Mine School at Nobi in September 1941, initially detecting a medium bomber at 97km (soon

extended to 110km). That is, at the experimental level the Japanese were not far behind the United States (except that their magnetron was much less powerful) at the beginning of the Pacific War. However, the connection between laboratory efforts and production and service was far poorer. Unfortunately Nakagawa does not discuss either Japanese radar intercept receivers or Japanese airborne radars, both of which were important tactically.

8. The 1.5m wavelength Mk 2 Mod 1 detected a single carrier-type aircraft flying at 3000m (about 10,000ft) at 55km range and a battleship at 20km. The 10cm sea-search set (Model 103) detected a battleship at 35km, but could not detect aircraft. The principal wartime air-search set was Type 2 Mk 2 Mod 1, work on which was completed in August 1943. It operated at 200 MHz, the same frequency as the US SK and SC series, but peak power was far lower (5kW). Pulse repetition rate was much higher (1000 pulses/seconds), so average power, which determines effective range, was not so much less. Typical range on a single aircraft was 70km.

9. Comment made by Shizuo Fukui, the Japanese warship historian and former naval constructor, to Alan Raven (courtesy of Alan Raven). The attempt failed because the Japanese did not recognise the British air-search antennas as radar. The Japanese did recover US and British army sets, but they do not see to have had much influence.

10. 'Jap radar appraised', *CIC* (an official Confidential magazine), April 1946.

11. The R/T section of the October 1944 Royal Navy fighter direction handbook, ADM 239/352 provides the full vocabulary then in use, in both R/T and W/T versions. *Rats* were identified enemy fighters and *See You* meant fleet in sight. *Tramlines* were a beam approach. Some of the phrases probably came from the US Navy: *Heads Up* (enemy got through) and *Hey Rube* (rendezvous over own ship).

12. This account of early British techniques is based largely on Lieutenant Commander R S Woolrych, 'Fighter Direction Material and Technique' in F A Kingsley (ed), *The Application of Radar and Other Electronic Systems in the Royal Navy in World War 2* (London: Macmillan, 1995).

13. In the British 1938 Summer Exercise the battleship *Rodney* detected emissions from the cruiser *Sheffield* at 200nm range, with a bearing accuracy of 2°. When she went to the Mediterranean in 1940, the carrier *Illustrious* was allowed only one radar sweep per hour until she made contact. She was not allowed to break radio silence to her fighters until the raid was 20nm from the ship. This was not an idle fear: *Bismarck* detected the emissions of the British cruiser shadowing her.

14. I have based this account largely on that given by J D Brown, *Carrier Fighters* (London: Macdonald and Janes, 1975). When he wrote it, Brown was head of the Royal Navy Historical Branch, with extensive access to official files. He was also a former FAA observer, with special knowledge of air tactics (he was first assigned to a carrier in 1945 in the Pacific).

15. Understanding that IFF might be ineffective, the convoy commander issued special instructions to aircraft to make stereotyped identification manoeuvres when rejoining the convoy: fighters should approach in a stepped-up line-astern formation from the side opposite to the sun. When five miles out, they would make a complete orbit to allow radar and visual 'de-lousing' (to insure against enemy aircraft following them home). The rules would be disregarded only by aircraft in hot pursuit. As an additional aid to identification, aircraft had the leading edges of their wings painted yellow. Forty years later IFF was still a problem and a senior US commander pointed to the need for returning aircraft not only to squawk but also to follow special identification manoeuvres.

16. *Eagle* had sixteen Sea Hurricanes and four spares. *Victorious* had sixteen Fulmar II and five Sea Hurricanes. *Indomitable* had twelve Sea Hurricanes, nine Martlet IIs and ten Sea Hurricanes.

17. The high cover was possible only because multiple carriers were operating together. The December 1942 Royal Navy fighter direction handbook describes a standard practice of maintaining a medium-altitude combat air patrol called an 'Umbrella' at 15,000ft or less. It might be supplemented by a 'Toadstool' patrol at about 3000ft, these latter fighters flying closer to the ship. The handbook cautioned against a tendency to expend fighter strength against ever-present shadowers, leaving too few fighters to face the subsequent attack. The revised version of this section of the handbook (January 1945) envisaged a series of alternative policies for an Umbrella carrier and a stand-by Umbrella carrier, plus perhaps other fighter carriers. Typically the Umbrella carrier would place one section on patrol and another at readiness on deck, the stand-by ship having two sections at readiness on deck. If air attack was probable (but unescorted), the Umbrella carrier would have two sections in the air and two on deck at readiness, the stand-by carrier two sections at readiness and the other fighter carriers two sections on deck (i.e. not warmed up or manned). If enemy fighters were likely to escort the attackers, the stand-by carrier would add its own two-section Umbrella patrol; it would match the Umbrella carrier. This list does not include the low-altitude patrol envisaged in 1942.

18. She was the second armoured carrier to be put out of action by Stuka dive bombers, *Victorious* having been the first, in January 1941. The Stukas were

using much heavier bombs than those against which the armoured decks had been designed (500lbs, the bomb used by the Royal Navy). There was no question of action repairs, as in a US lightweight flight deck.

19. ADM 239/352, CB 04262(1), *Notes on the Direction of Fighters by H.M. Ships, a Guard Book* for successive editions of the notes. The bulk of the book is the 1944 edition. The 1942 edition is mainly a discussion of RDF, with minimal comments about how to direct fighters.

20. This version of the handbook gave an example to show just how far in advance a fighter director had to act. It imagined an enemy closing at 210 knots and defending fighters flying out at 240 knots. The moment at which the fighter director had to order a turn onto a course similar to (parallel to) the enemy was when they were 11nm apart, because that allowed for a minute for the fighters to turn through 180°, half a minute transmitting R/T and the pilot beginning to turn and half a minute for the present (actual) position of each aircraft being ahead of its plotted position (on a Skiatron or PPI the half minute lag would not be needed).

21. The triangle consisted of the projected movement of the target and the projected movement of the intercepting aircraft attacking it. This is the same problem as that solved by a torpedo fire-control device, although of course the speeds and distances are radically different. It is also involved in gunnery. A surprising fact is that distances are not factors, only relative speeds and courses. Distances determine where the interception actually occurs.

22. The first PPI in a British carrier was an RAF unit (for ground-controlled interception) 'borrowed' by *Illustrious* in Ceylon in mid-1942. Trials of the standard naval PPI (designated JE) began on board the minesweeping sloop *Saltburn* in April 1943.

23. The higher the frequency, the larger the number of possible channels. HF normally supported only a single channel because the operating frequency had to be adjusted to atmospheric conditions. On the other hand, HF range extended beyond line of sight. That was an advantage for a fighter flying below the horizon, but a disadvantage if the enemy was listening. VHF was nearly line-of-sight and in theory its range was limited, so that an enemy would find it difficult to intercept from a distance (that was not always true). It operated at the lower end of the radar frequency range and thus required the sort of advanced radio technology employed by radars. An R/T section in the 1944 edition cautions that 'as a wholly VHF installation is not regarded as ideal for naval day fighters, arrangements are being made so that the present HF R/T installation is easily interchangeable with the proposed VHF installation'. Presumably this was a reference to the need to control fighters flying below the horizon at a distance. Naval night fighters would have VHF only. As in the US Navy, the VHF sets were crystal-controlled on four spot frequencies, the frequency selected by button. The projected standard naval fighter control set was the US SCR-522/542, a US version of the RAF TR.1143 with an extended frequency range (100–156 MHz rather than 100–120 or 100–124 MHz).

24. Brown, *Carrier Fighters*, p 146. He claims that this capability had already been demonstrated in the Mediterranean and by implication he contrasts it with US capability (and also argues for much better British R/T discipline, which was important in a melee).

25. This account of early US fighter direction experience is largely based on a post-war BuAer official history of fighter direction reprinted in the official Confidential *CIC* magazine, beginning with the April 1946 issue. A manuscript copy, giving the authors as Lieutenant William C Bryant and Lieutenant Keith I Hermans, is in the files of NHHC Aviation History. It provides footnotes.

26. Radar Doctrine, US Pacific Fleet came into effect shortly after Pearl Harbor as successor to previous tentative doctrines. Commander, Air Task Group was made responsible for maintaining a continuous plot of all radar information affecting air operations; evaluating plots and issuing alerts of impending air attacks; launching combat air patrols as necessary; utilising own radar to best advantage to supplement information from other radar ships; transmitting radar information to other ships; issuing standard instructions to fighter patrols; and directing interceptions of enemy aircraft.

27. The CXAM-1 antenna could tilt back to some degree in an abortive attempt to give height data. Anti-aircraft radars introduced from 1941 on could give height data, but only at short range.

28. In December 1941 CNO made IFF a priority second only to radar. The British already had an IFF system, but the US Navy wanted something more accurate and also secure against enemy interception. The US ABA offered bearing accuracy equal to that of the CXAM search radar, variable frequency and coded replies. The British Mk III was bought for use in the Atlantic.

29. Account from CNO Secret Information Bulletin No. 1; this raid was not included in the BuAer fighter direction history as a case in point of ineffective direction.

30. The summary of lessons learned included the comment that it would be good to have arrangements for returning aircraft land on either carrier;

'consideration should be given to the value of two carriers operating in mutual support of each other'. That would be particularly valuable if one of the carriers was damaged. This sort of full mutual support was not adopted until well into 1943 with the establishment of multi-carrier task groups.

31. The controller in *Enterprise* used true rather than magnetic bearings. That might seem trivial, but it meant that pilots had to convert them into magnetic bearings matching their magnetic compasses. This controller was working with all other ships which might not be aware of his methods. He also transmitted regularly without identifying himself. IFF was installed but ineffective.

32. The earlier aircraft used HF radio. VHF was just entering service, apparently not in the navy (the Royal Navy was in a similar position).

33. The new Fighter Direction School on Oahu developed a new 'X-Ray Formation'. The main body of the CAP would fly at a designated altitude, but as insurance against error one division (four fighters) would fly 5000ft above and one section (two fighters) 5000ft below. In practice fighter directors chose to stack their CAP sections at altitudes chosen to respond to current conditions. Stacking was a preferred alternative to the high-altitude technique (CAP at 20,000ft) proposed after Coral Sea. Pilots at that altitude needed oxygen and found flying more tiring and if they had to dive to deal with low-altitude attackers they used up much more fuel; they might also miss the bogey altogether.

34. The BuAer fighter direction history attributes this to a peculiarity of the CXAM display, which had alternative settings of 0–50nm, 50–100nm, 100–150nm and 150–200nm. The operator used a triggering device to determine in which segment the bogey was. The low end of each scale was partly filled with pips from accompanying ships and aircraft overhead. A target at the low end would therefore be largely masked. The history suggests that such masking precluded detection of the bogey between 119nm and 44nm; the later SC and SK radars eliminated the discontinuous-range problem.

35. According to the BuAer history, the commander of VF-62 reported that fighters were being continuously vectored in and out on many bearings and at varying distances and altitudes trying to find enemy aircraft. Too many instructions were sent and most apparently meant little or nothing to the pilots. The *Enterprise* fighter director gave only three vector orders in standard form, all at the beginning of the attack. None led to an interception. Many gave the bogey position in terms of the heading of the violently manoeuvring ship.

36. CICs had two distinct origins. One was air combat and fighter direction. The other was night surface warfare. In the latter, the CIC was a way of providing each ship with a meaningful picture of a complex situation, drastically reducing errors such as engaging friendly ships. In both cases, CIC was built around a single plot of the tactical situation, based both on radar and on other data (such as lookout reports and electronic intercepts). It might be supplemented by remote readouts of the pictures produced by particular radars, a method used in fighter control.

37. The heavy carriers were less and less available. *Saratoga* was damaged and put out of action and *Wasp* sunk by a Japanese submarine. About November 1942 the only US fleet carrier left in the Pacific was *Enterprise*, which had been badly damaged several times. The only other US fleet carrier was *Ranger*, which was not considered adequate for the Pacific.

38. The fighter direction history recounts a battle in which the heavy cruiser *Chicago* was sunk by aerial torpedoes. She was in a convoy covered by fighters from *Enterprise* and from the escort carriers *Chenango* and *Suwanee*. The fighter director was on board the cruiser *Wichita*. The force was shadowed on the morning and afternoon of 29 January and *Wichita* maintained a complete track, but the Officer in Tactical Command (OTC) refused to allow her to direct CAP at them. At this time the US Navy had no carrier night fighters, but some torpedo bombers (TBFs) carried radar. The OTC ordered two radar TBFs and a division of fighters launched to seek and destroy the shadowers without fighter direction. Part of the problem was that some of the bogeys were mis-identified as friendlies failing to use their IFF. That caused the OTC to doubt that enemy aircraft were about. Presumably he did not want fighter direction because he thought that chatter on the fighter net would give away the position of his force. Shortly after the CAP returned to the carriers for the night, the Japanese struck and hit *Chicago*. ComSouth Pacific saw the incident as proof that radio silence should always be broken for fighter-control. Had VHF radio been available, it would have been possible to break silence without any risk. Similarly, if friendly aircraft had consistently used their IFF, there would not have been any doubt about the identity of the snoopers. To make matters worse, the next day, when the damaged *Chicago* was under tow away from the main convoy and CAP was present, the Japanese were able to attack undetected. Cruisers were withdrawn from the fighter-control role, partly because they were wanted more urgently for bombardment.

39. Issued as USF-10A, dated 1 February 1944 and effective 10 April; PAC-10 was the Pacific Fleet draft version. It described the standard multi-carrier

circular formations used throughout the rest of the war. This book included a drawing of a multi-carrier British formation, probably as a way of popularising multi-carrier operations for the US fleet. It also pointed to earlier battle experience to show that concentrating an anti-aircraft screen around two carriers had proven effective at the Coral Sea and Midway. At the Coral Sea both carriers initially manoeuvred within a single screen, but separated as they operated their aircraft. According to USF-10A, of about 120 Japanese aircraft which attacked, about 60 per cent were destroyed. Although both carriers were damaged, each could still operate aircraft; *Lexington* sank later due to a fuel vapour explosion 'which is not apt to be repeated in carrier of new design'. At Midway, *Yorktown* operated in a separate task force from the other two carriers and her loss was attributed to lack of anti-aircraft support. At Santa Cruz, each of the two carriers operated in its own task force and both were damaged (*Hornet* was sunk). For this evolution see Dr Thomas C Hone, 'Replacing Battleships with Aircraft Carriers in the Pacific in World War II', *Naval War College Review* 66, 1 (Winter 2013), pp 56–76. Dr Hone sees Rear Admiral Frederick C Sherman, who had commanded *Lexington* at the Coral Sea, as the originator of the multi-carrier concept. The relevant version of PAC-10 was written by a special Pacific Fleet Board created on 13 April 1943, PAC-10 Change 3 (version 3) being issued in June 1943. The designation USF-10 had been used for the standard set of US Fleet orders since at least 1934.

40. The BuAer fighter direction history dates adoption of visual fighter control to 1944.

41. According to the BuAer fighter history, a night fighter version of the twin-engine F7F Tigercat was proposed in 1941 (ultimately F7Fs were built as night fighters). It was rejected because it would take far too long to enter service and because there were real questions as to whether the radar operator in the back seat was worthwhile.

42. The BuAer fighter history refers to numerous problems with initial F4U production, few aircraft having been built by November 1942. BuAer notified its representative at Vought that it was considering cancelling F4U production. That caused Vought to accelerate production and also to concentrate more on solving remaining problems with the aircraft.

43. AIA was in the same US Navy designation series as the SK and SC search radars. A stood for airborne and I for an intercept set; A indicated that it was the first of the type. Later naval radars of this type were designated in the now-familiar AN series, e.g., AN/APS-6, typically abbreviated as APS-6. In this series A was for airborne, P for radar (i.e. pulsed) and S was for search. The Navair History office of NHHC includes in its files a 2 September 1941 letter from BuAer to the navy representative to NRDC (which was responsible for the Rad Lab) stating an urgent need for a radar suited to a single-seat navy fighter. NRDC was already developing an AI-10 intercept radar, but its size and weight limited it to multi-engine aircraft. BuAer asked that the antenna be faired into the fuselage or wing, that the radar be accurate enough for gun-aiming (blind fire), that useful range be at least two miles at any altitude between 2000ft and 35,000ft, that minimum dependable range be less than 500ft and that the display should show relative target azimuth and elevation as an aid to manoeuvre by the intercepting fighter. Total installed weight, exclusive of the power supply, should not exceed 250lbs (preferably 200). A 28 November 1941 memo from the Special Assistant (Material) to the Director of (BuAer) Material stated that the requirement could be met with a 3cm (X-band) radar, but that as yet there was no adequate US source of the necessary tubes. A report dated 26 December 1942 showed that the first AIA had been delivered to the Naval Aircraft Factory for installation on an F4U-2.

44. According to the BuAer manuscript fighter history, II-18, the initial requirement was to use the F4U-2 to drive away Japanese snoopers in the form of four-engine bombers. They might be visible to search radar, but they might hide in clouds. With no F4U-2 yet completed, the test aircraft was a Beech JRB.

45. Of the two dots, the one on the right indicated target elevation. If it was above the left dot, so was the enemy aircraft. The B-scan was included for search, for example to find a surface target.

46. According to the BuAer fighter direction history (manuscript version), of 252 night interceptions attempted between 30 March and 17 May 1945, 116 resulted in radar contact by the fighter, but only eighteen led to a target being shot down (this may refer only to aircraft directed by ships in the amphibious area, where direction was by amphibious flagship AGC or radar picket destroyer). The same history mentions ninety-one enemy aircraft shot down by Task Force 58 night fighters between 18 March and 25 May.

47. BuAer fighter history, unpaginated, footnote referring to a 16 June 1945 CNO directive to chief of BuAer. Two FD-1s and two FJ-1s were each to have APS-19 radar installed. Since only three experimental prototypes of each type of jet fighter (F6U, FJ, F2D later redesignated F2H Banshee and FD two prototypes.) had been ordered, installation was deferred to production aircraft. The FJ-1 night fighter was cancelled in October 1945 because the prototype was 868lbs overweight and offered no promise as a night

fighter. The FD-1 project continued for a time but did not lead to any night fighter prototype.

48. ADR considered two alternative powerplants, two GE TG-100 turboprop and two or four Westinghouse 24-C turbojet. Armament would have been four 20mm cannon. The four 24-C design offered better performance except climb at 20,000ft, but both versions were too heavy for carrier operation and unfolded wing span was too great for the flight deck opposite the island. The aircraft were too near the size of carrier lifts and they did not meet desired spotting factors. The TG-100 version was superior to the two-24-C version in performance, offered good wave-off characteristics (which the two-24-C version lacked) and was smaller and lighter. Except for speed at sea level it had nearly the performance of the four-24-C version. It also used only one-third to half the fuel of the jet. In earlier studies the turboprop was superior to the jet except for high speed short range aircraft.

49. In RG 72 Entry P-1044F (Proposals), NARA II. This file includes the minutes of a 6 July 1942 conference between BuAer, Grumman and General Motors on the projected modification of the F4F for the new escort carriers. Production was to begin in about six months, i.e. in February 1943. Grumman presented its own study of what could be done and that seems to have been the basis of the BuAer order. BuAer developed two alternative versions, A and B, of which B had been chosen by early May 1942. The earliest memo in the file is from Class Desk 'A', dated 6 January 1942; it already mentions that the F2A-3 cannot be accepted because its wings do not fold and because its engine installation is already about as light as it can be.

50. In British service the FM-2 was the Wildcat VI. In British parlance the G-36A ordered for France became the Martlet I and then the Wildcat I. Martlet II (Wildcat II) was the G-36B with folding wings. Martlet III (Wildcat III) was the F4F-3 with fixed wings, some being G-36As originally ordered for Greece. Martlet IV (Wildcat IV) was the F4F-4B, which had an R-1820 rather than the standard US Navy R-1830. Martlet V (Wildcat V) was the FM-1, which differed from the F4F-4 mainly in having four rather than six wing guns.

51. Comments from an 18 June 1942 letter from John W. Meader to Assistant Secretary of the Navy for Air Artemus L Gates on 'The 1000 HP Fighter "XF8F"' quoted in the BuAer fighter history, not paginated. Meader was Special Assistant to Gates. The history emphasises that his letter did not reflect BuAer views, but that even within the bureau 'the situation was muddled', hence was worth quoting. Meader associated size with engine power and argued that all the combatants were using 1000hp fighters, whereas the United States had jumped to twice their size, hence twice their size. He thought that two 1000hp fighters could be produced with the same effort as one of 2000hp and that the smaller fighters could operate from 10,000 ton carriers (he may have included the *Independence* class). The 1000hp fighter, powered by a nine-cylinder radial engine (R-1820), would be slower than the new fighters, but I would have improved manoeuvrability and climb. Specifications should be limited to allow the manufacturer maximum ingenuity. The aircraft should have four 0.50-calibre guns, but no bomb racks, no armour, simplified radio (the history points out that how to simplify it was not specified), simplified instruments, self-sealing tanks and non-folding wings.

52. As described in the BuAer manuscript history, this aircraft would have been powered by a two-speed R-1830-90 engine (1200hp at take-off) and would have had strength reduced from 9 G to 7 G. It was expected to weigh 6150lbs compared to 5214lbs for a Zero and to attain 351mph at 15,300ft (compared to 316mph at 12,300ft). Rate of climb at sea level would have been 3280ft/min rather than 3100ft/min and service ceiling 33,900 rather than 32,000ft. Take-off run with 25 knots of wind over deck would have been 179ft rather than 105ft. The redesigned F4F was already being developed and the proposed fighter would be inferior to the other production fighters.

53. BuAer decided to use the same engine as in the SBD Dauntless dive bomber to simplify logistics (ultimately escort carriers generally did not employ SBDs, however). The BuAer fighter history dates the decision to use the R-1820-56 for this reason to August 1942. Grumman had already been asked in June or July 1942 to study modification of two F4Fs to use this engine. The F4F-8 was in flight tests by January 1943. It encountered problems: engine surging, excessive night visibility of the engine exhausts, marginal elevator effectiveness in the flare down (landing) condition and unacceptable rudder controls. Further improvements early in 1944 were water injection and VHF radio. In December 1944 some FM-2s were being fitted with rocket launchers for close air support. At about the same time bomb racks allowing an FM-2 to carry two 650lb depth bombs were being tested (they were completed in March 1945).

54. Memo 14 July 1944 in RG 72 Design Co-ordination Branch Correspondence 1934–1959 Box 23 (RG 72 Entry P 1044-E, NARA II). The memo mentions that the study had been initiated by Admiral Radford, hence that it should be given a high priority. A 15 July memo mentions a 12 July 1944 conference attended by Vice Admiral McCain and Rear

Admiral Radford which approved installation of APS-6 radars on all VF(N) and APS-3 on all VT(N) of 'Night Carrier Groups'.

55. Early steps towards an F8F night fighter were described at a 5 April 1945 BuAer meeting to determine characteristics of a projected jet night fighter, in NHHC Aviation History files. An F8F was being prototyped with an APS-4 radar 'bomb', the type the British were using in their Firefly. If that proved successful, the next step would be an APS-6, but Grumman studies already showed that would be unsatisfactory (the situation might be saved by reducing the pilot's back armour). When it became available, an APS-19 would be installed. If either the APS-6 or -19 could be installed, a night version of the F8F would replace all existing carrier night fighters (F6F-5N and F4U-4N). At this time production of the APS-6 version of the F7F Tigercat had ended and Grumman was completing a prototype equipped with the more powerful army SCR-720.

56. Grumman records include a 24 September 1943 proposal letter which indicates that the aircraft responded to an informal BuAer approach.

57. Memo dated 21 March 1946, Aer-R-RED VF CVE/VV in NHHC Navair History division files.

58. This enormously oversimplifies aero-engine development, which went through numerous versions of each engine denoted by a dash number, as in R-1820-6. Much of what follows is from the engine section of the BuAer *Ten Year History and Programme of Future Research and Development (Naval Aircraft Equipment and Support Facilities)*. It was prepared in response to an August 1945 request from the Senate Special Committee Investigating the National Defense Programme and therefore is sometimes defensive in tone. Pratt & Whitney developed a series of engines named after insects: the R-1690 Hornet (nine cylinders, 700hp by 1935), the Wasp Junior (R-985, 450hp in 1935) and the Twin Wasp (R-1535, fourteen cylinders in two rows). The Twin Wasp powered the Grumman F2F-1 and F3F-1. Of these engines the Hornet was probably the most significant because it sold the navy on air-cooled engines; in the T4M torpedo bomber it replaced a Packard liquid-cooled engine but was just half its weight. The much more significant R-1830 Twin Wasp used a new enlarged cylinder. The initial version produced 750hp, but at the beginning of 1935 it was rated at 800hp. At that time it was the most powerful available fighter engine. In June 1935 the navy contracted for an improved -64 version to produce 900hp on take-off; it was first used on the PBY-1 Catalina. At the same time the navy contracted for a version with a two-stage supercharger, to develop 800hp at 15,000ft (earlier Pratt & Whitney engines had single-stage superchargers). This -70 powered most Grumman Wildcats. Improvement continued; in June 1936 the navy contracted for a 1050hp version, which ultimately developed 1200hp. A contract for a two-stage supercharged version was let in June 1938 (1000hp at 19,000ft). Pratt & Whitney's next step was a more powerful eighteen-cylinder two-row engine, the R-2800 Double Wasp. Development began in 1936 and the engine was bought for F4U Corsair prototype in June 1938 at a rated output of 1800hp at take-off. In February 1939 the navy contracted for a version (-4) with a two-stage supercharger. The take-off rating was raised to 1850hp. In June 1941 the navy contracted for -8 test engines rated at 1650hp at 22,500ft using a two-stage supercharger (2000hp at take-off). This was the B series, ultimately rated at 200hp at take-off. The C series was redesigned to develop 2100hp at altitude (at 2800rpm rather than 2700rpm), with a single- or two-stage supercharger. Experimental engines were ordered in October 1943. Extra power did cost weight: the B version weighed 2480lbs, the C version 2560lbs. Output at altitude was 1650hp at 21,000ft for the B version, 1800hp at 25,000ft for the C version. Fuel consumption fell from 0.430lbs/hp per hour to 0.405lbs/hp per hour. The two-stage -18W powered the F4U-4 Corsair. The single-stage -34W powered the F7F Tigercat and the F8F Bearcat and was about to enter service as the war ended. With water injection it could develop 2900hp at sea level and about 2400hp at 16,000ft. A contract for an E series was let in June 1944. The BuAer history associates the change from two- to one-stage supercharging with the progress of the Pacific War. At the outset, when the United States was on the defensive, the emphasis was on high-altitude performance, despite the weight and drag of the auxiliary stage supercharger and intercooler. Once the United States was on the offensive, the emphasis was on medium altitudes, up to 20,000ft and one supercharger stage was enough. By 1936 the navy was pressing for a 2300hp engine, which it thought would have to be liquid-cooled. In 1939 Pratt & Whitney designed the air-cooled 28-cylinder (four row) R-4360 Wasp Major, in effect its alternative to Wright's R-3350. It used R-2800 cylinders. It was qualified at 3000hp in June 1942 and at 3500hp by August 1945.
Curtiss-Wright (the two firms merged in 1929) was the other major supplier of US naval piston engines. Its R-1820 Cyclone was first installed in naval service aircraft in 1929; by that time it developed 575hp, weighed 940lbs and had a rated altitude of 500ft. It was a single-row nine-cylinder engine. Versions in service in 1935 produced 700hp or 750hp. By 1945 a test version of the R-1820 weighed 1400lbs (because it incorporated a supercharger), developed 1425hp and had a rated altitude of 11,600ft.

Wright denoted successive versions by suffix letters, the Cyclone F appearing in 1932. The G-series (R-1820-22), initially designed for 850hp (at take-off), was first delivered to the navy in 1935. A two-speed supercharger was later added (R-1820-34). In 1940 the navy accepted the 1200hp R-1820-40 for Brewster F2A fighters (the -42 was a version with left-hand propeller rotation to be combined with the right-hand version for the F5F Skyrocket twin-engine fighter). By 1945 typical output was 1350hp in the -56, -62, -66 and -72 engines, which had turbochargers. A further late-war development added water injection. In November 1935 Wright began work on the successor two-row fourteen-cylinder R-2600 Cyclone 14, using cylinders similar to those in the R-1820 but with a shorter stroke. It was initially intended to produce 1500hp. The prototype R-2600-2, rated at 1500hp for take-off, was delivered for initial tests in May 1937, the first production engines being delivered in the spring and summer of 1938. The R-2600-6 (1600hp at take-off) was first delivered in April 1939 and the standard wartime version delivered 1700hp at take-off. Later versions (-20 and -22) produced 1900hp at take-off and were used in wartime attack aircraft, among others. In effect the R-2600 was Wright's alternative to the more successful R-2800. During the war Wright decided to concentrate on its more powerful R-3350 Duplex Cyclone or Cyclone 18 rather than on improving the R-2600. The new engine used eighteen cylinders of the same bore and stroke as the fourteen of the R-2600. The initial A series engines (2000hp) were delivered for testing in 1938. The first production BA series produced 2200hp and powered, among others, the B-29. The later BB series (2300hp) was developed for the navy and the BD version (2500hp, R-3350-24) was released for production in June 1945. The R-3350 was an important post-war naval engine. Navy interest in high-power liquid-cooled engines led to a December 1939 contract with Lycoming for the H-2470, a 24-cylinder liquid-cooled H engine (two sets of opposing cylinders); that company had already developed the necessary technology in its O-1230, a horizontally-opposed twelve-cylinder engine. The H-2470 was planned for the Curtiss XF14C and the army P-54. This engine nearly completed its 100-hour test in January 1942, but no production followed.

59. The XF4U required excessive stick forces, so it was fitted with larger ailerons. Tests showed poor spin and dive recovery characteristics and poor lateral stability as it landed. Initial tests demonstrated its high speed and its superior service ceiling, but also its excessive landing speed, 78mph (which would increase once it was loaded with the newly-required protection for pilot and fuel). The aircraft also had to be modified to reduce landing speed to 75mph and take-off run to no more than 200ft with 25 knots of wind over deck. Wing flaps were added to reduce the take-off run and also to improve manoeuvrability. Like other fighters in the 1938 competition, the F4U-1 had two 0.50-calibre wing guns and two fuselage guns (one 0.30, one 0.50-calibre) firing through its propeller. The initial production version eliminated the fuselage guns and added two 0.50-calibre guns to each wing. The navy wanted six 0.50s and provision for 20mm cannon. The March 1942 delivery date envisaged in January 1941 assumed that the production F4U-2 would be very similar to the XF4U-1 prototype, lessons learned from wind tunnel and flight tests being incorporated in later production aircraft. This further development was to have a two-speed propeller, improved engine ducting and Zap or other high-lift full-span flaps. Speed would be well over 400mph and take-off would be shorter.

60. According to the BuAer manuscript history, lack of vision over the nose was considered a serious problem. After a visit to Europe in the autumn of 1942, Commander J S Thach (of the 'Thach weave') commented that 'both the British and the Germans – by comparison with our carrier fighters – know very little about fixed gunnery [i.e., deflection shooting] . . . Because RAF representatives in the Bureau of Aeronautics insisted that it wasn't necessary to see downward over the nose of a fighter, the manufacturers of the F4U were allowed to do away with this important angle downward and almost ruined the F4U for deflection shooting. I believe it would help the British very much if one of our properly trained navy carrier fighter squadrons could operate intact with the British over Europe. It would open their eyes. It is regrettable that the US Army pursuit squadrons in England cannot fill the bill' (report dated 21 November 1942 in BuAer VF Vol 7, RG 72 confidential correspondence, 1922–1944). The fifth production Corsair had a raised cockpit, raised pilot's seat and raised line of sight, but early production aircraft had the original low canopy and cockpit. The version with the raised seat was placed in production in the spring of 1943; by September all production had been converted to this version. The raised cabin improved ground handling, which was further improved by extending the tail wheel (modification tested August 1943, released for production November 1943). In 1943 the Army Air Force modified both of its major fighters (P-47 and P-51) with bubble canopies offering far better all-round vision. A Goodyear-built FG-1 (F4U-1) was similarly modified, but the modified version was not placed in production because the existing raised canopy offered good rear vision and also because BuAer did not want to delay production. A turbocharged version designated F4U-

3 was being discussed by April 1942. A decision to use a production rather than an experimental turbocharger delayed the project, as did congestion (i.e., limited design personnel) at Vought. The aircraft was tested in late 1944 and plans were made to convert twenty-seven F4U-1Ds to F4U-3s. Later the Goodyear Corsair (FG-1) was ordered converted instead (as FG-3), but only one aircraft was completed. Meanwhile substitution of four 20mm cannon for the previous 0.50s was also being studied. At the end of the war plans called for mounting 20mm cannon in production aircraft beginning in March 1946. However, many F4U-1s were given 20mm cannon under the designation F4U-1C. A version with two underwing pylons, either capable of supporting either a 165-gallon drop tank or a 1000lb bomb, was designated F4U-1D (summer 1944 tests showed that the pylons could carry 1600lb or 2000lb bombs, although in that case the aircraft had to be flown with some restrictions). This aircraft retained a provision for a centreline drop tank (100 gallons). Another major change was water injection. At critical altitude an F4U-1 made 417mph without water injection and 431mph with it; production of aircraft with water injection had begun by October 1943

61. The Grumman history archive drawing is dated 4 May 1938. The nose guns were 0.30s, the wing guns 0.50s. Span was 37ft, length 28ft 4in. Fully-loaded weight was 6850lbs (7090lbs with bombs). Wing loading was 26.75ft^2. Grumman based its performance estimate on a geared R-2600 engine offering 1350hp at 13,000ft. This file does not include further details, but the result was clearly far inferior to the Vought submission.

62. According to the BuAer manuscript fighter history, p 74, Grumman was unenthusiastic about the Design S modification of the F4F proposed in July 1940. It suggested instead that the two-stage R-2600 be mounted in a redesigned F4F. However, it soon concluded that such an aircraft still would not be competitive with the F4U, that design would be lengthy and that it would be considerably heavier than the F4F. BuAer's plant representative Commander L C Stevens apparently considered the R-2600 project a valuable fall-back against possible problems with the F4U (which were soon evident). He explained as much to BuAer in a July 1940 memo, unfortunately now lost, which probably described Grumman's unwillingness to develop the S design. Work on the R-2600 version of the F4F probably continued through early December 1940. That month Stevens personally explained to company president Leroy Grumman and to chief engineer William T Schwendler that BuAer was not interested in an equivalent to the F4U. It wanted quantity production of a fighter capable of at least 350mph. War was imminent. Stevens' 16 December 1940 memo to BuAer explaining the situation is included in the Navair History (NHHC) file on the Hellcat. This file also includes a lecture by Frank L Greene on the history of the Hellcat given at the annual meeting of the Northeast Aero Historians on 28 October 1967. Greene dated the beginning of the R-2600 project to June or July 1940, which jibes with the BuAer history account. Schwendler and his engineering team decided to move the F4F wing down and use wing-mounted landing gear, a combination which raised the nose and made it possible to use a larger-diameter propeller better able to absorb increased engine power. Grumman was also already interested in substituting the R-2800 for the R-2600, having initially proposed the larger engine. Added weight made it necessary to increase wing span by 4ft and length by 24in. Estimated maximum speed was 380mph. Redesign produced a new aircraft, although the result broadly resembled the F4F. BuAer favoured the R-2600 because it feared a shortage of R-2800s, but Grumman preferred the more powerful engine and sized its fighter to use it. Grumman received a prototype contract on 30 June 1941 and the navy ordered quantity production of the version powered by the R-2800 before the prototype of the R-2600 version even flew on 26 June 1942. Similarity to the existing Wildcat made it relatively easy for Grumman to begin large-scale production. The R-2600 version was designated F6F-1. A turbocharged version was the F6F-2, which did not enter production. The production version with the R-2800 was designated F6F-3. The second production version, incorporating detail improvements (including a Mk 23 lead-computing gun sight), was the F6F-5. The final version was the F6F-6, which exceeded 400mph using a 'C' series R-2800 engine and a four-bladed propeller. It did not enter production (the Navair History file includes a 1 December 1944 report describing the F6F-6 and stating that production has been 'postponed indefinitely'. Greene wrote that Grumman was also considering a version powered by an R-4360 and one with a jet booster engine, but he had no details. In 1941 there was some BuAer interest in a Brewster project paralleling the F6F, rebuilding the Buffalo around an R-2600, but it seems not to have gone very far. According to the BuAer fighter design history, p 132, the F6F was a relatively simple redesign of the F4F with a much more powerful engine, but a year was spent deciding on details; hence the lengthy run-up to the 30 June 1941 contract signing. The new aircraft was so similar to the F4F, according to the BuAer history, that no mock-up of the entire aircraft was required, only a cockpit mock-up.

63. According to the BuAer fighter history, the choice was between a conven-

tional programme using scale models of progressively larger size and a riskier programme in which a prototype would be built at once. The navy compromised, seeking the least expensive possible full-scale model (but still strong enough for flight tests) and a wind tunnel model. The V-173, which was completed in the spring of 1941, could test controllability (albeit at low speed) but lacked sufficient power for a near-vertical take-off. Vought also made 24in and 32in scale models for wind tunnel tests at the NACA free-flight tunnel at Langley.

64. The 21 December 1940 BuAer letter is in the Grumman History Archives file on the F7F Tigercat, as this was the competition the F7F won. The initial Type Specification was dated 3 September 1940. It was quite general and as usual it included blanks that Grumman had to fill out, describing its submission. The engines listed in September 1940 did not include the R-2800, which at this point was considered too experimental. Listed engines were the Cyclone H with two-speed or two-stage supercharger (1200hp at take-off), the R-1820-48 with two-stage supercharger (1200hp for take-off), the R-2600-B with two-stage supercharger (1800hp for take-off), the ultimately abortive Wright R-2170-A with two-speed or two-stage supercharger (1500hp) and the R-3350-B with two-speed or two-stage supercharger (2300hp). However, the R-2800 appeared on another list dated 12 October 1940, credited with 2000hp at take-off. On this list the R-2170 was crossed off.

65. Grumman won the 1940 award in June 1941. As with its twin-engine F5F, the army was interested and, according to the BuAer history, it would have bought a version had the war not intervened. As it was, the programme was delayed because of the high priority accorded the F6F, which received a contract at the same time. Work actually began in the spring of 1942, the mock-up being postponed from June to mid-September 1942. In November 1942 the first flight was expected in July 1943, but it actually occurred that November. By that time BuAer wanted to replace the planned R-2600-14 engines with the new R-2800-C, because no other aircraft was using the R-2600-14. It did so, the first prototype receiving R-2800-Bs, the second R-2800-Cs. In January 1944 it was decided that the first 200 would be completed as night fighters. Production was scheduled to begin in July. However, production was delayed by deficiencies, such as poor stability in the wave-off condition, revealed in tests. *Randolph* (CV 15) was the first *Essex* class carrier to be completed with the required high-capacity arresting gear. However, the increased size (hence reduced carrier capacity) of the F7F was a more serious problem. An *Essex* could accommodate twenty-five F7F on her hangar deck and thirty-three on her flight deck, for a total of fifty-eight, compared to sixty and seventy-two Corsairs and Hellcats, for a total of 132 fighters. Against that, the F7F was expected to be 30mph faster than an F4U at sea level, but only 10mph faster at 12,000ft and no faster at 20,000ft (both would make 411mph). Above 21,000ft the F4U enjoyed a slowly increasing advantage. At low altitude the F7F had a much greater rate of climb than either single-engine fighter, but this advantage disappeared above 18,000ft. The F7F did carry a much more powerful armament, four 20mm in its wings and four 0.50-calibre machine guns in its nose. Like a Hellcat, it could carry a bomb or torpedo on its centreline. It needed a 300-gallon drop tank to match the combat radius of an F6F-3. In November 1944 the single-seat version was designated F7F-1, the night fighter F7F-2N and a strengthened night fighter F7F-3N (the N suffix may not initially have been used). There was also a night fighter version of the -1. By March 1945 the F7F-3 was in production. The first 175 were to be day fighters with additional internal fuel and no radar. The BuAer fighter history mentions that catapult hooks and tail hooks were planned for the 201st and later aircraft. The rest were presumably intended from the outset for land-based Marine units, although the F7F had been conceived as a carrier fighter.

66. The first US naval expansion act was the Vinson-Trammell Act of 1934, calling for a total of 2150 naval aircraft. It was superseded by a 1938 Act calling for a minimum of 3000 to be available within five years (1943). In the spring of 1940 the programme called for 4500 aircraft to help enforce US neutrality and also to fill an enlarged carrier force. In the spring of 1940 the 'Two-Ocean Navy' Act intended to deal with the threat of French and perhaps even British ships falling under German control (in addition to the usual Japanese threat) raised numbers to 10,000; in July the programme grew to 15,000 aircraft.

67. BuAer manuscript fighter history, p 75, citing a 24 January 1941 BuAer memo on the fighter development programme.

68. It contracted with Curtiss to build a fighter based on ADR Design No. 201, powered by a liquid-cooled Lycoming XH-2470 engine: the XF-14C. About November 1941 BuAer asked for a second aircraft (XF14C-2) powered by an R-3350 radial. In February 1942 Curtiss was told to deliver the R-3350 aircraft first, followed by the XH-2470 aircraft with turbocharger and contraprops and then an R-3350 aircraft with a turbocharged R-3350 and a pressure cabin (XF14C-3). The two R-3350 aircraft were the only Navy fighters under development capable of operating at 33,000–37,000ft. When BuAer asked Curtiss to begin pro-

duction engineering of the F14C-2, the company replied that it had recently taken a production order from the army for the P-60 (in the end, another abortive aircraft) and did not have the capacity to produce the F14C. The XF14C-2 flew in October 1943, but navy interest was evaporating, as the mixed-power F15C was more important. The Lycoming engine, the reason for the whole project, was not completed and the XF14C-1 was cancelled in the summer of 1943.

69. RG 72 BuAer confidential correspondence 1922-1944, VF Vol 7, a letter from Chief of BuAer to Inspector of Naval Aircraft at Vought, dated 23 November 1942 quoting a 5 November report (in the same file) of comparative tests. It began 'When the F6F was first flown in July 1942, it was apparent that it possessed none of the particular deficiencies which have caused so much concern in the F4U . . . Further preliminary tests of the F6F have so strongly reemphasised this comparison that it is believed advisable to present certain general conclusions.'

70. The BuAer Corsair correspondence file includes a 24 August 1943 message (sent before the *Bunker Hill* trials) stating that these aircraft would be sent only to the Marines. However, the aircraft was kept carrier-capable in case (as happened) it was issued to carriers later on. *Bunker Hill* took VF-17 on her shakedown cruise, reporting back in December 1943. The ship had already recommended (in August) a raised cockpit and a modified tail hook; both were completed after the shakedown. At 30 knots or more relative wind, the accident rate on landing was normal; below 30 knots it increased and was probably worse than with the Hellcat. The ship's CO wrote that it was acceptable as a carrier aircraft, the new cockpit permitting a normal approach with the signal officer in sight at all times. There was some difficulty in landing because the aircraft reacted quickly to a change in throttle setting. Landing speed was about the same as that of the Hellcat, but the approach was flatter and there was less margin of error because of the Corsair's more limited visibility and tendency to bounce on the deck. In view of its excellent fighting qualities, the CO considered the Corsair a satisfactory carrier fighter. These comments were in response to a 20 October 1943 BuAer request for full data on Corsair carrier operations (the CO letter included full accident statistics). Corsairs had also been tested briefly (9–12 May 1943) on board the carrier *Enterprise*, during a brief post-refit refresher cruise. A 5 April 1943 report from the training carrier *Wolverine* had described the Corsair as 'an excellent carrier type, very easy to land aboard'. The British certainly found the Corsair perfectly acceptable. The British designated the F4U-1 the Corsair I; the F4U-1A became Corsair II, the Brewster-built F3A-1A becoming Corsair III and the Goodyear FG-1D the Corsair IV. The British received 2012 Corsairs which served with nineteen squadrons; the Royal New Zealand Air Force received another 370. Of these versions, the F4U-1A had the raised cockpit and higher tail wheel plus a small spoiler on the leading edge of the starboard wing. British aircraft had clipped wing tips so that they could be stowed in British carrier hangars. Corsair Is were fitted with bulged canopies so that a pilot could raise his seat for a better view on landing (not the type later standardised by the US Navy).

71. According to the BuAer manuscript fighter history, the experimental F6F-6 attained 420mph at 20,000ft on military power and 430mph at 23,300ft on war emergency power.

72. According to the BuAer manuscript fighter history, the Eglin demonstrations led to adaptation of the F6F and F4U as fighter-bombers. Brewster, which by this time was making Corsairs, began work on what turned out to be an abortive torpedo installation. Grumman was more successful: its centreline hardpoint could carry a drop tank or a 500lb or 1000lb bomb or a torpedo. This installation was tested at Patuxent River in a 45° dive. Three squadrons had been equipped by the end of July 1943. By that time Patuxent River was also testing a wing hardpoint capable of carrying a 1000lb bomb. With a hardpoint under each wing, a Hellcat could carry both a drop tank and a 1000lb bomb. Detailed conclusions of the 1942 trials are in the BuAer Corsair file, dated 29 December 1942.

73. According to the BuAer fighter history, in a test by Atlantic Fleet Air Force Carrier Aircraft Service Unit 23 (CASU-23), the F6F required 1.245 man-hours per flight hour, the F4U 1.65 man-hours, nearly a third more. Ordnance and communication gear were more difficult to service and the F4U had considerably more landing accidents.

74. The question of whether to replace the Hellcat with the Corsair was revived in 1944. An initial (unfortunately undated, but probably late 1943) memo argued that the Hellcat was superior in stability and low-speed control (for landing); in maintenance; in cooling characteristics; and in its cockpit arrangement. The Corsair was considerably faster (about 20mph in maximum speed); had better high-speed control; and offered better quiet and comfort in its cockpit. Patuxent River, which prepared the report, therefore recommended that the Corsair again be employed as a carrier fighter. This memo is in the BuAer VF4U1/F1-1 Vol I file. Further tests were carried out early in 1944. For example, on 1 February the training escort carrier *Charger* reported tests of landings under light wind conditions (as requested late in 1943). These tests and take-off tests showed that the

Corsair could operate from an escort carrier, but only with considerable wind over deck. It was clearly suitable for a larger carrier with higher speed. In April an improved F4U-1 was tested against an improved F6F-3 (equivalent to an F6F-5); the improvements in the Corsair were a new unframed canopy and improved oleo undercarriage. It proved entirely superior in speed and rate of climb and equally manoeuvrable and showed excellent landing characteristics. The test pilots considered it entirely satisfactory as a carrier aircraft (the landing signal officer agreed). The report was signed by Commander Fleet Air West Coast, Rear Admiral Frederick C Sherman, a future CNO. The tests also showed that the F6F-5 was sufficiently superior to the F6F-3 that the two should not operate together. The 28 April report of this trial seems to have led to a definite decision to place Corsairs on board carriers. The trials ship was the large escort carrier *Gambier Bay*. The 30 April 1944 chart of the current and projected US naval air organisation showed that the fighting squadrons of Air Groups 84 and 85 were to use Corsairs. They would operate from *Essex* class carriers. In May Quonset Point Air Station, which trained British pilots on the Corsair, reported to ComAirLant that its training experience with the Corsair showed that it was a superior fighter. The landing 'bounce' problem had been solved, so the Corsair now landed as smoothly as other carrier types; and the landing gear was so sturdy that it rarely suffered damage from hard landings. Its large flap area decelerated a landing Corsair more rapidly than a Hellcat, so that arresting wire runout was shorter. The Corsair carried more fuel, so it had a considerably greater cruising radius (and the fuel consumption of its engine was somewhat less at the same power setting). The Corsair was more manoeuvrable, lighter on the controls and was probably a better gun platform. Maintenance time was only slightly greater than for the Hellcat. The only drawback of the Corsair was a longer familiarisation period. In June, Commander Air Forces Pacific rejected replacement of the F6F-3 by the F4U-1 on logistical grounds. DCNO(Air) replied on 28 June that the coming F4U-4 was definitely desired for carriers if its performance came up to expectation. By this time the F4U-4 was definitely planned for the air groups of the new *Midway* class heavy carriers (CVBs) and ComAirPac proposed that it also equip four new fleet aircraft groups, together with related night-fighter squadrons. DCNO(Air) agreed that Air Groups 7, 84, 85 and a spare group (probably CVAG 98) should be equipped with F4U-4s by November 1944. Due to the special equipment and engineering required, DCNO(Air) rejected the request for night-fighting F4U-4s for the present (later an F4U-4N version was fielded, as well as an F4U-4E intended specifically for night attack). This correspondence in the BuAer VF4U1/A4 Vol 1 file is interesting because it shows that, contrary to the usual accounts, Corsairs were projected as carrier fighters before the Marine Corsair squadrons were brought on board as an emergency measure late in 1944. It is not clear from the correspondence when the initial decision was made to place Corsairs on board the CVBs.

75. BuAer manuscript fighter history, p 133, in the context of armament choices for the F6F. At this time the US Navy was building *Fletcher* class destroyers whose machinery spaces were protected against 0.50-calibre strafing fire. According to the BuAer history, immediately after the United States entered the war fighter armament was again reviewed. This time it seems to have been influenced by the British decision to replace the eight 0.303in guns in Spitfires with four 20mm, despite the cost of about 10mph (which BuAer thought could be overcome by proper fairing of the cannon). Work on a 20mm installation for the F4U was immediately ordered. According to the BuAer history, the British decision to adopt 20mm guns was based on the striking energy per second of various alternative armaments. BuAer changed the criterion to striking energy per second per pound of installation, on which basis one 20mm cannon was about equal to two 0.50-calibre machine guns. The BuAer history cites a 7 July 1942 report of the British Aircraft Commission to the Sub-Committee on Standardisation, 'Comparison of Effectiveness of Various Gun Calibres Installed in Fighter Aircraft', with US comments. Other factors in the BuAer choice were complete access to guns and ammunition, provision for arming guns when wings were folded, close grouping as near the centreline as possible (for aiming and to minimise the effect of wings flexing in flight), construction of ammunition containers and feed chutes so that they would not jam despite violent manoeuvres and provision of maximum downward angle over the forward cowling (a requirement evident pre-war, for deflection shooting).

76. BuAer VF4U1/A4 Vol 2 file, letter dated 29 November 1943. This file does not include any test results, nor does it include the order to Pratt & Whitney to install the engine. The F2G was originally intended as a Marine interceptor, the project being established by a 27 November 1943 BuAer letter. To expedite that, the programme was broken down into two phases, of which Phase 1 was the high-priority Marine interceptor. Phase 2 was a carrier version, secondary to Phase 1. The Phase 1 version was designated F2G-1, the Phase 2 version F2G-2. Phase 2 involved reinstalling wing folding and arresting gear in the basic Corsair as modified for the

more powerful engine. The original restriction to the Marine land-based version was made because it would need a larger-diameter propeller (too large for carrier operation) to absorb the 3000hp of the new engine and also to avoid additional structural strengthening to withstand carrier landings. However, the contractor was asked to keep the aircraft quickly adaptable to carrier operation. In carrier form it would use a 13ft 6in diameter propeller instead of the initial 14ft type. A 12 February 1944 memo from the BuAer Aircraft Section on pre-production F2Gs stated that the first two would be substantially the same as the F4U-1 in which Pratt & Whitney had installed an R-4360-4 engine; the other three pre-production aircraft would embody progressively more structural changes and refinements, the seventh being substantially a production aircraft. In March Goodyear received a contract for 418 F2G-1 and ten F2G-2. In September 1944 the Marines stated a new policy: all of their single-engine aircraft should be carrier-capable; the F2G therefore had to be developed as a carrier fighter. Delivery of the -1 was scheduled for November 1944 but was delayed by supercharger problems. The prototype was flying in October 1944, but it encountered substantial problems (for example, in May 1945 a dorsal fin had to be installed to counteract the torque of the new engine). The fully carrier-capable version was designated F2G-2. Development was justified by an October 1944 BuAer Design Co-ordination report, which compared the F2G-1 (modified for carrier operation) with the F8F Bearcat. The F2G-1 using military power would be substantially faster than the Bearcat using war emergency power and it was also superior to the Bearcat using the R-2800E engine, except at high altitude. The F2G-1 was superior in speed over the F8F with the E engine from sea level to 17,000ft. The F8F-E climbed faster. However, the F2G-1 had a much higher stalling speed (92mph vs 82.5mph), which made it impractical to use from escort carriers. The F8F had a substantially better take-off but a somewhat shorter combat radius (the F2G could carry two drop tanks rather than one to gain even more radius). Goodyear claimed that adapting the F2G to carriers would require only limited additional weight. Design Co-ordination recommended continuing development on the basis of the speed advantage the F2G would enjoy at low altitude over other conventional fighters. The F2G-1 programme was curtailed in May 1945, production of the F2G-1 being cut to ten aircraft (the cutback was planned about late April). When the programme was cancelled at the end of the war, five F2G-1s and five F2G-2s had been completed; they became known mainly as post-war racing aircraft.

77. Two FG-1As were modified with bubble canopies as possible production prototypes, but they were not placed in production. The BuAer F2G file includes an account of a bubble canopy conference held on 1 July 1944. Ultimately a somewhat different bubble canopy was chosen.

78. Naval Air Fighting Development Unit report dated 19 February 1944 in BuAer VF4U1 file, forwarded by the US Naval Air Attaché. This was a preliminary report, with a more extensive one expected (but not in this file).

79. BuAer manuscript fighter history.

80. BuAer manuscript fighter history, citing a 24 July 1944 memo by Military Requirements Branch.

81. BuAer manuscript fighter history, citing an 11 November 1944 memo from Commander W J Widhelm to BuAer on 'VF Aircraft for the Fleet'. According to the BuAer history, although Widhelm's requirements were unofficial, BuAer took them seriously. Desired characteristics for the day fighter were a speed of about 400mph at sea level and 450mph at 20,000ft and a radius of action of about 400nm. The only projected aircraft which met these requirements was the F2G, a modified Corsair with an R-4360 engine (435mph at sea level, 465mph at 19,500ft, combat radius 400nm). However, it would not be available until late 1945. Only the Ryan Fireball met the 400mph sea level requirement, but its maximum speed at higher altitude was 433mph at 18,000ft. Neither of the main operational fighters could meet the requirement: the F4U-4 was rated at 359mph at sea level and 425mph at 23,000ft. The new F8F was rated at 386mph at sea level and 424mph at 17,500ft. The F7F Tigercat offered 394mph at sea level and 427mph at 19,200ft and a combat radius of 435nm. The existing fighters generally failed the combat radius test: the F8F offered 313nm and the F4U-4 offered 345nm. Generally a 300nm combat radius had been specified because to demand more would cost climb, manoeuvrability and size (as demonstrated by the F7F).

82. BuAer manuscript fighter history, citing a 24 March 1945 memo from Military Requirements.

83. As shorthand and to provide easy comparison, in what follows I give the capacities of the British engines in the form of US designations, e.g. V-1650 for the Merlin. The naval fighter engines in service in 1940 were the 905hp Bristol Perseus (nine-cylinder R-1520) in the Skua and the Rolls-Royce Merlin (twelve-cylinder V-1650, 1030hp in 1937 but about 2000hp in 1945) in the Fulmar. The wartime engines were the Sabre (never operational with the Royal Navy; 24-cylinder H-2238; originally 2200hp, but 3055hp in 1944) and the more useful Centaurus (eighteen-cylinder R-3270) and Griffin (twelve-cylinder V-2239 originally 1500hp but later

2000hp or more, up to 2500hp). All of these engines gained considerable power as they were developed. Thus the Centaurus, which powered the Sea Fury and the Firebrand, was rated at 2000hp when first tested in 1939, but in 1942 it was cleared for production at 2520hp. Of the 2000hp engines, the Griffon at least was conceived specifically for the navy, as a possible torpedo bomber powerplant.

84. ADM 1/10749, a file on future FAA fighter policy (1940). The issue was illustrated by an exchange about the roles of 803 Squadron, which until December 1939 was solely responsible for the fighter defence of the Orkneys and Scapa Flow. Its CO wrote that in this role the Roc was considered slightly superior from an armament point of view. Writing in February 1940, he noted that enemy aircraft did not approach Scapa after 18 December 1939, so he had to deal with reports from further afield, including the need to deal with snoopers and shadowers over the Home Fleet. He had to place fighters on distant patrol and he found that if the section on patrol included a Roc, the Roc had to return to base due its short endurance (in some cases as low as 2.75 hours). In one case CinC Home Fleet asked for fighters 210nm away. Since the two three-fighter sections each contained a Roc, only four aircraft responded. By February 1940 the RAF was able to deploy interceptors to Scapa, so 803 Squadron was reassigned by Fighter Command to perform fighter duties at a distance over the sea. An outer patrol line might be set up, for which the Skua was adequate but the Roc was not. He therefore asked that the Rocs be withdrawn, which was approved by Fifth Sea Lord and DNAD on 27 March. On 16 February CinC Home Fleet Admiral Forbes agreed that it was sound policy to revert the Scapa Flow defensive squadron (803) to Skuas only: the Skua was unsuitable as an interceptor and was best used for long-range fighter patrol. 'It is, however, considered that the Roc as a free gun fighter is more than slightly superior to the Skua; it offers the only chance of effective action against an enemy aircraft of equal or superior performance. To be effective, the fixed gun fighter must have a superior performance and unless vastly superior, is confined in attack to a limited arc of approach, thus making the defensive armouring of the enemy comparatively easy. FAA fighters are never likely to have such superiority and it is therefore recommended that such fighters in future be either wholly free gun turret fighters or perhaps fitted with one large calibre fixed gun in addition.' As of February 1940 DNAD wanted a turret fighter included in the 1940 experimental programme. He had ordered external tanks for the Roc to counter its greatest perceived drawback, its limited endurance. He was reluctant to relieve the four Rocs in 803 Squadron (at Scapa Flow) with Skuas because they were the only available source of tactical experience with such aircraft (the squadron was due to replace its Skuas with Fulmars in June 1940 in any case). Meanwhile DNAD suggested reorganising the squadron into two sections (three Skuas each) for long-range work and two of one Skua and one Roc each for closer patrols. DAM, who was responsible for aircraft programmes, agreed. Meanwhile it turned out that the Rocs could not accommodate IFF sets, which were considered essential for operation within the UK radar defence system, so they had to be retired from 803 Squadron. In May 1940 DNAD was still interested in exploring the tactics of the turret fighter; on 31 May he asked the Fighter School to investigate the issue, noting the similarity between the Roc and the RAF's Defiant. Only in December 1940 did DNAD write that DNAD 'in view of the altered circumstances, in that it is now in the highest degree unlikely that the Roc will be used as a first-line fighter aircraft'. The Admiralty letters asking for the tactical investigation were finally cancelled.

85. AVIA 16/139, material collected for a type biography of the Firebrand. It extended only through 1940.

86. Among the tenders was Vickers' project for a Griffon Spitfire. Hawker offered fighters powered by the Hercules and Griffon engines. Blackburn seems to have been a late entrant, as its name was pencilled in to the list of tenders.

87. AIR 2/4255. In February 1940 Supermarine thought it could deliver a folding-wing prototype five months after a formal instruction to proceed, then two aircraft after thirteen months, fourteen after fourteen months and fifty after sixteen months, at the cost of seventy-five standard Spitfires. ADM1/10752 on FAA Fighter Aircraft Policy (1940) brings up the question of how to organise special high-performance fighters. For example, they might be in special squadrons waiting to be embarked in lieu of other squadrons for special operations. DNAD suspected that defence of shore bases would be a long-term commitment, as (in February 1940) for at least eighteen months he saw little chance of the RAF being in a position to relieve the fighter squadrons in the Shetlands that CinC Home Fleet wanted.

88. ADM 1/10572.

89. As the newest British fighter in the spring of 1940, the Fulmar briefly had the highest priority, but it was soon completely withdrawn from the priority list to give maximum effort for Spitfires and Hurricanes for the RAF. On 18 May 1940 special priority was given to the Hurricane, Spitfire, Blenheim, Whitley and Wellington, but firms making Fulmars, Albacores

and Walruses were ordered not to interfere with the flow of these aircraft to the FAA. The special instruction was cancelled on 13 June 1940. On 25 May 1940 First Sea Lord wrote to the Ministry of Aircraft Production agreeing not to ask for any increased production until 1 July 1940. The Prime Minister wrote to MAP Minister Lord Beaverbrook on 2 November 1940 that FAA expansion was not going properly, but nothing seems to have been done at the time. This Minute came to light when Prime Minister Churchill renewed the requirement for naval Spitfires in the autumn of 1941.

90. A crossed-out section of the minutes of the meeting recounted DAM's attempt, on the orders of the previous Fifth Sea Lord, to obtain Spitfires or Hurricanes. Without folding wings, they could be struck down only on board the two surviving old fleet carriers *Glorious* and *Furious*; later carriers had narrow lifts which could not take unfolded aircraft. Even if the design problem was solved, the RAF would be reluctant to release its first-line fighters.

91. Of the other two large pre-war carriers, *Courageous* was sunk by a U-boat in September 1939 and *Glorious* was sunk by the German battlecruisers *Scharnhorst* and *Gniesenau* in June 1940.

92. ADM 1/11207.

93. Later in the same document DNAD admitted that the requirement that aircraft be able to land on in in all weather (including windless days) at full load and with inexperienced pilots as well as experienced, did require a relatively low stall speed. However, now that the Royal Navy had adopted arresting gear and 'controlled' deck landing, the limit had been raised to a point where stall speed and deck landing had little effect on aircraft maximum speed compared to the effect of other requirements.

94. The table showed the Sea Gladiator, Skua, Fulmar, N5/40, F3F-2, F2A-1, F4F, F5F, Hurricane, Spitfire and the RAF's prospective Tornado. Of the RN fighters, the Sea Gladiator had four 0.303in guns, the Skua added one rear gun, the Fulmar had eight 0.303in and N5/40 had four 20mm. The Sea Gladiator was listed as not navigable. Nor was it fitted for homing (others were). Its maximum speed was given as 213 knots, compared to 195 knots for the Skua, 230+ knots for the Fulmar and 300+ knots for the N5/40. Endurance at maximum speed was about 45 minutes for the Sea Gladiator vs two hours for the Skua and Fulmar. At economical speed, endurance was six hours for RN two-seaters, 2.25 hours for the Sea Gladiator. The Sea Gladiator had no W/T, but the two-seaters had it. A note indicated that a single-seat version of N5/40 might also be built. It would not be navigable and would lack W/T but it would be faster. The Grumman F3F-2 was considered about contemporary with the Skua in design, with a maximum speed of 240 knots and dive-bombing capability. It could climb to 10,000ft in 3.5 minutes compared to 4.5 minutes for the Sea Gladiator and 12.25 minutes for the Skua. At something more than 10,000lbs, the Fulmar was the heaviest of the RN fighters. The table credited the F4F with two 0.30 and two 0.50 or four 0.30 guns and the F5F with two 0.30, two 0.50 or two 20mm. The Tornado would be armed with twelve 0.303in or four 20mm guns, but current RAF fighters had eight 0.303in.The Hurricane was credited with a climb to 10,000ft in 3.5–4 minutes, the Spitfire with 3.5 minutes. Speeds were given as, respectively, 280 knots and 300+ knots, but 350 knots for the Tornado.

95. According to ADM 1/10572, the Grummans were ordered (a) to insure against loss of Fulmar production due enemy action and (b) to provide a fighter of 'interceptor' characteristics (of necessity single seater) as distinct from the patrol and escorting class of fleet fighter represented by the Fulmar, to arm a proportion of the fighter units already in the programme. The first unit to receive Grummans would be 804 Squadron, currently equipped with twelve Gladiators. One section of Gladiators might have to be retained for night work. Once enough Grummans had been added, the squadron would be split, the second Grumman squadron (probably to be renamed 802) to be assigned to *Furious* in place of 801 Squadron (with Skuas), the latter to be assigned to Hatston as needed by CinC Home Fleet. Enough Grummans would be available for one of the fighter squadrons earmarked for *Indomitable* (880) to be rearmed with nine Grummans as it formed. One of the fighter squadrons planned for *Implacable* would similarly be armed with twelve Grummans. Up to about nine Grummans would go to the Fighter School, where they would ultimately replace Gladiators. At this time the British also took over Vought V-156 Vindicators (the US Navy's SB2Us) which France had ordered. They were considered potential Skua replacements as scout bombers, but except in speed and climb the Skua was superior. Moreover, after the rearming of 800 and 803 Squadrons with Grummans, there would be ample numbers of Skuas.

96. In October 1940, when Churchill made a general inquiry about Grummans, he was told that twenty-six were available and 181 more were on order, 140 of which would have folding wings. In fact 100 with folding wings were ordered in July 1940 and another 150 in December 1940, the first ten to be delivered in July 1940 and the rest following at twenty per month. The programme was badly delayed, so on 18 November 1941 none

of the folding-wing Grummans was available. In November 1941 Prime Minister Churchill personally asked President Roosevelt to accelerate deliveries and in December 1941 the US assigned the whole output of folding-wing Wildcats to date (twenty-nine) for the armoured carriers *Illustrious* and *Formidable*, then under repair in US yards. Meanwhile the United States was accelerating monthly production from sixty to seventy-five and the British were assigned twenty-five per month from April 1942 onwards. US authorities asked the British for a formal statement that carrier aircraft were more important to them than bombers. On 9 December Churchill asked that two US bomber factories be turned over to FAA production; he said that aircraft for the armoured carriers should have priority over everything else (aircraft for escort carriers were less urgent). Delivery became more difficult as the United States entered the war and its own priorities competed with those of the British.

97. ADM 1/12126, a 10 July 1941 summary of air requirements. The three armoured carriers had no two-seaters, only the twelve single-seaters plus twenty-one TBR each. *Indomitable*, with a larger hangar, had nine two-seaters and the two other armoured carriers had twelve two-seaters each. Projected new fleet carriers, beginning with *Ark Royal*, would carry twenty-four fighters. None of the older carriers had single-seat fighters (*Hermes* and *Eagle* had no fighters at all, only eighteen TBR). *Furious* had twelve two-seaters and eighteen TBR. By this time there were thirteen auxiliary carriers planned or built, seven of the *Empire Audacity* type (nine single-seat fighters each, no other aircraft) and six of the *Winchester Castle* type (each with two single-seat fighters and fourteen TBR). Six catapult ships would each carry two two-seat fighters (as yet no CAM ships with single fighters on board seem to have been planned).

98. CinC Home Fleet wrote on 18 July 1940 that neither the Swordfish nor the Skua was suitable, as each had insufficient endurance. On 21 June, when six Swordfish attacked the *Scharnhorst* at a distance of 240nm, those which returned to base at Hatston had only seven gallons of fuel left. That was despite the accurate navigation of the squadron, which found its objective on the Norwegian coast in the expected place. There would have been no margin at all if the enemy had not been found so readily or had been further afield. The Skuas could not get beyond Bergen. Moreover, long-range fighters were needed to cover torpedo bombers attacking Norwegian targets. The problem was exacerbated, as the Germans seemed to be able to find British ships in the North Sea too readily and then to shadow them efficiently. The shadower generally homed German bombers. Forbes wrote that it was almost impossible to make a surprise attack, as once aware of the British force the Germans quickly turned their fleet out of harm's way while subjecting the British fleet to heavy attack. It would improve matters very considerably if the British could shoot down shadowers. Forbes thought the solution would be efficient fighters (Brewsters or Grummans) on catapults on board battleships or cruisers. After shooting down a shadower, they would recover to a land base, as they had sufficient endurance to get there.

99. According to the official summary of British naval air activity through 3 February 1941 (ADM 239/196), this programme started with *Pegasus* carrying two Fulmars. *Springbank* was then fitted as a fighter catapult ship with one fighter from 804 Squadron. Other ships given rocket catapults were the Ocean Boarding Vessels *Maplin*, *Patria* and *Ariguani*. These ships were all classified as Fighter Catapult Ships. *Patria* was bombed and sunk before she had embarked her aircraft. As of 1941, the seaplane carrier *Albatross* was being fitted with a catapult for this purpose, but she apparently did not serve as a fighter convoy escort. In addition, thirty-five merchant ships were converted to CAM (Catapult Armed Merchant) ships. The CAM ships carried RAF fighters, fifty British and fifty Canadian-built Hurricanes being allocated (one merchant ship, the *Michael E*, carried a naval fighter). Note that these were not Sea Hurricanes. The US Navy's BuAer became interested in the catapult ship idea and in March 1943 ADR produced a study of a catapult fighter. By that time the catapult ship idea was obsolete. The configuration was unconventional, with powerplant and propeller abaft the pilot. It would have had a float wing and it would have been about half the gross weight of the existing F4F-3S floatplane and SC-1 scout. It does not appear that the float version of the F4F was conceived for this mission; the BuAer fighter historian could not explain its origin (it was probably inspired by the float version of the Zero). BuAer considered ADR's design estimates optimistic and its stall speed (73.5mph) too high for landing in rough water. On the other hand, the unusual configuration was thought to offer unusually light weight and work continued after the fighter was rejected on a possible catapult scout/observation aircraft.

100. ADM 1/12126, which includes memoranda through 1942.

101. The summary of British naval air activity through 13 July 1941 (ADM 239/197) records the supply of 210 Sea Hurricanes adapted for catapulting, some of them with arrester hooks. At this time they equipped 800 Squadron and were equipping 801 Squadron. More were later converted. The 100 CAM ship aircraft were designated Sea Hurricane IA and were also

known as Hurricats. Sea Hurricane IBs were for the FAA. Sea Hurricane IC was a later version with 20mm cannon. There were also a Sea Hurricane IIC and a Sea Hurricane XIIA (Canadian production). Work was done on a folding wing design, but it was not pursued. During the North African landings, the Sea Hurricane II operated successfully from escort carriers. Although it had insufficient performance to compete with the Ju-88, it was successful against French fighters of similar performance and it was considered valuable on the North Russia convoy run where it would encounter enemy long-range bombers and heavily-armoured shadowers (hence the importance of its 20mm guns). It would be retained for escort carriers after the Seafire II became standard on board fleet carriers.

102. Seafire designations are somewhat confusing, particularly since by 1944 there was a conscious effort to keep the Seafire Mark series separate from that of the Spitfire. A Spitfire VB was successfully landed on board Illustrious in 1941, demonstrating that its high landing speed (85mph) was not a problem. Orders were immediately given to convert forty-eight and then another 118 Mk VBs to hooked Seafire IBs, the main alterations being the arrester hook and arrangements for slinging for cranes (to load them onto carriers). The B indicated a B-series wing with one 20mm cannon and two 0.303in machine guns. The follow-on Seafire IIC was built as such, with the C ('universal') wing. Unlike the IB, it was reinforced so that it could be catapulted. Supermarine built IICs and Westland built the Seafire LF IIC with a cropped wing (262 Seafire IIC and 110 LF IIC were built). Seafire III had the folding wing (there were also an LF III and a photo-reconnaissance version; total production was 1220, by Westland by Cunliffe-Owen, which Supermarine had set up as a shadow producer of Spitfires). To avoid confusion with later Spitfires, the Griffon-engined version was designated Seafire XV rather than Seafire IV. It was a composite design with a Seafire III fuselage, a Spitfire VIII tail (to overcome the torque of the much more powerful engine) and a Spitfire XII engine mounting; its undercarriage was strengthened. Seafire XVI was a Seafire XV with a bubble canopy. In 1944 a completely redesigned Griffon-powered Spitfire XXI emerged. The initial naval version (Stage 1) was Seafire Mk 45, with non-folding wings, naval radio and a sting arrester hook. It had a two-stage Griffon engine and four 20mm cannon instead of the mixed armament of earlier Seafires. Seafire 46 (Stage 2) had contraprops, a bubble canopy, a 24-volt electrical system, wing drop (blister) tanks and two-point catapult attachments. Mk 47 (Stage 3) had folding wings and increased flap area. All three appeared post-war, Mk 47 entering fleet service.

103. The June 1942 MAP reply to Churchill's November 1941 demand that the carriers be given the highest-performing fighters listed the maximum speeds of current and prospective aircraft. Contrary to expectation, the Fulmar was credited with only 220/235 knots (the first figure represented aircraft with reconditioned Merlin engines). By way of comparison, the Firefly was expected to make 315 knots and the single-seat Firebrand 322 knots. The Seafire was credited with 300 knots and the Sea Hurricane with 278 knots. The US Martlet was credited with 230/280 knots and the new US F6F, which the British hoped to receive, with 322 knots (the Corsair, which the British actually received, was not listed).

104. When this was written, the Firefly prototype had just disintegrated in the air, but the problem was considered far more curable than that of the Firebrand.

105. Summary of British naval air activity from 1 July 1941 through 25 December 1941, ADM 239/198. This publication does not date the Admiralty conclusions about future naval aircraft.

106. Summary of British naval air activity from 1 July 1942 through 31 December 1942 (issued February 1943), ADM 239/200.

107. The reference to using US fighters as long-range escorts is from the summary of British naval air activity through 30 June 1943, ADM 239/201. In addition to Martlets (renamed Wildcats to standardise with the US Navy) the Royal Navy received large numbers of one of the two main standard US wartime carrier fighters, the Corsair; for a time, the Royal Navy was the only shipboard operator of the Corsair. British observers considered the Hellcat superior to the Corsair in landing and handling qualities, but also slower. In 1944 the British evaluation of the Corsair was that for air-to-air combat it was better than the Hellcat 'in all respects'. Because the US Navy largely standardised on the Hellcat, the British received it in limited numbers. The British considered it better than the Hellcat for escort carriers and they planned to replace all Wildcats on board assault escort carriers with Hellcats (Wildcats would be retained in the mixed TBR/fighter squadrons on board general purpose trade protection. escort carriers).

108. ADM 1/13593, Future Aircraft for the FAA, including material from the Naval Aircraft Design Sub-Committee of the Future Building Committee. The paper on fighters was dated 23 July 1943, from a meeting held on 15 July 1943. The situation was summarised in the semi-annual summary of British naval air activity through 31 December 1943 (ADM 239/202): until the end of 1942 the rigid limits on overall dimensions, all-up weight

and minimum take-off performance were so severe a handicap that development almost stopped. Engines 'were no real credit to current models'. Despite continued improvements in their power-to-weight ratio, the maximum permissible all-up weight limited the gross weight of the engines, so that the maximum for a single-seat fighter was 2000hp (1800hp for a two-seater). The situation now suddenly changed, as the Royal Navy was building larger carriers (the Ark Royals) and fighters could have much higher power either in single or multiple engines (the latter was presumably a reference to the twin-engine Sea Hornet). Within the next five years 4000hp in a single-seater and 5000hp in a two-seater could be expected (with two Merlins a Sea Hornet developed something close to 4000hp). These powers could be achieved by continued development along conventional lines, so long as the resulting drag and increased weight were accepted. In the short-term, within the next two years, engine power could be boosted by water and nitrous oxide injection. Water injected into a supercharger would evaporate and thus cool the air, so that a higher boost pressure could be used without knocking. This technique could be used only up to the full throttle height of the engine, i.e. where there was an excess of supercharger power. Above that the engine was starved of oxygen, so that any boost had to supply extra oxygen (hence nitrous oxide). New fuels with better anti-knock ratings could make higher boost pressure possible. At this point the coming naval engine was the 2500hp Centaurus radial, which was expected to attain 3000bhp in 1946. A two-stage supercharger was boosting the Merlin (which had produced 900bhp in 1939) to 1700bhp in service and the Griffon was now rated at 2100bhp. Using a new specially blended fuel, the Merlin had developed nearly 2000hp on a test-bed and the Griffon planned for the Firefly was expected to attain 2500bhp. Rolls-Royce was expected to put a 3500hp 'H' Eagle engine into production in 1945 for fighters and it was working on a 24-cylinder air-cooled X engine which was expected to produce over 3000hp and to enter production late in 1945. The latter engine was to be developed into 36- and then a 48-cylinder versions, to produce 4000 and 5000bhp. In 1944 the British government (MAP) reviewed the engine programme given the rapid development of jet and turbojet engines. The largest piston engines which survived were the Eagle and the Centaurus. The 32- and 48-cylinder in-line engines and the 28-cylinder radial were all shelved. Among the surprises of jet technology was that engines could be developed and produced in less than half the time required for piston engines (as noted in the December 1944 edition of the summary of British naval air activity).

109. This account of the post-Salerno conference is from ADM 1/16345, an extensive discussion of carrier grouping.

110. During the October 1943 conference on lessons of the Salerno operation, the CO of the participating escort carrier Hunter offered an estimate of the number of sorties which an escort carrier could mount, assuming it had twenty-four aircraft on board: fourteen in the hangar, four in the deck park and six6 spares in overhead storage. The stored aircraft could be put on deck in serviceable condition in half an hour. With no enemy opposition, it could fly forty-four sorties the first day, declining to thirty-eight on the second, thirty on the third and twenty-four on the fourth. With slight enemy opposition that would fall to forty, thirty-six, thirty-two and twenty. With heavy opposition, the carrier could fly thirty-seven sorties the first day and none afterwards, because on the second day the carrier would have only about eight serviceable aircraft and seven or eight repairable ones.

5. THE COLLAPSE OF RADAR CONTROL: OKINAWA

1. In 1944 US CAP fighters were accounting for about 60 per cent of attacking Japanese aircraft. Anti-aircraft fire would destroy about a third of attackers and the hitting rate was about 15 per cent. Thus to make twelve hits would require eighty surviving aircraft, which would mean that 120 would have to survive CAP fighters. Given the 60 per cent CAP figure, 300 aircraft would have to set out to make the twelve hits and 220 of them would be shot down. Kamikaze pilots were largely poorly trained, so in April 1945 the US Navy estimated that the Japanese were losing half of them, compared to 33.6 per cent of conventional attackers. However, the surviving half was likely to do far more damage. At that time the estimated hitting rate by conventional attackers was 10 per cent, but any Kamikaze which survived anti-aircraft fire was likely to hit. It might take only sixty Kamikazes to get the same twelve hits as the 300 conventional attackers: twenty-four would likely survive CAP, of which twelve would be shot down. That would cost sixty pilots rather than the 220 lost out of 300. The US goal in 1945 was to reduce Japanese effectiveness to its former level, which would mean costing them 220 aircraft to make twelve hits. In that case CAP and anti-aircraft fire would have to destroy 208 aircraft – a 95 per cent rate. That could mean, for example, raising the CAP rate to 78 per cent (172 aircraft) and the anti-aircraft rate to 75 per cent (thirty-six aircraft).

2. Probability of detection depends in part on how much radar energy is poured onto the target while the radar points at it. That is why air-search radars designed to work at long range typically scan more slowly than their

shorter-range cousins. The broader the radar beam, the longer the target stays within it as the radar scans, but in that case a target is not located as precisely and that complicates any form of plotting or fighter control. Other factors in radar detection include the size of the antenna (in wavelengths), as that determines how much of an echo the radar picks up, the echoing area of the target (which depends on frequency) and the ability of the radar receiver (and operator) to pick a signal out of noise.

3. Anti-Aircraft Study No 8, AA Defense of the Fast Carrier Task Force 24 October 1944 to 21 March 1945, as revised 11 September 1945. NHHC Operational Archives Post 1 January 1946 Command File. At this time OEG was the Special Defense Operations Research Group of the Office of Scientific Research and Development.

4. Anti-Aircraft Study No. 13, Anti-Aircraft Actions in the Okinawa Campaign, 18 March – 15 August 1945, dated 12 October 1945.

5. OEG 254, 6 March 1946, *A Study of CAP Operations From October 1944 through May 1945*, NHHC Operational Archives Post 1 January 1946 Command File.

6. There were a few old-style massed raids, including the first occasion when the rocket-powered 'Baka' bomb was used (21 March 1945). In this raid twenty-five missile-carrying G4M 'Betty' bombers were escorted by twenty-five fighters. This raid was intercepted and destroyed.

7. Memo for Assistant Secretary of the Navy for Air, A1-3/VV dated 7 June 1945.

8. This account of the origin of the US AEW programme is largely based on a manuscript on the subject in the files of the NHHC Aviation History branch. It was almost certainly written by Dr William Armstrong, who for many years was in charge of the (then) separate NAVAIR History office. The Aviation History files also include Chapter 8 of the NDRC Radar History written shortly after the end of the war. This history credits the idea for a relay radar to the Joint Committee on New Weapons, the navy picking up the idea. According to the NDRC history, the experimental relay using a borrowed RCA television link was demonstrated on the roof of a building at MIT on 14 August 1942 and by May 1943 PPI signals had been received at Boston Airport from an aircraft flying over Nantucket at 10,000ft. The radio link was considered reliable at 50 miles and a relay radar (APS-14) was demonstrated to naval officers in July 1943.A short film was made and Cominch asked that range be extended to 100 miles, which was done. NDRC tried to terminate the project in December because no production request had been made. In January the navy revived the project as an AEW system under the Rad Lab code name Cadillac.

9. 'The Wartime Origins of AEW', a Naval Air Systems Command paper dated December 1975, attached to the Armstrong history and almost certainly a version of the Armstrong history (differing from the main paper).

10. Dr Armstrong interpreted the beginnings of the project as a means of seeing low-flying aircraft and saw experience at Midway as a clear indication that it was badly needed. However, low fliers were not a major problem at the time and what Midway actually showed was that US scouting was badly deficient. Hence Rad Lab's initial approach using an air-to-surface radar.

11. Attachment to Armstrong history, a 30 December memo to the Director of the BuAer Engineering Division on the current status of the programme. The Armstrong history dates the revival of AEW to February or March 1944, noting a loss of interest on the part of Cominch. BuAer decided in May 1944 to have the Rad Lab build five systems for tests in two TBMs.

12. The choice seems to have been made at an 8 March 1944 BuAer conference, the minutes of which are in the Armstrong package. Aircraft considered were the PBJ (navy version of the B-25 medium bomber), the PB4Y-1 (navy version of the B-24 Liberator), PB4Y-2 (Privateer), B-17, TB2D (a huge torpedo bomber in the prototype stage), TBY (the largely abortive alternative to the TBM Avenger) and the TBM. At this time a 32ft² antenna had been specified; it was too massive for anything except a PB4Y or a B-17. Rad Lab now, however, said that the required range of 200nm on ships could be achieved with a 16ft² antenna 'provided maintenance and operation is well done'. At this time only forty aircraft were planned, so they could surely be provided with 'gilt edge maintenance and operators'. A carrier aircraft would assure co-ordination between task force and radar plane and reduce flight time (and hazards) in transit between a base and station. It also allowed deck testing of both ends of the relay system to ensure that it was working. The meeting concluded that the TBM was best, the scanner, 8ft wide, to be housed in a streamlined radome at the front of the bomb bay. A TBM-3 could loiter at 5000ft for about four hours, after which it could climb to 20,000ft for a short look before returning to the carrier. It would probably fly a 20-mile-square pattern above the task force, detecting a single plane at about 60nm. The memo concluded with requirements for pre-design studies, including wind tunnel tests of the proposed radome installation. Note that this memo demonstrates that the original B-17 proposal was for a radar relay aircraft, not an airborne CIC. A later memo dates the decision to convert one TBM into an AEW prototype to March 1944.

13. Rad Lab Report S-50, 15 June 1945, AEW Practical Tests at Brigantine (abstract only), in the package of Armstrong AEW papers.

14. The timing is uncertain. The NDRC radar history (*Radar: Summary Report and HARP Project*, 1946) dates the beginning of Cadillac II to June 1945 and to a perception that airborne early warning was needed in places unsuited to the operation of ships with AEW terminals. The idea had been considered much earlier but dropped because the basic Cadillac project was already so heavily engaged. The main new elements were large 12in off-centre PPIs. Plans initially called for eleven complete systems, for which eleven sets of Cadillac I equipment were to be diverted. The quantity was increased to thirteen, then seventeen and ultimately twenty-five, before being cut back to seventeen at the end of the war. Deliveries of the systems began in August 1945 and were completed by the end of October 1945. Note that this account does not mention the need to supplement or replace radar picket destroyers. Armstrong dates Cadillac II to 1944 because that is when engineering tests were conducted on a B-17G, but the March 1944 memo on installations clearly envisages various aircraft as airborne radars feeding their data to a surface terminal. Armstrong's paper on 'The Wartime Origins of AEW' dates the idea of an airborne CIC to successful 1944 tests of a B-17G, presumably some time late in the year. However, this history also states that during the spring and summer of 1945 those responsible for the programme realised that the flying CIC would be useful against Kamikazes and also to control some aspects (presumably fighter defence) of amphibious operations. The package of enclosures to the Armstrong history includes a letter from CNO (presumably DCNO Air, but the designation is obscured by the binding of the package) to the chief of BuAer (18 January 1945) responding to the latter's letter dated 9 December 1944 concerning engineering studies of installation of AEW in patrol aircraft. Enclosures from BuAer were studies of installation on a PBM-5 Mariner, on a PB2Y-3 Coronado (both seaplanes) and on a B-17F. CNO asked for an additional study of installation on board a P2V (later called Neptune). 'Because of circumstances regarding the present scheduled production and installation of AEW in carrier type aircraft, as well as related studies concerning availability of B-17 models, no further work on the subject project is desired at the present time'. The package includes a 20 February 1945 report on installation in a P2V. This report notes that the P2V can take only the radome developed for the TBM, but that a B-17 could handle a larger radome. Note that the Rad Lab description of AEW dated September 1944 (in the Armstrong package) describes *only* the TBM version of the system, not the B-17G.

15. It was clearly experimental, so on 15 May 1946 it was redesignated as an Aircraft Development Squadron (VX-4). The VPB-101 designation had been used at least once for another patrol bomber squadron operating in the Pacific. The squadron was commissioned before any of its aircraft were delivered, the first being an unmodified B-17 received on 9 September 1945. The second aircraft (15 November) had a radome and two drop tanks but no radar; it flew with ballast. Meanwhile aircraft were being modified at Johnsville. The first fully-equipped PB-1W was received on 5 January 1946.

16. The US Navy was aware of this experiment. It is described in the BuAer fighter direction history, with a reference to the minutes of the British Air Interception Meeting, summarised in *CIC* for April 1945, p 50. The Wellington had a radio altimeter and VHF radio as well as the radar.

17. ADM 1/17242, based on extracts from US reports, a summary dated 3 August 1945 and updated with later comments on possible countermeasures. The basic report written on 3 August 1945 claimed that suicide attacks were six to ten times as profitable to the enemy as conventional ones, as ten times as many ships had been sunk and six times as many damaged (per 100 aircraft lost to CAP and anti-aircraft). With current tactics, the chance of an aircraft hitting a ship once it began its dive was 40 to 50 per cent. A tabulation showed eighteen ships hit in October, twenty-eight in November, thirty-three in December, forty-two in January, nineteen in February/March (during the Japanese build-up for Okinawa) and a staggering 106 in April and seventy-six in May. On average a Kamikaze hit put a ship out of action for three months. The proportion of attackers making suicide dives increased to 35 per cent at the beginning of 1945 and might be higher later. If the Japanese produced 1000 fighters per month and all became Kamikazes, about 160 ships would be damaged each month. If on average ships were out of action for three months, that would be 480 ships requiring repairs, which might exceed what shipyards could do.

18. Commander J I Nichols and Commander J D Shea, NRL, 'CIC Track-Handling Capacity', *Combat Readiness* Vol V No 1 (Jan–March 1957), pp 30–1.

19. OEG 395, 'A Comparison of the Capabilities and Requirements of Broadcast Control and Close Control Methods of Interceptor Direction', 15 June 1949, in the DCNO (Air) formerly Secret files, RG 428, NARA II.

20. In this study the threat was a 500-knot bomber carrying a 30nm stand-off

missile represented by the Kingfisher then being developed by the US Navy. The defender was a 550-knot interceptor. A bomber detected 100nm from the task force would penetrate to 50–55nm before an interceptor on CAP managed to meet it and it had to be splashed outside the 30nm launch range. OEG envisaged rear-hemisphere attack tactics for the fighter, meaning that it had to be vectored out, manoeuvring into attack position once the bomber was sighted. Just as in gun fire control, the fighter and controller had to minimise errors along the line of flight (like the line of fire of a gun) and across it. The fighter could turn at 2G (turning radius about 4000 yds). It was assumed to have the same APS-21 search radar as an F3D Skyknight; if it was not vectored to within radar range, it would not see the target at all. For detection range OEG used the range at which a target would be detected half the time, taking into account the high closing speed of fighter and bomber, which would limit the number of radar scans. An APS-21 using a wide scanning window (offering limited dwell time on any place in the sky) would detect the bomber 3.5nm away. With a narrower scan effective range would be 10.5nm.

6. THE JET AGE BEGINS

1. ADM 116/5977.

2. The other fighters listed were the F5U 'pancake', the F7F, F8B, F2M and F8F, of which BuAer characterised the FD, FR, F8B, an F8F as interceptors. The others were listed as long-range fighters. BuAer considered the F2M a hedge against the failure of its other interceptors. The British representative was Commander D R F Campbell, later one of two inventors of the angled deck.

3. According to an Attacker history by DCNR(A) (Deputy Chief of Naval Requirements Air.) dated 24 February 1948 and attached to the notes of the 3 March 1948 committee meeting, E.10/44 was a hasty attempt to see what could be done to produce a single-seat fighter powered by the new Nene engine. While it was being developed, the Spiteful was test-flown. It proved to have unacceptable stalling characteristics and it was assumed that with the same wing the E.10/44 would have similar characteristics. Also, E.10/44 had a conventional tailwheel undercarriage, but by 1944–5 it was assumed that jets should have tricycle undercarriages. Despite a loss of naval interest, Supermarine pressed on with the project after the war and the Ministry of Supply (successor to the wartime MAP) considered it desirable to assist the firm where possible 'in spite of the fact that the Navy had expressed no interest in the type'. Preliminary deck landings in 1947 showed that a fast jet could be landed on a carrier using a conventional undercarriage and the design of the undercarriage was considered an improvement on anything previously tried. This aircraft also had the first lift spoilers, 'which were well reported on by the pilots and showed that this device is a very promising aid in deck landing a jet'. At this time the Attacker had been thoroughly evaluated, but the Sea Hawk was still in the early trial stage, suffering from vibration problems. The main objections to the Attacker were probably its high landing speed and long take-off run, but the latter could be discounted because in future all fighters would probably require assisted take-off. The 105-knot approach speed was comparable to that of the N.7. Attacker endurance was less than that of the N.7. At this time the Attacker had not yet been modified to fold its wings. Perhaps the key argument was that some jigs and tools were already available, presumably due to the wartime Spiteful/Seafang programme, so if production was ordered at once, aircraft would be available in 15 to 18 months.

4. Sea Vampires were built to production specifications 45/46P and 46/46P (production by English Electric). The latter were designated Sea Vampire F.20. The British Aircraft Specification List includes F.11/45 for a naval jet fighter. It was filled by the prototype Sea Vampire. It mentions an alternative Westland design powered by an AJ-65 (Avon) engine. This project does not appear in the committee file. The specially-modified Sea Vampire for flexible-deck landing was to N.18/47; three such aircraft were tested on board *Warrior* and ashore on a flexible deck built at Farnborough.

5. Some published sources indicate that in December 1945 the Royal Navy asked for tenders for a jet interceptor, but there is no indication of such action in the file of the committee quoted here. Sources for the tender are William Green and Roy Cross, *The Jet Aircraft of the World* (Garden City: Hannover House, 1956), p 70 (discussion of the Sea Hawk) and K J Meekoms and E B Morgan, *The British Aircraft Specification File* (Tonbridge: Air-Britain, 1994), pp 350–1. Meekoms and Morgan cite a failed Shorts tender, their S.41/S.A.3. The list of 1946 Specifications included E.38/46, a version of N.7/46 with a swept wing (Hawker P.1052) intended not as a possible naval fighter but as a research aircraft. This specification was issued to Hawker on 18 March 1947.

6. Some figures given at the 1 October meeting illustrate the problem. The new Hawker fighter would require an end speed of 108.5 knots with its normal load (113 knots with drop tanks). Against this, the BH III catapults in the existing fleet carriers had an end speed of 66 knots. At full speed (30 knots) that would offer an effective end speed of 96 knots, so the ship would need to head into a 12.5-knot wind to launch fighters in normal condition. The same BH III catapult equipped the *Colossus* class light fleet carriers, but they had a maximum speed of only 24 knots. As then designed, the new fleet carrier *Ark Royal* would have a maximum speed of 31 knots and its new BH V catapult had an end speed of 75 knots. The same catapult equipped the large light fleet carriers of the *Hermes* class, but their maximum speed was 28 knots. Thus at top speed *Ark Royal* could in theory launch the Hawker fighter when steaming into a 2.5-knot wind. Arresting speed was also a problem, as the maximum speed of entry into the gear on the fleet carriers was 60 knots (75 knots for *Ark Royal*, *Hermes* and the *Majestic* class light fleets). Although designed landing speed was 108.5 knots, that was an aerodynamic figure; at least 5 knots had to be added for errors by the average pilot.

7. According to a project history in the committee papers (pp 235–8), Supermarine was asked to design a prototype undercarriageless fighter in 1945 for operation from a flexible ('sprung') deck. That must have happened not long after RAE raised the idea in the first place. Eric Morgan and John Stevens, *The Scimitar File* (Tunbridge: Air Britain, 2000), p 13 describe Supermarine's Type 505 'carpet fighter' designed to an internally-generated Supermarine specification. Supermarine offered its Design 505 in the autumn of 1945. Dimensions were set after a meeting with the Admiralty (DACR) on 21 February 1946, at which carrier limits on dimensions were discussed. It was conceived as a mid-wing aircraft with a vee (butterfly) tail powered by a pair of Rolls-Royce AJ 65 axial turbojets. By this time Supermarine was well aware of the advantages of a swept wing, but it planned a thin, tapered straight wing to limit aircraft dimensions (it also knew that a thinner wing would have a higher compressibility limit). Work on the flexible deck slowed after the war and it was soon clear that there was not enough money to provide carriers with such decks in the near future. Hence the reorientation of the project; it had always been assumed that the flexible-deck concept could be tested using a modified conventional aircraft. The Supermarine fighter was not a way of testing the flexible deck but a way of exploiting it. At a 9 August 1946 meeting (presumably at MAP) it was decided that the development of an undercarriageless prototype could not be justified. Given the work Supermarine had already done, the project was reoriented as a fall-back against failure of the Hawker naval fighter. That would also ensure that the navy had a 'stand-in' undercarriageless fighter available for possible production should carriers be modified with flexible decks. Thus Supermarine was to develop a conventional fighter which could if necessary be converted to flexible-deck configuration. As redesigned it kept the same dimensions, but the wings were made somewhat thicker to meet naval requirements, but it was also expected to meet RAF interceptor requirements. The great power offered by the two Avon engines gave it a spectacular rate of climb (4.5 minutes to 45,000ft) and speed (575 knots [661mph] at sea level). Twin engines also offered greater reliability. It would land fast (107 knots at 15,340lbs, with a half-hour of fuel left) but high power would allow it to take off in only 375ft in a 27-knot wind, which could be halved using JATO. That gave it a take-off run comparable to that of conventional fighters. For catapulting it would need an 85-knot version of the BH V catapult on the *Ark Royal*.

8. As in the case of the Hawker N.7/46, Meekoms and Morgan, *The British Aircraft Specification File*, p 369, lists alternatives to the Supermarine design, in this case the Hawker P.1063 and probably the Blackburn B.74 and a Westland design. The file of the committee suggests no such competition.

9. According to the committee file, the other bidders for N.40/46 were Fairey, Blackburn and Westland. De Havilland was preferred because its design was far ahead of the others in sweep back and other elements of high-speed design; the Ministry considered that it alone had the knowledge to put a really modern aircraft into production in about five years. De Havilland was the only British firm with experience flying aircraft with swept wings, this configuration deemed essential to meet naval requirements. The Ministry of Supply considered de Havilland the leading British aircraft firm, with excellent knowledge of high-speed flight. A report appended to the minutes of the 7 July 1948 meeting described the N.40/46 requirement as very difficult: 500 knots (575mph) top speed, 85 knots landing speed, about four hours' endurance. De Havilland won with an adaptation of its tender to the contemporary RAF night fighter requirement (F.44/46). The design just met the Staff Requirement for all-up weight and endurance, range, etc were all barely acceptable. Landing speed was, however, about 90–95 knots, which was considered inevitable with this type of configuration. It was offset to some extent by the exceptional view afforded the pilot. Landing weight would be about 21,000lbs. Very powerful engines offered a short take-off run, 525ft into a 28-knot wind. Estimated maximum speed was 560 knots (645mph, Mach 0.85) at sea level (545 knots at 20,000ft, Mach 0.89) and the aircraft could climb to 20,000ft in 2.5 minutes. However, patrol endurance at 20,000ft allowing for take-off and combat was far less than desired, 2.3 hours. With maximum fuel that could be extended to 2.9 hours and with drop tanks it

would be four hours (but then take-off weight would be 30,832lbs). The main drawback was slow radar development; the first aircraft would have the AI Mk XI set which did not meet the Staff Requirement. According to Meekoms and Morgan, *The British Aircraft Specification File*, p 361, the other bidders for N.40/46 were Gloster, Fairey and Westland, of which Gloster offered its P-231 armed with three 30mm cannon and powered by two Rolls-Royce AJ-65 Avon engines. The Westland candidate was powered by two Metrovick Beryl engines.

10. The choice was between the British-made AI Mk 9C and the AI Mk 10 supplied by the United States during the war (presumably it was the army's SCR-720, used in aircraft such as the Black Widow fighter and some versions of the F7F Tigercat night fighter). In 1949 the RAF but not the Royal Navy used Mk 10 (the Firefly and Sea Hornet night fighters were equipped with the US ASH/APS-4). AI Mk 9C was slightly larger; it was estimated that aircraft using the American set could be supplied six months earlier. Both sets offered much greater performance than the wartime ASH (APS-4). The DH 110 was designed for the more advanced AI Mk 16, due in service in 1957. Data provided in 1950 credited ASH with a maximum range of 4–5nm, compared to 6–8nm for Mk 10. The current minimum range requirement of both RAF and RN was 14nm, recently confirmed by the Ministry of Defence Working Party on AI Mk 16 and endorsed by the Defence Research Projects Committee. Thus neither set was satisfactory, but Mk 10 gave twice the range of Mk 9C. The current joint requirement for minimum range was 300ft. Minimum range of Mk 9C was 450ft, of Mk 10, 200ft. Experience with Fireflies indicated that Mk 9C was now at the stage at which serviceability would fall due to its age. Current stocks would be exhausted about 1953 and it was unlikely that more could be obtained from the United States. The Air Ministry offered 136 sets of AI Mk 10 for the 100 or so naval Venoms contemplated.

11. British aircraft were designed to multiple official requirements, the numbering of which is somewhat confusing. Between 1920 and 1949 the Ministry of Aviation and then the Ministry of Supply used a numbering system for all aircraft specifications indicating the year and a sequence number, so that N.40/46 was the fortieth specification announced in 1946 (presumably the fiscal rather than the calendar year). The letter preceding the numbers indicated the aircraft role, for example O for a reconnaissance (observation) type, although O was also used for others. S indicated a scout. The post-war Royal Navy also used Staff Requirements in an NA (or NRA) series and three-digit project designations in an N or M series. Thus the Scimitar was N.9/47 but also N.113 from the outset. The N.14/49 night fighter satisfied the navy's NA.38 Staff Requirement. NA.39 was the Buccaneer bomber, but that aircraft was also referred to as N.139. Probably beginning in 1940 (the FAA experimental E.28/40 was OR.101) there were also Operational Requirements (OR) in a separate series covering all the services. Thus the E.10/44 Attacker was to OR.182 and the Wyvern (N.11/44) was to OR.174 (the RAF version was to F.13/44 and OR.194). The navalised attacker (E.1/45) was to OR.195. There is apparently no complete list of either OR or NA numbers. NA numbers include NA 9 (M.6/49 and OR.275) for the ASW version of the Sturgeon, NA 14 for the DH 110 night fighter, NA 17 for the N.9/47 Scimitar (also OR.254 and N.113), NA 18 for an abortive naval strike aircraft (N.8/49, for the DH 109), NA 21 for the navalised Sikorsky S-51 helicopter (to S.14/48 and OR.264), NA 27 for the production Attacker (19/48P), NA 31 (A.13/49, production of the Skeeter helicopter), NA 38 for the 1952 night fighter (filled by a modified version of the DH 110), NA 39 (the Buccaneer strike bomber) and NA 43 (an ASW general-purpose helicopter).

12. The key clause was that the Admiralty 'would prefer this aircraft to be produced by a Leading Fighter Firm with recent experience in the design and construction of Naval Fighter Aircraft'. There was some support for using 'require' rather than 'prefer' to limit bidders to those who had offered designs the previous year.

13. Bell Aircraft had proposed a naval version of its P-77 lightweight fighter, powered by an XV-770-7 engine (some of the proposal documents were marked 'F2L.' At about this time, too, ADR was studying a lightweight fighter as its D-23; a data sheet dated 25 July 1942 showed a 6150lb fighter powered by an R-1830-90 engine rated at 1200hp at take off. This study was presumably connected to proposals for a stripped-down fighter comparable to the Zero. Maximum speed would have been 351mph at 15,300ft.

14. BuAer (RG 72) Confidential correspondence 1927–44 VF Vol 7, NARA II. The Ryan project was discussed informally with the company at a 19 December 1942 meeting, the company offering an informal proposal dated 15 January 1943. Unfortunately the surviving BuAer file offers no description of the original discussion or its origin.

15. The centrifugal-flow engine was apparently selected to fit the limited space inside the fuselage. According to the BuAer history, maximum weight including accessories was 950lbs and maximum diameter was 46in. Comparable figures for the F15C were 1500lbs and 58in. In each case diameters greatly exceeded anything required for the axial-flow

Westinghouse engines, but engine length would have been a problem (centre of gravity could not be too far aft).

16. Plans called for changing the engine to the R-1820-74W (with a four-bladed propeller) in aircraft produced from August 1945 on, the aircraft gaining 150hp on take-off. A further development, the FR-3, was to have had an I-20 turbojet. Both versions were cancelled at the end of the war, Ryan turning to a version using the R-1820-74W engine and a Westinghouse 24C turbojet.

17. The proposal was submitted in December 1943. The next January, according to the BuAer fighter history, the bureau asked that the single H-1 be replaced by a pair of Westinghouse jets, presumably Type 19s. Curtiss protested that adopting two jet engines would cost 10mph. It won. This project superseded the experimental F14C that Curtiss had been developing. The BuAer history suggests that the F15C was effectively a modified version of the earlier fighter, which itself had been bought only as an experimental project.

18. For some time aircraft histories have claimed that nine companies submitted mixed-power designs, unfortunately without any list. BuAer confidential correspondence includes no widespread call for designs and the proposal file shows fewer than nine offers. That is not conclusive, because it seems clear that much correspondence referred to in the BuAer fighter manuscript is no longer in the files at NARA II and the NHHC aviation history section files on particular aircraft seem to include material taken directly from the BuAer files while they were still in navy custody. The BuAer proposal file does not include Grumman's G-57, which suggests that it was not formally submitted (it can be found in Grumman records). The BuAer file does include G-67, an F7F-2 with an I-20 jet engine in each nacelle, submitted in August 1943 The BuAer proposal file (RG 77 Entry 1044-F) does not include the McDonnell 18J, but it does include the McDonnell 17 turboprop. It does not, incidentally, include either of the two mixed-power fighters actually ordered. Goodyear submitted its GA-5 proposal (R-2800 plus 24C jet) in December 1944. It seems to have been designed in response to the 1944 jet fighter competition. BuAer compared it to the F15C and to the new jet fighters, but not to the Ryan Fireball. Similarly, McDonnell's Model 17A brochure was dated 6 September 1944. It did not include a pure jet engine, only a TG-100 turboprop (2430 equivalent shaft horsepower). The date suggests that it was an entry in the 1944 jet fighter competition; it is clear that at this time some within McDonnell saw turboprops as a better bet than pure turbojets. The Convair turboprop, using a TG-100 engine, incorporated a separate GE turbojet for take-off, climb and combat. It was submitted in July 1945, which places it outside the jet fighter competition and suggests that it was unsolicited. Convair claimed that it could make 539mph at sea level and 545mph at 15,000ft, with higher speeds available with water injection (130 per cent power). Vought actually developed a jet boost installation for the Corsair and flew it in 1943, but it does not appear to have been intended as the basis for an operational fighter.

19. Memo, 6 March 1944, in BuAer 1927–44 Confidential correspondence VF file Vol. 9. The larger diameter of a fuselage with a radial engine in the nose made it possible to use a larger-diameter jet engine. The limits imposed by the FR-1 were a diameter of about 46 inches and a weight not over 950lbs (for balance). The larger engine of the F15C allowed for a 58in jet engine weighing up to 1500lbs. Both had to burn aviation gasoline.

20. Jet engine design was so fluid at this time that an aircraft company, in this case McDonnell, could exert considerable influence on the engine builder. When replying to BuAers May 1944 query about the 23C engine, McDonnell asked for a slightly more powerful version of the B19 (or 19B) engine it was to use in the Phantom; it envisaged an engine producing 1680lbs of thrust, with a specific fuel consumption of 1.1lb per pound of thrust per hour. At this time the X19B engine was rated at 1300lbs of thrust, although the slightly later production J30-WE-20 was rated at 1600lbs. McDonnell's point was that its twin-engine design was well suited to take somewhat larger engines, since they occupied easily-enlarged wing root space. Typically engine builders offered series of engines in which the next engine was 1.8 to 2.0 times the power of the last (which was actually the case with the X24C compared to the production X19). Going further in one jump had often proven unsuccessful – which was not a bad prediction for Westinghouse's jump to the 40in J40.

21. The NHHC Naval Aviation history VF file shows how badly. It includes excerpts from BuAer progress reports. On 31 January 1944 progress had recently been accelerated and delivery of the two Westinghouse engines was due on 1 May and 1 June 1944. That turned out to mean delivery to Westinghouse test facilities, so McDonnell was expected to receive the engines on 1–15 June. On 1 July 1944 the first flight was expected in July. By 1 September that had slipped to October, the engines not yet having been delivered. McDonnell expected to begin ground tests ten days after receiving engines. A 1 October report stated that the first engine had been shipped; the second was due for delivery on 1 October (that expected date soon slipped to 30 October). Delivery of the second jet engine was

'imminent' in the 1 December 1944 report. In January 1944 BuAer commented that 'with the present indication of substantial increase in the output of the Westinghouse units within the next year, this aircraft compares favourably with pure jet aircraft of other services' (such as the P-80 Shooting Star).

22. BuAer 9 June 1944 memo, 'Future High Speed VF Development' in BuAer 1927–44 Confidential correspondence VF Vol 8, NARA II.

23. BuAer manuscript fighter history.

24. This choice was laid out in a 9 June 1944 BuAer memo on future high speed fighters, quoted in the BuAer history. The new catapult was H-8, the current hydraulic catapult being H-4; presumably the -8 meant 'double the previous type'. It was accepted that because of their high fuel consumption jet aircraft would be heavier than their predecessors, to carry enough fuel. They would also find wave-offs difficult because at low speed they could not accelerate rapidly and because they had no propeller slipstream to reduce stall speed. The proposed solution was to specify minimum allowable climbing angle in wave-off condition, which in turn would limit combat radius. According to the BuAer history, the take-off problem was that initial rate of climb in take-off condition would be low. In this condition flaps and landing gear were down, weight was at a maximum and catapult speed was estimated as 90mph plus 20mph head wind. In this state the Vought F6U, which won the 1944 competition, would climb at only 33ft/min. To maintain level flight it needed a lift coefficient of 1.94, which was 92 per cent of the estimated maximum. Retracting the flaps to 22° deflection would increase the climb rate to 113ft/min (still very low), but the necessary lift coefficient would be very close to the maximum available. The situation could be improved if take-off speed was increased. At 125mph (30mph wind over deck), with full flaps down, the aircraft would climb at 370ft/min and a lift coefficient of 1.50 (71 per cent of maximum) would have sufficed to keep the aircraft aloft. In that case flap deflection could be reduced to 22° (climb rate 500ft/min). Experience showed that estimated lift coefficients often were not met. This particular study led Chance Vought, which built the F6U, to increase wing span.

25. BuAer Request for Proposal in Grumman G-71 file.

26. Aircraft Design Research Branch memo to VF Design Branch, 24 January 1945, in files of NHHC Aviation History branch. The sketch design featured four 0.60-calibre machine guns, a type BuAer was then promoting (it never entered service, however).

27. Grumman memo of visit to BuAer, 16 January 1945, in the same internal memo describing alternatives investigated after the G-71 design was rejected. Grumman archives G-71 file.

28. Unlike the successful North American and Vought designs, G-71 used wing-root intakes. After the G-71 design was rejected, Grumman engineers considered three alternatives: an aircraft about the size of a Bearcat with a 19in Westinghouse engine (J30) in its tail; a G-71 with two J30s instead of a single J34; and an aircraft powered by two J34s. The latter project was attractive because the J34 (24in unit) was so much better than the 19in (J30) in thrust:weight ratio. Notes in Grumman Archive G-71 file.

29. The divergence began with the air force decision to substitute fuselage dive brakes for the wing dive brakes in the original design. That freed space in the wings for fuel and allowed elimination of saddle tanks in the belly, making for a slimmer fuselage. Given the delays, the design was incomplete when captured German data showed the value of swept wings. H L Elman, 'Curing Furious Headaches or Down to the Sea in Jets', *AAHS Journal* (Summer 1968). The navy was offered the modified design, but the prototype FJ-1 had already flown. FJ-1s tried for several speed records in 1948: the triple run from Seattle to either San Francisco, Los Angeles or San Diego; and victory in the jet division of the Bendix Trophy race. An FJ-1 set a Seattle to Los Angeles record (1 hour, 58 minutes, 7 seconds) and FJ-1s won all three top spots in the Bendix race despite being fully armed. Elman also credits the FJ with establishing numerous important jet operating and maintenance practices. The only carrier squadron to operate FJ-1s was VF-5A (redesignated VF-51 in August 1948).

30. Notes of 26 November 1944 conference to discuss North American fighter proposals in NHHC Aviation History FJ file. This conference also considered the company's offer of a carrier version of the P-51 Mustang. This project was attractive, but it was dropped so that North American could concentrate on the jet.

31. Memo from ADR, 30 January 1947, in NHHC Aviation History files (VF), in the context of evaluation of the Douglas D-571, which became the F4D Skyray. According to the memo, the ideas cited had already been widely discussed within BuAer and the paper was intended to crystallise thought.

32. Later the navy bought some air force F-80s as training aircraft designated TO-1s. As of November 1948 there were two jet squadrons in the Atlantic and three in the Pacific, of which two Pacific squadrons (VF-52 and VMF-311) had air force F-80Cs (which the navy designated TO-1s, meaning trainers). Another Pacific squadron had been allocated twenty-four FJ-1s, but attrition had already reduced that to seventeen. Similarly, VF-171

(Atlantic) had been allocated twenty-four FH-1s (cut to nineteen by attrition) and VMF-122 (Atlantic) had been allocated twelve FH-1s (cut to eleven by attrition). All of these aircraft were considered first-generation experiments. No more would be bought. As for the other single-engine fighter bought under the 1944 competition, the F6U-1 Pirate, only thirty were to be bought, plans for a much larger number (180) having been abandoned with the failure of its afterburner. ACNO (Aviation Plans) to CNO on introduction of new model jet aircraft and redeployment of existing ones, 26 November 1948, in BuAer Confidential Correspondence VV Vol 2 for 1948–9, NARA II.

33. According to the December 1955 BuAer note, the director of the Military Requirements Division, Rear Admiral R E Dixon, was particularly determined to develop a second source of engines.

34. The minutes of the 2 July 1946 conference are in NHHC Aviation History files, probably the F9F file. Metzger noted that two other categories, the turboprop escort fighter and the rocket interceptor, had not been funded and so would not be started this year.

35. BuAer December 1955 history, 17–18, based in part on minutes of the 2 July 1946 conference.

36. Secret letter, now declassified, in NHHC Aviation History file.

37. Procurement schedules in BuAer Confidential VV files Vol 1 for 1948–9, Correspondence Box 175 in NARA II.

38. BuAer to Op-504, 13 December 1949 in Vol 4 of BuAer Confidential VV Correspondence.

39. BuAer manuscript fighter history, unpaginated, describing a 29 December 1945 conference on automatic fire control equipment for fighters. The initial step was for Patuxent River to test theoretical pursuit path analysis using a P-80 (Shooting Star) it was then testing.

40. Chuck Hansen, 'The Emerson Aero X17A Roll-Traverse Nose Turret', *The Hook* (Fall 1984). It includes four photos of the Panther (BuNo 122562) in flight, with the four guns installed.

41. OEG Study 279, The Problem of Armament and Fire Control in a Fighter Plane Against a Very High Speed Bomber, 26 June 1946, in NHHC Post 1 January 1946 Command File. This study included the use of fixed offset guns which the Germans and the Japanese had used during the war (the German version was called Schrage Musik). Figures on buffeting and minimum range are from 'Armament for the High-Speed, High Altitude Interceptor' in BuAer Confidential Bulletin, October 1949. By the time this article appeared, the main BuAer interceptor weapon programme was the FFAR.

42. The October 1949 article included damage probabilities which showed just how little a fighter could expect to accomplish in a very short time. The probability of inflicting fatal ('A') damage on a B-25 with a single 20mm high-explosive incendiary (HEI) shell was 0.015, rising to 0.66 for ten hits. To get those ten hits at 1000 yds it would have to fire 357 rounds. Given a typical cyclic rate of 750 rounds/min, the fighter would have to stay on target for 28.6 seconds. The fighter could do better with multiple guns, but to achieve any useful results it would have to fire far too many rounds for far too long.

43. The DCNO (Air) Secret correspondence for 1948–51 (RG 428, NARA II) includes a March 1950 memo from OpNav informed BuAer that BuOrd had just been authorised to develop the necessary fire-control system as AAFCS Mk 8, under Operational Requirement AD-13503. Development by BuOrd had been approved in February 1950 pending resolution of the problem of cognisance (BuAer or BuOrd) of the fire-control problem by CNO; this memo presumably represented that resolution. On 1 February CNO had recommended that BuOrd proceed with development of AFCS Mk 8, production to depend on comparison with other similar systems (presumably that developed by BuAer) concurrently. The specification concentrated, as might be imagined, on fire control, but a provision that it be capable of automatic control of the interceptor during the intercept and attack phases suggests that it was equivalent to the BuAer system. Interceptor speed could be up to Mach 1.3 and target speed up to Mach 1. The pilot should be able to switch from manual to automatic control in less than a second. The requirements presumably indicate what was wanted in an interceptor radar at the time: a 90 per cent probability of detecting a $3m^2$ target at 15nm when closing at 1300 knots while scanning over a 50 x 30° area, tracking to begin at 8nm (95 per cent probability). The associated fire control computer was to yield a solution within 6 seconds. The system was to operate from the surface up to 60,000ft. At this time BuAer's Aero XIA and its APS-25 radar were scheduled for completion in June 1950, but AFCS Mk 8 was expected in January 1954. The DCNO(Air) file includes BuOrd's 23 August 1949 specification for Mk 8 as revised on 19 June 1950.

44. APS-25 was essentially a lighter-weight version of the existing APS-19, offering no range improvement. Plans were underway to adapt the APS-19 to use a larger dish (22in, 26in or 30in) for greater range. This radar acquired targets using a spiral scan and plans were underway to make its speed constant so that maximum range would no longer depend on

bearing. The APS-25 might also be adapted to use a larger dish. APS-25 was designed to provide search, intercept, automatic gun and rocket firing and range information for the A-1 sight. APS-21 was expected to be available in September 1948. At this time the Royal Navy's goals for an AI radar were a range of 15 to 18nm using a 40in dish, 180° azimuth coverage, elevation cover between plus 60° and minus 30° (as in APS-21) and a weight of 350lbs. Estimated development time was four to five years. APS-21 seemed superior to any day AI radar the British had or contemplated.

45. Undated memo from Director, Electronics Division to Director, Piloted Aircraft Division in NHHC Aviation History VF file, referring to a 4 November 1947 outlining the required radar characteristics.

46. Memo to Director, Piloted Aircraft Branch, 3 February 1950, in NHHC Aviation History files.

47. Letter in BuAer S83-2 Confidential series, Vol 8 of 1946. In a June 1946 letter Douglas Aircraft pointed out that an *Essex* could only barely launch the two navy aircraft for which it was responsible, the AD Skyraider attack bomber and the F3D Skyknight fighter. The XF3D was expected to weigh 22,200lbs and to stall at 107mph. Douglas was developing a new pilotless aircraft designated P/A V was expected to weigh 15,000lbs but to stall at 180mph. Maximum aircraft accelerations were 4.67G for the propeller-driven Skyraider and 3.69G for the Skyknight. Douglas estimated that a piloted version of P/A V could handle 4.5G at most; without a pilot it could accept 10G. The Douglas letter was signed by Chief Engineer E H Heinemann. His company's contract for P/A V included specific responsibility for launching.

48. Memo (formerly Secret) from Rear Admiral J H Cassidy, DCNO (Air), 6 June 1950, in RG 428 records of DCNO (Air) in NARA II. The relevant papers do not indicate the outcome. In his book on the role of nuclear weapons in US naval aviation, Admiral Miller wrote that the Banshee interception was never carried out. He pointed out that at the altitude involved, the Banshee would be on the edge of a stall and that its engine compressors might well be stalling. The magazine *The Hook* mentioned actual interceptions by Panthers in a brief history of the squadron involved. The CNO directive was dated 22 August 1949.

49. Data given in the 11 March 1952 summary of the navy missile programme, CNO Chron File, NHHC Operational Archives.

50. Semi-active missiles such as Sparrow III home on radiation reflected by a target, typically in the form of a continuous (fixed frequency) wave. A radar such as APQ-50 has a separate element which injects the required CW radiation into it, so that it can emit that radiation (in addition to its normal radiation) to support missile homing. One advantage of this type of homing is that the missile can receive the CW radiation from the fire-control radar at the same time that it receives the reflected radiation. The speed of the target causes the latter to shift frequency (Doppler shift), so the missile can be designed to measure target speed in the direction the missile is flying. Given that information, the missile can be programmed to lead the target rather than point directly towards it throughout its flight, and that adds significantly to its effective range.

51. Data on missiles from AVIA65/1814 of January 1960, a table of all current British operational and developmental missiles. It has been supplemented by some dates from Bill Gunston, *The Illustrated Encyclopaedia of the World's Rockets and Missiles* (London: Salamander, 1979). According to Gunston, the original 1956 requirement called for an IR missile not confined by the 15° cone within which first-generation IR missiles like Sidewinder could home. That required a more sensitive seeker. Gunston also claims that maximum speed was Mach 3.

52. The Joint Staff Requirement for Blue Sky was issued in 1949 (ADM 1/25429). The previous project, Red Hawk, required a capability to attack from all directions. On 18 June 1949 Director of Air Warfare wrote that he feared that would delay service introduction; given progress in the development of fast jet bombers, it might be necessary to intercept them as early as 1954. 'The possibility of a kill with the presently intended armament of Aden guns is remote . . . [because of] the short range to which the fighter must close before opening fire and the difficulty of doing this either against an armed modern bomber or against an unarmed bomber of high subsonic speed.' DAW therefore wanted to reduce the Red Hawk requirement to a 20° cone astern of the bomber, restating the Red Hawk staff requirement. The existing Staff Requirement would be changed into a Joint Staff Target, while a new Staff Requirement for a simplified Red Hawk to enter service by 1954 'or thereabouts' was written. The new Staff Requirement, renamed Blue Sky, was numbered A.W. 30/OR 1088. By 1953 estimated dates of initial delivery were early 1957 for Blue Sky and mid-1958 for Blue Jay, the latter offering considerable advantages. The beam-riding Blue Sky was a visual-only missile, comparable in theory to the US Sparrow I in its simplest form. Blue Jay was also lighter and offered less drag (Blue Sky had two large boosters, above and below, mounted in these positions to keep the receiver for the beam clear). Blue Sky offered some insurance against the failure of Blue Jay, but otherwise it would be wasted and the fifty-three aircraft which could be fitted with it before Blue Jay appeared would have

to be rebuilt, if they could be used at all. At this time the navy planned to develop the N.113 (Scimitar) into a day and night fighter-bomber and a two-seat day and night all-weather fighter-bomber. The radars on the two versions would differ, but that would not matter to a Blue Jay installation (it would matter enormously for Blue Sky). These arguments killed Blue Sky in the FAA. They were signed off on by Director Gunnery Division (21 June 1954) and by Director of Naval Air Warfare (16 June 1954). The Board formally agreed. The Scimitar was divided into a Mk 1 version with guns and a Mk 2 version with Blue Jay and reheat. The Admiralty file includes the 1952 version of the Blue Sky requirement, in which the target is a Tu-4 or a jet bomber. The potential platforms are the Swift, Hunter and N.113 (Scimitar).

53. Red Top was developed to meet the RAF's Operational Requirement OR 1117 (AVIA 65/544). The OR was originally written in 1951 to cover Blue Jay Mk 1. It pointed out that the beam-riding Blue Sky required rigid mounting of the radar antenna, modifications to the aircraft nose and precision installation, which would be extremely difficult on a retrospective basis. Active radar guidance could be used in restricted tactics, minimising the special equipment on the fighter, but such weapons would not become available until 1957 (which turned out to be grossly optimistic). The US air-to-air radar-guided missiles were expected to be in production by the end of 1953, but they required bulky onboard equipment. The British therefore chose IR for the simplest installation. It also offered better immunity to countermeasures and possible small size; and an IR missile was also likely to be better at low altitude. The only range requirement seems to have been that a fighter be able to fire from at least 2000 yds; this persisted in later versions of the OR. When Issue 3 (September 1957) was written, an additional all-aspect capability was desired. This Issue also pointed out that preliminary design work had shown that Red Top was suitable for radar as well as IR guidance. Presumably that was attractive because in itself it offered all-aspect homing, but such a version had to be usable by both the RN Sea Vixen (AI 18 radar) and the RAF Lightning (AI 23) it had to be able to home on radar pulses rather than on the CW which the US semi-active missiles used. However, there were strong arguments favouring CW and the Admiralty might not want to forego such advantages. The AI 18 radar could easily be modified for CW injection, but AI 23 could not. At the least, there was an obvious inconsistency between the pursuit-course weapon conceived in 1952 and the all-round attack weapon conceived five years later. Issue 4 of OR 1117 (Admiralty AW 274) was dated July 1958. It required that a target attacked by two weapons have a 10 per cent or less chance of surviving without losing control within one minute. The weapon was to deal with subsonic aircraft at heights of up to 55,000ft; 'the Naval Staff are particularly concerned that the weapon shall be fully effective when used against low flying aircraft.' At this stage Red Top was required to attack within a 30° wide (15° half-angle) cone astern of a Mach 0.95 target; there was no mention of all-aspect homing. Minimum range was given as 2000 yds. Minimum launch speed was Mach 0.7. This was the requirement for the original Blue Jay, which was to be in service by 1958. An attached sheet described an all-round attack IR missile, which would home anywhere outside the 40° wide ahead cone. Homing should not be affected by engine cooling, the use of bypass engines, or the use of flares. In this version, snap-up height was 15,000ft for a fighter flying at 20,000–50,000ft. Snap-up might be reduced to 8,000ft for a fighter flying between sea level and 20,000ft. The in-service date required was 1963. RAE also pointed out, about 1961, that a Sea Vixen was unlikely to be able to use Red Top against Mach 2 targets and that an alternative missile was needed. By December 1962 the homing requirement was that the missile should offer full all-round homing against large supersonic targets at speeds of Mach 1.7 or above and all-round except for a restricted cone (as noted) against supersonic targets with or without afterburning at speeds between Mach 1.3 and Mach 1.7, the extend of the excluded zone depending on the target. A reduced guidance zone would be accepted for targets flying slower than Mach 1.3. Nothing in the RAE file referred to the considerably increased range of Red Top, or to the need for a fighter computer to support it.

54. Like Red Top, the US Sparrow III used proportional navigation to find a collision course to its target. In its case, the missile received CW radiation from the guiding radar using rearward-pointing antennas. It gauged relative target speed by comparing the Doppler-shifted frequency of the CW reflection on which it homed with the basic frequency emitted by the guiding aircraft.

55. The Joint Staff Requirement is given in ADM1/28041. It is described as the missile for the A.W.406 aircraft and it is dated 19 November 1962 (elsewhere it is the missile for AW 406 and also for RAF's OR 356). It was expected to enter service in 1969–70. Director of Tactical and Weapons Policy pointed out that it was now necessary for studies of a new weapon to run parallel to those of the parent aircraft, which was much the path the US Navy took with Eagle-Missileer. Unfortunately no file on the planned weapon system surrounding the missile has surfaced. The requirement was

dated 21 November 1962 and approved 7 January 1963. At the time of formulation, it was expected that data to support a formal staff requirement would be available in April 1963. The missile was required to counter low-level attacks by fast (Mach 0.95) fighter-bombers as well as turboprop snoopers (250 knots or less) and enemy support aircraft overload, plus a high-altitude threat presented by bombers carrying stand-off missiles, launching from altitudes up to 65,000ft at Mach 2.5; the missile would also deal with high-flying reconnaissance aircraft. The defined high-altitude target, at least at the outset, was a $5m^2$ target manoeuvring at half applicable G at 60,000ft at Mach 2. Maximum missile weight was 800lbs. It was to be launchable from Mach 0.85 to Mach 2.5 (if possible, down to Mach 0.7). A jump-up capability of at least 25,000ft and a jump-down capability of at least 15,000ft were desirable. An aircraft was expected to carry up to four of the proposed weapons or four Red Tops. RAE studies had already shown that to meet the low level threat the missile had to have a low level aerodynamic range of about 10nm. For carrier operation, maximum length when assembled was 16ft (192in), with a desirable maximum of 162in.

56. Copy of 27 April OpNav letter from DCNO(Air) in SCB 6A papers, NHHC Aviation branch. Most of the twenty-six members were captains, of whom R B Pirie was later quite prominent. The letter setting up the Advisory Board mentioned advice on the characteristics of other aviation-related ships, such as seaplane tenders.

57. Confidential letter from BuAer to CNO, 11 December 1945, Aer-E-12-EEP, copy in SCB 6A file of NHHC Aviation branch. No correspondence at this level of classification mentioned nuclear weapons, but it seems obvious that after August 1945 heavy bombs included them. However, a 24 July 1946 letter from Acting Secretary of the Navy John L Sullivan to President Truman was explicit: the atomic bomb was 'the most effective single instrument of mass destruction ever developed' and the high mobility of a fast carrier task force made it 'a most suitable means of waging atomic warfare . . . particularly during the early phases of a war when fixed shore installations may be temporarily immobilised by planned surprise attacks in force'. Sullivan cited Truman's 19 August 1945 memo requiring specific Presidential approval for the navy to receive necessary nuclear information to enable it to prepare for use of nuclear weapons (this was the memo under which all three services could employ nuclear weapons, not only the air force). Truman discussed the letter with Secretary of the Navy James Forrestal (soon to become the first Secretary of Defense) at a cabinet meeting not long afterwards and wrote that no such memo from him was needed – in effect, he approved the carrier and bomber projects.

58. The initial study of special carrier bombers seems to have been submitted by the BuAer Engineering Division in August 1945. These 'maximum capacity dive bombers' to deliver 8000–12,000lb loads were to operate conventionally from carriers. The report suggested that it might be necessary to modify carriers or even to abandon the usual requirements for arrested landing and for dimensions limited by lifts. Unfortunately the 13 September 1945 BuAer memo (in VV Files Vol 5 of BuAer 1945 correspondence) does not include the ADR memo (dated 5 September) describing these aircraft. The later BuAer letter referred to more elaborate studies, perhaps inspired by the initial ones. In its letter to DCNO (Air), BuAer envisaged bombers normally capable of delivering 8000lb bombs but carrying 12,000lb bombs as an overload. The nominal weight of a nuclear bomb was 10,000lbs. It envisaged three categories, A, B and C. Bomber A, operable from a *Midway*, would take off at 30,000lbs weight, with a maximum speed of 362mph at sea level and a combat radius of 300nm. Bomber B, the limit of what a *Midway* could launch, would weigh 45,000lbs on take-off. It would make 500mph at 35,000ft and it would have a combat radius of 1000nm. Bomber C (100,000lbs) would have similar speed performance but its extra weight would provide enough fuel for a combat radius of 2800nm. These figures could be achieved only with turboprops. As a near-term possibility a Category B bomber powered by piston engines and jets could achieve 500mph at 35,000ft with jets on, but its combat radius would be only 300nm (take-off weight would be 41,000lbs). BuAer considered turboprops sufficiently mature to make design of a Category B bomber practicable. The design study for the 41,000lb bomber was submitted on 12 October 1945 (BuAer VV files Vol 5, RG 72 BuAer correspondence). It was designed to land at the current carrier weight limit of 30,000lbs and 90mph and to carry a 7000lb bomb. It would be powered by two R-2800 turbocharged piston engines and three 24C (J34) jets. Maximum speed would be 545mph at 10,000ft. Combat radius was 300nm. An attempt at a faster design using swept wings (to delay the drag rise due to compressibility) failed due to balance problems, but the idea was worth pursuing. This design was sketched in response to an (undated) verbal request by the Director of Engineering of BuAer.

59. The OpNav memo approving the BuAer proposal was dated 28 December 1945. The follow-up DCNO(Air) memo, signed by Vice Admiral Marc A Mitscher, who had commanded the wartime fast carrier task force, was

dated 8 January and approved by the Secretary of the Navy on 23 January. NHHC Naval Aviation branch, SCB 6A (United States) file. By May it was clear that the bombers would be too large to stow below, so all stowage would be on the flight deck; initially the new carrier would have no hangar at all or else a small hangar for utility aircraft. It would have a completely flush deck without any permanent protrusions (such as an island or uptakes) above the level of the flight deck. A quick initial study by Aircraft Design Research (ADR 42) showed a gross weight of 90,000lbs and a span of 116ft without tip tanks (128ft with them); width when folded would be 44ft. In this study the aircraft was armed with a quadruple tail turret and with two remote-controlled 20mm guns in each wing tip. Minimum take-off run using a catapult was about 400ft (660ft without a catapult). The length of deck required to stow three such aircraft abreast in itself made for a huge carrier, its minimum flight deck length with twenty-four aircraft set at 1125ft.

60. As then understood, elements of the project included a turboprop developing 3000 to 3500hp, a ten-bladed contraprop to absorb its power (to be developed under the FY48 programme), a radar bombsight (Bomb Director Mk 2 APB-2, making possible radar bombing up to 50,000ft altitude at speeds up to 700 knots) and a quadruple 20mm tail turret (already under contract).

61. Clarifying letter from VF branch, 25 November 1946, referring to a 21 November 1946 memo, in NHHC Aviation History file.

62. Memo from Fighter Branch to Director Military Requirements Division, 11 December 1946, answering his 25 November 1946 memo, in NHHC Aviation History File. The calculations for the F2R did not include use of a Ryan-developed afterburner, which would offer better performance in combat but reduce range. An attached note by the Aero Co-ordination Branch (Spangenburg) questioned the value of the slower F2R in combat; the claimed performance (518mph at 25,000ft and 496mph at 30,000ft) seemed low for a modern fighter. The problems (flight profiles) offered by the two manufacturers were different and not only in combat duration. The Banshee cruised out at 280mph, the F2R returned at 306mph. Spangenburg agreed with the basic idea, that no new aircraft was needed to support the AJ-1.

63. The history of the project is given in a 2 February 1949 memo from the Chief of BuAer, in NHHC Aviation History VF files.

64. Traces of others remain. McDonnell's designs are included in Tony Buttler's account of post-war US fighter projects. The BuAer files include its withdrawal from bidding. Lockheed submitted a design study, but not a formal proposal.

65. According to the December 1955 BuAer note, this study was written on 14 May 1945, before the competition was announced.

66. Companies invited to tender were Bell, Boeing, Convair, Chance Vought, Curtiss, Douglas, Grumman, Goodyear. Lockheed, North American and Northrop.

67. According to the December 1955 BuAer note, most of the designs could achieve the specified 450mph speed with one or more engines dead. The combat problem was changed to include five minutes at maximum speed and 20 minutes at the speed giving maximum endurance with all engines running. A new night intruder problem was added, but the Grumman design had insufficient fuel for the desired 350-mile combat radius (it had enough for only 142nm and with enough fuel for the longer radius it would have been too large for a carrier).

68. The December 1955 BuAer note cites a 13 December 1945 memo giving the performance of the two alternatives. Grumman's would have a maximum speed of 575mph and a rate of climb of over 7000ft/min at sea level; it could intercept any aircraft up to 100nm from the carrier. The Douglas intruder offered an operational radius of 350nm, a maximum speed of 530mph and a rate of climb of 4500ft/min. The tail warning radar was eliminated from the Grumman design and added to the F3D; the latter's nose had to be enlarged to provide space for the APS-21 radar. It was also given four 20mm cannon instead of the spin-stabilised rockets initially envisaged.

69. December 1955 BuAer note, 14.

70. Later the cancellation of the F9F night fighter was attributed to a change in requirements, but a December 1955 BuAer historical review suggested that the change was due to the F7F problem, as perceived both by Grumman and by BuAer (and OpNav). BuAer changed the Grumman contract to a day interceptor designated F9F-2.

71. Memo 28 February 1947 from Director, Military Requirements Division to Assistant Chief (of BuAer) for Design and Engineering, in NHHC Aviation History file. By June the F6U was in trouble; in a 9 June memo the Head, Fighter Branch pointed out to Director, Piloted Aircraft Division that preliminary studies of the F6U conversion showed that due to its inferior thrust it should be withdrawn in favour of night fighter versions of the F2H and F9F. At this time preliminary studies for an F2H-1N had been completed, but no preferred configuration had been chosen. Grumman had just been asked for a Panther night fighter design, but nothing came of it.

Fighter Branch argued further that turning a day fighter into a limited night fighter by installing a short-range radar was at best an interim solution; a night fighter needed a longer-range radar with adequate coverage, countermeasures equipment, radar homing and other equipment operated by a dedicated operator – as in the two-seat F3D. In August 1947 delivery of the prototype F2H-1N was expected in January 1949. The first F9F-2N was expected about November 1948.

72. Minutes enclosed in 17 March 1948 memo, NHHC Aviation History file. At this time the F7F-4N had just been carrier-qualified and was back in production.

73. On average in F8Fs and F7Fs maximum intercept range on an F6F target plane was 2nm dead ahead and half a mile when 60° off boresight. Aiming performance was unsatisfactory because the antenna had mechanical backlash and also because beam width was unsymmetrical or too wide. The indicator (screen) showed poor focus. Trials by VCN-1 showed that the problem was the antenna. The radar performed much better with an APS-6 dish, since it was more powerful than an APS-6. Early tests by the manufacturer, Sperry, using an AIA dish offered better than 8nm intercept range. Some of the APS-19 problems were traced to the lack of skilled technicians since the end of the war. The F8F night fighter was found to be so bad that Op-50 called for its replacement in a composite squadron (VCN-1) by night Hellcats (F6F-5N). This squadron and VCN-2 supplied detachments of night fighters to carriers. Each would retain eight F6F-5N for training. At this time the Marines were still using night Hellcats, as were the ASW carriers. F4U-5N night Corsair production was accelerated to make up for the failure of the F8F-2N Bearcat. The F8F was rejected because with the nacelle for an APS-19 its stability characteristics were so bad that it was difficult for a pilot to fly it on instruments while operating the radar.

74. Westinghouse viewed the J46 as the smaller companion to its J40 series (maximum diameter 40in, but length 300in vs 182in). J46 was a redesigned J34 intended to produce 4500lbs of thrust. It had a somewhat greater width, 31in rather than 28in in the most developed version of J34. Compared to J34, it had a twelve- rather than eleven-stage axial compressor and single rather than double annular combustion chambers. The basic J40 had the same configuration (in a larger diameter), but there was also a thirteen-stage version, J40-WE-10, which was expected to be more powerful. J46 could be accommodated in any aircraft designed for J34 by redesigning the engine installation (e.g., the nacelles in a Skynight). In 1949 BuAer expected the basic engine to produce 4200lbs of thrust (as much as some J34s with afterburner) and 6100lbs with an afterburner, in a version designated 24C-10D or J46-WE-8. The basic J34 produced 3000lb of thrust. With a short afterburner, J34-WE-11, -15, -32 and -42 all produced 4200lbs of thrust. J34-WE-30 (24C-4C) produced 3200lbs without an afterburner, J34-WE-34 (24C-4D) produced 3250lbs of thrust (early projected figures were 3500lbs without and 4900lbs with an afterburner) and J34-WE-36 (24C-4E) produced 3400lbs of thrust. The production F3D-1 used the J34-WE-32.

75. Confidential memo (now declassified) 28 September 1949 in NHHC Naval Aviation files; its inclusion in this file indicates that it was later considered important.

76. The other items listed as applicable were DR 1051, 'Some Particular Kinematic Studies of Pursuit'; DR 1056, 'Study of High Performance Interceptors;' DR 1081, 'Comparison of Power Plants for an Interceptor Problem'; RAE Report AERO 2300, 'Report of RAE Advanced Fighter Project Group'; and OEG Study 324, 'The Future Development of Military Aircraft'.

77. BuAer VF3D file for 1951, memo of programme recommendation dated 27 April 1951 based on a programme review suggesting re-examination of programme objectives.

78. US radar designations may seem confusing. The United States used a standardised system in which the first letter in a three-letter designation indicated the platform, the second the type of system and the third the function. A was for aircraft and P (pulse) for radar. S indicated search and G indicated fire control (gunnery). Q indicated multi-purpose. APS-25 was thus a search radar. Note that radars with the same number but different letter designators were not related: there was no connection between, for example, APQ-50 and APG-50.

79. A purely optical gunsight estimates the target speed across the line of sight as a change in target angle. The sight required a range to convert that into a required deflection. In a purely optical sight, the pilot typically supplied approximate range by inserting the apparent size of the target (the sight designer generally assumed that all targets were of about the same size). The faster the targets, the greater the need for accurate speed, hence the use of range-only radars beginning with APG-30.

80. BuAer was well aware of the conical-scan problem, so it sponsored the General Electric APQ-42 monopulse radar, earmarked for the F10F when that aircraft was repurposed as a general-purpose fighter. A monopulse radar continuously compares the radar echo as seen by four different receiving horns (the sheer size of the horns presents problems). The comparison shows whether the target is moving relative to the antenna axis and in which direction. There is no cycle and deception is very difficult. Even five decades later, monopulse radars of all kinds present a serious countermeasures problem. Because the intended aircraft was a general-purpose fighter, APQ-42 included an air-to-ground ranging function, to be used in a visual attack (later the F10F, F3H and F4D were all credited with a secondary surface-search radar designated APS-35). Like APS-25, APQ-42 could control FFARs for a collision-course attack. It was also connected to a 20mm gun fire-control computer. Like APQ-41 and APG-37, its peak power was 250kW. This radar was still included among current intercept radars in a 1955 BuAer summary, but it never entered service. The fighter radars of the 1950s, including the APQ-72 of the Phantom, all used conical scan to track their targets.

81. Memo from Head, Fighter Design Branch, 20 March 1951, to Assistant Chief for R&D, in BuAer VF2H Confidential file, RG 72, NARA II.

82. This account of the radar mess is based on documents in the BuAer Confidential VF2H2 file for 1951, NARA II, particularly a 1 May 1951 Memo for Assistant Chief of R&D from Commander N P Aurand of the Fighter Design Branch.

83. The BuAer file contains a strongly-worded memo from the Electronics Division supporting the APQ-41 as the most advanced airborne interceptor-control radar currently in production, pointing to BuAer's $3.4 million R&D investment in Westinghouse, the company's substantial current production run, the company's determination to meet the required delivery dates, the top priority it had given the navy programme and commonality with other Westinghouse radars offering economy of supply and maintenance. Adopting an air force radar would double the navy maintenance load. At this time Westinghouse had already produced 120 APQ-35A radars and was producing 210 APQ-35B, 140 APQ-41 (for the F2H-3) and sixteen APQ-43 plus about another 400 APQ-43 to meet British and Australian requirements.

84. The September 1955 edition of the BuAer radar handbook credits the F2H-4 with an APG-51 radar. It does not list APG-37, which most sources give as the F2H-4 radar; it may have been the designation for the navy adaptation of the Hughes radar.

85. Naval Aviation Logistics Summary, June 1953. By that time the day fighter versions of the Banshee were valued for their ability to deliver the new lighter-weight nuclear weapons (Mks 7 and 8); the bomber version of the F2H-2 was the -2B (all -3s could deliver these weapons).

86. From a December 1955 BuAer note on initial steps in the development of the F9F-2, F3D-1 and F10F-1 aircraft, referring to informal notes (9 April 1945) on an informal conference held on 5 April 1945. NHHC Aviation History files. The meeting was attended by personnel from the Fighter Design Branch, Military Requirements Division of DCNO (Air), Radio and Electrical Branch and a representative of the US Naval Attaché office in London, who presumably could discuss current British jet fighter developments. A copy of the memo describing the conference is in NHHC Aviation History files. The minutes merely refer to the need for a jet interceptor, without giving any proposed specific requirements.

87. The navy had already paid for ex-army P-39 Airacobras to be fitted with swept wings as L-39s to explore the low-speed performance of such aircraft and it was interested in a similar conversion of a T-6 trainer.

88. Memo from Director, Piloted Aircraft Division, 7 November 1947, in NHHC Aviation History VF file. He added that 'based upon performance of present Navy jet aircraft, this company might be one of the most reliable in the jet field' but it had no follow-on programme after the F2H Banshee.

89. This account of the origins of the Douglas D-571 is based on Nicholas M Williams, 'The X-Rays: Douglas' XF4D-1 Skyrays, Research Project 6923, *Journal of the American Aviation Historical Society* (Winter 1977), in the NHHC Naval Aviation files, F4D folder.

90. Memo of conference, 29 January 1948, in NHHC Aviation History VF files. This was not the F10F Jaguar (Grumman design G-83), work on which had begun in 1946. It was G-84. Grumman considered using either two Nenes or a Nene and a liquid-fuel rocket (for take-off and combat or just for combat, with JATO take-off) or a Nene with an afterburner and 'detachable boosters' for take-off. The last was considered best. The Grumman project was discussed at a 23 January 1948 conference in the BuAer Fighter Design office. Grumman doubted that the 1952 threat, as BuAer understood it, was likely to materialise: a 500-knot bomber at 40,000ft. It was equally emphatic that a fighter built now could much exceed Mach 1 in level flight. The company disliked any large heavy fighter even if it was needed to meet a particular flight profile (problem); a small fighter would meet high performance requirements more easily and would be less expensive. Hence their preference for the detachable booster. They liked the Nene IV (6200lbs thrust) better than the J40 because the latter seemed excessively long with its afterburner. The Grumman design weighed about 12,800lbs and had swept wings. It would climb to 40,000ft in 2.87 minutes after acceleration or 3.06 minutes including take-off. The boosters would add 6000lbs of thrust for 4.5 seconds and reduce take-off

roll to 250ft. An alternative 46,000lbs thrust booster (burning for three seconds) would simply fire the aircraft into the air from a 15° ramp, imposing 4G. Grumman expected its fighter to make Mach 0.98 at 40,000ft, where it could make 2.5G turns (180° in about 30 seconds). The problem (flight profile) Grumman thought its fighter could meet would be to take off and climb to 40,000ft in 3.06 minutes, then cruise there for 15 minutes, fight with afterburner for eight minutes and loiter at sea level for 30 minutes.

91. Memo from Director of Military Requirements Division to Director of Piloted Aircraft Division, 20 October 1947, in NHHC Aviation History VF file.

92. Minutes dated 11 December 1947 in NHHC Aviation History VF files, apparently copied from BuAer VV folder 1947 Vol 4 (but not in the folder at NARA II).

93. The conference was told that it would be ready for installation in an aircraft in July 1952, experimental air firing being scheduled for October 1951 .It would be ready for service in July 1952. At this stage it was 127in long with a diameter of 8in and 38in wings; maximum speed was given as Mach 2.4. The associated radar search range was 11nm against a $1m^2$ target, using an 18in dish and 250kW power (but the BuAer Electronics Division questioned the claimed range).

94. Memo 24 December 1947 from Captain J W Murphy, not otherwise identified but within BuAer, in NHHC Aviation History VF files, apparently from VV Vol 4 folder, 1947. Context places him in the Piloted Aircraft Division.

95. A December 1948 BuAer table showed wind over deck required by the McDonnell and Grumman alternatives, using various carrier catapults. With the H4B of unmodified *Essex* class carriers, the McDonnell design required 14 knots; Grumman required 43 knots. With the H4-1 of the *Midways*, the McDonnell fighter required 3 knots, the Grumman design 27 knots. With the more powerful H-8 planned for the *Oriskany* (conceived as a jet carrier), the McDonnell design could fly with 8 knots of wind blowing the wrong way; Grumman required 22 knots. Each carrier could reliably produce 30 knots, but the standard was a carrier speed of 25 knots.

96. The file on the V-366E/F includes an undated BuAer change order for Chance Vought ordering a study of modification of the F7U to include APS-25 radar (with space for APS-19 with 30in dish), J46 engines, an autopilot, four 20mm cannon or twenty-four FFARs and fuel for a combat radius of at least 600nm and an endurance of at least four hours. Another paper in the same file indicates that on 5 January 1949 BuAer asked for a cost quotation to determine general configuration and arrangement and limited performance information for an improved F7U-1. Vought seems to have submitted the studies in April 1949 as an argument for a more extensive study. This work was based on, but was not identical to, Vought's V-362 interceptor. In this report, V-366A was armed with thirty-two FFARs, V-366B with twenty-four FFARs and V-366C with four 20mm cannon.

97. The 6 April 1951 memo explaining the F7U-3 problem and setting out possible solutions is in the BuAer 1951 Confidential VF file in RG 72, NARA II. The engines were credited with 400lbs less afterburner thrust and 120lbs less military thrust and also with higher fuel consumption. These deficiencies affected mainly rate of climb (by 4900ft/min out of 17,500ft/min at sea level); speed at sea level was 7 knots less than originally calculated. This de-rated J46-WE-2 offered better performance than the J35 proposed as an alternative. This file includes a 25 April 1951 discussion of alternatives.

98. Memo, Director Aircraft Division to Chief of BuAer 21 November 1952 on replacement of J40-WE-10 by J40-WE-22, in BuAer Confidential VF files for 1952, RG 72 NARA II.

99. The ADR memo (which is undated) offered a typical combat problem (flight profile): five minutes of take-off at maximum power, then a climb with maximum power to 35,000ft, loiter there for 134 minutes, a 100nm fly-out at maximum power, 2.5 minutes of combat, a cruise back at the speed giving maximum range and then five minutes at maximum power for approach and landing. The combat radius was attained if loiter time was reduced to zero. Gross weight was 15,800lbs (11,972lbs empty); span was 31.4ft and length 37.9ft. A sketch showed an aircraft with swept wings and tail and with four tail surfaces at 45° angles. Each wing carried a pod at about one-third span, presumably containing rockets. A sketch of ADR-57 showed a more exotic configuration, with a vertical wing and a vee-tail plus a vertical lower tail.

100. AD-10502, issued 4 May 1950, in DCNO (Air) Formerly Secret records, RG 428, NARA II. OS-122, the specification issued to aircraft companies, was dated 10 July 1950. BuAer announced its intention to develop a VTO Convoy Fighter in a 28 April 1950 internal Secret letter and in May ADR asked to receive the formal statement of the competition, so that it could offer a design. Proposals were the Convair ZF-50-15002, Goodyear GA-28B, Lockheed L-200, Martin 262 and Northrop N-63. Designs were either conventional tailed types or tailless or delta. Delta designs had to

cruise using both engines, but straight-wing designs could shut down one of the two units in the T40 to cruise more economically. Lockheed and Martin selected the more conventional configuration, the former with a straight wing and Martin with a swept wing; both required elaborate deck equipment for landing. The other three selected configurations with sufficiently wide bases that they could land without any special equipment to provide sufficient stability on deck. Consolidated and Goodyear submitted modified deltas; Northrop offered a straight-wing design with a horizontal tail well below and almost under the wing; the horizontal surface was used for support rather than for control, so this was close to a delta in concept. As evaluated by BuAer, none of the designs met the speed and climb requirements. All but Goodyear were willing to guarantee speeds beyond the required 540 knots at 35,000ft, but these figures were based on calculations of compressibility that BuAer considered unrealistic. The Bureau's desired climb performance was apparently beyond the state of the art. Changes in equipment, powerplant and propeller characteristics since the initial BuAer studies all contributed. Level-flight performance, though not competitive with carrier-based jets, was considerably better than that of other propeller-driven fighters, hence sufficiently high for convoy protection. Lockheed offered the most complete proposal, including wind tunnel data and scale-model flight results. Stability and control were rated inferior to other designs due to margin stability in normal flight and some question of pitch control when hovering into a wind. The weight estimate was considered 1200lbs too low; Lockheed proposed designing to its proposed weight, then increasing strength to full design values at minimum cost in weight (BuAer thought it was still over-optimistic). The Lockheed design was rated best by the electronics, power plant, armament and production divisions. Performance was comparable to that of the other designs, except that turning radius was very high, due to high wing loading. Martin offered the best fighter performance (highest level speed, smallest level turning radius) but its landing method was considered impracticable, requiring greater precision than could be attained in practice. Northrop's was the only design which offered the desired two hours of loiter time. The quoted cost was the highest and although satisfactory it was not considered outstanding in any way. Goodyear offered a high wing arrangement with triple vertical tails, its arrangement apparently dictated by the belief that it should be capable of conventional as well as vertical take-offs. It thereby accepted considerable complication which offered no advantage if the aircraft were used for VTO only. It was the heaviest of all the designs, even though BuAer considered its weight estimate 1000lbs too low. All BuAer divisions considered Convair's delta satisfactory or better, its major deficiency being its low loiter time at 35,000ft (CAP). However, it could add 15 minutes by dropping down a few thousand feet and it had sufficient extra fuel capacity to approach the other designs in loiter time. It was considered best from a stability and control point of view and it was the only design with clearance provided for seat ejection in any seat position. It also had the best structure. It was 'easily the outstanding design in the competition' and also had the lowest quoted price. Also, Convair had more experience with delta wings than any other US manufacturer. Unfortunately all BuAer estimates (by ADR) had been based on conventional configurations, model flight tests at NACA giving the necessary assurances that suitable control was available. The short coupled delta was not tested in the hovering regime and its feasibility was doubted. As soon as it became clear that a delta was standing up well in the competition, NACA was asked to test a typical arrangement for comparison with a straight winged aircraft. Preliminary results were favourable. On this basis the Convair design won the competition. The R&D division proposed that Convair and Lockheed receive contracts, the latter to be modified to use a standard power plant and with other changes to improve stability and control.

101. As usual, ADR produced a sketch design, DR-72A. As described by ADR in a 1 August 1950 report, it would weigh 7255lbs gross (5672lbs empty), its gas turbine producing 2640 SHP plus 800lbs of thrust and driving an 8-blade contraprop 11.9ft in diameter. Maximum speed at sea level would be 475 knots (546mph). Combat radius would be 60nm. ADR pointed to a new possibility, that such an aircraft could operate in a forward area under direct control of a tactical field commander – foreshadowing the Marines' use of the Harrier. It could carry 500lbs of armament, which might be a single bomb or two 20mm guns. Much of the report is taken up with a detailed description of a landing and take-off system. The operational strike version of the DR-72A test aircraft was designated DR-94A (DR-94 was an ASW killer version of DR-72A). This report is in BuAer Confidential VV Vol 2 file for 1950 (RG 72, NARA II). The same file contains report DR-1226 dated November 1950, describing a VTO escort fighter (DR-95), a more exotic twin-boom design in which the fuselage pod contained the cockpit, electronics and some of the fuel. The booms contained the two T40-A-8 engines. Alternative armament was four 20mm cannon or four AAM-N-2 (Sparrow) missiles. Normal gross weight would be 28,000lbs (32,000lbs overload) and span would be 40ft. Maximum sea level speed would be 555 knots (638mph) with the 20mm guns (540 knots with the

missiles). At 35,000ft comparable figures would be 513 knots and 510 knots. Combat radius with the cannon would be 310nm at normal gross weight (186nm with the missiles, however). ADR chose a straight rather than swept-back wing to save structural weight (about 1400lbs) despite its much worse drag above Mach 0.9. At the same time ADR studied a conventional turboprop attack aircraft (DR-93); it commented that both aircraft could carry similar loads. DR-95 offered much better performance at sea level because it needed so much more power to take off.

102. Assistant Chief of BuAer for R&D to Chief of Bureau, 24 January 1951, describing the alternative designs and explaining the preferred choice, in BuAer VF Confidential file for 1951. This letter erroneously dates the DR-57 study 21 May 1945 rather than 1947. An enclosure describes the design alternatives.

103. 'BuAer Studies Air Defense Systems' in BuAer Confidential Bulletin, November 1953, reporting a study conducted by NADC Johnsville.

104. RG 72 Entry 1044F contains the initial EDO proposal, R-3 of December 1945. Estimated maximum speed at sea level was 515mph on military thrust. Gross weight was 6500lbs and armament was four 0.50-calibre machine guns instead of the later 20mm cannon. This design had swept wings (40°) with a span of 24ft 6in. It would have had two 19-XB engines, as in an FH-1 Phantom. A sketch showed the two engines side by side in a pod atop the fuselage. EDO offered a much larger Model 93 the following year. It was a high-wing seaplane with an unusually slender hull. A performance summary dated 9 September 1946 shows a maximum speed of 514mph at 10,000ft (512mph at sea level). Maximum range would be 1500 miles (combat radius would be 100 miles). The aircraft had a straight wing (span 47.5ft). The powerplant would be two Westinghouse 19XB-2B in the wings, near the roots, plus one Westinghouse 24C-4A in the tail (985lbs or 1720lbs thrust, respectively). The engine in the tail would improve the boundary layer over the hull and, EDO claimed, would materially assist in the landing condition by improving flow over the centre section. Normal weight would be 14,000lbs. In October 1946 EDO offered an alternative design with a swept wing, for which it claimed a maximum speed of 524 knots at sea level (BuAer estimated 501 knots [576mph]). This time the powerplant would have been two Westinghouse 24C turbojets (3000lbs thrust each). Combat radius would have been 100nm. The BuAer Fighter Design Branch held a conference on the EDO seaplane fighter study on 7 November 1946. It brought out serious doubts as to the seaworthiness of the design, as the wing was less than two feet from the water at its tip; one wing might well 'dig in' in anything but a flat calm. Flaps would be subject to the impact of heavy spray and solid water during take-off and landing. The swept-wing version would be unusually bad because the centre of buoyancy of the floats was abaft that of the hull, which would automatically cause the aircraft to water-loop. The soft (rounded) chines would throw excessive spray. Although it was impossible to analyse the aerodynamics of the hull in detail, available data indicated that the drag rise caused by the underbody would become critical before the wing, limiting terminal velocity to the maximum speed in level flight. The narrow hull, with its high waterline and its far-aft centre of buoyancy would probably cause it to 'dig in' during take-off or landing. This tendency would be aggravated by the lack of slipstream effect to raise the nose at low airspeed. The engine location was undesirable because spray coming over the wings would damage the engines. Water might well come in the tail-pipe and run forward into the engines. There were numerous more minor problems. EDO did not seem to have access to sufficient aerodynamic information. NACA was investigating hull forms up to Mach 0.9 and detailed results were expected within six months. The conference proposed that further action on seaplane fighters be held in abeyance until the NACA hull-drag data became available. This memo is in RG 72 Entry P7. BuAer finally wrote to EDO on 18 December 1946 (RG 72 Entry P7) advising the company that it was not interested; 'a seaplane fighter is of interest in the naval programme only if its air performance is approximately equal to that of carrier based aircraft and if its hydrodynamic characteristics are such that operations may be conducted with regularity in safety. At the present state of the art, sufficient information is not available on high speed hulls to either prove or disprove the practicability of meeting the above conditions'.

105. Memo, 20 August 1947, in NHHC Aviation History Branch file on Aircraft, Fighters, Seaplanes, R&D/Proposals.

106. The early Convair Skate work is described in a short statement on the Sea Dart programme prepared in 1958 for the Senate Preparedness Investigating Subcommittee (parallel statements were prepared for other naval aircraft cancelled before they became operational). The report is in the NHHC Aviation History Branch file on Aircraft, Fighters, Seaplanes, R&D/Proposals.

107. EDO memo, 12 November 1948, in NHHC Aviation History Branch file. In August 1949 ADR produced a report (DR-1143) on hydro-ski operation. It referred to a NACA hydro-ski, a retractable planning surface which could replace the usual flying boat forebody at planning speeds. It

was highly loaded, hence small and not too difficult to retract. At this time EDO was experimenting with a small flying boat equipped with a hydro-ski.

108. As verbally directed, according to a 30 July 1948 memo to the Chief of BuAer laying out the initial specification, in the BuAer VF file for 1948. Although an attempt had been made to comply with this directive, it was considered 'most unlikely that an aircraft designed to be a fighter will be suitable for giving a true indication of the characteristics or of the performance of a larger seaplane designed for other operational use'. To meet the intent as closely as possible, several provisions and compromises were accepted: the aircraft was to have two engines; a radar operator was added, making for a larger cockpit; armament was specified as FFARs, the lightest available; to stay near a weight of 30,000lbs and still have a 300nm radius of action, maximum speed was set at Mach 0.9 at 40,000ft; to reduce weight, strength factor was set at 6G; and operation was required in 3ft rather than 5ft waves in sheltered waters. Although this was not the ultimate seaplane fighter which could be built with existing knowledge, it would still have enough operational value to be worthwhile. The extent to which the seaplane fighter was seen as an aerodynamic test vehicle shows in a handwritten note on the July 1948 memo: 'if at any time definite requirements for an operational aircraft fighter develop, we will have to amend this contract appropriately and reschedule the project'.

109. The undated request for proposals is in the BuAer VF file for 1948. To limit cost, BuAer asked bidders to submit proposals for stripped prototypes with space and weight provision for armament, electronics and autopilot. Contracts would be awarded on a phase basis, the initial commitment covering only Phase I, preliminary design through mock-up. Phase II would cover design and construction of the stripped prototypes and Phase III flight testing and correction of defects. Phase I would be carried out between December 1948 and March 1949, Phase II between July and December 1950 and Phase III between July and December 1950. Engineering proposals were due by 18 October 1948 and cost proposals by 1 November 1948. The Outline Specification was dated 21 July 1948. It specified 3ft waves and a maximum speed of Mach 0.9 at 40,000ft at target gross weight (gross weight less 40 per cent fuel). The specified mission profile was five minutes at normal thrust for warm-up, take-off and rendezvous; climb at maximum rate to initial cruise-out altitude (not less than 25,000ft, not more than the altitude at which the aircraft could climb at 300ft/min on normal thrust), cruise-out to optimum range, then a descent to 15,000ft on military thrust, of which five minutes would be with afterburner if available, then a climb back to initial cruise-back altitude and cruise back, with 10 per cent fuel reserve. The list of allowable engines consisted of the J33, various versions of the J40, the J47 and the J48 (Nene). The radar was the APQ-35 of the F3D Skynight and the armament was twenty-four FFARs.

110. This report is in the BuAer VF file for 1948. ADR saw no problem in operating this aircraft in 3ft waves, despite its high take-off speed of 113 knots. Gross weight would be 24,500lbs. With afterburning, DR-67A could take off in 2100ft (without, in 3800ft). The powerplant would be two XJ-46-WE-2 engines. A data table showed a speed of 597 knots (Mach 0.9) at sea level. The table did not include dimensions.

111. Letter 1 September 1948 from Chief of BuAer to DCNO (Air) in BuAer VF file for 1948. This letter asked that the characteristics be approved so that a design competition could be held. These characteristics in turn were set at a 19–20 August 1948 BuAer internal conference (minutes in the same file, dated 23 August) which responded to a verbal directive to determine characteristics so that ADR could undertake a study to determine possible performance.

112. Memo on design competition, 5 April 1949, in NHHC Aviation History Branch file on Aircraft, Fighters, Seaplanes, R&D/Proposals. Both proposals are in RG 72 Entry P7.

113. Presentation on the F2Y to the Air Board, 7 July 1952, in NHHC Aviation History Branch file on Aircraft, Fighters, Seaplanes, R&D/Proposals. A chronology in this file shows a summary report on Skate testing, including the hydro-skis, dated 1 February 1950. A contract for two prototypes, which were clearly Y2-2s, was initiated on 1 April 1950. As of 1 May, a preliminary draft of the detail specification had been drawn up. The 1 June Monthly Progress Report of the Piloted Aircraft Division stated that 'in accordance with decisions of the Chief of the Bureau of Aeronautics a research jet seaplane programme will be undertaken on small piloted flight articles of a hydrodynamic configuration suitable for further VF seaplane applications'. The Y2-2 designation was adopted some time in June 1950.

114. Memo from Director, Piloted Aircraft Division to Chief of BuAer, 10 February 1950, in NHHC Aviation History file. Robert F Bradley, *Convair Advanced Designs II: Secret Fighters, Attack Aircraft, and Unique Designs 1929-1973* (Manchester: Crecy, 2013), p 82 describes both as attempts to obtain the desired long-range high speed attack performance in a seaplane, Cudda being transonic and Betta supersonic; the supersonic seaplane project embodied both the blended wing and the hydro-ski. Skate was a series of

scale models of blended-wing designs. In contrast to BuAer's explanation that Convair began with a hull and adapted it to high performance, Skate 1 was the company's B-46 medium bomber adapted as a seaplane. Skate 2 was a smaller aircraft (it modelled a 30,000lb aircraft). Skate 3 was a refined version and Skate 4 was a model of a 15,000lb fighter. Skate 5 was a twin-engine 30,000lb fighter, presumably a step towards the desired night fighter. Convair also produced a twin-engine design for an attack bomber. Skate 9 was the night fighter design.

115. According to Bradley, *Convair Advanced Designs II*, p 89, Convair numbered its seaplane designs in a Y series because Y was the company's designator in the navy system. Y2-1 was the seaplane night fighter; Y2-2 was its contractual successor, the single-seat delta seaplane. The Betta attack seaplane was sometimes known as Y4. Bradley does not indicate what Y1 or Y3 were to have been.

116. Detailed justifications were laid out in a 2 September 1953 presentation for Admiral Oftsie from Op-551C4 (an office within DCNO (Air)) in the NHHC Aviation History file.

117. A 21 September 1953 data sheet in the NHHC Aviation History file lists electronics for three alternative aircraft: the basic F2Y-1, a day interceptor and a day fighter. The two day fighters had APG-45 range-only radars and Mk 16 fire-control systems. The basic F2Y-1 was a night fighter with an APQ-50 radar and the Mk 16 system. It and the day interceptor would be armed with forty-four rockets. The day fighter would have three T-160 cannon instead. The military load of the night fighter would be 2319lbs, compared to 1523lbs for the day interceptor and 1412lbs for the day fighter. The effect of the much greater armament weight of the night fighter was to reduce its fuel load to the point where its combat radius would be 89nm, compared to 170nm for the day fighter. These figures were produced as a proposal to save the F2Y by cutting armament weight.

118. These were the original pair of XF2Y-1 prototypes, four YF2Y-1s for operational tests and twelve fully-configured F2Y-1s as initial production aircraft.

119. Captain George B Chafee, USN, Director of Ships Installation Division, 'Carrier Requirements for Future Aircraft', in *BuAer Confidential Bulletin* (July 1947). The projected *Oriskany* conversion was described in 'Some Aspects of the *Essex* Class Conversion', *BuAer Confidential Bulletin* (January 1949). According to the article, study showed that an intermediate step was needed before the next carrier could be designed. Barriers were a serious issue, because the existing wire barriers protecting the deck park at a carrier's bow were unsuited to jets. Instead of wrapping itself around a propeller to stop a bolting aircraft, the wire would ride up the nose of a jet and sometimes decapitate the pilot (that was already a problem if a propeller plane smashed its propeller, nosing down on the deck and then righting itself to hit the barrier). The solution to this particular problem was a nylon net.

120. The letter was sent to potential manufacturers early in December (the letter was written on 30 November). It is in BuAer S83-2 Confidential file for 1945, Vol 4 (new series; this is not the Vol 4 in the 1922–44 correspondence series) in RG 72 NARA II.

121. Letter, Naval Aircraft Factory to BuAer, 19 September 1946 in BuAer Confidential S83-2 file (Vol 9), BuAer Confidential correspondence 1945–7. Estimated weight was 675,000lbs. A 9 August letter from BuAer had recently authorised the design of the H9 (double H8) catapult, with much the same performance as the XC1 as then understood, but apparently it could not meet the new requirement.

122. XC-2 was a missile launcher intended to accelerate a ramjet to supersonic speed. XC-4, intended for anti-aircraft missiles, was stopped in March 1949 because the necessary high-acceleration components were not available. XC-6 was designed specifically for Grumman's XSSM-6 Rigel surface-to-surface missile. Other slotted cylinders were built to accelerate smaller missiles and targets.

123. On 31 May 1949, about six weeks after the heavy carrier was cancelled, BuAer sent BuShips via CNO a proposal to rebuild the Midways, so as to keep the Navy heavy attack programme alive.

124. Letter dated 13 March 1950, registered as Ser 3232992, in BuAer S83-2(C) 1950 Vol 1. C-7 was to launch aircraft weighing between 12,500lbs and 80,000lbs at a maximum end speed of 125 knots (average acceleration 3.25G, maximum 3.5G) and a minimum end speed of 60 knots. Specifications included a launching interval not to exceed 30 seconds for aircraft weighing up to 40,000lbs and not to exceed a minute for those weighing 40,000 to 80,000lbs.

125. C-10 was conceived as a modified C-1; C-8 and -9 were target catapults.

126. The cylinder had to be lined to protect it against explosion and it needed a zipper in its slot to limit the escape of the gas driving the piston. It also had to be cooled.

127. The most powerful catapult in current service, on board unmodified *Midway* class carriers, was H4-1, which could accelerate a 52,500lb aircraft to 61 knots or a 23,000lb aircraft to 87 knots. It achieved this performance because it had a much longer track than the H4B on board an unmodified

Essex class carrier (239ft vs 170ft): a 13,000lb aircraft to 87 knots and a 17,000lb aircraft to 78 knots. The substantially heavier H8, on modernised *Essex* class carriers (245ft track) could accelerate a 15,000lb aircraft, such as a jet fighter, to 104 knots or a 52,500lb aircraft to 66 knots, a bit over what the H4-1 on a *Midway* could do. By way of contrast, XC7 (360ft track) was expected to accelerate an 80,000lb aircraft to 125 knots.

128. It probably did not help that at this juncture BuAer decided to switch from powder to liquid propellant.

129. Undated attaché report in BuAer Ships Installation Division file on *Perseus* trials.

130. Steam was provided by a destroyer tied up alongside. An BuAer memo-taker wrote that 'if these tests should verify that the British catapult has approximately the capacity predicted and if BuShips will underwrite putting this catapult in our ships with the note, crossed out, something they have not previously done for any direct-drive catapult, the Ships Characteristics Board might well be requested ['directed' was crossed out] to examine the feasibility of employing British catapults in our carriers'. This must have been a sensitive proposition: the writer added that 'in making this recommendation, I do not wish to imply that our own catapult development programme will not yield thoroughly reliable catapults. In fact, if allowed to continue our own programme aggressively, we will produce catapults by about 1956 which are greatly superior to any possible extrapolation of the present British low pressure catapult.' He had to admit that the British were actually firing their catapult two months before development of the C10 even began.

131. That BuAer wanted them suggests that whatever had been forwarded earlier had been lost, since they included a cross-section through the catapult cylinder and various basic system diagrams.

132. The main exception was the radical technology the Germans introduced during the Second World War. For example, after a very successful demonstration of the new British Limbo ASW weapon in 1949, Americans apologised: they knew that BuOr would prefer its inferior Weapon Alfa. The British understood. The last foreign innovations BuOrd had willingly adopted had been the Swedish and Swiss anti-aircraft guns immediately before the United States entered the war and the German electric torpedo – all answers to very urgent operational problems.

133. AVIA 15/2134. The idea of eliminating undercarriages seems to have arisen with Director of Technical Development (DTD) N E Rowe. It begins with his 11 October 1944 memo to CNR of the Ministry of Aircraft Production mentioning a current line of thought at Farnborough towards operating a fast land aircraft without an undercarriage. Elsewhere in the file Rowe traced the idea to reports of the Me-163B, adding that 'most of us' have asked why not throw away the undercarriages of jets from time to time. In this particular case he was looking for a way to improve the performance of a land-based jet bomber. Rowe added that arresting gear on the deck of a carrier would help stabilise the aircraft as it landed. Initially the sprung deck was favoured over the flexible deck. About January 1945 the Admiralty was interested enough to be willing to build a dummy deck for trials. The project was slowed considerably by the loss of staff as the war ended. In April, the Admiralty was interested in operating undercarriage-less aircraft and saw an interceptor as a likely first step. It was not yet reasonable to design a new carrier, but Farnborough was invited to develop something which could be installed in a few months. Existing jets could be used with their undercarriages removed, to gain experience.

134. The project was to proceed in stages, four of which were proposed in 1945. Phase I was $1/8$-scale model tests, Phase II was full-scale experiments using surplus Hotspur gliders, Phase III was landings on the carrier and Phase IV was sea trials. This programme was completed in 1949, at which time two further stages were proposed: Stage V the design of a land-based aircraft and Stage VI the design of a future interceptor (30,000lbs, landing speeds of 200 and 150 knots).

135. Further trials were flown between 3 November 1948 and 31 May 1949, including a final series (20–31 May 1949) to test whether average pilots could land on the flexible deck. Nine pilots in all were involved; the average-pilot tests were conducted by three British pilots selected from operational squadrons and one US Navy Lieutenant Commander. These tests proved that as long as the pilot kept up his speed as he hit the single arresting wire he could get away perfectly safely if he failed to engage the wire, even if the aircraft touched down on the deck (as happened more than once). One pilot, making his first attempts, engaged the wire, parted his arrester hook, touched the deck and managed to fly off.

136. ADM 1/31003, on an award for the angled deck innovation, the individuals involved being Lewis Boddington of RAE, Rear Admiral D R F Campbell (in 1951 prospective CO of *Ark Royal*) and Lieutenant Commander K A B Macdonald. Macdonald had proposed a swivelled flight deck in February 1949, meaning that he envisaged landing at an angle to a ship's course. His idea was that the ship could turn the deck into the wind rather than turning into the wind herself. Boddington rejected it at the time as impracticable. Boddington claimed that he had conceived the idea

and submitted it to Campbell. Boddington's sketch of an *Ark Royal* arrangement was dated 28 August 1951. When the claim was adjudicated in 1953, Campbell and Boddington were given equal awards and Macdonald a third of the larger ones.

137. Questions from a paper Campbell circulated before the meeting, with the agenda, reproduced in ADM 1/31003. The original sketches included in this file showed the flexible deck either laid on top of a conventional flight deck or raised above it, with a barrier on it and a parking area forward (one sketch showed a trolley leading to the parking area). Raising the flexible deck made it possible to place the arresting wire at nearly its after end, since that is about where a landing aircraft would arrive. The sketch on the other side clearly shows the flexible deck placed at an angle to the main flight deck. It is marked 'briefly discussed at meeting 7/8/51'.

138. Minutes circulated 9 August, in ADM1/31003.

139. Paper dated 18 September 1951, in ADM1/31003. The key parameter was that aircraft typically passed the round-down of the carrier 10ft above the deck.

140. ADM 1/22418, a file on the proposal, which unfortunately does not include the original paper. The angled deck idea is attributed to RAE Farnborough, but the later paper on the award for the invention makes its origins clear.

141. Even then techniques differed. The US Navy had its aircraft approach in level flight, 15–20ft above the flight deck (however, records of actual landings showed that aircraft typically approached at a shallow glide angle). The 'cut' was given before the pilot reached the after end of the deck (what the British called the round-down), after which the pilot made his own landing. Between adopting LSOs and 1949, the British employed a very different technique in which the pilot approached in a fairly steep descent, aiming at a point just forward of the round-down (in one case, Seafires aboard the training carrier *Pretoria Castle* in 1944, at a 4–5° angle). The DLCO gave the 'cut' no more than a second before touch-down. The DLCO could signal for a slower descent, the pilot applying power. With this technique it was relatively easy for the DLCO to judge the point of arrival. The technique was abandoned because it was difficult for the pilot to judge where to start his descent and aircraft often touched down well up the deck. Inconsistent approaches and pilot problems judging the appropriate point at which to apply limited power for corrections, caused many aircraft to float over the wires. An RAE report (1952) blamed the British technique for high losses of Seafires in particular. The British adopted the US technique in 1949. G Lean, *A Review of Current Deck Landing Techniques* (RAE Technical Note AERO 2206, November 1952, AVIA6/23492).

142. In February 1949 BuAer assigned project TED PTR AC-210 to the Naval Air Test Center, Patuxent River, to develop new jet landing techniques. It is not clear whether the project anticipated later key developments or was used to pay for testing them. The sub-projects cited in a later account of the success of the angled deck in the US Navy were (1) power-on jet landing techniques, (2) glide-slope landing without an LSO (the mirror technique) and (3) the angled deck.

143. The US Navy found itself demanding that pilots obey far more detailed flight instructions, creating far more detailed flight handbooks (NATOPS) than in the past. Attention to this sort of detail eventually brought jet accident rates down to an acceptable level. This important story is outside the scope of this book.

144. From a 10 February 1956 report by ONI, based on a 3 February report from the US Naval Attaché, in the US flexible deck file.

145. ADM1/31003, the awards package. Note, however, that the US flexible-deck file dates disclosure to a US Naval Attaché report dated December 1951. The dating in the claims package would preclude the claim that the idea was brought to the United States by Captain Eric 'Winkle' Brown, although it certainly seems likely that he discussed it with fellow test pilots in the autumn of 1951 when seconded to Patuxent River. Brown remembered complaining that the US Navy was showing no interest in the new British concept, but the documents show that the opposite was true – the US Navy moved extremely fast. Commander Hal Buell, USN (Ret), 'The Angled Deck Concept – Savior of the Tailhook Navy', *The Hook* (Fall 1987). Unfortunately there are no source notes. I have assumed that the account of Brown's impact on the pilots at Patuxent River was his own.

146. BuShips Journal, December 1953, from NavAir History files. The angled (canted) deck was described in the August 1952 issue of the BuAer Confidential Bulletin, just after the successful tests.

147. The US Navy's flexible deck file is a separate group within RG 72 at NARA II, Records Relating to the Flexible Deck Project, 1951-8. This file includes the brochure-like final report of the air force's related ZELMAL project.

148. Research Division memo dated 22 September 1952, responding to a verbal request from Ship Installations, in the RG 72 Flexible Deck file. It examined the F3H-1 Demon, the A3D-1 Skywarrior and the Research Division's DR-122A fighter. The flexible-deck equivalents all showed dramatically reduced weights: 20,150lbs rather than 29,650lbs for the

Demon, 57,700lbs rather than 70,000lbs for the Skywarrior and 10,900lbs rather than 16,500lbs for the DR-122A fighter. In each case, performance was held constant. The report went on to give the examples in the main text. Given the weight savings, the report went on to emphasise that to take full advantage of the flexible deck it would be necessary to press development of small jet engines.

149. The Grumman summary report is in Box 1 of the RG 72 series on the Flexible Deck. The report, describing arrangements to use an F9F-7 Cougar, is dated 30 December 1954 (trials themselves are described in a 29 July 1955 report). The BuAer specification for a Type I Flexible Deck was dated 2 February 1953. Grumman envisaged a wheeled cart onto which the aircraft would be placed after it landed, for further handling. Other Grumman reports covered launching and deck handling of undercarriageless aircraft. The last Cougar landing was made on 6 June 1955.

150. The Convair contract in the Flexible Deck file is dated 30 June 1953. BuAer expected the test fighter to be delivered in July 1954 and thirteen more F2Y-1s to be procured in March through September 1955. In addition to the false structure under the aircraft (among other things, to increase flap clearance), Convair was to fit an arrester hook.

151. Undated memo, SI-41 to SI-10 within Ship Installation (SI) division. Rough dating is implied by references to the Air Force ZELMAL programme, completed at the end of 1954 and to the Grumman tests. The flexible deck file contains a 1 July 1955 BuAer memo from the Research Division to the Director of SI Division commenting on the Convair study of the use of CVEs in conjunction with a Seaward Early Warning Line.

152. Letter from BuAer representative to Bureau Chief, 24 February 1956.

153. AVIA6/23492.

154. This was Type 93, an aural version of the standard BABS (Type 257) radar beacon. The pilot used the standard carrier homing beacon receiver (ZBX or ZB/ARA). It indicated a narrow approach path. Trials in *Pretoria Castle* established procedure and the effect of yawing by the carrier in rough weather, a particular issue with escort carriers. An account is in the official summary of British naval air activity through 31 December 1944, ADM 239/204.

155. From the official British summaries of naval air activity, ADM 239/203 and 204.

156. Report, 1 June 1950, in RG 428 records of DCNO (Air) Box 693, NARA II.

157. This account of ACLS development is based on an official history in NHHC Naval Air Branch records. This file reproduces a series of progress reports on the system, as well as an article, John L Loeb (deputy project manager for ACLS), 'Automatic Landing Systems are Here', delivered at the 8th meeting of the Guidance and Control Panel, Advisory Group for Aerospace R&D, NATO, 20–22 May 1969. The Landing Control Central was under development by both Honeywell (XN-1 version) and Bell Aerosystems (XN-2 version). Honeywell used an X-band CW radar and Bell a Ka-band pulse radar. There are three operating modes: Mode I is fully automatic hands-off landing, the ultimate objective of development, operational in 1969; Mode II is an instrument landing system which provides the pilot with a display; and Mode III is a ground-controlled approach (GCA – the original CCA) which provides the pilot with instructions to change course and rate of descent. In Mode I the pilot uses his heads-up display to monitor the system.

158. In 1968 there was also a SPN-41 transmitting set and carrier approach control system with a complementary ARA-63 receiving-decoding set in the aircraft, making possible fully hands-off landings. SPN-42 used a pair of stabilised Ku-band antennas under the after end of the flight deck to provide information on the pilot's heads-up display. One antenna measures errors in elevation, the other errors in bearing.

159. By 1969 ACLS consisted of two independent elements, SPN-41 and SPN-42, of which -42 was the original system derived from SPN-10. SPN-42 used a dedicated digital computer of the same USQ-20 type used in NTDS, but not part of that system. SSW-1 was the encoder and SRC-31 the data link transmitter. The aircraft end of the data link was either ASW-25 (Link 4, as in the F-4J) or ASW-27. SPN-42 had two separate fire-control type antennas, hence could handle two aircraft at the same time. In 1969 there was interest in a phased array radar which could handle more, but it was not developed. Another limitation was inherent in the programmed digital computer controlling landing: it based its commands on a stored model of the approaching aircraft. If the aircraft was badly enough damaged, its behaviour would no longer match the model. The programme might also find it difficult to deal with turbulence.

160. Previously the emphasis had been on defeating jamming by using many different types of radar. The SPS-40 of the *Spruance* class and other destroyers was chosen for this reason, as was the original version of SPS-49. It is not clear to what extent the change was made because the Soviets were credited with a better ability to discriminate among radars they sensed.

161. JP-1 was a narrow-cut (i.e. low yield, because it could be obtained over only a narrow range of distillation temperatures) high-paraffin kerosene. JP-2

was a failed experimental fuel. JP-3 was so wide a cut that it had too many low-boiling point constituents.

162. As of 1953, estimated annual world expenditure for RN carriers during the first year of a war beginning in 1954 was 80,000 tons, rising to 128,000 for a war beginning in 1955 and to 162,000 tons for a war beginning in 1956 (the change was due to phase-out of piston engines). Even the 1956 figure amounted to only 6 per cent of total British RN and RAF fuel requirements.

163. ADM1/24628.

164. ADR 1772, November 1955.

165. The assumed air group for the three carriers was seventy-two F8U-1 for CAP, seventy-two F4H-1 for strike, thirty-six A3J and eighteen A3D.

166. The end of the Zip Fuel story is told in John D Clark, *Ignition! An Informal History of Liquid Rocket Propellants* (New Brunswick: Rutgers University Press, 1972), pp 122–4. Clark was a rocket fuel chemist working largely for the navy. The navy fuels were HiCal-3 and HiCal-4, the air force equivalents being HEF-3 and -4. The combustion product was boron trioxide, which below about 1800°C is either a solid or a very viscous liquid, either of which would cause gross damage to a turbine.

7. THE KOREAN WAR AND AIR SUPERIORITY

1. Comments based on a 2 October 1951 letter from ComAirLant to the BuAer chief. The carriers suited to the F9F-5 as of December 1951 would be *Oriskany*, *Essex*, *Wasp*, *Kearsage*, *Lake Champlain* and *Bennington*.

2. Statement of air groups for the Preparedness Subcommittee of the Senate Armed Service Committee for FY53 in Series III Box 2 of DCNO (Air) papers, NHHC Operational Archives.

3. Richard P Hallion, *The Naval Air War In Korea* (Baltimore: Nautical and Aviation, 1986), p 61.

4. Hallion, *The Naval Air War In Korea*, pp 160–3.

5. DCNO (Air) memo of 10 September 1952 and DCNO (Air) memo 16 December 1952 in BuAer Confidential VF3H1 file for 1952. Initially DCNO (Air) wanted the all-weather fighters delivered first; this memo changed that to simultaneous delivery.

6. As referenced in a 23 February 1951 memo from Director, Industrial Planning Division to Director, Maintenance Division about spares, in the BuAer Confidential VF9F6 file for 1951.

7. Report dated 6 June 1952 in BuAer Confidential VF3H1 file for 1952.

8. A 10 October 1952 conference established the configuration of the stripped-down fighter and also decided its F3H-2 designation. In addition to the radar change (APQ-50 replaced by APG-30), the radio altimeter and the auto pilot were eliminated. It was estimated that a 'stripped' Demon would cost $145,016 less than the all-weather version (which would cost $1,380,787 in FY54).

9. This APS-67 was a simple Magnavox search radar offering the range-tracking feature required for gun fire control (output included range rate as well as range). It did not confer blind-fire or all-weather interception capability because it did not lock onto the target.

10. Notes on the mixed programme in the 1952 BuAer Confidential VF3H1 file are marked 'programme greatly changed: see PC-2 Plans Directive dated 2 December 1954'. Unfortunately the 1954 BuAer Confidential correspondence has not yet been reviewed for declassification. It seems likely that, given the large number of interim day fighters already on order and the potential of the two upgraded Sapphire fighters, the stripped Demon no longer made sense. Korean War appropriations had also been cut back drastically. The fifty-six F3H-1s had the J40 engine. Of these twenty-nine were re-engined with J71s. They were followed by 239 F3H-2s, 125 F3H-2N (four Sidewinders) and ninety-five F3H-2M armed with Sparrow I missiles, a total of 515 aircraft, all with all-weather radars. There were no F3H-1Ps.

11. The navy had already considered the Sabre. According to a note card in the NHHC Aviation history fighter file, a 7 September 1948 memo to BuAer chief Admiral Moebus discussed possible adoption by each service of the other's fighters. The air force could use any navy fighter it found superior to its own, but only the F-86A Sabre, the new air force swept-wing fighter, could be adopted for carrier operation. That would add 4 per cent to its weight. The F7U-1 Cutlass was considered comparable to the F-86 in performance.

12. Memo 3 December 1951 from Director, Aircraft Division to Chief of BuAer via Assistant Chief discussing the FJ-3 project and comparing it with the other two prospective air-superiority fighters, in NHHC Aviation History FJ file.

13. A 20 March 1952 comparison sheet (in the 1952 BuAer VFJ3 file) showed that with the same fuel weight (5010lbs) the FJ-3 would have a combat radius of 419nm compared to 395nm for the FJ-2; on a two-hour mission, average speed would be 470 rather than 452 knots and CAP endurance would be 2.6 hours rather than 2.5 hours. Maximum speed at sea level would be 600 rather than 596 knots and at 35,000ft it would be 530 rather than 521 knots. The FJ-3 would gain 1120ft/min in rate of climb at sea

level (from 8050ft/min) and 1340ft/min at 35,000ft (from 1800ft/min); time to 35,000ft would be six rather than eight minutes. The sheet was attached to a memo from the Assistant Chief (of BuAer) for R&D, who recommended that two FJ-2s be converted immediately to FJ-3s; flight tests could begin as soon as March or April 1953. Conversion would be a normal production improvement, hence could be charged to production rather than R&D funds.

14. Memo describing the Grumman proposal from Director, Piloted Aircraft Division, 18 December 1950 in BuAer VF9F file for 1950.

15. The relationship between the FJ-4 and the G-98 is made apparent in a BuAer file comparing the two, in RG 72 Entry P7 Box 618, NARA II. This series of proposals also includes various proposed versions of the G-98. The Grumman archive contains an undated but elegiac history of the F11F by Harold Andrews, which gives 1951, roughly at the time the Cougar first flew, as the starting point for the design (the Grumman files do not give any date).

16. When Grumman began design work in 1951, the only Cougar was the F9F-6. Concurrently with work on the new design, a Cougar powered by the Allison J33-A-16 was built as the F9F-7. The F9F-6 was modified (as Grumman G-99) with a slightly extended fuselage (for more range) and a modified wing (outboard sections extended to form a dog-tooth, slats eliminated and an extended trailing edge). With greater chord, the same wing had a reduced thickness in terms of thickness vs. chord, so transonic performance was improved. The extended wing leading edge housed additional fuel, but it was mainly intended to improve performance at high angles of attack. The modified aircraft was designated F9F-8, hence the -9 designation for the radically modified G-97.

17. The BuAer comparison file includes a table of fighter performance, in each case with a specified fuel (avgas vs JP-4). Only the G-98 was listed with JP-4 and there was no indication of how it would have performed burning avgas.

18. This is the configuration in Grumman's undated brochure for a Sapphire Cougar (in RG 72 Entry P 7 in NARA II). In the brochure, the new aircraft was described as a refinement of the F9F-6 offering a substantial increase in performance while keeping the aircraft small and reducing its weight (italics in original). The drawing shows the wing higher than in the final design and the area-ruling later very evident is not so obvious. A transparent overlay of the F9F-6 over the new design makes it obvious that this is not merely a simple modification of the earlier aircraft. Speed in this brochure is Mach 0.95 (630 knots) at sea level and Mach 0.96 (553 knots) at 35,000ft, with a rate of climb of 13,400ft/min at sea level and a combat radius of 320nm. Claimed speed was without afterburner, Grumman offering supersonic speed (without further detail) and more than twice the rate of climb at 35,000ft with an afterburner. Two wing hardpoints were to be provided, the brochure showing a pair of Sparrow-like missiles carried above the wings. Take-off weight would be 15,807lbs compared to 18,309lbs for the F9F-6 Cougar.

19. Grumman's undated initial improvement proposal showed a wing fillet, an afterburner increasing exhaust temperature by 35°C to 690°C, a new asymmetric splitter gap in the air intake, a 20in afterburner extension of the fuselage, an extended windscreen and a stabiliser thinned from 6 per cent to 3 per cent. Figures were presented for the J65-W-18 engine, speed at 35,000ft being given as somewhat above Mach 1.3. The brochure also showed greatly improved supersonic turning performance.

20. Report dated 12 February 1953.

21. The 7600lb rating itself was optimistic; according to a BuAer memo dated 15 January 1953, in the comparison file, Armstrong Siddeley rated the engine at 7175lbs (30 minute limit). To get to the 8600lbs that Wright envisaged the company would have to do considerable development, which would be much more than it had taken to boost the engine to 7220–7800lbs thrust. The J65 programme had begun in 1950, the current version being J65-W-2. At this time the 7800lb version was expected to pass its 150-hour test by December 1950 and the afterburner version was to be complete by December 1954. The full 8500lb military thrust rating would be available in mid-1955. These dates were preliminary estimates. A 17 December 1952 sheet comparing all available day fighters, including the FJ series, shows engine performance as then understood. The J40-WE-22 was credited with 7250lbs of thrust (10,900 with afterburner). The J48-P-8 of the Cougar was credited with the same 7250lbs, but it had no afterburner. By way of comparison, the FJ-2's GE J47-GE-2 was credited with 6000lbs of thrust, which explains why the Sapphire seemed attractive. At this time both the FJ-3 and the FJ-4 were listed with Sapphires, the -3 with the J65-W-2 (7220lbs) and the -4 with the follow-on 7800lb version (the table included estimates for an FJ-4 with an 8500lb version). These figures show just how much more powerful the new engines were. The 57-P-7 chosen for the F4D offered 9220lbs (14,800lbs with afterburner) and the J71-A-7 offered 10,200lbs (14,500lbs with afterburner).

22. A Grumman list of projects shows G-98A, with the abortive J73 engine (October 1953); G-98B, a photo-reconnaissance version later designated G-

98P and planned as the F11F-1P; G-98C, with 45° sweep; G-98D, with the 45° sweep and a J79 engine, later developed as the Super Tiger (January 1954); G-98E, with beam-riding Sparrow I missile and APQ-51 radar (June 1954); G-98F with Sidewinder (September 1954); G-98G two-seater (August 1954); G-98H with Sparrow III missiles (November 1954); G-98I high-altitude interceptor with J79 engine (December 1954); G-98J Super Tiger (F11F-1F) flown 25 May 1956; G-98J1 for the air force; G-98J2 for the Navy; G-98J3 attack version; G-98J5 for NATO (with G-98J5P photo version); G98J7 two-seater for Germany; G-98J11 for Japan; G-98J11A for Canada; G-98K with the afterburning J65-W-12 (January 1955); G-98L with J-65-W-12, all-weather radar and Aero 19A fire-control system and a new wing; G-98L1 attempt to get -98L to 60,000ft (could not quite get there), June 1955; G-98L2, J79 with various 350ft² wings; G-98L3 with a J79 engine and three Sidewinders in a package under the cockpit with alternative gun package and Sparrow I with APS-67 search radar; there was also a May 1955 version leading to the abortive F12F ; G-98M with APQ-51 radar (May 1955); G-98N with 300ft² wing (September 1955); G-98O with a rocket (October 1953); G-98R with an 8000lb thrust booster rocket, February 1956; G-98R1 with 2000lbs of hydrogen peroxide in a saddle tank; G-98R2 with two tanks and the 8000lb RMI rocket; G-98S modified version, May 1956; and G-98U (ultimate version). There were also undesignated versions for Switzerland and with a Martin-Baker ejection seat. No other Grumman aircraft was designed in anything like as many versions, the Intruder coming closest. The navy brochure file includes brochures for G-98D, G-98J (including the version with the Aero 19), G-98L and G-98S. Undated clippings in the Grumman file record Canadian interest in the Super Tiger, which was described as the leading contender to fulfil the Canadian commitment to NATO to provide a fighter-bomber. The Japanese version of the Super Tiger was widely reported at the time as the leading contender for the Japanese requirement and it was clearly an alternative for the German NATO requirement. In the end, all three chose the Lockheed F-104. There was later widespread press speculation that Lockheed had won partly by corruption (charges were successfully brought in Belgium for the NATO programme. and in Japan).

23. Memo, Director of Aircraft Division to Bureau Chief, 16 July 1957 in NHHC Aviation History file, explaining changes pursuant to a 1956 DCNO (Air) order which the file does not contain. The DCNO (Air) order is not referenced. The memo states that the modification programme was very satisfactory. The nuclear mission is reflected in the list of weapon shapes for which separation was tested: Mk 7, Mk 12 and Mk 28 (air force shapes), all nuclear weapons. Of these the standard F2H-2B weapon was the Mk 7. The last of 221 FJ-4Bs was due for delivery in May 1958, compared to the planned total of 800 to 1000 A4Ds. The memo therefore ended with a proposal for further FJ-4B procurement, but none was bought (the usual figure of 222 presumably includes the prototype). Under the post-1962 designation system the FJ-4B was the AF-1C, the F-1 being the Fury fighter. Carrier trials were conducted on board *Saratoga*. FJ-4Bs served only with the Pacific Fleet, in attack (VA) rather than fighter (VF) squadrons

24. This idea seems to have arisen in a 16 May 1952 memo from the head of the attack design branch to the Chief of BuAer asking for a study of current fighters for possible modification as bombers to provide interim aircraft to fill a serious gap in the carrier-based attack force due to unexpected delays in the A2D/T40 programme. The A2D had been considered valuable not only as a fast attack bomber (to replace the AD Skyraider) but also as a possible escort for heavy attack aircraft. The mission was described as high altitude high speed special attack or interdiction. The memo had been sent at the verbal direction of the Assistant Bureau Chief for Research and Development. The VA Design Branch had surveyed all existing fighters for possible use both by carrier attack squadrons and by the Marines. The key requirement to carry a 3500lb store (i.e., a nuclear bomb) eliminated the F9F-5, F9F-6, F4D-1 and FJ-2. That seemed to leave the F3H-1 Demon, F10F-1 Jaguar, F7U-3 Cutlass, F3D-3 Skynight (which had just been cancelled) and the F2H-3 and F2F-2B Banshees. None was completely suitable and none could be modified to be completely suitable. Vought was already offering a bomber version of the Cutlass as the A2U-1 and that seemed to be the best alternative. The VA Branch head recommended it for the FY54 programme. The study really showed that no current aircraft was suitable. 'In this light the small minimised day attack proposal recently made by Mr E H Heinemann of Douglas Aircraft becomes even more attractive. For this reason Mr Heinemann's fifth study has been added to the comparison tables. Not only is this configuration completely carrier-suitable, but it will carry the same bomb a greater distance at attractive speeds and altitudes for half the gas load of the fighters. The striking potential of the carriers will be greatly increased and the maximum wind-over-deck requirement will be 10 knots.' Douglas had just made a formal cost proposal, the target date for the mock-up being December 1952, with a first flight in December 1953, if authority to proceed could be given prior to 15 August 1952. This was of course the wildly successful A4D Skyhawk.

On a cost basis, five Douglas bombers could be bought for each Cutlass and the first aircraft could be delivered to the fleet in August 1955, only eight months late for the FY54 shopping list. The recommendation was then to order a few A2U-1 in FY54 as a stop-gap. It seems likely that within a short time the problems of the Cutlass had made this choice unattractive and the FJ-4 and F9F-8 conversions were carried out instead as a minimum cost measure while the fleet waited for the A4D. This paper is in RG 72 Confidential Correspondence for 1952, coded VV. Note that the F3D-3 used in the study was a stripped-down version powered by a single J65 Sapphire engine, hence hardly likely to be available in FY54. The problem with the rejected aircraft was insufficient ground clearance, requiring asymmetrical carriage of the weapon under a wing.

25. Memo in BuAer VF file for 1951, RG 72 in NARA II. The memo added that the division was concerned that there was apparently no programme to develop appreciably more economical jet engines. It suggested that a bypass engine (a turbofan) would help solve the current problem of excessive fighter size required for long range. The ADR study was to be completed by about the end of February 1951.

26. This study was dated 15 August 1952, based on OS-130 requirements dated July 1952.

27. According to the Spangenberg oral history (p 122) the original specification reflected the belief of Captain Pete Aurand, then on the Fighter Desk, that high subsonic speed was good enough and that the key virtue was simplicity. Then Captain Aurand was detached and within a week all the bidders were told that instead of Mach 0.95 the navy wanted at least Mach 1.2.

28. OS-130 requirements from a Grumman design notebook for the G-97 fighter submitted in that competition, from Grumman History Archives. The Grumman copy is missing its dated covering sheet, but it seems to have been received in the spring of 1952 (an appendix on drag-producing devices was dated 1 February 1952).

29. From a NAVAIR chronology of the F-8 programme written in May 1969. The operational requirement was signed out on 9 July 1952, but the request for proposal was not issued until 12 September. Closing date was 9 January 1953. In October 1952 prospective bidders were informed that the minimum speed requirement had been increased to Mach 1.2 and that they could use afterburning engines. Closing date was moved to 8 March 1953 (Vought submitted its engineering proposal in February 1953).

30. Some of the evaluation data and also some 1954 comparisons with the McDonnell F3H-G and –H designs (which became the F4H Phantom) with general-purpose versions of the fighters, is in RG 72 Entry 1044-F. The design proposals and brochures are in RG 72 Entry P7. Both are in NARA II.

31. Spangenberg oral history, p 122. Note that this was *not* one of Vought's versions of its F-100.

32. Direct Lift Control made it possible for a pilot on approach to adjust his rate of descent directly. It was replaced by Boundary Layer Control in 136 F-8Es (the other aircraft in the programme were 89 F-8Ds).

33. In its report on the VFA design philosophy, Vought stated that it had considered alternative radar systems: E-10, APQ-42 (miniaturised), APQ-50, APQ-47 and APQ-51. That is, it had not followed a BuAer specification; the VFA was its own initiative. The APQ-50 had been specified for the general-purpose aircraft analysed by ADR slightly earlier. Size and weight limited the choice to the E-10, miniaturised APQ-42 (characterised as very good in this respect) and the APQ-47; Vought made no reference to which ones were navy-approved. Of these, the E-10 was available, the APQ-42 only marginally available and the APQ-47 was not available. All had selectable search capability and all were compatible with Sparrow (E-10 could handle all three types, the others only the beam-riding and self-guided versions).

34. ADR assumed that the Sparrow was the active version, Sparrow II, not the semi-active version BuAer ultimately used.

35. Sparrow was not yet in service. ADR assumed a kill probability (based on two-missile salvoes) of 0.8 and overall missile reliability of 0.66, the latter considered reasonable for 1960. Overall kill probability, counting reliability, was 0.52. The estimated kill probability of the heavy FFAR load on board such an aircraft (seventy-two rockets) was 0.45. System positioning success was counted as 0.8; the probability that an FFAR fighter would kill its opponent was only 0.17, compared to 0.52 for the Sparrow fighter. ADR pointed out that the 0.8 figure for the FFAR fighter was probably far too high, as such a fighter had to sight very accurately yet would be nearly 1000 yds from the target when firing. If the figure was reduced to a more realistic 0.5, the success rate for the FFAR fighters would be only 0.11 and the exchange rate would be 4.7 to 1. Even if missile kill probability was only 0.5 and the optimistic FFAR figures were used, the missile still offered an exchange rate of 1.3:1.

36. In his history of post-war US fighter projects, Tony Buttler writes that the navy assigned the project an attack designation because attack funds had not been obligated. He was clearly working from McDonnell company

records and the description of the F3H-G/H with far more hardpoints than the navy wanted (as indicated in the ADR papers) suggests that the idea was the company's.

37. This early history is based on a 15 December 1955 memo from Director, Aircraft Division to Deputy and Assistant Chief of Bureau on the programme history, in RG 72 Entry 1044-E Design Co-ordination Branch correspondence 1934–59.

38. The first paragraph in the 14 March 1955 DCNO (Air) letter calling the conference was 'the progress of the AH-1 development to date gives rise to considerable question as to its ultimate usefulness as a service aircraft'.

39. BuAer letter dated 15 April 1955 cited in DCNO (Air) letter specifying requirements. Unfortunately the file apparently does not include this letter. As designed the AH-1 had four 20mm cannon, the guns being deleted in May 1955. At this time other gunless fighters were the F8U-2 Crusader and the F8U-3 Super Crusader (at the time the F8U-2 had internally-mounted Sidewinders). As built, the F8U-2 did have the usual guns in blisters alongside its fuselage. A 4 February 1955 conference on future fighter armament agreed that all-weather fighters should have Sparrow and day fighters Sidewinder missiles. In each type of fighter the missile would be standardised to simplify logistics and training and for maximum kill probability. Elimination of guns was apparently not discussed.

40. Memo to Assistant Chief for R&D from Director, Aircraft Division, 11 October 1956, synopsis of F4H-1 Armament History, in RG 72 Entry 1044-E (Design Co-ordination Branch), correspondence 1934–59.

41. Memo, Assistant Chief for RDT& E to Assistant Chief for Programme Management, 1 February 1960, in RG 343 Test and Evaluation file, NARA II. The question had been reviewed most recently on 4 September 1959. The F4H could deliver bombs, but the A3J offered greater range and a more sophisticated bombing-navigational system. As of September 1959 it would cost $1.51 billion to buy 300 F4H and 100 A3J (FY60 and beyond) vs $1.29 billion for 400 F4H fighters. Thus substituting F4H fighters for the planned 100 A3Js would not save very much and the saving would shrink further because a new bombing system would have to be developed for the F4H. The idea of replacing the A3J with additional F4H fighters seems to have originated in an April 1959 McDonnell brochure (in the file cited) advertising a true dual-purpose aircraft it called the F4H-1A, with a solid-state bombing computer, a Ku-band terrain-avoidance and bombing radar and an APN-116 Doppler radar (plus the F4H-1 navigational computer). The company claimed that it had integrated these units into a package interchangeable with the usual AMFCS IA. It argued that the proper balance between attack and fighter aircraft would vary from place to place and from situation to situation, hence that a 'swing' aircraft was needed. In this case the shift required replacement of the modular nose/radar combination as well as the usual APQ-72 cockpit displays.

42. The F-4E reflected air force combat experience: the big Sparrow-guidance radar was replaced by a smaller-diameter APQ-120, leaving space for a 20mm gun. F-4F was a Luftwaffe version of the F-4E without the former's air-to-ground weapon system. There was no F-4H, as it would have been confused with the navy F4H designation. F-4N was the designation of 228 F-4Bs upgraded in 1971 with new avionics and a strengthened structure. F-4S was a corresponding upgraded F-4J with leading-edge slats.

43. Discussed at the 4 March 1952 meeting of the Naval Aircraft Sub-Committee.

44. The envisaged submarine strike force was twenty-three units, of which twelve would be nuclear (SSGN) and eleven new diesel SSG. The warships associated with the seaplane strike force were two new tenders (AVA rather than AV), two converted tenders and four converted AVPs; there would also be submarine tankers to fuel the seaplanes covertly. The entire submarine programme died when Polaris was adopted and the cost of the Polaris programme killed the seaplane strike plan.

45. As described in the 1955 report, this all-weather attack aircraft would have a maximum speed at sea level of about 500 knots when clean. It could deliver either a small atomic weapon to a target 600nm away (flying the nearest 300nm out and back on the deck) or 4000lbs of conventional ordnance. As a support aircraft with up to seven separate bombs or rocket packages or air-to-surface missiles, it would loiter for an hour 300nm from a likely objective, then attack as needed.

46. The BBGs would be the four *Iowa*s plus the *Kentucky* (BB 66), which had been retained incomplete. Each BBG would be armed with two Talos launchers and one Regulus/Triton launcher. It would have long-range search radar and would be capable of controlling aircraft.

47. The committee envisaged building fifteen entirely new nuclear-powered Talos cruisers, which would be supplemented by conversions of the three *Newport News* class cruisers and of two *Baltimore*s (or *Oregon City* class). Existing converted cruisers would apparently all be discarded as obsolete. The US Navy ended up building one nuclear missile cruiser (*Long Beach*) and converting three *Baltimore*s to the *Albany* class missile cruisers.

48. This policy called for building a nuclear cruiser (CGN) for each nuclear carrier and a total of sixteen large nuclear destroyers (DLGN, at the time

called frigates). The programme was cut to one nuclear carrier (*Enterprise*), one cruiser (*Long Beach*) and one DLGN (*Bainbridge*), others following later. The even number of DLGN suggests that plans called for two-carrier task groups.

49. The committee listed SAM ships, long-range surface-to-surface missiles, distant warning/surveillance against aircraft and transiting submarines (which meant the new SOSUS system), nuclear submarine propulsion, vertical assault and a jet attack seaplane force. These were exactly the areas the budgets of the next few years emphasised, the seaplane attack force dying only because funds went into Polaris instead. The plan showed a total of twenty-four carriers in the 1966 fleet (including ASW carriers), declining to twenty-two in 1971, when the first of a new class of light nuclear carriers (CVLN) would be ordered to replace the CVS. The plan assumed five carrier task groups, each with three attack carriers; plus two carriers for assignment as required, for a total of seventeen such ships. Another seven would be maintained for ASW.

50. However, the proposal file in RG 72 Entry P7 includes proposals from Avro Canada and from Lockheed. Avro offered a canard with a swivelling Bristol Orpheus 11 engine at each wingtip, the canards having slightly shorter span than the main wings near the tail. The proposal included a drawing showing that the proposed aircraft was about the size of a McDonnell Banshee, a fighter the Royal Canadian Navy was then operating. Lockheed's CL-349 was a series of design studies which the company claimed showed that the desired performance required either more advanced engines than had been permitted or a reduced thrust to weight margin (5 per cent rather than 10 per cent).

51. Programme description from memo from Director, Aircraft Division to Chief of BuAer 29 October 1956 describing the status of current competitions, in NHHC Aviation History branch files.

52. RG 72 Entry P7 includes an August 1951 Ryan brochure for a tail-sitting Model 38 delta powered by an XJ53-GE-X10 engine for which a maximum thrust of 24,900lbs was claimed (with afterburning). An existing version of the XJ53 produced a maximum of 21,000lbs and weighed 6500lbs (Ryan claimed 4900lbs for its engine). Neither engine ever entered service. Gross weight was 17,500lbs. Ryan claimed 661 knots at sea level and 871 knots at 35,000ft on afterburner, but BuAer analysts stated that the company had badly underestimated transonic drag, so that it would not be nearly so fast. BuAer apparently considered the Ryan aircraft far too small. In December 1951 ADR wrote that Ryan had been entirely too optimistic in its weight estimates, which were crucial. A forthcoming ADR report would estimate that a VTO interceptor should weigh at least 33,000lbs at take-off and then it could work only by using the highly restricted XJ53-GE-X10 engine Ryan planned to use. This included a 2315lb military load. ADR pointed to some possible weight savings. For example, if the sighting system was reduced to a bare minimum (APG-30 range-only radar plus visual), weight could be only 28,000lbs – which was still far more than Ryan proposed. It might also be possible to cut structural weight by careful design. Overall, ADR recommended that the jet VTO programme begin with a non-tactical test aircraft, to be followed by a tactical aircraft once handling problems had been resolved. The BuAer powerplant division pointed out that the XJ53-GE-X10 engine had been engineered for a high thrust/weight ratio which precluded full-throttle operation near sea level. It could gain power only by operating its afterburner at less than full throttle, to avoid putting too much stress on the engine proper. At sea level the best it could do would be 17,800lbs thrust, a kind of tailoring which would probably soon be common in high-performance engines. The engine might also never be produced; its only projected application was the 1956 air force interceptor. GE was therefore concentrating on the heavier (7500lb) J53-GE-1; the 50-hour test on the –GE-10 engine had been deferred to early 1955. Worse, Ryan could not use the –GE-10 engine as designed, because its accessories were in the wrong place; it would need a new engine, with a special diffuser-plenum chamber which would have to be specially developed.

53. As described in a 1 November 1956 Bell report, D-188 was powered in level flight by two J79s. A 'Verti-Pack' of nine vertically-mounted J85s would provide lift in combination with diverter valves for the two main engines. The J85s would always operate at maximum thrust, vertical power being modulated by throttling the two main engines. Eight of the J85s were paired, placed at equal distances fore and aft of the centre of gravity; the ninth engine was at the centre of gravity. In this brochure Bell specifically rejected rotating engines, which it had used in a test vehicle, as suitable only for short-light engines. It also rejected a rotating afterburner, which might be associated with a more powerful engine required for high level speed. This report did, however, mention as a rejected configuration a version with rotating wingtip engines (afterburning J85s in this case), the main propulsion engines having valves and piping allowing diversion of their thrust (without afterburning) downward.

54. From BuAer notes of weekly progress in various aircraft programmes, RG 72. As of April, Bell envisaged a six-engine aircraft with a maximum speed

of Mach 2 and a combat ceiling of 67,000ft. The presentation was made late in February 1957. Bell received a go-ahead letter about 18 March 1957. Both J83 and J85 were air force engines and the air force was expected to decide which would proceed. Since the Fairchild J83 was larger, Bell designed around it; the J85 would fit within those dimensions. The air force chose the General Electric J85 for its T38 trainer and thus decided the engine issue (the XJ83 never went into production). The chosen engine for the D-188A was the J85-GE-5.

55. The basic description in RG 72 Entry P7 is dated 4 September 1957.

8. A NEW KIND OF THREAT

1. We now know that the specification for KS was issued on 8 September 1947. The Tu-4 carrier flying at 400–1500m would detect a ship at a range of 100km (54nm) and it would launch the missile at 60km (32nm); the missile would reach a speed of 950km/hr (510 knots). The Komet project consisted of Kometa I (electronics on board the missile), Kometa II (the guidance system on board the aircraft and Kometa III (the missile itself). KS was first successfully fired at a ship on 21 November 1952 and it was accepted for service in 1953, the Black Sea Fleet beginning system integration in June. Its conducted its first operational tests in 1954–5, fourteen of eighteen missiles hitting their targets. When Khrushchev referred to the shock of learning of anti-ship missiles, which convinced him that the *Sverdlov* class cruisers were worthless, he was referring to these tests. He probably witnessed the sinking of the old cruiser *Krasni Kavkaz*, which had had been fitted with huge radar reflectors so that she would simulate the radar signature of a carrier. Some Russian writers have mentioned speculation that the demonstration was helped by placing large charges aboard the cruiser. Tests of the Tu-16KS missile carrier version began in 1954 and it entered operational service in June 1957; two missiles were launched simultaneously from a bomber in 1958. Because KS had been designed for the slower Tu-4 bomber, to fire it a Tu-16KS had to slow down to 420km/hr (initially to 360km/hr, but that was changed) to fire it. That was partly so that it could extend the radome of its Kobalt-M guidance radar, as KS flew down the radar beam. The aircraft also had to descend to 3000–4000m to fire. Effective range was 35–45nm, although rated range, which was used by the West, was 55nm (the range limit was set by the need for the guidance system to capture the missile in its radar beam). Because the missile was command-guided, the bomber had to stay with it, slowing further to 320km/hr and remaining on course for three to four minutes. The radar lacked frequency stability, so only one of a group of aircraft could launch at a time (launch aircraft had to be at least 90° apart). An improved KS-G had increased range (140–160km) and could be launched from greater altitude. It also had retractable wings to reduce air resistance. These limits seem not to have been known to Western navies at the time, but the 55nm figure was known. KS was developed as a coast defence missile and it was tested as a ship-to-ship missile from the cruiser *Admiral Nakhimov*.

2. The Soviets placed their version of FX-1400 in production. The Soviet Ministry of Agricultural Production tested Hs-293 from a Tu-2D bomber in 1948 and may have assisted the Czechs in their attempts to place it in production. Neither project was known in the West. The Ministry of Agricultural Production developed a follow-on to Hs-293 it called Shchuka (Pike), the initial version being the command-guided '1948 torpedo' (Shchuka-A). The '1949 torpedo' version had a radar seeker. These were light bomber weapons; the specification for Shchuka requiring a range of 15–20km at an altitude of 2km (about 6500ft), with a speed of 320m/seconds (about 620 knots). After tests in 1951–5, Shchuka was reoriented as an anti-ship weapon (Soviet KSSh, NATO SS-N-1).

3. Initial requirements were two or three times the launch range of KS, launch altitude closer to that of the carrier aircraft and double the missile speed. It was also to be capable of flying a complex path to the target, including a final low-altitude leg. The missile was developed by the MiG design bureau, which designated it K-10S (a parallel strategic missile for Tu-95 'Bear' bombers was K-20). Work on a KS follow-on was authorised on 3 February 1955, the K-10 project being approved on 16 November. K-10S (Snaryad) was the missile proper. Carriers would be both the Tu-16 and its supersonic follow-on, then designated Tu-105 (but built as the Tu-22 'Blinder'). As designed, the missile had a range of 180 to 250km (97–135nm) and a speed of 1700–2000km (up to 1250mph) carrying a 1000kg warhead (twice the weight of the KS warhead). Instead of diving directly to the target after being launched at 11,000m (about 36,000ft), it would dive 1000–1500m, then climb back up to the bomber's altitude. The bomber would order it into a second dive 105km from the target, the missile levelling off at about 1000m (3280ft). Its own active radar seeker would lock on at a range of 15 to 20km. The missile was first launched (unguided) on 28 May 1958 and the system was accepted into service on 12 August 1961. A total of 220 Tu-16K-10s was built, compared to about 100 Tu-16K.

4. On 2 April 1956, before K-10S had flown, Berezhniak was authorised to produce a version of KS using his rocket engine. That reduced body diameter enough to increase missile speed to 1200–1250km/hr, about Mach 1. The rocket left enough space for a 950kg K-10S warhead. The initial guidance system was that of the K-10S missile. The operational version (KSR-2) had an enlarged radar dish, adopted after problems were revealed in 1958 tests at Feodosiya. Range at high altitude was about twice that of KS, 180 to 230km. The entire system was designated K-16, 'Badgers' fitted with it being Tu-16K-16s. This version was accepted into service on 30 December 1961 and in February 1962 it was decided to re-equip 'Badgers' armed with KS. There was also an anti-radar version, authorised in 1957, which became the K-11 system ('Badger Gs' fitted to launch it were designated Tu-16K-11-16).

5. This system was developed by Raduga, the Berezhniak design bureau. The K-22 missile control system and the Tu-16K missile carrier projects were presented early in 1960 and approved in March. The prototype Kh-22 missile was completed in 1962. It was a true fire-and-forget missile, capable of locking onto a target before it was dropped by the bomber. Kh-22 was normally launched at 10–14km (36,000–46,000ft), climbing to a cruise altitude of 22.5km (about 75,000ft). The missile used a mid-course guidance autopilot and a terminal radar, which was normally activated about 80nm from the target. At that point the missile began a 3° terminal dive. Minimum range was 70nm (the missile had to distinguish its target in the 10nm it ran from seeker turn-on to minimum range). A bomber flying at 950km/hr (513 knots) at 10km altitude (33,000ft) could hit a target at a range of 350 or 400km (the latter was 216km). A supersonic bomber (1720km/hr [929 knots]) at 14km altitude (46,000ft) could hit at 550km (297nm).

6. Development was ordered in August 1962 and there was an anti-radar version (KSR-5P).

7. Information provided under the CFE (Conventional Forces in Europe) agreement credited Tu-22M2 and –M3 bombers with an ability to detect targets at 150 to 200km, but these may have been land rather than sea targets. The existence of the video data link associated with the Kh-22M missile was apparently first disclosed by a Russian account published about 2000. This version was typically launched at a low enough altitude to keep the attacking aircraft below the horizon of fleet air defences, climbing to 12,000m (39,000ft) and then approaching in a shallow supersonic (Mach 1.2) dive towards an attack altitude of 500m (1640ft).

8. Details of the WV-2 from Lockheed report MSR/103 of 1 February 1954 in RG 72 Entry P7, WV-2 Airborne Early Warning Aircraft – Aircraft Data.

9. APS-70 operated at 430 MHz, whereas an S-band radar like APS-20 operated at about 3000 MHz. APS-70A had twice the power of APS-20 (2 MW). With a 17ft x 4ft antenna (as in a WV-2) it could detect a 5m² target, a typical bomber, at 200nm. In 1956 plans called for a 30ft x 4ft antenna in the next- generation W2V-1 and a 24ft x 2ft antenna for a future carrier AEW aircraft of the mid-1960s, which became the E-2. As of December 1957, the single WV-2E was scheduled as the test platform for the automated ATDS system (the aerial node of the developmental NTDS fleet computer system), which ultimately was installed in the E-2 Hawkeye (it was to be returned to Lockheed for ATDS installation in mid-October 1958, evaluation being scheduled to begin in June 1959). Between December 1959 and June 1960 it was to be used to test the USC-2 air-to-air data link (Link 4) and a corresponding air-to-ground system.

10. RG 72 Entry P7 includes Lockheed's Report 9974-2 of 17 September 1954, a summary of its study of the CIC Patrol Aircraft problem. An earlier 1954 Report 9974 suggested the rotodome and the UHF radar. This report indicated, among other things, how a heightfinder could be integrated with the rotodome, as it was needed until the ultimate single ranging and heightfinding radar could be produced. The rotodome and its UHF radar were proposed as a solution to the early warning barrier problem rather than the fleet air defence problem, but the two were clearly related. The aircraft with the rotodome was designated CL-257-6, the -6A version having the heightfinding APS-45 integrated into the support for the rotodome. Lockheed proposed an interim arrangement in which two APS-20A antennas were mounted back to back in the rotodome while the ultimate UHF radar (APS-70) was developed.

11. A December 1956 prospective schedule in the BuAer compilation of weekly reports showed a planned first flight in July 1960, with Board of Inspection and Survey (BIS) trials between July 1962 and August 1963 and fleet deliveries beginning in October 1962.

12. BuAer Confidential VV correspondence Files Vol 6, 1946, NARA II. The basic letter includes the reference to the two OpNav letters, dated 4 August 1945 and 22 May 1946. It submitted an Aircraft Research Design branch feasibility study, ADR-39. A summary of characteristics was attached to the BuAer 17 July 1946 letter to OpNav. ADR envisaged a heavily-armed aircraft (a twin 20mm power mount in the nose and a quadruple 20mm power mount in the tail) capable of 421mph at 30,000ft using two 25D turboprops then under development. It would have a crew of seven, including pilot and co-pilot, a navigator and three fighter director and

control officers. The AEW radome would be retractable so that the aircraft could land on board a ship. Electronics would weigh 4063lbs, including the radar. With the radome retracted, stall speed would be 104.2mph, which was barely acceptable. Endurance at speed giving maximum range would be 9.9 hours; maximum range at 30,000ft would be 2810nm. This would be a large aircraft, with a folded span of 26ft6in (span 75ft) and a length of 53ft.

13. I have not found any account of a competition for this project and no proposals for these aircraft are included in the two proposal files in RG 72 in NARA II. The list of competitions kept by the NHHC Naval Air History branch does not include one for the AEW-CIC version of the single-package ASW aircraft. The S2U-1W is described in 'The Carrier Based Airborne CIC Problem' in *BuAer Confidential Bulletin* 2-51 (August 1951), pp 33–4. This article mentions a possible future stacked-beam AEW radar to solve the heightfinding problem. Bidders for the single-package ASW contract were Grumman, Central Aircraft, North American, Douglas, Convair, Chance Vought, Martin, McDonnell, Republic, Cessna, Northrop, Goodyear, Lockheed, Curtiss and Chase (which later made the C-123 transport). The number testifies to how thin the military market was before the outbreak of war in Korea. Bids were requested on 20 January 1950 and received on 17 April, the engineering recommendation following on 23 May and the award approved on 29 May 1950. The sixteen bidders offered twenty-four designs. The operational requirement (AS-04501) was issued on 8 August 1950, after the selection of the winner.

14. The RG 72 Mock-Up Report file includes a 1 December 1952 report on the mock-up of the XWF-1 and TF-1, both of which were based on the Grumman S2F. The mock-ups covered only the fuselages, since both used the S2F wing. A drawing of the WF-1, which was never built, shows a bulbous radome for its APS-20B radar above its cockpit. Its vertical tail has been somewhat enlarged and two smaller vertical fins have been added to balance the side area of the radome. The aircraft would also have carried an APR-9 radar intercept receiver. Two fighter controllers would have sat side by side behind the cockpit, looking aft, with APS-20B displays in front of them.

15. According to a US attaché report dated 30 November 1949 (in DCNO (Air) files, NARA II) the Admiralty and the Air Ministry were drawing up requirements for AEW, particularly to detect snorkels (the RAF had previously refused to consider buying such radars). In May 1949 the British had sent a mission to the United States to consider having BTH (British Thompson-Houston) make a version of the radar. By November that was no longer possible, as the British army had taken all BTH capacity for anti-aircraft fire-control radar. Hence the need to import aircraft and radars. At this point the AEW project still had to be approved by the Defence Research Policy Committee and it was unlikely to proceed unless it received an A-1 priority.

16. David Hobbs, *The British Carrier Strike Fleet After 1945* (Barnsley: Seaforth, 2015), 105–6. As a FAA pilot, Commander Hobbs flew AEW Gannets. His book includes a drawing (p 314) of a projected Gannet AEW.7 carrying a radome for the APS-82 radar used in the E-1B. It was associated with the project for a new carrier. There was also a much more ambitious proposal for an entirely new AEW aircraft carrying an FM interrupted CW radar.

9. A CRISIS IN FLEET AIR DEFENCE

1. *US Naval Policy for Fleet Air Defense*, 31 March 1948, issued by CNO, in CNO Chron File (Box 541), Operational Archives, NHHC. The 15 June 1950 edition is in Box 543. It did not change the basic policy, but it did include a directive that destroyers and larger ships should be capable of launching and guiding missiles and controlling aircraft. Apparently the missiles would be surface-to-surface weapons; a later clause singled out special ships using pilotless aircraft to destroy air targets.

2. Fleet Air Defense Priority, 7 November 1949, in CNO Chron File (Box 542), Operational Archives, NHHC. Further priorities, in order, were development of the Mk 65 target indication fire-control system; development of surface-to-air guided missiles (Terrier and Talos); continued development of air-to-air interceptor radars and controls for collision-course interception; increased effectiveness of existing air-to-air weapons and sights (including a lead collision sight); development of ECM; and development of the air-to-air Meteor missile (which was not pursued much further). Lower down the list were development of a carrier-based airborne CIC, which did not materialise for nearly a decade; the new Mk X IFF system; and IR sensors as a supplement to or replacement for radar.

3. Report of Queen Test 42 dated 14 May 1949 in RG 428 (OpNav records) formerly classified correspondence of DCNO 1948–51, Box 676. This file also includes the order (from OpDevFor) setting rules for the exercise, issued on 30 April. Planned participating aircraft were eight F4U-5 from VX-3 with APX-6 IFF transponders, available Banshees from AirLant and from Patuxent River, two PB-1W from VX-4, one P2B (B-29) from the Tactical Test unit at Patuxent, two P2V Neptunes and four air force B-50s or B-36s, but not all of them participated.

4. Fourth Partial Report dated 13 June 1950 in DCNO (Air) Formerly Secret file, RG 428 in NARA II.

5. With catapults set at 3100 psi, Banshee pilots did not consider launching safe with less than 35 knots of wind over the deck at a weight of 16,500lbs.

6. The plan sketched in OpDevFor report showed the CVL deployed towards the threat, with two command ships each 60nm away (and away from the threat), all three (and the main body, to the rear) receiving linked data from an AEW aircraft flying its racetrack path above the point between the four. Each command ship (and the CVL) was in touch with a radar picket destroyer (DDR) 80nm away. The station directly in the path of the threat would be occupied by two DDR. Between the DDRs and the threat would be AEW aircraft flying racetracks, down-linking radar data to them. Much further out would be four radar picket submarines, their radar coverage not overlapping either with each other's or with that of the task force; one was 200nm from the two-DDR station. This formation employed six DDR stations (two with two DDR each) and four submarines, plus three distant AEW (to cover the 180° threat sector) and another AEW over the force centre.

7. Report of Working Group for Review of OEG Report 61 to Air Defense Board in formerly Secret DCNO (Air) files, NARA II.

8. The DCNO (Air) file in NARA II contains a revised version of the planning figures as Annex A, Revised. The document is undated but surrounding documents show that it dates from 1949–50. It opened with the planning assumption that the Soviets could overrun Europe in 60 days.

9. OEG was later part of the present Center for Naval Analyses (CNA).

10. The 1955 results are from OEG Summary Report 3: *Fleet Air Defense Improvements*, 31 October 1956. It offered remedies which might be made before 1958, i.e. with existing technology. The first report was OEG Report 14, which extended analyses published in OEG 540 (1952 and 1953) and OEG 526 (air defence against low fliers).

11. *Combat Readiness* July–September 1953 issue, describing OpDevFor exercises against low fliers to support compilation of the forthcoming handbook (Naval Warfare Publication) NWP 23, *Air Defense*; NHHC Operational Archives.

12. *Combat Readiness* October-December 1955 issue, article on Fleet Air Defense, NHHC Operational Archives

13. The F2H-2 offered 2.9 hours directly overhead, the F9F-8 Cougar 3.3 hours (174 minutes on CAP overhead, 164 minutes at 100nm, 139 minutes at 380 knots). The F9F-5 offered 159 minutes directly overhead at 348 knots. The FJ-4 with four Sidewinders offered 2.4 hours endurance (124 minutes overhead, 106 minutes at 100nm and 75 minutes at 200nm, at 355 knots). On the other hand, the high-performance Skyray (F4D-1) offered only an hour endurance (51 minutes overhead, 31 minutes at 100nm and only five minutes at 200nm). It was the worst of the available fighters.

14. CNO memo dated 8 September 1949 in DCNO (Air) file, NARA II. It seems likely that the envisaged technology would have been a much-expanded equivalent to the Mk 65 fire-control (actually target-designation) system then under development. Mk 65 created a somewhat automated small-scale tactical picture as a basis for assigning weapons; assignment was to include an evaluation of whether the assigned weapon could hit the target. The associated special-purpose radar was the three-dimensional SPS-3. This combination was installed in the fleet command ship (actually command test ship) *Northampton*, the radar topping its after tower mast. The September 1949 memo listed references beginning in April 1946 as recommendations for aircraft intercept control and missile guidance systems. The AD number was part of a new system intended to maintain a systematic list of new development projects.

15. In 1958 CAL performed a Forward Pass study for BuAer. Forward Pass figured heavily in early studies of the Outer Air Battle, the idea being that the performance should go into the missile rather than the airborne radar platform – as in Eagle-Missileer. The problem was always bringing the missile into position for control to be handed over.

16. No IR system was envisaged, although in the early 1950s that had been advanced as a way of overcoming jamming.

17. Radar folder in RG 402 (BuWeps) RH-2 Fighter Design file, Box 3, Fighter Design Correspondence. A data sheet on the radar shows that, like other pulse-Doppler radars, it produced pulses at a very high rate, so its duty cycle (0.1) was much higher than that of a conventional pulse radar. As a consequence, its average power, which determined its effective detection range, was 2kW, but peak power on each pulse was only 20kW. For comparison, APS-20E, which was a very powerful conventional pulse radar, had a peak power of 2MW (a thousand times as much), but it produced 300 pulses per second, each two microseconds long – its duty cycle (the time it spent transmitting) was only 0.0006 and its average output was 600 watts, about a third of that of the APQ-81. APQ-81 produced 20kW pulses slightly wider (1.6 microseconds) than those of APS-20E, but at a rate of 62,500 per second.

18. The BuAer proposal file in RG 72 Entry P7 includes the June 1958 Bendix

brochure describing the missile and the supporting system, except for the radar.

19. The radars listed were the Westinghouse C-band pulse-Doppler radar (which became APQ-81), the North American APQ-75 and the Westinghouse APQ-72/74, of which only the APQ-72 entered service (on board the F-4 Phantom). As proposed by the Bendix/Grumman team, the tactical computer could accept either APQ-75 or -81 track-while-scan radar data (the arrangement with the -75 required an extra module). When the Bendix brochure was written in 1958, the Westinghouse radar was credited with the ability to track twelve targets simultaneously, but by 1959 that had grown to sixteen, presumably due to increasing computer capability.

20. This was actually a second round of proposals. In 1957 BuAer included a long-range missile fighter in its programme under the designation AWS-404. To help shape it, in July 1957 BuAer asked for comments from about twelve manufacturers; several replied. The series began with a meeting at Republic Aviation in December 1957. These contractor comments were presumably used to shape the requirements set for the long-range air-to-air missile, the competition Bendix and Grumman won.

21. Initially BuAer limited the competition to bidders with recent carrier aircraft experience: Chance Vought, Douglas, Grumman, McDonnell and North American. Boeing and Convair then asked to compete and were added to the list. Bell and Martin were later added. Six companies offered designs: Boeing, Chance Vought, Douglas, Grumman, McDonnell and North American. Three designs were modifications of existing aircraft: Douglas D-790 (modified A3D-2 with J79 engines and four external and two internal missiles), Grumman G-128E (an enlarged Intruder powered either by the J52 used in the Intruder or by the new TF 30 turbofan, with six underwing Eagles) and North American's modified A3J (high lift wing version with either a small-antenna Eagle system or a GAR-9 Falcon system). None was satisfactory. The A3D was considered too large, the modified Intruder too heavy and the modified A3J was considered entirely contrary to the Missileer concept. On flying qualities, Douglas and Chance Vought were preferred over Boeing and McDonnell, which in turn were better than Grumman and North American. Designs with internally-stowed missiles offered higher performance, but external stowage was preferred for access and for quick loading; performance was not as important. Of aircraft carrying their missiles externally, those which could leave the booster fins extended were preferred: Douglas and Grumman. A 12 April 1960 summary by the BuWeps Systems Analysis division indicated a general preference for straight wings (optimised for subsonic flight), missiles visible from the crew stations (who could be sure they had been launched correctly), rear-fuselage mounted engines, manually operated controls and avionics accessible during flight. Generally swept-back wings, internally-stowed missiles, pod-mounted engines, widely-spaced avionics (making for difficult maintenance) and tandem seating for the two-man crew were rejected. Only designs using the new TF30 turbofan came close to meeting the specification, particularly for loiter time. Three of them had 'Caravelle' engine arrangements (so-called after the French airliner, the first to have its engines under its tail; at this time it was also used in the Lockheed Jetstar and the North American Sabreliner). This is much the same arrangement as in the A-10. It offered simple installation and removal and flexibility for growth or change, as well as deck safety and less of a problem of ingesting missile exhaust gas. Of the Caravelle arrangements, McDonnell's Model 153A was eliminated because its weights were considered far too optimistic. Boeing's Caravelle configuration aircraft (its Model 835) used a swept wing, which was not needed for the Missileer mission but increased the potential for other missions (an early internal navy document indicated that the Missileer might also be used as an attack plane). Its mixed internal and external missile stowage was disliked. Missile ejection at a slight angle could cause problems, since the booster fins were not extended until after launch. Time on station was unacceptably low. Chance Vought's V-434 showed some good design features, including an excellent power plant installation, but they were overwhelmed by insufficient time on station. Extra fuel allowed for in the design would have increased loiter time only from 3.1 to 3.3 hours. Of the other three TF30 designs, North American Columbus offered CL-4166, a conventional straight-wing aircraft with two podded TF30s under a high wing. Grumman's G-128E was a modified A2F (A-6) with six underwing missiles. Douglas offered D-766, which easily won. Its high wing gave excellent access to the missiles and the fuel system was the simplest on offer. It required the least wind over deck. Only it and the Grumman design came close to the desired four hours on station.

10. THE COMPUTER AGE IN FLEET AIR DEFENCE

1. CDS is described in detail in its inventor's autobiography: Professor Ralph Benjamin, *Five Lives in One: An Insider's View of the Defence and Intelligence World* (Tunbridge Wells: Parapress, 1996). See also R V Alred (Admiralty Signal and Radar Establishment), 'Future Techniques for Displaying and Recording of Information in CIC', in 'American-British CIC'. C A Laws of Elliott Brothers, which made the equipment, gave a supplementary talk on the electro-electronic techniques used. See also Eric Grove, 'Naval Command and Control Equipment: The Birth of the Late Twentieth Century "Revolution in Military Affairs"' in Robert Bud and Philip Gummett (eds), *Cold War, Hot Science: Applied Research in Britain's Defence Laboratories 1945-1990* (Amsterdam: Harwood Academic Publishers, 1999). I am indebted to Peter Marland. See his 'Post-War AIO and Command Systems in the RN' in *Warship 2016* (London: Conway/Bloomsbury, 2016), pp 76–98.

2. The digital choice for DPT was probably inspired by successful Canadian demonstration of a digital link as part of their developmental DATAR digital combat direction system. DPT was Link I for the Royal Navy, it is probably why the US Navy's NTDS link was initially designated Link II and then Link 11 when Roman numerals for such systems were abandoned.

3. Target speed was not held in memory, but it was calculated and used for rate-aided tracking by the trackers.

4. The input portion of a CDS system was broken down into tracking groups each consisting of one detector, three trackers and one analyser, which together were considered capable of handling twenty-four tracks. The analysis display unit showed expanded parts of range-elevation and A-scan displays, making it possible to disentangle targets which might be close together.

5. An A-scope, the original type of radar scope, displayed only range but made it possible for an operator to see noise surrounding a target, which might otherwise obscure it. A B-scope showed range plotted against bearing (B-scopes were often used in gunnery).

6. The author remembers the pride with which the late J D Brown, who was a Royal Navy airborne radar operator at the time, recalled these trials. Brown was later head of the Royal Navy Historical Branch.

7. Despite its crudity, EDS was so badly needed that it was installed on board the four radar picket destroyers of DesDiv 262 at Norfolk between September 1958 and February 1959 (initial tests on board the destroyer *Willis A. Lee*, between 14 March 1956 and 10 May 1957 had failed). The associated SSN-21 data link could handle a 25-ship net. OpDevFor recommended that it be used only as an interim system, because the much better NTDS was coming. Operational Test and Evaluation Force report on EDS, Project Op/S480/S67 of 1 February 1960, Operational Archives. According to a contemporary ONR report, the advantages of EDS were faster detection (electronic feedback marked targets already being tracked) and faster and more accurate tracking (two operators could do thirty plots per minute and the board would display twenty-four plots in 24 seconds). The CIC using EDS was quieter, with less phone talk. As with CDS, the plot was immediately available to other stations: Flag Plot, CO Plot and Weapon Control Centers. Interceptors could be assigned rapidly. Perhaps above all, EDS could easily fit current CIC systems. Disadvantages were the 24-target limit and the requirement that auxiliary data be hand-plotted. In February 1955 CNO authorised procurement of twenty systems; soon EDS was seen as the interim predecessor to the new NTDS (in fact computers developed so rapidly that no such interim device was fielded).

8. The NORAD system was called SAGE (Semi-Automatic Ground Environment); it inspired numerous later NATO air-defence 'ground environments'. In each case the point of the system, as it had been with the filter rooms and the vertical plots, was to present the Command with a usable picture of the current tactical situation. SAGE helped launch the US commercial computer industry, because it required far more computers than any other application imagined at the time. Although solid-state electronics was coming into existence, the urgency of the SAGE system led to the use of much less reliable vacuum-tube machines.

9. There is apparently no declassified US report of LAMPLIGHT, but the report of the British delegation has survived as DEFE 7/2084.

10. The British LAMPLIGHT report describes the two-step EDS/DATAR plan. McNally probably submitted his NTDS concept to ONR after the conference. David L Boslaugh, *When Computers Went to Sea: The Digitisation of the US Navy* (Los Alamitos and Washington: IEEE Computer Society and ASNE, 1999) ascribes McNally's estimates to his knowledge of the Kamikaze problem, but more likely they were figures thrown out during LAMPLIGHT discussions.

11. Based on a 1999 interview with McNally recounted in Boslaugh, *When Computers Went to Sea*, p 121.

12. By 1960 work was proceeding to digitise WDS and fold it into NTDS.

13. The issue was how much data a single radio channel could carry. HF was limited by multipath: signals could take several alternative paths, the signals along them interfering at the receiver. The HF link was the primary 'A' link, using the HF surface wave extending out to about 180nm. Its messages consisted of computer commands (in machine language) and data. Some commands added or updated a track. Others were orders, e.g. to engage a given target. When the 'A: link was exported, governments objected that they did not want their ships taking commands from other

navies' ships. Computers on allied ships had some 'A' link commands disabled. The 'A' link required far more information capacity than a single HF channel (75 bits/seconds) could carry. The initial estimate of 1125 bits/seconds (fifteen channels) was doubled to provide overhead (control and management and error correction) to 2250 bits/seconds (thirty channels), but channels doubled up by using two polarizations. The link used 30-bit words to match those of the computers (six error-correcting bits and 24 message bits). These details were probably settled by 1958. The message technique required a computer to convert the radio signals into usable computer data and in turn the computer raised the cost of any 'A' link installation. The 'A' link was NATO Link II (Link 11). McNally was aware that older ships generally would not receive NTDS, so he proposed that the NTDS computer also generate formatted teletype messages for them (the 'B' link, later Link 14; the US Navy devised a means of turning these messages into automated plots). The TOR also envisaged a simplified UHF ship-to-ship link ('C' link, later Link 13). Limited to line-of-sight range, it did not require a complicated computer for reception, but it never entered service. A fourth link (later Link 4) controlled aircraft, as in SAGE. It used UHF and 70-bit words. The navy had become particularly interested in Link 4 because it could be used to command an aircraft into a blind landing, but it could also be used to control air strikes. Note that originally the NTDS data link was called TIDE (Tactical Interchange Data Equipment). A Canadian later wrote that the term was adopted because the Tide detergent used the motto that it would always clean up stains (TIDE would clean up the tactical picture). Captain (N) D N Macgillivray and Lieutenant (N) G Switzer, 'Canadian Naval Contribution to Tactical Data Systems and Data Link Development' in Commemorative Edition (1985) of (Canadian) *Maritime Warfare Bulletin*. The TIDE link was adopted for the British ADA system and also for the initial weaponised version, ADAWS after a 1954 British-Canadian-US conference on data links, at the time seen mainly as a way of connecting analogue systems with better (less noisy) links. Beginning in the autumn of 1962, the US Navy tried to convince NATO to adopt Link 11 as an alliance-wide standard. By 1967, when the NATO committee involved collapsed, the French, German and Italian navies had all adopted Link 11 and NTDS technology, in each case using their own software. The Royal Navy, which had been using Link 11 for ADA and ADAWS ships, became interested in a more austere link for ASW ships. Given the origins of the term TIDE, the British may have taken the name of their new link from the usual detergent commercial, in which the advertised brand beats 'Brand X'. In effect the British were saying that for many purposes Brand X – Link X – was good enough. Because the British used 24-bit computers, their Link X used 24-bit words. The Royal Navy adopted it as Link 10. The Dutch claimed that Link X was joint Dutch/British property because it used features they had adopted from the abortive Link 13. They adopted Link 10, as did the Royal Norwegian Navy and the Turkish Navy. Both the Dutch and the British had link ships with both Link 10 and Link 11 installations as gateways to Link 11 nets. Link X is historically significant because, unlike Link 11, it could be exported, becoming the first data link that many navies used (the export version was usually called Link Y).

14. Normally no one aboard ship would refer to particular targets by track numbers, which were not displayed. There was an unsuspected problem. Those on board a ship monitoring a situation would want to examine particular tracks, for example to see whether a particular aircraft was climbing or descending. That could not be seen on two-dimensional radar displays, but the system memory carried three-dimensional data. When *Vincennes* was in the Persian Gulf in 1988, she was monitoring air traffic out of Iran. Her CO asked what a particular aircraft, indicated by the track number his ship had assigned, was doing. By the time he was asking, that particular number had been reassigned (the aircraft in question had already been detected by the frigate *Sides* and both ships' computers adopted the number assigned by *Sides'* computer). It happened that a nearby battle group on the same Link 11 channel had used the same set of track numbers, contrary to accepted procedure (*Vincennes* had been assigned to the Gulf specifically to clean up Link 11 practice there). The number now referred to an A-6 landing on the carrier *Saratoga*, about 100 miles away. Told that this aircraft, identified only by track number, was descending rapidly (i.e. landing), the ship's CO thought the aircraft, approaching his ship on his display (which did not show track numbers) was about to crash his ship (he had been given reason to expect an Iranian attack). He engaged, with tragic consequences: he shot down an Iranian Airbus, which at the time was climbing, not diving at all. In the aftermath, there was considerable interest in new three-dimensional displays.

15. A list of planned 1962 installations is in Op-353/sjt Ser 060P35 of 8 May 1962 in Double Zero files, 9000 series, 1962, Box 10, Operational Archives. This list includes a description of an earlier policy paper, VCNO Ser 9456P34 of 23 January 1959. According to Boslaugh, the new-construction installation decisions listed here were made only in March 1962, when it was clear that NTDS was successful: three carriers (*Kitty Hawk*,

Constellation and *America*, all of which had Terrier missile batteries); the three *Albany*-class missile cruisers; the ten *Belknap/Truxtun* class missile frigates (DLG, later CG); and the nuclear frigate (DLGN) *Bainbridge*, which received NTDS in a post-completion refit.

16. 'Albany Recommissioned', *Naval Ordnance Bulletin* 1-69.

17. Based on a formerly Confidential paper in the NHHC Naval Aviation file on the WF-2 dated 27 February 1956, justifying procurement despite the ongoing AEW competition.

18. In the interviews making up his oral history, George Spangenberg talked angrily about what he considered an illegitimate political decision to award the contract to Grumman (p 170). Throughout, he was very concerned to maintain the honesty of the competitions. He accepted that sometimes the best technical proposal would be rejected on industrial grounds and its features handed over to the winner, but in his view the AEW competition went beyond what he would accept.

19. The BuAer compilation of weekly 'Items of Interest' clips in RG 72 includes a report of a 1957 redesign of the W2F to raise its rotodome and change it from a low-wing to a high-wing configuration (the new rotodome had to be partially retractable so that the aircraft could fit some carrier hangars). Raising the rotodome gave it very nearly its theoretical free-space (i.e. without any aircraft attached) range). Raising the rotodome made it possible to raise the entire wing, placing the engines much closer to the centre of gravity of the aircraft, eliminating the need to retract the landing gear into the wing (thus adding fuel space) and also clearing the fuselage for a more efficient arrangement. Another item in this file recounts the decision to replace the APS-70A radar initially specified with a General Electric radar capable of instantaneous heightfinding, which presumably became the APS-96 and its successors.

20. Data largely from the draft Programme Change Recommendation (PCR) for what became the E-2C, in the 'E-2 Background File' folder in Navair History Aircraft Collection Box 69. The PCR refers to this new programme as the E-2B, but it shows characteristic E-2C features.

21. C E Hutchinson and Edward J Thaubeld, 'E-2C/F-14A – A Formidable Team', Selected Readings for Naval Operations 1977 in NWC Archives RG 4. An E-2C could exchange data with NTDS on board a carrier at a rate equivalent to 28 targets/seconds.

22. A Naval Staff Requirement (NSR 7868) for ADA in all major ships was approved on 2 June 1959, with separate Staff Requirements for ADAWS in other ships. The CVA 01 version was NSR 7909, approved 15 November 1965.

23. *Eagle* had fifteen two-screen workstations (and one spare), three of which were used by direction officers. The latter could display AEW radar video. One console was in the general direction room, the others being in the operations and air defence rooms. There were four interception officers. Each screen could be switched to show raw radar video, markers, a combination of the two, remote AEW data or a tabular ('tote') display similar to that in CDS.

24. This version would have used three F1600 series computers and four drum memories supporting two plots, eighteen totes and twenty-four video displays (LPD: labelled plot displays). ADAWS 6 in *Invincible* and *Illustrious* had four plots, seven totes and eighteen video displays (*Illustrious* added three mini-totes). *Ark Royal* had ADAWS 10, which had ADAWS 6 displays plus eight mini-totes. Track capacity in ADAWS 6/10 was over 500. ADA capacity was probably 256, as in the contemporary NTDS. These were all central-computer systems like NTDS, all commands and data passing from consoles and sensors through the main computer. There were two types of console, a horizontal 22in LPD flanked by three keyboards, with a vertical 12in tote and a two-screen display (12in tote alongside 12in LPD) with one keyboard and a roller ball. A peculiarity of the British system was that most commands were entered using an alphabetical keyboard (in ABCD rather than QWERTY format) rather than (as in the US systems) by designated quick-reaction keys (the British special-action keys were programmed from the keyboard, if they were used at all). Reportedly the British human interface proved difficult to use under combat conditions in the Falklands. Ultimately ADAWS 6/10 was replaced by a distributed version called ADIMP or ADAWS Mod 1.

25. ADM 1/31081 refers to this paper and gives its chronology and its main results, but no copy seems to have surfaced.

26. ADM 1/26006, 'Diagrams for Defensive Fighters' dated 17 April 1955. This is a series of notes and diagrams prepared for Director of Navigation and Direction to support a study of requirements for the new carrier fighter.

27. This draft seems not to have surfaced. By this time RAE was studying defence against Mach 2 high-altitude bombers.

28. The 1955 paper gave a more expansive idea of what the Soviets might field in 1962–70, arguing that they would not be able to employ their best weapons against naval forces. Thus a threat section of the report predicted that they could have developed supersonic (Mach 2) bombers operating at up to 75,000ft, able to deliver nuclear weapons at a stand-off range of

400nm. Such aircraft might be expected by 1965. Bombers operating at lower altitudes would have subsonic speed. By 1965 the Soviets would also have Mach 2 reconnaissance aircraft, up to eight of which might be encountered in any one theatre.

29. It was assumed that one person could allocate six fighters per minute to targets. That would match the rate at which the carriers could launch fighters. The pilots of the first four fighters on each carrier would have to be in their cockpits on deck alert; pilots of the other eight would have to be ready but not yet in their cockpits.

30. Chronology in AVIA 65/731, for submission to the Americans in support of the project, but the original proposal was probably developed somewhat earlier.

31. This Staff Requirement (Issue 1) is bound in with the SR.177 specification file, AVIA 65/632. An October 1955 version increased climbing time to seven minutes.

32. The 1956 specification differed from the earlier ones in detail. The naval mission profile envisaged a 5.4-minute climb to 40,000ft, then a three-minute cruise at Mach 0.9, acceleration to Mach 1.4 in about a minute during a climb to 60,000ft, then the 2 G turn at Mach 1.4, a 1.5-minute run-in to attack at 60,000ft, a 60nm run back, descending from 60,000ft to 40,000ft in seven minutes, a further descent to sea level in five minutes and 20 minutes of loiter between sea level and 1000ft. Total sortie time would be 45 minutes. Time to climb from pressing the starter on the catapult to 60,000ft at Mach 1.4 was four minutes. Sustained speed was Mach 1.4 at 60,000ft, with a burst capability of Mach 2 at that altitude. As in the earlier specification, the aircraft was to be able to operate at 75,000ft for a minute. The parallel RAF specifications were similar, but distinguished between a case of 220nm early warning and one of 400nm early warning. In the latter case the aircraft would carry drop tanks. The two versions also differed in the fuel they would burn, AVCAT for the navy, AVTAG for the RAF.

33. The July 1955 draft specified only pursuit-course missiles, but one of the commentators on the draft indicated that Blue Jay Mk 3 should be specified. It was to be suitable for launching at up to Mach 1.7. It would have the best possible altitude capability, but just what that would be was not known. Mk 1 was capable of 15G at 45,000ft and 8G at 55,000; Mk 3 should operate higher, but until aircraft capable of flying above 50,000ft were available for trials, no figures could be given. At 75,000ft its turning capability should be very limited, however.

34. ADM 1/29134, 'Future of the P.177 Aircraft', file dated 16 November 1956. The comment on cancellation is from a 23 November note by Head of Air Branch in the Admiralty.

35. AVIA 65/731. US letters in the file mention a previous agreement to fund development of the Orpheus turbojet, which powered the Folland Gnat light fighter (not adopted by the British, but exported) and also the NATO light fighter contenders including the winning entry, the Fiat G-91 (ironically, the British later adopted the Gnat as a fighter trainer). The implication was that the US government was being used not to support British defence as such but rather to support British defence exports. Reference to the Germans cannot have helped. The project was ultimately submitted to the US Air Force, which had its own vested interest in the German order which eventually led to adoption of the F-104 by the German air force. Nothing in the British file suggests any suspicion that such motives were involved.

36. ADM 1/31081, which is labelled 1957 but includes the 1956 papers. The final report of the Working Party was dated 12 September 1956, when P 177 was in trouble but still very much alive.

37. Presented with the report, the Admiralty Board decided that it might be unwise to circulate it even among senior flag officers, because recent government decisions (the Sandys White Paper cuts) would preclude providing even the acceptable minimum system defined by the Working Party. The confidence of senior flag officers in the administration might be shaken and it might have a similar effect on the Commonwealth and US Navies. Worse, the Minister of Defence might conclude that since the navy would be unable to defend itself properly, it might be cut further. Board Minute 5222, 24 April 1958, in ADM 1/31081. The report itself was classified Top Secret Discreet UK Eyes Only.

38. The elements of the 1957 system which had survived the White Paper cuts were the Scimitar day fighter, the Sea Vixen all-weather fighter (with the Blue Jay missile), Skyraider and later Gannet carrier AEW aircraft, picket destroyers (converted from 1943 'Battles'), Type 984 radar with CDS (48/32 track versions) and the DPT data link, Sea Slug and various gun systems and the Green Light (Sea Cat) short-range missile, plus improved radio and ECM. Much of this equipment was expected to be in service about 1960. The report devoted considerable space to radio warfare in the ship-air battle.

39. According to the post-Defence Review preface to the Working Party report, 'if it is necessary on grounds of expense to fall below the standard of the 1970 Air-defence system, then . . . the effect of such a policy will be to

enable our enemies to deny increasing areas of the world to us by the mere threat of sophisticated air-borne weapons …it will not be possible for a reduced fleet of obvious ineffectiveness in war to maintain even an adequate level of police activity'. The Defence Review cancelled the only projected navy long-range surface-to-air missile, the Blue Envoy (Stage 1¾) and in 1957 there was no plan whatever to provide the fleet with a long-range guided weapon. The post-White Paper preface to the Working Party report does not make any connection between the Blue Envoy cancellation and the cancellation of the missile cruiser planned at that time. The post-war Royal Navy did not have the option, which the US Navy of this period enjoyed, of having large existing cruisers which could be converted into long-range air-defence missile ships. Its surviving Second World War cruisers were generally too small and the largest of them were badly needed for Third World operations, hence could not be spared for reconstruction. There is no evidence of projects for major missile conversions of existing cruisers during this period (cruisers had been considered and rejected as Sea Slug platforms). The decision (announced in the White Paper) to discard the four *King George V* class battleships eliminated them as a possibility and presumably they would have been too expensive (in manpower terms) to operate. Aside from some quick Sea Slug studies of the early 1950s, no studies of battleship missile conversions appear to have been made.

40. The Working Party assumed that AEW aircraft would have to be supplied by the United States. The existing APS-20E was inadequate. The options were a scaled-up Super Constellation (WV-2) or later turboprop design, with radar aerials perhaps 35ft across (presumably the W2V with its APS-70 radar) or a shipboard aircraft with aerials about 17ft6in across (presumably the new WF-2 with its APS-82 radar). A large shore-based aircraft could detect medium supersonic bombers at about 200nm at all heights and in all sea states, but it was susceptible to jamming by small light-weight jammers and heightfinding would normally be inadequate. It might have a supplementary 100nm centimetric heightfinder, but that would easily be saturated. A force of seven land-based aircraft would be needed to keep one continuously airborne, though four (three serviceable) would do for reasonably short operations. To the Working Party, pickets were far better, as it would be 'imprudent' to assume that they would be available when needed and also because they would need fighter protection. A carrier AEW aircraft, about a tenth the size and cost of the land-based type, was likely to be far better. However 'it could not be counted upon at this stage, even if we had the dollars to buy it or the resources to copy it; although feasible as a weight-lifting proposition, its controllability has not yet been studied'. Douglas was then claiming 200nm detection range for a 35,000lb carrier AEW aircraft, but the Working Party dismissed this 'sales' figure and estimated that carrier AEW detection range would not exceed 100nm under favourable conditions; 'American assessments cast doubt on the aircraft's ability to detect the Mach 2 bomber at all under unfavourable conditions. But at least it ought to detect BEAR, which is its most important task'. The Working Party dismissed the possibility of an airborne equivalent to CDS, which was exactly what the US Navy was then planning in the form of ATDS on its new AEW aircraft (E-2). Without it, but using simple intercept computers, an AEW aircraft could close-control two fighters per intercept position and it would probably have three of them.

41. AVIA 7/3699. The underlying Admiralty staff paper has not apparently surfaced. The request was dated 11 November 1958.

42. The Blue Parrot radar of the Buccaneer had a 30in dish, but the aircraft's nose did not provide for the scanning movement of the 30in AI 18 dish (50nm range). A possible development of the Blue Parrot radar on board the Buccaneer would give 25nm range. AVIA 7/3699 includes correspondence on alternative Cassegrain antennas which scanned by moving a secondary reflector, which in turn reflected the radar beam onto the main (fixed) dish. This file includes a summary of the current and near-term radar situation as of 1 June 1959, based on visits to RRE Malvern and to ASWE Portsdown, the latter being responsible for shipboard radars. It credits AI 18 (29in dish) with a clutter-free 75 per cent probability of picking up a Canberra viewed head-on at 28nm and more than 38nm had been achieved against a B-47. Studies indicated that AI 18 could be improved to the point of detecting such targets at 50nm in a clutter-free zone. The improved version would use a new antenna and an associated computer for multiple-target tracking (TWS). By 1970 a coherent pulse-Doppler or CW radar might be available using a 36in dish and a higher average power of 500 W (compared to 200 W for AI 18 and AI 23). A somewhat later note described a radar then being developed by Hughes with a much higher mean power (5kW – ten times that of the proposed radar) using pulse-Doppler techniques; the 25-fold increase was expected to improve detection range by a factor of 2.5. The Hughes radar also had a 40in dish, which was expected to offer a further factor of 2 improvement in range. That must have been the forerunner of the AWG-9 radar. A range of 90nm might be achieved over a land mass, the worst possible operating environment. In a clutter-free area range might be as great as 120nm. The

best existing AEW radar was the US APS-96 of the E-2A; the Admiralty was considering it for a future British AEW aircraft. It had moving target indication (MTI). On board an aircraft at 30,000ft, it was expected to detect a low-flying 15m^2 target at up to 185nm. With parametric amplifiers, which would be available in the expected time frame, it would gain 30–50 per cent in range, hence would be able to see a target all the way to the radar horizon (208nm from 30,000ft).

43. AVIA 7/3723, which is part 2 of the study of a future fighter/strike aircraft for the Royal Navy, includes the April 1959 Joint Staff Target (OR 346) for the variable-geometry (swing-wing) fighter.

44. The significance of the tail-less design was that a swing-wing normally pitched up because the centre of lift moved away from the centre of gravity as the wing sweep varied. A tail could be co-ordinated to balance this change. Vickers hoped to solve the problem in an aerodynamic way, which would yield a much better aircraft. No such tailless swing-wing aircraft was ever built. The US swing-wing aircraft, then being tested in wind tunnels, had a conventional tail and a simpler structural design. A British report characterised the US design as more flexible (presumably meaning it could accommodate a much wider range of loads) and therefore would meet various roles, i.e. high altitude fighter, high/low strike and ferry. 'They were a little frightened of the structural problems associated with the Vickers design'. A British representative to NASA had been told that a fixed wing (non-swing) design could be developed for some sorties, but not all with a single design. The Vickers design would weigh 48,000lbs in the strike role and 53,000lbs as an interceptor. A brochure was submitted in October 1959. There was a parallel US design, probably by NASA rather than an aircraft company. The US design had two J79s, the Vickers design four RB 153s (a scaled-down Spey: 6850lbs thrust or 11,645lbs with afterburning). At this time Vickers claimed that at Mach 1 the US engines had three times the specific weights (presumably fuel consumption) of the RB 153 and that at Mach 2 the factor was probably six. Time to accelerate from Mach 0.7 to Mach 2.5 was 2.6 minutes for the US design vs 4.5 minutes for Vickers (1.5–2 minutes for Vickers with rockets). The payload of the US design was 2000lbs of bombs and 4000 of equipment compared to 6000 and 4000lbs for Vickers. In limited war the US aircraft would carry weapons externally. The US design seems to have been a precursor to the F-111. In the interceptor role on CAP the Vickers design offered the required four-hour endurance at 40,000ft, with a dash to Mach 2.5 or 3. Take-off weight would be 51,000lbs (the navy wanted 50,000 as an upper limit). The endurance allowed for fuel for one wave-off and 20 min loiter. By early 1960 the Vickers design incorporated small lift engines to maintain trim.

45. ADM 1/29155.

46. In March, the Chief of Air Staff wrote to First Sea Lord rejecting the navy's position. This joint project had been brewing since at least 6 December 1961, when the Defence Committee discussed a supersonic development of the P1127 (the first Hawker VTOL) to meet the needs of both services. The Minister of Defence was to submit a formal requirement. In mid-December the Chiefs of Staff defined the projected aircraft as a supersonic fighter/ground attack type to meet the NMBR 3 NATO requirement and to enter service about 1969–70. NMBR 3 was a VTOL strike aircraft, the VTOL capability imposing about a 50 per cent penalty (increase) in all-up weight and a similar increase in cost (later that was changed to 30 to 80 per cent addition to weight and cost); the VTOL requirement also limited it to a single seat and to a short low-level radius, which the navy estimated would be only about 250nm with a 2000lb bomb load (at that range the Buccaneer would deliver four times the payload). Given the agreement reached in December, Chief of Air Staff argued that the navy staff had to co-operate in writing a joint requirement. The Ministry of Defence was already working with the Ministry of Aviation, a Working Group to develop a submission for NMBR 3 having been formed. At this point the most promising competitors for the NATO project were the Hawker P.1154 and the French Mirage IIIV, the latter using separate lift engines.

47. The Admiralty initially preferred the BAC Vickers 584 to the P.1154; but the Ministry of Aviation considered the P.1154 the best British competitor for NMBR 3 and it was the main subject of Admiralty attention. The other competitor was the Fokker Republic Alliance (sometimes listed as the Fokker Republic D24), which was derived from the Bell D-188A which had competed a few years earlier for the US Navy's VTOL fighter requirement. This aircraft was actually built and tested by Fokker-VFW as the VFW 191, with partial US Navy sponsorship. The P.1154 and Mirage IIIV were front-runners because they were closer to completion than the others. A mid-July comparison between the P.1154 and the Vickers 584 showed that the latter offered a greater strike radius with the same payload, more time on CAP with the same weapons load (with or without external fuel) and a much longer ferry range. The P.1154 could meet the four-hour CAP requirement only with full internal fuel plus drop tanks. RAE saw growth potential in the Vickers design but not in the P.1154. By this time there was so little real commonality between the RAF and RN versions of the P.1154 that the naval version was expected to cost 50 per cent more than

the RAF version.

48. A British analysis dated 3 August 1962 is in the ADM 1/29155 file. By this time the competition had narrowed to the P.1154 and the Mirage IIIV. The French had committed to the Mirage, but were worried because they could not afford to go on without partners. They were said to be alarmed by the American attitude and by the 'drift of European nations' towards the P.1154. Canada had no interest in an aircraft of this type and Italy wanted something simpler (like the P.1127). Belgium preferred the P.1154 on economic grounds, but had not made a firm commitment. Germany and the Netherlands were unable to choose at present, but expected to be able to do so later on; they wanted the NATO programme to survive. The United States had withdrawn its earlier offer to support an advanced NMBR 3 which had secured multi-national support. The stated reason was that neither aircraft met the full (over-ambitious) specification, but it seemed that they were stalling while clarifying their policy and their own national needs. As the British saw it, the threat to the P.1154 was more American than French, because the Americans were still wobbling from interest in the P.1154 to a redesign of the Fokker-Republic D 24 which had already been eliminated from the NMBR 3 competition. 'The hint of American funds implicit in this latter possibility inevitably dazzles the Dutch and perhaps also the Germans and Canadians. The Americans may thus find it convenient to let the French wreck NMBR 3, justifying their own desertion of it by organising support for a later, more sophisticated aircraft.'

49. The two requirements did not quite match, the OR 355 aircraft being considerably larger. It required a greater radius of action by about 400nm and twice the supersonic dash (400nm vs 200nm). It was also required to be able to land vertically and have a short take-off run (2500ft). Early in 1963 the Naval Air Department estimated that it would be about 20,000lbs heavier, so fewer would fit on board the 50,000-ton carrier, if indeed it could be made carrier-capable at all. DNAD thought that the 400nm requirement corresponded to expected European conditions and that it would not apply to the navy's main concern of overseas operations. It was possible that the Air Staff could be convinced that even in Europe the 400nm requirement was excessive, hence that the OR 355 aircraft could be pared down. Naval Air Department thought that by using variable geometry and blown flaps OR 355 could be made to operate from a carrier without any need for lift engines. The 400nm supersonic dash was also required for the US TFX and in both cases the desired run-in probably corresponded to the distance from the inter-German border to key Central European targets.

50. Memo to First Sea Lord, 12 June 1963, in ADM1/29154. CDS also said that the Minister had recognised that there was no money to be saved by cancelling the carrier programme 'if we are still going to have a world-wide military deployment. I hear however that Sir Burke Trend has, on his own initiative put in a paper to the Prime Minister which is weighted towards Little England and offering the cancellation of the carriers as one good way of saving money.'

51. When negotiating the Phantom purchase in March 1964, the British delegation sought compensating US purchases of British technology. At this point the P.1154 was offered as the planned replacement for the Hunter, but it was probably already dead as far as the RAF was concerned.

52. In January 1964, when the British fact-finding mission visited Washington, two further versions were being considered. The F-4K was an F-4J with an inertial navigations system (ASN-44) in place of the ASN-39 air data system, a dive toss bomb computer, a lead computing sight and a radar-warning and homing system. The F-4L was an F-4K with improved J79/J1B engines with higher thrust and better fuel economy, a new high lift wing with increased area and more boundary layer control and enlarged tailplane, 600-gallon internal wing tanks and reduced-pressure tires. It seemed unlikely that the US Navy would approve the F-4K, because the US Navy did not believe that a quick-reaction interceptor under close radar control needed an inertial navigation system, which would have to be aligned as the aircraft waited on the catapult if a high degree of accuracy was wanted. The British commented that the USN had not given much thought to the fighter in its autonomous role and that it accepted the accuracy of the F-4B Doppler navigation system (4 per cent of distance flown) for ground attack. The F-4L had not been given serious consideration and it seemed unlikely to receive any unless TFX ran into serious trouble. F-4L seems to have been an early version of the upgraded series of versions Navair explored using a contract with McDonnell. In the event, the F-4K designation was given to the British naval version of the Phantom, the F-4L designation was reserved and the F-4M was the RAF version.

53. The Royal Navy radar was designated AWG-11, the RAF equivalent being AWG-12. The original British report quoted the US Navy as crediting AWG-10 with 100nm detection range on another Phantom, with lock-on at 40nm. It had an alternative pulse mode for air-to-air interception and also for in-flight refuelling and for visual identification. There were also

air-to-ground mapping, terrain following and navigation modes. The radar also provided CW energy to guide the Sparrow missile. Fire control was by an analogue computer.

54. The F-4J deployment plan was limited to *Eagle* and *Hermes*, as in 1964 the Royal Navy was also operating *Victorious* and *Ark Royal* – the latter eventually operating Phantoms. The plan written in January 1964 envisaged operation from *Eagle* in 1970–2 prior to a special refit, then in *Hermes* from 1972 after a special refit, in the first of the new carriers (replacing *Ark Royal*) from 1973 and in 1974 from *Eagle* after her special refit, which would eliminate landing limitations. *Ark Royal* received a limited refit to allow her to operate Phantoms, but *Victorious* was discarded before that became an issue.

55. ADM 1/29055, covering Phantom acquisition. It includes the report of the first fact-finding mission. The report of the second is ADM 1/29048. Both included Captain Eric Brown RN, the famous test pilot, who at the time was Deputy Director of the Naval Air Division.

11. THE VIETNAM ERA

1. This account of the F-111 story is largely based on Robert F Coulam, *Illusions of Choice: The F-111 and the Problem of Weapons Acquisition Reform* (Princeton: Princeton University Press, 1977). Coulam worked largely from the reports of extensive Congressional Hearings and his deductions of technical issues were made partly on the basis of the aviation press and partly from a series of anonymous interviews. Unfortunately navy documentation of the F-111B story has not been released, apart from a few reports on the unsuccessful weight-saving programme. Interpretations are all the author's own.

2. Spangenberg, p 213, states that the TFX became Project 34 in an early list McNamara kept of vital projects. The driver was a claim that merging the air force and navy projects would save a billion dollars. In Spangenberg's account of the disaster, a recurring theme is the unfortunate results of an air force bureaucracy nearly always willing to tell McNamara what he wanted to hear. To Spangenberg, the air force also resisted compromises that might have made the programme work. McNamara had served in the Army Air Force during the Second World War and he may have been more comfortable (and much more familiar) with its culture than with the more free-wheeling one of the navy. Spangenberg also emphasises the gross ignorance of the aircraft development process on the part of McNamara and his staff. For example, during 1961 instead of the usual three months to write a specification, the navy was given two weeks and a total of one month to write the formal Request for Proposals. Also, the navy requirements were embodied in an air force 'work statement' rather than the usual naval form. As an example of bizarre bureaucratic procedure, two or three days before the Request for Proposals was due to go out (1 October 1961), Spangenberg was called by DCNO (Air) Rear Admiral Pirie and asked to attend a meeting DDR&E had called. It was to consist only of high-level civilians. Spangenberg was there only because the navy's Assistant Secretary for R&D was out of town. He was the most senior man. This meeting was, bizarrely, to approve the work statement; Spangenberg was the only one in the room who had seen it, because he was also the only man in the room from the working level. He suggested that the meeting be postponed until that evening to give the others a chance to read it, but the reality was that none of them could evaluate it. DDR&E himself, Dr Harold Brown, appeared about a half-hour late and his first words were 'Well, what have they done to us now,' meaning that 'they,' the services, had once again tried to derail the brilliant plans of the Office of the Secretary of Defense. As the most senior naval air technical man (and a key man in aircraft procurement), Spangenberg found himself at many of the critical meetings during the F-111B fiasco. He was called to testify during the first, classified, Congressional investigation but was never interviewed by authors writing about the F-111 mess. His main theme is outrage that a technical process was so badly politicised and therefore that the integrity of the procurement system was so badly damaged.

3. This possibility does not appear in Coulam's account and the thoroughness of his research suggests strongly that it was never suggested, at least publicly. Coulam does associate the high supersonic speed demanded of the TFX at high altitude with a requirement that it function as an air-superiority fighter, but that seems ludicrous given its sheer size; its smaller predecessor the F-105 was never used as an air-superiority fighter and it seems likely that by 1959 the air force no longer considered that mission very meaningful. By approaching its target at low level and high speed, the TFX would evade enemy fighter opposition altogether. The navy followed much the same logic when it bought the Intruder and on the eve of the Vietnam War it too had lost interest in air superiority.

4. Spangenberg explains VFAX as a navy attempt to find an alternative to a programme already obviously doomed. One possibility was to accept one F-111B squadron on a carrier for fleet air defence plus three OFR (Other Fighter Requirement) squadrons for roles such as fighter escort, close air support, etc. That in turn led to VFAX, which was defined as a fighter in

about the weight class of the F-4 with a variable sweep wing, matching the F-4 as a fighter and the A-7 as an attack plane. Cost-effectiveness studies showed that one squadron of F-111Bs and three of VFAX was better than two of F-111Bs and two of A-7s or two of F-111Bs and two of VFAX. The navy maintained the position favouring the F-111B/VFAX mix for about a year and a half.

5. According to Spangenberg, the first round eliminated four bidders. Both air force chief General Curtis LeMay and CNO Admiral Anderson wanted to retain the two surviving competitors. The evaluators were very unhappy with the designs. The Secretary of the Air Force (approved by higher authority in OSD) directed a second round. Contractors had been told their deficiencies on the first round, a standard practice so that they would improve their offers. By that time the air force had held its separate engine competition and had ruled out a GE engine, which was not even under contract. Unfortunately, without it the contractors had an even worse time. It did not help that standard air force practice in such competitions was to tell contractors that they had a problem in some area, but never to tell them what it was (for example, a contractor would not be told whether he was higher or lower than the expected cost). The second round was even worse. The services recommended separate aircraft, but unsurprisingly they were told to go to a third round. It was very short; they were to report the differences between their air force and navy aircraft to get something satisfactory. General Dynamics produced something thin, as might be expected given the available time. Boeing produced a new design, which offered much more to the navy. Unfortunately when this round ended the air force said that it wanted more low-altitude dash range, which it thought had been better in the initial round. The navy group knew that the air force would need more range and that it would end up adding fuel and weight, to the detriment of any navy version (that happened two or three months after the contract was signed, about 10,000lbs being added – which, in Spangenberg's words, 'sent shockwaves' through BuWeps). On the fourth round, Boeing's proposal was the same and it was acceptable to the navy. It was larger and heavier than the navy might have liked, but it was usable. According to Spangenberg, the navy expected the programme to fail and it did not want to be responsible. The air force officers from TAC also considered the Boeing design superior; 'we thought we had probably achieved our goals of letting the Air Force take credit for the selection decision. After all, they had responsibility for the management of the programme.' Unfortunately, the selection board reported not that it much preferred Boeing, but that it had no significant preference between the two. Spangenberg does not say why, only that he has long regretted signing that statement. It seems that he signed as a way of avoiding navy responsibility for the selection in the expectation that the air force members would choose the right aircraft. He wrote that the air force's culture of secrecy in contracting probably contributed to the selection reversal. That left open the possibility that senior air force officers were well aware that McNamara would favour General Dynamics. Throughout Spangenberg's description of what happened a consistent theme is that the air force always tried to agree with McNamara, to the extent that it buried disappointing reports.

6. The initial round of hearings was triggered when Senator 'Sco-op' Jackson of Washington, Boeing's home state, asked for an investigation of how the contract had been awarded. As he began the investigation, Senator McClellan, chairman of the Senate Permanent Subcommittee on Investigations of the Committee on Government Operations, asked Deputy Secretary of Defense Roswell Gilpatric not to sign the contract. Gilpatric told the air force to go ahead. The contracting officer who did sign was never told of McClellan's request. When McClellan asked service witnesses to testify, McNamara issued a directive telling them to co-operate with McClellan 'to the fullest degree'. That surprised Spangenberg, but he seems to have been naïve: McNamara expected the witnesses to understand that they should be anything but actually co-operative. He and other navy witnesses took McNamara at his word and, according to Spangenberg, 'Every time we co-operated we got SecDef into more trouble which then annoyed him no end. He had elected at the beginning of the [first series] hearing to have the services present their position and then he was going to come in on that fifth or sixth day and clear up all the confusion and expected to wind up with a laurel wreath, I guess.' This series of hearings was dropped when President Kennedy was shot. Failure to reach any conclusion about corruption led the committee to examine the logic of the TFX programme award. In Coulam's view, the hearings forced McNamara to defend the TFX programme more rigidly than he need have done and thus reinforced his determination to force a common air force-navy programme: Coulam, *Illusions of Choice*, p 63. Spangenberg pointed out that several of those who had testified and embarrassed McNamara found themselves moved out of Washington, though not demoted and therefore in no position to complain. Shortly after testifying that Boeing's aircraft was better, CNO Anderson resigned to become Ambassador to Portugal. DCNO (Air) Rear Admiral Ashworth was suddenly given command of the 6th Fleet. Spangenberg listed others and wondered whether the list repre-

sented McNamara's vindictiveness.

7. Spangenberg recalls writing a 5 February 1964 letter recommending that the navy stop work on the F-111B until it could be redesigned to meet its requirements (Spangenberg oral history, p 238). He was told that instead a weight improvement programme would be continued. Contractors were asked through the air force SPO (System Project Office) to provide studies for a fall-back design. General Dynamics offered four designs in the SWIP (Super Weight Improvement Category). Grumman offered more detail on a design they called CWIP (Colossal Weight Improvement Programme) with a new fuselage. It saved considerably more weight. The decision was to continue with SWIP as the least costly alternative and to hold the contractor to his schedule and make some management improvements.

8. Coulam, *Illusions of Choice*, p 241, quotes a breakdown of the added empty weight including 4608lbs of miscellaneous – unidentified – additions, presumably the additional weight inevitably added every time part of the aircraft turned out to be heavier than expected. The miscellaneous items amounted to about half of the overall weight growth.

9. Specified take-off weight was an already-heavy 62,788lbs, but the production version was expected to weigh 79,000lbs, 20 per cent overweight. As a consequence, it would have needed 19 knots of wind over deck to take off (compared to a -8-knot requirement allowing a carrier to steam away from the wind). To land on, the F-111B would have required 12 knots rather than 5 knots of wind over the deck. Loiter time would have been three rather than 3.5 hours and loiter altitude would have been 30,000 rather than 35,000ft. Coulam, *Illusions of Choice*, p 243, lists the take-off weights of contemporary naval aircraft for comparison: 47,000 to 56,000lbs for the F-4J; 70,000 to 73,000lbs for the A-3B; over 76,500lbs for the RA-5C; and 72,566lbs for the F-14 with maximum missile and bomb loads.

10. Grumman Anti-Air Warfare, Status Report No.1, covering the period 11 June through 11 September 1965, in RG 343 Entry UD-WW 301 Box 3. This box includes the sets of vu-graphs Grumman circulated (it is impossible to say who saw or received them).

11. Coulam, *Illusions of Choice*, p 75. This was the F-14 proposal.

12. RG 343 Entry UD-WW 301 Box 3, NARA II, with other General Dynamics slides.

13. The aircraft companies were Boeing (July 1964: High-Performance General Purpose Aircraft Study. State of the Art), Douglas (July 1964: High Performance General-Purpose Tactical Aircraft Study) and North American (October 1964: Preliminary Report, Attack vs. Multi-Mission Aircraft Study). Later McDonnell added a fourth study (April 1966: 1975–80 Fighter/Attack Aircraft Advanced Planning Study). The powerplant study was by United Aircraft (January 1965: Analytical Study of V/STOL Propulsion System Requirements). Despite its title, the United Aircraft report included conventional aircraft. At about the same time there were several analyses of the requirements of a new attack aircraft (VAX), which became the A-7. The North American report is not listed among VFAX documents, but its timing fits the claim that three aircraft companies submitted studies before 1965.

14. The programme was laid out in 1966 NAVAIR vu-graphs. At that time the plan was to form thirty VFA squadrons, eight VFS squadrons, fifteen Marine squadrons (VFMA), two navy training squadrons (CRAW) and two Marine training squadrons (VMT). The first procurement would be three aircraft in each of FY68 and FY69, followed by sixteen in FY70, 116 in FY71, 204 in FY72, 232 in FY73, 240 in FY74 and 228 in FY75, after which it would tail off to ninety-six in FY76 and twenty-six in FY77, for a total of 1164 aircraft. Nothing remotely like this happened.

15. Based on NAVAIR (AIR-503) papers prepared for the President's Science Advisory Committee (PSAC) in March 1967, in the RG 343 Test and Evaluation file. In retrospect it is extraordinary that by this time the navy could openly propose VFAX as a way of killing the odious F-111B and also that it could state that the original plans for F-111B procurement were already being cut back. NAVAIR also had to explain why VFAX was not a VSTOL; it cited studies showing that even when carrier decks were damaged VSTOL exacted too high a performance penalty.

16. VFAX material is in RG 343 (BuWeps) Test and Evaluation material (UD-WW441) Carton 6 in NARA II. This is from Technical Development Plan 11-06 for VFAX, 18 February 1966, Vol 1, formerly Confidential.

17. According to the TDP, the three engine contractors were GE, Pratt & Whitney and Curtiss-Wright. Because the engines were associated with a VTOL programme, all had high thrust-to-weight ratios (10.1:1 for GE, 9.74:1 for Pratt & Whitney, 9.83:1 for Curtiss–Wright). All were turbofans, though with low bypass ratios (respectively, 1.41, 1.27 and 1.5). Thrust (dry/afterburning) was, respectively, 8685lbs/15,330lbs, 7660lbs/14,850lbs and 7500lbs/13,600lbs. All had only seven compressor stages, two fan stages and high and low pressure turbine stages (two of each except for Curtiss-Wright, which had one high-pressure stage). As an example of greater efficiency, GE proposed to do the same amount of work in its compressor per pound of air flow as in the J79 in three fewer stages at 30 per cent less weight, with 5 to 6 per cent greater efficiency; it saved

weight by using titanium in all rotor stages. Pratt & Whitney's engine was derived from that planned for the US supersonic transport (SST), which in the end was not built.

18. The TDP was revised during 1967, which is why the design studies submitted that year were all labelled as tentative.

19. According to Spangenberg, this idea was first suggested by Fred Glockler of BuWeps. Spangenberg recalls a discussion with a group of Grumman people: 'the more you looked at the total situation the more you became convinced that a better solution would be to get a new fighter that would carry Phoenix and still have enough performance to do the other fighter missions.' That was VFAX plus Phoenix. Spangenberg recalls that Grumman came up with the initial studies and that they were attractive.

20. Although conceived, like other US naval fighters, as a dual-purpose interceptor and bomber, F-14 aerodynamics initially precluded bombing: bombs were reportedly sucked back up into the tunnel between the bottoms of the engines (some suggested that the bombing problem was exaggerated at the time, since ground attack was not really an important mission). Work to revive the F-14's conventional bombing capability began about 1989. Tests showed that the aerodynamic problems had been exaggerated and all aircraft had their four fuselage weapons stations modified so that they could carry bombs instead of Phoenix missiles. The result was called a 'Bombcat'. It became more important with the collapse of the A-12 and successor A/F-X programmes and with the 1993 decision to retire all A-6Es by 1999: the 'Bombcat' provided some of the long-range punch previously associated with the A-6. The first operational 'Bombcats' were two squadrons (VF-14 and -32) deployed in October 1992 to the Eastern Mediterranean aboard *John F Kennedy*.

21. RG 343 Entry UD-WWW 441, Box 10 (Test and Evaluation), Grumman Contract Definition Report for the F-14B (Installation of the Advanced Technology Engines in the F-14A), Section 3: Performance, undated (but this box includes a January 1970 Contract Definition Report). Note that the prototype F-14A first flew on 21 December 1970; the F-14B upgrade was planned from the outset. Both engines were lighter than the TF30 but more powerful. At sea level the TF30-P-412 engine was credited with a thrust (non-afterburning) of 9825lbs (19,493lbs afterburning). Comparable figures for the ATEs were 11,856lbs/26,321lbs for the F400 and 10,680lbs/26893lbs for the F401. With either engine, Grumman's guaranteed maximum speed with four Sparrow missiles was Mach 2.4. Supersonic combat ceiling was, respectively, 60,900ft and 61,400ft and constant altitude acceleration time from Mach 0.8 to Mach 1.8 at 35,000ft was 1.31 minutes. Manoeuvre capability for a buffet-free turn at 35,000ft at Mach 0.9 was 2.22G. The F-14B was expected to offer a fighter escort range of 500nm and a loiter endurance of more than two hours. Compared to the F-14A, it would be faster, with a greater ceiling. Maximum speed would be limited not by the engine but by the need to avoid major structural changes in the airframe.

22. The meaning of what was seen was somewhat obscured because Soviet ships stowed their missiles in closed canisters on deck. In 1970 the Soviets were beginning to deploy a new generation of surface combatants consisting of 'Krivak' class frigates and 'Kresta' class cruisers. Many of them had relatively short canisters which were assumed to contain a new short-range anti-ship missile, which NATO designated SS-N-10. In fact they contained an ASW missile comparable to the Anglo-Australian Ikara, though it did have a secondary anti-ship mode. The surface fleet's concentration on the growing Soviet surface fleet obscured the reality that the Soviet navy did have a kind of capital ship core in the form of the fleet of missile-carrying bombers – which could be dealt with only by long-range fighters carrying long-range air-to-air missiles.

23. Vu-graphs for a 1967 talk entitled 'What Should An Escort Fighter Be? Summary of Lessons Learned With Air-to-Air Engagements in Viet Nam' are in the VFAX folder in the RG 343 Test and Evaluation material in NARA II. Sources were Project Red Baron (Weapon System Evaluation Group), Nellis Air Force Base Tactical Analysis Bulletins, the DoD Operations Review Group and pilot interviews.

24. The vu-graphs included graphs comparing F-4C (air force version of the navy F-4B) performance with that of the MiG-17 and MiG-21 at various speeds and altitudes. Superiority or inferiority was measured in terms of excess thrust at two G-loadings, 1G and 5Gs. It appeared that the F-4C was clearly superior to the MiG-17 under 1G conditions. Under 5G conditions, it was still superior over a large area of subsonic speeds, particularly at low altitude and at all supersonic speeds (as the MiG-17 was subsonic). Under 1G conditions the F-4C had a considerable area of advantage at low altitude. Under 5G conditions, it still had a significant advantage at low altitude and high speed. Thus it was possible for F-4Cs to find combinations of speed and altitude at which they were always superior, though that was more difficult against a MiG-21 than against a MiG-17.

25. Probably the most prominent was Colonel John Boyd, who discovered energy-manoeuvrability as the key factor in air-to-air combat. He had been a fighter pilot in Korea and he also discovered the 'OODA Loop'

(Observation-Orientation-Decision-Action) cycle, which is widely used in the United States, as a description of warfare explaining such outcomes as the defeat of a stronger French army by the Germans in 1940. Also extremely important was Pierre Sprey, who claimed that he had invented the lightweight fighter. His December 1971 testimony before the Senate Armed Services Committee on the Weapon Acquisition Process is in the NAVAIR ACF file, marked 'very valuable F-18 history'. At this time Sprey was manager of the systems division of Enviro Control, Inc. He had worked for System Analysis in OSD for five years, between January 1966 and December 1970. He contrasted the rising cost in air-to-air fighter kills, from about $20 for 0.50-calibre machine guns in Korea to $7000 for a Sidewinder and $40,000 for a Sparrow; to the opposite trend in kills per attempt through Vietnam. He also noted that the very simple Sidewinder had performed far better than the complex Sparrow. Sprey felt that he had good data on Soviet fighter costs which showed that the United States was now paying about four times as much as the Soviets for a first-line fighter. The gap seemed to be opening further, which was disastrous, because the United States was trying to maintain something like parity in numbers of fighters in Europe. Sprey divided fighter cost into avionics, propulsion and airframe and he considered avionics the source of most of the problem: between 1945 and 1970 the factor of increase (in 1970 dollars) had been about 1000 (with additional maintenance costs) compared to about 50 for propulsion and 40 for airframe. Some of the avionics escalation was due to additional equipment not really essential in combat (as in a MiG-21 or a Mirage III); some was due to demands for military standards when commercial equipment would have done as well (and often far more reliably) at a much lower cost. He also charged that engine developers had pursued technology beyond the point at which it made for better aircraft performance. He thought adequate engines could be bought for a third of their current cost. Current military engines had about a quarter of the life of their commercial counterparts. Overall, in Sprey's view the pressure for the last 1 or 2 per cent of performance was driving prices. So was the cost of installing over-elaborate avionics, which might account for three-quarters of total avionics cost. Fighters were also expensive because of the demand for maximum speed, yet in combat fighters never flew at Mach 2, because that took too much fuel and gave the pilot too little time to fight. Sprey thought a viable fighter could be built for half the price per pound in half the size of current aircraft. He recalled his 1968 OSD project for an austere fighter called FXX, i.e. an alternative to the FX then being developed into the F-15. It offered 140 per cent better turning capability than the F-4 and 110 per cent better acceleration, where the normal steps in fighter development offered 20 to 40 per cent improvement and then in only one aspect. It was also considerably smaller at 25,000lbs (Sprey thought that it could have been pared to 15,000lbs). It was also considerably less expensive than an F-4, $2.2 million when produced in a quantity of 250. Testimony brought out the fact that Dr Sprey's version of optimisation was predicated on a single mission, shooting down MiG-21s. His austere fighter proposal was informally considered and rejected by both NAVAIR and its air force equivalent. At the Senate hearing, NAVAIR analysis was cited to show that Sprey's data were grossly overoptimistic, for example as to thrust-to-weight ratio and wing loading. At the hearing, Senator Howard Cannon of Nevada, a Second World War airman, attacked the austere fighter (as represented in Vietnam by the F-104) for serious drawback such as an inability to survive in the face of modern air defences (SAMs) and for insufficient range.

26. In his oral history, Spangenberg regarded the prototype idea as badly misguided. He considered the Corsair the last aircraft truly prototyped. All others had been developed concurrently – production engineering had been done while the prototypes were built and they were used for development, not to test whether a design was adequate. Spangenberg considered current engineering capacity quite sufficient to show whether an aircraft would work. However, elsewhere in his oral history he points to gross failures of Air Force engineering due to what he saw as an illogical vertical work structure (the most important SPO would gather the best in every discipline, ultimately leaving the dregs). Spangenberg's case in point was the very inexperienced weight estimator assigned to TFX, in which weight was so important. Spangenberg also suspected that the real point of the programme was to allow the air force to buy the lightweight fighter that the 'gum on the windshield' fighter enthusiasts wanted. Spangenberg was also strongly opposed to the high-low idea, arguing that it was actually more expensive to split the fighter force between two types. Buying fewer high-end aircraft would run up their cost and buying two types would add considerable logistical and training costs. However, high-low was intuitively attractive and it could not be killed. In a world in which politicians and some admirals wanted to kill what they saw as the gold-plated F-14, high-low kept it alive by offering them less expensive companion aircraft. To Spangenberg, that was merely a suicidal compromise, since the likely enemy was hardly going to build low-end aircraft to fight US low-end aircraft.

27. The Advanced Prototyping Programme was the subject of a special Senate Armed Services Committee Hearing held 9 September 1971, parts of the transcript of which are in the NAVAIR file on the Advanced Combat Fighter (which became the F/A-18). The programme seems to have been the particular brainchild of Deputy Secretary of Defense David Packard, who pointed to reliance on paper studies as one of two causes of excessively expensive and unsatisfactory programmes. The other was concurrency – the practice of beginning production before development was complete. The F-111 (not just the -111B) could be seen as the poster child for these problems. It had been ordered from a paper design, even though it embodied radical changes in aircraft practice, particularly the swing-wing and afterburning turbofans. Its really disastrous aerodynamic problems, which were mostly associated with its engines, had been completely unanticipated. The navy part of the FY72 programme was divided between ASW sensors, weaponisation of ships and VSTOL for the Sea Control Ship, of which the latter was more than half the total. Attractive future projects (presumably for the air force) were an advanced medium STOL transport (leading to the YC-14 and -15), a very low radar cross-section test vehicle, a small lightweight fighter and a quiet aircraft. Note that the reference to radar stealth was in the public version of the transcript. Its length (19ft) was public, but its wing span was deleted; the air force had demonstrated new radar-absorbing material in the laboratory but had not flight-tested it. The object at this point was not to build a manned aircraft but rather a stealthy drone. The air force prototyping budget for FY72 was $24 million, compared to the navy's $20 million and of that the allocation to the lightweight fighter, $10 million, was the same as the navy's allocation for the VTOL fighter.

28. Testimony by Under Secretary of Defense for R&E Dr Malcom Currie before the House Appropriations Committee, April 1974, in the NAVAIR Air Combat Fighter file in NARA II (RG 343 UD-WW-230). Other testimony in the package showed that the air force had not been particularly happy with the ACF idea; it doubted the value of a visual-only fighter and pointed out that the Soviets, the wartime enemy, had also recognised the need for longer detection and tracking range. An anonymous NAVAIR commentator wrote on the cover sheet that the programme had originated with OSD (Office of the Secretary of Defense) and not with the air force. It was by no means clear where the lightweight fighter would fit in the air force's structure.

29. In connection with the LTV challenge to the navy choice of the Northrop fighter, in June 1975 NAVAIR produced a chronology of the Naval Air Combat Fighter (NACF) programme. Its data are supplemented by some dates provided by Rear Admiral Feightner (NAVAIR) in a 1974 hearing. On 22 June 1973 Deputy Secretary of Defense Clements wrote to the Chairman of the House Armed Services Committee asking for approval for the navy to begin its own fighter prototype programme in FY74 (he turned the project down, but the parallel Senate committee was friendlier). A February 1976 NAVAIR memo reported that Clements had previously asked for prototypes of a stripped-down F-14X and a carrier-suitable F-15N, the latter apparently recommended by CNO Admiral Zumwalt (analysis showed that the F-15N would require sufficient changes to make it carrier-capable that it became quite expensive. The Senate Armed Services Committee rejected Clements' idea and instead recommended that the navy consider an entirely new aircraft as a complement to the F-14. In August 1973 the Secretary of Defense directed the navy to pursue a lower-cost alternative to the F-14 and the navy began the appropriate studies. This new aircraft was designated VFAX, indicating that it was envisaged both as a fighter and as an attack aircraft to replace the existing A-7E. A Specific Operational Requirement was written and the plane was designated VFX during the FY75 budget review cycle. In May 1974 the Deputy Secretary of Defense testified before the Tactical Air Power Subcommittee of the Senate Armed Services Committee describing VFAX as a supplement to the F-14, a replacement for the F-4 Phantom, and ultimately a replacement for the A-7E. The navy wanted 400 such aircraft to supplement the 313 F-14s the planned. The supplementary fighter had to be superior to the F-4J and also it had to have significantly better reliability and maintainability. An improved F-4 proposed at this time offered the same range as the F-4J, slightly less speed (by Mach 0.18, to Mach 2.02) and 20 to 25 per cent better lift coefficient (increased G capacity within the flight envelope) as well as significantly improved high angle of attack control. Compared to the lightweight fighters, the F-4 had significantly better ordnance load (the lightweights could carry 4000lbs of bombs) and ability to operate autonomously. The lightweight fighters generally had higher thrust-to-weight ratio and lower wing loading, hence better manoeuvrability; they were also superior in acceleration. The improved F-4 had a slight advantage in combat range and weapons control over any of the proposed lightweight fighters. They were likely to enjoy considerable advantages in reliability and maintainability. Testimony by Dr Currie (1974) mentioned a stripped-down F-14 without Phoenix as well as variants of the YF-16 and YF-17 and an entirely new fighter. At some point CNO Admiral Zumwalt

held out the possibility that the navy might buy a version of the air force F-15, but in Congressional testimony that was shot down; among other things the aircraft would need 35 per cent of its structure redesigned to take the stresses of carrier operation and as a result an F-15(N) would be far more expensive than an F-15. In 1974 the House Armed Services Committee wanted VFAX abandoned on the ground that the navy had not adequately justified a need to augment the F-14 and also that it had refused to adopt a derivative of one of the air force lightweight fighters. The committee was, however, willing to entertain an FY76 request (which would be made in 1975) if the navy could demonstrate both that it needed a new fighter and that the lightweight prototypes would not be adequate. In contrast, in June 1974 the Senate Armed Services Committee supported the whole $34 million the navy had requested. The conference committee left $30 million in VFAX funding in the FY75 Authorisation Act, so VFAX survived. In June 1974 the navy released a presolicitation notice to fourteen aerospace companies seeking a review and critique of its requirements; it expected to release a request for proposals in September 1974. Responders were General Dynamics (Convair), General Dynamics (Fort Worth), Grumman, LTV, McDonnell Douglas, Northrop and Rockwell International. The House Appropriations Committee soon recommended eliminating the $30 million because the navy was not buying one of the two air force prototypes and the final Appropriations Act passed in August 1974 eliminated VFAX. However, the Senate Appropriations Committee favoured VFAX and on 28 August 1974 CNO released a formal VFAX Operational Requirement. NAVAIR was directed to prepare a solicitation for Contract Definition and Full-Scale Development (FSD). On 3 September the air force solicited FSD proposals from its two lightweight fighter contenders. That month OSD directed the navy to limit itself to derivatives of the two air force designs. The FY 75 appropriations (as opposed to authorisation) Act included $20 million for the VFAX programme. McDonnell Douglas entered into a teaming agreement with Northrop on 2 October 1974 LTV and General Dynamics had a similar agreement on 25 October. In each case one company would be prime contractor if the air force selected its aircraft, the other if the navy but not the air force selected its aircraft. Since the lightweight fighter was an air force project, it was Air Force Systems Command which on 12 October 1974 asked for quotes for FSD of the navy's version. The navy received technical briefings from both navy fighter bidders on 10 January 1975.

30. This document is in the RG 343 file on the Naval Air Combat Fighter. Generally parameters were given as minimum (threshold) and goal. Fighter escort radius on internal fuel was to be 400–450nm, which compares to an earlier requirement for 300nm. No CAP endurance was specified. Strike mission radius with four Mk 83 bombs was 550nm. Usable subsonic load factor was 7G/7.5G. Specific excess power at Mach 0.9 and 10,000ft with maximum thrust was 750ft/sec/850ft/sec. Acceleration from Mach 0.8 to Mach 1.6 at 35,000ft at maximum thrust was 110/80 seconds. Service ceiling was 45,000ft/50,000ft. Approach speed for carrier suitability was set at 125/115 knots and deck spotting factor 1.1/1.0. Freefall weapons delivery accuracy was 8/6 mils. Armament would be two Sparrows, two Sidewinders and a gun. The fighter version would have a track-while-scan radar with non-co-operative identification capability. The strike version would need ground map and air-to-air search and track capability, manual terrain avoidance/following and beacon modes. Other strike sensors were to provide laser spot search and tracking; a passive sensor capable of detecting a 'Komar' (missile boat) size target at sufficient range to enable the pilot to identify and attack it on the first pass at night; and also a projected map display system (PMDS) to tell the pilot where he was. 'To enhance the multi-mission capability of the VFAX, it is essential that integrated multi-mode displays including a HUD be incorporated', flexible enough for upgrading and for use in various missions. The aircraft also needed a reliable inertial platform compatible with a data link carrier alignment system and with inflight alignment capability and it had to be compatible with the automatic carrier landing system. At this time the envisaged programme was more than 800 aircraft.

31. The schedule listed in a January-February 1972 Senate Armed Services Committee hearing on the FY72 programme called for a first flight testing 18 to 26 months after go-ahead, which would have meant between December 1973 and June 1974. The five companies were Boeing, Lockheed, Northrop, General Dynamics and LTV.

32. The only US user was the navy, which used the F-5 to train its pilots to fight dissimilar aircraft. As of April 1974 Northrop had sold 618 F-5As, 145 F-5Bs, eighty-nine RF-5As and eighty-four F-5Es. The version which would otherwise have been designated F-5G was designated F-20 instead; it found no buyers. The F-5 itself was a fighter version of the standard air force T-38 supersonic trainer. In 1974 Northrop was seeking customers for a next-generation fighter it called the P-530 Cobra. Its P-YF-17 was a developed version (its model P-600). The Congressional testimony compared average FY75 flyaway costs. An F-4E, the air force version of the Phantom, cost $4.2 million, as did the YF-16. The YF-17 was expected to

cost $5.2 million (costs were based on a 300-aircraft programme). By way of comparison, an F-5E cost $1.7 million. These figures made the two Air Combat Fighter alternatives direct replacements for the F-4 (though much less expensive, it was hoped, to operate). Costs and capabilities of the F-14 and F-15 were not listed. Speed data redacted from the public version of the hearings showed that the YF-16 could attain Mach 1.2 at sea level and Mach 2 at altitude; the YF-17 could make Mach 1.1 at sea level and Mach 2 at altitude. The F-4E was rated at Mach 1.15 at sea level and Mach 2.05 at altitude. As a measure of manoeuvrability, the wing loadings of the two prototypes were, respectively, 62lbs/ft^2 and 58lbs/ft^2, compared to 73lbs/ft^2 for the F-4E and 72.5lbs/ft^2 for the F-5E.

33. The Government Accounting Office (GAO) had reported that it was half the design life of the F-4 and F-15. At the hearing, the committee was told that the F-15 had a 4000-hour design life with a scatter factor of 4, so that it had to pass a 16,000 hour test to insure that it could fly for the 4000 hours. The air force version of the F-4 had a design life of 3000 hours with the same scatter factor, but was being strengthened to 4700 hours.

34. As stated in written testimony before the House of Representatives Appropriations Hearings for 1975, a copy of which is in the NAVAIR file on the Air Combat Fighter in NARA II.

35. Northrop marketed the fully land-based version as the F-18L and about 1978 it found a launch customer in Iran (which wanted 250 of them). The fall of the Shah the next year killed the programme. Customers (Canada and Switzerland) who have bought the Hornet for land use have bought the fully navalised version.

36. The VFAX type specification was TS-169, presumably in the same series as earlier OS and TS specifications. NAVAIR received technical proposals on 2 December 1974. In its rejoinder to LTV's claim that the evaluation had been biased, NAVAIR pointed to the sheer complexity of the process, as LTV submitted twenty-five volumes of technical details and McDonnell Douglas submitted thirty-one volumes. By way of contrast, a typical fighter submission of the early 1950s was about five volumes plus drawings. In the 1975 case, the evaluators reported problems which the two contestants were asked to solve. In the end, the unresolved problems of the F-18 were structural strength and suitability in the attack role; high approach speed; concurrent engine development; expensive R&D; and limited growth potential, of which limited growth potential was probably the most serious. For LTV the problems were far worse: few performance thresholds met, carrier suitability was considered a high risk, combat survivability was judged very poor, growth potential was limited (as in the F-18) and R&D would be expensive. LTV was invited to offer additional design data. Data already submitted on the V-1602 had been limited and LTV was invited to submit greater detail – which did not solve its problems. Ultimately the assessment was that the McDonnell Douglas 267 was acceptable in all areas except carrier suitability performance, which was judged marginal. The final V-1602 was considered unacceptable in combat performance (marginal in cruising performance) and in carrier suitability and mechanical systems. Its armament was considered marginal (the F-18's was acceptable) and its survivability was unacceptable (F-18 was rated unacceptable to marginal in this respect because there was no means of isolating damage to one engine from the other; NAVAIR also doubted the survivability of any pure fly-by-wire system).

37. The NAVAIR rejoinder to the LTV protest includes brief data on the alternatives offered by LTV/GD and by McDonnell Douglas/Northrop. At this point the McDonnell Douglas Model 267 (which became the F-18) was expected to weigh 20,583lbs empty compared to 16,940lbs for the F-17. It was slightly shorter but had longer-span wings (37.5ft vs 35ft) with substantially greater area (400ft^2 vs 350ft^2) but the same tail. Its flaps had considerably greater travel ($35°$ vs $25°$) for higher lift during a carrier landing and it had single $45°$ slotted flaps and drooped ailerons (the F-17 had plain flaps and no drooped ailerons). In place of the J101-GE-400 engine it had the developed equivalent, the F404-GE-400 (originally designated J101-GE-100). LTV offered V-1600, -1601 and -1602. Like the F-18, all would have been heavier than the F-16. The version actually offered to the navy, V-1602, would have weighed 20,311lbs empty, 32 per cent more than the F-16 (13,350lbs). It would have been considerably longer (53.92ft vs 48.23ft), with longer wings (35.94ft vs 28.98ft) of greater area (300ft^2 vs 260ft^2) and a considerably larger tail. The normal full-span leading-edge flaps of the F-16 would have been supplemented by full-span Krueger flaps and the usual trailing edge flaperons would have had more than twice the travel ($50°$ vs $20°$). All versions of the F-16 had blowing boundary layer control. Engines would have varied. The navy pointed to considerable differences between the LTV designs and the F-16 compared to relatively minor ones between F-17 and F-18 to belie LTV's argument that the navy had been constrained simply to adapt the air force lightweight fighter; surely a constrained dein would not have felt it necessary nearly to double the horizontal tail area of the F-16 to produce a naval fighter (LTV had justified the larger tail to provide sufficient longitudinal controllability in the event of a missed landing). Both air force prototypes had employed con-

ventional high-lift devices, such as flaps, for slow-speed operations such as landing and take-off. The F-18 design slightly modified the leading-edge flaps of the F-17 and it showed somewhat greater modification of the trailing edge flap. The modifications involved (slotted flaps, drooped ailerons) were much less radical than the very complex leading-edge Kreuger flaps of the LTV designs, which were considered a reliability and maintainability risk. The proposed blowing boundary layer control for the trailing edge was another radical change from the relatively simple F-16, requiring air bled from the engine. The navy viewed the V-1602 design as almost entirely different from the F-16, showing that LTV had never tried to produce the envisaged derivative of a lightweight fighter. The F-18 was far closer to the F-17; the navy described it as McDonnell Douglas' adaptation of the F-17 to resolve deficiencies the navy found in it.

38. The F/A-18 file in RG 343 (NARA II) includes Navy replies to a further LTV proposal, submitted in the autumn of 1975, to substitute a version of the A-7E powered by an afterburning version of the aircraft's TF41 engine (B-32K) for the F-18. The improved A-7 would attain about Mach 1, far from the F-18 capability. Using LTV data, NAVAIR estimated that the F-18 could develop 25 per cent more sustained Gs and more than twice the specific power of the improved A-7 (subsonic at 10,000ft, with combat loading). The main impact of the new engine would an ability to sustain high G above Mach 0.7, which the navy doubted would much improve survivability. Inherent F-18 design features also offered better survivability. For example, the A-7 had a long duct to its jet engine, surrounded by fuel tanks. The F-18 had shorter ducts whose surrounding fuel would be used up before it entered combat. If the A-7 tanks were punctured, a hydraulic ram effect would dump fuel into the engine via the duct.

39. Based on a 15 September 1977 programme review for the Assistant Secretary of the Navy for Research, Engineering and Systems in the RG 343 Naval Air Combat Fighter file. This file includes a 3 November 1976 F-18 Programme Review for OSD (R&D)/OMB by C M Mitchell, the deputy project manager, which shows the differences between the F-18 and A-18 cockpits and an undated review by Captain H L Halleland, the project manager. His diagram describes the radar as multi-mission. Commonality is apparent in an accompanying briefing on the planned FLIR (forward-looking IR) sensor of the A-18, which is to be installed in place of the left-hand Sparrow missile of the F-18.

40. McDonnell Douglas wanted the aircraft named Banshee II, after McDonnell's earlier very successful fighter, but the navy chose to name it the Hornet.

41. The F/A-18 also carried a much smaller payload than the A-7E, but proponents claimed that would not matter very much because an aircraft could not make more than two passes over a heavily-defended area, meaning two separate shots with the current laser-guided bomb (multiple bombs could not be used because the first bomb would throw up so much debris that a second would miss the laser spot used to guide it). If what counted was radius when carrying a pair of 1000lb smart bombs. In that case the A-7E had about 100nm greater strike radius. The new digitised aircraft was expected to be 40 per cent more available than the A-7E, reducing manning (for maintenance) by about 35 per cent. A combination of accuracy, improved survivability (due largely to much higher performance) and higher sortie rates would, it was claimed, allow an F-18 force to kill 30 per cent more targets than an equal force of A-7Es.

42. In 1987 McDonnell started a Hornet 2000 study looking towards a variant of the Hornet which could replace the ageing A-6. The navy resisted to protect the chosen A-6 successor, the A-12, but the Hornet 2000 returned after the A-12 was killed. The two main options developed by McDonnell had been Option IIIC, which was essentially the current Super Hornet and a more exotic Option IV called the Super Hornet Plus. It had a cranked-arrow wing, forward-swept canards and larger twin canted tail fins. The engines would have been two uprated F404-GE-400s. There would have been a new flight-control system and an upgraded tactical architecture. In 1987 McDonnell offered Option IV to France as a codevelopment project, but the French preferred their own Rafale. The aircraft was also offered to Japan and to the European fighter consortium as an alternative to the current Typhoon. However, Option IIIC was the obvious replacement for the A-6 and also a much better and longer-legged fighter than the earlier versions of the F/A-18. As of 2016 Boeing (which bought McDonnell Douglas) was offering a stealthier version to the navy as a much less expensive alternative to the F-35C. Data from Erik Simonsen, *A Complete History of US Combat Aircraft Fly-Off Competitions* (Forrest Lake: Specialty Press, 2016), pp 163–4.

43. Once NAVAIR asked for supersonic performance, Grumman modified its design (as G-607A) by replacing the supercritical airfoil of the original design with a thinner conventional wing. The wing was slightly enlarged to maintain the desired manoeuvrability at transonic speeds. To gain internal volume, the landing gear was changed to a bicycle type (as in the Harrier) with outriggers extending from the existing missile pylons. This would have been a 30,000lb aircraft using two lift engines and one lift/cruise engine, with a fly-by-wire control system (as in both of the lightweight fighters), in this case triply-redundant. Adopting a full fly-by-wire control system made it possible to make the tail smaller.

44. Details of the Grumman project are from that company's history files. Details of the Convair project are from Robert F Bradley, *Convair Advanced Designs II: Secret Fighters, Attack Aircraft and Unique Designs 1929-1973* (Manchester: Crecy, 2013), pp 158–63. Other projects are described in Tony Buttler, *American Secret Projects: Fighters and Interceptors 1945-1978* (Hinckley: Midland, 2007). Buttler includes the McDonnell 267 (AV-8C), the VAK-191 (ex-D-188A) left over from the 1956 competition, the de Havilland Canada DHC P-71-30 and a lightweight design from San Diego Engineering (Sandaire) called the Stinger, of which no details of the DHC design and the Stinger are given. Lift-plus-lift/cruise proposals were those from Grumman and Convair plus the Fairchild Republic FR-150 and the LTV V-517/520. Fairchild-Republic offered a conventional swept-wing aircraft; the paucity of details in the Buttler book suggests that it did not receive a Phase I contract (Buttler adds that it had excessive wing loading and did not include details of its control system). LTV offered a lift-plus-lift/cruise design with two or three J99s using a high swept wing it had already developed in detail for a proposed fighter. V-520 had two fold-out lift jets. It is unlikely that Vought received a Phase I contract. Buttler records that the company wrote (presumably in December 1971) that a February 1972 go-ahead would make possible a July 1974 first flight. Both the FR-150 and V-520 used swing-out lift engines and both offered inferior performance to the fixed-lift engine arrangements. The Boeing design was rejected for operational unsuitability: it would have required massive redesign of carriers and it could not use any existing support equipment.

45. Buttler, *American Secret Projects*, p 151 states that assessment began on 3 January 1972 followed sixteen days later by NAVAIR's recommendation for a VTOL fighter to be designated XFV-12A. He does not include the Grumman design in the list of NAVAIR evaluations, but it is clear from Grumman documents that its design received a Phase I contract.

46. Zumwalt's departure did not kill US Navy interest in VSTOL, because his successor as CNO, Admiral James Holloway III, was interested in dispersing naval air power among the maximum possible number of ships. He sponsored studies of VSTOL versions of supporting aircraft. The death of the FV-12 programme came later, when it became clear that money would be available for large-deck carriers.

12. THE FALKLANDS WAR

1. The Pegasus 15 was already funded to reach service in 1974–5 (Pegasus 11 was expected to enter service in 1972). Fitted with a zero-stage fan and compressor, it could increase thrust to 31,700lbs and reduce specific fuel consumption to 0.63; a further development, which might be available in 1978 (Pegasus 16-01) would increase that to 35,500lbs but at the cost of reduced fuel economy (SFC 0.73). Less ambitious alternatives were a zero stage compressor (27,600lbs thrust, increasable to 30,500lbs) and a zero stage fan (28,700lbs, increasable to 32,200lbs). The fan was the turbofan which fed air into the forward ducts to provide half the lift. It was driven by the LP turbine, so that too would have been replaced. The HP turbine would have driven a new compressor. It would have been able to withstand higher temperatures due to improved cooling.

2. Brochure in RG 343 Entry UD-WW 301 (Test and Evaluation) Box 1, NARA II. The programme was begun on 12 April 1973 when both organisations signed an MoU which authorised preliminary design effort and model tests by the participating aircraft and engine teams. The aircraft would meet the 'stated or anticipated needs' of the US Marine Corps, the RAF, the Royal Navy and the US Navy, a statement which implied that at this point the Royal Navy was already planning a VSTOL aircraft for its through-deck cruiser. It was hoped that the AV-8A could be substantially improved at a modest cost. The result would have a degree of performance 'normally associated with a full second generation development, but at much lower risk and cost.' The brochure outlining the programme was produced by the US manufacturer in the programme, McDonnell Douglas. This brochure describes the management structure of the project but not any performance or technical details. The project was initially designated AV-8C (this designation was later used for a remanufactured AV-8A) and then AV-16A. It would have a new fuselage, new supercritical wing and plenum chamber burning for much higher performance. It would also have more weapon stations under its wing. The British withdrew from the project in 1975. At that time the Royal Navy did not yet have its Harrier carriers, so the dominant voice was that of the RAF, which preferred to concentrate on Jaguar and what became Tornado. The US government was unwilling to pursue the project alone and the Marines began to see the AV-16 as far more sophisticated than they needed. That led to less ambitious projects which modified the basic Harrier with an enlarged wing and led to the AV-8B and to the RAF GR.6.

3. The Naval Staff paper (by VCNS) is in AIR /17247. It cites a series of reductions since the 1966 announcement that the carriers would be retired

(which had been brought forward to 1971): reduced capability of shore-based aircraft and reduced number of nuclear submarines. Plans announced in 1966 for a small surface-to-surface missile had been changed in favour of providing a small missile for helicopters. Meanwhile the Soviet surface fleet was increasingly capable and was being deployed on a much wider scale (the paper did not cite the appearance of the Soviet surface fleet in the Mediterranean after the 1967 Middle East War). According to the paper, the Naval Staff began fresh studies late in 1968.

4. The Naval Staff paper included in AIR 2/17247 includes the statement that potential foreign customers had already approached British firms about the naval use of VSTOL aircraft. 'In the absence of evidence that we intend to adapt the Harrier for maritime operations or to produce a successor aircraft that could be used effectively in the maritime role, is at present a source of embarrassment to British industry'. Chief of Air Staff wanted this statement deleted 'as a matter of principle', on the ground that export possibilities should not be allowed to shape policy, but the Royal Navy refused to do so. RAF comments on the VCNS paper show anxiety about the high costs of the various projects the navy was pressing: in addition to the naval Harrier, the helicopter-launched air-to-surface missile (which became Sea Skua) and the ship- and submarine-launched missiles, which ultimately became the Royal Navy Exocet and Sub-Harpoon.

5. By December 1969 an interim report had been produced, advocating procurement of a horizon-range anti-ship missile, Exocet being a candidate. The operations research paper seems not to have surfaced. The navy staff paper actually placed development of a submarine-launched anti-ship missile first in priority.

6. Paper for DOR3 and ACAS (OR) by Group Captain D C H Simmons RAF, Assistant to DOR1 (operational research), 3 December 1969, in AIR 2/17247. He mentioned that the current Harrier had only minimal air defence capability, even with the projected Tail Dog (presumably IR-guided) missile.

7. AIR 2/17247 contains a copy of this report, SAW/P(69)70, dated 23 September 1969. The reconnaissance and probe mission would usually be carried out by land-based aircraft, the maritime reconnaissance element of the 'V' bomber force and the SACLANT-dedicated Buccaneers. However, the Committee recognised that the 'V' bombers might not be available, as they might not be able to divert from their primary task and that in any case the increased reaction time of shore-based aircraft might sometimes not meet the needs of a naval force offshore. The report claimed that with aerial refuelling RAF Phantoms could provide continuous air cover over fleet units out to 750nm.

8. A record of this project, as seen by the RAF, is in AIR 2/17247.

9. This account of Harrier development and capability is based largely on Jon Lake, 'BAE Systems Sea Harrier and other first-generation Harriers' in *World Airpower Journal*, Summer 2000 (Number 41).

10. The number was limited by the requirement, typical of British carrier operations, that all aircraft be stowable below decks. The *Invincible* class hangar deck had an odd dumbbell-shape, as the gas-turbine uptake and down-take had to pass to either side of it amidships (some wags claimed that the shape was a deliberate attempt to limit aircraft capacity).

11. Thus a 6 July 1976 DNAW (Director Naval Air Warfare) memo (for RAE) on intercept calculations for the Sea Harrier calls out the 'Bear D' as the prime target. The Sea Harrier missile is to be the AIM-9L. The memo identifies other aircraft as secondary possibilities: 'Badger' and 'Backfire' bombers, 'Fencer' light bombers and the Yak-38 then being operated by the semi-carrier *Kiev*. This reply had been prompted by a 24 May RAE memo asking for target priorities. DEFE 69/622, a file on studies of Sea Harrier capabilities.

12. AVIA 6/25876, 'An Assessment of the Vectored Thrust Aircraft to AST 403 in the Maritime Intercept Role,' September 1978 (RAE [Farnborough] paper). AST 403 was intended as the basis for feasibility studies of Harrier and Jaguar replacements for the RAF; both VSTOL and conventional designs were considered and possible sketch designs were compared with foreign aircraft, including the notional F-18L. The main paper is DEFE 72/104. The Hawker Siddeley design was the only one offering VSTOL

capability. The study was initiated by the RAE Systems Assessment Department to test whether, if the RAF bought the aircraft, it would be a worthwhile naval interceptor. As such it gives some insight into the interception problem as then understood. The study was intended to indicate weaknesses which might be addressed in a Phase II feasibility study of AST 403. This aircraft would have been powered by a Pegasus 11D-43 engine rated at 22,050lbs thrust (23,400lbs with water injection) – and 30,100lbs (32,250lbs) with plenum chamber burning. Compared to other VSTOLs, AST 403 had a relatively large wing (380ft^2) and therefore it could lift an unusually large weight when launched from a ski-jump (over 40,000lbs, including a load of about 17,000lbs). Assessment was complicated by the fact that the design had been optimised for low-level strike. BAe Kingston offered a variant with a folding wing; RAE estimated that the existing hangar could accommodate about nine of the fighters and eight Sea King follow-on helicopters.

13. The version was the AIM-9L which was provided to the Royal Navy during the Falklands War. In 1978 the RAF was planning it as the main air-to-air weapon of the MRCA (which became the Tornado). At this time RAE estimated that its improved warhead gave it the same lethality against a Backfire as a Sparrow, about a 70 per cent chance of a mission kill with one hit. The 1978 study also addressed Skyflash, a British development of Sparrow, commenting that its semi-active homing technique made it impossible to fire at multiple targets in close succession, which the defending fighter would have to do. The interval between Sidewinder launches was determined by the burn-out time of the missile motor, as the next missile might lock onto the previous one. In the case of Skyflash, the determining factor was missile flight time. If the first missile was fired at maximum range (23.8nm), it would take 40 seconds to hit. A missile launched as soon as possible afterwards would be fired when the second target was 6.5nm away (but several factors made a distance of 4nm more plausible). Unless there were many targets, the fighter would not get a third chance. RAE assumed that the radar would be a pulse-Doppler type.

14. This point is made by Commander 'Sharkey' Ward in *A Maverick At War: Sea Harrier Over the Falklands* (Annapolis: Naval Institute Press, 1992), pp 172–3. According to Ward, a two-Sea Harrier CAP was sent urgently to investigate an intermittent contact, which had to be a fast jet popping up into radar cover and then down below it. They were recalled by the flagship *Hermes*, which ordered them to undertake a visual search for possible enemy surface ships, when a radar search from further back would have sufficed. Ward cites other examples of a staff unaware of how aircraft could and should function.

15. The dates of the projects and some details are taken from the Jon Lake article cited above and are not from any contemporary previously classified source.

13. THE OUTER AIR BATTLE

1. Existing A-6Es were ordered rewinged without the new radar or other new features. The A-6F would have had two additional stores stations suitable for AIM-120 AMRAAM missiles, generally described as defensive, and new F404-GE-400D turbofans. It was cancelled as part of FY89 budget cuts. An alternative A-6G proposed at that time would have had the new wing and the radar but not the new engines. It was not bought and instead some A-6s were reworked. The new radar would have guided Phoenix missiles and that in turn would have made the A-6 a contributor to the Outer Air Battle (with very good CAP endurance) rather than a liability which had to be confined to the carrier's hangar.

2. The A-6 was attractive because it carried more ordnance and was much more capable in adverse weather. Its known weakness, compared to the A-7, was inferior pinpoint bombing accuracy. It was known that the attack systems of the two aircraft were comparable in accuracy. The difference was that the A-7 displays were easier to follow to put a bomb on a target. The A-6 was a better area bomber (this was just before the advent of precision weapons such as GPS-guided bombs). Since the display was the difference, new displays were a feature of the A-6 upgrade. Another problem was the sheer cost of the A-6, which at one point forced closure of the assembly line.

BIBLIOGRAPHY

Archival Documents Not Cited in the Text

NOTE: The documents below are from the British national archive (PRO). The US National Archives, at least for the files for BuAer and its successors, is not organised as discrete documents. Instead they are in effect boxed-up office files containing thousands of pages. A typical file might be listed simply as a number of FRC (Federal Records Center) boxes, each a cubic foot of paper.

CB.04040A(39) *Naval Air Fighting Instructions 1939* (at NARA II).

CB.04040 (GB) *Naval Air Fighting Instructions 1942-46* (at NARA II, in one binder).

ADM 1/8602/52, Progress in Naval Aviation 1921 (draft).

ADM1/11207 Aircraft types for the Fleet Air Arm, 1940.

ADM 1/13615, Typhoon and Tempest as possible carrier fighters, 1943.

ADM 1/11980, Provision of fighters for carriers (War Cabinet), 1941–2.

ADM 1/13351, Fighter direction in the US Pacific Fleet, 1943.

ADM1/13384, HMS *Victorious* report on USS *Saratoga*, 1943.

ADM1/15576, Operational Grouping of Carriers, 1943–4.

ADM1/15722, Fighter tactical air support from escort carriers, 1944 (looks toward Pacific operations).

ADM 1/16021 Visit to USA to discuss carrier operations, March 1949.

ADM1/17484, British Pacific Fleet air operations including landing rate.

ADM1/17516, Vought F6U, February 1945.

ADM 1/22776, Air defence of convoys in the Mediterranean, 1951.

ADM1/22934, Fighter defence of convoys, 1951.

ADM1/23260, Sea Fury and Firefly vs MiG-15 in Korea, 1952.

ADM1/25254, Air Defence Against Fast Low-Level Attack, 1954.

ADM1/27827, Nuclear weapon for Scimitar, 1963.

ADM 116/5341, Reduction in supply of Corsairs to RN to provide more for US carriers, 1945.

ADM 116/5347, Supply of aircraft to Royal Navy under Lend-Lease.

ADM 116/6327 Exercise 'Mariner,' 1953.

ADM 213/41, Visit to USA September-October 1945 (on AEW).

ADM 213/1092, High-speed interception trials, HMS *Harrier* (FDO school), 1950.

ADM 220/75, Air Interception 1940–4.

ADM 220/586, Control of fighters for air defence, 1950 (use of Type 984).

ADM 239/489 and 490 Exercise TRIDENT, 1949, exhibition and war game including use of carriers with heavy bombers.

ADM 281/109, Visit to USA November 1948 (carrier facilities).

ADM 287/1, Visit to USA October-November 1948 (mainly problems of carrier operation).

AIR 20/3735, Fleet Air Arm request for cannon-armed fighters, 1943.

AIR 20/845 Fighter operation from carriers, 1944 (issue of Spitfire suitability, problems with transferred RAF pilots on escort carriers for assault missions).

AIR 20/7209, Mounting of an Air Offensive in 1957 – Use of Naval Carriers (RN proposal for carrier-based Canberras, and Air Staff rejection).

AIR 2/4255, Spitfire – RAF Investigation of Suitability for FAA, 1939.

AIR 9/194, Carrier-borne aircraft: problems of Spitfires on escort carriers, 1944 (possible use of RAF squadrons on escort carriers).

AIR 64/351: Central Fighter Establishment Visit to the United States September–October 1961 (this is the file in which the US Air Force describes the F4H Phantom as the best fighter in existence; it includes a very brief account of US Navy expectations for the F-111B fire-control system).

AVIA 6/14884, Effect of sweepback, higher wing loading, and single reheated engine on N.9/47.

AVIA 6/16021, RAE visit to US March 1949 to discuss carrier operating practices.

AVIA 15/1790 Policy for Fury and Sea Fury.

AVIA 45/159 Supermarine N.9/47 (Scimitar) general design.

AVIA 26/2185, RRE memo on visit to the United States concerning coherent radar, May 1961; includes data on APQ-81.

AVIA 65/633 Specification for AEW Gannet.

CAB 158/23, Joint Intelligence Committee papers for 1956, including a survey of the Soviet military; mentions dates of KS-1 development (but KS-1 does not figure in the June 1957 RN survey of Soviet naval aviation, and the advent of naval 'Badgers' is open to question).

CAB 158/39: Joint Intelligence Committee papers for 1961, including a survey of the Soviet military.

DEFE 7/679, Nuclear weapons on aircraft carriers, 1958. This is the file which gives the yield of the Scimitar weapon as 3kT.

DEFE 67/124, Harrier operations in the Falklands: gives numbers available day by day, but not results of air combat .

DEFE 67/126, Operation 'Corporate' (Falklands) overview for operational evaluation group, July 1982.

DEFE 72/257 Specification for Sea Harrier FRS.1.

DSIR 23/17889 Notes on US naval aircraft 1949.

RN Battle Summaries (accessed at NARA II)

    No. 18/32: Selected Convoys (Mediterranean) 1941–2, 1957.

    No. 31: Invasion of North Africa ('Torch'), 1948.

    No. 32: Malta Convoys, 1945.

    No. 35: Invasion of Sicily, 1946.

    No. 37: Invasion of Italy – landing at Salerno, 1946.

    No. 43: Invasion of the South of France, 1950.

    No. 45/46: Battles of Coral Sea and Midway (one volume), 1952.

    No. 47: Okinawa, 1950.

Published Books

Amet, Capt de Corvette, *Tactique des Forces de l'Aeronautique Navale* (2 vols, issued to the Ecole de Guerre Navale [School of Naval Warfare] in 1938, in the French tri-service archive at Vincennes). Captain Amet is not otherwise identified, except as Professor of Aeronautics at the school; this is a textbook in a series in the archives, produced in mimeograph form. The same series includes his notes on solving air security problems (for the 1936–7 term), but they are geometric solutions to scouting problems, not notes on fighter defence.

Bell, Dana, *F4U-1 Corsair* Vols 1 and 2 (Classic Warships Aircraft Pictorials Nos. 7 and 8, 2014 and 2015).

Bradley, Robert F, *Convair Advanced Designs II: Secret Fighters, Attack Aircraft, and Unique Designs 1929-1973* (Manchester: Crecy, 2013).

Brown, David, *Carrier Fighters* (London: Macdonald and Jane's, 1975).

Brown, Eric M 'Winkle', *Wings of the Navy: Testing British and US Carrier Aircraft* (Manchester: Hikoki, 2013).

Buttler, Tony, *British Secret Projects: Jet Fighters Since 1950* (Hinckley: Midland, 2000).

_____, *American Secret Projects: Fighters and Interceptors 1945-1978* (Hinckley: Midland, 2008).

_____, and Griffith, Alan, *American Secret Projects: Fighter, Bomber, and Attack Aircraft* (Manchester: Crecy, 2016): Second World War era.

Christianson, Paul J, *Westinghouse J40 Axial Turbojet Family: Development History and Technical Profiles* (Olney, MD: Bleeg, 2015).

Clark, John D, *Ignition! An Informal History of Liquid Propellants* (Rutgers University Press, 1972).

Cooper, Geoffrey, *Farnborough and the Fleet Air Arm* (Hersham: Midland, 2008).

Coulam, Robert F, *Illusions of Choice: The F-111 and the Problem of Weapons Acquisition Reform* (Princeton University Press, 1977).

Donald, David (ed), *Tupolev Bombers* (Norwalk, CT: AIRtime, 2002).

Elward, Brad, *Grumman F9F Panther/Cougar* (North Branch, MN: Specialty Press, 2010).

Francillon, René, *Japanese Aircraft of the Pacific War* (Annapolis: Naval Institute Press, 1987).

Frankel, Mark, *Killer Rays: Story of the Douglas F4D Skyray and F5D Skylancer* (North Branch, MN: Specialty Press, 2010).

Friedman, Norman, *Carrier Air Power* (London: Conway Maritime Press, 1981).

_____, *Naval Radar* (London: Conway Maritime Press, 1982).

_____, *Network-Centric Warfare: How Navies Learned to Fight Smarter in Three World Wars* (Annapolis: Naval Institute Press, 2009).

Gardner, Tom, *Vought F7U Cutlass: A Developmental History* (Atglen: Schiffer, 2010).

Gibson, Chris, and Buttler, Tony, *British Secret Projects: Hypersonics, Ramjets, and Missiles* (Hinckley: Midland, 2007).

Ginter, Steve, *Douglas F3D Skyknight* (Naval Fighters No. 4, Simi Valley, CA: Steve Ginter, 1982).

Gordon, Yefim, and Komissarov, Dmitriy, *Chinese Aircraft: China's Aviation Industry Since 1951* (Manchester: Hikoki, 2008).

_____, *Tupolev Tu-95/Tu-142* (Hinckley: Midland, 2009).

_____, *Soviet and Russian Military Aircraft in Asia* (Manchester: Hikoki, 2014).

_____, and Rigmant, Vladimir, *Tupolev Tu-4: The First Soviet Strategic Bomber* (Atglen: Schiffer, 2014).

Green, William, and Cross, Roy, *The Jet Aircraft of the World* (Garden City: Hanover House, 1956): for early jet engine development.

Gunston, Bill, *World Encyclopedia of Aero Engines* (5th ed, Phoenix Mill: Sutton, 2006).

Hallion, Richard P, *The Naval Air War in Korea* (Baltimore: Nautical & Aviation, 1986).

Hobbs, David, *The British Carrier Strike Fleet After 1945* (Barnsley: Seaforth, 2015).

Hone, Thomas C, Friedman, Norman, and Mandeles, Mark D, *American and British Carrier Development, 1919-1941* (Annapolis: Naval Institute Press, 1999).

_____, *Innovation in Carrier Aviation* (Newport, RI: Naval War College Press, Newport Paper No. 37, 2011).

Isby, David C, *The Decisive Duel* (Boston: Little, Brown, 2012).

Kingsley, F A (ed), *The Development of Radar Equipments for the Royal Navy 1935-45* (Macmillan, 1995)

_____, *Radar and Other Electronic Systems in the Royal Navy in World War 2* (Macmillan, 1995).

Lake, Jon (ed), *McDonnell F-4 Phantom: Spirit in the Skies* (London: Aerospace Publishing, 1992).

Lundstrom, John B, *The First Team: Naval Air Combat from Pearl Harbor to Guadalcanal* (Annapolis: Naval Institute Press, 2005).

McClelland, Tim, *Harrier* (Hersham: Classic [Ian Allan imprint], 2011).

Meekcoms, K J, and Morgan, E B, *The British Aircraft Specifications File* (Tonbridge: Air Britain, 1994).

Mikesh, Robert C, and Abe, Shorzoe, *Japanese Aircraft 1910-1941* (Annapolis: Naval Institute Press, 1990).

Miller, Jerry, *Nuclear Weapons and Aircraft Carriers: How the Bomb Saved Naval Aviation* (Washington: Smithsonian, 2001).

Morgan, Eric, and Stevens, John, *The Scimitar File* (Tunbridge Wells: Air-Britain, 2000).

Moulin, Jean, Morareau, Lucien, and Picard, Claud, *Le Béarn et le Commandant Teste* (Bourg en Bresse: Marine Editions, ND).

Myer, Corky, *Grumman XF10F-1 Jaguar Swing-Wing* (Naval Fighters No. 26; Simi Valley, CA: Steve Ginter, 1993). Myer was the only pilot to have flown the XF10F.

Parshall, Jonathan, and Tully, Anthony, *Shattered Sword: The Untold Story of the Battle of Midway* (Dulles, VA: Potomac, 2005).

Peattie, Mark R, *Sunburst: The Rise of Japanese Naval Air Power, 1909-1941* (Annapolis: Naval Institute Press, 2001).

Rivas, Santiago, *Wings of the Malvinas: The Argentine Air War over the Falklands* (Manchester: Hikoki, 2012).

Simonsen, Erik, *A Complete History of US Combat Aircraft Fly-Off Competitions: Winners, Losers, and Might-Have-Beens* (North Branch, MN: Specialty Press, 2016).

Swanborough, Gordon, and Bowers, Peter M, *United States Naval Aircraft Since 1911* (3rd ed, Annapolis: Naval Insitute Press, 1990).

Thetford, Owen, *British Naval Aircraft Since 1912* (London: Putnam, 1977).

Thomason, Tommy H, *US Naval Air Superiority: Development of Shipborne Jet Fighters, 1943-1962* (North Branch, MN: Specialty Press, 2007).

Wagner, Ray, *American Combat Planes of the 20th Century* (Reno: Jack Bacon, 2004).

Ward, Commander 'Sharkey', *A Maverick at War: Sea Harrier Over the Falklands* (Annapolis: Naval Institute Press 1992).

Wolters, Timothy S, *Information at Sea: Shipboard Command and Control in the U.S. Navy, from Mobile Bay to Okinawa* (Baltimore: Johns Hopkins, 2013).

Articles

Delaney, Jason M, 'RCN Jet Fighter Procurement 1950-1964', in Gimblett, R H, and Mayne, R O (eds), *People, Policy, and Programmes: Proceedings of the 7th Maritime Command (MARCOM) Historical Conference (2005)* (RCN, 2008).

Gates, Thomas F, 'Down to the Sea in Jets (VF-51)', *The Hook* 24, 3 (1996) (includes the anti-B-36 project; pt II, in the next issue, described air combat over Korea).

Hansen, Chuck, 'The Emerson Aero X17A Roll-Traverse Nose Turret', *The Hook* 12, 3 (1984).

Jacobs, Jan, 'Follow The Bouncing Cougar: The Flexdeck Program', *The Hook* 12, 1 (1984).

LeCompte, Malcolm A, 'Naval Air Supremacy and the Development of the Brewster Buffalo', *AAHS* 41, 4 (1990).

Long, B J, 'Seadart (US Navy XF2Y-1 and YF2Y-1 Experimental Supersonic Seaplanes)', *AAHS* 24, 1 (1979).

O'Rourke, Jerry, 'The Douglas Navy F4D Ford', *AAHS* 24, 2 (1979).

Powell, Robert R, 'Vee Ess Eff – Very Small Fighters', *The Hook* 34, 1 (Spring 2006).

Rochefort, Garry L, 'The Republic XF-91 (Short-Lived Thunder in the Sky)', *AAHS* 34, 1 (1989).

Whitby, Michael, 'Fouled Deck: The Pursuit of an Augmented Aircraft Carrier Capability for the Royal Canadian Navy', Pt. 1, 1945–56, *Canadian Air Force Journal* Vol 3, 3 (Summer 2010); Part 2, 1956–64, *Canadian Air Force Journal* Vol 3, 4 (Autumn 2010).

Williams, Nicholas M, 'The X-RAYS Douglas' XF4D-1 Skyrays', *AAHS* 22, 4 (1977).

AIRCRAFT DATA

Data are in Imperial units (feet, inches, pounds), but British aircraft fuel tanks are in Imperial gallons, whereas US drop tanks are in US gallons (4 Imperial gallons equal 5 US gallons). Metric data for Japanese aircraft have been converted into Imperial units for ease of comparison and in some cases sources did not provide precise data in terms of feet and inches. Speeds are all in knots (1 knot is 1nm/hr and a nautical mile is 1.15 statute miles). Thus a speed of 300 knots is equivalent to 345mph. Distances are all in nautical miles (6080ft rather than 5280ft for a statute mile, frequently taken as 6000ft or 2000 yds). Roll means the distance the fighter must roll before taking off and the figures given here show how it is affected by the amount of wind flowing over the flight deck (Wind Over Deck, WOD). The take-off distances for jets show why catapults were so important. Wing loading is weight per square foot of wing, expressed as pounds per square foot. The lower the wing loading, the more manoeuvrable the aircraft. The figures make it clear how much lighter and hence more manoeuvrable biplanes were, but the reader should keep in mind that manoeuvrability depends on much more. Engine ratings are in horse-power for piston engines and in pounds of static thrust for jets; at 375mph 1lb of thrust equals 1hp, but above that the equivalent horse-power increases in proportion to the speed. In piston engine ratings, 'dash' power is war emergency (WE) water injection output, which could not be maintained for more than five minutes (for US engines, the W suffix indicated water injection). In jets the equivalent is the afterburner. AB indicates performance with afterburner lit, i.e., using the dash rating of the engine. All weights are take-off weights. Stall speeds are at landing weight, so that they approximate carrier approach speed. Speeds are indicated as a speed in knots at a stated altitude, so that 250/15,000 means 250 knots at 15,000ft. In ranges, the figure after diagonal mark is the speed in knots for that range. Rate of climb is in feet per minute. For piston engine aircraft, the service ceiling is the altitude at which the rate of climb is reduced to 100ft/min. For US jets, the service ceiling quoted is the combat ceiling, at which the rate of climb is reduced to 500ft/min.

In a few cases quoted in these tables, US official data (SACC [Standard Aircraft Characteristics Charts]) give speed in Mach numbers rather than knots. In a dry atmosphere, Mach 1 at sea level is 768mph (667 knots). The speed of sound decreases at altitude, because the air is thinner (sound travels as a pressure wave in the air and the denser the medium, the faster it travels). For a wetter atmosphere in which Mach 1 at sea level is 661 knots, at 5000ft it is 650 knots, at 20,000ft it is 614 knots, at 35,000 it is 574 knots and between 40,000 and 60,000ft it is 573 knots. Thus Mach 0.9 at sea level is about 598 knots, the precise figure depending on humidity.

Data for US fighters are generally taken from official ACP (Aircraft Characteristics and Performance) booklets or their post-war successors (after about 1949), the SACCs. For pre-1939 aircraft I have used official BuAer multi-aircraft charts equivalent to ACPs. The important exceptions are the XF4U-1, F6D-1 and XFV-1. F4U-1 data are based on published numbers plus the relevant BuAer correspondence file.

F6D data are from the file on the Missileer competitors (performance data are the BuWeps versions, not the contractor's, describing Douglas Model 766). FV-1 data are from Ray Wagner, *American Combat Planes of the 20th Century* (Reno: Jack Bacon, 2004) and he in turn probably used a SACC chart. Data for the F/A-18 and F-35C are entirely unofficial.

A. FIGHTERS WITHOUT RADAR
United Kingdom

	FLYCATCHER I	OSPREY III	NIMROD IIS
ARMAMENT	2 x 0.303in	2 x 0.303in	2 x 0.303in
ENGINE	Jaguar IV	Kestrel IIMS[1]	Kestrel IIS
RATING (NORMAL)	400	630	590
(TAKE-OFF)	N/A	N/A	N/A
(DASH)	N/A	N/A	N/A
SPAN	29-0	37-0	33-7
SPAN (FOLDED)	N/A	15-7	N/A
WING AREA	288	339	301
LENGTH	23-0	29-4	26-7
HEIGHT	12-0	10-4	9-10
WEIGHT	3028	4950	4258
WING LOADING	10.5	14.6	13.5
MAXIMUM SPEED			
LOW	117/SL	N/A	141[2]
HIGH	112.5/10,000	153/5000	170/14,000
CLIMB RATE AT SL	1090	1400	1640
SERVICE CEILING	20,600	23,500	26,900
RANGE	191.3/112.5	401/130[3]	396[4]
RANGE WITH TANKS	N/A	N/A	N/A
RADIUS OF ACTION	98	N/A	N/A
ROLL (0 WOD)	N/A	450[5]	300
ROLL (25kts WOD)	N/A	185 (20kts)	N/A
STALL SPEED	48.0	N/A	N/A

[1]. MS indicated a Moderately Supercharged engine, as opposed to an S (Supercharged) engine. The Admiralty indicated that fighters would operate at 10,000ft, where the MS engine offered better performance. Originally the 21/26 prototypes had S engines.
[2]. As tested in 1935 with a 600hp Kestrel V engine, at a weight of 4069lbs. Take-off distance is with this engine. Service ceiling was 28,800ft and initial rate of climb was 2738ft/min.
[3]. According to the April 1939 edition of the official list of British ship and aircraft characteristics, Nimrod range was 231nm in peacetime, but 330nm in war, in each case at a cruising speed of 110 knots; in war the aircraft would carry 76 rather than 53 gallons of fuel.
[4]. According to the April 1939 edition of the official list of British ships and aircraft characteristics, Osprey range was 282nm in peacetime, but 341nm in war, in each case at a cruising speed of 110 knots; in war the aircraft would carry 94 gallons rather than 77 gallons of fuel.
[5]. The Osprey Specification gave maximum and landing speeds (the latter was 45 knots) but not a required take-off distance. Maximum catapult take-off speed was 55 knots. The figure here was estimated in 1931 for an aircraft powered by a Kestrel IIMS, weighing 4650lbs. With a Kestrel IIS, take-off distance was 100ft, but speed at 5000ft was reduced to 146 knots. This engine gave greater power above 10,000ft, e.g. 164 vs 145 knots at 15,000ft.

	SKUA	SEA GLADIATOR	FULMAR II
ARMAMENT	5 x 0.303in	4 x 0.303in	8 x 0.303in
	500lb bomb	–	–
ENGINE	Perseus XII	Mercury VIIA	Merlin 30
RATING (NORMAL)	620	840	1300
(TAKE-OFF)	830	N/A	N/A
(DASH)	905	N/A	N/A
SPAN	46-2	32-3	46-4½
SPAN (FOLDED)	16-2	N/A	17-10
WING AREA	312	323	342
LENGTH	35-7	27-5	40-3
HEIGHT	14-2	10-7	10-8
WEIGHT	8230	5420	9672
WING LOADING	26.4	15.5	27.5
MAXIMUM SPEED			
LOW	177/SL	182.6/SL	230/1750
HIGH	195/6700[1]	213/15,000	237/7250
CLIMB RATE AT SL	740	2300	1320
SERVICE CEILING	19,100	32,000	27,200
RANGE	720/120[2]	315/140	695.6/152
RANGE WITH TANKS	N/A	361/191	N/A
		(1 x 83-gal)	
ROLL (0 WOD)	N/A	N/A	420[3]
ROLL (25kts WOD)	N/A	195 (30kts)	260 (30kts)
STALL SPEED	66	47.6	56

[1] In 1934, estimated maximum speed with a Perseus IIS engine (835hp at 15,000ft) was 203 knots at 15,000ft, with a service ceiling of 30,000ft and a range of 527nm. Estimated range with a drop tank instead of a bomb was 635nm.

[2] According to the April 1939 official British list of ship and aircraft characteristics, Skua range as a fighter dive bomber was 470nm in peace but 640nm in war, at a cruising speed of 135 knots. As a pure fighter, corresponding ranges were 665nm and 685nm and cruising speed was 140 knots.

[3] In 1940 tests at 9000lbs, take-off run in zero wind was 420ft. The specification required 225ft take-off distance in 20 knots wind, but more could be accepted if the engine was incapable of attaining this figure.

United States

	F3B-1	F4B-4	FF-2
ARMAMENT	1 x 0.30in, 1 x 0.50	2 x 0.30in	2 x 0.30in
ENGINE	R-1340B	R-1340-16	R-1820-78
RATING (NORMAL)	450	550	700
(TAKE-OFF)	N/A	N/A	N/A
(DASH)	N/A	N/A	N/A
SPAN	33-0/26-6	30-0/26-4	34-6/31-6
SPAN (FOLDED)	N/A	N/A	N/A
WING AREA	275	227.5	310
LENGTH	24-9	20-4	24-6
HEIGHT	10-1	9-9	11-1
WEIGHT	2950	3178	4826
WING LOADING	10.7	14.0	15.6
MAXIMUM SPEED			
LOW	136/SL	N/A	179.8/4000
HIGH	123/15,000	147.8/15,000	160.9/15,000
CLIMB RATE AT SL	2020	–[1]	–[2]
SERVICE CEILING	20,900	26,900	21,100
RANGE	327	331.3	673
RANGE WITH TANKS	687	654.8	N/A
	(1x 50-gal)		

	ROLL (0 WOD)	272	430	585
	ROLL (25kts WOD)	72	139	202
	STALL SPEED	46	51.7	51.3

[1] No initial rate given; 2.7 minutes to 5000ft.
[2] No initial rate given; 2.9 minutes to 5000ft.

	F2F-1	F3F-3	F2A-3
ARMAMENT	2 x 0.30in	1 x 0.30in, 1 x 0.50in	4 x 0.50in
ENGINE	R-1535-72	R-1820-22	R-1820-40
RATING (NORMAL)	650	850	1000
(TAKE-OFF)	N/A	950	1200
(DASH)	N/A	N/A	N/A
SPAN	28-6/26-0	32-0/29-5	35-0
SPAN (FOLDED)	N/A	N/A	N/A
WING AREA	230	260.6	209
LENGTH	21-5	23-4⅜	26-5
HEIGHT	11-2	11-2	12-0
WEIGHT	3787	4535	6538
WING LOADING	16.5	17.4	31.3
MAXIMUM SPEED			
LOW	176.5	207.8	252/SL
HIGH	200.9/7500	198.3/10,000	258.3/4500
CLIMB RATE AT SL	2050	2840	2290
SERVICE CEILING	27,100	33,200	33,200
RANGE	985/107.8	979/109.6	839
RANGE WITH TANKS	N/A	N/A	1330/143
			(1 x 53-gal)
ROLL (0 WOD)	360	322	508
ROLL (25kts WOD)	126	189	230
STALL SPEED	52.3	54.7	66.4

	F4F-3A
ARMAMENT	4 x 0.50in
ENGINE	R-1830-90
RATING (NORMAL)	1100/SL
(TAKE-OFF)	1200
(DASH)	N/A
SPAN	38-0
SPAN (FOLDED)	N/A
WING AREA	260
LENGTH	28-11
HEIGHT	11-11
WEIGHT	7425
WING LOADING	28.6
MAXIMUM SPEED	
LOW	244/SL
HIGH	279/16,100
CLIMB RATE AT SL	2680 (mil power)
SERVICE CEILING	33,000
RANGE	1060/139
RANGE WITH TANKS	N/A
ROLL (0 WOD)	600
ROLL (25kts WOD)	253
STALL SPEED	64

	F4F-4	FM-2	F2M-1[1]
ARMAMENT	6 x 0.50in	4 x 0.50in	4 x 0.50in
ENGINE	R-1830-86	R-1820-56	R-1820-70W
RATING (NORMAL)	1100	1200	1200
(TAKE-OFF)	1200	1350	1350
(DASH)	N/A	1360	1500
SPAN	38-0	38-0	37-6
SPAN (FOLDED)	14-4	14-4	16-8
WING AREA	260	260	235
LENGTH	29-0	28-10⅝	30-6
HEIGHT	10-0	13-6½	13-2
WEIGHT	7975	7487	7515
WING LOADING	30.7	28.5	32.0
MAXIMUM SPEED			
LOW	238.3/SL	258/SL	264/SL
HIGH	278.3/18,800	284/10,700 (WE)	354/26,000 (WE)
CLIMB RATE AT SL	–[2]	2890	3390
SERVICE CEILING	34,000	35,600	37,400
RANGE	722/140	830/140	1050/146
RANGE WITH TANKS	1109/133	1275/133	1570/131
	(2 x 58-gal)	(2 x 58-gal)	(2 x 58-gal)
COMBAT RADIUS	105	180	85
		(1 drop tank)	
ROLL (0 WOD)	610	423	399
ROLL (25kts WOD)	278	178	164
		(WE: 301/201)	
STALL SPEED	66.7	62.3	57

[1.] Estimated data from an ACP dated 1 May 1944: this aircraft was never completed.
[2.] XF4F-4 with R-1830-76 engine had a climb rate of 2050ft/min at sea level; the aircraft characteristics chart for the F4F-4 does not give a rate of climb. The FM-1, a modified F4F-4 with four rather than six machine guns, had a climb rate of 3650ft/min.

Japan

	A4N1	A5M4 'Claude'	A6M2 'Zero'
ARMAMENT	2 x 7.7mm	2 x 7.7mm	2 x 7.7mm, 2 x 20mm
ENGINE	Hikari I	Kotobuki 41[1]	Sakae 12
RATING (NORMAL)	730	680	830
(TAKE-OFF)	N/A	N/A	940
(DASH)	N/A	785 (mil rating)	950 (mil rating)
SPAN	32-9.5	36-1	39-5
SPAN (FOLDED)	N/A	N/A	N/A
WING AREA	246.4	192	241.5
LENGTH	21-9.25	24-10	29-7
HEIGHT	10-1	10-6	11-6
WEIGHT	3880	3684	5538
WING LOADING	15.7	19.2	22.1
MAXIMUM SPEED			
LOW	N/A	N/A	N/A
HIGH	190/10,500	233.5/10,365	275/14,432
CLIMB RATE AT SL			4527
SERVICE CEILING	25,390	32,100	32,800
RANGE	457		1026[2]
RANGE WITH TANKS	N/A	648/216 knots (1 x 42-gal)	1810/160 knots (1 x 87-gal)

ROLL (0 WOD)	N/A	N/A	649
ROLL (25kts WOD)	N/A	N/A	269 (23kts)
STALL SPEED	N/A	N/A	60.0

1. License-built British Jupiter, for comparison with other aircraft
2. With fuel for 10 minutes' combat; with fuel for 30 minutes, range is 774nm. Range and take-off data from a Japanese manual captured in 1944.

	A6M5[1] 'Zero'	A7M2 'Sam' (Reppu)
ARMAMENT	2 x 20mm, 2 x 7.7mm	4 x 20mm
ENGINE	Sakae 31A	MK9A
RATING (NORMAL)	830	2200
(TAKE-OFF)	1120	2200
(DASH)	1210	N/A
SPAN	36-1	45-11
SPAN (FOLDED)	N/A	N/A
WING AREA	230	332
LENGTH	29-9½	36-1
HEIGHT	9.2	14-1
WEIGHT	6026	10,384
WING LOADING	26.2	31.3
MAXIMUM SPEED		
LOW	256/SL(WE)	N/A
HIGH	304/23,100 (WE: 310/22,000)	339/21,650 N/A
CLIMB RATE AT SL	3140	N/A
SERVICE CEILING	35,100	35,750
RANGE	1600/126	N/A
RANGE WITH TANKS	NA	N/A
ROLL (0 WOD)	975	N/A
ROLL (25kts WOD)	NA	N/A
STALL SPEED	NA	70

[1.] Performance data were taken from a 1944 TAIC publication reflecting flight tests. Take-off is airfield not flight deck, data presumably including sufficient distance to get over a 50ft obstacle.

B. SECOND WORLD WAR FIGHTERS
United Kingdom

	SEA HURRICANE	SEAFIRE LIIC	FIREFLY I
ARMAMENT	4 x 20mm	2 x 20mm, 2 x 0.303in	4 x 20mm
ENGINE	Merlin III	Merlin 46	Griffon II
RATING (NORMAL)	1030	1415/14,000ft	N/A
(TAKE-OFF)	N/A	N/A	1735
(DASH)	N/A	N/A	N/A
SPAN	40.0	32-7	44.5
SPAN (FOLDED)	N/A	N/A	13.5
WING AREA	258	232	328
LENGTH	31.4	30-0	37.0
HEIGHT	13.0	13-0	12.3
WEIGHT	7015	7006	12,131
WING LOADING	27.2	30.2	37.0
MAXIMUM SPEED			

LOW	N/A	275/SL	N/A
HIGH	267.8/18,000	295/6000	257.4/3500
CLIMB RATE AT SL	N/A	4380	1930
SERVICE CEILING	32,700	24,000	29,700
RANGE	482.6/180.9	440/192	671.3/187.8
RANGE WITH TANKS	957/181	660/190	1186/188
	(1 x 90-gal)	(1 x 45-gal)	(2 x 50-gal)
COMBAT RADIUS	N/A	N/A	N/A
ROLL (0 WOD)	400 (20kts)	N/A	490 (20kts)
ROLL (25kts WOD)	270 (30kts)	225 (30kts)	330 (30kts)
STALL SPEED	N/A	N/A	62.0

	SEA HORNET F20	FIREFLY FR4	SEA FURY FB11
ARMAMENT	4 x 20mm	4 x 20mm	4 x 20mm
ENGINE	2 x Merlin 130	Griffon 74	Centaurus 18
RATING (NORMAL)	N/A	2245/9250ft	1845
(TAKE-OFF)	2030	2750	2480
	(1890 supercharged)		
(DASH)	N/A	N/A	2550
SPAN	45-0	41.0	38-5
SPAN (FOLDED)	27.5	16-0	N/A
WING AREA	361	330	280
LENGTH	36-8	37-8	34-8
HEIGHT	14-2	15-6	15-11
WEIGHT	18,250	13,927	12,350
WING LOADING	50.5	42.2	44.1
MAXIMUM SPEED			
LOW	375/10,000	287/SL	N/A
HIGH	406/22,000	319/14,000	400/18,000
CLIMB RATE AT SL	4000	_[1]	4320
SERVICE CEILING	35,000	31,900	35,800
RANGE	1000/231.3	506/203	609
RANGE WITH TANKS	1678/231	930/198	904
	(2 x 100 gal)	(2 x 90 gal)	(2 x 90 gal)
COMBAT RADIUS	N/A	N/A	626
ROLL (0 WOD)	N/A	N/A	960
ROLL (25kts WOD)	N/A	N/A	500 (27 knots)
STALL SPEED	68.0	N/A	N/A

[1] To 10,000ft in 7 minutes 9 seconds; to 5000ft in 3 minutes 36 seconds.

	FIREBRAND TF5	SEAFIRE 47
ARMAMENT	4 x 20mm, 1 torpedo	4 x 20mm
ENGINE	Centaurus IX	Griffon 88
RATING (NORMAL)	1975	1490/13,000ft
(TAKE-OFF)	2520	2145/16,000ft
(DASH)	2225 (Mil Rating)	2375/1250ft
SPAN	51-4	36-11
SPAN (FOLDED)	16-10	19-1
WING AREA	383	244
LENGTH	38-11½	34-4
HEIGHT	14-11½	12-9
WEIGHT	16,700	10,200
WING LOADING	43.6	41.8
MAXIMUM SPEED		
LOW	278/SL	332/SL

HIGH	304/13,000ft	393/20,500
CLIMB RATE AT SL	2600[1]	4800
SERVICE CEILING	28,500	43,100
RANGE	643/222	348/187
RANGE WITH TANKS	N/A	817
		(1 x 90, 2 x 22.5-gal)
COMBAT RADIUS	N/A	217
ROLL (0 WOD)	N/A	N/A
ROLL (25kts WOD)	540	378 (27kts)
STALL SPEED	N/A	N/A

[1] With torpedo, 2200ft/min. Speed with torpedo is 297 knots at 13,000ft.

United States

	CORSAIR XF4U-1	CORSAIR F4U-1	CORSAIR F4U-1D
ARMAMENT	2 x 0.50in, 2 x 0.30in	6 x 0.50in	4 x 20mm
ENGINE	R-2800-4	R-2800-8W	R-2800-8W
RATING (NORMAL)	1460/21,500	1675	1675
(TAKE-OFF)	1850	2000	2000
(DASH)	N/A	2135	2250
SPAN	41-0	41-0	40-11²³⁄₃₂
SPAN (FOLDED)	16-	17-0⅜	17-0⅜
WING AREA	314	314	314
LENGTH	32-6	33-4	33-4⅛
HEIGHT	15-0	15-3	14-8½
WEIGHT	9374	12,039	12,175
WING LOADING	29.9	38.3	38.8
MAXIMUM SPEED			
LOW	271.3/SL	312/SL	311.3/SL
HIGH	345.2/23,000	362.6/19,900	355.7/19,900
CLIMB RATE AT SL	3250	2890	3370
SERVICE CEILING	39,900	36,900	40,000
RANGE	940	1015/158	980/158.3
RANGE WITH TANKS	N/A	1685/161.7	1500/153
	–	(1 x 150-gal)	(1 x 150-gal)
COMBAT RADIUS	N/A	125	100
ROLL (0 WOD)	N/A	710[1]	621
ROLL (25kts WOD)	230[2]	340	267
STALL SPEED	65.2	71.1	71.5

[1] Data from 1 March 1944 ACP. As tested in 1942 at 11,194lbs, take-off distances were 560ft and 240ft. This was the original low-cockpit version of the F4U-1, with an R2800 rated at 1800hp military power (2000hp for take-off). Speed at 22,800ft was 343.5 knots.
[2] Guaranteed figure as of June 1940; guaranteed maximum speed was 359.6mph (312.7 knots). Guaranteed service ceiling was 35,500ft.

	CORSAIR F4U-4
ARMAMENT	6 x 0.50in
ENGINE	R-2800-18W
RATING (NORMAL)	1700
(TAKE-OFF)	2100
(DASH)	2380
SPAN	41-0
SPAN (FOLDED)	17-2
WING AREA	314
LENGTH	33-8
HEIGHT	16-4
WEIGHT	12,420
WING LOADING	39.6
MAXIMUM SPEED	
LOW	331.3/SL
HIGH	387.8/26,200 (WE)
CLIMB RATE AT SL	3870
SERVICE CEILING	38,400
RANGE	1005/187
RANGE WITH TANKS	300/180
	(2 x 150-gal)
ROLL (0 WOD)	410
ROLL (25kts WOD)	288
STALL SPEED	73.2

	CORSAIR F4U-5N	HELLCAT F6F-3	HELLCAT F6F-5
ARMAMENT	6 x 0.50in	6 x 0.50in	2 x 20mm, 4 x 0.50in
ENGINE	R-2800-32W	R-2800-10W	R-2800-10W
RATING (NORMAL)	900	1675	1675
(TAKE-OFF)	2300	2000	2000
(DASH)	2675	2250	2135
SPAN	40-1¾	42-10	42-10
SPAN (FOLDED)	17-0⅝	16-2	16-2
WING AREA	314	334	334
LENGTH	34-0	33-7	33-7
HEIGHT	14-9	14-5	14-5
WEIGHT	15,105	12,575	13.797
	(with 150-gal tank)		
WING LOADING	48.1	37.6	41.3
MAXIMUM SPEED			
LOW	309/SL	273/SL	276/SL
HIGH	384/30,000	323.5/18,000	330/23,400
CLIMB RATE AT SL	4340	3250	2980
SERVICE CEILING	43,000	38,800	35,100
RANGE	N/A	955/139	950
RANGE WITH TANKS	710/210	1340/140	1339/148.7
	(1 x 150-gal)	(1 x 150-gal)	(1 x 150-gal)
COMBAT RADIUS	200	120	340
	–	–	(1 x 150-gal)
ROLL (0 WOD)	1000	640	799
ROLL (25kts WOD)	520	294	384
STALL SPEED	71.2	71.1	72

	BEARCAT F8F-1	CORSAIR F2G-2	TIGERCAT F7F-3
ARMAMENT	4 x 20mm	4 x 0.50in	4 x 20mm, 4 x 0.50in
ENGINE	R-2800-34W	R-4360-4	2 x R-2800-34W
RATING (NORMAL)	1700	2500	1700
(TAKE-OFF)	2100	3000	2100
(DASH)	2750	N/A	2380
SPAN	35-6	40-11¾	51-6
SPAN (FOLDED)	23-9½	17-0½	32-4
WING AREA	244	314	455
LENGTH	27-8	33-10	45-5¼
HEIGHT	13-0	10-7¾	17-0
WEIGHT	10,674	13,346	21,720
WING LOADING	43.7	42.5	47.7
MAXIMUM SPEED			
LOW	366/SL	347/SL	318/SL
HIGH	372/18,800	375/16,900	378/22,200
CLIMB RATE AT SL	3230	4400	4530
SERVICE CEILING	34,700	38,800	40,700
RANGE	1230/217	1190/190	1200/180
RANGE WITH TANKS	1810/207	1610/188	1365/193
	(1 x 150, 2 x 100-gal)	(1 x 150-gal)	(1 x 300-gal)
COMBAT RADIUS	216/203	125	110
ROLL (0 WOD)	544 (with 150-gal tank)	577	650
ROLL (25kts WOD)	250 (with 150-gal tank)	259	312
STALL SPEED	67.9	73.9	81.4

	TIGERCAT F7F-4N (APS-19 radar)
ARMAMENT	4 x 20mm
ENGINE	2 x R-2800-34W
RATING (NORMAL)	1700
(TAKE-OFF)	2100
(DASH)	2100
SPAN	51-6
SPAN (FOLDED)	32-4
WING AREA	455
LENGTH	46-11
HEIGHT	16-7
WEIGHT	24,139 (with tank)
WING LOADING	53.0
MAXIMUM SPEED	
LOW	328/SL
HIGH	381/22,100
CLIMB RATE AT SL	4460
SERVICE CEILING	37,600
RANGE	N/A
RANGE WITH TANKS	1055/210
	(1 x 300-gal)
COMBAT RADIUS	N/A
ROLL (0 WOD)	902
ROLL (25kts WOD)	355
STALL SPEED	83.7

C. EARLY JETS

United Kingdom

	ATTACKER F1	SEA HAWK FGA6
ARMAMENT	4 x 20mm	4 x 20mm
ENGINE	Nene 3	Nene 103
RATING (NORMAL)	5100	5400
(TAKE-OFF)	N/A	N/A
(DASH)	N/A	N/A
SPAN	36-11	39-0
SPAN (FOLDED)	30-11	13-4
WING AREA	226	278
LENGTH	37-6	39-8
HEIGHT	9-11	8-8
WEIGHT	11,500	16,200
WING LOADING	50.9	58.3
MAXIMUM SPEED		
LOW	513/SL	450/SL
HIGH	468/30,000	465/35,000[1]
CLIMB RATE AT SL	6350	4720
SERVICE CEILING	45,000	44,500
RANGE	513/309	860
RANGE WITH TANKS	1035/309	1050
	(1 x 270-gal)	(2 x 100-gal)
COMBAT RADIUS	N/A	250-370
ROLL (0 WOD)	N/A	N/A
ROLL (25kts WOD)	N/A	N/A
STALL SPEED	N/A	105

[1]. Also given as 486 knots at 36,000ft clean and 460.8 knots at 36,000ft with drop tanks. The 250nm combat radius is without drop tanks.

United States

	FIREBALL FR-1
ARMAMENT	4 x 0.50in
ENGINE	R-1820
	I-16 jet (parens)
RATING (NORMAL)	1200 (1425)
(TAKE-OFF)	1350 (1610)
(DASH)	1400
SPAN	40-0
SPAN (FOLDED)	15-10 9/16
WING AREA	275
LENGTH	32-3¾
HEIGHT	13-11
WEIGHT	9958
WING LOADING	36.2
MAXIMUM SPEED	
LOW	328.7/SL
HIGH	351.3/17,800
CLIMB RATE AT SL	4650
SERVICE CEILING	43,100
RANGE	930/160
RANGE WITH TANKS	N/A
COMBAT RADIUS	55 (interceptor)
ROLL (0 WOD)	620
ROLL (25kts WOD)	300
STALL SPEED	74.6

	XF15C-1	PHANTOM FH-1	FURY FJ-1
ARMAMENT	4 x 20mm	4 x 0.50in	4 x 20mm
ENGINE	R-2800-30W	J30-WE-2	J35-A-2
	Plus Halford H-1B	–	–
	(jet data in parentheses)	–	–
RATING (NORMAL)	1800 (2700lbs)	1285	3350
(TAKE-OFF)	2120	1560	4000
(DASH)	2360	N/A	N/A
SPAN	48-0	40-9	38-2½
	–	–	40-11 7/16
	–	–	(tip tanks)
SPAN (FOLDED)	20-5	16-3	N/A
WING AREA	400	274	221.37
LENGTH	43-8½	38-9	34-3¾
HEIGHT	15-3	17-2	14-1½
WEIGHT	16,660	11,292	15,115
	–	–	(with tip tanks)
WING LOADING	41.7	41.2	59.3
MAXIMUM SPEED			
LOW	376/SL	410/SL	510
HIGH	408/25,300	421/15,000	475/20,000
CLIMB RATE AT SL	5020	4800	4690
SERVICE CEILING	41,800	34,500	47,400
RANGE	1385/163	670/271	860/296
RANGE WITH TANKS	1745/161	790/267	1300/375
	(1 x 150-gal)	(1 x 295-gal)	(tip tanks)
COMBAT RADIUS	130	320	530/375
ROLL (0 WOD)	865 (571)	1520	2635
ROLL (25kts WOD)	404 (268)	785	1604
STALL SPEED	69	83	105.5

	PIRATE F6U-1	BANSHEE F2H-2	BANSHEE F2H-3
ARMAMENT	4 x 20mm	4 x 20mm	4 x 20mm
ENGINE	J34-WE-30A	2 x J34-WE-34	2 x J34-WE-34
RATING (NORMAL)	2640	2650	2650
(TAKE-OFF)	3150	3250	3250
(DASH)	4100	N/A	N/A
SPAN	32-10	41-7.4	41-8.8 (no tanks)
		44-10.49	
	–	(over tip tanks)	–
SPAN (FOLDED)	N/A	18-5	18-5
WING AREA	204	294	294
LENGTH	37-8	40-2	48-2
HEIGHT	12-11	14-6	14-6
WEIGHT	12,874	19,602	21,013 (no tanks)
	(tip tanks)	–	23,507 (tip tanks)
WING LOADING	62.3	66.6	71.5 (no tanks)
MAXIMUM SPEED			
LOW	518/SL	506/SL	503/SL
HIGH	N/A	462/35,000	455/35,000
CLIMB RATE AT SL	8060	7140	6000
SERVICE CEILING	46,300	46,600	46,600
RANGE	N/A	790/430	1015
RANGE WITH TANKS	1015/375	1655/400	1490
	(2 x 140-gal tip tanks)	(2 x 200-gal)	(2 x 200-gal)
COMBAT RADIUS	390/375	715/400	655/395 (tip tanks)

ROLL (0 WOD)	1805(AB)	2150	3210 (tip tanks)
	–	–	2490 (no tanks)
ROLL (25kts WOD)	1035(AB)	1300	2100 (tip tanks)
	–	–	1560 (no tanks)
STALL SPEED	98	86	122 (tip tanks, power off)
	–	–	115 (no tanks, power off)

[1.] Data from a SACC dated 1 September 1952, before the aircraft flew. Data in Ray Wagner, *American Combat Planes of the 20th Century* (2004) are probably taken from a later SACC chart reflecting actual performance; they are considerably worse: maximum sea level speed was 412 knots; maximum at 24,000ft was 425.2 knots. Climb rate at sea level was 9980ft/min. Gross weight was 14,250lbs.

[2.] Loiter time 1.17 hours at 35,000ft.

[3.] Loiter one hour at 35,000ft.

	PANTHER F9F-5	SKYNIGHT F3D-2
ARMAMENT	4 x 20mm	4 x 20mm
ENGINE	J48-P-6	2 x J34-WE-36
RATING (NORMAL)	5000	3400
(TAKE-OFF)	6250 (dry)	3400
(DASH)	7000 (wet)	N/A
SPAN	38-0	50-0
SPAN (FOLDED)	23-9	26-10
WING AREA	250	400
LENGTH	38-10	45-0
HEIGHT	12-3	16-1
WEIGHT	17,766 (tip tanks)	24,614
WING LOADING	71.1	61.5
MAXIMUM SPEED		
LOW	525/SL	458/SL
HIGH	472/35,000	428/35,000
CLIMB RATE AT SL	6000	3570
SERVICE CEILING	42,800	35,500
RANGE	N/A	995/395
RANGE WITH TANKS	1130/418	1195/395
	(2 x 120-gal)	(2 x 150-gal)
COMBAT RADIUS	420/418	415/395
ROLL (0 WOD)	2257 (dry)	2080
ROLL (25kts WOD)	1435 (dry)	1270
STALL SPEED	94	80.6

	XFV-1	XFY-1[1]
ARMAMENT	4 x 20mm	4 x 20mm
ENGINE	XT-40-A16	XT40-A-16
RATING (NORMAL)	5775	5775
(TAKE-OFF)	6825	6955
(DASH)	6825 (mil rating)	6825
	(in each case this HP is supplemented by jet thrust: respectively, 1280/1363/1685lbs)	
SPAN	27-5	27-8
SPAN (FOLDED)	N/A	N/A
WING AREA	246	355
LENGTH	37-6	35-0
HEIGHT	N/A	N/A
WEIGHT	16,221	16,250
WING LOADING	66.0	45.8
MAXIMUM SPEED		
LOW	488.7/SL	506/SL
HIGH	517.4/35,000	517/35,000
CLIMB RATE AT SL	11,840	11,500
SERVICE CEILING	43,600	44,000
RANGE	_[2]	_[3]
RANGE WITH TANKS	N/A	N/A
ROLL (0 WOD)	N/A	N/A
ROLL (25kts WOD)	N/A	N/A
STALL SPEED	N/A	N/A

D. LATER JETS
United Kingdom

	SEA VENOM FAW.22	SCIMITAR F.1	SEA VIXEN FAW.2
ARMAMENT	4 x 20mm	4 x 30mm	4 x Red Top
ENGINE	Ghost 105	2 x Avon 202	2 x Avon 208
RATING (NORMAL)	5300	11,250	11,230
(TAKE-OFF)	N/A	N/A	N/A
(DASH)	N/A	N/A	20,515
SPAN	42-10	51-0	51-0
	(over tip tanks)	–	–
SPAN (FOLDED)	N/A	22-3	22-3
WING AREA	280	485	648
LENGTH	36-8	55-7	55-7
HEIGHT	8-6	15-3	15-0
WEIGHT	15,400	40,000	41,575
WING LOADING	55	82.5	64.2
MAXIMUM SPEED			
LOW	460/SL	610/SL	600/SL
HIGH	480/30,000	535-565/45,000	520/46,000
CLIMB RATE AT SL	5900	20,000	N/A
SERVICE CEILING	40,000	50,000	48,000
RANGE	N/A	N/A	N/A
RANGE WITH TANKS	613	1400-1650/495-515	1110-1350
	(2 x tip tanks)	(2 x 250, 2 or 4 x 150-gal)	(2 x 150-gal)
COMBAT RADIUS	250	440/610	250
ROLL (0 WOD)	N/A	N/A	N/A
ROLL (25kts WOD)	N/A	N/A	N/A
STALL SPEED	N/A	N/A	N/A

	SEA HARRIER FRS.1
ARMAMENT	2 x 30mm, 2 x Sidewinder
ENGINE	Pegasus 104
RATING (NORMAL)	21,500
(TAKE-OFF)	N/A
(DASH)	N/A
SPAN	25-32[1]
SPAN (FOLDED)	N/A
WING AREA	202.1
LENGTH	47-7
HEIGHT	12-2
WEIGHT	21,700
WING LOADING	107.4
MAXIMUM SPEED	
LOW	639+
HIGH	716[2]
CLIMB RATE AT SL	50,000 approx
SERVICE CEILING	51,000
RANGE	N/A

RANGE WITH TANKS	N/A		
COMBAT RADIUS	100[3]		
ROLL (0 WOD)	N/A		
ROLL (25kts WOD)	N/A		
STALL SPEED	N/A		

[1.] Span 29-8 with ferry tips. The weight given is that in the specification, but later maximum take-off weight was 26,200lbs.
[2.] Maximum 'never exceed' speed, as in a dive.
[3.] Requirements included 90 minutes CAP at 100nm at 30,000ft. Other performance data are unofficial. However, combat radius was later given unofficially as 400nm in a hi-hi-hi intercept mission with four Sidewinders, or 250nm on a hi-lo-hi attack mission.

LOW	568/SL	570/SL	617/SL
HIGH	530/35,000	588/18,000	549/35,000
		(max 632/35,000)	
CLIMB RATE AT SL	5850	16,300	13,350
SERVICE CEILING	41,400	49,000	45,800
RANGE	N/A	1108/502	1450/415
RANGE WITH TANKS	995/470	1146/466	1815/413
	(2 x 200-gal)	(2 x 150-gal)	(2 x 300-gal)
COMBAT RADIUS	700	310	550/415
ROLL (0 WOD)	5350	4260	1630
ROLL (25kts WOD)	3920	3100	930
STALL SPEED	107.0	103.3	97

[1.] From SACC dated 1 May 1951, before the XF10F-1 flew.

United States

	COUGAR	FURY		DEMON
	F9F-6	FJ-3		F3H-1
ARMAMENT	4 x 20mm	4 x 20mm	ARMAMENT	4 x 20mm
ENGINE	J48-P-8	J65-W-2	ENGINE	J40-WE-10
RATING (NORMAL)	5600	6400	RATING (NORMAL)	8330
(TAKE-OFF)	7250	7220	(TAKE-OFF)	9275
(DASH)	N/A	N/A	(DASH)	13,700
SPAN	34-6	37-1	SPAN	35-4
SPAN (FOLDED)	14-2		SPAN (FOLDED)	25-4
WING AREA	300	288	WING AREA	442
LENGTH	40-11	38-7	LENGTH	59-0
HEIGHT	12-4	13-8	HEIGHT	14-7
WEIGHT	18,450	19,360	WEIGHT	29,550
WING LOADING	61.5	67.2	WING LOADING	66.9
MAXIMUM SPEED			MAXIMUM SPEED	
LOW	561/SL	599/SL	LOW	636/SL
HIGH	505/35,000	530/35,000	HIGH	562/35,000
CLIMB RATE AT SL	5400	9400	CLIMB RATE AT SL	19,940
SERVICE CEILING	44,500	47,000	SERVICE CEILING	47,000
RANGE	780/442	995/470	RANGE	1025/485
RANGE WITH TANKS	N/A	N/A	RANGE WITH TANKS	N/A
COMBAT RADIUS	260/442	385 (JP-4)	COMBAT RADIUS	315/485
ROLL (0 WOD)	2100	2050	ROLL (0 WOD)	1850(AB)
ROLL (25kts WOD)	1360	1380	ROLL (25kts WOD)	1225(AB)
STALL SPEED	93	94.4	STALL SPEED	92.5

	FURY	TIGER	JAGUAR[1]		DEMON
	FJ-4B	F11F-1	F10F-1		F3H-2M
ARMAMENT	4 x 20mm	4 x 20mm	4 x 20mm	ARMAMENT	4 x Sparrow I
ENGINE	J65-W-16A	J65-W-18	J40-WE-8	ENGINE	J71-A-2B
RATING (NORMAL)	6780	6470	6700	RATING (NORMAL)	8700
(TAKE-OFF)	7700	7450	7400	(TAKE-OFF)	10,000
(DASH)	N/A	10,500	10,900	(DASH)	14,400
SPAN	39-1	31-7.5	50-7 (straight)	SPAN	35-4
			36-8 (straight)		
SPAN (FOLDED)	22-11	27-4	N/A	SPAN (FOLDED)	25-3
WING AREA	338.66	250	467 (straight)	WING AREA	519
			450 (swept)		
LENGTH	36-4	44-10	54-5	LENGTH	58-11.5
HEIGHT	13-11	13-3	16-3	HEIGHT	14-6.6
WEIGHT	25,037	21,035	31.255	WEIGHT	34,641
WING LOADING	73.9	84.1	67.0	WING LOADING	66.7
MAXIMUM SPEED				MAXIMUM SPEED	
				LOW	Mach 0.78/SL
				HIGH	Mach 0.95/31,600

CLIMB RATE AT SL	12,030[1]	
SERVICE CEILING	43,550	
RANGE	861/Mach 0.73	
RANGE WITH TANKS	1295/Mach 0.74	
	(2 x 285-gal)	
COMBAT RADIUS	302	
ROLL (0 WOD)	2330	
ROLL (25kts WOD)	1550	
STALL SPEED	93	

[1]. Climb rate without Sparrows was 15,430ft/min.

	CUTLASS F7U-1	CUTLASS F7U-3M	SKYRAY F4D-1
ARMAMENT	4 x 20mm	4 x 20mm, 4 x Sparrow I	4 x 20mm
ENGINE	2 x J34-WE-32	2 x J46-WE-8	J57-P-2
RATING (NORMAL)	3020	3620	8000
(TAKE-OFF)	3370	4020	9220
(DASH)	4900	5725	14,800
SPAN	38-8	39-8.6	33-6
SPAN (FOLDED)	21-3.2	22-3.8	28-1⅛
WING AREA	496	535	557
LENGTH	39-7.2	44-3	45-7⅞
HEIGHT	11-10	14-7.44	12-11⅞
WEIGHT	20,038	31,050	20,500
WING LOADING	40.4	58.1	36.8
MAXIMUM SPEED			
LOW	602/SL	501/SL[1][A]	645/SL
HIGH	544/35,000	513/15,000	565/50,000
CLIMB RATE AT SL	15,100	4100	23,640
SERVICE CEILING	50,000	33,400	56,500
RANGE	975/400	760/450	645/518
RANGE WITH TANKS	1490/391	665/380	915/510
	(2 x 250-gal)	(2 x 220-gal)	(2 x150-gal)
COMBAT RADIUS	290/400	230/450	225/518
ROLL (0 WOD)	1250 (AB)	3000	1205
ROLL (25kts WOD)	725 (AB)	2050	800
STALL SPEED	82.2	105	98.9

[1]. Performance for basic fighter without missiles.

	SEA DART F2Y-1[1]	SKYLANCER F5D-1	CRUSADER F8U-1(F-8A)
ARMAMENT	N/A	4 x 20mm or 2 x Sparrow II or 72 x FFAR	4 x 20mm, 32 x FFAR
ENGINE	2 x J46-WE-2	J57-P-8	J-57-P-4
RATING (NORMAL)	3670	8700	8700
(TAKE-OFF)	4080	10,200	10,200
(DASH)	6100	16,000	16,000
SPAN	33-8	33.5	35-8
SPAN (FOLDED)	N/A	28.5	22-6
WING AREA	563	557	375
LENGTH	52-7	32.8	54-2.75
HEIGHT	16-2	14.8	15-9.1
WEIGHT	15,327	28,072	26,969
WING LOADING	29.6	50.4	71.9

MAXIMUM SPEED			
LOW	683/SL(AB)	651 (Mach 0.986)	637/SL
HIGH	863/35,000(AB)	591/16,000 (AB: 828/35,000)	880/35,000
CLIMB RATE AT SL	32,700(AB)	5560 (AB: 20,790)	20,000
SERVICE CEILING	54,800	38,700	51,500
RANGE	446/450	523	1280/494
RANGE WITH TANKS	N/A	N/A	N/A
COMBAT RADIUS	N/A	340	345
ROLL (0 WOD)	N/A	4000	5200
ROLL (25kts WOD)	N/A	2850	3920
STALL SPEED	102	106.4	108.2

[1]. Estimated data dated 1 September 1951, giving unrealistically high speed. This was for the instrumented but entirely unarmed aircraft. Actual maximum speed was 563.4 knots at 35,000ft (stall speed 118.3 knots).

	CRUSADER F8U-2	CRUSADER F8U-2N[1]	CRUSADER F8U-3[2]
ARMAMENT	4 x 20mm	4 x 20mm, 2/4 x Sidewinder	3 x Sparrow III, 2 x Sidewinder
ENGINE	J57-P-16	J57-P-20	J75-P-6
RATING (NORMAL)	9150	9150	14,900
(TAKE-OFF)	10,700	10,700	16,500
(DASH)	16,900	18,000	26,000
SPAN	35-8	35-8	39-11.4
SPAN (FOLDED)	22-6	22-6	25-3.2
WING AREA	375	375	450
LENGTH	54-2.75	54-2.75	56-8.884
HEIGHT	15-9.1	15-9.1	16-4.5 (ventral fins up)
WEIGHT	27,938	29,472	37,701
WING LOADING	74.5	78.6	83.8
MAXIMUM SPEED			
LOW	653/SL	656/SL	693/SL
HIGH	960/35,000	1005/35,000	1267/35,000
CLIMB RATE AT SL	25,400	29,200	39,250
SERVICE CEILING	52,500	52,750	55,800
RANGE	1295/495	1263/495	1755/500
RANGE WITH TANKS	N/A	N/A	N/A
COMBAT RADIUS	320	355/787	582
ROLL (0 WOD)	7560	6980	5880
ROLL (25kts WOD)	4130	5160	6650
STALL SPEED	110.4	119.4	108.8

[1]. Data for fighter with four Sidewinders.
[2]. Data with Sparrows, no Sidewinders.

	D-188A[1]
ARMAMENT	4 x Sidewinders or 1000lb store
ENGINE	6 x J85-GE-5 with AB; 2 x J85-GE-5 without AB
RATING (NORMAL)	2140
(TAKE-OFF)	2455
(DASH)	3660
SPAN	23-8
SPAN (FOLDED)	N/A

FIGHTERS OVER THE FLEET

WING AREA	194
LENGTH	54-11
HEIGHT	12-3
WEIGHT	22,670
WING LOADING	116.9
MAXIMUM SPEED	
LOW	661/SL
HIGH	1147/35,000
CLIMB RATE AT SL	42,800
SERVICE CEILING	50,000 (100ft/min)
RANGE	1105/525
RANGE WITH TANKS	N/A
COMBAT RADIUS	225/525
ROLL (0 WOD)	N/A
ROLL (25kts WOD)	N/A
STALL SPEED	208

[1.] Bell data, not verified by BuAer.

	PHANTOM F-4B	PHANTOM F-4J	MISSILEER F6D-1
ARMAMENT	4 x Sparrow III	4 x Sparrow III	6 x Eagle
ENGINE	2 x J79-GE-8	2 x J79-GE-10	2 x TF30-P-2
RATING (NORMAL)	10,300	11,110	7750
(TAKE-OFF)	10,900	11,870	10,000
(DASH)	17,000	17,459	N/A
SPAN	38.4	38.4	70-0
SPAN (FOLDED)	27.6	27.6	37-6
WING AREA	530	530	630
LENGTH	58.2	58.3	53-0
HEIGHT	16.3	15.8	18-1
WEIGHT	43,907	46,833	49,500
WING LOADING	82.8	88.4	76.6
MAXIMUM SPEED			
LOW	734/SL	760/SL	Mach 0.715/SL
HIGH	1279/45,000	1230/36,089	Mach 0.763/35,000
CLIMB RATE AT SL	40,800	41,350	6325
SERVICE CEILING	56,850	54,700	40,400
RANGE	1126/505	981/489	Loiter 4hr/Mach 0.5[1]
RANGE WITH TANKS	1496/505	1308/490	N/A
		(1 x 370-gal)	(1 x 600-gal)
COMBAT RADIUS	410	351	N/A
ROLL (0 WOD)	2085	2490(AB)	2430
ROLL (25kts WOD)	1510	1830(AB)	N/A
STALL SPEED	133	120	93.3

[1.] 150nm from carrier. SL speed was about 440 knots. A speed of 472 knots has also been quoted; it was probably the Douglas rather than the official estimate.

	TFX F-111B
ARMAMENT	1 x 20mm, 6 x Phoenix
ENGINE	2 x TF30-P-1A
RATING (NORMAL)	8500
(TAKE-OFF)	10,750
(DASH)	18,500

SPAN	33-11(swept)
	70-0 (unswept)
SPAN (FOLDED)	N/A
WING AREA	550
LENGTH	66-9.5
HEIGHT	16-7.3
WEIGHT	77,566
WING LOADING	141.0
MAXIMUM SPEED	
LOW	678/SL
HIGH	1260/40,000
CLIMB RATE AT SL	21,300
SERVICE CEILING	44,900
RANGE	1830
RANGE WITH TANKS	N/A
COMBAT RADIUS	475
ROLL (0 WOD)	3070[1]
ROLL (25kts WOD)	N/A
STALL SPEED	99.6

[1.] Take-off roll to clear 50ft obstacle with afterburner lit, not the usual flight deck requirement, which would be somewhat shorter. Data included, unusually, time to accelerate from cruising speed to combat speed, 10.2 minutes (other SACC charts did not include this data).

	TOMCAT F-14A[1]	TOMCAT F-14D[2]	HORNET F/A-18A[3]
ARMAMENT	1 x 20mm,	1 x 20mm,	1 x 20mm,
	6 x Phoenix	6 x Phoenix	2 x Sparrow,
			2 x Sidewinder
ENGINE	2 x TF30-P-412A	2 x F110-GE-400	2 x F404-GE-400
RATING (NORMAL)	10,800	11,800	10,608
(TAKE-OFF)	12,350	16,333	N/A
(DASH)	20,900	26,950	16,016
SPAN	38-2.4 (swept)	38-2.4 (swept)	40-4
	64-1.5 (unswept)	64-1.5 (unswept)	–
SPAN (FOLDED)	N/A	N/A	27-6
WING AREA	565	565	400
LENGTH	61-10.6	61-10.6	56-0
HEIGHT	16-0	16-0	15-4
WEIGHT	68,649	72,465	35,690
WING LOADING	121.5	128.6	89.2
MAXIMUM SPEED			
LOW	708/SL	692/SL	691.3/SL
HIGH	AB: 1090/35,000	1052/35,000	991/35,000
CLIMB RATE AT SL	34,200	34,000	44,300
SERVICE CEILING	48,200	40,500	54,450
RANGE	N/A	N/A	N/A
RANGE WITH TANKS	1375	1226	N/A
COMBAT RADIUS	150	150	563[4]
ROLL (0 WOD)	3000	3200	N/A
ROLL (25kts WOD)	2000	2230	N/A
STALL SPEED	101	112	107[5]

[1.] Performance given for fleet air defence mission, with six Phoenix and two 267-gallon drop tanks. Speeds are without drop tanks. Stall speed is with approach power.
[2.] Performance given for fleet air defence mission, with four Phoenix, two Sparrow and two Sidewinders, plus two 280-gallon drop tanks. Speeds are without drop tanks. Max effort take-off in zero wind is 1690ft.
[3.] F/A-18C has the F404-GE-402 engine, 17,750lbs thrust on afterburner and

gross weight is 37,708lbs; maximum speed is 1183 knots at 35,000ft.
Reported F/A-18C/D combat radius is 1089nm with only two Sidewinders;
reported range is 1546nm with three 330-gallon drop tanks. Figures for F/A-18A should be slightly different.
4. Also given as typically over 470nm, probably with missiles on board; interception radius of action typically over 400nm. No CAP endurance figure has been published.
5. Approach speed given unofficially as 134 knots. The same source gives take-off distance as less than 1400ft, but it is not clear whether this is a deck take-off (zero obstacle) or an airfield take-off over a 50ft obstacle.

	HORNET F/A-18E	LIGHTNING II F-35C
ARMAMENT	1 x 20mm, missiles	1 x 27mm, missiles
ENGINE	2 x F414-GE-400	F135-PW-100
RATING (NORMAL)	N/A	N/A
(TAKE-OFF)	13,000	28,000
(DASH)	22,000	43,000
SPAN	44-10	43.0
SPAN (FOLDED)	N/A	N/A
WING AREA	500	668
LENGTH	60-2	51.5
HEIGHT	16-0	14.2
WEIGHT	47,881	70,000[1]
WING LOADING	95.8	104.8
MAXIMUM SPEED		
LOW	Mach 1.6[2]	N/A
HIGH	1035/40,000[3]	N/A
CLIMB RATE AT SL	44,882	N/A
SERVICE CEILING	50,000+	N/A
RANGE	1275	over 1200nm
RANGE WITH TANKS	–[4]	N/A
COMBAT RADIUS	390	N/A
ROLL (0 WOD)	N/A	N/A
ROLL (25kts WOD)	N/A	N/A
STALL SPEED	125[5]	N/A

1. This may be maximum take-off weight; a gross weight of 49,540lbs has been given for the F-35A version, which has shorter wings and is slightly shorter.
2. Unofficial figure; no altitude given.
3. Mach 1.8. Combat radius is for an interdiction mission. Reported increase in interdiction range over F/A-18C is 41 per cent.
4. Three 480-gal vs three 330-gal drop tanks in earlier versions. Reported range with tanks is 1660nm.
5. Approach speed, slightly higher than stall speed.

E. AEW AIRCRAFT

	SKYRAIDER AD-5W	TRACER WF-2 (E-1B)
ENGINE	R-3350-26-WA	2xR-1820-8
RATING (NORMAL)	2300	1275
(TAKE-OFF)	2700	1525
(DASH)	N/A	N/A
SPAN	50-0	72-3.892
SPAN (FOLDED)	24-0	30-5
WING AREA	400.3	506
LENGTH	40-0	45-4
HEIGHT	15-9	16-10
WEIGHT	18,037	26,594
WING LOADING	45.1	52.6
MAXIMUM SPEED		
LOW	250	201
HIGH	267/15,000	199/10,000
CLIMB RATE AT SL	2740	1580
SERVICE CEILING	24,400	15,800
RANGE	685/160	875
ENDURANCE	4.4hr	3.46hr/15,000ft
ROLL (0 WOD)	1025	1960
ROLL (25kts WOD)	540	1380
STALL SPEED	77.1	73

	HAWKEYE AEW 3	GANNET E-2C
ENGINE	2 x T46-A-8/8A	Double Mamba 112
RATING (NORMAL)	3730	3875
(TAKE-OFF)	4050	N/A
(DASH)	N/A	N/A
SPAN	80-7	54-4
SPAN (FOLDED)	29-4	19-11
WING AREA	700	483
LENGTH	56-4	43-0
HEIGHT	18-3.75	13-9
WEIGHT	50,920	19,600
WING LOADING	72.7	40.6
MAXIMUM SPEED		
LOW	291/SL	235/SL
HIGH	289/25,050	270/5000ft
CLIMB RATE AT SL	2930	2000
SERVICE CEILING	26,500	25,000
RANGE	N/A	609
ENDURANCE	4hr	5hr
ROLL (0 WOD)	1590	N/A
ROLL (25kts WOD)	N/A	N/A
STALL SPEED	71	N/A

INDEX